Essentials of Time Series for Financial Applications

Essentials of Time Series for Financial Applications

Massimo Guidolin
Professor of Finance, Bocconi University and Research Fellow, BAFFI-CAREFIN Centre

Manuela Pedio
Teaching Fellow, Bocconi University and Fellow, BAFFI-CAREFIN Centre

ELSEVIER

ACADEMIC PRESS
An imprint of Elsevier

Academic Press is an imprint of Elsevier
125 London Wall, London EC2Y 5AS, United Kingdom
525 B Street, Suite 1650, San Diego, CA 92101-4495, United States
50 Hampshire Street, 5th Floor, Cambridge, MA 02139, United States
The Boulevard, Langford Lane, Kidlington, Oxford OX5 1GB, United Kingdom

Notices

Knowledge and best practice in this field are constantly changing. As new research and experience broaden our understanding, changes in research methods, professional practices, or medical treatment may become necessary.

Practitioners and researchers must always rely on their own experience and knowledge in evaluating and using any information, methods, compounds, or experiments described herein. In using such information or methods they should be mindful of their own safety and the safety of others, including parties for whom they have a professional responsibility.

To the fullest extent of the law, neither the Publisher nor the authors, contributors, or editors, assume any liability for any injury and/or damage to persons or property as a matter of products liability, negligence or otherwise, or from any use or operation of any methods, products, instructions, or ideas contained in the material herein.

British Library Cataloguing-in-Publication Data
A catalogue record for this book is available from the British Library

Library of Congress Cataloging-in-Publication Data
A catalog record for this book is available from the Library of Congress

ISBN: 978-0-12-813409-2

Publisher: Candice Janco
Acquisition Editor: Scott Bentley
Editorial Project Manager: Jaclyn Truesdell
Production Project Manager: Anusha Sambamoorthy
Cover Designer: Mark Rogers

Typeset by MPS Limited, Chennai, India

Contents

List of Figures ix
List of Tables xiii
Preface xv

1. Linear Regression Model 1

1.1 Inference in Linear Regression Models 1

1.1.1 The Ordinary Least Squares Estimator 3
1.1.2 Goodness of Fit Measures 5
1.1.3 The Generalized Least Squared Estimator 7
1.1.4 Maximum Likelihood Estimator 9
1.1.5 Hypotheses Testing, Confidence Intervals, and Predictive Intervals 10
1.1.6 Linear Regression Model With Stochastic Regressors 15
1.1.7 Asymptotic Theory for Linear Regressions 16

1.2 Testing for Violations of the Linear Regression Framework 18

1.2.1 Linearity 18
1.2.2 Structural Breaks and Parameter Stability Test 23

1.3 Specifying the Regressors 25

1.3.1 How to Select the Regressors 26
1.3.2 Multicollinearity 29
1.3.3 Measurement Errors in the Regressors 31

1.4 Issues With Heteroskedasticity and Autocorrelation of the Errors 32

1.4.1 Heteroskedastic Errors 32
1.4.2 Autocorrelated Errors 34

1.5 The Interpretation of Regression Results 34

References 36

Appendix 1.A 36

Appendix 1.B Principal Component Analysis 38

2. Autoregressive Moving Average (ARMA) Models and Their Practical Applications 41

2.1 Essential Concepts in Time Series Analysis 41

2.1.1 Time Series and Their Properties 41
2.1.2 Stationarity 42
2.1.3 Sample Autocorrelations and Sample Partial Autocorrelations 45

2.2 Moving Average and Autoregressive Processes 49

2.2.1 Finite Order Moving Average Processes 49
2.2.2 Autoregressive Processes 52
2.2.3 Autoregressive Moving Average Processes 58

2.3 Selection and Estimation of AR, MA, and ARMA Models 61

2.3.1 The Selection of the Model and the Role of Information Criteria 61
2.3.2 Estimation Methods 65
2.3.3 Residual Diagnostics 67

2.4 Forecasting ARMA Processes 71

2.4.1 Standard Principles of Forecasting 71
2.4.2 Forecasting an AR(p) Process 71
2.4.3 Forecasting the Future Value of an MA(q) Process 72
2.4.4 Evaluating the Accuracy of a Forecast Function 73

References 75

Appendix 2.A 75

3. Vector Autoregressive Moving Average (VARMA) Models 77

3.1 Foundations of Multivariate Time Series Analysis 77

3.1.1 Weak Stationarity of Multivariate Time Series 77
3.1.2 Cross-Covariance and Cross-Correlation Matrices 78
3.1.3 Sample Cross-Covariance and Cross-Correlation Matrices 79
3.1.4 Multivariate Portmanteau Tests 81
3.1.5 Multivariate White Noise Process 82

3.2 Introduction to Vector Autoregressive Analysis 82

3.2.1 From Structural to Reduced-Form Vector Autoregressive Models 82
3.2.2 Stationarity Conditions and the Population Moments of a VAR(1) Process 86
3.2.3 Generalization to a VAR(p) Model 89
3.2.4 Estimation of a VAR(p) Model 91
3.2.5 Specification of a Vector Autoregressive Model and Hypothesis Testing 94
3.2.6 Forecasting With a Vector Autoregressive Model 97

3.3 Structural Analysis With Vector Autoregressive Models 100

3.3.1 Impulse Response Functions 100
3.3.2 Variance Decompositions 105
3.3.3 Granger Causality 108

3.4 Vector Moving Average and Vector Autoregressive Moving Average Models 110

3.4.1 Vector Moving Average Models 110
3.4.2 Vector Autoregressive Moving Average Models 111

References 112

4. Unit Roots and Cointegration 113

4.1 Defining Unit Root Processes 113

4.1.1 What Happens If One Incorrectly Detrends a Unit Root Series? 118
4.1.2 What Happens If One Incorrectly Applies Differencing to (Deterministic) Trend-Stationary Series? 119
4.1.3 What Happens If One Incorrectly Applies Differencing to a Stationary Series? 120
4.1.4 What Happens If One Incorrectly Applies Differencing $d+r$ Times to an $I(d)$ Series? 121

4.2 The Spurious Regression Problem 121

4.3 Unit Root Tests 124

4.3.1 Classical Dickey–Fuller Tests 124
4.3.2 The Augmented Dickey–Fuller Test 126
4.3.3 Other Unit Root Tests 131
4.3.4 Testing for Unit Roots in Moving-Average Processes 132

4.4 Cointegration and Error-Correction Models 133

4.4.1 The Relationship Between Cointegration and Economic Theory 133
4.4.2 Definition of Cointegration 134
4.4.3 Error-Correction Models 135
4.4.4 Testing for Cointegration 138

References 149

5. Single-Factor Conditionally Heteroskedastic Models, ARCH and GARCH 151

5.1 Stylized Facts and Preliminaries 151

5.1.1 The Stylized Facts of Conditional Heteroskedasticity 153

5.2 Simple Univariate Parametric Models 157

5.2.1 Rolling Window Forecasts 157
5.2.2 Exponential Smoothing Variance Forecasts: RiskMetrics 160
5.2.3 ARCH Models 161
5.2.4 Comparing the Performance of Alternative Variance Forecast Models: Do We Need More Than ARCH? 168
5.2.5 Generalized ARCH Models and Their Statistical Properties 171
5.2.6 A Few Additional, Popular ARCH Models 181

5.3 Advanced Univariate Volatility Modeling 190

5.3.1 Non-Gaussian Marginal Innovations 190
5.3.2 GARCH Models Augmented by Exogenous (Predetermined) Factors 197

5.4 Testing for ARCH 198

5.4.1 Lagrange Multiplier ARCH Tests 199
5.4.2 News Impact Curves and Testing for Asymmetric ARCH 202

5.5 Forecasting With GARCH Models 205

5.5.1 Long-Horizon, Point Forecasts 206
5.5.2 Forecasts of Variance for Sums of Returns or Shocks 208

5.6 Estimation of and Inference on GARCH Models 210

5.6.1 Maximum Likelihood Estimation 212
5.6.2 The Properties of MLE 214
5.6.3 Quasi MLE 218
5.6.4 Misspecification Tests 221
5.6.5 Sequential Estimation and QMLE 221
5.6.6 Data Frequency in Estimation and Temporal Aggregation 223

References 225

Appendix 5.A Nonparametric Kernel Density Estimation 226

6. Multivariate GARCH and Conditional Correlation Models 229

6.1 Introduction and Preliminaries 229

6.2 Simple Models of Covariance Prediction 230

6.3 Full, Multivariate GARCH Models 238

6.4 Constant and Dynamic Conditional Correlation Models 250

6.5 Factor GARCH Models 257
6.6 Inference and Model Specification 264
References 266

7. Multifactor Heteroskedastic Models, Stochastic Volatility 267
7.1 A Primer on the Kalman Filter 268
7.1.1 A Simple Univariate Example 268
7.1.2 The General Case 270
7.2 Simple Stochastic Volatility Models and their Estimation Using the Kalman Filter 271
7.2.1 The Economics of Stochastic Volatility: The Normal Mixture Model 271
7.2.2 One Benchmark Case: The Log-Normal Two-Factor Stochastic Volatility Model 272
7.3 Extended, Second-Generation Stochastic Volatility Models 281
7.4 GARCH versus Stochastic Volatility: Which One? 282
7.4.1 Some GARCH Models Are (Asymptotically) Stochastic Volatility Models 282
7.4.2 Stressing the Differences: What Have We Learned So Far? 284
References 285

8. Models With Breaks, Recurrent Regime Switching, and Nonlinearities 287
8.1 A Primer on the Key Features and Classification of Statistical Model of Instability 287
8.2 Detecting and Exploiting Structural Change in Linear Models 290
8.2.1 Chow Tests for Given Break Dates 291
8.2.2 CUSUM and CUSUM Square Tests 293
8.2.3 Andrews and Quandt's Single-Break Test 294
8.2.4 Bai and Perron's Multiple, Endogenous Breaks Test 297
8.2.5 Testing for Breaks When Testing for Unit Roots and Cointegration, and Vice Versa 302
8.3 Threshold and Smooth Transition Regime Switching Models 307
8.3.1 Threshold Regression and Autoregressive Models 308
8.3.2 Smooth Transition Regression and Autoregressive Models 316
8.3.3 Testing (Non-)Linearities 322
References 326

9. Markov Switching Models 329
9.1 Definitions and Classifications 329
9.2 Understanding Markov Switching Dynamics Through Simulations 337
9.2.1 Markov Switching Models as Normal Mixtures and Density Approximation 340
9.3 Markov Switching Regressions 341
9.4 Markov Chain Processes and Their Properties 344
9.5 Estimation and Inference for Markov Switching Models 350
9.5.1 Maximum Likelihood Estimation and the Expectation-Maximization Algorithm 350
9.5.2 Tests of Hypotheses 359
9.5.3 Testing and Selecting the Number of Regimes and the Nuisance Parameters Problem 362
9.6 Forecasting With Markov Switching Models 365
9.7 Markov Switching ARCH and DCC Models 369
9.8 Do Nonlinear and Markov Switching Models Work in Practice? 372
References 374
Appendix 9.A Some Notions Concerning Ergodic Markov Chains 376
Appendix 9.B State-Space Representation of an Markov Switching Model 377
Appendix 9.C First-Order Conditions for Maximum Likelihood Estimation of Markov Switching Models 378

10. Realized Volatility and Covariance 381
10.1 Measuring Realized Variance 381
10.1.1 Quadratic Variation and Its Estimators 381
10.1.2 Microstructure Noise and the Choice of the Sampling Frequency 383
10.1.3 Other Bias-Adjusted Measures of Realized Volatility 385
10.1.4 Jumps and Bipower Variation 387
10.2 Forecasting Realized Variance 388
10.2.1 Stylized Facts About Realized Variance 388
10.2.2 Forecasting Realized Variance: Heterogeneous Autoregressions 390

10.2.3 Range-Based Variance Forecasts 392
10.3 Multivariate Applications **395**
10.3.1 Realized Covariance Matrix Estimation 395
10.3.2 Range-Based Covariance Estimation 396
References **396**

Appendix A: Mathematical and Statistical Appendix 399

Index 409

List of Figures

Figure 1.1	Simulated scatter plots for a bivariate case. (A) 100 simulated observations linear relation; (B) 100 simulated observations linear relation; (C) 100 simulated observations independent variables; (D) 100 simulated observations quadratic relation	19
Figure 1.2	Scatter plots to investigate the linearity assumption. (A) Scatter plot between the dependent variable and the fitted values; (B) scatter plot between the dependent variable and the residuals	20
Figure 1.3	Scatter plot matrix	21
Figure 1.4	Output of a CUSUM for a break in the market Model Beta	25
Figure 2.1	Plots of two times series with alternative persistence properties and their comparison	44
Figure 2.2	Plot of data simulated from a Gaussian WN process	44
Figure 2.3	Correlograms of two times series with alternative persistence properties	46
Figure 2.4	Plots and correlogram of MA(1) simulated data with $\mu = 0$ and $\theta_1 = 0.3$	51
Figure 2.5	Plots and correlogram of MA(1) simulated data with $\mu = 0$ and $\theta_1 = 0.8$	51
Figure 2.6	Plots and sample correlogram of MA(2) simulated data with $\mu = 0$, $\theta_1 = 0.8$, and $\theta_2 = 0.3$	52
Figure 2.7	Plots and correlogram of AR(1) simulated data with $\mu = 0$ and $\phi_1 = 0.3$	56
Figure 2.8	Plots and correlogram of AR(1) simulated data with $\mu = 0$ and $\phi_1 = 0.7$	57
Figure 2.9	Plots and correlogram of AR(2) simulated data with $\mu = 0$, $\phi_1 = 0.7$, and $\phi_2 = -0.3$	57
Figure 2.10	Plots and correlogram of ARMA(1,1) simulated data with $\phi_1 = 0.7$ and $\theta_1 = -0.3$	61
Figure 2.11	Plot of the monthly percentage changes in US CPI from January 2001 to December 2016	62
Figure 2.12	The residuals, the standardized residuals, and the empirical distribution of the residuals of an ARMA(2,1) model for US CPI inflation data	69
Figure 2.13	Rolling one-step-ahead forecasts for US inflation based an ARMA(2,1) model	74
Figure 2.14	Rolling one-step-ahead forecasts for US inflation based an AR(2) model	75
Figure 3.1	Plot of weekly yields for 1-month and 10-year US Treasury bond	80
Figure 3.2	One-week ahead forecasts of 1-month, 1-, 5-, and 10-year US Treasury yields from a VAR(2)	99
Figure 3.3	IRFs to shocks to 1-month and 10-year yields, ordered on the basis of a Cholesky triangular scheme that places shocks to the 1-month at the top of the ordering	102
Figure 3.4	IRFs to a one standard deviation positive shocks to the 1-month Treasury yield	104
Figure 4.1	(A) Comparing trend-stationary series and stochastic trends. (B) Estimated deterministic trends and estimated random walk	114
Figure 4.2	(A) Detrended and first-differenced series. (B) Sample ACF of detrended and first-differenced series	118
Figure 4.3	Incorrect polynomial detrending of a random walk	119
Figure 4.4	Incorrect first-differencing of a trend-stationary series	120
Figure 4.5	Excessive differencing of a $I(1)$ series	121
Figure 4.6	Two simulated random walk processes	123
Figure 4.7	ACF of the residuals from regressing one RW walk on another RW and of regressing the same series in first differences	124
Figure 4.8	SACF of the first difference of S&P real prices and aggregate earnings. (A) Real S&P prices and (B) real earnings	128
Figure 4.9	Four simulated series based on identical shocks	129
Figure 4.10	Time series of real S&P equity index prices, aggregate earnings and dividends	131
Figure 4.11	Fitted values and cointegrating regression residuals of real S&P equity index prices regressed on aggregate earnings	141
Figure 4.12	Real S&P equity index prices/aggregate earnings ratio	141
Figure 4.13	Deviations from long-run equilibrium cointegrating relation between real S&P equity index prices and aggregate earnings	145
Figure 4.14	US riskless, annualized nominal treasury rates at maturities 1 month, 6 months, 1, 3, 7, and 10 years	147
Figure 4.15	$\lambda_{trace}(r)$ and $\lambda_{max}(r, r+1)$ tests applied to US riskless, annualized nominal treasury rates	147
Figure 4.16	Estimated normalized $\boldsymbol{\Pi} = \boldsymbol{\Lambda K}'$ decompositions	148
Figure 5.1	Time series plots and associated histograms for two series. (A) US stock returns. (B) US long-term treasury yields	153
Figure 5.2	Plots of daily US excess returns, their squares, and cubes	154
Figure 5.3	Scatter plots of squares versus levels for two series	156
Figure 5.4	Time series and scatter plots of squared returns/yield changes. (A) Treasury yields. (B) International stock returns	157

Figure 5.5	Plots of rolling window forecasts of mean and variance	160
Figure 5.6	Plot of 1-day ARCH(6) volatility forecasts	166
Figure 5.7	Plot of 1-day ARCH(6) and RiskMetrics volatility forecasts	170
Figure 5.8	Plots of CH model variance forecasts versus squared residuals	171
Figure 5.9	Predicted conditional volatility from a GARCH(1,1) model and four alternative simulated scenarios	177
Figure 5.10	Comparing GARCH and EGARCH volatility predictions	181
Figure 5.11	In-sample volatility forecasts from T-GARCH and PARCH	185
Figure 5.12	In-sample volatility forecasts from C-GARCH versus GARCH	188
Figure 5.13	Volatility forecasts from asymmetric component GARCH(1,1,1)	189
Figure 5.14	Kernel density estimators of model residuals	191
Figure 5.15	Volatility forecasts from Gaussian versus *t*-Student threshold GARCH(1,1) applied to Singapore's monthly returns in USD	194
Figure 5.16	Empirical estimates of the distribution of 1-year T-bill rates. (A) Histogram and sample statistics. (B) Quantile–quantile plot	196
Figure 5.17	NICs from alternative GARCH models. (A) Symmetric NIC. (B) Threshold GARCH-induced asymmetric NIC. (C) EGARCH-induced asymmetric NIC	203
Figure 5.18	Empirical nonparametric impact curve for HML returns	204
Figure 5.19	Empirical nonparametric impact curve for US equity returns	205
Figure 5.20	Mean and variance forecasts computed as of December 2016	208
Figure 5.21	Recursive, in-sample mean and variance forecasts	208
Figure A.1	Alternative KDEs versus normal density	228
Figure 6.1	Rolling window versus RiskMetrics stock–bond covariances	232
Figure 6.2	Rolling window and RiskMetrics stock–bond correlations	232
Figure 6.3	Rolling window and RiskMetrics stock–bond correlation forecasts under restrictions to keep them in [− 1,1]	233
Figure 6.4	One-week-ahead predictions of US stock and bond return variances, covariances, and correlations	237
Figure 6.5	One-week-ahead predictions of US stock and bond return variances, covariances, and correlations	243
Figure 6.6	One-week-ahead predictions of US Stock–bond return correlations under diagonal VECH and full rank multivariate GARCH(1,1)	245
Figure 6.7	One-week-ahead predictions of US stock and bond return variances, covariances, and correlations	248
Figure 6.8	One-week-ahead predictions of US stock and bond return correlations with and without asymmetric effects in VECH and BEKK models. (A) Models with asymmetries. (B) Symmetric models	249
Figure 6.9	One-week-ahead predictions of US stock and bond return variances, covariances, and correlations from RiskMetrics/DCC(1) model	253
Figure 6.10	One-week-ahead predictions of US stock and bond return variances, covariances, and correlations from GARCH/DCC(1) model	253
Figure 6.11	One-week-ahead predictions of US stock and bond return covariances with and without asymmetric effects in a threshold GARCH/CCC	255
Figure 6.12	MLE output from E-Views for a Gaussian VAR(1) threshold VECH-GARCH(1,1,1) for 17 monthly series of stock returns	256
Figure 6.13	One-week-ahead predictions of Italian and Swiss stock return variances, covariances, and correlations from GARCH/DCC(1) model	257
Figure 6.14	One-week predictions of variance for US excess stock returns and changes in the slope (10-year–3-month rates) of the riskless yield curve	260
Figure 6.15	One-week predictions of US size and value mimicking portfolio return variances, covariances, and correlations from a two-factor model	260
Figure 6.16	One-week predictions of US size and value mimicking portfolio variances, covariances, and correlations from a threshold BEKK(1,1,1)	261
Figure 6.17	Predictions of variance for a 50–50 stock–bond balanced portfolio and of its correlation with HML returns from the two-factor model	261
Figure 6.18	One-weekly predictions of US size and value mimicking portfolio variances, covariances, and correlations of regression residuals	262
Figure 7.1	Comparing volatility filtered and smoothed from a SVM versus GARCH(1,1) filtered volatility	275
Figure 7.2	Observed and fitted log-squared S&P 500 returns	275
Figure 7.3	Comparing 1-day-ahead predicted variance from two alternative SVMs	277
Figure 7.4	One-day-ahead predicted variance from three models	277
Figure 7.5	Comparing 1-day-ahead predicted variance from two alternative SVMs	279
Figure 8.1	In-sample performance of linear versus breaking models	293
Figure 8.2	CUSUM and CUSUM square tests applied to a predictive linear model for Fama-French portfolio returns. (A) Excess market returns. (B) SMB factor. (C) HML portfolio	295
Figure 8.3	Andrews–Quandt Sup-LR tests over the subinterval fractions [0.15, 0.85]	297
Figure 8.4	In-sample performance of a linear model subject to two breaks	302
Figure 8.5	In-sample fit of linear versus threshold regression models	313
Figure 8.6	Regime classification from threshold regression model	314
Figure 8.7	Back-tested actual and forecast excess returns	314

Figure 8.8	Estimated logistic transition function and time series of estimated $F(\text{FFR}_t)$	320
Figure 8.9	Estimated exponential transition function and time series of estimated $F(\text{FFR}_{t-2})$	321
Figure 8.10	In-sample fit of an exponential smooth threshold regression	321
Figure 8.11	Estimated cumulative normal self-exciting transition function and time series of estimated $F(x_{t-2})$	324
Figure 9.1	State probabilities from three univariate MSIH models	335
Figure 9.2	Comparing single- and two-state MS models	337
Figure 9.3	Comparing two alternative MSI(2,0) models	338
Figure 9.4	Comparing two alternative MSIH(2,0) models	338
Figure 9.5	Comparing two alternative MSIARH(2,0) models	339
Figure 9.6	Comparing linear versus nonlinear persistence in MSIAR(2,1) models	339
Figure 9.7	Unconditional density implied by an MSIAR(2,1) model	341
Figure 9.8	Unconditional density implied by an MSI(2,0) model	341
Figure 9.9	Unconditional density implied by an MSIARH(2,1) model	342
Figure 9.10	Constant versus time-varying transition probabilities	348
Figure 9.11	Filtered state probabilities under constant versus time-varying transition probabilities	349
Figure 9.12	Filtered and smoothed state probabilities from two-state MS heteroskedastic regression	357
Figure 9.13	One-month predicted state probabilities from two-state MS heteroskedastic regression	357
Figure 9.14	Filtered and smoothed state probabilities of regime 1 from two-state MS heteroskedastic regression	362
Figure 9.15	In-sample predictions of 10-year treasury excess returns from three alternative models	365
Figure 9.16	Smoothed probabilities from MSIH(2) model with time-varying probabilities	368
Figure 9.17	Time-varying probabilities from MSIH(2) model	368
Figure 9.18	In-sample forecasts from MSIH(2) model with time-varying probabilities	368
Figure 9.19	Forecasts from three-state MSIVAR(2)-VECH ARCH(2) model	371
Figure 10.1	S&P 500 realized volatility at 5- and 10-min sampling frequency	384
Figure 10.2	S&P 500 realized volatility at 10-min frequency versus average realized volatility at 10-min with 1-min subsampling	385
Figure 10.3	Distribution of the logarithm of S&P 500 5-min RV	389
Figure 10.4	Distribution of standardized S&P 500 returns using 5-min RV	390
Figure 10.5	Plots of realized volatility forecasts for NYSE returns from HAR versus AR(1) models	392
Figure 10.6	Range-based volatility and square root of squared returns for S&P 500 data	393
Figure 10.7	Empirical distribution of the logarithm of a range-based variance proxy versus squared returns	394
Figure A.1	PDF of a standard normal variable	400
Figure A.2	CDF of a standard normal variable	401

List of Tables

Table 1.1	Output of a Linear Regression Model With Three Regressors	7
Table 1.2	Fama–French Linear Regression Model for US Oil Stock Returns	12
Table 1.3	Fama–French Linear Regression Model for US Oil Stock Returns	15
Table 1.4	Output of a RESET Test With $m = 2$	22
Table 1.5	Output of a RESET Test With $m = 2$—Estimates of the Unrestricted Model	23
Table 1.6	Output of a Chow Breakpoint Test	25
Table 1.7	Estimated p-Values From a Backward Elimination Algorithm	29
Table 1.8	Correlation Matrix of Regressors	30
Table 1.9	Variance Inflation Factors (VIFs)	31
Table 1.10	VIFs After Dropping One Regressor	31
Table 1.11	White Test for Heteroskedasticity	33
Table 1.12	Estimated Regression to Perform a White Test for Heteroskedasticity	33
Table 1.13	Results of a Breusch–Godfrey Test of Autocorrelation	35
Table 2.1A	Serial Correlation Structure of Simulated AR(1) Data	47
Table 2.1B	Serial Correlation Structure of Simulated WN Data	48
Table 2.2	A Summary of the Characteristics of AR, MA, and ARMA Models	62
Table 2.3	Serial Correlation Structure of the Changes in the US CPI	63
Table 2.4	Information Criteria for Alternative Models Used to Describe CPI Inflation	64
Table 2.5	Estimates of an ARMA(2,1) Model for the US CPI Inflation Rate	67
Table 2.6A	The SACF of Residuals and Squared Residuals of an ARMA(2,1) Model for US CPI Inflation Data	70
Table 2.6B	The SACF of Residuals and Squared Residuals of an ARMA(2,1) Model for US CPI Inflation Data	70
Table 3.1	Descriptive Statistics of the 1-Month and 10-Year US Treasury Yield Series	80
Table 3.2	Sample Cross-Correlations Between 1-Month and 10-Year Treasury Yields	81
Table 3.3	Estimation Output of a VAR(1) Model for the 1-Month, 1-, 5-, and 10-Year Yields of the US Treasury Bonds	93
Table 3.4	VAR Selection Criteria Applied to 1-Month, 1-, 5-, and 10-Year US Treasury Yields	97
Table 3.5	Forecast Accuracy Measures for a VAR(2) Model of 1-Month, 1-, 5-, and 10-Year US Treasury Yields	99
Table 3.6	Forecast Accuracy Measures for a VAR(11) Model of 1-Month, 1-, 5-, and 10-Year US Treasury Yields	99
Table 3.7	Forecast Error Variance Decomposition of 1-Month, 1-, 5-, 10-Year Treasury Yields When the Cholesky Ordering Is 1-Month, 1-, 5-, 10-Year Yields	106
Table 3.8	Forecast Error Variance Decomposition of the 10-Year Treasury Yields (10-Year Yield on the Top of the Cholesky Ordering)	108
Table 3.9	Granger Causality Tests	110
Table 4.1	Sample ACF and Estimated AR(p) Models on RW Series	116
Table 4.2	Engle–Granger Tests of Trivariate Cointegration	142
Table 4.3	Phillips–Ouliaris Tests of Trivariate Cointegration	142
Table 4.4	Unit Root Tests Applied to US Nominal Treasury Rates	147
Table 5.1	Sample ACF and PACF for Squared Stock Returns and Cross-Sample Correlogram of Levels and Cubes of Returns	155
Table 5.2	Worked Out Calculations for Rolling Window Variance Forecasts	159
Table 5.3	Sample ACF and PACF for US Excess Stock Returns	165
Table 5.4	Sample ACF and PACF for Squared Residuals	166
Table 5.5	Calculations of RiskMetrics and ARCH Variance Forecasts	167
Table 5.6	Sample ACF/PACF for Squared Residuals and Cross-Correlogram Between Standardized Residuals and Their Squares, RiskMetrics Model	170
Table 5.7	Sample ACF/PACF for Squared Residuals and Cross-Correlogram Between Standardized Residuals and Their Squares, ARCH(6) Model	171
Table 5.8	Calculations for RiskMetrics and GARCH Variance Forecasts	173
Table 5.9	ACF/PACF for Residuals and Squared Standardized Residuals	176
Table 5.10	ACF/PACF of Squared Standardized Residuals from GARCH(1,1)	176
Table 5.11	Information Criteria-Based Model Selection	181
Table 5.12	Information Criteria-Based Model Selection for Different Data	185

Table 5.13	Information Criteria-Based Model Selection	189
Table 5.14	Comparing ML Estimates of Gaussian Versus *t*-Student GARCH	193
Table 8.1	Results of Chow Break Tests for Three Selected Dates	292
Table 8.2	Results of Bai–Perron's Sequential Multiple Break Tests	301
Table 8.3	Results of Standard ADF Tests Applied to Aggregate US Dividends and Earnings	305
Table 8.4	Results of Breakpoint-Modified ADF Tests for Aggregate Dividends and Earnings—Innovational Outliers	305
Table 8.5	Results of Breakpoint-Modified ADF Tests for Aggregate Dividends and Earnings—Additive Outliers	306
Table 8.6	Threshold Specification Analysis Based on Sequential Tests	313
Table 8.7	Threshold Specification Analysis Based on the SBIC	314
Table 8.8	Linearity Tests Based on (up to) the Fourth-Order Taylor Expansion	324
Table 8.9	Additional Nonlinearity Tests Based on (up to) the Fourth-Order Taylor Expansion	325
Table 9.1	Univariate MS Model Selection	333
Table 9.2	Multivariate MS Model Selection	335
Table 9.3	MS Regression Model Selection	343
Table 10.1	SACF and SPACF of S&P 500 RV at 5-min Sampling Frequency	388

Preface

This textbook is the result of more than 10 years spent in the classroom, teaching MSc-level financial econometrics to a very diverse crowd of students, at Bocconi University, Italy and University of Manchester, United Kingdom. During these years, one of the authors has managed to change side of the classroom and blossom in a well-liked instructor. The other author proudly claims to be responsible of such an awesome shift of her role. In any event, we have both retained and developed over time a keen awareness of the fact that similarly to Stephen Hawking's famous quote—and contrary to what students and colleagues may think before approaching applied statistics—also in econometrics "there is no unique picture of reality." As a result, in *Essentials of Time Series for Financial Applications* we have wholeheartedly applied this principle and—intentionally and unintentionally—presented a range of models and inferential techniques that just aim at providing different and concurring answers to three basic questions: Can we forecast the conditional mean of one or more time series? Can we forecast the conditional variances and covariances of the same series? What are the trade-offs between these two key applications and approaches? As simple as these questions may sound, the book witnesses the existence of a wide variety of methods and techniques and therefore a range of potential answers. These all represents different, equally valid and faithful pictures of the same reality, the data—in our case, financial time series data.

In our treatment, this feature is greatly emphasized by the constant interplay between theoretical definitions and results and a large number of fully developed examples that are used to either illustrate the methodologies at work or to openly discuss of their limitations in actual cases. In fact, additional examples that could not find space in the book have been available in the book's website (at http://essentialoftimeseries.wordpress.com), where also the data and EViews worksheets are made available to a Reader. In fact, practitioners and researchers in empirical finance approaching *Essentials of Time Series for Financial Applications* may even find it productive to work through the book backwards, i.e., past some introductory notions and definitions in each chapter, to focus first on the examples to then better understand the theoretical concepts.

The book has a rather linear structure and goes from simple and introductory topics, such as Chapter 1 on the linear regression model and Chapter 2 on ARMA models, to more advanced but still MSc-level topics, such as Vector autoregressions in Chapter 3 and ARCH models in Chapter 5, to more advanced topics in multivariate (like in Chapter 6 on conditional heteroskedastic models) and nonlinear (like in Chapters 8 and 9, on threshold and Markov switching models with regimes) econometrics analysis. The latter set of topics and chapters may find use in advanced, elective MSc courses in financial econometrics or even as a background Reader in a first-year doctoral course in the econometrics of finance. However, the book is sufficiently rich and structured in a modular fashion to allow a use that could be either mostly focused on models of the conditional mean under stationary linear processes (Chapters 2 on ARMA and 3 on VARMA), followed by cointegrated vector error correction models (Chapter 4), and finally by nonlinear regime switching models (Chapters 8 and 9). Alternatively, one can imagine a pedagogical path focused instead on modeling and forecasting conditional variances and covariances, and more generally conditionally higher-order moments, and therefore centered on Chapters 5 (on ARCH), 6 (on multivariate GARCH and dynamic conditional correlation approaches), 7 (on stochastic volatility), 9 (on Markov switching variances and correlations), and 10 (on realized variance). Both these keys to potentially read and present the material in *Essentials of Time Series for Financial Applications* are strengthened by a number of additional "concept boxes" including additional material and explanations that, for pure reasons of space, could not be included but that are available at the book's website (at http://essentialoftimeseries.wordpress.com).

The book developed out of our lectures, tutorials, and thesis supervisions. We are grateful first and foremost to many students over the years whose questions, detailed error-hunting, and comments have shaped the course of the manuscript and helped us to put in greater focus the trickiest points. We are grateful to Elena De Gioannis, Serena De

Lorenzi, and Valentina Massagli for their precious work as research assistants and to Beatrice Franzolini for her help with Chapter 1 that reflects portion of her background research and notes. We also thank Federico Mainardi for volunteering to proofread a large portion of the book. All errors remain our own of course. As for Bocconi's unparalleled research and teaching environment, our praise cannot escape quoting Frederik Nietsche's from his 1889 *Twilight of the Idols, or, How to Philosophize with a Hammer*: "Was dich nicht umbringt, macht dich starker."

Chapter 1

Linear Regression Model

The roots of education are bitter, but the fruit is sweet.

Aristotle

In this chapter, we present one of the basic, essential tools of applied time series analysis, the linear regression model and a range of statistical tools that can be used to investigate (linear) relations among two or more random variables, both in time series and in cross-sectional frameworks. To provide an intuitive set up to the problem, a linear regression model is characterized by the selection of one variable, y, called the *dependent variable* (or regressand), and by one or more *explanatory variables* $x_1, x_2, \ldots, x_K$, also called *independent variables* (or regressors). The aim of a regression model (when there is little ambiguity, we shall drop the reference to its linear nature) is to explain (or predict) the values assumed by the dependent variable exploiting the information summarized by the values taken by the regressors.

Despite the arguable simplicity of the model, it is crucial to consider which underlying hypotheses are routinely made to make inference possible and to appreciate the different properties of alternative inferential approaches. In fact, there is little doubt that a superficial use of the model may often lead to misguided or at least unreliable conclusions.

Therefore, in this chapter, we present the basic structure of a classical regression model and a range of suitable estimation methods along with their properties. In addition, in order to retain a strong applied orientation, we also provide some pointers as to how to safely interpret the results of an analysis based on the estimation of linear regression models.

1.1 INFERENCE IN LINEAR REGRESSION MODELS

Common statements reported by average users of econometric modeling strategies are that they would like to understand from the observed data, say, daily returns on a stock portfolio, "from where they came" or better "how they have been generated." Such a language is not completely random, because also in a technical sense, when we collect and observe samples of data, we interpret their values as realizations of an unobservable *data generating process* (DGP), which is the object we are really interested in (the *population*). In simpler words, the underlying, albeit often implicit, assumption is that there exists a stochastic process, which is a sequence (or collection) of random variables from which the data came, so that every sample value that we observe simply represents a single realization of a random variable. Therefore, we cannot directly observe the random variables themselves but—for each of them—only a number of their realizations (often only one). For instance, when it comes to the closing S&P 500 index price on August 4, 2017, we can collect (at most, assuming the market has not been halted or closed out of extraordinary circumstances, as it occasionally happens) one observation: we have no way to rewind history or to ponder different realizations of alternative histories. However, if we consider the random variable defined as "the price of the first security traded at market open on every first day of the week," then we have multiple realizations for the same random variable.

Our goal is therefore to investigate the nature of the DGP, that is, to capture the features of the (collection or sequence of) random variables from which the data were generated. To perform this task, first, some assumptions on the DGP have to be cautiously introduced (i.e., we say that we select a *statistical model*); second, a sample of data—often a simple random sample made of independent and identical random variables, although other, more complex circumstances may also be addressed—must be collected to estimate the parameters in the model using inferential procedures.

Essentials of Time Series for Financial Applications. DOI: https://doi.org/10.1016/B978-0-12-813409-2.00001-7

From this point onward, we shall assume to work with time series variables and to have collected the data concerning both the dependent variable y and the K regressors, $x_1, x_2, \ldots, x_K$ over a sampling period of length T.[1] A linear regression model is then:

$$\mathbf{y} = \mathbf{X\beta} + \boldsymbol{\varepsilon} \qquad \boldsymbol{\varepsilon} \sim (\mathbf{0}, \sigma^2\mathbf{I}_T), \tag{1.1}$$

where $\mathbf{y}$ is the $T \times 1$ vector collecting the values assumed by the dependent variable, $\mathbf{X}$ is a $T \times (K+1)$ matrix with a first column of ones and collecting in the remaining columns the values assumed by every of the K explanatory variables, $\boldsymbol{\beta}$ is a $(K+1)$-dimensional vector of parameters called *regression coefficients* and $\boldsymbol{\varepsilon}$ is a $T \times 1$ vector of error terms, which represent all the unobservable, random factors and shocks (such as omitted regressors or measurement errors) that contribute to the realized value of $\mathbf{y}$. Note that Eq. (1.1) does not commit to any specific assumption on the distribution of the errors, assumption that is therefore not used in what follows. However, if Eq. (1.1) is extended to introduce an explicit assumption on the normal nature of the disturbances, $\boldsymbol{\varepsilon} \sim N(\mathbf{0}, \sigma^2\mathbf{I}_T)$, the model is called the *classical linear regression model*.

To make Eq. (1.1) more transparent, we can rewrite in its extended, algebraic form to provide the following system of equations:

$$\begin{aligned}
y_1 &= \beta_0 + \beta_1 x_{1,1} + \beta_2 x_{2,1} + \cdots + \beta_K x_{K,1} + \varepsilon_1 \\
y_2 &= \beta_0 + \beta_1 x_{1,2} + \beta_2 x_{2,2} + \cdots + \beta_K x_{K,2} + \varepsilon_2 \\
&\vdots \\
y_t &= \beta_0 + \beta_1 x_{1,t} + \beta_2 x_{2,t} + \cdots + \beta_K x_{K,t} + \varepsilon_t \\
&\vdots \\
y_T &= \beta_0 + \beta_1 x_{1,T} + \beta_2 x_{2,T} + \cdots + \beta_K x_{K,T} + \varepsilon_T,
\end{aligned} \tag{1.2}$$

where $\varepsilon_t \sim N(0, \sigma^2)$ for every t and $Cov(\varepsilon_t, \varepsilon_s) = 0$ for every t and s with $t \neq s$. As shown in Eq. (1.2), in a linear regression model, the value of y at time t can be expressed as a linear combination of the observable values assumed by the explanatory variables plus an unobserved, zero-mean error term.

EXAMPLE 1.1

Suppose that you have collected daily returns on a stock portfolio over the two most recent months. A way to perform a quantitative analysis of the performance of this portfolio is to estimate a regression that explains stock returns using the returns of the market portfolio. This is the well-known market model: a simple statistical regression in which the dependent variable is the return of a security of interest and there is only one explanatory variable, the return on the market portfolio. The assumption behind the market model is that the performance of any security can be additively factored as a component related to the movement of the market and a residual portion, uniquely related to the behavior or properties of the specific firm (sometimes called idiosyncratic risk).

As anticipated, we are interested in the DGP of the dependent variable y_t. Clearly, while stating the basic equation of the model in Eq. (1.1), we are already making specific (in fact, restrictive) assumptions listed below over the functional form of the process.

- *Linearity*: The correct functional form is linear, that is, the expected value of y_t is just a linear combination of the values of the regressors.
- *Zero-mean errors*: The errors have mean equal to 0, that is, $E[\varepsilon_t] = 0$. Thus, the effects of the unobservable or omitted factors can be either positive or negative for a single observation, but their expected value is 0.
- *Homoskedasticity*: The error term is a random variable with constant variance over time, $Var[\varepsilon_t] = \sigma^2$.
- *Zero serial correlation*: The error term does not depend on its own past values, $Cov[\varepsilon_t, \varepsilon_{t-k}] = E[\varepsilon_t \varepsilon_{t-k}] = 0$, where $k \neq 0$.
- *Normally distributed errors:* The errors are normally distributed. This assumption is needed mostly to perform hypothesis testing and to compute confidence intervals in small samples but, as we shall see later in this chapter, this can be generalized or even removed, at the cost of either introducing alternative assumptions or resorting to large-sample (only asymptotically valid) results.

1. The case in which we deal with cross-sectional data can be analyzed in a similar way. We would select a sample of N contemporaneous observations, instead of T observations collected over time, from a population composed by many more statistical units, from which we sample.

Finally, we also introduce the (rather implausible) assumption below.

- *Correctly selected regressors* (i.e., no omitted explanatory variables): The matrix $\mathbf{X}$ collects all the relevant regressors, which means that we are neither forgetting any relevant observable regressor that contributes to explain the dependent variable nor including any redundant regressor.

In addition to this condition, for the time being, we also assume that all regressors are non-stochastic, which means that unlike y_t, they are not a realization of a random variable. However, this restriction shall be removed in Section 1.1.6.

From Eq. (1.1) it follows that the dependent variable $\mathbf{y}$ is normally distributed with expected value equal to $\mathbf{X\beta}$ and a diagonal covariance matrix where all the elements on the main diagonal are equal to σ^2 (we also call it scalar matrix):

$$\mathbf{y} \sim N(\mathbf{X\beta}, \sigma^2\mathbf{I}_T). \tag{1.3}$$

In order to gain knowledge on the features of the DGP, of the random time series $\mathbf{y}$, we first estimate the $K+2$ regression coefficients collected in the vector $\boldsymbol{\beta}$ and the variance parameter, σ^2. Moreover, on the basis of the estimated vector of regression coefficients ($\hat{\boldsymbol{\beta}}$), we are able to compute the estimates of the dependent variable resulting from the model in Eq. (1.1), the so-called *fitted values*, $\hat{y}_t = \mathbf{x}_t'\hat{\boldsymbol{\beta}}$. In matrix notation, we denote by $\hat{\mathbf{y}}$ the T-dimensional vector that collects all the fitted values at time t, with $t = 1, ..., T$. Using the estimated fitted values, it is also possible to compute the sample counterpart of the error term, the vector of *residuals*, defined as $\hat{\boldsymbol{\varepsilon}} = \mathbf{y} - \mathbf{X}\hat{\boldsymbol{\beta}} = \mathbf{y} - \hat{\mathbf{y}}$. Based on this framework, we are now able to introduce a few key inference tools.

1.1.1 The Ordinary Least Squares Estimator

The most widely used estimation method applied to a regression is the *ordinary least squares (OLS)* procedure, which displays many desirable properties, listed and discussed below. Numerically, the estimates resulting from this method are the ones—assumed to be unique—that minimize the squared distance between the observed values $\mathbf{y}$ and the fitted values $\hat{\mathbf{y}}$ computed from the model (over the available sample) in correspondence to a vector of coefficients, $\boldsymbol{\beta}$:

$$\hat{\boldsymbol{\beta}}^{OLS} = \arg\min_{\boldsymbol{\beta}} (\mathbf{y} - \hat{\mathbf{y}})'(\mathbf{y} - \hat{\mathbf{y}}). \tag{1.4}$$

The logic is that, if you accept to measure the distance between the sample values of the dependent variable and the fitted values produced by the model with their squared difference, then Eq. (1.4) is simply searching for the vector $\boldsymbol{\beta}$ that allows the model to fit as well as possible. The advantage of identifying "distance" with squared differences is that the square function is always positive (i.e., it prevents negative $y_t - \hat{y}_t$ to be compensated by positive ones), it is symmetric (i.e., it does not favor any sign), and it is everywhere differentiable, what we sometimes refer to as being a *smooth function*. Note that because $\hat{\boldsymbol{\varepsilon}}(\boldsymbol{\beta}) \equiv \mathbf{y} - \hat{\mathbf{y}} = \mathbf{y} - \mathbf{X}\hat{\boldsymbol{\beta}}$, the OLS estimator also minimizes the sum of the squared residuals,

$$\hat{\boldsymbol{\beta}}^{OLS} = \arg\min_{\boldsymbol{\beta}} \hat{\boldsymbol{\varepsilon}}(\boldsymbol{\beta})'\hat{\boldsymbol{\varepsilon}}(\boldsymbol{\beta}). \tag{1.5}$$

To derive the expression for $\hat{\boldsymbol{\beta}}^{OLS}$, we minimize the scalar objective sum of squared residuals (SSR) function $\text{SSR}(\boldsymbol{\beta})$ with respect to $\boldsymbol{\beta}$:

$$\begin{aligned} \text{SSR}(\hat{\boldsymbol{\beta}}) &= (\mathbf{y} - \hat{\mathbf{y}})'(\mathbf{y} - \hat{\mathbf{y}}) = (\mathbf{y} - \mathbf{X}\hat{\boldsymbol{\beta}})'(\mathbf{y} - \mathbf{X}\hat{\boldsymbol{\beta}}) \\ &= \mathbf{y}'\mathbf{y} - 2\hat{\boldsymbol{\beta}}'\mathbf{X}'\mathbf{y} + \hat{\boldsymbol{\beta}}'\mathbf{X}'\mathbf{X}\hat{\boldsymbol{\beta}}. \end{aligned} \tag{1.6}$$

To find the (hopefully global) minimum, we start out by first equating the vector of first (partial) derivatives of $\text{SSR}(\boldsymbol{\beta})$ (also called the *gradient*) with respect to $\boldsymbol{\beta}$ to a vector of zeros:

$$\frac{\partial \ell(\boldsymbol{\beta})}{\partial \boldsymbol{\beta}} = -2\mathbf{X}'\mathbf{y} + 2\mathbf{X}'\mathbf{X}\boldsymbol{\beta} \Rightarrow -2\mathbf{X}'\mathbf{y} + 2\mathbf{X}'\mathbf{X}\hat{\boldsymbol{\beta}}^{OLS} = \mathbf{0}. \tag{1.7}$$

It follows that the OLS estimator is:

$$\hat{\boldsymbol{\beta}}^{OLS} = (\mathbf{X}'\mathbf{X})^{-1}\mathbf{X}'\mathbf{y}. \tag{1.8}$$

The OLS estimator $\hat{\boldsymbol{\beta}}^{OLS}$ presents the following properties:

- It is *linear*, in the sense that it is a linear combination $\hat{\boldsymbol{\beta}}^{OLS} = \mathbf{L}'\mathbf{y} = \underbrace{(\mathbf{X}'\mathbf{X})^{-1}\mathbf{X}'}_{\mathbf{L}}\mathbf{y}$ of the values of the dependent variable.
- It is *unbiased*, meaning that its expected value equals the true (and yet unknown) parameter, that is,

$$\begin{aligned} E\left[\hat{\boldsymbol{\beta}}^{OLS}\right] &= (\mathbf{X}'\mathbf{X})^{-1}\mathbf{X}'E[\mathbf{y}] = (\mathbf{X}'\mathbf{X})^{-1}\mathbf{X}'(E[\mathbf{X}\boldsymbol{\beta}] + E[\boldsymbol{\varepsilon}]) \\ &= (\mathbf{X}'\mathbf{X})^{-1}(\mathbf{X}'\mathbf{X})\boldsymbol{\beta} = \boldsymbol{\beta}. \end{aligned} \tag{1.9}$$

- Its covariance matrix is $\sigma^2(\mathbf{X}'\mathbf{X})^{-1}$, that is,

$$\begin{aligned} Var\left[\hat{\boldsymbol{\beta}}^{OLS}\right] &= Var\left[(\mathbf{X}'\mathbf{X})^{-1}\mathbf{X}'\mathbf{y}\right] = (\mathbf{X}'\mathbf{X})^{-1}\mathbf{X}'Var[\mathbf{y}]\mathbf{X}(\mathbf{X}'\mathbf{X})^{-1} \\ &= (\mathbf{X}'\mathbf{X})^{-1}\mathbf{X}'Var[\mathbf{X}\boldsymbol{\beta} + \boldsymbol{\varepsilon}]\mathbf{X}(\mathbf{X}'\mathbf{X})^{-1} \\ &= (\mathbf{X}'\mathbf{X})^{-1}\mathbf{X}'\sigma^2\mathbf{I}_T\mathbf{X}(\mathbf{X}'\mathbf{X})^{-1} = \sigma^2(\mathbf{X}'\mathbf{X})^{-1} \end{aligned} \tag{1.10}$$

because $Var[\mathbf{X}\boldsymbol{\beta} + \boldsymbol{\varepsilon}] = Var[\boldsymbol{\varepsilon}]$.

- It is normally distributed, being a linear combination of the random variables that compose the random sample on the dependent variable, each of which is normally distributed, that is,

$$\hat{\boldsymbol{\beta}}^{OLS} \sim N(\boldsymbol{\beta}, \sigma^2(\mathbf{X}'\mathbf{X})^{-1}). \tag{1.11}$$

- It is the *best linear unbiased estimator (BLUE)*, meaning that among the class of linear unbiased estimators for $\boldsymbol{\beta}$, $\hat{\boldsymbol{\beta}}^{OLS}$ has the minimum variance; this last property is usually referred to as the *Gauss–Markov theorem*; equivalently, we also say that $\hat{\boldsymbol{\beta}}^{OLS}$ is the (uniformly) minimum variance estimator within the linear class, that is, the simplest possible class.

RESULT 1.1 (Gauss–Markov theorem)

If in the linear regression model (1.1), the matrix of regressors is correctly specified, and the error terms of the model have zero expectations, are uncorrelated, and homoskedastic, then the OLS estimator $\hat{\boldsymbol{\beta}}^{OLS}$ is BLUE.

Proof (sketch): Our strategy consists in first computing the covariance matrix of a generic linear unbiased estimator for $\boldsymbol{\beta}$ and then in comparing this result with the covariance matrix of the OLS estimator.

Consider a generic estimator $\tilde{\boldsymbol{\beta}}$ for $\boldsymbol{\beta}$. First, we impose that $\tilde{\boldsymbol{\beta}}$ is linear, so there exists a non-random matrix $\mathbf{C}$ and a non-random vector $\mathbf{d}$ such that $\tilde{\boldsymbol{\beta}} = \mathbf{C}\mathbf{y} + \mathbf{d}$. Therefore, we have that $E[\tilde{\boldsymbol{\beta}}] = E\left[\mathbf{C}\mathbf{y} + \mathbf{d}\right] = \mathbf{C}\mathbf{X}\boldsymbol{\beta} + \mathbf{d}$. We now want to consider the class of unbiased estimators only, and as such we impose that $E[\tilde{\boldsymbol{\beta}}] = \boldsymbol{\beta}$ holds, so that:

$$E\left[\tilde{\boldsymbol{\beta}}\right] = \mathbf{C}\mathbf{X}\boldsymbol{\beta} + \mathbf{d} = \boldsymbol{\beta}. \tag{1.12}$$

To satisfy Eq. (1.12), $\mathbf{CX}$ must be the identity matrix and $\mathbf{d}$ a vector of zeros. We now define a matrix $\mathbf{R} \equiv \mathbf{C} - (\mathbf{X}'\mathbf{X})^{-1}\mathbf{X}'$. By construction we have that $\mathbf{C} = \mathbf{R} + (\mathbf{X}'\mathbf{X})^{-1}\mathbf{X}'$ and from the condition $\mathbf{CX} = \mathbf{I}_T$, it follows that $\mathbf{RX} = \mathbf{O}$, a matrix of zeros, because $\mathbf{CX} = \mathbf{RX} + (\mathbf{X}'\mathbf{X})^{-1}(\mathbf{X}'\mathbf{X}) = \mathbf{I}_T$. Putting these facts together, we have:

$$\begin{aligned} Var[\tilde{\boldsymbol{\beta}}] &= Var[\mathbf{C}\mathbf{y}] = [\mathbf{R} + (\mathbf{X}'\mathbf{X})^{-1}\mathbf{X}']Var[\mathbf{y}][\mathbf{R} + (\mathbf{X}'\mathbf{X})^{-1}\mathbf{X}']' \\ &= \sigma^2\left[\mathbf{R}\mathbf{R}' + \underbrace{\mathbf{R}\mathbf{X}}_{=\mathbf{O}}(\mathbf{X}'\mathbf{X})^{-1} + (\mathbf{X}'\mathbf{X})^{-1}\underbrace{\mathbf{X}'\mathbf{R}'}_{=\mathbf{O}} + \underbrace{(\mathbf{X}'\mathbf{X})^{-1}(\mathbf{X}'\mathbf{X})}_{=\mathbf{I}_T}(\mathbf{X}'\mathbf{X})^{-1}\right] \\ &= \sigma^2\left[\mathbf{R}\mathbf{R}' + (\mathbf{X}'\mathbf{X})^{-1}\right] = Var\left[\hat{\boldsymbol{\beta}}^{OLS}\right] + \sigma^2\mathbf{R}\mathbf{R}'. \end{aligned} \tag{1.13}$$

This shows that the covariance matrix of any linear unbiased estimator can be expressed as the sum of the variance of the OLS estimator plus the matrix $\sigma^2\mathbf{RR}'$. To conclude the proof, it is sufficient to remark that $\sigma^2\mathbf{RR}'$ is a semipositive definite quadratic form because it is the product between a positive scalar and matrix multiplied by its transpose, a sort of "matrix squared." In conclusion, because $Var[\hat{\boldsymbol{\beta}}^{OLS}]$ can always be

(Continued)

RESULT 1.1 (Continued)

decomposed as $Var[\tilde{\boldsymbol{\beta}}]$ minus a semipositive definite matrix, $Var[\hat{\boldsymbol{\beta}}^{OLS}]$ is always smaller than the covariance matrix of any other linear unbiased estimator (even though only in a matrix form). When $K = 1$, then it also follows that $Var[\tilde{\beta}] = Var[\hat{\beta}^{OLS}] + \sigma^2 R^2 \Rightarrow Var[\hat{\beta}^{OLS}] \leq Var[\tilde{\beta}]$. Hence, the covariance of $\hat{\boldsymbol{\beta}}^{OLS}$ is the lower bound of the variance for all linear unbiased estimators of $\boldsymbol{\beta}$. Moreover, $Var[\tilde{\boldsymbol{\beta}}] = Var[\hat{\boldsymbol{\beta}}^{OLS}]$, if and only if $\mathbf{R} = \mathbf{0}$, but when $\mathbf{R} = \mathbf{0}$, $\mathbf{C} = (\mathbf{X}'\mathbf{X})^{-1}\mathbf{X}'$ and $\tilde{\boldsymbol{\beta}} = \hat{\boldsymbol{\beta}}^{OLS}$.

Along with these important properties of the OLS estimator, the least squares procedure ensures also three additional, desirable algebraic properties of the sample residuals, provided that the model has an intercept:

- The sample average of the OLS residuals is 0, $T^{-1}\sum_{t=1}^{T}\hat{\varepsilon}_t = 0$.
- The sample covariance between the OLS residuals and the regressors is 0, $T^{-1}\sum_{t=1}^{T} x_{k,t}\hat{\varepsilon}_t = 0$ for every $k = 1, 2, ..., K$.
- The sample covariance between the OLS residuals and the fitted values for the dependent variable equals 0, $T^{-1}\sum_{t=1}^{T}\hat{y}_t\hat{\varepsilon}_t = 0$.

To prove these properties is fairly easy as it only requires algebraic manipulations, and therefore this is left as an exercise for the Reader.

Also note that from the definition of the residuals, we can express every realization of y as a sum of the correspondent fitted value and the OLS residual:

$$y_t = \hat{y}_t + \hat{\varepsilon}_t. \tag{1.14}$$

It is straightforward to prove that Eq. (1.14) and the earlier result on the sample average of the residuals imply that the sample average of the dependent variable y is equal to the sample average of the fitted values. These results will be soon very important when we will define and measure the goodness of fit of a model.

To complete the estimation of all parameters in the model, we also need to define an estimator for σ, as the function minimized according to the OLS criterion in Eq. (1.4) does not depend on it. The OLS estimation of the residual variance parameter is simply

$$\hat{s}^2_{OLS} = \frac{\hat{\boldsymbol{\varepsilon}}'\hat{\boldsymbol{\varepsilon}}}{T-K-1}, \tag{1.15}$$

where $\hat{\boldsymbol{\varepsilon}}$ is the OLS residual obtained using $\hat{\boldsymbol{\beta}}^{OLS}$ as the estimator of $\boldsymbol{\beta}$. The OLS estimator $\hat{s}^2_{OLS}$ is characterized by the following, useful properties:

- $\hat{s}^2_{OLS}$ is unbiased, that is,

$$\hat{\boldsymbol{\varepsilon}} = \mathbf{y} - \mathbf{X}\hat{\boldsymbol{\beta}}^{OLS} = \mathbf{y} - \mathbf{X}(\mathbf{X}'\mathbf{X})^{-1}\mathbf{X}'\mathbf{y} = [\mathbf{I}_T - \mathbf{X}(\mathbf{X}'\mathbf{X})^{-1}\mathbf{X}']\mathbf{y} \tag{1.16}$$

- its variance is $2\sigma^4/(T-K-1)$.
- It has minimum variance within the class of unbiased estimators for the variance parameter σ^2.
- It is a quadratic form that involves normally distributed variables and as a result:

$$(T-K-1)\frac{\hat{s}^2_{OLS}}{\sigma^2} \sim \chi^2_{T-K-1}. \tag{1.17}$$

Notably, the OLS method does not require the introduction of any assumption on the distribution of the error term. In particular, we have not used the normal distribution hypothesis to derive either the estimator in Eq. (1.8) or the one in Eq. (1.15). In other words, the normality assumption only helped us to characterize the distribution of the estimators, not their identity or formulation.

1.1.2 Goodness of Fit Measures

Suppose now that we have estimated the model and computed the fitted values $\hat{\mathbf{y}}$ and the residuals $\hat{\boldsymbol{\varepsilon}}$. As already emphasized by Eq. (1.14), every realization of $\mathbf{y}$ is the sum of two variables $\mathbf{y} = \hat{\mathbf{y}} + \hat{\boldsymbol{\varepsilon}}$. The fitted value represents the component of $\mathbf{y}$ that we are able to explain (and predict) using the information provided by the explanatory variables in $\mathbf{X}$, while the residuals are the components of $\mathbf{y}$ that we are not able to explain (and predict). An ideal result would be then that all the information contained in the dependent variable $\mathbf{y}$ could be perfectly represented by the fitted values only and all the residuals were exactly 0. On the contrary, the worst case would emerge when all the fitted values were equal to some uninformative constant—which indicates that $\mathbf{X}$ has no information content—while all the variability in $\mathbf{y}$ would be left to the residual terms. To measure how much of the variability of $\mathbf{y}$ the model can explain, we use as a measure of variability the *sum of the squared deviations from the mean*. Clearly, such a measure is sensible because built in a way consistent with the objective function in Eq. (1.4). When this measure is computed with reference to the dependent variables in $\mathbf{y}$, it is called *total sum of squares (SST)*:

$$\mathrm{SST} = \sum_{t=1}^{T} (y_t - \bar{y})^2 \text{ where } \bar{y} = \frac{1}{T}\sum_{t=1}^{T} y_t. \tag{1.18}$$

When we compute the same measure on the fitted values and the residuals, we obtain the *explained sum of squares (SSE)* and the *residual sum of squares (SSR)*, which are defined respectively as:

$$\mathrm{SSE} = \sum_{t=1}^{T} (\hat{y}_t - \bar{y})^2. \tag{1.19}$$

$$\mathrm{SSR} = \sum_{t=1}^{T} \hat{\varepsilon}_t^2. \tag{1.20}$$

It is easy to prove that SST can be expressed as the sum of SSE and SSR, SST = SSR + SSE:

$$\begin{aligned}\mathrm{SST} &= \sum_{t=1}^{T}(y_t-\bar{y})^2 = \sum_{t=1}^{T}(y_t-\bar{y}+\hat{y}_t-\hat{y}_t)^2 \\ &= \sum_{t=1}^{T}\left[\hat{\varepsilon}_t+(\hat{y}_t-\bar{y})\right]^2 = \sum_{t=1}^{T}\left[\hat{\varepsilon}_t^2 + 2\hat{\varepsilon}_t(\hat{y}_t-\bar{y}) + (\hat{y}_t-\bar{y})^2\right] \\ &= \sum_{t=1}^{T}\hat{\varepsilon}_t^2 + 0 + \sum_{t=1}^{T}(\hat{y}_t-\bar{y})^2 = \mathrm{SSR} + \mathrm{SSE}.\end{aligned} \tag{1.21}$$

To measure what fraction of the variability in $\mathbf{y}$ can be explained through its linear relation with the regressors, we can compute the R^2 (also called *coefficient of determination*) of the model, which is defined as:

$$R^2 = \frac{\mathrm{SSE}}{\mathrm{SST}} = 1 - \frac{\mathrm{SSR}}{\mathrm{SST}}. \tag{1.22}$$

The ratio in Eq. (1.22) is often multiplied by 100 to obtain the percentage of variability of the dependent variable explained by the model. Thus, from Eq. (1.21) and from the positivity of the sum of squared deviation from the mean, it follows that the R^2 can only take values between 0 and 1. The higher the R^2, the better is the fit of the model. Even though this is completely sensible, this measure presents an important limitation: it never decreases when the number of regressors increases, even if the added regressors are (almost) irrelevant and they happen to pick up some variability in $\mathbf{y}$ by pure chance. Therefore, R^2 does not provide a reliable index to compare models built on a different number of explanatory variables. To overcome this limitation, it is common to apply a correction to Eq. (1.22) to obtain the *adjusted* R^2:

$$R^2_{\mathrm{Adj}} = \left(R^2 - \frac{K}{T-1}\right)\frac{T-1}{T-K-1}. \tag{1.23}$$

The adjusted R^2 varies between 0 and 1, but it can no longer be interpreted as the percentage of explained variability to the adjusted R^2 penalizes the standard R^2 measure so that it declines when weak, almost-irrelevant regressors are added. Of course, the penalization applied to the R^2 is based on a sensible but arbitrary functional modification. In Chapter 2 we shall introduce additional indices of goodness fit that are based on similar principles. Eq. (1.23) is then commonly used to compare the goodness of fit of alternative models, based on a different number of regressors.

EXAMPLE 1.2

Table 1.1 shows the results of OLS estimation of a linear regression model, in which the dependent variable is the daily excess return on a portfolio composted by stocks of US firms operating in the food industry and where the regressors are the so-called Fama–French factors, which are supposed to pick up systematic influences of general aggregate economic conditions on the equity prices and hence returns. The returns are in excess of the daily return on the 1-month Treasury Bill. In the table, the regressors are labeled as Excess MKT, SMB (Small Minus Big), and HML (High Minus Low).

The OLS estimates of the regression coefficients are reported in the column *Coefficient*, meaning that the estimated regression is:

$$(R_t - R^f) = 0.018 + 0.747(R_{MKT,t} - R^f) - 0.246\,\text{SMB}_t + 0.015\,\text{HML}_t + \hat{\varepsilon}_t,$$

where $(R_t - R^f)$ is the excess return on the food portfolio at time t, $(R_{MKT,t} - R^f)$ is the excess return on the market portfolio at time t, SMB_t is the return of a portfolio long on small caps and short on large ("big") caps, and HML_t is the return of a portfolio long on firms with high book-to-market value and short on firms with low book-to-market value.

The R^2 of the model is 0.672, meaning that the three Fama–French factors explain roughly 67% of the variability of the excess returns on food portfolio, while the remaining 33% is captured by the error terms. The adjusted R^2 is almost identical, and, in any case, it would be useful only to compare alternative linear models. In Table 1.1, the statistics reported in the column *S.E.* are the square root of the estimates that appear on the main diagonal of $\widehat{Var}\left[\hat{\boldsymbol{\beta}}^{OLS}\right] = \hat{\sigma}^2(\mathbf{X}'\mathbf{X})^{-1}$; in particular, $\hat{\sigma}$ happens to be estimated at 0.453 in this application. The output also informs us that:

$$\text{SSR} = \sum_{t=1}^{T}(\hat{y}_t - \bar{y})^2 = 102.579 \quad \text{SST} = \sum_{t=1}^{T}(y_t - \bar{y})^2 = (0.788)^2 \times 504 = 312.96 \; \bar{y} = 0.042.$$

Indeed, it turns out that 102.579/312.96 gives the 32.8% fraction of total variation that is left unexplained by the three regressors assumed here. Other portions of this output will be explained as we move on with our presentation of the material.

TABLE 1.1 Output of a Linear Regression Model With Three Regressors

Dependent Variable: Excess Food
Method: Least Squares
Sample: 1/02/2014 12/31/2015
Included Observations: 504

Variable	Coefficient	S.E.	*t*-Statistic	Probability
C	0.018	0.020	0.913	0.362
Excess MKT	0.747	0.024	31.668	0.000
SMB	−0.246	0.041	−6.061	0.000
HML	0.015	0.047	0.309	0.757
R^2	0.672	Mean dependent variable		0.042
Adjusted R^2	0.670	SD dependent variable		0.788
S.E. of regression	0.453	Akaike information criterion		1.262
SSR	102.579	Schwarz criterion		1.295
Log-likelihood	−313.975	Hannan–Quinn criterion		1.275
F-statistic	340.883	Durbin–Watson statistic		2.056
p (*F*-statistic)	0.000			

1.1.3 The Generalized Least Squared Estimator

Up to this point, we have always assumed that the variance–covariance matrix of the error terms was "spherical," that is, a diagonal matrix with all the elements on the main diagonal identical, also known as a *scalar matrix*, $\sigma^2\mathbf{I}_T$. Although in many empirical applications this is a plausible assumption, OLS estimation method is impractical in many other situations in which we would have reasons—either theoretical or empirical, on the basis of the behavior of the data—to believe that autocorrelation and/or heteroskedasticity (which means that the variances and covariances of the error terms are not constant over time and across different observations) in the error terms may exist. To start taking these aspects into consideration, we now extend the model to the case in which the covariance matrix is some *known* general matrix. Later, we shall further extend the resulting estimation tools to the case of unknown covariance matrix. Moreover, Chapters 5 and 6, will be devoted to models of *conditional heteroskedasticity*.

When the known, $T \times T$ covariance matrix is some general, positive definite matrix $\boldsymbol{\Sigma}$, the (*classical*) linear regression model becomes:

$$\mathbf{y} = \mathbf{X}\boldsymbol{\beta} + \boldsymbol{\varepsilon} \qquad \boldsymbol{\varepsilon} \sim \text{IID}(\mathbf{0}, \boldsymbol{\Sigma}). \tag{1.24}$$

This model requires all the assumptions of the classical, linear regression model presented before, except the ones concerning the covariance matrix of the residuals, of course. Once we relax this assumption, the OLS estimator, $\hat{\boldsymbol{\beta}}^{OLS}$, will fail to display all the properties that we have listed and proven in Section 1.1.1: more precisely, if it were to be adopted, $\hat{\boldsymbol{\beta}}^{OLS}$ would still be unbiased, but it will not have minimum variance. Indeed, under Eq. (1.24), the BLUE estimator is no longer the OLS, but instead the so-called *generalized least squared (GLS)* estimator, which we are now going to derive.

Because $\boldsymbol{\Sigma}$ is symmetric, we can express it through its so-called "spectral" decomposition $\boldsymbol{\Sigma} = \mathbf{UDU}'$, where $\mathbf{D}$ is a diagonal matrix that presents on the main diagonal the eigenvalues of $\boldsymbol{\Sigma}$ and $\mathbf{U}$ is an *orthogonal matrix*, that is, $\mathbf{U}' = \mathbf{U}^{-1}$ (see Appendix 1.B for a detailed discussion). Note that also the inverse of $\boldsymbol{\Sigma}$ can be expressed in terms of the matrices $\mathbf{U}$ and $\mathbf{D}$: $\boldsymbol{\Sigma}^{-1} = \mathbf{UD}^{-1}\mathbf{U}'$. We also define a third standardization matrix $\mathbf{T} \equiv \mathbf{D}^{-1/2}\mathbf{U}'$. It is straightforward to prove that $\mathbf{T}'\mathbf{T} = \boldsymbol{\Sigma}^{-1}$. Premultiplying by $\mathbf{T}$ on both sides of the model in Eq. (1.24), we obtain:

$$\mathbf{Ty} = \mathbf{TX}\boldsymbol{\beta} + \mathbf{T}\boldsymbol{\varepsilon}. \tag{1.25}$$

At this point, if we define $\tilde{\mathbf{y}} \equiv \mathbf{Ty}$, $\tilde{\mathbf{X}} \equiv \mathbf{TX}$, and $\tilde{\boldsymbol{\varepsilon}} = \mathbf{T}\boldsymbol{\varepsilon}$, we have:

$$\tilde{\mathbf{y}} = \tilde{\mathbf{X}}\boldsymbol{\beta} + \tilde{\boldsymbol{\varepsilon}} \qquad \tilde{\boldsymbol{\varepsilon}} \sim \text{IID } N(\mathbf{0}, \mathbf{I}_T), \tag{1.26}$$

where the interesting statement is that the transformed residuals, $\tilde{\boldsymbol{\varepsilon}}$, are now Gaussian independently and identically distributed (IID) with identity covariance matrix because:

$$\begin{aligned} &E[\tilde{\boldsymbol{\varepsilon}}] = E[\mathbf{T}\boldsymbol{\varepsilon}] = \mathbf{T}E[\boldsymbol{\varepsilon}] = \mathbf{T}\cdot\mathbf{0} = \mathbf{0} \\ &E[\tilde{\boldsymbol{\varepsilon}}\tilde{\boldsymbol{\varepsilon}}'] = \mathbf{T}E[\boldsymbol{\varepsilon}\boldsymbol{\varepsilon}']\mathbf{T}' = (\mathbf{D}^{-1/2}\underbrace{\mathbf{U}')\mathbf{U}}_{\mathbf{I}_T}\mathbf{D}\underbrace{\mathbf{U}'(\mathbf{U}}_{\mathbf{I}_T}\mathbf{D}^{-1/2}) = \mathbf{D}^{-1/2}\mathbf{D}\mathbf{D}^{-1/2} = \mathbf{I}_T. \end{aligned} \tag{1.27}$$

The model in Eq. (1.26) is the regression in Eq. (1.1) for the new variables $\tilde{\mathbf{y}}, \tilde{\mathbf{X}}$, and $\tilde{\boldsymbol{\varepsilon}}$, where all the assumptions of the classical linear model are satisfied: in particular, the error terms now display a spherical covariance matrix. Moreover, this model contains a vector of parameters $\boldsymbol{\beta}$ identical to the one of the more general models in Eq. (1.24). Therefore, to obtain a BLUE estimator of $\boldsymbol{\beta}$, it is sufficient to apply the OLS estimation procedure to the model in Eq. (1.26), deriving:

$$\hat{\boldsymbol{\beta}}^{OLS} = (\tilde{\mathbf{X}}'\tilde{\mathbf{X}})^{-1}\tilde{\mathbf{X}}'\tilde{\mathbf{y}}. \tag{1.28}$$

To re-express this estimator as a function of the variables originally appearing in the generalized model Eq. (1.24), we simply substitute the definitions of $\tilde{\mathbf{y}}$ and $\tilde{\mathbf{X}}$, obtaining what is normally called the (theoretical, because it assumes that $\boldsymbol{\Sigma}$ is known) GLS estimator:

$$\hat{\boldsymbol{\beta}}^{GLS} = (\mathbf{X}'\mathbf{T}'\mathbf{TX})^{-1}(\mathbf{X}'\mathbf{T}'\mathbf{Ty}) = (\mathbf{X}'\boldsymbol{\Sigma}^{-1}\mathbf{X})^{-1}(\mathbf{X}'\boldsymbol{\Sigma}^{-1}\mathbf{y}). \tag{1.29}$$

In summary, the estimator in Eq. (1.29) is derived from a more general model where $Var[\boldsymbol{\varepsilon}]$ can be any positive definite matrix $\boldsymbol{\Sigma}$. When $\boldsymbol{\Sigma}$ is known, we can use it to define a transformation of the variables appearing in the general model in such a way that this can be transformed into the classical model satisfying all the assumptions needed to apply the OLS method, so to obtain a BLUE estimator for the vector of parameters $\boldsymbol{\theta}$. This strategy works because when we go from Eq. (1.24) to Eq. (1.26), $\boldsymbol{\theta}$ is left unchanged after the transformation.

The GLS estimator $\hat{\boldsymbol{\beta}}^{GLS}$ is linear, normally distributed and unbiased:

$$E[\hat{\boldsymbol{\beta}}^{GLS}] = E[(\mathbf{X}'\boldsymbol{\Sigma}^{-1}\mathbf{X})^{-1}\mathbf{X}'\boldsymbol{\Sigma}^{-1}\mathbf{y}] = (\mathbf{X}'\boldsymbol{\Sigma}^{-1}\mathbf{X})^{-1}\mathbf{X}'\boldsymbol{\Sigma}^{-1}\mathbf{X}\boldsymbol{\beta} = \boldsymbol{\beta}. \tag{1.30}$$

Moreover, it has the minimum variance among the class of the linear unbiased estimator. The proof is identical to the Gauss–Markov theorem of Result 1.1, when one recognizes that the $\hat{\boldsymbol{\beta}}^{GLS}$ is just the OLS estimator for Eq. (1.26).

However, the GLS estimator in Eq. (1.29) is often called the *unfeasible* GLS because its use would require a complete knowledge of the matrix $\boldsymbol{\Sigma}$; clearly, this is a very unlikely situation when working with empirical data. The most common situation when conducting an analysis is instead that we do not know $\boldsymbol{\Sigma}$, and we only entertain a series of doubts concerning the hypotheses of homoskedasticity and zero-autocorrelation. To solve this problem, it is usually advised to perform a few tests to assess whether the suspicion of heteroskedasticity and/or autocorrelation of the errors finds any empirical backing and, if needed, to proceed to:

- either adopt feasible versions of Eq. (1.29) that, however, require some first-step estimates of $\boldsymbol{\Sigma}$ and a clear understanding of whether and how the resulting feasible GLS estimator may be valid in practice, being at least unbiased and consistent, given that such a two- or multi-step estimator is by construction unlikely to be the most efficient one;
- or retain $\hat{\boldsymbol{\beta}}^{OLS}$ as the estimator of choice, but adopting estimators of the variance of the estimator—$\widehat{Var}\left[\hat{\boldsymbol{\beta}}^{OLS}\right]$, also called heteroskedasticity/autocorrelation-consistent (HAC) estimators—which take into account the effects of heteroskedasticity and autocorrelation on the efficiency of $\hat{\boldsymbol{\beta}}^{OLS}$.

We shall return to these options with more details later, in Section 1.4 of this chapter, when we will consider the role played by violations of the hypotheses concerning the errors in a more practical perspective.

1.1.4 Maximum Likelihood Estimator

The independence from any hypothesis over the distribution of the error terms that characterizes both the OLS and GLS estimators can be desirable when we do not have any specific information on the distribution of the errors and/or we refrain from imposing any such, strong assumptions. However, it may occasionally occur that some information on the distribution of $\boldsymbol{\varepsilon}$ is available; or, alternatively, that a researcher may be ready to impose such an assumption. When this is sensible, then an additional estimation method—in fact, one guaranteed to return the *uniformly most efficient estimator*—becomes available, the *maximum likelihood estimator (MLE)*.

The basic idea of MLE is that some realizations of the dependent variable $\mathbf{y}$ are most likely to occur than others and that in reality—in the available random sample drawn from some underlying population—it is most likely that we have observed exactly the data to which it is associated the highest probability. Therefore, MLE aims at finding the values for the vector of parameters $\boldsymbol{\theta}$ that maximizes the probability of observing the sample data we have in fact collected. Such values represent the maximum likelihood (ML) estimates of $\boldsymbol{\theta}$ (and arguably, also σ^2).

The first-step to derive ML estimators is to define the probability distribution of an observed sample of data. Differently from what we have done so far, we assume that $\mathbf{y}$ is normally distributed with expected value equal to $\mathbf{X}\boldsymbol{\beta}$ and a diagonal variance and covariance matrix, where all the elements on the diagonal are equal to σ^2: $\mathbf{y} \sim N(\mathbf{X}\boldsymbol{\beta}, \sigma^2\mathbf{I}_T)$. Note that other assumptions could be made at this point, but the normal benchmark is crucial to define the classical normal regression model. As a result, the joint density function of $\mathbf{y}$ is given by:

$$f\left(\mathbf{y}|\boldsymbol{\beta}, \sigma^2\right) = \left(2\pi\sigma^2\right)^{-\frac{T}{2}} \exp\left[-\frac{(\mathbf{y}-\mathbf{X}\boldsymbol{\beta})'(\mathbf{y}-\mathbf{X}\boldsymbol{\beta})}{2\sigma^2}\right]. \tag{1.31}$$

For the purpose of ML estimation, we shall consider Eq. (1.31) as a function of the $K+2$ parameters $\boldsymbol{\theta}$ and σ^2, obtaining the so-called *likelihood function*, and find its maximum with respect to exactly those parameters. The likelihood function is therefore defined as:

$$L(\boldsymbol{\beta}, \sigma^2|\mathbf{y}) = \left(2\pi\sigma^2\right)^{-\frac{T}{2}} \exp\left[-\frac{(\mathbf{y}-\mathbf{X}\boldsymbol{\beta})'(\mathbf{y}-\mathbf{X}\boldsymbol{\beta})}{2\sigma^2}\right], \tag{1.32}$$

where $\mathbf{y}$ no longer represents a random variable of which we care of the joint density function as in Eq. (1.31), but instead a fixed and given vector containing the realized data over the sampling period. Indeed, the likelihood in Eq. (1.32) is based on the parameters $\boldsymbol{\theta}$ and σ^2 being the variables with respect to which the maximization needs to be performed. To simplify the calculations, it is common to perform the maximization not of Eq. (1.32) as such but of the logarithm of the likelihood function (called *log-likelihood function*):

$$\ell\left(\boldsymbol{\beta}, \sigma^2|\mathbf{y}\right) = -\frac{T}{2}\ln\left(2\pi\sigma^2\right) - \frac{1}{2\sigma^2}(\mathbf{y}-\mathbf{X}\boldsymbol{\beta})'(\mathbf{y}-\mathbf{X}\boldsymbol{\beta}). \tag{1.33}$$

Following standard principles of (free) optimization of a real function $\mathbb{R}^{K+1} \to \mathbb{R}$, to find a maximum we now compute the *score function*,

$$S(\boldsymbol{\beta}, \sigma^2) = \begin{bmatrix} \dfrac{\partial \ell(\boldsymbol{\beta}, \sigma^2|\mathbf{y})}{\partial \boldsymbol{\beta}} \\ \dfrac{\partial \ell(\boldsymbol{\beta}, \sigma^2|\mathbf{y})}{\partial \sigma^2} \end{bmatrix} = \begin{bmatrix} (-2\sigma^2)^{-1}(-2\mathbf{X}'\mathbf{y} + 2\mathbf{X}'\mathbf{X}\boldsymbol{\beta}) \\ -T(2\sigma^2)^{-1} + (2\sigma^4)^{-1}(\mathbf{y} - \mathbf{X}\boldsymbol{\beta})'(\mathbf{y} - \mathbf{X}\boldsymbol{\beta}) \end{bmatrix} \tag{1.34}$$

and equate it to 0 to obtain a system of necessary first-order conditions (FOCs):

$$\begin{bmatrix} -\mathbf{X}'\mathbf{y} + \mathbf{X}'\mathbf{X}\hat{\boldsymbol{\beta}}^{ML} \\ -T(2\hat{s}^2_{ML})^{-1} + \dfrac{1}{2}(\hat{s}^2_{ML})^{-2}\left(\mathbf{y} - \mathbf{X}\hat{\boldsymbol{\beta}}^{ML}\right)'\left(\mathbf{y} - \mathbf{X}\hat{\boldsymbol{\beta}}^{ML}\right) \end{bmatrix} = \begin{bmatrix} 0 \\ 0 \end{bmatrix}. \tag{1.35}$$

Solving this system of $K + 2$ equations in $K + 2$ unknowns, we obtain:

$$\hat{\boldsymbol{\beta}}^{ML} = (\mathbf{X}'\mathbf{X})^{-1}\mathbf{X}'\mathbf{y} = \hat{\boldsymbol{\beta}}^{OLS} \tag{1.36}$$

$$\hat{s}^2_{ML} = \frac{\hat{\boldsymbol{\varepsilon}}'\hat{\boldsymbol{\varepsilon}}}{T}. \tag{1.37}$$

The result in Eq. (1.36) is intriguing: by assuming a normal distribution for the error terms and, as consequence, for the dependent variable, the ML estimator of the regression coefficients coincides with the OLS estimator, while the ML estimator for the variance differs from the OLS estimator $\hat{s}^2_{OLS}$. Hence, the ML estimator presents all the desirable properties of $\hat{\boldsymbol{\beta}}^{OLS}$ as stated by the Gauss–Markov theorem, while $\hat{s}^2_{ML}$ is biased:

$$E\left[\hat{s}^2_{ML}\right] = E\left[\frac{\hat{\boldsymbol{\varepsilon}}'\hat{\boldsymbol{\varepsilon}}}{T}\right] = \frac{T-K-1}{T}\sigma^2 \neq \sigma^2 = E\left[\frac{\hat{\boldsymbol{\varepsilon}}'\hat{\boldsymbol{\varepsilon}}}{T-K-1}\right] = E\left[\hat{s}^2_{OLS}\right]. \tag{1.38}$$

Although in general an ML estimator $\hat{\boldsymbol{\theta}}^{ML}$ for some vector of parameters $\boldsymbol{\theta}$ could be biased, one can prove that MLE always presents the following properties:[2]

- *Invariance*: If $\hat{\boldsymbol{\theta}}^{ML}$ is the MLE for $\boldsymbol{\theta}$, then the ML estimator for $g(\boldsymbol{\theta})$ is $g(\hat{\boldsymbol{\theta}}^{ML})$, provided the function $g(\boldsymbol{\theta})$ satisfies a few conditions (such as being one-to-one, or being at least continuous).
- *Consistency*: As the sample size T increases (technically, over a sequence of random samples of increasing size T), the ML estimator converges (in probability) to the unknown vector of parameter, $\boldsymbol{\theta}$.
- *Asymptotic normality*: As the sample size T increases, $\sqrt{T}(\hat{\boldsymbol{\theta}}^{ML} - \boldsymbol{\theta})$ has an approximately normal distribution $N(\mathbf{0}, \mathbf{V})$, where $\mathbf{V}$ is the *asymptotic covariance matrix*.
- *Asymptotic efficiency*: The matrix $\mathbf{V}$ is equal to the *Cramér–Rao lower variance bound*, and therefore the MLE is the uniformly most efficient estimator among the ones that asymptotically are characterized by a zero bias.[3]

1.1.5 Hypotheses Testing, Confidence Intervals, and Predictive Intervals

In Sections 1.2.1–1.2.3, we have shown how to derive point estimates of the parameters in the linear regression model, under a variety of different assumptions. However, in empirical analyses, it is often crucial to combine point estimates of coefficients with some indicators of the associated degree of confidence in this very point estimates, that is, how reliable and accurate the point estimate we have found may be. To this purpose, it is typical to compute *confidence intervals*, which are intervals for the unknown parameters, to which it is possible to associate a probability such that the true but unknown parameter value falls in the interval defined around some point estimate with the stated confidence; this can also be interpreted as frequency of the intervals including the true parameters over a long sequence of samples of identical size T.[4] To fully grasp what follows, let us remind ourselves that a point estimator is nothing but a random

2. The case of the estimation of the coefficients of linear regression models offers an exception because the Gauss–Markov theorem guarantees that the MLE of some of the coefficients (those in $\boldsymbol{\theta}$) are also unbiased.

3. The Cramér–Rao Bound is the lower bound on the (co) variance among all (asymptotically) unbiased estimators for a given vector of parameters, $\boldsymbol{\theta}$. See Rao (1945) and Cramér (1946) for details.

4. Because the distribution of an estimator is typically continuous, it is not possible to associate a probability directly to a point estimate. In fact, the probability of observing a specific value from a continuous distribution is always equal to 0, by construction.

variable (with an expected value and a variance). When we compute a point estimated value, we substitute the observed values of the dependent and explanatory variables in the appropriate formula (e.g., Eq. 1.36) and obtain a value that is however just one specific realization of the random variable.

In the case of the OLS estimator for $\boldsymbol{\beta}$, we know that if the errors are normally distributed then $\hat{\boldsymbol{\beta}}^{\text{OLS}} \sim N(\boldsymbol{\beta}, \sigma^2(\mathbf{X}'\mathbf{X})^{-1})$. Because a joint, multivariate normal distribution for $\hat{\boldsymbol{\beta}}^{\text{OLS}}$ implies that each of the coefficients in $\boldsymbol{\beta}$ have a marginal normal distribution, $\hat{\beta}_k^{\text{OLS}} \sim N(\beta_k, \sigma^2(\mathbf{X}'\mathbf{X})_{kk}^{-1})$ for every $k = 0, 1, \ldots, K$, where $(\mathbf{X}'\mathbf{X})_{kk}^{-1}$ is the $(k+1)$th element on the main diagonal of $(\mathbf{X}'\mathbf{X})^{-1}$. Standardizing $\hat{\beta}_k^{\text{OLS}}$, we have: $(\hat{\beta}_k^{\text{OLS}} - \beta_k)/[\sigma^2(\mathbf{X}'\mathbf{X})_{kk}^{-1}] \sim N(0, 1)$ and therefore:

$$P\left\{ -z_{\alpha/2} < \frac{\hat{\beta}_k^{\text{OLS}} - \beta_k}{\sigma\sqrt{(\mathbf{X}'\mathbf{X})_{kk}^{-1}}} < z_{\alpha/2} \right\} = 1 - \alpha, \tag{1.39}$$

where $z_{\alpha/2}$ is the quantile of the standard normal distribution of order $1 - \alpha/2$, $\alpha \in [0, 1]$. At this point, from Eq. (1.39) it follows that:

$$P\left\{ \hat{\beta}_k^{\text{OLS}} - z_{\alpha/2}\sigma\sqrt{(\mathbf{X}'\mathbf{X})_{kk}^{-1}} < \beta_k < \hat{\beta}_k^{\text{OLS}} + z_{\alpha/2}\sigma\sqrt{(\mathbf{X}'\mathbf{X})_{kk}^{-1}} \right\} = 1 - \alpha. \tag{1.40}$$

This formula defines a $(1-\alpha)$-percent confidence interval for the parameter β_k, indeed we can state that the true parameter belongs to $[\hat{\beta}_k^{\text{OLS}} - z_{\alpha/2}\sigma\sqrt{(\mathbf{X}'\mathbf{X})_{kk}^{-1}}, \hat{\beta}_k^{\text{OLS}} + z_{\alpha/2}\sigma\sqrt{(\mathbf{X}'\mathbf{X})_{kk}^{-1}}]$ with a confidence of $1 - \alpha$.[5]

Note that it is in principle necessary to know the true value of σ to compute the lower and upper bounds, and once more this appears odd, that while $K + 1$ parameters are unknown, the $(K + 2)$th is instead known. Yet, it can be shown that:

$$\frac{\hat{\beta}_k^{\text{OLS}} - \beta_k}{\hat{s}_{\text{OLS}}\sqrt{(\mathbf{X}'\mathbf{X})_{kk}^{-1}}} \sim t_{T-K-1}, \tag{1.41}$$

where t_{T-K-1} is a t-student random variate with $T - K - 1$ degrees of freedom. The estimated value $\hat{s}_{\text{OLS}}\sqrt{(\mathbf{X}'\mathbf{X})_{kk}^{-1}}$ is called the *standard error (S.E.)*, and it represents the most efficient estimate of the standard deviation (SD) of $\hat{\beta}_k^{\text{OLS}}$. Thus, for every chosen value of the probability α, the estimated $(1-\alpha)$-percent confidence interval is:

$$\left[\hat{\beta}_k^{\text{OLS}} - t_{T-K-1,\alpha/2}\hat{s}_{\text{OLS}}\sqrt{(\mathbf{X}'\mathbf{X})_{kk}^{-1}}, \hat{\beta}_k^{\text{OLS}} + t_{T-K-1,\alpha/2}\hat{s}_{\text{OLS}}\sqrt{(\mathbf{X}'\mathbf{X})_{kk}^{-1}} \right], \tag{1.42}$$

where $t_{T-K-1,\alpha/2}$ is the quantile of a t-student with $T - K - 1$ degrees of freedom of order $1 - \alpha/2$.

EXAMPLE 1.3

Table 1.2 shows the output from OLS estimation of a linear regression model, where the dependent variable is the monthly excess return series on a portfolio composed by stocks of US firms operating in the Oil market and where the regressors are the Fama–French factors, similarly to Example 1.2.

To compute confidence intervals for the estimated coefficients, we use the information shown in the columns *Coefficient* and *S.E.* of Table 1.2. The number of observations is $T = 96$, the number of regressors is $K = 3$. Using Eq. (1.40), the 95% confidence for the coefficient associated with excess market returns (Excess MKT) is:

$$\left[1.374 - t_{92,0.025}0.210, 1.374 + t_{92,0.025}0.210\right]$$

and because $t_{92,0.025} \cong 2.28$, the confidence interval is $[0.895, 1.853]$. Therefore, possibly with a 95% confidence interval, the beta of oil stock returns may in fact be equal to 1.

5. The confidence level can be seen as a probability in the sense that if we were to repeat the sample selection infinitely many times and each time forms this very confidence interval, we would obtain that the estimated confidence intervals include the true parameter value $(1-\alpha)$-percent of the time, see Neyman (1937).

TABLE 1.2 Fama–French Linear Regression Model for US Oil Stock Returns

Dependent Variable: Excess Oil
Method: Least Squares
Sample: 2009M01 2016M12
Included Observations: 96

Variable	Coefficient	S.E.	*t*-Statistic	Probability
C	− 1.260	0.785	− 1.605	0.112
Excess MKT	1.374	0.210	6.539	0.000
SMB	0.750	0.345	2.178	0.032
HML	0.625	0.295	2.116	0.037

R^2	0.520	Mean dependent variable	0.602
Adjusted R^2	0.505	SD dependent variable	10.392
S.E. of regression	7.315	Akaike information criterion	6.859
SSR	4923.191	Schwarz criterion	6.965
Log-likelihood	− 325.212	Hannan–Quinn criterion	6.902
F-statistic	33.245	Durbin–Watson statistic	1.832
p (*F*-statistic)	0.000		

The same argument can be applied to derive the $(1-\alpha)$-percent confidence interval for the parameter σ^2. Because $(T-K-1)(\hat{s}^2_{\text{OLS}}/\sigma^2) \sim \chi^2_{T-K-1}$, we have:

$$P\left\{\frac{(T-K-1)\hat{s}^2_{\text{OLS}}}{\chi^2_{T-K-1,1-\alpha/2}} < \sigma^2 < \frac{(T-K-1)\hat{s}^2_{\text{OLS}}}{\chi^2_{T-K-1,\alpha/2}}\right\} = 1-\alpha, \tag{1.43}$$

where $\chi^2_{T-K-1,\,\alpha/2}$ is the quantile of a chi-squared random variable with $T-K-1$ degree of freedom of order $1-\alpha/2$.

EXAMPLE 1.4

Consider again the outputs in Table 1.2, where the square root of the OLS estimated variance is indicated as *S.E. of regression*, here $\hat{s}^2_{\text{OLS}} = 7.315^2 = 53.509$. Alternatively, $\hat{s}^2_{\text{OLS}}$ can be computed dividing the entry in SSR by $T-K-1$, in this case 92. Using Eq. (1.43), the 95% confidence interval for the residual variance coefficient is:

$$\left[\frac{(T-K-1)\hat{s}^2_{\text{OLS}}}{\chi^2_{T-K-1,1-\alpha/2}}, \frac{(T-K-1)\hat{s}^2_{\text{OLS}}}{\chi^2_{T-K-1,\alpha/2}}\right] = \left[\frac{92\times 53.509}{\chi^2_{92,0.975}}, \frac{92\times 53.509}{\chi^2_{92,0.025}}\right]$$

and, because $\chi^2_{92,0.975} \cong 120.4$ and $\chi^2_{92,0.025} \cong 67.36$, the confidence interval turns out to be approximately [40.88, 73.08].

When applying linear regression in practice, we are often interested in computing *predictions* for the values of the dependent variable, given certain, chosen values for the regressors. Such values may represent either exogenous forecasts of the regressors (for instance, financial analysts' predictions) or values obtained from some other model that we take as given. In this case, our question is "what value we could expect for $\mathbf{y}$ if the values of the regressors are $\mathbf{x}_f$?." In general, $\mathbf{x}_f$ does not belong to our sampling period and may simply represent a simulation value of particular meaning to the researcher. There are two alternative ways to answer this question. The first is to compute the point estimate for the expected value of y_f corresponding to $\mathbf{x}_f$, $E[y_f] = \mathbf{x}_f'\boldsymbol{\beta}$, which is called a *mean response*. The second is to compute the point estimate for $y_f = \mathbf{x}_f'\boldsymbol{\beta} + \varepsilon_f$, which is called a *news response*. However, when the regression coefficients are not known, the point estimates of the two objects coincide and they are given by the *point prediction* $\hat{y}_f = \mathbf{x}_f'\hat{\boldsymbol{\beta}}^{\text{OLS}}$, which is nothing, but the fitted value computed in correspondence to $\mathbf{x}_f$. The prediction $\hat{y}_f$ is an unbiased estimator of both $E[y_f]$ and y_f.

Interestingly, the two quantities come to diverge again when we aim at computing confidence intervals for such predictions, which seems to be necessary to quantify the uncertainty surrounding the forecasts, which are random by their very nature. If we want to compute a confidence interval for the mean response, we have to take into account the distribution of $\hat{y}_f = \mathbf{x}_f'\hat{\boldsymbol{\beta}}^{\text{OLS}}$; it is straightforward to prove that:

$$\hat{y}_f = \mathbf{x}_f'\hat{\boldsymbol{\beta}}^{\text{OLS}} \sim N(\mathbf{x}_f'\boldsymbol{\beta}, \mathbf{x}_f'\sigma^2(\mathbf{X}'\mathbf{X})^{-1}\mathbf{x}_f). \tag{1.44}$$

Therefore, the $(1-\alpha)$-percent confidence interval for the mean response $E[y_f]=\mathbf{x}_f'\boldsymbol{\beta}$ is:

$$\left[\hat{y}_f \pm t_{T-K-1,\alpha/2}\hat{s}_{\text{OLS}}\sqrt{\mathbf{x}_f'(\mathbf{X}'\mathbf{X})^{-1}\mathbf{x}_f}\right]. \tag{1.45}$$

However, to compute the $(1-\alpha)$-percent confidence interval for the news response, we need to consider that $y_f = E[y_f]+\varepsilon_f$, so that there are two sources of variability concerning the value of y_f. The first is the one resulting from the estimation of $\boldsymbol{\beta}$ and it is already taken into account in the confidence interval in Eq. (1.45), for the mean response; the second is the uncertainty coming from the variance of ε_f. The confidence interval for y_f is then:

$$\left[\hat{y}_f \pm t_{T-K-1,\alpha/2}\hat{s}_{\text{OLS}}\sqrt{(\mathbf{x}_f'(\mathbf{X}'\mathbf{X})^{-1}\mathbf{x}_f+1)}\right]. \tag{1.46}$$

A topic which is closely related to confidence intervals is the testing of hypotheses. The *theory of hypothesis testing* helps to develop procedures to verify the plausibility of conjectures made by a user over the parameters of the model or over some linear combinations of them. Before proceeding, we shall briefly remind the reader that the key idea behind hypothesis testing consists of assuming as true the hypothesis we are traditionally *not* interested in (which is called the *null hypothesis* and it is indicated with H_0) and evaluate how likely our observations are under such a hypothesis. For instance, a researcher who wants to support her claim that past price-dividend ratios may forecast future excess market returns will adopt as her null hypothesis the one that there is no empirical link between the two variables, which goes contrary to her conjecture; she will then investigate whether the available sample data support the null hypothesis (possibly hoping this is not the case). We will reject the null when what we have observed in the sample is unlikely to have occurred under the null hypothesis. More precisely, we are going to fix an a priori small probability value $\alpha \in [0,1]$ (that is the same α that we have introduced above, but with a different role), and we will *reject the null* if the probability of observing the value of some *test statistic* or a more extreme one is smaller than α under H_0. When the test statistic takes values that occur under H_0 with a probability of α or in excess, then we shall *not reject the null hypothesis*, that is deemed to be consistent with sample evidence. Note that nowhere we have used the expression "to accept the null hypothesis" that is in fact not admissible in a frequentist style test.

Before presenting the details of a frequentist testing procedure in detail, let us consider once again the distribution of the estimator $\hat{\boldsymbol{\beta}}^{\text{OLS}}$: $\hat{\boldsymbol{\beta}}^{\text{OLS}} \sim N(\boldsymbol{\beta}, \sigma^2(\mathbf{X}'\mathbf{X})^{-1})$. If we define a non-stochastic $(K+1)\times Q$ matrix $\mathbf{K}$ and a Q-dimensional vector $\mathbf{k}$, we have:

$$\mathbf{K}'\hat{\boldsymbol{\beta}}^{\text{OLS}} - \mathbf{k} \sim N(\mathbf{K}\boldsymbol{\beta}-\mathbf{k}, \sigma^2\mathbf{K}'(\mathbf{X}'\mathbf{X})^{-1}\mathbf{K}) \tag{1.47}$$

which is a general form for the distribution of any set of Q linear combinations of the estimators of the regression coefficients. For instance, if we choose $\mathbf{K}=[1\ 0\ \ldots\ 0]'$ and $k=0$, then $\hat{\beta}_0^{\text{OLS}}=0$, that is, the intercept only, where $Q=1$. Another example with $Q=1$ is $\mathbf{K}=[1\ \ -2\ 0\ \ldots\ 0]$ and $k=1$, then $\mathbf{K}'\hat{\boldsymbol{\beta}}^{\text{OLS}} - k = \hat{\beta}_0^{\text{OLS}} - 2\hat{\beta}_1^{\text{OLS}} - 1$. Finally, a case with $Q=2$ could be:

$$\mathbf{K}' = \begin{bmatrix} 1 & -1 & 0 & 0 & \cdots & 0 \\ 0 & 0 & 1 & 0 & \cdots & 0 \end{bmatrix}, \quad \mathbf{k}=\mathbf{0} \Rightarrow \mathbf{K}'\hat{\boldsymbol{\beta}}^{\text{OLS}} - \mathbf{k} = \mathbf{0} \Rightarrow \begin{cases} \hat{\beta}_0^{\text{OLS}} = \hat{\beta}_1^{\text{OLS}} \\ \hat{\beta}_2^{\text{OLS}} = 0 \end{cases}. \tag{1.48}$$

By simple properties of products of vectors and matrices, all null hypotheses concerning linear combinations of the parameters can be expressed as $\mathbf{K}'\boldsymbol{\beta}-\mathbf{k}=\mathbf{0}$, where the number of restrictions imposed under the null equals the rank of $\mathbf{K}$.[6] For concreteness, consider another example, the hypothesis of the intercept β_0 being equal to the coefficient of the first regressor β_1. In this case, we can express the constraint by setting $\mathbf{K}=[1\ \ -1\ 0\ \ldots 0]'$ and $\mathbf{k}=\mathbf{0}$, to get that $\mathbf{K}'\boldsymbol{\beta}-\mathbf{k}=\mathbf{0}$ is equivalent to $\beta_0=\beta_1$.

Equipped with these tools, we are now ready to build a statistical test for a linear hypothesis H_0:$\mathbf{K}'\boldsymbol{\beta}-\mathbf{k}=\mathbf{0}$. If H_0 is true, the expected value of $\mathbf{K}'\hat{\boldsymbol{\beta}}^{\text{OLS}}-\mathbf{k}$ should be a vector of zeros and Eq. (1.47) becomes:

$$\mathbf{K}'\hat{\boldsymbol{\beta}}^{\text{OLS}} - \mathbf{k} \sim N(\mathbf{0}, \sigma^2\mathbf{K}'(\mathbf{X}'\mathbf{X})^{-1}\mathbf{K}) \tag{1.49}$$

6. The rank of a matrix is the maximum number of linearly independent rows or columns in the matrix. If $\mathbf{K}$ is $Q\times(K+1)$, $\text{rank}(\mathbf{K})=\min[Q,K+1]$.

from which—because the square of a Q-variate normal distribution is a chi-square with Q degrees of freedom—it follows that:

$$(\mathbf{K}'\hat{\boldsymbol{\beta}}^{\text{OLS}} - \mathbf{k})'[\sigma^2\mathbf{K}'(\mathbf{X}'\mathbf{X})^{-1}\mathbf{K}]^{-1}(\mathbf{K}'\hat{\boldsymbol{\beta}}^{\text{OLS}} - \mathbf{k}) \sim \chi^2_Q. \tag{1.50}$$

Moreover, because we know already that $(T-K-1)(\hat{s}^2_{\text{OLS}}/\sigma^2) \sim \chi^2{}_{T-K-1}$ and that the ratio of two chi-squared distributions divided by their corresponding degrees of freedom is distributed as an F random variable, it is possible to show that:

$$F_T \equiv \frac{(\mathbf{K}'\hat{\boldsymbol{\beta}}^{\text{OLS}} - \mathbf{k})'[\sigma^2\mathbf{K}'(\mathbf{X}'\mathbf{X})^{-1}\mathbf{K}]^{-1}(\mathbf{K}'\hat{\boldsymbol{\beta}}^{\text{OLS}} - \mathbf{k})/Q}{\hat{s}^2_{\text{OLS}}/\sigma^2} \sim F_{Q,T-K-1}. \tag{1.51}$$

If the hypothesis $H_0{:}\mathbf{K}'\boldsymbol{\beta} - \mathbf{k} = \mathbf{0}$ were true, then the test statistics F_T would be distributed as a Snedecor's F random variable with Q and $T-K-1$ degrees of freedom; if H_0 were false, then the ratio in Eq. (1.51) would have another, unknown distribution. To complete the algorithm, we use Eq. (1.51) to compute the p-value of the test, that is, the probability of observing exactly the value of the test statistic or a more extreme one under the null hypothesis:

$$p\text{-value}\ (F_T) = P(F \geq F_T | H_0). \tag{1.52}$$

We reject the null if p-value $(F_T) < \alpha$. Of course, we will reach the same conclusion by confronting the critical value $F_{Q,T-K-1,1-\alpha}$, that is, the quantile of an F random variable with Q and $T-K-1$ degrees of freedom of order $1-\alpha$. If $F_T > F_{Q,T-K-1,1-\alpha}$, we shall reject the null hypothesis for a fixed *size of the test*, equal to α.

The test statistic in Eq. (1.51) can be used for testing any linear hypothesis on the regression coefficients. Some special attention is normally paid to the case of the null $H_0{:}\beta_k = 0$, $k = 0, 1, \ldots, K$, because testing this hypothesis is fundamental, any time we need to choose whether to include a regressor in our model. In this case, $\mathbf{K}$ is a vector of all zeros except for a 1 in correspondence to the $(k+1)$th element and k is a scalar equal to 0, so that $\mathbf{K}'\hat{\boldsymbol{\beta}}^{\text{OLS}} - k = \beta_k$, $\mathbf{K}'(\mathbf{X}'\mathbf{X})^{-1}\mathbf{K} = (\mathbf{X}'\mathbf{X})^{-1}_{kk}$, and

$$F_T \equiv \frac{(\hat{\beta}_k^{\text{OLS}})^2(\mathbf{X}'\mathbf{X})^{-1}_{kk}}{\hat{s}^2_{\text{OLS}}} = \left(\frac{\hat{\beta}_k^{\text{OLS}}}{\hat{s}_{\text{OLS}}\sqrt{(\mathbf{X}'\mathbf{X})^{-1}_{kk}}}\right)^2 \sim F_{1,T-K-1}. \tag{1.53}$$

However, because the squared root of an F random variable with 1 and g degrees of freedom is also distributed as a standard t-student with g degrees of freedom, we could define a new test statistic,

$$t_T \equiv \frac{\hat{\beta}_k^{\text{OLS}}}{\hat{s}_{\text{OLS}}\sqrt{(\mathbf{X}'\mathbf{X})^{-1}_{kk}}} \sim t_{T-K-1} \tag{1.54}$$

which under $H_0{:}\beta_k = 0$ is distributed as a t-student with $T-K-1$ degrees of freedom. This result should not be surprising: in fact, it will be also obtained considering the result in Eq. (1.47) when the variance is unknown under the null hypothesis.

Because they are based on Eq. (1.50), the tests presented above are all *two-sided tests*. These differ from *one-sided tests*. To distinguish between these two kinds of tests, we have to introduce the concept of *alternative hypothesis* H_1, which can be seen as the logical alternative to H_0 and therefore represents the hypothesis/conjecture favored by a researcher. When we perform a two-sided test for $H_0{:}\beta_k = 0$, we are assuming as alternative hypothesis $H_1{:}\beta_k \neq 0$, $k = 0, 1, \ldots, K$, meaning that under the alternative hypothesis, the parameter can be either positive or negative. In this case, the p-value of the test will be:

$$p\text{-value}\ (t_T) = p(|t| \geq t_T; H_0). \tag{1.55}$$

Instead, when we perform a one-sided test for $H_0{:}\beta_k = 0$, we are assuming as an alternative hypothesis $H_1{:}\beta_k > 0$ (or $H_1{:}\beta_k < 0$), meaning that we exclude a priori one direction of inequality. In this case, the p-value of the test is defined as:

$$p\text{-value}\ (t_T) = p(t \geq t_T; H_0) \quad \text{if } H_1 : \beta_k > 0 \tag{1.56}$$

or

$$p\text{-value}\ (t_T) = p(t \leq t_T; H_0) \quad \text{if } H_1 : \beta_k < 0. \tag{1.57}$$

In all these cases, we reject the null hypothesis if p-value $(t_T) < \alpha$.

EXAMPLE 1.5

We extend Example 1.4, which was based on the following estimation output from OLS estimation of a linear regression model, where the dependent variable is the monthly excess return series on a portfolio composed by stocks of US firms operating in the Oil industry (Table 1.3).

The table shows the results of two-sided *t*-student tests of the null of each of the coefficients being individually 0. For instance, in the case of the "loading" of the returns on the oil industry on the value-sorted HML portfolio, we have:

$$t_{96}^{\beta_{\mathrm{HML}}=0} = \frac{0.625}{0.295} = 2.116$$

which, under a t_{92}, implies a *p*-value of 0.037. If we had set a size of the test equal to the standard 0.05, because 0.037 is below such a value, we would reject the null of $\beta_{\mathrm{HML}} = 0$. However, if we wanted to test the null of $\beta_{\mathrm{excessMKT}} = 1$, which means that oil sector returns have the same average systematic risk as the market portfolio, we obtain:

$$t_{96}^{\beta_{\mathrm{ExcessMKT}}=1} = \frac{1.374 - 1}{0.210} = 1.781$$

which, under a t_{92} implies a *p*-value of 0.078. If we had set a size of the test equal to the standard 0.05, because 0.078 exceeds such a value, we would fail reject the null of $\beta_{\mathrm{excessMKT}} = 1$, that is, oil stock returns do have the same systematic risk as the market portfolio. Finally, the very regression output reveals that the *F*-statistic associated with the composite null hypothesis that all the regression coefficients but the constant are 0, gives a test static of 33.245, which, under an $F_{3,92}$ returns a *p*-value which is essentially 0, which would lead to reject the null that the model does not explain anything of the oil industry returns.

TABLE 1.3 Fama–French Linear Regression Model for US Oil Stock Returns

Dependent Variable: Excess Oil
Method: Least Squares
Sample: 2009M01 2016M12
Included Observations: 96

Variable	Coefficient	S.E.	*t*-Statistic	Probability
C	−1.260	0.785	−1.605	0.112
Excess MKT	1.374	0.210	6.539	0.000
SMB	0.750	0.345	2.178	0.032
HML	0.625	0.295	2.116	0.037

R^2	0.520	Mean dependent variable	0.602
Adjusted R^2	0.505	SD dependent variable	10.392
S.E. of regression	7.315	Akaike information criterion	6.859
SSR	4923.191	Schwarz criterion	6.965
Log-likelihood	−325.212	Hannan–Quinn criterion	6.902
F-statistic	33.245	Durbin–Watson statistic	1.832
p (*F*-statistic)	0.000		

1.1.6 Linear Regression Model With Stochastic Regressors

Up to this point we have treated the explanatory variables as if they were given and fixed (in repeated samples). Of course, in reality it is difficult to find a reason to justify this assumption. In fact, there is no substantial difference between the nature—fixed versus random—of the dependent variable $\mathbf{y}$ and of the regressors $\mathbf{x}_1, \mathbf{x}_2, \ldots, \mathbf{x}_K$, if not any differences that are artificially set out by a researcher while choosing the regression linear model as tool to investigate the relation among the variables. Moreover, all the theory underlying classical inferential statistics is based on the idea that the values assumed by time series data are simply realizations of random variables and as such it is hard to justify considering the explanatory variables as fixed. The problem is also felt when working on cross-sectional data, when we should randomly draw a sample from a population and collect information for every unit in the sample, at some specific point in time. In this case, it is even problematic to justify the choice of considering some of the information, as represented by variables, to be stochastic while other being deterministic.

As a reaction to these problems, we now provide an extension of the model in which all the variables are stochastic. The basic linear regression model becomes:

$$\mathbf{y} = \mathbf{X}\boldsymbol{\beta} + \boldsymbol{\varepsilon} \quad \boldsymbol{\varepsilon}|\mathbf{X} \sim N(\mathbf{0}, \sigma^2 \mathbf{I}_T). \tag{1.58}$$

In Eq. (1.58), both the dependent variable and the regressors are random variables with a joint density function $f(\mathbf{y}, \mathbf{x}_1, \ldots, \mathbf{x}_K)$. The assumptions implied by Eq. (1.58) are:

- The model is correctly specified, that is, the relationship between y and the regressors is actually linear and the identity of the regressors is correctly specified.
- The conditional expected value of the errors is 0, $E[\boldsymbol{\varepsilon}|\mathbf{X}] = \mathbf{0}$.
- The errors are conditionally homoskedastic, $E[\boldsymbol{\varepsilon}\boldsymbol{\varepsilon}'|\mathbf{X}] = \sigma^2 \mathbf{I}_T$.
- The conditional distribution of the errors is normal, $\boldsymbol{\varepsilon}|\mathbf{X} \sim N(\mathbf{0}, \sigma^2 \mathbf{I}_T)$.

If we focus our interest on the distribution of $\mathbf{y}$ conditional to the values of the regressors in $\mathbf{X}$, all the results presented so far in this chapter will hold, because $\mathbf{y}|\mathbf{X} \sim N(\mathbf{X}\boldsymbol{\beta}, \sigma^2 \mathbf{I}_T)$. Moreover, also the properties of the OLS estimators still hold, conditional on $\mathbf{X}$:

$$\hat{\boldsymbol{\beta}}^{OLS}|\mathbf{X} \sim N(\boldsymbol{\beta}, \sigma^2 (\mathbf{X}'\mathbf{X})^{-1}) \tag{1.59}$$

$$(T - K - 1)\frac{\hat{s}^2_{OLS}}{\sigma^2}|\mathbf{X} \sim \chi^2_{T-K-1}. \tag{1.60}$$

Therefore, also the distribution of the test statistics shown in Eqs. (1.53) and (1.54) remains unchanged, when they are derived conditional to $\mathbf{X}$.

Although this may seem reassuring, as the message seems to be that what we have learned fully applies and no changes are needed, it is also true that in practice we will be often (if not predominantly) interested in the unconditional distributions of the test statistics, and, as a consequence, of the estimators, for instance

$$\hat{\boldsymbol{\beta}}^{OLS} \sim \int_{-\infty}^{\infty} \int_{-\infty}^{\infty} \cdots \int_{-\infty}^{\infty} \underbrace{\phi_K(\boldsymbol{\beta}, \sigma^2 (\mathbf{X}'\mathbf{X})^{-1})}_{K\text{-dimensional Gaussian PDF}} \, d\mathbf{x}_1 d\mathbf{x}_2 \ldots d\mathbf{x}_K \tag{1.61}$$

while the results in Eqs. (1.59) and (1.60) are strictly conditional distributional results. To relax the hypothesis of the regressors being non-stochastic while retaining the possibility of studying their unconditional distributions, we will rely on asymptotic theory, the essentials of which are presented in the next section.

1.1.7 Asymptotic Theory for Linear Regressions

All the results obtained so far, especially the ones concerning the distributions of the estimators and the resulting test statistics, were based on rather strong assumptions on the error terms and on the non-randomness of the regressors. However, in many circumstances it may be difficult for these assumptions to appear realistic. In those cases, asymptotic theory can help us, in the sense that it is possible to derive the asymptotic distribution of many random statistics of interest under a variety of assumptions and then use the results as an approximation to finite-sample distributions. Let us start by rewriting the linear regression model as:

$$y_t = \mathbf{x}_t{}'\boldsymbol{\beta} + \varepsilon_t, \tag{1.62}$$

where the moments of each error are restricted below.[7] Note that in Eq. (1.62), y_t and ε_t are scalar random variables, while $\mathbf{x}_t$ and $\boldsymbol{\beta}$ are $(K + 1)$-dimensional vectors. No assumption is made either on the unconditional distribution or the conditional distribution of the errors. The only assumptions imposed on the model in Eq. (1.62) are that:

- y_t is IID over time.
- $\mathbf{x}_t$ is IID over time with finite first and second moments, in particular: $E[\mathbf{x}_t\mathbf{x}'_t] = \boldsymbol{\Sigma}_{xx}$ with $\|\boldsymbol{\Sigma}_{xx}\| < \infty$.
- The conditional expected value of the errors is 0, $E[\varepsilon_t|\mathbf{x}_t] = 0$ for every t.
- The errors display constant conditional variance and zero-autocorrelation for every t, $Var[\varepsilon_t|\mathbf{x}_t] = \sigma^2$ and $E[\varepsilon_t\varepsilon_{t-k}|\mathbf{x}_t] = 0$ for $k > 0$.

7. These assumptions on the conditional moments of the errors are even less restrictive than the ones made in the previous sections, as $E[\boldsymbol{\varepsilon}|\mathbf{X}] = \mathbf{0}$ implies $E[\varepsilon_t|\mathbf{x}_t] = 0$, but not vice versa.

From the last two assumptions and the law of iterated expectations, it follows that all the regressors and the errors have zero correlation:

$$\begin{aligned} Cov(\mathbf{x}_t, \varepsilon_t) &= E[\mathbf{x}_t\varepsilon_t] - E[\mathbf{x}_t]E[\varepsilon_t] = E_{\mathbf{x}_t}[E[\mathbf{x}_t\varepsilon_t|\mathbf{x}_t]] - E[\mathbf{x}_t]E_{\mathbf{x}_t}[E[\varepsilon_t|\mathbf{x}_t]] \\ &= E_{\mathbf{x}_t}[\mathbf{x}_t E[\varepsilon_t|\mathbf{x}_t]] - E[\mathbf{x}_t]E_{\mathbf{x}_t}[0] = E[\mathbf{x}_t \cdot 0] - E[\mathbf{x}_t]\cdot 0 = \mathbf{0}. \end{aligned} \tag{1.63}$$

Before studying the asymptotic distribution of the estimators and of the test statistics, we need to introduce a few additional definitions and tools, stated in the form of lemmas.

DEFINITION 1.1 (Convergence in probability)

A sequence of random variables z_t with $t = 1, 2, ...$ converges in probability to a value z, if $\lim_{t\to\infty} p(|z_t - z| < \varepsilon) = 1$, for every $\varepsilon > 0$, or $\lim_{t\to\infty} p(|z_t - z| > \varepsilon) = 0$. It this case, we also write $p \lim z_t = z$ or $z_t \overset{p}{\to} z$.

DEFINITION 1.2 (Convergence in distribution)

A sequence of random variables z_t with $t = 1, 2, \ldots$ converges in distribution to a random variable z, if $\lim_{t\to\infty} F(z_t) = F(z)$, in this case, we write $z_t \overset{D}{\to} z$.

RESULT 1.2 (Law of large numbers)

(Under some weak technical conditions) the sample mean of a sequence of IID variables z_t converges in probability to the expected value, $E[z_t]$,

$$\frac{1}{T}\sum_{t=1}^{T} z_t \overset{p}{\to} E[z_t]. \tag{1.64}$$

RESULT 1.3 (Lindeberg–Lévy's central limit theorem)

If a sequence of IID variables z_t has an expected value of μ and a variance $\sigma^2 < \infty$, then as $T \to \infty$, the standardized sum of the variables z_t converges in distribution to a standard normal distribution:

$$\frac{1}{\sqrt{T}} \frac{\sum_{t=1}^{T} z_t - \mu}{\sigma} \overset{D}{\to} N(0, 1). \tag{1.65}$$

RESULT 1.4 (Slutsky's theorem)

If a sequence of IID variables z_t converges in distribution to a random variable z and a sequence of random variables w_t converges in probability to some deterministic value w, then $g(z_t, w_t)$ converges in probability to $g(z, w)$.

We are now ready to state (and derive, in appropriate appendices at the end of the chapter) three fundamental results concerning the asymptotic behavior of the OLS estimators $\hat{\boldsymbol{\beta}}^{OLS}$ and $\hat{s}^2_{OLS}$ under the flexible and generally weak assumptions 1–4 listed above.

RESULT 1.5 (Consistency of OLS estimator of regression coefficients)
$\hat{\boldsymbol{\beta}}^{OLS}$ is a consistent estimator for $\boldsymbol{\beta}$: $p\lim \hat{\boldsymbol{\beta}}^{OLS} = \boldsymbol{\beta}$.

Of course, this result is far from surprising, given that it confirms what we have obtained above, but it is reassuring to see that modeling stochastic regressors makes no difference to our goals.

RESULT 1.6 (Consistency of OLS estimator of residual variance)
$\hat{s}^2_{OLS}$ is a consistent estimator for σ^2: $p\lim(\hat{s}^2_{OLS}) = \sigma^2$.

RESULT 1.7 (Asymptotic normality of OLS estimator of regression coefficients)
$\hat{\boldsymbol{\beta}}^{OLS}$ has an asymptotic normal distribution.

From Results 1.5 and 1.6, it can easily be shown that the t-test in Eq. (1.54) has a normal asymptotic distribution and that the F-test in Eq. (1.51) has a chi-squared asymptotic distribution with Q degrees of freedom:

$$t_T \equiv \frac{\hat{\beta}_k^{OLS}}{\hat{s}_{OLS}\sqrt{(\mathbf{X}'\mathbf{X})^{-1}_{kk}}} \xrightarrow{D} N(0,1) \tag{1.66}$$

$$F_T \equiv \frac{(\boldsymbol{K}'\hat{\boldsymbol{\beta}}^{OLS} - \boldsymbol{k})'\left[\sigma^2\boldsymbol{K}'(\mathbf{X}'\mathbf{X})^{-1}\boldsymbol{K}\right]^{-1}(\boldsymbol{K}'\hat{\boldsymbol{\beta}}^{OLS} - \boldsymbol{k})/Q}{\hat{s}^2_{OLS}} \xrightarrow{D} \chi^2_Q. \tag{1.67}$$

1.2 TESTING FOR VIOLATIONS OF THE LINEAR REGRESSION FRAMEWORK

1.2.1 Linearity

When choosing a linear regression model to fit data, the first assumption we are making is that there exists a linear relationship between the dependent variable and the regressors and that, as a result, the expected value of $\mathbf{y}$ can be expressed as a linear, weighted combination of the regressors, $\mathbf{x}_1$, $\mathbf{x}_2$, ..., $\mathbf{x}_K$ subject to random disturbances. Implicitly, this means that we do not directly consider any different (and usually more complex) type of functional relationship between the variables. For instance, let us consider the case of two explanatory variables for y_t. In the first case, assume that the DGP is $y_t = \beta_0 + \beta_1 x_{1,t} x_{2,t} + \varepsilon_t$, that is, the effect of the explanatory variables is multiplicative instead of additive; or, alternatively, consider $y_t = \beta_0 + \beta_1 x_{1,t}{}^2 + \beta_2 x_{2,t}{}^3 + \varepsilon_t$ (where the relation is not linear). Both models for the DGP seem quite simple and yet, using a linear regression model on data generated by these processes could let us wrongly conclude that the relationship between the dependent and the explanatory variables is weak. Paradoxically, even if we were to set $\varepsilon_t = 0$ at all times, the resulting simulated data would generate a regression R^2 well below 100%. To avoid using a linear model in all those cases in which the correct functional form is different from the classical $y_t = \beta_0 + \beta_1 x_{1,t} + \cdots + \beta_K x_{K,t} + \varepsilon_t$, there are two cautions that is always useful to consider: first, we should always plot the data and inspect the relationship between variables in pairs, composed of an explanatory variable and the dependent variable; second, we can perform formal tests of the hypothesis of linearity.

For concreteness, let us consider graphical methods applied to the bivariate case in which the variables under investigation are y_t and x_t. Having collected T observations on both, we can represent them with a *scatter plot*, which is a graph on the Cartesian-plan where every point has coordinates (x_t, y_t). If there exists a linear relation between y_t and x_t, the collection of points will be well approximated by a straight line, as in Fig. 1.1A and B. On the contrary, when there is no linear relation between the variables, the points will assume other shapes, as in Fig. 1.1C and D, which show how

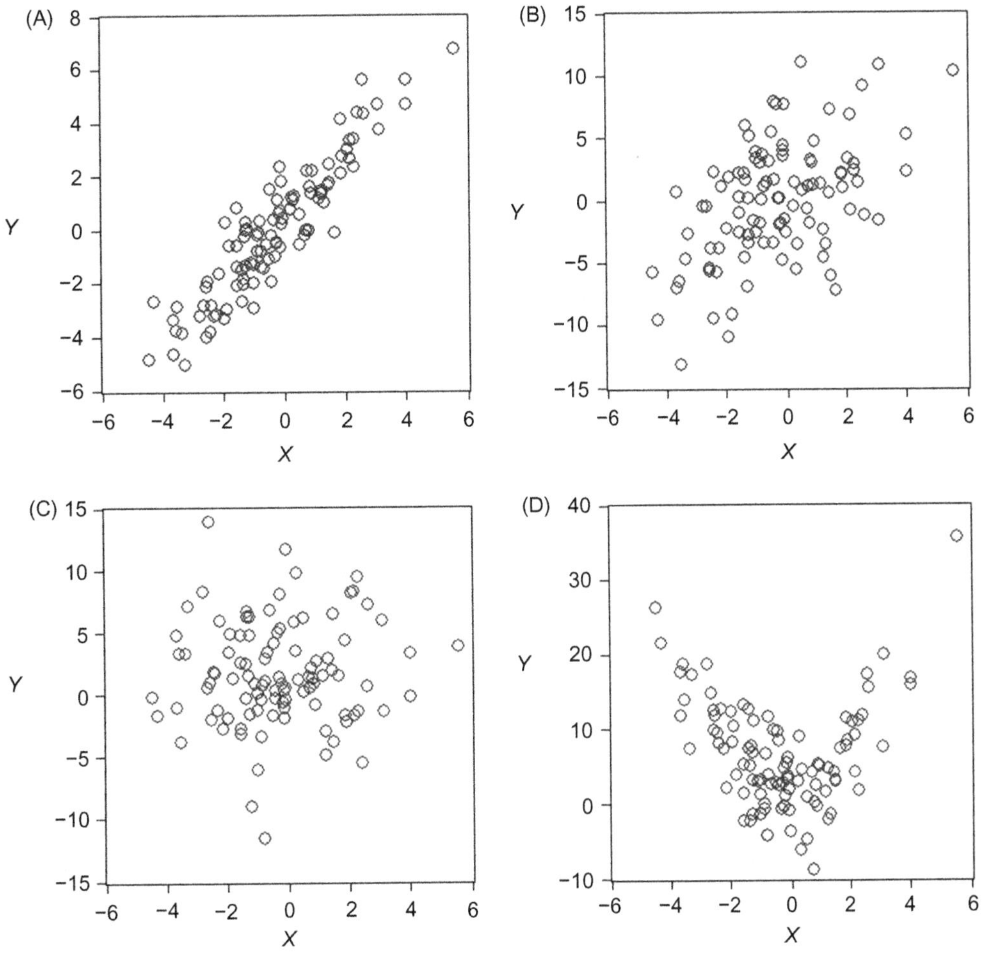

FIGURE 1.1 Simulated scatter plots for a bivariate case. (A) 100 simulated observations linear relation; (B) 100 simulated observations linear relation; (C) 100 simulated observations independent variables; (D) 100 simulated observations quadratic relation.

a scatter plot looks like, respectively in case of no relation at all between y_t and x_t, and in the case of a quadratic relationship, when the cloud of points assumes a U-shape.

In the bivariate case, the simple scatter plot between the dependent and the explanatory variable may provide a preliminary idea over the functional form of the relation. The multivariate case is instead more complicated and requires one of the techniques below:

- The scatter plot matrix, which consists in K^2 scatter plots between each pair of variables potentially used in the model. We shall be especially interested in the first column of this matrix, where one can find the pairwise scatter plots between the dependent variable and each of the regressors. To interpret the plots within this matrix, keep in mind that the pairwise relationships between the regressors x_k, $k = 1, 2, ..., K$, and y are linear keeping fixed the value of the other regressors. Therefore, if the regressors are correlated with each other, we will not always observe a collection of point approximating a straight line (as in the bivariate case), even if a linear functional form were to be correctly specified. Therefore, for a high number of regressors, this representation is often unsatisfactory because the linearity of the relationship may fail to turn up in visual terms.
- The scatter plot of observed y_t and fitted values $\hat{y}_t$. Contrary to what has been said about the scatter plot matrix, the scatter plot between y_t and $\hat{y}_t$ must always approximate a straight line if the functional form is linear.
- The scatter plot between observed values y_t and residuals $\hat{\varepsilon}_t$, which represents the same information between observed values and fitted values, but it can sometimes be more immediate to interpret, because, if the function form is linear, we would observe a collection of point distributed around a horizontal line, instead of around a diagonal (either upward or downward sloping) line.

EXAMPLE 1.6

Consider the following model for US aggregate excess stock returns (x_t):

$$x_t = \beta_0 + \beta_1 \text{dp}_t + \beta_2 \text{ep}_t + \beta_3 \text{svar}_t + \beta_4 \text{inf}_t + \varepsilon_t,$$

where dp_t is the dividend price ratio, ep_t is the earnings-price ratio, svar_t is the realized variance of stock returns, and inf_t is the inflation rate. The data used are monthly and the sample goes from January 2009 to November 2016.

As anticipated, when so many variables are involved, the best choice for the graphical representation of the information are scatter plots between the observed and the fitted values and between the observed dependent variable and the residuals, which are presented in Fig. 1.2A and B. From those graphs, it can be clearly inferred that there is no linear relation among the dependent variable and the regressors: indeed, in Fig. 1.2A, all the points are distributed on a horizontal line around −0.01, which is approximately the mean of the dependent variable; moreover, in Fig. 1.2B, there is a distinct upward sloping pattern because the largest residuals are associated with the largest values of the dependent variable, while the two should be approximately unrelated.

Moreover, although the scatter plot matrix presented in Fig. 1.3 can be quite difficult to interpret, looking at the first column, we can easily infer that there are no strong linear relationships between excess equity returns and any of the regressors.

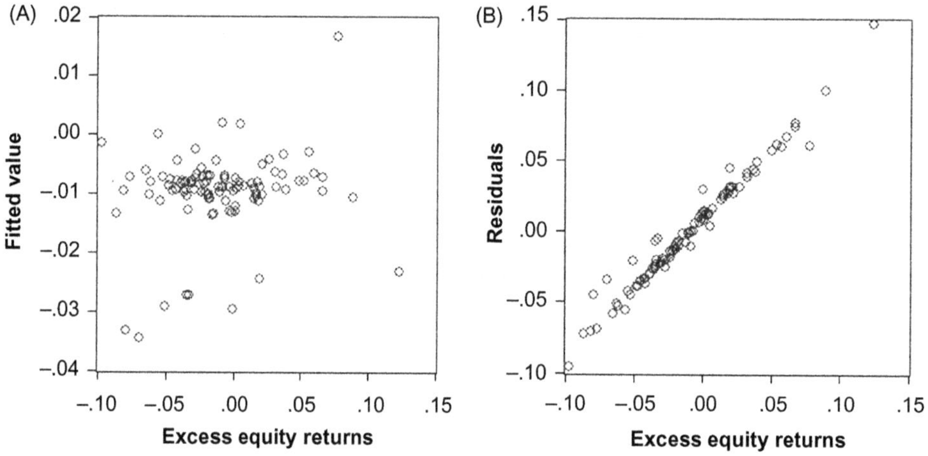

FIGURE 1.2 Scatter plots to investigate the linearity assumption. (A) Scatter plot between the dependent variable and the fitted values; (B) scatter plot between the dependent variable and the residuals.

However, using scatter plots does not allow us to derive a well-specified decision rule whether to reject or not the linearity hypothesis. Therefore, it is wise to also perform a few formal statistical tests of hypothesis. In what follows we present the *Regression Specification Error Test* (RESET) test, a famous test for linearity, first proposed by Ramsey (1969). In this test, the null hypothesis is that the model is correctly specified: therefore, under the null, not only we assume linearity but also we are not omitting any relevant explanatory variables. This composite nature of the null hypothesis represents the major challenge to practical use of RESET. The test is then applied by performing the following steps:

1. Estimate the coefficients and the residuals from the linear model:

$$y_t = \beta_0 + \beta_1 x_{1,t} + \beta_2 x_{2,t} + \cdots + \beta_K x_{K,t} + \varepsilon_t. \tag{1.68}$$

2. Collect the fitted values $\hat{y}_t$ and the residuals $\hat{\varepsilon}_t$ from the previous step and compute the residuals sum of squares SSR_ε as in Eq. (1.20).
3. Estimate the model:

$$y_t = \beta_0 + \beta_1 x_{1,t} + \cdots + \beta_K x_{K,t} + \alpha_1 \hat{y}_t^{\,2} + \alpha_2 \hat{y}_t^{\,3} + \cdots + \alpha_m \hat{y}_t^{\,m+1} + u_t, \tag{1.69}$$

where m powers of the fitted values are added as regressors.

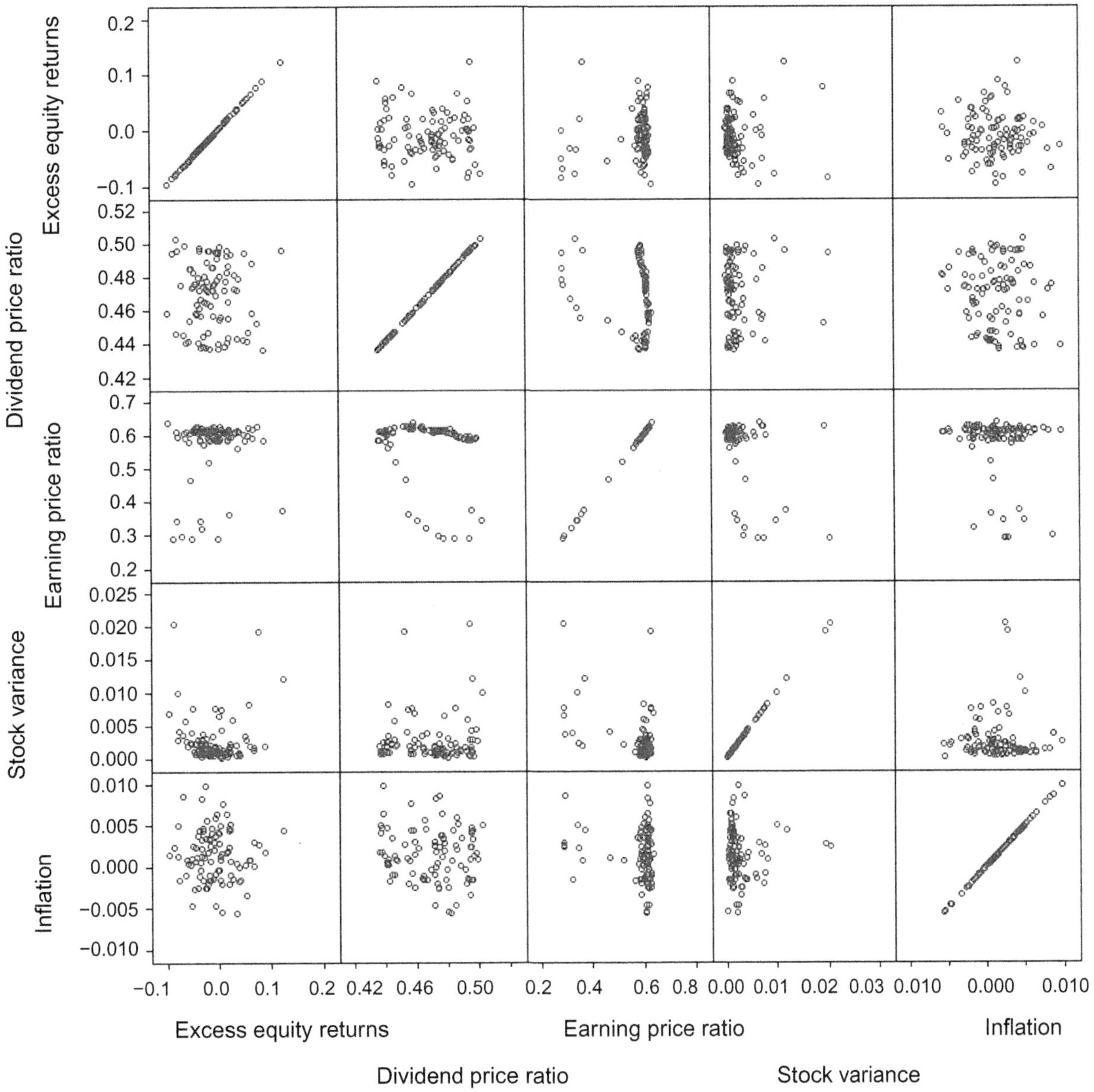

FIGURE 1.3 Scatter plot matrix.

4. Collect the residuals $\hat{u}_t$ from the estimation in the previous step and compute the corresponding residual sum of squares SSR_u.
5. Compute the test statistic:

$$F = \frac{(\mathrm{SSR}_\varepsilon - \mathrm{SSR}_u)/m}{\mathrm{SSR}_u/(T-K-1-m)}. \tag{1.70}$$

Under the hypothesis of correct specification, the F-statistic above is distributed according to an F-distribution with m and $T-K-1-m$ degrees of freedom. The null hypothesis of correct model specification can be written as $H_0{:}\alpha_1 = \alpha_2 = \cdots = \alpha_m = 0$. Intuitively, this comes from the fact that if the model in Eq. (1.68) were correctly specified, then the values for the powers of the fitted values could not represent relevant explanatory variables and, hence, their coefficients should not be significantly different from 0. Moreover, if H_0 were true, the model in Eq. (1.69) would fail to provide a better fit than the original model and therefore the difference $\mathrm{SSR}_\varepsilon - \mathrm{SSR}_u$ would be close to 0.

The RESET test is useful to detect specification errors; however, it does not give any suggestion about an alternative functional form in case the test leads to a rejection. Finally, it may occur that a linear functional form appears to be rejected not only or mostly because the linear model is deficient but simply because one or more explanatory variables have been incorrectly omitted from the model in Eq. (1.68).

EXAMPLE 1.7

Table 1.4 presents the result of a RESET test (with $m=2$, i.e., squared and cubic fitted values used as test variables in Eq. 1.69) applied to the estimated regression:

$$x_t = \beta_0 + \beta_1 \text{dp}_t + \beta_2 \text{ep}_t + \beta_3 \text{svar}_t + \beta_4 \text{dm}_t + \beta_5 \text{df}_t + \beta_6 \text{inf}_t + \varepsilon_t,$$

where the variables are the ones of Examples 1.5 and 1.6 with the addition of bm_t, the aggregate book-to-market ratio, and df_t, the default yield spread (the difference between the rates of Baa and Aaa corporate bonds, as per Moody's rating classifications). Because the p-value for the test (which is indicated as *Probability* in the last column, the first row of Table 1.4) is 0.008 and therefore it is lower than standard size levels of 1% and 5%, we reject the null hypothesis of correct specification.

Table 1.4 shows also the SSR for the model in Eq. (1.68) as *Restricted* SSR and for the model Eq. (1.69) as *Unrestricted* SSR.

Table 1.5 actually displays the estimated unrestricted model in Eq. (1.69). Looking at the column *Probability*, which contains the p-values of the t-tests on each coefficient, we note that at a significance level of 95% (also 99%, or equivalently at sizes of the test as low as 5% and 1%), none of the coefficients of the original regression is statistically significant, while both powers of the fitted values carry coefficients significantly different from 0. This result, along with the overall RESET test statistic, strongly indicates misspecification in the model and a potential for nonlinear relations between excess equity returns and the selected regressors.

TABLE 1.4 Output of a RESET Test With $m=2$

Ramsey RESET test
Omitted Variables: Powers of Fitted Values From 2 to 3

	Value	*df*	Probability
F-statistic	5.182	(2, 86)	0.008
F-test summary			
	Sum of Squares	***df***	**Mean Squares**
Restricted SSR	0.145	88	0.002
Unrestricted SSR	0.130	86	0.002

In general, there is not an obvious or unique solution to deal with the presence of nonlinearities in the relationships of interest. If we believe that some relation among the variables exists, but that it is likely to be nonlinear, a first approach could be to include in our model some transformations of the explanatory variables, such as their powers or their logarithms, either in replacement or in addition to their levels. In this case, after transforming the variables, we can conduct the analysis using an OLS estimator with no additional efforts or concerns required. Of course, any such transformations should then be taken into account when reporting and interpreting the results. For instance, regressing a dependent variable on the log of some explanatory variable will take us to estimate a semielasticity; regressing logs of the dependent on logs of the explanatory variables would take us to obtain an elasticity.

To estimate more complex models that cannot be expressed in a linear form, that is, when there is nonlinearity in the way the parameters enter the relationship, we have to rely on the *nonlinear least squares* (NLS) estimator. NLS is based on the same criterion of the OLS estimator, that is, the minimization of the sum of the squared residuals, but it can also be applied to nonlinear functional forms and therefore is suitable to a much larger class of models versus standard linear regressions. To derive the general formulation of NLS, first we have to define the functional form of our

TABLE 1.5 Output of a RESET Test With $m = 2$—Estimates of the Unrestricted Model

Unrestricted Model Estimate
Dependent Variables: Equity Premium
Method: Least Squares
Sample: 2009M01 2016M11
Included Observations: 95

Variable	Coefficient	S.E.	t-Statistic	Probability
C	−0.010	0.125	−0.079	0.937
Dividend price ratio	−0.220	0.222	−0.988	0.326
Earning price ratio	0.159	0.175	0.906	0.367
Stock variance	−1.129	1.941	−0.581	0.562
Book to market	−0.069	0.147	−0.466	0.643
Default yield spread	1.756	1.713	1.025	0.308
Inflation	−1.075	1.393	−0.772	0.442
FITTED^2	304.010	98.741	3.079	0.003
FITTED^3	9084.435	2881.859	3.152	0.002

R^2	0.135	Mean dependent variable	−0.010
Adjusted R^2	0.055	SD dependent variable	0.040
S.E. of regression	0.039	Akaike information criterion	−3.568
SSR	0.130	Schwarz criterion	−3.327
Log-likelihood	178.504	Hannan–Quinn criterion	−3.471
F-statistic	1.678	Durbin–Watson statistic	2.018
p (F-statistic)	0.115		

model, that means specifying some nonlinear real-valued function $f(\cdot):\mathbb{R}^K \to \mathbb{R}$ (but recall that after all also linear functions are just degenerate cases of nonlinear ones):

$$y_t = f(\mathbf{x}_t; \boldsymbol{\beta}) + \varepsilon_t. \tag{1.71}$$

This is usually the most complex part of the modeling procedure because, unless we can base our analysis over a specific theoretical, economic, or financial model, we will have to select a functional form for the relationship between the dependent variables and a set of K explanatory variables, when in principle there exist infinite different specifications. In other words, once we understand that the model cannot simply be of a linear type as in Eq. (1.68), there are many ways in which the variables and the parameters can be concocted in a nonlinear functional representation.

Once we have selected $f(\cdot)$, the estimator $\hat{\boldsymbol{\beta}}^{\text{NLS}}$ can be derived as:

$$\hat{\boldsymbol{\beta}}^{\text{NLS}} \equiv \arg\min_{\boldsymbol{\beta}} \sum_{t=1}^{T} [y_t - f(\mathbf{x}_t; \boldsymbol{\beta})]^2, \tag{1.72}$$

which is of course just another SSR, $\varepsilon_t \equiv y_t - f(\mathbf{x}_t; \boldsymbol{\beta})$, minimization. The minimization problem defined by Eq. (1.72) admits interior solutions if the function $f(\mathbf{x}_t; \boldsymbol{\beta})$ is twice continuously differentiable in the second argument. Moreover, the problem rarely admits a closed-form analytical solution for the parameters, differently from the famous OLS expression in Eq. (1.8), and this is the reason for why NLS often imply considerable computational costs and technical issues. To compute $\hat{\boldsymbol{\beta}}^{\text{NLS}}$ it is often necessary to use an *iterative numerical algorithm* that often approach a solution (that may yet be a local maximum only) rather slowly.[8]

1.2.2 Structural Breaks and Parameter Stability Test

Another implicit assumption that we are making in the baseline linear regression model is that it holds identically over the entire sample period—equivalently, that the sample comes from the same population—and specifically that the values of the parameters remain unchanged over time. However, economic theories and empirical analysis often suggest

8. We refer the interested reader to the introductory treatment in Davidson and McKinnon (2004) for additional details.

that the relationships among variables may change over time. Therefore, the assumption of stable, time-invariant parameters may prove to be too restrictive, especially when we work with long samples of data. When we detect (e.g., using statistical tests) a change in the parameters of a DGP, we say that there is evidence of a *structural break* (sometimes we shall say we were unable to find evidence against the presence of a break). Even though this topic will be studied in greater depth in Chapter 8, here we just describe a few typical tests that can be performed with reference to the results of a regression analysis. To detect structural breaks, different *tests of parameter stability* have been developed. Here we present two alternative approaches that differ because the former will require to make an a priori assumption on the date(s) of the structural break(s), while the latter does not.

Imagine dealing with a sample period in which a financial crisis or a major macroeconomic event has occurred. A good practice is then to test whether this event has had relevant effects on the relationship among the variables under investigation and therefore on the values of the parameters. This is the case in which we knew a priori the date of the potential break, that is, the date of the event. The most naive way to test for parameter stability is to compare the results from a restricted model,

$$y_t = \mathbf{x}'_t\,\boldsymbol{\beta} + \varepsilon_t \tag{1.73}$$

and the unrestricted model,

$$\begin{aligned} y_t &= \mathbf{x}'_t\boldsymbol{\beta}_1 + \varepsilon_t \qquad \textit{if}\ \ t<T_1 \\ y_t &= \mathbf{x}'_t\boldsymbol{\beta}_2 + \varepsilon_t \qquad \textit{if}\ \ t\geq T_1, \end{aligned} \tag{1.74}$$

where T_1 is the date in which the structural break is conjectured to have occurred. Under the null hypothesis $H_0{:}\boldsymbol{\beta}_1 = \boldsymbol{\beta}_2$, that is, there is no structural break and the following ratio is distributed as an F-distribution with $K+1$ and $T-2K-2$ degrees of freedom:

$$F_T \equiv \frac{(\mathrm{SSR} - \mathrm{SSR}_1 - \mathrm{SSR}_2)/(K+1)}{(\mathrm{SSR}_1 + \mathrm{SSR}_2)/(T-2K-2)}, \tag{1.75}$$

where SSR, SSR_1, and SSR_2 are the residual sums of squares of the model in Eq. (1.73) and of the two submodels in Eq. (1.74), respectively. Such a test is often referred to as a *known break date, Chow test*. An analogous test can be performed by adding to the regressors a dummy variable which assumes a value of 0 before the structural break and of 1 after this date and then using a t-statistic to check for the significance of the parameter associated to the dummy variable.

In other situations, we may also be concerned with the stability of the parameters but have no a priori information or even conjectures concerning the time in which a break may take place. In this case, we can rely on the results of a *CUSUM test*, developed by Page (1954). The test is based on a statistic computed from the values assumed by recursive regression residuals, which are defined as:

$$w_t = y_t - \mathbf{x}'_t\hat{\boldsymbol{\beta}}_{t-1}^{\mathrm{OLS}} \qquad t = K+2,\ldots,T, \tag{1.76}$$

where $\hat{\boldsymbol{\beta}}_{t-1}^{\mathrm{OLS}}$ is the OLS estimate of the parameters obtained using only the first $t-1$ observations of the sample. Therefore, the point of Eq. (1.76) is to perform a one-step-ahead prediction of the dependent variable using OLS estimates obtained from data that do not contain that value. The test is then implemented by computing the values for $t = K+2,\ldots,T$ of the following statistics:

$$W_t \equiv \tilde{s}^{-1}\sum_{i=K+2}^{t} w_i, \tag{1.77}$$

where $\tilde{s}$ is the estimated SD of the recursive residuals. Under the null hypothesis of the absence of structural breaks, the values from Eq. (1.77) are distributed according to a special distribution, the CUSUM distribution, whose expected value is 0 and whose variance increases as t increases. After having fixed a size of the test and having computed the upper and lower bounds according to the CUSUM distribution for W_t we shall reject the null hypothesis of no breaks if any value of W_t over $t = K+2,\ldots,T$ falls outside such bounds.

EXAMPLE 1.8

Table 1.6 presents the result of a known break date, Chow test applied to a linear regression model in which the dependent variable is the daily return on a portfolio composted by stocks of US firms operating in the clothing industry and the regressor is simply the aggregate, value-weighted market return (what we sometimes call *market model*). The sample period is January 2000–December 2015. The p-value of the test in correspondence to an assumed break date on January 1, 2008, equals 0.000 and leads to a rejection of the null hypothesis of the absence of structural breaks. The interpretation is that the exposure to market risk by the stocks of firms in the clothing industry has significantly changed after 2008.

On the contrary, if we perform on the same model and with the same data a CUSUM test, we obtain the results shown in Fig. 1.4. Under this different breakpoint test methodology, the standardized recursive residuals never exceed the 95% confidence bounds pointing to a failure to reject the null hypothesis. This different result emphasizes that different methodologies may lead to different conclusions (this is trivially often the case), but especially that by assuming a known break date, one may get more power from a test, at the cost of incurring in the perils of the assumed date being incorrect.

TABLE 1.6 Output of a Chow Breakpoint Test

Chow Breakpoint Test: 1/01/2008
Null Hypothesis: No Breaks at Specified Breakpoints
Varying regressors: All Equation Variables
Equation Sample: 1/03/2000 12/31/2015

***F*-statistic**	16.518	***p*(*F*(2,4021))**	0.000

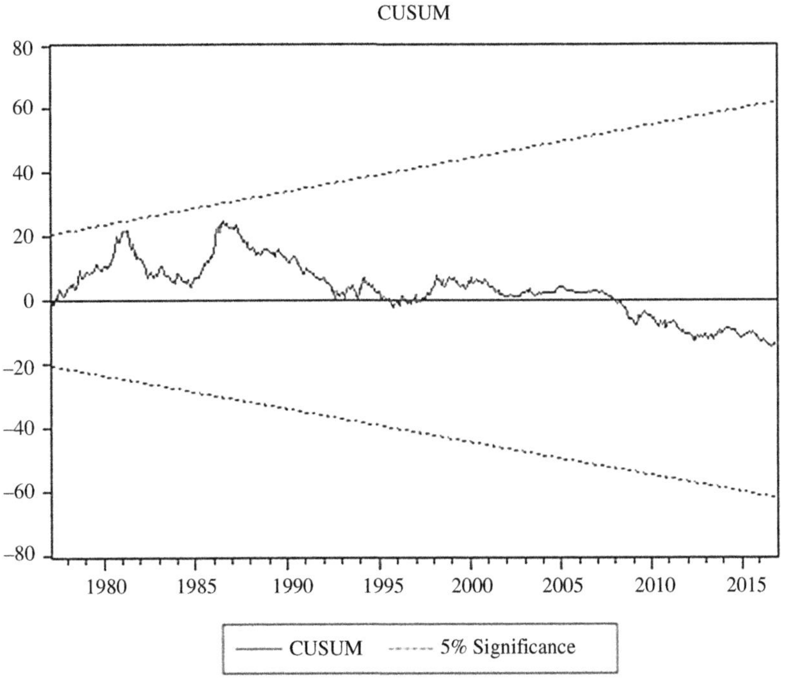

FIGURE 1.4 Output of a CUSUM for a break in the market Model Beta.

1.3 SPECIFYING THE REGRESSORS

We now consider three important aspects regarding the selection and properties of explanatory variables. The first aspect concerns the choice of the most appropriate regressors for a model and the consequence of variable misspecifications (omissions or inclusions of irrelevant variables) at this stage; the second is related to (linear) admissible and non-admissible relationships among sets of regressors; the final aspect deals with the issues arising from collecting observations on the regressors that contain random measurement errors.

1.3.1 How to Select the Regressors

We already had the opportunity to emphasize that assuming that a regression model is correctly specified means both that the functional form is actually linear and that the model includes all and only the relevant regressors. Moreover, recall that a Ramsey's test (see Section 1.2.1) can easily be used for detecting misspecification errors due to a poor choice of the functional form of the model, but that the test assumes that the explanatory variables had been correctly selected. Here, we are going to investigate in detail why it is so important to carefully select the appropriate regressors and what are the consequences of omitting some otherwise relevant regressors (i.e., that ought to be included in the model, even though we have no way to know that) or of including some irrelevant regressors that should not have been included. Because it is rather natural to do so, we will conclude by providing some operational insights on how to effectively select the regressors.

Suppose that the actual DGP is represented in matrix form as:

$$\mathbf{y} = \mathbf{X}\boldsymbol{\beta} + \boldsymbol{\varepsilon} \quad \boldsymbol{\varepsilon}|\mathbf{X} \sim N(\mathbf{0}, \sigma^2\mathbf{I}_T). \tag{1.78}$$

The $T \times (K+1)$ matrix $\mathbf{X}$, which contains the observations on the explanatory variables, can be rewritten as $\mathbf{X} = [\mathbf{Z}\ \mathbf{Q}]$, where $\mathbf{Z}$ is a $T \times H$ matrix and $\mathbf{Q}$ is a $T \times L$ matrix, with $H + L = K + 1$. The two matrices will respectively contain the observations on the first H and on the last L explanatory variables. Accordingly, it also possible to split the vector $\boldsymbol{\beta}$ in two vectors $\boldsymbol{\beta}_1$ and $\boldsymbol{\beta}_2$, which are H- and L-dimensional, such that $\boldsymbol{\beta} \equiv [\boldsymbol{\beta}_1'\boldsymbol{\beta}_2']'$. Writing Eq. (1.78) in terms of $\mathbf{Z}$, $\mathbf{Q}$, $\boldsymbol{\beta}_1$, and $\boldsymbol{\beta}_2$, we get:

$$\mathbf{y} = \mathbf{Z}\boldsymbol{\beta}_1 + \mathbf{Q}\boldsymbol{\beta}_2 + \boldsymbol{\varepsilon} \quad \boldsymbol{\varepsilon}|\mathbf{Z}, \mathbf{Q} \sim N(\mathbf{0}, \sigma^2\mathbf{I}_T). \tag{1.79}$$

Suppose now that we have estimated a linear regression for $\mathbf{y}$ that correctly includes all the regressors in $\mathbf{Z}$, but that incorrectly omits all the variables in the submatrix $\mathbf{Q}$. Because $\mathbf{Z}$ is the only recognized matrix of regressors, the OLS estimate of our model will be $\hat{\boldsymbol{\beta}}_1^{OLS} = (\mathbf{Z}'\mathbf{Z})^{-1}\mathbf{Z}'\mathbf{y}$. The expected value of the OLS estimator is then:

$$\begin{aligned} E\left[\hat{\boldsymbol{\beta}}^{OLS}|\mathbf{X}\right] &= E\left[(\mathbf{Z}'\mathbf{Z})^{-1}\mathbf{Z}'\mathbf{y}|\mathbf{X}\right] = (\mathbf{Z}'\mathbf{Z})^{-1}\mathbf{Z}'(\mathbf{Z}\boldsymbol{\beta}_1 + \mathbf{Q}\boldsymbol{\beta}_2) \\ &= (\mathbf{Z}'\mathbf{Z})^{-1}\mathbf{Z}'\mathbf{Z}\boldsymbol{\beta}_1 + (\mathbf{Z}'\mathbf{Z})^{-1}\mathbf{Z}'\mathbf{Q}\boldsymbol{\beta}_2 = \boldsymbol{\beta}_1 + (\mathbf{Z}'\mathbf{Z})^{-1}\mathbf{Z}'\mathbf{Q}\boldsymbol{\beta}_2. \end{aligned} \tag{1.80}$$

Crucially, the term $(\mathbf{Z}'\mathbf{Z})^{-1}\mathbf{Z}'\mathbf{Q}\boldsymbol{\beta}_2$ is generally different from 0, meaning that $\hat{\boldsymbol{\beta}}_1^{OLS}$ is a biased estimator for $\boldsymbol{\beta}_1$, the vector of coefficients of the regressors that have been correctly included. In fact, $(\mathbf{Z}'\mathbf{Z})^{-1}\mathbf{Z}'\mathbf{Q}\boldsymbol{\beta}_2$ equals a vector of zeros only when all the pairwise correlations between the included and the omitted regressors are 0, which seems unlikely, at least as a matter of sheer luck. In all other situations, the sign and the magnitude of the bias of the individual coefficient estimates collected in $\hat{\boldsymbol{\beta}}_1^{OLS}$ will depend both on the values of the parameters in $\boldsymbol{\beta}_2$ and on the covariances between the included regressors (in $\mathbf{Z}$) and the omitted ones (in $\mathbf{Q}$). This result on the existence of a bias in $\hat{\boldsymbol{\beta}}_1^{OLS}$ when some relevant regressors are omitted is known as an *omitted variable bias* and—whether perceived as such or not—it tends to appear in many regression models. Moreover, in the case of omitted regressors, because there is no reason to think that $(\mathbf{Z}'\mathbf{Z})^{-1}\mathbf{Z}'\mathbf{Q}\boldsymbol{\beta}_2$ will vanish asymptotically, as $\mathbf{Q}$ has simply been ignored, it can be shown also that:

$$p\lim(\hat{\boldsymbol{\beta}}_1^{OLS}) \neq \boldsymbol{\beta}_1. \tag{1.81}$$

Therefore, the bias persists also in large (asymptotic) samples and $\hat{\boldsymbol{\beta}}_1^{OLS}$ is an inconsistent estimator of $\boldsymbol{\beta}_1$.

Summing up the results obtained so far, we can state that every time we forget to include in the model an important variable that significantly contributes to determine the value of the dependent variable, not only we will be failing to investigate the correct DGP but we will also obtain unreliable estimates and forecasts regarding the effect of the included regressors, because the OLS estimator is biased and inconsistent. The coefficients will be overestimated or underestimated (i.e., the bias will be positive or negative) depending on the sign of the product between the coefficient of the omitted variable and the covariance between the included and the omitted regressors.

Let now consider the opposite case, that is, suppose that the correct model is:

$$\mathbf{y} = \mathbf{X}\boldsymbol{\beta} + \boldsymbol{\varepsilon} \quad \boldsymbol{\varepsilon}|\mathbf{X} \sim N(\mathbf{0}, \sigma^2\mathbf{I}_T) \tag{1.82}$$

and that we are incorrectly including some irrelevant explanatory variables, that is, such that $E[\mathbf{R}'\mathbf{y}] = \mathbf{0}$, and therefore estimating the following:

$$\mathbf{y} = \mathbf{X}\boldsymbol{\beta}^* + \mathbf{R}\boldsymbol{\beta}_R + \boldsymbol{\varepsilon}, \tag{1.83}$$

where R stands for "redundant" here. Defining $\mathbf{Z} = [\mathbf{XR}]$, Eq. (1.83) becomes:

$$\mathbf{y} = \mathbf{Z}\boldsymbol{\beta} + \boldsymbol{\varepsilon}, \tag{1.84}$$

where $\boldsymbol{\beta} \equiv [\boldsymbol{\beta}^{*\prime}\ \boldsymbol{\beta}_R{}']'$. The OLS estimator of $\boldsymbol{\beta}$ will be $\hat{\boldsymbol{\beta}}^{OLS} = (\mathbf{Z}'\mathbf{Z})^{-1}\mathbf{Z}'\mathbf{y}$. It can be shown that the estimates resulting from $\hat{\boldsymbol{\beta}}^{OLS}$ remain unbiased even though these are by construction different from those that should have been obtained for $\hat{\boldsymbol{\beta}}^{*,OLS} = (\mathbf{X}'\mathbf{X})^{-1}\mathbf{X}'\mathbf{y} \neq (\mathbf{Z}'\mathbf{Z})^{-1}\mathbf{Z}'\mathbf{y}$. The reason is that $E[\mathbf{R}'\mathbf{y}] = \mathbf{0}$. However, the variance of the estimator will increase when compared to the case in which only the relevant regressors are included. With higher S.E.s, OLS is no longer the most efficient estimation method, that is, $\hat{\boldsymbol{\beta}}^{OLS}$ is not BLUE (in principle, GLS might be used to take into account of the effects caused by the inclusion of the redundant regressors on the errors).

Clearly bias and inconsistency are much more undesirable than some loss in efficiency, that is often anyway hard to measure. Therefore, in general, we can say that, when facing any doubts as to whether a specific variable should be or should not be included in a regression model, including it appears to be the best option. However, when this way of proceeding is interpreted as a rule of selection for all sorts of reasonable and less reasonable explanatory variables, it may result in the so-called kitchen-sink regressions, which are models in which an extremely large number of variables are included without any economic foundation or reason; as a result, they require to estimate a large number of parameters and eventually may lead—also because multicollinearity problems (see Section 1.3.2 for additional details) will often lurk in the background—to confusing, often hard-to-interpret, empirical results.

Because some middle ground must be stroke between the risk of omitting some variables and the perils of kitchen sinks, with the increase in computational power, it has become increasingly popular to use *automatic variable selection procedures* that we now briefly summarize. Suppose we have selected a set of all the possible M regressors that may provide a sensible explanation—this is therefore more than mere correlation, even though we are not yet discussing the issue of causality (see Chapter 3, for a definition and details)—for a given dependent variable of interest. Clearly, the most efficient way to select among such regressors will be to form all possible subsets of regressors, estimate all the possible, resulting linear regression models, and compare their results in term of adjusted R^2 and possibly of significance of all or subsets of key estimated coefficients. However, this is rarely an open option, due to the high number of models that could be estimated and the consequent computational costs. For instance, try to imagine how large the set of all the possible variables that can explain the performance (say, profitability) of a firm can be. Moreover, once we have selected M possible variables, all the resulting possible linear regression models will be 2^M; for instance, when $M = 10$, the number of possible alternative models is 1024; however, when $M = 20$, this becomes 1,048,576. Therefore, the actual chances to have the resources to estimate and compare all the possible specifications and then to find the absolute, optimal model are thin (but see, for instance, Sala-i-Martin, 1997). The automatic variable selection procedures are algorithms that help instead to find a relative, optimal subset of regressors while limiting the implied computational cost of estimating all possible models. The most commonly employed variable selection algorithms are:

- forward selection,
- backward elimination,
- stepwise regression.

The *forward selection* algorithm is the simplest among the three procedures and it consists of the following steps:

1. Estimating an initial, linear regression model with no regressors, that is, a model with only the intercept (of course, this is equivalent to just estimating the sample mean of the dependent variable).
2. Choose as the first candidate regressor (among the set of all possible M explanatory variables minus the already added regressors) the one that will produce the highest increase in the R^2.
3. Estimate the model after adding the candidate regressor (and keeping all the previously selected ones).
4. Keep the candidate regressor in the model only if the p-value associated with the corresponding t-test in the regression is lower than α_{in}, where α_{in} is an arbitrarily chosen test size value (e.g., 5%, 10%, or 20%).
5. Repeat steps from 2 to 4, until it found a candidate regressor that cannot be added or until all the M regressors are included in the model.

Along with its simplicity—in fact, the algorithm is simply automatizing a common-sense approach to the problem—the advantage of this procedure is that it can be applied also in those cases in which the number of explanatory variables is higher than the number of observations.[9] Sometimes, the forward selection algorithm is also described as an empiricist going "from simple to general" in building her model. This is often praised as a way to maximize the chances to end up with a relatively parsimonious and simple model. The obvious limitation of the forward selection method is that once a regressor has been added, it will remain in the model for good, even if its significance were to decline and the p-value of the corresponding t-test to increase above α_{in}, after the addition of other additional regressors among the original M.

The *backward elimination* algorithm is structured in the opposite way compared to the forward selection. In fact, its steps are:

1. Estimate an initial, linear regression model including all the available regressors.
2. Choose one candidate variable to be eliminated, to be identified with the regressor that implies the highest p-value in the regression.[10]
3. Drop a candidate regressor only if its p-value exceeds α_{out}, where α_{out} is an arbitrarily chosen test size (e.g., 5%, 10%, or 20%).
4. Repeat steps from 2 to 3, until no additional regressor can be eliminated or no regressor is left in the model, which at this point will just consist of the sample mean.

Differently from the forward selection methodology, here the final model will include only regressors with a p-value smaller than α_{out}. However, we have no way to verify whether some of the eliminated regressors will come to imply a p-value smaller than α_{out}, after removing other variables. In fact, once we have eliminated one regressor, it cannot be added again to the model. Therefore, variations of the backward elimination algorithms exist that take pause to verify whether any regressors discarded in earlier steps may be included back later on.

The *stepwise regression* method is a mix of the two previous algorithms and consists of the following steps:

1. Estimating an initial, linear regression model with no regressors, that is, a model with only the intercept.
2. Choose as a candidate regressor the one that yields the highest increase in the R^2 (among the set of potential explanatory variables not yet considered).
3. Estimate the model adding to it the candidate regressor.
4. Keep the candidate regressor in the model only if the p-value is lower than some fixed threshold α_{in}.
5. Apply a backward elimination subroutine starting from the model defined at Step 4:
   - **5.a** Choose as a candidate to be eliminated, the regressor with the highest p-value.
   - **5.b** Drop the candidate regressor only if the p-value of the t-statistic exceeds α_{out}, where α_{out} is an arbitrarily chosen test size threshold (e.g., 5%, 10%, or 20%).
   - **5.c** Repeat Steps 5.a and 5.b, until no regressor can be eliminated.
6. Repeat steps from 2 to 5, until the algorithm finds a first candidate explanatory variable that cannot be added or until all the regressors are included in the model.

Using this approach, if the significance of a variable previously added declines and its p-value exceeds α_{out}, the variable is removed from the model. Although it is possible to choose different values for α_{in} and α_{out}, it is wise to fix them to the same level. In fact, when $\alpha_{\text{in}} > \alpha_{\text{out}}$ the algorithm is more likely to drop the just added regressors and the computational cost of the algorithm increases as it may become slower and erratic, while when $\alpha_{\text{in}} < \alpha_{\text{out}}$, the methodology turns less likely to drop the added regressors, reducing the effectiveness of Step 5.

EXAMPLE 1.9

Table 1.7 shows the steps of a backward elimination procedure applied to the same linear regression model of Example 1.7. Each column reports the p-values of each of the regressors for a different model specification. The symbol "x" indicates that the regressor has been excluded in the model specification provided in the columns. Fixing a threshold $\alpha_{\text{out}} = 0.05$, none of the regressors would be included in the final model, while for a value of α_{out} equal to 0.20, the selected model would be the one with only the earning price ratio as explanatory variable.

9. Although this may appear obvious, let us remind ourselves that it is not possible to estimate a linear regression model where $K > T$. Algebraically, this derives from the fact that in order to invert the matrix $\mathbf{XX}'$ it is necessary that rank($\mathbf{X}$) $= K$, while rank($\mathbf{X}$) $= \min[K, T]$.

10. An alternative implementation is based on selecting regressors to be dropped that have the lowest t-statistic. Of course, because p-values come from t-tests, the two criteria give identical results. However, there are variations of the algorithm in which in each single step all explanatory variables implying t-statistics above some fixed threshold are simultaneously dropped. A similar caveat applies to the forward algorithm, in the sense that only regressors with t-statistics above some thresholds will be added.

TABLE 1.7 Estimated p-Values From a Backward Elimination Algorithm

Variable	p-values	p-values	p-values	p-values	p-values	p-values	p-values
Dividend price ratio	0.744	0.742	0.754	x	x	x	x
Earning price ratio	0.303	0.145	0.123	0.111	0.120	0.174	x
Stock variance	0.409	0.372	0.355	0.352	0.444	x	x
Book to market	0.611	0.584	0.563	0.575	x	x	x
Default yield spread	0.985	x	x	x	x	x	x
Inflation	0.880	0.879	x	x	x	x	x

1.3.2 Multicollinearity

Another key issue regarding the selection of regressors is the so-called *multicollinearity* problem, which alludes to the presence of relatively high linear relationships (and, therefore, large correlations in absolute value) among (linear combinations, besides pairs of) regressors. The first aspect to clarify is that in order to compute the estimator $\hat{\boldsymbol{\beta}}^{OLS}$, $\mathbf{X}$ must have a full column rank (i.e., rank($\mathbf{X}$) $= K + 1$); otherwise, the matrix $\mathbf{X}'\mathbf{X}$ would not be invertible. This algebraic condition is satisfied as long as none of the regressors can be obtained exactly as a linear combination of the remaining ones. When $\mathbf{X}$ fails to have full column rank, we say that we have *perfect multicollinearity* and in this case, not only we cannot invert the matrix $\mathbf{X}'\mathbf{X}$ but also from a formal perspective; the problem is that we are representing the same information more than once and using more variables that what is actually needed. However, the most common situation encountered in empirical research is that we will not find perfectly aligned linear combinations among the regressors but only some relationships strong enough to come close to a strong linear fit, which usually means high absolute values of the correlations among regressors.[11] When this occurs, $\mathbf{X}'\mathbf{X}$ will be invertible, but the values in $(\mathbf{X}'\mathbf{X})^{-1}$ will tend to be very high in absolute value, and, as consequence, the S.E.s resulting from $\widehat{Var}\left[\hat{\boldsymbol{\beta}}^{OLS}\right] = \hat{\sigma}^2(\mathbf{X}'\mathbf{X})^{-1}$ will be excessively large, so that the confidence intervals are wider, and the t-tests will be likely not to reject the null of the coefficients being equal to 0: their estimates will lack most or all precision for anything meaningful being learnable from the sample. Therefore, in order to avoid poor efficiency of the estimator and in practice the inability to perform any accurate inferences on the model, it is important to check for multicollinearity and correct the problem, before interpreting the results or drawing any conclusions based on tests of hypotheses.

The typical signs of multicollinearity in a given data set are:

- high p-values of the individual t-tests on the individual coefficients, accompanied by an overall high R^2 of the regression;
- high p-values from t-tests on the individual coefficients, but a low p-value from the F-test applied to the regression as whole (because asymptotically, the F-statistic can be approximated as TR^2, this is of course less than surprising);
- the estimates of the coefficients considerably change (for instance, they abruptly switch sign and their p-values jump discontinuously) when some specific regressors are included or excluded from the model.

A first way to investigate multicollinearity is to compute the correlation matrix among all regressors or to look at the scatter plot matrix. Both these tools permit to identify the strongest pairwise linear relationships between pairs of explanatory variables. However, multicollinearity may be created by the existence of strong linear relationships among

11. Technically this is sufficient but not necessary for multicollinearity to become problematic because $\mathbf{X}'\mathbf{X}$ may become close to being singular (it is also said to be ill-conditioned in this case) when there are combinations of regressors that turn out to have high absolute value of their correlation with any other linear combination of the variables. For instance, when $K = 4$, it may happen that even though no pairs of variables are highly correlated per se, a weighted sum of $\mathbf{x}_1$ and $\mathbf{x}_3$ (say) implies a high absolute value correlation with a weighted sum of $\mathbf{x}_2$ and $\mathbf{x}_4$ (say).

sets of regressors. To study the multivariate relationships among variables, we could use instead one of the following indicators:

1. The *partial* R^2 *coefficients* R_k^2, which are the R^2 from linear regressions of the kth regressor on all the other $K-1$ candidate explanatory variables. R_k^2 should be computed for each regressor, $k=1,2,...,K$. Values higher than a threshold typically in the range 0.8–0.9 are indicative of multicollinearity.
2. The *variance inflation factors* (VIF), defined as:

$$\mathrm{VIF}_k \equiv \frac{1}{1-R_k^2}, \tag{1.85}$$

where R_k^2 is defined above; VIF values higher than 10 (or 5) indicate worrisome multicollinearity.

EXAMPLE 1.10

Table 1.8 shows the correlation matrix and the *p*-values associated (under the estimated correlations) to the null hypothesis of zero correlation among the six regressors of the model in Example 1.7.

Table 1.8 shows that the correlations that are the most significant and the highest in absolute value are the ones associated with the variables Earning Price Ratio and Default Yield Spread. The absolute value of the correlation coefficient between these two variables is a worrisome 0.76. This may represent a first indicator of multicollinearity. To analyze in greater depth the issue, we compute also the VIFs, presented in Table 1.9. VIFs computed according to Eq. (1.85) are the values in the column *Centered VIF*. All values in Table 1.9 are below the threshold of 5, although the VIF for the Earning Price Ratio, equal to 4.03, falls close to it. Not surprisingly the highest VIF is the one associated with the Earning Price Ratio and the second highest is the one of the Default Yield Spread, of 3.73. In Table 1.10, we drop the Earning Price Ratio from the model and compute again the VIFs for the remaining five variables. All values have decreased, and the most relevant reduction is the one associated to the Default Yield Spread, for which the VIF goes from 3.73 to 1.83. Table 1.10 represents an example of a desirable situation for a regression analysis as it identifies a set of regressors for which multicollinearity is not a reason for concern.

TABLE 1.8 Correlation Matrix of Regressors

Covariance Analysis
Sample: 2009M01 2016M11
Included Observations: 95

Correlation	**Dividend price ratio**	**Earning price ratio**	**Stock variance**	**Book to market**	**Default yield spread**	**Inflation**
Dividend price ratio	1.000					
	–					
Earning price ratio	−0.180	1.000				
	0.082	–				
Stock variance	0.053	−0.459	1.000			
	0.611	*0.000*	–			
Book to market	−0.143	0.415	0.163	1.000		
	0.167	*0.000*	*0.115*	–		
Default yield spread	0.191	−0.757	0.635	−0.008	1.000	
	0.064	*0.000*	*0.000*	*0.939*	–	
Inflation	−0.110	−0.154	0.010	0.031	0.113	1.000
	0.288	*0.137*	*0.920*	*0.768*	*0.274*	–

Note: *p*-values are in italics.

TABLE 1.9 Variance Inflation Factors (VIFs)

Variance Inflation Factors
Sample: 2009M01 2016M11
Included Observations: 95

Variable	Coefficient variance	Centered VIF
Dividend price ratio	0.05	1.085
Earning price ratio	0.01	4.033
Stock variance	2.822	1.817
Book to market	0.017	1.807
Default yield spread	2.814	3.731
Inflation	1.955	1.073

TABLE 1.10 VIFs After Dropping One Regressor

Variance Inflation Factors
Sample: 2009M01 2016M11
Included Observations: 95

Variable	Coefficient variance	Centered VIF
Dividend price ratio	0.05	1.085
Stock variance	2.771	1.783
Book to market	0.01	1.068
Default yield spread	1.378	1.826
Inflation	1.901	1.042

Once multicollinearity has been detected, there are no completely satisfying procedures to eradicate the problem: when the regressors are suggested by a model, they are what they are. An alternative could be to perform a *principal component analysis* (PCA, more properly known as eigenvalue decomposition) on the regressors and to use the resulting component as regressors. PCA is a statistical procedure that uses an orthogonal transformation to convert a set of observations of possibly correlated variables into a set of values of linearly uncorrelated variables called principal components (see Appendix 1.B for details). However, PCA only rarely represents a valid solution to multicollinearity. Indeed, principal components—except for a few lucky situations—make it almost impossible to interpret the results and do not allow a researcher to investigate the relationship among the dependent and the original regressors, which is in general the main objective in finance and economic applications. The cleverest solution to deal with multicollinearity seems instead to be dropping the variables with high VIF value, as it has been done in Table 1.10. Such an act of dropping candidate variables may often be informative of the underlying economic phenomenon and as such it should be treated.

1.3.3 Measurement Errors in the Regressors

Another potential reason of concern is the possibility that the regressors may be poorly measured. To see what the problem is about, let us consider the following, simple DGP:

$$y_t = \beta_0 + \beta_1 z_t + \varepsilon_t \qquad \varepsilon_t | z_t \sim N(0, \sigma^2). \tag{1.86}$$

Suppose now that we have collected data on the only regressor that contains some random errors, that is, that we actually observe $x_t = z_t + u_t$, where u_t is the measurement error, which can be due to poorly constructed or measured data. Being an error, this should be random and therefore (ruling out the worst cases of systematic biases in data collection), we can assume that its expected value is 0, its variance is a constant positive value, σ_u^2, and that it is uncorrelated with both z_t and y_t. Substituting z_t with $x_t - u_t$ in Eq. (1.86), we get:

$$y_t = \beta_0 + \beta_1(x_t - u_t) + \varepsilon_t = \beta_0 + \beta_1 x_t + \varepsilon_t - \beta_1 u_t. \tag{1.87}$$

Therefore, if we estimate the model using x_t as regressor instead of the appropriate explanatory variable z_t, the errors in the model will be $w_t = \varepsilon_t - \beta_1 u_t$. Indeed, Eq. (1.87) can also be written as:

$$y_t = \beta_0 + \beta_1 x_t + w_t. \tag{1.88}$$

Eq. (1.88) may appear to be a well-specified classical linear regression model, but if we look more closely, we note that the error term is correlated with the regressor:

$$\begin{aligned} E[x_t w_t] &= E\left[(z_t + u_t)(\varepsilon_t - \beta_1 u_t)\right] \\ &= E[z_t\varepsilon_t] - \beta_1 E[z_t u_t] + E[u_t\varepsilon_t] - \beta_1 E\left[u_t^2\right] = -\beta_1\sigma_u^2. \end{aligned} \tag{1.89}$$

Therefore, the resulting OLS estimation will be biased and inconsistent, as shown in Section 1.1.

Moreover, when these results are extended to a multiple linear regression model in which there are $K > 1$ explanatory variables, it is important to observe that even if we include only one regressor x_k that is affected by measurement errors, all the resulting OLS estimators in $\hat{\boldsymbol{\beta}}^{OLS}$ will be biased and inconsistent even though the remaining variables are measured correctly and even display zero correlation with the only regressor that is being measured with error.

1.4 ISSUES WITH HETEROSKEDASTICITY AND AUTOCORRELATION OF THE ERRORS

There is one more set of assumptions that we have made and that concern the properties of the regression errors. In the basic linear regression model of Sections 1.1 and 1.2, we have assumed that $Var[\varepsilon_t] = \sigma^2$ for every t, that is, that the errors are homoskedastic, and that $Cov[\varepsilon_t, \varepsilon_s] = 0$ for every $t \neq s$, that is, the errors are not autocorrelated. In what follows, we study the consequences of these two assumptions breaking down, and, when this occurs, we propose alternative estimators for the OLS covariance matrix and therefore for the S.E.s and present two related test statistics.

1.4.1 Heteroskedastic Errors

In Section 1.1, we have seen that the OLS estimator is unbiased and consistent even in the presence of heteroskedastic errors. However, we have already clarified that in this case, the OLS is no longer the most efficient estimator. One way to understand this problem is trying to compute the variance of $\hat{\boldsymbol{\beta}}^{OLS}$ in the presence of heteroskedasticity, that is, of a full matrix $\boldsymbol{\Sigma} \equiv Var[\mathbf{y}|\mathbf{X}]$:

$$\begin{aligned} Var\left[\hat{\boldsymbol{\beta}}^{OLS}|\mathbf{X}\right] &= Var\left[(\mathbf{X}'\mathbf{X})^{-1}\mathbf{X}'\mathbf{y}|\mathbf{X}\right] \\ &= (\mathbf{X}'\mathbf{X})^{-1}\mathbf{X}'\, Var[\mathbf{y}|\mathbf{X}]\mathbf{X}(\mathbf{X}'\mathbf{X})^{-1} = (\mathbf{X}'\mathbf{X})^{-1}\mathbf{X}'\boldsymbol{\Sigma}\mathbf{X}(\mathbf{X}'\mathbf{X})^{-1}. \end{aligned} \tag{1.90}$$

Even when the error terms are just heteroskedastic but still uncorrelated, $\boldsymbol{\Sigma}$ will be a diagonal matrix with different elements on the main diagonal, and the expression in Eq. (1.90) will not coincide with the classical covariance matrix estimator, $\sigma^2(\mathbf{X}'\mathbf{X})^{-1}$. If we had a reason to believe that this is the case in our analysis and we estimated a linear regression using OLS, the resulting S.E.s will be biased and inconsistent, because we would compute them simply as $\hat{s}_{OLS}\sqrt{(\mathbf{X}'\mathbf{X})^{-1}_{kk}}$, incorrectly assuming homoskedasticity. White (1980) proposed an alternative estimator for the covariance matrix of $\hat{\boldsymbol{\beta}}^{OLS}$ in Eq. (1.90) that is consistent in the case of heteroskedasticity, known as the *White covariance estimator*:

$$\widehat{Var}(\hat{\boldsymbol{\beta}}^{OLS})_W = \left(\sum_{t=1}^{T}\mathbf{x}_t\mathbf{x}_t'\right)^{-1}\left(\sum_{t=1}^{T}\varepsilon_t^2\mathbf{x}_t\mathbf{x}_t'\right)\left(\sum_{t=1}^{T}\mathbf{x}_t\mathbf{x}_t'\right)^{-1}. \tag{1.91}$$

Considering the square root of the elements on the main diagonal of the matrix in Eq. (1.91), we obtain the *heteroskedasticity-consistent S.E.s* that should be used to perform t-tests, for instance on the single coefficients.

In the same paper, White (1980) also presented a test statistic to perform the famous *White test* that can (and should) be used to test the null hypothesis of the absence of heteroskedasticity in the residuals of a regression. The null hypothesis is H_0: $\sigma_1^2 = \sigma_2^2 = \cdots = \sigma_T^2$, where $\sigma_t^2 = Var[\varepsilon_t]$. The test statistic is given by TR_W^2, where T is the sample size and R_W^2 is the R^2 of the regression of the squared residuals on the squared regressors and their pairwise products:

$$\hat{\varepsilon}_t^2 = \alpha_0 + \alpha_1 x_{1,t}^2 + \cdots + \alpha_K x_{K,t}^2 + \alpha_{K+1} x_{1,t} x_{2,t} + \cdots + \alpha_M x_{K-1,t} x_{K,t} + v_t. \tag{1.92}$$

The TR_W^2 statistic is distributed as a chi-square with M degrees of freedom. This test is only one among many others, such as Goldfeld and Quandt's (1965) and Breusch and Pagan's (1979), that all take the structure of regression-based tests on powers and cross-products.

EXAMPLE 1.11

Tables 1.11 and 1.12 present the result of a White heteroskedasticity test and the estimates of the linear regression of the squared residuals from a first-step regression on the squared regressors and all possible pairwise products of the same. The errors concern the regression of monthly excess returns on a portfolio of US firms operating in the oil market and in which the regressors are the Fama–French factors, as in Example 1.3.

The p-value associated with the White test is 0.095. If we had fixed a test size of 10%, we would reject the null hypothesis of homoskedasticity of the error terms. Therefore, if we wanted to estimate the model and then perform tests on the coefficients, we should use White's S.E.s.

TABLE 1.11 White Test for Heteroskedasticity

Heteroskedasticity Test: White			
F-statistic	1.749	$p(F(9,86))$	0.09
Obs*R^2	14.853	$p(\chi^2(9))$	0.095
Scaled explained SS	23.607	$p(\chi^2(9))$	0.005

TABLE 1.12 Estimated Regression to Perform a White Test for Heteroskedasticity

Test Equation
Dependent Variable: RESID^2
Method: Least Squares
Sample: 2009M01 2016M12
Included Observations: 96

Variable	Coefficient	S.E.	t-Statistic	Probability
C	29.216	14.86	1.966	0.053
Excess MKT	4.399	3.051	1.442	0.153
Excess MKT^2	0.159	0.575	0.275	0.784
Excess MKT × SMB	−2.966	1.516	−1.957	0.054
Excess MKT × HML	−0.742	1.174	−0.632	0.529
SMB	−4.215	4.705	−0.896	0.373
SMB^2	3.058	1.698	1.801	0.075
SMB × HML	0.401	1.614	0.248	0.804
HML	−7.297	3.964	−1.841	0.069
HML^2	1.634	0.928	1.760	0.082

R^2	0.155	Mean dependent variable	51.283
Adjusted R^2	0.066	SD dependent variable	95.911
S.E. of regression	92.679	Akaike information criterion	11.994
SSR	738686.438	Schwarz criterion	12.262
Log-likelihood	−565.736	Hannan–Quinn criterion	12.102
F-statistic	1.749	Durbin–Watson statistic	1.405
p (F-statistic)	0.090		

1.4.2 Autocorrelated Errors

The second assumption on the covariance matrix of the errors is that its off-diagonal elements were all equal to zeros, meaning that the error terms are not serially correlated. When this assumption is not satisfied on the available data, the OLS estimator $\hat{\boldsymbol{\beta}}^{OLS}$ will still be unbiased, but neither the classical S.E.s nor the ones resulting for White's estimator will be valid. Indeed, both types of covariance matrix estimators would be inconsistent as they assume zero autocorrelations. This limitation is overcome using the *Newey−West covariance estimator* of $Var[\hat{\boldsymbol{\beta}}^{OLS}|\mathbf{X}]$ (Newey and West, 1987), defined as:

$$Var[\hat{\boldsymbol{\beta}}^{OLS}|\mathbf{X}]_{NW} = \left(\sum_{t=1}^{T} \mathbf{x}_t\mathbf{x}_t'\right)^{-1} \hat{\Omega} \left(\sum_{t=1}^{T} \mathbf{x}_t\mathbf{x}_t'\right)^{-1}, \tag{1.93}$$

where $\hat{\Omega}$ is an estimator of the *long-run covariance* of the random vector $\mathbf{x}_t\hat{\varepsilon}_t$. The resulting S.E.s are called *HAC S.E.s*, and these should be used when we have reason to believe that the errors terms are serially correlated. Interestingly, even though the HAC S.E.s shield a researcher against serial correlation in the errors, the HAC covariance estimator provides S.E.s that are robust also to the presence of heteroskedasticity.

There is a rather dated but still popular test that can help us to investigate the presence of autocorrelation in the residuals, the Breusch−Godfrey's test (see Breusch, 1978 and Godfrey, 1978). It is just one among many options that have appeared in the literature to test for the presence of serial correlation in data and/or regression residuals, among them the famous but less and less employed test procedure proposed by Durbin and Watson (1950, 1951) and the portmanteau Q test by Box and Pierce (1970), which will be presented in detail in Chapter 2. The null hypothesis of the *Breusch−Godfrey test* is the absence of autocorrelation in the errors terms. Also in this case, the test statistic is given by $T_\varepsilon R^2_\varepsilon$, where R^2_ε is the R^2 of the regression of the residuals $\hat{\varepsilon}_t$ on the regressors $x_1, x_2, \ldots, x_K$ and the lagged value of the residuals themselves:

$$\hat{\varepsilon}_t = \gamma_0 + \gamma_1 x_{1,t} + \cdots + \gamma_K x_{K,T} + \delta_1\hat{\varepsilon}_{t-1} + \cdots + \delta_L\hat{\varepsilon}_{t-L} + \eta_t \tag{1.94}$$

while T_ε is the number of observations used to estimate Eq. (1.94) on the first-step regression residuals, $T_\varepsilon \equiv T - L$. Under the null hypothesis of zero serial correlation, $T_\varepsilon R^2_\varepsilon$ is asymptotically distributed as a chi-square with L degrees of freedom, where L influences the power of the test and has to do with the number of lags for which serial correlation is suspected.

EXAMPLE 1.12

Table 1.13 presents the results of a Breusch−Godfrey test on the residuals of the linear model:

$$R_t = \beta_0 + \beta_1 \mathrm{dp}_t + \beta_2 \mathrm{ep}_t + \beta_3 \mathrm{svar}_t + \beta_4 \mathrm{dm}_t + \beta_5 \mathrm{df}_t + \beta_6 \mathrm{inf}_t + \varepsilon_t,$$

where the variables are the same as in Example 1.6 but when the sample is selected to be January 1985−November 2016.

Table 1.13 shows the value of the test statistic $T_\varepsilon R^2_\varepsilon$ (Obs*R^2) and the corresponding p-value; below, we see the estimates of the auxiliary regression Eq. (1.94) of the residuals on the regressors and their lagged value. We choose $L = 2$ and, having fixed the size of the test α to be 5%, we reject the null hypothesis of zero autocorrelations, because the p-value of the test equals 0.043.

1.5 THE INTERPRETATION OF REGRESSION RESULTS

In this final section, we provide some intuition that we hope may prove useful to correctly interpret the results of a linear regression model and to avoid many pitfalls commonly encountered in this phase. In fact, also a correctly set up and coherent analysis may turn out to be completely worthless or even misleading when a researcher fails to pay sufficient attention to the interpretation of the results obtained. In Section 1.1.5, we have already discussed how to interpret the results of the t- and F-tests. Here, we shall focus on the estimates of the coefficients. In strict statistical terms, if a researcher had previously set fixed threshold to perform tests of hypotheses—which we note is not always the case, especially when the empirical analyses are performed in the exploratory stage—the estimated coefficients should be used and interpreted only when the associated p-values from the corresponding t-tests are smaller than the preselected α (generally set to 0.05, but also to sizes of 0.10 or 0.01 are popular). In fact, it may turn out to be problematic to

TABLE 1.13 Results of a Breusch–Godfrey Test of Autocorrelation

Breusch–Godfrey Serial Correlation LM Test			
F-statistic	3.130	*p* (*F*(2,374))	0.045
Obs*R^2	6.305	Obs. ($\chi^2(2)$)	0.043

Test Equation
Dependent Variable: RESID
Method: Least Squares
Sample: 1985M01 2016M11
Included Observations: 383
Presample Missing Value Lagged Residuals set to 0.

Variable	Coefficient	S.E.	*t*-Statistic	Probability
C	−0.001	0.027	−0.025	0.98
Dividend price ratio	0.004	0.092	0.044	0.965
Earning price ratio	−0.001	0.061	−0.024	0.981
Stock variance	−0.174	0.411	−0.424	0.672
Book to market	0.002	0.019	0.083	0.934
Default yield spread	−0.043	0.753	−0.057	0.955
Inflation	−0.097	0.652	−0.148	0.882
RESID(−1)	−0.116	0.052	−2.223	0.027
RESID(−2)	−0.073	0.052	−1.409	0.160

R^2	0.016	Mean dependent variable	0.000
Adjusted R^2	−0.005	SD dependent variable	0.039
S.E. of regression	0.039	Akaike information criterion	−3.637
SSR	0.563	Schwartz criterion	−3.544
Log-likelihood	705.492	Hannan–Quinn criterion	−3.600
F-statistic	0.782	Durbin–Watson statistic	1.994
p (*F*-statistic)	0.618		

discuss the sign or the size of a coefficient that is not "statistically different from 0," as it is often written with language that borrows from both hypothesis testing and from confidence interval theory. Assuming these have turned out to be the statistically significant, we have then to distinguish between the meaning of the intercept and of the other coefficients:

- The intercept represents the expected value of the dependent variable when all other regressors are equal to 0. However, it is important to remark that this interpretation is valid only if the hypothesis of all regressors being equal to 0 is economically meaningful; otherwise, the intercept may have no sensible economic interpretation and yet be needed in mathematical terms to ensure that the other estimates are unbiased.
- The coefficient associated to each explanatory variable tells which is the expected change in the dependent variable due to a unitary increase in the regressor, while holding the other variables in the model constant. Indeed:

$$\frac{\partial}{\partial x_k} E[\mathbf{y}|\mathbf{X}] = \frac{\partial}{\partial x_k} (\beta_0 + \beta_1 x_{1,t} + \cdots + \beta_K x_{K,t}) = \beta_K. \tag{1.95}$$

Therefore, the statement "$\hat{\beta}_k^{OLS}$ is the expected change in $\mathbf{y}$ for a unitary increase in $\mathbf{x}_k$" is generally incorrect: if the regressors are correlated with each other, an increase in x_1 will on average cause some movements also in the other regressors, resulting in a change in $\mathbf{y}$ different from $\hat{\beta}_k^{OLS}$. The only case in which the statement above would be correct is when we have perfect independence among the regressors, in all possible pairs. As such, it may be important to reformulate the proposition as "$\hat{\beta}_k^{OLS}$ is the expected change in $\mathbf{y}$ for a unitary increase in $\mathbf{x}_k$, keeping fixed all the other variables." Another way to emphasize this point is to consider that the estimate $\hat{\beta}_k^{OLS}$ in a multiple linear regression model will be in general different from the estimate of the same coefficient from a simple, univariate regression (i.e., the regression in which only $\mathbf{x}_k$ would be the explanatory variable). In fact, it can be shown that the estimate $\hat{\beta}_k^{OLS}$ resulting from a multiple linear regression model equals the estimate of the slope of the model where $\mathbf{y}$ is regressed on a single variable $\mathbf{v}$, where $\mathbf{v}$ is the residual of the regression of $\mathbf{x}_k$ on all the other regressors.

Additionally, recall that the absolute value of the coefficient clearly depends on the unit of measurement of the associated regressor and, as consequence, no conclusion can be inferred on the relative importance of the regressors just by comparing the estimated point values of such coefficients. If we seriously wanted to compare the importance of two explanatory variables, we should compute the *partial* R^2, which represents the contribution of each of the regressors to explain the same dependent variable. The partial R^2 of the kth regressor is given by:

$$R_k^2 = \frac{\text{SSE} - \text{SSE}_{-k}}{\text{SSR}_{-k}} \quad k = 1, 2, ..., K, \tag{1.96}$$

where SSE_{-k} and SSR_{-k} are, respectively, the explained sum of squares and the residual sum of squares of a model obtained excluding the kth regressor, while keeping all other explanatory variables. The partial R^2 represents the proportion of variability explained by the kth regressor alone, that cannot be explained by the other explanatory variables. Clearly, the higher the partial R^2, the higher the importance of a regressor.

One final consideration on the point estimates of the coefficients regards the choice of the units of measurement, say, the choice between a proportion/fractional number (e.g., a return of 0.1) or a percentage (e.g., a return of 10%) or between measures in dollars or thousands of dollars. The choice of unit of measurement has no effect on the interpretation of the results, but it will obviously change the estimated values of the regression coefficients. Specifically, if the dependent variable is multiplied by a constant c, all the estimated coefficients will be transformed as if they are multiplied by the same constant c. If an individual regressor is multiplied by a constant c, then the corresponding coefficient will be transformed as if it had been multiplied by $1/c$, while all others would remain unchanged. Finally, it is easy to prove that changes in the units of measurement will not affect either the R^2 or the results of the test statistics concerning the coefficients.

REFERENCES

Box, G.E.P., Pierce, D.A., 1970. Distribution of residual autocorrelations in autoregressive-integrated moving average time series models. J. Am. Stat. Assoc. 65, 1509–1526.

Breusch, T.S., 1978. Testing for autocorrelation in dynamic linear models. Aust. Econ. Pap. 17, 334–355.

Breusch, T.S., Pagan, A.R., 1979. A simple test for heteroskedasticity and random coefficient variation. Econometrica 47, 1287–1294.

Cramér, H., 1946. Mathematical Methods of Statistics. Princeton University Press, Princeton, NJ.

Davidson, R., MacKinnon, J.G., 2004. Econometric Theory and Methods. Oxford University Press, New York.

Durbin, J., Watson, G.S., 1950. Testing for serial correlation in least squares regression, I. Biometrika 37, 409–428.

Durbin, J., Watson, G.S., 1951. Testing for serial correlation in least squares regression, II. Biometrika 38, 159–179.

Godfrey, L.G., 1978. Testing against general autoregressive and moving average error models when the regressors include lagged dependent variables. Econometrica 46, 1293–1301.

Goldfeld, S.M., Quandt, R.E., 1965. Some tests for homoscedasticity. J. Am. Stat. Assoc. 60, 539–547.

Newey, W.K., West, K.D., 1987. A simple, positive semi-definite, heteroskedasticity and autocorrelation consistent covariance matrix. Econometrica 55, 703–708.

Neyman, J., 1937. Outline of a theory of statistical estimation based on the classical theory of probability. Philos. Trans. Royal Soc. A. 236, 333–380.

Page, E.S., 1954. Continuous inspection scheme. Biometrika 41, 100–115.

Rao, C.R., 1945. Information and the accuracy attainable in the estimation of statistical parameters. Bulletin of the Calcutta Mathematical Society 37, 81–89.

Ramsey, J., 1969. Tests for specification errors in classical linear least squares regression analysis. J. Royal Stat. Soc. 31, 350–371.

Sala-i-Martin, X., 1997. I just ran two million regressions. Am. Econ. Rev. 87, 178–183.

White, H., 1980. A heteroskedasticity-consistent covariance matrix estimator and a direct test for heteroskedasticity. Econometrica 48, 817–838.

APPENDIX 1.A

Proof of Unbiasedness of the OLS Estimator for the variance

Denoting the matrix $[\mathbf{I}_T - \mathbf{X}(\mathbf{X}'\mathbf{X})^{-1}\mathbf{X}']$ with $\mathbf{M}$, we get:

$$\begin{aligned}\mathbf{MM} &= [\mathbf{I}_T - \mathbf{X}(\mathbf{X}'\mathbf{X})^{-1}\mathbf{X}'][\mathbf{I}_T - \mathbf{X}(\mathbf{X}'\mathbf{X})^{-1}\mathbf{X}'] \\ &= \mathbf{I}_T - \mathbf{X}(\mathbf{X}'\mathbf{X})^{-1}\mathbf{X}' - \mathbf{X}(\mathbf{X}'\mathbf{X})^{-1}\mathbf{X}' + \mathbf{X}(\mathbf{X}'\mathbf{X})^{-1}\overbrace{(\mathbf{X}'\mathbf{X})(\mathbf{X}'\mathbf{X})^{-1}}^{\mathbf{I}_K}\mathbf{X}' \\ &= \mathbf{I}_T - \mathbf{X}(\mathbf{X}'\mathbf{X})^{-1}\mathbf{X}' = \mathbf{M}.\end{aligned} \tag{A1}$$

So, $\mathbf{M}$ is an idempotent $T \times T$ matrix such that $\mathbf{MM} = \mathbf{MM}' = \mathbf{M}'\mathbf{M} = \mathbf{M}$, and substituting $\mathbf{y}$ with the basic equation of the model, we get:

$$\hat{\boldsymbol{\varepsilon}} = \left[\mathbf{I}_T - \mathbf{X}(\mathbf{X}'\mathbf{X})^{-1}\mathbf{X}'\right]\mathbf{y} = \mathbf{M}(\mathbf{X}\boldsymbol{\beta} + \boldsymbol{\varepsilon}) = \mathbf{MX}\boldsymbol{\beta} + \mathbf{M}\boldsymbol{\varepsilon}. \tag{A2}$$

Indeed, exploiting the properties of the trace operator, it can be shown that the trace of $\mathbf{M}$ equals $T - K - 1$ and $\mathbf{MX} = \mathbf{O}$:

$$\begin{aligned} tr(\mathbf{M}) &= tr\left[\mathbf{I}_T - \mathbf{X}(\mathbf{X}'\mathbf{X})^{-1}\mathbf{X}'\right] = tr(\mathbf{I}_T) - tr\left[\mathbf{X}(\mathbf{X}'\mathbf{X})^{-1}\mathbf{X}'\right] \\ &= T - tr\left[(\mathbf{X}'\mathbf{X})^{-1}(\mathbf{X}'\mathbf{X})\right] = T - tr(\mathbf{I}_{K+1}) = T - K - 1 \\ \mathbf{MX} &= \left[\mathbf{I}_T - \mathbf{X}(\mathbf{X}'\mathbf{X})^{-1}\mathbf{X}'\right]\mathbf{X} = \mathbf{X} - \mathbf{X}(\mathbf{X}'\mathbf{X})^{-1}(\mathbf{X}'\mathbf{X}) = \mathbf{X} - \mathbf{X} = \mathbf{O}. \end{aligned} \tag{A3}$$

It follows from Eq. (A3) and from the properties of $\mathbf{M}$ that $\hat{\boldsymbol{\varepsilon}} = \mathbf{M}\boldsymbol{\varepsilon}$ and $\hat{\boldsymbol{\varepsilon}}'\hat{\boldsymbol{\varepsilon}} = \boldsymbol{\varepsilon}'\mathbf{M}'\mathbf{M}\boldsymbol{\varepsilon} = \boldsymbol{\varepsilon}'\mathbf{M}\boldsymbol{\varepsilon}$. Therefore,

$$E\left[\frac{\hat{\boldsymbol{\varepsilon}}'\hat{\boldsymbol{\varepsilon}}}{T-K-1}\right] = \frac{1}{T-K-1}E[\boldsymbol{\varepsilon}'\mathbf{M}\boldsymbol{\varepsilon}]. \tag{A4}$$

Because $\boldsymbol{\varepsilon}'\mathbf{M}\boldsymbol{\varepsilon}$ is a scalar, we can rewrite the expected value of the estimator as:

$$\begin{aligned} E[\hat{s}^2_{\text{OLS}}] &= \frac{1}{T-K-1}E[tr(\boldsymbol{\varepsilon}'\mathbf{M}\boldsymbol{\varepsilon})] = \frac{1}{T-K-1}E[tr(\mathbf{M}\boldsymbol{\varepsilon}'\boldsymbol{\varepsilon})] \\ &= \frac{1}{T-K-1}tr(\mathbf{M}E[\boldsymbol{\varepsilon}'\boldsymbol{\varepsilon}]) = \frac{T-K-1}{T-K-1}\sigma^2 = \sigma^2. \end{aligned} \tag{A5}$$

Proof of Result 1.5 (Consistency of OLS) Define $\mathbf{S}_{xx} \equiv T^{-1}\mathbf{X}'\mathbf{X} = T^{-1}\sum_{t=1}^{T}\mathbf{x}_t\mathbf{x}_t'$, $\mathbf{S}_{xy} \equiv T^{-1}\mathbf{X}'\mathbf{y} = T^{-1}\sum_{t=1}^{T}\mathbf{x}_t\mathbf{y}_t$ and $\mathbf{S}_{x\varepsilon} \equiv T^{-1}\mathbf{X}'\boldsymbol{\varepsilon} = T^{-1}\sum_{t=1}^{T}\mathbf{x}_t\boldsymbol{\varepsilon}_t$ and write the OLS estimator as a function of $\mathbf{S}_{xx}$ and $\mathbf{S}_{xy}$: $\hat{\boldsymbol{\beta}}^{\text{OLS}} = (\mathbf{X}'\mathbf{X})^{-1}\mathbf{X}'\mathbf{y} = \mathbf{S}_{xx}{}^{-1}\mathbf{S}_{xy}$. It follows that:

$$\begin{aligned} \hat{\boldsymbol{\beta}}^{\text{OLS}} &= \mathbf{S}_{xx}^{-1}\left(T^{-1}\sum_{t=1}^{T}\mathbf{x}_t y_t\right) = \mathbf{S}_{xx}^{-1}T^{-1}\left[\sum_{t=1}^{T}\mathbf{x}_t(\mathbf{x}_t'\boldsymbol{\beta} + \varepsilon_t)\right] \\ &= \mathbf{S}_{xx}^{-1}\mathbf{S}_{xx}\boldsymbol{\beta} + \mathbf{S}_{xx}^{-1}\mathbf{S}_{x\varepsilon} = \boldsymbol{\beta} + \mathbf{S}_{xx}^{-1}\mathbf{S}_{x\varepsilon}. \end{aligned} \tag{A6}$$

Therefore, $\hat{\boldsymbol{\beta}}^{\text{OLS}} - \boldsymbol{\beta} = \mathbf{S}_{xx}^{-1}\mathbf{S}_{x\varepsilon}$. By the law of large numbers, we know that $plim\,(\mathbf{S}_{xx}) = \boldsymbol{\Sigma}_{xx}$, and therefore, by Slutsky's theorem: $plim\,(\mathbf{S}_{xx}^{-1}) = \boldsymbol{\Sigma}_{xx}^{-1}$. Moreover, because $\boldsymbol{\Sigma}_{x\varepsilon} = E[\mathbf{x}_t\varepsilon_t] = \mathbf{0}$, it follows that $plim\,(\mathbf{S}_{x\varepsilon}) = \boldsymbol{\Sigma}_{x\varepsilon} = \mathbf{0}$.

Therefore, $plim\,(\hat{\boldsymbol{\beta}}^{\text{OLS}} - \boldsymbol{\beta}) = plim\,(\mathbf{S}_{xx}^{-1})\,plim\,(\mathbf{S}_{x\varepsilon}) = \boldsymbol{\Sigma}_{xx}^{-1}\cdot\mathbf{0} = \mathbf{0}$ which establishes the result.

Proof of Result 1.6 (Consistency of OLS estimator for the variance)
Recall that:

$$\begin{aligned} \hat{s}^2{}_{\text{OLS}} &= \frac{1}{T-K-1}\sum_{t=1}^{T}\hat{\varepsilon}_t^2 = \frac{1}{T-K-1}\sum_{t=1}^{T}(y_t - \mathbf{x}_t'\hat{\boldsymbol{\beta}}^{\text{OLS}})^2 \\ &= \frac{1}{T-K-1}\sum_{t=1}^{T}(\mathbf{x}_t'\boldsymbol{\beta} + \varepsilon_t - \mathbf{x}_t'\hat{\boldsymbol{\beta}}^{\text{OLS}})^2 = \frac{1}{T-K-1}\sum_{t=1}^{T}[\varepsilon_t - \mathbf{x}_t'(\hat{\boldsymbol{\beta}}^{\text{OLS}} - \boldsymbol{\beta})]^2 \\ &= \frac{1}{T-K-1}\left[\sum_{t=1}^{T}\varepsilon_t^2 - 2\sum_{t=1}^{T}\varepsilon_t\mathbf{x}_t'(\hat{\boldsymbol{\beta}}^{\text{OLS}} - \boldsymbol{\beta}) + \sum_{t=1}^{T}(\hat{\boldsymbol{\beta}}^{\text{OLS}} - \boldsymbol{\beta})'\mathbf{x}_t\mathbf{x}_t'(\hat{\boldsymbol{\beta}}^{\text{OLS}} - \boldsymbol{\beta})\right] \\ &= \frac{1}{T-K-1}\sum_{t=1}^{T}\varepsilon_t^2 - \frac{2T}{T-K-1}\mathbf{S}_{x\varepsilon}'\mathbf{S}_{xx}^{-1}\mathbf{S}_{x\varepsilon} + \frac{T}{T-K-1}\mathbf{S}_{x\varepsilon}'\mathbf{S}_{xx}^{-1}\mathbf{S}_{xx}\mathbf{S}_{xx}^{-1}\mathbf{S}_{x\varepsilon} \\ &= \frac{1}{T-K-1}\sum_{t=1}^{T}\varepsilon_t^2 - \frac{T}{T-K-1}\mathbf{S}_{x\varepsilon}'\mathbf{S}_{xx}^{-1}\mathbf{S}_{x\varepsilon}, \end{aligned} \tag{A7}$$

where by the law of large numbers, $(T-K-1)^{-1}\sum_{t=1}^{T}\varepsilon_t^2$ converges in probability to σ^2 and $T/(T-K-1)\mathbf{S}_{x\varepsilon}'\mathbf{S}_{xx}^{-1}\mathbf{S}_{x\varepsilon}$ converges in probability to 0. Thus, $\hat{s}^2{}_{\text{OLS}}$ converges in probability to σ^2.

Proof of Result 1.7 (Asymptotic normality)
From the proof of Result 1.5 we know that: $\hat{\boldsymbol{\beta}}^{OLS} - \boldsymbol{\beta} = \mathbf{S}_{xx}{}^{-1}\mathbf{S}_{x\varepsilon}$ and $plim(\mathbf{S}_{xx}^{-1}) = \boldsymbol{\Sigma}_{xx}^{-1}$. Then

$$\sqrt{T}(\hat{\boldsymbol{\beta}}^{OLS} - \boldsymbol{\beta}) = \mathbf{S}_{xx}{}^{-1}\left(\frac{1}{\sqrt{T}}\sum_{t=1}^{T}\mathbf{x}_t\varepsilon_t\right). \tag{A8}$$

Let's study the properties of the IID variable $\mathbf{x}_t\varepsilon_t$. Its expected value is 0 and its covariance matrix is $\boldsymbol{\Sigma}_{xx}\sigma^2$, so that, by the central limit theorem:

$$\sqrt{T}\mathbf{S}_{x\varepsilon} \xrightarrow{p} N(\mathbf{0}, \boldsymbol{\Sigma}_{xx}\sigma^2) \tag{A9}$$

and $\sqrt{T}(\hat{\boldsymbol{\beta}}^{OLS} - \boldsymbol{\beta}) \sim N(\mathbf{0}, \boldsymbol{\Sigma}_{xx}^{-1}\sigma^2)$.

APPENDIX 1.B PRINCIPAL COMPONENT ANALYSIS

Given an N-dimensional random vector $\mathbf{y} \equiv [y_1 y_2 ... y_N]'$ with covariance matrix $\boldsymbol{\Sigma}_y$ and correlation matrix $\boldsymbol{\rho}_y$, PCA is concerned with using a few linear combinations of the variables y_i ($i = 1, 2, \ldots, N$) to explain the structure of $\boldsymbol{\Sigma}_y$ or ρ_y.

Let $\mathbf{c}_i = [c_{i,1}, c_{i,2}, \ldots, c_{i,N}]'$ be an N-dimensional vector, where $i = 1, 2, \ldots, N$. Then

$$\mathrm{PC}_i = \mathbf{c}_i'\mathbf{y} = \sum_{j=1}^{k} c_{ij}y_j. \tag{B1}$$

Using properties of a linear combination of random variables, we have:

$$Var(\mathrm{PC}_i) = \mathbf{c}_i'\boldsymbol{\Sigma}_y\mathbf{c}_i \quad i = 1, \ldots, k \tag{B2}$$

$$Cov(\mathrm{PC}_i, \mathrm{PC}_j) = \mathbf{c}_i'\boldsymbol{\Sigma}_y\mathbf{c}_j \quad i, j = 1, \ldots, k. \tag{B3}$$

The idea of PCA is to find linear combinations $\boldsymbol{c}_i$ such that PC_i and PC_j are uncorrelated for $i \neq j$ and the variances of PC_i are as large as possible. More specifically:

1. The first principal component of $\boldsymbol{r}$ is the linear combination $\mathrm{PC}_1 = \mathbf{c}_1'\mathbf{y}$ that maximizes $Var(\mathrm{PC}_1)$ subject to the constraint $\mathbf{c}_1'\mathbf{c}_1 = 1$.
2. The second principal component of $\boldsymbol{r}$ is the linear combination $\mathrm{PC}_2 = \mathbf{c}_2'\mathbf{y}$ that maximizes $Var(\mathrm{PC}_2)$ subject to the constraints $\mathbf{c}_2'\mathbf{c}_2 = 1$ and $Cov(\mathrm{PC}_2, \mathrm{PC}_1) = 0$.
3. The ith principal component of the data $\mathbf{y}$ is the linear combination $\mathrm{PC}_i = \mathbf{c}_i'\mathbf{y}$ that maximizes $Var(\mathrm{PC}_i)$ subject to the constraints $\mathbf{c}_i'\mathbf{c}_i = 1$ and $Cov(\mathrm{PC}_i, \mathrm{PC}_j) = 0$ for $j = 1, \ldots, i-1$.

Because the covariance matrix $\boldsymbol{\Sigma}_y$ is positive definite, it has a *spectral decomposition*. This term refers to the factorization of a matrix into a canonical form, whereby the matrix is represented in terms of its eigenvalues and eigenvectors.

Given a square matrix $\boldsymbol{\Sigma}_y$, an *eigenvalue* of $\boldsymbol{\Sigma}_y$ is a number λ which, when subtracted from each of the diagonal entries of $\boldsymbol{\Sigma}_y$, converts $\boldsymbol{\Sigma}_y$ into a singular matrix. Subtracting a scalar λ from each diagonal entry of $\boldsymbol{\Sigma}_y$ is the same as subtracting λ times the identity matrix $\mathbf{I}$ from $\boldsymbol{\Sigma}_y$. Therefore, λ is an eigenvalue of $\boldsymbol{\Sigma}_y$ if and only if $\boldsymbol{\Sigma}_y - \lambda\mathbf{I}$ is a singular matrix. This means that the system of equations $(\boldsymbol{\Sigma}_y - \lambda\mathbf{I})\mathbf{x} = \mathbf{0}$ has a solution other than $\mathbf{x} = \mathbf{0}$.

When λ is an eigenvalue of $\boldsymbol{\Sigma}_y$, a nonzero vector $\mathbf{x}$ such that:

$$(\boldsymbol{\Sigma}_y - \lambda\mathbf{I})\mathbf{x} = \mathbf{0} \tag{B4}$$

is called an *eigenvector* of $\boldsymbol{\Sigma}_y$ corresponding to eigenvalue λ. Multiplying Eq. (B5), we get that if λ is an *eigenvalue* and $\mathbf{x}$ is a corresponding *eigenvector*, so that $\boldsymbol{\Sigma}_y\mathbf{x} = \lambda\mathbf{x}$. Additionally, we know that $\mathbf{x}_i'\mathbf{x}_i = 1$ and $\mathbf{x}_i'\mathbf{x}_j = 0$ (i.e., the eigenvectors are orthogonal to each other).

Useful properties of a positive definite matrix $\boldsymbol{\Sigma}_y$ include (1) all eigenvalues of $\boldsymbol{\Sigma}_y$ are real and positive and (2) the matrix can be decomposed as:

$$\boldsymbol{\Sigma}_y = \mathbf{P}\boldsymbol{\Lambda}\mathbf{P}, \tag{B5}$$

where $\boldsymbol{\Lambda}$ is a diagonal matrix consisting of all eigenvalues of $\boldsymbol{\Sigma}_y$ and $\mathbf{P}$ is an $m \times m$ matrix consisting of the m right eigenvectors of $\boldsymbol{\Sigma}_y$.

Let $(\lambda_1, \mathbf{x}_1), \ldots, (\lambda_k, \mathbf{x}_k)$ be the eigenvalue-eigenvector pairs of $\boldsymbol{\Sigma}_y$, where $\lambda_1 \geq \lambda_2 \geq \cdots \geq \lambda_k \geq 0$. Then one can prove the following result.

Result 1B. 1: The ith principal component of $\boldsymbol{y}$ is $\mathrm{PC}_i = \mathbf{e}_i'\mathbf{y} = \sum_{j=1}^{k} x_{ij}y_j$ for $i = 1, \ldots, k$. Moreover,

$$Var(\mathrm{PC}_i) = \mathbf{x}_i'\boldsymbol{\Sigma}_y\mathbf{x}_i = \lambda_i \quad i = 1, \ldots, k \tag{B6}$$

$$Cov(\mathrm{PC}_i, \mathrm{PC}_j) = x_i'\boldsymbol{\Sigma}_y x_j = 0 \quad i \neq j. \tag{B7}$$

In addition, we have

$$\sum_{i=1}^{N} Var(y_i) = tr(\boldsymbol{\Sigma}_y) = \sum_{i=1}^{N} \lambda_i = \sum_{i=1}^{N} Var(\mathrm{PC}_i). \tag{B8}$$

The result of Eq. (B8) says that

$$\frac{Var(\mathrm{PC}_i)}{\sum_{i=1}^{N} Var(y_i)} = \frac{\lambda_i}{\lambda_1 + \cdots + \lambda_k}. \tag{B9}$$

Consequently, the proportion of total variance of $\boldsymbol{y}$ explained by the ith principal component is simply the ratio between the ith eigenvalue and the sum of all eigenvalues of $\boldsymbol{\Sigma}_y$. One can also compute the cumulative proportion of total variance explained by the first M principal components (i.e., $(\sum_{j=1}^{M} \lambda_j)/(\sum_{j=1}^{N} \lambda_j)$). In practice, one selects a small M such that the prior cumulative proportion is large. Since $tr(\boldsymbol{\rho}_y) = N$, the proportion of variance explained by the ith principal component is then λ_i/N when the correlation matrix is used to compute PCA. A by-product of the PCA is that a zero eigenvalue of $\boldsymbol{\Sigma}_y$, or $\boldsymbol{\rho}_y$, indicates the existence of an *exact* linear relationship between the components of $\boldsymbol{y}$. For instance, if the smallest eigenvalue $\lambda_N = 0$, then by Result 1.B1 $Var(\mathrm{PC}_N) = 0$. Therefore, $y_N = \sum_{j=1}^{N} x_{kj}r_j$ is a constant and there are only $N - 1$ linearly independent random variables in $\boldsymbol{y}$. In this case, the dimension of $\boldsymbol{y}$ can be reduced. For this reason, PCA has been used in the literature as a tool for *dimensionality reduction*.

In applied work, the covariance matrix $\boldsymbol{\Sigma}_y$ and the correlation matrix $\boldsymbol{\rho}_y$ are unknown, but they can be estimated consistently by the sample covariance and correlation matrixes under some regularity conditions. Assuming that the data are weakly stationary, we have the following estimates:

$$\hat{\boldsymbol{\Sigma}}_y \equiv \left[\hat{\sigma}_{ij,y}\right] = \frac{1}{T-1}\sum_{t=1}^{T}(\mathbf{y}_t - \overline{\mathbf{y}})(\mathbf{y}_t - \overline{\mathbf{y}})' \quad \overline{\mathbf{y}} = \frac{1}{T}\sum_{t=1}^{T}\mathbf{y}_t \tag{B10}$$

$$\hat{\boldsymbol{\rho}}_y = \hat{\mathbf{D}}^{-1}\hat{\boldsymbol{\Sigma}}_y\hat{\mathbf{D}}^{-1}, \tag{B11}$$

where $\hat{\mathbf{D}} \equiv \mathrm{diag}\left\{\sqrt{\hat{\sigma}_{11,y}}, \ldots, \sqrt{\hat{\sigma}_{NN,y}}\right\}$ is the diagonal matrix of sample S.E.s of $\boldsymbol{y}_t$. Most statistical packages now have the capability to perform PCA.

Chapter 2

Autoregressive Moving Average (ARMA) Models and Their Practical Applications

Study the past, if you would divine the future.

Confucio

Undisputedly, one of the deepest desires of human beings is to be able to predict the future. Of course, finance professionals (no matter whether they are analysts, traders, asset managers, or risk managers) are very from being immune to this temptation. In Chapter 1, we have introduced linear regression models, where the values of a dependent (random) variable are explained by a number of independent variables, the regressors. Instead, in this chapter, we introduce linear time series models in which past information is used to forecast future values of a random variable (e.g., the 1-week-ahead return on the S&P 500 index or the 1-month-ahead yield on 10-year US Treasury notes). Given this goal, in this chapter, we shall limit our discussion to univariate time series analysis, while in Chapter 3, we will introduce multivariate models.

We start the chapter by introducing some basic concepts, including the definition of stationarity, a key foundation of linear time series analysis, and the computation of sample autocorrelations (i.e., the correlations between the current value of the variable of interest and its own past), which provide an important tool to study the structure of stationary time series. Next, we introduce some widely used linear time series models and their basic statistical properties: the moving average (MA) and the autoregressive (AR) models, mixed, autoregressive moving average (ARMA) models. Then, following the seminal work of Box and Jenkins (1976), we discuss the three steps to build ARMA models from the data:

- Identification (i.e., specifying the lag order required to capture the features of the data based on a visual inspection of different types of sample autocorrelations.
- Selection (through information criteria, often shortened to IC) and estimation of the model that best fits the data.
- Diagnostic checking of a model's fit to the data.

Finally, we show how the models illustrated in the chapter can be used in forecasting applications.

2.1 ESSENTIAL CONCEPTS IN TIME SERIES ANALYSIS

2.1.1 Time Series and Their Properties

Before we introduce time series models, it is useful to recall (and refine) the definition of *time series* that we have given in Chapter 1. As we said, a time series consists of a sequence of random variables, $y_1, y_2, \ldots, y_T$, also known as a stochastic process $\{y_t\}_{t=1}^{T}$, of which we only observe the empirical realizations. When the observations are recorded continuously over some time interval, we speak of continuous time series; conversely, when the observations are recorded at equally spaced time intervals, we refer to them as *discretely sampled time series*. In the rest of this chapter (and in the entire book, with occasional exceptions at most), we will only deal with discrete time series. The earnings reported by a company at the end of each quarter, the daily closing price of the S&P 500 index, the number of tourists that visit the Colosseum in Rome every month, and the points scored by Kobe Bryant in the matches he played during his last NBA season are all examples of discretely, regularly sampled time series. An attentive reader may object that the daily closing prices of the S&P 500 are not precisely equally spaced because of weekends and holidays and that the basketball calendar is not always regularly spaced—Kobe sometimes did play back-to-back and occasionally enjoyed breathers of

Essentials of Time Series for Financial Applications. DOI: https://doi.org/10.1016/B978-0-12-813409-2.00002-9

a few days. However, the discussion on how to treat missing values and/or irregularly spaced time series is far beyond the scope of this book and we shall limit ourselves to mention that there exists a specialized literature that specifically deals with this issue (see, e.g., Jones, 1980, and Ansley and Kohn, 1983, for an introductory treatment).

An observed time series $\{y_t\}_{t=1}^{T}$ (for instance, the sequence of daily returns of the S&P 500 index over the last 2 years) is a selection (technically, a subsequence because limited to a finite sample) of the realized values of a family of random variables $\{y_t\}_{-\infty}^{+\infty}$ defined on an appropriate probability space. Noticeably, the relationship between a stochastic process and its realizations is analogous to the one between a population and a sample. For the sake of brevity, in the rest of this chapter, we shall use the term time series to refer to both the data and the stochastic process that has originated them.

A time series model for the observations $\{y_t\}_{t=1}^{T}$ is a specification of the joint distribution of the set of random variables of which the sampled data are a realization. Because a complete probabilistic time series model for the process that generated the data would be impractical, as it may include a very large number of parameters, we often specify only the first- and second-order moments of such a joint distribution, that is, the mean, variances, and covariances of $\{y_t\}$ and we focus mainly (at least, initially, but see Chapters 5–8 for examples of exceptions to this principle) on the properties of $\{y_t\}$ that depend on these (namely, on its second-order moments). However, under the assumption that the joint distribution of the variables in the random sequence $\{y_t\}$ is multivariate normal, the second-order moments of the process will be sufficient to give a complete statistical characterization of $\{y_t\}$. Although one may object that this is not the case for a number of financial time series, when the stochastic process can be assumed to be *linear*, that is, the current value of the process is generated by a linear combination of the past values of the process itself and current and past values of any other linearly related process, its second-order characterization may still be sufficient. Indeed, the theory of minimum mean squared error linear prediction depends only on the second-order moment properties of the process (the interested reader may refer to Brockwell and Davis, 2002, Chapter 2, for a proof). A more precise characterization of linearity is featured in the following definition.

DEFINITION 2.1 (Linear process)

A time series $\{y_t\}$ is said to be a linear process if it has the representation

$$y_t = \mu + \sum_{j=-\infty}^{\infty} \phi_j z_{t-j} \tag{2.1}$$

for all t, where μ is a constant, $\{\phi_j\}$ is a sequence of constant coefficients where $\phi_0 = 1$ and $\sum_{j=-\infty}^{\infty} |\phi_j| < \infty$, and $\{z_t\}$ is a sequence of independent and identically distributed (IID) random variables with a defined distribution function. In particular, we assume that the distribution of z_t is continuous, with $E[z_t] = 0$ and $Var(z_t) = \sigma_z^2$. Noticeably, if $\sigma_z^2 \sum_{i=1}^{\infty} \phi_i^2 < \infty$, then y_t is weakly stationary, with the meaning that we shall see later.

Due to their practical value and their mathematical ease of manipulation, such linear models represent the focus of the rest of this chapter.

2.1.2 Stationarity

In order to use past realizations of a variable of interest to forecast its future values, it is necessary for the stochastic process that has originated the observations to be *stationary*. Loosely speaking, a process is said to be stationary if its statistical properties do not change over time. However, a more formal definition may be precious in what follows.

DEFINITION 2.2 (Strict stationarity)

A process is *strictly stationary* if the joint distribution of the variable associated to any subsequence of times $t_1, t_2, \ldots, t_n$ is the same as the joint distribution of the sequence of all times $t_{1+k}, t_{2+k}, \ldots, t_{n+k}$ (where k is an arbitrary time shift). In other words, a strictly stationary time series $\{y_t\}$ has the following properties:

- The random variables y_t are identically distributed.
- The two random vectors $[y_t, y_{t+1}]'$ and $[y_{t+k}, y_{t+1+k}]'$ have the same joint distribution for any t and k.

Strict stationarity requires that all the moments of the distribution are time invariant, which is quite a strong assumption. However, in many applications (including linear time series analysis), a weaker form of stationarity generally provides a useful sufficient condition.

DEFINITION 2.3 (Weak stationarity)

A stochastic process $\{y_t\}$ is *weakly stationary* (or, alternatively, *covariance stationary*) if it has time invariant first and second moments, that is, if for any choice of $t = 1, 2, \ldots, \infty$, the following conditions hold:

$$\mu_y \equiv E(y_t), \quad \text{with } |\mu_y| < \infty \tag{2.2}$$

$$\sigma_y^2 \equiv E\left[\left(y_t - \mu_y\right)\left(y_t - \mu_y\right)\right] = E\left[\left(y_t - \mu_y\right)^2\right] < \infty \tag{2.3}$$

$$\gamma_h \equiv E\left[\left(y_t - \mu_y\right)\left(y_{t-h} - \mu_y\right)\right] \quad \forall h, \text{ with } |\gamma_h| < \infty, \tag{2.4}$$

where $h = \ldots, -3, -2, -1, 1, 2, 3, \ldots$.

In practice, Eqs. (2.2) and (2.3) state that the time series has a constant (and finite) mean and variance, respectively. Eq. (2.4) implies that the covariance of y_t and y_{t-h} (where h is a positive integer) does not vary over time, but only depends on the length of the lag displacement (denoted by h), that is, $Cov(y_t, y_{t-h}) = Cov(y_{t-j}, y_{t-j-h}) = \gamma_h$.

Importantly, $\gamma_h \equiv Cov(y_t, y_{t-h})$ for $h = \ldots, -3, -2, -1, 1, 2, 3, \ldots$ is generally defined as the *autocovariance function* of the time series. Instead, $\rho_h = \gamma_h / \gamma_0$ (where γ_0 is the variance) is called autocorrelation function (ACF), for $h = \ldots, -3, -2, -1, 1, 2, 3, \ldots$. Obviously, being pure numbers that by construction fall in the interval $[-1, 1]$, autocorrelations convey more useful information than autocovariance coefficients do, as the latter depend on the units of measurement of y_t. For stationary processes, both the functions $\gamma(\cdot)$ and $\rho(\cdot)$ should eventually decay to 0. Therefore, the autocovariance and ACFs are important for the characterization and classification of time series. We will turn our attention to autocorrelations in Section 2.1.3.

Unsurprisingly, strict stationarity implies weak stationarity (provided that the first and the second moments exist) while the reverse is generally not true. In the remainder of this chapter, when we refer to stationarity we shall mean its weak form, unless differently stated. In addition, we will routinely assume that our time series are stationary (or have been suitably transformed to make them stationary, as we will discuss in detail in Chapter 4).

EXAMPLE 2.1

A time series generated by a stationary process fluctuates around a constant mean, because its memory of past shocks decays over time. Fig. 2.1 visually compares a stationary process with a nonstationary one.

The data plotted in Fig. 2.1A are 1000 realizations of a first-order AR process of the type $y_t = \phi_0 + \phi_1 y_{t-1} + \varepsilon_t$, with $\phi_0 = 0$ and $\phi_1 = 0.2$. We shall discuss AR models in detail later in this chapter. For the time being, we are just interested in the fact that this process is stationary. This is visually obvious: the process reverts back in time to its zero mean and shows no sign of either an explosive or drifting behavior. In Fig. 2.1B the same stationary data as in Fig. 2.1A are plotted in comparison to a nonstationary time series that has been generated from a random walk process (that we shall discuss in more detail in Chapter 4) of the type $y_t = \mu + y_{t-1} + \varepsilon_t$ (in fact, in Fig. 2.1B μ has been set equal to, i.e., we have simulated a random walk without drift). To allow an exact comparison, both series have been generated using the same normal, IID random shocks. Visually, nonstationary data wander around aimlessly and they appear to be in no hurry to revert back to their mean (which, in fact, does not even exist, as we shall emphasize later). The explosive behavior of the series generated from a random walk in Fig. 2.1B is evident by a simple inspection of the simulated data: these have a minimum value at −10.80 and a maximum at 1.60; conversely, the simulated AR(1) data range between −0.70 and 0.76 only!

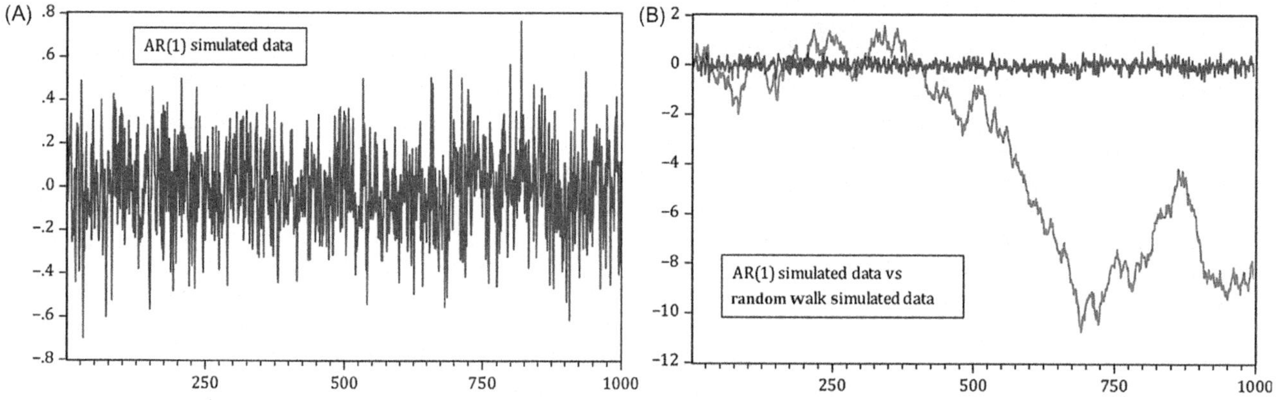

FIGURE 2.1 Plots of two times series with alternative persistence properties and their comparison.

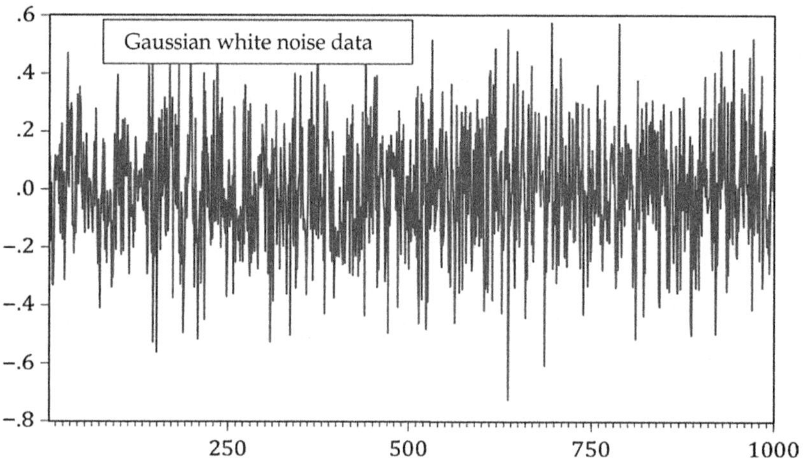

FIGURE 2.2 Plot of data simulated from a Gaussian WN process.

Before we move on, we shall introduce a fundamental class of stationary processes; in some ways, one may even argue that these are fundamental building blocks of all (covariance) stationary processes: the *white noise* (WN).

DEFINITION 2.4 (White noise)

A WN process is a sequence of random variables $\{z_t\}$ with mean equal to 0, constant variance equal to σ^2, and zero autocovariances (and autocorrelations) except at lag 0. If $\{z_t\}$ is normally distributed, we shall speak of a Gaussian WN.

Fig. 2.2 shows an example of Gaussian WN, from which 1000 simulations have been generated with a standard deviation of 0.2. Clearly, the process in Fig. 2.2 represents pure noise in the sense that—apart from lucky patterns that may accidentally appear (and not always it will be clear whether this occurs in the plot or in the mind of the observer)—there is no appreciable structure in the plotted data, either in terms of its levels or in terms of its tendency to randomly fluctuate. In fact, Definition 2.4 implies that a WN process corresponds to an AR(1) process in which $\phi_1 = 0$.

We may also want to add that it is not trivial to visually distinguish the process plotted in Fig. 2.2 from the AR(1) model with a low AR coefficient ($\phi_1 = 0.2$) presented in Fig. 2.1A. Therefore, in Section 2.1.3, we proceed to discuss how we can formally test whether there is evidence of serial correlation in the data, which will allow us, at least in principle, to tell AR(p) processes apart from simpler WN models.

2.1.3 Sample Autocorrelations and Sample Partial Autocorrelations

Example 2.1 has shown a case where it was fairly easy to visually assess the stationarity of the simulated series plotted in Fig. 2.1A. However, plotting the data is not always sufficient to determinate whether the *data generating process* (henceforth, DGP) is stationary or not. Autocorrelations may represent a good tool to further investigate the properties of the data. Indeed, as discussed earlier, for a series that originates from a stationary process, the autocorrelations tend to die out quickly as the length of the lag (h) that is examined increases. More generally, the sample ACF (SACF) reflects important information about the degree of *linear dependence* of a time series at different times or, in other words, the length and the strength of the memory of the process (and thus the predictive power of lagged values for future realizations of the series). However, it is important to understand that, because we only observe one of the possible realized and necessarily finite sequences of sample data from the process $\{y_t\}$, we shall only be able to compute *sample* autocorrelations, which therefore only provide estimates of the true and unobserved autocorrelations of $\{y_t\}$ and that may contain large sample variation and substantial uncertainty: both ought to be taken in due account when mapping the properties of an SACF into the characterization of the underlying DGP.

DEFINITION 2.5 (Sample autocorrelations)

Given a sample of T observations of the variable y_t, $y_1, y_2, \ldots, y_T$, the estimated or sample ACF $\hat{\rho}_h$ (where h is a positive integer) is computed as:

$$\hat{\rho}_h = \frac{\sum_{t=h+1}^{T}(y_t-\hat{\mu})(y_{t-h}-\hat{\mu})}{\sum_{t=1}^{T}(y_t-\hat{\mu})^2} = \frac{\hat{\gamma}_h}{\hat{\gamma}_0}, \tag{2.5}$$

where $\hat{\mu}$ is the sample mean computed as $\hat{\mu} = T^{-1}\sum_{t=1}^{T} y_t$.

Noticeably, the sample autocorrelation $\hat{\rho}_h$ is equal to the sample autocovariance $\hat{\gamma}_h$ divided by the sample variance $\hat{\gamma}_0$. If $\{y_t\}$ is an identically and independently distributed process with finite variance, then for a large sample, the estimated autocorrelations will be asymptotically normally distributed with mean 0 and variance $1/T$ (where T is the size of the sample). This result allows us to conduct tests of hypotheses on the autocorrelation coefficients to determine whether they are significantly different from 0. For instance, the 95% confidence interval (most commonly used in the literature) is simply given by $\hat{\rho}_h \pm 1.96/\sqrt{T}$. More generally, if $\{y_t\}$ is a weakly stationary time series satisfying $y_t = \mu + \sum_{j=0}^{q}\phi_j z_{t-j}$, where $\phi_0 = 1$ and $\{z_j\}$ is a Gaussian WN, then $\hat{\rho}_h$ will asymptotically be:

$$\hat{\rho}_h \overset{a}{\sim} N\left(0, T^{-1}\left(1 + 2\sum_{j=1}^{q}\rho_j^2\right)\right). \tag{2.6}$$

Further discussion of the statistical properties of sample autocorrelations is beyond the scope of this book and may be found in Fuller (1976, Chapter 6) and Brockwell and Davis (1991, Chapter 7). However, it is important to mention that in finite samples $\hat{\rho}_h$ is a biased estimator of ρ_h. The bias is of the order of $1/T$ and therefore while it can be large for small samples, it becomes less and less relevant as the number of observations increases.

EXAMPLE 2.2

Fig. 2.3 plots the sample ACFs of the two simulated time series introduced in Example 2.1. These plots are also known as sample correlograms. The bars are the autocorrelations up to lag 24 while the upper and lower dashed bands represent their 95% confidence intervals computed using the formula in Eq. (2.5). Indeed, as a rule of thumb, the correlations are deemed to be significant if they lie outside the $\pm 1.96 \times 1/\sqrt{T}$ bands. The correlograms give us a wealth of important information on the linear properties of the data. First, it is very easy to guess which data came from a nonstationary process: the correlogram in Fig. 2.3B shows autocorrelation coefficients (almost) equal to 1 that fail to decay as the lag order increases. Notably, the theoretical autocorrelation coefficients for a random walk process shall be exactly one at all lags. However, we shall not be completely surprised that the sample autocorrelations do not exactly match the theoretical values that ought to obtain: as discussed earlier, the sample autocorrelations are downward biased estimates of the true and unobserved ones; such an effect gets stronger as the number of displacement lags h grows, and this is the reason why the SACF of the random walk process in Fig. 2.3B declines below 1 in a visible manner for h larger than 12.

On the contrary, Fig. 2.3A, in addition to clearly showing the stationary nature of the process that originated the data (because the autocorrelations quickly die off to 0, with one isolated exception at lag $h = 22$), entails useful information about the underlying lag structure of the AR process. In fact, we notice that autocorrelations turn to near zero after the first lag. In fact, all

(Continued)

EXAMPLE 2.2 (Continued)

the correlation coefficients at lags higher than 1 lie inside the 95% confidence interval, meaning that the hypothesis that each individual coefficient is equal to 0 cannot be rejected at a 5% size. This is not surprising, because the data have been truly generated from a first-order AR process. We shall return to the discussion of how the SACF can be used to specify the unknown lag order of an AR-type process (which is generally unobserved) in Section 2.3.1.

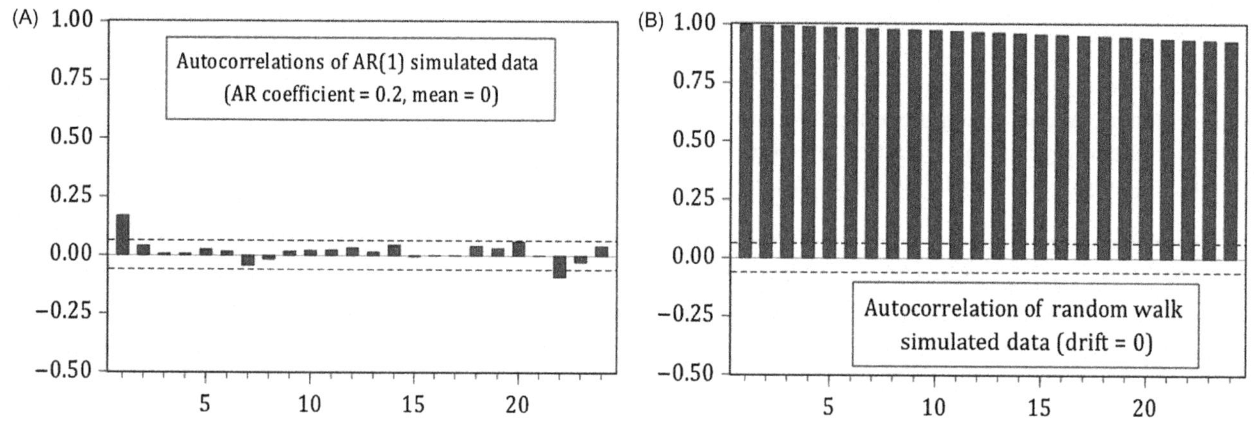

FIGURE 2.3 Correlograms of two times series with alternative persistence properties.

It is also possible to jointly test whether several (say, M) consecutive autocorrelation coefficients are equal to 0. To this purpose, Box and Pierce (1970) developed a well-known portmanteau test based on the Q-statistic:

$$Q(M) \equiv T\sum_{h=1}^{M}\hat{\rho}_h^2 \overset{a}{\sim} \chi_M^2, \tag{2.7}$$

where T is the sample size and M is the maximum lag length that we want to entertain in the test. The Q-statistic is asymptotically distributed as a χ_M^2 under the null hypothesis that the M autocorrelation coefficients are jointly 0 (i.e., we test $H_0:\rho_1 = \rho_2 = \cdots = \rho_M = 0$ against the alternative hypothesis that $H_1:\rho_i \neq 0, \;$ for some $i \in \{1, 2, \ldots, M\}$). Therefore, if the Q-statistic exceeds the critical value from the χ^2 distribution with M degrees of freedom at a probability $1-\alpha$, then the hypothesis that the first M autocorrelation coefficients are equal to 0 can be rejected in a test of size α (meaning that at least one autocorrelation coefficient must have been significantly different from 0). However, the Box-Pierce test has poor small sample properties, that is, it leads to the wrong decision too often when the sample size is small. Consequently, Ljung and Box (1978) developed a variant of the Q-statistic that has better small sample properties:

$$Q^*(M) = T(T+2)\sum_{h=1}^{M}\frac{\hat{\rho}_h^2}{T-h} \sim \chi_M^2. \tag{2.8}$$

Finally, in addition to autocorrelations, we can also compute *partial autocorrelations*. The partial autocorrelation between y_t and y_{t-h} is the autocorrelation between the two random variables in the time series, *conditional on* $y_{t-1}, \ldots, y_{t-h+1}$, that is, the autocorrelation measured after netting out the portion of the variability linearly explained already by the lags between $t-1$ and $t-h+1$.

DEFINITION 2.6 (Sample partial autocorrelations)

Formally, the partial autocorrelation a_h is defined as:

$$a_h = Corr(y_t, y_{t-h}|y_{t-1}, \ldots, y_{t-h+1}). \tag{2.9}$$

The sequence $a_1, a_2, \ldots, a_T$ as a function of $h = 1, 2, \ldots$ of partial autocorrelations is called partial autocorrelation function (PACF). The sample estimate $\hat{a}_h$ of the partial autocorrelation at lag h is obtained as the ordinary least square (OLS) estimator of ϕ_h in an AR model $y_t = \phi_0 + \phi_1 y_{t-1} + \cdots + \phi_h y_{t-h} + \varepsilon_t$ (that we shall discuss formally in Section 2.3.2).

While the meaning of autocorrelations is quite obvious, as they simply measure the strength of the linear relationship between y_t and the lagged values of the series (the higher the autocorrelation coefficient, the stronger the linear predictive relationship between past and future values of the series), the interpretation of partial autocorrelations is a bit less intuitive. Broadly speaking, partial autocorrelations measure the "added" predictive power of the hth lag of the series, y_{t-h}, when $y_{t-1},\ldots,y_{t-h+1}$ are already accounted for in the predictive regression. Indeed, the partial autocorrelation between y_t and y_{t-h} is nothing else than the regression coefficient of y_{t-h} in a regression where $y_{t-1},\ldots,y_{t-h+1}$ are also used as predictors of y_t.

EXAMPLE 2.3

Table 2.1A and B compares the sample autocorrelations (SACF) and partial autocorrelations (SPACF) functions of the data simulated from the AR(1) process already introduced in Examples 2.1 and 2.2, with those of the WN process depicted in Fig. 2.2. In addition, this table also shows the Ljung–Box test statistic (Q) for $M = 1,2,\ldots,24$ (penultimate column) and the p-value for the test (last column). The null that all the (population) autocorrelations coefficients are equal to 0 can always be rejected at any level of significance (because all the p-values are essentially nil) for the AR(1) generated data, meaning that at least one coefficient (the first one, as we can see from the plot) is significantly different from 0. On the contrary, as one would expect, we cannot reject the same null hypothesis for the WN data. Therefore, it would be incorrect to specify a linear model (soon to be defined to be of the ARMA type) for these second generated samples. Such crucial information is hardly obtainable from a simple visual comparison of the two plots in Figs. 2.1A and 2.2A.

TABLE 2.1A Serial Correlation Structure of Simulated AR(1) Data

Autocorrelation	Partial correlation		AC	PAC	Q-statistic	Probability
		1	0.168	0.168	28.433	0.000
		2	0.039	0.010	29.925	0.000
		3	0.006	−0.002	29.961	0.000
		4	0.006	0.005	29.997	0.000
		5	0.025	0.024	30.646	0.000
		6	0.015	0.007	30.873	0.000
		7	−0.045	−0.052	32.956	0.000
		8	−0.018	−0.003	33.282	0.000
		9	0.018	0.024	33.594	0.000
		10	0.020	0.013	34.001	0.000
		11	0.023	0.016	34.531	0.000
		12	0.032	0.028	35.566	0.000
		13	0.014	0.005	35.764	0.001
		14	0.045	0.038	37.802	0.001
		15	−0.005	−0.022	37.828	0.001
		16	−0.001	0.002	37.829	0.002
		17	−0.001	−0.000	37.829	0.003
		18	0.040	0.042	39.502	0.002
		19	0.029	0.016	40.336	0.003
		20	0.059	0.051	43.884	0.002
		21	−0.001	−0.018	43.884	0.002
		22	−0.094	−0.099	52.881	0.000
		23	−0.028	−0.001	53.672	0.000
		24	0.038	0.046	55.161	0.000

TABLE 2.1B Serial Correlation Structure of Simulated WN Data

Autocorrelation	Partial correlation		AC	PAC	Q-statistic	Probability
		1	0.022	0.022	0.4673	0.494
		2	−0.010	−0.010	0.5598	0.756
		3	0.051	0.051	3.1776	0.365
		4	0.027	0.025	3.9294	0.416
		5	−0.056	−0.056	7.1017	0.213
		6	0.033	0.034	8.2260	0.222
		7	0.004	−0.001	8.2428	0.312
		8	0.006	0.011	8.2735	0.407
		9	−0.011	−0.012	8.4026	0.494
		10	0.028	0.024	9.2163	0.512
		11	−0.033	−0.032	10.308	0.503
		12	−0.051	−0.050	12.961	0.372
		13	−0.031	−0.031	13.937	0.378
		14	0.008	0.008	13.996	0.450
		15	0.059	0.069	17.483	0.291
		16	0.010	0.008	17.584	0.349
		17	−0.013	−0.015	17.752	0.405
		18	0.020	0.013	18.143	0.446
		19	0.014	0.013	18.333	0.500
		20	0.051	0.059	21.024	0.396
		21	−0.009	−0.014	21.100	0.453
		22	−0.037	−0.041	22.539	0.428
		23	−0.033	−0.039	23.667	0.422
		24	−0.037	−0.042	25.038	0.404

Before moving on, it is important to stress once again that ACFs (and PACFs), despite being a very useful tool to identify the order of AR, MA, and ARMA models (as we shall see in Section 2.3), can only measure the degree of *linear* association between y_t and y_{t-k} for $k \geq 1$ and thus they may fail to detect important nonlinear dependence relationships in the data. Consider the following example:

$$y_t = \varepsilon_{t-1}^2 + \varepsilon_t, \tag{2.10}$$

where $\{\varepsilon_t\}$ is a normally distributed WN process. Since y_{t-1} is a function of ε_{t-1}, the value of y_t is dependent on the value of y_{t-1}, $y_t = (y_{t-1} - \varepsilon_{t-2}^2)^2 + \varepsilon_t$. Nevertheless, with simple algebra it is possible to demonstrate that all the autocorrelations are equal to 0. Taking the expectation of y_t, we get $E[y_t] = E[\varepsilon_{t-1}^2] = E[y_{t-1}] = E[\varepsilon_{t-2}^2] = \sigma^2$, where σ^2 is the variance of the homoskedastic process $\{\varepsilon_t\}$. Thus, the autocorrelations are:

$$\begin{aligned}\rho_i &= E\left[\left(y_t - \sigma^2\right)\left(y_{t-i} - \sigma^2\right)\right] = E\left[\left(\varepsilon_{t-1}^2 + \varepsilon_t - \sigma^2\right)\left(\varepsilon_{t-1-i}^2 + \varepsilon_{t-i} - \sigma^2\right)\right] \\ &= E\left[\varepsilon_{t-1}^2\varepsilon_{t-1-i}^2 + \varepsilon_{t-1}^2\varepsilon_{t-i} - \varepsilon_{t-1}^2\sigma^2 + \varepsilon_t\varepsilon_{t-1-i}^2 + \varepsilon_t\varepsilon_{t-i} - \varepsilon_t\sigma^2 - \sigma^2\varepsilon_{t-1-i}^2 - \sigma^2\varepsilon_{t-i} + \sigma^2\sigma^2\right].\end{aligned} \tag{2.11}$$

Note that $E[\varepsilon_{t-i}^2\varepsilon_{t-j}^2] = \sigma^2\sigma^2 = \sigma^4$, $E[\varepsilon_t\varepsilon_{t-i}^2] = 0$, and $E[\varepsilon_t\sigma^2] = 0$. Therefore

$$\rho_i = \sigma^2\sigma^2 + E\left[\varepsilon_{t-1}^2\varepsilon_{t-i}\right] - \sigma^2\sigma^2 - \sigma^2\sigma^2 + \sigma^2\sigma^2 = E\left[\varepsilon_{t-1}^2\varepsilon_{t-i}\right]. \tag{2.12}$$

Clearly, all the values of $E[\varepsilon_{t-1}^2\varepsilon_{t-i}] = 0$ for $i \neq 1$; even when $i = 1$, because ε_t is normally distributed, its third moment $E[\varepsilon_t^3] = E[\varepsilon_{t-i}^3] = 0$. As a result, $\rho_i = 0$ for any $i \neq 0$, that is, all the autocorrelations are equal to 0. Therefore, if one analyzes the correlogram of a long sample of data coming from a process such the one in Eq. (2.10), he/she may incorrectly infer that the data come from a WN process (as all the autocorrelations will not be significantly different from 0). However, y_t is clearly dependent on y_{t-1}, although the relationship is nonlinear.

2.2 MOVING AVERAGE AND AUTOREGRESSIVE PROCESSES

2.2.1 Finite Order Moving Average Processes

In Section 2.1.2 we have defined a simple stationary process, the WN. A linear combination of WN processes is generally known as an MA process.

DEFINITION 2.7 (Moving average process)

A qth order MA, denoted as MA(q), is a process that can be represented as:

$$y_t = \mu + \varepsilon_t + \theta_1 \varepsilon_{t-1} + \theta_2 \varepsilon_{t-2} + \cdots + \theta_q \varepsilon_{t-q}, \tag{2.13}$$

where the process of $\{\varepsilon_t\}$ is an IID WN with mean 0 and constant variance equal to σ_ε^2. More compactly, the process is often written as:

$$y_t = \mu + \varepsilon_t + \sum_{j=1}^{q} \theta_j \varepsilon_{t-j}. \tag{2.14}$$

Importantly, MA(q) models are always stationary as they are finite, linear combination of WN processes for which the first two moments are time invariant. More precisely, an MA(q) process has constant mean, variance, and autocovariances (hence, autocorrelations) that may be different from 0 up to lag q, but are equal to 0 afterward. Formally, the moment properties of an MA(q) can be summarized as follows:

$$E(y_t) = \mu \tag{2.15}$$

$$Var(y_t) = \gamma_0 = (1 + \theta_1^2 + \theta_2^2 + \cdots + \theta_q^2)\sigma^2 \tag{2.16}$$

$$\begin{aligned} \gamma_h &= Cov(y_t, y_{t-h}) = (\theta_h + \theta_{h+1}\theta_1 + \theta_{h+2}\theta_2 + \cdots + \theta_q\theta_{q-h})\sigma^2 && \text{for } h = 1, 2, \ldots, q \\ \gamma_h &= 0 && \text{for } h > q. \end{aligned} \tag{2.17}$$

As an example, we shall verify those properties for the MA(1) and MA(2) models, and leave the extensions to higher orders as an exercise for the reader.

Consider the following MA(1) model:

$$y_t = \mu + \varepsilon_t + \theta_1 \varepsilon_{t-1} \tag{2.18}$$

as well as the MA(2) model

$$y_t = \mu + \varepsilon_t + \theta_1 \varepsilon_{t-1} + \theta_2 \varepsilon_{t-2}, \tag{2.19}$$

where in both cases, ε_t IID $N(0, \sigma_\varepsilon^2)$. Taking expectations of both sides of Eq. (2.18), we obtain:

$$E(y_t) = E(\mu + \theta_1 \varepsilon_{t-1} + \varepsilon_t) = E(\mu) + \theta_1 E(\varepsilon_{t-1}) + E(\varepsilon_t) = \mu \tag{2.20}$$

because we know that the expected value of a constant is equal to the constant itself and that $E(\varepsilon_t) = E(\varepsilon_{t-1}) = 0$ by the definition of an MA process. The result is identical when we consider the MA(2) in Eq. (2.19) because also $E(\varepsilon_{t-2})$ is equal to 0.

Without loss of generality, in order to simplify the rest of the computations, in what follows we assume $\mu = 0$. We are now ready to compute the variance of y_t under simple MA models. Let us first consider the model in Eq. (2.18), that is,

$$Var(y_t) = E[(y_t - E(y_t))^2], \tag{2.21}$$

where, assuming $E(y_t) = 0$, Eq. (2.21) simplifies to:

$$Var(y_t) = E[y_t^2] = E[(\varepsilon_t + \theta_1 \varepsilon_{t-1})^2] = E[\varepsilon_t^2] + \theta_1^2 E[\varepsilon_{t-1}^2] + 2\theta_1 E[\varepsilon_t \varepsilon_{t-1}]. \tag{2.22}$$

Because we know that ε_t and ε_{t-1} are uncorrelated, that is, $Cov(\varepsilon_t, \varepsilon_{t-1}) = E[\varepsilon_t \varepsilon_{t-1}] = 0$ and that $E[\varepsilon_t^2] = E[\varepsilon_{t-1}^2] = \sigma_\varepsilon^2$, then

$$Var(y_t) = \sigma_\varepsilon^2 + \theta_1^2 \sigma_\varepsilon^2 = (1 + \theta_1^2)\sigma_\varepsilon^2. \tag{2.23}$$

It is straightforward to extend these computations to the MA(2) model in Eq. (2.19), considering that: $Cov(\varepsilon_t, \varepsilon_{t-j}) = 0$ for any $j \geq 0$:

$$Var(y_t) = E[y_t^2] = E[(\varepsilon_t + \theta_1\varepsilon_{t-1} + \theta_2\varepsilon_{t-2})^2] = \sigma_\varepsilon^2 + \theta_1^2\sigma_\varepsilon^2 + \theta_2^2\sigma_\varepsilon^2 = (1 + \theta_1^2 + \theta_2^2)\sigma_\varepsilon^2. \quad (2.24)$$

Finally, we compute the autocovariances and the autocorrelations of these two processes. Again, we first consider the MA(1) model and compute the autocovariance at lag 1:

$$\gamma_1 = E[(y_t - E[y_t])(y_{t-1} - E[y_{t-1}])]. \quad (2.25)$$

Again, we assume $E[y_t] = E[y_{t-1}] = 0$, so that we are left with

$$\gamma_1 = E[y_t y_{t-1}] = E[(\varepsilon_t + \theta_1\varepsilon_{t-1})(\varepsilon_{t-1} + \theta_1\varepsilon_{t-2})]. \quad (2.26)$$

Because $Cov(\varepsilon_t, \varepsilon_{t-j}) = 0$ for any $j \geq 0$, all the cross products (i.e., $E[\varepsilon_t\varepsilon_{t-1}]$, $E[\varepsilon_t\varepsilon_{t-2}]$, and $E[\varepsilon_{t-1}\varepsilon_{t-2}]$) are all equal to 0, we obtain:

$$\gamma_1 = \theta_1 E[\varepsilon_{t-1}^2] = \theta_1\sigma_\varepsilon^2. \quad (2.27)$$

It is easy to verify that the autocovariance at lag 2 is equal to 0, as all the cross products are equal to 0:

$$\gamma_2 = E[y_t y_{t-2}] = E[(\varepsilon_t + \theta_1\varepsilon_{t-1})(\varepsilon_{t-2} + \theta_1\varepsilon_{t-3})] = 0. \quad (2.28)$$

The same applies to all autocovariances of order equal to or higher than 2, because $E[\varepsilon_{t-i}\varepsilon_{t-i-j}] = 0$ for all $i + j > i \geq 0$ so that $\gamma_j = E[y_t y_{t-j}] = E[(\varepsilon_t + \theta_1\varepsilon_{t-1})(\varepsilon_{t-j} + \theta_1\varepsilon_{t-j-1})] = 0$.

Now we move to consider the MA(2) process and we obtain that the autocovariance at lag 1 is equal to:

$$\gamma_1 = E[y_t y_{t-1}] = E[(\varepsilon_t + \theta_1\varepsilon_{t-1} + \theta_2\varepsilon_{t-2})(\varepsilon_{t-1} + \theta_1\varepsilon_{t-2} + \theta_2\varepsilon_{t-3})] = \theta_1 E[\varepsilon_{t-1}^2] + \theta_2\theta_1[\varepsilon_{t-1}^2] = (1 + \theta_2)\theta_1\sigma_\varepsilon^2. \quad (2.29)$$

We can now verify that the autocovariance at lag 2 of an MA(2) process is not 0 (while the autocovariances at lags higher than the MA order will be equal to 0):

$$\gamma_2 = E[y_t y_{t-2}] = E[(\varepsilon_t + \theta_1\varepsilon_{t-1} + \theta_2\varepsilon_{t-2})(\varepsilon_{t-2} + \theta_1\varepsilon_{t-3} + \theta_2\varepsilon_{t-4})] = \theta_2 E[\varepsilon_{t-2}^2] = \theta_2\sigma_\varepsilon^2. \quad (2.30)$$

Finally, the autocorrelation coefficients are simply obtained by dividing the autocovariance coefficient by the variance. Therefore, for an MA(1) model we have:

$$\rho_1 = \frac{\gamma_1}{\gamma_0} = \frac{\theta_1\sigma_\varepsilon^2}{(1 + \theta_1^2)\sigma_\varepsilon^2} = \frac{\theta_1}{1 + \theta_1^2} \quad (2.31)$$

while $\rho_h = 0$ for $h > 1$. Instead, for an MA(2) model, the autocorrelation coefficients of orders 1 and 2 are different from 0 and equal to:

$$\rho_1 = \frac{(1 + \theta_2)\theta_1\sigma_\varepsilon^2}{(1 + \theta_1^2 + \theta_2^2)\sigma_\varepsilon^2} = \frac{(1 + \theta_2)\theta_1}{(1 + \theta_1^2 + \theta_2^2)} \quad (2.32)$$

$$\rho_2 = \frac{\theta_2\sigma_\varepsilon^2}{(1 + \theta_1^2 + \theta_2^2)\sigma_\varepsilon^2} = \frac{\theta_2}{(1 + \theta_1^2 + \theta_2^2)} \quad (2.33)$$

EXAMPLE 2.4

In this example, we show the plots and the sample correlogram for 1000 observations simulated from a set of alternative MA(1) and MA(2) processes. To simulate all these processes, we have assumed ε_t IID$N(0, 0.04)$. The left panel of both Figs. 2.4 and 2.5 shows how hard it can be to "eyeball" the MA order of the process, even when the coefficients that have been used to simulate the data are in fact rather different: in Fig. 2.5, θ_1 is more than twice the value taken by θ_1 in Fig. 2.4.

Figs. 2.4 and 2.5 illustrate the characteristics of data simulated from two alternative MA(1) processes with 0 mean and θ_1 equal to 0.3 and 0.8, respectively. As one should expect, only the autocorrelation coefficient at the first lag is statistically significant in both cases. This is unsurprising, because, as we have demonstrated in Eq. (2.28), when the data are generated from an MA(1) process, autocovariance and autocorrelations of order higher than the first one will be 0. Applying Eqs. (2.27) and (2.31), we can compute the theoretical autocovariance and autocorrelation at lag 1 for the two models (of which the sample autocorrelation plot in panel (B) are just sample estimates). In the case of the simulations appearing in Fig. 2.4, the theoretical autocovariance at lag 1 is $\gamma_1 = \theta_1\sigma_\varepsilon^2 = 0.3 \times 0.04 = 0.012$ and the theoretical autocorrelation is:

$$\rho_1 = \frac{\theta_1}{1 + \theta_1^2} = \frac{0.3}{1 + 0.3^2} = 0.275.$$

(Continued)

EXAMPLE 2.4 (Continued)

In the case of the data in Fig. 2.5, the theoretical autocovariance at lag 1 is $\gamma_1 = \theta_1\sigma_\varepsilon^2 = 0.8 \times 0.04 = 0.032$ and the theoretical autocorrelation is:

$$\rho_1 = \frac{\theta_1}{1+\theta_1^2} = \frac{0.8}{1+0.8^2} = 0.49.$$

As it is visible from a comparison of the plots in Figs. 2.4B and 2.5B, respectively, data generated from a process in which shocks are more persistent (i.e., $\theta_1 = 0.8$) are more volatile than the data originating from a process with lower shock persistence ($\theta_1 = 0.3$). We can verify this intuition by computing the variance of the two processes using Eq. (2.23). We find that the variance for the MA(1) process with $\theta_1 = 0.3$ is $Var(y_t) = (1+\theta_1^2)\sigma_\varepsilon^2 = (1+0.3^2) \times 0.04 = 0.0436$, which implies a standard deviation of 20.9%. Instead, the variance for the MA(1) process with $\theta_1 = 0.8$ is $Var(y_t) = (1+\theta_1^2)\sigma_\varepsilon^2 = (1+0.8^2) \times 0.04 = 0.0656$, implying a standard deviation of 25.6%. Such a disparity is completely consistent with the observed differences in the dynamics of the two simulated series.

Finally, Fig. 2.6 plots and shows the statistical properties of data generated from an MA(2) model with $\theta_1 = 0.8$ and $\theta_2 = 0.3$. To save space, from now on we limit our computations to the autocorrelation coefficients and leave the calculation of variance and autocovariances to the reader. The first-order autocorrelation coefficient is:

$$\rho_1 = \frac{(1+\theta_2)\theta_1}{1+\theta_1^2+\theta_2^2} = \frac{(1+0.3)\times 0.8}{1+0.8^2+0.3^2} = 0.601$$

while the second-order coefficient is:

$$\rho_2 = \frac{\theta_2}{1+\theta_1^2+\theta_2^2} = \frac{0.3}{1+0.8^2+0.3^2} = 0.173.$$

As already discussed, all the autocorrelation coefficients at lags higher than 2 in an MA(2) model should be equal to 0. In the correlogram, this corresponds to sample coefficients that are not statistically significant (see Fig. 2.6B with the only minor exception of the sample estimate of the 21st-order coefficient that touches the lower edge of the 95% confidence band).

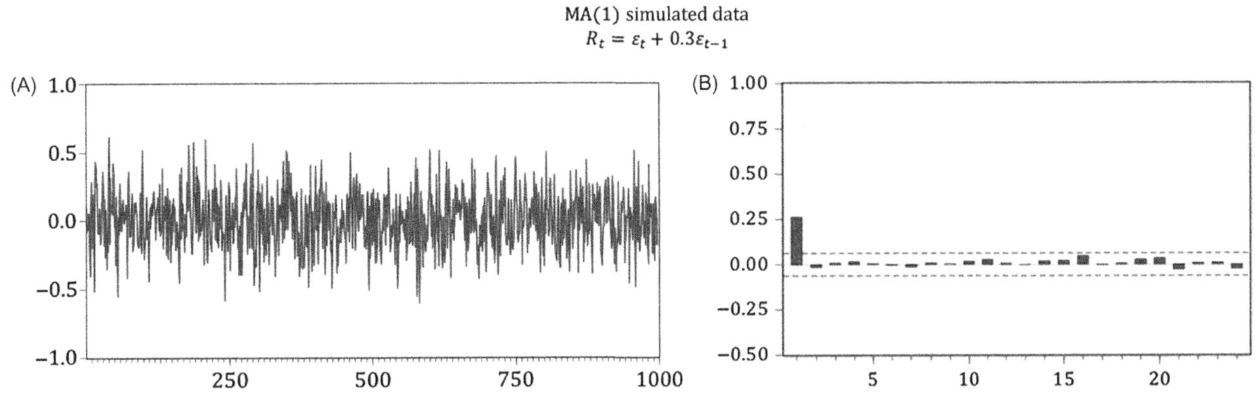

FIGURE 2.4 Plots and correlogram of MA(1) simulated data with $\mu = 0$ and $\theta_1 = 0.3$.

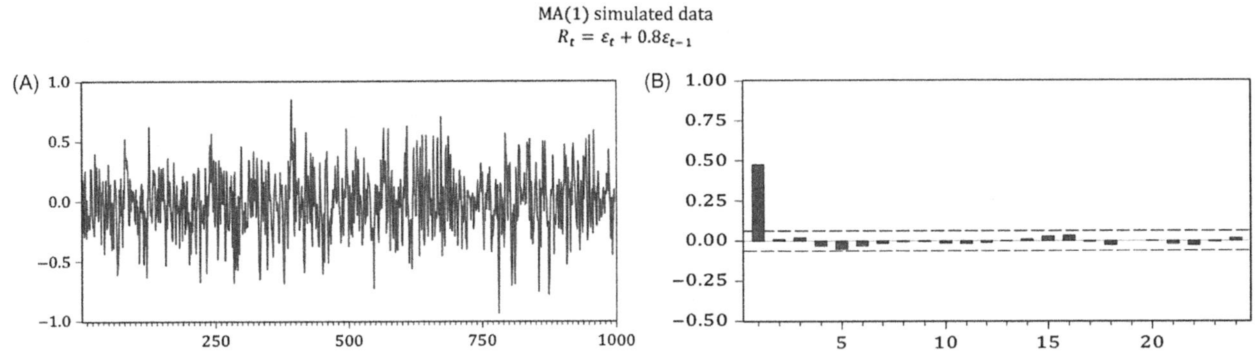

FIGURE 2.5 Plots and correlogram of MA(1) simulated data with $\mu = 0$ and $\theta_1 = 0.8$.

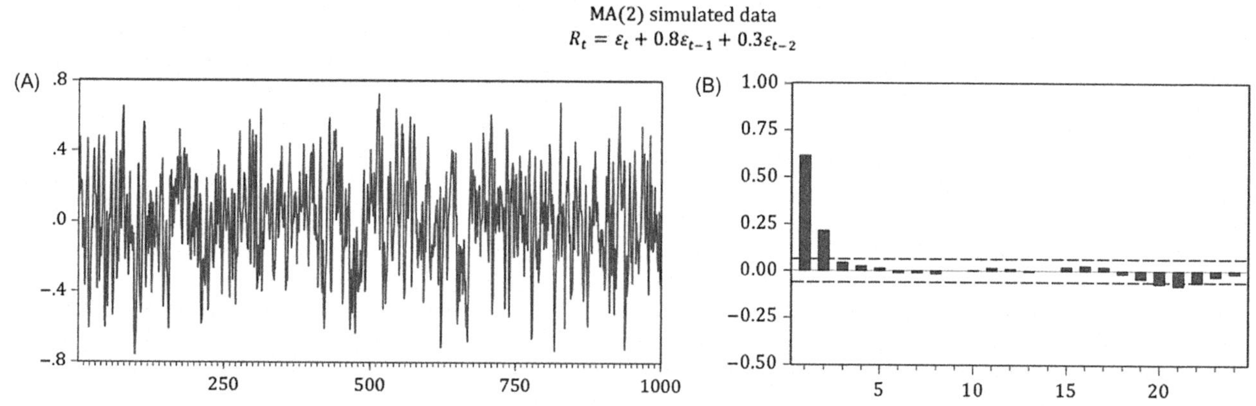

FIGURE 2.6 Plots and sample correlogram of MA(2) simulated data with $\mu = 0$, $\theta_1 = 0.8$, and $\theta_2 = 0.3$.

2.2.2 Autoregressive Processes

An Autoregressive (AR) process of order p is a process in which the random variable y_t is a weighted sum of p past variables in the series $(y_{t-1}, y_{t-2}, \ldots, y_{t-p})$ plus a WN error term, ε_t. AR(p) models are simple univariate devices to capture the often-observed *Markovian nature* of financial and macroeconomic data, that is, the fact that the series tends to be influenced at most by a finite number of past values of the same series, which is often also described as the series only having a finite memory, of p periods at most.

DEFINITION 2.8 (Autoregressive process)

A pth order AR process, denoted as AR(p), is a process that can be represented by the pth order stochastic *difference equation*

$$y_t = \phi_0 + \phi_1 y_{t-1} + \phi_2 y_{t-2} + \cdots + \phi_p y_{t-p} + \varepsilon_t, \quad (2.34)$$

where the process of $\{\varepsilon_t\}$ is an IID WN with mean 0 and constant variance σ_ε^2. More compactly, we can write:

$$y_t = \phi_0 + \sum_{j=1}^{p} \phi_j y_{t-j} + \varepsilon_t. \quad (2.35)$$

For notational convenience, we shall now introduce the lag (sometimes also known as *backward shift*) and the *difference operators*. The lag operator, generally denoted by L (or, alternatively, by B), shifts the time index of a variables regularly sampled over time backward by one unit. Therefore, applying the lag operator to a generic variable y at time t, we obtain the value of the variable at time, $t-1$, that is, $Ly_t = y_{t-1}$. Equivalently, applying L^2 means lagging the variable twice, that is, $L^2 y_t = L(Ly_t) = y_{t-2}$ and so on, that is, $L^k y_t = L(L^{k-1} y_t) = L(L^{k-1}(L^{k-2} y_t)) = \cdots = L(L^{k-1}(L^{k-2} \cdots (Ly_t) \cdots)) = y_{t-k}$, with $k \geq 1$.

The difference operator Δ is used to express the difference between consecutive realizations of a time series. Indeed, with Δy_t we denote the first-order difference $\Delta y_t = y_t - y_{t-1}$, with $\Delta^2 y_t$ we denote the second-order difference, that is, $\Delta^2 y_t = \Delta(\Delta y_t) = \Delta(y_t - y_{t-1})$ and so on. Clearly, $\Delta y_t = y_t - y_{t-1}$ can also be rewritten using the lag operator, that is, $\Delta y_t = y_t - Ly_t = (1-L)y_t$. More generally, we can write a difference equation of any order, $\Delta^k y_t$, as $\Delta^k y_t = (1-L)^k y_t$, with $k \geq 1$. More details on the lag operator and the way it can be used to provide solutions to difference equations can be found in Appendix 2.A.[1] Back to the AR model in Eq. (2.34), we now know that, because it is a stochastic difference equation, it can be rewritten using the lag operator as:

$$(1 - \phi_1 L - \phi_2 L^2 - \cdots - \phi_p L^p) y_t = \phi_0 + \varepsilon_t, \quad (2.36)$$

1. The focus on difference equations is justified by the fact that, even though the model in Eq. (2.35) is a stochastic difference equation owing to the presence of the random shocks ε_t, useful information on its solution can be obtained by dropping ε_t and simply solving the resulting, deterministic difference equation.

or, more compactly, as:

$$\phi(L)y_t = \phi_0 + \varepsilon_t, \tag{2.37}$$

where $\phi(L)$ is the polynomial of order p, $(1 - \phi_1 L - \phi_2 L^2 - \cdots - \phi_p L^p)$. Replacing in the polynomial $\phi(L)$ the lag operator L by a variable λ and setting it equal to 0, that is, $\phi(\lambda) = 0$, we obtain the (reverse) *characteristic equation* associated with the difference equation in Eq. (2.34). Any value of λ that satisfies the polynomial equation $\phi(\lambda) = 0$ is called a *root* of the polynomial $\phi(L)$. A polynomial of degree p has p roots, which are often complex numbers. The roots of the polynomial associated with the difference equation are important determinants of the behavior of the time series. Indeed, if the absolute value of all the roots of the (reverse) characteristic equations is higher than 1, the process is said to be *stable*. It can be demonstrated that a stable process is always weakly stationary. Even if stability and stationarity are conceptually different (and stability is not necessary for stationarity), stability conditions are commonly referred to as stationarity conditions.

In order to discuss the basic properties of AR models, we focus on AR(1) and AR(2) processes and then generalize the discussion to AR(p) models. Let us consider the simple AR(1) model

$$y_t = \phi_0 + \phi_1 y_{t-1} + \varepsilon_t, \tag{2.38}$$

where ε_t IID $N(0, \sigma_\varepsilon^2)$. Taking the expectation of Eq. (2.38), we obtain:

$$E(y_t) = \phi_0 + \phi_1 E(y_{t-1}). \tag{2.39}$$

Under the stationarity condition, we know that it must be $E(y_t) = E(y_{t-1}) = \mu$ and hence:

$$E(y_t) = \mu = \phi_0 + \phi_1 \mu, \tag{2.40}$$

which solved for the unknown unconditional mean gives:

$$\mu = \frac{\phi_0}{1 - \phi_1}. \tag{2.41}$$

Intuitively, it is necessary that $\phi_1 \neq 1$ for the mean of y_t to exist and be constant;[2] indeed, in the case $\phi_1 = 1$ the mean will diverge to infinity and the process will show an explosive behavior. If we now substitute $\phi_0 = (1 - \phi_1)\mu$ from Eq. (2.41) in Eq. (2.38), we obtain that:

$$y_t - \mu = \phi_1(y_{t-1} - \mu) + \varepsilon_t. \tag{2.42}$$

Of course, because the AR dynamics must govern all times t, it must also be the case that:

$$y_{t-1} - \mu = \phi_1(y_{t-2} - \mu) + \varepsilon_{t-1}, \tag{2.43}$$

and therefore

$$y_t - \mu = \phi_1(\phi_1(y_{t-2} - \mu) + \varepsilon_{t-1}) + \varepsilon_t. \tag{2.44}$$

By a process of infinite backward substitution, we obtain:

$$y_t - \mu = \varepsilon_t + \phi_1 \varepsilon_{t-1} + \phi_1^2 \varepsilon_{t-2} + \cdots = \sum_{i=0}^{\infty} \phi_1^i \varepsilon_{t-i}. \tag{2.45}$$

This result leads us to introduce and use one of the most important results in time series analysis, known as *Wold's decomposition theorem* (by Wold, 1960).

RESULT 2.1 (Wold's decomposition)

Every weakly stationary, purely nondeterministic, stochastic process $(y_t - \mu)$ can be written as an infinite, linear combination of a sequence of WN components:

$$y_t - \mu = \sum_{i=0}^{\infty} \psi_i \varepsilon_{t-i}. \tag{2.46}$$

---

2. We are about to see that such a condition is necessary but not sufficient because, as it will turn out, one needs $|\phi_1| < 1$ for weak stationarity to hold.

Of course, Eq. (2.46) is exactly what we obtained in Eq. (2.45). The references to purely non-deterministic series in our statement of Wold's theorem refers to the fact that any linearly deterministic component should have been subtracted from the process already, before applying the decomposition as a weighted sum of WN components, which is the reason why we consider $(y_t - \mu)$ and not y_t. In other words, Wold's theorem states that only an AR process of order p with no constant and no other predetermined, fixed terms can be expressed as an infinite order moving average process, MA(∞). As long as the process is stationary, the sum $\sum_{i=0}^{\infty} \psi_i \varepsilon_{t-i}$ will converge. This result is useful for deriving the ACF of an AR process and it creates an interesting, and possibly not completely expected link between the AR(p) processes of this section and the MA processes of Section 2.2.1.

More generally, and following algebraic steps similar to those that have led to Eq. (2.41) (they are just more tedious), the (unconditional) mean of an AR(p) model can be proven to be equal to:

$$\mu = \frac{\phi_0}{1 - \phi_1 - \phi_2 - \cdots - \phi_p}. \tag{2.47}$$

It is easy to derive that the necessary and sufficient condition for the mean of this general AR(p) process to exist and be finite is that the sum of the AR coefficients is less than 1 in absolute value, $|\phi_1 + \phi_2 + \cdots + \phi_p| < 1$.

From Eq. (2.42), we can also compute the variance of an AR(1) process as:

$$E[(y_t - \mu)^2] = \phi_1^2 E[(y_{t-1} - \mu)^2] + E[\varepsilon_t^2] \tag{2.48}$$

that under the stationarity assumption $E[(y_t - \mu)^2] = E[(y_{t-1} - \mu)^2] = Var[y_t]$ turns out to be:

$$Var[y_t] = \phi_1^2 \, Var[y_t] + \sigma_\varepsilon^2 \tag{2.49}$$

and therefore

$$Var[y_t] = \frac{\sigma_\varepsilon^2}{1 - \phi_1^2} \tag{2.50}$$

provided that $\phi_1^2 < 1$ (as the variance needs to be positive, and this can also formally be proven to be necessary and sufficient for the infinite sums defining the unconditional means and variances to converge). Therefore, putting all the conditions derived before together, for an AR(1) model, weak stationarity requires $|\phi_1| < 1$. In general, the variance of an AR(p) process must be computed from Yule-Walker equations written in the recursive form. For example, in case of AR(2) we obtain:

$$Var[y_t] = \frac{(1 - \phi_2)\sigma_\varepsilon^2}{(1 + \phi_2)(1 - \phi_1 - \phi_2)(1 + \phi_1 - \phi_2)}. \tag{2.51}$$

Unfortunately, for higher order AR models, the corresponding characteristic polynomials are rather convoluted to the point that it becomes infeasible to define simple restrictions on the AR coefficients that ensure covariance stationarity. However, the *Schur criterion* provides an alternative to check the covariance stationarity of a process. For an AR(p) polynomial $\phi(L) = 1 - \phi_1 L - \phi_2 L^2 - \cdots - \phi_p L^p$, the criterion requires the construction of two lower-triangular matrices, $\mathbf{A}_1$ and $\mathbf{A}_2$ of the form:

$$\mathbf{A}_1 \equiv \begin{bmatrix} 1 & 0 & \cdots & 0 & 0 \\ -\phi_1 & 1 & & & 0 \\ -\phi_2 & -\phi_1 & \ddots & & \vdots \\ \cdots & -\phi_2 & & & \\ & \cdots & & \ddots & 0 \\ -\phi_{p-1} & -\phi_{p-2} & \cdots & -\phi_1 & 1 \end{bmatrix}, \quad \mathbf{A}_2 \equiv \begin{bmatrix} -\phi_p & 0 & \cdots & 0 & 0 \\ -\phi_{p-1} & -\phi_p & & & 0 \\ -\phi_{p-2} & -\phi_{p-1} & \ddots & & \vdots \\ \cdots & -\phi_{p-2} & & \ddots & \\ & \cdots & & & 0 \\ -\phi_1 & -\phi_2 & \cdots & -\phi_{p-1} & -\phi_p \end{bmatrix}. \tag{2.52}$$

Schur's criterion states that the AR(p) process is covariance stationary if and only if the matrix

$$\mathbf{S} = \mathbf{A}_1\mathbf{A}_1' - \mathbf{A}_2\mathbf{A}_2' \tag{2.53}$$

is positive definite.

Finally, also the autocovariances and autocorrelations of AR(p) processes can be computed by solving a set of simultaneous equations known as *Yule–Walker equations*. For instance, consider the AR(2) process

$$y_t = \phi_1 y_{t-1} + \phi_2 y_{t-2} + \varepsilon_t, \tag{2.54}$$

where μ has been set equal to 0 as it has no effect on the ACF. We multiply Eq. (2.54) by y_{t-s} with $s = 1, 2, \ldots$ and take the expectation of each resulting stochastic difference equation, obtaining:

$$\begin{aligned}
E[y_t y_t] &= \phi_1 E[y_{t-1} y_t] + \phi_2 E[y_{t-2} y_t] + E[y_t \varepsilon_t] \\
E[y_t y_{t-1}] &= \phi_1 E[y_{t-1} y_{t-1}] + \phi_2 E[y_{t-2} y_{t-1}] + E[y_{t-1} \varepsilon_t] \\
E[y_t y_{t-2}] &= \phi_1 E[y_{t-1} y_{t-2}] + \phi_2 E[y_{t-2} y_{t-2}] + E[y_{t-2} \varepsilon_t] \\
\vdots \quad & \quad \vdots \\
E[y_t y_{t-s}] &= \phi_1 E[y_{t-1} y_{t-s}] + \phi_2 [y_{t-2} y_{t-s}] + E[y_{t-s} \varepsilon_t].
\end{aligned} \tag{2.55}$$

By definition, the autocovariances of a stationary series are such that $E[y_t y_{t-s}] = E[y_{t-k} y_{t-k-s}] = \gamma_s$. We also know that $E[\varepsilon_t y_t] = \sigma^2$ and $E[y_{t-s}\varepsilon_t] = 0$. Therefore, we can use Eq. (2.55) to write:

$$\gamma_0 = \phi_1 \gamma_1 + \phi_2 \gamma_2 + \sigma^2 \tag{2.56}$$

which is the equation for the variance that we already found in Eq. (2.50), and moreover:

$$\gamma_1 = \phi_1 \gamma_0 + \phi_2 \gamma_1 \tag{2.57}$$

$$\vdots \quad \vdots$$

$$\gamma_s = \phi_1 \gamma_{s-1} + \phi_2 \gamma_{s-2}, \quad s \geq 2. \tag{2.58}$$

Dividing Eqs. (2.57) and (2.58) by γ_0, we obtain:

$$\rho_1 = \phi_1 \rho_0 + \phi_2 \rho_1 \tag{2.59}$$

$$\vdots \quad \vdots$$

$$\rho_s = \phi_1 \rho_{s-1} + \phi_2 \rho_{s-2}, \quad s \geq 2. \tag{2.60}$$

Because by construction ρ_0, that is, the correlation of one realization of the series with itself is equal to 1, we are able to solve Eq. (2.59) obtaining:

$$\rho_1 = \frac{\phi_1}{1 - \phi_2} \tag{2.61}$$

and, consequently, we can solve by recursive substitution Eq. (2.60) for any $s \geq 2$. For instance, ρ_2 can be now computed as:

$$\rho_2 = \phi_1 \rho_1 + \phi_2 \rho_0. \tag{2.62}$$

and therefore, it is equal to:

$$\rho_2 = \phi_1 \frac{\phi_1}{1 - \phi_2} + \phi_2 = \frac{\phi_1^2}{1 - \phi_2} + \phi_2. \tag{2.63}$$

Importantly, for a stationary AR(p) model, the ACF will decay geometrically to 0 because the leading term will also take the form of powers of sums of the coefficients that—as we have seen, in order to ensure stationarity—need to be restricted to absolute sums that are less than 1.

While it is possible to use the SACF to identify the order of an MA(q) model, also the sample PACF function turns useful in the case of an AR(p) model. From Definition 2.6, we know that the PACF is obtained by estimating the following AR models in the sequence reported here:

$$\begin{aligned}
y_t &= \phi_{0,1} + \phi_{1,1} y_{t-1} + e_{1t} \\
y_t &= \phi_{0,2} + \phi_{1,2} y_{t-1} + \phi_{2,2} y_{t-2} + e_{2t} \\
y_t &= \phi_{0,3} + \phi_{1,3} y_{t-1} + \phi_{2,3} y_{t-2} + \phi_{3,3} y_{t-3} + e_{3t}, \\
\vdots \quad & \quad \vdots
\end{aligned} \tag{2.64}$$

where $\phi_{0,j}$, $\phi_{i,j}$, and $\{e_{j,t}\}$ are, respectively, the constant term, the coefficient associated to y_{t-i}, and the error term of an AR(j) model. These models are in the form of multiple linear regressions and can be estimated by simple least squares. The estimate $\hat{\phi}_{1,1}$ is the sample first-order PACF of y_t; $\hat{\phi}_{2,2}$ is the sample second-order PACF of y_t, and so on. By construction and Definition 2.8 of an AR(p) model, $\hat{\phi}_{j,j}$ should converge to 0 for all orders $j > p$.

EXAMPLE 2.5

In this example, we show the plots of the generated series, the computed SACFs and SPACFs for 1000 observations simulated from a set of alternative AR(1) and AR(2) processes. To simulate these processes, we have assumed ε_t IID $N(0, 0.04)$. For both the AR(1) models represented in Figs. 2.7 and 2.8, only the first partial autocorrelation coefficient is significant (as one should expect considering that the data come from two alternative AR(1) processes). However, the AR(1) model represented in Fig. 2.8 is visibly much more persistent than the one in Fig. 2.7, because the ACF dies away very slowly.

Finally, the AR(2) model displayed in Fig. 2.9 has a sample PACF that suddenly levels off at the second lag, as expected. However, this process is much less persistent than the one presented in Fig. 2.8. As an additional exercise, we compute the theoretical autocorrelations up to lag 3 using the Yule–Walker equations. Of course, we know that $\rho_0 = 1$. Consequently, we solve:

$$\rho_1 = \phi_1\rho_0 + \phi_2\rho_1 = 0.7 \times 1 - 0.3\rho_1,$$

obtaining

$$\rho_1 = \frac{0.7}{1.3} = 0.54.$$

Now, knowing the value of ρ_1, we are able to compute:

$$\rho_2 = \phi_1\rho_1 + \phi_2\rho_0 = 0.7 \times 0.54 - 0.3 \times 1 = 0.08.$$

Again, using the value obtained for ρ_2 we calculate:

$$\rho_3 = \phi_1\rho_2 + \phi_2\rho_1 = 0.7 \times 0.08 - 0.3 \times 0.54 = -0.11.$$

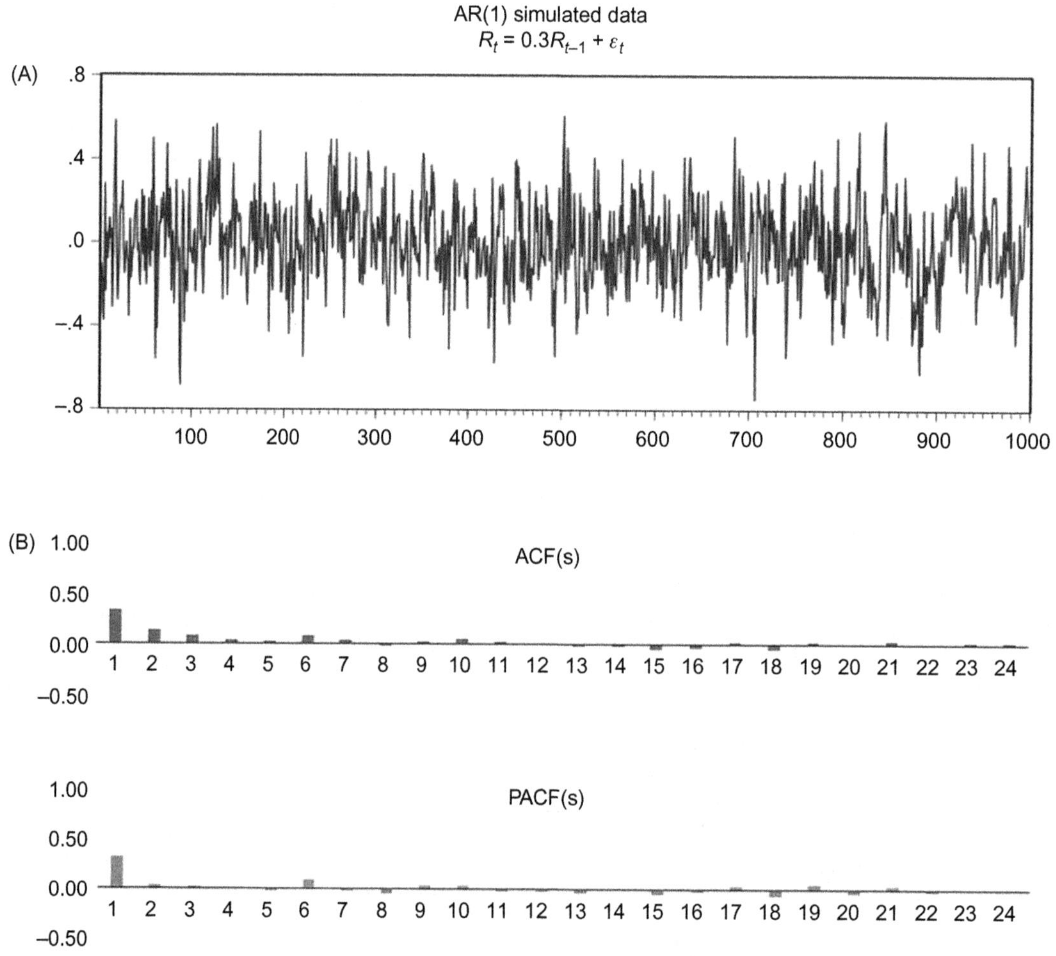

FIGURE 2.7 Plots and correlogram of AR(1) simulated data with $\mu = 0$ and $\phi_1 = 0.3$.

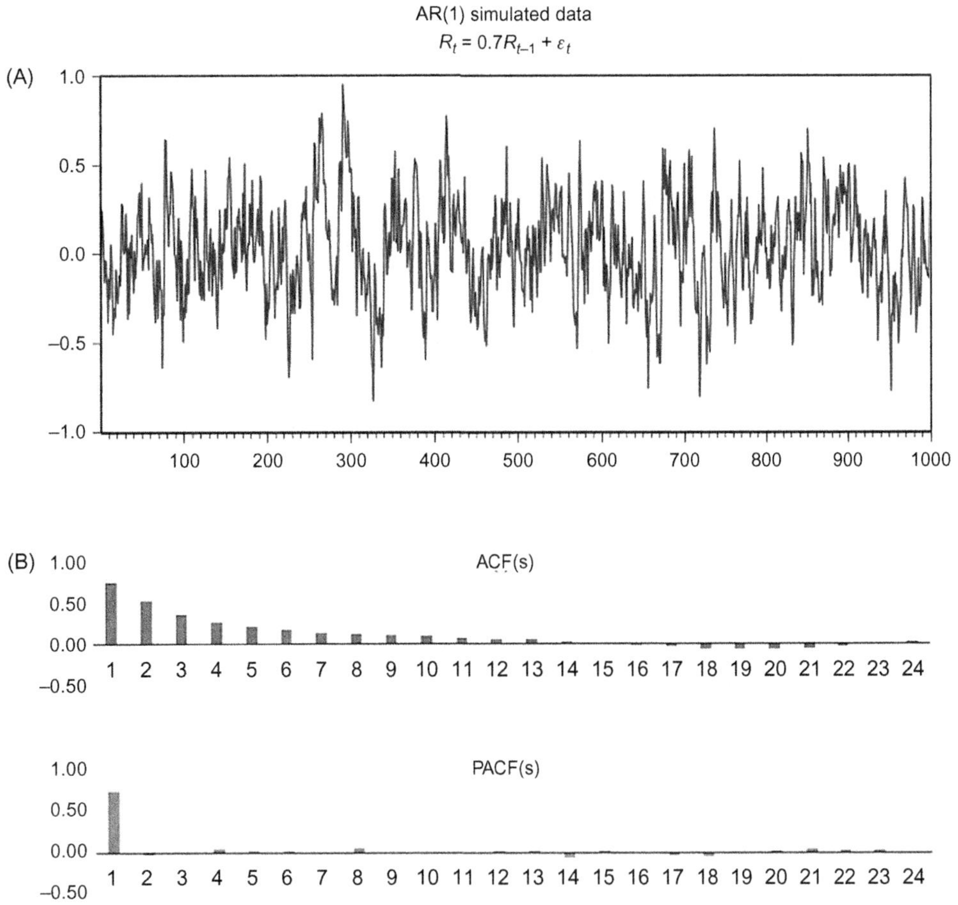

FIGURE 2.8 Plots and correlogram of AR(1) simulated data with $\mu = 0$ and $\phi_1 = 0.7$.

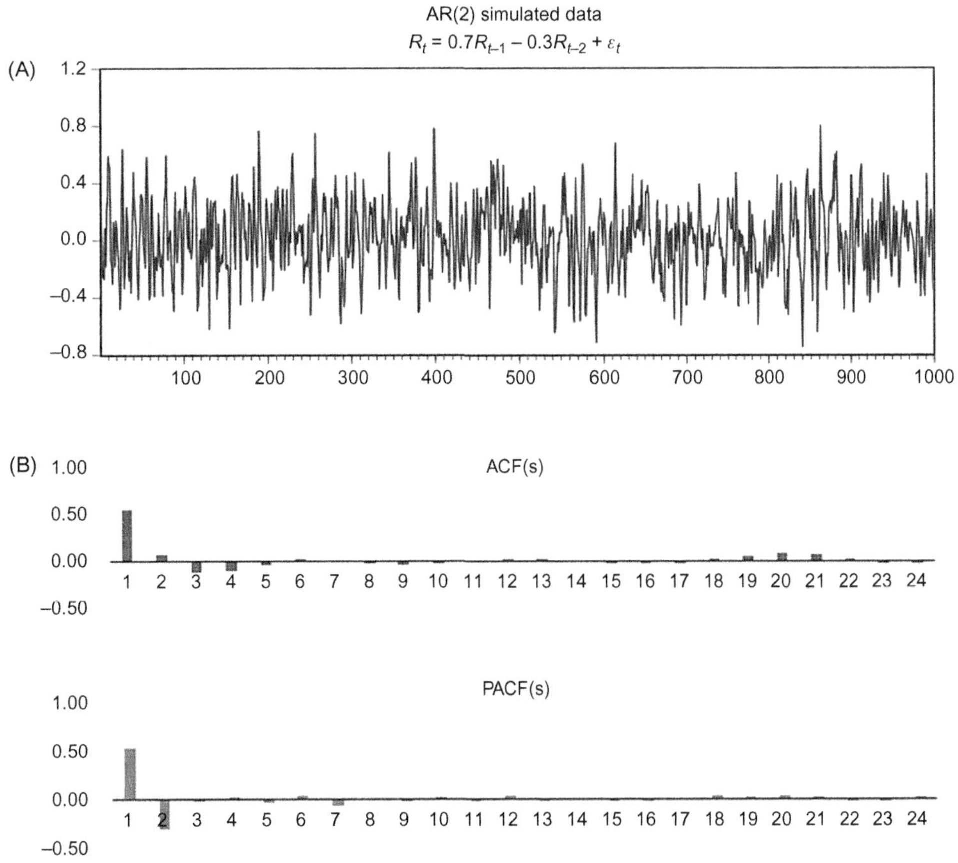

FIGURE 2.9 Plots and correlogram of AR(2) simulated data with $\mu = 0$, $\phi_1 = 0.7$, and $\phi_2 = -0.3$.

Before moving to combinations of AR and MA models, what we shall call ARMA models, we take some additional space to compare the characteristics of MA(q) and AR(p) models. An AR(p) process is described by an AFC that may slowly tail off at infinity and a PACF that is 0 for lags larger than p. Conversely, the AFC of an MA(q) process cuts off after lag q (i.e., the memory of the process lasts q periods while the observations that are distant in time by more than q periods are uncorrelated), while the PACF of the process may slowly tail off at infinity. This becomes quite unsurprising once we introduce the *invertibility condition* for MA(q) models.

DEFINITION 2.9 (Invertibility)

An invertible MA(q) model can be expressed as an AR(∞):

$$y_t = \sum_{i=0}^{\infty} \phi_i L^i y_{t-i} + u_t. \tag{2.65}$$

An MA(q) is invertible when the magnitude of all the roots of the MA polynomial exceeds 1.

Therefore, it is evident that in an invertible MA(q) process, the value of y_t depends on all its previous values, so that the PACF of an MA(q) model will decline geometrically. More in general, the ACF of an MA model has the same shape of the PACF of an AR model, and the PACF of an MA model has the same shape of an AR model.

2.2.3 Autoregressive Moving Average Processes

In some applications, the adequate empirical description of the dynamic structure of the data would require us to specify high-order AR or MA models, hence with many parameters. To overcome this problem, the literature has introduced the class of the ARMA models (see Box et al., 1994), which are a combination of AR and MA models combined in a compact form so that the number of parameters used is kept small. At this point, it must be clarified that for the series that we usually encounter in financial applications (returns or interest rates), in our experience, ARMA models are rarely needed to fit the most commonly used data. However, ARMA models are highly relevant in volatility modeling. As a matter of fact, the generalized autoregressive conditional heteroskedastic (GARCH) model, that we shall introduce in Chapter 5, can be regarded as an ARMA model, albeit this will concern not the series itself but its time-varying, random variance.

DEFINITION 2.10 (ARMA process)

A time series is said to follow an ARMA(p,q) if it satisfies

$$y_t = \phi_0 + \phi_1 y_{t-1} + \phi_2 y_{t-2} + \cdots + \phi_p y_{t-p} + \theta_1 \varepsilon_{t-1} + \theta_2 \varepsilon_{t-2} + \cdots + \theta_q \varepsilon_{t-q} + \varepsilon_t, \tag{2.66}$$

where the process of $\{\varepsilon_t\}$ is an IID WN with mean 0 and constant variance equal to σ_ε^2. More compactly,

$$y_t = \phi_0 + \sum_{i=1}^{p} \phi_i y_{t-i} + \sum_{i=0}^{q} \theta_i \varepsilon_{t-i}, \tag{2.67}$$

with $\theta_0 = 1$.

We can also write the ARMA(p,q) process using the lag operator

$$\left(1 - \sum_{i=1}^{p} \phi_i L^i\right) y_t = \phi_0 + \sum_{i=0}^{q} \theta_i \varepsilon_{t-i}, \tag{2.68}$$

with $\theta_0 = 1$, so that the solution for y_t is equal to:

$$y_t = \frac{\left(\phi_0 + \sum_{i=0}^{q} \theta_i \varepsilon_{t-i}\right)}{\left(1 - \sum_{i=1}^{p} \phi_i L^i\right)}. \tag{2.69}$$

Therefore, the ARMA(p,q) model will have a stable solution (seen as a deterministic difference equation) and will be covariance stationary if the roots of the polynomial $(1-\phi_1 L-\phi_2 L^2-\cdots-\phi_p L^p)$ lie outside the unit circle.

The statistical properties of an ARMA process will be a combination of those its AR and MA components. For illustrative purposes, we shall first use an ARMA(1,1) model to provide a concrete case and extend the reasoning to the general ARMA(p,q) case. An ARMA(1,1) model is represented as follows:

$$y_t=\phi_0+\phi_1 y_{t-1}+\theta_1\varepsilon_{t-1}+\varepsilon_t. \tag{2.70}$$

Taking the expectation of both the sides of Eq. (2.70), we obtain:

$$E[y_t]=\phi_0+\phi_1 E[y_{t-1}]+\theta_1 E[\varepsilon_{t-1}]+E[\varepsilon_t]. \tag{2.71}$$

Because we know that $E[\varepsilon_{t-1}]=E[\varepsilon_t]=0$, then the mean of the process, μ, is equal to:

$$\mu=\frac{\phi_0}{1-\phi_1}, \tag{2.72}$$

which is the same as an AR(1) model. More generally, the unconditional expectation of an ARMA(p,q) is equal to:

$$\mu=\frac{\phi_0}{1-\phi_1-\phi_2-\cdots-\phi_p}. \tag{2.73}$$

In order to simplify the calculations and without loss of generality in what follows we will assume that ϕ_0 (and thus μ) is equal to 0. We now compute the autocorrelations by solving the Yule–Walker equations that we already presented in Section 2.2.2:

$$E[y_t y_t]=\phi_1 E[y_{t-1}y_t]+\theta_1 E[\varepsilon_{t-1}y_t]+E[\varepsilon_t y_t] \tag{2.74}$$

$$E[y_t y_{t-1}]=\phi_1 E[y_{t-1}y_{t-1}]+\theta_1 E[\varepsilon_{t-1}y_{t-1}]+E[\varepsilon_t y_{t-1}] \tag{2.75}$$

$$E[y_t y_{t-2}]=\phi_1 E[y_{t-1}y_{t-2}]+\theta_1 E[\varepsilon_{t-1}y_{t-2}]+E[\varepsilon_t y_{t-2}] \tag{2.76}$$

$$E[y_t y_{t-s}]=\phi_1 E[y_{t-1}y_{t-s}]+\theta_1 E[\varepsilon_{t-1}y_{t-s}]+E[\varepsilon_t y_{t-s}]. \tag{2.77}$$

Solving Eqs. (2.74)–(2.77), we find:

$$\gamma_0=\phi_1\gamma_1+\theta_1(\phi_1+\theta_1)\sigma_\varepsilon^2+\sigma_\varepsilon^2, \tag{2.78}$$

$$\gamma_1=\phi_1\gamma_0+\theta_1\sigma_\varepsilon^2 \tag{2.79}$$

$$\gamma_2=\phi_1\gamma_1 \tag{2.80}$$

$$\vdots \qquad \vdots$$

$$\gamma_s=\phi_1\gamma_{s-1}. \tag{2.81}$$

Plugging Eq. (2.79) into Eq. (2.78), the result is:

$$\gamma_0=\phi_1(\phi_1\gamma_0+\theta_1\sigma_\varepsilon^2)+\theta_1(\phi_1+\theta_1)\sigma_\varepsilon^2+\sigma_\varepsilon^2, \tag{2.82}$$

and thus

$$\gamma_0=\frac{(1+\theta_1^2+2\theta_1\phi_1)\sigma_\varepsilon^2}{1-\phi_1^2}. \tag{2.83}$$

Now, substituting Eq. (2.83) into Eq. (2.79) we obtain that the first autocovariance is equal to:

$$\gamma_1=\frac{(1+\gamma_1\phi_1)(\gamma_1+\phi_1)}{(1-\phi_1^2)}\sigma_\varepsilon^2, \tag{2.84}$$

so that the autocorrelations are:

$$\rho_1=\frac{\gamma_1}{\gamma_0}=\frac{(1+\theta_1\phi_1)(\theta_1+\phi_1)}{(1+\theta_1^2+2\theta_1\phi_1)}, \quad \rho_s=\frac{\gamma_s}{\gamma_0}=\phi_1\rho_{s-1} \tag{2.85}$$

for any $s \geq 2$. Therefore, after the first lag, the ACFs of an ARMA(1,1) will decline geometrically at a rate that depends on ϕ_1. This means that after the first lag, it is the AR component of the process that determines the behavior of the ACF, as one would intuitively expect.

For a general ARMA(p,q) model, beginning with lag q the values of ρ_s will satisfy:

$$\rho_s = \frac{\gamma_s}{\gamma_0} = \phi_1 \rho_{s-1} + \phi_2 \rho_{s-2} + \cdots + \phi_p \rho_{s-p}. \tag{2.86}$$

It is easy to see that after the qth lag, the ACF of an ARMA model is geometrically declining, similarly to the one of a pure AR(p) model. The initial p-values for the series of interest can be treated as initial conditions that satisfy the Yule–Walker equations. For these initial p lags, the shape of the ACF is determined by the characteristic equation. It is also important to study the PACF as this is useful for distinguishing between an AR(p) process and an ARMA(p,q) process: indeed, while both have geometrically declining ACFs, the former will have a PACF that cuts off to 0 after p lags, while the latter will have a PACF that declines geometrically.

A simple method to build the PACF of an ARMA(p,q) model is to use the Yule–Walker equations and compute the partial autocorrelation coefficients from the autocorrelations as:

$$\phi_{1,1} = \rho_1 \quad \phi_{2,2} = \frac{\rho_2 - \rho_1^2}{1 - \rho_1^2} \tag{2.87}$$

and, for the additional lags, we have:

$$\phi_{3,3} = \frac{\rho_s - \sum_{j=1}^{s-1} \phi_{s-1,j} \rho_{s-j}}{1 - \sum_{j=1}^{s-1} \phi_{s-1,j} \rho_j}, \tag{2.88}$$

where $\phi_{s,j} = \phi_{s-1,j} - \phi_{s,s} \phi_{s-1,s-j}$ with $j = 1, 2, \ldots, s-1$.

EXAMPLE 2.6

In this example, in Fig. 2.10, we plot the series, the ACFs and PACFs for 1000 observations simulated from an ARMA(1,1) process. In line with the other examples presented in this chapter, we have assumed ε_tIID $N(0, 0.04)$ to simulate the process.

As one would expect of an ARMA process, both the ACF and the PACF decline geometrically: the ACF as a result of the AR part and the PACF as a result of the MA part. However, as the coefficient of the MA part is quite small, the PACF becomes insignificant after only two lags. Instead, the AR coefficient is higher (0.7) and thus the AFC dies away after nine lags and rather slowly. Using formula (2.85), we can compute the first-order autocorrelation of this ARMA(1,1) process:

$$\rho_1 = \frac{(1+\theta_1\phi_1)(\theta_1+\phi_1)}{(1+\theta_1^2+2\theta_1\phi_1)} = \frac{(1+(-0.3\times 0.7))\times(-0.3+0.7)}{1+(-0.3)^2+2\times(-0.3\times 0.7)} = 0.47.$$

Consequently, the other autocorrelations are computed as follows:

$$\rho_2 = \phi_1\rho_1 = 0.7 \times 0.47 = 0.33$$
$$\rho_3 = \phi_1\rho_2 = 0.7 \times 0.33 = 0.23,$$

and so on. The partial autocorrelations can be computed from the autocorrelations as $\phi_{1,1} = \rho_1 = 0.47$ and

$$\phi_{2,2} = \frac{\rho_2 - \rho_1^2}{1-\rho_1^2} = \frac{0.33 - 0.47^2}{1 - 0.47^2} = 0.14.$$

Before computing the third-order partial autocorrelation coefficient following the formula (2.87), we need to compute $\phi_{2,1}$ that is equal to:

$$\phi_{2,1} = \phi_{1,1} - \phi_{2,2,}\phi_{1,1} = 0.47 - 0.14 \times 0.47 = 0.4042.$$

Now we use this result to obtain:

$$\phi_{3,3} = \frac{\rho_s - \sum_{j=1}^{s-1}\phi_{s-1,j}\rho_{s-j}}{1-\sum_{j=1}^{s-1}\phi_{s-1,j}\rho_j} = \frac{\rho_3 - \sum_{j=1}^{2}\phi_{2,j}\rho_{s-j}}{1-\sum_{j=1}^{2}\phi_{2,j}\rho_j} = \frac{0.23-(0.4042\times 0.33+0.14\times 0.47)}{1-(0.4042\times 0.33+0.14\times 0.47)} = 0.038.$$

We leave the computation of the remaining autocorrelation and partial autocorrelation coefficients as an exercise for the reader.

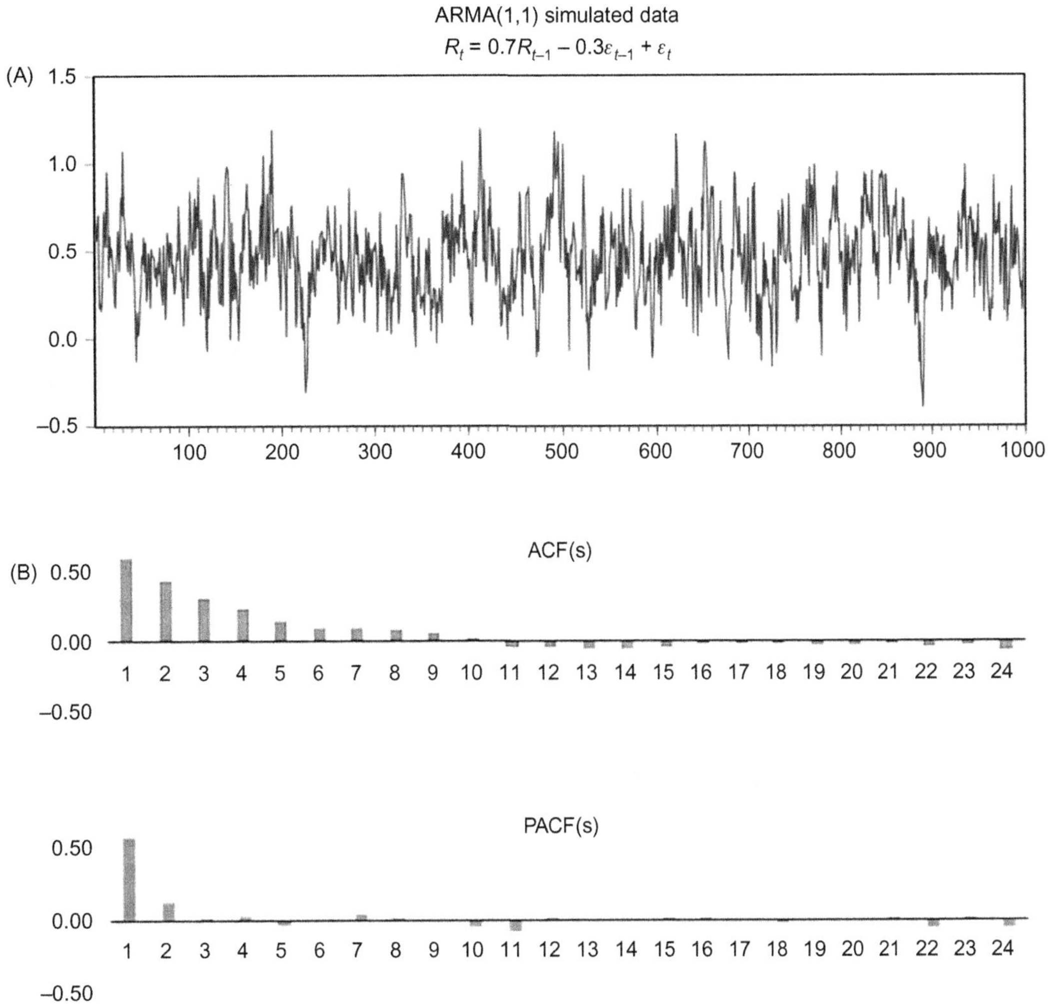

FIGURE 2.10 Plots and correlogram of ARMA(1,1) simulated data with $\phi_1 = 0.7$ and $\theta_1 = -0.3$.

2.3 SELECTION AND ESTIMATION OF AR, MA, AND ARMA MODELS

2.3.1 The Selection of the Model and the Role of Information Criteria

Now that we have discussed the main properties of the AR, the MA, and of mixed ARMA models, we are able to perform the first step of the procedure suggested by Box and Jenkins (1976), that is, visual inspection of sample autocorrelation and partial autocorrelation coefficients (that they call "identification" of the model, although this term can sometimes be confusing). More concretely, Box and Jenkins suggest computing the SACF and PACF of the observed time series (using the formulas outlined in Section 2.1.3 or with the help of a software package such as Eviews) and compare the results with the theoretical shape of the ACF and PACF of the alternative models, illustrated in Sections 2.2.1–2.2.3. This procedure allows us to understand, at least as a first approximation, which model is most likely to be the one that best fits the available data. For a quick reference, Table 2.2 summarizes the properties expected of AR, MA, and ARMA models.

Example 2.7 shows how the SACF and PACF can help to identify the model that best fits the data.

TABLE 2.2 A Summary of the Characteristics of AR, MA, and ARMA Models

	ACF	PACF
AR(p)	Decays toward 0	Cut off after lag p
MA(q)	Cuts off after lag q	Decays toward 0
ARMA(p,q)	Decays toward 0 starting at lag q	Decays toward 0 starting at lag p

EXAMPLE 2.7

Fig. 2.11 plots the monthly percentage changes in US Consumer Price Index (CPI, i.e., the inflation rate) from January 2001 to December 2016 for a total of 192 observations.

Table 2.3 shows the autocorrelations and the partial autocorrelations of the data at 24 lags (with the corresponding, standard confidence bands), the Ljung–Box test statistics (Q), and the p-value associated with them (in the rightmost column).

Looking at the table, it is evident at a first glance that the data are serially correlated. Indeed, all the p-values associated with the Ljung–Box test statistics are equal to 0, meaning that the null hypothesis of no autocorrelation can be rejected at any meaningful level of confidence (this is of course unsurprising given that the first autocorrelation coefficient is highly significant). While the interpretation of the PACF is rather clear, because it seems to cut off after lag 2 (apart from an odd spike at lag 24, which may be simply due to the relatively small sample under consideration), the ACF is more difficult to interpret: it does not seem to geometrically decay (as one would expect instead of an AR model), but it does not abruptly drop to 0 either, as it should do if the model were of an MA type. Indeed, the first coefficient of the ACF is highly significant, while the second one is not. Then, the following seven coefficients are all mildly significant but negative. Indeed, they are significant if we look at the 95% confidence interval that is shown in the table, but many of them are not significant if we build a more conservative 99% confidence interval (which will be delimited by the $\pm 2.57 \times 1/\sqrt{T}$ bands, i.e., ± 0.185). Based on this evidence, one can expect the process to be of some ARMA type, but it remains quite difficult to determinate its precise order (especially of the MA component). In order to gain further insight on the type of model potentially driving US consumer price inflation, we now introduce the definition of IC.

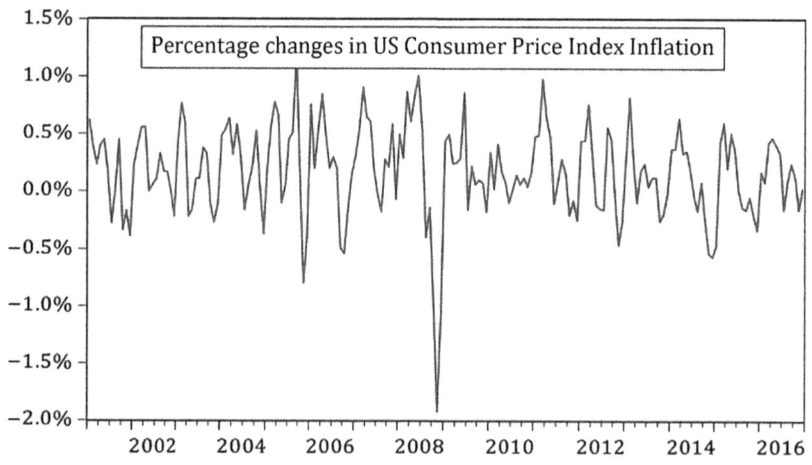

FIGURE 2.11 Plot of the monthly percentage changes in US CPI from January 2001 to December 2016.

TABLE 2.3 Serial Correlation Structure of the Changes in the US CPI

Autocorrelation	Partial correlation		AC	PAC	Q-statistic	Probability
		1	0.510	0.510	50.792	0.000
		2	0.069	−0.259	51.714	0.000
		3	−0.147	−0.085	55.976	0.000
		4	−0.156	−0.011	60.806	0.000
		5	−0.181	−0.152	67.340	0.000
		6	−0.190	−0.085	74.574	0.000
		7	−0.193	−0.114	82.082	0.000
		8	−0.221	−0.183	92.008	0.000
		9	−0.149	−0.027	96.518	0.000
		10	0.070	0.123	97.530	0.000
		11	0.275	0.120	113.09	0.000
		12	0.301	0.049	131.88	0.000
		13	0.171	−0.022	137.95	0.000
		14	0.066	0.035	138.87	0.000
		15	−0.008	−0.014	138.89	0.000
		16	−0.059	−0.018	139.63	0.000
		17	−0.099	−0.014	141.70	0.000
		18	−0.122	−0.009	144.90	0.000
		19	−0.116	0.035	147.82	0.000
		20	−0.163	−0.107	153.58	0.000
		21	−0.110	−0.005	156.23	0.000
		22	0.019	0.015	156.30	0.000
		23	0.148	0.040	161.16	0.000
		24	0.326	0.271	184.78	0.000

As seen in Example 2.7, the interpretation of the ACF and PACF can be difficult and sometimes even subjective. Therefore, one usually conducts a thorough specification search by the means of the so-called *IC*. These criteria essentially trade off the goodness of (in-sample) fit and the parsimony of the model and provide a (cardinal, even if specific to an estimation sample) summary measure. In fact, an obvious criterion to measure the goodness of fit of competing models would be the sample residual variance, routinely computed as:

$$\hat{\sigma}^2 = \frac{1}{T}\sum_{i=1}^{T}\hat{\varepsilon}_t^2, \tag{2.89}$$

where the residuals of the estimated model are denoted as $\hat{\varepsilon}_t$. However, a comparison of the residual variance of alternative models would systematically favor larger models as they tend to provide a better in-sample fit, because each estimated parameter provides additional flexibility in approximating a data set of a given size.[3] Nonetheless, we are normally interested in forecasting time series out-of-sample: when we use too many parameters we will end up fitting noise and not the dependence structure in the data, thus reducing the forecasting power of the model (a phenomenon that is known as *overfitting*). Consequently, IC always include in rather simple mathematical formulations two terms: one which is a function of the *sum of squared residual* (SSR, or the associated log-likelihood kernel, as we discussed in Chapter 1), supplemented by a *penalty* for the loss of degrees of freedom from the number of parameters that the

3. This claim may seem overly weak to readers used to apply simple linear regression models, where adding regressors and hence parameters leads to a noninferior in-sample fit as a matter of definition (i.e., one can always see smaller, more parsimonious regressions as resulting from restrictions placed on larger models and we know that unconstrained optimizations cannot result in a worse fit that unconstrained ones). However, when it comes to nonlinear models, starting with nonlinear regressions, the fact that adding parameters or even explanatory variables in a model leads to a better in-sample fit stops being a necessity, but remains a generally likely outcome.

model implies. In this way, adding a new variable (or a lag of a shock or of the series itself, in our specific case) to the model will have two opposite effects on the IC: it will reduce the residual sum of squares but increase the value of the penalty term. The best performing (possibly, promising in out-of-sample terms) model will be the one that minimizes the IC.

The most common IC are Akaike's (1973) information criterion (AIC), Schwarz's (1978) Bayesian information criterion (SBIC), and Hannan-Quinn's (1979) information criterion (HQIC). Mathematically, the three criteria are computed as follows:

$$\text{AIC} = \ln(\hat{\sigma}^2) + \frac{2k}{T}, \tag{2.90}$$

$$\text{SBIC} = \ln(\hat{\sigma}^2) + \frac{2k}{T}\ln(T), \tag{2.91}$$

$$\text{HQIC} = \ln(\hat{\sigma}^2) + \frac{2k}{T}\ln(\ln(T)), \tag{2.92}$$

where T is the sample size, $\hat{\sigma}^2$ is the residual variance computed as in Eq. (2.89) (which is equal to SSR divided by the number of observations), and k is the total number of parameters to be estimated. It is important to note that the SBIC is the IC that imposes the strongest penalty ($\ln(T)$) for each additional parameter that is included in the model. The HQIC embodies a penalty that is somewhere in between the one typical of AIC and the SBIC. Just to provide an example, suppose that we have collected 30 observations and we want to estimate a model that contains five parameters. The AIC will impose a penalty of $2k/T$, equal to 0.33. In the SBIC, this term will be multiplied by $\ln(T)$ and thus the penalty will be 1.13 ($>$0.33). Finally, in the HQIC 0.33 will be multiplied by $\ln(\ln(T))$ and thus it will be equal to 0.41. If we add one parameter to the model, the residual variance will (most likely) decrease lowering the three criteria by the same quantity. However, the penalty would be 0.4 for the AIC, 1.36 for the SBIC, and 0.49 for the HQIC. As a result, the three IC may select different models, leaving us with the issue of which criteria should be followed when they lead to different results.

The SBIC is a consistent criterion, that is, it determinates the true model asymptotically, meaning that, as the sample size approaches infinity, it will select the correct model order (Schwarz, 1978); conversely, the AIC asymptotically overestimates the order/complexity of a model with positive probability. However, one should bear in mind that no criteria will always outperform the others. For this reason, Box et al. (1994) suggested using the ICs only to obtain supplementary guidance and not as a substitute the visual inspection of SACFs and PACFs.

EXAMPLE 2.8

In Example 2.7, we have tried to select the appropriate model for the US CPI inflation rate by investigating its sample correlogram. However, the interpretation of the outputs turned out to be difficult (especially when applied to the ACF). Therefore, we now compute the IC for a number of alternative model specifications to help us to decide which model we shall estimate (Table 2.4).

From Table 2.4, we see that both the Akaike and the Hannan–Quinn criteria are minimized by selecting an ARMA(2,1) model (the winning model according to each criterion are boldfaced). Conversely, the SBIC selects a more parsimonious AR(2) model. As discussed earlier, it is not uncommon that different criteria lead to select different models. However, using the guidance that we derived from the inspection of the correlogram, we believe that an ARMA model is more likely, given that the ACF does not show signs of geometric decay, which we shall expect in case of an AR model. Therefore, we could be inclined to conclude in favor of a ARMA(2,1) for the monthly CPI inflation rate.

TABLE 2.4 Information Criteria for Alternative Models Used to Describe CPI Inflation

	Log-Likelihood	AIC	SBIC	HQIC
AR(1)	817.289	−8.4822	−8.4313	−8.4616
AR(2)	823.9792	−8.5415	**−8.474**	−8.514
AR(3)	824.6745	−8.5383	−8.4534	−8.5039
AR(4)	824.6798	−8.5279	−8.4261	−8.4867
MA(1)	818.3171	−8.4929	−8.442	−8.4723

(Continued)

TABLE 2.4 (Continued)

	Log-Likelihood	AIC	SBIC	HQIC
MA(2)	823.7956	−8.5395	−8.4717	−8.5121
MA(3)	824.3971	−8.5354	−8.4506	−8.501
MA(4)	824.8733	−8.5299	−8.4281	−8.4887
ARMA(1,1)	821.745	−8.5182	−8.4503	−8.4907
ARMA(2,1)	826.4089	**−8.556**	−8.4715	**−8.522**
ARMA(2,2)	826.9914	−8.552	−8.4502	−8.5108
ARMA(3,2)	827.0005	−8.5417	−8.4229	−8.4936
ARMA(3,3)	827.6836	−8.5384	−8.4026	−8.4834

Note: Winning model according to each criterion are boldfaced.

2.3.2 Estimation Methods

The second step of the Box–Jenkins procedure concerns the estimation of the model. We will start with the estimation of an AR model because it can be performed simply by (conditional) OLS. However, when an MA component is included, the estimation becomes more complicated and requires more sophisticated techniques. The regression equation through which an AR model can be estimated is:

$$y_t = \phi_0 + \phi_1 y_{t-1} + \phi_2 y_{t-2} + \cdots + \phi_p y_{t-p} + \varepsilon_t, \tag{2.93}$$

where $\phi_0 = (1 - \phi_1 - \phi_2 - \cdots - \phi_p)\hat{\mu}$ which is a restriction that guarantees that the estimated AR(p) process yields an unconditional mean equal to $\hat{\mu} \equiv T^{-1}\sum_{t=1}^{T} y_t$.[4] Assuming that presample values $y_{1-p}, \ldots, y_0$ are available in addition to the sample values $y_1, \ldots y_T$, the OLS estimator of $\varphi = [\phi_0, \phi_1, \ldots, \phi_p]'$ is

$$\hat{\varphi} = \left(\sum_{t=1}^{T} \mathbf{x}_{t-1}\mathbf{x}_{t-1}'\right)^{-1} \sum_{t=1}^{T} \mathbf{x}_{t-1} y_t, \tag{2.94}$$

where $\mathbf{x}_{t-1} = [1, y_{t-1}, \ldots, y_{t-p}]'$. The fitted model is:

$$y_t = \hat{\phi}_0 + \hat{\phi}_1 y_{t-1} + \hat{\phi}_2 y_{t-2} + \cdots + \hat{\phi}_p y_{t-p} + \hat{\varepsilon}_t, \tag{2.95}$$

and the associated residuals are

$$\hat{\varepsilon}_t = y_t - \hat{y}_t. \tag{2.96}$$

From the residual series, we obtain

$$\hat{\sigma}_\varepsilon^2 = \frac{\sum_{t=p+1}^{T} \hat{\varepsilon}_t^2}{T - 2p - 1}. \tag{2.97}$$

Noticeably, the OLS estimation of the model (2.93) is equivalent to maximum likelihood estimation (MLE) conditional on initial values if the process is normally distributed. In this case, the estimators have the asymptotically optimal properties that were discussed in Chapter 1; moreover, also additional details about OLS estimation methods have been presented in Chapter 1.

Unfortunately, when the model contains MA terms, estimation by simple OLS is not possible and MLE or, in case the conditional distributions of the observations are not known, quasi-MLE (QMLE) is required to obtain valid

4. Otherwise, we know that $\mu = \phi_0/(1 - \phi_1 - \phi_2 - \cdots - \phi_p)$ so that if the estimation of ϕ_0 were to be left unconstrained, it would be possible for the implied unconditional mean to differ from the sample mean of the data.

estimates. To avoid overwhelming the reader with a large and unnecessary amount of details, we go straight to the estimation of the parameters of a mixed ARMA model. As discussed in Chapter 1, the likelihood maximization procedure searches for the parameter values that make the set of observations collected the most likely under the selected ARMA model (the selection will essentially concern p and q, in our case). Therefore, the first step in deriving the ML estimator consists of defining the probability distribution of the observed data. The joint density of the random variable generating the sample may be written as a product of conditional densities so that the log-likelihood function of an ARMA(p,q) process $\phi(L)y_t = \theta(L)\varepsilon_t$ has the form

$$\ln L(\phi_1, \ldots, \phi_p, \ldots, \theta_1, \ldots, \theta_q) = \sum_{t=1}^{T} \ell_t(\cdot), \tag{2.98}$$

where

$$\ell_t(\cdot) = -\frac{1}{2}\ln 2\pi - \frac{1}{2}\ln \sigma_\varepsilon^2 - \frac{(\theta(L)^{-1}\phi(L)y_t)^2}{2\sigma_\varepsilon^2}, \tag{2.99}$$

which clearly exploits an assumption that the conditional distributions of y_t are normally distributed.[5] Under general conditions, the resulting estimators will then be consistent and have an asymptotic normal distribution, which may be used for inference.

Given that iterative numerical algorithms (see Chapter 5 for a brief discussion) usually have to be used to optimize the log-likelihood function, start-up values for the parameters are required. Different procedures may be used for this purpose and it is often the case that the estimates reported by standard software packages may turn out to strongly depend on the methods used to set such starting conditions (however, a thorough discussion is beyond the scope of this chapter). As an example of the importance of such choices of starting conditions, consider that for an ARMA model one may consider first fitting a pure AR model by OLS. In a second step, denoting the first-step AR residuals by $\hat{\varepsilon}_t^{(1)} (t = 1, 2, \ldots, T)$, one may obtain OLS estimates of the parameters from

$$y_t = \phi_0 + \phi_1 y_{t-1} + \cdots + \phi_p y_{t-p} + \theta_1 \hat{\varepsilon}_{t-1}^{(1)} + \cdots + \theta_q \hat{\varepsilon}_{t-q}^{(1)}. \tag{2.100}$$

These estimates may be used for starting up an iterative maximization of the log-likelihood function that will deliver either ML or QML estimates of the parameters. As an example, we now estimate an ARMA(2,1) for the monthly US CPI inflation rate already used in Examples 2.7 and 2.8.

EXAMPLE 2.9

In Example 2.8, we have concluded that an ARMA(2,1) is the most likely process that has generated the US CPI inflation data presented in Examples 2.7 and 2.8. Table 2.5 contains the estimates of the parameters of the model, which have been obtained using Eviews by means of the (Q)ML method.

In practice, the model that we specified is estimated to be the following (p-values are in parenthesis underneath the coefficient estimates):

$$\text{CPInfl}_t = \underset{(0.000)}{0.002} + \underset{(0.000)}{1.285}\,\text{CPInfl}_{t-1} - \underset{(0.000)}{0.555}\,\text{CPInfl}_{t-2} - \underset{(0.000)}{0.731}\,\varepsilon_{t-1} + \varepsilon_t,$$

where CPInfl_t represents the percentage change in the CPI registered at time t with respect to the previous month. The output of the estimation is remarkably similar to the ones that have been already shown in Chapter 1. Indeed, Table 2.5 also shows the standard errors and the t-statistics for each coefficient (including the intercept) and the associated p-values (that we are already able to interpret from Chapter 1. In this example, the intercept and all the coefficients are significantly different from 0 at any conventional level of confidence as indicated by p-values that are virtually indistinguishable from 0.

In addition, this table also contains a number of residual-based regression statistics—such as the regression (unadjusted and adjusted) R^2, the standard error of regression, and the Durbin–Watson statistic (that we shall discuss in Section 2.3.3). These statistics have been computed using the estimated one-period-ahead forecast (or prediction) errors $\hat{\varepsilon}_t$. These terms represent the

(Continued)

5. Of course, MLE can be applied to any parametric distribution even when different from the normal; however, QMLE replaces by construction any unknown parametric distribution for the time series process with a normal assumption, see Chapter 5 for additional details.

EXAMPLE 2.9 (Continued)

forecast errors that you would incur if you computed forecasts using a prediction of the inflation series based upon past values of the data, both directly and indirectly, through the lagged impact of past prediction errors (i.e., the MA component).

Finally, the output above reports the reciprocal roots of the AR and MA polynomials (inverted AR roots and inverted MA roots). We know that the modulus of these roots should lie inside the unit circle, that is, simply be less than 1 in modulus (note that for real numbers, their modulus is the same as their absolute value), which is the case in our example (the AR roots are imaginary numbers, but their modulus, which is equal to 0.747, is less than 1).

TABLE 2.5 Estimates of an ARMA(2,1) Model for the US CPI Inflation Rate

Variable	Coefficient	Std. Error	*t*-Statistic	Probability
C	0.001717	0.000257	6.681979	0.0000
AR(1)	1.285087	0.082165	15.64032	0.0000
AR(2)	− 0.555030	0.055236	− 10.04829	0.0000
MA(1)	− 0.730921	0.107332	− 6.809925	0.0000
SIGMASQ	1.07E-05	9.63E-07	11.06491	0.0000
R^2	0.330274	Mean dependent var.		0.001716
Adjusted R^2	0.315948	SD dependent var.		0.003999
S.E. of regression	0.003308	Akaike info criterion		− 8.556343
Sum squared resid.	0.002046	Schwarz criterion		− 8.471513
Log-likelihood	826.4089	Hannan-Quinn criter.		− 8.521986
F-statistic	23.05464	Durbin–Watson stat.		1.919884
p (*F*-statistic)	0.000000			
Inverted AR roots	0.64−0.38*i*	0.64 + 0.38*i*		
Inverted MA roots	0.73			

2.3.3 Residual Diagnostics

After the model has been specified, the last step of the procedure outlined by Box and Jenkins is to check its adequacy. Intuitively, if the model has been specified correctly, all the structure in the (mean of the) data ought to be captured and the residuals shall not exhibit any predictable pattern. Therefore, most diagnostic checks involve the analysis of the residuals of the estimated model.

First of all, a fast and intuitive way to identify potential problems with a ARMA model is to plot the residuals or, better, the standardized residuals, obtained by subtracting the predicted mean for time t and dividing by the standard deviation of the residuals (which in this case is just the estimated standard error of the model), that is, $\hat{\varepsilon}_t^s = (\hat{\varepsilon}_t^s - \hat{\bar{\varepsilon}})/\hat{\sigma}_\varepsilon$. If the residuals are normally distributed with 0 mean (as we shall expect if the model was properly specified, again assuming that normality had been specified in the first instance) and unit variance, then approximately 95% of the standardized residuals should fall in an interval of ± 2 around 0. It is also useful to plot the squared (standardized) residuals. Such a plot is helpful in distinguishing between periods of lower and higher volatility. If the model is correctly specified, such a plot of squared standardized residuals should not display any clusters, that is, the tendency of high (low) squared residuals to be followed by other high (low) squared standardized residuals.

A more formal way to test for normality of the residuals is the *Jarque–Bera test*. This test is based on the third and fourth moments of the residuals from the estimated ARMA model. Because the normal distribution is symmetric, the third central moment, denoted by μ_3, should be 0; and the fourth central moment μ_4, should satisfy $\mu_4 = 3\sigma_\varepsilon^4$, where σ_ε^2 is the variance (of the residuals). At this point, a typical index of asymmetry based on the third moment (the *skewness*), that we denote by $\hat{S}$, of the distribution of the residuals is:

$$\hat{S} = \frac{1}{T}\sum_{t=1}^{T}\frac{\hat{\varepsilon}_t^3}{\hat{\sigma}_\varepsilon^3}, \tag{2.101}$$

while the most commonly employed index of tail thickness based on the fourth moment (*excess kurtosis*), denoted by $\hat{K}$, is

$$\hat{K} = \frac{1}{T}\sum_{t=1}^{T}\frac{\hat{\varepsilon}_t^4}{3\hat{\sigma}_\varepsilon^4} - 3, \tag{2.102}$$

where T is the number of observations and $\hat{\sigma}_\varepsilon^2$ is the estimated variance of the residuals. Note that in Eq. (2.101), kurtosis is measured in excess of the tail thickness index of a normal benchmark, that is equal to 3. If the residuals were normal, $\hat{S}$ and $\hat{K}$ would have a zero-mean asymptotic distribution, with variances $6/T$ and $24/T$, respectively. The Jarque–Bera test concerns the composite null hypothesis:

$$H_0 : \frac{\mu_3}{\sigma^3} = 0 \quad \text{and} \quad H_0 : \frac{\mu_4}{\sigma^4} - 3 = 0. \tag{2.103}$$

Jarque and Bera simply prove that because the sample statistics

$$\lambda_1 = \frac{1}{\sqrt{6T}}\sum_{t=1}^{T}\frac{\hat{\varepsilon}_t^3}{\hat{\sigma}_\varepsilon^3}, \tag{2.104}$$

and

$$\lambda_2 = \frac{1}{\sqrt{24T}}\sum_{t=1}^{T}\left(\frac{\hat{\varepsilon}_t^4}{\hat{\sigma}_\varepsilon^4} - 3\right) \tag{2.105}$$

are both $N(1)$ distributed, the null hypothesis consists of a joint test that λ_1 and λ_2 are 0 and can be tested as $H_0 : \lambda_3 = 0$, where

$$\lambda_3 = \lambda_1^2 + \lambda_2^2, \tag{2.106}$$

which is asymptotically distributed as a $\chi^2(2)$. However, it should be noted that the small sample properties of the sample moments may deviate considerably from their theoretical counterparts. Thus, for small samples, any results derived from a Jarque–Bera test should always be interpreted with caution.

Once we have verified that the residuals of the chosen model specification are normally distributed, it is also important to compute their sample autocorrelations and to perform corresponding tests of hypotheses to assess whether there is any remaining serial dependence in them. If the residuals were truly uncorrelated (in the population), we would expect 95% of the sample autocorrelations to fall inside the approximate (asymptotically valid) confidence interval $\pm 2/\sqrt{T}$ around 0. Needless to say, the same portmanteau tests based on the Q-statistic discussed in Section 2.1.3 can be applied here to test the null hypothesis that there is no remaining autocorrelation in the residuals at orders up to h, against the alternative that at least one of the autocorrelations is nonzero.

Finally, the Durbin–Watson (DW) test can be applied to assess the presence of first-order serial correlation in the residuals of an estimated ARMA model. The DW statistic measures the linear association between adjacent residuals from a regression model and can be formally used in a test of the hypothesis

$$H_0 : \rho = 0 \tag{2.107}$$

versus the alternative $H_1 : \rho > 0$, in the specification

$$\varepsilon_t = \rho\varepsilon_{t-1} + u_t. \tag{2.108}$$

Given a residual series $\hat{\varepsilon}_t$ with T observations, the Durbin–Watson statistic is:

$$\text{DW} = \frac{\sum_{t=2}^{T}(\hat{\varepsilon}_t - \hat{\varepsilon}_{t-1})^2}{\sum_{t=1}^{T}\hat{\varepsilon}_t^2}. \tag{2.109}$$

It is possible to show that the DW statistic is approximately equal to $2(1 - \hat{\rho}_1)$, where $\hat{\rho}_1$ is the one-lag ACF of $\{\hat{\varepsilon}_t\}$ (the interested reader may find a proof of this in Brooks, 2008, Chapter 4). Therefore, if there is no serial correlation (and thus $\hat{\rho}_1$ is near 0), the DW statistic is approximately 2 (while a positive correlation shall imply $\text{DW} < 2$). Unfortunately, the DW test does not follow a standard statistical distribution and thus we must compare it with two sets of critical values, that are usually labeled as d_U (upper) and d_L (lower). If $\text{DW} < d_L$ we reject H_0 in favor of H_1; if

DW $> d_U$ we fail to reject H_0. Finally, if $d_L \leq \text{DW} \leq d_U$ the test is inconclusive. The critical values d_u and d_L depend on the chosen level of significance, on the number of observations and of explanatory variables and have been tabulated by Durbin and Watson (1951).

EXAMPLE 2.10

Fig. 2.12 plots the residuals and, most importantly, the standardized residuals (with the associated ± 2 approximate 95% confidence bands) for the ARMA(2,1) specified and estimated in Example 2.9. Visually, although most of the residuals lie within the ± 2 bands, there are some notable exceptions, for instance in correspondence to mid-2008. In Fig. 2.12B, we can clearly observe that the empirical distribution of the residuals shows signs of departure from normality both in terms of their nonzero skewness and positive excess kurtosis. Indeed, a Jarque–Bera test leads us to reject the null hypothesis of normality of the residuals at any conventional confidence level, as the p-value is less than 0.01.

Table 2.6A and B shows instead the sample autocorrelation and partial autocorrelation of the residuals (on the rightmost side of panel (A)) and of the squared residuals (on the leftmost side of panel (B)). If there is no serial correlation in the residuals (squared residuals), the autocorrelations and partial autocorrelations at all lags should be nearly 0, and all Q-statistics should be insignificant with large p-values. We can see that, while there is no evidence of autocorrelation left in the residuals (as one should expect after a successful ARMA modeling exercise, with only some doubts concerning the 11th-order autocorrelation, that may be, however, just attributable to the relatively short sample), squared residuals show at least two significant autocorrelation coefficients, at the first two lags. This fact together with the nonnormality of the residuals may indicate the presence of heteroskedasticity in the residuals. Tests for heteroskedasticity and methods to model it will be discussed in detail in Chapter 5.

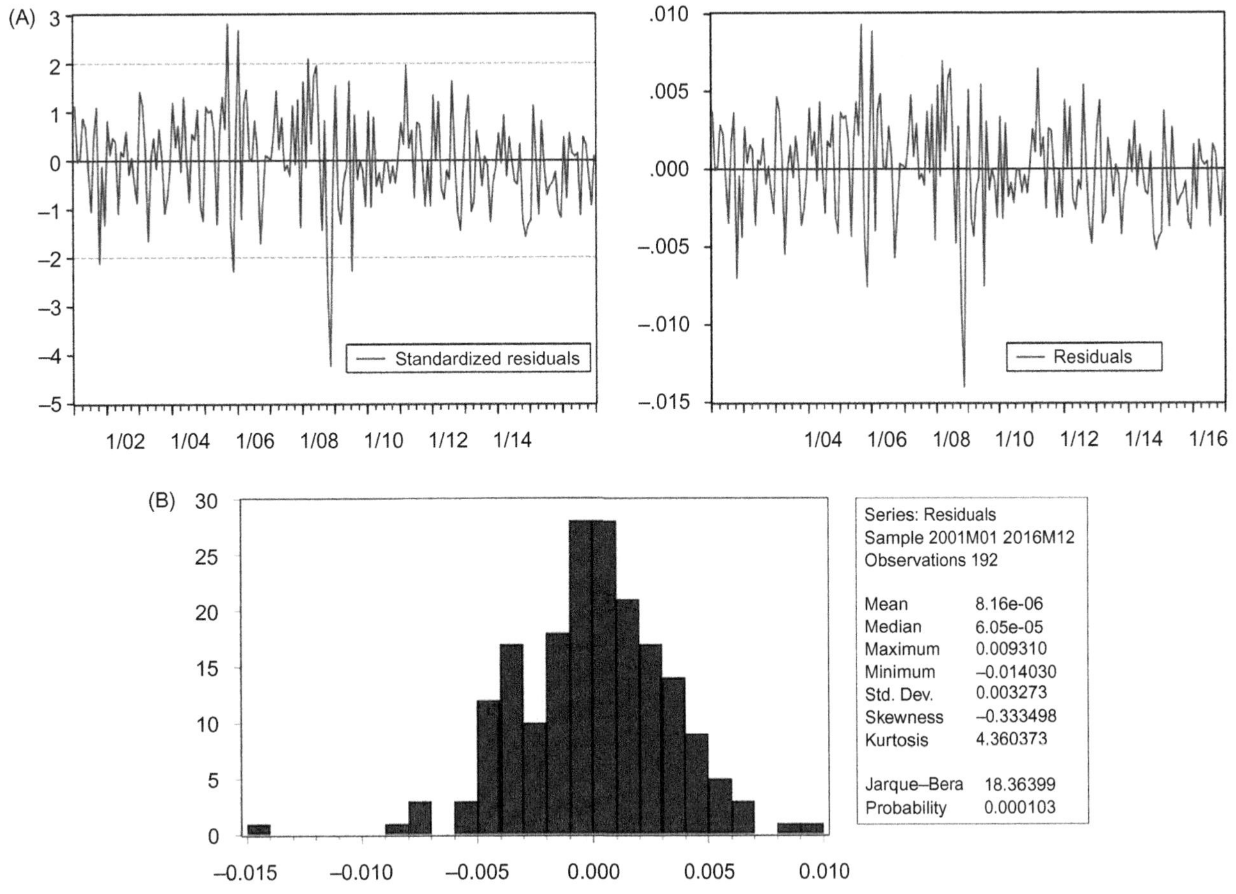

FIGURE 2.12 The residuals, the standardized residuals, and the empirical distribution of the residuals of an ARMA(2,1) model for US CPI inflation data.

TABLE 2.6A The SACF of Residuals and Squared Residuals of an ARMA(2,1) Model for US CPI Inflation Data

Autocorrelation	Partial correlation		AC	PAC	Q-statistic	Probability
		1	0.037	0.037	0.2610	0.609
		2	−0.062	−0.064	1.0145	0.602
		3	−0.059	−0.054	1.6911	0.639
		4	0.100	0.101	3.6570	0.454
		5	0.014	−0.001	3.6943	0.594
		6	−0.004	0.004	3.6982	0.717
		7	0.020	0.034	3.7819	0.805
		8	−0.088	−0.102	5.3392	0.721
		9	−0.120	−0.114	8.2665	0.508
		10	0.019	0.022	8.3397	0.596
		11	0.164	0.139	13.826	0.243
		12	0.148	0.154	18.319	0.106
		13	−0.005	0.034	18.324	0.146
		14	0.004	0.030	18.327	0.192
		15	0.003	−0.016	18.329	0.246
		16	0.002	−0.040	18.330	0.305
		17	−0.016	−0.046	18.387	0.365
		18	−0.039	−0.062	18.712	0.410
		19	0.046	0.079	19.170	0.446
		20	−0.084	−0.026	20.683	0.416
		21	−0.045	−0.003	21.113	0.452
		22	0.028	0.022	21.286	0.503
		23	−0.034	−0.108	21.543	0.548
		24	0.175	0.173	28.309	0.247

TABLE 2.6B The SACF of Residuals and Squared Residuals of an ARMA(2,1) Model for US CPI Inflation Data

Autocorrelation	Partial correlation		AC	PAC	Q-statistic	Probability
		1	0.182	0.182	6.4907	0.011
		2	0.188	0.160	13.450	0.001
		3	0.078	0.022	14.661	0.002
		4	0.094	0.052	16.425	0.002
		5	0.112	0.080	18.945	0.002
		6	0.053	0.001	19.508	0.003
		7	0.059	0.018	20.215	0.005
		8	0.244	0.230	32.264	0.000
		9	0.012	−0.087	32.294	0.000
		10	0.040	−0.038	32.625	0.000
		11	−0.025	−0.032	32.754	0.001
		12	−0.000	−0.022	32.754	0.001
		13	−0.028	−0.058	32.917	0.002
		14	0.013	0.040	32.953	0.003
		15	−0.071	−0.081	34.016	0.003
		16	−0.032	−0.072	34.228	0.005
		17	−0.125	−0.074	37.566	0.003
		18	−0.033	0.022	37.793	0.004
		19	−0.100	−0.056	39.938	0.003
		20	0.028	0.093	40.113	0.005
		21	−0.102	−0.073	42.361	0.004
		22	−0.091	−0.091	44.195	0.003
		23	−0.095	−0.005	46.169	0.003
		24	−0.042	0.035	46.552	0.004

2.4 FORECASTING ARMA PROCESSES

2.4.1 Standard Principles of Forecasting

Forecasting, that is, the attempt to predict which value of a random variable is most likely to take in the future, is of course one of the most important applications of time series analysis. Before moving on to linear predictions, which are the focus of this section, it is important to define some essential terminology in forecasting. *In-sample forecasts* are those generated with reference to the same data that were used to estimate the parameters of the model. The R^2 of the model, that has been discussed in Chapter 1, is a measure of in-sample goodness of fit, in the sense that a R^2 close to 1 means that the model is able to explain most of the variability in the data. Of course, ARMA models are time series models in which the past of a series is used to explain the behavior of the series, so that using the R^2 to quantify the quality of a model faces considerable limitations. Moreover, one is generally more interested in how well the model performs when it is used *to forecast out-of-sample*, that is, to predict the value of observations that were not used initially to specify and estimate the model.

Forecasts can be one-step-ahead or multistep-ahead. A one-step-ahead forecast $\hat{y}_t(1)$ is simply the forecast (computed at time t on the basis of the information then available) of the value that a random variable y_t is likely to assume in the next period, while a multistep-ahead forecast $\hat{y}_t(h)$ is the forecast (again at time t) that the same random variable is likely to assume at time $h > 1$, y_{t+h}.

In order to evaluate the usefulness of a forecast, we need to specify a *loss function* that defines how concerned we are if our forecast were to be off relative to the realized value, by a certain amount. Very convenient results are obtained if one assumes a quadratic loss function, that is, if we choose a forecast $\hat{y}_t(h)$ that minimizes

$$\text{MSFE}[\hat{y}_t(h)] \equiv E\left[\left(y_{t+h} - \hat{y}_t(h)\right)^2\right]. \tag{2.110}$$

Expression (2.110) is known as the *mean square forecast error* (MSFE) associated to the forecast $\hat{y}_t(h)$. It is possible to demonstrate that MSFE$[\hat{y}_t(h)]$ is minimized when $\hat{y}_t(h)$ is equal to $E[y_{t+h}|\Im_t]$, where $\Im_t$ is the information set available to the forecaster. In other words, the conditional mean of y_{t+h} given its past observations is the best estimator of $\hat{y}_t(h)$ in terms of MSFE. A detailed, formal proof of this claim can be found in Hamilton (1994), while the intuition is shown in the following. With a little bit of manipulation (i.e., adding and subtracting the same quantity, $E[y_{t+h}|\Im_t]$ to Eq. (2.110)), we obtain:

$$\text{MSFE}[\hat{y}_t(h)] = E\left[\left(y_{t+h} - E[y_{t+h}|\Im_t] + E[y_{t+h}|\Im_t] - \hat{y}_t(h)\right)^2\right]. \tag{2.111}$$

Squaring the expression in brackets and using the fact that $E[(y_{t+h} - E[y_{t+h}|\Im_t])(E[y_{t+h}|\Im_t] - \hat{y}_t(h))] = 0$, due to the fact that $y_{t+h} - E[y_{t+h}|\Im_t]$ only depends on $\varepsilon_{t+1}, \ldots, \varepsilon_{t+h}$ and $E[y_{t+h}|\Im_t] - \hat{y}_t(h)$ only depends on $y_t, y_{t-1}, y_{t-2}, \ldots$, then we obtain:

$$\text{MSFE}\left[\hat{y}_t(h)\right] = \text{MSFE}(E[y_{t+h}|\Im_t]) + E\left[\left(E[y_{t+h}|\Im_t] - \hat{y}_t(h)\right)^2\right], \tag{2.112}$$

which is clearly minimized when $\hat{y}_t(h) = E[y_{t+h}|\Im_t]$. We are now ready to apply this result to prediction of AR, MA, and ARMA processes.

2.4.2 Forecasting an AR(p) Process

From the AR(p) model in Eq. (2.34), we know that:

$$y_{t+1} = \phi_0 + \phi_1 y_t + \cdots + \phi_p y_{t+1-p} + \varepsilon_{t+1}. \tag{2.113}$$

Under the MSFE loss function, the point forecast y_{t+1} given the model and observations up to time t is the conditional expectation

$$\hat{y}_t(1) = E[y_{t+1}|y_t, y_{t-1}, y_{t-2}, \ldots] = \phi_0 + \sum_{i=1}^{p} \phi_i y_{t+1-i}, \tag{2.114}$$

and the associated forecast error is:

$$u_t(1) = y_{t+1} - \hat{y}_t(1) = \varepsilon_{t+1}. \tag{2.115}$$

Consequently, the variance of the one-step-ahead forecast is $Var[u_t(1)] = Var[\varepsilon_{t+1}] = \sigma_\varepsilon^2$. Therefore, at least when ε_t is normally distributed, the confidence interval for the point forecast y_{t+1} is equal to $\hat{y}_t(1) \pm 1.96 \times \sigma_\varepsilon$. It is important to consider that, in practice, we use estimated parameters of the model (and not the true, unobserved ones) in order to compute the forecasts. Consequently, our forecasts fail to consider the uncertainty in the parameter estimates. Potentially, one could take into account parameter uncertainty when forecasting, but this would be much more complex, and it is out of the scope of this book. However, when the sample size used in the estimation of the model is large, the forecast based on estimated parameters should be close to the true one.

In general, the h-step-ahead forecast of y_{t+h} based on the minimum square error loss function is the conditional expectation of y_{t+h} given $\{y_{t-i}\}_{i=0}^{\infty}$ which can be obtained as:

$$\hat{y}_t(h) = E[y_{t+h}|y_t, y_{t-1}, \ldots] = \phi_0 + \sum_{i=1}^{p} \phi_i \hat{y}_t(h-i), \tag{2.116}$$

where $\hat{y}_t(i) = y_{t+i}$ if $i < 1$. This forecast can be computed recursively using forecasts $\hat{y}_t(i)$ for $i = 1, 2, \ldots, h-1$. The h-step-ahead forecast error is then $u_t(h) = y_{t+h} - \hat{y}_t(h)$. It can be shown that for a stationary AR(p) model, $\hat{y}_t(h)$ converges to $E[y_t]$ as h approaches infinity. This property, generally known as *mean reversion*, implies that when the forecast horizon is long enough, the best prediction of an AR(p) process is its unconditional mean and the variance of the forecast error is equal to the unconditional variance of the process.

2.4.3 Forecasting the Future Value of an MA(q) Process

The forecasts of an MA process are very easy to obtain. Notably, because the model has a memory limited to q periods only, the resulting point forecasts may converge to the mean of the series quickly and they are forced to do so when the forecast horizon exceeds q periods. In other words, q delimits the forecast horizon over which the resulting prediction differs from the unconditional mean of the process. This result is fairly easy to be demonstrated in practice. For instance, let us consider the MA(2) model:

$$y_t = \mu + \varepsilon_t + \theta_1 \varepsilon_{t-1} + \theta_2 \varepsilon_{t-2}. \tag{2.117}$$

Given the parameter constancy over time is assumed, if this relationship holds for the series y at time t, it is also assumed to hold for y at time $t+1$, $t+2, \ldots$, so that 1 can be added to each of the time subscripts in Eq. (2.117) obtaining:

$$y_{t+1} = \mu + \varepsilon_{t+1} + \theta_1 \varepsilon_t + \theta_2 \varepsilon_{t-1} \tag{2.118}$$

$$y_{t+2} = \mu + \varepsilon_{t+2} + \theta_1 \varepsilon_{t+1} + \theta_2 \varepsilon_t. \tag{2.119}$$

Suppose that all information up to and including time t is available and that forecasts for $1, 2, \ldots, h$ steps ahead are desired. To obtain the one-step-ahead forecast is easy: taking the conditional expectation of Eq. (2.118), we have:

$$\hat{y}_t(1) = E[y_{t+1}|y_t, y_{t-1}, \ldots] = \mu + \theta_1 \varepsilon_t + \theta_2 \varepsilon_{t-1}, \tag{2.120}$$

where ε_t has already been observed and thus it is known. The forecast error is:

$$u_t(1) = y_{t+1} - \hat{y}_t(1) = \varepsilon_{t+1}, \tag{2.121}$$

and thus, the variance of the one-step-ahead forecast error is again equal to $Var[u_t(1)] = Var[\varepsilon_{t+1}] = \sigma_\varepsilon^2$. Obviously, because ε_{t+1} has not yet been observed at time t, and its expectation at time t is 0, the two-step-ahead forecast obtained by taking condition expectation of Eq. (2.119) at time t is equal to:

$$\hat{y}_t(2) = E[y_{t+2}|y_t, y_{t-1}, \ldots] = \mu + \theta_2 \varepsilon_t. \tag{2.122}$$

It is then easy to see that the forecast of

$$y_{t+3} = \mu + \varepsilon_{t+3} + \theta_1\varepsilon_{t+2} + \theta_2\varepsilon_{t+1} \tag{2.123}$$

is simply

$$\hat{y}_t(3) = E[y_{t+3}|y_t, y_{t-1}, \ldots] = \mu \tag{2.124}$$

as $\varepsilon_{t+1}, \varepsilon_{t+2}$ and ε_{t+3} are not known at time t.

By induction, this shows that the forecasts of an ARMA(p,q) model can be obtained simply using the formula

$$\hat{y}_t(h) = \phi_0 + \sum_{i=1}^{p} \phi_i\hat{y}_t(h-i) + \sum_{j=1}^{q} \theta_j E[\varepsilon_{t+h-j}], \tag{2.125}$$

and applying the rules that have been illustrated earlier for each of their terms.

2.4.4 Evaluating the Accuracy of a Forecast Function

In Section 2.4.1, we have defined the MSFE, that is, the squared difference between the actual value of an observation at time $t+h$ and the forecast computed at time t, as a measure of the accuracy of the prediction. Of course, the MSFE statistics of two different models can be compared and, obviously, the model with the lowest MSFE will be deemed to be the most accurate. In practice, the MSFE is computed as follows:

$$\text{MSFE}(h) = \frac{1}{T-(T_1-1)}\sum_{t=T_1}^{T} \left(y_{t+h} - \hat{y}_t(h)\right)^2, \tag{2.126}$$

where T is the total sample size (in-sample plus out-of-sample) and T_1 is the first out-of-sample observation. However, MSFE is based on a quadratic loss function that may be realistic only when large forecast errors are considered disproportionately more serious than smaller errors are. On the contrary, this feature can also be viewed as a disadvantage if large errors are not disproportionately more costly.[6]

As a result of these flaws, Makridakis (1993) has proposed the *mean absolute percentage error* (MAPE) as a relative prediction accuracy measure that incorporates the best characteristics among a variety of prediction accuracy criteria. The MAPE is calculated as:

$$\text{MAPE}(h) = \frac{100}{T-(T_1-1)}\sum_{t=T_1}^{T} \left|\frac{y_{t+h} - \hat{y}_t(h)}{y_{t+h}}\right|, \tag{2.127}$$

where T and T_1 have the same meaning as earlier. The MAPE has an attractive property compared to MSFE: it can be interpreted as an average percentage error, and furthermore, its value is bounded from below by 0. In addition, MAPE has another advantage: in the case of a random walk in log levels (i.e., one that implies a constant zero forecast), the criterion will take the value 1 (or 100 if we multiply the formula by 100 to get a percentage). Therefore, if a forecasting model gives an MAPE that is lower than 1, this model should be deemed superior to the random walk.

However, in many financial applications, the fact that a model is the most accurate in terms of statistical criteria does not imply that it will always help to produce superior profits when used to implement appropriate trading strategies. Often, in a practical trading application of a forecasting model, being able to correctly predict the sign of future

6. By the same token, the same critique could also be applied to the whole least squares methodology.

returns is much more important than accurately forecasting its magnitude. Consequently, Pesaran and Timmerman (1992) have suggested computing the percentage of correct signs prediction statistic, defined as:

$$\% \text{ of correct sign predictions} = \frac{1}{T-(T_1-1)}\sum_{t=T_1}^{T} q_{t+h}, \tag{2.128}$$

where $q_{t+h}=1$ if the sign of the prediction is correct and $q_{t+h}=0$ otherwise. They also develop adequate inferential methods to test hypotheses concerning the statistic. A developing literature, started by Leitch and Tanner (1991), has shown in a number of applications that the statistic (2.128) has a much stronger connection to the profitability of a forecasting signal/model than MSFE or MAPE have.

EXAMPLE 2.11

Consider again the model for CPI inflation data that has been estimated in Example 2.9. A policymaker (among many others) may be interested in using this model to forecast inflation in subsequent periods. Fig. 2.13 shows a sequence of 1-month-ahead forecasts of the percentage change in the US CPI index obtained for an out-of-sample period that goes from January 2001 to December 2016. The forecasts are obtained rolling the sample forward one observation after each forecast to use actual rather than predicted values for the lagged dependent variables. The forecasts are represented by the solid line, while the 95% confidence interval is given by the two dotted lines. In the box, some measures of out-of-sample forecasting accuracy such as the MAPE that we have discussed earlier are also presented.

It is interesting to compare the out-of-sample forecasting accuracy of the ARMA(2,1) model with that of alternative models that we decided not to select according to IC in Example 2.9. As an example, we compare the out-of-sample predictive performance of the ARMA(2,1) with the one of the AR(2) model, that was selected by the more parsimonious SBIC, but not by the HQIC and the AIC (Fig. 2.14).

The results of the comparison are extremely interesting: we find that the AR(2) model that we rejected based on our specification search displays higher forecasting accuracy than the ARMA(2,1), because it has a lower average percentage error (represented by the MAPE). In conclusion, if our objective were simply forecasting—based on our (of course limited)—recursive backtesting, we should have preferred the AR(2) model (as isolated by the SBIC) over the ARMA(2,1).

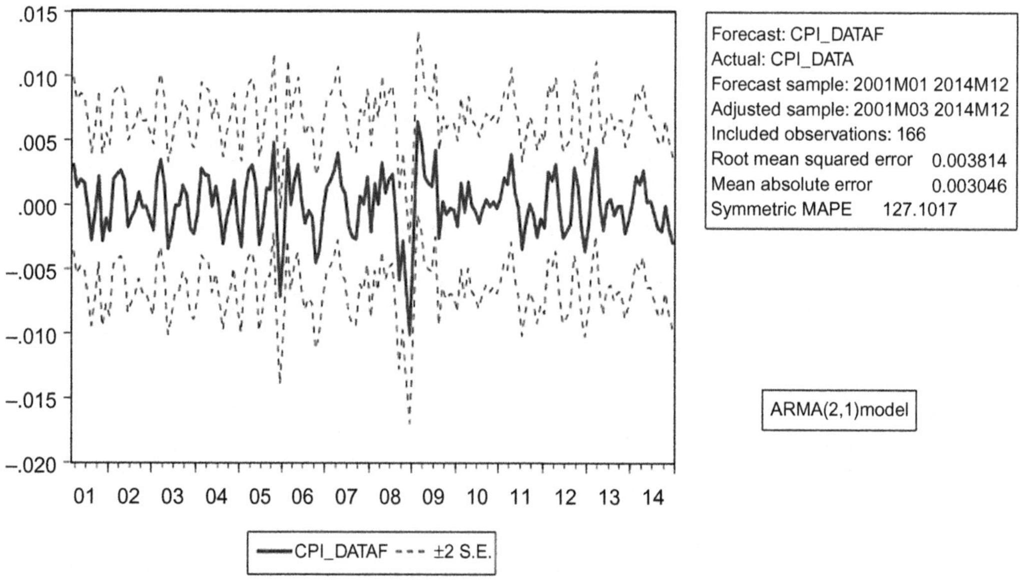

FIGURE 2.13 Rolling one-step-ahead forecasts for US inflation based an ARMA(2,1) model.

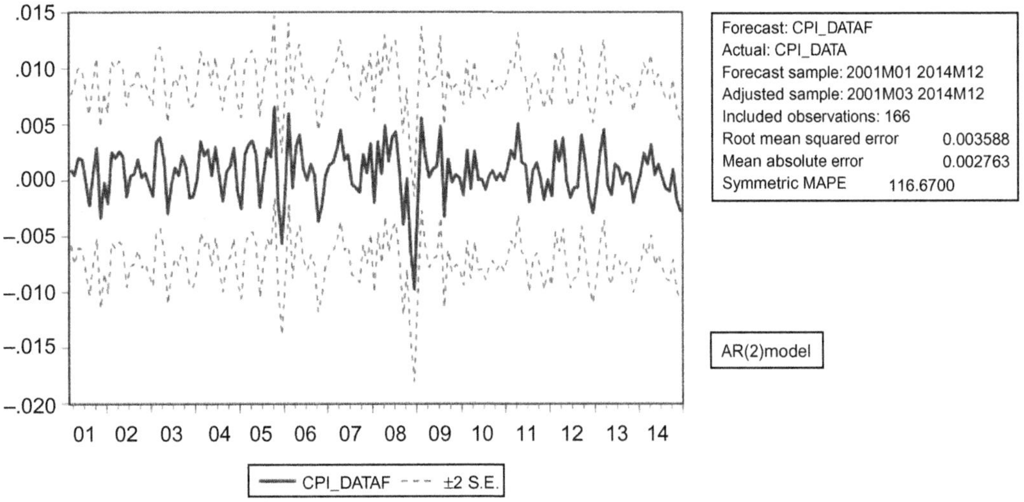

FIGURE 2.14 Rolling one-step-ahead forecasts for US inflation based an AR(2) model.

REFERENCES

Akaike, H., 1973. Information theory and an extension of the maximum likelihood principle. In: Petrov, B., Csàki, F. (Eds.), 2nd International Symposium on Information Theory. Acadèmiai Kiadò, Budapest, pp. 267–281.

Ansley, C.F., Kohn, R., 1983. Exact likelihood of vector autoregressive-moving average process with missing or aggregated data. Biometrika 70, 275–278.

Box, G.E.P., Jenkins, G.M., 1976. Time Series Analysis: Forecasting and Control. Holden-Day, San Francisco, CA.

Box, G.E.P., Pierce, D.A., 1970. Distribution of residual autocorrelations in autoregressive-integrated moving average time series models. J. Am. Stat. Assoc. 65 (332), 1509–1526.

Box, G.E.P., Jenkins, G.M., Reinsel, G.C., 1994. Time Series Analysis; Forecasting and Control, third ed. Prentice Hall, Englewood Cliff, NJ.

Brockwell, P.J., Davis, R.A., 1991. Time Series: Theory and Methods. Springer, New York.

Brockwell, P.J., Davis, R.A., 2002. Introduction to Time Series and Forecasting, second ed. Springer, New York.

Brooks, C., 2008. Introductory Econometrics for Finance. Cambridge University Press, New York.

Durbin, J., Watson, G.S., 1951. Testing for serial correlation in least squares regression. II. Biometrika 38 (1/2), 159–177.

Fuller, W.A., 1976. Introduction to Statistical Time Series. Wiley, New York.

Hamilton, J.D., 1994. Time Series Analysis. Princeton University Press, Princeton, NJ.

Hannan, E.J., Quinn, B.G., 1979. The determination of the order of an autoregression. J. R. Statis. Soc. Ser. B 41, 190–195.

Jones, R.H., 1980. Maximum likelihood fitting of ARMA models to time series with missing observations. Technometrics 22, 389–395.

Leitch, G., Tanner, J.E., 1991. Economic forecast evaluation: profits versus the conventional error measures. Am. Econ. Rev. 81, 580–590.

Ljung, G.M., Box, G.E.P., 1978. On a measure of lack of fit in time series models. Biometrika 65, 297–303.

Makridakis, S., 1993. Accuracy measures: theoretical and practical concerns. Int. J. Forecast. 9 (4), 527–529.

Pesaran, M.H., Timmermann, A., 1992. A simple nonparametric test of predictive performance. J. Bus. Econ. Stat. 10 (4), 461–465.

Schwarz, G., 1978. Estimating the dimension of a model. Ann. Stat. 6, 461–464.

Wold, H., 1960. A generalization of causal chain models. Econometrica 28, 443–463.

APPENDIX 2.A

Lag Operators. The lag operator L is defined as a linear operator such that for any value y_t,

$$L^i y_t \equiv y_{t-i}. \tag{A1}$$

Therefore, L^i preceding y_t means that y_t needs to be lagged by i periods. The lag operator has the following properties:

- The lag operator applied to a constant gives a constant: $Lc \equiv c$.
- The distributive law holds, that is, $(L^i + L^j)y_t = L^i y_t + L^j y_t = y_{t-i} + y_{t-j}$.
- The associative law of multiplication holds, $(L^i L^j)y_t = L^{i+j} y_t = y_{t-i-j}$.

- L raised to a negative power is actually a lead operator, $L^{-i}y_t \equiv y_{t+i}$.
- For $|a| < 1$, the infinite sum $(1 + aL + a^2L^2 + \cdots)y_t = y_t/(1 - aL)$ (this property follows directly from the second and the third properties).

Proof: Multiply each side by $(1 - aL)$ to get $(1 - aL)(1 + aL + a^2L^2 + \cdots)y_t = y_t$. Multiply the two equations to obtain $(1 - aL + aL - a^2L^2 + a^2L^2 \cdots)y_t = y_t$. Given that $|a| < 1$, the expression $a^nL^ny_t$ converges to 0 as $n \to \infty$. Therefore, the two sides of the equation are equal.

- For $|a| > 1$, the infinite sum $[(1 + (aL)^{-1} + (aL)^{-2} + \cdots)]y_t = -aLy_t/(1 - aL)$, so that $y_t/(1 - aL) = -(aL)^{-1}\sum_{i=0}^{\infty}(aL)^{-i}y_t$.

Proof: Multiply each side by $(1 - aL)$ to form $(1 - aL)[(1 + (aL)^{-1} + (aL)^{-2} + \cdots]y_t = -aLy_t$. Perform the multiplication to obtain:

$$[1 - aL + (aL)^{-1} - 1 + (aL)^{-2} - (aL)^{-1} + (aL)^{-3} \cdots]y_t = -aLy_t. \tag{A2}$$

Given that$|a| > 1$, the expression $a^{-n}L^{-n}y_t$ converges to 0 as $n \to \infty$. Therefore, the two sides of the equation are equal.

The lag operator provides a concise notation for writing difference equations. Using the lag operator, we can write a pth order equation $y_t = a_0 + a_1y_{t-1} + \cdots + a_py_{t-p} + \varepsilon_t$ as:

$$(1 - a_1L - a_2L^2 - \cdots - a_pL^p)y_t = a_0 + \varepsilon_t \tag{A3}$$

or, more compactly, as:

$$A(L)y_t = a_0 + \varepsilon_t, \tag{A4}$$

where $A(L)$ is the polynomial $(1 - a_1L - a_2L^2 - \cdots - a_pL^p)$.

It is straightforward to use the lag operator to solve linear difference equations. Again, consider the first-order equation $y_t = a_0 + a_1y_{t-1} + \varepsilon_t$ where $|a| < 1$. Use the definition of L to form

$$y_t = a_0 + a_1Ly_t + \varepsilon_t. \tag{A5}$$

Solving for y_t, we obtain:

$$y_t = \frac{a_0 + \varepsilon_t}{1 - a_1L}. \tag{A6}$$

From Property 1 earlier, we know that $La_0 = a_0$, so that $a_0/(1 - a_1L) = a_0 + a_1a_0 + {a_1}^2a_0 + \cdots = a_0/(1 - a_1)$. From Property 5, we know that $\varepsilon_t/(1 - a_1L) = \varepsilon_t + a_1\varepsilon_{t-1} + {a_1}^2\varepsilon_{t-2} + \cdots$. Combining these two properties, we obtain the solution above.

Chapter 3

Vector Autoregressive Moving Average (VARMA) Models

In every action, we must look beyond the action at our past, present and future state, and at others whom it affects, and see the relations of all these things.

Blaise Pascal, The Thoughts of Blaise Pascal

In Chapter 2, we have focused our attention on univariate time series models. However, because markets and institutions are highly intercorrelated, in financial applications we often need to jointly model a number of different time series to study the dynamic relationship among them. Therefore, in this chapter, we introduce econometric models for *multivariate time series analysis*. Loosely speaking, instead of focusing on the time series realization of a single variable, as we did in Chapter 2, now we consider a set of variables (e.g., the log-returns of N assets or the yields of Treasury bonds for N different maturity buckets), $\mathbf{y}_t = [y_{1,t}, y_{2,t}, \ldots, y_{N,t}]'$ with $t = 1, 2, \ldots, T$, where T is the number of observations in the series. The resulting sequence is called a N-dimensional (discrete) vector stochastic process.

In particular, we devote most of our attention to the *vector autoregressive* (VAR) models popularized by Sims (1980) that have come to be commonly used in financial applications. These are very flexible models where a researcher needs to know very little ex ante theoretical information about the relationship among the variables to guide the specification of the model and all variables are treated as a priori endogenous. In fact, as we shall see throughout this chapter, a VAR allows each variable to depend not only on its own lags (and/or combinations of white noise terms) but also on the lags of the other variables in the model.

In the rest of the chapter, we proceed as follows. First, we generalize the concepts of (weak) stationarity to the case of N-dimensional vector time series and discuss how to compute the first two moments of the resulting multivariate distribution. Second, we introduce VAR models in their structural and reduced forms and their applications, including impulse response function (IRF) analysis and variance decomposition. Third, we introduce the concept of Granger causality and show how to test for it. Finally, we briefly introduce vector moving average (VMA) and vector autoregressive moving average (VARMA) models. In this chapter, we focus as much as possible on the intuition and on the applications and as little as possible on the algebra and related technicalities. Of course, these remain important to any rigorous approach: an in-depth review of the statistical theory underlying multivariate time series analysis can be found in Lütkepohl (2005) and Reinsel (1993).

3.1 FOUNDATIONS OF MULTIVARIATE TIME SERIES ANALYSIS

3.1.1 Weak Stationarity of Multivariate Time Series

In Chapter 2, we have introduced the concept of stationarity of a time series as a necessary condition to be able to use past observations of a variable to forecast its future realizations. In particular, we said that a time series is (strictly) stationary if its statistical properties do not change over time and that it is *weakly stationary* if its first two moments are time-invariant. These definitions still apply when we generalize them to multivariate time series.

Essentials of Time Series for Financial Applications. DOI: https://doi.org/10.1016/B978-0-12-813409-2.00003-0

DEFINITION 3.1 (Weak stationarity)

Consider a N-dimensional time series $\mathbf{y}_t = [y_{1,t}, y_{2,t}, \ldots, y_{N,t}]'$. Formally, this is said to be weakly stationary if its first two unconditional moments are finite and constant through time, that is,

- $E[\mathbf{y}_t] \equiv \boldsymbol{\mu} < \infty$ for all t;
- $E[(\mathbf{y}_t - \boldsymbol{\mu})(\mathbf{y}_t - \boldsymbol{\mu})'] \equiv \boldsymbol{\Gamma}_0 < \infty$ for all t;
- $E[(\mathbf{y}_t - \boldsymbol{\mu})(\mathbf{y}_{t-h} - \boldsymbol{\mu})'] \equiv \boldsymbol{\Gamma}_h$ for all t and h;

where the expectations are taken element-by-element over the joint distribution of $\mathbf{y}_t$. In particular, $\boldsymbol{\mu}$ is the vector of the means, $\boldsymbol{\mu} = [\mu_1, \mu_2, \ldots, \mu_N]$, and $\boldsymbol{\Gamma}_0$ is the $N \times N$ covariance matrix where the ith diagonal element is the variance of $y_{i,t}$ and the (i, j)th element is the covariance between $y_{i,t}$ and $y_{j,t}$. Finally, $\boldsymbol{\Gamma}_h$ is the cross-covariance matrix at lag h.

Of course the definition of weak stationarity provided previously is completely analogous to the one discussed in Chapter 2 (as it is a corresponding definition of strict stationarity that is omitted here to save space), but it requires the computation of cross-covariance and cross-correlation matrices, that we shall discuss in Section 3.1.2.

3.1.2 Cross-Covariance and Cross-Correlation Matrices

While a reader should be familiar with the computation of the covariance matrix at lag 0, we provide a primer on how to get the correlation matrix (at lag 0) from the covariance matrix $\boldsymbol{\Gamma}_0$. Let $\mathbf{D}$ be a $N \times N$ diagonal matrix collecting (on its main diagonal) the standard deviations of $y_{i,t}$ for $i = 1, \ldots, N$. The concurrent (i.e., at lag 0), correlation matrix of $\mathbf{y}_t$ is defined as

$$\boldsymbol{\rho}_0 = \mathbf{D}^{-1}\boldsymbol{\Gamma}_0\mathbf{D}^{-1}, \tag{3.1}$$

where the (i, j)th element of $\boldsymbol{\rho}_0$ is the correlation coefficient between $y_{i,t}$ and $y_{j,t}$ at time t:

$$\rho_{i,j}(0) = \frac{Cov[y_{i,t}, y_{j,t}]}{\sigma_{i,t}\sigma_{j,t}}. \tag{3.2}$$

Because $\rho_{i,j}(0) = \rho_{j,i}(0)$, $-1 \leq \rho_{i,j} \leq 1$, and $\rho_{i,i} = 1$ for $1 \leq i$ and $j \leq N$, $\boldsymbol{\rho}_0$ is a symmetric matrix with unit diagonal elements.

We are now interested in computing the cross-covariance and cross-correlation matrices at lags different from 0. More specifically the lag-h cross-covariance matrix of $\mathbf{y}_t$ is defined as

$$\boldsymbol{\Gamma}_h = E[(\mathbf{y}_t - \boldsymbol{\mu})(\mathbf{y}_{t-h} - \boldsymbol{\mu})'], \tag{3.3}$$

where $\boldsymbol{\mu}$ is the mean vector of $\mathbf{y}_t$. Therefore, the (i, j)th element of $\boldsymbol{\Gamma}_h$ is the covariance between $y_{i,t}$ and $y_{j,t-h}$. From Definition 3.1, for a weakly stationary time series, the cross-covariance matrix is time-invariant, that is, it only depends on the lag length h and not on the temporal index t.

The lag-h cross-correlation matrix is defined as

$$\boldsymbol{\rho}_h = \mathbf{D}^{-1}\boldsymbol{\Gamma}_h\mathbf{D}^{-1}, \tag{3.4}$$

where, as previously, $\mathbf{D}$ is the diagonal matrix of standard deviations of the individual series $y_{i,t}$. Therefore, the (i, j)th element of $\boldsymbol{\rho}_h$ is the correlation coefficient between $y_{i,t}$ and $y_{j,t-h}$:

$$\rho_{i,j}(h) = \frac{Cov[y_{i,t}, y_{j,t-h}]}{\sigma_{i,t}\sigma_{j,t}}. \tag{3.5}$$

Interestingly, when $h > 0$, the correlation coefficient $\rho_{i,j}(h)$ measures the *linear dependence* of $y_{i,t}$ on $y_{j,t-h}$. Similarly, $\rho_{j,i}(h)$ measures the linear dependence of $y_{j,t}$ on $y_{i,t-h}$. Finally the diagonal element $\rho_{i,i}(h)$ is simply the lag-h autocorrelation coefficient of $y_{i,t}$. Notably, one has to recognize that $\rho_{j,i}(h) \neq \rho_{i,j}(h)$ for any $i \neq j$, as these coefficients measure different linear relationships. Therefore, $\boldsymbol{\Gamma}_h$ and $\boldsymbol{\rho}_h$ do not need to be symmetric. In summary the cross-correlation matrices of a weakly stationary vector time series summarize in a compact and easy-to-use way, the following information:

- if $\rho_{i,j}(0) \neq 0$, $y_{i,t}$ and $y_{j,t}$ are *contemporaneously linearly correlated*;
- if $\rho_{i,j}(h) = \rho_{j,i}(h) = 0$ for all $h \geq 0$, then $y_{i,t}$ and $y_{j,t}$ share no linear relationship;
- if $\rho_{i,j}(h) = 0$ and $p_{j,i}(h) = 0$ for all $h > 0$, then $y_{i,t}$ and $y_{j,t}$ are said to be linearly *uncoupled*;
- if $\rho_{i,j}(h) = 0$ for all $h > 0$, but $\rho_{j,i}(q) \neq 0$ for at least some $q > 0$, then there is a *unidirectional (linear) relationship* between $y_{i,t}$ and $y_{j,t}$ where $y_{i,t}$ does not depend on $y_{j,t}$, but $y_{j,t}$ linearly depends on (some) lagged values of $y_{i,t}$;
- if $\rho_{i,j}(h) \neq 0$ for at least some $h > 0$, and $\boldsymbol{\rho}_{j,i}(q) \neq 0$ for at least some $q > 0$ then there is a *linear feedback (bi-directional) relationship* between $y_{i,t}$ and $y_{j,t}$.

The concepts of unidirectional versus feedback linear relationships among variables will be further developed in the so-called Granger–Sims causality tests (see Section 3.3).

3.1.3 Sample Cross-Covariance and Cross-Correlation Matrices

Now that we have discussed what cross-covariance and cross-correlation matrices are, we are ready to discuss how they can be computed in practice from the data. In fact, as we already know from Chapter 2, we only observe empirical realizations of a time series and thus we can only compute *sample cross-covariances* and *cross-correlations*, which (under some conditions) will provide consistent but biased estimates of their true, unobserved counterparts (see Fuller, 1976, for a technical discussion of the asymptotic properties of sample cross-covariances and cross-correlations).

Given a sample $\{\mathbf{y}_t | t = 1, \ldots, T\}$, the cross-covariance matrix can be estimated by

$$\hat{\boldsymbol{\Gamma}}_h = \frac{1}{T}\sum_{t=h+1}^{T}(\mathbf{y}_t - \bar{\mathbf{y}})(\mathbf{y}_{t-h} - \bar{\mathbf{y}})' \quad \text{with } h \geq 0, \tag{3.6}$$

where $\bar{\mathbf{y}}$ is the vector of sample means, that is, $\bar{\mathbf{y}} = [\bar{y}_1, \bar{y}_2, \ldots, \bar{y}_N]'$ and $\bar{y}_i = T^{-1}\sum_{t=1}^{T} y_{i,t}$ with $i = 1, \ldots, N$. The cross-correlation matrix can be then estimated as

$$\hat{\boldsymbol{\rho}}_h = \hat{\mathbf{D}}^{-1}\hat{\boldsymbol{\Gamma}}_h\hat{\mathbf{D}}^{-1}, \quad \text{with } h \geq 0, \tag{3.7}$$

where $\hat{\mathbf{D}}$ is the $N \times N$ diagonal matrix of the sample standard deviations of each of the component series.

EXAMPLE 3.1

Consider the weekly yields of US 1-month Treasury bills and 10-year US Treasury bonds, for the sample January 1990–December 2016, as plotted in Fig. 3.1.

These yields form a bivariate time series $\mathbf{y}_t = [y_{1,t}, y_{2,t}]'$, where $y_{1,t}$ is the 1-month Treasury bill yield and $y_{2,t}$ is the 10-year yield. First, we compute the vector of sample means of the series and the contemporaneous correlation matrix, which are reported in Table 3.1. All the values reported in Table 3.1, with the exceptions of the correlation coefficient (which is by construction a pure number, i.e., without a scale), are percentages (e.g., 3.04 should be read as 3.04%). It is easy to see that the two series have a high contemporaneous correlation coefficient, $\rho_{1,2}(0) = 0.87$ and thus they are concurrently linearly correlated. However, cross-correlations at different lags can give us additional useful information about the dynamic relationship between the series.

Table 3.2 presents the cross-correlations between the series. In particular the first set of bins (in the first column) shows the correlations between the 1-month Treasury yield and the lagged values of 10-year US Treasury yields (for

(Continued)

EXAMPLE 3.1 (Continued)

increasing lags, h). The set of bins in the second column shows the correlation between the 1-month Treasury yield and the leading values of the 10-year US Treasury yield, which are equivalent (because of the definition of stationarity) to the correlation between 10-year US Treasury yields and lagged values of 1-month bill yields (for increasing lags, h). According to the definition given previously the two series display a strong feedback relationship, as both $\rho_{i,j}(h) \neq 0$ and $\rho_{j,i}(q) \neq 0$ hold.

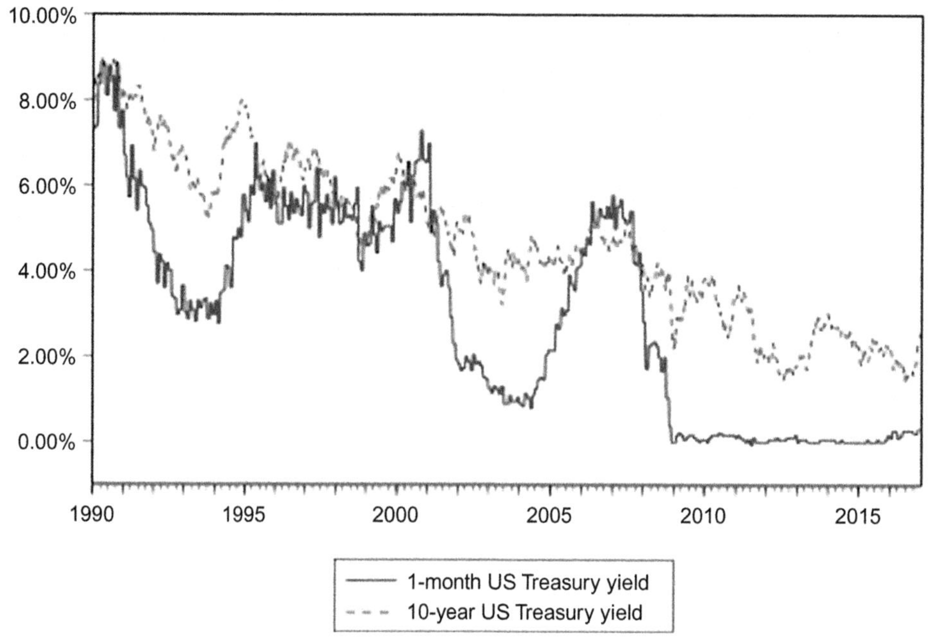

FIGURE 3.1 Plot of weekly yields for 1-month and 10-year US Treasury bond.

TABLE 3.1 Descriptive Statistics of the 1-Month and 10-Year US Treasury Yield Series

(A) Summary Statistics

	Mean	Standard Deviation	Skewness	Kurtosis	Minimum	Maximum
1-month Treasury yield	3.04	2.51	0.18	1.75	− 0.05	8.89
10-year Treasury yield	4.74	1.89	0.14	2.15	1.38	9.02

(B) Correlation Matrix

	1-Month Treasury Yield	10-Year Treasury Yield
1-month Treasury yield	1	
10-year Treasury yield	0.87	1

TABLE 3.2 Sample Cross-Correlations Between 1-Month and 10-Year Treasury Yields

One-month yield,10-year yield(−h)	One-month yield,10-year yield(+h)	h	Lag	Lead
		0	0.8681	0.8681
		1	0.8672	0.8657
		2	0.8663	0.8631
		3	0.8653	0.8606
		4	0.8641	0.8581
		5	0.8627	0.8556
		6	0.8610	0.8530
		7	0.8590	0.8504
		8	0.8567	0.8476
		9	0.8537	0.8447
		10	0.8505	0.8416
		11	0.8474	0.8387
		12	0.8442	0.8360
		13	0.8411	0.8333
		14	0.8377	0.8304
		15	0.8342	0.8275
		16	0.8307	0.8242
		17	0.8272	0.8211
		18	0.8232	0.8182
		19	0.8191	0.8156
		20	0.8150	0.8131
		21	0.8109	0.8104
		22	0.8072	0.8075
		23	0.8035	0.8047
		24	0.7999	0.8019

3.1.4 Multivariate Portmanteau Tests

In Chapter 2, we have introduced the Ljung and Box's (1978) Q-statistic to jointly test whether several (M) consecutive autocorrelation coefficients were equal to 0. As far as multivariate time series are concerned, we are interested in testing whether there are both no auto- and cross-correlations in a vector series $\mathbf{y}_t$. A simple, multivariate version of the Ljung–Box statistic to test the null hypothesis $H_0 : \rho_1 = \cdots = \rho_M = 0$ versus the alternative hypothesis $H_1 : \rho_i \neq 0$ for some $i \in \{1, \ldots, M\}$ is

$$Q(M) = T\sum_{h=1}^{M}\frac{1}{T-h}tr\left(\hat{\boldsymbol{\Gamma}}_h\hat{\boldsymbol{\Gamma}}_0^{-1}\hat{\boldsymbol{\Gamma}}_h\hat{\boldsymbol{\Gamma}}_0^{-1}\right), \tag{3.8}$$

where T is the sample size, N is the dimension of $\mathbf{y}_t$, M is the maximum lag length that we wish to test and $tr(\mathbf{A})$ is the *trace* of some matrix $\mathbf{A}$, simply defined as the sum of the diagonal elements of $\mathbf{A}$. Under the null hypothesis, $Q(M)$ is asymptotically distributed as a χ^2 distribution with N^2M degrees of freedom. For practical purposes, it is important to note that the χ^2 approximation to the distribution of the test statistic may be misleading for small values of T. In addition, not knowing the small sample distribution is clearly a shortcoming, because infinite samples are not available. Using Monte Carlo techniques, it was found that in small samples the nominal size of the portmanteau test tends to be lower than the significance level chosen (see, e.g., Hosking, 1980). Moreover, the test has low power against many alternatives.

To overcome this drawback, both Hosking (1980, 1981) and Li and McLeod (1981) have proposed adjusted versions of the multivariate Ljung–Box statistic that, despite being asymptotically equivalent to the original one, have better finite-sample performance. The test statistic proposed by Hosking (1980) has the expression

$$Q^*(M) = T^2 \sum_{h=1}^{M} \frac{1}{T-h} tr\left(\hat{\boldsymbol{\Gamma}}_h \hat{\boldsymbol{\Gamma}}_0^{-1} \hat{\boldsymbol{\Gamma}}_h \hat{\boldsymbol{\Gamma}}_0^{-1}\right), \tag{3.9}$$

while the test statistic proposed by Li and McLeod (1981) is instead

$$Q^{**}(M) = T \sum_{h=1}^{M} \frac{1}{T-h} tr\left(\hat{\boldsymbol{\Gamma}}_h \hat{\boldsymbol{\Gamma}}_0^{-1} \hat{\boldsymbol{\Gamma}}_h \hat{\boldsymbol{\Gamma}}_0^{-1}\right) + \frac{N^2 M(M+1)}{2T}. \tag{3.10}$$

Both Li and McLeod (1981) and Hosking (1981) provided simulation experiments to demonstrate the improvement of their suggested modified portmanteau test with respect to the original multivariate version of Ljung–Box statistic. Li (2004) has noted that a comparison of these two modified tests with the original one shows that both modifications work equally well and are better than the original multivariate portmanteau test. Kheoh and McLeod (1992) have suggested that the variance of the Li-McLeod modified portmanteau test is less than Eq. (3.8).

3.1.5 Multivariate White Noise Process

Before we move on to the discussion of VAR models, we introduce the concept of multivariate white noise, which will be useful in the rest of the chapter to define a few classes of multivariate models.

DEFINITION 3.2 (Multivariate white noise)

Let $\mathbf{z}_{i,t} = [z_{1,t}, z_{2,t}, \ldots, z_{N,t}]$ be a $N \times 1$ vector of random variables. This multivariate time series is said to be a *multivariate white noise* if it is a stationary vector with zero mean, and if the values of $\mathbf{z}_t$ at different times are uncorrelated, that is, $\boldsymbol{\Gamma}_h$ is an $N \times N$ matrix of zeros at all $h \neq 0$.

Definition 3.2 implies that each component of $\mathbf{z}_t$ simply behaves like a univariate white noise; additionally the individual white noises are uncoupled in a linear sense. It is important to understand that the assumption that the values of $\mathbf{z}_t$ are uncorrelated does not necessarily imply that they are independent (while we know that independence implies zero correlation, see the Mathematical and Statistical Appendix at the end of the book). However, independence can be inferred by the lack of correlations at all leads and lags among the random variables that enter $\mathbf{z}_t$, when the random vector follows a multivariate normal distribution.

3.2 INTRODUCTION TO VECTOR AUTOREGRESSIVE ANALYSIS

3.2.1 From Structural to Reduced-Form Vector Autoregressive Models

VAR models are a natural generalization of the univariate AR model that already discussed in Chapter 2. In practice a VAR is a system regression model that treats all the variables as endogenous and allows each of them to depend on p lagged values of itself and of all the other variables in the system. Formally a VAR(p) model can be defined as follows.

DEFINITION 3.3 (Vector autoregressive model)

A VAR model of order p (in short VAR(p)) is a process that can be represented as

$$\mathbf{y}_t = \mathbf{a}_0 + \mathbf{A}_1 \mathbf{y}_{t-1} + \mathbf{A}_2 \mathbf{y}_{t-2} + \cdots + \mathbf{A}_p \mathbf{y}_{t-p} + \mathbf{u}_t = \mathbf{a}_0 + \sum_{j=1}^{p} \mathbf{A}_j \mathbf{y}_{t-j} + \mathbf{u}_t, \tag{3.11}$$

where $\mathbf{y}_t$ is a $N \times 1$ vector containing N endogenous variables, $\mathbf{a}_0$ is a $N \times 1$ vector of constants, $\mathbf{A}_1, \mathbf{A}_2, \ldots, \mathbf{A}_p$ are the p $N \times N$ matrices of autoregressive coefficients, and $\mathbf{u}_t$ is a $N \times 1$ vector of white noise disturbances.

To help the reader familiarize with the concepts, we start our discussion introducing a bivariate VAR(1) model, while in Section 3.2.3 we generalize it to a VAR(p) model with N endogenous variables (hence, equations). Consider the following bivariate, first-order Markovian system

$$y_{1,t} = b_{1,0} - b_{1,2}y_{2,t} + \varphi_{1,1}y_{1,t-1} + \varphi_{1,2}y_{2,t-1} + \varepsilon_{1,t} \tag{3.12}$$

$$y_{2,t} = b_{2,0} - b_{2,1}y_{1,t} + \varphi_{2,1}y_{1,t-1} + \varphi_{2,2}y_{2,t-1} + \varepsilon_{2,t}, \tag{3.13}$$

where both the variables $y_{1,t}$ and $y_{2,t}$ are assumed to be stationary and the *structural error terms* $\varepsilon_{1,t}$ and $\varepsilon_{2,t}$ are uncorrelated white noise disturbances with standard deviation σ_1 and σ_2, respectively. The system in Eqs. (3.12) and (3.13) can also be rewritten in a more compact form using matrix notation:

$$\begin{bmatrix} 1 & b_{1,2} \\ b_{2,1} & 1 \end{bmatrix} \begin{bmatrix} y_{1,t} \\ y_{2,t} \end{bmatrix} = \begin{bmatrix} b_{1,0} \\ b_{2,0} \end{bmatrix} + \begin{bmatrix} \varphi_{1,1} & \varphi_{1,2} \\ \varphi_{2,1} & \varphi_{2,2} \end{bmatrix} \begin{bmatrix} y_{1,t-1} \\ y_{2,t-1} \end{bmatrix} + \begin{bmatrix} \varepsilon_{1,t} \\ \varepsilon_{2,t} \end{bmatrix} \tag{3.14}$$

or,

$$\mathbf{B}\mathbf{y}_t = \mathbf{Q}_0 + \mathbf{Q}_1\mathbf{y}_{t-1} + \boldsymbol{\varepsilon}_t, \tag{3.15}$$

where

$$\mathbf{B} \equiv \begin{bmatrix} 1 & b_{1,2} \\ b_{2,1} & 1 \end{bmatrix}, \quad \mathbf{y}_t \equiv \begin{bmatrix} y_{1,t} \\ y_{2,t} \end{bmatrix}, \quad \mathbf{Q}_0 = \begin{bmatrix} b_{1,0} \\ b_{2,0} \end{bmatrix}, \quad \mathbf{Q}_1 = \begin{bmatrix} \varphi_{1,1} & \varphi_{1,2} \\ \varphi_{2,1} & \varphi_{2,2} \end{bmatrix}, \quad \mathbf{y}_{t-1} \equiv \begin{bmatrix} y_{1,t-1} \\ y_{2,t-1} \end{bmatrix}, \quad \text{and} \quad \boldsymbol{\varepsilon}_t \equiv \begin{bmatrix} \varepsilon_{1,t} \\ \varepsilon_{2,t} \end{bmatrix}.$$

In this system, that is also known as a *structural VAR* (or *VAR in primitive form*), $y_{1,t}$ depends on its own lag and on one lag of $y_{2,t}$, but also on the current value of $y_{2,t}$; similarly, $y_{2,t}$ depends on its own lag and on one lag of $y_{1,t}$, but also on the current value of $y_{1,t}$. Therefore, a VAR in its structural form captures *contemporaneous feedback effects*: $-b_{1,2}$ measures the contemporaneous effect of a unit change of $y_{2,t}$ on $y_{1,t}$ and $-b_{2,1}$ measures the contemporaneous effect of a unit change of $y_{1,t}$ on $y_{2,t}$.

Unfortunately, structural VARs are not very practical for applied purposes because standard estimation techniques require the regressors to be uncorrelated with the error terms, which is clearly not the case of the VAR in its structural form. This is due to the presence of contemporaneous feedback effects: obviously, each contemporaneous variable is correlated with its own error term. From Eqs. (3.12) and (3.13), it is clear that when $-b_{1,2}$ is nonzero, $y_{2,t}$ depends on $y_{1,t}$ from the second equation and therefore on $\varepsilon_{1,t}$, and it will be correlated with it; when $-b_{2,1}$ is nonzero, $y_{1,t}$ depends on $y_{2,t}$ from the first equation and therefore on $\varepsilon_{2,t}$. As an additional drawback of the structural model, contemporaneous terms cannot be used in forecasting, that is, exactly where VAR models tend to be largely popular. As a result, in time series analysis, it is common to manipulate the VAR in its structural form to make it more directly useful. Premultiplying both sides of Eq. (3.15) by $\mathbf{B}^{-1}$ we obtain

$$\mathbf{y}_t = \mathbf{a}_0 + \mathbf{A}_1\mathbf{y}_{t-1} + \mathbf{u}_t, \tag{3.16}$$

where $\mathbf{a}_0 = \mathbf{B}^{-1}\mathbf{Q}_0$, $\mathbf{A}_1 = \mathbf{B}^{-1}\mathbf{Q}_1$, and $\mathbf{u}_t = \mathbf{B}_t^{-1}\boldsymbol{\varepsilon}_t$. Denoting by $a_{i,0}$ the element in row i of the vector $\mathbf{a}_0$, by $a_{i,j}$ the element in row i and column j of the matrix $\mathbf{A}_1$, and by $u_{i,t}$ the element in row i of the vector $\mathbf{u}_t$, we can rewrite Eq. (3.16) in the equivalent form:

$$y_{1,t} = a_{1,0} + a_{1,1}y_{1,t-1} + a_{1,2}y_{2,t-1} + u_{1,t} \tag{3.17}$$

$$y_{2,t} = a_{2,0} + a_{2,1}y_{1,t-1} + a_{2,2}y_{2,t-1} + u_{2,t}. \tag{3.18}$$

This system is called *reduced-form* VAR or, alternatively, it is said to describe a VAR in its *standard form*. The model in Eq. (3.16) only features *lagged* endogenous variables (i.e., it does not contain contemporaneous feedback terms) and it can be estimated equation-by-equation using ordinary least square (OLS) (as we shall see in detail in Section 3.2.4). Clearly the new, *reduced-form error terms*, $u_{1,t}$ and $u_{2,t}$, are composites of the two original (also called pure or structural) shocks $\varepsilon_{1,t}$ and $\varepsilon_{2,t}$. This is easy to see if we solve $\mathbf{u}_t = \mathbf{B}^{-1}\boldsymbol{\varepsilon}_t$ to get:

$$u_{1,t} = \frac{\varepsilon_{1,t} - b_{1,2}\varepsilon_{2,t}}{1 - b_{1,2}b_{2,1}}, \tag{3.19}$$

$$u_{2,t} = \frac{\varepsilon_{2,t} - b_{2,1}\varepsilon_{1,t}}{1 - b_{1,2}b_{2,1}}. \tag{3.20}$$

Recalling that $\varepsilon_{1,t}$ and $\varepsilon_{2,t}$ are white noise processes, we can easily derive the properties of the reduced-form errors $u_{1,t}$ and $u_{2,t}$. First, taking the expected value of Eqs. (3.19) and (3.20) (and recalling that, based on the definition of a white noise, $E[\varepsilon_{1,t}] = 0$ and $E[\varepsilon_{2,t}] = 0$), we obtain that

$$E[u_{1,t}] = E\left[\frac{\varepsilon_{1,t} - b_{1,2}\varepsilon_{2,t}}{1 - b_{1,2}b_{2,1}}\right] = 0, \tag{3.21}$$

$$E[u_{2,t}] = E\left[\frac{\varepsilon_{2,t} - b_{2,1}\varepsilon_{1,t}}{1 - b_{1,2}b_{2,1}}\right] = 0. \tag{3.22}$$

In addition, because $\varepsilon_{1,t}$ and $\varepsilon_{2,t}$ are uncorrelated, that is, $Cov[\varepsilon_{1,t}, \varepsilon_{2,t}] = 0$, we find that the variance of $u_{1,t}$ is

$$\begin{aligned} Var[u_{1,t}] &= \frac{Var[\varepsilon_{1,t} - b_{1,2}\varepsilon_{2,t}]}{(1-b_{1,2}b_{2,1})^2} = \frac{Var[\varepsilon_{1,t}] + b_{1,2}^2 Var[\varepsilon_{2,t}] - 2b_{1,2}Cov[\varepsilon_{1,t}, \varepsilon_{2,t}]}{(1-b_{1,2}b_{2,1})^2} \\ &= \frac{\sigma_{\varepsilon,1}^2 + b_{1,2}^2\sigma_{\varepsilon,2}^2}{(1-b_{1,2}b_{2,1})^2}, \end{aligned} \tag{3.23}$$

and, similarly,

$$Var[u_{2,t}] = \frac{\sigma_{\varepsilon,2}^2 + b_{2,1}^2\sigma_{\varepsilon,1}^2}{(1-b_{1,2}b_{2,1})^2}. \tag{3.24}$$

It easy to see that the variances of $u_{1,t}$ and $u_{2,t}$ are constant over time. Finally the covariance between the two structural errors is equal to

$$Cov[u_{1,t}, u_{2,t}] = \frac{E[(\varepsilon_{1,t} - b_{1,2}\varepsilon_{2,t})(\varepsilon_{2,t} - b_{2,1}\varepsilon_{1,t})]}{(1-b_{1,2}b_{2,1})^2} = \frac{-(b_{2,1}\sigma_{\varepsilon,1}^2 + b_{1,2}\sigma_{\varepsilon,2}^2)}{(1-b_{1,2}b_{2,1})^2}. \tag{3.25}$$

Noticeably, while the reduced-form error terms remain serially uncorrelated (i.e., autocorrelations are equal to 0) as the structural errors were, they are cross-correlated unless $b_{1,2} = b_{2,1} = 0$ (i.e., there are no contemporaneous effects of $y_{1,t}$ on $y_{2,t}$ and vice versa). The variances and covariances of the reduced-form errors can be collected in the matrix $\mathbf{\Sigma}_u$:

$$\mathbf{\Sigma}_u = \begin{bmatrix} Var[u_{1,t}] & Cov[u_{1,t}, u_{2,t}] \\ Cov[u_{1,t}, u_{2,t}] & Var[u_{2,t}] \end{bmatrix} = \begin{bmatrix} \sigma_1^2 & \sigma_{1,2} \\ \sigma_{1,2} & \sigma_2^2 \end{bmatrix}. \tag{3.26}$$

The reduced-form VAR in Eqs. (3.17) and (3.18) is very practical and easy to estimate (this can be done by simple OLS), but it is important to understand that, *in general*, it is not possible to *identify* the structural parameters and errors (i.e., the sample estimates of the coefficients and the residuals of the primitive system) from the OLS estimates of the parameters and the residuals of the standard form VAR. This lack of identification (because the model is linear, the problem is both local and global, see Chapter 8 for a differentiation of the two concepts) may be overcome if one is prepared to impose appropriate restrictions on the primitive system. This is unsurprising: the structural VAR in Eqs. (3.12) and (3.13) contains eight coefficients and two variances of the error terms, for a total of 10 parameters; the VAR in its standard form only contains nine parameters (six coefficients, two variances, and one covariance of the error terms). Therefore, and this occurs for a rather intuitive accounting, back-of-the-envelope reason, it is not possible to recover all the information that was present in the primitive system unless we are able to restrict one of its parameters. To this purpose a popular identification scheme is the one proposed by Sims (1980), based on a *recursive Cholesky triangularization*.

Suppose that you are willing to impose a restriction on the primitive system in Eqs. (3.12) and (3.13) such that $b_{1,2}$ is equal to 0, meaning that $y_{1,t}$ has a contemporaneous effect on $y_{2,t}$, but $y_{2,t}$ only affects $y_{1,t}$ with a one-period lag:

$$y_{1,t} = b_{1,0} + \varphi_{1,1}y_{1,t-1} + \varphi_{1,2}y_{2,t-1} + \varepsilon_{1,t} \tag{3.27}$$

$$y_{2,t} = b_{2,0} - b_{2,1}y_{1,t} + \varphi_{2,1}y_{1,t-1} + \varphi_{2,2}y_{2,t-1} + \varepsilon_{2,t}. \tag{3.28}$$

This corresponds to imposing a Cholesky decomposition on the covariance matrix of the residuals of the VAR in its standard form. Indeed, now we can rewrite the relationship between the pure shocks (from the structural VAR) and the regression residuals as

$$u_{1,t} = \varepsilon_{1,t}, \tag{3.29}$$

$$u_{2,t} = \varepsilon_{2,t} - b_{2,1}\varepsilon_{1,t}. \tag{3.30}$$

Practically, imposing the restriction $b_{1,2}=0$ means that $\mathbf{B}^{-1}$ is given by

$$\mathbf{B}^{-1} \equiv \begin{bmatrix} 1 & 0 \\ -b_{2,1} & 1 \end{bmatrix},$$

and thus premultiplication of the primitive system (3.12) and (3.13) by the lower diagonal matrix $\mathbf{B}^{-1}$ yields

$$\begin{bmatrix} y_{1,t} \\ y_{2,t} \end{bmatrix} = \begin{bmatrix} 1 & 0 \\ -b_{2,1} & 1 \end{bmatrix}\begin{bmatrix} b_{1,0} \\ b_{2,0} \end{bmatrix} + \begin{bmatrix} 1 & 0 \\ -b_{2,1} & 1 \end{bmatrix}\begin{bmatrix} \varphi_{1,1} & \varphi_{1,2} \\ \varphi_{2,1} & \varphi_{2,2} \end{bmatrix}\begin{bmatrix} y_{1,t-1} \\ y_{2,t-1} \end{bmatrix} + \begin{bmatrix} 1 & 0 \\ -b_{2,1} & 1 \end{bmatrix}\begin{bmatrix} \varepsilon_{1,t} \\ \varepsilon_{2,t} \end{bmatrix}, \tag{3.31}$$

which results in

$$\begin{bmatrix} y_{1,t} \\ y_{2,t} \end{bmatrix} = \begin{bmatrix} b_{1,0} \\ b_{2,0} - b_{1,0}b_{2,1} \end{bmatrix} + \begin{bmatrix} \varphi_{1,1} & \varphi_{1,2} \\ \varphi_{2,1} - b_{2,1}\varphi_{1,1} & \varphi_{2,2} - b_{2,1}\varphi_{1,2} \end{bmatrix}\begin{bmatrix} y_{1,t-1} \\ y_{2,t-1} \end{bmatrix} + \begin{bmatrix} \varepsilon_{1,t} \\ \varepsilon_{2,t} - b_{2,1}\varepsilon_{1,t} \end{bmatrix}. \tag{3.32}$$

The system has now only nine parameters that can be identified using the OLS estimates from Eqs. (3.17) to (3.18). Indeed, using simple algebra we can see that: $a_{1,0}=b_{1,0}$; $a_{2,0}=b_{2,0}-b_{1,0}b_{2,1}$; $a_{1,1}=\varphi_{1,1}$; $a_{1,2}=\varphi_{1,2}$; $a_{2,1}=\varphi_{2,1}-b_{2,1}\varphi_{1,1}$; $a_{2,2}=\varphi_{2,2}-b_{2,1}\varphi_{1,2}$. In addition, since we know from Eqs. (3.29) to (3.30) that $u_{1,t}=\varepsilon_{1,t}$ and $u_{2,t}=\varepsilon_{2,t}-b_{2,1}\varepsilon_{1,t}$, we can compute:

$$\sigma_1^2 \equiv Var\left[u_{1,t}\right] = \sigma_{\varepsilon,1}^2, \tag{3.33}$$

$$\sigma_2^2 \equiv Var\left[u_{2,t}\right] = \sigma_{\varepsilon,2}^2 - b_{2,1}^2\sigma_{\varepsilon,1}^2, \tag{3.34}$$

$$Cov\left[u_{1,t}, u_{2,t}\right] = -b_{2,1}\sigma_{\varepsilon,1}^2. \tag{3.35}$$

The implication of the identification restriction that we just imposed is that, while both the $\varepsilon_{1,t}$ and $\varepsilon_{2,t}$ shocks affect the contemporaneous value of $y_{2,t}$, only $\varepsilon_{1,t}$ impacts the contemporaneous value of $y_{1,t}$. In practice, the observed values of $u_{1,t}$ are completely attributed to pure (structural) shocks to $y_{1,t}$. This technique of decomposing the residuals in a triangular fashion is called Cholesky decomposition (or triangularization). Put in other words, we see that the covariance matrix of the residuals is forced to be equal to

$$\mathbf{\Sigma}_u = \mathbf{W}\mathbf{\Sigma}\mathbf{W}' = \mathbf{\Sigma}^{1/2}(\mathbf{\Sigma}^{1/2})', \tag{3.36}$$

where $\mathbf{W}=\mathbf{B}^{-1}$, $\mathbf{\Sigma}$ is the diagonal covariance matrix of the structural innovations, and $\mathbf{\Sigma}^{1/2}$ is the triangular "square root" of the covariance matrix $\mathbf{\Sigma}_u$. Eq. (3.36) is easily checked:

$$\mathbf{\Sigma}_u = \begin{bmatrix} 1 & 0 \\ -b_{2,1} & 1 \end{bmatrix}\begin{bmatrix} \sigma_{\varepsilon,1}^2 & 0 \\ 0 & \sigma_{\varepsilon,2}^2 \end{bmatrix}\begin{bmatrix} 1 & 0 \\ -b_{2,1} & 1 \end{bmatrix}' = \begin{bmatrix} 1 & 0 \\ -b_{2,1} & 1 \end{bmatrix}\begin{bmatrix} \sigma_{\varepsilon,1}^2 & 0 \\ 0 & \sigma_{\varepsilon,2}^2 \end{bmatrix}\begin{bmatrix} 1 & -b_{2,1} \\ 0 & 1 \end{bmatrix} = \begin{bmatrix} \sigma_{\varepsilon,1}^2 & -b_{2,1}\sigma_{\varepsilon,2}^2 \\ -b_{2,1}\sigma_{\varepsilon,1}^2 & \sigma_{\varepsilon,2}^2 - b_{2,1}^2\sigma_{\varepsilon,1}^2 \end{bmatrix}, \tag{3.37}$$

which is exactly what we found in Eqs. (3.33)–(3.35). The decomposition in Eq. (3.36) is what we call the Cholesky decomposition of the symmetric matrix $\mathbf{\Sigma}_u$. Needless to say the task that one usually wants to accomplish is to go back from the estimated $\mathbf{\Sigma}_u$ to the original (and unobserved) diagonal matrix $\mathbf{\Sigma}$. With a little bit of algebra, we understand that this is equivalent to

$$\mathbf{\Sigma} = \mathbf{W}^{-1}\mathbf{\Sigma}_u(\mathbf{W}')^{-1}. \tag{3.38}$$

This technique can be generalized to a VAR system with any number N of equations. In particular, in a N-variate VAR, exact identification requires us to impose $(N^2-N)/2$ to retrieve the N structural shocks from the residual of the OLS estimate. Being based on a triangular structure, a Cholesky decomposition forces exactly $(N^2-N)/2$ values of the matrix $\mathbf{B}$ to be 0 (or to some other constant).

Let us pause for a moment to understand the meaning (and the implications) of the Cholesky decomposition for a less simplistic model, for instance a VAR(1) with three endogenous variables (and therefore three equations). The parameters in the structural model consist of three intercept terms, six (two for each equation) coefficients that map the contemporaneous effect of each variable on the other two, nine autoregressive coefficients (contained in a 3×3 matrix), and the three variance coefficients of the error terms, for a total of 21 parameters. The VAR in its reduced form contains 12 estimated coefficients (three intercepts and six autoregressive coefficients), three variances and three covariances, for a total of 18 coefficients. Therefore, we shall need to impose three restrictions to identify the parameters of the primitive system from the OLS estimates of the VAR in its standard form, which is exactly $(3^2-3)/2=3$

restrictions. Indeed, imposing a triangular (Cholesky) decomposition on the structural residuals is equivalent to premultiplying the structural VAR by the lower triangular matrix

$$\mathbf{B}^{-1} = \begin{bmatrix} 1 & 0 & 0 \\ -b_{1,2} & 1 & 0 \\ -b_{1,3} & -b_{2,3} & 1 \end{bmatrix}, \tag{3.39}$$

which yields the reduced form residuals:

$$\mathbf{u}_t = \mathbf{B}^{-1}\boldsymbol{\varepsilon}_t = \begin{bmatrix} 1 & 0 & 0 \\ -b_{2,1} & 1 & 0 \\ -b_{3,1} & -b_{3,2} & 1 \end{bmatrix} \begin{bmatrix} \varepsilon_{1,t} \\ \varepsilon_{2,t} \\ \varepsilon_{3,t} \end{bmatrix} = \begin{bmatrix} \varepsilon_{1,t} \\ \varepsilon_{2,t} - b_{2,1}\varepsilon_{1,t} \\ \varepsilon_{3,t} - b_{3,1}\varepsilon_{1,t} - b_{3,2}\varepsilon_{2,t} \end{bmatrix}. \tag{3.40}$$

Because the Cholesky decomposition is based on premultiplying by a (lower) triangular matrix, it follows that when we decide the ordering of the variables in a VAR system, we are also deciding which kind of restrictions the decomposition will impose on the contemporaneous effects of each variable on the others. For example, in the trivariate case of Eq. (3.39) earlier, $b_{2,1}, b_{3,1}$, and $b_{3,2}$ are set to 0, meaning that the first variable in the system is forced not to be contemporaneously affected by shocks to any of the other variables; the second variable in the system is only contemporaneously affected by shocks to the first variable; the last variable is contemporaneously affected by the shocks to both the other variables. It is easy to generalize this reasoning to the N-variable case.

It should be evident that there are as many Cholesky decompositions as all the possible orderings of the variables, which are therefore a combinatorial factor of N. Therefore, we shall need to be aware that any time that we apply a Cholesky triangular identification scheme to a VAR model that results in a specific ordering, we will be introducing a number of (potentially arbitrary) assumptions on the contemporaneous relationships among the variables. Therefore, despite being very practical, Cholesky decompositions are quite deliberate in the restrictions that they place and tend not to be based on any theoretical assumptions regarding the nature of the economic relationships among the variables. Alternative identification schemes are possible (although they are more popular in the macroeconomics literature than in applied finance). A review of some commonly used restriction schemes to achieve identification based on a theoretical background can be found in Lütkepohl (2005, Chapter 9).

3.2.2 Stationarity Conditions and the Population Moments of a VAR(1) Process

Let us now discuss the properties of a reduced-form, standard VAR(1) model such as the one in Eq. (3.16). Assume that $\mathbf{y}_t$, $\mathbf{a}_0$, $\mathbf{y}_{t-1}$, and $\mathbf{u}_t$ are $N \times 1$ vectors and $\mathbf{A}_1$ is a $N \times N$ matrix and that the process is weakly stationary, according to Definition 3.1. By taking the expectation of $\mathbf{y}_t$ and using the fact that $E[\mathbf{u}_t] = \mathbf{0}$, we obtain:

$$E[\mathbf{y}_t] = \mathbf{a}_0 + \mathbf{A}_1 E[\mathbf{y}_{t-1}]. \tag{3.41}$$

Because we are assuming stationarity, $E[\mathbf{y}_t]$ is time-invariant so that $E[\mathbf{y}_t] = E[\mathbf{y}_{t-1}]$ and thus

$$\boldsymbol{\mu} \equiv E[\mathbf{y}_t] = (\mathbf{I}_N - \mathbf{A}_1)^{-1}\mathbf{a}_0, \tag{3.42}$$

provided that the matrix $\mathbf{I}_N - \mathbf{A}_1$ is nonsingular, where $\mathbf{I}_N$ is the $N \times N$ identity matrix. Clearly the unconditional mean vector $\boldsymbol{\mu}$ in Eq. (3.42) must be contrasted with the conditional mean vector:

$$\boldsymbol{\mu}_{t|t-1} \equiv E[\mathbf{y}_t|\mathfrak{I}_{t-1}] = E[\mathbf{y}_t|\mathbf{y}_{t-1}] = \mathbf{a}_0 + \mathbf{A}_1\mathbf{y}_{t-1}. \tag{3.43}$$

Using $\mathbf{a}_0 = (\mathbf{I}_N - \mathbf{A}_1)\boldsymbol{\mu}$, the VAR(1) model can be rewritten as

$$\mathbf{y}_t - \boldsymbol{\mu} = \mathbf{A}_1(\mathbf{y}_{t-1} - \boldsymbol{\mu}) + \mathbf{u}_t. \tag{3.44}$$

If we let $\tilde{\mathbf{y}}_t \equiv \mathbf{y}_t - \boldsymbol{\mu}$ be the mean-corrected time-series, or equivalently the vector process expressed in deviations from its unconditional mean, we can write the model as:

$$\tilde{\mathbf{y}}_t = \mathbf{A}_1\tilde{\mathbf{y}}_{t-1} + \mathbf{u}_t. \tag{3.45}$$

Clearly, it is possible to substitute $\tilde{\mathbf{y}}_{t-1} = \mathbf{A}_1\tilde{\mathbf{y}}_{t-2} + \mathbf{u}_{t-1}$ in the expression (3.45), obtaining

$$\tilde{\mathbf{y}}_t = \mathbf{A}_1(\mathbf{A}_1\tilde{\mathbf{y}}_{t-2} + \mathbf{u}_{t-1}) + \mathbf{u}_t = \mathbf{A}_1^2\tilde{\mathbf{y}}_{t-2} + \mathbf{A}_1\mathbf{u}_{t-1} + \mathbf{u}_t. \tag{3.46}$$

We can now substitute $\tilde{\mathbf{y}}_{t-2} = \mathbf{A}_1\tilde{\mathbf{y}}_{t-3} + \mathbf{u}_{t-2}$ in the expression (3.46), and then keep iterating till we obtain:

$$\tilde{\mathbf{y}}_t = \mathbf{u}_t + \mathbf{A}_1\mathbf{u}_{t-1} + \mathbf{A}_1^2\mathbf{u}_{t-2} + \mathbf{A}_1^3\mathbf{u}_{t-3} + \cdots = \sum_{i=1}^{\infty}\mathbf{A}_1^i\mathbf{u}_{t-i} + \mathbf{u}_t. \tag{3.47}$$

Notice that $\tilde{\mathbf{y}}_t = \mathbf{y}_t - \boldsymbol{\mu}$, so that Eq. (3.47) can also be rewritten as

$$\mathbf{y}_t = \boldsymbol{\mu} + \sum_{i=1}^{\infty}\mathbf{A}_1^i\mathbf{u}_{t-i} + \mathbf{u}_t. \tag{3.48}$$

If we define $\boldsymbol{\Theta}_i \equiv \mathbf{A}_1^i$, we can rewrite Eq. (3.48) as

$$\mathbf{y}_t = \boldsymbol{\mu} + \sum_{i=1}^{\infty}\boldsymbol{\Theta}_i\mathbf{u}_{t-i} + \mathbf{u}_t, \tag{3.49}$$

which is the *VMA infinite representation* of the VAR(1) model and that it is immediately useful to discuss its properties. First, because $\mathbf{u}_t$ is serially uncorrelated, it is also uncorrelated with the past values of $\mathbf{y}_t$, that is, $Cov[\mathbf{u}_t, \mathbf{y}_{t-1}] = \mathbf{0}$. For this reason, $\mathbf{u}_t$ is often referred to as the vector of *innovations* of the series at time t. Second, postmultiplying the expression (3.48) by $\mathbf{u}_t'$, taking the expectation, and exploiting again the fact that $\mathbf{u}_t$ is serially uncorrelated, we obtain $Cov[\mathbf{y}_t, \mathbf{u}_t] = \boldsymbol{\Sigma}_u$. Third, Eq. (3.48) implies that in a VAR(1) model, $\mathbf{y}_t$ depends on the past innovations $\mathbf{u}_{t-j}$ with a coefficient matrix $\mathbf{A}_1^j$, that is, with coefficients that are collected in increasing powers of the VAR(1) matrix. For such dependence to fade progressively away as the time distance between $\mathbf{y}_t$ and past innovations grows—which seems to be a sensible condition, in the sense that in the VAR(1) model past shocks are gradually forgotten in a typical geometric decaying fashion—$\mathbf{A}_1^j$ must converge to 0 as j goes to infinity. In practice, this means that all the N eigenvalues of the matrix $\mathbf{A}_1$ must be less than 1 in modulus, to avoid that $\mathbf{A}_1^j$ will either explode or converge to a nonzero matrix as j goes to infinity. Therefore, provided that the covariance matrix of $\mathbf{u}_t$ exists, the requirement that all the eigenvalues of $\mathbf{A}_1$ are less than one in modulus is a necessary and sufficient condition for $\mathbf{y}_t$ to be *stable* (and, thus, *stationary*, as stability implies stationarity as discussed in Chapter 2), that is, the roots of the equation below must lie outside the unit circle:[1]

$$\det(\mathbf{I}_N - \mathbf{A}_1 z) = 0. \tag{3.50}$$

Of course, you will recognize that Eq. (3.49) represents the multivariate extension of the *Wold's representation* theorem already stated in Chapter 2 for multivariate stationary time series. Finally, using expression (3.48), we have that

$$Cov[\mathbf{y}_t] \equiv \Gamma_0 = \boldsymbol{\Sigma}_u + \mathbf{A}_1\boldsymbol{\Sigma}_u\mathbf{A}'_1 + \mathbf{A}_1^2\boldsymbol{\Sigma}_u(\mathbf{A}_1^2)' + \cdots = \sum_{i=0}^{\infty}A_1^i\boldsymbol{\Sigma}_u(\mathbf{A}_1^i)', \tag{3.51}$$

where $\mathbf{A}_1^0$ is an $N \times N$ identity matrix $\mathbf{I}_N$. Also in this case, this is to be contrasted with the conditional covariance matrix for $\mathbf{y}_t$:

$$Cov[\mathbf{y}_t|\Im_{t-1}] = Cov[\mathbf{y}_t|\mathbf{y}_{t-1}] = \mathbf{A}_1 Cov[\mathbf{y}_{t-1}|\mathbf{y}_{t-1}]\mathbf{A}'_1 + \boldsymbol{\Sigma}_u = \boldsymbol{\Sigma}_u, \tag{3.52}$$

because $Cov[\mathbf{y}_{t-1}|\mathbf{y}_{t-1}] = O$. Interestingly, while the *unconditional* covariance matrix is a complex function of both the covariance matrix of the residuals, $\boldsymbol{\Sigma}_u$, and of the matrix of VAR coefficients $\mathbf{A}_1$, conditioning on past information, the covariance matrix of $\mathbf{y}_t$ is the same as the covariance matrix of the residuals, $\boldsymbol{\Sigma}_u$; therefore, when the residuals are simultaneously uncorrelated (i.e., $\boldsymbol{\Sigma}_u$ is diagonal), then also $Cov[\mathbf{y}_t|\mathbf{y}_{t-1}]$ will be diagonal.

To find a more useful expression in place of Eq. (3.51), note that it can alternatively be written as

$$\Gamma_0 = \sum_{i=0}^{\infty}\boldsymbol{\Theta}_i\boldsymbol{\Sigma}_u\boldsymbol{\Theta}_i', \tag{3.53}$$

1. The condition in Eq. (3.50) is simply states that all the eigenvalues of the matrix A must be less than 1 in modulus. In fact, all the eigenvalues of matrix $\mathbf{A}_1$ are less than 1 in modulus if and only if the polynomial $\det(\mathbf{I}_N - \mathbf{A}_1 z)$ has no roots in and on the complex unit circle.

where the coefficients $\boldsymbol{\Theta}_i$ are simply the coefficients of the moving average representations of the VAR. This way of representing Eq. (3.51) is quite convenient because these coefficients can be easily recovered once we write the VAR (1) process in *lag operator* notation, that is,

$$\mathbf{y}_t = \boldsymbol{\mu} + \mathbf{A}(L)\mathbf{y}_t + \mathbf{u}_t, \tag{3.54}$$

or, alternatively,

$$\tilde{\mathbf{A}}(L)\mathbf{y}_t = \boldsymbol{\mu} + \mathbf{u}_t, \tag{3.55}$$

where L is the lag operator discussed in Chapter 2 and $\tilde{\mathbf{A}}(L) \equiv \mathbf{I}_N - \mathbf{A}(L)$. At this point, let $\boldsymbol{\Theta}(L) \equiv \sum_{i=0}^{\infty} \boldsymbol{\Theta}_i L^i$ be an operator such that $\boldsymbol{\Theta}(L)\tilde{\mathbf{A}}(L) = \mathbf{I}_N$ and postmultiply Eq. (3.55) by $\boldsymbol{\Theta}(L)$ to obtain

$$\mathbf{y}_t = \boldsymbol{\Theta}(L)\boldsymbol{\mu} + \boldsymbol{\Theta}(L)\mathbf{u}_t, \tag{3.56}$$

that is,

$$\mathbf{y}_t = \sum_{i=0}^{\infty} \boldsymbol{\Theta}_i\boldsymbol{\mu} + \sum_{i=0}^{\infty} \boldsymbol{\Theta}_i\mathbf{u}_{t-i}. \tag{3.57}$$

This means that the operator $\boldsymbol{\Theta}(L)$ is the inverse of $\tilde{\mathbf{A}}(L)$. With a modicum of additional but tedious algebra (that the interested reader can find in Lütkepohl, 2005), it is possible to prove that

$$\boldsymbol{\Theta}_i = \sum_{j=1}^{i} \boldsymbol{\Theta}_{i-j}\mathbf{A}_1, \tag{3.58}$$

where $\boldsymbol{\Theta}_0 = \mathbf{I}_N$. Finally, postmultiplying by $\tilde{\mathbf{y}}_{t-h}$ in Eq. (3.45), taking expectation, and exploiting the fact that $Cov\left[\mathbf{u}_t, \mathbf{y}_{t-j}\right] = E\left[\mathbf{u}_t\mathbf{y}'_{t-j}\right] = \mathbf{0}$ for $j > 0$, we obtain

$$E(\tilde{\mathbf{y}}_t\tilde{\mathbf{y}}_{t+1-h}) = \mathbf{A}_1 E(\tilde{\mathbf{y}}_t\tilde{\mathbf{y}}_{t-h})' \quad \text{for } h > 0. \tag{3.59}$$

Therefore, the cross-correlation matrices $\boldsymbol{\Gamma}_h$ can be computed as

$$\boldsymbol{\Gamma}_h = \mathbf{A}_1\boldsymbol{\Gamma}_{h-1} \quad \text{for } h > 0. \tag{3.60}$$

By repeated substitution, it is easy to show that

$$\boldsymbol{\Gamma}_h = \mathbf{A}_1^h\boldsymbol{\Gamma}_0 \quad \text{for } h > 0, \tag{3.61}$$

and thus once $\boldsymbol{\Gamma}_0$ has been computed, all the other cross-correlation matrix for $h > 0$ can be calculated by recursive substitution.

Finally, by pre- and postmultiplying Eq. (3.60) by $\mathbf{D}^{-1/2}$ we can also work out the expression of the cross-correlation matrix, that is,

$$\boldsymbol{\rho}_h = \mathbf{D}^{-1/2}\mathbf{A}_1\boldsymbol{\Gamma}_{h-1}\mathbf{D}^{-1/2} = \mathbf{D}^{-1/2}\mathbf{A}_1\mathbf{D}^{1/2}\mathbf{D}^{-1/2}\boldsymbol{\Gamma}_{h-1}\mathbf{D}^{-1/2} = \boldsymbol{\Psi}\boldsymbol{\rho}_{h-1}, \tag{3.62}$$

where $\boldsymbol{\Psi} = \mathbf{D}^{-1/2}\mathbf{A}_1\mathbf{D}^{-1/2}$. Again, by recursive iteration we obtain

$$\boldsymbol{\rho}_h = \boldsymbol{\Psi}_h\boldsymbol{\rho}_0 \quad \text{for } h > 0, \tag{3.63}$$

and thus once $\boldsymbol{\rho}_0$ has been computed, it is trivial to obtain all the other correlation matrices.

EXAMPLE 3.2

Let us suppose that we have estimated the following VAR(1) model for the 1-month and the 10-year US Treasury yields that were already plotted in Example 3.1. Without entering into the details of the estimation, that we shall discuss in Section 3.2.4 (we shall provide a complete sample output in Example 3.3), we only report the estimated coefficients (*t*-statistics are in square brackets),

$$\begin{bmatrix} y_{1M,t} \\ y_{10Y,t} \end{bmatrix} = \begin{bmatrix} \underset{[-2.5382]}{-0.0490} \\ \underset{[0.8711]}{0.0080} \end{bmatrix} + \begin{bmatrix} \underset{[210.6540]}{0.9819} & \underset{[0.4077]}{0.0209} \\ \underset{[3.3784]}{0.0009} & \underset{[240.0320]}{0.9970} \end{bmatrix} \begin{bmatrix} y_{1M,t-1} \\ y_{10Y,t-1} \end{bmatrix} + \begin{bmatrix} u_{1M,t} \\ u_{10Y,t} \end{bmatrix},$$

(Continued)

EXAMPLE 3.2 (Continued)

and the estimated covariance matrix of the reduced-form residuals is

$$\hat{\Sigma}_u = \begin{bmatrix} 0.0476 & 0.0013 \\ 0.0013 & 0.0110 \end{bmatrix}.$$

We also compute the unconditional first and second moments of the series. Let us start from the mean, that can be computed quite easily by applying the formula in Eq. (3.42):

$$\mu = (\mathbf{I}_2 - \mathbf{A}_1)^{-1}\mathbf{a}_0 = \left(\begin{bmatrix} 1 & 0 \\ 0 & 1 \end{bmatrix} - \begin{bmatrix} 0.9819 & 0.0209 \\ 0.0009 & 0.9970 \end{bmatrix} \right)^{-1} \begin{bmatrix} -0.0490 \\ 0.0080 \end{bmatrix} = \left(\begin{bmatrix} 0.1801 & -0.0209 \\ -0.0009 & 0.0030 \end{bmatrix} \right)^{-1} \begin{bmatrix} -0.0490 \\ 0.0080 \end{bmatrix}$$
$$= \begin{bmatrix} 84.53 & 588.90 \\ 25.36 & 510.00 \end{bmatrix} \begin{bmatrix} -0.0490 \\ 0.0080 \end{bmatrix} = \begin{bmatrix} 0.5692 \\ 2.8374 \end{bmatrix}.$$

Therefore, the 1-month Treasury yield has an unconditional mean of approximately 57 bps, while the 10-year US Treasury yield has an unconditional mean of approximately 284 bps, which implies an average riskless yield spread of 227 bps per year. Knowing that the 1-month Treasury yield on September 30, 2016 was 0.26%, and the 10-year US Treasury yield was 1.58%, we can also compute their *conditional* expectations:

$$\mu_{t|09/30/16} = E\left[\mathbf{y}_t | \mathbf{y}_{09/30/16}\right] = \mathbf{a}_0 + \mathbf{A}_1 \mathbf{y}_{09/30/16} = \begin{bmatrix} -0.0490 \\ 0.0080 \end{bmatrix} + \begin{bmatrix} 0.9819 & 0.0209 \\ 0.0009 & 0.9970 \end{bmatrix} \begin{bmatrix} 0.16 \\ 1.58 \end{bmatrix} = \begin{bmatrix} 0.1411 \\ 1.5834 \end{bmatrix}.$$

For completeness, we note that, at least in hindsight, on October 7, 2016, that is, one period (week) later, the 1-month Treasury yield turned out to be 0.21% and the 10-year US Treasury yield was 1.70%. The differences between the conditional expectations of the yields and their realized value, approximately 7 and 12 bps, respectively, are the forecast errors, that we shall discuss in Section 3.2.6.

We now compute the unconditional covariance matrix of the two series, $\mathbf{\Gamma}_0$:

$$\hat{\mathbf{\Gamma}}_0 = \hat{A}_1 \hat{\mathbf{\Gamma}}_0 \hat{A}_1' + \hat{\Sigma}_u \Rightarrow \text{vec}(\hat{\mathbf{\Gamma}}_0) = \text{vec}(\hat{A}_1 \hat{\mathbf{\Gamma}}_0 \hat{A}_1') + \text{vec}(\hat{\Sigma}_u)$$
$$\text{vec}(\hat{\mathbf{\Gamma}}_0) = (\hat{A}_1 \otimes \hat{A}_1)\text{vec}(\hat{\mathbf{\Gamma}}_0) + \text{vec}(\hat{\Sigma}_u)$$
$$\Rightarrow [\mathbf{I}_4 - (\hat{A}_1 \otimes \hat{A}_1)]\text{vec}(\hat{\mathbf{\Gamma}}_0) = \text{vec}(\hat{\Sigma}_u) \Rightarrow \text{vec}(\hat{\mathbf{\Gamma}}_0) = [\mathbf{I}_4 - (\hat{A}_1 \otimes \hat{A}_1)]^{-1}\text{vec}(\hat{\Sigma}_u).$$

Plugging in the estimates reported previously, we find:

$$\text{vec}(\hat{\Gamma}_0) = [\mathbf{I}_4 - \hat{\mathbf{A}}_1 \otimes \hat{\mathbf{A}}_1]^{-1}\text{vec}(\hat{\Sigma}_u) = \left(I_4 - \begin{bmatrix} 0.9641 & 0.0205 & 0.0205 & 0.0004 \\ 0.0009 & 0.9790 & 1.88e{-}05 & 0.0208 \\ 0.0009 & 1.88e{-}05 & 0.9790 & 0.0208 \\ 8.10e{-}0.7 & 0.0009 & 0.0009 & 0.9940 \end{bmatrix} \right)^{-1}$$

$$\times \begin{bmatrix} 0.0476 \\ 0.0013 \\ 0.0013 \\ 0.0110 \end{bmatrix} = \begin{bmatrix} 29.9370 & 41.6850 & 41.6850 & 292.152 \\ 1.7951 & 60.0539 & 12.5807 & 252.762 \\ 1.7951 & 12.5807 & 60.0539 & 252.762 \\ 0.5418 & 10.8845 & 10.8845 & 242.671 \end{bmatrix} \begin{bmatrix} 0.0476 \\ 0.0013 \\ 0.0013 \\ 0.0110 \end{bmatrix} = \begin{bmatrix} 4.7461 \\ 2.9602 \\ 2.9602 \\ 2.7235 \end{bmatrix},$$

which gives the unconditional covariance matrix:

$$\hat{\mathbf{\Gamma}}_0 = \begin{bmatrix} 4.746 & 2.960 \\ 2.960 & 2.724 \end{bmatrix} \neq \hat{\Sigma}_0 = \begin{bmatrix} 0.0476 & 0.0013 \\ 0.0013 & 0.0110 \end{bmatrix}.$$

Clearly, conditional ($\hat{\Sigma}_u$) and unconditional second moments are radically different: the residuals, also because both series are highly serially correlated, have very low variances and a correlation of 0.057 ($=0.0013/(0.0476 \times 0.0110)^{1/2}$). In unconditional terms, 1-month and 10-year rates are characterized by rather large standard deviations (2.179% and 1.650% per year) and a correlation of 0.823 ($=2.960/(4.746 \times 2.724)^{1/2}$). The latter is more in line with reality and asset pricing expectations, of course.

3.2.3 Generalization to a VAR(p) Model

Now that we have analyzed the properties of a VAR(1) model, their generalization to the VAR(p) model $\mathbf{y}_t = \mathbf{a}_0 + \mathbf{A}_1\mathbf{y}_{t-1} + \mathbf{A}_2\mathbf{y}_{t-2} + \cdots + \mathbf{A}_p\mathbf{y}_{t-p} + \mathbf{u}_t$, that we presented in Eq. (3.11) should be quite obvious.

Using again the lag operator L as we did for the VAR(1), Eq. (3.11) can be rewritten as

$$(\mathbf{I}_N - A_1 L - \cdots - A_p L^p)\mathbf{y}_t = \mathbf{a}_0 + \mathbf{u}_t, \tag{3.64}$$

where $\mathbf{I}_N$ is the $N \times N$ identity matrix. More compactly, Eq. (3.64) can be rewritten as

$$\tilde{\mathbf{A}}(L)\mathbf{y}_t = \mathbf{a}_0 + \mathbf{u}_t, \tag{3.65}$$

where now $\tilde{\mathbf{A}}(L) = \mathbf{I}_N - \mathbf{A}_1 L - \cdots - \mathbf{A}_p L^p$. Assuming that $\mathbf{y}_t$ is weakly stationary, we obtain that

$$\boldsymbol{\mu} = E[\mathbf{y}_t] = (\mathbf{I}_N - \mathbf{A}_1 - \cdots - \mathbf{A}_p)^{-1}\mathbf{a}_0, \tag{3.66}$$

provided that the inverse of the matrix $(\mathbf{I}_N - \mathbf{A}_1 - \cdots - \mathbf{A}_p)$ exists. Also in this case the conditional mean vector has expression $\boldsymbol{\mu}_{t|t-1} \equiv E[\mathbf{y}_t|\mathbf{y}_{t-1}] = \mathbf{a}_0 + \sum_{j=1}^{p} \mathbf{A}_j \mathbf{y}_{t-j}$. Again, for notational convenience, we can transform Eq. (3.11) by defining $\tilde{\mathbf{y}}_t = \mathbf{y}_t - \boldsymbol{\mu}$:

$$\tilde{\mathbf{y}}_t = \mathbf{A}_1\tilde{\mathbf{y}}_{t-1} + \mathbf{A}_2\tilde{\mathbf{y}}_{t-2} + \cdots + \mathbf{A}_p\tilde{\mathbf{y}}_{t-p} + \mathbf{u}_t. \tag{3.67}$$

Using this equation and applying the same techniques that we have applied in the case of the VAR(1) in Section 3.2.2, it is possible to show that:

- $Cov[\mathbf{y}_t, \mathbf{u}_t] = \boldsymbol{\Sigma}_u$, the covariance matrix of $\mathbf{u}_t$;
- $Cov[\mathbf{y}_{t-h}, \mathbf{u}_t] = \mathbf{0}$ for any $h > 0$;
- $\boldsymbol{\Gamma}_h = \mathbf{A}_1\boldsymbol{\Gamma}_{h-1} + \cdots + \mathbf{A}_p\boldsymbol{\Gamma}_{h-p}$ for $h > 0$;
- $\boldsymbol{\rho}_h = \boldsymbol{\Psi}_1\boldsymbol{\rho}_{h-1} + \cdots + \boldsymbol{\Psi}_p\boldsymbol{\rho}_{h-p}$ for $h > 0$, where $\boldsymbol{\Psi}_i = \mathbf{D}^{-1/2}\mathbf{A}_i\mathbf{D}^{-1/2}$.

Naturally, all the considerations that we have expressed with references to a VAR(1) can easily be generalized to a VAR(p) model. Such an effort simplifies if we consider that a VAR(p) model can be represented as a Np-dimensional VAR(1). To this end, define

$$\underset{(Np)\times 1}{\boldsymbol{\xi}_t} \equiv \begin{bmatrix} \tilde{\mathbf{y}}_t \\ \tilde{\mathbf{y}}_{t-1} \\ \vdots \\ \tilde{\mathbf{y}}_{t-p+1} \end{bmatrix}, \quad \underset{(Np\times Np)}{\mathbf{F}_1} \equiv \begin{bmatrix} \mathbf{A}_1 & \mathbf{A}_2 & \cdots & \mathbf{A}_p \\ \mathbf{I}_N & \mathbf{0} & \cdots & \mathbf{0} \\ \mathbf{0} & \mathbf{I}_N & \cdots & \mathbf{0} \\ \vdots & \vdots & \cdots & \vdots \\ \mathbf{0} & \mathbf{0} & \cdots & \mathbf{0} \end{bmatrix}, \tag{3.68}$$

which is also known as the *companion matrix* of the VAR(p) system, and $\mathbf{U}_t \equiv [\mathbf{u}_t, \mathbf{0}\cdots\mathbf{0}]'$. Then a VAR($p$) model can be written as

$$\boldsymbol{\xi}_t = \mathbf{F}_1\boldsymbol{\xi}_{t-1} + \mathbf{U}_t, \tag{3.69}$$

where

$$E[\mathbf{U}_t\mathbf{U}'_t] = \begin{bmatrix} \boldsymbol{\Sigma}_u & \mathbf{0} & \cdots & \mathbf{0} \\ \mathbf{0} & \mathbf{0} & \cdots & \mathbf{0} \\ \vdots & \vdots & \cdots & \vdots \\ \mathbf{0} & \mathbf{0} & \cdots & \mathbf{0} \end{bmatrix} \quad \text{and} \quad E[\mathbf{U}_t\mathbf{U}'_{t-h}] = \mathbf{0} \text{ for } h > 0. \tag{3.70}$$

Clearly, Eq. (3.69) can be represented in the same form of Eq. (3.48), that is, in its VMA representation,

$$\boldsymbol{\xi}_t = \mathbf{U}_t + \mathbf{F}_1\mathbf{U}_{t-1} + \mathbf{F}_1^2\mathbf{U}_{t-2} + \cdots = \sum_{i=1}^{\infty} \mathbf{F}_1^i\mathbf{U}_{t-i} + \mathbf{U}_t, \tag{3.71}$$

that is, denoting $\boldsymbol{\Pi}_i \equiv \mathbf{J}\mathbf{F}_1^i\mathbf{J}'$, where $\mathbf{J} \equiv [\mathbf{I}_N, \mathbf{0}, \ldots, \mathbf{0}]'$, we have:

$$\boldsymbol{\xi}_t = \sum_{i=1}^{\infty} \boldsymbol{\Pi}_i\mathbf{U}_{t-i} + \mathbf{U}_t. \tag{3.72}$$

It follows that a VAR(p) model is stable (and thus stationary) as long as the eigenvalues of the *companion matrix* $\mathbf{F}_1$ defined in Eq. (3.68) are all less than one in modulus, which implies that the roots of the equation below must lie outside the unit circle:

$$\det(\mathbf{I}_N - \mathbf{A}_1 z - \cdots - \mathbf{A}_p z^p) = 0. \tag{3.73}$$

In other words, this condition states that the roots of the reverse characteristic polynomial associated with the matrix should all exceed one in modulus (i.e., they should lie *outside the unit circle*) or, equivalently, that the (inverse) roots from the characteristic polynomial should all lie inside the unit circle, as we already discussed in Chapter 2 for univariate AR models.

3.2.4 Estimation of a VAR(p) Model

Let us consider an unrestricted, stationary VAR(p) model similar to the one specified in Eq. (3.11) and suppose that we want to estimate its parameters.[2] Following the notation in Lütkepohl (2005), we can write Eq. (3.11) as

$$\mathbf{Y} = \mathbf{BZ} + \mathbf{U}, \tag{3.74}$$

where $\mathbf{Y} \equiv [\mathbf{y}_1, \mathbf{y}_2, \ldots, \mathbf{y}_t]$, $\mathbf{B} \equiv [\mathbf{a}_0, \mathbf{A}_1, \mathbf{A}_2, \ldots, \mathbf{A}_p]$, $\mathbf{U} \equiv [\mathbf{u}_1, \mathbf{u}_2, \ldots, \mathbf{u}_T]$, and $\mathbf{Z} \equiv [\mathbf{Z}_0, \mathbf{Z}_1, \ldots, \mathbf{Z}_{T-1}]$ with $\mathbf{Z}_t \equiv [\mathbf{1}', \mathbf{y}'_{t-1}, \mathbf{y}'_{t-2}, \ldots, \mathbf{y}'_{t-p+1}]'$. Also consider that $\mathbf{y} \equiv vec(\mathbf{Y})$, $\boldsymbol{\beta} \equiv vec(\mathbf{B})$, and $\mathbf{u} \equiv vec(\mathbf{U})$, where "vec" is the column stacking operator that stacks the columns of a matrix in a column vector. Also recall that the covariance matrix of the residuals is $\boldsymbol{\Sigma}_u$.

The *multivariate LS estimator* (here a GLS estimator) of $\boldsymbol{\beta}$ minimizes the quantity:

$$S(\boldsymbol{\beta}) = \mathbf{u}'(\mathbf{I}_T \boldsymbol{\Sigma}_u)^{-1}\mathbf{u}. \tag{3.75}$$

Although we shall skip the details of the computation of the estimator (which the interested reader may find in Lütkepohl, 2005), it is useful to report the solution to the problem:

$$\hat{\boldsymbol{\beta}} = \left((\mathbf{ZZ}')^{-1} \otimes \boldsymbol{\Sigma}_u\right)(\mathbf{Z} \otimes \boldsymbol{\Sigma}_u^{-1})\mathbf{y} = \left((\mathbf{ZZ}')^{-1}\mathbf{Z} \otimes \mathbf{I}_N\right)\mathbf{y}. \tag{3.76}$$

Notably, the GLS estimator in Eq. (3.76) is identical to the OLS estimator obtained by minimizing:

$$S(\boldsymbol{\beta}) = \mathbf{u}'\mathbf{u} = [\mathbf{y} - (\mathbf{Z}' \otimes \mathbf{I}_N)\boldsymbol{\beta}]' \, [\mathbf{y} - (\mathbf{Z}' \otimes \mathbf{I}_N)\boldsymbol{\beta}], \tag{3.77}$$

as demonstrated by Zellner (1962). Therefore as mentioned before, a *standard, unrestricted VAR(p) can be simply estimated equation-by-equation by OLS*. We shall call such an estimator $\hat{\mathbf{B}}$: by construction, being obtained by stacking rows of $\hat{\boldsymbol{\beta}}$ OLS estimators obtained equation-by-equation, $\hat{\mathbf{B}}$ is a $N \times (p+1)$ matrix.

The finite-sample properties of the LS estimator are difficult to derive analytically given the complexity of the expression in Eq. (3.76) and therefore we only discuss its asymptotic properties here. Under standard assumptions (see Lütkepohl, 2005, for details), the OLS estimator $\hat{\mathbf{B}}$ is consistent and asymptotically normally distributed,

$$\sqrt{T}\ \mathrm{vec}(\hat{\mathbf{B}} - \mathbf{B}) \xrightarrow{D} N(0, \boldsymbol{\Sigma}_{\hat{\mathbf{B}}}), \tag{3.78}$$

where the vec of $\hat{\mathbf{B}}$ needs to be taken to turn the estimator into a vector. Indeed, this result can also be written more intuitively as

$$\mathrm{vec}(\hat{\mathbf{B}}) \overset{a}{\sim} N(\mathrm{vec}(\mathbf{B}), \boldsymbol{\Sigma}_{\hat{\mathbf{B}}}/T), \tag{3.79}$$

where the "a" on the top of distribution symbol means "asymptotically distributed as" and $\boldsymbol{\Sigma}_{\hat{\mathbf{B}}} = \mathrm{plim}(\mathbf{ZZ}'/T)^{-1} \otimes \boldsymbol{\Sigma}_u$. Intuitively, this means that as $T \to \infty$, the covariance matrix of the OLS estimator converges (in the sense that deviations from the right-hand side of the formula carry a very small probability) to a complex web of inverse average cross-products between lagged values of the endogenous variables, $p\lim(\mathbf{ZZ}'/T)^{-1}$, multiplied by each of the elements of the covariance matrix of the structural residuals, $\boldsymbol{\Sigma}_u$. A few readers will note the analogy with the $\sigma_u^2(\mathbf{X}'\mathbf{X})^{-1}$ expression in Chapter 1.

The covariance matrix $\boldsymbol{\Sigma}_u$ can be estimated as

$$\hat{\boldsymbol{\Sigma}}_u = \frac{1}{T - Np}\sum_{t=1}^{T} \hat{\mathbf{u}}_t \hat{\mathbf{u}}'_t \quad \text{or } \tilde{\boldsymbol{\Sigma}}_u = \frac{1}{T}\sum_{t=1}^{T} \hat{\mathbf{u}}_t \hat{\mathbf{u}}'_t \tag{3.80}$$

where $\hat{\mathbf{u}}_t = \mathbf{y}_t - \mathbf{BZ}_{t-1}$. Both estimators are consistent and asymptotically normally distributed independently of $\hat{\mathbf{B}}$. The first estimator is sometimes referred to as the "degree-of-freedom adjusted" version of the covariance matrix estimator.

Alternatively, one may estimate a VAR(p) model using maximum likelihood (ML) methods. Given a sample of T observations on the N-variate variable $\mathbf{Y}$ defined as previously and a presample of p initial conditions $y_{-p+1}, y_{-p+2}, \ldots, y_0$, under the assumption that the process is stationary and that innovations are a Gaussian multivariate white noise, the variables $\mathbf{Y} = [\mathbf{y}_1, \mathbf{y}_2, \ldots, \mathbf{y}_T]'$ will also be jointly normally distributed (although the assumption of normal distribution is not necessary to use ML methods, see Chapter 5). In addition, because the multivariate

2. A model is said to be unrestricted when the estimation process is allowed to determinate any possible value for the unknown parameters; on the contrary, a model is restricted if the estimation procedure restricts the parameters in some way (for instance, by imposing that some of them is equal to constant values).

white noise is assumed to be Gaussian, the innovations at different times will be independent (which allows for considerable simplification when computing the likelihood function). The noise error terms are assumed to be independent with covariance matrix $\boldsymbol{\Sigma}_u$ and, as an implication, $\mathbf{u}$ (that is the vectorization of $\mathbf{U}$ as discussed previously) has a covariance matrix $\boldsymbol{\Sigma}_U = \mathbf{I}_T \otimes \boldsymbol{\Sigma}_u$. As a cumulative result of all these assumptions, $\mathbf{u}$ has the following NT-variate normal density:

$$f_{\mathbf{u}}(\mathbf{u}) = (2\pi)^{-\frac{NT}{2}}|\mathbf{I}_T \otimes \boldsymbol{\Sigma}_u|^{-\frac{1}{2}}\exp\left(-\frac{1}{2}\mathbf{u}'(\mathbf{I}_T \otimes \boldsymbol{\Sigma}_u^{-1})\mathbf{u}\right). \quad (3.81)$$

The density function in Eq. (3.81) can also be expressed in terms of the endogenous variables:

$$f_y(\mathbf{y}) = (2\pi)^{-\frac{NT}{2}}|\mathbf{I}_T \otimes \boldsymbol{\Sigma}_u|^{-\frac{1}{2}}\exp\left(-\frac{1}{2}(\mathbf{Y}-\mathbf{BZ})'(\mathbf{I}_T \otimes \boldsymbol{\Sigma}_u^{-1})(\mathbf{Y}-\mathbf{BZ})\right). \quad (3.82)$$

Therefore, the log-likelihood that should be maximized can be represented as follows:

$$\begin{aligned}\ell(\mathbf{B}, \boldsymbol{\Sigma}_u; \mathbf{Y}, \mathbf{Z}) = \ln f_y(\mathbf{Y}) &= -\frac{NT}{2}\ln(2\pi) - \frac{T}{2}\ln|\boldsymbol{\Sigma}_u| - \frac{1}{2}(\mathbf{Y}-\mathbf{BZ})'(\mathbf{I}_T \otimes \boldsymbol{\Sigma}_u^{-1})(\mathbf{Y}-\mathbf{BZ}) \\ &= -\frac{NT}{2}\ln(2\pi) - \frac{T}{2}\ln|\boldsymbol{\Sigma}_u| - \frac{1}{2}\mathrm{tr}\left(\mathbf{U}'\boldsymbol{\Sigma}_u^{-1}\mathbf{U}\right).\end{aligned} \quad (3.83)$$

Importantly, under the assumption of Gaussian innovations, the OLS estimator in Eq. (3.76) is equivalent (conditional on the initial values, i.e., the equivalence is in fact to a quasi-ML because of this form of conditioning, see Chapter 5, for additional details) to the ML estimator of the coefficients. Moreover, the ML estimator of the matrix $\boldsymbol{\Sigma}_u$ is

$$\tilde{\boldsymbol{\Sigma}}_u = \frac{1}{T}\sum_{t=1}^{T}\hat{\mathbf{u}}_t\hat{\mathbf{u}}_t', \quad (3.84)$$

which is nothing else than the average cross-vector product of the OLS residuals. Substituting the expression for the matrix $\tilde{\boldsymbol{\Sigma}}_u$ that maximizes the likelihood, in the class of all symmetric positive definite matrices, back into Eq. (3.83), we obtain

$$\ell(\mathbf{B}, \boldsymbol{\Sigma}_u; \mathbf{Y}, \mathbf{Z}) = -\frac{NT}{2}\ln(2\pi) - \frac{T}{2}\ln\left|\tilde{\boldsymbol{\Sigma}}_u\right| - \frac{1}{2}NT. \quad (3.85)$$

This object is also known as the concentrated log-likelihood of the VAR(p) model. Optimizing Eq. (3.83) in one pass or maximizing over Eqs. (3.84) and (3.85) iterating between the two objects until convergence is achieved will return identical results. Example 3.3 shows the typical estimation outputs of OLS estimation of a VAR model.

EXAMPLE 3.3

Consider the weekly yields of the 1-month, 1-year, 5-year, and 10-year US Treasury bonds between January 1990 and December 2016 (for a total of 1408 observations). Suppose that we specify a VAR(1) model for the series. Using E-Views, we have estimated the following model:

$$\begin{bmatrix} y_{1M,t} \\ y_{1Y,t} \\ y_{5Y,t} \\ y_{10Y,t} \end{bmatrix} = \begin{bmatrix} \underset{(0.775)}{-0.008} \\ \underset{(0.042)}{0.021} \\ \underset{(0.527)}{0.009} \\ \underset{(0.217)}{0.016} \end{bmatrix} + \begin{bmatrix} \underset{(0.000)}{0.835} & \underset{(0.000)}{0.219} & \underset{(0.035)}{-0.083} & \underset{(0.288)}{0.032} \\ \underset{(0.000)}{-0.031} & \underset{(0.000)}{1.023} & \underset{(0.028)}{0.034} & \underset{(0.010)}{-0.031} \\ \underset{(0.012)}{-0.016} & \underset{(0.059)}{0.022} & \underset{(0.000)}{0.993} & \underset{(0.960)}{-0.001} \\ \underset{(0.260)}{-0.007} & \underset{(0.456)}{0.008} & \underset{(0.703)}{0.008} & \underset{(0.000)}{0.988} \end{bmatrix} \begin{bmatrix} y_{1M,t-1} \\ y_{1Y,t-1} \\ y_{5Y,t-1} \\ y_{10Y,t-1} \end{bmatrix} + \begin{bmatrix} u_{1M,t} \\ u_{1Y,t} \\ u_{5Y,t} \\ u_{10Y,t} \end{bmatrix},$$

where p-values are reported in brackets. The estimated covariance matrix of the residuals is:

$$\hat{\boldsymbol{\Sigma}}_u = \begin{bmatrix} 0.043 & 0.001 & 0.001 & 0.001 \\ 0.001 & 0.007 & 0.007 & 0.005 \\ 0.001 & 0.007 & 0.012 & 0.011 \\ 0.001 & 0.005 & 0.011 & 0.012 \end{bmatrix}.$$

(Continued)

EXAMPLE 3.3 (Continued)

The complete estimation output is reported in Table 3.3. Below each estimated coefficient the reader finds the standard errors and the associated *p*-values (in brackets). The coefficients that are statistically significant at a size of the test lower or equal to 5% are boldfaced.

Each column of Table 3.3 represents one equation of the system; because usually equations are written as rows, this implies that they have been flipped around to populate the columns. For instance, the first column corresponds to the first equation of the VAR(1):

$$y_{1M,t} = \underset{(0.775)}{-0.008} + \underset{(0.000)}{0.835}\, y_{1M,t-1} + \underset{(0.022)}{0.219}\, y_{1Y,t-1} - \underset{(0.039)}{0.083}\, y_{5Y,t-1} + \underset{(0.288)}{0.032}\, y_{10Y,t-1} + u_t.$$

As we have discussed, each equation can be estimated separately by OLS. Therefore, the second panel of Table 3.3 presents standard OLS regression statistics for each equation (including the R^2 and the adjusted R^2), to which we can attribute the same meaning that has been attached to them in Chapter 1. For example the *F*-statistic refers to the null hypothesis that all the lags of the endogenous variables are jointly nonsignificant in each of the system equations. The numbers at the very bottom of the table are instead the summary statistics for the VAR system as a whole. For instance, because an overall, multivariate R^2 statistic is not obviously defined, while for each single equation we do report one R^2, in overall terms it makes sense to report the maximized log-likelihood, also because we know that the OLS and ML estimators are identical when the errors are multivariate normal.

In this example, we have assumed that one lag of the endogenous variables was sufficient to explain the key features of the data. However, this assumption was rather arbitrary. Therefore, in Section 3.2.5, we shall discuss how we can decide the appropriate lag length for a general VAR model.

TABLE 3.3 Estimation Output of a VAR(1) Model for the 1-Month, 1-, 5-, and 10-Year Yields of the US Treasury Bonds

	Yield 1 Month	Yield 1 Year	Yield 5 Years	Yield 10 Years
Yield 1 month (−1)	**0.835**	**−0.031**	**−0.016**	−0.007
	0.012	0.005	0.007	0.006
	(0.000)	(0.000)	(0.012)	(0.26)
Yield 1 year (−1)	**0.219**	**1.023**	0.022	0.008
	0.022	0.009	0.012	0.011
	(0.000)	(0.000)	(0.059)	(0.456)
Yield 5 years (−1)	**−0.083**	**0.034**	**0.993**	0.008
	0.039	0.015	0.021	0.020
	(0.035)	(0.028)	(0.000)	(0.703)
Yield 10 years (−1)	0.032	**−0.031**	−0.001	**0.988**
	0.030	0.012	0.016	0.015
	(0.288)	(0.01)	(0.96)	(0.000)
C	−0.008	0.021	0.009	0.016
	0.027	**0.010**	0.014	0.013
	(0.775)	(0.042)	(0.527)	(0.217)
R^2	0.993	0.999	0.997	0.997
Adj. R^2	0.993	0.999	0.997	0.997
Sum sq. resids	59.956	9.306	16.509	15.014

(Continued)

TABLE 3.3 (Continued)

	Yield 1 Month	Yield 1 Year	Yield 5 Years	Yield 10 Years
S.E. equation	0.207	0.081	0.108	0.103
F-statistic	51,568.215	303,363.793	139,899.774	117,486.468
Log-likelihood	224.179	1535.678	1132.122	1198.978
Akaike AIC	− 0.311	− 2.174	− 1.601	− 1.696
Schwarz SC	− 0.293	− 2.156	− 1.582	− 1.677
Mean dependent	3.035	3.166	4.155	4.735
S.D. dependent	2.512	2.393	2.166	1.893
Determinant resid. covariance (dof adj.)		0.000		
Determinant resid. covariance		0.000		
Log-likelihood		6215.082		
Akaike information criterion		− 8.800		
Schwarz criterion		− 8.725		

Before we move on, we shall summarize below two extremely important results that we have discussed (although we have not provided the proofs) in this section:

- when a reduced-form VAR is unconstrained, the GLS estimator is the same as the OLS estimator and therefore an *unconstrained VAR* can be estimated equation-by-equation by OLS;
- for an unconstrained VAR, the ML and OLS estimators are the same *under the assumption of Gaussian innovations* (further discussion of this topic is provided in on-line supplementary material).

3.2.5 Specification of a Vector Autoregressive Model and Hypothesis Testing

In Section 3.2.4, we have discussed how to estimate a VAR model of order p, but we have not explained how a researcher may go about deciding the appropriate number of lags to be included. In general, increasing the order of a VAR model reduces the (absolute) size of the residuals and improves the fit of the model, but also damages its forecasting power. Equivalently, as it is often the case in applied econometrics, by increasing the number of parameters of the model, we generally improve its in-sample accuracy, at expenses of its out-of-sample predictive power. This occurs because in a VAR, long lag lengths quickly consume degrees of freedom in the individual regression equations (i.e., the number of observations minus the number of parameters to be estimated): if the lag length is specified to be p, each of the N equations will contain Np coefficients plus the intercept term. Therefore, appropriate lag selection is usually crucial to the usefulness of VAR(p) models. In the following, we discuss the selection of the common lag length parameter p to apply to all equations of the VAR model. This prevents us from considering the case of *restricted, standard VAR* models in which the structure and number of lags included in each equation may vary across different equations. These models can be useful but tend to be less frequently used in applied finance.[3]

3. This has a simple justification: when the VAR includes restrictions, then the numerical equivalence between ML, GLS, and OLS estimators breaks down, and consistent estimation needs to be performed using ML methods applied to the full multivariate model. As for their specification, the number of lags in each of the individual equations is often specified using simple t- or F-tests to either go general-to-simple, or simple-to-general. Moreover, there is an inner incoherence between estimating a multivariate model by MLE and performing lag length specification tests at an equation-by-equation level.

A first method that can be used to select the appropriate lag length is the *likelihood ratio (LR) test.* To understand how this works when applied to the selection of p, suppose that we want to test the hypothesis that a set of variables was generated from a Gaussian VAR with p_0 lags against the alternative specification of $p_1 > p_0$ lags. For instance, assume that we aim at testing whether four lags are appropriate, against an alternative specification with five lags. Under the assumption of normally distributed shocks entertained earlier (or when the VAR is assumed to be correctly specified under the quasi-maximum likelihood estimation (MLE) principle), the LR statistic is

$$\mathrm{LRT}(p_0, p_1) = T\left(\ln\left|\tilde{\Sigma}_u^{p_0}\right| - \ln\left|\tilde{\Sigma}_u^{p_1}\right|\right), \tag{3.86}$$

where T is the number of usable observations, $|\tilde{\Sigma}_u^{p_0}|$ is the determinant of the covariance matrix estimated under the hypothesis that the VAR model includes p_0 (say, 4) lags of all the variables and $|\tilde{\Sigma}_u^{p_1}|$ is the determinant of the covariance matrix estimated under the alternative hypothesis that the VAR model contains p_1 (say, 5) lags.

As an alternative, Sims (1980) has proposed a small sample modification of the LR statistic in Eq. (3.87) that consists of using $T-(Np+1)$ rather than T as its scale factor, where $Np+1$ is the number of parameters per equation under the alternative hypothesis:

$$\mathrm{LRT}'(p_0, p_1) = (T - Np - 1)\left(\ln\left|\tilde{\Sigma}_u^{p_0}\right| - \ln\left|\tilde{\Sigma}_u^{p_1}\right|\right). \tag{3.87}$$

Both statistics have an asymptotic χ^2 distribution with degrees of freedom equal to the number of restrictions in the system, $N^2(p_1-p_0)$. In our example, there are N restrictions in each of the N equation, for a total number of N^2 restrictions. Large values of the test statistics in Eqs. (3.86) and (3.87) trigger a rejection of the null hypothesis that p_0 lags are sufficient to capture the key features of the (conditional mean function of the) data. On the contrary, if the calculated value of the statistic is less than the critical value of the χ^2 corresponding to the specified size of the test, we will not be able to reject the null that p_0 lags are sufficient. When this occurs, we may think of restricting the model even more, and calculate the LR statistic under the null that less than p_0 (say, $p_0 - 1 \geq 1 = 3$) are adequate, against the alternative of p_0 and to iterate this procedure until we cannot reject the null hypothesis. This way of specifying the model by sequential LR testing the lag order of a VAR(p) is said to represent a *general-to-simple approach.*[4]

On the one hand, LR tests are quite intuitive, and they are applicable to any type of cross- and within-equation restrictions. For instance, let Σ_u^U and Σ_u^R be the covariance matrices of the residuals of the unrestricted system and of the restricted one, respectively, for whatever types of restrictions (e.g., that the covariances between alternative pairs of reduced-form residuals be identical). Then the statistic

$$T\left(\ln\left|\tilde{\Sigma}_u^R\right| - \ln\left|\tilde{\Sigma}_u^U\right|\right) \tag{3.88}$$

can be compared to a χ^2 distribution characterized by a number of degrees of freedom equal to the number of restrictions in the system. In case the resulting sample statistic is less than the critical value under a χ^2 at the specified size level, we do not reject the null hypothesis that the restricted model is adequate to fit the data.

On the other hand, LR tests can only be used to perform a pairwise comparison of two VAR systems, one that is obtained as a restricted version of the other. We also say that the smaller VAR with fewer lags is *nested inside* the bigger VAR with a larger number of lags. As a consequence, if we want to determine the appropriate number of lags that are needed to best characterize a sample, we have first to specify the largest VAR and then proceed to pair it down until we cannot reject the null hypothesis, meaning that while in some applications going simple-to-general may be logically appealing, sequential LR testing is inconsistent with it. A further drawback of the LR test approach is that, as already emphasized, the χ^2 distribution of the test statistic will be valid in finite samples only under the assumption that errors from each equation are normally distributed. In general, without distributional assumptions, it is unclear whether performing LR tests may have any merit. Finally, when the sample size is small, it remains unclear whether LR tests may display reasonable power without being subject to substantial size distortions (see Hoffman and Schlagenhauf, 1982, for a discussion).

---

4. Technically, a general-to-simple approach should impose that the size of the tests be adjusted because—being based on a common sample—the tests fail to be independent. However, this issue tends to be disregarded in practice.

An alternative approach to the selection of the appropriate lag length is to minimize a multivariate version of the information criteria that were firstly presented in Chapter 2, namely:

$$(M)\text{AIC} = \ln\left|\tilde{\Sigma}_u\right| + 2\frac{k}{T}, \tag{3.89}$$

$$(M)\text{SBC} = \ln\left|\tilde{\Sigma}_u\right| + \frac{k}{T}\ln(T), \tag{3.90}$$

$$(M)\text{HQIC} = \ln\left|\tilde{\Sigma}_u\right| + 2\frac{k}{T}\ln(\ln(T)), \tag{3.91}$$

where (M) stands for multivariate (to signal that this is a multivariate generalization of the univariate versions proposed in Chapter 2), $\tilde{\Sigma}_u$ is the estimated covariance matrix of the residuals, T is the number of observations in the sample, and k is the total number of regressors across all equations in the VAR(p) (i.e., $N^2p + N$, where N is the number of equations and p is the number of lags).[5] The intuition behind the criteria and the properties that we discussed in Chapter 2 fully apply to their multivariate generalizations.

Finally, it is interesting to introduce one additional criterion to determine the model order/lag length proposed by Akaike (1969), namely, the *final prediction error* (FPE) measure:

$$\text{FPE}(p) = \left[\frac{T+Np+1}{T-Np+1}\right]^N \left|\tilde{\Sigma}_u\right|, \tag{3.92}$$

where $\left|\tilde{\Sigma}_u\right|$ is the determinant of the estimated covariance matrix of the residuals from a given VAR(p) model. Example 3.4 shows how these criteria can be used and compared to select the best fitting VAR(p) model.

EXAMPLE 3.4

In Example 3.3, we have specified a VAR(1) model for the weekly yields of 1-month, 1-year, 5-year, and 10-year US Treasury bonds. However, we have failed to check whether a larger VAR model could be more appropriate to fit the data.

Table 3.4 presents the values of the information criteria that we have just discussed for a number of lags ranging between 0 and 15. It also reports the maximized log-likelihood associated with each model and the sequential (modified, in the sense that it is computed applying Sims' small sample adjusted in Eq. (3.87)) log-likelihood test outcomes. Therefore, the second row reports the LR test of $p = 1$ versus the alternative $p = 2$, the third row tests the null of $p = 2$ versus the alternative $p = 3$, and so on. In general the kth row uses an LR statistic to test the null of $p = k - 1$ versus the alternative of $p = k$. The model selected by each criterion is boldfaced.

Unsurprisingly, as we have already observed in Chapter 2, different criteria may lead to different lag selections. In this case the AIC and the FPE select quite a large VAR(11) model, while the Schwarz and the Hannan-Quinn (HQ) criteria favor a more parsimonious VAR(2) model. However, a VAR(11) model for the four Treasury yield series requires the estimation of a 180 parameters ($N^2p + N = 4^2 \times 11 + 4 = 180$) with a *saturation ratio* (i.e., the number of observations available across the entire model per each parameter that has to be estimated) of only 7.8. Instead, a VAR(2) model implies the estimation of only 36 parameters, with a much safer saturation ratio of 39.1 parameters. Therefore, we elect to specify and estimate the VAR(2) model later (p-values are in parentheses):

$$\begin{bmatrix} y_{1M,t} \\ y_{1Y,t} \\ y_{5Y,t} \\ y_{10Y,t} \end{bmatrix} = \begin{bmatrix} \underset{(0.725)}{-0.001} \\ \underset{(0.168)}{0.014} \\ \underset{(0.793)}{0.004} \\ \underset{(0.236)}{0.016} \end{bmatrix} + \begin{bmatrix} \underset{(0.000)}{\mathbf{0.877}} & \underset{(0.110)}{0.170} & \underset{(0.515)}{-0.118} & \underset{(0.796)}{0.042} \\ \underset{(0.039)}{\mathbf{-0.021}} & \underset{(0.000)}{\mathbf{1.185}} & \underset{(0.149)}{0.010} & \underset{(0.456)}{-0.046} \\ \underset{(0.400)}{-0.012} & \underset{(0.800)}{-0.014} & \underset{0.000}{\mathbf{1.270}} & \underset{(0.431)}{0.066} \\ \underset{(0.727)}{-0.005} & \underset{(0.327)}{-0.051} & \underset{(0.157)}{0.126} & \underset{(0.000)}{\mathbf{1.098}} \end{bmatrix} \begin{bmatrix} y_{1M,t-1} \\ y_{1Y,t-1} \\ y_{5Y,t-1} \\ y_{10Y,t-1} \end{bmatrix}$$

$$+ \begin{bmatrix} \underset{(0.057)}{0.049} & \underset{(0.591)}{0.059} & \underset{(0.865)}{0.031} & \underset{(0.965)}{-0.007} \\ \underset{(0.000)}{\mathbf{-0.044}} & \underset{(0.000)}{\mathbf{-0.167}} & \underset{(0.240)}{-0.081} & \underset{(0.649)}{-0.028} \\ \underset{0.068}{-0.024} & \underset{(0.507)}{-0.037} & \underset{(0.002)}{\mathbf{1.270}} & \underset{(0.357)}{0.077} \\ \underset{(0.454)}{-0.010} & \underset{(0.258)}{-0.061} & \underset{(0.153)}{-0.127} & \underset{(0.191)}{-0.104} \end{bmatrix} \begin{bmatrix} y_{1M,t-2} \\ y_{1Y,t-2} \\ y_{5Y,t-2} \\ y_{10y,t-2} \end{bmatrix} + \begin{bmatrix} u_{1M,t} \\ u_{1Y,t} \\ u_{5Y,t} \\ u_{10y,t} \end{bmatrix},$$

(Continued)

5. When a VAR is estimated equation-by-equation by OLS, the covariance matrix is just computed residually as a result of the estimation process, as we know from Chapter 1. However, when a VAR model is estimated by MLE (and this must occur when it is restricted and thus OLS is not a consistent estimator), we should in principle take into account also the $N(N + 1)/2$ elements of the covariance matrix as parameters to be estimated.

EXAMPLE 3.4 (Continued)

with estimated covariance matrix of residuals equal to

$$\hat{\Sigma}_u = \begin{bmatrix} 0.043 & 0.001 & 0.001 & 0.001 \\ 0.001 & 0.006 & 0.006 & 0.005 \\ 0.001 & 0.006 & 0.011 & 0.010 \\ 0.001 & 0.005 & 0.010 & 0.010 \end{bmatrix}.$$

The coefficients that are significant at a confidence level lower or equal than 5% have been highlighted.

TABLE 3.4 VAR Selection Criteria Applied to 1-Month, 1-, 5-, and 10-Year US Treasury Yields

Lag	Log *L*	LR	FPE	AIC	SC	HQ
0	−4979.73	NA	0.014977	7.150265	7.165301	7.155887
1	6156.06	22191.71	1.77E-09	−8.803535	−8.728357	−8.775426
2	6258.44	203.4223	1.56E-09	−8.927455	**−8.792134**	**−8.876858**
3	6278.01	38.77297	1.55E-09	−8.932576	−8.737112	−8.859491
4	6293.26	30.13075	1.55E-09	−8.931501	−8.675895	−8.835930
5	6348.24	108.3155	1.47E-09	−8.987436	−8.671686	−8.869376
6	6369.05	40.86544	1.46E-09	−8.994331	−8.618439	−8.853784
7	6384.72	30.68329	1.46E-09	−8.993854	−8.557819	−8.830819
8	6400.32	30.47299	1.46E-09	−8.993288	−8.497111	−8.807766
9	6413.26	25.19834	1.47E-09	−8.988902	−8.432582	−8.780893
10	6436.94	45.96209	1.45E-09	−8.999917	−8.383454	−8.769420
11	6454.65	34.26402	**1.45E-09**	**−9.002361**	−8.325756	−8.749377
12	6467.35	24.52523	1.45E-09	−8.997640	−8.260892	−8.722168
13	6484.71	33.38878	1.45E-09	−8.999583	−8.202692	−8.701623
14	6498.44	26.33077	1.46E-09	−8.996321	−8.139288	−8.675874
15	6509.84	21.81540	1.47E-09	−8.989731	−8.072555	−8.646797

3.2.6 Forecasting With a Vector Autoregressive Model

Similarly to what we have discussed in Chapter 2, for AR models, one obvious application of VAR models is forecasting. Analogously to what we have discussed with reference to univariate models, also in the context of VAR models, loss functions that lead to the minimization of the mean squared forecast error (MSFE) are the most widely used. Evidence in favor of using the MSFE as key forecasting index is given, for instance, by Granger (1969b) and Granger and Newbold (1986), who show that minimum MSFE forecasts also minimize a range of loss functions other than the MSFE. Moreover, for many loss functions, the optimal prediction function is a simple function of minimum MSFE predictions.

Consider a (stationary) N-dimensional VAR(p) process similar to the one in Eq. (3.11). Assume that $\mathbf{u}_t$ is an independent multivariate white noise, such that $\mathbf{u}_t$ and $\mathbf{u}_s$ are independent for $t \neq s$ and thus $E_t[\mathbf{u}_{t+h}|\Im_t] = 0$ for $h > 0$. The minimum time t MSFE prediction at a forecast horizon h is the conditional expected value

$$E_t[\mathbf{y}_{t+h}|\Im_t] = E_t[\mathbf{y}_{t+h}|\{\mathbf{y}_s|s \leq t\}], \tag{3.93}$$

where $\Im_t$ is the information set containing the variables up to and including period t. This prediction minimizes the MSFE of each component of the vector $\mathbf{y}_t$. Therefore,

$$E_t\left[\mathbf{y}_{t+h}|\Im_t\right] = \mathbf{a}_0 + \mathbf{A}_1 E_t\left[\mathbf{y}_{t+h-1}|\Im_t\right] + \cdots + \mathbf{A}_p E_t\left[\mathbf{y}_{t+h-p}|\Im_t\right], \tag{3.94}$$

is the optimal h-step-ahead predictor of a VAR(p) process. The formula in Eq. (3.94) can be used recursively to compute h-step-ahead predictions starting with $h = 1$. For instance, let us consider the case of a VAR(1) model. The one-step-ahead forecast of $\mathbf{y}_t$ with origin at time t is

$$E_t[\mathbf{y}_{t+1}|\Im_t] = \mathbf{a}_0 + \mathbf{A}_1 E_t[\mathbf{y}_t|\Im_t] = \mathbf{a}_0 + \mathbf{A}_1 \mathbf{y}_t, \tag{3.95}$$

where $E_t[\mathbf{y}_t|\Im_t] = \mathbf{y}_t$, given that we are at time t. Then, to obtain the two-step-ahead forecast we can simply use the value $E_t[\mathbf{y}_{t+1}|\Im_t]$ that we have just computed. Through this iterative process, we can compute the h-step-ahead forecast. The conditional expectation that turns out to provide the minimum MSFE has the following properties:

- it is an unbiased predictor, meaning that $E[\mathbf{y}_{t+h} - E_t[\mathbf{y}_{t+h}|\Im_t]] = 0$;
- if $\mathbf{u}_t$ is an independent white noise vector (that, as we shall recall, is a stronger assumption than being uncorrelated), $\text{MSFE}\left[E_t\left[\mathbf{y}_{t+h}\right]\right] = \text{MSFE}\left[E_t\left[\mathbf{y}_{t+h}|\mathbf{y}_t, \mathbf{y}_{t-1}\ldots\right]\right]$, meaning that MSFE of the prediction equals the conditional MSFE given $\mathbf{y}_t, \mathbf{y}_{t-1}, \ldots$.

In case $\mathbf{u}_t$ is not an independent white noise, additional assumptions are required to find the optimal prediction of a VAR(p) process. However, without these assumptions it is still possible to find the minimum MSFE predictor among those that are linear functions of $\mathbf{y}_t, \mathbf{y}_{t-1}, \ldots$. Without going into the details of the proof (which can be found in Lütkepohl, 2005), it can be shown that the best linear predictor in terms of MSFE minimization is:

$$E_t\left[\mathbf{y}_{t+h}|\Im_t\right] = \mathbf{a}_0 + \mathbf{A}_1 E_t\left[\mathbf{y}_{t+h-1}|\Im_t\right] + \cdots + \mathbf{A}_p E_t\left[\mathbf{y}_{t+h-p}|\Im_t\right]. \tag{3.96}$$

For the sake of simplicity we analyze again the case of a VAR(1) model, where the prediction function is

$$E_t[\mathbf{y}_{t+h}|\Im_t] = \mathbf{a}_0 + \mathbf{A}_1 E[\mathbf{y}_{t+h-1}|\Im_t]. \tag{3.97}$$

The one-step forecast error $\tilde{\mathbf{u}}_t(1)$ is simply:

$$\tilde{\mathbf{u}}_t(1) = \mathbf{y}_{t+1} - E_t\left[\mathbf{y}_{t+1}|\Im_t\right] = \mathbf{u}_{t+1}, \tag{3.98}$$

and the associated covariance matrix of forecast errors is $\boldsymbol{\Sigma}_u$. By iterating over this formula, we can obtain that the h-step forecast error $\tilde{\mathbf{u}}_t(h)$ as

$$\tilde{\mathbf{u}}_t(h) = \mathbf{y}_{t+h} - E_t\left[\mathbf{y}_{t+h}|\Im_t\right] = \sum_{i=0}^{h-1} \mathbf{A}_1^i \mathbf{u}_{t+h-i}, \tag{3.99}$$

where $\mathbf{A}^0 = \mathbf{I}_N$. The covariance matrix of the forecast errors is therefore $\sum_{i=0}^{h-1} \mathbf{A}_1^i \boldsymbol{\Sigma}(\mathbf{A}_1^i)'$. The generalization to a VAR(p) model is straightforward although computations are nontrivial (the interested reader is referred to Lütkepohl, 2005). Example 3.5 shows VAR models in action when it comes to prediction.

EXAMPLE 3.5

Fig. 3.2 shows the 1-week ahead forecasts of the 1-month, 1-, 5-, and 10-year US Treasury bond yields obtained from the VAR (2) model estimated in Example 3.4.

Table 3.5 reports the forecast accuracy measures that have been discussed in Chapter 2, namely, the root mean squared error (RMSE, which is just the square root of the mean square forecast error), the mean absolute error (MAE), and the mean absolute percentage error (MAPE). Clearly the lower these prediction error measures are the higher the practical usefulness of a model.

Obviously, these accuracy measures are useful when we would like to compare the predictive power of different models. For example, we may want to compare the forecast accuracy of the VAR(2) versus the VAR(11) model that was selected by the FPE and AIC criteria in Example 3.4. Table 3.6 displays the forecast accuracy measures for the VAR(11) model. It is evident that the VAR(2) and the VAR(11) models display very similar predictive power although the VAR(11) slightly outperforms the VAR(2) according to some specific indicators.

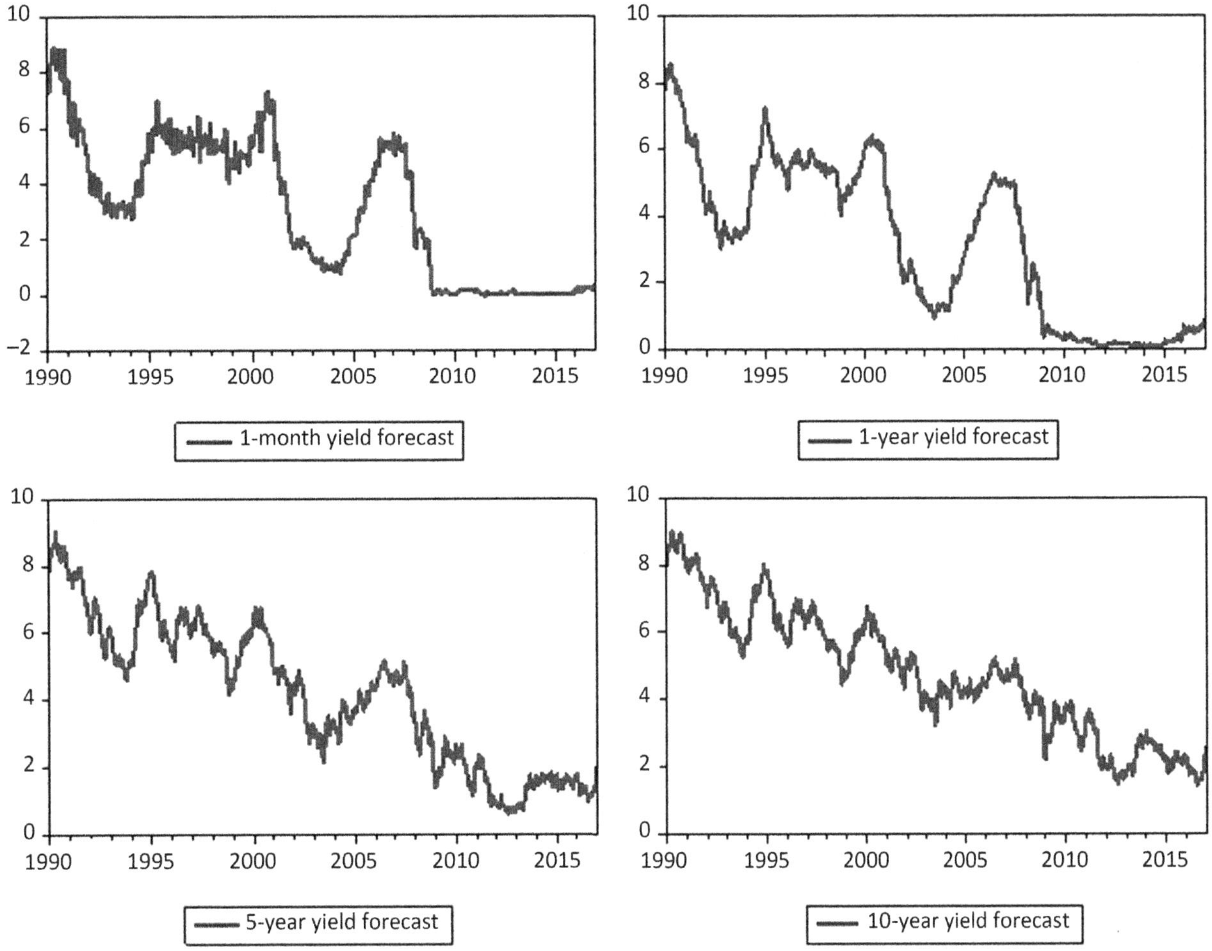

FIGURE 3.2 One-week ahead forecasts of 1-month, 1-, 5-, and 10-year US Treasury yields from a VAR(2).

TABLE 3.5 Forecast Accuracy Measures for a VAR(2) Model of 1-Month, 1-, 5-, and 10-Year US Treasury Yields

Variable	Inc. obs.	RMSE	MAE	MAPE
1-month yield	1409	0.21	0.10	35.18
1-year yield	1409	0.08	0.05	3.63
5-year yield	1409	0.11	0.08	2.74
10-year yield	1409	0.10	0.08	1.99

RMSE, root mean square error; *MAE*, mean absolute error; *MAPE*, mean absolute percentage error.

TABLE 3.6 Forecast Accuracy Measures for a VAR(11) Model of 1-Month, 1-, 5-, and 10-Year US Treasury Yields

Variable	Inc. obs.	RMSE	MAE	MAPE
1-month yield	1409	0.19	0.10	48.40
1-year yield	1409	0.08	0.05	3.96
5-year yield	1409	0.10	0.08	2.79
10-year yield	1409	0.10	0.08	1.99

RMSE, root mean square error; *MAE*, mean absolute error; *MAPE*, mean absolute percentage error.

3.3 STRUCTURAL ANALYSIS WITH VECTOR AUTOREGRESSIVE MODELS

3.3.1 Impulse Response Functions

In Section 3.2, we have discussed the statistical properties of a VAR(p) model, how it can be estimated, and how it can be used in forecasting applications. However, VAR models are often used in practice with the goal of understanding the *dynamic relationships* between the variables of interest. For instance, in Example 3.4, we have estimated a VAR(2) model for the 1-month, 1-, 5-, and 10-year US Treasury yield series and then, in Example 3.5, we have computed and assessed one-step-ahead forecasts. However, a researcher may also be interested in studying the effects that a sudden increase (decrease) in the 1-month rate, for instance as a result of a tight (expansive) monetary policy, may have on the other yields in the system (when these four specific maturity buckets are used to summarize the term structure of the Treasury yield curve). In other words a researcher may be interested in the effects that a shock to one (or more) variable(s) produces over the others. Therefore, in this section, we introduce IRFs. A general definition of IRF is as follows.

DEFINITION 3.4 (Impulse response function)

In the context of a VAR model, the IRFs trace out the time path of the effects of an exogenous shock to one (or more) of the endogenous variables on some or all of the other variables in a VAR system.

To simplify, let us start our discussion from the simple VAR(1) model (written in reduced form) discussed in Section 3.2.1, namely:

$$\begin{bmatrix} y_{1,t} \\ y_{2,t} \end{bmatrix} = \begin{bmatrix} a_{1,0} \\ a_{2,0} \end{bmatrix} + \begin{bmatrix} a_{1,1} & a_{1,2} \\ a_{2,1} & a_{2,2} \end{bmatrix} \begin{bmatrix} y_{1,t-1} \\ y_{2,t-1} \end{bmatrix} + \begin{bmatrix} u_{1,t} \\ u_{2,t} \end{bmatrix}. \tag{3.100}$$

We already know that a stationary VAR(p) model has a moving average representation, and, in particular this also applies to the VAR(1), that is, using a compact notation,

$$\mathbf{y}_t = \mathbf{a}_0 + \mathbf{A}_1 \mathbf{y}_{t-1} + \mathbf{u}_t, \tag{3.101}$$

can be rewritten as

$$\mathbf{y}_t = \boldsymbol{\mu} + \sum_{i=0}^{\infty} \mathbf{A}_1^i \mathbf{u}_{t-i}, \tag{3.102}$$

or, alternatively, recalling the algebraic steps that we have discussed in Section 3.2.2, to

$$\mathbf{y}_t = \boldsymbol{\mu} + \sum_{i=0}^{\infty} \boldsymbol{\Theta}_i \mathbf{u}_{t-i}, \tag{3.103}$$

that is,

$$\begin{bmatrix} y_{1,t} \\ y_{2,t} \end{bmatrix} = \begin{bmatrix} \mu_1 \\ \mu_2 \end{bmatrix} + \sum_{i=0}^{\infty} \begin{bmatrix} \theta_{1,1(i)} & \theta_{1,2(i)} \\ \theta_{2,1(i)} & \theta_{2,2(i)} \end{bmatrix} \begin{bmatrix} u_{1,t-i} \\ u_{2,t-i} \end{bmatrix}. \tag{3.104}$$

You will also recall from our discussion in Section 3.2.1 that the two error processes, $\{u_{1,t}\}$ and $\{u_{2,t}\}$ can be also represented in terms of the two sequences $\{\varepsilon_{1,t}\}$ and $\{\varepsilon_{2,t}\}$, that is, the structural (or pure), unobserved innovations:

$$\begin{bmatrix} u_{1,t} \\ u_{2,t} \end{bmatrix} = \frac{1}{1 - b_{1,2}b_{2,1}} \begin{bmatrix} 1 & -b_{1,2} \\ -b_{2,1} & 1 \end{bmatrix} \begin{bmatrix} \varepsilon_{1,t} \\ \varepsilon_{2,t} \end{bmatrix}. \tag{3.105}$$

Therefore, plugging Eq. (3.105) into (3.104), we obtain a 2×2 matrix $\boldsymbol{\Phi}_i$ equal to

$$\boldsymbol{\Phi}_i = \frac{\mathbf{A}_1^i}{1 - b_{1,2}b_{2,1}} \begin{bmatrix} 1 & -b_{1,2} \\ -b_{2,1} & 1 \end{bmatrix} = \frac{\boldsymbol{\Theta}_i}{1 - b_{1,2}b_{2,1}} \begin{bmatrix} 1 & -b_{1,2} \\ -b_{2,1} & 1 \end{bmatrix}, \tag{3.106}$$

and therefore

$$\mathbf{y}_t = \boldsymbol{\mu} + \sum_{i=0}^{\infty} \boldsymbol{\Phi}_i \boldsymbol{\varepsilon}_{t-i}. \tag{3.107}$$

It is now easy to see how the moving average representation of the VAR can be useful: the coefficients of the matrix $\mathbf{\Phi}_i$, that is, each $\phi_{i,j}$ can be used to generate the effects of shocks to the innovations $\varepsilon_{1,t}$, $\varepsilon_{2,t}$ on the entire time path of the $\{y_{1,t}\}$ and $\{y_{2,t}\}$ series. In other words the four coefficients $\phi_{1,1(i)}$, $\phi_{1,2(i)}$, $\phi_{2,1(i)}$, and $\phi_{2,2(i)}$ for each i can be regarded as *impact multipliers*. For instance, $\phi_{1,2(0)}$ represents the instantaneous impact on $y_{1,t}$ of a one-unit change in $\varepsilon_{2,t}$ (i.e., the structural innovation to $y_{2,t}$), while $\phi_{1,2(1)}$ is the one-period response of $y_{1,t}$ to the same unit change in $\varepsilon_{2,t-1}$. The cumulative effects of a one-unit shock (or impulse) to $\varepsilon_{2,t}$ on the variable $y_{1,t}$ after H periods can then be obtained by computing the sum $\sum_{i=0}^{H} \phi_{1,2(i)}$. Clearly the same result holds for the cumulative effects of a unit shock to $\varepsilon_{1,t}$ on $y_{2,t}$, which can be computed as $\sum_{i=0}^{H} \phi_{2,1(i)}$, and so on. Interestingly, if we let the horizon H approach to infinity, we obtain the so-called *long-run multipliers*. Indeed, as the sequences $\{y_{1,t}\}$ and $\{y_{2,t}\}$ are assumed to be stationary, it follows that $\sum_{i=0}^{\infty} \phi_{j,k(i)}^2$ for j, $k = 1, 2, \ldots, N$, is finite. Put into other words, because a VAR model can be easily generalized to contain N variables instead of two, the element $\phi_{j,k(i)}$, that is, the (j,k)th of the matrix $\mathbf{\Phi}_i$ represents the reaction of the jth variable of the system to a one-unit shock in a variable k, i periods ago. Therefore given Definition 3.4, the set of elements $\phi_{j,k(i)}$ with $i = 1, 2, \ldots, H$ can be easily seen as the *IRF* of the jth variable of the system, up to the period H. The sum $\sum_{i=0}^{H} \phi_{j,k(i)}$, that represents the cumulative effects of a shock to variable k on the variable j after H periods, is also known as the *cumulative response* of the variable j to a shock to the variable k.

What is the problem with the VAR representation in Eq. (3.107)? If the VAR system were identified, that is, if it were possible to recover all the parameters of the structural VAR model from the estimates of the VAR in its standard form, it would be possible to trace out the effects of a shock to one (or more) of the structural innovations to the variables. However, we already know from Section 3.2.1 that a VAR in its reduced form is under-identified by construction and therefore we are not able to compute the coefficients $\phi_{j,k(i)}$ from the OLS estimates of the VAR in its standard form unless we impose adequate restrictions. As we have seen in Section 3.2.1, one method to place these restrictions consists of the application of a Cholesky decomposition. In practice, by using a Cholesky decomposition, we can rewrite the VMA representation of a VAR(1) in Eq. (3.103) (note that this also applies to a VAR(p), because a VAR(p) can be rewritten as a VAR(1)) such that

$$\mathbf{y}_t = \boldsymbol{\mu} + \sum_{i=0}^{\infty} \mathbf{\Theta}_i \mathbf{W}\mathbf{W}^{-1}\mathbf{u}_{t-i}, \tag{3.108}$$

where $\mathbf{\Sigma}_u = \mathbf{W}\mathbf{\Sigma}\mathbf{W}'$, $\boldsymbol{\varepsilon}_t = \mathbf{W}^{-1}\mathbf{u}_{t-1}$, and $\mathbf{\Phi}_i = \mathbf{\Theta}_i\mathbf{W}$. It is easy to recognize that Eq. (3.108) is equivalent to Eq. (3.107). However, it should be already clear from Section 3.2.1 that a Cholesky decomposition allows only the shock to the first variable to contemporaneously affect all the other variables in the system. A shock to the second variable will produce a contemporaneous effect on all the variables in the system, but the first one (this may of course be impacted in the subsequent period, through the transmission effects mediated by the autoregressive coefficients). A shock to the third variable will affect all the variables in the system, but the first two, and so on. Therefore, it is important to recognize that this identification scheme forces a potentially important *identification asymmetry* on the system that is typical of Cholesky ordering schemes. For instance, in our initial bivariate example, a shock to $\varepsilon_{1,t}$ has a contemporaneous effect on both $u_{1,t}$ and $u_{2,t}$ (and thus on $y_{1,t}$ and $y_{2,t}$), but a shock to $\varepsilon_{2,t}$ does not contemporaneously impact $u_{1,t}$ (and thus $y_{1,t}$). For this reason, $y_{1,t}$ is said to be "casually prior" to $y_{2,t}$, a bit of language that will be better explained later on. Of course, as already emphasized in Section 3.2.1, a different ordering of the variables in the system would have been possible, implying a reverse ordering of the shocks and that $y_{2,t}$ would have been "casually prior" to $y_{1,t}$. To make our reasoning clearer, in Example 3.6 we see how the decomposition works in practice.

EXAMPLE 3.6

Let us consider a VAR(1) for the 1-month US Treasury bill and the 10-year US Treasury bond yields (the same series for the January 1990–December 2016 sample that we have estimated in Example 3.2):

$$\begin{bmatrix} y_{1M,t} \\ y_{10Y,t} \end{bmatrix} = \begin{bmatrix} \underset{[-2.5382]}{-0.0490} \\ \underset{[0.8711]}{0.0080} \end{bmatrix} + \begin{bmatrix} \underset{[210.6540]}{0.9819} & \underset{[0.4077]}{0.0209} \\ \underset{[3.3784]}{0.0009} & \underset{[240.0320]}{0.9970} \end{bmatrix} \begin{bmatrix} y_{1M,t-1} \\ y_{10Y,t-1} \end{bmatrix} + \begin{bmatrix} u_{1M,t} \\ u_{10Y,t} \end{bmatrix},$$

with estimated covariance matrix of the reduced-form residuals:

$$\hat{\mathbf{\Sigma}}_u \begin{bmatrix} 0.0476 & 0.0013 \\ 0.0013 & 0.011 \end{bmatrix}.$$

As we shall recall from Section 3.2.1, applying a Cholesky decomposition we get that $Var[u_{1M,t}] = \sigma_1^2$, $Var[u_{10Y,t}] = \sigma_2^2 - b_{2,1}\sigma_1^2$, $Cov[u_{1M,t}, u_{10Y,t}] = -b_{2,1}\sigma_1^2$. Therefore, $b_{2,1}$ is equal to,

$$b_{2,1} = -\frac{\hat{\sigma}_{1,2}}{\hat{\sigma}_1^2} = -\frac{0.0013}{0.4762} = -0.0027,$$

(*Continued*)

EXAMPLE 3.6 (Continued)

and Eqs. (3.29) and (3.30) become

$$u_{1M,t} = \varepsilon_{1,t}$$
$$u_{10Y,t} = \varepsilon_{2,t} - b_{2,1}\varepsilon_{1,t} = \varepsilon_{2,t} - 0.0027\varepsilon_{1,t}.$$

This means that a shock to $\varepsilon_{1,t}$ equal to one standard deviation (0.218, that is $\sqrt{0.0476}$) causes an immediate change by 0.218 in $u_{1M,t}$ (and thus in $y_{1M,t}$); in addition, it will also cause an immediate increase (albeit very small) of $0.218 \times 0.0027 = 0.0006$ in $u_{10Y,t}$ (and thus in the 10-year US Treasury yield) because of the implicit correlation structure that is admissible under the selected Cholesky scheme. At time $t+1$ the lagged value of the 1-month yield enters the first equation with a coefficient 0.9819 and thus after one period the 1-month yield will grow by $0.9819 \times 0.218 = 0.214$ (i.e., approximately 21 basis points, henceforth bps) above what it would have been without the shock. The 10-year yield would have been $0.9970 \times 0.0006 = 0.000598$ higher because of the effect of its own lag. In addition, the lagged value of the 1-month yield also enters the second equation with a coefficient 0.0009, and thus the 10-year US Treasury yield will rise by an additional $0.0009 \times 0.218 = 0.000196$; in total the 10-year US Treasury yield would be approximately 0.00079 higher with respect to what it would have been without a shock to the 1-month yield. Therefore, one period after the one standard deviation shock to the 1-month Treasury yield has occurred, the *cumulative response* of the 1-month Treasury yield to its own shock would have been $0.218 + 0.214 = 0.432$, that is, 43 bps. In addition, the accumulated response of the 10-year US Treasury yield to the one standard deviation shock to the 1-month Treasury yield would have been $0.0006 + 0.00079 = 0.00139$. The process then progresses further over subsequent rounds of impulse and reaction.

Alternatively, it is easy to see what happens if we give a one standard deviation shock to $\varepsilon_{2,t}$ (equal to 0.105): $u_{10Y,t}$ immediately increases by 0.105 (and so does $y_{10Y,t}$), but nothing happens to $u_{1M,t}$. Therefore, at time $t+1$ the 10-year yield would be higher by $0.9970 \times 0.105 = 0.10469$ (i.e., approximately 10 bps) because of the effect of its own lag (for an accumulated response of 0.209). In addition, the lag of the 10-year yield now affects the 1-month yield with a coefficient of 0.0209 and therefore the 1-month Treasury yield will be $0.0209 \times 0.10469 = 0.0021$ higher than it would have been without a shock happening to the 10-year US Treasury yield.

Fig. 3.3 depicts the IRFs to a one standard deviation shock to the 1-month yield and to the 10-year yield on the basis of a Cholesky triangular scheme that places the 1-month yield at the top of the variable ordering.

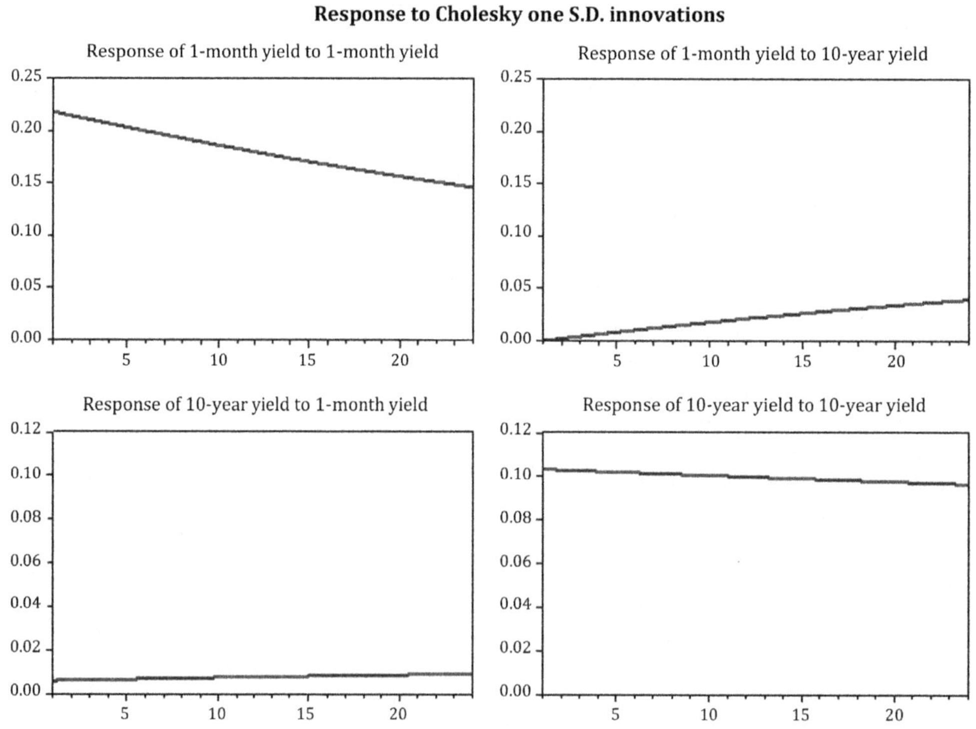

FIGURE 3.3 IRFs to shocks to 1-month and 10-year yields, ordered on the basis of a Cholesky triangular scheme that places shocks to the 1-month at the top of the ordering.

Notably, as we have seen in Example 3.6, it is not compulsory to give simple one standard deviation shocks. A researcher is free to give to the system all kinds of shocks that she is interested in or that she feels are economically plausible. However, it is quite common in practice to study the effects of a shock equal to one standard deviation, especially when the variables have different scales. Such a rescaling may sometimes give a better picture of the dynamic relationships among variables because the average scale of the innovations occurring in a system depends on their standard deviation.

Summing up, two points should be clear:

- a reduced-form VAR, although commonly employed in applied finance, is under-identified and it is not possible to recover the structural parameters from its estimates unless we impose some restrictions, that is, identification forces the researcher to impose some structure on the system;
- Cholesky decompositions provide a minimal set of restrictions concerning the simultaneous relationships among variables that can be used to identify the structural model (however, other identification schemes, based on a theoretical background, are of course possible but appear to be less common in finance).

It should be also clear that under a Cholesky decomposition the ordering of the variables in the system is important: it is indeed crucial which of the variables is placed first and which one is placed second, and so on. In addition, the relevance of the ordering depends on the magnitude of the correlation coefficients between the innovations $u_{1,t}$, $u_{2,t}, \ldots$, $u_{N,t}$: in our example, when $Cov[u_{1,t}, u_{2,t}] \simeq 0$, it must be that $b_{1,2} \simeq 0$, in which case none of the variables is simultaneously associated and the reduced-form VAR is practically isomorphic to the structural VAR, so that all standard shocks are also structural shocks. When the reduced-form shocks are instead highly correlated, as it is often the case, unfortunately, the ordering of the variables cannot be determined with statistical methods but has to be selected by the researcher. Therefore, as suggested by Sims (1981), it is often warmly suggested that a researcher tries different orderings of the variables to understand what are the implications to choose some restrictions instead of others in terms of the resulting estimates of the IRFs.

Another important issue with IRFs is that they are constructed using the estimated coefficients. Given that each coefficient is estimated with uncertainty (due to a variety of factors, such as small sample sizes and measurement error), the IRFs will contain sampling error as well, that is, they will be highly nonlinear transformations of the sample parameter estimates. Therefore, it is often advisable, after having computed and plotted the IRFs of interest, to also construct confidence intervals around them to account for the uncertainty that derives from parameter estimation. Although under some assumptions, confidence bands can be constructed relying on asymptotic theory that implies that OLS (equal to ML) parameter estimates are normally distributed, recently it has become common to use *bootstrapping methods*, see the Mathematical and Statistical Appendix at the end of this book for a brief introduction. The bootstrap is based on resampling from either the distribution of parameter estimates obtained from the true, original data (*parametric* bootstrap), or directly from the data with replacement to obtain blocks of consecutive observations (*nonparametric* bootstrap); in both cases the final goal is to generate a large number of alternative pseudo-samples then used to approximate the distribution of one or more sample statistics of interest—for instance, the IRFs of a VAR—computed across the pseudo-samples (see, for instance, Efron and Tibshirani, 1986). When applied to IRFs, bootstrapping techniques have two major advantages: first, they produce confidence intervals that are more reliable than those based on asymptotic theory (see Kilian, 1998); second, this methodology avoids the computation of exact expressions for the asymptotic variance of the IRF coefficients, which is otherwise rather complex (see Lütkepohl, 1991). The bootstrap method consists in the implementation of the following steps.

- Each equation is estimated by OLS/MLE and the vector series $\{\mathbf{u}_t^b\}$ of T errors (with T equal to the original sample size) is constructed by randomly sampling with replacement from the estimated residuals. Random sampling with replacement from an initial dataset means that T observations are drawn, randomly from the original sample. After each drawn the observation is replaced in the sample, so that any observation can be drawn more than once. Importantly, when drawing the observations, one has to properly consider the fact that the error terms are correlated across the equations, which implies that horizontal blocks of N different structural residuals are jointly drawn.
- The series $\{\mathbf{u}_t^b\}$ and the estimated coefficients are then used to construct a pseudo-vector of endogenous variable series, $\{\mathbf{y}_t^b\}$.
- The coefficients used to generate $\{\mathbf{y}_t^b\}$ are discarded and new coefficients are estimated from $\{\mathbf{y}_t^b\}$. The IRFs are computed from the newly estimated coefficients and saved, also indexed by the bootstrap iteration b.

When this procedure is repeated a sufficiently large number of times, $b = 1, 2, \ldots, B$, the resulting IRFs can be used to construct the confidence bands. As an example, a 95% confidence interval is the one that excludes the highest and the lowest bootstrapped, resampled 5% observations: for each horizon $h = 1, 2, \ldots, H$ the lowest (highest) 2.5% IRFs are excluded, and the interval is set to contain the remaining 95% IRFs. An IRF is considered to be statistically significant if 0 is not included in the bootstrapped confidence interval.

EXAMPLE 3.7

We are now ready to return to Example 3.4. In case of a positive shock to the short end of the yield curve (a tightening of conventional monetary policy), what can we expect to happen to the rest of the curve, on average? Let us consider the VAR(2) model estimated in Example 3.4 and compute the IRFs to a one standard deviation positive shock (equal to approximately 21 bps) to the 1-month yield. Fig. 3.4 shows the responses of each of the variables in the system over 52 weeks, that is, for $h = 1, 2, \ldots, 52$. The dotted lines represent the 95% bootstrapped confidence intervals.

Unsurprisingly the response of the 1-month yield to its own shock is positive and quite persistent. However, after approximately 18 weeks such an effect turns negative and statistically significant. Conversely the other Treasury yields display weak or no effects: the responses of the 5- and 10-year yields to the shock are never significant (as 0 is always in the confidence interval, the null hypothesis that the IRF is equal to 0 cannot be rejected). The 1-year yield is mildly positively affected by the shocks, but after 2 weeks the response turns negative (small, but significant). If one takes a 1-month US T-bills positive shock as indicative of a monetary policy tightening, the figure gives rather attenuated indications of policy transmission to longer-term riskless rates.

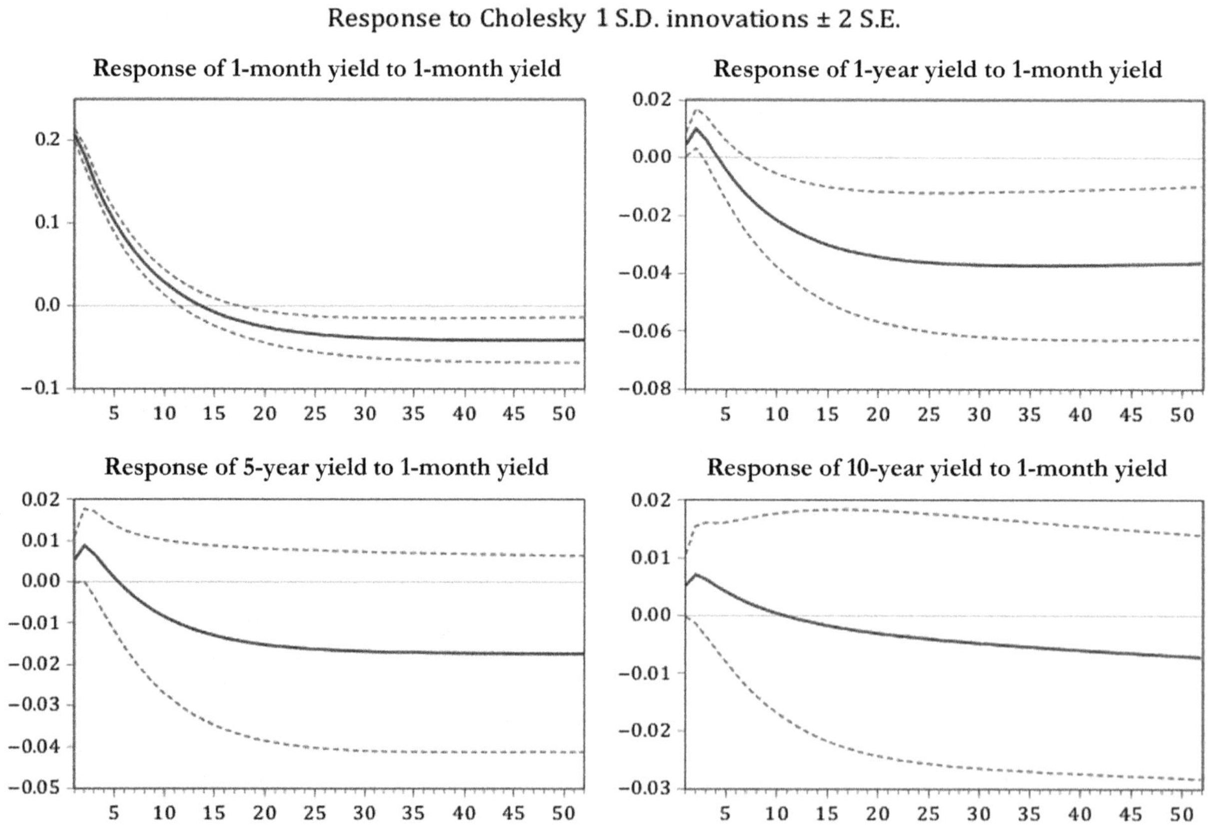

FIGURE 3.4 IRFs to a one standard deviation positive shocks to the 1-month Treasury yield.

3.3.2 Variance Decompositions

In Section 3.2.6, we have discussed how a VAR model can be used in forecasting. However, irrespective of the actual accuracy of the predictions, understanding the properties of forecast errors is helpful to assess the interrelationships among the variables in the system. In Eq. (3.99), we have provided the formula to compute the forecast error for a VAR(1) model. It is possible to reformulate such an equation exploiting the VMA representation of the model, so that the h-step-ahead forecast error is

$$\mathbf{u}_t(h) = \mathbf{y}_{t+h} - E_t\left[\mathbf{y}_{t+h}\right] = \sum_{i=0}^{h-1} \mathbf{\Phi}_i \boldsymbol{\varepsilon}_{t+h-i}. \tag{3.109}$$

To help our understanding, we apply Eq. (3.109) to the bivariate VAR model that we have discussed in Section 3.3.1 and, focusing only on the series $\{y_{1,t}\}$, we note that

$$\begin{aligned} u_{y1}(h) = y_{1,t+h} - E[y_{1,t+h|t}] = \phi_{1,1}(0)\varepsilon_{1,t+h} + \phi_{1,1}(1)\varepsilon_{1,t+h-1} + \cdots + \phi_{1,1}(h-1)\varepsilon_{1,t+1} + \phi_{1,2}(0)\varepsilon_{2,t+h} \\ + \phi_{1,2}(1)\varepsilon_{2,t+h-1} + \cdots + \phi_{1,2}(h-1)\varepsilon_{2,t+1}. \end{aligned} \tag{3.110}$$

Consequently, if we denote by $\sigma^2_{y1}(h)$ the h-step-ahead variance of the forecast of $y_{1,t+h}$, we obtain:

$$\sigma^2_{y1}(h) = \sigma^2_{\varepsilon_1}[\phi^2_{1,1}(0) + \phi^2_{1,1}(1) + \cdots + \phi^2_{1,1}(h-1)] + \sigma^2_{\varepsilon_2}[\phi^2_{1,2}(0) + \phi^2_{1,2}(1) + \cdots + \phi^2_{1,2}(h-1)]. \tag{3.111}$$

Interestingly, because all the coefficients $\phi^2_{j,k}$ are nonnegative as they are squared, the variance of the forecast error increases as the forecast horizon h increases.

It is possible to decompose the h-step-ahead forecast error variance in Eq. (3.111) into the proportion due to each of the (structural) shocks. In particular the proportion of the forecast error variance due to the shocks in the sequence $\{\varepsilon_{1,t}\}$ is

$$\frac{\sigma^2_{\varepsilon 1}\left[\phi^2_{1,1}(0) + \phi^2_{1,1}(1) + \cdots + \phi^2_{1,1}(h-1)\right]}{\sigma^2_{y_1}(h)}, \tag{3.112}$$

while the proportion of forecast error variance due to the shocks in the sequence $\{\varepsilon_{2,t}\}$ is

$$\frac{\sigma^2_{\varepsilon 2}\left[\phi^2_{1,2}(0) + \phi^2_{1,2}(1) + \cdots + \phi^2_{1,2}(h-1)\right]}{\sigma^2_{y_1}(h)}. \tag{3.113}$$

It is easy to see how this result can be generalized to a VAR including N variables instead of the two in our example. The computation of the proportion of the forecast error variance due to each shock is often referred to as *forecast error variance decomposition*. In practice, variance decompositions determine how much of the h-step-ahead forecast error variance of a given variable is explained by innovations to each explanatory variable for $h = 1, 2, \ldots$. For instance, in our bivariate example, if the $\varepsilon_{2,t}$ shocks explain none of the forecast variance of $y_{1,t}$ at all forecast horizons, we would say that the series $\{y_{1,t}\}$ is *exogenous*, that is, it evolves independently of the $\varepsilon_{2,t}$ shocks and of the $\{y_{2,t}\}$ sequence. Conversely, if $\varepsilon_{2,t}$ shocks explain all the forecast variance of $\{y_{1,t}\}$ at all forecast horizons, then $\{y_{1,t}\}$ is said to be completely endogenous. In most practical applications, it is common for $\varepsilon_{1,t}$ ($\varepsilon_{2,t}$) to explain most of the forecast variance of $y_{1,t}$ ($y_{2,t}$) at short-term horizons, while the importance of shocks to $y_{2,t}$ ($y_{1,t}$) on the forecast variance of $y_{1,t}$ ($y_{2,t}$) grows with the forecast horizon.

Importantly, like in IRF analysis, forecast error variance decompositions of reduced-form VARs require identification (because otherwise we would be unable to go from the coefficients in $\mathbf{\Theta}_i$ to their counterparts in $\mathbf{\Phi}_i$); therefore Cholesky decompositions (or other restriction schemes) are typically imposed. As we recall from Section 3.3.1, in the bivariate model examined in this section, this means that all the one-period forecast error variance of $y_{1,t}$ is attributed to $\varepsilon_{1,t}$. It is important to emphasize again that assuming a particular ordering is necessary to compute the impulse responses and variance decompositions from a VAR although the restrictions underlying the ordering used may not be supported by the data because they may be decided by the researcher on an a priori basis. As already discussed in the case of IRFs, when possible economic theory should give some guidance on what is a plausible ordering of the variables (i.e., to point out that when the movement in a variable is likely to temporally precede rather than follow the movements by the other variables this variable should be placed at the top of the ordering). Once more, however, the lower the pairwise cross-correlations among the errors are the weaker the impact of the ordering on the results.

In conclusion, both forecast error variance decomposition and IRF analyses entail similar information from the time series under analysis and are often used in combination (such a combined approach is called *innovation accounting*) to uncover the dynamic interrelationships among the endogenous variables.

EXAMPLE 3.8

We present the variance decompositions for the forecast error variance of the 1-month, 1-, 5-, and 10-year US Treasury yields from the VAR(2) estimated in Example 3.4 at forecast horizons between 1 and 12 weeks. In particular, panel (A) of Table 3.7 presents in which proportion the innovations to each variable in the system contribute to the forecast error variance of the 1-month T-bill yield at different horizons. The variance decompositions of the 1-year, 5-year, and 10-year US Treasury yields can be found in panels (B), (C), and (D), respectively.

Notably the forecast error variance of the 1-month yield at a 1-week horizon is entirely explained by its own innovations. By construction, this derives from the specific Cholesky triangularization that entails placing the 1-month yield on the top of the ordering. However, even at a forecast horizon of 12 weeks, the own innovations continue to contribute as much as 70% of the forecast variance of the 1-month yield.

Interestingly the movements in the 10-year yield seem to explain little of the forecast error variance of the other riskless yield series and even of its own error variance. However, to understand why the ordering of the variable is often crucial, Table 3.8 presents how the variance decomposition of the 10-year yield changes when the 10-year yield is placed at the top of the ordering in a different Cholesky identification scheme.

Under this new ordering, most of the forecast error variance at all the 12 horizons considered is explained by its own 10-year yield innovations. Indeed the estimated correlation coefficients among the innovations of the variables in the VAR(2) are:

$$\hat{\rho} = \begin{matrix} 1M \\ 1Y \\ 5Y \\ 10Y \end{matrix} \begin{bmatrix} 1 & 0.059 & 0.051 & 0.050 \\ 0.051 & 1 & 0.734 & 0.612 \\ 0.051 & 0.734 & 1 & 0.938 \\ 0.050 & 0.612 & 0.938 & 1 \end{bmatrix}.$$

Interestingly the correlation between the innovations to 10-year and the 5-year yields is very close to one, while for a few additional pairs of reduced-form yield residuals display substantial correlations. As we have learned, when correlation coefficients between the innovation are high, the ordering that a researcher selects to achieve identification may be of crucial importance.

TABLE 3.7 Forecast Error Variance Decomposition of 1-Month, 1-, 5-, 10-Year Treasury Yields When the Cholesky Ordering is 1-Month, 1-, 5-, 10-Year Yields

(A) Variance Decomposition of 1-Month Yield

Period	S.E.	1-Month Yield	1-Year Yield	5-Year Yield	10-Year Yield
1	0.207	100.000	0.000	0.000	0.000
2	0.275	99.897	0.061	0.039	0.003
3	0.315	99.377	0.504	0.110	0.008
4	0.340	98.241	1.544	0.199	0.016
5	0.359	96.425	3.254	0.299	0.022
6	0.373	93.943	5.625	0.405	0.027
7	0.386	90.867	8.591	0.512	0.030
8	0.398	87.309	12.045	0.615	0.031
9	0.409	83.405	15.854	0.710	0.030
10	0.421	79.300	19.879	0.793	0.029
11	0.433	75.127	23.985	0.861	0.027
12	0.445	70.998	28.060	0.915	0.028

(B) Variance Decomposition of 1-Year Yield					
Period	S.E.	1-Month Yield	1-Year Yield	5-Year Yield	10-Year Yield
1	0.079	0.348	99.652	0.000	0.000
2	0.126	0.784	99.110	0.092	0.015
3	0.164	0.609	99.201	0.153	0.037
4	0.197	0.425	99.325	0.188	0.063
5	0.226	0.358	99.341	0.210	0.091
6	0.254	0.406	99.244	0.228	0.122
7	0.280	0.543	99.057	0.243	0.156
8	0.304	0.741	98.806	0.258	0.195
9	0.328	0.978	98.512	0.274	0.236
10	0.351	1.237	98.191	0.291	0.282
11	0.373	1.506	97.855	0.308	0.330
12	0.394	1.778	97.513	0.328	0.382
(C) Variance Decomposition of 5-Year Yield					
Period	S.E.	1-Month Yield	1-Year Yield	5-Year Yield	10-Year Yield
1	0.106	0.261	53.622	46.117	0.000
2	0.166	0.391	53.547	46.045	0.017
3	0.212	0.341	53.959	45.674	0.026
4	0.251	0.267	54.526	45.180	0.027
5	0.284	0.209	55.120	44.646	0.025
6	0.314	0.174	55.695	44.109	0.022
7	0.341	0.158	56.235	43.588	0.019
8	0.366	0.159	56.737	43.087	0.017
9	0.390	0.173	57.200	42.612	0.015
10	0.412	0.197	57.629	42.161	0.013
11	0.433	0.227	58.026	41.735	0.012
12	0.454	0.263	58.393	41.333	0.011
(D) Variance Decomposition of 10-Year Yield					
Period	S.E.	1-Month Yield	1-Year Yield	5-Year Yield	10-Year Yield
1	0.101	0.260	37.242	51.653	10.845
2	0.158	0.306	36.977	52.897	9.820
3	0.202	0.285	37.053	53.316	9.345
4	0.237	0.253	37.265	53.389	9.093
5	0.268	0.221	37.527	53.311	8.941
6	0.296	0.194	37.805	53.163	8.839
7	0.321	0.170	38.086	52.981	8.763
8	0.344	0.150	38.363	52.784	8.703

(D) Variance Decomposition of 10-Year Yield					
Period	S.E.	1-Month Yield	1-Year Yield	5-Year Yield	10-Year Yield
9	0.365	0.134	38.633	52.580	8.653
10	0.385	0.120	38.896	52.375	8.608
11	0.404	0.109	39.151	52.171	8.568
12	0.422	0.100	39.399	51.971	8.530

TABLE 3.8 Forecast Error Variance Decomposition of the 10-Year Treasury Yields (10-Year Yield on the Top of the Cholesky Ordering)

Variance Decomposition of 10-Year Yield					
Period	S.E.	10-Year Yield	1-Month Yield	1-Year Yield	5-Year Yield
1	0.101	100.00	0.000	0.000	0.000
2	0.158	99.939	0.003	0.001	0.057
3	0.202	99.902	0.002	0.001	0.096
4	0.237	99.879	0.004	0.001	0.116
5	0.268	99.860	0.010	0.005	0.125
6	0.296	99.840	0.020	0.010	0.130
7	0.321	99.818	0.032	0.018	0.132
8	0.344	99.794	0.047	0.027	0.132
9	0.365	99.767	0.063	0.039	0.132
10	0.385	99.738	0.079	0.051	0.132
11	0.404	99.707	0.097	0.065	0.131
12	0.422	99.676	0.115	0.080	0.130

3.3.3 Granger Causality

Another tool that is useful to investigate the dynamic relationships among the variables in a VAR system is *Granger causality* (see Granger, 1969a). Formally the definition of Granger causality is as follows.

DEFINITION 3.5 (Granger causality)

Let $\Im_t$ be the information set containing all the relevant information available up to and including time t. In addition, let $\mathbf{y}_t(h|\Im_t)$ be the optimal (minimum MSFE) h-step-ahead prediction of the process $\{\mathbf{y}_t\}$ at the forecast origin t, based on the information set $\Im_t$. The vector time series process $\{\mathbf{x}_t\}$ is said to (Granger-) cause $\{\mathbf{y}_t\}$ in a Granger sense if and only if $MSFE_{yt}(h|\Im_t) < MSFE_{yt}(h|\Im_t \; \{\mathbf{x}_s|s \leq t\})$.

Alternatively, it is possible to define Granger causality using its "its complement" (or lack thereof), that is, $\{\mathbf{x}_t\}$ does not cause $\{\mathbf{y}_t\}$ in a Granger sense at horizon h, if taking into account present and past values of $\{\mathbf{x}_t\}$ does not improve the accuracy of the h-step-ahead prediction of the future realizations of $\{\mathbf{y}_t\}$. Finally, if and only if $\{\mathbf{x}_t\}$ causes $\{\mathbf{y}_t\}$ and $\{\mathbf{y}_t\}$ causes $\{\mathbf{x}_t\}$, then the joint process $\{\mathbf{x}'_t, \mathbf{y}'_t\}'$ is said to represent a *feedback system*.

Notably, because the information set $\Im_t$ of all the existent relevant information is rarely available to the forecaster, the optimal prediction given $\Im_t$ cannot be determined. Therefore, instead of considering the entire set $\Im_t$, we only consider the information in the past and present values of the process under examination. In addition, instead of comparing optimal predictors, we compare the optimal linear predictors that we have discussed in Section 3.2.6. Therefore, we can rewrite Definition 3.5 as follows.

DEFINITION 3.6 (Granger causality—restricted)

Let $\mathbf{y}_t(h|\{\mathbf{x}_s, \mathbf{y}_s|s \leq t\})$ be the optimal linear (minimum MSFE) h-step-ahead prediction function of the process $\{\mathbf{y}_t\}$ at the forecast origin t, based on the information $\{\mathbf{x}_s, \mathbf{y}_s|s \leq t\}$. The process $\{\mathbf{x}_t\}$ is said to Granger cause $\{\mathbf{y}_t\}$ if $\text{MSFE}(E[\mathbf{y}_t|\mathbf{x}_{t-1}, \mathbf{x}_{t-2}, \ldots, \mathbf{y}_{t-1}, \mathbf{y}_{t-2}, \ldots]) \leq \text{MSFE}(E[\mathbf{y}_t|\mathbf{y}_{t-1}, \mathbf{y}_{t-2}, \ldots])$.

To discuss the Granger causal relationship among the variables in a VAR system, let us go back to our bivariate example, and, in particular, to its VMA representation:

$$\begin{bmatrix} y_{1,t} \\ y_{2,t} \end{bmatrix} = \begin{bmatrix} \mu_1 \\ \mu_2 \end{bmatrix} + \sum_{i=0}^{\infty} \begin{bmatrix} \theta_{1,1(i)} & \theta_{1,2(i)} \\ \theta_{2,1(i)} & \theta_{2,2(i)} \end{bmatrix} \begin{bmatrix} u_{1,t-i} \\ u_{2,t-i} \end{bmatrix}. \tag{3.114}$$

It can be proven (see Lütkepohl, 2005) that

$$y_{1,t}(1|\{y_{1,s}, y_{2,s}|s \leq t\}) = y_{1,t}(1|\{y_{1,s}|s \leq t\}) \Leftrightarrow \theta_{1,2}(i) = 0 \tag{3.115}$$

for $i = 1, 2, \ldots$. In addition, equality of the one-step-ahead predictors implies the equality of the h-step-ahead predictors, for $h = 2, 3, \ldots$. Therefore, the fact that $\theta_{1,2(i)} = 0$, for $i = 1, 2, \ldots$ provides a necessary and sufficient condition for $y_{1,s}$ *not* being caused by $y_{2,t}$ in a Granger sense. Therefore, the lack of Granger causality can be easily verified from the VMA representation of the model. In addition, it is worthwhile noting that for a stationary, stable VAR(p) process

$$\begin{bmatrix} y_{1,t} \\ y_{2,t} \end{bmatrix} = \begin{bmatrix} a_{1,0} \\ a_{2,0} \end{bmatrix} + \begin{bmatrix} a_{1,1(1)} & a_{1,2(1)} \\ a_{2,1(1)} & a_{2,2(1)} \end{bmatrix} \begin{bmatrix} y_{1,t-1} \\ y_{2,t-1} \end{bmatrix} + \cdots + \begin{bmatrix} a_{1,1(p)} & a_{1,2(p)} \\ a_{2,1(p)} & a_{2,2(p)} \end{bmatrix} \begin{bmatrix} y_{1,t-p} \\ y_{2,t-p} \end{bmatrix} + \begin{bmatrix} u_{1,t} \\ u_{2,t} \end{bmatrix} \tag{3.116}$$

the condition in Eq. (3.115) is satisfied if and only if $a_{1,2(i)} = 0$ for $i = 1, 2, \ldots, p$. This implies that the lack of causality can be assessed simply by looking at the representation of the VAR in its standard form. This means that in this context the lack of Granger causality can be easily verified by performing a standard F-test (like the one discussed in Chapter 1) of the restriction $a_{1,2(1)} = a_{1,2(2)} = \cdots = a_{1,2(p)} = 0$.

A multivariate generalization of Granger causality leads to *block-exogeneity tests* (or *block-causality tests*, a slightly more precise definition) which are useful to check whether adding a variable into a VAR may increase the accuracy of the forecasts produced by the model. In other words the test aims at verifying whether one variable, call it $y_{n,t}$, Granger causes any other variables in the system, that is, whether taking into account the lagged value of $y_{n,t}$ helps forecasting any of the other variables in the VAR.

From a practical point of view, block-causality tests simply consist of LR tests like the one discussed in Section 3.2.5:

$$(T - m)(\ln|\tilde{\Sigma}_u^R| - \ln|\tilde{\Sigma}_u^U|), \tag{3.117}$$

where $\tilde{\Sigma}_u^R$ is the covariance matrix of the residuals from a model that has been restricted to have all the coefficients of the lags of the variable $y_{n,t}$ set to 0 and $\tilde{\Sigma}_u^U$ is the residual covariance matrix of the unrestricted model. For instance, let us consider a trivariate VAR(1) model

$$\begin{bmatrix} y_{1,t} \\ y_{2,t} \\ y_{3,t} \end{bmatrix} = \begin{bmatrix} a_{1,0} \\ a_{2,0} \\ a_{3,0} \end{bmatrix} + \begin{bmatrix} a_{1,1} & a_{1,2} & a_{1,3} \\ a_{2,1} & a_{2,2} & a_{2,3} \\ a_{3,1} & a_{3,2} & a_{3,3} \end{bmatrix} \begin{bmatrix} y_{1,t-1} \\ y_{2,t-1} \\ y_{3,t-1} \end{bmatrix} + \begin{bmatrix} u_{1,t} \\ u_{2,t} \\ u_{3,t} \end{bmatrix}. \tag{3.118}$$

Suppose that we want to test whether $y_{3,t}$ Granger causes either $y_{2,t}$ or $y_{1,t}$. In practice, we need to test the restricted model

$$\begin{bmatrix} y_{1,t} \\ y_{2,t} \\ y_{3,t} \end{bmatrix} = \begin{bmatrix} a_{1,0} \\ a_{2,0} \\ a_{3,0} \end{bmatrix} + \begin{bmatrix} a_{1,1} & a_{1,2} & 0 \\ a_{2,1} & a_{2,2} & 0 \\ a_{3,1} & a_{3,2} & a_{3,3} \end{bmatrix} \begin{bmatrix} y_{1,t-1} \\ y_{2,t-1} \\ y_{3,t-1} \end{bmatrix} + \begin{bmatrix} u_{1,t} \\ u_{2,t} \\ u_{3,t} \end{bmatrix}, \tag{3.119}$$

versus the unrestricted model in Eq. (3.118) using an LR test. Failure to reject the null hypothesis that the restricted model is sufficient to fit the data (i.e., if the calculated value of the statistic is less than the critical value of the χ^2 at a prespecified size level) means that $y_{3,t}$ Granger causes at least one of the other two variables in the system. Of course, additional tests may be implemented to separately test whether $y_{3,t}$ Granger causes $y_{1,t}$, $y_{2,t}$, or both.

EXAMPLE 3.9

To conclude the analysis of the VAR(2) model for the 1-month, 1-, 5-, and 10-year US Treasury yields that we have estimated in previous examples, we test Granger causality for all the variables in the model. In particular, Table 3.9 considers one dependent variable at a time and tests whether the lags of each of the other variables help to predict it. In other words, in this case, the χ^2 statistics refer to a test in which the null is that the lagged coefficients of the "excluded" variable are equal to 0 (i.e., the "excluded" variable does not help to forecast the selected dependent variable).

Notably the only lead-lag interactions that seem to be significant at conventional size levels are the following:

- the 1-year yield (and 5-year yield, at 10% confidence level) Granger causes the 1-month yield;
- the 1-month yield Granger causes the 1-year and the 5-year yields.

Therefore, there is a feedback effect (or two-way causality) between 1-month and 1-year Treasury yields; however, the 5-year yield seems to be exogenous to 1-month rates.

TABLE 3.9 Granger Causality Tests

(A) Dependent Variable: 1-Month Yield				(B) Dependent Variable: 1-Year Yield			
Excluded	χ^2	df	Probability	Excluded	χ^2	df	Probability
1-year yield	102.054	2	0.000	1-month yield	33.950	2	0.000
5-year yield	4.965	2	0.084	5-year yield	3.236	2	0.198
10-year yield	1.309	2	0.520	10-year yield	2.714	2	0.257
All	180.123	6	0.000	All	43.161	6	0.000
(C) Dependent Variable: 5-Year Yield				**(D) Dependent Variable: 10-Year Yield**			
Excluded	χ^2	df	Probability	Excluded	χ^2	df	Probability
1-month yield	5.630	2	0.060	1-month yield	0.940	2	0.625
1-year yield	3.976	2	0.137	1-year yield	1.638	2	0.441
10-year yield	1.238	2	0.539	5-year yield	2.051	2	0.359
All	7.535	6	0.274	All	4.579	6	0.599

3.4 VECTOR MOVING AVERAGE AND VECTOR AUTOREGRESSIVE MOVING AVERAGE MODELS

3.4.1 Vector Moving Average Models

Although less common in financial applications, a researcher could also specify a VMA model

$$\mathbf{y}_t = \boldsymbol{\mu} + \mathbf{u}_t + \boldsymbol{\Theta}_1 \mathbf{u}_{t-1} + \boldsymbol{\Theta}_2 \mathbf{u}_{t-2} + \cdots + \boldsymbol{\Theta}_q \mathbf{u}_{t-q}. \tag{3.120}$$

where $\mathbf{y}_t = [y_{1,t}, y_{2,t}, \ldots, y_{K,t}]'$, $\mathbf{u}_t$ is a zero mean multivariate white noise with nonsingular covariance matrix $\boldsymbol{\Sigma}_u$ and $\mu = [\mu_1, \mu_2, \ldots, \mu_K]'$ is the mean vector of $\mathbf{y}_t$. It is possible to verify that, exactly as a VAR has an infinite VMA representation, a VMA model potentially has an infinite-order VAR representation. For concreteness, let us consider a VMA(1) model with zero mean (i.e., $\boldsymbol{\mu} = \mathbf{0}$):

$$\mathbf{y}_t = \mathbf{u}_t + \boldsymbol{\Theta}_1 \mathbf{u}_{t-1}. \tag{3.121}$$

It follows that

$$\mathbf{u}_t = \mathbf{y}_t - \boldsymbol{\Theta}_1 \mathbf{u}_{t-1}, \tag{3.122}$$

and thus

$$\mathbf{u}_{t-1} = \mathbf{y}_{t-1} - \boldsymbol{\Theta}_1 \mathbf{u}_{t-2}. \tag{3.123}$$

Therefore, we can rewrite Eq. (3.121) as

$$\mathbf{y}_t = \mathbf{u}_t + \boldsymbol{\Theta}_1 (\mathbf{y}_{t-1} - \boldsymbol{\Theta}_1 \mathbf{u}_{t-2}). \tag{3.124}$$

By iterative substitution, we eventually show that

$$\mathbf{y}_t = -\sum_{i=1}^{\infty} (-\boldsymbol{\Theta}_1)^i \mathbf{y}_{t-i} + \mathbf{u}_t, \tag{3.125}$$

which is the infinite-order VAR representation of the process. Note that this is only potentially infinite, because it may be that $(-\boldsymbol{\Theta}_1)^i$ may be equal to 0 for some i greater than some finite number p, so that the VAR representation may in fact turn out to be of finite order p. For this representation to be meaningful, $\boldsymbol{\Theta}_1^i$ must approach 0 as i approaches to infinity, which requires that the eigenvalues of $\boldsymbol{\Theta}_1$ are less than one in modulus, that is:

$$\det(\mathbf{I}_K - (-\boldsymbol{\Theta}_1)z) = \det(\mathbf{I}_K + \boldsymbol{\Theta}_1 z) = 0, \quad \textit{with } z \in \mathbb{C}, \ |z| > 1. \tag{3.126}$$

This is the same condition that we have discussed for the stability of a VAR(1) model.

In general, a VMA(q) process similar to the one in Eq. (3.120) with $\boldsymbol{\mu} = \mathbf{0}$ has a pure VAR representation

$$\mathbf{y}_t = \sum_{i=1}^{\infty} \Pi_i \mathbf{y}_{t-i} + \boldsymbol{\varepsilon}_t, \tag{3.127}$$

if the roots of det $(\mathbf{I}_K + \boldsymbol{\Theta}_1 z + \cdots + \boldsymbol{\Theta}_q z^q) = 0$, lie outside the unit circle. Such a VMA(q) is said to be *invertible*.

We can also examine the first and second moments of a VMA(q). As the multivariate white noise $\boldsymbol{\varepsilon}_t$ has zero mean vector, the mean of $\mathbf{y}_t$ is simply the vector $\boldsymbol{\mu} = [\mu_1, \mu_2 \ldots, \mu_N]$. For the sake of simplicity, in what follows we assume $\boldsymbol{\mu} = \mathbf{0}$. The autocovariance matrices are then

$$\boldsymbol{\Gamma}(h) = E(\mathbf{y}_t \mathbf{y}'_{t-h}) = \sum_{i=0}^{q-h} \boldsymbol{\Theta}_{i+h} \boldsymbol{\Sigma}_\varepsilon \boldsymbol{\Theta}'_i, \quad \text{for } h = 0, 1, \ldots, q, \tag{3.128}$$

and $\mathbf{O}$ for $h > q$. Clearly, $\boldsymbol{\Gamma}(0)$ is simply the covariance matrix of the series.

Unlikely VAR models, VMA processes can never be simply estimated equation-by-equation by OLS. One way to estimate them is the ML approach, more precisely by a maximum conditional-likelihood (that assumes $\mathbf{u}_t$ to be equal to 0 for $t \leq 0$) or alternatively by exact-likelihood (that treats $\mathbf{u}_t$ for $t \leq 0$ as additional parameters of the model). However, a detailed review of these methods is out of the scope of this book. The interested reader can find a treatment in Lütkepohl (2005).

3.4.2 Vector Autoregressive Moving Average Models

For the sake of completeness, we finally introduce VARMA processes, which are VAR models that are allowed to include finite order MA process. The general form of a VARMA(p,q) process with VAR order p and MA order q is

$$\mathbf{y}_t = \mathbf{a}_0 + \mathbf{A}_1 \mathbf{y}_{t-1} + \cdots + \mathbf{A}_p \mathbf{y}_{t-p} + \mathbf{u}_t + \boldsymbol{\Theta}_1 \mathbf{u}_{t-1} + \boldsymbol{\Theta}_2 \mathbf{u}_{t-2} + \cdots + \boldsymbol{\Theta}_q \mathbf{u}_{t-q}, \tag{3.129}$$

where $\boldsymbol{\varepsilon}_t$ is a white noise process with nonsingular covariance matrix Σ_u.

A little bit of algebraic manipulation may be worthy to better understand the nature of this process. Let us now define υ_t such as

$$\upsilon_t = \mathbf{u}_t + \mathbf{\Theta}_1\mathbf{u}_{t-1} + \mathbf{\Theta}_2\mathbf{u}_{t-2} + \cdots + \mathbf{\Theta}_q\mathbf{u}_{t-q}. \tag{3.130}$$

If we substitute Eq. (3.130) into (3.129), we obtain:

$$\mathbf{y}_t = \mathbf{a}_0 + \mathbf{A}_1 y_{t-1} + \cdots + \mathbf{A}_p y_{t-p} + \upsilon_t. \tag{3.131}$$

If this process is stable, that is, if det $(\mathbf{I}_K + \mathbf{A}_1 z + \cdots + \mathbf{A}_p z^p) = 0$ has all the roots outside the unit circle, it is also invertible and can be rewritten in its infinite VMA representation as

$$\mathbf{y}_t = \boldsymbol{\mu} + \sum_{i=0}^{\infty} \mathbf{D}_i \upsilon_{t-i} = \boldsymbol{\mu} + \sum_{i=0}^{\infty} \mathbf{\Theta}_i \mathbf{u}_{t-i}, \tag{3.132}$$

that is, a pure VMA process where $\boldsymbol{\mu} = (\mathbf{I}_K - \mathbf{A}_1 - \cdots - \mathbf{A}_p)^{-1}\mathbf{a}_0$.

Again, to compute the autocovariance matrices of a VARMA model, we will assume that $\boldsymbol{\mu} = 0$ to simplify the algebra; then we postmultiply Eq. (3.131) by $\mathbf{y}'_{t-h}$ and taking its expectation, we have

$$E\left[\mathbf{y}_t\mathbf{y}'_{t-h}\right] = \mathbf{A}_1 E\left[\mathbf{y}_{t-1}\mathbf{y}'_{t-h}\right] + \cdots + \mathbf{A}_p E\left[\mathbf{y}_{t-p}\mathbf{y}'_{t-h}\right] + E[\mathbf{u}_t\mathbf{y}'_{t-h}] + \mathbf{\Theta}_1 E[\mathbf{u}_{t-1}\mathbf{y}'_{t-h}] + \cdots + \mathbf{\Theta}_q E\left[\mathbf{u}_{t-q}\mathbf{y}'_{t-h}\right]. \tag{3.133}$$

given that $E[\mathbf{u}_{t-1}\mathbf{y}'_s] = \mathbf{O}$ for any $s < t$. Hence, for $h > q$ we can show that:

$$\mathbf{\Gamma}(h) = \mathbf{A}_1\mathbf{\Gamma}(h-1) + \cdots + \mathbf{A}_p\mathbf{\Gamma}(h-p). \tag{3.134}$$

If $p > q$ and $\mathbf{\Gamma}(0), \ldots, \mathbf{\Gamma}(p-1)$ are known, the relationship in Eq. (3.134) can be used to compute the autocovariance matrices recursively from$h = p, p+1, \ldots$.

Noticeably, as for the VMA model, also a VARMA model cannot be simply estimated by OLS, but it requires MLE. The interested reader may find more details about the estimation of VARMA models in Lütkepohl (2005).

REFERENCES

Akaike, H., 1969. Fitting autoregressive models for prediction. Ann. Inst. Stat. Math. 21, 243–247.

Efron, B., Tibshirani, R., 1986. Bootstrap methods for standard errors, confidence intervals, and other measures of statistical accuracy. Stat. Sci. 1, 54–75.

Fuller, W.A., 1976. Introduction to Statistical Time Series. John Wiley, New York.

Granger, C.W.J., 1969a. Investigating causal relations by econometric models and cross-spectral methods. Econometrica 37, 424–438.

Granger, C.W.J., 1969b. Prediction with a generalized cost of error function. Oper. Res. Quart. 20, 199–207.

Granger, C.W.J., Newbold, P., 1986. Forecasting Economic Time Series, second ed. Academic Press, New York.

Hoffman, D.L., Schlagenhauf, D., 1982. An econometric investigation of the monetary neutrality and rationality propositions from an international perspective. Rev. Econ. Stat. 64, 562–571.

Hosking, J.R.M., 1980. The multivariate portmanteau statistic. J. Am. Stat. Assoc. 75, 602–608.

Hosking, J.R.M., 1981. Equivalent forms of the multivariate portmanteau statistic. J. R. Stat. Soc. B43, 261–262.

Kheoh, T.S., McLeod, A.I., 1992. Comparison of two modified portmanteau tests for model adequacy. Comput. Stat. Data Anal. 14, 99–106.

Kilian, L., 1998. Small-sample confidence intervals for impulse response functions. Rev. Econ. Stat. 80, 218–230.

Li, W.K., 2004. Diagnostic Checks in Time Series. Chapman and Hall/CRC, New York.

Li, W.K., McLeod, A.I., 1981. Distribution of the residual autocorrelations in multivariate ARMA time series models. J. R. Stat. Soc. B43, 231–239.

Ljung, G.M., Box, G.E.P., 1978. On a measure of lack of fit in time series models. Biometrika 65, 297–303.

Lütkepohl, H., 1991. Introduction to Multiple Time Series Analysis. Springer, Berlin.

Lütkepohl, H., 2005. New Introduction to Multiple Time Series Analysis. Springer, Berlin.

Reinsel, G.C., 1993. Elements of Multivariate Time Series Analysis. Springer, New York.

Sims, C.A., 1980. Macroeconomics and reality. Econometrica 48, 1–48.

Sims, C.A., 1981. An autoregressive index model for the U.S. 1948–1975. In: Kmenta, J., Ramsey, J.B. (Eds.), Large-Scale Macro-Econometric Models. North-Holland, Amsterdam, pp. 283–327.

Zellner, A., 1962. An efficient method of estimating seemingly unrelated regressions and tests of aggregation bias. J. Am. Stat. Assoc. 57, 348–368.

Chapter 4

Unit Roots and Cointegration

All that is gold does not glitter, Not all those who wander are lost; The old that is strong does not wither, Deep roots are not reached by the frost.

J.R.R. Tolkien

In this chapter, we investigate the consequences of nonstationarity (in the form of unit roots in the assumed autoregressive moving average (ARMA), representation of a time series) for the econometric methodologies that we have been developing in Chapters 1–3. We also go beyond the simple definition and sample autocorrelation function/partial autocorrelation function (SACF/PACF) characterizations of a failure of weak stationarity provided in Chapter 2, to develop formal tests of unit roots in time series data. In Section 4.2, we discuss the problems that unit roots may cause in standard regression analysis when applied to time series data. Such problems represent the "dark side" of nonstationary series: in general, unit roots make standard inference invalid. In Section 4.3, we therefore discuss how one would go about formally testing for the presence of unit roots. We shall see that there are a variety of complementary approaches to perform the task, each with its strengths, which makes it smart to use many alternative tests in applied work. In Section 4.4, we define the notion of cointegration, whose very nature and characterization represents the very advantage, in terms of efficient use of the information in the data, that the presence of unit roots in standard regression and vector autoregressive (VAR) analysis may provide. In this section, we discuss both simple univariate methods to test for cointegration as well as more complex multivariate, VAR-style cointegration tests.

4.1 DEFINING UNIT ROOT PROCESSES

Time series often contain a *trend*, whose naïve meaning can be identified with the one used in common language. The key feature of a trend is that it has a permanent effect on a series. As we know from Chapter 2, shocks to a stationary time series without any trend are necessarily temporary; over time the effects of the shocks will dissipate and the series will revert to its long-run mean. In statistics two kinds of trends exist:

- *Deterministic trends*, which in general are functions (linear or nonlinear) of time, t, $y_t = f(t) + \varepsilon_t$; for instance, polynomial functions like

$$y_t = \sum_{j=0}^{Q} \delta_j t^j + \varepsilon_t, \tag{4.1}$$

where $\{\varepsilon_t\}$ is a white noise process, are deterministic trends. In this case the trending effect caused by functions of t is permanent and hence impresses a trend because time is obviously irreversible, for instance when $Q = 1$, $\Delta y_t = y_t - y_{t-1} = \delta_1 + (\varepsilon_t - \varepsilon_{t-1})$. In fact, suppose that a series always changes by the same fixed amount δ_1 from one period to the next, $\Delta y_t = \delta_1$. Basic principles deliver that the solution to this linear difference equation is $y_t = y_0 + \delta_1 t + \sum_{\tau=1}^{t} \eta_\tau$, where y_0 is the initial value and $\{\eta_t\}$ is a stationary process. In Eq. (4.1), y_t can differ from its trend value by the amount ε_t and because this deviation is stationary, the series will exhibit only temporary departures from the trend. As such, the long-term forecast of y_t will converge to the trend line $\sum_{j=0}^{Q} \delta_j t^j$. Because of this property, this type of model is said to be *trend stationary*.
- *Stochastic trends*, which characterize all series that can be written as:

$$y_t = y_0 + \mu t + \sum_{\tau=1}^{t} \varepsilon_\tau, \tag{4.2}$$

Essentials of Time Series for Financial Applications. DOI: https://doi.org/10.1016/B978-0-12-813409-2.00004-2

where $Var[\varepsilon_t] = \sigma^2$, which, because $y_{t+1} = y_0 + \mu t + \sum_{\tau=1}^{t} \varepsilon_\tau + \mu + \varepsilon_{t+1} = \mu + y_t + \varepsilon_{t+1}$, is equivalent to say that the series follows a *random walk (RW) with drift process.*[1]

More generally, y_t contains a stochastic trend if and only if it can be decomposed as $y_t = y_0 + \mu t + \sum_{\tau=1}^{t} \eta_\tau$, where η_τ follows any ARMA(p, q) stationary process, for instance $\eta_\tau = \phi\eta_{\tau-1} + \theta\varepsilon_{\tau-1} + \varepsilon_\tau$. Interestingly, this expression is centered on the first differences of y_t and we shall see later exactly why.

Note that the distinction is far from stark: all deterministic trends can be converted into stochastic trends. However, the opposite is not true, in the sense that stochastic trends can be defined on their own and have actually proven useful in characterizing the properties of a number of financial time series. To see this, note that given the decomposition of a linear time trend series as $y_t = y_0 + \delta_1 t + \sum_{\tau=1}^{t} \varepsilon_\tau$, we can think of $\sum_{\tau=1}^{t} \varepsilon_\tau$ as a stochastic intercept term. In the absence of any shocks the intercept is y_0, and each shock represents a shift in the intercept. Since all values of ε_τ have a coefficient of unity, the effect of each shock on the intercept term is permanent, which is indeed the intrinsic nature of a stochastic trend.

Because formal unit root tests are sensitive to the presence of deterministic time trends, this distinction is not just a matter of classification. In fact, useful unit root tests will manage to tell deterministic time trends apart from stochastic ones to generate decompositions of a series $\{y_t\}$ in the stochastic trend versus time trend-stationary components:

$$\begin{aligned} y_t &= \textit{trend} + \textit{stationary component} + \textit{noise} \\ &= (\textit{deterministic trend} + \textit{stochastic}\ \text{trend}) + \textit{stationary component} + \textit{noise}. \end{aligned} \tag{4.3}$$

Because Chapters 1 and 2 have already explained how to model the stationary component of a time series (say, using the Box–Jenkins methodology), in this chapter our attention is entirely devoted to trends. Fig. 4.1 compares simulated deterministic (linear, quadratic, and cubic) trends to (RW) stochastic trend series (with no drift and with positive/

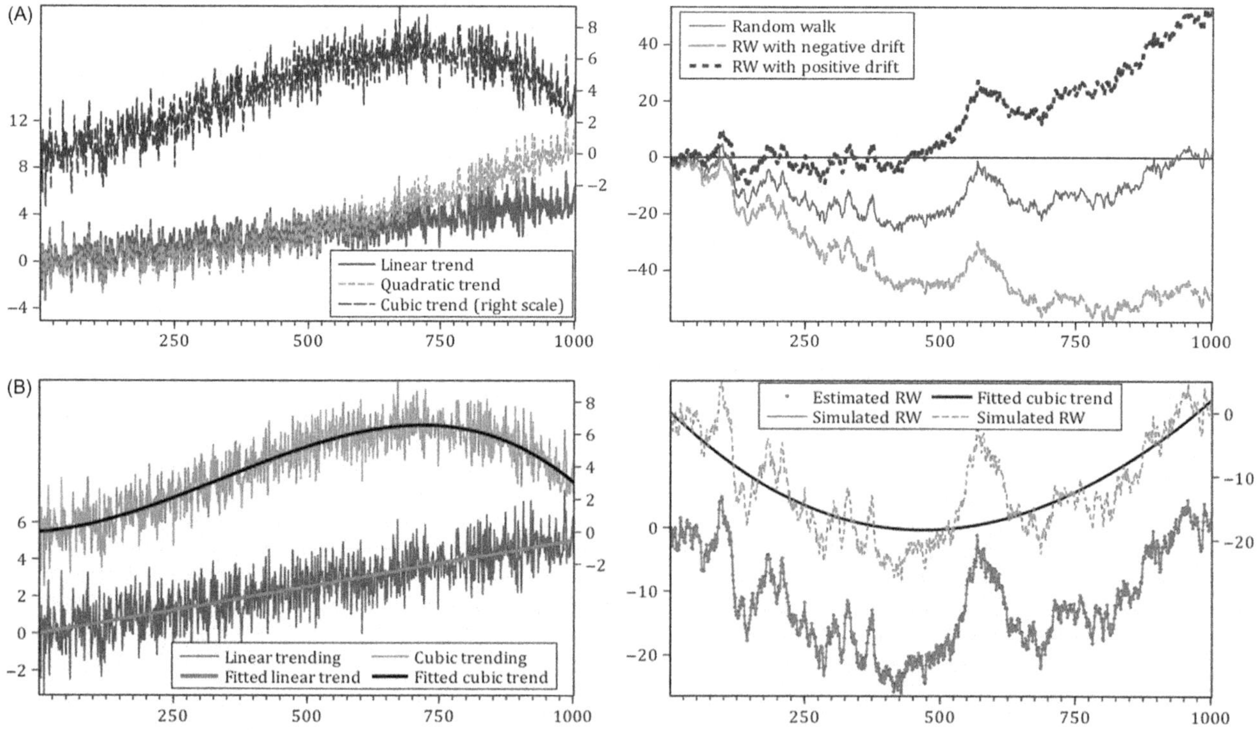

FIGURE 4.1 (A) Comparing trend-stationary series and stochastic trends. (B) Estimated deterministic trends and estimated random walk.

1. This model has carried a strong appeal to financial economists for centuries: suppose we are betting on the outcome of a coin toss, such that a head toss adds 1 to our wealth while a tail costs 1. Therefore we can say $\varepsilon_t = +1$ if a head appears and $\varepsilon_t = -1$ when we get a tail outcome; as a result, current wealth y_t equals last period's wealth y_{t-1} plus the realized value of ε_t. If we play again, our wealth in $t+1$ will be $y_{t+1} = y_t + \varepsilon_{t+1}$, and so on. Such a *fair game* endogenously generates random walk dynamics that describes the wealth process.

negative drift). In both cases, we show both the simulated series for 1000 periods (Fig. 4.1A) and a model fitted by simple ordinary least square (OLS) (Fig. 4.1B). All series use identical, identically and independently distributed (IID) standard normal shocks. In both panels, there is no pronounced tendency by any of the series to revert to a long-run mean. Clearly the deterministic time trend, induced by the drift component, dominates the time series. In a very large sample, asymptotic theory suggests that this will always be the case. However, we cannot conclude that it is always easy to discern the difference between a driftless RW and a model with drift. In a small sample, either by increasing the variance of the errors or by decreasing the absolute value of the drift parameter, chance might cloud the long-run properties of the resulting series.

Clearly, while in Fig. 4.1B OLS can do a fairly good job at fitting deterministic trends, provided flexible polynomials are allowed and the same occurs (subject to caveats that will be discussed later) to OLS estimates of an AR(1) process that as we know from Chapter 2, nests the RW, even flexible deterministic time trends provide a rather poor fit to data generated from a RW.

Consider now the case of a driftless RW ($\mu = 0$); taking expectations, we have $E[y_t] = E[y_{t+s}] = y_0 + E\left[\sum_{\tau}\varepsilon_{\tau}\right] = y_0 + \sum_{\tau}E[\varepsilon_{\tau}] = y_0$, a constant equal to the initial value. However, all stochastic shocks have nondecaying effects on the series. Given the initial value of the process the conditional mean is:

$$\begin{aligned} E_t[y_{t+1}] &= E_t[y_t + \varepsilon_{t+1}] = E_t[y_t] + E_t[\varepsilon_{t+1}] = y_t \\ E_t[y_{t+s}] &= E_t[y_{t+s-1} + \varepsilon_{t+s}] = E_t[y_{t+s-2} + \varepsilon_{t+s} + \varepsilon_{t+s-1}] = \cdots = E_t[y_t] + E_t\left[\sum_{i=1}^{s}\varepsilon_{t+i}\right] = y_t. \end{aligned} \tag{4.4}$$

For any $s \geq 2$ the conditional means for all values of y_{t+s} are equivalent, and the current y_t represents the minimum mean-squared loss function forecast of all future values of the series. If the drift was not 0, then, from Eq. (4.2), $E[y_t] = E_t[y_0 + \mu t + \sum_{\tau=1}^{t}\varepsilon_{\tau}] = y_0 + \mu t$ and $E_t[y_{t+s}] = E_t[y_0 + \mu(t+s) + \sum_{\tau=1}^{t}\varepsilon_{\tau}] = y_0 + \mu(t+s)$, so that the forecast function is no longer a constant, but changes deterministically with time.

It is also easy to show that the variance is time-dependent and therefore that a RW is not covariance stationary even when $\mu = 0$:

$$\begin{aligned} Var[y_t] &= Var\left[y_0 + \sum_{\tau=1}^{t}\varepsilon_{\tau}\right] = \sum_{\tau=1}^{t}Var[\varepsilon_{\tau}] = t\sigma^2 \\ Var[y_{t+s}] &= Var\left[y_0 + \sum_{\tau=1}^{t+s}\varepsilon_{\tau}\right] = \sum_{\tau=1}^{t+s}Var[\varepsilon_{\tau}] = (t+s)\sigma^2. \end{aligned} \tag{4.5}$$

Obviously, as $s \to \infty$, the variance approaches infinity. Thus a driftless RW meanders without exhibiting any tendency to increase or decrease. In fact, it can be shown that for any fixed real number M, the RW and its absolute will exceed M with probability 1 as the series lengthens. It is also useful to compute the covariance and correlation between y_t and y_{t+s}: exploiting the fact that the mean is constant, such a covariance is simply:

$$\begin{aligned} E[(y_t - y_0)(y_{t+s} - y_0)] &= E\left[\sum_{\tau=1}^{t}\varepsilon_{\tau}\cdot\sum_{\tau=1}^{t+s}\varepsilon_{\tau}\right] = E\left[\sum_{\tau=1}^{t}\varepsilon_{\tau}^2\right] = t\sigma^2 \\ Corr[y_t, y_{t+s}] &= \frac{E[(y_t - y_0)(y_{t+s} - y_0)]}{\sqrt{Var[y_t]Var[y_{t+s}]}} = \frac{t\sigma^2}{\sqrt{t\sigma^2(t+s)\sigma^2}} = \sqrt{\frac{t}{t+s}}. \end{aligned} \tag{4.6}$$

Interestingly the first few autocorrelations will be characterized by a very small s, so that for sufficiently large samples, $Corr[y_t, y_{t+s}] \simeq 1$, but as s grows $Corr[y_t, y_{t+s}]$ will decline below 1. Therefore as already discussed in Chapter 2, the population autocorrelation function (ACF) for a RW will show, especially in small samples, a slight tendency to decay that would make one think of a stationary AR(p) process with a sum of the AR coefficients close to 1. Thus at least in realistic samples, it will not be possible to simply use the ACF to distinguish between a unit root process and a stationary process with an autoregressive coefficient that is close to unity (often called a *near-unit root*). Table 4.1 presents the SACF of the driftless RW data generated on the rightmost panel of Fig. 4.1: even though the sample autocorrelations are close to 1, they visibly decay possibly instilling the doubt that we may be facing a highly persistent AR(1) process. To the right of the sample autocorrelogram, we also report the OLS estimates of the AR(1) and AR(2) processes: confirming the illusion that we may be facing a stationary process. In the AR(2) case the coefficients take the typical pattern of identical standard errors, the estimate of ϕ_1 exceeding 1 and the one of ϕ_2 negative, compensating ϕ_1

TABLE 4.1 Sample ACF and Estimated AR(p) Models on RW Series

Autocorrelation	Partial Correlation		AC	PAC	Q-Stat	Prob
		1	0.988	0.988	980.19	0.000
		2	0.976	-0.007	1937.8	0.000
		3	0.965	0.027	2874.5	0.000
		4	0.954	-0.014	3790.3	0.000
		5	0.942	0.002	4685.5	0.000
		6	0.931	-0.002	5560.7	0.000
		7	0.920	-0.007	6416.0	0.000
		8	0.910	0.030	7253.1	0.000
		9	0.901	0.036	8073.9	0.000
		10	0.892	0.015	8879.5	0.000
		11	0.883	0.003	9670.1	0.000
		12	0.874	-0.009	10446.	0.000

with a sum less than 1. Such typical patterns are in fact caused by near-singularity problems occurring when we attempt to estimate stationary ARMA models on nonstationary data:

$$y_{t+1} = \underset{(0.0023)}{0.9974}\, y_t + \underset{(0.0000)}{1.0116}\, z_{t+1}$$
$$y_{t+1} = \underset{(0.0317)}{1.0312}\, y_t - \underset{(0.0317)}{0.0339}\, y_{t-1} + \underset{(0.0000)}{1.0115}\, z_{t+1}$$

(standard errors in parentheses)

True DGP: $y_{t+1} = y_t + z_{t+1}$.

Before being able to provide a formal definition of a (stochastically) trending, unit root process, we need to examine the consequences of *differencing* both stochastically and deterministically trending series. While series containing (only) a deterministic time trend can be made stationary by *appropriately detrending* them, series containing (also) unit roots will require *appropriate* differencing.

DEFINITION 4.1 (Deterministic detrending)

Detrending entails regressing a variable on a deterministic (polynomial) function of time and saving the residuals, $\{\hat{\varepsilon}_t\}$, that come then to represent the new, detrended series:

$$\hat{y}_t = \sum_{j=0}^{Q} \hat{\delta}_j t^j + \hat{\varepsilon}_t, \tag{4.7}$$

where the coefficients can be simply estimated by OLS.

The appropriate degree of the polynomial can be set by standard t-tests, F-tests, and/or information criteria. The common practice is to estimate the regression in Eq. (4.7) using the largest value of Q considered reasonable in the light of the type of data or their frequency. The detrended process can then be modeled using traditional methods (such as ARMA).

As for stochastic trends, consider the RW with drift process and take its first difference:

$$\Delta y_{t+1} \equiv y_{t+1} - y_t = (\mu + y_t + \varepsilon_{t+1}) - y_t = \mu + \varepsilon_{t+1}. \tag{4.8}$$

The result of differencing is then a white noise series plus a constant intercept (equal to its mean and to the drift of the RW). This concept can be generalized as follows.

DEFINITION 4.2 (Unit root process and *d*th order integration)

When a time series process $\{y_t\}$ needs to be differenced d times before being reduced to the sum of constant terms plus a white noise process, $\{y_t\}$ is said to contain d unit roots or to be *integrated of order d*; we also write that $y_t \sim I(d)$.

Note that while $\{y_t\}$ containing d unit roots implies that $\{y_t\}$ is nonstationary, the opposite does not hold: there are types of nonstationary series that are not simply of the unit root type. Simply think of the case $y_{t+1} = \mu + \phi y_t + \varepsilon_{t+1}$ with $|\phi| > 1$, which is an *explosive* (possibly with oscillatory behavior) *autoregressive process*.

Typically, however, this case is ignored and $\phi = 1$ is used to characterize nonstationarity because $|\phi| > 1$ does not describe many data series in economics and finance, but $\phi = 1$ has been found to describe accurately many such time series. Moreover, $|\phi| > 1$ has the intuitively unappealing property that shocks to the process are not only persistent through time, they are instead propagated so that a given shock will have an increasingly large influence, which seems rather odd (this is equivalent to ask, say, "what explains the most of interest rates movements today?," receiving as a pondered answer "easy enough—unexpected monetary policy decisions taken two centuries ago").

The RW with drift in Eq. (4.8) is then $I(1)$ and it contains one unit root. Of course, as seen in Chapter 2, a white noise process is stationary, it contains no unit roots (i.e., it just contains stationary roots), and we can write $\varepsilon_t \sim I(0)$. To visualize what a general $I(d)$ process with $d > 1$ may look like, consider Example 4.1.

EXAMPLE 4.1

Consider the process $y_{t+1} = 2y_t - y_{t-1} + \varepsilon_{t+1}$, where ε_{t+1} is a white noise process. Note that:

$$\begin{aligned}\Delta y_{t+1} &= 2y_t - y_{t-1} + \varepsilon_{t+1} - y_t = y_t - y_{t-1} + \varepsilon_{t+1}\\ &= \Delta y_t + \varepsilon_{t+1}\end{aligned}$$

which shows that just differencing once is not sufficient to make the series stationary. In fact, differencing again, we have:

$$\Delta(\Delta y_{t+1}) \equiv \Delta^2 y_{t+1} = \Delta y_{t+1} - \Delta y_t = \Delta y_t - \Delta y_t + \varepsilon_{t+1} = \varepsilon_{t+1}.$$

Therefore, twice differencing the process delivers a stationary series, which is equivalent, by Definition 4.2 to the fact that $y_{t+1} = 2y_t - y_{t-1} + \varepsilon_{t+1}$ is I(2). In fact, note that using the lag operator introduced in Chapter 2, this process can be written as:

$$y_{t+1} - 2y_t + y_{t-1} = (1 - L)(1 - L)y_{t+1} = (1 - L)\Delta y_{t+1} = \Delta^2 y_{t+1} = \varepsilon_{t+1},$$

where $(1 - L)(1 - L) = 1 - 2L + L^2$, which reveals the need to differentiate twice. Following this lead, it is then clear that the process

$$\begin{aligned}(1 - L)(1 - L)y_{t+1} &= (1 - L)(y_{t+1} - 2y_t + y_{t-1})\\ &= (y_{t+1} - y_t) - 2(y_t - y_{t-1}) + (y_{t-1} - y_{t-2}) = y_{t+1} - 3y_t + 3y_{t-1} - y_{t-2} = \varepsilon_{t+1}\end{aligned}$$

is an I(3) process.

Note instead that the process $y_{t+1} = 2y_t - 2y_{t-1} + \varepsilon_{t+1}$ is not I(2):

$$\begin{aligned}\Delta y_{t+1} &= 2y_t - 2y_{t-1} + \varepsilon_{t+1} - y_t = y_t - y_{t-1} - y_{t-1} + \varepsilon_{t+1}\\ &= \Delta y_t - y_{t-1} + \varepsilon_{t+1}\end{aligned}$$

but then

$$\Delta(\Delta y_{t+1}) \equiv \Delta^2 y_{t+1} = \Delta y_{t+1} - \Delta y_t = \Delta y_t - y_{t-1} - \Delta y_t + \varepsilon_{t+1} = y_{t-1} + \varepsilon_{t+1}$$

is not a stationary process unless y_{t-1} is itself stationary, when then no differencing would be required in the first instance. Although we shall not take an interest in this extension in this book, $y_{t+1} = 2y_t - 2y_{t-1} + \varepsilon_{t+1}$ happens to be more than I(2) but less than I(3), that is, it is nonstationary and it contains more than two unit roots but it belongs to a class even more general than I(2) processes.

Example 4.1 delivers an important lesson: all $I(d)$ processes (with $d > 0$) are nonstationary, but there are nonstationary processes that do not fit Definition 4.2.[2]

2. Enders (2008) contains an entertaining treatment of seasonal unit roots, which can be defined using the lag operator as cases in which $(1 - L^s)A(L)y_t = B(L)\varepsilon_t$ for $s \geq 2$, where $A(L)$ and $B(L)$ are polynomials with roots inside the unit circle, and such that $(1 - L)A(L)y_t = B(L)\varepsilon_t$ is *not* stationary. For instance, when $y_t = \mu + y_{t-4} + \varepsilon_t$, note that $\Delta y_t = \mu + (y_{t-4} - y_{t-1}) + \varepsilon_t$ will not be stationary. However, rather interestingly, note that incorrectly applying seasonal differentiation to a random walk will make it stationary:

$$(1 - L^4)y_t = \mu + y_{t-1} - y_{t-4} + \varepsilon_t = \mu + (y_{t-1} - y_{t-2}) + (y_{t-2} - y_{t-3}) + (y_{t-3} - y_{t-4}) + \varepsilon_t = \mu + \Delta y_{t-1} + \Delta y_{t-2} + \Delta y_{t-3} + \varepsilon_t.$$

(A)

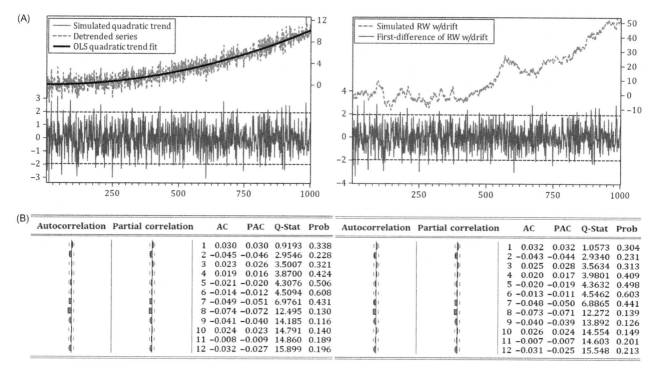

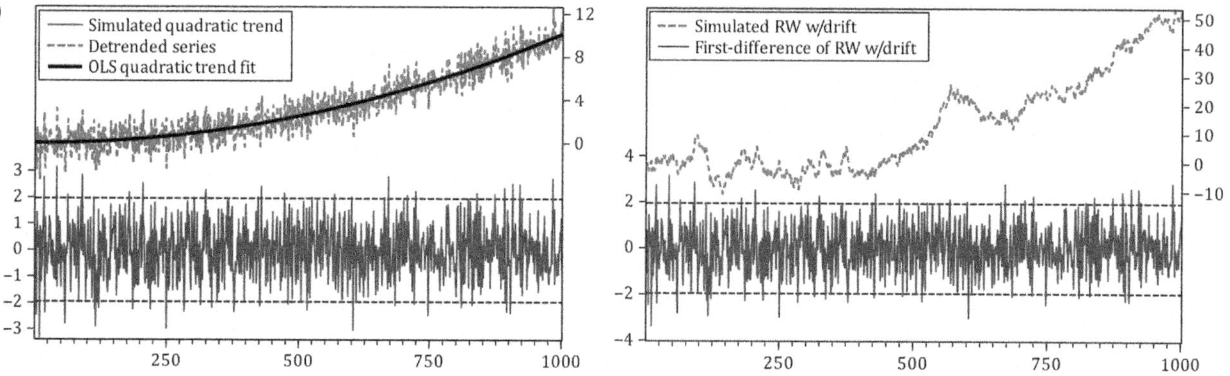

(B)

Autocorrelation	Partial correlation		AC	PAC	Q-Stat	Prob
		1	0.030	0.030	0.9193	0.338
		2	-0.045	-0.046	2.9546	0.228
		3	0.023	0.026	3.5007	0.321
		4	0.019	0.016	3.8700	0.424
		5	-0.021	-0.020	4.3076	0.506
		6	-0.014	-0.012	4.5094	0.608
		7	-0.049	-0.051	6.9761	0.431
		8	-0.074	-0.072	12.495	0.130
		9	-0.041	-0.040	14.185	0.116
		10	0.024	0.023	14.791	0.140
		11	-0.008	-0.009	14.860	0.189
		12	-0.032	-0.027	15.899	0.196

Autocorrelation	Partial correlation		AC	PAC	Q-Stat	Prob
		1	0.032	0.032	1.0573	0.304
		2	-0.043	-0.044	2.9340	0.231
		3	0.025	0.028	3.5634	0.313
		4	0.020	0.017	3.9801	0.409
		5	-0.020	-0.019	4.3632	0.498
		6	-0.013	-0.011	4.5462	0.603
		7	-0.048	-0.050	6.8865	0.441
		8	-0.073	-0.071	12.272	0.139
		9	-0.040	-0.039	13.892	0.126
		10	0.026	0.024	14.554	0.149
		11	-0.007	-0.007	14.603	0.201
		12	-0.031	-0.025	15.548	0.213

FIGURE 4.2 (A) Detrended and first-differenced series. (B) Sample ACF of detrended and first-differenced series.

Fig. 4.2 shows the results of detrending the quadratic determinist trend and of first-differencing (and demeaning) the positively drifting RW in Fig. 4.2A. Fig. 4.2A shows the resulting stationary series: in this case, we have generated the data and therefore we know by construction that regression-based polynomial detrending and first-differencing will work. Fig. 4.2B shows the corresponding sample ACF and confirms that in these two simulated cases, the procedures in Definitions 4.1 and 4.2 actually work.[3]

We now ask a few questions that are practically important. Serious damage—in a statistical sense—can be done when the inappropriate method is used to eliminate a trend.[4]

4.1.1 What Happens If One Incorrectly Detrends a Unit Root Series?

This occurrence used to be popular when formal tests for stochastic trends were at their beginnings and less well-known and easily accessible compared to what they are now. For instance, an analyst is given the 1000 observations plotted in the right-upper portion of Fig. 4.2A, and decides to try and make the series stationary by fitting and removing a deterministic trend. If this happens, damage will result:

RESULT 4.1 (Detrending a unit root process)

When a time series process $\{y_t\}$ is $I(d)$ but an attempt is made to remove its stochastic trend by fitting deterministic (often polynomial, spline type) time trend functions, the resulting OLS residuals will still contain one or more unit roots. Equivalently, deterministic detrending does not remove the stochastic trends.

Although the result holds more generally, let us examine the case of a RW with drift process in Eq. (4.2) that, just for the sake of argument, we shall try to detrend using a simple linear time trend, that is, subtracting $\hat{\delta}_0 + \hat{\delta}_1 t$:

3. In case you wonder, the ACF for the simulated quadratic determinist trend data looks very similar to the ACF concerning generated random walk data in Table 4.1.

4. Adherents to the Box–Jenkins methodology recommend differencing both nonstationary and variables with a near-unit root. For very short-term forecasts, differencing all types of trends away has proven not to be crucial. However, as the forecast horizon expands, the precise form of the trend becomes increasingly important: stationarity implies the absence of a trend and long-run mean reversion; a deterministic trend implies steady increases (or decreases) into the infinite future; forecasts of a series with a stochastic trend converge to a steady level.

(A)

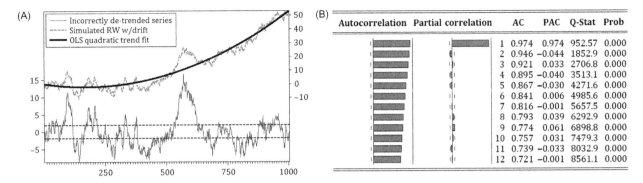

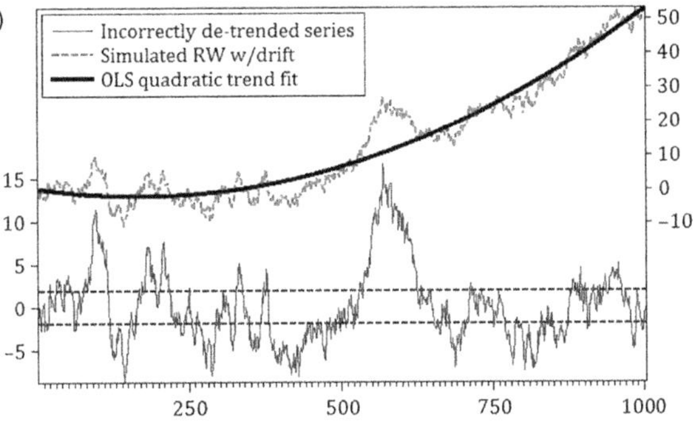

(B)

Autocorrelation	Partial correlation		AC	PAC	Q-Stat	Prob
		1	0.974	0.974	952.57	0.000
		2	0.946	−0.044	1852.9	0.000
		3	0.921	0.033	2706.8	0.000
		4	0.895	−0.040	3513.1	0.000
		5	0.867	−0.030	4271.6	0.000
		6	0.841	0.006	4985.6	0.000
		7	0.816	−0.001	5657.5	0.000
		8	0.793	0.039	6292.9	0.000
		9	0.774	0.061	6898.8	0.000
		10	0.757	0.031	7479.3	0.000
		11	0.739	−0.033	8032.9	0.000
		12	0.721	−0.001	8561.1	0.000

FIGURE 4.3 Incorrect polynomial detrending of a random walk.

$$
\begin{aligned}
y_t - \hat{y}_t^{detrend} &= y_0 + \mu t + \sum_{\tau=1}^{t} \varepsilon_\tau - \hat{\delta}_0 - \hat{\delta}_1 t \\
&= (y_0 - \hat{\delta}_0) + (\mu - \hat{\delta}_1)t + \sum_{\tau=1}^{t} \varepsilon_\tau
\end{aligned}
\tag{4.9}
$$

Visibly, nothing has been achieved: even in the almost impossible case in which the estimated coefficients happen to be such that $\hat{\delta}_0 = y_0, \hat{\delta}_1 = \mu$ (and there is no reason why this should happen), the resulting expression for $y_t - \hat{y}_t^{detrend}$ still equals $\sum_{\tau=1}^{t} \varepsilon_\tau$, which is evidence that source of unit roots and hence the stochastic trend has not been removed. For instance, Fig. 4.3 illustrates such outcomes—by plotting the series $y_t - \hat{y}_t^{detrend}$ on the left, and the ACF of $y_t - \hat{y}_t^{detrend}$ on the right—when we attempt to make the positively drifting RW of Fig. 4.2 stationary, by incorrectly fitting and subtracting a quadratic determinist trend.

Clearly, the ACF in the right panel is not the ACF of an obviously stationary process while exactly because we know how the series were generated, we would expect to recover observations on $\{\varepsilon_t\}$ in this case. On the contrary, we recover at best observations from $\left\{\sum_{\tau=1}^{t} \varepsilon_\tau\right\}_{t=1}^{1000}$, that is, cumulants of white noise realizations, not white noise realizations. Because we are working with series that we think are approximately white noise, while they are in fact cumulants of white noise, this may lead to grossly incorrect inferences or even financial decisions. Therefore correctly detecting stochastic trends and unit roots as such is of key importance.

4.1.2 What Happens If One Incorrectly Applies Differencing to (Deterministic) Trend-Stationary Series?

This problem is still pretty much widespread and we trust it can be still wreaking havoc in many statistical analyses of financial and economic data: an analyst is assigned the 1000 observations plotted in the left-upper portion of Fig. 4.2A, and, because some trend is clearly detectable, she simply decides to make the series stationary by taking first differences. If this happens, other damage will result:

RESULT 4.2 (Differentiating a trend-stationary processes)

When a time series process $\{y_t\}$ contains a deterministic time trend but it is otherwise I(0) (i.e., it is trend stationary), and an attempt is made to remove the deterministic trend by differentiating the series *d* times, the resulting differentiated series will contain *d* unit roots in its moving-average components and will therefore be not invertible. Equivalently, differentiating a trend-stationary series creates new stochastic trends that are shifted inside the shocks of the series.

To see why this is the case, consider the process in Eq. (4.1) and take its first difference:

$$
\begin{aligned}
\Delta y_t \equiv y_t - y_{t-1} &= \left(\sum_{j=0}^{Q} \delta_j t^j + \varepsilon_t\right) - \left(\sum_{j=0}^{Q} \delta_j (t-1)^j + \varepsilon_{t-1}\right) \\
&= \sum_{j=0}^{Q} \delta_j \left[t^j - (t-1)^j\right] + (\varepsilon_t - \varepsilon_{t-1}).
\end{aligned}
\tag{4.10}
$$

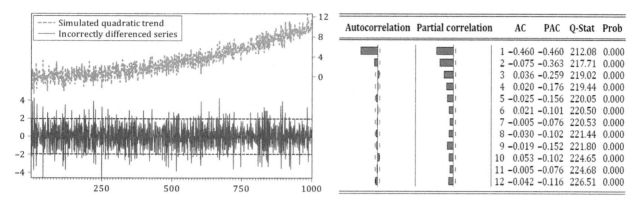

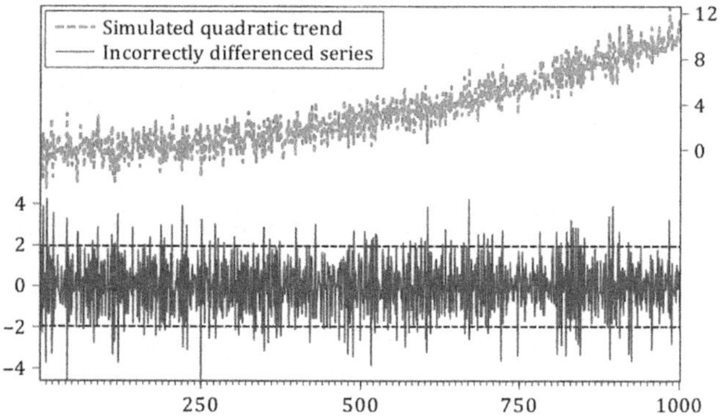

Autocorrelation	Partial correlation		AC	PAC	Q-Stat	Prob
		1	-0.460	-0.460	212.08	0.000
		2	-0.075	-0.363	217.71	0.000
		3	0.036	-0.259	219.02	0.000
		4	0.020	-0.176	219.44	0.000
		5	-0.025	-0.156	220.05	0.000
		6	0.021	-0.101	220.50	0.000
		7	-0.005	-0.076	220.53	0.000
		8	-0.030	-0.102	221.44	0.000
		9	-0.019	-0.152	221.80	0.000
		10	0.053	-0.102	224.65	0.000
		11	-0.005	-0.076	224.68	0.000
		12	-0.042	-0.116	226.51	0.000

FIGURE 4.4 Incorrect first-differencing of a trend-stationary series.

This process is now an moving average of order one (MA(1)) with a complex time trend, with one glaring feature: the coefficient in front of the MA term equals −1 and such we are dealing with a unit root in the MA component. For instance, when $Q=1$, the expression in Eq. (4.10) becomes $\Delta y_t = \delta_1 + (\varepsilon_{t+1} - \varepsilon_t)$, an *integrated moving-average of order 1*. What happens if we try to differentiate Eq. (4.10) again? Will matters get any better? Unfortunately not:

$$\begin{aligned}\Delta^2 y_t \equiv \Delta y_t - \Delta y_{t-1} &= \left(\sum_{j=0}^{Q}\delta_j\left[t^j - (t-1)^j\right] + \varepsilon_t - \varepsilon_{t-1}\right)\\ &\quad - \left(\sum_{j=0}^{Q}\delta_j\left[(t-1)^j - (t-2)^j\right] + \varepsilon_{t-1} - \varepsilon_{t-2}\right)\\ &= \sum_{j=0}^{Q}\delta_j\left\{\left[t^j - (t-1)^j\right] - \left[(t-1)^j - (t-2)^j\right]\right\} + \varepsilon_t - 2\varepsilon_{t-1} + \varepsilon_{t-2}.\end{aligned} \tag{4.11}$$

This is an integrated MA(2) process with two clearly visible roots in excess of 1, and an increasingly complex time trend function. Yet, this is exactly what Result 4.2 states: the more you differentiate a trend-stationary process, the higher the number of unit roots in the resulting MA process. Fig. 4.4 illustrates such outcomes—by plotting the series Δy_t on the left, and the ACF of Δy_t on the right—when we attempt to make the quadratic trend series in the leftmost plot in Fig. 4.2 stationary, by first-differencing.

Although the plot of the first-differenced series to the left may not reveal dramatic problems (but closer inspection reveals that more than 13% of the differenced data exceed ±1.96, which should not occur if one has recovered the Gaussian white noise series ε_{t+1}), the ACF on the right illustrates clear signs of the first-differenced series being of MA(1) or MA(2) type with negative coefficients, which is indeed expected. Section 4.3 will give an account of how we can formally test for unit roots in MA processes.

4.1.3 What Happens If One Incorrectly Applies Differencing to a Stationary Series?

In modern times, when scores of formal tests of unit roots are always a few clicks of our computer mouse device away, it is not clear why we could end up misdiagnosing a stationary series as I(1) and therefore mistreating it by taking first differences. However, if one deals with quantitative empirical analyses long enough, she will end up encountering cases in which a range of unit root tests all give indecisive evidence, so that it will remain unclear whether the data at hand are either $I(0)$ or $I(1)$. Should we incorrectly decide the series is $I(1)$, while it is actually $I(0)$, what harm will we be doing?

The answer is that—even when the trend-stationary component is absent—Result 4.2 applies: when a time series is $I(0)$ but it is differenced d times, the resulting differentiated series will contain d unit roots in its moving-average components and will therefore be not invertible. Paradoxically, we would start out with a fine stationary series and by incorrectly applying the "right cure" to remove stochastic trends we would end up with a noninvertible MA series, in which the unit roots have been moved inside the MA components. It is therefore fair to ask why, when in doubt as to the $I(0)$ versus $I(1)$ nature of a series, would a well-prepared analyst ever risk such an outcome. The answer lies in perils of using potentially $I(1)$ series in otherwise standard analyses that have been developed instead with reference to weakly stationary series, that we are about to discuss in Section 4.2.

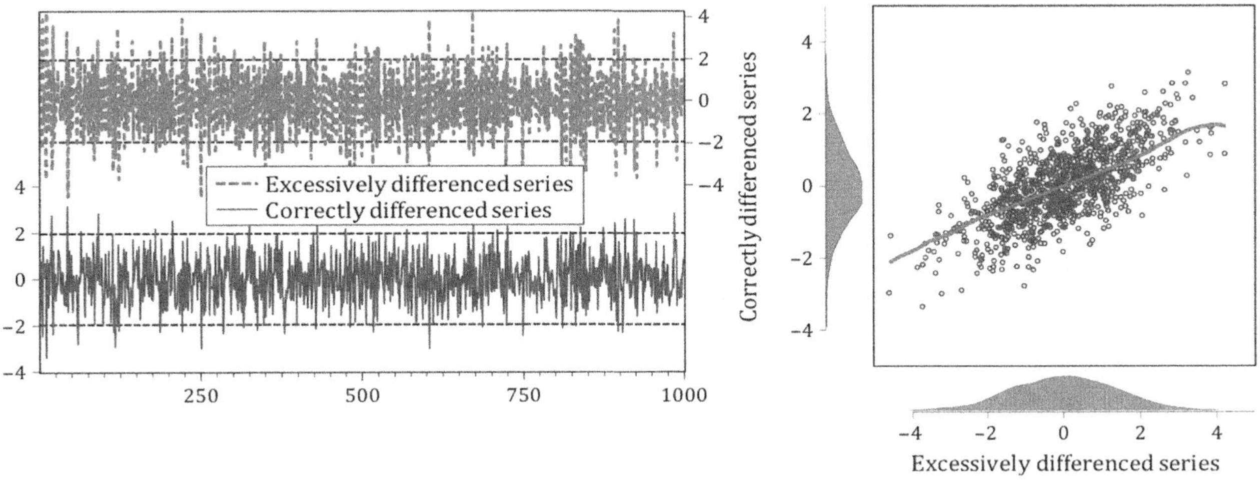

Autocorrelation	Partial correlation		AC	PAC	Q-Stat	Prob
		1	-0.460	-0.460	212.11	0.000
		2	-0.075	-0.364	217.77	0.000
		3	0.037	-0.260	219.14	0.000
		4	0.020	-0.176	219.56	0.000
		5	-0.024	-0.154	220.12	0.000
		6	0.020	-0.099	220.54	0.000
		7	-0.004	-0.073	220.56	0.000
		8	-0.030	-0.098	221.47	0.000
		9	-0.019	-0.148	221.84	0.000
		10	0.053	-0.099	224.69	0.000
		11	-0.005	-0.072	224.72	0.000
		12	-0.041	-0.111	226.45	0.000

FIGURE 4.5 Excessive differencing of a $I(1)$ series.

4.1.4 What Happens If One Incorrectly Applies Differencing $d+r$ Times to an $I(d)$ Series?

This last case is in fact a generalization of the cases in Sections 4.1.2–4.1.3: in Section 4.1.2, we were differencing $d=r$ times an $I(0)$ series that contained a deterministic trend; in Section 4.1.3, we were just differencing $d=r$ times a I(0) series. Now, we generalize such cases to envision situations in which $y_t \sim I(d)$ but by mistake we differentiate it $d+r$ times, $r \neq 0$. We can think of two cases:

- If $r>0$, we are over-differencing the series, and as such Result 4.2 applies, that is, when a time series is $I(d)$ but it is differenced more than d times, the resulting differentiated series will contain r unit roots in its moving-average components and will therefore be not invertible.
- If $r<0$, we are simply not differencing the series enough (think of the intermediate steps in Example 4.1) and therefore if the original time series had been $I(d)$ but it is differenced less than d times, the resulting differentiated series will still contain $d+r<d$ unit roots and will therefore remain nonstationary.

Fig. 4.5 gives one example of the damages caused by differencing twice the $I(1)$ RW with positive drift series of Fig. 4.3. Working through the pictures in a clock-wise direction, we can see that the over-differenced integrated MA series tends to be spikier and more volatile than the correctly differenced white noise series should be. This is confirmed by the scatter plot and the ACF that validates our expectations and in fact turns out to be very similar to the one in Fig. 4.4, which is unsurprising because the IID shocks on which the two series of generated data are based were selected to be the same.

4.2 THE SPURIOUS REGRESSION PROBLEM

Why do we care so much to find ways to turn series that contain a trend into stationary series? In this section, we describe the perils that nonstationary trending series pose in regression analysis. On the surface the reason is simple and revealed in Result 4.3.

RESULT 4.3 (Sums of stationary and nonstationary series)

Consider N time series, $y_{1,t} \sim I(d_1), y_{2,t} \sim I(d_2), \ldots, y_{N,t} \sim I(d_N)$. Then, *unless special conditions occur* (see Section 4.4), their weighted sum will be integrated with an order that is the maximum across all integration orders:

$$\sum_{i=1}^{N} w_i y_{i,t} \sim I(\max(d_1, d_2, \ldots, d_N)). \tag{4.12}$$

We do not care for proving this result here, but in the case of three series, say $y_t \sim I(1), x_t \sim I(1)$, and η_t, with y_t and x_t independent, a heuristic proof may be instructive. First, note that a regression of y_t on x_t, $y_t = a + bx_t + \eta_t$, can be equivalently written as $\eta_t = y_t - a - bx_t$. Therefore η_t is:

$$\begin{aligned}\eta_t &= \left(y_0 + \mu_y t + \textstyle\sum_{\tau=1}^{t} \varepsilon_\tau^y\right) - a - b\left(x_0 + \mu_x t + \textstyle\sum_{\tau=1}^{t} \varepsilon_\tau^x\right) \\ &= (y_0 - a - bx_0) + \left(\mu_y - b\mu_x\right)t + \textstyle\sum_{\tau=1}^{t}(\varepsilon_\tau^y - b\varepsilon_\tau^x).\end{aligned} \tag{4.13}$$

Because ε_t^x and ε_t^y are in general independent white noise errors so that their sum is also a white noise, Eq. (4.13) shows that η_t is a unit root process itself and

$$\begin{aligned}\eta_t &= \left(y_0 + \mu_y t + \textstyle\sum_{\tau=1}^{t} \varepsilon_\tau^y\right) - a - b\left(x_0 + \mu_x t + \textstyle\sum_{\tau=1}^{t} \varepsilon_\tau^x\right) = \left[(\mu_y - b\mu_x) + \varepsilon_t^y - b\varepsilon_t^x\right] + \\ &+ \underbrace{\left(y_0 - a - bx_0\right) + \left(\mu_y - b\mu_x\right)(t-1) + \textstyle\sum_{\tau=1}^{t-1}(\varepsilon_\tau^y - b\varepsilon_\tau^x)}_{\eta_{t-1}} = (\mu_y - b\mu_x) + \eta_{t-1} + (\varepsilon_t^y - b\varepsilon_t^x),\end{aligned} \tag{4.14}$$

another RW with drift. Of course, this is just Result 4.3 specialized to the case of a sum of two $I(1)$ variables: η_t is their weighted sum minus a constant, which is a degenerate $I(0)$ random variable. Therefore $\eta_t \sim I(1)$, which is indeed the highest integration order of the variables that we are combining.

This heuristic proof is also instructive on a different account: we have started from what seemed to be a standard regression, $y_t = a + bx_t + \eta_t$. Yet, when the regressand and regressor are both $I(1)$, it turns out that the regression errors must then also contain, *unless special conditions occur* (see Section 4.4), a unit root. This is of course problematic: the assumptions of the classical regression model necessitate that both the y_t and x_t variables be stationary and that the errors have a zero mean and a finite variance, which will not be the case with η_t that is instead a RW with drift. In the presence of nonstationary variables, we may face what Granger and Newbold (1974) call a *spurious regression*. A spurious regression has the following features:

- The residuals are $I(1)$ and as such any shock has a permanent effect on the regression, being equivalent to a permanent change of the intercept of the model.
- As a result, standard OLS estimators are inconsistent and the associated inferential procedures are invalid and statistically meaningless (because they assume stationarity of the regressand and of all the regressors).
- The regression has a high R^2 and t-statistics that appear to be significant, but the results are void of any economic meaning.

In short, estimating spurious regressions represents a misuse of energy and (often polluting) electricity while reporting and discussing results from a spurious regression is a criminal waste of time. Using our example in Eqs. (4.13) and (4.14) with $y_0 = x_0 = 0$ and $\mu_y = \mu_x = 0$, Granger and Newbold generated a large number of alternative series expecting to find $b = 0$ on average in the regressions they implemented, because y_t and x_t were generated independently. On the opposite, they reported that, at a 5% test size, they were able to reject the null hypothesis of $b = 0$ in approximately 75% of the simulations; moreover, most regressions displayed very high R^2 coefficients and the residuals exhibited a high degree of positive autocorrelation, consistently with their coming from a RW process. Importantly, this is not a small sample problem; in fact, these issues worsen as the sample size grows (see Phillips, 1986). The cure of the problem is also self-evident: to work with stationary first differences of the variables. Of course, these ideas generalize, at the cost of increasing technical complexity when one would try and regress an $I(d)$ series on another $I(d)$ series, without first taking the dth differentials. Example 4.2 shows these problems in action.

EXAMPLE 4.2

We generate two independent sets of IID white noise variables, ε_t^x and ε_t^y, and use them to simulate 1000 observations from two driftless RWs. Fig. 4.6 shows both series, in levels, and in first differences, which of course makes them stationary. Because the two RWs are generated from two independent sets of shocks and they have no drift, we expect them to be unrelated. In case you object the series seem to be trending in similar directions, you know that it is not—it is just chance and a good dose of visual illusion. However, the second plot in Fig. 4.6 (reading in counter clock-wise direction) shows that two RW series are seemingly related, through their stochastic trends that end up impressing similar trending shapes in portions of the sample.

In fact the estimated regression of one RW on the other gives (p-values are in parentheses):

$$y_t = \underset{(0.000)}{7.497} + \underset{(0.000)}{0.538}\, x_t + \underset{(0.000)}{12.184}\, z_t \qquad R^2 = 0.101$$

which poses the usual dilemma: given two independent RWs, how can one explain the other with a precisely estimated coefficient, with an R^2 in excess of 10%? As we now understand, this is due to the nature of the implied residuals, which are $I(1)$ and deprive the inference and the R^2 of any meanings. The left plot in Fig. 4.7 shows that the residuals do indeed contain glaring evidence of a unit root.

The last, rightmost plot in Fig. 4.6 shows that when the series are differentiated, a regression of one differentiated series on the other provides—as it is sensible to expect—no explanatory power:

$$\Delta y_t = \underset{(0.536)}{0.019} + \underset{(0.771)}{0.009}\, \Delta x_t + \underset{(0.000)}{0.976}\, z_t' \qquad R^2 = 0.000.$$

For once despite the absolute lack of any significance, such a result is "good" and sensible: any predictive power would be an artifact deriving from the spurious nature of the regression. The rightmost plot in Fig. 4.7 shows that the residuals from this second regression are approximately stationary.

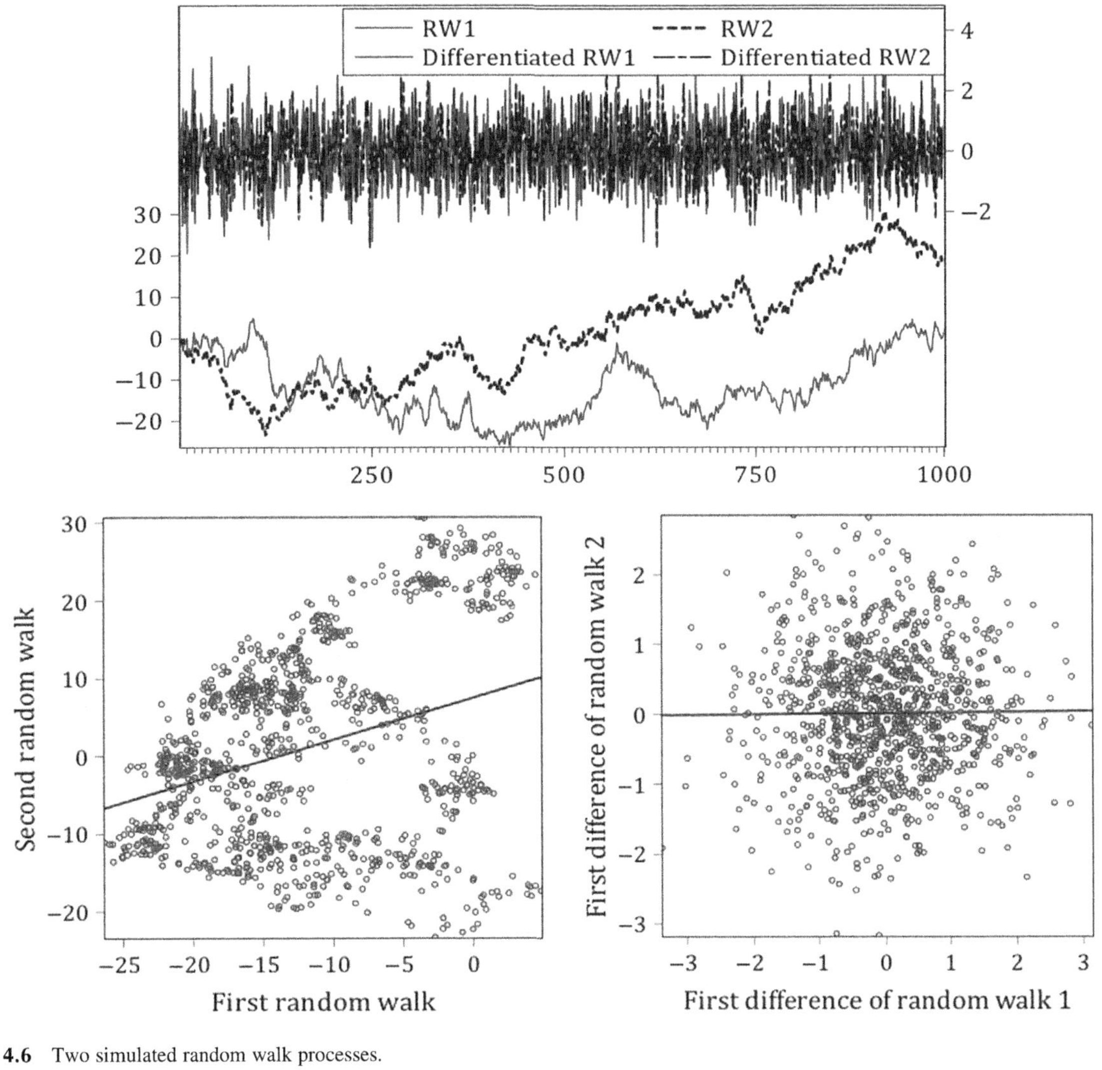

FIGURE 4.6 Two simulated random walk processes.

(A)

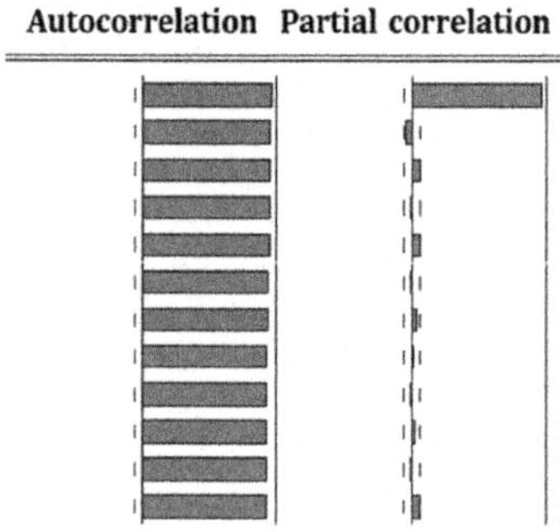

Lag	AC	PAC	Q-Stat	Prob
1	0.995	0.995	994.58	0.000
2	0.990	−0.042	1980.0	0.000
3	0.986	0.072	2957.8	0.000
4	0.981	−0.004	3927.8	0.000
5	0.978	0.060	4891.3	0.000
6	0.974	−0.010	5848.2	0.000
7	0.970	0.044	6799.2	0.000
8	0.967	0.016	7744.6	0.000
9	0.964	−0.014	8684.2	0.000
10	0.960	0.032	9618.4	0.000
11	0.957	−0.015	10547.	0.000
12	0.954	0.058	11471.	0.000

(B)

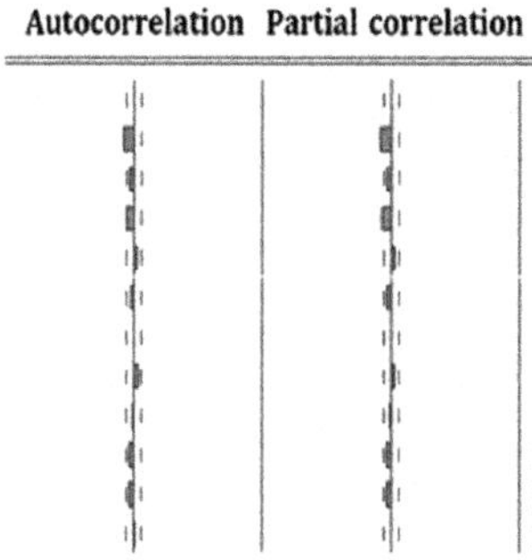

Lag	AC	PAC	Q-Stat	Prob
1	0.004	0.004	0.0124	0.911
2	−0.080	−0.080	6.4859	0.039
3	−0.030	−0.030	7.4005	0.060
4	−0.060	−0.067	11.063	0.026
5	0.032	0.027	12.088	0.034
6	−0.021	−0.033	12.517	0.051
7	0.001	0.002	12.518	0.085
8	0.037	0.031	13.912	0.084
9	−0.005	−0.003	13.937	0.125
10	−0.032	−0.030	14.944	0.134
11	−0.032	−0.030	16.005	0.141
12	0.008	0.007	16.076	0.188

FIGURE 4.7 ACF of the residuals from regressing one RW walk on another RW and of regressing the same series in first differences.

Note that problems will also arise in regression analysis when the regressand and the regressors are integrated of different orders. Regression equations using such variables are meaningless. For instance, if in Eq. (4.13) only x_t were to be $I(1)$, the resulting regression errors

$$\begin{aligned}\eta_t' &= (\mu_y + \varepsilon_t^y) - a - b\left(x_0 + \mu_x t + \textstyle\sum_{\tau=1}^{t} \varepsilon_\tau^x\right) \\ &= (\mu_y - a - bx_0) - b\mu_x t - b\textstyle\sum_{\tau=1}^{t} \varepsilon_\tau^x + \varepsilon_t^y,\end{aligned} \tag{4.15}$$

would still be $I(1)$. Although more complex, one could replace $\mu_y + \varepsilon_t^y$ in Eq. (4.15) with any stationary ARMA model, obtaining the same result because the sum between an invertible MA and an MA with unit roots is always an MA process with unit roots.

Finally, what are the special conditions mentioned in Result 4.3 that would make it possible for the weighted sum of $y_{1,t} \sim I(d), y_{2,t} \sim I(d), \ldots, y_{N,t} \sim I(d)$ to be of an order that is less than d or even 0, that is, stationary? This is the case of *cointegrated* nonstationary series of order up to d that shall be discussed in Section 4.4.

4.3 UNIT ROOT TESTS

4.3.1 Classical Dickey–Fuller Tests

As we saw in Section 4.1, especially in small samples, a $I(1)$ process will generate SACFs that start out at $Corr[y_t, y_{t-1}] < 1$ but close to 1 and then decline as the lag order grows. Because of these patterns, a researcher can be easily misled into thinking that the data, which were actually generated by a RW, may be stationary. Formally, because the estimated AR(1) coefficient equals $Corr[y_t, y_{t-1}]$, this means that any attempt to recover a unit root from generated RW data will fail because the OLS estimate of the unit root coefficient will contain a downward bias. Dickey and Fuller (1979) were the first researchers to offer a procedure to formally test for the presence of a unit root that takes this bias in due account, based on a *Monte Carlo design*. They generated a large number *of RW sequences* and for each of them they calculated the estimated value of the AR(1) coefficient. The larger is the number of simulation trials, the more precise the resulting distribution of the statistic is, by a simple application of the *Law of Large Numbers*. Although most of the estimates were close to one, some were further from one than others. For instance, Dickey and Fuller (henceforth DF) found that in the presence of an intercept:

- 10% of the estimated values of the AR(1) coefficient were less than 2.58 standard errors below one.
- 5% of the estimated values of the AR(1) coefficient were less than 2.89 standard errors below one.
- 1% of the estimated values of the AR(1) coefficient were less than 3.51 standard errors below one.

Because these critical values were generated by assuming a RW, it is clear that *DF operated under the null hypothesis of a RW*.

This suggests a natural way to formally test for a unit root in a given series. Because an AR(1) model can be equivalently written as:

$$y_{t+1} - y_t \equiv \Delta y_{t+1} = \mu + \underbrace{(\phi - 1)}_{\alpha} y_t + \varepsilon_{t+1}, \tag{4.16}$$

we can simply obtain the OLS estimate of α, the corresponding t-statistic (which is just how many standard deviations the estimate of ϕ deviates from 1), and compare it with the critical value found by DF in *a one-sided t-test.*[5] For instance, if the estimated value of ϕ was 0.962 with a standard error of 0.013, then the estimated coefficient α would be -0.038 and the corresponding t-statistic of $-0.038/0.013 = -2.923$ would indicate that such value falls 2.923 standard deviations below unity. According to DF's simulations, this happens in less than 5% of the time, under the null of a RW, but in more than 1% of the simulations. Therefore this represents a rather unlucky event under the null of a RW and this may lead to a rejection of the hypothesis, with a p-value between 0.01 and 0.05.

Interestingly, in this way, we are using a standard t-test taking into account that under the null of a RW, its distribution is nonstandard and cannot be analytically evaluated. In fact, *it would be incorrect to simply use the standard t-student because standard inference is invalid when the assumed stochastic process is nonstationary.*[6] For instance, if the estimated value of ϕ was 0.912 (a value even more distant from 1 that we had obtained previously), with a standard error of 0.042, then the estimated coefficient α would be -0.088 and the corresponding t-statistic would be $-0.088/0.042 = -2.095$. Using standard inference, this would lead to a rejection of the null of a RW with a p-value below 0.05 (in a one-side test of $\alpha < 1$). However, this would be misleading because from DF simulations we know that such a t-ratio occurs with a frequency that largely exceeds 10% and hence provides no ground to reject the null hypothesis of a unit root. Of course, it is possible to test for unit roots under a null of stationarity and we shall investigate later in the chapter how that can be performed. Interestingly, it is possible to reject the null of stationarity in favor of a unit root under the null of stationarity and also reject the null of nonstationarity in favor of stationary process under the null of a unit root although one hopes to encounter such an event as rarely as possible.

Dickey and Fuller (1979) actually considered two additional regression equations that can be used to test for the presence of a unit root, in addition to Eq. (4.16):

$$\Delta y_{t+1} = \alpha y_t + \varepsilon_{t+1} \tag{4.17}$$

$$\Delta y_{t+1} = \mu + \delta t + \alpha y_t + \varepsilon_{t+1}. \tag{4.18}$$

Eq. (4.17) drops the constant from Eq. (4.16), while Eq. (4.18) adds a deterministic time trend to Eq. (4.16). Dickey et al. (1986) have also shown that the limiting distribution for α is not affected by the removal of any *deterministic S seasonal components*, through dummy variables inserted in Eqs. (4.16)–(4.18), like in:

$$\Delta y_{t+1} = \mu + \delta t + \sum_{s=1}^{S-1} \lambda_s D_s + \alpha y_t + \varepsilon_{t+1}, \tag{4.19}$$

where D_s are the standard seasonal dummies in a number equal to $S-1$ (because the equation already contains an intercept). However, the parameter of interest in all the regression test equations remains α and the tests work in the same way, comparing the t-ratio of α, which still has a nonstandard (finite sample) distribution, with critical values that need to be approximated by simulation, using null models that are adjusted to either exclude the drift (in case of Eq. 4.16) or include a time trend (in case of Eq. 4.17).[7] Of course, it should also be economic theory or financial models to guide us through the decision as to whether to include a drift term and/or a determinist time trend, not only a matter of statistical robustness of the results.

The augmented Dickey-Fuller (ADF) critical values depend on which deterministic regressors, as they are called, are included, if any: the confidence intervals around $\alpha = 0$ dramatically expand if a drift and a time trend are included in the model. This is quite different from the case in which the series is stationary: in this case, as we know, the distribution of the t-statistic does not depend on the presence of the other regressors. However, one cannot even arbitrarily make the opposite choice: inappropriately omitting the intercept or time trend can cause the power of the test to go to 0.

5. More recently, MacKinnon (1991) has implemented a much larger set of simulations than those tabulated by Dickey and Fuller.

6. Sims et al. (1990) proved that if the DGP contains any deterministic regressors (i.e., an intercept and/or a time trend) and the estimating equation does contain these deterministic regressors, inference on all coefficients can be conducted using a t-test or an F-test. This is because a test involving a single restriction across parameters with different rates of convergence is dominated asymptotically by the parameters with the slowest rates of convergence. Therefore the simulated ADF distributions are needed only when you include deterministic regressors not in the actual DGP process.

7. Dickey and Fuller (1981) also provided (by simulation) critical values for three additional F-statistics to test joint hypotheses on the coefficients, for instance $\mu = \delta = \alpha = 0$ in the case of Eq. (4.18). These statistics are constructed in exactly the same way as ordinary F-tests, by comparing and scaling restricted and unrestricted sum of squared residuals, but the critical values need to be simulated by Monte Carlo under the null of a random walk. However, rejecting the joint null of $\mu = \delta = \alpha = 0$ will not carry information as to whether the data come from a trend-stationary process ($\delta \neq 0, \alpha < 0$) or a process that contains both deterministic and stochastic trends ($\delta \neq 0, \alpha = 0$).

For example, if, as in Eq. (4.18), the data generating process (DGP) process includes a function of time, omitting the term $\sum_{j=1}^{Q} \delta_j t^j$ will impress an upward bias in the estimated value of α.

4.3.2 The Augmented Dickey–Fuller Test

The classical DF test is flexible and easy to reproduce now that computers are cheap and largely available. However, it suffers from one obvious rigidity: given the null hypothesis of a RW, the alternative hypothesis is specified as an AR(1) stationary process. Of course, not all stationary time series variables can be well represented by an AR(1) process. It is however possible to use the DF tests in more general cases. Consider the AR(p) process:

$$y_{t+1} = \phi_0 + \phi_1 y_t + \phi_2 y_{t-1} + \cdots + \phi_{p-1} y_{t-p+2} + \phi_p y_{t-p+1} + \varepsilon_{t+1}, \tag{4.20}$$

where the errors are white noise and hence homoskedastic. Now add and subtract $\phi_p y_{t-p+2}$ to obtain:

$$y_{t+1} = \phi_0 + \phi_1 y_t + \phi_2 y_{t-1} + \cdots + (\phi_{p-1} + \phi_p) y_{t-p+2} - \phi_p \Delta y_{t-p+1} + \varepsilon_{t+1}. \tag{4.21}$$

Next, add and subtract $(\phi_{p-1} + \phi_p) y_{t-p+3}$ to get to:

$$y_{t+1} = \phi_0 + \phi_1 y_t + \cdots + (\phi_{p-2} + \phi_{p-1} + \phi_p) y_{t-p+3} - (\phi_{p-1} + \phi_p)\Delta y_{t-p+2} - \phi_p \Delta y_{t-p+1} + \varepsilon_{t+1}. \tag{4.22}$$

Repeating this step p times, we end up with:

$$\begin{aligned} \Delta y_{t+1} &= \phi_0 + \alpha y_t + \sum_{i=1}^{p} \gamma_i \Delta y_{t-i+1} + \varepsilon_{t+1} \quad \text{where} \\ \alpha &\equiv -\left(1 - \sum_{i=1}^{p} \phi_i\right) \qquad \gamma_i \equiv -\sum_{j=i}^{p} \phi_j, \end{aligned} \tag{4.23}$$

and the coefficient of interest remains α: if $\alpha = 0$, the equation is entirely in first differences and so it has a unit root; if $\alpha < 1$, this is indication of stationarity because taking first differences, one cannot remove y_t which is a sign of over-differencing. Given Eq. (4.23), we can test for the presence of a unit root using the same DF test discussed previously. This is an *augmented Dickey–Fuller (ADF) test*, that is valid for general AR(p) processes.[8] The ADF test implements a parametric correction for higher-order correlation. DF show that the asymptotic distribution of the t-ratio for α is independent of the number of lagged first differences included in the regression (4.23). Clearly, when $p = 1$, the ADF test boils down to a classical DF test because by construction we set $\sum_{i=2}^{1} \gamma_i \Delta y_{t-i+1} = 0$. Again the appropriate statistic to use depends on the deterministic components included in the regression equation, that is, whether a researcher would estimate Eq. (4.23) or any of the following:

$$\Delta y_{t+1} = \alpha y_t + \sum_{i=1}^{p} \gamma_i \Delta y_{t-i+1} + \varepsilon_{t+1} \text{ (no intercept)} \tag{4.24}$$

$$\Delta y_{t+1} = \phi_0 + \sum_{j=1}^{Q} \delta_j t^j + \alpha y_t + \sum_{i=1}^{p} \gamma_i \Delta y_{t-i+1} + \varepsilon_{t+1} \text{ (deterministic trend).} \tag{4.25}$$

Of course, we cannot properly estimate α and its standard error unless all of the autoregressive terms are included in the estimating equation, through correct specification of p. Too few lags will imply that the regression residuals do

8. The ADF test considers only a single unit root. However, a pth order autoregression may have $m \le p$ unit roots; if there are m unit roots, the series needs to be differenced m times to achieve stationarity and the test will have to be applied after each successive differentiation, starting with the highest order of differentiation, as suggested by Dickey and Pantula (1987). For instance, if two unit roots are suspected, one first estimates $\Delta^2 y_{t+1} = \alpha_1 \Delta y_t + \sum_{i=1}^{p_1} \gamma_{1,i} \Delta^2 y_{t-i+1} + \varepsilon^1_{t+1}$ to test the null that $\alpha_1 = 0$ using a DF test. If we cannot reject the null, we conclude that the series is I(2). If α_1 does differ from 0, we go on to determine whether there is a single unit root by estimating $\Delta^2 y_{t+1} = \alpha_1 \Delta y_t + \alpha_2 y_{t-1} + \sum_{i=1}^{p_1} \gamma_{1,i} \Delta^2 y_{t-i+1} + \sum_{i=1}^{p_1} \gamma_{1,i} \Delta y_{t-i+1} + \varepsilon^2_{t+1}$.
Because there are not two unit roots, we should find that α_1 and/or α_2 differ from 0. Under the null hypothesis of a single unit root, $\alpha_1 < 0$ and $\alpha_2 = 0$; under the alternative hypothesis the series is stationary so that α_1 and α_2 are both negative. In general, there is little or no empirical evidence that economic time series may need to be differenced more than twice.

not behave like a white noise process. The model will not appropriately capture the actual error process, so that α and its standard error will not be correctly estimated. Including too many lags reduces the power of the test to reject the null of a unit root since the increased number of lags necessitates the estimation of additional parameters and a loss of degrees of freedom (we lose one observation for each additional lag included in the autoregression).[9] In fact an ADF test may indicate a unit root for some lag lengths but not for others.

One approach is to start with a relatively long lag length and pare down the model by the usual t- and/or F-tests. In the pure AR(p) case, such a procedure will yield the true lag length with an asymptotic probability of one, provided the initial choice of lag length includes the true length, that is, that p_{max} is sufficiently high. Once a tentative lag length has been determined, diagnostic checks should be conducted. There should be no strong evidence of structural change (see Chapter 8) or of residual serial correlation, see Chapters 1 and 2. Unfortunately, Sims et al. (1990) noted that in regressions containing a mixture of $I(1)$ and $I(0)$ variables, t- and F-tests applied to the coefficients of the stationary variables will be (asymptotically) valid only when the residuals are white noise. In the case of Eqs. (4.23)–(4.25) the problem is that under the null hypothesis, the regression includes among its regressors y_t which is I(1). Therefore, applied researchers often resort to information criteria to select p, as we have already explained in Chapters 2 and 3.

It is of course ambiguous whether it is most appropriate to use Eq. (4.23), (4.24), or (4.25) when testing for unit roots. Elementary logic may suggest it is reasonable to test the hypothesis using the most general of the models, Eq. (4.25). Unfortunately the practice of econometrics disagrees: the presence of the additional estimated parameters may reduce the degrees of freedom and the power of the test. Because in the presence of extraneous deterministic components, the ADF test has low power to reject the null hypothesis, if the null hypothesis of a unit root were rejected in the most general specification Eq. (4.25), there would be no reason for concern: a unit root would be extremely unlikely. However, if the null hypothesis were not rejected, it would be necessary to determine whether too many deterministic regressors were included in Eq. (4.25), since the presence of these regressors may have reduced the power of the test. As such, we could test for the significance of the trend term(s) by testing the hypothesis $\delta_1 = \delta_2 = \cdots = \delta_Q$ and keep proceeding to simplify the testing model in the direction of Eqs. (4.24) and (4.23).

Note that Eq. (4.20) assumes an AR(p) process, but in reality the DGP may contain both autoregressive and moving-average components. However, because an invertible MA model can be transformed into an AR model, the procedure can be generalized to allow for moving-average components. Here the delicate issue is that an invertible MA corresponds in principle to an infinite-order AR that cannot be estimated using a finite data set. Fortunately, Said and Dickey (1984) have shown that an unknown autoregressive integrated moving average (ARIMA(p,1,q)) process can be well approximated by an ARIMA(n,1,0) where $n \leq \sqrt[3]{T}$. Therefore, we can simply use:

$$\Delta y_{t+1} = \phi_0 + \alpha y_t + \sum_{i=1}^{[T^{1/3}]} \gamma_i \Delta y_{t-i+1} + \varepsilon_{t+1}, \tag{4.26}$$

where $[T^{1/3}]$ denotes the integer part of $T^{1/3}$. Example 4.3 shows ADF tests in action on key financial series.

EXAMPLE 4.3

We investigate the presence of a unit root in long time series of monthly, January 1871–December 2016 data on the real Standard & Poors' (S&P) equity index (P_t) and aggregate real earnings (E_t) paid by the S&P companies. The data have been kindly made available by Bob Shiller at http://www.econ.yale.edu/~shiller/data.htm. Real prices and earnings are computed by deflating nominal series using the US consumers' price index. We separately examine each of the two series even though important financial models imply they are related, what we shall explore later on this chapter.

Starting out with the real price series a classical DF test reveals that the estimated α coefficient is +2.977 standard deviations away from 0, which actually implies an AR(1) estimate in excess of 1. Such a t-ratio of course does not fall below the DF one-sided critical values (these are negative!) and as a result one would fail to reject the null of a unit root. However, it is doubtful that such a simple DF test may have adequate power: in the long run, because they are risky and holding stocks needs to be compensated on average, the process for S&P index prices is likely to contain a positive drift. Moreover, the SACF of the first difference in equity prices reveals the existence of residual structure that should be picked up to make the resulting ADF test more powerful. Therefore we also perform an ADF test that includes an intercept (a trend would instead violate a number of deep finance principles) and that specifies the number of lags in the test equation by minimizing the modified Schwarz Bayesian information criterion (SBIC) (defined as $-2(L/T) + (dim(\theta) + adjf)\ln(T)/T$ where L is the maximized log-likelihood function, $dim(\theta)$

(Continued)

9. Recall that the power of a test is equal to the probability of rejecting a false null hypothesis (i.e., 1 minus the probability of a type II error).

EXAMPLE 4.3 (Continued)

is the number of parameters to be estimated in the model, and $+adjf$ is an adjustment factor described in Ng and Perron, 2001), with a maximum of 24 lags determined with the commonly used data-dependent criterion

$$p_{\max} = \left[\min(T/3, 12) \cdot \sqrt[4]{T/100}\right].$$

The resulting ADF regression is (t-ratios in squared brackets):

$$P_{t+1} = \underset{[0.639]}{0.499} + \underset{[0.565]}{0.001}\, P_t + \underset{[9.291]}{0.223}\, \Delta P_t - \underset{[-3.201]}{0.079}\, \Delta P_{t-1} + \underset{[1.475]}{0.036}\, \Delta P_{t-2} + \underset{[1.418]}{0.035}\, \Delta P_{t-3}$$
$$+ \underset{[5.444]}{0.133}\, \Delta P_{t-4} - \underset{[-3.242]}{0.080}\, \Delta P_{t-5} + \underset{[0.364]}{0.009}\, \Delta P_{t-6} + \underset{[3.772]}{0.091}\, \Delta P_{t-7} + \varepsilon_{t+1},$$

Clearly, with a t-statistic of $+0.565$ the null of a unit root cannot be rejected and in fact the p-value computed under the simulated ADF distribution is 0.989. If we use t-statistics to select the number of lags (again with a maximum of 24), we obtain an ADF test based on $p = 21$, but the estimate of α remains 0.001 and the t-statistic even increases, now to $+0.710$. Hence, there is no doubt whatsoever that the main historical stock price index in the United States contains a unit root, which as we know is also consistent with the efficient market hypothesis in finance theory. Fig. 4.8A shows the SACF of the first differences in real stock prices, which confirms that real prices did contain a unit root. In any event, just to be on the safe side, we apply an ADF test also to the first difference of real S&P prices with an intercept and number of lags determined using the modified SBIC. In this case, we find an estimate of α of -0.56 which is -7.789 standard deviations away from 0 and hence leads to a rejection of the null of a unit root with a p-value of 0.000.

In the case of real earnings, a classical DF test reveals that the estimated α coefficient is $+2.217$ standard deviations away from 0, which implies an AR(1) estimate in excess of 1. Again the resulting t-ratio does not fall below the DF one-sided critical values, and we fail to reject the null of a unit root. Because it is doubtful that a simple DF test may have adequate power, also because in the long run, we may expect real earnings to grow as the economy expands, the earnings process for S&P companies is likely to contain a positive drift. Also in this case the SACF of the first differences of real earnings reveals the existence of residual structure that should be picked up to make the resulting ADF test sufficiently powerful. Therefore we also perform an ADF test that includes an intercept and that specifies the number of lags in the test equation by using a variety of criteria, with a maximum of 24 lags determined with the same used data-dependent criterion as before. The ADF regression gives an estimate of α essentially equal to 0 with a t-ratio of $+0.196$ which, being positive, leads to a failure to reject the null of a unit root. In this case, we do not show the estimated ADF regression because under all criteria, the maximum number of 24 lags was always selected and this would take too much space.

Because in the case of earnings the presence of a time trend cannot be ruled out on theoretical grounds, we reapply the ADF test also including a linear time trend, obtaining a significant estimate of the linear deterministic trend (p-value is 0.020) and an estimate of α of -0.002 which is -1.900 standard deviations away from 0 and that does not allow us to reject the null of a unit root. Also in this case, we do not report the estimated ADF regression because under all criteria, the maximum number of 24 lags was always selected. Also in this case the failure to reject the null of a unit root is rather powerful, or so it seems. Fig. 4.8B shows the SACF of the first differences in real earnings, which is stationary even though some persistence remains. We apply an ADF test also to the first difference of real S&P prices with an intercept and number of lags determined using the modified SBIC. In this case, we find an estimate of α of -0.155 which is -10.30 standard deviations away from 0 and hence leads to a rejection of the null of a unit root with a p-value of 0.000.

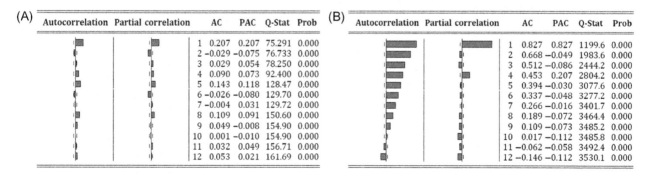

(A)

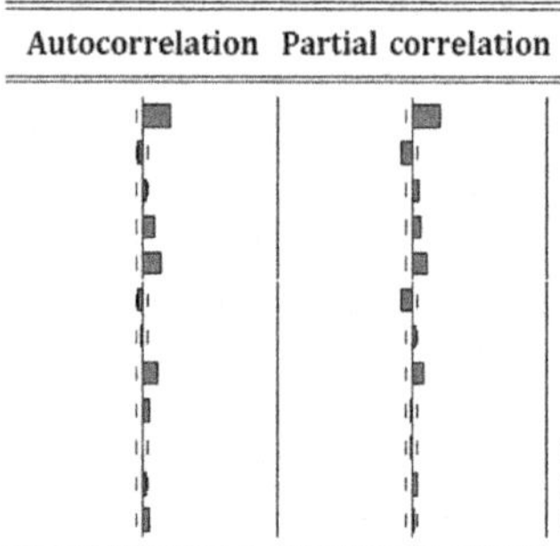

	AC	PAC	Q-Stat	Prob
1	0.207	0.207	75.291	0.000
2	-0.029	-0.075	76.733	0.000
3	0.029	0.054	78.250	0.000
4	0.090	0.073	92.400	0.000
5	0.143	0.118	128.47	0.000
6	-0.026	-0.080	129.70	0.000
7	-0.004	0.031	129.72	0.000
8	0.109	0.091	150.60	0.000
9	0.049	-0.008	154.90	0.000
10	0.001	-0.010	154.90	0.000
11	0.032	0.049	156.71	0.000
12	0.053	0.021	161.69	0.000

(B)

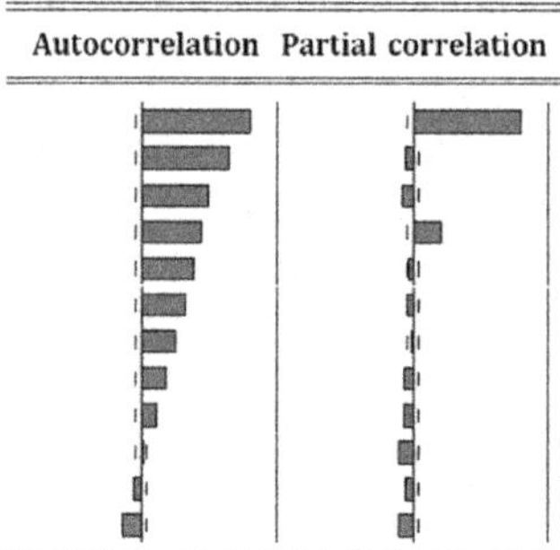

	AC	PAC	Q-Stat	Prob
1	0.827	0.827	1199.6	0.000
2	0.668	-0.049	1983.6	0.000
3	0.512	-0.086	2444.2	0.000
4	0.453	0.207	2804.2	0.000
5	0.394	-0.030	3077.6	0.000
6	0.337	-0.048	3277.2	0.000
7	0.266	-0.016	3401.7	0.000
8	0.189	-0.072	3464.4	0.000
9	0.109	-0.073	3485.2	0.000
10	0.017	-0.112	3485.8	0.000
11	-0.062	-0.058	3492.4	0.000
12	-0.146	-0.112	3530.1	0.000

FIGURE 4.8 SACF of the first difference of S&P real prices and aggregate earnings. (A) Real S&P prices and (B) real earnings.

ADF tests for unit roots suffer from low-power issues because they are not particularly good at distinguishing between:

- a series with a characteristic root that is close to unity and a true unit root process and
- trend stationary and stochastic trend processes, as in finite samples, any trend stationary process can be arbitrarily well approximated by a unit root process, and a unit root process can be arbitrarily well approximated by a trend stationary process.

Such a lack of power should not be too surprising after examining Fig. 4.9. The plot on the left compares 180 generated values from the two models:

$$\begin{aligned} y_{t+1} &= 1.1y_t - 0.1y_{t-1} + \varepsilon_{t+1} \ \text{(Nonstationary AR(2))} \\ z_{t+1} &= 1.1z_t - 0.15z_{t-1} + \varepsilon_{t+1} \ \text{(Stationary AR(2))} \end{aligned} \tag{4.27}$$

both initialized at $y_0 = y_1 = 0$, in which the errors are Gaussian IID and kept identical across simulated values.

If we had not known the actual DGP in Eq. (4.27), it would be difficult to tell that only the continuous series $\{z_t\}$ in the plot is stationary. There is a literature (surveyed by Enders, 2008, among others) that has conducted Monte Carlo experiments to assess the power of ADF tests. In practice, they have simulated a large number of series for stationary processes to determine the power of ADF tests to reject the null of a single unit root. In a Monte Carlo set up, power is simply the fraction of generated samples for which a rejection occurs, presumably as a function of the assumed stationary root $|\phi_1| < 1$. Of course, we would expect the test to have the least power when $|\phi_1|$ is close to 1. Typically, it has been reported that when $|\phi_1|$ is 0.8, the test does reasonably well. For example, at the 5% test size the false null hypothesis of a unit root is typically rejected in almost 90% of the Monte Carlo replications. However, already for $|\phi_1| = 0.95$ the power of the ADF test is estimated to be below 20% at the 5% size. Paradoxically, when $|\phi_1| = 0.99$, the power of the ADF test is 2% at the 1% size, that is, a stationary process becomes almost impossible to tell apart from a unit root. All in all the ADF test has very low power to detect near-unit root series.

Similarly, as illustrated in the rightmost plot of Fig. 4.9, it can be difficult to distinguish between a trend stationary and a RW with drift process. Using the same 180 realizations of the Gaussian IID errors, we have generated the series:

$$\begin{aligned} y_{t+1} &= 0.034 + y_t + 0.6\varepsilon_{t+1} \ \text{(Random walk with drift)} \\ w_{t+1} &= 0.05 + 0.03t + \varepsilon_{t+1} \ \text{(Trend stationary linear process).} \end{aligned} \tag{4.28}$$

Just as it is difficult for us to perceive the differences in the series in Fig. 4.9, it is difficult for ADF tests to select the correct specification. In fact, it can be shown that a trend stationary process can be made to mimic a unit root process arbitrarily well (see Enders, 2008 for a heuristic proof).

Recently, Elliott, Rothenberg, and Stock (1996, henceforth ERS) have proposed an ADF version in which instead of modeling a constant and/or time trends in the test regression, the data are detrended so that the deterministic explanatory variables are "taken out" of the data prior to estimating the test regression. ERS define a *quasi-differenced series*

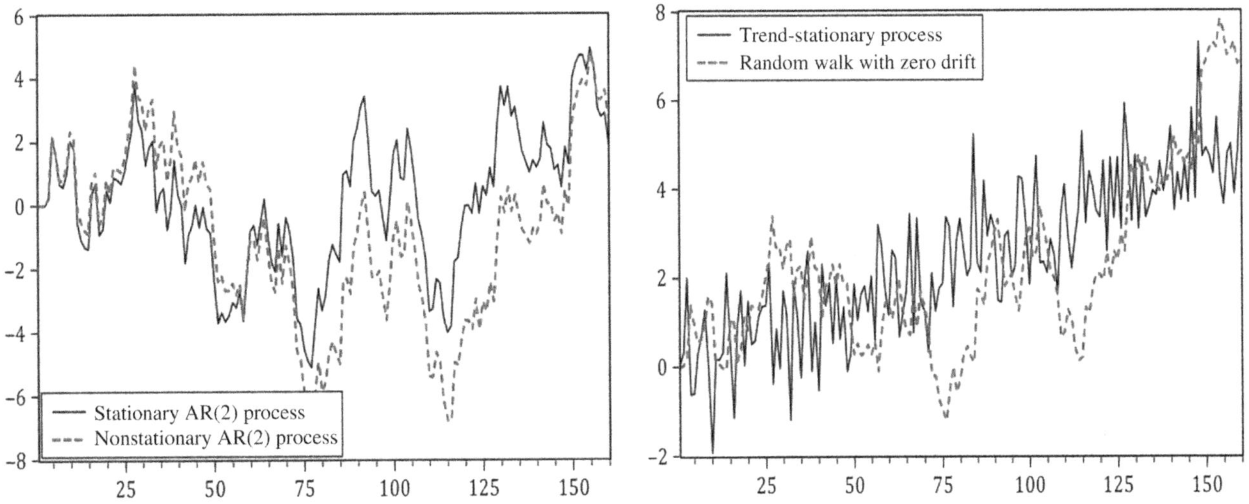

FIGURE 4.9 Four simulated series based on identical shocks.

that depends on a parametric value choice a representing the specific point alternative against which we wish to test the null, $\Delta_a y_{t+1} = y_{t+1} - a y_t$ for $t = 2, \ldots, T$ (also set $\Delta_a y_1 = y_1$). Next, they estimate an OLS regression of the quasi-differenced data on the quasi-differenced deterministic regressors

$$\Delta_a y_{t+1} = \Delta_a \mathbf{x}'_{t+1} \boldsymbol{\delta}(a) + v_{t+1}, \tag{4.29}$$

for instance $\Delta_a t = t - at$, $\Delta_a t^2 = t^2 - at^2$, etc. Although criteria exist to optimally select a, ERS recommend the use of $\tilde{a} = 1 - (7/T)$ when there is only an intercept, and $\tilde{a} = 1 - (13.5/T)$ when there is also a linear time trend. The last step consists of *applying standard ADF tests to the estimated quasi-differenced (generalized least squares, GLS) detrended data* from Eq. (4.29), $\hat{y}_t(\tilde{a}) = y_t - \mathbf{x}'_t \hat{\boldsymbol{\delta}}(\tilde{a})$:

$$\Delta \hat{y}_{t+1}(\tilde{a}) = \alpha \hat{y}_t(\tilde{a}) + \sum_{i=1}^{p} \gamma_i \Delta \hat{y}_{t+1-i}(\tilde{a}) + \varepsilon_{t+1}. \tag{4.30}$$

As with the ADF test, we consider the t-ratio for α from this test equation although its asymptotic distribution differs from DF. We now extend Example 4.3 to include one more key series and to implement ERS-style GLS-detrended ADF tests.

EXAMPLE 4.3 (continued)

Besides historical data on S&P real stock prices and aggregate earnings, we extend our evidence to aggregate S&P real dividends (over a 1872:01–2016:12 sample) and apply ERS tests. When it comes to dividends, instead of directly selecting the number of AR lags p , E-Views allows us to clean the estimate of the standard error of the residuals (hence the standard error of the coefficient α) from Eq. (4.30) by controlling the lag length or bandwidth used in the so-called "spectral estimator," which is a nonparametric kernel estimator of the residual variance. For instance, we have used a Bartlett–Kernel estimation method:

$$\hat{\sigma}^2_{Spectral} = \sum_{j=-(T-1)}^{T-1} \sum_{t=j+1}^{T} \frac{\hat{\varepsilon}_t \hat{\varepsilon}_{t-j}}{T} \cdot K(j/b_T) \qquad K(j/h) = \begin{cases} 1 - |j/b_T| & \text{if } |j/b_T| \leq 1 \\ 0 & \text{otherwise} \end{cases}$$

(which acts as a lag truncating function) in which the optimal bandwidth b_T is selected to be of a Newey–West's (1994) automatic, data-driven type, such that $b_T \to \infty$ and $b_T/T \to 0$ as $T \to \infty$:

$$b_T^{NW} = 1.1447 \left(\frac{\sum_{i=[-T^{2/9}]}^{[T^{2/9}]} |i|(T-i)^{-1} \sum_{t=i+1}^{T} \hat{\varepsilon}_t \hat{\varepsilon}_{t-i}}{\sum_{i=[-T^{2/9}]}^{[T^{2/9}]} (T-i)^{-1} \sum_{t=i+1}^{T} \hat{\varepsilon}_t \hat{\varepsilon}_{t-i}} \right)^{1/3} \sqrt[3]{T}.$$

This is of course just a weighted sum of autocovariances of the residuals that has been proven to provide a heteroskedasticity and autocorrelation-consistent estimate of the variance not simply centered on $T^{-1} \sum_{t=1}^{T} \hat{\varepsilon}_t^2$ (that would be instead a valid estimator if the residuals were truly IID). On the basis of these choices, we find a ERS test statistic associated with the estimated α of 21.492 which exceeds the critical values at all size levels of the one-sided test (e.g., 5.62 in the case of a 5% test size): this leads to a failure to reject the null of a unit root in aggregate dividends. Such a nonrejection occurs also from ERS GLS-detrended test when the linear trend is omitted: according to ERS test, which is supposed to have considerably more power than a standard ADF test, aggregate US real dividends contain a stochastic trend. Similarly a standard ADF test would lead to a failure to reject the null hypothesis of a unit root: when five lags of real dividend changes are selected using a modified SBIC criterion, this leads to an estimate of α of -0.001 to which it is associated with a t-ratio of -0.347 which is obviously consistent with the null hypothesis.

We also apply the ERS GLS-detrended unit root test to real stock prices and aggregate earnings. In the case of the S&P index, we find a test statistic (for the case of only a deterministic intercept) of 28.404 which grossly exceeds all critical values provided and leads to conclude that prices contain a unit root. In the case of real earnings the ERS test statistic (for the case of an intercept and linear trend) is 4.799 which leads to a rejection of the null at sizes 5% and 10%, but not 1%. However, the rejection strongly depends on the assumption that real earnings may contain a linear trend, because when the ERS test is applied only under a deterministic intercept, the test statistic is 8.598 and leads to a failure to reject the null of a RW with drift for all sizes of the test. Fig. 4.10 shows the three series under investigation. Although it is always difficult (in fact, dangerous) to eye-ball results, in the case of real earnings, it is difficult to see a clear linear trend, for instance because the deviations from the trend become increasingly volatile over time.

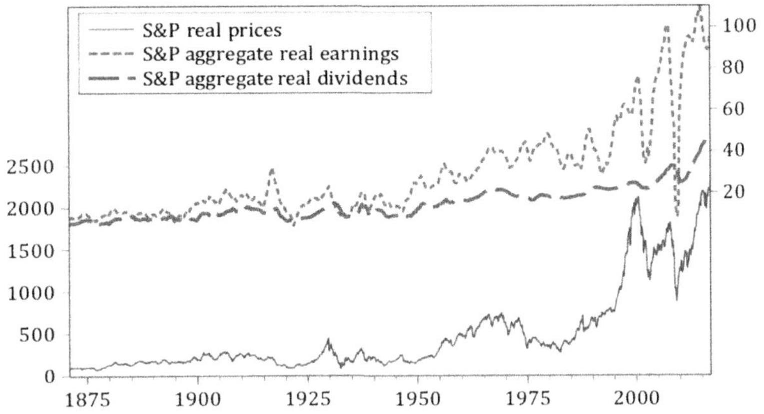

FIGURE 4.10 Time series of real S&P equity index prices, aggregate earnings and dividends.

4.3.3 Other Unit Root Tests

Phillips and Perron (1988, henceforth PP) have proposed a *nonparametric method of controlling for serial correlation* when testing for a unit root that is an alternative to the ADF test. The PP method estimates the classical DF test Eqs. (4.16)–(4.18) and modifies the t-ratio of the coefficient α so that serial correlation in the residuals does not affect the asymptotic distribution of the test statistic. The PP test is based instead on the statistic:

$$t_{\alpha}^{PP} = t_{\alpha}^{DF}\varsigma - \psi = \frac{\hat{\alpha}}{se(\hat{\alpha})}\sqrt{\frac{\frac{T-m}{T}\frac{1}{T}\sum_{t=1}^{T}\hat{\varepsilon}_t^2}{\sum_{i=[-T^{2/9}]}^{[T^{2/9}]}\frac{1}{T-i}\sum_{t=i+1}^{T}\hat{\varepsilon}_t\hat{\varepsilon}_{t-i}}} + \\ - \frac{se(\hat{\alpha})T\left(\sum_{i=[-T^{2/9}]}^{[T^{2/9}]}\frac{1}{T-i}\sum_{t=i+1}^{T}\hat{\varepsilon}_t\hat{\varepsilon}_{t-i} - \frac{T-m}{T}\sum_{t=1}^{T}\hat{\varepsilon}_t^2\right)}{2\sqrt{\left(\sum_{i=[-T^{2/9}]}^{[T^{2/9}]}\frac{1}{T-i}\sum_{t=i+1}^{T}\hat{\varepsilon}_t\hat{\varepsilon}_{t-i}\right)\left(\frac{1}{T}\sum_{t=1}^{T}\hat{\varepsilon}_t^2\right)}}, \quad (4.31)$$

where m is the number of deterministic regressors included, and $se(\hat{\alpha})$ is the OLS standard error of the estimated coefficient. Because $\varsigma, \psi > 0$, even when $\varsigma > 1$, it is possible for $t_{\alpha}^{PP} < t_{\alpha}^{DF}$, so that while a DF test would not reject the null of a unit root, the PP test will. The nonparametric nature of the test consists of the fact that instead of "whitening" the test regression residuals by fitting some AR(p), PP propose to directly adjust the test statistic in "HAC-way" (see Chapter 1 for an introduction to these issues). The asymptotic distribution of the PP modified t-ratio is the same as that of the ADF statistic, and the test is also performed under the null of a unit root.

Kwiatkowski, Phillips, Schmidt, and Shin (1992, henceforth KPSS) have proposed a testing strategy that differs from the other unit root tests described here in that *the series is assumed to be (trend-) stationary under the null*. The KPSS statistic is based on the residuals from the OLS regression of the series on the exogenous, deterministic factors:

$$y_{t+1} = \boldsymbol{x}'_t\boldsymbol{\delta} + u_{t+1}, \quad (4.32)$$

where $\boldsymbol{x}_t$ may contain the intercept and a polynomial time trend. KPSS test is then an Lagrange multiplier (LM) test:

$$\text{KPSS}_T \equiv \frac{\sum_{t=1}^{T}\left(\sum_{i=1}^{t}\hat{u}_i\right)^2}{T^2\sum_{i=[-T^{2/9}]}^{[T^{2/9}]}\frac{1}{T-i}\sum_{t=i+1}^{T}\hat{\varepsilon}_t\hat{\varepsilon}_{t-i}}, \quad (4.33)$$

where the denominator is an estimator of the residual spectrum at frequency 0, in this case written already to reflect a Newey–West automatic, data-driven bandwidth choice as in Example 4.3.[10] Example 4.4 shows the PP and KPSS tests at work.

EXAMPLE 4.4

We re-examine whether S&P real stock prices, aggregate earnings, and aggregate dividends give evidence of a unit root.

As far as the PP tests are concerned, we estimate the three simple, DF-style models with an intercept:

$$P_{t+1} = \underset{[0.146]}{0.118} + \underset{[2.044]}{0.002}\, P_t + \varepsilon_{t+1} \qquad t_\alpha^{PP} = 0.905 \text{ with } p\text{-value } 0.996$$

$$E_{t+1} = \underset{[0.400]}{0.017} + \underset{[1.057]}{0.001}\, E_t + \varepsilon_{t+1} \qquad t_\alpha^{PP} = -1.535 \text{ with } p\text{-value } 0.516$$

$$D_{t+1} = \underset{[-4.394]}{-0.0037} + \underset{[8.136]}{0.004}\, D_t + \varepsilon_{t+1} \qquad t_\alpha^{PP} = 1.760 \text{ with } p\text{-value } 0.999.$$

In all cases, we have selected a spectral estimation method based on a Bartlett kernel with Newey–West data-driven bandwidth. For all three series, we cannot reject the null of a unit root. However, when we performed afresh the tests also including a linear time trend, the p-value for dividends remains 0.998 while in the case of real earnings, we obtain:

$$E_{t+1} = \underset{[-0.665]}{-0.034} + \underset{[1.647]}{0.144}\frac{t}{1000} - \underset{[-0.741]}{0.001}\, E_t + \varepsilon_{t+1} \qquad t_\alpha^{PP} = -3.743 \text{ with } p\text{-value } 0.020.$$

Also in this case the null of a unit root can be rejected with a p-value inferior to 5%, which is consistent with the finding in Example 4.3.

Next, we apply KPSS tests, mindful of the fact that in this case, the null hypothesis is that the series is I(0). We apply the same spectral estimation methods as under the PP tests. In the case of prices, we obtain a LM test statistic of 3.372 that exceeds the 1% critical value of 0.739 and makes us reject the null of stationarity; in the case of real earnings, we obtain a test statistic of 3.969, which also commands a p-value close to 0; finally, as far dividends are concerned, the LM test gives 4.205, and the null is again rejected. Interestingly, in this case even when the deterministic variables include a linear time trend, the LM statistics remains 0.695 and exceeds the 1% critical value of 0.216. Under a KPSS test, there is little doubt that also real earnings contain a unit root.

Indirectly, Example 4.4 helps us to make an interesting point with reference to the case of US aggregate real earnings: in this case, when testing is performed including a deterministic time trend, we have found that ADF, ERS GLS-detrended, and PP unit root tests all led to rejections—even though of varying strength—of the null hypothesis of a unit root. Our intuition was that there is sufficient evidence in the data that real earnings may be stationary around a trend, without requiring the further contribution of a stochastic trend. Yet, in the example, we also saw that for the same data, a KPSS test also rejected the null of stationarity in favor of a unit root even when a time trend is present. Although we must remind ourselves that rejecting the null of a unit root does *not* imply "accepting" the alternative hypothesis of stationarity, one feels trapped in a conundrum. Unfortunately, there is no easy way out to such a situation: the tests applied, and in particular the ADF-type variations and KPSS, are sufficiently different that these indecisive and seemingly contradicting outcomes may turn up.

4.3.4 Testing for Unit Roots in Moving-Average Processes

In Section 4.2, we saw that unit roots may also characterize the MA(q) components of a time series process, which made it noninvertible. In fact, we have documented two interesting results:

- Testing for a unit root in the MA polynomial is equivalent to testing that a time series has been over-differenced.
- Testing for a unit root in the MA polynomial gives a chance to distinguish between trend-stationary and stochastically trending processes, because we know that while the dth difference of an I(d) process is I(0), the dth difference of a trend stationary process will contain d unit roots in the MA polynomial.

10. The kernel-based estimator of the frequency zero spectrum is based on a weighted sum of the autocovariances, with the weights are defined by a kernel function. An alternative that is offered by a few statistical packages consists of using an autoregressive spectral density estimator at frequency 0, which is based upon the residual variance from the testing model and estimated coefficients from an auxiliary regression that is identical to the ADF regression in Eq. (4.24).

At least in the case of MA(1) processes—that is practically also the most interesting one (the general case of MA(q) polynomials is considerably more complicated and not fully resolved)—the statistical literature contains a few simple, useful results. Let $\{\varepsilon_t\}$ be observations from an MA(1) model:

$$\varepsilon_{t+1} = \theta\eta_t + \eta_{t+1} \quad \eta_{t+1} \ \text{IID}(0, \sigma_\eta^2). \tag{4.34}$$

Davis and Dunsmuir (1996) have shown that under the null of $\theta = -1$, the statistic $T(\hat{\theta} + 1)$ based on the maximum likelihood estimator (MLE) $\hat{\theta}$ converges to a distribution that they have characterized. A one-sided test of the null H_0: $\theta = -1$ versus H_1: $\theta > -1$ can be shaped on this limiting result by rejecting the null when $\hat{\theta} > -1 + c_{size}/T$, where c_{size} is the (1-*size*)-quantile of the limit distribution of $T(\hat{\theta} + 1)$ (for instance, $c_{0.01} = 11.93$, $c_{0.05} = 6.80$, and $c_{0.10} = 4.90$).

4.4 COINTEGRATION AND ERROR-CORRECTION MODELS

4.4.1 The Relationship Between Cointegration and Economic Theory

As hinted at early on in this chapter, the presence of (especially, stochastic) trends in a time series is not only a source of problems that may force a researcher into action, for instance by removing such trends to make the series stationary and ready to Box–Jenkins techniques, but also a source of opportunities. However, to harvest such opportunities, one needs to consider multivariate, joint modeling of $N \geq 2$ $I(d)$ series, where d should be identical across the series. Here the important concept is that *there are situations in which the choice to simultaneously difference all nonstationary variables to transform them into a set of stationary variables may represent a mistake*, in the sense that this will imply a major loss of information, possibly invalid inference, and suboptimal predictive performance. Put very simply, what we shall be looking for is the existence of linear combinations of integrated variables that are stationary. When this happens, such N variables are said to be *cointegrated*, so that transforming these very variables to be $I(0)$ would represent a mistake: if a linear relationship is already stationary, differencing it entails a misspecification error.[11]

The appropriate way to treat nonstationary variables is not so straightforward in a multivariate context but for once in our treatment of time series modeling, we will be sometimes able to exploit the fact that economic models imply equilibrium relationships among sets of nonstationary variables that restrict their stochastic trends to be linked. For instance, a variety of no-arbitrage relationships typically imply that N variables cannot move independently of each other. As a point in case, consider the standard *discounted dividend/earnings growth model*, often traced back to Gordon (1959):

$$P_{t+1} = \frac{(1+g)F_{t+1}}{(r-g)} + \varepsilon_{t+1} \quad \varepsilon_{t+1} \ IID(0, \sigma^2) \Rightarrow P_{t+1} - \kappa F_{t+1} = \varepsilon_{t+1}, \tag{4.35}$$

where $\kappa \equiv (1+g)/(r-g) > 0$, P_{t+1} is the (real) stock price (or an equity index), F_{t+1} is some fundamental real quantity (such as cash dividends or earnings) that investors discount when pricing stocks, r is a fixed real discount rate that reflects the riskiness of stocks, and g is a constant real rate of growth of fundamentals. In Eq. (4.35), ε_{t+1} captures noise, that is, temporary deviations of market prices from what is justified by fundamentals, sometimes called the fair value of the stock index. Because the time series of mispricings, $\{\varepsilon_{t+1}\}$, represents temporary deviations, we expect them to be stationary, or even to be white noise. If $\{\varepsilon_{t+1}\}$ were a I(1) series, this would mean that pricing errors would never be corrected and on the contrary could diverge forever, which would make the very model useless. This is the sense in which Eq. (4.35) would hold, helping on average to organize market price data. However, if we think that the time series $\{P_{t+1}\}$ and $\{F_{t+1}\}$ are I(1)—either because of theoretical reasons, such as the efficient market hypothesis, or because this is revealed by the data—then Eq. (4.35) implies indeed that a coefficient κ exists such that a weighted sum of real prices and fundamentals yields a stationary variable:

$$I(1) - \kappa I(1) \sim I(0). \tag{4.36}$$

Eq. (4.36) represents of course an open violation of Result 4.3 and this at last vindicates our need to add the caution "unless special conditions occur" when the result was stated. Thus the model in Eq. (4.35) necessitates that the time paths of the two nonstationary variables $\{P_{t+1}\}$ and $\{F_{t+1}\}$ be closely linked. Of course, Eq. (4.35) represents just one

11. To be sure, however the first difference of a I(0) variable will be still I(0), but information on the "level" of the phenomenon will be obviously lost, often with some economic intuition. For instance, the first-difference of asset returns relates to the speed of change in prices, a kind of acceleration, and it is rarely used or useful in finance.

example: there are many models offering examples of equilibrium frameworks in which deviations from equilibrium must be temporary.[12] Section 4.4 will provide another interesting example.

4.4.2 Definition of Cointegration

Consider a set of economic variables in a *long-run equilibrium* when

$$\kappa_1 y_{1t} + \kappa_2 y_{2t} + \cdots + \kappa_N y_{Nt} = 0, \tag{4.37}$$

or compactly, $\boldsymbol{\kappa}'\mathbf{y}_t = 0$. The deviation from the long-run equilibrium, called the equilibrium error, is a scalar random variable $\varepsilon_t = \boldsymbol{\kappa}'\mathbf{y}_t$. *If the equilibrium is meaningful, it must be the case that the equilibrium error process is stationary.* This set up suggests a natural definition:

DEFINITION 4.3 (Cointegrated system)

The components of the N-dimensional random vector $\mathbf{y}_t \equiv [y_{1t}, y_{2t}, \ldots, y_{Nt}]'$ are said to be cointegrated of order d, b, denoted by $\mathbf{y}_t \sim CI(d, b)$, if all components of $\mathbf{y}_t$ are integrated of order d, and there exists a vector $\boldsymbol{\kappa} \equiv [\kappa_1, \kappa_2, \ldots, \kappa_N]'$ such that the *linear* combination $\boldsymbol{\kappa}'\mathbf{y}_t$ is integrated of order $(d-b) \geq 0$ where $b > 0$. The vector $\boldsymbol{\kappa}$ is called the *cointegrating vector.*

Although the definition is completely general, in practice, we shall be very interested in the case $\mathbf{y}_t \sim CI(1,1)$, when the linear combination defined by the cointegrating vector is simply stationary because $d - b = 1 - 1 = 0$. The reason is that traditional time series analysis applies when variables are $I(0)$ while very few economic variables are integrated of an order higher than unity (only money demand and a few other monetary aggregates come to mind, see Haldrup, 1994). Note that what we have just stated is a definition and not a result: *in general*, given a set of N integrated variables, these will not be cointegrated. Such *a lack of cointegration in a set of N I(1) variables implies that there is no long-run equilibrium among the variables, so that they can wander arbitrarily far from each other.*

In terms of Eq. (4.35), if real stock prices and fundamentals are both $I(1)$ and the linear combination $P_{t+1} - \kappa F_{t+1} = \varepsilon_{t+1}$ is stationary, then the variables are cointegrated of order (1, 1). In this case, the cointegrating vector is $[1, -\kappa']$. Note that Definition 4.3 refers only to a linear combination of nonstationary variables. Theoretically, it is quite possible that nonlinear long-run relationships exist among a set of integrated variables, an aspect that will be discussed again in Chapter 8. Moreover, the cointegrating vector is not unique: if $[\kappa_1, \kappa_2, \ldots, \kappa_N]'$ is a cointegrating vector, then for any nonzero value of ξ, $[\xi\kappa_1, \xi\kappa_2, \ldots, \xi\kappa_N]'$ is also a cointegrating vector, which is therefore not unique. Therefore typically, one of the variables is used to normalize the cointegrating vector by fixing its coefficient at unity, for instance $[1\ (\kappa_2/\kappa_1),\ (\kappa_3/\kappa_1), \ldots, (\kappa_N/\kappa_1)]'$ is a cointegrating vector standardized with respect to the first series. However, clearly also $[(\kappa_1/\kappa_N),\ (\kappa_2/\kappa_N),\ (\kappa_3/\kappa_N), \ldots, 1]'$ represents an equally valid cointegrating vector, now standardized with respect to the Nth series. Also note that the definition requires that all the variables are integrated of the same order. Therefore if two or more variables are integrated of different orders, they cannot be cointegrated. In fact, we know from Result 4.3 that a weighted sum of variables with different orders of integration will be integrated with order equal to the maximum order of integration in the set. Combining series that wildly fluctuate in heter/ogeneous ways, will simply generate a new random variable with "maximum tendency" to also fluctuate endlessly.[13]

Matters are a bit more complicated however. Even though this fact may be self-evident to some readers, we collect it here in the form of a result to give it some emphasis.

---

12. Another celebrated example in financial economics is the implication of the efficient market hypothesis by which the forward (or futures) price of an asset should equal the expected value of that asset's spot price in the future.

13. Nevertheless, it is possible to find equilibrium relationships among *groups* of variables that are integrated of different orders. Suppose that y_{1t} and y_{2t} are $I(2)$ and cointegrated, $[y_{1t},\ y_{2t}]' \sim CI(2,1)$. If there is a third variable $y_{3t} \sim I(1)$, even though there cannot be any cointegration within the vectors $[y_{1t},\ y_{2t},\ y_{3t}]'$, $[y_{1t},\ y_{3t}]'$, and $[y_{2t},\ y_{3t}]'$, it is possible that the cointegrated (2,1) combination of y_{1t} and y_{2t} is cointegrated with $y_{3t} \sim I(1)$. Granger and Lee (1989) defined this phenomenon *multicointegration*.

RESULT 4.4 (Multiplicity of cointegrating vectors)

If $\boldsymbol{y}_t$ has N nonstationary components, there may be as many as $(N-1)$ linearly independent cointegrating vectors. The number of cointegrating vectors is called the *cointegrating rank* of $\boldsymbol{y}_t$.

Clearly, if $\boldsymbol{y}_t$ contains only two variables, there can be at most one independent cointegrating vector. Finally, note that because, for instance:

$$\begin{aligned} \kappa_1 y_{1t} + \kappa_2 y_{2t} + \cdots + \kappa_N y_{Nt} &= \varepsilon_t \sim I(0) \\ \Rightarrow \kappa_2 y_{2t} + \cdots + \kappa_N y_{Nt} &= \varepsilon_t - \kappa_1 y_{1t} \sim I(1) \end{aligned}, \tag{4.38}$$

it follows that $[y_{1t}, y_{2t}, \ldots, y_{Nt}]' \sim \mathrm{CI}(d,b)$ does not imply that a subset of the same N variables needs to be also $CI(d,b)$ although some other order of cointegration may remain possible.

One useful way to understand cointegration is to note that *cointegrated variables are such because they share common stochastic trends*. To see this point, consider the dividend growth model in Eq. (4.35). Suppose that $\{P_t\}$ and $\{F_t\}$ are constructed as two RWs plus a stationary noise process:

$$P_t = RW_t^P + \varepsilon_t^P \quad F_t = RW_t^F + \varepsilon_t^F. \tag{4.39}$$

If prices and fundamentals are CI(1,1), there must be nonzero values of some coefficients κ_1 and κ_2 such that $\kappa_1 P_t + \kappa_2 F_t$ is stationary. However, this weighted sum is:

$$\begin{aligned} \kappa_1 P_t + \kappa_2 F_t &= \kappa_1 (RW_t^P + \varepsilon_t^P) + \kappa_2 (RW_t^F + \varepsilon_t^F) \\ &= (\kappa_1 RW_t^P + \kappa_2 RW_t^F) + (\kappa_1 \varepsilon_t^P + \kappa_2 \varepsilon_t^F). \end{aligned} \tag{4.40}$$

Therefore for $\kappa_1 P_t + \kappa_2 F_t$ to be stationary, because $\kappa_1 \varepsilon_t^P + \kappa_2 \varepsilon_t^F$ is stationary by construction, the term $\kappa_1 RW_t^P + \kappa_2 RW_t^F$ must vanish, $\kappa_1 RW_t^P + \kappa_2 RW_t^F = 0$. However, RW_t^P and RW_t^F are random variables whose realized values will be continually changing over time that cannot be simply set to 0. Therefore $\kappa_1 P_t + \kappa_2 F_t$ can be stationary if and only if:

$$RW_t^P = -\frac{\kappa_2}{\kappa_1} RW_t^F, \tag{4.41}$$

that is, the two stochastic trends are identical up to a scalar, $-\kappa_2/\kappa_1$.

This result generalizes to the case of N variables. Consider the vector representation

$$\boldsymbol{y}_t = \boldsymbol{RW}_t + \boldsymbol{\varepsilon}_t, \tag{4.42}$$

where $\boldsymbol{RW}_t$ is a $N \times 1$ vector of RW components and $\boldsymbol{\varepsilon}_t$ has an equivalent definition for white noise processes. If one trend can be expressed as a linear combination of the other trends in the system, it means that there exists a vector $\boldsymbol{\kappa}$ such that $\boldsymbol{\kappa}'\boldsymbol{RW}_t = 0$, so that:

$$\boldsymbol{\kappa}'\boldsymbol{y}_t = \boldsymbol{\kappa}'\boldsymbol{RW}_t + \boldsymbol{\kappa}'\boldsymbol{\varepsilon}_t = \boldsymbol{\kappa}'\boldsymbol{\varepsilon}_t \sim I(0). \tag{4.43}$$

Because the series in $\boldsymbol{y}_t$ share one or more common stochastic trends, they cannot drift "too far apart."

4.4.3 Error-Correction Models

A key feature of cointegrated variables is that their dynamics are influenced by the magnitude of any departures from the long-run equilibrium: if the system is to return to the equilibrium, the movements of at least some of the variables must respond to the magnitude of the recorded disequilibrium. For example, Gordon's growth model of equity valuation implies a long-run relationship between stock prices and earnings (or dividends): if the gap between stock prices and (some multiple of) fundamentals gets "large" relative to their long-run relationship—for instance in the form of some equilibrium, steady-state price-dividend or price-earnings ratio—then the stock price must ultimately decline, given the level of fundamentals. Of course, empirically at least, the gap could also be closed by an increase in fundamentals for given equity valuations, but this is not the way experts in business valuation think about these dynamics. In any event, without a full dynamic specification of the model, it is not possible to determine (estimate) which of the possible adjustments will occur. Nevertheless, the short-run dynamics must be influenced by the deviations from the long-run relationship in a *dynamic error-correction model*:

$$
\begin{aligned}
\Delta P_{t+1} &= \lambda_P(P_t - \kappa F_t) + u_t^P \quad \lambda_P \leq 0 \\
\Delta F_{t+1} &= -\lambda_F(P_t - \kappa F_t) + u_t^F \quad \lambda_F \leq 0,
\end{aligned} \tag{4.44}
$$

where u_t^P and u_t^F are the white noise disturbance terms which may be correlated, and λ_P and λ_F are the estimable parameters. As already shown, the unique long-run equilibrium is attained when $P_t = \kappa F_t$. Moreover, because we have assumed that prices and fundamentals are all $I(1)$, we know that ΔP_{t+1} and ΔF_{t+1} are $I(0)$. For Eq. (4.44) to be sensible the right-hand side must be $I(0)$ as well. Given that u_t^P and u_t^F are stationary, it follows that the linear combination $P_t - \kappa F_t$ must also be stationary, so that prices and fundamentals must be cointegrated with the cointegrating vector $[1, -\kappa]'$. This is therefore necessary for Eq. (4.44) to hold. This result is unaltered if we formulate a more general model by introducing the lagged changes of each variable in both equations:

$$
\begin{aligned}
\Delta P_{t+1} &= \lambda_P(P_t - \kappa F_t) + \textstyle\sum_{i=1}^{p} \phi_i^{PP} \Delta P_{t+1-i} + \sum_{i=1}^{p} \phi_i^{PF} \Delta F_{t+1-i} + u_t^P \quad \lambda_P \leq 0 \\
\Delta F_{t+1} &= -\lambda_F(P_t - \kappa F_t) + \textstyle\sum_{i=1}^{p} \phi_i^{FP} \Delta P_{t+1-i} + \sum_{i=1}^{p} \phi_i^{FF} \Delta F_{t+1-i} + u_t^F \quad \lambda_F \leq 0.
\end{aligned} \tag{4.45}
$$

In essence, Eq. (4.45) is a bivariate VAR(p) in first differences that contains error-correction terms, and in which λ_P *and* λ_F *can be interpreted as speed of adjustment parameters*: the larger these parameters are in absolute value, the greater the response of current values of the variables to the previous period's deviation from the long-run equilibrium. Of course, at least one of the speed of adjustment terms must be nonzero (i.e., $|\lambda_P| + |\lambda_F| > 0$): if both λ_P and λ_F were equal to 0, the long-run equilibrium relationship would not appear and the model would not be one of error-correction or cointegration.[14]

This result that identifies cointegration with error-correction models and vice versa, holds more generally, as shown in Definition 4.4.

DEFINITION 4.4 (Vector error-correction representation)

If the N I(1) variables in $\boldsymbol{y}_t$ have a vector error-correction model (VECM) representation,

$$
\Delta \boldsymbol{y}_{t+1} = \boldsymbol{\pi}_0 + \boldsymbol{\Pi} \boldsymbol{y}_t + \sum_{i=1}^{p} \boldsymbol{\Pi}_i \Delta \boldsymbol{y}_{t+1-i} + \boldsymbol{u}_{t+1}, \tag{4.46}
$$

(where the error vectors $\boldsymbol{u}_{t+1}$ can be serially correlated) then, because the vector equation will need to be balanced, $\boldsymbol{\Pi}\boldsymbol{y}_t \sim I(0)$ will imply that the variables in $\boldsymbol{y}_t$ are $CI(1,1)$. Because the $N \times N$ matrix $\boldsymbol{\Pi} \neq \boldsymbol{O}$ contains only constants, each row of this matrix is a cointegrating vector of $\boldsymbol{y}_t$ and *rank*($\boldsymbol{\Pi}$) is the cointegrating rank of $\boldsymbol{y}_t$.

Interestingly, the only case in which a VECM fails to imply a cointegrating relationship is when $\boldsymbol{\Pi} = \boldsymbol{O}$ so that Eq. (4.46) boils down to a traditional reduced-form VAR(p) in first differences. Of course, because $\boldsymbol{\Pi} = \boldsymbol{O}$, in this case $\boldsymbol{y}_{t+1}$ will not respond to previous period's deviation from the long-run equilibrium.

A fact sometimes ignored, which instead provides a compelling reply to the practically relevant question "Can we ignore cointegration and simply proceed to take first differences of all interesting variables?," is that when $\boldsymbol{\Pi} \neq \boldsymbol{O}$, $\boldsymbol{y}_{t+1}$ will respond to the previous period's deviations from the long-run equilibrium and therefore estimating Eq. (4.46) as a VAR(p) in first differences is inappropriate if $\boldsymbol{y}_{t+1}$ has instead a VECM representation. The omission of the term $\boldsymbol{\Pi}\boldsymbol{y}_t$ entails a rather severe misspecification. Equivalently, we say that in a model in which the error-correction terms have been unduly dropped, $\Delta \boldsymbol{y}_{t+1} = \boldsymbol{\pi}_0 + \sum_{i=1}^{p} \boldsymbol{\Pi}_i \Delta \boldsymbol{y}_{t+1-i} + \boldsymbol{u}_{t+1}$ has no long-run solution and it therefore has nothing to say about whether the variables have an equilibrium relationship. Given the misspecification error, all of the coefficient estimates, t-tests, F-tests, tests of cross-equation restrictions, impulse responses and variance decompositions would not be representative of the true process. Hence, there is a substantial penalty to pay if you estimate a VAR in first differences when the data are actually cointegrated; differencing "throws away" information contained in the cointegrating relationship(s). As a result, it is also natural to then ask: "Why not simply estimate all VARs in levels?", given the perils of differentiating cointegrated variables? The answer is that it is preferable to use the first differences if the N $I(1)$ variables are not cointegrated, at least for three reasons:

---

14. In case one or more of the adjustment coefficients were to have the "wrong" sign, then the system could be explosive and cointegration would fail.

- If cointegration is incorrectly assumed, tests lose power because you estimate N^2 additional parameters.
- For a VAR in levels, tests of Granger causality conducted on the $I(1)$ variables do not have a standard F-distribution.
- The impulse responses at long horizons would also lead to inconsistent estimates of the true responses; in particular, impulse response functions (IRFs) may not decay, and any imprecision in the coefficient estimates will have a permanent impact on the responses.

Going back to the dividend growth model example, a good way to examine the relationship between cointegration and VECM is to study the properties of a simple VAR(1) model, when financial markets are efficient (and hence, there are no-arbitrage opportunities):

$$\begin{aligned} P_{t+1} &= a_{11}P_t + a_{12}F_t + \varepsilon^P_{t+1} \\ F_{t+1} &= a_{20} + a_{22}F_t + \varepsilon^F_{t+1} \end{aligned}, \tag{4.47}$$

where $a_{12} \neq 0$, $|a_{11}| < 1$, and ε^P_{t+1}, and ε^F_{t+1} are possibly correlated white noise processes. We drop an intercept from the price equation to prevent the presence of a drift that would cause arbitrage opportunities. Note that if $a_{22} = 1$, the equation for fundamentals is a RW with drift and as such taking the first difference of both equations gives:[15]

$$\begin{aligned} \Delta P_{t+1} &= (a_{11} - 1)P_t + a_{12}F_t + \varepsilon^P_{t+1} = -a_{12}\left[\frac{1-a_{11}}{a_{12}}P_t - F_t\right] + \varepsilon^P_{t+1} \\ \Delta F_{t+1} &= a_{20} + \varepsilon^F_{t+1}. \end{aligned} \tag{4.48}$$

Eq. (4.48) shows that the first equation is balanced, in the sense that both its left- and right-hand sides are $I(0)$, if and only if $\left[\frac{1-a_{11}}{a_{12}}P_t - F_t\right] \sim I(0)$, and this independently of the value taken by a_{12}. Two additional restrictions are usefully imposed on the VAR in Eq. (4.48):

- $a_{12} > 0$, which guarantees a valid error-correction dynamic, because when $((1 - a_{11})/a_{12})P_t < F_t$ and the price is too low, then $-a_{12}\left[((1 - a_{11})/a_{12})P_t - F_t\right] > 0$, i.e., prices will have to increase, as expected.
- $a_{11} < 1$ because Eq. (4.48) implies a cointegrating vector $\left[((1 - a_{11})/a_{12}),\ -1\right]'$ and therefore the model underlying Eq. (4.48) reaches its long-run equilibrium when $F_t = ((1 - a_{11})/a_{12})P_t$ or $F_t/P_t = (1 - a_{11})/a_{12}$, where $(1 - a_{11})/a_{12}$ acts as an equilibrium fundamental-price level.

All these restrictions are required for a VECM representation such as the one in Eq. (4.48) to imply that prices and fundamentals are CI(1,1). More generally, *all VECMs can be interpreted as special, restricted VAR models*, similar to Eq. (4.47) concerning sets of N I(1) variables, $\Delta \boldsymbol{y}_{t+1} = \boldsymbol{\pi}_0 + \boldsymbol{\Pi} \boldsymbol{y}_t + \boldsymbol{\varepsilon}_{t+1}$. Therefore, it would be inappropriate to estimate a VAR of cointegrated variables using only first differences.

Considering again the bivariate VAR in Eq. (4.47):

$$\begin{aligned} P_{t+1} &= a_{11}P_t + a_{12}F_t + \varepsilon^P_{t+1} \\ F_{t+1} &= a_{20} + a_{22}F_t + \varepsilon^F_{t+1}, \end{aligned} \tag{4.49}$$

note that when $a_{11} = a_{22} = 1$ (it makes little sense to think of economic quantities as nonstationary oscillatory variables, so we shall not consider $a_{11} = a_{22} = -1$), both prices and fundamentals are RW processes, but while fundamentals contain one stochastic trend, prices will contain two:

$$\begin{aligned} P_{t+1} &= (P_0 + a_{12}F_0) + a_{12}a_{20}t + a_{12}\sum_{\tau=1}^{t}\varepsilon^F_\tau + \sum_{\tau=1}^{t+1}\varepsilon^P_\tau \\ F_{t+1} &= F_0 + a_{20}(t+1) + \sum_{\tau=1}^{t+1}\varepsilon^F_\tau. \end{aligned} \tag{4.50}$$

Therefore, prices will be $I(2)$ and because fundamentals are just $I(1)$, it will be impossible for prices and fundamentals to be cointegrated.

Finally, when in Eq. (4.50) we record $|a_{22}| > 1$ and/or $|a_{11}| > 1$, then both variables are nonstationary and explosive and therefore no cointegration exists. Mechanically, this derives from the fact that in Eq. (4.48), first-differencing fails to make the variables stationary.

15. Assuming $a_{22} = 1$ is vital, in the sense that if $|a_{22}| < 1$, then both processes are stationary by construction and no cointegration will be possible.

Although this is just an example (that could be generalized at the cost of additional algebra), the finding that a VECM for $I(1)$ variables necessarily implies cointegration illustrates the following.

RESULT 4.5 (Granger's representation theorem)

For any set of N $I(d)$ variables with identical integration order, error-correction and cointegration are equivalent representations.

4.4.4 Testing for Cointegration

There are two alternative and fundamental ways to test for cointegration:

- *Univariate, regression-based tests*—such as Engle and Granger's (1987)—that go back to Definition 4.3 and essentially exploit the simple idea that a regression could be used to find at least one (the least mean-squared error one) cointegrating relationship (i.e., vector) such that a weighted linear combinations of the variables of interest is $I(0)$.
- *Multivariate, VECM-based tests*, basically Johansen's (1988, 1995) and Stock and Watson's (1988), that exploit instead Granger–Engle's representation theorem and the equivalence between the existence of a VECM and cointegration; their idea is that a restricted, reduced-form VAR can be used to perform hypotheses tests that, under the null of $r < N$ cointegrating relationships among N variables, the transformation of a VAR into a VECM is supported by the data.

Engle and Granger's univariate methodology simply seeks to determine whether the residuals of an estimated equilibrium relationship are stationary. For concreteness, we describe their test for the special case of the dividend/earnings growth model and then briefly indicate how the methodology can be generalized to the case of N variables. Supposes that, by using appropriate unit root tests as documented in Section 4.3, we have already successfully determined that $\{P_t\}$ and $\{F_t\}$ are both $I(1)$. By definition, cointegration needs that two variables be integrated of the same order. For instance, if one or both variables were stationary, then cointegration would be logically impossible. At this point, we estimate the long-run equilibrium relationship:[16]

$$P_t = \kappa_0 + \kappa_1 F_t + e_t. \tag{4.51}$$

If the variables are cointegrated, an OLS regression yields a *superconsistent estimator* of the cointegrating parameters κ_0 and κ_1, in the sense that the OLS estimator converges faster (at rate proportional to T) than in OLS models using stationary variables, where the convergence rate is traditionally $\sqrt{T}$; intuitively, this is due to the fact that correlations between stochastic trends, which always underlie the OLS estimates of a regression slope coefficient, tend to be stronger than correlations between pairs of $I(0)$ variables.[17]

At this point, to determine whether prices and fundamentals are actually cointegrated, denote the series of residuals $\hat{e}_t = P_t - \hat{\kappa}_0 - \hat{\kappa}_1 F_t$, which (assuming cointegration) is also the time series of estimated deviations from the long-run relationship. If these deviations are found to be stationary, say using one of the unit root tests in Section 4.3, then prices and fundamentals will be cointegrated of order (1,1). It is just worthwhile to add that when (augmented) Dickey–Fuller type tests are applied, for instance as in the regression:

$$\hat{e}_t = \alpha \hat{e}_{t-1} + \sum_{i=2}^{p} \gamma_i \Delta \hat{e}_{t+1-i} + \eta_t, \tag{4.52}$$

there will be no need to include an intercept term because these are already zero-mean OLS residuals. Also, due attention should be paid to the logic of the test, which has implications for the language to be used: failure to reject the null of a unit root (i.e., H_0: $\alpha = 0$ in (4.52)) should be expressed as the *impossibility to reject the null of a unit root in the residuals of the Engle–Granger's regression which, in its turn, implies that we cannot reject the null hypothesis that*

16. One is often confronted with the choice between estimating a potentially cointegrating regression using the levels of the variables versus the logarithms of the levels of the variables. Although financial modeling may provide an answer as to the more appropriate functional form, fortunately Hendry and Juselius (2001) have noted that if a set of series is cointegrated in levels, they will also be cointegrated in log levels.

17. Interestingly, even if prices and fundamentals were cointegrated, in general we will not be able to make inferences concerning κ_0 and κ_1 using standard t- and F-tests. This occurs because while OLS estimates of the coefficients are super consistent, the same is not true of their standard errors. Methods to adjust inferential procedures to take this into account exist, but we shall not deal with them here. The interested reader may find an introduction in Hayashi (2000).

prices and fundamentals are not cointegrated.[18] In this case the appropriate modeling strategy would be to take first differences of all the variables. Such a model would have no long-run equilibrium solution, but this would not matter since no cointegration implies that there is no long-run relationship anyway. Finally, note that the critical value of ADF tests will need to be adjusted to reflect the fact that the residuals used in the test are generated from Eq. (4.51): by construction OLS estimates the parameters minimizing the sum of squared residuals and since residual variance is made as small as possible, using standard ADF critical values in Engle–Granger tests will contain a bias toward finding a stationary error process. In fact, besides focusing on the t-ratio statistic, $\hat{t}_\alpha \equiv \hat{\alpha}/se(\hat{\alpha})$, it is also typical to perform tests on the *normalized autocorrelation coefficient* from Eq. (4.52) (see Hayashi, 2000):

$$\hat{z}_\alpha \equiv \frac{T\hat{\alpha}}{1-\sum\limits_{i=2}^{p}\hat{\gamma}_i^2}. \tag{4.53}$$

Of course, it is also possible to use the Durbin–Watson (DW) test statistic (see Chapter 1) or the PP approach (see Section 4.3) to test for nonstationarity of the cointegrating regression residuals. If the DW test is applied to the residuals of the cointegrating regression, it is known as the *cointegrating regression Durbin–Watson (CRDW) test*. Under the null hypothesis of a unit root in the errors, CRDW will be close to 0, so the null of a unit root is rejected if the CRDW statistic is larger than the relevant critical value (which is approximately 0.5).

In the literature a PP test applied to the residuals of the cointegrating regression in Eq. (4.51) is called a *Phillips-Ouliaris' (1990) test*, which *uses the nonparametric PP methodology* to deal with serial correlation in the regression residuals, in the sense that $\{\hat{e}_t\}$ under $p = 0$ are used to compute estimates of the long-run variance ($\hat{V}_0$) to perform the adjustment to the estimated autocorrelation coefficient given by $\hat{\alpha}^{PP} = \hat{\alpha} - T\hat{V}_0\left(\sum_{t=2}^{T}\hat{e}_t^2\right)^{-1/2}$, so that $\hat{z}_\alpha^{PP} = T\hat{\alpha}^{PP}$. As with the PP statistic, the asymptotic distributions of the Phillips–Ouliaris statistics are nonstandard and depend on the deterministic regressor specification (intercept, time trends, etc.) that may appear in Eq. (4.51), so that critical values for the statistics are obtained from simulation results, such as those in MacKinnon et al. (1999).

At this point, when the null of no cointegration is rejected, it will be possible to estimate (usually by OLS) the VECM, which in this case will simply consist of a VAR(p) (this lag order p does not need to be the same as in Eq. (4.52)), in which the error-correction terms directly use the stationary estimated residuals from Eq. (4.51):

$$\begin{aligned}\Delta P_{t+1} &= \lambda_P\hat{e}_t + \sum_{i=1}^{p} a_{1i}^P \Delta P_{t+1-i} + \sum_{i=1}^{p} a_{2i}^P \Delta F_{t+1-i} + \varepsilon_{t+1}^P \\ \Delta F_{t+1} &= \lambda_F\hat{e}_t + a_0^F + \sum_{i=1}^{p} a_{1i}^F \Delta P_{t+1-i} + \sum_{i=1}^{p} a_{2i}^F \Delta F_{t+1-i} + \varepsilon_{t+1}^F.\end{aligned} \tag{4.54}$$

Because all terms in Eq. (4.54) are stationary, the test statistics and model diagnostic checks used in traditional VAR analysis are appropriate. Moreover, Lutkepohl and Reimers (1992) have shown that standard innovation accounting (i.e., impulse responses and variance decomposition analysis) can be used to extract information on the dynamic linkages among the variables. As a practical matter, the two innovations ε_{t+1}^P and ε_{t+1}^F may be contemporaneously correlated, so that in obtaining IRFs and variance decompositions, methods such as the Cholesky decomposition of Chapter 3 must be used to orthogonalize the innovations. Example 4.5 shows how the Engle–Granger and Phillips–Ouliaris tests are applied to long series of real stock prices, dividends and earnings.

EXAMPLE 4.5

We test whether S&P real stock prices, aggregate earnings, and aggregate dividends give any evidence of cointegration. We start by performing bivariate tests, considering first real prices and dividends—which represents the very classical Gordon's (1959) model—and then extend it to real prices and earnings. Last, we perform joint, trivariate tests of prices, dividends, and earnings. Because dividends are basically paid-out earnings, to have a trivariate joint relationship is less implausible than it may sound. From the analysis in Section 4.3, we know that asking whether the series are cointegrated is sensible because they all are I(1) (in spite of some reservations concerning the real aggregate earnings series).

(Continued)

18. This is a bit different from stating that, because we cannot reject the null of a unit root in the OLS residuals of Eq. (4.51), we reject the null hypothesis of cointegration. The reason is that in Eq. (4.51), the null hypothesis is that there is cointegration since OLS regressions are estimated under the null of stationarity of the residuals.

EXAMPLE 4.5 (Continued)

As far as real prices and dividends go, we start by applying a Engle–Granger cointegrating regression test. We estimate Eqs. (4.51)–(4.52) with no exogenous regressors given the structure of the model in Eq. (4.35), using a number of lags specified according to a modified SBIC, with a maximum number of lags equal to 12 (they turn out to be 6). In a regression of residuals from "prices on dividends," we find $\hat{\alpha} = -0.005$, $\hat{t}_\alpha = -2.176$ (p-value is 0.175), $\hat{z}_\alpha = -11.164$ (p-value is 0.138), which leads to not rejecting the null of a unit root in the cointegrating regression residuals and therefore to a nonrejection of the null of no cointegration between the series. In a regression of residuals from "dividends on prices," we find $\hat{\alpha} = -0.005$, $\hat{t}_\alpha = -2.354$ (p-value is 0.125), $\hat{z}_\alpha = -11.361$ (p-value is 0.132), which again leads to a nonrejection of the null of no cointegration. This evidence represents an outright rejection of the dividend growth model in the case of the United States, when stated in real terms: the two series do not share a common stochastic trend. A portion of the literature has interpreted this finding as evidence of bubbles in US stock prices, because prices may drift away from dividends without any correction mechanism pulling them back. We have repeated these tests when the number of lagged changes in residuals in Eq. (4.52) is specified using general-to-simple t-statistics for the γ_i coefficients, with a p-value threshold of 10%. In this case, eight lags were specified, the implied p-values declined to values between 0.080 and 0.111, but the null of no cointegration keeps not being rejected, which means that there are different stochastic trends in the two series.

We have also applied Phillips–Ouliaris tests. When prewhitening is applied to the residuals of Eq. (4.51) on the basis of a modified SBIC (this gives just one lag), the long-run variance is nonparametrically estimated using a Bartlett's kernel with Newey–West bandwidth selection, for the residuals from a regression of P_t on D_t, we find $\hat{\alpha} = -0.003$, $\hat{t}_\alpha^{PP} = -2.196$ (p-value is 0.169), $\hat{z}_\alpha^{PP} = -10.979$ (p-value is 0.143), which leads to a rejection of the null of no cointegration between the series; for residuals from a regression of dividends on prices, we find $\hat{\alpha} = -0.003$, $\hat{t}_\alpha^{PP} = -2.359$ (p-value is 0.124), $\hat{z}_\alpha^{PP} = -11.135$ (p-value is 0.139), which leads to the same conclusion. Also a Phillips–Ouliaris test gives evidence against a discounted dividend model for pricing US stocks.

Next, in the case of real prices and earnings, we follow the same steps but reach opposite conclusions:

- In a Engle–Granger regression of real prices on real earnings, $\hat{\alpha} = -0.009$, $\hat{t}_\alpha = -3.102$ (p-value is 0.021), $\hat{z}_\alpha = -22.319$ (p-value is 0.011), which leads to rejecting the null of a unit root in the cointegrating regression residuals and therefore to a rejection of the null of no cointegration between the series.
- In a Engle–Granger regression of residuals from "E_t on P_t," $\hat{\alpha} = -0.009$, $\hat{t}_\alpha = -3.510$ (p-value is 0.006), $\hat{z}_\alpha = -25.977$ (p-value is 0.005), which leads to rejecting the absence of cointegration.
- In a Phillips–Ouliaris regression of residuals from "real prices on earnings," we obtain $\hat{\alpha} = -0.009$, $\hat{t}_\alpha^{PP} = -3.102$ (p-value is 0.021), $\hat{z}_\alpha^{PP} = -22.319$ (p-value is 0.011), which leads to a rejection of the null of no cointegration.
- In a Phillips–Ouliaris regression of residuals from "real E_t on P_t," we retrieve $\hat{\alpha} = -0.009$, $\hat{t}_\alpha^{PP} = -3.510$ (p-value is 0.006), $\hat{z}_\alpha^{PP} = -25.977$ (p-value is 0.005), which also leads to a rejection of the null of no cointegration.

The results on P_t and E_t are robust to a range of checks, concerning how prewhitening of the residuals is performed, the type of kernel function and bandwidth selection in the nonparametric calculation of long-run variance: real US stock prices and earnings are cointegrated, which is consistent with a pricing model that implies the existence of a long-run, equilibrium price-earnings ratio:

$$P_{t+1} = \frac{(1+g_E)E_{t+1}}{(r-g_E)} + \varepsilon_{t+1} \Rightarrow E\left[\frac{P_t}{E_t}\right] = \frac{1+g_E}{r-g_E}.$$

For this case, we have also computed the cointegrating regression residuals (from regressing real P_t on E_t) that are also displayed in Fig. 4.11. The top portion is striking: according to a discounted earnings model, there was no stock market bubble in 2006–07, there is a well-evident bubble in 1997–99 and, at least possibly, in 2015–16 at the time we are writing; on the contrary the 2008–09 stock market collapse should have been deeper, based on the dynamics of earnings.

The estimated cointegrating regression is:

$$P_{t+1} = \underset{(0.000)}{18.057}\, E_{t+1} + \varepsilon_{t+1} \Rightarrow E\left[\frac{P_t}{E_t}\right] = 18.057 \Rightarrow \frac{r-g_E}{1+g_E} = 0.0554,$$

that is, with these data the cointegrating vector is (proportional to) [1,−18.057]′ and such a multiple is a rather plausible one. This requires an expected stock return of at least 5.5% per year, for the long-run multiple of 18.1 to make sense. Fig. 4.12 shows the time series of the S&P price-earnings ratio and does indeed show some tendency to revert toward a long-run average of 18.1.

At this point, we close by estimating the corresponding VECM. All criteria available indicate the need to include a large number of lags in the model, in this case equal to the maximum allowed, 12. We do not report estimates of the coefficients associated with the lags, but we obtain (t-statistics are in squared brackets):

$$\Delta P_{t+1} = -\underset{[2.575]}{0.0069}(P_t - E_t) + \text{lags of } \Delta P_{t+1} + \text{lags of } \Delta E_{t+1} + \varepsilon_{t+1}^P \quad R^2 = 0.131$$

$$\Delta E_{t+1} = \underset{[1.164]}{0.0001}(P_t - E_t) + \text{lags of } \Delta P_{t+1} + \text{lags of } \Delta E_{t+1} + \varepsilon_{t+1}^F \quad R^2 = 0.736.$$

(*Continued*)

EXAMPLE 4.5 (Continued)

The estimates of the adjustments coefficients are rather small, which is consistent with the sluggish reversion toward the long-run average displayed in Fig. 4.12. Note that the late 2008 spike is not a bubble episode, but corresponds to the fact that during a severe and quickly prevailing recession that savagely reduced corporate profitability, stock prices plummeted by less than the model implies. The estimates reveal that all the burden of the adjustment falls on equity valuations which display a negative and statistically significant coefficient of −0.0069; as one would expect, it is not earnings that adjust (when $N = 2$ using a t-test on the adjustment coefficient is formally appropriate although in general this is not the case).

We close with a brief analysis of the chances of trivariate cointegration. In this case, we copy here the typical outputs offered by E-Views.

Table 4.2 concerns Engle–Granger tests and offers an example in which the variable selected in the regression as the dependent one affects results. When we regress P_t on D_t and E_t, there is no evidence of cointegration. However, if one regresses either D_t or E_t on the remaining variables, the null of no cointegration is sharply rejected.

Results almost align in favor of trivariate cointegration when Phillips–Ouliaris tests are used in Table 4.3 although the most natural cointegration regression of P_t on D_t and E_t returns p-values between 0.07 and 0.10 that may trigger a failure to not reject the null of no cointegration.

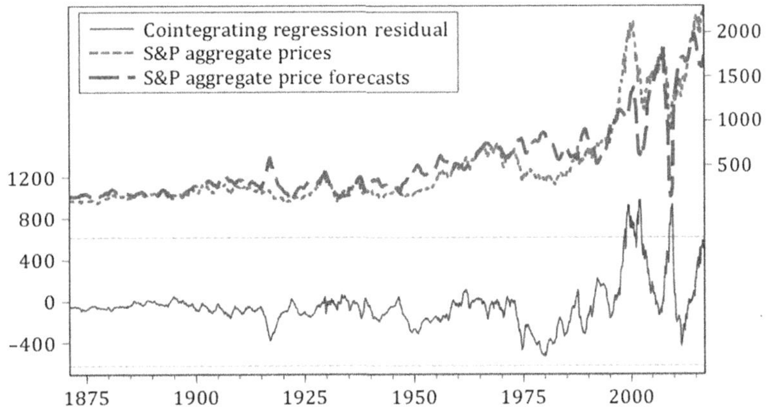

FIGURE 4.11 Fitted values and cointegrating regression residuals of real S&P equity index prices regressed on aggregate earnings.

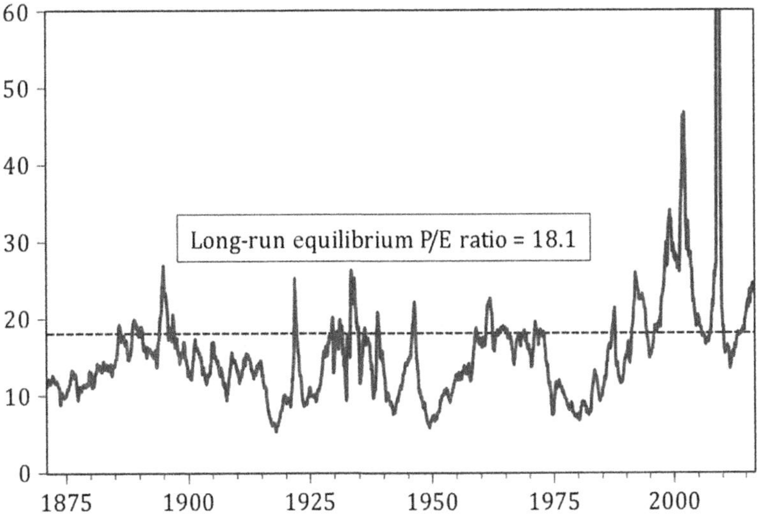

FIGURE 4.12 Real S&P equity index prices/aggregate earnings ratio.

TABLE 4.2 Engle–Granger Tests of Trivariate Cointegration

Series: Prices dividends earnings
Sample: 1871M01, 2016M12
Included observations: 1752
Null hypothesis: Series are not cointegrated
Automatic lags specification based on modified Schwarz criterion (maxlag = 12)

Dependent	ADF-Style *t*-Ratio	Probability	*z*-Statistic	Probability
Prices	− 2.6844	0.1894	− 17.2511	0.1275
Dividends	− 4.5945	0.0007	− 49.3258	0.0002
Earnings	− 6.1117	0.0000	− 76.4985	0.0000

Intermediate Results

	Prices	Dividends	Earnings
Estimated alpha coefficient	− 0.0073	− 0.0065	− 0.0142
S.E. of alpha coefficient	0.0027	0.0014	0.0023
Residual variance	631.0963	0.0591	0.6524
Long-run residual variance	1146.28	1.118226	6.184435
Number of lags	2	12	1

MacKinnon (1996) *p*-values.

TABLE 4.3 Phillips–Ouliaris Tests of Trivariate Cointegration

Series: Prices dividends earnings
Sample: 1871M01, 2016M12
Included observations: 1752
Null hypothesis: Series are not cointegrated
Long-run variance estimate (prewhitening with lags = −1 from SIC maxlags = 12, Bartlett kernel, Newey–West fixed bandwidth

Dependent	ADF-Style *t*-Ratio	Probability	*z*-Statistic	Probability
Prices	− 2.9938	0.1023	− 20.4728	0.0704
Dividends	− 4.2477	0.0028	− 36.3153	0.0028
Earnings	− 5.4785	0.0000	− 61.3360	0.0000

Intermediate Results

	Prices	Dividends	Earnings
Estimated alpha coefficient	− 0.0053	− 0.0047	− 0.0078
Bias corrected alpha	− 0.0117	− 0.0207	− 0.0350
S.E. of alpha coefficient	0.0039	0.0049	0.0064
Residual variance	687.8981	0.2108	1.1954
Long-run residual variance	1311.8110	0.9186	4.9677

MacKinnon (1996) *p*-values.

Although Engle and Granger's (1987) approach is easily implemented, it faces important drawbacks:

- The estimation of the long-run equilibrium regression requires that the researcher places one variable on the left-hand side and uses the others as regressors. For instance, in our example, shall we estimate Eq. (4.51) or

$$F_t = \kappa'_0 + \kappa'_1 P_t + e'_t \ ? \tag{4.55}$$

As the sample size grows, asymptotic theory indicates that the tests for a unit root using the residuals from Eq. (4.51) or (4.55) will become equivalent, but this is not helpful when we have finite samples, that is, always. In practice, similarly to Example 4.5, it is possible to find that one regression indicates that the variables are cointegrated, whereas reversing the order of dependent versus independent variables will reveal no cointegration, which is puzzling, almost to imply that, say, while there exists a long-run equilibrium price-earnings or price-dividend ratio, there is instead no long-run equilibrium for the earnings-price or dividend-price ratios! The problem is obviously compounded using three or more variables since any of the variables can be selected as the left-hand side variable, that is, should we be regressing y_{1t} on $\{y_{2t}, y_{3t}, \ldots, y_{Nt}\}$, y_{2t} on $\{y_{1t}, y_{3t}, \ldots, y_{Nt}\}$, etc., or y_{Nt} on $\{y_{1t}, y_{2t}, \ldots, y_{N-1,t}\}$?
- The Engle–Granger procedure relies on a two-step estimator, in which the first step regression residuals are used in the second step to estimate an ADF (or PP)-type regression, which causes errors and contamination deriving from a *generated regressors problem.*
- Finally, even more problematic is the fact that in tests using three or more variables, we know that there may be more than one cointegrating vector. Engle and Granger's method has no systematic procedure to perform the separate estimation of multiple cointegrating vectors.

On the contrary, multivariate methods naturally take the potential existence of multiple cointegrating vectors into account in a straightforward way, by using single-step full information maximum likelihood estimation. In practice, Johansen's (1995) procedure is nothing more than a multivariate generalization of the Dickey–Fuller tests from Section 4.3. Consider a reduced-form VAR(p) model for N variables of interest (adding an intercept is immaterial and we shall drop it to simplify matters):[19]

$$\boldsymbol{y}_{t+1} = \sum_{i=1}^{p} \boldsymbol{A}_i \boldsymbol{y}_{t+1-i} + \boldsymbol{\varepsilon}_{t+1} \quad \boldsymbol{\varepsilon}_{t+1} \text{ IID } (\boldsymbol{0}, \boldsymbol{\Sigma}_\varepsilon). \tag{4.56}$$

The model can be turned into a more revealing form following steps similar to those already employed in the case of the ADF test. First add and subtract $\boldsymbol{A}_p \boldsymbol{y}_{t-p+2}$ to the right-hand side, to obtain:

$$\boldsymbol{y}_{t+1} = \sum_{i=1}^{p-2} \boldsymbol{A}_i \boldsymbol{y}_{t+1-i} + (\boldsymbol{A}_{p-1} + \boldsymbol{A}_p)\boldsymbol{y}_{t-p+2} + \boldsymbol{A}_p \Delta \boldsymbol{y}_{t-p+1} + \boldsymbol{\varepsilon}_{t+1}. \tag{4.57}$$

Next, add and subtract $(\boldsymbol{A}_{p-1} + \boldsymbol{A}_p)\boldsymbol{y}_{t-p+3}$ and keep proceeding in this way. If we perform this operation p times, the final outcome is:[20]

$$\Delta \boldsymbol{y}_{t+1} = \boldsymbol{\Pi} \boldsymbol{y}_t + \sum_{i=1}^{p-1} \boldsymbol{\Gamma}_i \Delta \boldsymbol{y}_{t+1-i} + \boldsymbol{\varepsilon}_{t+1} \quad \boldsymbol{\Pi} \equiv -\left(\boldsymbol{I}_N - \sum_{i=1}^{p} \boldsymbol{A}_i\right), \quad \boldsymbol{\Gamma}_i \equiv -\sum_{j=i+1}^{p} \boldsymbol{A}_j. \tag{4.58}$$

Result 4.6 plays a key role in what follows.

RESULT 4.6

For a set of N variables $\boldsymbol{y}_{t+1}$ that can be represented as in Eq. (4.58), the rank of $\boldsymbol{\Pi}$ equals the number of cointegrating vectors, r. If $\boldsymbol{\Pi}$ consists of all 0's, so that $rank(\boldsymbol{\Pi}) = 0$, then all the variables in the vector $\boldsymbol{y}_{t+1}$ contain a unit root and there is no cointegrating relationship. If $rank(\boldsymbol{\Pi}) = N$, Eq. (4.58) represents a convergent system of difference equations so that all variables are stationary. If $N > rank(\boldsymbol{\Pi}) > 0$, then $\boldsymbol{\Pi}\boldsymbol{y}_t$ is the error-correction term such that:

(Continued)

---

19. The effect of including a vector of intercepts in a model for $\Delta \boldsymbol{y}_{t+1}$ is to allow for the possibility of linear time trends in the DGP. This can be easily accommodated but it will change the critical values of the tests described in the text.

20. Regardless of the rank of $\boldsymbol{\Pi}$, because $\Delta \boldsymbol{y}_t, \Delta \boldsymbol{y}_{t-1}, \ldots, \Delta \boldsymbol{y}_{t-p+1}$ are stationary variables, the number of lags can be established using classical t- and F-tests exploiting a result by Sims et al. (1990) that the coefficients on zero-mean stationary variables can be subject to hypothesis testing using a normal distribution. Yet, we cannot perform Granger causality tests in a cointegrated system using a standard F-test because these would involve coefficients in $\boldsymbol{\Pi}$ that multiply nonstationary variables.

RESULT 4.6 (Continued)

$$\mathbf{0} = E[\Delta \mathbf{y}_{t+1}] = \boldsymbol{\Pi}\mathbf{y}_t + \sum_{i=1}^{p-1} \boldsymbol{\Gamma}_i E[\Delta \mathbf{y}_{t+1-i}] + E[\boldsymbol{\varepsilon}_{t+1}] \Rightarrow \boldsymbol{\Pi}\mathbf{y}_t = \mathbf{0}. \quad (4.59)$$

and $\boldsymbol{\Pi} = \boldsymbol{\Lambda}\mathbf{K}'$, where $\mathbf{K}$ is the $N \times r$ matrix of cointegrating vectors and $\boldsymbol{\Lambda}$ is the $N \times r$, the matrix of weights with which each cointegrating vector enters the N equations of the VAR. $\boldsymbol{\Lambda}$ can also be interpreted as containing r different $N \times 1$ vectors of adjustment coefficients.

Johansen's method consists of the estimation of the matrix $\boldsymbol{\Pi}$ from an unrestricted VAR for N nonstationary series and of tests of whether we can reject the restrictions implied by the reduced rank of $\boldsymbol{\Pi}$. We know (see the mathematical and statistical Appendix for a review of the concept) that the rank of a matrix is equal to the number of its (inverse) characteristic roots (λ_i, $i = 1, 2, \ldots, N$, also called *eigenvalues*) that differ from 0. Suppose we have estimated the matrix $\boldsymbol{\Pi}$ and ordered the N eigenvalues such that $\lambda_1 > \lambda_2 > \cdots > \lambda_N$. Because when there is at least one cointegrating relationship, $\boldsymbol{\Pi}\mathbf{y}_t = \mathbf{0}$, it turns out that $\lambda_1 < 1$. If the variables in $\mathbf{y}_{t+1}$ are not cointegrated, the rank of $\boldsymbol{\Pi}$ is 0 and all of these characteristic roots will equal 0 and $\ln(1 - \lambda_i) = \ln 1 = 0$ $i = 1, 2, \ldots, N$. Similarly, if the rank of $\boldsymbol{\Pi}$ is one, then $1 > \lambda_1 > 0$, $\ln(1 - \lambda_1) < 0$ and $\ln(1 - \lambda_i) = \ln 1 = 0$ for $i = 2, 3, \ldots, N$; if the rank of $\boldsymbol{\Pi}$ is two, then $1 > \lambda_1 > \lambda_2 > 0$, $\ln(1 - \lambda_1) < \ln(1 - \lambda_2) < 0$, and $\ln(1 - \lambda_i) = \ln 1 = 0$ for $i = 3, 4, \ldots, N$, etc.

Johansen (1988) proposed that to test for the number of eigenvalues that are insignificantly different from unity can be conducted using the following two test statistics:

$$\lambda_{trace}(r) \equiv -T \sum_{i=r+1}^{N} \ln(1 - \hat{\lambda}_i) \quad (4.60)$$

$$\lambda_{\max}(r, r+1) \equiv -T\ln(1 - \hat{\lambda}_{r+1}), \quad (4.61)$$

where the $\hat{\lambda}_1 > \hat{\lambda}_2 > \cdots > \hat{\lambda}_N$ are the estimated values of the eigenvalues obtained from $\hat{\boldsymbol{\Pi}}$. $\lambda_{trace}(r)$ tests the null hypothesis that the number of distinct cointegrating vectors is less than or equal to r against a general alternative of a number exceeding r. The further the estimated eigenvalues are from 0, the larger is the trace statistic. $\lambda_{\max}(r, r+1)$ tests the null that the number of cointegrating vectors is r against the alternative of $r + 1$ cointegrating vectors. Again, if the estimated value of the eigenvalue is large, $\lambda_{\max}(r, r+1)$ will be large.

The critical values of the $\lambda_{trace}(r)$ and the $\lambda_{\max}(r, r+1)$ statistics are obtained using a Monte Carlo approach as in Johansen and Juselius (1990). The distribution of the test statistics is nonstandard, and the critical values depend on the value of $N - r$, the number of nonstationary components, and whether deterministic terms (such constants or trends) are included in each of the equations.[21] If the test statistic is greater than the appropriate critical value, we will reject:

- the null hypothesis that there are at most r cointegrating vectors in favor of the alternative that there are $r + 1$ vectors, in the case of the $\lambda_{trace}(r)$ test, or
- the null hypothesis that there are r cointegrating vectors in favor of the alternative that there are $r + 1$ vectors, in the case of $\lambda_{\max}(r, r+1)$.

Of course, the tests based on $\lambda_{trace}(0)$ and $\lambda_{\max}(0, 1)$ are key, because they are implicitly cointegration tests. Given their rather heterogeneous functional form, it is possible for Eqs. (4.60) and (4.61) to give different results. In fact, $\lambda_{\max}(r, r+1)$ has the sharper alternative hypothesis and as a result it is usually preferred when trying to pin down the number of cointegrating vectors.

Finally, it is important to emphasize that the VECM in Eq. (4.58) cannot be estimated by OLS because it is necessary to impose cross-equation restrictions on the $\boldsymbol{\Pi}$ matrix. Therefore, multivariate cointegration testing tends to rely on ML estimation methods. We are now ready to ask whether our historical times series of monthly real S&P stock prices, dividends, and earnings are cointegrated using multivariate, rank-based MLE tests.

21. Intercepts can be included either in the cointegrating vectors themselves or as additional terms in the VAR. The latter is equivalent to including a trend in the DGP for the levels of the series. The critical values of the $\lambda_{trace}(r)$ and the $\lambda_{\max}(r, r+1)$ statistics tend to become smaller without any deterministic regressors and larger with an intercept term included in the cointegrating vector.

EXAMPLE 4.6

We start out once more performing simpler, bivariate tests. If the variables are I(1), because $N = 2$, in this case there can be at most one cointegrating relationship between pairs of variables. In the case of real stock prices and dividends, $\boldsymbol{y}_t \equiv [P_t,\ D_t]'$, we perform the $\lambda_{trace}(0)$ and the $\lambda_{max}(0,1)$ tests while specifying an intercept in both the testing VAR and in the cointegrating vector. An intercept in the VAR accommodates a likely drift in real dividends, while an intercept in the cointegrating vector also allows the stationary relationships between variables to trend over time, as in $\boldsymbol{\Pi y}_t + \boldsymbol{Dx}_{t+1} = \boldsymbol{A}(\boldsymbol{K}'\boldsymbol{y}_t + \kappa_0)$, where $\boldsymbol{Dx}_{t+1}$ captures determinist regressors (such as drifts, polynomial trends, and seasonal factors) in an extended version of Eq. (4.58). The number of lags in Eq. (4.58) is set to 12. Because the estimated eigenvalues are rather small, $\hat{\lambda}_1 = 0.0073$ and $\hat{\lambda}_1 = 0.0008$, we obtain that $\lambda_{trace}(0) = 14.173$ (with p-value 0.078) and $\lambda_{max}(0,1) = 12.762$ (p-value 0.085) which do not allow us to reject the null hypothesis of no cointegration, that is, that $rank(\boldsymbol{\Pi}) = 0$. This conclusion echoes the one reached in Example 4.5: even though in this case, because of p-values between 5% and 10%, the failure to reject is not empirically overwhelming, there is enough evidence to conclude that our 1872–2016 sample is inconsistent with a dividend growth model for aggregate equity valuations.

We repeat these tests with reference to $\boldsymbol{y}_t \equiv [P_t,\ E_t]'$ using identical options in terms of deterministic regressors and selection of the number of lags. The estimated eigenvalues from $\hat{\boldsymbol{\Pi}}$ are 0.0115 and 0.0002, and the first eigenvalue appears to be large enough to give evidence that $rank(\boldsymbol{\Pi}) = 1$. In fact, $\lambda_{trace}(0) = 20.345$ (with p-value 0.009) and $\lambda_{max}(0,1) = 20.020$ (p-value 0.006) which lead us to reject the null of no cointegration in favor of $r = 1$. However, the variables are not stationary either, as we have reported in Section 4.3: $\lambda_{trace}(1) = 0.325$ (p-value 0.569) and $\lambda_{max}(1,2) = 0.325$ (p-value 0.569), so that $r = 2$ is rejected. Once more, real stock prices and earnings are cointegrated and this is evidence consistent with a discounted fundamentals model of equity valuations. When the cointegrating vector is normalized to have $\kappa_1 = 1$, we obtain (standard errors are in parenthesis):

$$\hat{\boldsymbol{A}} = [\underset{(0.0025)}{-0.0062},\ \underset{(0.0001)}{0.0002}]' \qquad \hat{\boldsymbol{K}} = [1,\ \underset{(2.343)}{-25.785}] \qquad \hat{\kappa}_0 = 264.27.$$

These estimates imply a long-run equilibrium cointegrating equation that, plugging in the point estimates, we can write as $P_t = 264.27 + 25.785E_t$, that is, a price-earnings ratio that asymptotically converges to 25.8. This value is substantially larger than what we had found using univariate cointegration tests, and the discrepancy between 18.1 and 25.8 will be of considerable importance to investors, asset managers, and academics debating whether and when a bubble in stock valuations may be forming. The estimates of the adjustment coefficients suggest once more that the error-correction is rather slow—given that $P_t - 264.27 - 25.785E_t = 1$, only 0.0062 of it is corrected by the price declining between two consecutive months—and that the correction is almost entirely supported by equity price changes given that the correction coefficient of earnings has the right sign but it is essentially 0. This is confirmed by a plot of the ECM deviations which we may interpret as mispricings, in Fig. 4.13. For instance, a major over-pricing of S&P stocks has occurred between 1997 and 2001, which somebody has then dubbed the "dot-com tech bubble." Interestingly, while Fig. 4.11 seemed to suggest some evidence of equity over-pricing between 2015 and 2016, this is not the case here.

Finally, we have also performed trivariate cointegration tests for $\boldsymbol{y}_t \equiv [P_t\ D_t\ E_t]'$. Both the $\lambda_{trace}(0)$ and $\lambda_{max}(0,1)$ tests lead to reject the null of no cointegration; however, $\lambda_{trace}(1)$ and $\lambda_{max}(1,2)$ establish that the data contain evidence of one cointegrating relationship at most. However, when we normalize the estimated cointegrating vector on prices, we obtain:

$$\hat{\boldsymbol{A}} = [\underset{(0.0007)}{0.0004},\ \underset{(3.8E-06)}{-1.77E\text{-}05},\ \underset{(1.7E-05)}{6.12E\text{-}05}]' \qquad \hat{\boldsymbol{K}} = [1,\ \underset{(48.821)}{268.13},\ \underset{(17.762)}{-128.44}] \qquad \hat{\kappa}_0 = -701.34.$$

This result is troublesome in economic terms because it is hard to make sense of the −268 loading of prices on real dividends as well as of the negative estimated intercept in the cointegrating relationship; additionally, it seems that in this VECM, prices stop correcting the disequilibrium so that the burden is left entirely upon real earnings. Of course, more in-depth research would be needed before ruling out a fundamental-based equity valuation model on either economic or statistical grounds.

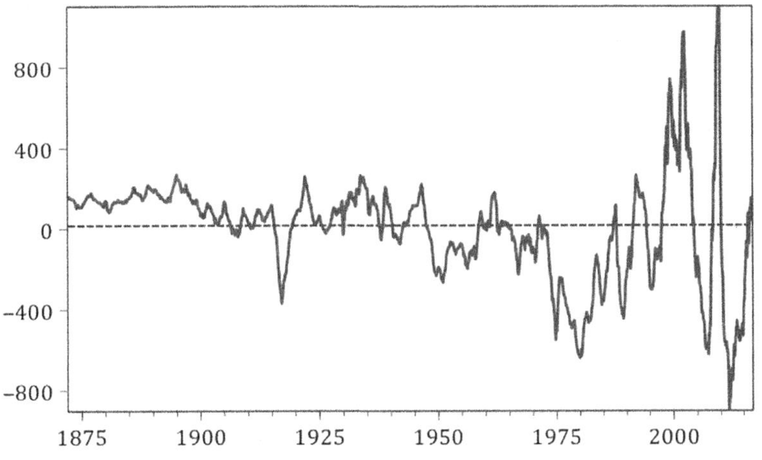

FIGURE 4.13 Deviations from long-run equilibrium cointegrating relation between real S&P equity index prices and aggregate earnings.

Example 4.6 shows that with ML multivariate cointegration tests and the corresponding VECM, estimation complexity may quickly grow as N exceeds just a pair of variables. To provide an even sharper taste of the issues involved, Example 4.7 closes the chapter emphasizing the strong connections between cointegration and the expectations hypothesis of (default) risk-free interest rates.

EXAMPLE 4.7

Consider weekly, constant-maturity US Treasury nominal rates for the maturities 1- and 6-month, 1-, 3-, 7-, and 10-years. The sample period is January 8, 1982–December 30, 2016. We care for cointegration because according to the expectation hypothesis (henceforth EH) of the term structure of interest rates, *at least over the long-run* it should happen that appropriately scaled sums of q expected rates with horizon of m months should equal the current rate with maturity of $qm > m$ months, minus a constant risk premium that rewards habitat effects or a liquidity preference in favor or shorter-term bonds. For instance, the 10-year rate should equal some constant (probably, positive) plus the current 6-month rate and the sum of appropriately weighted expected, future 6-month rates.

The clause "at least over the long run" means that in each week of the sample, deviations of the observed rates from the EH-implied rates are possible, but such deviations should not be permanent or deterministically trending. In other words, all mispricings should be temporary and as such they should be I(0). At this point, we are one step short from a cointegration statement: if it were the case that the tested rates were all I(1), and if future short rates were easily predictable to the point to equal on average their future realized value, then the EH implies that one or more weighted sums of the m I(1) rates exist, such that the result is a I(0) variable plus a constant (the risk premium).

As a first step, we proceed to plot the data in Fig. 4.14. All US rates fluctuate together and they never drift too far part one from the others. As a next step, we proceed to test whether all the six rates are $I(1)$, which is a necessary condition for a cointegration-based test of the EH. Here the critical choice turns out to be whether the unit root regressions should include a time trend. When this is the case, depending on subtle testing choices, we occasionally reject the null of nonstationarity. On the one hand, the data favor the inclusion of a deterministic trend, which is unsurprising in the light Fig. 4.14. On the other hand the presence of a time trend makes no economic sense: while the data seem to require a simple downward linear trend, if we were to extrapolate out-of-sample this feature, we should contemplate very negative rates that may even tend to −100%. When we test for a unit root in each of the six series just including an intercept (i.e., the null is a RW with drift). Table 4.4 presents that, under both ADF and PP tests, we cannot reject the null of a unit root (p-values below 5% have been boldfaced). Marginal doubts only exist in the case of 1-year rates and only under the ADF test. KPSS tests based on a null of stationarity lead to the specular conclusion: we always reject the null of I(0) interest rates.

At this point, we are ready to test for cointegration and hence, implicitly, for the EH using Johansen's method. We use two figures to show the typical outputs that the E-Views software package returns. We use 26 lags to increase the power of the test and we just specify a constant in the testing VAR equation, to capture the presence of any risk premia. Even though the $\lambda_{trace}(r)$ and $\lambda_{\max}(r, r+1)$ point toward a different number of cointegrating vectors, in Fig. 4.15 there is no doubt that $r > 1$, and this is consistent with the EH. Moreover, it also seems clear that $r < 6$, which is consistent with the nonstationarity of the series.

The remaining output, presented in Fig. 4.16, shows the structure of the $\hat{\boldsymbol{\Pi}} = \hat{A}\hat{K}'$ matrix at least for the cases of one and two cointegrating relationships.

The unrestricted coefficient values are the estimated values of coefficients in the cointegrating vector. However, because in any case the cointegrating vector is not uniquely determined, it is useful to normalize the coefficients to set the coefficient value on one of them to unity, as it occurs naturally in the Engle–Granger approach. In Fig. 4.16, we start off normalizing with respect to the first variable, in this case the 10-year Treasury rate, which seems a natural choice, given its importance in financial markets. The estimated adjustment coefficients, or loadings, in each regression (i.e., the "amount of the cointegrating vector" in the equation of each interest rate series) are provided in Fig. 4.16. Next the same format is used (i.e., the normalized cointegrating vectors are presented and then the adjustment parameters) but under the assumption that there are two cointegrating vectors. We omit outputs for the cases of 3 and 4 cointegrating relationships.

Can we claim not to have rejected the EH in US weekly data for the sample 1982–2016? Here we note that cointegration between the rates is a necessary but not sufficient condition for the EH to be supported by the data. The validity of the EH would also require that a combination of rates should be found to cointegrate with a cointegrating vector with structure $[1,\ \kappa_{7Y},\ \kappa_{3Y}, \ldots,\ \kappa_{1m}]'$ where $\kappa_{Y}, \kappa_{3Y}, \ldots, \kappa_{1m}$ should be all negative and satisfy precise constraints concerning the parameter m and q defined previously (see, e.g., Cuthbertson and Nitzsche, 2005, for an introduction). The very fact that all the estimated, normalized cointegrating vectors include large, positive values on the short-term rates indicates that appropriate restrictions do not seem to hold for these data.

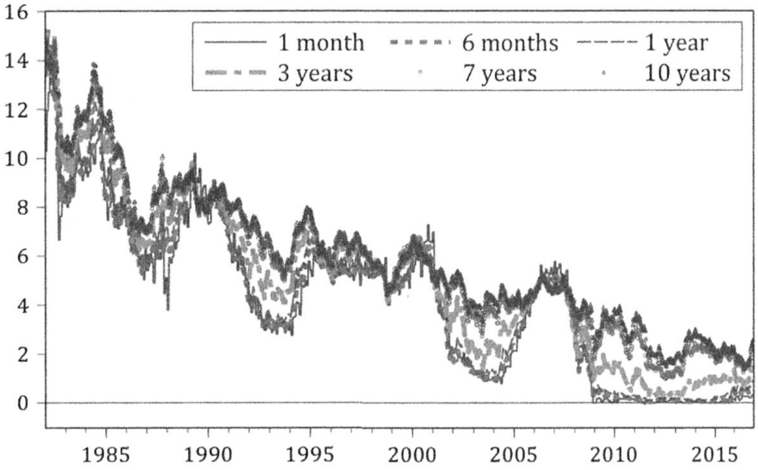

FIGURE 4.14 US riskless, annualized nominal treasury rates at maturities 1 month, 6 months, 1, 3, 7, and 10 years.

TABLE 4.4 Unit Root Tests Applied to US Nominal Treasury Rates

	ADF Test			PP Test			KPSS Test	
	No. of Lags	Est. Alpha	*p*-Value	Bandwidth	Est. Alpha	*p*-Value	LM Test	Outcome
1-month	5	− 0.005	0.206	32	− 0.005	0.315	4.245	Reject *I*(0) at 1%
6-month	10	− 0.003	0.059	13	− 0.003	0.104	4.330	Reject *I*(0) at 1%
1-year	1	− 0.003	**0.035**	16	− 0.003	0.093	4.423	Reject *I*(0) at 1%
3-year	1	− 0.003	0.055	17	− 0.003	0.101	4.715	Reject *I*(0) at 1%
7-year	1	− 0.003	0.057	14	− 0.003	0.086	4.870	Reject *I*(0) at 1%
10-year	1	− 0.003	0.053	13	− 0.003	0.082	4.888	Reject *I*(0) at 1%

Sample (adjusted): 7/16/1982 12/30/2016
Included observations: 1799 after adjustments
Trend assumption: No deterministic trend
Lags interval (in first differences): 1 to 26

Unrestricted Cointegration Rank Test (Trace)

No. of CE(s)	Eigenvalue	Trace-Eigenvalue Statistic	Critical Value	Prob.**
None *	0.0391	154.5082	83.9371	0.0000
At most 1 *	0.0172	82.8136	60.0614	0.0002
At most 2 *	0.0146	51.6783	40.1749	0.0024
At most 3 *	0.0083	25.1920	24.2760	0.0383
At most 4	0.0036	10.1201	12.3209	0.1137
At most 5	0.0020	3.5823	4.1299	0.0693

Trace test indicates 4 cointegrating eqn(s) at the 0.05 level
* denotes rejection of the hypothesis at the 0.05 level
**MacKinnon-Haug-Michelis (1999) P-values

Unrestricted Cointegration Rank Test (Maximum Eigenvalue)

No. of CE(s)	Eigenvalue	Max-Eigenvalue Statistic	Critical Value	Prob.**
None *	0.0391	71.6946	36.6302	0.0000
At most 1 *	0.0172	31.1354	30.4396	0.0409
At most 2 *	0.0146	26.4862	24.1592	0.0238
At most 3	0.0083	15.0719	17.7973	0.1228
At most 4	0.0036	6.5378	11.2248	0.2925
At most 5	0.0020	3.5823	4.1299	0.0693

Max-eigenvalue test indicates 3 cointegrating eqn(s) at the 0.05 level
* denotes rejection of the hypothesis at the 0.05 level
**MacKinnon-Haug-Michelis (1999) P-values

FIGURE 4.15 $\lambda_{\text{trace}}(r)$ and $\lambda_{\max}(r, r+1)$ tests applied to US riskless, annualized nominal treasury rates.

Unrestricted Cointegrating Coefficients

10 years	7 years	3 years	1 year	6 months	1 month
-0.175	0.520	-2.630	-17.754	15.109	4.713
-3.353	5.069	-3.454	-3.930	7.492	-1.963
-10.375	18.438	-16.751	-8.736	17.271	0.237
10.138	-15.116	5.730	-0.762	0.215	-0.103
-1.356	1.425	-0.226	-2.316	1.943	0.692
2.199	-0.942	-3.103	-1.531	3.473	-0.035

Unrestricted Adjustment Coefficients (alpha):

10 years	0.0028	−0.0039	0.0013	0.0009	−0.0061	-0.0011
7 years	0.0031	−0.0034	0.0007	0.0019	−0.0066	-0.0004
3 years	0.0039	−0.0004	0.0012	−0.0007	−0.0067	0.0006
1 year	0.0085	0.0064	−0.0023	−0.0009	−0.0046	-0.0007
6 months	0.0046	0.0028	−0.0035	−0.0020	−0.0055	0.0000
1 month	−0.0410	0.0145	0.0059	0.0040	−0.0029	-0.0022

1 Cointegrating Equation(s): Log Likelihood 15206.24

Normalized Cointegrating Coefficients (Standard Error in Parentheses)

10 years	7 years	3 years	1 year	6 months	1 month
1	-2.972	15.045	101.573	-86.443	-26.964
	(2.420)	(6.831)	(13.512)	(14.416)	(3.612)

Adjustment Coefficients (Standard Error in Parentheses)

10 years	-0.00049
	(0.0005)
7 years	-0.00054
	(0.0005)
3 years	-0.00069
	(0.0005)
1 year	-0.00148
	(0.0005)
6 months	-0.00080
	(0.0004)
1 month	0.00716
	(0.0011)

2 Cointegrating Equations: Log Likelihood 1522.81

Normalized Cointegrating Coefficients (Standard Error in Parentheses)

10 years	7 years	3 years	1 year	6 months	1 month
1	0	-13.475	-102.744	84.922	29.100
		(2.464)	(13.354)	(12.389)	(3.772)
0	1	-9.596	-68.744	57.657	18.863
		(1.616)	(8.756)	(8.123)	(2.473)

Adjustment Coefficients (Standard Error in Parentheses)

10 years	0.01270	-0.01847
	(0.0092)	(0.0140)
7 years	0.01072	-0.01542
	(0.0096)	(0.0146)
3 years	0.00077	-0.00016
	(0.0095)	(0.0144)
1 year	-0.02309	0.03708
	(0.0086)	(0.0130)
6 months	-0.01010	0.01644
	(0.0085)	(0.0129)
1 month	-0.04139	0.05211
	(0.0207)	(0.0314)

FIGURE 4.16 Estimated normalized $\Pi = \Lambda K'$ decompositions.

REFERENCES

Cuthbertson, K., Nitzsche, D., 2005. Quantitative Financial Economics: Stocks, Bonds and Foreign Exchange. John Wiley & Sons, Hoboken, NJ.

Davis, R.A., Dunsmuir, W.T., 1996. Maximum likelihood estimation for MA(1) processes with a root on or near the unit circle. Econometr. Theory 12, 1–29.

Dickey, D.A., Fuller, W.A., 1981. Likelihood ratio statistics for autoregressive time series with a unit root. Econometrica 33, 1057–1072.

Dickey, D.A., Fuller, W.A., 1979. Distribution of the estimators for autoregressive time series with a unit root. J. Am. Stat. Assoc. 74, 427–431.

Dickey, D.A., Pantula, S.G., 1987. Determining the order of differencing in autoregressive processes. J. Bus. Econ. Stat. 5, 455–461.

Dickey, D.A., Bell, W.R., Miller, R.B., 1986. Unit roots in time series models: tests and implications. Am. Stat. 40, 12–26.

Elliott, G., Rothenberg, T.J., Stock, J.H., 1996. Efficient tests for an autoregressive unit root. Econometrica 64, 813–836.

Enders, W., 2008. Applied Econometric Time Series. John Wiley & Sons, Hoboken, NJ.

Engle, R.F., Granger, C.W., 1987. Co-integration and error correction: representation, estimation, and testing. Econometrica 55, 251–276.

Gordon, M.,J., 1959. Dividends, earnings and stock prices. Rev. Econ. Stat. 41, 99–105.

Granger, C.W., Lee, T.H., 1989. Investigation of production, sales and inventory relationships using multicointegration and non-symmetric error correction models. J. Appl. Econometr. 4 (S1), S145–S159.

Granger, C.W., Newbold, P., 1974. Spurious regressions in econometrics. J. Econometr. 2, 111–120.

Haldrup, N., 1994. The asymptotics of single-equation cointegration regressions with I(1) and I(2) variables. J. Econometr. 63, 153–181.

Hayashi, F., 2000. Econometrics. Princeton University Press, Princeton, NJ.

Hendry, D.F., Juselius, K., 2001. Explaining cointegration analysis: Part II. Energy J. 22, 75–120.

Johansen, S., 1988. Statistical analysis of cointegration vectors. J. Econ. Dyn. Control 12, 231–254.

Johansen, S., 1995. Likelihood-Based Inference in Cointegrated Vector Autoregressive Models. Oxford University Press, Oxford.

Johansen, S., Juselius, K., 1990. Maximum likelihood estimation and inference on cointegration—with applications to the demand for money. Oxford Bull. Econ. Stat. 52, 169–210.

Kwiatkowski, D., Phillips, P.C., Schmidt, P., Shin, Y., 1992. Testing the null hypothesis of stationary against the alternative of a unit root. J. Econometr. 54, 159–178.

Lütkepohl, H., Reimers, H.E., 1992. Impulse response analysis of cointegrated systems. J. Econ. Dyn. Control 16, 53–78.

MacKinnon, J.G., 1991. Critical values for cointegration tests. In: Engle, R.F., Granger, C.W.J. (Eds.), Long-Run Economic Relationships: Readings in Cointegration. Oxford University Press, Oxford.

MacKinnon, J.G., 1996. Numerical Distribution Functions for Unit Root and Cointegration Test. J. Appl. Econometr. 11, 601–618.

MacKinnon, J.G., Haug, A.A., Michelis, L., 1999. Numerical distribution functions of likelihood ratio tests for cointegration. J. Appl. Econometr. 14, 563–577.

Newey, W., West, K., 1994. Automatic lag selection in covariance matrix estimation. Rev. Econ. Stud. 61, 631–653.

Ng, S., Perron, P., 2001. Lag length selection and the construction of unit root tests with good size and power. Econometrica 69, 1519–1554.

Phillips, P.C., 1986. Understanding spurious regressions in econometrics. J. Econometr. 33, 311–340.

Phillips, P.C., Ouliaris, S., 1990. Asymptotic properties of residual based tests for cointegration. Econometrica 58, 165–193.

Phillips, P.C., Perron, P., 1988. Testing for a unit root in time series regression. Biometrika 75, 335–346.

Said, S.E., Dickey, D.A., 1984. Testing for unit roots in autoregressive-moving average models of unknown order. Biometrika 71, 599–607.

Sims, C.A., Stock, J.H., Watson, M., 1990. Inference in linear time series models with some unit roots. Econometrica 58, 113–144.

Stock, J.H., Watson, M.W., 1988. Testing for common trends. J. Am. Stat. Assoc. 83, 1097–1107.

Chapter 5

Single-Factor Conditionally Heteroskedastic Models, ARCH and GARCH

I think it's much more interesting to live not knowing than to have answers which might be wrong. I have approximate answers and possible beliefs and different degrees of uncertainty about different things, but I am not absolutely sure of anything and there are many things I don't know anything about, such as whether it means anything to ask why we're here. I don't have to know an answer. I don't feel frightened not knowing things, by being lost in a mysterious universe without any purpose, which is the way it really is as far as I can tell.

Richard Feynman

One can easily argue that modern finance is about *risk*: defining it, measuring it, forecasting it, and managing it (often through trading of appropriate derivative securities). Traders care for risk because they usually operate under a strict budget concerning the exposures they are allowed to take; hence, to a trader it is of the utmost importance to accurately measure risk. Portfolio managers care for predicting risk because they aim at trading it off with expected performance, to adhere to their mandate and/or to track an assigned benchmark. Of course, risk managers deal with the difficult task of defining and forecasting risk because, by managing its amount and composition, risk impacts on the capital requirements of their firms. In this chapter, we first review a range of empirical regularities that motivate the models and techniques to be developed. After providing the key details and basic intuition for the autoregressive conditional heteroskedastic (ARCH) family (to be defined below), we proceed to propose more elaborate, state-of-the-art models that are being increasingly called for by the practical experience with financial data. In terms of applications, we devote considerable care to explain how conditional heteroskedastic models may be useful in forecasting. We conclude with a digression on how these models should be specified and estimated, that is, on how optimal inferences should be conducted on them.

5.1 STYLIZED FACTS AND PRELIMINARIES

Since the late 1980s and the seminal work by Engle (1982) and Bollerslev (1986), financial econometrics has witnessed a powerful drive toward developing methods to specify, estimate, and forecast (from) models concerning quantities that are useful to define risk. Such a drive has marked an important shift: until 30 years ago the focus of most financial time series modeling centered on the conditional first moment, with any temporal dependencies in higher order moments treated as a nuisance that required at best adjustments to estimation algorithms. The increased importance played by risk considerations in finance, however, has required the development of new econometric time series techniques that allow for the modeling of time-varying higher order moments, chiefly (but not only) variances and covariances.[1] In particular, when the data display patterns of time-varying variances and covariances, they are said to be *conditionally heteroskedastic* (henceforth, CH).

Although such an identification is far from trivial, in much of empirical finance, risk has been identified with *variance* or its square root, the standard deviation, often called *volatility*. In fact, any measure of uncertainty—such as

1. The standard caution is that, in the presence of heteroskedasticity, the regression coefficients of an ordinary least squares regression are still unbiased, but the standard errors and confidence intervals estimated by conventional procedures will be invalid. Instead of considering this as a problem to be corrected, ARCH models treat heteroskedasticity as an occasion to model variance. As a result, not only are the deficiencies of least squares corrected but also can a prediction be computed for the variance of each error term.

Essentials of Time Series for Financial Applications. DOI: https://doi.org/10.1016/B978-0-12-813409-2.00005-4

variance—becomes a *proper measure of risk* only when coupled with an assumption on the (predictive) density of the quantities of interest (see Poon and Granger, 2003). A proper measure of risk is one that allows to rank alternative portfolios, trades, projects, etc., according to its risk as perceived by the decision-maker. For instance, variance is a proper measure of risk when returns are generated from a Normal distribution; however, distributions can be found such that this is not the case and alternative measures (such as the mean absolute deviation or the interquartile range) ought to be used instead. Also on purely logical grounds, the use of variance presents some drawbacks. For instance, in asset management, it seems odd that variance would weight above and below mean outcomes in symmetric ways, even though, for an obvious mathematical reason, when portfolio returns have a normal distribution, to focus either on variance or on (negative) semivariance (just below-the-mean variance), will yield an identical ranking of portfolios. Finally, variances, covariances, and similar measures are characterized by one additional limitation: such *higher order moments* are not directly observable—unlike market prices, they are *latent variables*. Variances, covariances, etc. must therefore be inferred by looking at how much market prices move. For instance, if prices fluctuate a lot, we know volatility is high, but we cannot ascertain precisely how high. One reason is that we cannot distinguish whether a large shock to prices is transitory or permanent.

When risk is identified with variance or similar statistical measures, all finance practitioners and applied econometricians will report widespread evidence of a first *stylized fact* (i.e., a recurring empirical regularity arising with most data): while some average, long-run unconditional measure of risk exists and it represents a useful empirical focus, *over time risk tends to fluctuate widely*. For instance, traders understand very well that sometimes it is very important to estimate risk only using recent information, basing their algorithms only on recent data; at other times, instead, it is appropriate to base forecasts on long-run patterns and far-dating time series. Moreover, it is common experience in the market that price moves in a typical direction (e.g., large negative stock returns or quick exchange rate depreciations) may induce stronger reactions in subsequent higher order moments than other price moves do. One parsimonious way to describe what market participants often perceive is that asset price movements (often, returns) fail to be *identically and independently distributed* (IID). Large (small) shocks tend to be often followed by other large (small) shocks and hence fail to be independent over time; as a result, the (predictive) distributions typical of quant work in finance are not identically distributed over time.

Given these stylized facts, it would be ideal to resort to well-developed economic theories or financial models that would explain the variation in higher order moments. Unfortunately, with rare exceptions (see, e.g., the asset pricing models discussed by Timmermann, 1996, or Veronesi, 2000), theorists have traditionally lacked to offer a sufficiently complete understanding of the phenomena. Of course, a plausible, ever-green explanation for conditional heteroskedasticity, which seems to be an almost universal feature of asset return series in finance, is that the information arrivals which drive price changes themselves occur in clusters rather than being evenly spaced over time. For instance, from as early as the seminal paper by Patell and Wolfson (1979), we know that individual firms' stock return volatility is high around earnings announcements. There are also predictable changes in volatility across the trading day: since the paper by Harris (1986), we know that volatility is much higher at the open and close of exchange trading than during the middle of the day; the increase in volatility at the open can be partially imputed to the flow of traded motivated by information accumulated while the market was closed. According to the *mixture of distributions hypothesis* (see, e.g., Tauchen and Pitts, 1983), the evolution of returns and trading volume are both determined by the same latent mixing variable that reflects the amount of new information that arrives to the market. If the news arrival process is serially dependent, volatility and trading volume will be jointly serially correlated. However, although it is clear that information flows matter, such awareness just moves the issue one step further down the road: why would the process of news arrival display systematic and recurrent clusters? A related puzzle is that because many asset prices are closely tied to the health, the state of the economy, it would be natural to expect that measures of macroeconomic uncertainty such as the conditional variances of industrial production, money growth, and the inflation rate should help explain changes in asset return volatility. However, since the seminal research by Schwert (1989), massive empirical evidence has piled up to show that although asset volatility rises sharply during recessions and financial crises and drops during expansions, the relation between macroeconomic uncertainty and stock volatility is surprisingly weak, and in any event much more complex than one would think.

Such a vacuum of theoretical understanding has therefore been filled by statistical models from the *ARCH* class that capture the time variation and clustering in conditional variance using stylized mathematical representations. This class of models has become prominent in econometrics because of its tractability as well as in applications because of its strong forecasting power. Their success is easy to account for: ARCH models introduce parsimonious parametric specifications that, through a small set of parameters, solve the typical problem faced by the practitioners in finance:

- How many past observations to use and the weights to attribute to them, when it comes to predict variances (and covariances).
- Whether and how some types of price moves may differentially affect forecasts of higher order moments.

Equivalently, it turns out that *ARCH models* and their spin-offs do *capture departures* of financial price changes or returns *from IID-ness*. The ARCH framework, being based on a statistical modeling strategy, offers one additional bonus: the latent nature of higher order moments means that they must be predicted using statistical methods, and the ARCH literature has solved this problem in a very simple way that we shall soon describe.

5.1.1 The Stylized Facts of Conditional Heteroskedasticity

Similar to Chapter 2, we proceed first to motivate the structure of the CH models to be introduced by taking a bird's eye view on the key empirical regularities typical of a variety of financial data. In what follows, we generally write about "asset returns," even though a number of related quantities in finance—such as fixed income yields, yield spreads, changes in these yields and spreads, and exchange rate changes—display similar features.

First, asset returns tend to be *leptokurtic*, that is, their "average," unconditional density (for the time being, just think about the empirical histogram of a long-time series) tends to be characterized by tails that are "thicker" than a normal distribution as well as by more probability mass collected just around the mean (or the mode) of the data. Clearly, if "excessive" data frequencies are to be found both in the tails and just around the mean, there must exist some "intermediate" region in their support, where the empirical frequencies fall below those typical of a Gaussian density.

EXAMPLE 5.1

Two typical examples of leptokurtic distributions are illustrated below. Both histogram plots to the right compare the empirical distribution of the data with a matching normal distribution that has the same mean and variance as the data.

Both histograms collect excessive density just around their approximately zero means, but also display fat tails, as emphasized by the dashed, vertical lines that we have drawn in correspondence to the isolated bins in the two tails. Interestingly, Fig. 5.1B concerns not returns but changes in 10-year Treasury rates. Yet, the properties of the data seem to be similar.

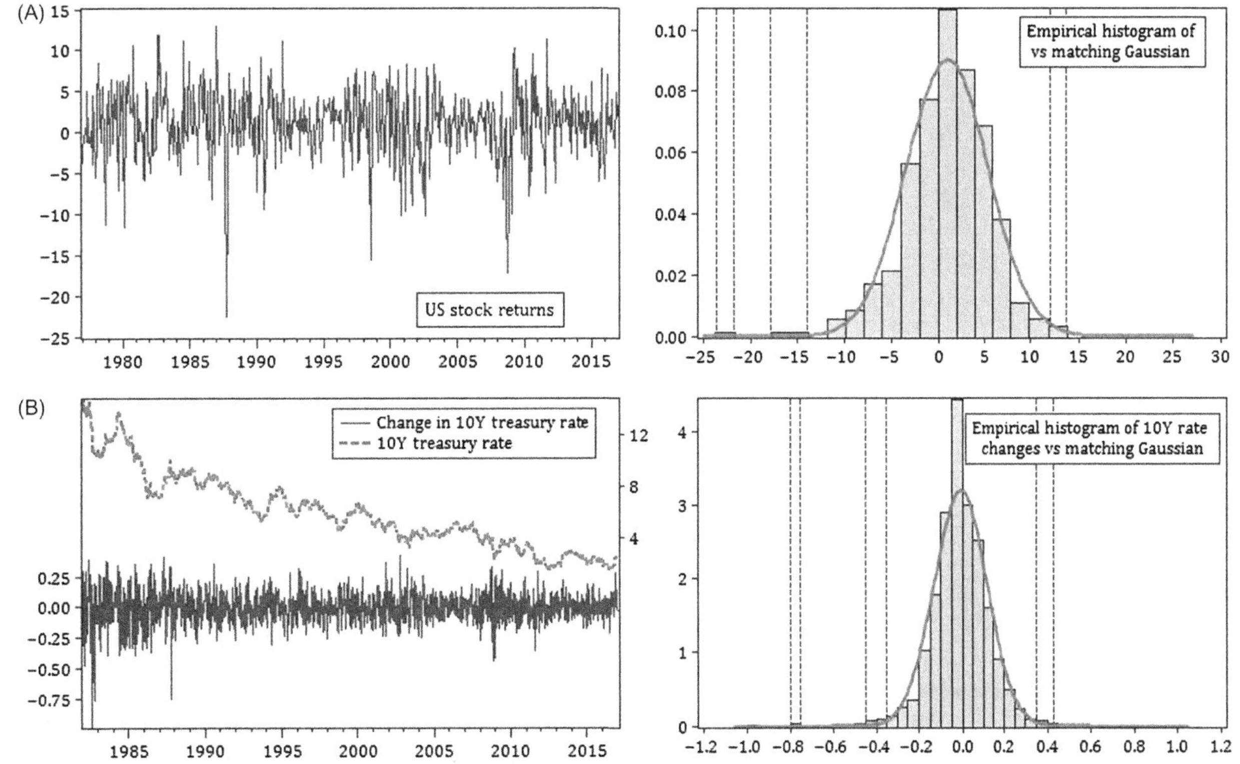

FIGURE 5.1 Time series plots and associated histograms for two series. (A) US stock returns. (B) US long-term treasury yields.

Second, asset returns are characterized by *clusters* in higher order moments, especially in volatility: large changes in prices or values (e.g., interest rates) tend to be followed by large changes, of either sign, and small changes tend to be followed by small changes.

EXAMPLE 5.2

Fig. 5.2 plots in the top panel the percentage daily US excess stock returns over a 1963–2016 sample, showing that the scale of returns clusters in rather specific, turbulent periods, such as 1974–75, 1997–2001, and 2008–09. The plots in the lower panel show instead the square and the cube of returns. To favor visibility, the values of the squares and cubes have been trimmed, even though this hides a few large spikes. The left lower panel gives indications consistent with volatility clustering, because when returns are squared, large returns tend to be followed by other large returns, when their sign is disregarded. The right panel shows that a similar phenomenon occurs with reference to third power of stock returns, with visible clusters between 1996 and 2002, and again between 2008 and 2010. Interestingly, there are periods in which the third power of returns clusters while squared returns only mildly do so.

One typical way in which volatility clustering is analyzed is by conducting Box–Jenkins analysis on either the squared residuals of some conditional mean function model (or on returns themselves) or by studying the cross-serial correlation patterns of different powers of the data, for instance, the level of returns with their third power.

The leftmost panel of Table 5.1 shows that past squared returns do forecast—with large and highly statistically significant autocorrelation function (ACF) coefficients—current and future squared stock returns. Identical indications are given by the Box–Pierce's portmanteau test, as explained in Chapter 2.[2] Therefore, large asset price movements, irrespective of their sign, forecast subsequent large price movements. As we shall examine below, any significant evidence of serial correlation between transformations of the original time series (apart for the case of the trivial, identity function) implies that the series departs from IID-ness. This is the case of squared stock returns. In fact, in the light of Chapter 2, a few readers will be tempted to interpret the leftmost panel of Table 5.1 as evidence of an autoregressive moving average, ARMA(p,q) process, possibly a simple ARMA(1,1), fitting squared stock returns. The rightmost plot reports similar evidence with reference to cross correlations between the level and the third power of daily returns, even though such significance is limited to the first two lags of the cube of returns predicting subsequent returns in level.

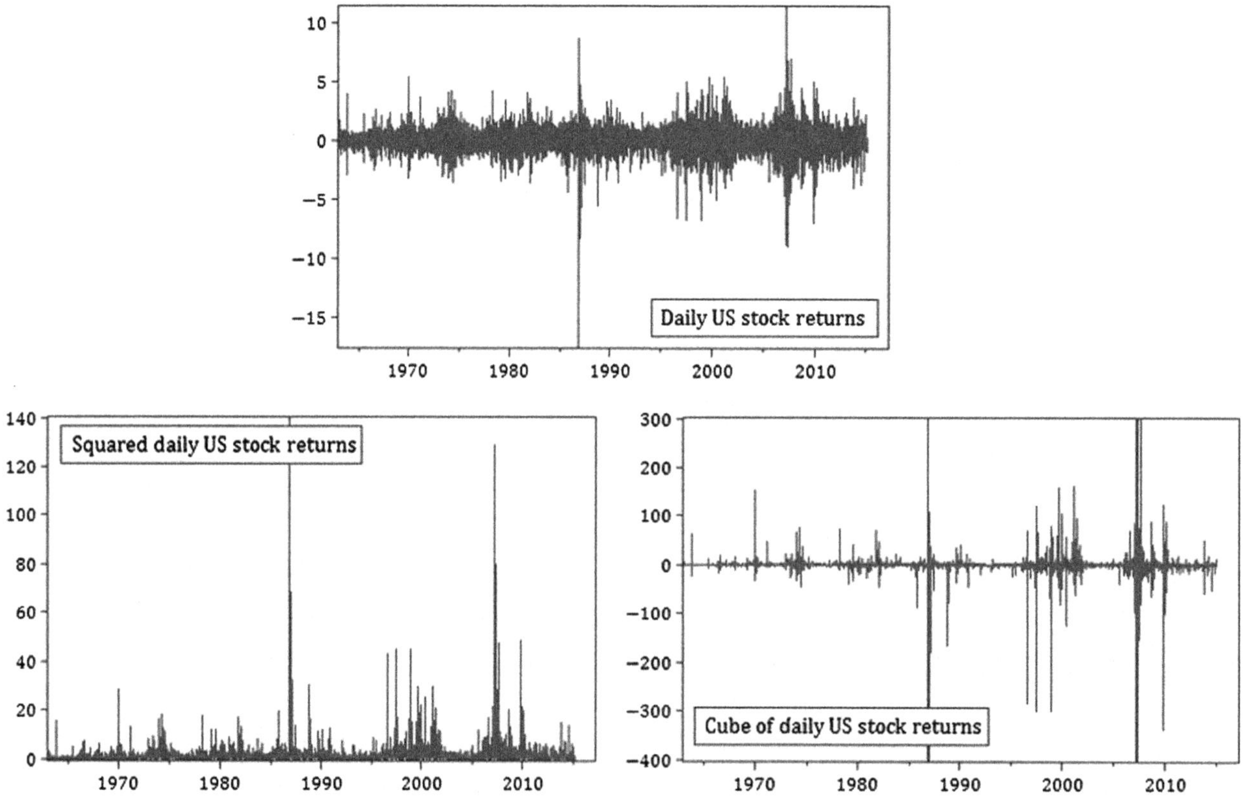

FIGURE 5.2 Plots of daily US excess returns, their squares, and cubes.

2. The asymptotic distribution of the Box–Pierce statistic applies if and only if the levels of the returns themselves are serially uncorrelated; this means that if we were uncertain about the specification of the conditional mean that makes residuals serially uncorrelated, we could not uncritically apply portmanteau tests for ARCH, because the validity of the test would be questionable.

TABLE 5.1 Sample ACF and PACF for Squared Stock Returns and Cross-Sample Correlogram of Levels and Cubes of Returns

Sample ACF and PACF for Squared Daily US Returns							Serial Correlation Btw. Level and Cube of Daily US Stock Returns				
Autocorrelatio...	Partial Correlation		AC	PAC	Q-Sta...	Prob	Level,Cube(-i)	Level,Cube(+i)	i	lag	lead
		1	0.152	0.152	315.69	0.000			1	−0.0296	0.0297
		2	0.303	0.287	1567.7	0.000			2	−0.0884	−0.0291
		3	0.176	0.111	1991.0	0.000			3	0.0369	0.0093
		4	0.159	0.051	2335.9	0.000			4	−0.0038	−0.0306
		5	0.260	0.184	3256.5	0.000			5	0.0644	−0.0057
		6	0.165	0.071	3627.6	0.000			6	−0.0030	0.0240
		7	0.161	0.015	3978.6	0.000			7	−0.0139	0.0037
		8	0.148	0.035	4278.3	0.000			8	−0.0174	0.0148
		9	0.165	0.070	4649.4	0.000			9	−0.0367	0.0178
		10	0.138	0.016	4907.5	0.000			10	−0.0201	−0.0058
		11	0.185	0.074	5373.6	0.000			11	0.0164	−0.0075
		12	0.134	0.031	5619.0	0.000			12	0.0236	0.0058
		13	0.120	−0.008	5814.0	0.000			13	−0.0209	−0.0102
		14	0.082	−0.041	5904.9	0.000			14	0.0030	−0.0012
		15	0.119	0.031	6098.5	0.000			15	0.0186	−0.0301
		16	0.130	0.043	6327.2	0.000			16	0.0327	0.0104
		17	0.128	0.031	6551.6	0.000			17	−0.0250	0.0122
		18	0.130	0.035	6782.4	0.000			18	−0.0273	−0.0283
		19	0.104	0.017	6929.4	0.000			19	0.0189	−0.0115
		20	0.109	0.005	7090.3	0.000			20	0.0081	0.0139
		21	0.124	0.031	7299.0	0.000			21	−0.0137	−0.0183
		22	0.097	−0.001	7426.6	0.000			22	−0.0053	0.0046
		23	0.130	0.034	7655.7	0.000			23	0.0198	−0.0009
		24	0.095	0.009	7779.7	0.000			24	−0.0048	0.0052

From a simple inspection of Fig. 5.2, it is clear that returns may not be IID through time. The first two stylized facts we have illustrated—volatility clustering and leptokurtic returns—are intimately related. To see this, let us start introducing a modicum of formalism. Call $\{\varepsilon_t(\theta)\}$, a time series process with zero conditional mean and variance function $\sigma_t^2(\theta) \equiv Var_t[\varepsilon_{t+1}] = E_t[\varepsilon_{t+1}^2]$ parameterized by the finite dimensional vector $\theta \in \Theta \subseteq \mathbb{R}^K$, where K is the number of parameters. In practice, the zero mean property implies that $\varepsilon_{t+1} = R_{t+1} - \mu_t(\varphi)$, where $\mu_t(\varphi) \equiv E_t[R_{t+1}]$, that is, $\{\varepsilon_t(\theta)\}$ defines the process of the news, or unexpected returns implied by a given selection of the conditional mean function $\mu_t(\varphi)$ parameterized by φ. Interestingly, if

$$R_{t+1} = \mu_{t+1|t} + \varepsilon_{t+1} = \mu_{t+1|t} + \sigma_{t+1|t} z_{t+1} \quad z_{t+1} \text{ IID } (0,1) \tag{5.1}$$

then $E_t[R_{t+1}] = E_t[\mu_{t+1|t}] + E_t[\sigma_{t+1|t}]E_t[z_{t+1}] = \mu_{t+1|t} + \sigma_{t+1|t} \times 0 = \mu_{t+1|t}$ and

$$Var_t[R_{t+1}] = Var_t[\mu_{t+1|t}] + \sigma_{t+1|t}^2 Var_t[z_{t+1}] + 2Cov_t[\mu_{t+1|t}, \sigma_{t+1|t} z_{t+1}] = \sigma_{t+1|t}^2 \tag{5.2}$$

from the fact that $Var_t[\mu_{t+1|t}] = Cov_t[\mu_{t+1|t}, \sigma_{t+1|t} z_{t+1}] = 0$.

These definitions give a standardized news process defined as:

$$z_t(\theta) \equiv \frac{\varepsilon_t(\theta)}{\sigma_t(\theta)} \tag{5.3}$$

and characterized by zero mean and a time-invariant conditional variance of unity. If the conditional distribution for $z_t(\theta)$ is furthermore assumed to be time invariant with a finite fourth moment, it follows from $\varepsilon_t(\theta) = \sigma_t(\theta) z_t(\theta)$ and by Jensen's inequality that:

$$\begin{aligned} kurt(\varepsilon_t) &\equiv \frac{E[\varepsilon_t^4]}{\left(E[\varepsilon_t^2]\right)^2} = \frac{E[(z_t\sigma_t)^4]}{\left(E[\varepsilon_t^2]\right)^2} = \frac{E[z_t^4\sigma_t^4]}{\left(E[\varepsilon_t^2]\right)^2} \\ &\geq \frac{E[z_t^4]\left(E[\sigma_t^2]\right)^2}{\left(E[\varepsilon_t^2]\right)^2} = E\left[z_t^4\right] = 3, \end{aligned} \tag{5.4}$$

where the last two equalities hold for a constant conditional variance only. Given a normal distribution for the standardized innovations in Eq. (5.1), z_{t+1} IID $N(0,1)$, the unconditional distribution for ε_t is therefore leptokurtic when there is

CH. *Excess kurtosis* in the empirical distribution of asset returns may therefore arise simply from randomness in conditional variance, that is, the fact that $E[z_t^4\sigma_t^4] = E[z_t^4]E[\sigma_t^4] + Cov[z_t^4, \sigma_t^4] \geq E[z_t^4]E[\sigma_t^4]$ without any necessity for any excess kurtosis in the distribution of the shocks z_{t+1}.

Before this point slips through, let us emphasize that as in earlier chapters, we shall be modeling asset or portfolio returns, and *never prices*! Interestingly, the absence of serial correlation in returns means that a good model for returns is indeed (ignoring any dividends or interim cash flows) $R_{t+1} = \mu + \sigma_{t+1|t}z_{t+1}$, which implies that when continuously compounded returns are considered and the mean is constant, then:

$$R_{t+1} \equiv \ln V_{t+1} - \ln V_t = \mu + \varepsilon_{t+1} \Rightarrow \ln V_{t+1} = \mu + \ln V_t + \varepsilon_{t+1}, \tag{5.5}$$

that is, (the log of) asset/portfolio prices (V_t) follow a *random walk with drift process*. Because (log-)asset prices are then $I(1)$ processes, they contain a *stochastic trend* (see Chapter 4). To analyze them without first removing the trend is therefore unwieldy and often plainly incorrect. Incorrect here means that most of the tests and inferential procedures you shall encounter in this chapter apply only—except for major and complicated corrections, if any—to stationary series, not to $I(1)$ series.

The third stylized fact is the so-called *leverage effect*, first reported by Black (1976), who noted the tendency for changes in (stock) prices to be negatively correlated with changes in subsequent (stock) volatility. Fixed costs such as financial and operating leverage provide a partial explanation for this phenomenon. A firm with debt and equity outstanding becomes more highly leveraged when the value of the firm falls; this mechanical effect, due to the fact that the value of debt is constant while equity valuations decline, raises equity returns volatility if the returns on the firm as a whole need to remain constant. Of course, such a mechanism is rather simplistic. For instance, it is not clear that the exact causal chain through which a higher leverage should translate in higher risk and hence higher equity return volatility. On the one hand, CH models are routinely applied to returns and other valuation indicators (such as changes in yields or exchange rates) that pertain to assets that are not equities and for which the leverage story put forth by Fisher Black cannot apply as such. However, in such cases we do speak of *asymmetric CH effects* revealed by the data and still endeavor to model and predict such effects. On the other hand, exactly because the underlying mechanism appears to be rather specific, there are a number of asset classes as well stocks and equity indices, for which leverage cannot be empirically identified: changes in past asset prices are essentially uncorrelated with subsequent changes in volatility.

EXAMPLE 5.3

The scatter diagrams in Fig. 5.3 give a feeling for the potential of correlation between lagged asset price changes and subsequent conditional variance, here proxied by squared returns (yield changes).

The thick curves in each of the two scatter plots are kernel regression fit lines that approximate the (possibly, nonlinear) relationship between the two variables on the axes. Clearly, while in the case of stocks, an asymmetric relationship is obvious and indicates that stock volatility is affected by leverage even when equities are aggregated into a broad index, in the case of long-term Treasuries, almost no leverage appears and the relationship between squared changes in rates and one lag of their level is almost perfectly symmetric.

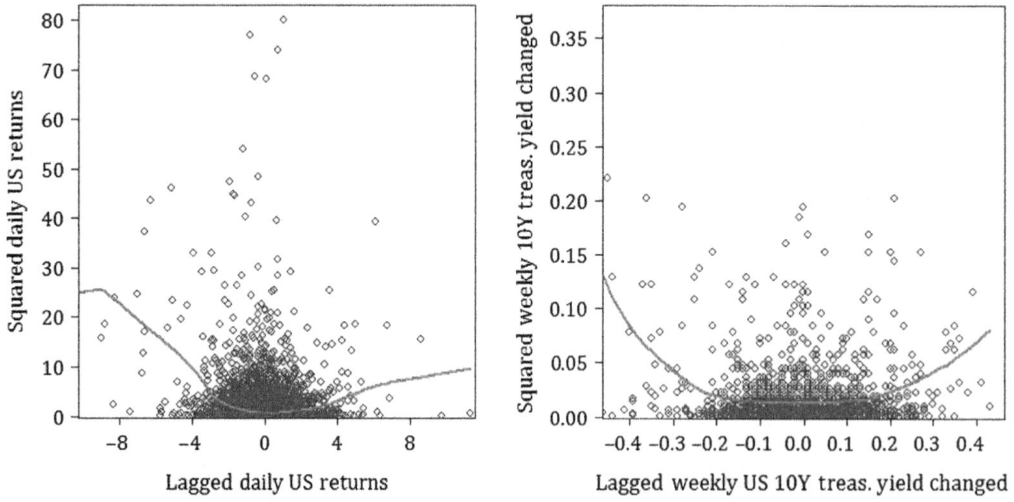

FIGURE 5.3 Scatter plots of squares versus levels for two series.

Fourth, there are considerable co-movements in volatilities across returns on different stocks, different maturities of the bonds issued by the same company or institution (e.g., the same government), exchange rates concerning different pairs of currencies, and even across alternative markets or asset classes. This has motivated a strand of research on common factors in volatilities and covariances that we shall briefly examine in Chapter 6.

EXAMPLE 5.4

For two different pairs of series—the weekly changes in 1- and 10-year US Treasury rates and monthly aggregate French and German stock returns—the following plots assess the relationships between squared return/yield changes across maturities and markets.

In the two scatter plots of Fig. 5.4, along the axes, we have also visualized a (kernel) estimate of the empirical density of the squared values of the series and (as boldfaced curve) a fourth-order polynomial kernel regression of the squares of one series on the squares of the other series. Clearly, if we take squared values to represent an instantaneous proxy of variance, the volatility of each pair of series tends to visibly co-move over time: even though exceptions can be found, spikes in the variance of one series often come when also the variance of other series is spiking. This is confirmed by the nonparametric regressions performed in the two scatter plots.

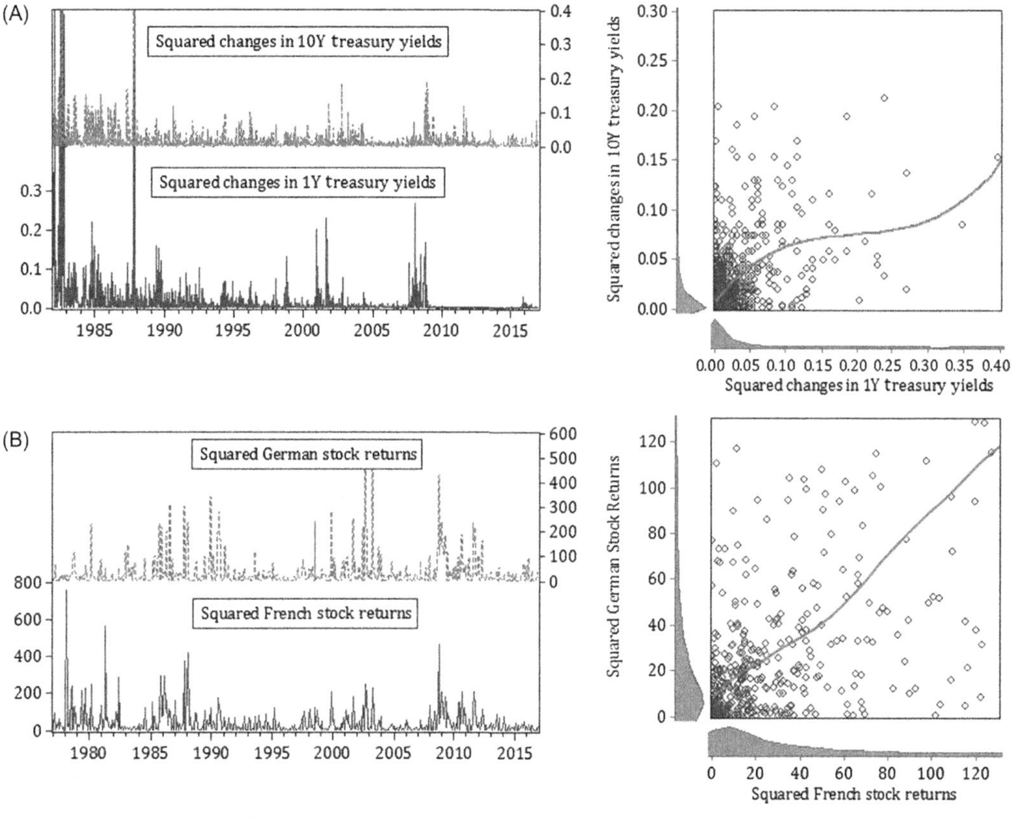

FIGURE 5.4 Time series and scatter plots of squared returns/yield changes. (A) Treasury yields. (B) International stock returns.

5.2 SIMPLE UNIVARIATE PARAMETRIC MODELS

5.2.1 Rolling Window Forecasts

The most naïve and yet surprisingly widespread models among practitioners are simple *rolling window models* of the conditional variance of $\{\varepsilon_t\}$, a time series process with zero conditional mean and conditional variance function $\sigma^2_{t+1|t} \equiv Var_t[\varepsilon_{t+1}] = E_t[\varepsilon^2_{t+1}]$ parameterized by the finite dimensional vector $\boldsymbol{\theta} \in \Theta \subseteq \mathbb{R}^K$. In practice, the series $\{\varepsilon_t\}$ will consist of the empirical residuals of some conditional mean function model. According to such a forecast framework, we have:

$$\sigma^2_{t+1|t}(W) = \frac{1}{W}\sum_{\tau=1}^{W}\varepsilon^2_{t+1-\tau} = \sum_{\tau=1}^{W}\left(\frac{1}{W}\right)\varepsilon^2_{t+1-\tau}, \tag{5.6}$$

where W, the rolling (also called moving) window length, is the only parameter in $\Theta \subseteq \mathbb{R}^K$. Eq. (5.6) simply computes an equally weighted average over a sample of W current and past observations of the squared residuals from some conditional mean model for the series of interest, say an asset returns series. Alternatively, Eq. (5.6) represents a *moving average model for squared residuals*. Note that it is the selection of $W \ll T$ (much smaller than the sample size) that allows the model in Eq. (5.6) to capture the time variation in conditional variance and that therefore endows it with some predictive power that responds to market conditions. Notice in fact that:

$$\lim_{W\to T^-}\sigma^2_{t+1|t}(W) = \lim_{W\to T^-}\frac{1}{W}\sum_{\tau=1}^{W}\varepsilon^2_{t+1-\tau} = \frac{1}{T}\sum_{\tau=1}^{T}\varepsilon^2_{t+1-\tau} \equiv \tilde{\sigma}^2_T, \tag{5.7}$$

where $\tilde{\sigma}^2_T$ is the maximum likelihood (ML) sample variance estimator. Interestingly, while the notation $\sigma^2_{t+1|t}(W)$ stresses that under a moving average model for variance, forecasts change over time as new data arrive, the notation $\tilde{\sigma}^2_T$ emphasizes that all the sample information has been used. Eq. (5.7) emphasizes that when all the data in the sample are used, the rolling window variance estimator simply becomes sample variance. Interestingly, though, notice that in general:

$$\frac{1}{T-W+1}\sum_{t=R}^{T}\sigma^2_{t+1|t}(W) = \frac{1}{(T-W+1)W}\sum_{t=W}^{T}\sum_{\tau=1}^{W}\varepsilon^2_{t+1-\tau} \neq \frac{1}{T}\sum_{\tau=1}^{T}\varepsilon^2_{t+1-\tau} \tag{5.8}$$

that is, the average of the rolling window variance forecasts is in general different from the sample variance estimator.

Example 5.5 illustrates how easy it is to compute variance forecasts using a rolling window model, but also its limitations. First, all squared errors are given the same weight, $1/W$, irrespective of how old they are. Even in our simple example, a trader at the end of December 2016 might question the exact rationale of giving the same weight (of 20%, under $W = 5$) to both the large 9.56% shock faced during that month and to the 2.22% from August 2016. She may have in fact perceived much more volatility in the market and felt that the old 2.22% from 5 months before could prevent an accurate forecasting of the uncertainty faced.

EXAMPLE 5.5

Consider the following series of 12 Italian market stock returns obtained over the last 12 months of 2016. Assume a very simple conditional mean function model: $\mu_t(\varphi) \equiv E_t[R_{t+1}] = \phi_0$, that is, a constant mean. Then, for three alternative choices of the rolling window length W, we obtain the results reported in Table 5.2. Note that in the table, also the mean has been computed as a moving average, but fixing the rolling parameter to 4 months, for simplicity. Of course, it is possible, if not preferable, to adapt the rolling window parameter used to compute the mean to be the same as W, used in the right portion of the table to compute variance forecasts.

Clearly, even in this simple example, alternative selections of the rolling window length, W, imply that—given identical past information—at each point in time rather different forecasts may be derived. For instance, a trader who wanted to forecast at the end of October 2016 the variance over the following month of November 2016 would find forecasts of 1.68 using $W = 3$, 8.48 using $W = 4$, and of 22.93 using $W = 5$! The last value is more than 13 times the first, and this maps into a volatility forecast using a long rolling window that is almost 370% larger than with a short window. Additionally, note that also the resulting averages of the computed forecasts differ somewhat, which is a bit odd given that the same information has been used three times. Yet, in all cases, the same formula in Eq. (5.6) has been applied. In this case, it is easy to check that while the sample variance of these data is 27.18, none of the averages of the conditional variance forecasts for the different values of W equals or falls close to this value.

Second, and as a consequence of some of the erratic results in Example 5.5, it is unclear how we should go about selecting the window length W. Technically, it is a parameter that affects the variance forecasts from the model in Eq. (5.6), but practically, its estimation does not appear to be obvious because if you pay close attention, W does not only enter the model Eq. (5.6) as a coefficient but it also represents the upper limit of a sum. Therefore, the selection of the rolling window length is often left to subjective assessments, with the paradox that different users, all endowed with the same data, the same formula in Eq. (5.6), and the same theoretical explanations, will end up delivering very different forecasts, as in the last three columns of Table 5.2.

Third, the rolling window variance model suffers by construction of a problem: especially when W is small, the forecasts tend to generate frequent spikes. When the forecast spikes up, this may be due to two facts: either some very small

TABLE 5.2 Worked Out Calculations for Rolling Window Variance Forecasts

Month	Return	MW Mean	Residual	Squared Residual	MW Variance Forecasts		
		$W=4$	$W=4$	$W=3$	$W=3$	$W=4$	$W=5$
January	− 11.55						
February	− 4.35						
March	8.36						
April	2.65	− 1.22	3.873	14.996			
May	− 2.52	1.04	− 3.555	12.638			
June	− 9.15	− 0.17	− 8.985	80.730	36.122		
July	4.16	− 1.22	5.375	28.891	40.753	34.314	
August	0.46	− 1.76	2.223	4.940	38.187	31.800	28.439
September	− 1.60	− 1.53	− 0.067	0.005	11.278	28.641	25.441
October	1.39	1.10	0.288	0.083	1.676	8.479	22.930
November	− 4.32	− 1.02	− 3.303	10.907	3.665	3.983	8.965
December	11.24	1.68	9.563	91.441	34.144	25.609	21.475
				Unconditional average	23.689	22.138	21.450

MW, moving window.

squared residual from $W-1$ periods before has been dropped or at time t some large squared residual has been recorded and enters the calculation. While the latter event represents the perfect reason for a variance forecast to increase signaling a state of elevated uncertainty, the former event would be very hard to rationalize—should an asset manager (say) decrease today her allocation to a risky asset because of data from $W-1$ periods before having been dropped from her worksheet? Similarly, when the variance forecast rapidly declines, this may be due to two facts: either some very large squared residual from $W-1$ periods before has been dropped or at time t the squared residual is small or 0. While the latter occurrence represents once again a strong motivation to understand why a variance forecast has declined, the former event would be hard to make sense—should an options market maker (say) increase its current offer price because the data point of $W-1$ periods before has been forgotten? Such *"box-shaped" effects* are in fact very prominent in Example 5.6.

EXAMPLE 5.6

The following plots in Fig. 5.5 concern monthly US aggregate stock returns, for which we have computed rolling window forecasts of conditional mean and variance under four alternative choices of the rolling window length parameter, W: 12-, 24-, 60-, and 120-months. In this case, we have aligned the values of W used to compute rolling window means and variances. Of course, this implies the loss of $2W$ observations: for instance, when $R=60$ months, the first 60 observations are used to forecast the mean between $t=60$ and 61; then squared residuals are derived and an additional amount of 60 observations are lost to compute to forecast conditional variances starting with observation 120. This is way 120-month rolling window forecasts for conditional variance in the bottom panel start out as late as 1996.

Clearly, short-term rolling window forecasts display much more variation than long-term ones. In fact, both the 120-month rolling forecasts of means and variances are very close to the unconditional sample estimates of mean and variance. Equivalently, the choice of a large W, besides "eating up" many initial observations, delivers very smooth forecasts that hardly react to the arrival of new information. When W is instead relatively small, especially $W=12$ and 24 months, the box-shaped effects are quite visible. For instance, when $W=12$, in mid-2010, the conditional variance forecast in the plots drops from 70 to less than 30. However, there was no evidence or perception of quickly disappearing uncertainty then—the rolling window forecasts just reflect the fact that all the large squared US stock return errors recorded during late 2008 and early 2009 left the rolling sample 12 months later, in late 2009 and 2010.

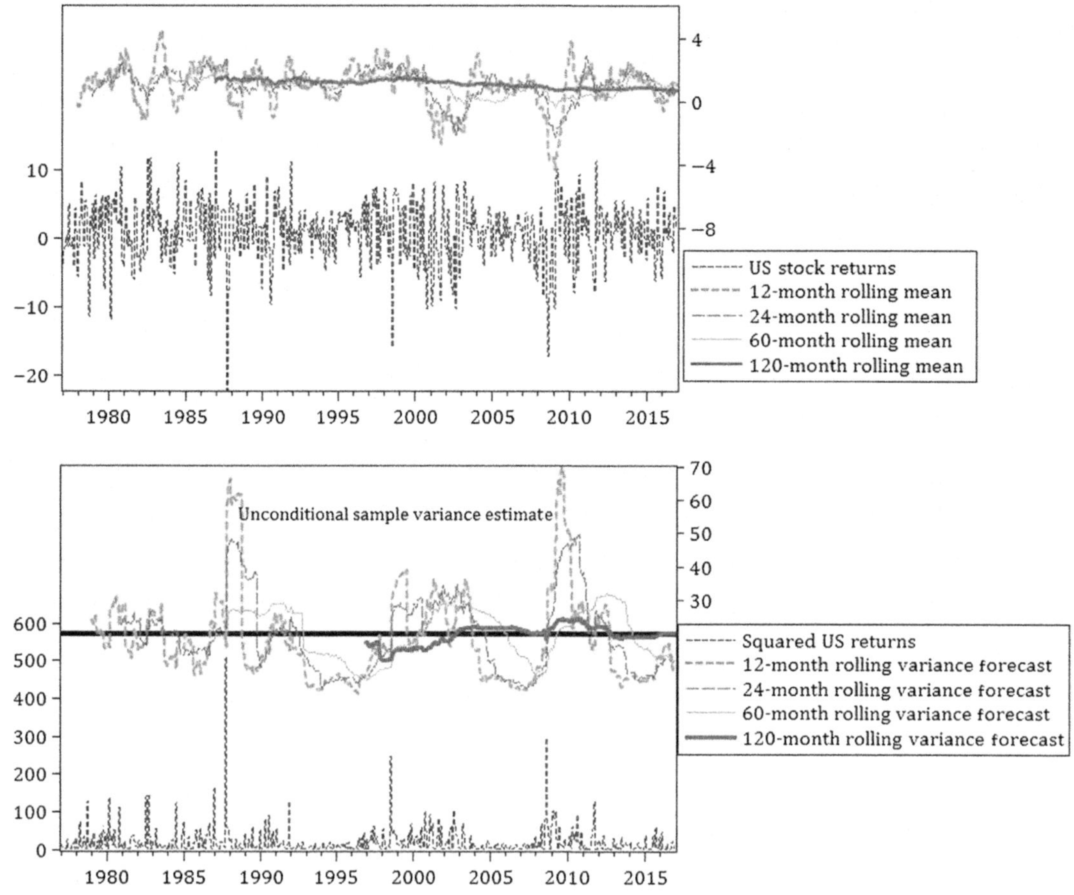

FIGURE 5.5 Plots of rolling window forecasts of mean and variance.

5.2.2 Exponential Smoothing Variance Forecasts: RiskMetrics

In spite of its intuitive simplicity, the three problems described in Section 5.2.1 severely limit (hopefully, they should!) the practical usefulness of the rolling variance forecast model. However, how one remedy to such limitations offers itself rather naturally if one carefully thinks of what are the issues plaguing Eq. (5.6): we need to find a way to use the entire history of a time series but at the same time to weight each past observation as a decreasing function of its distance to the forecast origin. The solution to this search for a better model is offered by one of the classical tools used by professional forecasters, *exponential smoothing models* (henceforth, ESM):

$$\sigma^2_{t+1|t}(\lambda) = (1-\lambda)\sum_{\tau=1}^{\infty}\lambda^{\tau-1}\varepsilon^2_{t+1-\tau}, \tag{5.9}$$

where $\lambda \in (0,1)$ so that increasing powers of the $\lambda^{\tau-1}$ factor assign a declining weight to past squared residuals: $\lambda^0 = 1 > \lambda > \lambda^2 > \cdots > \lambda^{\tau-1}$ for $\tau = 1, 2, \ldots$ The presence of the factor $(1-\lambda)$ that premultiplies the infinite sum guarantees that the sum of the weights equals 1, as it should:

$$(1-\lambda)\sum_{\tau=1}^{\infty}\lambda^{\tau-1} = (1-\lambda)\sum_{\tau=0}^{\infty}\lambda^{\tau} = (1-\lambda)\frac{1}{(1-\lambda)} = 1, \tag{5.10}$$

using the fact that $\sum_{\tau=0}^{\infty}\lambda^{\tau} = 1/(1-\lambda)$. Of course, the sum in the ESM formula is infinite, but in practice it is normally truncated in correspondence to the size of the available sample T, which usually does not cause problems when T is sufficiently large.

In the late 1980s, researchers at J.P. Morgan Chase realized that this rather simple and already famous forecasting device could be rewritten in an even simpler and considerably more elegant way:

$$\begin{aligned}\sigma^2_{t+1|t} &= (1-\lambda)\sum_{\tau=1}^{\infty}\lambda^{\tau-1}\varepsilon^2_{t+1-\tau} = (1-\lambda)\varepsilon^2_t + (1-\lambda)\sum_{\tau=2}^{\infty}\lambda^{\tau-1}\varepsilon^2_{t+1-\tau} \\ &= (1-\lambda)\varepsilon^2_t + \underbrace{\lambda(1-\lambda)\sum_{\tau=2}^{\infty}\lambda^{\tau-1}\varepsilon^2_{t+1-\tau}}_{\sigma^2_{t|t-1}(\lambda)} = (1-\lambda)\varepsilon^2_t + \lambda\sigma^2_{t|t-1}.\end{aligned} \tag{5.11}$$

Eq. (5.11) is called *RiskMetrics model.* It is characterized by just one parameter that can in principle be estimated from the data, and it consists of a simple, convex (in the sense that $\lambda \in (0, 1)$ and the two weights sum to 1) linear combinations of:

- the most recent squared residual, and
- the most recently saved forecast of the variance at time $t-1$ for time t, $\sigma^2_{t|t-1}$.

In the RiskMetrics model, λ plays a role similar to the choice of the rolling window parameter W in Eq. (5.6): the larger is λ, the slower is the speed at which past squared innovations are forgotten by the conditional variance model, which is similar to picking a relatively large value of W in the rolling window model. An interesting property of the RiskMetrics model is that:

$$\lim_{\lambda\to 1^-}\sigma^2_{t+1|t} = \lim_{\lambda\to 1^-}(1-\lambda)\varepsilon^2_t + \lim_{\lambda\to 1^-}\lambda\sigma^2_{t|t-1} = \sigma^2_{t|t-1}, \tag{5.12}$$

that is, today's forecast of time $t+1$ variance is simply yesterday's variance forecast. However, solving then the model backward, we would have $\sigma^2_{t+1} = \sigma^2_t = \sigma^2_{t-1} = \cdots = \sigma^2_0$, that is, the process for variance becomes constant and we obtain the standard homoskedastic case. The naive idea that one can simply identify the forecast of time $t+1$ variance with the squared return of the residuals corresponds instead to the case of $\lambda \to 0^+$, that is, a limit from the right:

$$\lim_{\lambda\to 0^+}\sigma^2_{t+1|t} = \lim_{\lambda\to 0^+}(1-\lambda)\varepsilon^2_t + \lim_{\lambda\to 0^+}\lambda\sigma^2_{t|t-1} = \varepsilon^2_t. \tag{5.13}$$

Of course, this represents a rather special parameterization, since it is the limit as $\lambda \to 0^+$ from the right.

The fact that the RiskMetrics model contains only one parameter is one of its most attractive features. We shall postpone discussing the methods of estimation of Eq. (5.11) after we introduce ARCH and GARCH models but emphasize one interesting feature of Eq. (5.11). Even though in many practical applications λ is actually estimated by ML, it turns out that for a variety of high-frequency data sets (for instance, when data are sampled at daily frequencies), it has become typical to obtain estimated values for λ that tend to be close to 0.94, which is the value originally estimated and proposed by J.P. Morgan. An illustration of this result can be found as an online example.

5.2.3 ARCH Models

The key idea that led Nobel Prize Winner Rob Engle (1982) to introduce ARCH models is that conditional forecasts are generally vastly superior to unconditional forecasts. For concreteness, consider the case of a simple *stationary* AR (1) process, $y_{t+1} = \phi_0 + \phi_1 y_t + \varepsilon_{t+1}$ with IID white noise errors and $|\phi_1| < 1$, for which:

$$E_t[y_{t+1}] = \phi_0 + \phi_1 y_t \quad \text{and} \quad E[y_{t+1}] = \frac{\phi_0}{1-\phi_1} \tag{5.14}$$

as we know from Chapter 2. The *mean-squared forecast error* (MSFE) of the *conditional* forecast is then:

$$E\left[\{y_{t+1} - \phi_0 + \phi_1 y_t\}^2\right] = E\left[\varepsilon^2_{t+1}\right] = \sigma^2 \tag{5.15}$$

while the MSFE of the *unconditional* forccast is:

$$\begin{aligned} E\left[\left\{y_{t+1} - \frac{\phi_0}{1-\phi_1}\right\}^2\right] &= E\left[\left\{\frac{\phi_0}{1-\phi_1} + \sum_{\tau=1}^{\infty}\phi_1^{\tau-1}\varepsilon_{t+1-\tau} - \frac{\phi_0}{1-\phi_1}\right\}^2\right] \\ &= E\left[\sum_{\tau=1}^{\infty}(\phi_1^2)^{(\tau-1)}\varepsilon^2_{t+1-\tau}\right] = \sigma^2\sum_{\tau=0}^{\infty}(\phi_1^2)^{\tau} = \frac{\sigma^2}{1-\phi_1^2}. \end{aligned} \tag{5.16}$$

The second equality derives, as we have seen in Chapter 2, from Wold's theorem for stationary processes. From Eq. (5.16), it is now clear that unless $\phi_1 = 0$ (i.e., unless we are truly dealing with a white noise process), we have that:

$$\text{Unconditional MSFE} = \frac{\sigma^2}{1-\phi_1^2} > \sigma^2 = \text{Conditional MSFE}. \tag{5.17}$$

A conditional forecast always produces a smaller MSFE than an unconditional one, at least on average. This example is of course referred to a conditional mean process. However, the intuition extends to variances, where intuitively one may try to forecast variance with $\sigma^2_{t+1|t} \equiv E_t[\varepsilon^2_{t+1}] \neq \overline{\sigma}^2$, say:

$$\begin{aligned}\sigma^2_{t+1|t} &= \overline{\sigma}^2 + \alpha_1(\varepsilon_t^2 - \overline{\sigma}^2) + \alpha_2(\varepsilon_{t-1}^2 - \overline{\sigma}^2) + \cdots + \alpha_p(\varepsilon^2_{t-p+1} - \overline{\sigma}^2) \\ &= \overline{\sigma}^2 + \sum_{i=1}^{p} \alpha_i(\varepsilon^2_{t-i+1} - \overline{\sigma}^2),\end{aligned} \tag{5.18}$$

where $\overline{\sigma}^2 = \alpha_0 / \left(1 - \sum_{i=1}^p \alpha_i\right) \geq 0$ for some intercept parameter α_0 and assuming the restriction $\sum_{i=1}^p \alpha_i < 1$ is satisfied. We shall see later in this section that exactly under this restriction, $\overline{\sigma}^2$ can be interpreted as the long-run, ergodic variance of the ARCH process. Moreover, it is common to also impose that $\alpha_0 > 0$ and $\alpha_1, \alpha_2, \ldots, \alpha_p \geq 0$ to ensure (these are clearly just sufficient conditions and therefore in practice they may turn out to be overly restrictive) that the variance forecasts are strictly positive at all points in time. Following steps similar to those that have led to Eq. (5.17), it is possible to show that when at least one of the $\alpha_1, \alpha_2, \ldots, \alpha_p$ coefficients is positive, then forecasting the variance as $E_t[\varepsilon^2_{t+1}] = \sigma^2$ will always produce a higher MSFE than forecasting with Eq. (5.18). In fact, Eq. (5.18) is called an ARCH(p) model, where p denotes the number of lags of past squared shocks that are included in the conditional variance model.

How does an ARCH(p) confront the key stylized facts of second moments that we have discussed above? Because the model is based on the decomposition $\varepsilon_{t+1} = \sigma_{t+1|t} z_{t+1}$ and $\sigma_{t+1|t}$ is time-varying provided that at least one of the coefficients $\alpha_1, \alpha_2, \ldots, \alpha_p$ is positive, similar to Section 5.2.1, by Jensen's inequality, we have that $kurt(\varepsilon_{t+1}) > E[z_t^4] = 3$, that is, conditional heteroskedasticity generates excess kurtosis. Because, as we shall see, an ARCH(p) generates however a symmetric return distribution and—to integrate to 1—the inflated tails must be compensated by the absence of probability mass in the intermediate range of the support of the distribution of returns, ARCH models capture the leptokurtic nature of asset returns. The mechanics through which the forecast function in Eq. (5.18) helps in capturing volatility clustering is clear: large past squared innovations will lead to large forecasts of subsequent variance; because many such lags show up on the right-hand side of Eq. (5.18), provided p is sufficient large and all or most $\alpha_1, \alpha_2, \ldots, \alpha_p$ coefficients are positive and non-negligible, this effect will persist over time and cause clustering. This of course captures the empirical fact that large movements in asset prices tend to follow large movements, of either sign. Conversely, past returns near the (conditional) mean $\mu_{t+1|t}$ imply lower than average future volatility and this effect may persist over time. In fact, these effects will be noticeable when $\sum_{i=1}^p \alpha_i$ is close to 1, when conditional variance becomes very volatile and also its average level (for a given $\alpha_0 > 0$) tends to increase.

However, ARCH models cannot capture the existence of asymmetric reaction of conditional variance to positive versus negative shocks; moreover, being of a simple univariate nature, ARCH models per se cannot capture the tendency of conditional variances to co-move across assets and maturities. In fact, multivariate ARCH models shall be needed to that purpose, see Chapter 6.

Because $\overline{\sigma}^2 = \alpha_0 / \left(1 - \sum_{i=1}^p \alpha_i\right)$, simple algebra shows that Eq. (5.18) may be equivalently rewritten as in the following.

DEFINITION 5.1 (ARCH)

In a ARCH(p) for conditional variance, forecasts depend on a (non-negatively) weighted sum of past squared residuals from some conditional mean function model:

$$\sigma^2_{t+1|t} = \alpha_0 + \sum_{i=1}^{p} \alpha_i \varepsilon^2_{t-i+1}, \tag{5.19}$$

where $\alpha_0 > 0$, $\alpha_1, \alpha_2, \ldots, \alpha_p \geq 0$, and $\sum_{i=1}^p \alpha_i < 1$ is necessary and sufficient for covariance stationarity.

This formulation will allow us to perform straightforward comparisons with models presented later on in this chapter. However, one aspect becomes immediately clear: an ARCH(p) model, in particular an ARCH(1) in which $\sigma^2_{t+1|t} = \alpha_0 + \alpha_1\varepsilon^2_t$, differs from a RiskMetrics model in two ways:

- It features no memory for recent, past variance forecasts, in the sense that no lags of $\sigma^2_{t+1|t}$ appear on its right-hand side.
- It features a constant coefficient α_0 that was absent in the RiskMetrics model, $\sigma^2_{t+1|t} = (1-\lambda)\varepsilon^2_t + \lambda\sigma^2_{t|t-1}$.

Moreover, when in Eq. (5.19) we set $\alpha_0 = 0$ and $\alpha_i = 1/W$, then an ARCH(W) model simply becomes a rolling window variance model. Clearly, also in this case the model will be nonstationary, because $\overline{\sigma}^2 = \alpha_0/\left(1 - \sum_{i=1}^{W} 1/W\right) = 0/[1 - W(1/W)] = 0/0$ gives an indeterminate form.

To get better familiarized with the *statistical properties* of ARCH models, let us examine the details of one specific example. A more general treatment of such properties based on the fact that ARCH represents a special case within the general ARCH family will appear in Section 5.2.5.

EXAMPLE 5.7

Consider a generic, stationary Gaussian AR(1)-ARCH(1) process for an excess return series, $\{x_t\}_{t=1}^{\infty}$:

$$x_{t+1} = \phi_0 + \phi_1 x_t + \varepsilon_{t+1} = \phi_0 + \phi_1 x_t + \sigma^2_{t+1|t} z_{t+1} \quad z_{t+1} \text{ IID } N(0,\ 1)$$
$$\sigma^2_{t+1|t} = \alpha_0 + \alpha_1\varepsilon^2_t \quad \text{with } |\phi_1| < 1, \alpha_0 > 0,\ 1 > \alpha_1 > 0.$$

Note that by construction z_{t+1} is uncorrelated with ε^2_t because z_{t+1} is IID and $\sigma^2_{t+1|t}$ only depends on past information. Therefore, the process of $\{\varepsilon_{t+1}\}$ has zero mean and is serially uncorrelated:

$$\begin{aligned} E[\varepsilon_t\varepsilon_{t-i}] &= E\left[\sqrt{\alpha_0 + \alpha_1\varepsilon^2_{t-1}}\, z_t z_{t-i}\sqrt{\alpha_0 + \alpha_1\varepsilon^2_{t-i-1}}\right] \\ &= E\left[\sqrt{\alpha_0 + \alpha_1\varepsilon^2_{t-1}}\sqrt{\alpha_0 + \alpha_1\varepsilon^2_{t-i-1}}\right] E[z_t z_{t-i}] = 0 \quad \text{for all } i = 1, 2, \ldots, \end{aligned}$$

which derives from z_{t+1} IID $N(0,\ 1)$. This property is important because it provides guarantees (necessary and sometimes sufficient conditions) to proceed to the estimation of the conditional mean function with standard methods. Moreover, this result means that once the AR(1) process has been correctly specified, the resulting errors are serially uncorrelated and their ACF ought to show that.

However, the process of $\{\varepsilon_{t+1}\}$ is not IID. To prove this point, start noting that the conditional process $\{\varepsilon_{t+1}|\varepsilon_t, \varepsilon_{t-1}, \varepsilon_{t-2}, \ldots\}$ has a zero conditional mean and a conditional variance of $\alpha_0 + \alpha_1\varepsilon^2_t$:

$$\begin{aligned} E[\varepsilon_{t+1}|\varepsilon_t, \varepsilon_{t-1}, \varepsilon_{t-2}, \ldots] &= E_t[\sqrt{\alpha_0 + \alpha_1\varepsilon^2_t}\, z_{t+1}] = \sqrt{\alpha_0 + \alpha_1\varepsilon^2_t}\, E_t[z_{t+1}] \\ &= \sqrt{\alpha_0 + \alpha_1\varepsilon^2_t} \times 0 = 0 \end{aligned}$$

$$\begin{aligned} E[\varepsilon^2_{t+1}|\varepsilon_t, \varepsilon_{t-1}, \varepsilon_{t-2}, \ldots] &= E_t[(\alpha_0 + \alpha_1\varepsilon^2_t) z^2_{t+1}] = (\alpha_0 + \alpha_1\varepsilon^2_t) E_t[z^2_{t+1}] \\ &= (\alpha_0 + \alpha_1\varepsilon^2_t) Var_t[z_{t+1}] = (\alpha_0 + \alpha_1\varepsilon^2_t) \times 1 = \alpha_0 + \alpha_1\varepsilon^2_t. \end{aligned}$$

Because the conditional expectation of ε^2_{t+1} depends on ε^2_t, we have that squared innovations are indeed auto-correlated, and as such the process of $\{\varepsilon_{t+1}\}$ is not IID. The fact that $E[\varepsilon^2_{t+1}|\varepsilon_t, \varepsilon_{t-1}, \varepsilon_{t-2}, \ldots] = \alpha_0 + \alpha_1\varepsilon^2_t$ implies:

$$\varepsilon^2_{t+1} = \alpha_0 + \alpha_1\varepsilon^2_t + \eta_{t+1},$$

where η_{t+1} is white noise, that is, the process followed by squared residuals equals its conditional expectation plus a white noise error; moreover, $\varepsilon^2_{t+1} = \alpha_0 + \alpha_1\varepsilon^2_t + \eta_{t+1}$ means that the squared residuals themselves follow an AR(1) process.

To develop the next set of properties, it is useful to recall that, by Wold's representation theorem, any AR(1) process can be represented as an infinite MA process:

$$\varepsilon^2_{t+1} = \alpha_0 + \alpha_1\varepsilon^2_t + \eta_{t+1} = \alpha_0 \sum_{i=0}^{t} \alpha_1^i + \alpha_1^{t+1}\varepsilon^2_0 + \sum_{i=0}^{t} \alpha_1^i \eta_{t-i}.$$

If the return series had started in the sufficiently "distant" past or, equivalently, when $t \to \infty$, this is indeed an MA(∞) process with:

$$\lim_{t\to\infty} \varepsilon^2_{t+1} = \frac{\alpha_0}{1-\alpha_1} + \sum_{i=0}^{\infty} \alpha_1^i \eta_{t-i},$$

where the convergence of the series derives from the assumption $0 < \alpha_1 < 1$. This proves in a very simple way that if the ARCH process is stationary, then:

$$\overline{\sigma}^2 \equiv Var[\varepsilon_{t+1}] = E\left[\varepsilon^2_{t+1}\right] = \frac{\alpha_0}{1-\alpha_1} + \sum_{i=0}^{\infty} \alpha_1^i E[\eta_{t-i}] = \frac{\alpha_0}{1-\alpha_1}.$$

Even though under ARCH(1) the forecasts of conditional variance may change over time, assuming stationarity, a finite long-run, average, unconditional variance exists, although it diverges to $+\infty$ as $\alpha_1 \to 1^-$. Finally, because

(Continued)

EXAMPLE 5.7 (Continued)

$\lim_{t\to\infty}\varepsilon_{t+1}^2 = \alpha_0/(1-\alpha_1) + \sum_{i=0}^{\infty}\alpha_1^i\eta_{t-i}$, this implies that the ACF of the series of squared shocks implied by an ARCH(1) decays at speed α_1^i.

One last property of this model that we state without proof (left as an exercise) is that for any integer number r, the 2rth moment exists if and only if $\alpha_1^r\prod_{k=1}^{r}(2k-1)<1$. For $r=1$ this gives the standard condition $\alpha_1<1$ for existence of the unconditional variance; however, for $r=2$ (existence of kurtosis), the condition is $3\alpha_1^2<1$ or $\alpha_1<\sqrt{1/3}$ which is quite restrictive. In particular, under this restriction, the kurtosis of an ARCH(1) process is given by:

$$kurt(\varepsilon_{t+1}) = 3\frac{1-\alpha_1^2}{1-3\alpha_1^2} > 3 \quad \text{if and only if } \alpha_1 > 0.$$

Because $E[\varepsilon_{t+1}^3] = E\left[\sqrt[2]{(\alpha_0+\alpha_1\varepsilon_t^2)^3}z_{t+1}^3\right] = E\left[\sqrt[2]{(\alpha_0+\alpha_1\varepsilon_t^2)^3}\right]E[z_{t+1}^3] = 0$ as a result of the fact that z_{t+1} is uncorrelated with all powers of ε_t and of the symmetric nature of the Gaussian white noise shocks z_{t+1}, the skewness implied by an ARCH(1) model is 0 and the model cannot induce any asymmetries in the unconditional density of the shocks.

Finally, we now work backward from the statistical properties of $\{\varepsilon_{t+1}\}$ to those of the underlying, original series, $\{x_{t+1}\}$. Trivially, the series x_{t+1} has conditional mean $\mu_{t+1|t} = \phi_0 + \phi_1 x_t$ and a conditional variance $\sigma_{t+1|t}^2 = \alpha_0 + \alpha_1\varepsilon_t^2$. Moreover, from basic properties of stationary AR(1) process examined in Chapter 2, we have that:

$$E[x_{t+1}] = \frac{\phi_0}{1-\phi_1} \quad Var[x_{t+1}] = \frac{Var[\varepsilon_{t+1}]}{1-\phi_1^2} = \frac{\alpha_0}{(1-\phi_1^2)(1-\alpha_1)}.$$

This shows that while the conditional variance function does not affect the mean (unconditional or conditional) of the return process, the conditional mean process affects the unconditional variance of returns. This is important: sometimes applied finance researcher and practitioners seem to operate under the assumption that—if you care for the variance—you can forget about specifying a careful conditional mean model. The result above shows how dangerous this may be. Equivalently, note that when the conditional mean is $\mu_t(\varphi) \equiv E_t[R_{t+1}]$ and $R_{t+1} - \mu = (R_{t+1} - \mu_t(\varphi)) + (\mu_t(\varphi) - \mu)$, then because $Var[R_{t+1}] = E[(R_{t+1}-\mu)^2]$, it follows that $Var[R_{t+1}] = Var[\varepsilon_{t+1}] + Var[\mu_t(\varphi)]$, which therefore includes the variance of the conditional mean function. Of course, occasionally paying little attention to the mean function may be correct, but not because the mean of observed asset returns is small but because the corresponding conditional mean function has no structure, that is, when $\phi_1 \simeq 0$. However, in general, note that $Var[x_{t+1}]$ may become very large not only because $\phi_1 \to 1^-$ but also because $\alpha_1 \to 1^-$.

Algebra similar to the one in Example 5.7 (see Section 5.2.5 for details) establishes that the long-run, ergodic variance from an ARCH(p) model is:

$$\bar{\sigma}^2 = \frac{\alpha_0}{1-\sum_{i=1}^{p}\alpha_i}. \tag{5.20}$$

Even though we have already discussed some of the limitations of ARCH models with regard to the key stylized facts concerning clustering in the higher order moments of asset returns, overall, this class of CH models appears to represent progress versus the simple rolling window model and to have properties that differ from those under RiskMetrics. However, ARCH models present an important limitation: in many applications, their specification gives rise to too richly parameterized frameworks, that is, to large-dimensional specifications, and this may be costly in terms of estimation and awkward in terms of the resulting interpretation of the estimates. Of course, given the substantial empirical success that we have claimed for RiskMetrics models, a pervasive need to pick a large p does not come as surprise, because such a selection obviously surrogates the role played by $\sigma_{t|t-1}^2$ on the right-hand side of RiskMetrics that is absent in ARCH models.

EXAMPLE 5.8

Consider 1963–2016 Center for Research in Security Prices (CRSP) stock excess daily return data. We start by plotting the sample ACF and partial autocorrelation function (PACF). Both the ACF and PACF are statistically significant at Lag 1 only (Table 5.3).

This suggests the usefulness of an MA(1) model. In fact, the Bayesian information criterion (BIC) for a simple constant expected return model is 2.8093, the one for an MA(1) model is 2.8070, the one for an AR(1) model is 2.8072, and the one for an ARMA(1,1) model is again 2.8070.[3] In the presence of ARCH, the portmanteau test for serial correlation in the level of the

(Continued)

3. Standard model selection criteria such as Akaike's and Schwartz's have been widely used in the literature, though their statistical properties in the ARCH context are unknown, particularly when the validity of the distributional assumptions underlying the likelihood is in doubt.

EXAMPLE 5.8 (Continued)

series will tend to over-reject. We decide in favor of an MA(1) model. The MA(1) model is estimated as (p-values are in parenthesis):

$$x_{t+1} = \underset{(0.004)}{0.025} + \underset{(0.000)}{0.057}\,\varepsilon_t + \varepsilon_{t+1} \quad \varepsilon_{t+1} \quad \text{IID } N(0, \sigma^2_{t+1|t}).$$

Next, we plot the sample ACF and PACF of the squared residuals (Table 5.4).

The plot gives a rather difficult picture: all ACF lags are individually and collectively significant; the first five to six lags of the PACF are also individually and collectively significant and one can find partial autocorrelations that are significant at a 5% size up to Lag 11 or 14 at least, before decaying to 0. All these indications point toward an appropriate fit by a large-scale ARCH model, as minimum as large as an ARCH(6). In fact, the BIC criterion for MA(1)–ARCH(6) is 2.4426 and the one for an MA(1)–ARCH(5) is 2.4513. Therefore, we select the former model. Note that such a BIC is considerably lower versus the 2.8070 BIC obtained from a homoskedastic MA(1) model. The MA(1)–ARCH(6) model estimated by ML in E-Views is:

$$\sigma^2_{t+1|t} = \underset{(0.000)}{0.219} + \underset{(0.000)}{0.116}\,\varepsilon_t^2 + \underset{(0.000)}{0.139}\,\varepsilon_{t-1}^2 + \underset{(0.000)}{0.142}\,\varepsilon_{t-2}^2 + \underset{(0.000)}{0.161}\,\varepsilon_{t-3}^2 + \underset{(0.000)}{0.134}\,\varepsilon_{t-4}^2 + \underset{(0.000)}{0.092}\,\varepsilon_{t-5}^2.$$

Each of the estimated coefficients is positive and statistically significant and their sum is 0.784 which establishes stationarity, but one naturally wonders if a more parsimonious way can be found to estimate a conditional heteroskedastic model with less parameters. In any event, the resulting forecast of conditional volatility over time is shown below. Basically, the plot emphasizes that only when all or most shocks are small over a 6-month window, the subsequent forecast of conditional volatility is modest, generally below 0.6% per day; otherwise volatility easily exceeds 1% per day, with spikes of 2%–3% (Fig. 5.6).

TABLE 5.3 Sample ACF and PACF for US Excess Stock Returns

Sample ACF and PACF for Daily US Stock Returns

Autocorrelation	Partial Correlation		AC	PAC	Q-Stat	Prob
		1	0.053	0.053	38.661	0.000
		2	−0.027	−0.030	48.674	0.000
		3	0.005	0.008	49.015	0.000
		4	−0.007	−0.008	49.592	0.000
		5	−0.019	−0.018	54.305	0.000
		6	−0.003	−0.001	54.427	0.000
		7	−0.016	−0.017	57.933	0.000
		8	0.004	0.006	58.191	0.000
		9	−0.010	−0.012	59.581	0.000
		10	0.010	0.011	60.898	0.000
		11	−0.011	−0.013	62.555	0.000
		12	0.034	0.035	77.978	0.000
		13	0.010	0.006	79.401	0.000
		14	−0.005	−0.004	79.686	0.000
		15	−0.015	−0.014	82.556	0.000
		16	0.033	0.034	97.153	0.000
		17	0.000	−0.003	97.154	0.000
		18	−0.029	−0.028	108.81	0.000
		19	−0.001	0.003	108.83	0.000
		20	0.015	0.012	111.78	0.000
		21	−0.023	−0.022	118.90	0.000
		22	−0.003	−0.001	118.99	0.000
		23	0.001	0.000	119.00	0.000
		24	0.016	0.015	122.38	0.000

TABLE 5.4 Sample ACF and PACF for Squared Residuals

Sample ACF and PACF for Squared Daily Residuals

Autocorrelation	Partial Correlation		AC	PAC	Q-Stat	Prob
		1	0.168	0.168	384.62	0.000
		2	0.303	0.283	1637.1	0.000
		3	0.188	0.117	2120.1	0.000
		4	0.162	0.050	2475.4	0.000
		5	0.268	0.187	3453.8	0.000
		6	0.173	0.073	3862.1	0.000
		7	0.165	0.015	4233.8	0.000
		8	0.156	0.035	4562.9	0.000
		9	0.167	0.068	4943.8	0.000
		10	0.145	0.017	5228.2	0.000
		11	0.194	0.079	5738.0	0.000
		12	0.140	0.030	6005.2	0.000
		13	0.127	-0.007	6224.1	0.000
		14	0.084	-0.045	6319.6	0.000
		15	0.125	0.032	6532.5	0.000
		16	0.132	0.039	6768.0	0.000
		17	0.134	0.032	7012.6	0.000
		18	0.135	0.036	7261.4	0.000
		19	0.110	0.020	7427.4	0.000
		20	0.114	0.006	7605.0	0.000
		21	0.130	0.032	7834.3	0.000
		22	0.103	-0.002	7977.5	0.000
		23	0.135	0.034	8225.2	0.000
		24	0.104	0.012	8373.0	0.000

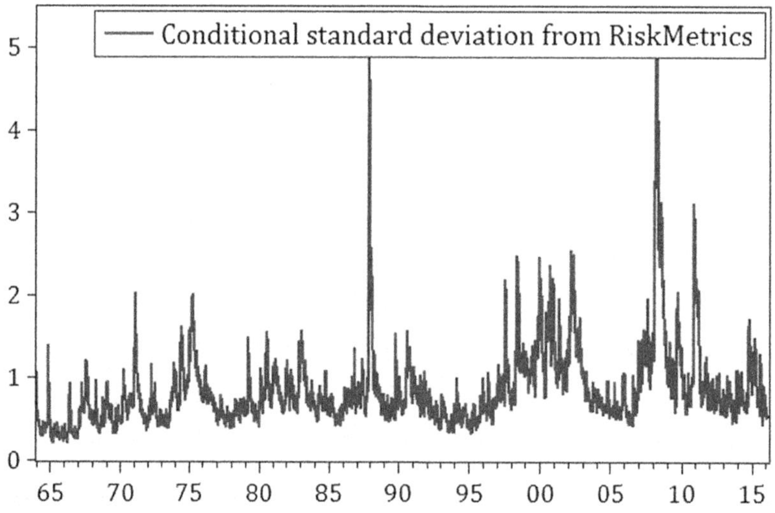

FIGURE 5.6 Plot of 1-day ARCH(6) volatility forecasts.

Example 5.8 exploits the result that the sample ACFs of the squared residuals contain a lot of information about the appropriate order p of ARCH models.

The large order p required by most financial data series has traditionally represented the main weakness of ARCH models. While nowadays this feature may simply interfere with our aesthetic sense and a quest for parsimonious models, in the 1980s the rich parameterization of ARCH together with the need to estimate them by maximizing the log-likelihood (see Section 5.6) subjects to the constraints that $\sum_{i=1}^{p} \alpha_i < 1$, $\alpha_0 > 0$, and $\alpha_1, \alpha_2, \ldots, \alpha_p \geq 0$ meant that estimation often proved slow and unreliable because of the interaction between the presence of local maxima and the effect of constraints. Early on, ARCH(p) models were specified by imposing prespecified structures of declining weight, for example, one would estimate only α_0 and α_1 but under the declining-weights structure:

$$\sigma^2_{t+1|t} = \alpha_0 + \alpha_1 \sum_{i=1}^{p} \frac{p-i+1}{10} \varepsilon^2_{t-i+1} \quad \alpha_0 > 0,\ 1 > \alpha_1 \geq 0. \tag{5.21}$$

Example 5.9 briefly illustrates the mechanics of a simple ARCH(1) model in comparison with a RiskMetrics.

EXAMPLE 5.9

Consider the same series of 12 Italian market stock returns obtained over the last 12 months of 2016 as in Example 5.5. Assume a very simple conditional mean function model: $\mu_t(\varphi) \equiv E_t[R_{t+1}] = \phi_0$, that is, a constant mean estimate ($\hat{\mu} = -0.436\%$) on the full sample. The following table reports two 1-month-ahead variance forecasts, from ARCH(1) with fixed parameter $\alpha_1 = 0.2$,

$$\sigma^2_{t+1|t} = \left[\frac{1}{12}\sum_{\tau=1}^{12}(R_\tau - (-0.436))^2\right](1-0.2) + 0.2(R_t - (-0.436))^2,$$

and an implicit constant α_0 such that $\overline{\sigma}^2 = \left[(12)^{-1}\sum_{\tau=1}^{12}(R_\tau - (-0.436))^2\right]$, and RiskMetrics with $\lambda = 0.94$ when the initial variance is set to $\sigma^2_{1|0} = (12)^{-1}\sum_{\tau=1}^{12}(R_\tau - (-0.436))^2$ (Table 5.5).

TABLE 5.5 Calculations of RiskMetrics and ARCH Variance Forecasts

Month	Return	Sample Mean	Residual	Squared Residual	Variance Forecasts		
					MWR = 4	RiskMetrics	ARCH(1)
January	−11.55	−0.436	−11.114	123.521		45.328	56.974
February	−4.35	−0.436	−3.914	15.319		43.527	35.333
March	8.36	−0.436	8.796	77.370		45.558	47.743
April	2.65	−0.436	3.086	9.523	56.433	43.396	34.174
May	−2.52	−0.436	−2.084	4.343	26.639	41.053	33.138
June	−9.15	−0.436	−8.714	75.934	41.792	43.145	47.456
July	4.16	−0.436	4.596	21.123	27.731	41.824	36.494
August	0.46	−0.436	0.896	0.803	25.551	39.363	32.430
September	−1.60	−0.436	−1.164	1.355	24.804	37.082	32.540
October	1.39	−0.436	1.826	3.334	6.654	35.057	32.936
November	−4.32	−0.436	−3.884	15.085	5.144	33.859	35.286
December	11.24	−0.436	11.676	136.329	39.026	40.007	59.535

One aspect of Example 5.9 is of general interest. When one sets:

$$\alpha_0 = \left[\frac{1}{T}\sum_{t=1}^{T}(R_t - \hat{\mu}_{t|t-1})^2\right]\left(1 - \sum_{i=1}^{p}\alpha_i\right) \tag{5.22}$$

we have that by construction $\overline{\sigma}^2 = \frac{1}{T}\sum_{t=1}^{T}(R_t - \hat{\mu}_{t|t-1})^2$, the sample variance of the data set. Such a restriction, called *variance targeting*, is often imposed in practical applications because it guarantees that, for a given data set, the ARCH (p) process will yield an unconditional variance that is exactly equal to the sample variance, which seems a sensible outcome. Note that this need stems from the common practice of estimating ARCH models using ML methods: under ML, the constrained optimization algorithm will aim at maximizing the probability that the data in the sample came from the assumed model and not in particular any of the sample moments characterizing the data. We shall return on these issues in Section 5.6.

5.2.4 Comparing the Performance of Alternative Variance Forecast Models: Do We Need More Than ARCH?

The tendency of ARCH models to imply richly parameterized models led researchers to explore more parsimonious alternatives already during the 1980s. In Section 5.2.5, we shall examine in detail how ARCH has been "generalized" in a very natural way. However, there is more to this operation than a simple desire to build more lightly parameterized models. To investigate such a deep motivation, we need first to develop methods to compare the performance of variance forecasts. In this section, we entertain two approaches. First, if a CH model is correctly specified, then the standardized residuals from the model should reflect any assumptions that have been made when the model has been specified and estimated. The logic is that because these assumptions have supported the way in which the model has been applied to the data, these have to be validated by the same data. Second, because the CH models we entertain in this section are time series models to be used in forecasting, a good CH model should be able to "adequately" predict future variance.

Under the first perspective, each of the models analyzed so far can be expressed as a model for the conditional variance function $\sigma^2_{t+1|t}(\theta,\varphi) \equiv Var_t[\varepsilon_{t+1}]$ of the process $\{\varepsilon_{t+1}\}$, where $\varepsilon_{t+1} = R_{t+1} - \mu_{t+1|t}(\varphi)$ and $\mu_{t+1|t}(\varphi) \equiv E_t[R_{t+1}]$ so that the overall process is:

$$R_{t+1} = \mu_{t+1|t} + \varepsilon_{t+1} = \mu_{t+1|t} + \sigma_{t+1|t}z_{t+1} \quad z_{t+1}\ \text{IID}\ (0,1), \tag{5.23}$$

where z_t is a standardized residual. Therefore, assuming the conditional variance and mean functions have been correctly specified and estimated, it is useful to check whether $\hat{z}_{t+1}$ IID (0, 1) holds, that is, whether these are identically distributed over time (e.g., not subject to structural breaks or regime shifts in their distributional properties), and especially whether they are independently distributed over time. The latter property may be checked by testing whether for a few sensible and commonly employed choices of the functions $h(\cdot):\mathbb{R}\to\mathbb{R}$ and $g(\cdot):\mathbb{R}\to\mathbb{R}$ (not necessarily identical), $E[h(\hat{z}_t)g(\hat{z}_{t-i})] = 0$ holds for all $i = 1, 2, \ldots$. In practice, it is common to focus on the case $h(\hat{z}_t) = g(\hat{z}_t) = \hat{z}_t^2$, which means checking whether the squared standardized residuals are serially uncorrelated.[4]

Under the second perspective, let us ask instead what it means that some CH models yield "good" forecasts of future variance. A minimal requirement seems that because $\sigma^2_{t+1|t} \equiv E_t[\varepsilon^2_{t+1}]$, on average the realized squared residuals must equal the variance forecasts that a model offers:

$$\sigma^2_{t+1|t} \equiv E_t[\varepsilon^2_{t+1}] = \varepsilon^2_{t+1} - e_{t+1|t} \Rightarrow \varepsilon^2_{t+1} = \sigma^2_{t+1|t} + e_{t+1|t}, \tag{5.24}$$

where $e_{t+1|t}$ is zero-mean, white noise forecast error. Note that Eq. (5.24) derives in practice from the very definition of a conditional variance forecast. However, empirically, it implies that two simple restrictions must be satisfied in a regression of squared residuals on the variance forecasts from a model, that is:

$$\varepsilon^2_{t+1} = a + b\sigma^2_{t+1|t} + e_{t+1|t}, \tag{5.25}$$

where a and b are constant coefficients such that:

- $a = 0$ and $b = 1$, *jointly* (sometimes we write that when this occurs, $\sigma^2_{t+1|t}$ offers an *unbiased predictor of squared residuals*, here used as a proxy of realized, instantaneous variance).
- The forecast errors must be "small," for instance, in the sense that their sum of squares must be small relative to the sum of the squares of the dependent variable (ε^4_{t+1})—we usually report this requirement by stating the *coefficient of determination* from the regression in Eq. (5.25) (i.e., its R^2) must be "large".

The adverb "jointly" emphasizes that while it may appear trivial to perform Wald (i.e., standard t) tests on the estimated coefficients a and b separately, it is usually informative to also perform a Wald test (by necessity, an F-test) of the composite null hypothesis of $a = (b-1) = 0$.[5]

---

4. The fact that a time series process is independently distributed implies that all the autocorrelation coefficients for all functions of the data will be uncorrelated; because this extends to the identity function, $h(z_t) = z_t$, independence implies the absence of serial (also known as auto-) correlation. However, the opposite is not true: a time series may be serially uncorrelated and yet be dependent over time (see the Mathematical and Statistical Appendix).

5. With reference to the R-square, also recall that under certain conditions, the regression statistic TR^2 has an asymptotic F distribution and provides a way to formally test the adequacy of the overall fit of the model.

Let us also mention a commonly reported problem with Eq. (5.25): the process $\{\varepsilon_{t+1}^2\}$ invariably provides a very poor proxy for the process followed by the true but unobserved time-varying variance, $\{\sigma_{t+1|t}^2\}$. The reason can be seen from rather simple algebra:

$$\begin{aligned} Var_t[\varepsilon_{t+1}^2] &= E_t[(\varepsilon_{t+1}^2 - \sigma_{t+1|t}^2)^2] = E_t[(\sigma_{t+1|t}^2 z_{t+1}^2 - \sigma_{t+1|t}^2)^2] \\ &= \sigma_{t+1|t}^4 E_t[(z_{t+1}^2 - 1)^2] = \sigma_{t+1|t}^4 E_t[1 + z_{t+1}^4 - 2z_{t+1}^2] \\ &= \sigma_{t+1|t}^4 (1 + kurt(z_{t+1}) - 2) = \sigma_{t+1|t}^4 (kurt(z_{t+1}) - 1). \end{aligned} \tag{5.26}$$

Therefore, when either the predicted variance $\sigma_{t+1|t}^2$ (hence, $\sigma_{t+1|t}^4$) or the kurtosis of the standardized residuals are high, $Var_t[\varepsilon_{t+1}^2]$ will be large, and using squared residuals to proxy instantaneous variances exposes a researcher to a lot of noise and this choice is almost surely guaranteed to yield low regression R^2. Equivalently, if we take the *coefficient of variation* (defined as $E[\hat{\theta}]/\sqrt{Var[\hat{\theta}]}$) to be a measure of the variability of an estimator, then:

$$\frac{E_t[\varepsilon_{t+1}^2]}{Var_t[\varepsilon_{t+1}^2]} = \frac{\sigma_{t+1|t}^2}{\sqrt{\sigma_{t+1|t}^4 (kurt(z_{t+1}) - 1)}} = \frac{1}{\sqrt{kurt(z_{t+1}) - 1}} \tag{5.27}$$

and this coefficient declines as $kurt(z_{t+1})$ increases. In Chapter 10, we shall examine a few suggested remedies for this problem, but for the time being, we shall adopt the regression in Eq. (5.25) as a useful tool. Note that while the first type of tests described is applied as tests of whether the squared *standardized* residuals carry any serial correlation in them, the regression-based test in Eq. (5.25) concerns directly the squared residuals.

EXAMPLE 5.10

To see CH model comparisons in action, let us return to the 1963–2016 CRSP stock excess daily return data. We start by plotting and comparing conditional variance forecasts from the RiskMetrics and an ARCH(6) models, as obtained from the ML estimation performed in Example 5.8. Although the general patterns of the two series are similar, a few differences stand out. ARCH forecasts are more "spiky" but tend to revert back quickly to a baseline variance that is slightly higher than that predicted from RiskMetrics; however, only the latter model is able to generate occasional predictions (such as in late 1987 and late 2008) of structurally elevated variance (Fig. 5.7).

In Tables 5.6 and 5.7 we ask whether there is evidence of significant departures from IID-ness in the squared standardized residuals from any of the models. The left panel of Table 5.6 shows that there is small but statistically significant serial correlation left in the z_{t+1} from the RiskMetrics model; worse, the correlation between 1- and 2-day lagged standardized residuals and the subsequent squares appears to be strong and highly significant, an indication that $\hat{z}_{t+1}$ IID (0, 1) fails at least in the independence part. In particular, it seems that past US equities losses lead to subsequent higher variance, which we know to be called leverage effect.

In Table 5.7 we investigate instead any evidence of departures from IID-ness of the standardized residuals inferred from the ARCH(6) model. Here the ACF of the squared residuals gives less reasons for concern, even though at Lag 3 there seems to be some (faint) evidence of omitted conditional heteroskedasticity. However, in the rightmost panel, we note once more that there is non-negligible cross-correlation between 1- and 2-day lagged standardized residuals and the subsequent squares. Also in Table 5.7, there is then evidence of deviations from IID-ness that are hard to ignore.

Finally, we estimate and visually represent the regression in Eq. (5.25) (Fig. 5.8).

Clearly, the two scatter plots show that there is a linear relationship between realized squared residuals and predicted variances. However, too many observations fall far off the regression lines, as confirmed by the two regressions (robust *standard errors* are reported in parentheses):

$$\text{RiskMetrics: } \varepsilon_{t+1}^2 = \underset{(0.037)}{0.142} + \underset{(0.018)}{0.854}(\sigma_{t+1|t}^{RiskMetrics})^2 + e_{t+1|t} \quad R^2 = 13.8\%$$

$$\text{ARCH(6): } \varepsilon_{t+1}^2 = \underset{(0.036)}{0.197} + \underset{(0.017)}{0.791}(\sigma_{t+1|t}^{ARCH})^2 + e_{t+1|t} \quad R^2 = 13.8\%.$$

In this case, it is crucial to have reported the standard errors and not simply the p-values. The reason is that the simple null hypothesis of $b = 1$ requires that we calculate the t ratios:

$$\text{RiskMetrics: } t_{b=1}^{RiskMetrics} = \frac{0.854 - 1}{0.018} = -\frac{0.146}{0.018} = -8.111$$

$$\text{ARCH(6): } t_{b=1}^{ARCH} = \frac{0.791 - 1}{0.017} = -\frac{0.209}{0.017} = -12.29.$$

(Continued)

EXAMPLE 5.10 (Continued)

Moreover, it is obvious that the null hypothesis of $a = 0$ may be rejected with p-values close to 0.000 in both cases. Given the individual rejections from both coefficients, it seems pointless to apply F-tests of the joint hypothesis. Therefore, even though the two R^2 reported are low but not completely irrelevant, the problem is that positive and significant estimates of the regression intercept indicate that predicted variance is on average too low versus realized variance; the two slope coefficients significantly less than 1 further emphasize that realized variance moves over time less than what is predicted in terms of change of variances by both models.

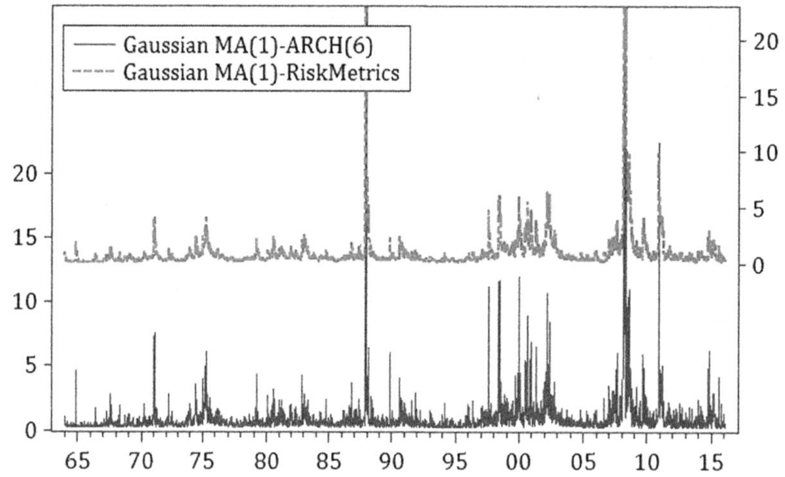

FIGURE 5.7 Plot of 1-day ARCH(6) and RiskMetrics volatility forecasts.

TABLE 5.6 Sample ACF/PACF for Squared Residuals and Cross-Correlogram Between Standardized Residuals and Their Squares, RiskMetrics Model

Sample ACF and PACF for Squared Standardized Residuals							Cross-Correlogram of Levels and Squared Std. Residuals				
Autocorrelatio...	Partial Correlation		AC	PAC	Q-Stat	Prob	Level, Squared(-i)	Level, Squared(+i)	i	lag	lead
		1	0.035	0.035	16.684	0.000			0	−0.2348	−0.2348
		2	0.024	0.023	24.545	0.000			1	0.0120	−0.0757
		3	0.009	0.007	25.643	0.000			2	0.0065	−0.0752
		4	0.008	0.006	26.426	0.000			3	0.0031	−0.0396
		5	0.003	0.002	26.526	0.000			4	0.0052	−0.0345
		6	−0.007	−0.008	27.229	0.000			5	0.0028	−0.0285
		7	−0.011	−0.010	28.778	0.000			6	0.0004	−0.0259
		8	0.004	0.005	28.946	0.000			7	0.0069	−0.0224
		9	0.007	0.008	29.699	0.000			8	−0.0021	−0.0140
		10	−0.002	−0.003	29.775	0.001			9	0.0036	−0.0182
		11	−0.000	−0.001	29.778	0.002			10	−0.0195	−0.0137
		12	−0.009	−0.009	30.976	0.002			11	0.0031	−0.0029
		13	−0.006	−0.006	31.470	0.003			12	0.0002	−0.0119
		14	−0.003	−0.002	31.568	0.005			13	0.0037	0.0032
		15	−0.012	−0.011	33.615	0.004			14	0.0045	−0.0174
		16	−0.010	−0.009	34.926	0.004			15	0.0053	0.0022
		17	−0.010	−0.009	36.321	0.004			16	−0.0054	0.0042
		18	−0.014	−0.013	39.081	0.003			17	0.0023	0.0109
		19	−0.000	0.001	39.081	0.004			18	0.0049	0.0134
		20	−0.014	−0.013	41.851	0.003			19	−0.0084	0.0027
		21	−0.016	−0.015	45.376	0.002			20	0.0117	−0.0000
		22	−0.012	−0.011	47.459	0.001			21	−0.0019	−0.0071
		23	−0.010	−0.008	48.789	0.001			22	0.0023	0.0054
		24	0.001	0.002	48.800	0.002			23	−0.0057	0.0144
									24	0.0045	−0.0023

TABLE 5.7 Sample ACF/PACF for Squared Residuals and Cross-Correlogram Between Standardized Residuals and Their Squares, ARCH(6) Model

Sample ACF and PACF of Squared Standardized Residuals								Cross-Correlogram of Levels and Squares of Std. Residuals				
Autocorrelation	Partial Correlation		AC	PAC	Q-Stat	Prob	Level, Squared(-i)	Level, Squared(+i)	i	lag	lead
		1	-0.000	-0.000	0.0004	0.984			0	-0.1913	-0.1913
		2	-0.007	-0.007	0.7142	0.700			1	0.0100	-0.0598
		3	-0.019	-0.019	5.4936	0.139			2	0.0100	-0.0602
		4	-0.028	-0.028	15.958	0.003			3	0.0095	-0.0240
		5	-0.027	-0.028	26.105	0.000			4	0.0103	-0.0165
		6	-0.029	-0.030	37.831	0.000			5	0.0080	-0.0110
		7	0.009	0.007	38.946	0.000			6	0.0025	-0.0082
		8	0.022	0.020	45.481	0.000			7	0.0048	-0.0040
		9	0.024	0.022	53.466	0.000			8	-0.0108	-0.0074
		10	0.021	0.020	59.719	0.000			9	0.0088	-0.0108
		11	0.020	0.020	65.132	0.000			1...	-0.0138	-0.0122
		12	0.013	0.015	67.456	0.000			1...	0.0043	0.0092
		13	0.018	0.022	71.907	0.000			1...	0.0058	-0.0065
		14	0.025	0.029	80.141	0.000			1...	0.0052	0.0054
		15	0.013	0.017	82.329	0.000			1...	0.0067	-0.0222
		16	0.011	0.014	83.879	0.000			1...	0.0112	-0.0054
		17	0.013	0.016	86.007	0.000			1...	-0.0091	-0.0046
		18	0.017	0.020	89.976	0.000			1...	0.0013	0.0025
		19	0.026	0.029	99.287	0.000			1...	0.0134	-0.0011
		20	0.008	0.010	100.07	0.000			1...	-0.0108	-0.0096
		21	0.005	0.006	100.44	0.000			2...	0.0137	-0.0065
		22	0.008	0.008	101.26	0.000			2...	-0.0014	-0.0181
		23	0.011	0.011	102.82	0.000			2...	0.0071	0.0078
		24	0.022	0.022	109.14	0.000			2...	-0.0002	0.0087
									2...	0.0086	-0.0111

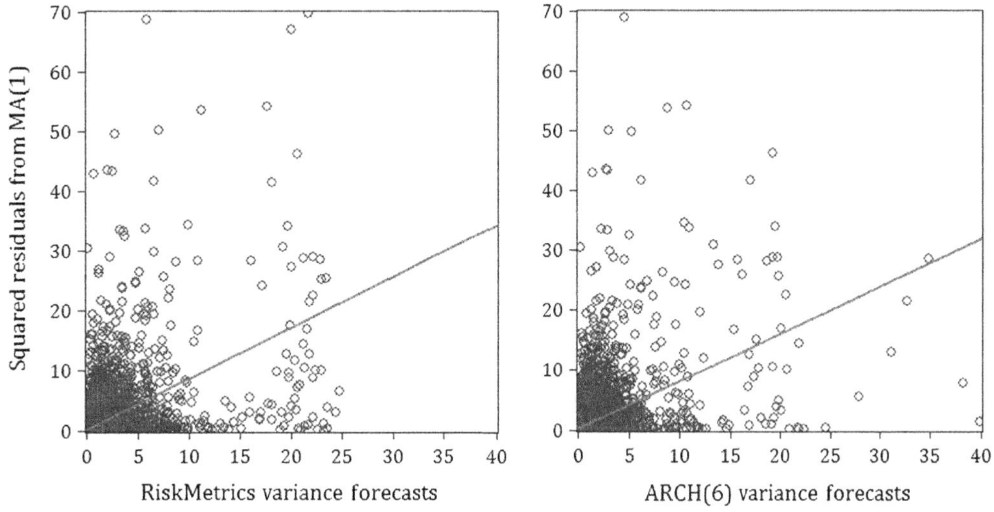

FIGURE 5.8 Plots of CH model variance forecasts versus squared residuals.

Any differences between the assumed process for the errors and the process of actual residuals, as well as the inability to predict subsequent realized squared residuals in an unbiased fashion, represent the real issues with the models presented so far. In what follows we therefore proceed to generalize the ARCH class not only or even mostly as a matter of formal elegance but especially because better models appear to be needed in practice.

5.2.5 Generalized ARCH Models and Their Statistical Properties

Generalizing through similar algebra one fact shown in Example 5.7, we know that because in an ARCH(p) model $E[\varepsilon_{t+1}^2|\varepsilon_t, \varepsilon_{t-1}, \varepsilon_{t-2}, \ldots] = \alpha_0 + \sum_{i=1}^{p} \alpha_i \varepsilon_{t-i+1}^2$, we have:

$$\varepsilon_{t+1}^2 = \omega + \sum_{i=1}^{p} \alpha_i \varepsilon_{t-i+1}^2 + \eta_{t+1}, \tag{5.28}$$

where η_{t+1} is a serially uncorrelated forecast error. Hence, the squared residuals themselves follow an AR(p) process. Note we have changed the notation of α_0 in ω, without loss of generality and for consistency with the bulk of the literature. Bollerslev (1986) observed that it is rather natural to think that in many applications the data may require that squared residuals be modeled as an ARMA(p,q) process, not a simple AR(p). In this case, Eq. (5.28) can be generalized to:

$$\varepsilon_{t+1}^2 = \omega + \sum_{i=1}^{\max(p,q)} (\alpha_i + \beta_i)\varepsilon_{t-i+1}^2 - \sum_{j=1}^{q} \beta_j \eta_{t+1-j} + \eta_{t+1}. \tag{5.29}$$

Eq. (5.29) features an ARMA(max[p, q], q) process. Observe now that $\beta_1(\varepsilon_t^2 - \eta_t) = \beta_1 \sigma_{t|t-1}^2$, $\beta_2(\varepsilon_{t-1}^2 - \eta_{t-1}) = \beta_2 \sigma_{t-1|t-2}^2$, ..., $\beta_q(\varepsilon_{t-q+1}^2 - \eta_{t-q+1}) = \beta_q \sigma_{t-q+1|t-q}^2$. The fact that the first sum on the right-hand side of Eq. (5.29) runs up to q when $q > p$ is important to ensure that for all $j = 1, 2, \ldots, q$, one such term $\beta_j \sigma_{t-j+1|t-j}^2$ can be constructed. Then Eq. (5.29) can simply be rewritten as a *generalized autoregressive conditional heteroskedasticity* model (GARCH(p, q)):

DEFINITION 5.2 (GARCH)

In a GARCH(p,q) model for conditional variance, forecasts depend on a (non-negatively) weighted sum of past squared residuals (from some conditional mean function model) and past variance forecasts:

$$\varepsilon_{t+1}^2 - \eta_{t+1} = \sigma_{t+1|t}^2 = \omega + \sum_{i=1}^{p} \alpha_i \varepsilon_{t-i+1}^2 + \sum_{j=1}^{q} \beta_j \sigma_{t-j+1|t-j}^2, \tag{5.30}$$

where $\omega > 0$, $\alpha_1, \alpha_2, \ldots, \alpha_p \geq 0$, $\beta_1, \beta_2, \ldots, \beta_q \geq 0$, and $\sum_{i=1}^{p} \alpha_i + \sum_{j=1}^{q} \beta_j < 1$ is necessary and sufficient for covariance stationarity.

One way to understand how and why we would set up a model such as Eq. (5.30) is to think that an ARCH(p) can be simply written, using the lag operator that we have introduced in Chapter 2, as:

$$\sigma_{t+1|t}^2 = \omega + \sum_{i=1}^{p} \alpha_i \varepsilon_{t-i+1}^2 = \omega + \sum_{i=1}^{p} \alpha_i L^i \varepsilon_{t+1}^2 = \omega + \boldsymbol{\alpha}(L)\varepsilon_{t+1}^2. \tag{5.31}$$

Of course, nothing prevents the lagged polynomial in Eq. (5.31) to be an infinite order, $\sigma_{t+1|t}^2 = \kappa + \boldsymbol{\pi}(L)\varepsilon_{t+1}^2$. At this point, assuming weak stationarity of the process for the squared residuals, an idea is to parameterize $\boldsymbol{\pi}(L)$ as the ratio of two finite-order polynomials:

$$\boldsymbol{\pi}(L) = \frac{\boldsymbol{\alpha}(L)}{1 - \boldsymbol{\delta}(L)} = \frac{\alpha_1 L + \alpha_2 L^2 + \cdots + \alpha_p L^p}{1 - \delta_1 L - \delta_2 L^2 - \cdots - \delta_q L^q}, \tag{5.32}$$

where we assume that the roots of $1 - \boldsymbol{\delta}(L) = 0$ are outside the unit circle. If $\sigma_{t+1|t}^2 = \kappa + \boldsymbol{\pi}(L)\varepsilon_{t+1}^2$ is multiplied by $1 - \boldsymbol{\delta}(L)$, the result is:

$$\begin{aligned} [1 - \boldsymbol{\delta}(L)]\sigma_{t+1|t}^2 &= \kappa[1 - \boldsymbol{\delta}(1)] + \boldsymbol{\alpha}(L)\varepsilon_{t+1}^2 \\ &= \overbrace{\kappa[1 - \delta_1 - \delta_2 - \cdots - \delta_q]}^{\omega} + \sum_{i=1}^{p} \alpha_i L^i \varepsilon_{t+1}^2 \end{aligned} \tag{5.33}$$

or

$$\sigma_{t+1|t}^2 = \omega + \sum_{i=1}^{p} \alpha_i L^i \varepsilon_{t+1}^2 - \sum_{j=1}^{q} \delta_j L^i \sigma_{t+1|t}^2 = \omega + \sum_{i=1}^{p} \alpha_i L^i \varepsilon_{t+1}^2 + \sum_{j=1}^{q} \beta_j L^i \sigma_{t+1|t}^2, \tag{5.34}$$

where $\beta_j = -\delta_j$ for $j = 1, 2, \ldots, q$. Eq. (5.34) is just a version of Eq. (5.29) and displays a clear analogy to a ARMA(p,q) process, of which it inherits a number of key properties:

- The process is well defined if $\omega > 0$, $\alpha_1, \alpha_2, \ldots, \alpha_p \geq 0$, and $\beta_1, \beta_2, \ldots, \beta_q \geq 0$, although this is only sufficient; under some technical conditions on the lag polynomials characterized by the coefficients $\alpha_1, \alpha_2, \ldots, \alpha_p$ and $\beta_1, \beta_2, \ldots, \beta_q$, provided that the roots of the polynomial defined by the coefficients $\beta_1, \beta_2, \ldots, \beta_q$ lie outside the unit circle, this positivity constraint is satisfied if and only if all the coefficients in the infinite power series expansion for $\alpha(L)/(1-\delta(L))$ are non-negative.
- As in the case of all ARMA(max[p, q], q) processes, Eq. (5.29) will be covariance stationary if and only if all the roots of the characteristic polynomial associated to the coefficients $(\alpha_1 + \beta_1), (\alpha_2 + \beta_2), \ldots, (\alpha_{\max(p,q)} + \beta_{\max(p,q)})$ lie outside the unit circle (see Bollerslev, 1986, for a formal proof).

Interestingly, the statistical properties of the GARCH process in Eq. (5.30) depend not on ARCH and "generalized" coefficients (say, the αs and the βs) separately but also on their sum. Just as an ARMA model in Chapter 2 often led to a more parsimonious representation of the temporal dependencies in the conditional mean than an AR model could, the GARCH(p,q) formulation in Eq. (5.30) provides a similar flexibility over the ARCH(p) model when parameterizing the conditional variance. This analogy with the ARMA class also allows for the usage of standard time series, Box–Jenkins type techniques in the identification of the orders p and q, when applied to the squared residuals of some conditional mean model. However, because of the higher order dependencies in the $\{\eta_{t+1}\}$ process, standard Box–Jenkins inference procedures will generally turn out to be very inefficient (see the discussion in Bollerslev, 1988).

As far *strict stationarity* goes, at least in the case of a GARCH(1,1), we know that the condition $E[\ln(\alpha z_t^2 + \beta)] < 0 \ \forall t \geq 1$ is sufficient (see Lumsdaine, 1996). However, because $E[\ln(\alpha z_t^2 + \beta)] < \ln E[(\alpha z_t^2 + \beta)] = \ln(\alpha E[z_t^2] + \beta) = \ln(\alpha + \beta) < \ln(1) < 0$ under covariance stationarity, we have that at least for a GARCH(1,1), covariance stationarity always guarantees strict stationarity.[6]

EXAMPLE 5.11

To better investigate the mechanics of GARCH, we return to the same data as in Example 5.9, assume a constant mean ($\hat{\mu} = -0.436\%$), and compare 1-month-ahead variance forecasts, from RiskMetrics under $\lambda = 0.94$ when the initial variance is set to $\sigma^2_{1|0} = (12)^{-1}\sum_{\tau=1}^{12}(R_\tau - (-0.436))^2$, from one GARCH(1,1), with $\alpha_1 = 0.1$, $\beta_1 = 0.88$, and a GARCH(2,2) with $\alpha_1 = 0.30$, $\alpha_2 = 0.20$, $\beta_1 = 0.28$, and $\beta_2 = 0.20$. For both GARCH models, the variance initialization is identical to RiskMetrics, and the constant is set to $\omega = \sigma^2_{1|0}(1 - 0.1 - 0.88) = \sigma^2_{1|0}(1 - 0.2 - 0.3 - 0.28 - 0.20)$.

Table 5.8 shows that while GARCH(1,1) and RiskMetrics give rather similar forecasts (this is due to the fact that in the former model $\alpha_1 + \beta_1 = 0.98$ is close to the unit root featured by RiskMetrics) and their distribution tilts in the direction of over-weighting recent variance forecasts as is typical of RiskMetrics, the GARCH(2,2) features an identical persistence $\alpha_1 + \alpha_2 + \beta_1 + \beta_2 = 0.98$ but loads heavily on recent squared residuals, more than on past variance. As a result, the GARCH (2,2) yields less smooth forecasts and allows an investigator to perceive a drop in predicted variance between October and December that the other two models miss out.

TABLE 5.8 Calculations for RiskMetrics and GARCH Variance Forecasts

Month	Return	Sample Mean	Residual	Squared Residual	Conditional Variance Forecasts		
					RiskMetrics	GARCH (1,1)	GARCH (2,2)
January	−11.55	−0.436	−11.114	123.521	45.328	48.655	57.225
February	−4.35	−0.436	−3.914	15.319	43.527	45.155	54.197
March	8.36	−0.436	8.796	77.370	45.558	48.280	53.702

(Continued)

6. Because ARCH processes are fat-tailed, the conditions for weak stationarity are often more stringent than the conditions for strict stationarity. For instance, the simple ARCH(1) model with normal errors of Example 5.8 with $\alpha_1 = 1/3$ is strictly- but not covariance-stationary.

TABLE 5.8 (Continued)

Month	Return	Sample Mean	Residual	Squared Residual	Conditional Variance Forecasts		
					RiskMetrics	GARCH (1,1)	GARCH (2,2)
April	2.65	−0.436	3.086	9.523	43.396	44.246	45.014
May	−2.52	−0.436	−2.084	4.343	41.053	40.177	27.358
June	−9.15	−0.436	−8.714	75.934	43.145	43.756	41.119
July	4.16	−0.436	4.596	21.123	41.824	41.424	39.315
August	0.46	−0.436	0.896	0.803	39.363	37.340	24.504
September	−1.60	−0.436	−1.164	1.355	37.082	33.802	16.098
October	1.39	−0.436	1.826	3.334	35.057	30.886	11.486
November	−4.32	−0.436	−3.884	15.085	33.859	29.495	12.435
December	11.24	−0.436	11.676	136.329	40.007	40.395	50.502

Obviously, the ARCH(p) models discussed in Section 5.2.3 are simply GARCH(p,0) models in which there is no memory in the process for past conditional variance predictions. Also because in forecasting applications it has proven to be very hard to beat (see Hansen and Lunde, 2005), unless special needs are felt, practitioners usually resort to simple GARCH(1,1) models:

$$\sigma^2_{t+1|t} = \omega + \alpha\varepsilon^2_t + \beta\sigma^2_{t|t-1}. \tag{5.35}$$

This is of course the same model as a ARMA(1,1) for squared errors.

In the case of GARCH(1,1), positivity comes from the restrictions $\omega > 0$, $\alpha \geq 0$, $\beta \geq 0$, and stationarity from the simple characteristic equation $(\alpha + \beta)L^* = 1$, which implies the constraint $\alpha + \beta < 1$. Exploiting its equivalence to an ARMA(1,1), we also derive in a straightforward way the stationary, long-run variance:

$$\overline{\sigma}^2 = \frac{\omega}{1 - \alpha - \beta}. \tag{5.36}$$

Note that we should not be misled by the naive notion that because second moments change over time, this implies that the time series process characterized by such moments becomes nonstationary. On the contrary, under appropriate technical conditions, we have just shown that *even though the conditional variance may change in heteroskedastic fashion, the time series process may still be stationary*. In practice, this means that even though the variance of a series may go through high and low periods, the unconditional (long-run, average) variance may still exist and be constant. Of course, when the unconditional variance of a time series is not constant, then the time series will not be stationary (see the definition in Chapter 2).

Because under the restriction $\beta \leq \alpha + \beta < 1$ the ARMA(1,1) process is stationary, if we recursively substitute the lagged variance on the right-hand side of Eq. (5.35), we can express conditional variance as a weighted average of all of infinite lagged squared residuals:

$$\begin{aligned}
\sigma^2_{t+1|t} &= \omega + \alpha\varepsilon^2_t + \beta\sigma^2_{t|t-1} = \omega + \alpha\varepsilon^2_t + \beta(\omega + \alpha\varepsilon^2_{t-1} + \beta\sigma^2_{t-1|t-2}) \\
&= (1+\beta)\omega + \alpha(\varepsilon^2_t + \beta\varepsilon^2_{t-1}) + \beta^2\sigma^2_{t-1|t-2} \\
&= (1+\beta)\omega + \alpha(\varepsilon^2_t + \beta\varepsilon^2_{t-1}) + \beta^2(\omega + \alpha\varepsilon^2_{t-2} + \beta\sigma^2_{t-2|t-3}) \\
&= (1+\beta+\beta^2)\omega + \alpha(\varepsilon^2_t + \beta\varepsilon^2_{t-1} + \beta^2\varepsilon^2_{t-2}) + \beta^3\sigma^2_{t-2|t-3} \\
&= \cdots = \omega\sum_{\tau=1}^{\infty}\beta^{\tau-1} + \alpha\sum_{\tau=1}^{\infty}\beta^{\tau-1}\varepsilon^2_{t-\tau+1} + \lim_{\tau\to\infty}\beta^{\tau}\sigma^2_{t-\tau+1|t-\tau} \\
&= \frac{\omega}{1-\beta} + \alpha\sum_{\tau=1}^{\infty}\beta^{\tau-1}\varepsilon^2_{t-\tau+1},
\end{aligned} \tag{5.37}$$

which shows that under covariance stationarity a GARCH(1,1) has an invertible MA(∞) representation, as implied by Wold's theorem. Moreover, from Eq. (5.37), we can see that the GARCH(1,1) variance specification is analogous to a sample variance estimator but one that downweighs more distant lagged squared errors. Moreover, there is one more interesting implication: the reason for the success of simple GARCH(1,1) models over often-complex ARCH(p) with relatively large p is that GARCH(1,1) can be shown to be equivalent to an ARCH(∞) model! In fact, from Eq. (5.37), we can see that a GARCH(1,1) is just an ARCH(∞) model with a special structure of decaying weights, $\alpha_\tau = \beta^\tau$ for $\tau = 1, 2, \ldots$

The result in Eq. (5.36) implies one additional way to rewrite Eq. (5.35) that is easily interpreted in a financial context, where a risk manager or a trader predicts next period's variance by forming a weighted average of the long-term variance (the constant), the forecast variance from the most recent period (the GARCH term), and information about volatility observed in the previous period (the ARCH term). Because Eq. (5.36) implies that $\omega = \overline{\sigma}^2(1-\alpha-\beta)$, Eq. (5.35) is equivalent to:

$$\sigma^2_{t+1|t} = \overline{\sigma}^2(1-\alpha-\beta) + \alpha\varepsilon_t^2 + \beta\sigma^2_{t|t-1} = \overline{\sigma}^2 + \alpha(\varepsilon_t^2 - \overline{\sigma}^2) + \beta(\sigma^2_{t|t-1} - \overline{\sigma}^2). \tag{5.38}$$

If the asset return was unexpectedly large in either the upward or the downward direction, then an analyst will increase the estimate of the variance for the next period. Of course, more generally, Eq. (5.30) can be written as:

$$\sigma^2_{t+1|t} = \overline{\sigma}^2 + \sum_{i=1}^{p} \alpha_i(\varepsilon^2_{t-i+1} - \overline{\sigma}^2) + \sum_{j=1}^{q} \beta_j(\sigma^2_{t-j+1|t-j} - \overline{\sigma}^2). \tag{5.39}$$

It seems now an appropriate time to provide a realistic example, also to see in action this meta-law that often the data seem to prefer a rather simple GARCH(1,1) model over more complex alternatives.

EXAMPLE 5.12

Let us study the weekly 1982–2016 returns (here approximated by the negative of the changes in yields, see Shiller, 1979, for a better approximation formula) of 10-year US Treasury notes. The first issue is to investigate the sample ACF and PACF of the data to derive some indications as to the likely order of the required ARMA model for their conditional mean. A quick BIC-based model specification search reveals that a simple AR(1) model for returns guarantees the best trade-off between fit and parsimony with a BIC of −1.372 (against −1.370 for MA(1) and −1.317 for a constant mean model).

Table 5.9 shows that a simple AR(1) for the mean does an excellent job at capturing any linear structure characterizing the data. However, both the SACF and SPACF of squared residuals are characterized by a slow and irregular decay that—even though it cannot be taken as a fail-proof indication of the need of ARMA model for squared residuals—is often associated with simple ARMA(1,1) or ARMA(2,2) dynamics. Moreover, note that any attempt to use a simpler ARCH model to capture the dynamics revealed by the sample ACF would lead to a very large, possibly ARCH(11) specification!

An unreported selection exercise based on information criteria confirms our feeling that ARMA models are needed to fit the squared residuals from an AR(1) mean model: it is indeed a classical GARCH(1,1) that offers the best trade-off between its simplicity and the in-sample fit provided. Of course, richer, more heavily parameterized models increase the maximized log-likelihood to even higher values (for instance, 1430.7 for a GARCH(3,3) versus 1425.6 for a GARCH(2,2)), but also the number of parameters to be estimated increases. We therefore proceed to estimate by ML a GARCH(1,1) model, obtaining (p-values are in parentheses):

$$R_{t+1} = \underset{(0.169)}{0.003} + \underset{(0.000)}{0.230}R_t + \varepsilon_{t+1} \quad \varepsilon_{t+1} \text{ IID } N(0, \sigma^2_{t+1|t})$$

$$\sigma^2_{t+1|t} = \underset{(0.003)}{0.0002} + \underset{(0.000)}{0.073}\varepsilon_t^2 + \underset{(0.000)}{0.910}\ \sigma^2_{t|t-1}.$$

The AR(1) coefficient is well below 1 in module and sum of the coefficients of the GARCH(1,1) model is 0.983, which corroborates the (covariance) stationarity of the model. At least for these data, the evidence in favor of GARCH(1,1) is strong. For instance, in Table 5.10, the sample ACF of squared standardized residuals is characterized by the absence of additional structure.

Finally, the standard regression that tests whether the GARCH(1,1) model can forecast squared residuals gives (robust standard errors in parentheses):

$$\varepsilon^2_{t+1} = \underset{(0.0013)}{0.0017} + \underset{(0.067)}{0.878}(\sigma^{GARCH}_{t+1|t})^2 + e_{t+1|t} \quad R^2 = 8.69\%.$$

In this case, the intercept is not statistically significant, while

$$t^{GARCH}_{b=1} = \frac{0.878-1}{0.067} = -\frac{0.122}{0.067} = -1.821,$$

which fails to be significant at a test size of 5%; moreover, a F-test of the joint hypothesis of $a = (b-1) = 0$ gives a statistic of 1.687 that with (2, 1822) degrees of freedom, implies a p-value of 0.185 and leads to a failure to reject. The GARCH(1,1) seems to perform really well, even though the predictive regression for squared returns gives a rather low R^2.

TABLE 5.9 ACF/PACF for Residuals and Squared Standardized Residuals

Sample ACF and PACF of AR(1) Residuals

Autocorrelation	Partial Correlation		AC	PAC	Q-Stat	Prob
		1	0.004	0.004	0.0348	0.852
		2	−0.023	−0.023	1.0310	0.597
		3	0.047	0.047	5.1115	0.164
		4	0.001	−0.000	5.1125	0.276
		5	0.037	0.039	7.5778	0.181
		6	0.014	0.011	7.9302	0.243
		7	−0.005	−0.004	7.9804	0.334
		8	0.027	0.024	9.2955	0.318
		9	−0.042	−0.044	12.525	0.185
		10	−0.019	−0.018	13.186	0.213
		11	0.011	0.005	13.390	0.269
		12	−0.019	−0.016	14.077	0.296
		13	0.055	0.056	19.561	0.107
		14	−0.012	−0.012	19.826	0.136
		15	0.019	0.026	20.477	0.154
		16	−0.015	−0.023	20.913	0.182
		17	−0.015	−0.009	21.302	0.213
		18	0.008	0.001	21.414	0.259
		19	0.000	−0.002	21.414	0.314
		20	0.013	0.015	21.727	0.355
		21	0.001	−0.003	21.731	0.415
		22	−0.036	−0.029	24.093	0.342
		23	−0.032	−0.032	25.929	0.304
		24	−0.019	−0.020	26.589	0.324

Sample ACF and PACF of Squared Residuals from AR(1) Model

Autocorrelation	Partial Correlation		AC	PAC	Q-Stat	Prob
		1	0.130	0.130	31.051	0.000
		2	0.136	0.121	64.968	0.000
		3	0.179	0.153	123.76	0.000
		4	0.100	0.051	141.93	0.000
		5	0.150	0.102	182.94	0.000
		6	0.111	0.050	205.51	0.000
		7	0.143	0.088	242.94	0.000
		8	0.238	0.177	346.54	0.000
		9	0.123	0.043	374.28	0.000
		10	0.057	−0.041	380.31	0.000
		11	0.131	0.043	412.07	0.000
		12	0.055	−0.024	417.60	0.000
		13	0.059	−0.018	423.93	0.000
		14	0.061	−0.013	430.85	0.000
		15	0.045	−0.020	434.58	0.000
		16	0.056	−0.024	440.36	0.000
		17	0.056	0.009	446.19	0.000
		18	0.070	0.042	455.25	0.000
		19	0.041	−0.009	458.35	0.000
		20	0.076	0.047	468.93	0.000
		21	0.064	0.038	476.52	0.000
		22	0.048	0.012	480.80	0.000
		23	0.057	0.022	486.78	0.000
		24	0.026	−0.010	487.99	0.000

TABLE 5.10 ACF/PACF of Squared Standardized Residuals from GARCH(1,1)

ACF and PACF of Squared Std. Residuals from GARCH(1,1)

Autocorrelation	Partial Correlation		AC	PAC	Q-Stat	Prob
		1	−0.017	−0.017	0.5367	0.464
		2	−0.013	−0.013	0.8249	0.662
		3	0.043	0.043	4.1959	0.241
		4	0.000	0.002	4.1963	0.380
		5	−0.004	−0.003	4.2248	0.518
		6	0.013	0.011	4.5334	0.605
		7	0.018	0.018	5.1207	0.645
		8	0.035	0.036	7.3509	0.499
		9	0.009	0.010	7.5054	0.585
		10	0.012	0.012	7.7847	0.650
		11	−0.028	−0.031	9.2487	0.599
		12	−0.009	−0.011	9.4020	0.668
		13	−0.020	−0.023	10.172	0.680
		14	−0.013	−0.013	10.502	0.725
		15	−0.061	−0.063	17.436	0.294
		16	−0.023	−0.026	18.387	0.302
		17	−0.001	−0.003	18.391	0.365
		18	−0.017	−0.012	18.907	0.398
		19	−0.044	−0.040	22.480	0.261
		20	0.013	0.013	22.797	0.299
		21	0.003	0.008	22.816	0.354
		22	−0.001	0.008	22.816	0.412
		23	−0.026	−0.021	24.022	0.403
		24	−0.031	−0.030	25.804	0.363

Because the persistence index of a GARCH(p, q) model is given by $\sum_{i=1}^{p} \alpha_i + \sum_{j=1}^{q} \beta_j$, obviously large values of both the coefficients α_i $i = 1,\ldots,p$ and β_j $j = 1,\ldots,q$ act to increase the conditional volatility; however, they do so in different ways. The larger are the α_is, the larger is the response of $\sigma^2_{t+1|t}$ to new information; the larger are the β_js, the longer and stronger is the memory of conditional variance to past (forecasts of) variance. This means that for any given, fixed persistence index, it is possible for different stationary GARCH models to behave rather differently and therefore yield heterogeneous economic insights on the perceptions of uncertainty and risk, depending on the "fraction" of a fixed $\sum_{i=1}^{p}\alpha_i + \sum_{j=1}^{q}\beta_j$ brought about by $\sum_{i=1}^{p}\alpha_i$ and $\sum_{j=1}^{q}\beta_j$, respectively. Example 5.13 further elaborates on this point.

EXAMPLE 5.13

Let us fit a simple Gaussian ARMA(p_m, q_m)–GARCH(p, q) to monthly UK stock returns over a sample 1977–2016. To try an alternative strategy, we simply apply information criteria (with a preference for the BIC) to select the best model for a relatively wide range of choices of p_m, q_m, p, and q, including zeros and homoskedastic models. We obtain that a very simple constant mean ARMA(0,0)–GARCH(1,1) model brings the BIC down to 6.158, and this is sensibly inferior to the 6.170 of an AR(1)–GARCH(1,1) and the 6.172 of a more complex ARMA(1,1)–GARCH(1,1). In particular, ARCH models as well as bigger GARCH models never succeed in reducing the BIC below 6.158. The estimated model is then (p-values in parentheses):

$$R_{t+1} = \underset{(0.000)}{1.087} + \varepsilon_{t+1} \quad \varepsilon_{t+1} \quad \text{IID} \quad N(0, \sigma^2_{t+1|t})$$

$$\sigma^2_{t+1|t} = \underset{(0.095)}{0.540} + \underset{(0.000)}{0.086}\varepsilon_t^2 + \underset{(0.000)}{0.898}\ \sigma^2_{t|t-1}.$$

The implied persistence index is then 0.984, which is in fact relatively high considering that these are monthly returns.

At this point, we perform the following experiment: holding constant the same time series of standardized residuals that we have obtained from the actual estimation of the model, we simulate four alternative series of both returns and variance predictions:

- α set to 1/4 of the estimated coefficient (0.022) with β set in such a way that their sum still equals 0.984, that is, to 0.962.
- α set to 1/2 of the estimated coefficient (0.043) with β set in such a way that their sum still equals 0.984, that is, to 0.943.
- α set to be 50% higher than the estimated coefficient (0.129) with β set in such a way that their sum still equals 0.984, that is, to 0.855.
- α set to be four times the estimated coefficient (0.344) with β set in such a way that their sum still equals 0.984, that is, to 0.640 (Fig. 5.9).

In all cases, the constant coefficient in the conditional variance model is held fixed to the estimated 0.540 and the series are initialized at the same value of 33.322, to favor comparability. Clearly, the first two cases illustrate the behavior of stationary, persistent GARCH models that react weakly to shocks; the last two cases concern GARCH models in which news tend to yield large impacts. Fig. 5.11 shows the resulting five implicit monthly *volatility* series, just because these enter more frequently the jargon of traders and researchers.

Of course, all series but one are just counter-factual simulations derived from the only, actual estimated process. However, the key role played by the structure of a GARCH model is easily detected. Even though, by construction, all processes have the same long-run, ergodic volatility of approximately 5.8% per month, the predicted volatility series characterized by high α and low β tend to fall most of the time below their long-run average, to then suddenly spike in short-lived volatility bursts that are however as high as three to four times the average. In our case, such models really make the turbulence of the 2007–09 Great Financial Crisis (henceforth GFC) look unprecedented. Note that risk managers and practitioners may then be induced into some degree of "Black Swan" type of complacency, when the numbers turn in the red or defaults occur. On the opposite, under GARCH models with low α and high β, volatility tends to be a rather smooth process that hovers around its long-run mean, to the point (in extreme cases in which β falls below 0.7) that extreme events such as the GFC may look hardly significant, in retrospect. In any event, the case stands: ML estimation has picked one and only one combination of α and β (among the infinite combinations such that $\alpha + \beta = 0.984$), because this one maximizes the likelihood that the sample of monthly UK returns does come from the model specified.

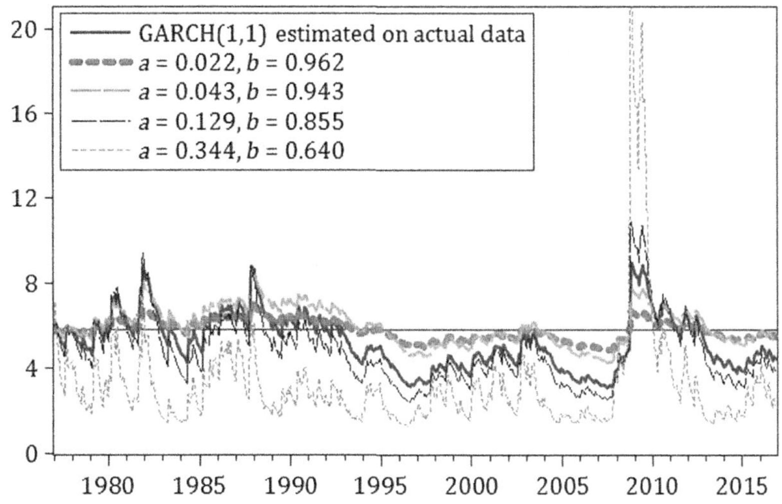

FIGURE 5.9 Predicted conditional volatility from a GARCH(1,1) model and four alternative simulated scenarios.

In many applications to high-frequency financial data, the estimate of $\sum_{i=1}^{\max(p,q)}(\hat{\alpha}_i + \hat{\beta}_i)$ turns out to be close to unity. This provides an empirical motivation for the so-called *integrated GARCH*(p, q), or IGARCH(p, q), model introduced by Engle and Bollerslev (1986). In the IGARCH class of models, the autoregressive polynomial in Eq. (5.35) has a unit root, and consequently a shock to the conditional variance is persistent in the sense that it remains equally important for future forecasts at all horizons. In fact, IGARCH is a class of models that may be strictly stationary (under appropriate conditions) but is not covariance stationary. In fact, because by Jensen's inequality, $E[\ln(\alpha z_t^2 + \beta)] < \ln(E[\alpha z_t^2 + \beta]) = \ln(\alpha E[z_t^2] + \beta) = \ln(\alpha + \beta)$, in the case of IGARCH(1,1) we have $\ln(\alpha + \beta) = \ln 1 = 0$, which always ensures stationarity. Yet, this does not mean that the IGARCH process does not have ANY finite moment: for instance, Nelson (1990) shows that in the IGARCH(1,1) model $E_s[\sigma_t^{2\eta}]$ converges to a finite limit independent of time s information as $t \rightarrow \infty$, whenever $\eta < 1$.[7] However, this is not new to us. To see why, consider for concreteness a GARCH(1,1) model when $\alpha + \beta = 1$ or $\alpha = 1 - \beta$. Then,

$$\sigma^2_{t+1|t} = \omega + (1-\beta)\varepsilon_t^2 + \beta\sigma^2_{t|t-1}. \tag{5.40}$$

Yet, upon reflection, Eq. (5.40) has been encountered already in Section 5.2.2: *IGARCH(1,1) is just a RiskMetrics model* in which the parameter λ has been relabeled β and in which a constant intercept ω has appeared. If we flip our argument around, we obtain one important insight: RiskMetrics is just a special case of GARCH(1,1) in which

- there is no intercept;
- the sum of the coefficients is one so that the model is not covariance stationary, and as such
- the long-run, ergodic variance $\overline{\sigma}^2 = \omega/(1-\alpha-\beta) = 0/0$ and therefore it does not exist (one may say that $\overline{\sigma}^2$ diverges, even though this would require a $\omega > 0$).

Therefore, RiskMetrics ought to be used with extreme caution for two reasons. First, because it is a special case of a more general model that has been investigated for its good empirical properties but that in general includes an intercept $\omega > 0$ and is characterized by ARMA "complexity dimensions" p and q that should be either estimated or at least selected on the basis of the data: RiskMetrics instead imposes $\omega = 0$ and $p = q = 1$. Second, because, as we shall see in Section 5.4, using a nonstationary model (in the covariance sense) to forecast has clear limitations, and one should adopt this choice only when sharply demanded by the data.

One may wonder how is it possible that IGARCH models are estimated using the same methods as standard stationary GARCH models (see Section 5.6), even though they are nonstationary. Although the exact answer has a technical nature, the intuition can be grasped by the fact that given that $\alpha + \beta = 1$ (to be concrete, consider the (1,1) case), and that:

$$\begin{aligned}
\sigma^2_{t+1|t} &= \omega + (1-\beta)\varepsilon_t^2 + \beta\sigma^2_{t|t-1} = \omega + (1-\beta)\varepsilon_t^2 + \beta[\omega + (1-\beta)\varepsilon_{t-1}^2 + \beta\sigma^2_{t-1|t-2}] \\
&= \omega(1+\beta) + (1-\beta)[\varepsilon_t^2 + \beta\varepsilon_{t-1}^2] + \beta^2\sigma^2_{t-1|t-2} \\
&= \cdots = \omega\sum_{j=0}^{\infty}\beta^j + (1-\beta)\sum_{j=0}^{\infty}\beta^j\varepsilon_{t-j}^2 = \frac{\omega}{1-\beta} + (1-\beta)\sum_{j=0}^{\infty}\beta^j\varepsilon_{t-j}^2,
\end{aligned} \tag{5.41}$$

unlike a genuinely nonstationary process, conditional variance is a geometrically declining function of the current and past realizations of the sequence of past shocks, that will make it possible for a IGARCH model to be at least *ergodic*, that is, to have the dependence between increasingly distant past shocks that fades to 0 sufficiently fast, for the properties of generally used estimation methods (such as ML) to hold as for any other GARCH model.

GARCH(p, q) models are extended ARCH models that deliver the same advantages as ARCH but require a lower number of parameters to be estimated under inequality constraints. Therefore, similarly to ARCH, GARCH successfully captures thick-tailed returns and volatility clustering. However, it is not well suited to capture what we have called the "leverage effect" because the conditional variance in Eq. (5.40) is a function only of the magnitudes of the lagged squared residuals and not of their signs.

In the *exponential GARCH (EGARCH)* model of Nelson (1991), $\sigma^2_{t+1|t}$ depends on both the size and the sign of lagged residuals. The model is set up to directly express forecasts not of future conditional variance, but of *future conditional log-variance*. When estimation is performed by ML, from the invariance property of maximum likelihood

7. In fact, when the support of the shocks z_t is unbounded, Nelson (1990) proves that in any stationary and ergodic GARCH(1,1) model, $E_s[\sigma_t^{2\eta}]$ diverges for all sufficiently large η and converges for all sufficiently small η.

estimator (MLE) (by which, under technical conditions, the MLE of some transformation $g(\boldsymbol{\theta})$ is simply $g(\hat{\boldsymbol{\theta}}^{ML})$), we know that the forecast of conditional variance is simply the exponential of the forecast of log-variance, because the exponential is a monotone increasing function. Moreover, modeling the log of conditional variance appears to be a good idea because no constraints will have to be imposed, because even though $\ln \sigma^2_{t+1|t} \leq 0$, we know that $\exp(\ln \sigma^2_{t+1|t}) > 0$ by construction. One formulation of the model is provided in Definition 5.3.

DEFINITION 5.3 (Exponential GARCH)

In a EGARCH(p, q) model for the conditional log-variance, forecasts depends on a (non-negatively) weighted sum of past standardized errors (from some conditional mean function model, both in levels and in absolute values) and past log-variance forecasts:

$$\ln \sigma^2_{t+1|t} = \omega + \sum_{i=1}^{p} \alpha_i [z_{t-i} + \theta(|z_{t-i}| - E|z_{t-i}|)] + \sum_{j=1}^{q} \beta_j \ln \sigma^2_{t-j+1|t-j}. \tag{5.42}$$

The sequences (for fixed $i = 1, 2, \ldots, p$) $\{z_{t-i} + \theta(|z_{t-i}| - E|z_{t-i}|)\}$ are zero-mean, IID random sequences in which, assuming $\theta < 0$):

- if $z_{t-i} > 0$, $z_{t-i} + \theta(|z_{t-i}| - E|z_{t-i}|) = const + (1+\theta)z_{t-i}$, a linear function with slope $(1+\theta) < 1$;
- if $z_{t-i} < 0$, $z_{t-i} + \theta(|z_{t-i}| - E|z_{t-i}|) = const + (1-\theta)z_{t-i}$, a linear function with slope $(1-\theta) > (1+\theta)$.

Thus, $\{z_{t-i} + \theta(|z_{t-i}| - E|z_{t-i}|)\}$ is function of both the magnitude and the sign of past standardized residuals, and it allows the conditional variance process to respond asymmetrically to rises and falls in asset prices compared to their mean. Indeed, it can be rewritten as:

$$const + [1 + ((I_{z_{t-i} \geq 0}) - (I_{z_{t-i} < 0}))\theta]|z_{t-i}|. \tag{5.43}$$

Therefore, EGARCH is an ideal framework—albeit not the only one, as we shall see in Section 5.2.6—to capture the leverage effect and, more generally, the existence of asymmetries in conditional variance. For the reasons explained above, no restrictions on the parameters are necessary to ensure non-negativity of the conditional variances. Moreover, albeit unusual, it is possible to find cases in which either negative or positive past shocks end up decreasing the forecast of variance instead of increasing it, which would represent an extreme type of asymmetric effect.

An alternative version of EGARCH—here simply stated for the typical (1,1) case is:

$$\ln \sigma^2_{t+1|t} = \omega + \xi|z_t| + \delta z_t + \beta \ln \sigma^2_{t|t-1} = \omega + \xi\left|\frac{\varepsilon_t}{\sigma_{t|t-1}}\right| + \delta z_t + \beta \ln \sigma^2_{t|t-1}. \tag{5.44}$$

In this case, the potential role of the asymmetries is captured by the coefficient δ: when $\delta < 0$, then a negative residual increases the forecast of conditional variance more than a positive residual does. The model in Eq. (5.44) is easy to generalize to the case in which there are p lags of the standardized residuals and q lags of past variance forecasts on the right-hand side. Nelson (1991) argued that writing a CH model in terms of standardized residuals allows for a more natural interpretation of the size and persistence of the shocks because standardized residuals are unit-free measures.

Nelson's EGARCH has another key advantage. In a GARCH, we know that the parameter restrictions needed to ensure moment existence become increasingly stringent as the order of the moment grows. For instance, even in the simple case of an ARCH(1), that is, a GARCH(1,0), we have seen that for a given integer r, the 2rth moment exists if and only if $\alpha_1^r \prod_{k=1}^{r}(2k-1) < 1$. Already in the case of $r = 2$, we have discovered that existence of the unconditional kurtosis requires $\alpha_1 < \sqrt{1/3}$. Instead, in a EGARCH(p,q) case, if the error process $\{\eta_{t+1}\}$ in the ARMA representation of the model has all moments and the sum of the squares of the beta coefficients does not exceed or equal 1, $\sum_{j=1}^{q} \beta_j^2 < 1$, then all moments for the EGARCH process will exist.

How far better can EGARCH fare versus a standard GARCH model? Indirectly, this question can also be reinterpreted as how important are asymmetries in conditional variance? Of course, the first and most obvious answer is that "it depends on the data under investigation". Having said this, the next example gives a fairly typical insight on this problem.

EXAMPLE 5.14

Let us return to the 1963–2016 CRSP daily stock excess return data of Example 5.10. From Example 5.8, we know that a simple and yet effective conditional mean model is an MA(1), that we also adopt here. A model specification search based on information criteria in the space of GARCH(p, q) and EGARCH(p, q) models yields Table 5.11. Models selected by each criterion are boldfaced.

To some surprise, given what the literature has typically reported, in this case the information criteria tend to select relatively large models: a GARCH(2,2) in the GARCH family and even a more complex EGARCH(3,3) in the exponential family. However, as signaled by the stars next to these models, the unconstrained ML estimation routines in E-Views gave negative coefficients very often in the case of GARCH models.[8] We have therefore excluded these models from consideration. In fact, the frequency with which these cases of negatively estimated ML coefficients tend to show up, even with reference to this long and famous sample of daily stock returns, may be taken as a powerful indication of the true usefulness of EGARCH. If one compares the two "champions" from both families—which is doable and technically correct when information criteria are used—then EGARCH is massively preferred over GARCH, as one would expect of data—such as equity returns—that are commonly thought to feature asymmetric effects.

The estimated GARCH(1,1) model is:

$$x_{t+1} = \underset{(0.000)}{0.046} + \underset{(0.000)}{0.125}\,\varepsilon_t + \varepsilon_{t+1} \quad \varepsilon_{t+1} \text{ IID } N(0, \sigma^2_{t+1|t})$$

$$\sigma^2_{t+1|t} = \underset{(0.000)}{0.008} + \underset{(0.000)}{0.090}\,\varepsilon^2_t + \underset{(0.000)}{0.904}\,\sigma^2_{t|t-1}$$

implying $\overline{\sigma}^2 = 0.008/(1-0.090-0.904) = 1.339$, that is, a volatility of 1.157% per day. The estimated EGARCH(3,3) model of course cannot have problems caused by negatively signed coefficients:

$$x_{t+1} = \underset{(0.000)}{0.023} + \underset{(0.000)}{0.121}\,\varepsilon_t + \varepsilon_{t+1} \quad \varepsilon_{t+1} \text{ IID } N(0, \sigma^2_{t+1|t})$$

$$\begin{aligned}\ln \sigma^2_{t+1|t} = &- \underset{(0.000)}{0.006} + \underset{(0.000)}{0.108}|z_t| - \underset{(0.000)}{0.063}|z_{t-1}| - \underset{(0.000)}{0.037}|z_{t-2}| - \underset{(0.000)}{0.171}z_t + \underset{(0.000)}{0.180}z_{t-1} \\ &- \underset{(0.208)}{0.011}z_{t-2} + \underset{(0.000)}{1.792}\ln \sigma^2_{t|t-1} - \underset{(0.000)}{0.693}\ln \sigma^2_{t-1|t-2} - \underset{(0.000)}{0.099}\ln \sigma^2_{t-2|t-3}.\end{aligned}$$

This process implies an odd, mixed leverage effect, because negative returns from the previous business day increase predicted variance, but negative returns from two previous business days depress it.

In Fig. 5.10, we compare in two different ways the predicted 1-day-ahead volatility filtered from the two different models.

Clearly, the variance forecasts are not radically different. However, the rightmost scatter plot (especially the kernel regression that we have plotted as a boldfaced curve) shows that when volatility is predicted to be high, then often GARCH(1,1) predicts a higher level than EGARCH(3,3) does. It is not clear whether this may be sensible, of course. As usual, we have therefore tested the two models for their ability to predict squared realized residuals, obtaining:

$$\text{GARCH}(1,1):\ \varepsilon^2_{t+1} = \underset{(0.037)}{0.131} + \underset{(0.018)}{0.841}\,(\sigma^{GARCH}_{t+1|t})^2 + e_{t+1|t} \quad R^2 = 13.6\%$$

$$\text{EGARCH}(3,3) = \varepsilon^2_{t+1} = -\underset{(0.039)}{0.221} + \underset{(0.025)}{1.303}\,(\sigma^{EGARCH}_{t+1|t})^2 + e_{t+1|t} \quad R^2 = 16.5\%.$$

Interestingly, while in the case of GARCH(1,1), we obtain a result virtually identical to Example 5.10— that is, the intercept is significantly positive, the slope coefficient significantly different from one, and the regression R^2 mediocre—in the case of EGARCH the R^2 increases somewhat, but the results on the intercept and slope are qualitatively similar, even though now the intercept is negative and the EGARCH predictions seem to underreact to the arrival of information versus what realized squared residuals do. Such a difference, that is, the fact that the estimated slope coefficient increases from 0.84 to 1.30 when going from GARCH to EGARCH derives from the tendency of forecasts in the latter model to be smoother and to vary less, probably insufficiently. Finally, also in these results we can read evidence of how difficult it is to improve over a simple GARCH(1,1) model, the point made by Hansen and Lunde (2005).

---

8. Unfortunately, the E-Views environment offers a rich selection of commands to estimate GARCH models, but in no case constraints (either to ensure positivity or to enforce covariance stationarity) can be imposed. Interestingly, Nelson's (1991) original application to daily excess stock returns had returned an EGARCH(2,2) as the best fitting one.

TABLE 5.11 Information Criteria-Based Model Selection

Conditional Mean Model	Conditional Variance Model	p	q	Total Number of Parameters	Saturation Ratio	Maximized Log-Likelihood	BIC	Hannan–Quinn	AIC
MA(1)	Homoskedastic	0	0	3	4531.3	− 19069.6	2.8070	2.8063	2.8059
MA(1)	RiskMetrics	1		3	4531.3	− 16359.7	2.4090	2.4079	2.4073
MA(1)	*GARCH(1,1)*	*1*	*1*	*5*	*2718.8*	− 16255.1	*2.3950*	*2.3932*	*2.3922*
MA(1)	GARCH(2,1)**	2	1	6	2265.7	− 16254.0	2.3956	2.3933	2.3922
MA(1)	GARCH(1,2)	1	2	6	2265.7	− 16254.5	2.3956	2.3934	2.3923
MA(1)	GARCH(2,2)**	2	2	7	1942.0	− 16216.6	2.3907	2.3882	2.3869
MA(1)	GARCH(3,3)**	3	3	9	1510.4	− 16215.5	2.3920	2.3887	2.3870
MA(1)	EGARCH(1,1)	1	1	6	2265.7	− 16060.5	2.3671	2.3649	2.3638
MA(1)	EGARCH(2,1)	2	1	8	1699.3	− 16027.1	2.3636	2.3606	2.3592
MA(1)	EGARCH(1,2)	1	2	8	1699.3	− 16054.6	2.3669	2.3643	2.3630
MA(1)	EGARCH(2,2)	2	2	9	1510.4	− 16057.5	2.3687	2.3654	2.3638
MA(1)	**EGARCH(3,3)**	**3**	**3**	**12**	**1132.8**	− 15933.4	**2.3526**	2.3482	2.3459
MA(1)	EGARCH(4,4)	4	4	15	906.3	**− 15922.3**	2.3530	**2.3475**	**2.3448**

**Some of the ML estimates of GARCH coefficients turned out to be negative.

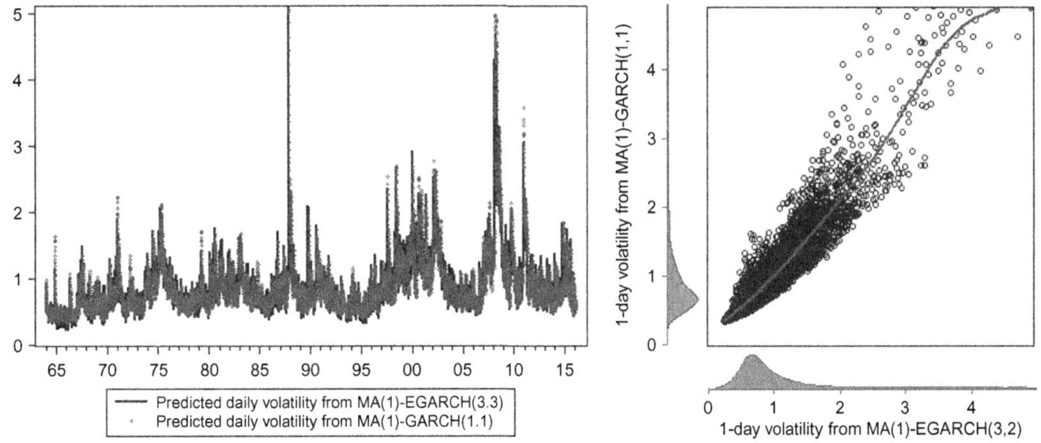

FIGURE 5.10 Comparing GARCH and EGARCH volatility predictions.

5.2.6 A Few Additional, Popular ARCH Models

Before closing this section presenting and offering examples concerning a few more ARCH-type models, we hasten to emphasize that not only listing and discussing all possible GARCH models would deserve an entire book (and in fact a few such books exist, see, among others Francq and Zakoïan, 2011, and Gouriéroux, 1997) but also that probably such a task would even be impossible because of the sheer number of models that have been developed and presented in the literature. For instance, Bollerslev (2009) published a simple glossary that compiled a list of 139 different GARCH-type models, when also a few "multivariate" twists and strands were included! In addition, since 2009, of course, a few more types of GARCH models have appeared. In the interest of parsimony, we shall organize this section in a series of short subsections keeping details and technicalities to the bare minimum.

5.2.6.1 The Threshold GARCH (TARCH) Model

Threshold ARCH and Threshold GARCH(p,d,q), introduced independently by Zakoïan (1994) and Glosten et al. (1993), are described by the definition that follows.

DEFINITION 5.4 (Threshold GARCH)

In a threshold GARCH(p, d, q) model for conditional variance, forecasts depend on a (non-negatively) weighted sum of the sign and the size of past squared errors and on past variance forecasts:

$$\sigma^2_{t+1|t} = \omega + \sum_{i=1}^{p} \alpha_i \varepsilon^2_{t-i+1} + \sum_{l=1}^{d} \delta_l I\{\varepsilon_{t-l+1} < 0\} \varepsilon^2_{t-l+1} + \sum_{j=1}^{q} \beta_j \sigma^2_{t-j+1|t-j}$$
$$I\{\varepsilon_{t-l+1} < 0\} = \begin{cases} 1 & \text{if } \varepsilon_{t-l+1} < 0 \\ 0 & \text{if } \varepsilon_{t-l+1} \geq 0 \end{cases}, \tag{5.45}$$

where $\omega > 0$, $\alpha_1, \alpha_2, \ldots, \alpha_p \geq 0$, $\delta_1, \delta_2, \ldots, \delta_d \geq 0$, $\beta_1, \beta_2, \ldots, \beta_q \geq 0$, and $\sum_{i=1}^{p} \alpha_i + \frac{1}{2}\sum_{l=1}^{d} \delta_l + \sum_{j=1}^{q} \beta_j < 1$ is necessary and sufficient for covariance stationarity.

Assuming for simplicity $p = d$, in this model good news and bad news have differential effects on conditional variance; past good news ($\varepsilon_{t-l+1} \geq 0$) at a lag of l periods has an impact of α_i, while bad news ($\varepsilon_{t-l+1} < 0$) has an impact of $\alpha_i + \delta_i$. Of course, p could differ from d but when $p = q = 1$, as typical, of course, there is little space for additional action. If $\delta_i > 0$, bad news increases volatility, and we say that there is a leverage effect of the ith order. Clearly, the standard GARCH(p, q) is a special case of the Threshold GARCH model where the number of threshold terms, d, is set to 0.

Under Eq. (5.45), the ARMA structure implied by the model becomes a nonlinear one and the unconditional variance of the process, *under covariance stationarity*, has a slightly different formula when compared to Eq. (5.36). For instance, in the threshold GARCH(1,1,1) case, we have:

$$\begin{aligned} &\sigma^2_{t+1|t} = \omega + \alpha\varepsilon^2_t + \delta I_{\{\varepsilon_t < 0\}}\varepsilon^2_t + \beta\sigma^2_{t|t-1} \\ &\Rightarrow \overline{\sigma}^2 \equiv E[\sigma^2_{t+1|t}] = \omega + \alpha E[\varepsilon^2_t] + \delta E[I_{\{\varepsilon_t < 0\}}\varepsilon^2_t] + \beta E[\sigma^2_{t|t-1}] \\ &\Rightarrow \overline{\sigma}^2 = \omega + \alpha\overline{\sigma}^2 + \frac{1}{2}\delta\overline{\sigma}^2 + \beta\overline{\sigma}^2 \Rightarrow \overline{\sigma}^2 = \frac{\omega}{1 - \alpha - 0.5\delta - \beta}, \end{aligned} \tag{5.46}$$

where $E[I_{\{\varepsilon_t < 0\}}\varepsilon^2_t] = E[I_{\{\varepsilon_t < 0\}}]E[\varepsilon^2_t] = 0.5\overline{\sigma}^2$ holds for all symmetric distributions with zero mean, for which the magnitude of ε_t and therefore of its square does not depend on the sign of ε_t and

$$E\left[I_{\{\varepsilon_t < 0\}}\right] = \Pr(\varepsilon_t < 0) = \frac{1}{2}. \tag{5.47}$$

More generally, a simple extension of the algebra shown above, leads to:

$$\overline{\sigma}^2 = \frac{\omega}{1 - \sum_{i=1}^{p} \alpha_i - \frac{1}{2}\sum_{l=1}^{d} \delta_l - \sum_{j=1}^{q} \beta_j}. \tag{5.48}$$

One online example compares the different degree of estimated exposure to asymmetries of different asset classes. The example finds that stock return data contain strong evidence of a need to incorporate asymmetries in GARCH models; bond returns data do not, and economically it would be more complex to find any justification for such asymmetries. On the opposite, the frequency of the data does not seem to be crucial: stock index returns data contain leverage both at daily and monthly frequency and over two quite different time periods.

5.2.6.2 The Power ARCH and NAGARCH Models

Taylor (1986) and Schwert (1989) introduced a standard deviation GARCH model, where it is the standard deviation to be modeled rather than the variance:

$$\sigma_{t+1|t} = \omega + \sum_{i=1}^{p} \alpha_i |\varepsilon_{t-i+1}| + \sum_{j=1}^{q} \beta_j \sigma_{t-j+1|t-j}. \tag{5.49}$$

This model was generalized by Ding et al. (1993) to a flexible *Power ARCH* specification. In the Power ARCH (p,d,q) model, the power parameter of the standard deviation can be estimated rather than imposed, and additional terms/parameters are added to capture asymmetry of up to order $d \leq p$:

$$\sigma^{\gamma}_{t+1|t} = \omega + \sum_{i=1}^{p} \alpha_i (|\varepsilon_{t-i+1}| - \delta_i \varepsilon_{t-i+1})^{\gamma} + \sum_{j=1}^{q} \beta_j \sigma^{\gamma}_{t-j+1|t-j}, \tag{5.50}$$

where $\gamma > 0$, $|\delta_i| \leq 1$ for $i = 1, 2, \ldots, d$ and $\delta_i = 0$ for $i > d$ (this allows to place a cap on the number of asymmetric terms that the model contains). For $\gamma = 1$ and $d = 0$, one obtains the symmetric standard deviation model of Taylor and Schwert; for $\gamma = 2$ and $d = 0$, this is a standard GARCH(p,q) model; for $\gamma = 2$ and $d \geq 1$, this becomes a threshold GARCH(p,d,q) model, called *quadratic ARCH* (QARCH). When $\gamma = 1$ and $p = d$, this is similar to the Zakoïan's (1994) threshold GARCH, which is often written as:

$$\begin{aligned}\sigma_{t+1|t} = \omega &+ \sum_{i=1}^{p} [\alpha_i I\{\varepsilon_{t-l+1} \geq 0\} |\varepsilon_{t-i+1}| + \delta_i I\{\varepsilon_{t-i+1} < 0\} |\varepsilon_{t-i+1}|] \\ &+ \sum_{j=1}^{q} \beta_j \sigma_{t-j+1|t-j}.\end{aligned} \tag{5.51}$$

Clearly, in Eq. (5.51) variance forecasts depend on both the size and the sign of past residuals, thereby allowing for the leverage effect in return volatility. Higgins and Bera (1992) dealt with the case:

$$\sigma^{\gamma}_{t+1|t} = \omega + \sum_{i=1}^{p} \alpha_i |\varepsilon_{t-i+1}|^{\gamma} + \sum_{j=1}^{q} \beta_j \sigma^{\gamma}_{t-j+1|t-j}, \tag{5.52}$$

and called this model nonlinear ARCH or NARCH. Another related example is Heston and Nandi's (2000) *nonlinear asymmetric GARCH or NAGARCH*:

$$\begin{aligned}\sigma^2_{t+1|t} &= \omega + \sum_{i=1}^{p} \alpha_i (\varepsilon_{t-i+1} - \delta_i \sigma_{t-i+1|t-i})^2 + \sum_{j=1}^{q} \beta_j \sigma^2_{t-j+1|t-j} \\ &= \omega + \sum_{i=1}^{p} \alpha_i (\sigma_{t-i+1|t-i} z_{t-i+1} - \delta_i \sigma_{t-i+1|t-i})^2 + \sum_{j=1}^{q} \beta_j \sigma^2_{t-j+1|t-j} \\ &= \omega + \sum_{i=1}^{p} \alpha_i \sigma^2_{t-i+1|t-i} (z_{t-i+1} - \delta_i)^2 + \sum_{j=1}^{q} \beta_j \sigma^2_{t-j+1|t-j},\end{aligned} \tag{5.53}$$

which features a mix of past squared standardized residuals multiplied by past forecasts of variance on the right-hand side. For instance, in the empirically popular NAGARCH(1,1) case, we have:

$$\begin{aligned}\sigma^2_{t+1|t} &= \omega + \alpha(\varepsilon_t - \delta\sigma_{t|t-1})^2 + \beta\sigma^2_{t|t-1} = \omega + \alpha\sigma_{t|t-1}(z_t - \delta)^2 + \beta\sigma^2_{t|t-1} \\ &= \omega + \alpha\sigma^2_{t|t-1} z_t^2 + \alpha\delta^2\sigma^2_{t|t-1} - 2\alpha\delta\sigma^2_{t|t-1} z_t + \beta\sigma^2_{t|t-1} \\ &= \omega + \alpha\varepsilon_t^2 + (\beta + \alpha\delta^2 - 2\alpha\delta z_t)\sigma^2_{t|t-1} \\ &= \omega + \alpha\varepsilon_t^2 + \beta'\sigma^2_{t|t-1} - 2\alpha\delta z_t \sigma^2_{t|t-1} \quad \beta' \equiv \beta + \alpha\delta^2,\end{aligned} \tag{5.54}$$

where $\beta' > \beta$ when $\alpha > 0$. NAGARCH(1,1) is:

- *Asymmetric*, because if $\delta \neq 0$, then the impact of a past squared standardized shock (for given $\sigma^2_{t|t-1} = \sigma^2$) is proportional to $\alpha\sigma^2 z_t^2 - 2\alpha\delta\sigma^2 z_t$ which is no longer a simple, symmetric quadratic function of standardized residuals, differently from a plain vanilla GARCH(1,1); equivalently, and assuming $\delta > 0$, while $\varepsilon_t \geq 0$ impacts conditional variance only as $(\varepsilon_t - \delta\sigma_t)^2 < \varepsilon_t^2$, $\varepsilon_t < 0$ impacts conditional variance by $(\varepsilon_t - \delta\sigma_t)^2 > \varepsilon_t^2$.[9]

9. When $\delta < 0$, the asymmetry remains, but in words, while $\varepsilon_t < 0$ impacts conditional variance only by $(\varepsilon_t - \delta\sigma_t)^2 < \varepsilon_t^2$, $\varepsilon_t \geq 0$ impacts conditional variance in the measure $(\varepsilon_t - \delta\sigma_t)^2 > \varepsilon_t^2$. This means that $\delta > 0$ captures a left asymmetry consistent with a leverage effect and in which negative returns increase variance more than positive returns do; $\delta < 0$ captures instead a right asymmetry that we shall encounter soon in our examples.

- *Nonlinear*, because NAGARCH(1,1) may be written as:

$$\sigma^2_{t+1|t} = \omega + \alpha\varepsilon_t^2 + (\beta' - 2\alpha\delta z_t)\sigma^2_{t|t-1} = \omega + \alpha\varepsilon_t^2 + \beta(z_t)\sigma^2_{t|t-1}, \quad (5.55)$$

where $\beta(z_t) \equiv \beta' - 2\alpha\delta z_t$ is a function that makes the beta coefficient of the GARCH dependent on lagged standardized residuals. Here the claim of nonlinearity follows from the fact that a model that is written using a linear affine functional form (i.e., $f(x) = a + bx$) but in which some or all coefficients depend on their turn on the conditioning variables or information (i.e., $f(x) = a_x + b_x x$, in the sense that $a_x = a(x)$ and/or $b_x = b(x)$) is a nonlinear model, to be precise, a *time-varying coefficient model*.[10]

NAGARCH plays a key role in option pricing with stochastic volatility because it allows us to derive closed-form expressions for European option prices in spite of its rich, asymmetric volatility dynamics. Because a NAGARCH may be written as $\sigma^2_{t+1|t} = \omega + \alpha\sigma^2_{t|t-1}(z_t - \delta)^2 + \beta\sigma^2_{t|t-1}$ and, at least when $z_t \sim N(0, 1)$, z_t is independent of $\sigma^2_{t|t-1}$ as $\sigma^2_{t|t-1}$ just depends on an infinite number of *past* squared returns, it is possible to easily derive the long-run, unconditional variance under NAGARCH(1,1) and the assumption of stationarity:[11]

$$\begin{aligned} E[\sigma^2_{t+1|t}] &= \bar{\sigma}^2 = \omega + \alpha E[\sigma^2_{t|t-1}(z_t - \delta)^2] + \beta E[\sigma^2_{t|t-1}] \\ &= \omega + \alpha E[\sigma^2_{t+1|t}]E[z_t^2 + \delta^2 - 2\delta z_t] + \beta E[\sigma^2_{t+1|t}] \\ &= \omega + \alpha\bar{\sigma}^2(1 + \delta^2) + \beta\bar{\sigma}^2, \end{aligned} \quad (5.56)$$

where $\bar{\sigma}^2 = E[\sigma^2_{t+1|t}]$ and $E[\sigma^2_{t+1|t}] = E[\sigma^2_{t|t-1}]$ because of stationarity. Therefore,

$$\bar{\sigma}^2\left[1 - \alpha(1 + \delta^2) - \beta\right] = \omega \Rightarrow \bar{\sigma}^2 = \frac{\omega}{1 - \alpha(1 + \delta^2) - \beta}, \quad (5.57)$$

which exists and is positive if and only if $\alpha(1 + \delta^2) + \beta < 1$. This has two implications: (1) the persistence index of a NAGARCH(1,1) is $\alpha(1 + \delta^2) + \beta$ and not simply $\alpha + \beta$; (2) a NAGARCH(1,1) model is stationary if and only if $\alpha(1 + \delta^2) + \beta < 1$.

Example 5.15 shows how arbitrary it may be to impose a typical quadratic, conditional variance-centered structure instead of letting the data express themselves through power ARCH models.

EXAMPLE 5.15

In this example, we start by estimating a simple, asymmetric Gaussian PARCH(1,1,1) model for daily 1963–2016 excess returns data, obtaining (the *p*-values for γ are reported to the right of the point estimate):

$$x_{t+1} = \underset{(0.001)}{0.022} + \underset{(0.000)}{0.126}\varepsilon_t + \varepsilon_{t+1} \quad \varepsilon_{t+1}\ \text{IID}\ N(0, \sigma^2_{t+1|t})$$

$$\sigma_{t+1|t}^{1.187(0.000)} = \underset{(0.000)}{0.012} + \underset{(0.000)}{0.078}(|\varepsilon_t| - \underset{(0.000)}{0.596}\varepsilon_t)^{1.187(0.000)} + \underset{(0.000)}{0.922}\sigma_{t+1|t}^{1.187(0.000)}.$$

The two plots in Fig. 5.11 show the differences between a standard threshold GARCH(1,1,1) and a power GARCH(1,1,1) model in which γ is estimated to be $1.187 < 2$ (in fact, the standard error of the estimate is 0.054, which means that the estimate significantly differs from both 1, that is, Taylor's standard deviation GARCH, and 2, which is the classical GARCH). As one may expect, as past shocks are here raised to a power which is much less than 2, PARCH volatility forecasts are less spiky versus those from a threshold GARCH; as a result, in the rightmost plot, a range of dots corresponding to GARCH volatility forecasts between 2% and 3% per day are matched by PARCH predictions of about 2%. However, once the differences in parameter estimates and functional form are factored in, we find that the two sets of forecasts are not so different (their correlation is 0.987).

(Continued)

10. While in a standard linear model the derivatives with respect to the regressors are constant, $df(x)/dx = b$, in a time-varying coefficient model this is potentially not the case as $df(x)/dx = [da(x)/dx] + [db(x)/dx]\cdot x + b(x)$ which may not be constant.

11. The claim that $\sigma^2_{t|t-1}$ is a function of an infinite number of past squared returns derives from the fact that under GARCH, we know that the process of squared returns follows (under appropriate conditions) a stationary ARMA. You know from Chapter 2 that any ARMA has an autoregressive infinite representation.

EXAMPLE 5.15 (Continued)

After performing a by-now standard model specification search based on information criteria, Table 5.12 documents instead the type of heterogeneity that exists across different series and portfolios. For a change, we also investigate power ARCH estimates for daily 1963–2016 returns on three additional factor portfolios commonly used in asset pricing research and asset management: small minus big (SMB) that represents the return of a strategy that buys large stocks and short small ones; high minus low (HML) that buys value (as captured by a high book-to-market ratio) stocks and short growth ones (as captured by a low book-to-market ratio); momentum that buys past 12-month winner stocks to sell losing stocks.

Table 5.12 shows that power GARCH also dominates over standard GARCH models, including threshold GARCH. Moving from the top to the bottom of the table, models of increasing complexity and including asymmetric effects yield the best trade-off between in-sample fit (an increasing maximized log-likelihood) and parsimony, as captured by the penalty terms of the information criteria. In the case of SMB, a PARCH(2,1,1) prevails in which $\hat{\gamma} = 1.626$ (standard error is 0.070); in the case of HML returns, we report evidence in favor of PARCH(2,2,1) model in which $\hat{\gamma} = 1.981$ (standard error is 0.104 which implies that we cannot reject the null that a quadratic, GARCH-type model, called NARCH(2,1), would be appropriate in this case); finally, when it comes to returns on the momentum-sorted portfolio, we report evidence in favor of an even richer PARCH(2,2,2) with $\hat{\gamma} = 1.281$ (standard error is 0.074).

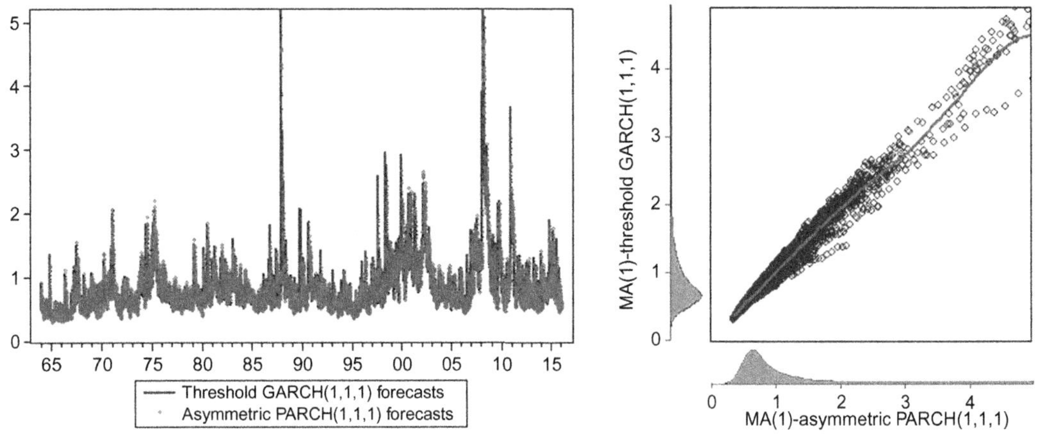

FIGURE 5.11 In-sample volatility forecasts from T-GARCH and PARCH.

TABLE 5.12 Information Criteria-Based Model Selection for Different Data

Conditional Mean Model	Conditional Variance Model	*p*	*d*	*q*	Maximized Log-Likelihood	BIC	Hannan–Quinn	AIC
				SMB Portfolio Returns From CRSP				
ARMA(1,1)	Homoskedastic	0	0	0	−10407.8	1.5335	1.5323	1.5318
ARMA(1,1)	GARCH(1,1)	1	0	1	−8245.2	1.2174	1.2151	1.2140
ARMA(1,1)	T-GARCH(1,1)	1	1	1	−8234.4	1.2174	1.2151	1.2140
ARMA(1,1)	SYMM PARCH(1,0,1)	1	0	1	−8244.2	1.2179	1.2153	1.2140
ARMA(1,1)	ASYMM PARCH(1,1,1)	1	1	1	−8232.3	1.2169	1.2139	1.2124
ARMA(1,1)	*ASYMM PARCH(2,1,1)*	*2*	*1*	*1*	*−8205.2*	*1.2136*	*1.2103*	1.2086
ARMA(1,1)	ASYMM PARCH(2,2,1)	2	2	1	−8203.9	1.2141	1.2104	1.2086
ARMA(1,1)	ASYMM PARCH(2,2,2)	2	2	2	−8201.8	1.2145	1.2104	*1.2084*
ARMA(1,1)	ASYMM PARCH(3,3,3)**	3	3	3	−8170.1	1.2119	1.2068	1.2042

(Continued)

TABLE 5.12 (Continued)

Conditional Mean Model	Conditional Variance Model	p	d	q	Maximized Log-Likelihood	BIC	Hannan–Quinn	AIC
				HML Book-to-Market Portfolio Returns From CRSP				
MA(1)	Homoskedastic	0	0	0	−9737.2	1.4348	1.4337	1.4331
MA(1)	GARCH(1,1)	1	0	1	−5974.7	0.8833	0.8811	0.8800
MA(1)	T-GARCH(1,1)	1	1	1	−5969.8	0.8833	0.8807	0.8794
MA(1)	SYMM PARCH(1,0,1)	1	0	1	−5974.6	0.8840	0.8814	0.8801
MA(1)	ASYMM PARCH(1,1,1)	1	1	1	−5969.4	0.8839	0.8810	0.8795
MA(1)	ASYMM PARCH(2,1,1)	2	1	1	−5940.5	0.8804	0.8770	0.8754
MA(1)	*ASYMM PARCH(2,2,1)*	*2*	*2*	*1*	*−5936.3*	*0.8804*	*0.8767*	*0.8749*
MA(1)	ASYMM PARCH(2,2,2)**	2	2	2	−5923.0	0.8792	0.8751	0.8731
MA(1)	ASYMM PARCH(3,3,3)**	3	3	3	−5918.3	0.8806	0.8754	0.8729
				Winner-Minus-Losers Portfolio Returns From CRSP				
AR(1)	Homoskedastic	0	0	0	−14169.2	2.0862	2.0855	2.0851
AR(1)	GARCH(1,1)	1	0	1	−9100.7	1.3426	1.3407	1.3398
AR(1)	T-GARCH(1,1)	1	1	1	−9100.4	1.3432	1.3410	1.3399
AR(1)	SYMM PARCH(1,0,1)	1	0	1	−9082.3	1.3405	1.3383	1.3372
AR(1)	ASYMM PARCH(1,1,1)	1	1	1	−9082.2	1.3412	1.3386	1.3373
AR(1)	ASYMM PARCH(2,1,1)	2	1	1	−9063.3	1.3391	1.3362	1.3347
AR(1)	ASYMM PARCH(2,2,1)	2	2	1	−9055.0	1.3386	1.3353	1.3336
AR(1)	*ASYMM PARCH(2,2,2)*	*2*	*2*	*2*	*−9042.2*	*1.3374*	*1.3337*	*1.3319*
AR(1)	ASYMM PARCH(3,3,3)**	3	3	3	−9020.7	1.3364	1.3316	1.3292

**Some of the ML estimates of GARCH coefficients turned out to be negative.

Finally, note that in the (1,1,1) and $\gamma = 2$ case, the power GARCH model in Eq. (5.50) simplifies to:

$$\begin{aligned}\sigma^2_{t+1|t} &= \omega + \alpha(|\varepsilon_t| - \delta\varepsilon_t)^2 + \beta\sigma^2_{t|t-1} \\ &= \omega + \alpha\sigma^2_{t|t-1}(|z_t| - \delta z_t)^2 + \beta\sigma^2_{t|t-1},\end{aligned} \tag{5.58}$$

which is a special case of NAGARCH. Therefore, Example 5.15 is also about NAGARCH, although in the example, we never find evidence of an estimate of exactly $\gamma = 2$.

5.2.6.3 *The Component GARCH Model and the Differences Between Transitory and Permanent Variance Components*

The conditional variance process in a plain vanilla GARCH(1,1) model shows mean reversion to $\overline{\sigma}^2 = \omega/(1 - \alpha - \beta)$, which is a constant at all times. Engle and Lee (1999) have generalized GARCH to a *component GARCH (C-GARCH) model* that allows mean reversion to a varying level or—equivalently—that incorporates a distinction between transitory and permanent conditional variance dynamics:

$$\begin{aligned}\sigma^2_{t+1|t} &= v^2_{t+1|t} + \alpha(\varepsilon^2_t - v^2_{t|t-1}) + \beta(\sigma^2_{t|t-1} - v^2_{t|t-1}) \\ v^2_{t+1|t} &= \omega + \psi(v^2_{t|t-1} - \omega) + \zeta(\varepsilon^2_t - \sigma^2_{t|t-1}),\end{aligned} \tag{5.59}$$

(here the model is presented with reference to the simple (1,1) case, but see below for a different interpretation). In Eq. (5.59), the first equation represents the dynamics of the *transitory variance component* which, by construction, converges to $v^2_{t+1|t}$. The second equation therefore represents the dynamics of the *long-term or permanent variance component*. Simple algebra shows that Eq. (5.59) may be rewritten as:

$$\begin{aligned}(\varepsilon^2_{t+1} - v^2_{t+1|t}) &= (\alpha + \beta)(\varepsilon^2_t - v^2_{t|t-1}) - \beta\eta_t + \eta_{t+1} \quad \alpha + \beta < 1, \alpha, \beta \geq 0 \\ (v^2_{t+1|t} - \omega) &= \psi(v^2_{t|t-1} - \omega) + \zeta\eta_t \quad \omega > 0, \quad 0 \leq \psi < 1, \zeta \geq 0.\end{aligned} \tag{5.60}$$

This shows that the transitory component for ε^2_{t+1} is the usual ARMA(1,1) process that converges to $v^2_{t+1|t}$ at the persistence rate given by the index $\alpha + \beta < 1$. The permanent component is instead an AR(1)-type process, the persistence of which depends on ψ.

Interestingly, one can combine the transitory and permanent component to write:

$$\begin{aligned}
\sigma^2_{t+1|t} &= v^2_{t+1|t} + \alpha(\varepsilon^2_t - v^2_{t|t-1}) + \beta(\sigma^2_{t|t-1} - v^2_{t|t-1}) \\
&= v^2_{t+1|t} - (\alpha+\beta)v^2_{t|t-1} + \alpha\varepsilon^2_t + \beta\sigma^2_{t|t-1} \\
&= (1-\psi)\omega - (\alpha+\beta)(1-\psi)\omega + \psi\underbrace{\left[v^2_{t|t-1} - (\alpha+\beta)v^2_{t-1|t-2}\right]}_{\sigma^2_{t|t-1} - \alpha\varepsilon^2_{t-1} - \beta\sigma^2_{t-1|t-2}} \\
&\quad + \zeta(\varepsilon^2_t - \sigma^2_{t|t-1}) - (\alpha+\beta)\zeta(\varepsilon^2_{t-1} - \sigma^2_{t-1|t-2}) + \alpha\varepsilon^2_t + \beta\sigma^2_{t|t-1} \\
&= (1-\alpha-\beta)(1-\psi)\omega + \psi[\sigma^2_{t|t-1} - \alpha\varepsilon^2_{t-1} - \beta\sigma^2_{t-1|t-2}] + (\alpha+\zeta)\varepsilon^2_t \\
&\quad + (\beta-\zeta)\sigma^2_{t|t-1} - (\alpha+\beta)\zeta(\varepsilon^2_{t-1} - \sigma^2_{t-1|t-2}) \\
&= (1-\alpha-\beta)(1-\psi)\omega + (\alpha+\zeta)\varepsilon^2_t - [\psi\alpha + (\alpha+\beta)\zeta]\varepsilon^2_{t-1} \\
&\quad + (\psi+\beta-\zeta)\sigma^2_{t|t-1} - [\psi\beta + (\alpha+\beta)\zeta]\sigma^2_{t-1|t-2},
\end{aligned} \tag{5.61}$$

which shows that the component model is a (nonlinear) restricted GARCH(2,2) model, $\sigma^2_{t+1|t} = \lambda_0 + \lambda_1\varepsilon^2_t + \lambda_2\varepsilon^2_{t-1} + \lambda_3\sigma^2_{t|t-1} + \lambda_4\sigma^2_{t-1|t-2}$ in which

$$\begin{aligned}
&\lambda_0 = (1-\alpha-\beta)(1-\psi)\omega > 0 \quad \lambda_1 = (\alpha+\zeta) \geq 0 \quad \lambda_2 = -[\psi\alpha + (\alpha+\beta)\zeta] < 0 \\
&\lambda_3 = (\psi+\beta-\zeta) \quad \lambda_4 = -[\psi\beta + (\alpha+\beta)\zeta] < 0.
\end{aligned} \tag{5.62}$$

We go from Eqs. (5.59) to (5.61) simply by plugging the function for the permanent variance component inside the temporary variance component and noting the recurring relationship $v^2_{t|t-1} - (\alpha+\beta)v^2_{t-1|t-2} = \sigma^2_{t|t-1} - \alpha\varepsilon^2_{t-1} - \beta\sigma^2_{t-1|t-2}$. This is interesting because one often wonders about the actual use of GARCH(p, q) when $p \geq 2$ and $q \geq 2$. In fact, higher-order GARCH models are rarely used in practice, and this GARCH(2,2) case represents one of the few cases in which—even though it is subject to constraints coming from the structure of Eq. (5.60)—implicitly, through the component GARCH case, a (2,2) model has been used in many practical applications. Even though by construction the corresponding GARCH(2,2) always gives positive variance components, its coefficients in Eq. (5.62) are not all positive (in fact, two out of five are guaranteed to be negative). Apart from the case at hand, this is a powerful proof of the fact that setting all coefficients to be non-negative in GARCH(p, q) is certainly sufficient but never necessary to guarantee that the resulting variance forecast be positive at all times.

In the literature, we have had also variations of C-GARCH(p, d, q) models that have included leverage-type asymmetric effects in the short-run conditional variance equation:

$$\begin{aligned}
\sigma^2_{t+1|t} &= v^2_{t+1|t} + \textstyle\sum_{i=1}^{p^T} \alpha_i(\varepsilon^2_{t-i+1} - v^2_{t-i+1|t-i}) + \sum_{i=1}^{d} \delta_i I_{\{\varepsilon_{t-i+1}<0\}}(\varepsilon^2_{t-i+1} - v^2_{t-i+1|t-i}) \\
&\quad + \textstyle\sum_{j=1}^{q^T} \beta_j(\sigma^2_{t-j+1|t-j} - v^2_{t-j+1|t-j}) \\
v^2_{t+1|t} &= \omega + \textstyle\sum_{j=1}^{q^P} \psi_j(v^2_{t-j+1|t-j} - \omega) + \sum_{i=1}^{p^P} \zeta_i(\varepsilon^2_{t-i+1} - \sigma^2_{t-i+1|t-i}),
\end{aligned} \tag{5.63}$$

where the superscript "T" refers to the transitory components of conditional variance and the transcript "P" to the permanent component. This model combines the component model with the asymmetric threshold GARCH model, introducing asymmetric effects in the transitory equation.

Example 5.16 shows practical implementations of component GARCH models.

EXAMPLE 5.16

In this example, we compare the importance of distinguishing between transitory and permanent GARCH components using two of the key series that we have been analyzing up to this point. We start with weekly 1982–2016 data on the negative of the differences in 10-year US Treasury rates. As we know, in this case the data contain no evidence of leverage effects: past negative and positive news affect subsequent variance in the same way. Therefore, we start off by comparing a plain vanilla GARCH(1,1) model—that in Example 5.12 turned out to provide a good fit to these data—with a CGARCH(1,1). The ML estimate of the Gaussian GARCH(1,1) was (p-values are in parentheses):

$$\begin{aligned}
R_{t+1} &= \underset{(0.169)}{0.003} + \underset{(0.000)}{0.230}R_t + \varepsilon_{t+1} \quad \varepsilon_{t+1} \text{ IID } N(0, \sigma^2_{t+1|t}) \\
\sigma^2_{t+1|t} &= \underset{(0.003)}{0.0002} + \underset{(0.000)}{0.073}\varepsilon^2_t + \underset{(0.000)}{0.910}\,\sigma^2_{t|t-1}.
\end{aligned}$$

(Continued)

EXAMPLE 5.16 (Continued)

The component model estimates are instead:

$$R_{t+1} = \underset{(0.212)}{0.003} + \underset{(0.000)}{0.231} R_t + \varepsilon_{t+1} \quad \varepsilon_{t+1} \text{ IID } N(0, \sigma^2_{t+1|t})$$
$$\sigma^2_{t+1|t} = v^2_{t+1|t} - \underset{(0.010)}{0.055}(\varepsilon^2_t - v^2_{t|t-1}) + \underset{(0.491)}{0.275}(\sigma^2_{t|t-1} - v^2_{t|t-1})$$
$$v^2_{t+1|t} = \underset{(0.000)}{0.014} + \underset{(0.000)}{0.977}(v^2_{t|t-1} - \underset{(0.000)}{0.014}) + \underset{(0.000)}{0.096}(\varepsilon^2_t - \sigma^2_{t|t-1}).$$

Interestingly, while the permanent component features a standard and precisely estimated GARCH(1,1), the transitory variance component is rather weak. The left panel of Fig. 5.12 shows both series of predicted variances. In this case, most of the variance on government bond returns is estimated to come from the permanent component, with transitory variance generally small, scarcely persistent, and in an economic perspective, used to fit occasional weeks of low volatility, when the temporary component gives a negative contribution. Of course, $\sigma^2_{t+1|t} - v^2_{t+1|t} = -0.055(\varepsilon^2_t - v^2_{t|t-1}) + 0.275(\sigma^2_{t|t-1} - v^2_{t|t-1})$ is a scarcely persistent ARMA(1,1) process, so that the high-frequency movements in the temporary component in the leftmost plot do not come as a surprise. The rightmost panel shows instead that, even though a CGARCH(1,1) model is in fact a restricted GARCH(2,2) model, it gives forecasts that are very hard to be told apart from a plain vanilla GARCH(1,1). A further look clarifies why GARCH(1,1), GARCH(2,2), and CGARCH(1,1) (that as we know is a restricted GARCH(2,2)) give maximized log-likelihoods of 1425.64, 1426.922, and 1426.921, respectively, that is, the improvement we can achieve using models more complex than a GARCH(1,1) are modest; in fact, a BIC criterion that penalizes complexity scores −1.5426, −1.5358, and −1.5358 again, so that the choice clearly falls on the simplest of the models.

This first portion of the example may lead us to think that component GARCH models are of dubious practical relevance. However, when estimation is applied to 1963–2016 US daily excess stock returns data, the model selection in Table 5.13 makes us think differently:

On the one hand, the component GARCH model is not clearly rejected, especially when asymmetries are taken into account (the BIC declines from 2.3908 to 2.3837). On the other hand, the CGARCH still has problems outperforming a simpler threshold GARCH(2,1,1).[12] Therefore, if any, a preference for a component GARCH must come from the existence of economic reasons. Before tackling this issue, we present ML estimates of the CGARCH(1,1,1):

$$x_{t+1} = \underset{(0.000)}{0.037} + \underset{(0.000)}{0.117}\varepsilon_t + \varepsilon_{t+1} \quad \varepsilon_{t+1} \text{ IID } N(0, \sigma^2_{t+1|t})$$
$$\sigma^2_{t+1|t} = v^2_{t+1|t} + \underset{(0.000)}{0.017}(\varepsilon^2_t - v^2_{t|t-1}) + \underset{(0.000)}{0.112} I_{\{\varepsilon_t < 0\}}(\varepsilon^2_t - v^2_{t|t-1})$$
$$+ \underset{(0.000)}{0.889}(\sigma^2_{t|t-1} - v^2_{t|t-1})$$
$$v^2_{t+1|t} = \underset{(0.000)}{0.558} + \underset{(0.000)}{0.995}(v^2_{t|t-1} - \underset{(0.000)}{0.558}) + \underset{(0.000)}{0.033}(\varepsilon^2_t - \sigma^2_{t|t-1}),$$

which shows that the asymmetric effect is precisely estimated.

Fig. 5.13 shows in-sample predicted standard deviation from the model. In this case, temporary variance deviations from long-run variance show some persistence. A few well-known volatility spikes such as the Fall of 1987, the Fall of 2008, and again the sovereign debt jitters of the Fall 2010 are mainly captured as temporary spikes in volatility.

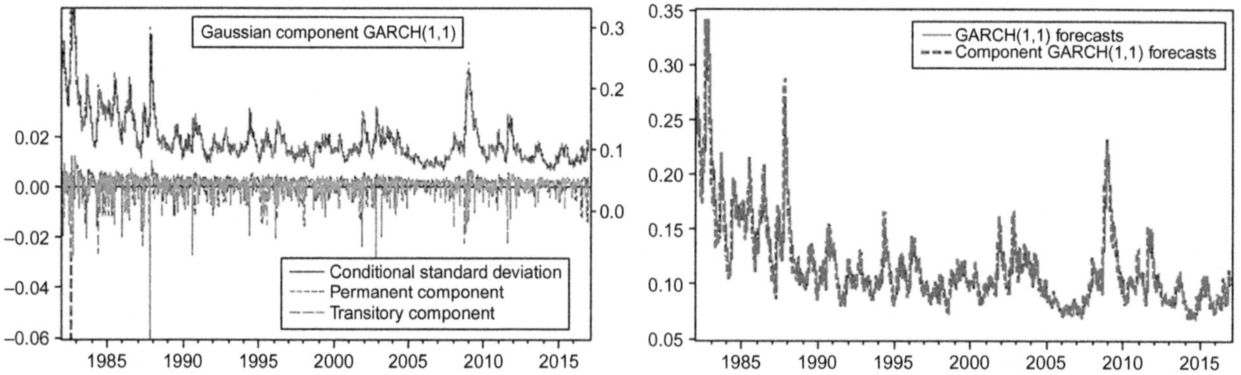

FIGURE 5.12 In-sample volatility forecasts from C-GARCH versus GARCH.

12. Our attempt to estimate richer, asymmetric CGARCH(2,2,1) and (2,2,2) models with custom-written algorithms has met with hard-to-overcome numerical convergence issues.

TABLE 5.13 Information Criteria-Based Model Selection

Conditional Mean	Conditional Variance Model	*p*	*d*	*q*	No. of Parameters	Saturation Ratio	Maximized Log-Likelihood	BIC	Hannan–Quinn	AIC
MA(1)	Homoskedastic	0	0	0	3	4531.3	− 19069.6	2.8070	2.8063	2.8059
MA(1)	GARCH(1,1)	1	0	1	5	2718.8	− 16255.1	2.3950	2.3932	2.3922
MA(1)	GARCH(2,2)	2	0	2	6	2265.7	− 16216.6	2.3907	2.3882	2.3869
MA(1)	T-GARCH (1,1,1)	1	1	1	6	2265.7	− 16103.9	2.3735	2.3713	2.3702
MA(1)	*T-GARCH (2,2,1)*	*2*	*2*	*1*	*8*	*1699.3*	*− 16091.2*	*2.3730*	*2.3700*	*2.3686*
MA(1)	Comp. GARCH(1,1)	1	0	1	7	1942.0	− 16217.1	2.3908	2.3882	2.3870
MA(1)	Component Asymmetry. GARCH(1,1,1)	1	1	1	8	1699.3	− 16163.6	2.3837	2.3807	2.3792

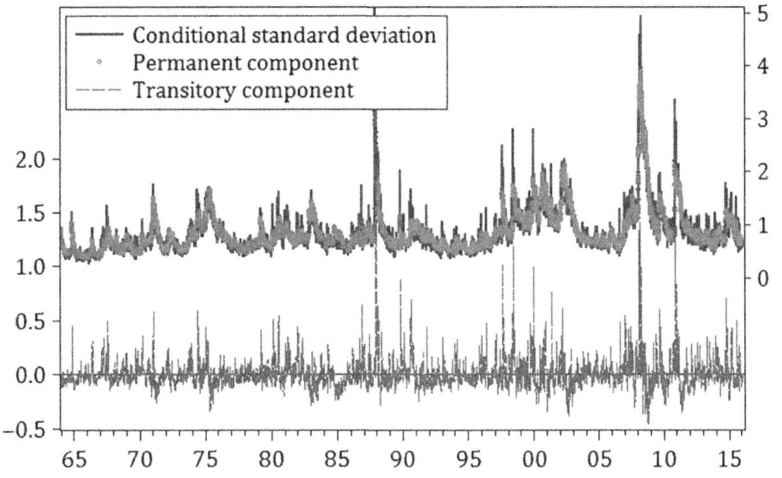

FIGURE 5.13 Volatility forecasts from asymmetric component GARCH(1,1,1).

Even though they may not always represent the best fitting models, CGARCH may have a crucial asset pricing justification: it may be often optimal that the fair price of certain securities (think of long-term options, sometimes called *leaps*) and a few types of financial decisions (such as portfolio weights for the long-run) may not be made to depend on short-run spikes and alterations in predicted conditional variance. In this case, a CGARCH model that maintains a distinction between $\sigma^2_{t+1|t}$ and $v^2_{t+1|t}$ may serve the purpose, as in the recent option pricing application by Christoffersen et al. (2008).

5.2.6.4 *The GARCH-In-Mean Model*

So far, we have rigidly and somewhat artificially kept distinct the conditional variance from the conditional mean specifications, apart from one obvious fact: the residuals that a conditional variance model uses must be estimated by subtracting from the available time series some estimates of their conditional mean. On the contrary, Engle et al. (1987) introduced a specification that ought to capture one of the basic tenets of modern finance: many theories call for an explicit linear relationship between the expected returns and variance, or at least the covariance among returns and some notion of benchmark or market portfolio. For instance, in Merton's (1973) *intertemporal capital asset pricing model (CAPM) model*, the expected excess return on the market portfolio is linear in its conditional *variance* under the assumption of a representative agent with log utility. In more general settings, the conditional covariance with an appropriately defined benchmark portfolio often serves to price all assets. For example, according to the traditional CAPM the excess returns on all risky assets are proportional to the non-diversifiable risk as measured by their covariances with market portfolio returns. This implies that the expected excess return on the market portfolio is simply proportional to its own conditional variance as in the univariate Merton (1973) model.

The ARCH in mean, or ARCH-M, model was designed to capture such relationships.

DEFINITION 5.5 (ARCH-in mean)

In a ARCH-M model the conditional mean is an explicit function of the conditional variance,

$$R_{t+1} = \underbrace{\mu'_{t+1|t} + g(\sigma^2_{t+1|t})}_{\mu_{t+1|t}} + \sigma_{t+1|t} z_{t+1} \quad z_{t+1} \text{ IID } (0, 1) \tag{5.64}$$

with $g(\sigma^2_{t+1|t})$ possibly linear, like in $g(\sigma^2_{t+1|t}) = \gamma\sigma^2_{t+1|t}$ or nonlinear as in $g(\sigma^2_{t+1|t}) = \gamma'\sigma_{t+1|t}$, with the former model supported by Merton's intertemporal CAPM.

For $\gamma \neq 0$, the risk premium will be time-varying and could even change sign if $\sigma^2_{t+1|t} < -\mu'_{t+1|t}/\gamma$ but $\mu'_{t+1|t} < 0$. Moreover, under an ARCH-M model, any time variation in $\sigma^2_{t+1|t}$ will result in serial correlation in the process for returns, which is often realistic. We often expect the coefficients γ and γ' to be positive, what has been often dubbed a "first fundamental law of finance," even though as early as in Backus and Gregory (1993), examples were given of a negative relation between return and variance that is consistent with equilibrium.

Because of the explicit dependence of the conditional mean on the conditional variance and/or covariance, several unique problems arise in the estimation and testing of ARCH-M models. For instance, while in Section 5.6 we shall explain that estimation of ARCH model may sometimes be performed sequentially by QMLE, consistent estimation of the parameters in ARCH-M models generally requires that both the conditional mean and variance functions be correctly specified and estimated simultaneously.

As first noted by French et al. (1987), GARCH-in mean effects provide a second explanation, along with the leverage effect, for volatility asymmetries. If volatility risk is priced, an anticipated increase in volatility will raise the required rate of return and necessitate an immediate asset price decline in order to allow for higher future returns. This causality from volatility to prices has been labeled the *volatility feedback effect.* Although it suggests a causal effect opposite to the leverage effect, which involves the reverse causality from returns to volatility, the two may be observationally equivalent if the causality lag is smaller than the time between observations.

5.3 ADVANCED UNIVARIATE VOLATILITY MODELING

5.3.1 Non-Gaussian Marginal Innovations

Up to this point, we have specified and estimated only GARCH models characterized by normal standardized errors. Although this is prevalent in practice (the exact reasons will be explained in Section 5.6 that deals with estimation methods), this is often not optimal. One way to see it is that when the data have been truly generated by:

$$R_{t+1} = \mu_{t+1|t} + \varepsilon_{t+1} = \mu_{t+1|t} + \sigma_{t+1|t} z_{t+1}, \quad z_{t+1} \text{ IID } D(0, 1; \boldsymbol{\delta}), \tag{5.65}$$

(where $\boldsymbol{\delta}$ is a vector of unknown parameters and for some generic distribution D with zero mean and unit variance, that is, that has been standardized), even though the conditional mean and variance functions $\mu_{t+1|t}$ and $\sigma^2_{t+1|t}$ were correctly specified, estimating instead:

$$R_{t+1} = \mu_{t+1|t} + \varepsilon_{t+1} = \mu_{t+1|t} + \sigma_{t+1|t} z_{t+1}, \quad z_{t+1} \text{ IID } N(0, 1), \tag{5.66}$$

where the generic distribution $D(0, 1; \boldsymbol{\delta})$ is incorrectly specified to be Gaussian (or, equivalently, $\boldsymbol{\delta}$ has been incorrectly set to values such that the generic distribution D collapses to a Normal) cause the resulting ML estimates to be inefficient or even inconsistent.

One way to see this is with reference to Fig. 5.14 in which for a typical time series of financial returns (these are daily value-weighted excess US returns), we present two *kernel density plots* (see Appendix A).

The leftmost plot concerns the original data and—by comparison with the dashed normal density with the same mean and variance as the data—clearly shows their leptokurtic nature. The rightmost plot shows that the standardized residuals from a threshold GARCH(1,1,1) with Gaussian shocks follow a distribution that is much closer to a normal

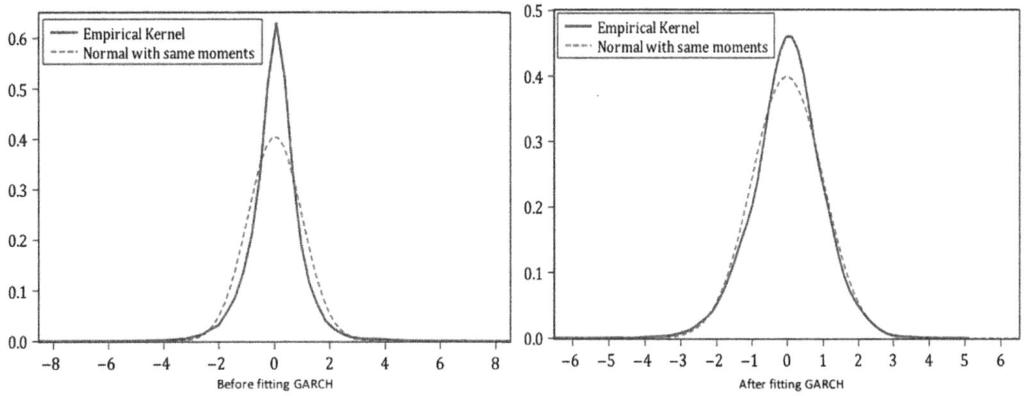

FIGURE 5.14 Kernel density estimators of model residuals.

density than the original data. Yet, the differences between the estimated empirical kernel density and the dashed Gaussian benchmark remain visible and illustrate that a simple GARCH modeling strategy may be inadequate, without further adjustments to the assumed marginal density of the errors.

The issue is then whether the data may require (i.e., be generated from a process that features) errors drawn from a non-normal distribution, and of what kind this distribution may be. One robust but technically involved idea is that one may escape the full specification of $D(0,1;\boldsymbol{\delta})$ to be replaced instead by a *nonparametric or semiparametric GARCH model*. Among a few other cases, Engle and Gonzalez-Rivera (1991) have proposed a two-step procedure in which in the first step, they obtain QML estimates of the parameters of the model using the Gaussian likelihood. In the second step, the density of the residuals standardized by their estimated conditional standard deviations is estimated using a linear spline with smoothness priors. However, kernel estimators could have been used as well. The estimated density is then taken to be the true density and the new likelihood function is maximized. In a Monte Carlo study, they show that this approach improves the efficiency beyond QMLE, particularly when the density was highly non-normal and skewed.

A more classical option consists instead in proposing an alternative *parametric specification*. Already in the 1990s the financial econometrics literature (see Francq and Zakoïan, 2011) has often advocated the advantages of assuming that the standardized residuals from CH models follow a *symmetric t-Student*, with density:

$$f_t(z_{t+1};\nu)=\frac{\Gamma\left(\frac{\nu+1}{2}\right)}{\Gamma(\nu/2)\sqrt{\pi(\nu-2)}}\left(1+\frac{z_{t+1}^2}{\nu-2}\right)^{-\frac{\nu+1}{2}}, \tag{5.67}$$

where $\nu>2$ (a parameter often referred to as the number of "degrees of freedom," although in our application it will be allowed to be a real number) and $\Gamma(\cdot)$ is the gamma function,

$$\Gamma(\nu)=\int_0^\infty e^{-l}l^{\nu-1}dl \tag{5.68}$$

with well-known recursive properties, that is, $\Gamma(\nu+1)=\nu\Gamma(\nu)$, and $\Gamma(1)=1$, so that $\Gamma(2)=2$, $\Gamma(3)=6$, etc., or $\Gamma(\nu+1)=\nu!$ in the case of positive integers. Because of the very definition of Nepero's number "e" and the continuity of $1+1/n$, one has that:

$$\lim_{\nu\to\infty}\left(1+\frac{1}{\nu}\right)^{-\nu}=\left[\lim_{\nu\to\infty}\left(1+\frac{1}{n}\right)^{\nu}\right]^{-1}=e^{-1}, \tag{5.69}$$

and

$$\begin{aligned}\lim_{\nu\to\infty}f_t(z_{t+1};\nu)&=\frac{\Gamma\left(\frac{\nu}{2}+\frac{1}{2}\right)}{\Gamma\left(\frac{\nu}{2}\right)\sqrt{\pi(\nu-2)}}\left[\left(1+\frac{z_{t+1}^2}{\nu-2}\right)^{\nu+1}\right]^{-\frac{1}{2}}\\&=\frac{1}{\sqrt{2\pi}}\exp\left(-\frac{1}{2}z_{t+1}^2\right)=\phi(z_{t+1}),\end{aligned} \tag{5.70}$$

where $\phi(z_{t+1})$ is the standard normal distribution: as the number of degrees of freedom diverges to infinity, a *t*-Student distribution converges to a standard Gaussian; therefore, the *t*-Student nests the Gaussian, that is, in practice the data may be informative enough to tell us whether their underlying DGP was (approximately) normal or not. In practice, a useful rule-of-thumb is that when ν is large and exceeds 20, then for applied purposes $f_t(z_{t+1};\nu)$ may be well approximated by a normal distribution.

The comparison between the *t*-Student probability density function (PDF) in Eq. (5.67) and the limit standard normal density in Eq. (5.70) allows us to make a further point. As a modeling strategy, adopting the PDF in Eq. (5.67) gives an advantage over Eq. (5.70) for a mechanical reason: the former is a negative power function, the tails of which decay to 0 at a speed that is given by the power $-\nu/2$; the lower is ν, the slower is the rate at which the tails decay to 0 as $z_{t+1} \to \pm\infty$. The latter PDF is instead of a well-known negative exponential type: because of the famous result in Eq. (5.69), a negative exponential represents the functional specification, the tails of which go to 0 faster among all functions. Indeed, we obtain Eq. (5.70) as a limit of Eq. (5.67) as $\nu \to \infty$. For instance, for $z=4$ (which may be interpreted as meaning four standard deviations away from the mean) while $exp[-0.5\times(4)^2]=0.000336$, under a negative power function with $\nu=10$, we have $[1+(4)^2/8]^{-11/2}=0.002376$. The latter probability is then $(0.002376/0.000336)\cong 7.08$ times larger. If we repeat this experiment considering a really large, extreme realization, say some (standardized) return 12 times away from the sample mean (say a -9.5% return on a given day), then $exp[-0.5\times(12)^2]=5.38E-32$ which is basically 0 (this means impossible, and yet how many -10% did we really see in the Fall of 2008?), while $[1+(12)^2/8]^{-11/2}=9.27E-08$. Although also the latter number is definitely small, the ratio between the two probabilities $(9.27E-08/5.38E-32)$ becomes astronomical $(1.72E-24)$: events that are impossible under a Gaussian distribution become rare but billions of billions of times more likely under a fat-tailed, *t*-Student distribution. Therefore, switching from a normal to a *t*-Student distribution represents a natural and relatively costless way to capture the leptokurtic nature of financial data.

EXAMPLE 5.17

In this example, we consider a flexible model, a threshold GARCH(1,1,1) that clearly also nests symmetric GARCH(1,1) models, to show what difference it makes in empirical applications the specification of the distribution of the shocks as either normally or *t*-Student distributed, with ν degrees of freedom. We do this with reference to a variety of time series, to offer an overview of the implications of assuming z_{t+1}IID $t(\nu)$. Table 5.14 documents a few key results. Below the coefficient estimates, we report *p*-values but we also boldface the significant estimates.

Table 5.14 contains interesting findings and debunks a few common beliefs that do not seem to find support in the data. First, both the accurately estimated values for v—always below 20 and often below 5—and (unreported) information criteria confirm that all the data under consideration require a *t*-Student assumption for their innovations in place of a classical Gaussian structure. Second, contrary to what is sometimes reported, it is not true that as the frequency of data declines (from daily, to weekly, to monthly), the need for *t*-Student innovation disappears. It may be instead the type of financial series to drive such a feature: for instance, intermediate- and long-term government bond returns seem to display less thick tails and hence they demand with less strength a *t*-Student assumption. However, 1-year Treasury bill returns imply an estimate of ν of 5.5 only. Third, it is often argued that modeling *t*-Student shocks would be useful to capture volatility spikes and returns in the extreme tails without forcing GARCH models to become near-integrated, displaying an excessive persistence, close to 1. In Table 5.14, this does not occur: the last column calculates the differential in estimated persistence when going from Gaussian to *t*-Student shocks; although according to popular beliefs, we should only find negative values in this column and these are expected to be substantial (to give an idea, at least 10% of a typical GARCH persistence, that tends to range between 0.90 and 0.99), the data give us frequent evidence of a persistence that *increases* in *t*-Student models (consider the US monthly equity returns), while also the negative differentials are modest at best. Fourth, as it should be expected under an ML estimation strategy, changing the assumptions on the distribution of the shocks affects all parameter estimates and their *p*-values, even though—with limited exceptions—in Table 5.14, we find only modest differences; for instance, there is only weak evidence of leverage in monthly stock returns and in weekly bond returns, and this does not appear to depend on whether the shocks are assumed to be normal or not.

How different will the variance forecasts be under normality versus *t*-Student errors? In a few cases shown in Table 5.14, an inspection makes it obvious that the differences will be modest at most: the estimated ML coefficients are very similar independently of the assumption on the distribution of the shocks, even though the estimate of ν is consistently below 10. However, in other cases—think of the case of Singapore's stock returns (in USD)—we observe rather different parameter estimates and a loss in implied persistence that we cannot easily map into a perception of heterogeneity in variance forecasts. For the case of Singapore, Fig. 5.15 offers additional evidence. We note that differences are not major, but especially in correspondence to volatility spikes (in excess of 14%–15% per month), a *t*-Student GARCH tends to forecast slightly larger volatility surges than GARCH does.

TABLE 5.14 Comparing ML Estimates of Gaussian Versus *t*-Student GARCH

Data	ML Estimates of threshold Gaussian GARCH(1,1)							ML Estimates of threshold t-Student GARCH(1,1)								Δ Persistence
	ϕ_0	ϕ_1	θ	ω	α	δ	β	ϕ_0	ϕ_1	θ	ω	α	δ	β	υ	
Daily Excess Equity Returns, 1963–2016																
Excess market	**0.023**	0.083	0.047	**0.009**	**0.023**	**0.113**	**0.911**	**0.040**	−0.027	**0.149**	**0.007**	**0.024**	**0.111**	**0.914**	**7.809**	0.003
	0.000	0.218	0.481	0.000	0.000	0.000	0.000	0.000	0.710	0.034	0.000	0.000	0.000	0.000	0.000	
SMB (size)	0.000	**0.882**	**−0.811**	**0.002**	**0.066**	**0.030**	**0.916**	0.001	**0.912**	**−0.848**	**0.001**	**0.052**	**0.029**	**0.930**	**9.105**	−0.0005
	0.614	0.000	0.000	0.000	0.000	0.000	0.000	0.060	0.000	0.000	0.000	0.000	0.000	0.000	0.000	
HML (value)	**0.009**	**0.430**	**−0.246**	**0.002**	**0.097**	**−0.019**	**0.905**	**0.007**	**0.445**	**−0.259**	**0.001**	**0.081**	**−0.015**	**0.920**	**9.083**	0.001
	0.000	0.000	0.000	0.000	0.000	0.000	0.000	0.001	0.000	0.000	0.000	0.000	0.017	0.000	0.000	
Momentum	**0.025**	**0.342**	**−0.076**	**0.002**	**0.123**	−0.005	**0.879**	**0.031**	**0.374**	**−0.110**	**0.003**	**0.121**	**−0.002**	**0.879**	**7.465**	−0.0005
	0.000	0.000	0.019	0.000	0.000	0.418	0.000	0.000	0.000	0.001	0.000	0.000	0.861	0.000	0.000	
Weekly Approximate Treasury Returns, 1982–2016																
1 year	−0.001	0.145	0.109	3.1E-06	**0.137**	0.020	**0.876**	−0.001	0.163	0.106	5.9E-06	**0.121**	0.043	**0.876**	**5.521**	−0.0045
	0.560	0.141	0.278	0.108	0.000	0.129	0.000	0.517	0.064	0.233	0.105	0.000	0.112	0.000	0.000	
5 years	0.002	0.108	0.149	**1.5E-05**	**0.068**	0.002	**0.922**	0.002	0.159	0.108	**1.5E-05**	**0.060**	0.001	**0.929**	**10.13**	−0.0015
	0.407	0.251	0.121	0.006	0.000	0.872	0.000	0.361	0.077	0.236	0.017	0.000	0.966	0.000	0.000	
10 years	0.004	−0.023	0.267	**2.5E-05**	**0.074**	0.006	**0.905**	0.004	0.026	0.224	**2.4E-05**	**0.066**	0.001	**0.915**	**13.72**	−0.0005
	0.198	0.811	0.005	0.003	0.000	0.674	0.000	0.135	0.786	0.018	0.008	0.000	0.931	0.000	0.000	
Monthly Equity Returns, 1977–2016																
United States	0.563	0.427	−0.352	**7.994**	0.068	**0.482**	**0.424**	0.250	**0.775**	**−0.756**	**4.235**	0.042	**0.337**	**0.655**	**7.684**	0.1325
	0.262	0.380	0.487	0.000	0.065	0.000	0.001	0.377	0.002	0.005	0.009	0.163	0.008	0.000	0.000	
United Kingdom	0.008	**0.988**	**−0.996**	**1.066**	0.051	**0.073**	**0.877**	0.006	**0.991**	**−0.996**	**1.557**	0.057	0.090	**0.845**	**8.141**	−0.0175
	0.237	0.000	0.000	0.013	0.111	0.035	0.000	0.316	0.000	0.000	0.050	0.261	0.173	0.000	0.000	
Italy	**1.310**	−0.520	**0.592**	5.366	**0.089**	0.023	**0.801**	**1.291**	**−0.558**	**0.636**	2.786	**0.082**	0.042	**0.851**	**9.558**	0.0525
	0.027	0.140	0.078	0.085	0.013	0.577	0.000	0.019	0.039	0.012	0.166	0.027	0.417	0.000	0.029	
Singapore	0.513	0.468	−0.370	**1.787**	**0.204**	−0.022	**0.795**	0.343	**0.689**	**−0.624**	**2.868**	**0.182**	0.077	**0.753**	**5.035**	−0.0145
	0.147	0.141	0.273	0.001	0.000	0.646	0.000	0.243	**0.007**	**0.027**	0.027	0.017	0.432	0.000	0.000	

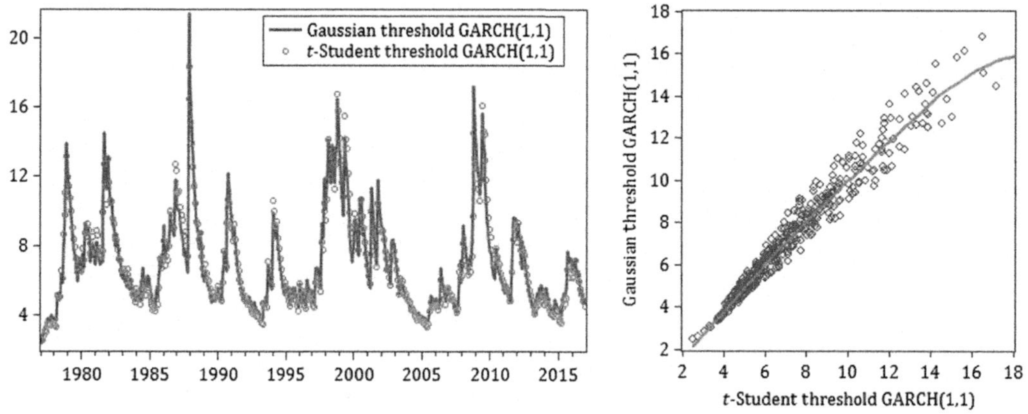

FIGURE 5.15 Volatility forecasts from Gaussian versus *t*-Student threshold GARCH(1,1) applied to Singapore's monthly returns in USD.

Assuming the moments exist, the *t*-Student distribution is characterized by the following moments:

$$E[z_{t+1};\nu]=0, \quad Var[z_{t+1};\nu]=\frac{\nu}{\nu-2}$$
$$Skew[z_{t+1};\nu]=0, \quad Kurt[z_{t+1};\nu]=3+\frac{6}{\nu-4}. \tag{5.71}$$

Visibly, it is a zero-mean, symmetric distribution, the variance of which exists if and only if ν exceeds 2, as assumed. More interestingly, the fourth moment exists if and only if $\nu>4$.[13] In general, given $\nu>2$, only the first $\text{int}(\nu-\varepsilon)$ moments exist, where $int(\bullet)$ is the integer part of a real number, $\varepsilon>0$ is a number as small as we like, and considering the integer part of $\nu-\varepsilon$ ensures that if ν is already an integer, then only the first $\nu-1$ moments exist. For instance, if $\nu=3$, then only mean and variance exist and skewness is not 0, it is simply not defined; if $\nu=3.001$, then mean, variance, and skewness exist, with both mean and skewness equal to 0.

Because of the moments in Eq. (5.71), note that when in Eq. (5.65) $D(0,1;\boldsymbol{\delta})$ corresponds to a *t*-Student with ν degrees of freedom (so that $\boldsymbol{\delta}=\nu$), then:

$$E_t[R_{t+1}]=E_t[\mu_{t+1|t}]+E_t[\sigma_{t+1|t}z_{t+1}]=\mu_{t+1|t}+\sigma_{t+1|t}\underbrace{E_t[z_{t+1}]}_{=0}=\mu_{t+1|t}$$

$$Var_t[R_{t+1}]=\underbrace{Var_t[\mu_{t+1|t}]}_{=0}+Var_t\left[\sigma_{t+1|t}z_{t+1}\right]=\sigma^2_{t+1|t}Var_t[z_{t+1}]=\frac{\nu}{\nu-2}\sigma^2_{t+1|t}$$

$$Skew_t[R_{t+1}]\equiv\frac{E_t[R^3_{t+1}]}{\sigma^3_{t+1|t}}=\underbrace{Skew_t[\mu_{t+1|t}]}_{=0}+\underbrace{Skew_t[z_{t+1}]}_{=0}=0$$

$$Kurt_t[R_{t+1}]\equiv\frac{E_t[R^4_{t+1}]}{(Var_t[R_{t+1}])^2}=\frac{1}{(Var_t[R_{t+1}])^2}\underbrace{E_t[\mu^4_{t+1|t}]}_{=0}+\frac{\sigma^4_{t+1|t}}{(Var_t[R_{t+1}])^2}E_t\left[z^4_{t+1|t}\right]$$
$$=\frac{\sigma^4_{t+1|t}E_t[z^4_{t+1|t}]}{(\sigma^2_{t+1|t}Var_t[z_{t+1}])^2}=\frac{E_t[z^4_{t+1|t}]}{(Var_t[z_{t+1}])^2}=Kurt_t[z_{t+1}]=3+\frac{6}{\nu-4}. \tag{5.72}$$

13. Existence of moments is equivalent to the fact that the expression for the moment does not diverge to $\pm\infty$. Clearly, for $\nu<2$ both variance and kurtosis appear to be negative, which cannot be and indicates that these formulas should not be used. For $\nu=2$, variance explodes to $+\infty$ and kurtosis is zero, which cannot be. For $2<\nu<4$, variance exists but kurtosis is negative (but the formula remains meaningless). For $\nu=4$, variance exists (it equals 2) but kurtosis diverges to $+\infty$. Finally, for $\nu>4$, all the four moments exist.

There are three sets of interesting implications:

- In the case of a t-Student conditional variance model, it is no longer the case that $\sigma^2_{t+1|t}$ measures a time-t forecast of one-step-ahead variance: although $\sigma^2_{t+1|t}$ is proportional to conditional variance $Var_t[R_{t+1}]$ and it drives its variation over time, conditional variance exceeds $\sigma^2_{t+1|t}$:

$$Var_t[R_{t+1}] = \frac{\nu}{\nu-2}\sigma^2_{t+1|t} > \sigma^2_{t+1|t}. \tag{5.73}$$

The larger such a difference is, the closer the parameter ν is to 2 (from the right).

- When $\nu > 4$, $Kurt_t[R_{t+1}] = 3 + \frac{6}{\nu-4} > 3$ and the adoption of a t-Student marginal density for the shocks in a GARCH model ends up creating excess kurtosis versus a Gaussian benchmark.
- When ν diverges to $+\infty$ and the t-Student converges to a normal distribution, then:

$$\begin{aligned} &E_t[R_{t+1}] = \mu_{t+1|t} \quad \lim_{\nu\to\infty} Var_t[R_{t+1}] = \lim_{\nu\to\infty}\frac{\nu}{\nu-2}\sigma^2_{t+1|t} = \sigma^2_{t+1|t} \\ &Skew_t[R_{t+1}] = 0 \quad \lim_{\nu\to\infty} Kurt_t(R_{t+1}) = \lim_{\nu\to\infty}\left(3+\frac{6}{\nu-4}\right) = 3, \end{aligned} \tag{5.74}$$

which is exactly the classical result under a standard normal distribution.

Importantly, adopting a t-Student distribution as the marginal density for the IID shocks of a GARCH model ends up creating *positive conditional excess kurtosis* and not only positive unconditional kurtosis. Formally:

$$\begin{aligned} Kurt(R_{t+1}) &\equiv \frac{E[\sigma^4_{t+1|t} z^4_{t+1}]}{(Var[R_{t+1}])^2} \geq \frac{E[z^4_{t+1}]\left(E[\sigma^2_{t+1|t}]\right)^2}{\bar{\sigma}^4} \\ &= \left(3+\frac{6}{\nu-4}\right) = Kurt_t(R_{t+1}) > 3, \end{aligned} \tag{5.75}$$

which means that t-Student GARCH models create unconditional kurtosis both directly, through the conditional excess kurtosis implied by the very shocks assumed in the model, and indirectly, because of the time variation of conditional variance that is typical of GARCH models. As a result, unconditional excess kurtosis will be even higher than conditional excess kurtosis, even though they will be both positive.

An online example documents both the difference between conditional and unconditional excess kurtosis, and how such moments come to depend on the parameters of the process that here are simply assumed instead of being estimated. Using numerical examples, it becomes visible how in practice the sources of excess kurtosis, volatility clustering, and fat-tailed shocks may compound to give massively thick tails and that there are powerful interaction effects between the thick tails generated by GARCH and the tails of the marginal density that characterizes the assumed t-Student shocks. Here the peril is that by incorrectly assuming Gaussian shocks in all circumstances, a researcher may force her GARCH model to express too high a persistence just because implicitly the parameter ν is forced to diverge to infinity while the data would often "prefer" smaller values.

Another common alternative distribution for shocks in the GARCH literature is the *Generalized Error Distribution* (GED, also called generalized normal distribution), whose standardized density is:

$$f_t(z_{t+1}; \lambda) = \frac{\lambda}{\sqrt{2}\Gamma(1/\lambda)}\exp(-|z_{t+1}|)^{\lambda} \quad \lambda > 0, \tag{5.76}$$

where λ is the tail parameter. Clearly, because $\Gamma(1/\lambda) = \sqrt{\pi}$, when $\lambda = 2$, Eq. (5.76) becomes the PDF of a standard normal distribution (apart from a scaling factor). In fact, Eq. (5.76) turns into the Laplace distribution for $\lambda = 1$, and as limiting cases it includes all continuous uniform distributions on bounded intervals of the real line (when $\lambda \to \infty$ and on the interval $[-\sqrt{2}, \sqrt{2}]$). This family allows for tails that are either heavier than normal (when $\lambda < 2$) or lighter than normal (when $\lambda > 2$).

The GED implies an excess kurtosis of:

$$ExKurt_t(z_{t+1}) = \frac{\Gamma(5/\lambda)\Gamma(1/\lambda)}{\Gamma(3/\lambda)^2} - 3. \tag{5.77}$$

When $\lambda = 2$, one notes that:

$$ExKurt_t(z_{t+1}) = \frac{1.5\Gamma(3/2)\Gamma(1/2)}{[\Gamma(3/2)]^2} - 3 = \frac{1.5\Gamma(1/2)}{0.5\Gamma(1/2)} - 3 = 0, \tag{5.78}$$

which derives from $\Gamma(n+1) = n\Gamma(n)$. Note that the GED distribution remains however symmetric and implies zero skewness. Interestingly, also the GED nests the normal distribution, as the *t*-Student distribution does. However, while in the case of Eq. (5.67) for all $\nu > 2$, the adoption of a *t*-Student will inflate the tails (only as ν diverges this stops being the case); under a GED, there is enough flexibility for λ to be estimated to be below 2.

EXAMPLE 5.18

In this example, we estimate GARCH models under a variety of distributional assumptions for the standardized shocks of the weekly series of 1-year US Treasury bill annualized *rates* (and not returns, unless an investor has a 1-year horizon). The reason of such a choice is easily seen in Fig. 5.16.

One-year Treasury rates display a distribution with a long, right-tail (sample skewness is 0.46, highly statistically significant) but have no left tail in a classical sense. As a result, the excess kurtosis is slightly negative (−0.29) and any attempt to fit a distribution that is approximately Gaussian or symmetric *t*-Student, may fail as these PDFs cannot fit asymmetries and excessively thin tails. The plot to the right (panel (b)) is a typical quantile–quantile (QQ) plot: if the two distributions represented on the axis were the same, or equivalently, if the data on the horizontal axis came from the theoretical distribution named on the vertical axis, then all dots (each representing the $(1/T)$ *th* percentile, T being the sample size) would fall on the 45-degree line. Clearly, in the case of this series, no values are negative, while under a normal distribution with mean 4.46% and standard deviation of 3.33%, we would expect that approximately 9% of the observations would be negative. Therefore, the left tail of the empirical distribution is too thin. However, too many values do fall between 0% and 0.5%, as shown by a large portion of the low percentiles falling below the 45-degree line. In the right tail, we also detect too high a frequency of rates exceeding 14%, versus what a normal distribution would imply.

Next, we proceed to estimate by ML a GARCH(1,1) model with GED errors, expecting to find an estimate of λ very different from the Gaussian benchmark of 2. Note that this step of the analysis is sensible because standard augmented Dickey–Fuller tests (see Chapter 4) allow us to reject the null hypothesis of a unit root with a *p*-value of 0.035, even though the overall covariance stationarity of this series may remain questionable. The estimated model turns out to be (here y_t represents yields, *p*-values are in parentheses):

$$y_{t+1} = \underset{(0.688)}{0.000} + \underset{(0.000)}{0.999}y_t + \underset{(0.000)}{0.247}\varepsilon_t + \varepsilon_{t+1} \quad \varepsilon_{t+1} \ \text{IID GED}(0, \sigma^2_{t+1|t}; \underset{(0.000)}{1.288})$$
$$\sigma^2_{t+1|t} = \underset{(0.154)}{0.000} + \underset{(0.000)}{0.122}\varepsilon_t^2 + \underset{(0.000)}{0.875}\ \sigma^2_{t|t-1}.$$

As one would expect, the GED parameter λ is estimated to be only 1.29; unsurprisingly such a value differs from 2, even though it turns out to give indication of thicker, not lighter tails versus a normal distribution. This is probably driven by the large frequency mass of data at around 0%.

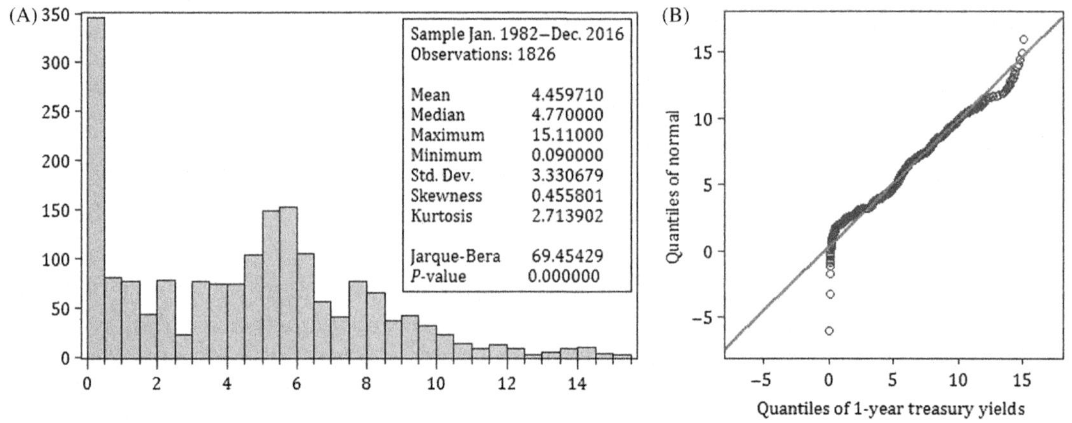

FIGURE 5.16 Empirical estimates of the distribution of 1-year T-bill rates. (A) Histogram and sample statistics. (B) Quantile–quantile plot.

5.3.2 GARCH Models Augmented by Exogenous (Predetermined) Factors

There is also an applied literature that has connected time-varying volatility not only to pure time series features but also to observable economic phenomena, especially at high frequencies, such as daily or weekly. For instance, days where no trading takes place and days of halted trading in the middle of the week will affect the forecast of variance differently when compared to days when trading resumes, that is, days that follow a weekend or a holiday. News tend to cumulate during weekend and holidays and to generate trades, hence price movements and volatility, only when regular trading resumes. For instance, Taylor and Xu (1997) have fit 120 different seasonal factors (representing hours, days, and weeks) to the conditional variance of the log-change in exchange rates. In particular, a rather popular CH model they specify is

$$\begin{aligned}\sigma^2_{t+1|t} &= \omega + \alpha\varepsilon^2_t + \beta\sigma^2_{t|t-1} + \lambda PWH_{t+1} \\ &= \omega + \alpha\sigma^2_{t|t-1}z^2_t + \beta\sigma^2_{t|t-1} + \lambda PWH_{t+1},\end{aligned} \tag{5.79}$$

where PWH (which stands for "post-weekend or holiday") is a (deterministic, hence perfectly predictable on the basis of the exchange trading calendar) *dummy variable* that takes a unit value in correspondence of a day that follows a weekend or a holiday. Note that in this model, the plain vanilla GARCH(1,1) portion (i.e., $\omega + \alpha\varepsilon^2_t + \beta\sigma^2_{t|t-1}$) has been rewritten in a different but completely equivalent way, exploiting the fact that $\varepsilon^2_t = \sigma^2_{t|t-1}z^2_t$ by definition.

Obviously, many alternative models including predetermined variables different from PWH could have been proposed. Other exogenous variables could be last period's trading volume or prescheduled news announcement dates such as company earnings and FOMC (Federal Open Market Committee at the U.S. Federal Reserve) meeting dates. For example, suppose that you want to detect whether the terrorist attacks of September 11, 2001, increased the volatility of stock index returns in the following 3 months. One way to accomplish the task would be to create a dummy variable $D^{09/11}_t$ that equals 0 before September 11, 2001, and equals 1 on that day and until December 10, 2001, and then returns back to a zero value.

EXAMPLE 5.19

Let us try and put at work these ideas to see whether they materially affect either the values of the variance predictions for value-weighted US daily stock *excess* returns over a 1963–2016 sample, or—more importantly—the quality of such predictions as measured (with all the problems and limitations that we have discussed above) by the resulting (in-sample) *root mean squared prediction error* (RMSPE) for squared returns at horizon H:

$$RMSPE(H) = \sqrt{T^{-1}\sum_{t=1}^{T}(R^2_{t+H} - \sigma^2_{t+H|t})^2}.$$

Because this is the most common and useful horizon, in what follows, we shall set $H = 1$ and compute $RMSPE(1)$ for a range of models. These RMSPE measures will be in any event in-sample measures because they are based on full-sample estimates of the parameters of the augmented GARCH(1,1) models. Because we have appreciated in Section 5.3.1 its importance, in this example, we always allow the innovations to be z_{t+1} IID $t(\nu)$. Following earlier findings, we model the conditional mean process as a MA(1) process. For consistency (but this choice could be subject to specification tests), we allow all dummies to appear in the same way both in the conditional mean and the conditional variance processes.

We consider a t-Student GARCH(1,1) model in which the volatility of the 3 months following October 19, 1987 (Black Monday's market crash), September 11, 2001, and the 3 months following the Lehman's Chapter 11 filing (September 15, 2008) are treated as special and therefore "dummied out" within the GARCH volatility process, using specific dummies (p-values are in parentheses):

$$\begin{aligned}x_{t+1} &= \underset{(0.000)}{0.054} + \underset{(0.000)}{0.120}\varepsilon_t + \underset{(0.623)}{0.076}D^{Oct87}_t - \underset{(0.095)}{0.359}D^{Sept01}_t + \underset{(0.977)}{0.006}D^{GFC}_t + \varepsilon_{t+1} \\ \sigma^2_{t+1|t} &= \underset{(0.000)}{0.005} + \underset{(0.000)}{0.082}\varepsilon^2_t + \underset{(0.000)}{0.915}\sigma^2_{t|t-1} + \underset{(0.737)}{0.004}D^{Oct87}_t + \underset{(0.124)}{0.086}D^{Sept11}_t + \underset{(0.694)}{0.010}D^{GFC}_t \\ \varepsilon_{t+1} &\quad \text{IID } t(0, \sigma^2_{t+1|t}; \underset{(0.000)}{7.176}).\end{aligned}$$

In spite of much popular press, there is no compelling statistical evidence that any of these three famous episodes of market disruption have altered the behavior of market excess returns in structural ways. At the margin, there is weak evidence (with p-value around 10%) that in the 3 months following the September 2001 attacks, the market declined in anomalous ways while volatility was structurally high. In fact, while the *RMSPE* when all dummies are ignored is 3.287 (this is expressed in variance units), it increases to 3.826 when the dummies are added, that is, they hurt the ability of the augmented GARCH model to forecast variance, as proxied by squared market excess returns.

A few researchers, see, for example, Poon and Granger (2005), have proposed to use dummy variables to capture particular, known events that may unduly bias the estimation of the classical conditional mean and variance functions because they may generate *outliers*, that is, rare observations that come from a different density versus the bulk of the available observations (i.e., from a different regime, see Chapters 8 and 9 for details). This seems superior to the other, often-practiced solution of omitting outliers from the calculation of the log-likelihood function (i.e., a form of *trimming* or pre-estimation "winsorizing" of the data).

More generally, consider the model (say, for asset returns R_{t+1})

$$R_{t+1} = k_t z_{t+1}, \tag{5.80}$$

where z_{t+1} is IID $D(0, 1)$, D is some distribution left unspecified, and k_t is a random variable observable at time t. Note that while if $k_t = k_0$ $\forall t \geq 1$, R_{t+1} is also $D(0, k_0^2)$ and homoskedastic, when $\{k_t\}_{t=1}^{T}$ is a random process, then $Var_t[R_{t+1}] = k_t^2$. Because we can observe k_t at time t, one can forecast the variance of returns conditioning on the realized value of k_t. Furthermore, if $\{k_t\}_{t=1}^{T}$ were positively serially correlated, then the conditional variance of returns will exhibit positive serial correlation.

The issue is then what variable(s) may enter the model with the role envisioned above. One approach is to try and empirically discover what such variable(s) $\mathbf{K}_t$ may be by using standard regression analysis: we modify the basic model by introducing the coefficients α_0 and $\boldsymbol{\alpha}_1$ (the latter is a vector) and estimate the resulting predictive regression equation in logarithmic form as:

$$\ln(1 + R_{t+1}) = \alpha_0 + \boldsymbol{\alpha}_1 \ln \mathbf{K}_t + e_{t+1}. \tag{5.81}$$

This procedure is simple to implement since the logarithmic transformation results in a linear regression equation; if one ignores issues with the definition of the distributional properties of the original error term (that, for instance, may be advised to be log-normal instead of normally distributed), ordinary least squares (OLS) can be used to estimate α_0 and $\boldsymbol{\alpha}_1$ directly. A major difficulty with this strategy is that it assumes a specific cause for the changing variance. The empirical literature has had a hard time coming up with convincing choices of variables capable to affect the conditional variance of returns. For instance, was it the oil price shocks, a change in the conduct of monetary policy, and/or the breakdown of the Bretton Woods system that was responsible for the volatile exchange rates during the 1970s? On these issues, the jury still seems to be out in spite of decades of intense research efforts (see, e.g., Flood and Rose, 1999).

Among the large number of predetermined variables that have been proposed in the empirical literature, one (family) has recently acquired considerable importance in exercises aimed at forecasting variance: *option implied volatilities*, and in particular the (square of the) CBOE's (Chicago Board Options Exchange) VXO and VIX indices as well as other functions and transformations of the same. In general, models that use explanatory variables to capture time variation in variance are represented as:

$$\sigma_{t+1|t}^2 = \omega + g(\mathbf{X}_t) + \alpha\sigma_{t|t-1}^2 z_t^2 + \beta\sigma_{t-1|t}^2, \tag{5.82}$$

which is one more case of augmented GARCH and in which $\mathbf{X}_t$ is a vector of predetermined variables that may as well include implied volatility. More details on this model, together with an example, can be found online.

5.4 TESTING FOR ARCH

In Section 5.2.4 and Example 5.10, we have introduced and used two common methods to assess the appropriateness of a CH model. While the second of such methods implied the specification and estimation of one regression, the first approach—based on the idea that under correct specification of the CH framework, the standardized residuals ought to be IID—also lends itself to a different, more primitive usage: testing whether the residuals from some conditional mean model contain empirical deviations from IID-ness that a GARCH-type approach may take care of.[14] Because

14. In fairness, variance regression tests could also be used to decide on whether GARCH modeling ought to be evaluated: it is possible to formally test whether simple, primitive GARCH models (say, GARCH(1,1) or even ARCH(1)) provide better forecasts of squared realized residuals than simply a constant, which of course corresponds to the homoskedastic case. Formally, this implies testing whether in the regression $\varepsilon_{t+1}^2 = a + b\sigma_{t+1|t}^2 + e_{t+1|t}$, where $\sigma_{t+1|t}^2$ comes from some CH model, the adjusted R-square exceeds that from $\varepsilon_{t+1}^2 = a + e_{t+1|t}$. Such a test has clearly low power and poses the additional logical challenge that if the null of incremental predictive power cannot be rejected, this may be entirely due to a poor selection of the model that has originated the $\sigma_{t+1|t}^2$ forecasts.

Box–Pierce asymptotic Q tests may be applied to functions that involve the own and cross-serial correlation properties of residuals, these tests can also be turned into formal tests of ARCH-related hypotheses.

5.4.1 Lagrange Multiplier ARCH Tests

A more popular and better formalized approach, the *Lagrange multiplier (LM) test* for (G)ARCH has been proposed by Engle (1982). The methodology involves the following three steps.

1. Estimate the most appropriate conditional mean function model (e.g., some ARMA model or a regression suggested by practice or theory), letting $\{\hat{z}_t^2\}_{t=1}^T$ be the squared standardized residuals. Of course, when one approaches yet unexplored data, it may be the case that the original model is homoskedastic so that $\hat{z}_t^2 = \hat{\varepsilon}_t^2/\hat{\sigma}^2$.
2. Regress these squared standardized residuals on a constant and on m lagged values $\hat{z}_{t-1}^2, \hat{z}_{t-2}^2, \ldots, \hat{z}_{t-m}^2$,
$$\hat{z}_t^2 = \xi_0 + \xi_1 \hat{z}_{t-1}^2 + \xi_2 \hat{z}_{t-2}^2 + \cdots + \xi_m \hat{z}_{t-m}^2 + e_t, \tag{5.83}$$
where e_t is a white noise shock. Here we call the number of lags on the right-hand side m and not p because we want to emphasize that in principle testing for ARCH does not assume previous knowledge of the correct order, p.
3. Because in the absence of ARCH the estimated values of ξ_1 through ξ_m should be 0, $\xi_1 = \xi_2 = \cdots = \xi_m = 0$, this regression will have little explanatory power so that its coefficient of determination (the R^2) will be low; therefore, under the null hypothesis of no ARCH, the test statistic TR^2 converges to a χ_m^2 so that if TR^2 is sufficiently large, the rejection of the null hypothesis that $\xi_1 = \xi_2 = \cdots = \xi_m = 0$ is equivalent to rejection of the null hypothesis of no ARCH errors.[15]

Crucially, this result is obtained when the conditional mean function is correctly specified; otherwise, it will be likely that the LM test will reject as any misspecification errors may induce serial correlation in the squared errors. Interestingly, the individual t-type (*Wald*) statistics associated to each of the coefficients in Eq. (5.83), ξ_1, ξ_2, and ξ_m, have a nonstandard, non-t-Student distribution, and they should be used with caution.[16]

A straightforward extension of Eq. (5.83) can be used to test alternative specifications of (G)ARCH models. For instance, to test for ARCH(p_1) against ARCH(p_2), with $p_2 > p_1$, we would simply estimate Eq. (5.83) by regressing the standardized squared residuals from the ARCH(p_1) model on $p_2 - p_1$ lags of the same-squared residuals and then use an F-test for the null hypothesis that $\xi_{p1} = \xi_{p1+1} = \cdots = \xi_{p2} = 0$ in:

$$\hat{z}_t^2 = \xi_0 + \xi_{p_1} \hat{z}_{t-p_1-1}^2 + \xi_{p_1+1} \hat{z}_{t-p_1-2}^2 + \cdots + \xi_{p_2} \hat{z}_{t-p_2}^2 + e_t. \tag{5.84}$$

Note that these tests will be valid in small samples only if all the competing ARCH models have been estimated on the same data sets, in the sense that the total number of observations should be identical even though $p_2 > p_1$. In practice, this implies that p_2 initial observations should be removed also when estimating the ARCH(p_1) model, which is of course a partial ML approach to estimation. A regression such as Eq. (5.83) is said to be an *auxiliary regression* because it simplifies the calculation of a complex test statistic that—formally speaking at least—ought to depend on the value of the LM of a constrained ML estimation problem, where the constraints derive from the hypotheses to be tested (see Davidson and MacKinnon, 2004, Chapter 10, for a formal equivalence proof).

It is also possible to test for GARCH effects by performing a LM regression–based test. For instance, if one has initially estimated an ARCH(p) model and wants to test for q additional generalized ARCH terms, then a valid auxiliary regression is:

$$\hat{\varepsilon}_t^2 = \varsigma_0 + \varsigma_1 \hat{\sigma}_{t-1|t-2}^{2,\,ARCH(p)} + \varsigma_2 \hat{\sigma}_{t-2|t-3}^{2,\,ARCH(p)} + \cdots + \varsigma_q \hat{\sigma}_{t-q|t-q-1}^{2,\,ARCH(p)} + e_t, \tag{5.85}$$

where $\hat{\sigma}_{t|t-1}^{2,\,ARCH(p)}$ is the time series of filtered, in-sample ARCH(p) conditional variances obtained in the first-stage estimation step. Note that the auxiliary regression in Eq. (5.85) features squared residuals and not standardized residuals as its dependent variable. This is because the scale of the regressand and the regressors would be otherwise different. If there were no GARCH effects, the estimated values of ς_1 through ς_q should be 0, $\varsigma_1 = \varsigma_2 = \cdots = \varsigma_q = 0$. Hence, this

15. If TR^2 were sufficiently low, it would be possible to conclude that there are no ARCH effects. With the samples typically used in applied work, an F-test of the null hypothesis $\xi_1 = \xi_2 = \cdots = \xi_m = 0$ has been shown to be superior (more powerful) to a χ_m^2 test.

16. Also the likelihood ratio test statistics that will be featured prominently in Chapter 9 may be examined, although they have an uncertain distribution under the null. However, Bollerslev et al. (1994) note that practical experience "(...) suggests that the latter is a very powerful approach to testing for GARCH effects." (p. 2975).

regression will have little explanatory power and its R^2 would be low. Under the null hypothesis of no GARCH, the statistic TR^2 converges to a χ^2_q. As before, in small samples, an F test may have superior power.

Another formal test for CH that is routinely applied is Brock et al.'s (1996) (*BDS*) *portmanteau test for independence*, that can be used for testing against a variety of possible deviations from independence including linear dependence, nonlinear dependence, or chaos. When used to test for ARCH, it plays an important role because it can detect CH in the absence of volatility clustering. To perform the test, we first choose a *distance parameter*, δ. We then consider any pair of residuals from some previously estimated conditional mean function.[17] If the observations of the series truly are IID, then for any pair of points, the probability of the distance between these points being less than or equal to δ will be constant. We denote this probability by $C_1(\delta)$. We can also consider sets consisting of multiple pairs of points. One way we can choose sets of pairs is to move through the consecutive residuals of the sample in order. That is, given two residuals ε_s and ε_t, we can construct a set of pairs of the form $(\varepsilon_s, \varepsilon_t)$, $(\varepsilon_{s+1}, \varepsilon_{t+1})$, $(\varepsilon_{s+2}, \varepsilon_{t+2})$, …, $(\varepsilon_{s+m-1}, \varepsilon_{t+m-1})$, where m is the number of consecutive points used in the set, or *embedding dimension*. We denote the joint probability of every pair of points in the set satisfying the delta condition by $C_m(\delta)$. The intuition behind the BDS test is based on the fact that under the assumption of independence, this probability will simply be the product of the individual probabilities for each pair, $C_m(\delta) = [C_1(\delta)]^m$. When working with sample data, we do not directly observe $C_1(\delta)$ or $C_m(\delta)$, we can simply estimate them; as a result, we do not expect this relationship to hold exactly, but only with some error. The larger the error, the less likely it is that the error is caused by random sample variation. The BDS test provides a formal basis for judging the size of this error.

To estimate the probability for a particular dimension, we simply go through all the possible sets of that length that can be drawn from the sample and count the number of sets which satisfy the e_t condition. The ratio of the number of sets satisfying the condition divided by the total number of sets provides the estimate of the probability:

$$C_{m,T}(\delta) = \frac{2}{(T-m+1)(T-m)} \sum_{s=1}^{T-m+1} \sum_{t=s+1}^{T-m+1} \prod_{j=0}^{m-1} I_\delta(\varepsilon_{s+j}, \varepsilon_{t+j}) \quad I_\delta(x,y) = \begin{cases} 1 & \text{if } |x-y| \le \delta \\ 0 & \text{otherwise} \end{cases}. \tag{5.86}$$

The coefficient $2/[(T-m+1)(T-m)]$ derives from the fact that under an embedding dimension of length m that defines m histories, there are a total of $(T-m+1)(T-m)/2$ such histories. These statistics are often referred to as *correlation integrals*. We can use their sample estimates to construct the BDS test statistic:

$$BDS_{m,T}(\delta) = C_{m,T}(\delta) - [C_{1,T-m+1}(\delta)]^m, \tag{5.87}$$

where the second term discards the last observations from the sample so that it is based on the same number of terms as the first statistic. Under the assumption of independence, we would expect this statistic to be close to 0. In fact, Brock et al. (1996) show that:

$$\sqrt{T-m+1}\frac{BDS_{m,T}(\delta)}{\sqrt{4\left(K^m + 2\sum_{j=1}^{m-1} K^{m-j}[C_{1,T}(\delta)]^{2j} + (m-1)^2[C_{1,T}(\delta)]^{2m} - m^2K[C_{1,T}(\delta)]^{2(m-1)}\right)}} \overset{asy}{\sim} N(0,1), \tag{5.88}$$

where K is the probability of any triplet of points lying within each other and is estimated by counting the number of sets satisfying the sample condition:

$$K_T(\delta) = \frac{2}{m(T-1)(T-2)} \sum_{t=1}^{T} \sum_{s=t+1}^{T} \sum_{r=s+1}^{T} [I_\delta(\varepsilon_t, \varepsilon_s)I_\delta(\varepsilon_s, \varepsilon_r) + I_\delta(\varepsilon_t, \varepsilon_r)I_\delta(\varepsilon_r, \varepsilon_s) + I_\delta(\varepsilon_s, \varepsilon_t)I_\delta(\varepsilon_t, \varepsilon_r)]. \tag{5.89}$$

In practical implementations of the test, the most common way to select δ is to ensure that a certain fraction of the total number of pairs of points in the sample lies within of each other. This way of setting δ has been proven to be robust to different distributions of the underlying series. As for the choice of the embedding dimension, it is typical to examine the test results for m that grows between 2 and some upper bound, under the expectation that under the null, no rejection should be encountered. However, when m is increased, also δ should be increased accordingly, to improve the power of the test. Monte Carlo experiments suggest that δ should be between 1/2 and

17. However, we recommend that BDS p-values be bootstrapped when one is assessing the IID-ness of standardized residuals estimated from some first-pass GARCH model.

2 standard deviations of the data, and that T/m should be greater than 200 with m no greater than 5 or 6. For the asymptotic distribution to be a good approximation to the finite-sample behavior of the test, samples of at least 500 observations are required.

The BDS test has power against many, though not all, departures from IID-ness; however, ARCH is among such departures, even though Hsieh (1991) has shown that its power against ARCH alternatives is close to a standard LM test. For other CH alternatives, the power of the BDS test may be superior. For instance, a famous example is the deterministic chaotic ("tent") process by which $\sigma_{t+1}^2 = 1 - 2|\sigma_t^2 - 0.5|$ (with $\sigma_0^2 \in (0,1)$): this model is trivially CH but does not exhibit volatility clustering, because its population ACF is flat at 0 at all lags. BDS works very well in this case, that is, it manages to detect a deviation from IID-ness due to pure CH even in the absence of volatility clustering.

EXAMPLE 5.20

Consider testing for ARCH in the residuals of a Gaussian AR(1) model for (approximate) weekly returns on 5-year Treasury notes. As in previous examples, the model is selected on the basis of the minimization of the BIC criterion. We then proceed to apply a regression-based LM test with $m = 4$ obtaining:

$$\hat{z}_t^2 = \underset{(0.000)}{0.010} + \underset{(0.001)}{0.079}\,\hat{z}_{t-1}^2 + \underset{(0.000)}{0.093}\,\hat{z}_{t-2}^2 + \underset{(0.000)}{0.125}\,\hat{z}_{t-3}^2 + \underset{(0.010)}{0.079}\,\hat{z}_{t-4}^2 + \hat{e}_t.$$

Clearly, all four lags of squared residuals are statistically significant: past squared residuals do forecast future squared residuals. The regression R^2 is 0.045. Such an evidence would have also emerged from using a standard sample ACF/PACF plot and from inspecting the Box–Pierce Q-statistics. Here, we have available a formal test: with 1820 observations, $TR^2 = 82.54$, that under a χ_4^2 commands a p-value of 0.000 and leads to rejecting the null of no ARCH, when $q = 4$. Similarly, even though the sample size is relatively large, we have that under the F-statistic of 21.557, an $F(4,1815)$ implies a p-value of 0.000 and leads to a rejection of the null.

We also apply a BDS test with δ selected to be 1 standard deviation of the residuals and a maximum $m = 6(T/m = 303 > 200)$. We find that for all values of m between 2 and 6, the null hypothesis of IID-ness is always rejected with p-values of 0.000, with the BDS test statistic ranging from $BDS_{2,1820}(0.127) = 0.012$ to $BDS_{6,1820}(0.127) = 0.023$. In the latter case, even computing $BDS_{6,1820}(0.252) = 0.075$ confirms a low p-value. We have also tried to set δ so that 70% of the total number of pairs of points in the sample lies within of each other (this gives $\delta = 0.171$), but the results hardly change: there is evidence of nonlinearities that cause departures from IID-ness and this is compatible with ARCH.

Suppose now to estimate a Gaussian ARCH(4) model and to then wonder whether there would be any additional need of generalized ARCH terms, that is, of a GARCH(4,4), say. On the one hand, an LM test of (say) order 8 immediately shows that there is heteroskedastic structure that an ARCH(4) model has failed to pick up:

$$\hat{z}_t^2 = \underset{(0.000)}{0.906} - \underset{(0.522)}{0.015}\hat{z}_{t-1}^2 - \underset{(0.305)}{0.024}\hat{z}_{t-2}^2 - \underset{(0.170)}{0.032}\hat{z}_{t-3}^2 - \underset{(0.184)}{0.031}\hat{z}_{t-4}^2$$
$$+ \underset{(0.277)}{0.025}\hat{z}_{t-5}^2 + \underset{(0.032)}{0.050}\hat{z}_{t-6}^2 + \underset{(0.017)}{0.056}\hat{z}_{t-7}^2 + \underset{(0.009)}{0.061}\hat{z}_{t-8}^2 + \hat{e}_t.$$

The resulting R^2 is 0.013 so that 1820×0.013 gives a $TR^2 = 22.84$ that under a χ_8^2 commands a p-value of 0.004 and still leads to a rejection. On the other hand, because we doubt that the best approach could be to switch to an ARCH(8) model, it also makes sense to directly test whether any generalized ARCH terms could help forecast squared residuals:

$$\hat{\varepsilon}_t^2 = \underset{(0.518)}{0.001} + \underset{(0.052)}{0.333}\hat{\sigma}_{t-1|t-2}^{2,\,ARCH(4)} + \underset{(0.037)}{0.655}\hat{\sigma}_{t-2|t-3}^{2,\,ARCH(4)} - \underset{(0.000)}{0.472}\hat{\sigma}_{t-3|t-4}^{2,\,ARCH(4)}$$
$$+ \underset{(0.000)}{1.401}\hat{\sigma}_{t-4|t-5}^{2,\,ARCH(4)} + \hat{e}_t.$$

The auxiliary regression R^2 is 0.087 and the resulting TR^2 is $1820 \times 0.087 = 158.3$ which implies a zero p-value under a χ_4^2. Even though the negative estimate of one of the coefficients in the regression may be disturbing, these results establish the usefulness of extending our modeling effort to GARCH(p, q) models.

These results, by which a Gaussian ARCH(4) would not be sufficient to capture the CH in the data, are not supported by BDS tests with δ selected to be 1 standard deviation of the residuals and a maximum $m = 6$. Because we apply the tests to the standardized errors of a first-step ARCH modeling effort, we compute p-values using a bootstrap with 20,000 repetitions. We find that for all values of m between 2 and 6, the null hypothesis of IID-ness is never rejected, with the smallest p-value of 0.092 for $m = 5$.

5.4.2 News Impact Curves and Testing for Asymmetric ARCH

Even though in Section 5.1.1 we have tried to elaborate a story for the origins of asymmetric—often called leverage—effects in ARCH models, to applied econometricians, what matters is only that returns on most assets seem to be characterized by an asymmetric *news impact curve* (henceforth, NIC), which we define next.[18]

DEFINITION 5.6 (News impact curve)

The NIC measures how new information, as measured by shocks (residuals), is incorporated into volatility, that is, it measures the relationship between the current shock ε_t and conditional variance one-period-ahead $\sigma^2_{t+1|t}$, holding constant all other past and current information. Formally,

$$\sigma^2_{t+1|t} = \text{NIC}\ (\varepsilon_t|\sigma^2_t = \sigma^2_{t-1} = \cdots = \sigma^2, \varepsilon_{t-1} = \varepsilon_{t-2} = \cdots = 0). \tag{5.90}$$

Note that the NIC should be defined and estimated with reference to shocks to returns, that is, *news*. In general terms, news is defined as the unexpected component of returns, that is, $\varepsilon_{t+1} = R_{t+1} - \mu_{t+1|t}$. To provide some concreteness to our definition, in the case of a plain vanilla GARCH(1,1) model we have:

$$\text{NIC}\ (\varepsilon_t|\sigma^2_t = \sigma^2) = \omega + \alpha\varepsilon^2_t + \beta\sigma^2 = A + \alpha\varepsilon^2_t, \quad A \equiv \omega + \beta\sigma^2 > 0, \tag{5.91}$$

which is the equation of a quadratic function (a parabola) with shift parameter $A > 0$ and convexity parameter $\alpha > 0$. This function is a quadratic function of ε_t and therefore symmetric around $\varepsilon_t = 0$ (with intercept A).

As an additional example, consider a EGARCH(1,1) model in Eq. (5.42), $\ln \sigma^2_{t+1|t} = \omega + \alpha[z_t + \theta(|z_t|\text{-}E|z_t|)] + \beta \ln \sigma^2_{t|t-1}$. A simple transformation reveals that:

$$\begin{aligned}\text{NIC}\ (\varepsilon_t|\ln \sigma^2_t = \sigma^2) &= \exp[\omega]\exp[\alpha(\varepsilon_t/\sigma^2) + \theta(|\varepsilon_t/\sigma^2| - E|\varepsilon_t/\sigma^2|)] \\ &\times \exp(\beta)\sigma^2 = A'\exp[\alpha(\varepsilon_t/\sigma^2) + \theta(|\varepsilon_t/\sigma^2| - E|\varepsilon_t/\sigma^2|)],\end{aligned} \tag{5.92}$$

where $A' \equiv \exp(\omega + \beta)\sigma^2 > 0$. Such a function is clearly not symmetric around $\varepsilon_t = 0$. Obviously, the type of asymmetry will depend on the sign of θ, as already discussed in Section 5.2.5.

EXAMPLE 5.21

Let us consider the asymmetry properties of conditional heteroskedastic models of daily *value* (as proxied by HML) returns over a 1963–2016 sample. We estimate three models with GED errors (from a AR(1) model, as in earlier examples), to gain the necessary flexibility: GARCH(1,1), threshold GARCH(1,1), and EGARCH(1,1), obtaining the following outputs.

In panel (a), by construction, the NIC is restricted to be symmetric because of the very nature of the plain vanilla GARCH. In panels (b) and (c) instead, the models may acquire enough flexibility to reproduce any asymmetries in the data. Even though the NICs from the threshold GARCH and EGARCH models are rather different (the EGARCH kink is caused by the absolute value appearing in the model specification), they display the same type of asymmetry: *positive* news implies a higher reaction of subsequent predicted variance than negatives news does. This is consistent with the signs of the coefficients in the terms $-0.015I(\varepsilon_t < 0)\varepsilon^2_t$ and $+0.011z_t$ in the threshold GARCH(1,1) and EGARCH(1,1), respectively. Note that even though these coefficients are relatively small in absolute value, they are both estimated precisely and they do affect in visible ways the structure of the two NICs in Fig. 5.17. Importantly, the type of asymmetries that HML portfolio returns reveals are far different from the classical leverage effect asymmetries that stock index and individual stock returns typically show: it is positive news that drive volatility higher than negative ones, even though—because HML is a long-short portfolio—these can then be interpreted as better news on value stocks than on growth stocks on a given day.

---

18. Intuitively, both negative and positive news should increase conditional volatility because they trigger trades by market operators. This is another flaw of our earlier presentation of asymmetries in the NIC as leverage effects: in this story, positive news ought to reduce company leverage, reduce risk, and volatility. In practice, all kinds of news tend to generate trading and hence volatility, even though negative news often increase variance more than positive news do.

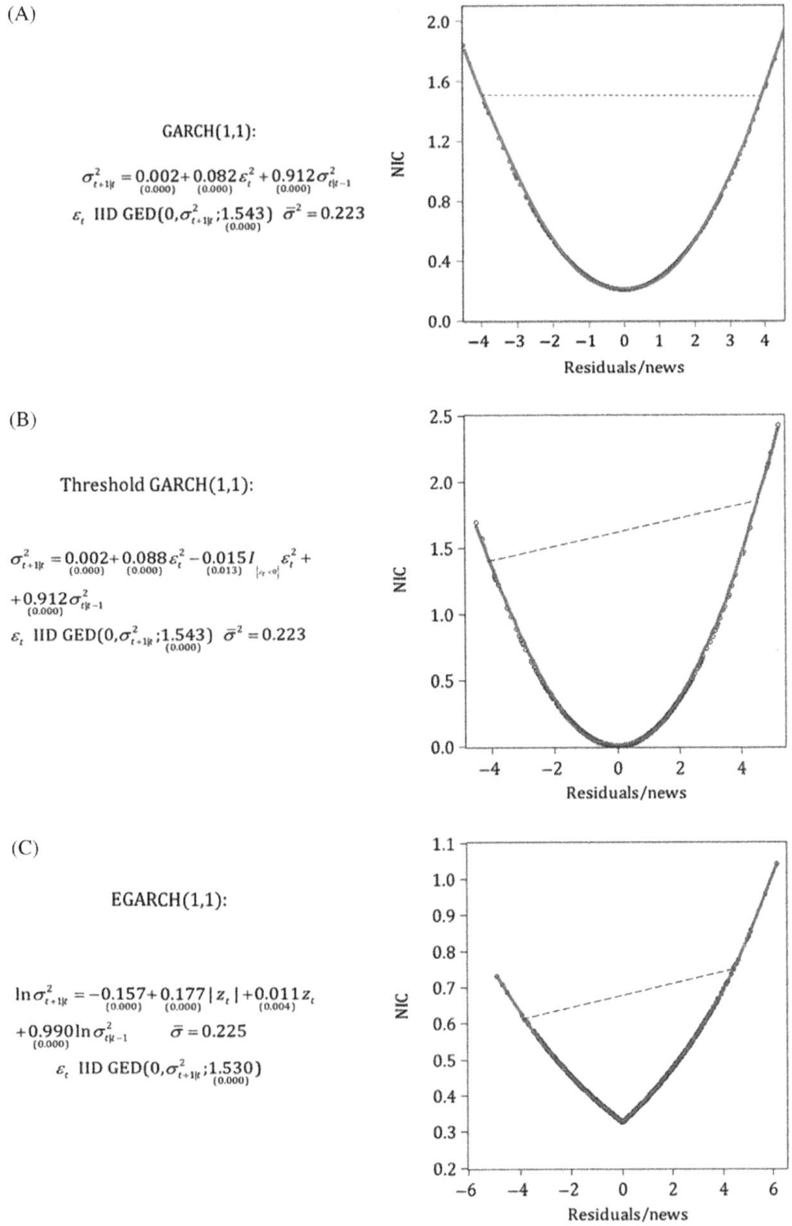

FIGURE 5.17 NICs from alternative GARCH models. (A) Symmetric NIC. (B) Threshold GARCH-induced asymmetric NIC. (C) EGARCH-induced asymmetric NIC.

One last aspect raised by Example 5.21 is whether any of these models, that are rather typical in the toolkit of applied econometricians in finance and that we have made additionally flexible through the GED innovation distributional assumption, may be sufficiently rich to fit the *empirical NIC* that is hidden in the data. In fact, NICs can be *computed* in a mathematical sense from the estimates of a given CH model, as we have done in Fig. 5.17 or they can be *empirically estimated* from the data.

In Fig. 5.18, we have applied a simple nonparametric kernel regression-type estimator to locally approximate the complex and nonlinear nature of the relationship between squared residuals and lagged residuals using the same data as in Example 5.21. In Section 5.2.4, we have already discussed the problems with identifying realized variance with squared residuals, and this explains why the scatter of points in Fig. 5.18 looks like a cloud in which it is hard to imagine a specific shape. However, the kernel regression reveals an empirical NIC that has the expected behavior and that approximately displays the same type of asymmetry shown in Fig. 5.17. We emphasize however that through the threshold GARCH and EGARCH models in Fig. 5.17, we have obtained just a "rough" fit to the empirical NIC in Fig. 5.18: a careful observer will note that the NIC of HML portfolio returns is essentially symmetric between −2% and +2%

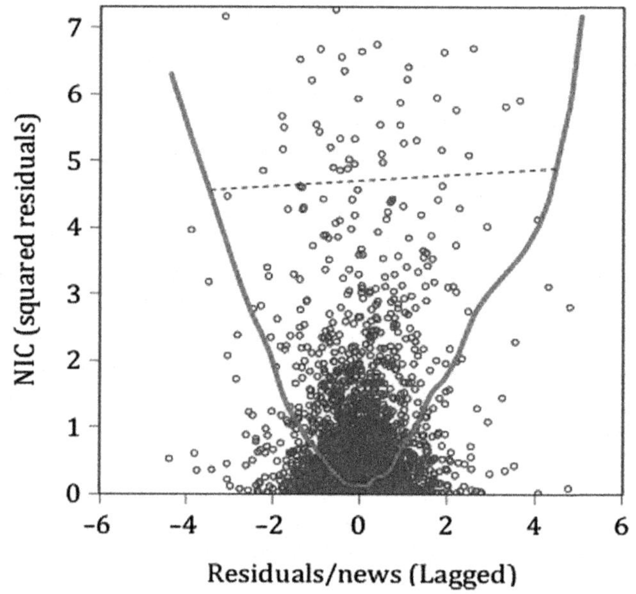

FIGURE 5.18 Empirical nonparametric impact curve for HML returns.

and then tilts to the right, to capture the regularity that only relatively large, positive shocks to HML returns do increase subsequent variance more than negative shocks do.

Before a reader may fall under the impression that empirical NICs tilting toward the right, that is, with a negative (positive) leverage (feedback) effect may represent the norm, we remind of the evidence in Fig. 5.3 for daily US excess equity returns, in which a classical leverage effect, that is, a left asymmetry, was visible.

From a score of empirical papers that contain evidence similar to Example 5.21 and Figs. 5.3 and 5.18, we now understand that for most asset return and interest rate series, the empirical NIC fails to be symmetric. How do you actually test whether there are asymmetric effects in conditional heteroskedasticity? In Figs. 5.3 and 5.18, we have employed a deceivingly simple method: nonparametric regressions. Leaving aside the fact that their introduction here is beyond our goals (see, e.g., Altman, 1992, for a brief introduction), the careful reader will have noticed that in Figs. 5.3 and 5.18, there are no confidence intervals that would allow us to decide, for instance, whether this point estimation evidence of asymmetries derives from mere over-fitting of the data or is a robust finding in the light of the statistical uncertainty that is inherent in the inferential problem on the NIC. Obviously, we need more classical and in some ways more approachable methods to perform formal tests for asymmetries in volatility clustering.

The simplest and most common approach consists of using LM ARCH-type tests similar to those introduced in Section 5.4.1. After having fitted to the data some appropriate combination of conditional mean and CH models, call $\{\hat{z}_t\}_{t=1}^{T}$ the corresponding time series of standardized residuals. For simplicity, we shall ignore any initial observations lost because of the ARMA structure in the conditional moment functions, so that $\{\hat{z}_t\}_{t=1}^{T}$ starts at $t = 1$. Then simple regressions may be performed to assess whether the NIC is actually asymmetric: if tests of the null hypothesis that the coefficients $\gamma_1, \gamma_2, \ldots, \gamma_d, \phi_1, \phi_2, \ldots, \phi_d$ are all equal to 0 (jointly or individually) in the regressions:

$$\hat{z}_t^2 = \gamma_0 + \gamma_1 \hat{z}_{t-1} + \gamma_2 \hat{z}_{t-2} + \cdots + \gamma_d \hat{z}_{t-d} + e_t, \tag{5.93}$$

or

$$\hat{z}_t^2 = \gamma_0 + \gamma_1 I_{\{\hat{z}_t-1<0\}} + \cdots + \gamma_d I_{\{\hat{z}_{t-d}<0\}} + \phi_1 I_{\{\hat{z}_{t-1}<0\}} \hat{z}_{t-1} + \cdots + \phi_d I_{\{\hat{z}_{t-d}<0\}} \hat{z}_{t-d} + e_t, \tag{5.94}$$

this is evidence of the need of modeling asymmetric conditional variance effects. This occurs because either the signed level of past estimated shocks ($\hat{z}_{t-1}, \hat{z}_{t-2}, \ldots, \hat{z}_{t-d}$), dummies that capture such signs, or the interaction between their signed level and sign dummies show explanatory power for squared standardized residuals.

Asymmetries in volatility clustering play an important practical role. Consider the pricing of 30-day index options after a large, 6 standard deviation shock to index returns. As we shall see in Section 5.5.2, a trader that relies on a GARCH model estimated on daily data will forecast the variance of the underlying asset over the life of the contract using a formula that, at least qualitatively, will be similar to:

$$\sigma_{t+1:t+30}^2 = 29\overline{\sigma}^2 + \sum_{h=1}^{29} PI^{h-1}(\sigma_{t+1|t}^2 - \overline{\sigma}^2). \tag{5.95}$$

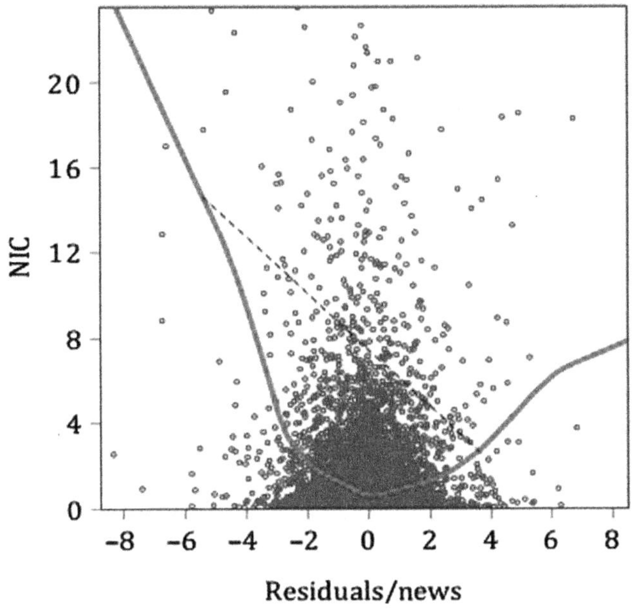

FIGURE 5.19 Empirical nonparametric impact curve for US equity returns.

Here *PI* stands for *persistence index*, the formula of which will naturally depend on the specific type of CH model the trader uses. Whatever the exact expression for *PI*, a crucial role will be played by the sign and magnitude of $\sigma^2_{t+1|t} - \overline{\sigma}^2$. Suppose now the trader faces a NIC like the one in Fig. 5.3, which is copied here for convenience and numbered as Fig. 5.19.

It then becomes of vital importance for the trader to find out whether today's index return has given a standardized deviation from the mean of either -6% (in which case the variance on the following day is predicted to exceed 17) or $+6\%$ (when the variance on the following day is predicted to be just above 6, almost one-third). Because of such importance, one recent enhancement in the ARCH literature has consisted of developing ARCH models that are directly based on the specification and estimation of *statistical parametric models of the NIC*. At this point, we have to stop and note the difference among:

- empirical NICs directly estimated from asset return data, usually using nonparametric methods;
- implied, theoretical NICs, computed on the basis of the estimated parameters of selected CH models; and
- statistical parametric NICs, that are directly estimated on the data on the basis of selected functional forms.

The most famous of such functional forms are derived by simply extending the GARCH NIC, $NIC(z_t|\sigma_t^2 = \sigma^2) = A + \alpha\sigma^2 z_t^2$ (where $A \equiv \omega + \beta\sigma^2 > 0$) to a family of volatility models parameterized by θ_1, θ_2, and θ_3 that can be written as follows:

$$NIC(z_t) = \alpha[|z_t - \theta_1| - \theta_2(z_t - \theta_1)]^{2\theta_3}. \tag{5.96}$$

The objective is then to estimate the parameters (θ_1, θ_2, θ_3, and β) of models with the structure:

$$\sigma^2_{t+1|t} = NIC(z_t) + \beta\sigma^2_{t|t-1} = \omega + \alpha[|z_t - \theta_1| - \theta_2(z_t - \theta_1)]^{2\theta_3} + \beta\sigma^2_{t|t-1}. \tag{5.97}$$

One can retrieve a standard, plain vanilla GARCH(1,1) by setting $\theta_1 = 0$, $\theta_2 = 0$, and $\theta_3 = 1$. Another important case that we have already encountered in Section 5.2.6, the NAGARCH(1,1) model, can be obtained from Eq. (5.96) by setting $\theta_1 = 0$ and $\theta_3 = 1$, as we detail in one online example.

5.5 FORECASTING WITH GARCH MODELS

We have emphasized in several occasions that the point of GARCH models is to allow the calculation of forecasts of future variance. Even though they are also frequently used in hindsight to offer and test economic stories and hypotheses for why variance may be time-varying, both academics and practitioners consider them more as a tool than as a philosophical achievement. It is therefore important to devote some more space to how one should forecast conditional variance with a GARCH model.[19]

At one level, the answer is very simple because the one-step (1-day)-ahead forecast of variance, $\sigma^2_{t+1|t}$, is given directly by the model, say in Eq. (5.30),

$$\sigma^2_{t+1|t} = \omega + \alpha\varepsilon^2_t + \beta\sigma^2_{t|t-1}, \tag{5.98}$$

where the notation $\sigma^2_{t+1|t} \equiv E_t[\sigma^2_{t+1}]$ stresses that such a prediction for time $t+1$ is obtained on the basis of information up to time t, that is, $\sigma^2_{t+1|t}$ is a short-hand for $Var[\varepsilon_{t+1}|\Im_t] = E[\varepsilon^2_{t+1}|\Im_t]$, where $\Im_t$ is the information set and the equality derives from the fact that residuals are defined to have zero mean.

5.5.1 Long-Horizon, Point Forecasts

However, we are rarely interested in just forecasting one step ahead of variance. Consider a generic forecast horizon, $H \geq 1$. In this case, it is easy to show that, from Eq. (5.38), when the GARCH is stationary,

$$\begin{aligned}\sigma^2_{t+H|t} - \bar{\sigma}^2 &= E_t[\sigma^2_{t+H}] - \bar{\sigma}^2 = \alpha E_t[\varepsilon^2_{t+H-1} - \bar{\sigma}^2] + \beta E_t[\sigma^2_{t+H-1} - \bar{\sigma}^2]\\ &= \alpha(E_t[\varepsilon^2_{t+H-1}] - \bar{\sigma}^2) + \beta(E_t[\sigma^2_{t+H-1}] - \bar{\sigma}^2)\\ &= \alpha(\sigma^2_{t+H-1|t} - \bar{\sigma}^2) + \beta(\sigma^2_{t+H-1|t} - \bar{\sigma}^2)\\ &= (\alpha+\beta)(\sigma^2_{t+H-1|t} - \bar{\sigma}^2).\end{aligned} \tag{5.99}$$

This establishes a *recursive relationship*: the predicted deviations of $t+H$ forecasts from the unconditional, long-run variance on the left-hand side equal $(\alpha+\beta) < 1$ times the predicted deviations of the $t+H-1$ forecasts from the unconditional variance. All the forecasts are computed conditioning on time t information. However, we know from the recursion that $\sigma^2_{t+H-1|t} - \bar{\sigma}^2 = (\alpha+\beta)(\sigma^2_{t+H-2|t} - \bar{\sigma}^2)$, and

$$\sigma^2_{t+H|t} - \bar{\sigma}^2 = (\alpha+\beta)\left[\underbrace{(\alpha+\beta)(\sigma^2_{t+H-2|t} - \bar{\sigma}^2)}_{\sigma^2_{t+H-1|t} - \bar{\sigma}^2}\right] = (\alpha+\beta)^2(\sigma^2_{t+H-2|t} - \bar{\sigma}^2). \tag{5.100}$$

Working backward this way $H-1$ times, it is easy to see that:

$$\sigma^2_{t+H|t} - \bar{\sigma}^2 = (\alpha+\beta)^{H-1}(\sigma^2_{t+1|t} - \bar{\sigma}^2). \tag{5.101}$$

RESULT 5.1 (*H*-horizon GARCH forecasts)

Assuming a stationary GARCH(1,1) model, the H-horizon variance forecast is:

$$\begin{aligned}\sigma^2_{t+H|t} &= \bar{\sigma}^2 + (\alpha+\beta)^{H-1}(\sigma^2_{t+1} - \bar{\sigma}^2)\\ &= \bar{\sigma}^2 + (\alpha+\beta)^{H-1}[\alpha(\varepsilon^2_t - \bar{\sigma}^2) + \beta(\sigma^2_t - \bar{\sigma}^2)].\end{aligned} \tag{5.102}$$

As the forecast horizon H grows, because $(\alpha+\beta) < 1$, the limit of $(\alpha+\beta)^{H-1}$ is 0 and

$$\lim_{H\to\infty} \sigma^2_{t+H|t} = \bar{\sigma}^2, \tag{5.103}$$

that is, the very long horizon forecast is the long-run variance.

---

19. For concreteness, in what follows we focus on the case of a simple GARCH(1,1) model. All these results, at the cost of tedious algebra, may be generalized to the GARCH(p, q) case. This is a useful (possibly, boring) exercise. We shall also ignore all estimation issues that will be dealt with in Section 5.6, i.e., for the time being we assume that all parameters are known.

Practically, this means that because stationary GARCH models are mean-reverting, any long-run forecast will simply exploit this fact, that is, use $\overline{\sigma}^2$ as the prediction. Of course, for finite but large H, it is easy to see that when $\alpha+\beta$ is relatively small, then $\sigma^2_{t+H|t}$ will be close to $\overline{\sigma}^2$ for relatively modest values of H; when $\alpha+\beta$ is instead close to 1, $\sigma^2_{t+H|t}$ will depart from $\overline{\sigma}^2$ even for large values of H. Eq. (5.102) has another key implication: because in a GARCH we also restrict both α and β to be positive, $(\alpha+\beta)\in(0,\ 1)$ implies that $(\alpha+\beta)^{H-1}>0$ for all values of the horizon $H\geq 1$. Therefore, it is clear that $\sigma^2_{t+H|t}>\overline{\sigma}^2$ when $\sigma^2_{t+1|t}>\overline{\sigma}^2$, and vice versa. This means that the H-step-ahead forecasts of the variance will exceed long-run variance if one-step-ahead forecasts exceed long-run variance, and vice versa.

As you have understood at this point, the coefficient sum $\alpha+\beta$ plays a crucial role in all matters concerning forecasting with GARCH models and is commonly called the *persistence level/index* of the model: a high persistence $\alpha+\beta$, close to 1, implies that shocks which push variance away from its long-run average will persist for a long time, even though eventually the long-horizon forecast will be the long-run average variance, $\overline{\sigma}^2$.

EXAMPLE 5.22

We examine a t-Student AR(1) GARCH(1,1)-in-mean model for (approximate) weekly returns on 5-year Treasury notes, over a sample 1982–2016. As in previous examples, the model is selected on the basis of the minimization of the BIC criterion: the t-Student specification for the errors minimizes the BIC compared to the Gaussian case. We find the estimates:

$$R_{t+1} = \underset{(0.533)}{-0.003} + \underset{(0.000)}{0.257}R_t + \underset{(0.189)}{0.440}\sigma^2_{t|t-1} + \varepsilon_{t+1} \quad \varepsilon_{t+1}\ \text{IID t}(0, \sigma^2_{t+1|t}; \underset{(0.000)}{10.16})$$

$$\sigma^2_{t+1|t} = \underset{(0.017)}{0.0002} + \underset{(0.000)}{0.060}\varepsilon^2_t + \underset{(0.000)}{0.930}\sigma^2_{t|t-1}.$$

The GARCH-in mean term is not accurately estimated. However, the 0.44 coefficient estimate is economically not negligible and, as we shall see, it will affect forecasts of the mean. Consistently with earlier examples, the number of degrees of freedom estimated for the t-Student process implies significant departures from normality. We now proceed to compute two types of forecasts. First, we place ourselves at the end of the sample and we produce point forecasts of variance for the 52 weeks of 2017 with horizon H that varies between 1 week and 52 weeks.

We plot both mean and variance forecasts from the model. Mean forecasts are relatively uninteresting because essentially constant, even though some upward sloping behavior is detectable. This result is fairly general: since the mean of any GARCH process is 0, the optimal H-step-ahead point forecast (i.e., mean prediction) does not depend on the presence of CH; however, the size of any confidence interval surrounding the forecasts does depend on conditional volatility. In fact, also because the coefficient estimates were imprecise, the bootstrapped predicted confidence bands that take into account of GARCH effects are extremely wide and reveal that the mean forecast is uninformative. Variance forecasts are also upward sloping (which may be driving the modest increase in bond return forecasts) and this is entirely driven by the formula

$$\hat{\sigma}^2_{t+H|t} = \overline{\sigma}^2 + (\hat{\alpha}+\hat{\beta})^{H-1}(\hat{\sigma}^2_{t+1|t} - \overline{\sigma}^2) = [1-(\hat{\alpha}+\hat{\beta})^{H-1}]\overline{\sigma}^2 + (\hat{\alpha}+\hat{\beta})^{H-1}\hat{\sigma}^2_{t+1|t}$$

when $\hat{\sigma}^2_{t+1|t}<\overline{\sigma}^2$, that is, starting from a relatively low level of predicted variance (0.0095), as it was the case in US bond markets at the end of 2016. Because in this example, the estimated persistence index $\hat{\alpha}+\hat{\beta}=0.99$ is relatively high, the convergence of predicted variance to $\overline{\sigma}^2=0.0144$ takes many weeks, approximately 250 (e.g., $1-(0.06+0.93)^{250}=0.92$, when the weight is almost entirely assigned to the long-run variance) (Fig. 5.20).

Next, we recursively compute—using full-sample estimates of the parameters—1-week-ahead forecasts of mean and variance. Of course, it would be possible to perform such calculations for horizons $H>1$ week, thus obtaining a three-dimensional surface, but usually such plots are complex to interpret. Because these forecasts are computed using full-sample estimates but are applied backward in time recursively, initializing each forecast at time t between January 1982 and December 2016 using the actual, realized past returns and estimated shocks, this type of forecasts are sometimes called *in-sample forecasts*.

Fig. 5.21 shows the results. In this recursive application, the predicted mean oscillates quite a bit, between −0.06% and 0.14% per week, that are not negligible values in the US Treasury markets. The uncertainty surrounding the forecasts remains considerable, and it tends to reflect also the CH in the data, as shown by the correspondence between the RHS plot of $\hat{\sigma}^2_{t+1|t}$ and the width of the 95% confidence interval to the left.

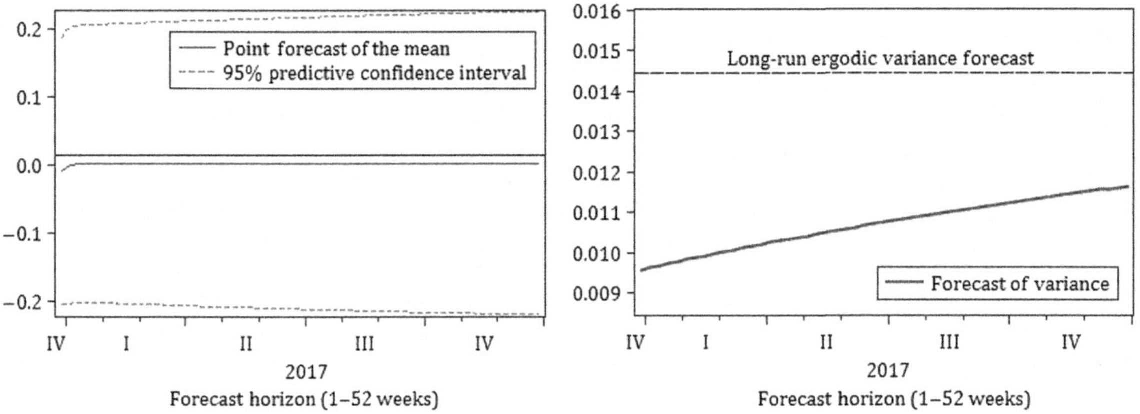

FIGURE 5.20 Mean and variance forecasts computed as of December 2016.

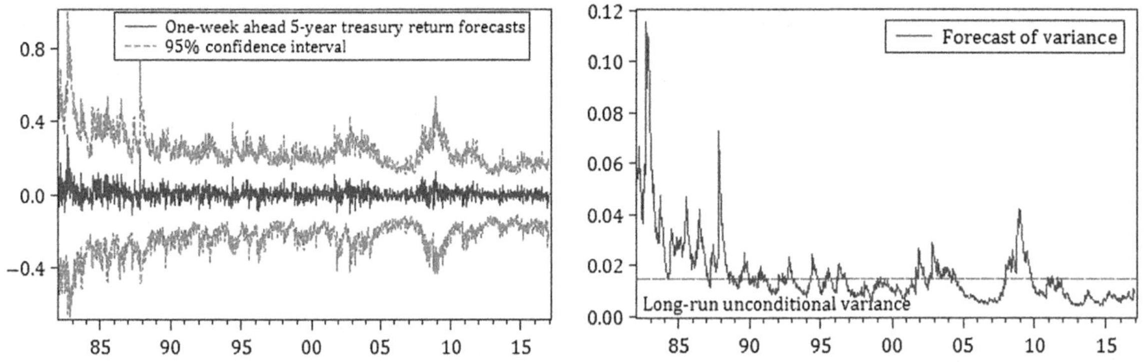

FIGURE 5.21 Recursive, in-sample mean and variance forecasts.

Because under RiskMetrics we know that $(\alpha + \beta) = 1$, it follows that

$$\sigma^{2,RiskMtcs}_{t+H|t} = \overline{\sigma}^2 + 1^{H-1}(\sigma^2_{t+1|t} - \overline{\sigma}^2) = \sigma^{2,RiskMtcs}_{t+1|t}, \tag{5.104}$$

which means that any shock to current variance is destined to persist forever and impact the forecast accordingly: if today is a high (low)-variance day, then the RiskMetrics model predicts that all future days will be high (low)-variance days, which is clearly rather unrealistic. Sometimes we say that under RiskMetrics (more generally, IGARCH) conditional variance follows a random walk. In fact, this can be dangerous: assuming the RiskMetrics model holds despite the data truly look more like a stationary GARCH will give users—especially risk managers and derivative pricers—a false sense of calmness of the market in the future, when the market is calm today and $\sigma^2_{t+1|t} < \overline{\sigma}^2$. A stationary GARCH-type more realistically assumes that eventually, in the future, variance will revert to its average value, $\overline{\sigma}^2$.

5.5.2 Forecasts of Variance for Sums of Returns or Shocks

In asset allocation problems, we sometimes care for the variance of *long-horizon returns* that (assuming continuous compounding) are defined as:

$$R_{t+1:t+H} \equiv \sum_{h=1}^{H} R_{t+h}, \tag{5.105}$$

where $R_{t+1\,:\,t+H}$ indicates the returns summed over the interval $[t+1, t+H]$. For instance, a portfolio manager with a mandate over $H > 1$ periods will hardly care for the point forecast of the variance of returns in H periods from now, given the information available at time t, $\overline{\sigma}^2_{t+H|t}$ (or $Var[R_{t+H}|\Im_t]$); she will instead care for $Var[R_{t+1\,:\,t+H}|\Im_t]$. Therefore, in this section, we investigate conditional forecasts (expectations) of the variance of long-horizon returns.

Because of the model $R_{t+1} = \mu_{t+1|t} + \sigma_{t+1|t}z_{t+1} = \mu_{t+1|t} + \varepsilon_{t+1}$, $z_{t+1} \sim \text{IID}\,(0,1)$ (recall that normality is frequently assumed but in no way necessary) implies that the residuals have zero autocorrelations, the variance of the cumulative H-day return is:

$$\begin{aligned}\sigma^2_{t+1:t+H} &\equiv Var_t\left[\sum_{h=1}^{H} R_{t+h}\right] = E_t\left[\left(\sum_{h=1}^{H} R_{t+h} - \mu_{t+1|t}\right)^2\right] = E_t\left[\sum_{h=1}^{H} \varepsilon^2_{t+h}\right] \\ &= \sum_{h=1}^{H} E_t[\varepsilon^2_{t+h}] = \sum_{h=1}^{H} \sigma^2_{t+h|t}.\end{aligned} \tag{5.106}$$

Note that $E_t \sum_{h=1}^{H} \varepsilon^2_{t+h} = \sum_{h=1}^{H} E_t[\varepsilon^2_{t+h}]$ because the absence of autocorrelation in the shocks, due to the IID-ness assumption, leads to all the conditional expectations of the cross-products, $E_t[\varepsilon_{t+\tau}\varepsilon_{t+\tau+k}] (k \neq 0)$ to vanish by construction. Substituting the appropriate forecasts in Eq. (5.106) for the GARCH(1,1) case, we obtain the result below.

RESULT 5.2 (*H*-horizon return GARCH forecasts)

Assuming a stationary GARCH(1,1) model, the variance forecast for the H-horizon return $R_{t+1:t+H} \equiv \sum_{h=1}^{H} R_{t+h}$, is:

$$\begin{aligned}\sigma^2_{t+1:t+H} &= \sum_{h=1}^{H} \overline{\sigma}^2 + \sum_{h=1}^{H} (\alpha+\beta)^{h-1}(\sigma^2_{t+1|t} - \overline{\sigma}^2) \\ &= H\overline{\sigma}^2 + \sum_{h=1}^{H} (\alpha+\beta)^{h-1}(\sigma^2_{t+1|t} - \overline{\sigma}^2) \neq H\overline{\sigma}^2.\end{aligned} \tag{5.107}$$

In particular, $\sigma^2_{t+1:t+H} \gtreqless H\overline{\sigma}^2$ when $\sum_{h=1}^{H} (\alpha+\beta)^{h-1}(\sigma^2_{t+1|t} - \overline{\sigma}^2) \gtreqless 0$, which requires that $\sigma^2_{t+1|t} \gtreqless \overline{\sigma}^2$.

Note that the variance of the (log-)long horizon return is not simply H times their unconditional, long-run variance: the term $H\overline{\sigma}^2$ needs to be adjusted to take into account transitory effects, concerning each of the shocks ε_{t+h} contributing to $R_{t+1:t+H}$. Given this result, the *per-period variance* from a GARCH model is:

$$\frac{\sigma^2_{t+1:t+H}}{H} = \overline{\sigma}^2 + \frac{1}{H}\sum_{h=1}^{H} (\alpha+\beta)^{h-1}(\sigma^2_{t+1|t} - \overline{\sigma}^2) \tag{5.108}$$

so that, as the forecast horizon grows, the per-period long run variance simply boils down to the long-run unconditional variance. However, the shorter the horizon is, the stronger will be the influence of the terms $H^{-1}\sum_{h=1}^{H} (\alpha+\beta)^{h-1}(\sigma^2_{t+1|t} - \overline{\sigma}^2)$, the sign of which depends as usual on the sign of $\sigma^2_{t+1|t} - \overline{\sigma}^2$, that is, whether the current forecast of variance exceeds or not the long-run, average variance.

Under RiskMetrics, the variance of long-horizon returns is:

$$\begin{aligned}\sigma^{2,RiskMtcs}_{t+1:t+H} &= \sum_{h=1}^{H} \overline{\sigma}^2 + \sum_{h=1}^{H} 1^{h-1}(\sigma^{2,RiskMtcs}_{t+1|t} - \overline{\sigma}^2) \\ &= H\sigma^{2,RiskMtcs}_{t+1|t} = H(1-\lambda)\varepsilon^2_t + H\lambda\sigma^{2,RiskMtcs}_{t|t-1},\end{aligned} \tag{5.109}$$

which is just H times the most recent forecast of future variance. Consequently, the per-period long-run variance is:

$$\frac{\sigma^{2,RiskMtcs}_{t+1:t+H}}{H} = \sigma^{2,RiskMtcs}_{t+1|t} = (1-\lambda)\varepsilon^2_t + \lambda\sigma^{2,RiskMtcs}_{t|t-1} \tag{5.110}$$

which is simply the standard RiskMetrics forecast at time t for $t+1$. An extension of Example 5.22 to the computation of the weekly cumulative variance forecasts of approximate 5-year Treasury note returns is available as an online example.

5.6 ESTIMATION OF AND INFERENCE ON GARCH MODELS

In a frequentist statistical perspective, to estimate the parameters of a GARCH model means that, given a random sample of data, one wants to select a vector of parameters $\boldsymbol{\theta} \in \mathbb{R}^K$(let K be the total number of parameters to be estimated) in a way that maximizes some criterion function that measures how *plausible* each possible value for $\boldsymbol{\theta}$ is with reference to the recorded sample. As we recall from Chapter 1, the choice of the criterion and of a method to maximize it defines the (point) *estimation method* and as such one specific type of *estimator*.

Even though this general principle will be made clearer later on, to gain some intuition, consider two examples. First, we may look for a unique $\hat{\boldsymbol{\theta}} \in \mathbb{R}^K$ such that the probability that the observed data sample has been generated by the assumed stochastic process is maximized when $\boldsymbol{\theta} = \hat{\boldsymbol{\theta}}$, where for simplicity $\hat{\boldsymbol{\theta}}$ is assumed to be unique. One such estimator will be the *MLE*. Second and alternatively, we may look for a unique $\tilde{\boldsymbol{\theta}} \in \mathbb{R}^K$ such that some *statistical features* implied by the data-generating process—for instance, some interesting moments, such as unconditional means and variances, or the impulse-response functions—are the same when computed from the assumed stochastic process under the condition $\boldsymbol{\theta} = \tilde{\boldsymbol{\theta}}$ as in the sample of data; one such estimator, based on matching the sample with population moments, is the *method-of-moment (MM) estimator*.

The MMs relies on the idea of estimating any unknown parameters by simply matching the sample moments in the data with the theoretical (population) moments implied by a statistical model. The intuition is simple: if the data came from the assumed model—which will represent a family of joint PDF functions—parameterized by $\boldsymbol{\theta}$, then the best among the members of such a family will be characterized by a choice of $\tilde{\boldsymbol{\theta}}^{MM}$ that generates population moments that are identical or at least close to the observed sample moments. Example 5.23 provides a brief introduction to such methods, applied to a case of interest.

EXAMPLE 5.23

Define the noncentral and central sample moments of order $n \geq 1$ (where n is a natural number) as:[20]

$$\hat{m}_n \equiv \frac{1}{T}\sum_{t=1}^{T}(z_t)^n \quad \hat{\overline{m}}_n \equiv \frac{1}{T}\sum_{t=1}^{T}(z_t - \hat{m}_1)^n.$$

Similar to Eq. (5.67), assume that asset returns follow the constant mean, homoskedastic process $R_{t+1} = \mu + \sigma z_{t+1}$, z_{t+1} IID $t(0, 1; \nu)$. The MM principle consists then in equating sample and theoretical moments (see the expressions in Eq. 5.72) to derive the following system of equations to be solved with respect to the unknown parameters μ, σ, and ν:

$$\overbrace{\hat{m}_1 = \frac{1}{T}\sum_{t=1}^{T}R_t}^{\text{sample}} = \overbrace{E[R_t] = \mu}^{\text{population}}$$

$$\overbrace{\hat{\overline{m}}_2 = \frac{1}{T}\sum_{t=1}^{T}(R_t - \hat{m}_1)^2}^{\text{sample}} = \overbrace{Var[R_t] = \sigma^2\frac{\nu}{\nu - 2}}^{\text{population}}$$

$$\overbrace{\hat{\overline{m}}_3/(\hat{\overline{m}}_2)^{1.5} = \frac{T^{-1}\sum_{t=1}^{T}(R_t - \hat{m}_1)^3}{\left[T^{-1}\sum_{t=1}^{T}(R_t - \hat{m}_1)^2\right]^{1.5}}}^{\text{sample}} = \overbrace{Skew[R_t] = 0}^{\text{population}}$$

$$\overbrace{\hat{\overline{m}}_4/(\hat{\overline{m}}_2)^2 = \frac{T^{-1}\sum_{t=1}^{T}(R_t - \hat{m}_1)^4}{\left[T^{-1}\sum_{t=1}^{T}(R_t - \hat{m}_1)^2\right]^2}}^{\text{sample}} = \overbrace{Kurt[R_t] = 3 + \frac{6}{\nu - 4}}^{\text{population}}.$$

This is a system with four equations. However, the third equation is redundant because it just states that the population skewness is 0 and therefore does not depend on any parameters. Moreover, all the quantities on the left-hand side of this system will turn into

(Continued)

20. Sample moments are sample statistics because they depend on a random sample and as such they are estimators. Instead population moments are parameters that characterize the entire data-generating process. Clearly, $\hat{m}_1 = \hat{\overline{m}}_1 = \hat{E}[z_t]$, while $\hat{\overline{m}}_2 = \widehat{Var}[z_t]$.

EXAMPLE 5.23 (Continued)

numbers when we are given a sample of data. Why these three moments (given that skewness cannot contribute in any way)? They make a lot of sense given our characterization of $R_{t+1} = \mu + \sigma z_{t+1}$ under *t*-Student errors. Yet, their choice remains arbitrary. Of course, one needs to pick at least three moments and hence three equations, given that three coefficients had to be estimated. The one above is a system of three equations in three unknowns (with a recursive block structure) that is easy to solve to find:

$$\tilde{\mu}^{MM} = T^{-1}\sum_{t=1}^{T} R_t = \text{sample mean} \quad \tilde{\nu}^{MM} = 4 + \frac{6}{\hat{\bar{m}}_4/(\hat{\bar{m}}_2)^2 - 3} \quad \tilde{\sigma}^{2,MM} = \frac{\tilde{\nu}^{MM} - 2}{\tilde{\nu}^{MM}}\hat{\bar{m}}_2.$$

In practice, one first goes from the sample excess kurtosis to estimate the number of degrees of freedom of the *t*-Student, $\tilde{\nu}^{MM}$; then to the estimate of the variance coefficient (also called diffusive coefficient), $\tilde{\sigma}^{2,MM}$, and finally and independently to compute an estimate of the mean (which is just the sample mean). Interestingly, while under more classical estimation methods, we are used to the fact that one possible variance estimator is $\hat{\bar{m}}_2$ itself, in the case of returns that follow a *t*-Student process, we know from Eq. (5.73) that $Var_t[R_{t+1}] = \nu/(\nu-2)\sigma^2 > \sigma^2$. An online example shows one practical application of these simple expressions.

Besides being very intuitive, is MM a good estimation method? Because MM does not exploit the entire empirical density of the data but only a few sample moments, it is clearly not as efficient as other methods, that we are about to introduce. This means that in general MM tends to yield standard errors that are larger than necessary. In some empirical applications, for instance when we are assessing models on the basis of tests of hypotheses of some of their parameter estimates, we shall care for standard errors.

GARCH models can be estimated with methods that extend the MMs, called the *generalized method of moments* (henceforth, GMM). Because the model in Eq. (5.65) can be simply characterized by the assumptions that the residuals in the conditional mean function are uncorrelated with the explanatory variables and/or their own past,

$$E_t[R_{t+1} - \mu_{t+1|t}(\boldsymbol{\theta})] = E[(R_{t+1} - \mu_{t+1|t}(\boldsymbol{\theta}))|\Im_t] = 0 \tag{5.111}$$

and that the implicit error in forecasting the squared residual is uncorrelated with lagged squared residuals,

$$E_t[\varepsilon^2_{t+1} - \sigma^2_{t+1|t}(\boldsymbol{\theta})] = E[(\varepsilon^2_{t+1} - \sigma^2_{t+1|t}(\boldsymbol{\theta}))|\Im_t] = 0, \tag{5.112}$$

where $\Im_t$ contains all past information in returns, the model residuals, and any possible transformation applied to them, Bates and White (1990) (but see also the treatment in Hamilton, 1994) noted that the parameters of a GARCH model could be estimated by generalizing the MMs, choosing its parameters (say, collected in the vector $\boldsymbol{\theta}$) so as to minimize (at least in a numerical sense) the objective (we disregard the identification of any required pre-sample values):

$$\mathbf{g}(\boldsymbol{\theta}; \Im_T)'\mathbf{W}_T\mathbf{g}(\boldsymbol{\theta}; \Im_T), \tag{5.113}$$

where

$$\mathbf{g}(\boldsymbol{\theta}; \Im_T) = \begin{bmatrix} T^{-1}\sum_{t=1}^{T}(R_{t+1} - \mu_{t+1|t}(\boldsymbol{\theta}))\mathbf{x}_t^{\mu} \\ T^{-1}\sum_{t=1}^{T}(\varepsilon^2_{t+1} - \sigma^2_{t+1|t}(\boldsymbol{\theta}))\mathbf{x}_t^{\sigma} \end{bmatrix}, \tag{5.114}$$

$\mathbf{x}_t^{\mu}, \mathbf{x}_t^{\sigma} \in \Im_t$ are the so-called *instruments* (variables in the information set with which residuals and squared residuals should be uncorrelated). $\mathbf{g}(\boldsymbol{\theta}; \Im_T)$ is therefore a vector of M empirical, sample moment conditions, and $\mathbf{W}_T$ is a $M \times M$ (potentially full) weighting matrix that potentially depends on the sample size. $\mathbf{W}_T$ has the purpose to weigh different moment conditions and that can be shown (under some technical conditions) to optimally equal the estimated sample covariance matrix of the M moment conditions $\mathbf{g}(\tilde{\boldsymbol{\theta}}; \Im_T)$ themselves, evaluated at some previous stage optimum vector of parameters. Eqs. (5.111) and (5.112) are called the *orthogonality conditions* of the GMM estimating a generic GARCH model. The same comment made before also applies here: even though these are GMM, they often remain rather inefficient.

In the bulk of our exposition, we focus however on MLE of $\boldsymbol{\theta}$.[21] Here $\boldsymbol{\theta}$ collects all the parameters of interest, for instance ϕ_0, ϕ_1, ω, α, and β in the case of a Gaussian AR(1), plain vanilla GARCH(1,1) model. In this case, $K = 5$ and $\boldsymbol{\theta} \equiv [\phi_0\ \phi_1\ \omega\ \alpha\ \beta]' \in \mathbb{R}^5$. When one takes into account the usual stationarity constraints, that is, $|\phi_1| < 1$, $\omega > 0$, $\alpha \geq 0$, $\beta \geq 0$, and $\alpha + \beta < 1$, in fact we have that $\boldsymbol{\theta}' \equiv [\phi_0\ \phi_1\ \omega\ \alpha\ \beta]' \in \mathbb{R} \times (-1, 1) \times \mathbb{R}_+ \times [0, 1) \times [0, 1 - \alpha)$, where $\mathbb{R}_+$ is the subset of strictly positive real numbers. Later, specific notation (Θ) to accommodate any constraints will be introduced.

21. Yet ML estimators can all be viewed as GMM estimators in which the orthogonality conditions are that the expectations of some special sample statistics (called the scores) are zero (see Hamilton, 1994). Of course, because just in this case, GMM and MLE are identical, GMM will be asymptotically efficient.

5.6.1 Maximum Likelihood Estimation

As we already know from Chapter 1, MLE is based on knowledge of the *likelihood function* implied by the data-generating process, to be numerically evaluated in correspondence to the available sample of data called $L(R_1, R_2, \ldots, R_T; \boldsymbol{\theta})$. Such an object is in general equivalent (i.e., at least for practical purposes) to the *joint PDF of the data*:

$$L(R_1, R_2, \ldots, R_T; \boldsymbol{\theta}) = \Pr(R_1, R_2, \ldots, R_T; \boldsymbol{\theta}). \tag{5.115}$$

The goal is to maximize such a probability that the data actually came from the assumed data-generating process.

DEFINITION 5.7 (MLE, I)

Assuming a unique maximizer, the MLE of the parameter vector $\boldsymbol{\theta} \in \Theta$, where Θ is the subset of admissible parameters, is defined as:

$$\hat{\boldsymbol{\theta}}_t^{ML} = \underset{\theta \in \Theta}{\arg\max}\, L(R_1, R_2, \ldots, R_T; \boldsymbol{\theta}), \tag{5.116}$$

where T is the sample size.

In general, models that are estimated by MLE are fully specified *parametric models*, in the sense that once the parameter values are known, all necessary information is available either to compute the probability of each observation in the sample under the joint PDF or to simulate the (dependent) variable(s) of interest; yet, if one can simulate the process, this means that the PDF must be known, both for each observation as a scalar random variable and for the full sample as a random vector.

In what follows, for concreteness, we shall refer to the MLE of a standard Gaussian AR(1)−GARCH(1,1) model, when $\boldsymbol{\theta} \equiv [\phi_0\ \phi_1\ \omega\ \alpha\ \beta]'$. The specification of the AR(1) process for the mean—even though it is clearly just an example—is very important to remind us that under MLE, *the parameters that enter the conditional mean and variance functions are jointly and simultaneously estimated.* However, it should be clear that these concepts easily generalize to all CH models covered in this chapter and therefore to any possible structure for $\boldsymbol{\theta} \in \Theta$. Specifically, the assumption of IID normal shocks (z_{t+1}),

$$R_{t+1} = \left(\phi_0 + \phi_1 R_t\right) + \sigma_{t+1|t} z_{t+1} \quad z_{t+1} \sim \text{IID } N(0,1) \tag{5.117}$$

implies (from normality and identical distribution of z_{t+1}) that the conditional density—also called *contribution to the total likelihood of the sample*, l_t—of the time t observation, given the information up to time $t-1$, is:

$$\begin{aligned} l_{t|t-1} \equiv \Pr(R_t;\ \boldsymbol{\theta}|R_{t-1}, \sigma^2_{t-1|t-2}) &= \frac{1}{\sigma_{t|t-1}(\boldsymbol{\theta})\sqrt{2\pi}}\exp\left[-\frac{1}{2}\frac{(R_t - \mu_{t|t-1}(\boldsymbol{\theta}))^2}{\sigma^2_{t|t-1}(\boldsymbol{\theta})}\right] \\ &= \frac{1}{\sqrt{2\pi}\sqrt{\omega + \alpha(R_t - \phi_0 - \phi_1 R_{t-1})^2 + \beta\sigma^2_{t-1|t-2}}} \\ &\quad \times \exp\left[-\frac{1}{2}\frac{(R_t - \phi_0 - \phi_1 R_{t-1})^2}{\omega + \alpha(R_t - \phi_0 - \phi_1 R_{t-1})^2 + \beta\sigma^2_{t-1|t-2}}\right], \end{aligned} \tag{5.118}$$

where the notations $\mu_{t|t-1}(\boldsymbol{\theta})$ and $\sigma^2_{t|t-1}(\boldsymbol{\theta})$ emphasize that conditional mean and variance depend on $\boldsymbol{\theta} \in \Theta$. Note that the expression after the first equality is completely general, as it depends on the two functions $\mu_{t|t-1}(\boldsymbol{\theta})$ and $\sigma^2_{t|t-1}(\boldsymbol{\theta})$. Because each shock is *conditionally independent of others* (from independence over time of z_{t+1}), by a standard *prediction error decomposition* argument, the total PDF of the entire sample is then the product of T such densities:

$$\begin{aligned} L(R_1, R_2, \ldots, R_T; \boldsymbol{\theta}) &\equiv \prod_{t=1}^{T} l_{t|t-1} = l_1 \\ &\times \prod_{t=2}^{T} \frac{1}{\sigma_{t|t-1}(\boldsymbol{\theta})\sqrt{2\pi}}\exp\left[-\frac{1}{2}\frac{(R_t - \mu_{t|t-1}(\boldsymbol{\theta}))^2}{\sigma^2_{t|t-1}(\boldsymbol{\theta})}\right]. \end{aligned} \tag{5.119}$$

Here $l_1 \equiv \Pr(R_1;\boldsymbol{\theta})$ is the probability of the very first observation that—by construction—cannot depend on previous information. As we shall see below, such l_1 contribution is often set to be equal to the average, unconditional probability of any given observation in the sample. The $1/\sigma_{t|t-1}(\boldsymbol{\theta})$ is a *Jacobian term* that arises in the transformation from the standardized innovations, $(R_t - \mu_{t|t-1}(\boldsymbol{\theta}))/\sigma_{t|t-1}(\boldsymbol{\theta})$ to the observable returns. We emphasize how crucial it is the role played by IID-ness of the shocks in driving the result in Eq. (5.119) that the total joint probability of the sample is equal to the product of the contribution of each of the observations.

The expression in Eq. (5.119) is our first, Gaussian-type likelihood function. However, because it is computationally more convenient, one usually prefers to deal with the natural logarithm of the likelihood function,

$$\ell(R_1,\ldots, R_T;\ \boldsymbol{\theta}) \equiv \ln L(R_1,\ \ldots,\ R_T;\ \boldsymbol{\theta}) = \ln \prod_{t=1}^{T} l_{t|t-1} = \ln l_1 + \sum_{t=2}^{T} \ln l_{t|t-1}, \tag{5.120}$$

called the *log-likelihood function* of the sample. However, nothing prevents us from seeing the log-likelihood as a function that simply depends on the unknown parameters in $\boldsymbol{\theta}\in\Theta$. In this case, it is not uncommon to find the notation $\ell(\boldsymbol{\theta}; R_1,\ \ldots,\ R_T)$ or simply $\ell(\boldsymbol{\theta})$. Because to maximize a given function of $\boldsymbol{\theta}\in\Theta$ and to maximize any monotone increasing transformation of the same function always gives the same maximizer, we have the following.

DEFINITION 5.8 (MLE, II)

Assuming a unique maximizer, the MLE of the parameter vector $\boldsymbol{\theta}\in\Theta$, where Θ is the subset of admissible parameters, is defined as:

$$\hat{\boldsymbol{\theta}}_T^{ML} = \arg\max_{\boldsymbol{\theta}\in\Theta} \ln L(R_1,\ R_2,\ldots,\ R_T;\ \boldsymbol{\theta}) = \arg\max_{\boldsymbol{\theta}\in\Theta} \ell(R_1,\ R_2,\ldots,\ R_T;\ \boldsymbol{\theta}), \tag{5.121}$$

where T is the sample size.

In the special case in Eq. (5.119), we have that the log-likelihood function that will be maximized is:

$$\begin{aligned}
\ell(R_1,\ldots,R_T;\boldsymbol{\theta}) &= \ln l_1 + \sum_{t=2}^{T}\left[-\ln \sigma_{t|t-1}(\boldsymbol{\theta}) - \ln\sqrt{2\pi} - \frac{1}{2}\frac{(R_t - \mu_{t|t-1}(\boldsymbol{\theta}))^2}{\sigma^2_{t|t-1}(\boldsymbol{\theta})}\right] \\
&= \ln l_1 - \frac{T-1}{2}\ln 2\pi - \frac{1}{2}\sum_{t=2}^{T}\ln \sigma^2_{t|t-1}(\boldsymbol{\theta}) - \frac{1}{2}\sum_{t=2}^{T}\frac{(R_t - \mu_{t|t-1}(\boldsymbol{\theta}))^2}{\sigma^2_{t|t-1}(\boldsymbol{\theta})} \\
&= \ln l_1 - \frac{T-1}{2}\ln 2\pi - \frac{1}{2}\sum_{t=2}^{T}\ln[\omega + \alpha(R_t - \phi_0 - \phi_1 R_{t-1})^2 + \beta\sigma^2_{t-1|t-2}] \\
&\quad - \frac{1}{2}\sum_{t=2}^{T}\frac{(R_t - \phi_0 - \phi_1 R_{t-1})^2}{\omega + \alpha(R_t - \phi_0 - \phi_1 R_{t-1})^2 + \beta\sigma^2_{t-1|t-2}},
\end{aligned} \tag{5.122}$$

where we have used several obvious properties of natural logarithms, including the fact that $\ln\sqrt{x} = \ln x^{1/2} = 0.5\ln x$ and $\ln \sigma_{t|t-1}(\boldsymbol{\theta}) = \ln\sqrt{\sigma^2_{t|t-1}(\boldsymbol{\theta})} = 0.5\ln \sigma^2_{t|t-1}(\boldsymbol{\theta})$. Therefore, the MLE is simply based on the idea of performing a function optimization, once the functional form of Eq. (5.119) has been written down, for instance setting

$$\begin{aligned}
\ln l_1 &= -\ln \bar{\sigma}(\boldsymbol{\theta}) - \frac{1}{2}\ln 2\pi - \frac{1}{2}\frac{(R_1 - \bar{\mu}(\boldsymbol{\theta}))^2}{\bar{\sigma}^2(\boldsymbol{\theta})} = -\ln\sqrt{\omega/(1-\alpha-\beta)} \\
&\quad - \frac{1}{2}\ln 2\pi - \frac{1}{2}\frac{(R_1 - \phi_0/(1-\phi_1))^2}{\omega/(1-\alpha-\beta)},
\end{aligned} \tag{5.123}$$

which means that both mean and variance are initialized at their long-run average unconditional values (more generally, at $\overline{\mu}(\boldsymbol{\theta})$ and $\overline{\sigma}^2(\boldsymbol{\theta})$). However, also $\ln l_1$ depends on the unknown, estimable parameters, $\boldsymbol{\theta}$.[22] Therefore, the ML estimator $\hat{\boldsymbol{\theta}}_T^{ML}$ shall solve—under appropriate constraints represented by the subset Θ—the maximization problem:

$$\max_{\boldsymbol{\theta}\in\Theta}\left\{-\frac{1}{2}\ln 2\pi-\ln\sqrt{\omega/(1-\alpha-\beta)}-\frac{1}{2}\frac{(R_1-\phi_0/(1-\phi_1))^2}{\omega/(1-\alpha-\beta)}+\right.$$
$$-\frac{T-1}{2}\ln 2\pi-\frac{1}{2}\sum_{t=2}^{T}\ln\left[\omega+\alpha(R_t-\phi_0-\phi_1R_{t-1})^2+\beta\sigma^2_{t-1|t-2}\right] \tag{5.124}$$
$$\left.-\frac{1}{2}\sum_{t=2}^{T}\frac{(R_t-\phi_0-\phi_1R_{t-1})^2}{\omega+\alpha(R_t-\phi_0-\phi_1R_{t-1})^2+\beta\sigma^2_{t-1|t-2}}\right\}.$$

Note that Eq. (5.120) has a recursive structure: $\ln l_{2|1}$ involves $\mu_{2|1}(\boldsymbol{\theta})$ and $\sigma^2_{2|1}(\boldsymbol{\theta})$ that depend on R_2 and R_1; $\ln l_{3|2}$ involves $\mu_{3|2}(\boldsymbol{\theta})$ and $\sigma^2_{3|2}(\boldsymbol{\theta})$ that depend on R_3 and R_2, etc. until $\ln l_{T|T-1}$ that depends on $\mu_{T|T-1}(\boldsymbol{\theta})$ and $\sigma^2_{T|T-1}(\boldsymbol{\theta})$ that depend on R_T and R_{T-1}.

The model so far has been specified under Gaussian shocks. However, *MLE applies whenever the distribution of the shocks is fully specified* in a parametric sense.

How do we actually proceed to maximize the log-likelihood function of a sample by selecting the optimizing parameters, subject to $\boldsymbol{\theta}\in\Theta$? Surely enough, not by using paper and pencil! Note that even in our short description of the recursive structure of the log-likelihood function calculation, that was done only for a given choice of the parameters $\boldsymbol{\theta}\in\Theta$ in $\ell(\boldsymbol{\theta})$: infinite, such choices remain possible. Therefore, at least in principle, to maximize $\ell(\boldsymbol{\theta})$ you will then need to repeat this operation an infinite number of times to span all the vectors of parameters in $\boldsymbol{\theta}\in\Theta$. Needless to say, it takes an infinite amount of time to "search over" all of Θ, a needle in a dense, infinite-dimensional haystack. Therefore, appropriate *methods of numerical, constrained optimization* need to be implemented: this is what packages such as Matlab, Gauss, E-Views, or Stata are for.

For instance (i.e., other, better but more complex methods are feasible), *Newton's method* uses the *Hessian*, which is a $K\times K$ matrix $H(\boldsymbol{\theta})\equiv\partial^2\ell(\boldsymbol{\theta})/\partial\boldsymbol{\theta}\partial\boldsymbol{\theta}'$ that collects second partial derivatives of the log-likelihood function with respect to each of the parameters in $\boldsymbol{\theta}$. A review of how this method works can be found among online supplementary material.

5.6.2 The Properties of MLE

What about the desired good properties of the estimator? *Assuming correct specification* of both the functional forms estimated (e.g., for conditional mean and conditional variance) and the assumed parametric density function for the errors, ML estimators have very strong theoretical properties:

- They are *consistent* estimators, meaning that as the sample size $T\to\infty$, the probability that the estimator $\hat{\boldsymbol{\theta}}_T^{ML}$ (in repeated samples) shows a large divergence from the true (unfortunately unknown) parameter values $\boldsymbol{\theta}$, goes to 0.
- They are the *most efficient* estimators (i.e., those that give estimates with the smallest standard errors, in repeated samples) among all the (asymptotically) unbiased estimators.[23]

Asymptotic normality of the MLE (and of quasi-MLE, see Section 5.6.3) has been proven in the univariate case under low-level assumptions; one of them is the existence of moments of the errors of order four or higher (see Lee and Hansen, 1994).[24]

22. Other choices for the initial $t=1$ contribution $\ln l_1$ to the log-likelihood would be possible. Even though initializing $\ln l_1$ in this way guarantees good numerical properties in applications, asymptotically the choice of $\ln l_1$ has no bearing. Occasionally, researchers ignore $\ln l_1$ and practically compute the log-likelihood effectively losing the first observation.

23. An asymptotically unbiased estimator is not a consistent estimator but for the time being, we may ignore the details of the differences between the two concepts. One indirect but equivalent way to state that the MLE is the most efficient estimator is that it achieves the *Crámer–Rao lower bound* for the variance of the estimator. The famous bound represents the least possible covariance matrix among all possible asymptotically unbiased estimators, $\hat{\boldsymbol{\theta}}$. This result derives from the fact that while MLE exploits knowledge of the density of the data, other methods (e.g., MM) do not.

24. Failing such an assumption, Hall and Yao (2003) show that the asymptotic distribution of the (Q)MLE in the univariate GARCH(p,q) model is not normal but is a stable distribution (with fatter tails than the normal) if the innovations are in the domain of attraction of a stable law with exponent smaller than two (implying nonexisting fourth moments).

All these properties can be summarized as:

RESULT 5.3 (Properties of the MLE)

Assuming a unique maximizer that solves the problem

$$\hat{\boldsymbol{\theta}}_T^{ML} = \underset{\boldsymbol{\theta}\in\Theta}{\text{argmax}} \ln L(R_1, R_2, \ldots, R_T; \boldsymbol{\theta}) = \underset{\boldsymbol{\theta}\in\Theta}{\text{argmax}}\ \ell(R_1, R_2, \ldots, R_T; \boldsymbol{\theta}), \tag{5.125}$$

$\hat{\boldsymbol{\theta}}_T^{ML}$ is consistent, asymptotically normal, and the most efficient among all asymptotically unbiased estimators for $\boldsymbol{\theta}\in\Theta$.

The concept of efficiency begs the question of how can one compute standard errors for the MLEs, in particular with reference to GARCH. If the econometric model is *correctly specified*, such an operation is based on the concept of *information matrix*:

$$I(\boldsymbol{\theta}) \equiv \lim_{T\to\infty} -E\left[\frac{1}{T}\frac{\partial^2 L(\boldsymbol{\theta})}{\partial\boldsymbol{\theta}\partial\boldsymbol{\theta}'}\right]. \tag{5.126}$$

The information matrix is just the opposite of the (expected) *Hessian of the likelihood function*.[25]

Correct specification means that the conditional mean and variance functions (i.e., $\mu_{t|t-1}(\boldsymbol{\theta})$ and $\sigma^2_{t|t-1}(\boldsymbol{\theta})$) should be correct and that the parametric distribution of the shocks (here, so far it was $z_{t+1}\sim$ IID $N(0,1)$, $z_{t+1}\sim$ IID $t(0,1;\nu)$, or $z_{t+1}\sim IID\ GED(0,1;\lambda)$ but any parametric specification for the marginal PDF of the shocks would do) is also correct. In fact, under the assumption of correct specification, the result in Eq. (5.126) is called *information matrix equality* (to the Hessian). In particular, it is the inverse of the information matrix, $I^{-1}(\boldsymbol{\theta})$ that will provide the asymptotic covariance matrix of the estimates.

RESULT 5.4 (Asymptotic Distribution of the MLE)

Assuming a unique maximizer solving the problem $\underset{\boldsymbol{\theta}\in\Theta}{\text{argmax}}\ \ell(R_1, R_2, \ldots, R_T; \boldsymbol{\theta})$, and correct specification, under some technical conditions (such as the existence of fourth-order moments),

$$\sqrt{T}(\hat{\boldsymbol{\theta}}_T^{ML} - \boldsymbol{\theta}) \overset{D}{\to} N(\mathbf{0}, I^{-1}(\boldsymbol{\theta})), \tag{5.127}$$

where $\overset{D}{\to}$ denotes convergence in distribution.

Obviously, this result implies that $\hat{\boldsymbol{\theta}}_T^{ML} \overset{a}{\to} \boldsymbol{\theta}$ and $Var[\hat{\boldsymbol{\theta}}_T^{ML}] = I_T^{-1}(\hat{\boldsymbol{\theta}}_T^{ML})$.[26] Consistent estimates of the information matrix may be calculated from T sample observations as:

$$I_T(\hat{\boldsymbol{\theta}}_T^{ML}) = -\frac{1}{T}\sum_{t=1}^{T}\left[\frac{\partial^2 L(R_t;\boldsymbol{\theta})}{\partial\boldsymbol{\theta}\partial\boldsymbol{\theta}'}\Big|_{\boldsymbol{\theta}=\hat{\boldsymbol{\theta}}_T^{ML}}\right], \tag{5.128}$$

25. For instance, when the likelihood only depends on two parameters, say θ_1 and θ_2, the Hessian is:

$$\frac{\partial^2 L(\boldsymbol{\theta})}{\partial\boldsymbol{\theta}\partial\boldsymbol{\theta}'} = \begin{bmatrix} \dfrac{\partial^2 L(\theta_1,\theta_2)}{\partial\theta_1^2} & \dfrac{\partial^2 L(\theta_1,\theta_2)}{\partial\theta_1\partial\theta_2} \\ \dfrac{\partial^2 L(\theta_1,\theta_2)}{\partial\theta_2\partial\theta_1} & \dfrac{\partial^2 L(\theta_1,\theta_2)}{\partial\theta_2^2} \end{bmatrix}.$$

The Hessian is a symmetric matrix because $\frac{\partial^2 L(\theta_1,\theta_2)}{\partial\theta_1\partial\theta_2} = \frac{\partial^2 L(\theta_1,\theta_2)}{\partial\theta_2\partial\theta_1}$.

26. Technically, under adequate assumptions, this may be stated as $\hat{\boldsymbol{\theta}}_T^{ML}$ converging to $\boldsymbol{\theta}$ *almost surely*, meaning that the event in which asymptotically $\hat{\boldsymbol{\theta}}_T^{ML} \neq \boldsymbol{\theta}$ has probability zero. See Chapter 1 for details.

where, for instance, in a Gaussian PDF case, the log-likelihood contribution $L(R_t;\ \boldsymbol{\theta})$ is:

$$L\left(R_t;\ \hat{\boldsymbol{\theta}}_T^{ML}\right) = \exp\left[-\ln \sigma_{t|t-1}\left(\hat{\boldsymbol{\theta}}_T^{ML}\right) - \ln\sqrt{2\pi} - \frac{1}{2}\frac{\left(R_t - \mu_{t|t-1}\left(\hat{\boldsymbol{\theta}}_T^{ML}\right)\right)^2}{\sigma^2_{t|t-1}\left(\hat{\boldsymbol{\theta}}_T^{ML}\right)}\right]. \tag{5.129}$$

The information matrix measures the average amount of information about the parameters that is contained in the observations of the sample. As $T \to \infty$, the asymptotic distribution of $\hat{\boldsymbol{\theta}}_T^{ML}$ allows us to approximate its covariance matrix as:

$$Var\left[\hat{\boldsymbol{\theta}}_T^{ML}\right] \simeq \left\{-\frac{1}{T}\sum_{t=1}^{T}\left[\frac{\partial^2 L(R_t;\ \boldsymbol{\theta})}{\partial\boldsymbol{\theta}\partial\boldsymbol{\theta}'}\bigg|_{\boldsymbol{\theta}=\hat{\boldsymbol{\theta}}_T^{ML}}\right]\right\}^{-1}. \tag{5.130}$$

The inverse of this matrix can be used for hypothesis testing by constructing the usual z-ratio statistic:

$$z_{\theta_j} = \frac{\mathbf{e}_j'(\hat{\boldsymbol{\theta}}_T^{ML} - \boldsymbol{\theta}^*)}{\sqrt{\mathbf{e}_j' Var[\hat{\boldsymbol{\theta}}_T^{ML}]\mathbf{e}_j}} \quad j = 1, 2, \ldots, K, \tag{5.131}$$

where $\mathbf{e}_j$ is a $K \times 1$ vector with zeros everywhere but in the jth position, where a 1 appears, for instance $\mathbf{e}_2 = [0100]'$; therefore $\mathbf{e}_j'(\hat{\boldsymbol{\theta}}_T^{ML} - \boldsymbol{\theta}^*)$ is the jth element of the vector of differences between estimated values and assumed values $(\hat{\boldsymbol{\theta}}_T^{ML} - \boldsymbol{\theta}^*)$ under the null hypothesis, and $\sqrt{\mathbf{e}_j' Var[\hat{\boldsymbol{\theta}}_T^{ML}]\mathbf{e}_j}$ is the square root of the jth element on the main diagonal of the covariance matrix of $\hat{\boldsymbol{\theta}}_T^{ML}$. Asymptotically valid tests of hypothesis are built exploiting the fact the z_{θ_j} ratios have a structure similar to t-ratios, although their distribution obtains only asymptotically, as $T \to \infty$, $z_{\theta_j} \to^D N(0, 1)$.

For instance, consider testing the null hypothesis that in a GARCH(1,1) model, $\alpha = \alpha^*$ (note that α^* is not necessarily 0, even though the null hypothesis of $\alpha^* = 0$ is very common), that is, $H_0 : \alpha = \alpha^*$. The first step is to find the ML estimate $\hat{\alpha}_T^{ML}$. Second, we compute an estimate of the standard error of this estimate from the covariance matrix, that is, $\sqrt{\mathbf{e}_j' Var[\hat{\boldsymbol{\theta}}_T^{ML}]\mathbf{e}_j}$ where j equals the index associated with α within the vector $\boldsymbol{\theta}$. Third, define the ratio

$$\hat{z}_{\alpha^*} = \frac{\hat{\alpha}_T^{ML} - \alpha^*}{S.E.[\hat{\alpha}_T^{ML}]} \overset{asy}{\sim} N(0, 1) \tag{5.132}$$

and compare it with a chosen critical value under a $N(0, 1)$, assuming α^* belongs to the feasible set, $\Theta \subseteq \mathbb{R}^K$.[27] If instead we wanted to test whether in a threshold GARCH(1,1,1) model $\alpha + \delta = const$, then the corresponding z-ratio would be:

$$\begin{aligned}\hat{z}_{\alpha+\delta} &= \frac{\boldsymbol{r}_{\alpha+\delta}'(\hat{\boldsymbol{\theta}}_T^{ML} - \boldsymbol{\theta}^*)}{\sqrt{\boldsymbol{r}_{\alpha+\delta}' Var[\hat{\boldsymbol{\theta}}_T^{ML}]\boldsymbol{r}_{\alpha+\delta}}} = \qquad \text{where } \boldsymbol{r}_{\alpha+\delta} = [0\ldots 1\ 1\ldots 0]' \\ &= \frac{\hat{\alpha}^{ML} + \hat{\delta}^{ML} - const}{\sqrt{Var[\hat{\alpha}^{ML}] + Var[\hat{\delta}^{ML}] + 2Cov[\hat{\alpha}^{ML}, \hat{\delta}^{ML}]}} \overset{a}{\sim} N(0, 1),\end{aligned} \tag{5.133}$$

where we assume that α and δ occupy adjacent places in $\boldsymbol{\theta} \in \Theta$. Interestingly, in this case $\boldsymbol{r}_{\alpha+\delta}' Var[\hat{\boldsymbol{\theta}}_T^{ML}]\boldsymbol{r}_{\alpha+\delta} = Var[\hat{\alpha}^{ML}] + Var[\hat{\delta}^{ML}] + 2Cov[\hat{\alpha}^{ML}, \hat{\delta}^{ML}]$, exactly as one would expect from first principles. Therefore, $z_{\alpha+\delta}' = (\hat{\alpha}^{ML} + \hat{\delta}^{ML} - const)/(S.E.[\hat{\alpha}^{ML}] + S.E.[\hat{\delta}^{ML}])$ would then represent an invalid test because it ignores the covariance between the ML estimators of α and δ.

27. For instance, assuming a Type I error of 5%, if $|\hat{z}_{\alpha^*}| \geq 1.96$, the null hypothesis of $\hat{\alpha}_T^{ML} = \alpha^*$ is rejected; if $|\hat{z}_{\alpha^*}| < 1.96$ the null cannot be rejected.

EXAMPLE 5.24

Let us return to estimating GARCH models for daily, value-weighted US excess equity returns over a long sample 1963–2016. We have so many observations (13,595) that even ignoring the very first one and maximizing the (partial) log-likelihood that sums between $t=2$ and $T=13{,}595$ should not make much difference. We assume an MA(1) conditional mean and estimate by MLE, using E-Views, a threshold GARCH(1,1,1) with Gaussian innovations:

$$x_{t+1} = \underset{(0.000)}{0.026} + \underset{(0.000)}{0.129}\,\varepsilon_t + \varepsilon_{t+1} \quad \varepsilon_{t+1}\text{IID } N(0,\sigma^2_{t+1|t})$$

$$\sigma^2_{t+1|t} = \underset{(0.000)}{0.009} + \underset{(0.000)}{0.024}\,\varepsilon_t^2 + \underset{(0.000)}{0.112}\, I_{\{\varepsilon_t<0\}}\varepsilon_t^2 + \underset{(0.000)}{0.911}\,\sigma^2_{t|t-1},$$

with an estimated persistence index of $0.024+0.5\times 0.112+0.911=0.991$. The estimation is performed setting the tolerance threshold at 0.0001, which is rather typical. The initial values are obtained by a first-round estimation performed on the OLS residuals of the model and are 0.025, 0.005, 0.631, 0.150, 0.050, and 0.600, for the parameters in $\boldsymbol{\theta}\equiv[\kappa_0\ \kappa_1\ \omega\ \alpha\ \delta\ \beta]'$, respectively. E-Views informs us after printing the estimation output that only 18 iterations were required to achieve convergence. The maximized log-likelihood is -16103.88. The covariance matrix for the ML parameter estimates corresponding to the output above is then:

$$Var[\hat{\boldsymbol{\theta}}_T^{ML}] = \begin{bmatrix} 4.5E-05 & 1.4E-06 & -3.9E-07 & 5.6E-07 & -5.9E-06 & -4.2E-07 \\ 1.4E-06 & 8.0E-05 & 2.0E-07 & -1.0E-06 & 3.7E-06 & -9.6E-07 \\ -3.9E-07 & 2.0E-07 & 3.9E-07 & 3.7E-07 & 4.7E-07 & -1.3E-06 \\ 5.6E-07 & -1.0E-06 & 3.7E-07 & 9.8E-06 & -8.1E-06 & -5.8E-06 \\ -5.9E-06 & 3.7E-06 & 4.7E-07 & -8.1E-06 & 2.1E-05 & -1.1E-06 \\ -4.2E-07 & -9.6E-07 & -1.3E-06 & -5.8E-06 & -1.1E-06 & 8.3E-06 \end{bmatrix}.$$

Clearly, because at least asymptotically, $Var[\hat{\boldsymbol{\theta}}_T^{ML}] \overset{asy}{\to} I_T^{-1}(\hat{\boldsymbol{\theta}}_T^{ML})$, we have:

$$I_T(\hat{\boldsymbol{\theta}}_T^{ML}) \cong \begin{bmatrix} 32305 & -688.7 & 366459 & 123594 & 57978 & 154270 \\ -688.7 & 12570 & -1085.8 & -36.4 & -2388.5 & 888.1 \\ 366459 & -1085.8 & 16709810 & 4289531 & 1734009 & 5914460 \\ 123594 & -36.4 & 4289531 & 1666943 & 699248 & 1951148 \\ 57979 & -2388.5 & 1734009 & 699248 & 345230 & 815227 \\ 154270 & 888.1 & 5914460 & 1951148 & 815227 & 2546055 \end{bmatrix}.$$

We then proceed to reestimate the same model, starting from a different set of initial conditions, that is, a rather special $\boldsymbol{\theta}_0\equiv[0\ 0\ 0\ 0\ 0\ 0]'$. We find identical ML estimates and maximized log-likelihood function. We then apply a more restrictive convergence criterion, 0.000001 instead of 0.0001. E-Views now takes a bit longer, iterates 26 times, but achieves an identical optimum and yields identical ML estimates. In fact, the same occurs under a very lax convergence tolerance criterion of 0.001 only. This builds a strong case for the $\hat{\boldsymbol{\theta}}_T^{ML}$ reported above representing a true global maximizer.

Finally, we repeat the estimation assuming *t*-Student innovations for the shocks and obtain, starting from initial conditions 0.025, 0.005, 0.971, 0.150, 0.050, 0.600, and 20.00 for $\boldsymbol{\theta}\equiv[\kappa_0\ \kappa_1\ \omega\ \alpha\ \delta\ \beta\ \nu]'$, the following ML estimates:

$$x_{t+1} = \underset{(0.000)}{0.039} + \underset{(0.000)}{0.122}\,\varepsilon_t + \varepsilon_{t+1} \quad \varepsilon_{t+1}\text{ IID } t(0,\sigma^2_{t+1|t};\underset{(0.000)}{7.823})$$

$$\sigma^2_{t+1|t} = \underset{(0.000)}{0.007} + \underset{(0.000)}{0.024}\,\varepsilon_t^2 + \underset{(0.000)}{0.111}\, I_{\{\varepsilon_t<0\}}\varepsilon_t^2 + \underset{(0.000)}{0.914}\,\sigma^2_{t|t-1},$$

with an estimated persistence index of $0.024+0.5\times 0.111+0.914=0.993$, that once more goes to show that even a very fat-tailed *t*-distribution not always goes to reduce the persistence of a GARCH model. Also note that the MA(1) estimates have changed too, which is expected when under full MLE all coefficients are jointly and simultaneously estimated. Only 13 iterations were required to achieve convergence and the maximized log-likelihood is -15844.05. However, because it is computed under a radically different ($\hat{\nu}=7.823\ll 20$) parametric model for the PDF, such a maximized log-likelihood value is not strictly comparable, in terms of judging whether a global maximum has been achieved, with the -16013.88 reported above. The covariance matrix for the ML parameter estimates corresponding to the output above is then:

$$Var[\hat{\boldsymbol{\theta}}_T^{ML}] = \begin{bmatrix} 3.9E-05 & 1.5E-07 & -4.1E-07 & -1.3E-08 & -5.8E-06 & 3.6E-07 & -1.0E-04 \\ 1.5E-07 & 8.0E-05 & -2.3E-08 & -1.1E-06 & 4.1E-06 & -1.0E-06 & -2.9E-06 \\ -4.1E-07 & -2.3E-08 & 7.4E-07 & 2.8E-07 & 1.3E-06 & -2.1E-06 & 1.7E-05 \\ -1.3E-08 & -1.1E-06 & 2.8E-07 & 2.3E-05 & -1.5E-05 & -1.3E-05 & -6.4E-05 \\ -5.8E-06 & 4.1E-06 & 1.3E-06 & -1.5E-05 & 5.8E-05 & -1.0E-05 & -3.8E-04 \\ 3.6E-07 & -1.0E-06 & -2.1E-06 & -1.3E-05 & -1.0E-05 & 1.9E-05 & -4.4E-05 \\ -1.0E-04 & -2.9E-06 & 1.7E-05 & -6.4E-05 & -3.8E-04 & -4.4E-05 & 1.9E-01 \end{bmatrix}.$$

Apart from the newly estimated $Var[\hat{\nu}^{ML}]=0.186$ and related covariances, also the variances and covariances of all remaining parameter estimates have now changed, as one expects of a differently specified parametric model. For instance, $Var[\hat{\alpha}^{ML}]$ was

(Continued)

EXAMPLE 5.24 (Continued)

9.78E−06 under Gaussian errors and it becomes 2.29E−05 under *t*-Student errors, more than doubling. Finally, if we wanted to test the null hypothesis $\alpha + \delta = 0.15$ (which is the 1-day delayed impact of the square of a negative shock on subsequent variance), because

$$\sqrt{Var[\hat{\alpha}^{ML}] + Var[\hat{\delta}^{ML}] + 2Cov[\hat{\alpha}^{ML}, \hat{\delta}^{ML}]} = \sqrt{0.000023 + 0.000058 - 2 \cdot 0.000015}$$

and this equals 0.00226, then:

$$\hat{z}_{\alpha+\delta} = \frac{0.024 + 0.111 - 0.150}{0.00226} = -0.664 \overset{asy}{\sim} N(0,1),$$

and we conclude that the null cannot be rejected as $|\hat{z}_{\alpha+\delta}| < 1.96$.

Although in practice they are used less often than they could or should, it is clear how one would proceed from Eqs. (5.130) and (5.131) to form *confidence intervals with confidence level* $(1-p)\%$ for each of the estimated coefficients, $j = 1, 2, \ldots, K$:

$$\begin{aligned}
z_{\theta_j} &= \frac{\boldsymbol{e}'_j(\hat{\boldsymbol{\theta}}_T^{ML} - \boldsymbol{\theta})}{\sqrt{\boldsymbol{e}'_j Var[\hat{\boldsymbol{\theta}}_T^{ML}]\boldsymbol{e}_j}} \overset{asy}{\sim} N(0,1) \Rightarrow \Pr\left(|z_{\theta_j}| = \left|\frac{\boldsymbol{e}'_j(\hat{\boldsymbol{\theta}}_T^{ML} - \boldsymbol{\theta})}{\sqrt{\boldsymbol{e}'_j Var[\hat{\boldsymbol{\theta}}_T^{ML}]\boldsymbol{e}_j}}\right| < z_{1-p/2}\right) = 1-p \\
&\Rightarrow \Pr\left(-z_{1-p/2} < \frac{\boldsymbol{e}'_j(\hat{\boldsymbol{\theta}}_T^{ML} - \boldsymbol{\theta})}{\sqrt{\boldsymbol{e}'_j Var[\hat{\boldsymbol{\theta}}_T^{ML}]\boldsymbol{e}_j}} < z_{1-p/2}\right) = 1-p \\
&\Rightarrow \Pr\left(-S.E.[\hat{\boldsymbol{\theta}}_T^{ML}]z_{1-p/2} < \boldsymbol{e}'_j\hat{\boldsymbol{\theta}}_T^{ML} - \boldsymbol{e}'_j\boldsymbol{\theta} < S.E.[\hat{\boldsymbol{\theta}}_T^{ML}]z_{1-p/2}\right) = 1-p \\
&\Rightarrow \Pr\left(-\boldsymbol{e}'_j\hat{\boldsymbol{\theta}}_T^{ML} - S.E.[\hat{\boldsymbol{\theta}}_T^{ML}]z_{1-p/2} < -\boldsymbol{e}'_j\boldsymbol{\theta} < -\boldsymbol{e}'_j\hat{\boldsymbol{\theta}}_T^{ML} + S.E.[\hat{\boldsymbol{\theta}}_T^{ML}]z_{1-p/2}\right) = 1-p \\
&\Rightarrow \Pr\left(\boldsymbol{e}'_j\hat{\boldsymbol{\theta}}_T^{ML} - S.E.[\hat{\boldsymbol{\theta}}_T^{ML}]z_{1-p/2} < \boldsymbol{e}'_j\boldsymbol{\theta} < \boldsymbol{e}'_j\hat{\boldsymbol{\theta}}_T^{ML} + S.E.[\hat{\boldsymbol{\theta}}_T^{ML}]z_{1-p/2}\right) = 1-p,
\end{aligned} \tag{5.134}$$

where $z_{1-p/2}$ is the critical value under the standard normal PDF that leaves $p/2\%$ probability in each of the two tails. An example on the computation of confidence intervals based on the same point estimates as in Example 5.24 can be found in an online appendix.

5.6.3 Quasi MLE

Arguably, the idea of trying and finding a unique $\hat{\boldsymbol{\theta}}_T^{ML} \in \Theta$ that maximizes the joint probability that the sample of data actually came from the process parameterized by $\boldsymbol{\theta} \in \Theta$ is rather intuitive. It follows a layman's drive to give an assumed model (e.g., a GARCH) its best chance to make it as consistent as possible to what we see out there in real life, in financial markets. Importantly "as consistent as possible" hardly means "perfectly consistent," that is, a poorly specified model, even though it is estimated by MLE, may still yield a very poor fit to the available data. However, one detail that should not go unnoticed is the fact that MLE requires knowledge of all the elements that enter

$$R_{t+1} = \mu_{t+1|t} + \sigma_{t+1|t}z_{t+1} \quad z_{t+1} \sim \text{IID } D(0,\ 1; \boldsymbol{\theta}_D), \tag{5.135}$$

which means to know with perfect certainty:

- The parametric and functional form of the conditional mean, $\mu_{t+1|t}$, for instance some ARMA(p,q) or regression model.
- The parametric and functional form of the conditional variance, $\sigma_{t+1|t}$, for instance some variant of GARCH(p,q) model.
- The IID nature of the shocks, z_{t+1}.
- The parametric PDF $D(0,\ 1; \boldsymbol{\theta}_D)$ from which the errors are drawn, where $\boldsymbol{\theta}_D$ is the subset of the $K \times 1$ vector of parameters $\boldsymbol{\theta}$ that just collects parameters that enter the distribution of the errors (e.g., ν in the case of a *t*-Student); for instance, $D(0,\ 1; \boldsymbol{\theta}_D)$ could be a Normal, a *t*-Student, a GED, etc.

In fact, as we have seen in Section 5.6.1, both the IID nature of z_{t+1} and the fact that $z_{t+1} \sim D(0, 1; \theta_D)$ have been repeatedly exploited in building the log-likelihood function. What if we were not positive about the fact that Eq. (5.135) adequately describes our data? For instance, what if all we can say is that $R_{t+1} = \mu_{t+1|t} + \sigma_{t+1|t} z_{t+1}$ where $z_{t+1} \sim$ IID (0, 1) but with no precise idea on the parametric, functional form of the distribution from which the shocks are drawn? Possibly, in many applications, it will feel that we understand well what types of parametric distributions are not adequate to describe the data—for instance, that a standard Gaussian density for $z_{t+1} \sim$ IID N (0, 1) may simply *not* work because its symmetry and relatively thin tails are inadequate—but we are clueless as to which exact type may perform well. Can we then still somehow perform the estimation procedure that we have described in Section 5.6.1 and count on *some* of the good properties of ML estimators stated in Section 5.6.2? The answer is a qualified—because *it holds only subject to specific but possibly verifiable conditions*—"yes" and the resulting estimator is called a *quasi (or pseudo) maximum likelihood estimator* (QMLE). Interestingly, the underlying statistical proof is one of the most useful and frequently exploited findings in modern econometrics—in a way, as close to magic as econometrics can get!

The key finding concerning the QML estimator is that even though the conditional distribution of the shocks z_{t+1} is *non-normal* (i.e., z_{t+1} is *not* IID $N(0, 1)$), *under some conditions*, an application of MLE based on $z_{t+1} \sim$ IID N (0, 1)—where *normality is anyway assumed to hold*—will yield estimators of the conditional mean and variance parameters which converge to the true parameters as the sample gets infinitely large, that is, that are *consistent.*[28] What are these conditions? Apart from some technical requirements, you will need that:

- *The conditional variance function,* $\sigma^2_{t+1|t}$, seen as a function of all information up to time t, *must be correctly specified.*
- *The conditional mean function,* $\mu_{t+1|t}$, seen as a function of all information up to time t, *must be correctly specified.*

DEFINITION 5.9 (QMLE)

Assuming a unique maximizer and the conditional mean and variance functions, $\mu_{t+1|t}$ and $\sigma^2_{t+1|t}$, are both correctly specified in terms of their functional dependence of $\boldsymbol{\theta} \in \Theta$, the QMLE of the parameter vector $\boldsymbol{\theta} \in \Theta$, where Θ is the subset of admissible parameters, is defined as:

$$\hat{\boldsymbol{\theta}}_T^{QML} = \underset{\boldsymbol{\theta}\in\Theta}{\text{argmax}} \ \ln L(R_1, R_2, \ldots, R_T; \boldsymbol{\theta}) = \underset{\boldsymbol{\theta}\in\Theta}{\text{argmax}} \ \ell(R_1, R_2, \ldots, R_T; \boldsymbol{\theta}),$$

where T is the sample size and

$$\begin{aligned} L(R_1, R_2, \ldots, R_T; \boldsymbol{\theta}) &= l_1(R_1; \boldsymbol{\theta}) \bullet \prod_{t=2}^{T} \frac{1}{\sigma_{t|t-1}(\boldsymbol{\theta})\sqrt{2\pi}} \exp\left[-\frac{1}{2} \frac{(R_t - \mu_{t|t-1}(\boldsymbol{\theta}))^2}{\sigma^2_{t|t-1}(\boldsymbol{\theta})} \right] \\ \ell(R_1, R_2, \ldots, R_T; \boldsymbol{\theta}) &= \ln l_1(R_1; \boldsymbol{\theta}) + \sum_{t=2}^{T} \left[-\ln \sigma_{t|t-1}(\boldsymbol{\theta}) - \ln\sqrt{2\pi} - \frac{1}{2} \frac{(R_t - \mu_{t|t-1}(\boldsymbol{\theta}))^2}{\sigma^2_{t|t-1}(\boldsymbol{\theta})} \right]. \end{aligned} \tag{5.136}$$

Two aspects need to be clarified. First, the expression "correctly specified" means that the functional specification of the models for the conditional mean and variance are the right ones among many possible. In practice, most of this chapter may be taken as a survey of alternative and increasingly complex conditional variance functions. Chapters 2–4 can be read as a survey of a range of potential models for the conditional mean function. Of course, based on a reader's past econometrics sequence and studies, we can imagine an unlimited number of regressions that can be used to pin down the dynamics of conditional means. For instance, under correct specification, it will be the case that no past value of the variables or the residuals will be able to forecast subsequent residuals as well as squared standardized residuals.

One example of what it means to *misspecify a model* will help understanding what correct specification means. Suppose the world as we know it, is actually ruled—as far as the conditional variance of the returns of some portfolio of interest goes (say the market portfolio of the CAPM)—by a EGARCH(1,1) process, say:

$$\ln \sigma^2_{t+1|t} = \omega + \beta \ln \sigma^2_{t|t-1} + g(z_t) \qquad g(z_t) = \theta z_t + \delta(|z_t| - E|z_t|). \tag{5.137}$$

---

28. Such conditions and technical details are presented in Bollerslev and Wooldridge (1992).

However, we do not know it (how could we, given that until a few days or weeks ago we had not ever heard of such a EGARCH gadget?) and just out of lack of better ideas, we proceed to estimate a plain vanilla GARCH(1,1) model, $\sigma^2_{t+1|t} = \omega + \alpha\varepsilon^2_t + \beta\sigma^2_{t|t-1}$. Therefore, the very functional form that we use is incorrect; not to mention that the very fact that we should be estimating four parameters (ω, β, θ, and δ in the EGARCH) and not just the three featured by the GARCH (ω, α, and β), this represents a violation of the needed assumptions to operationalize the QMLE.

Second, note that the set of assumptions needed for the properties of QMLE to obtain includes the correct specification of the conditional mean function, $\mu_{t+1|t}$. This applies also when our main interest lies with the estimation of the conditional variance process. This represents an important note of caution when QMLE is invoked in applied volatility work and an analyst may be tempted—usually with daily data—to assume either a zero mean or a very simplistic, "off-the-shelf" ARMA model, without performing adequate misspecification tests.

The QML result that delivers consistency of the estimator under correct specification of the conditional mean and variance may feel as the classical case of "Too good to be true," and in some ways this is true. In fact, QMLE methods imply a cost, in a statistical sense: *QMLE will in general be less efficient than ML estimators are*. Under QMLE, the optimal estimator of $Var[\hat{\boldsymbol{\theta}}_T^{QML}]$ is:

$$Var\left[\hat{\boldsymbol{\theta}}_T^{QML}\right] \simeq \left\{-\frac{1}{T}\sum_{t=1}^{T}\left[\frac{\partial^2 L(R_t;\boldsymbol{\theta})}{\partial\boldsymbol{\theta}\partial\boldsymbol{\theta}'}\bigg|_{\boldsymbol{\theta}=\hat{\boldsymbol{\theta}}}\right]\right\}^{-1} \times\left\{-\frac{1}{T}\sum_{t=1}^{T}\left[\frac{\partial L(R_t;\boldsymbol{\theta})}{\partial\boldsymbol{\theta}}\bigg|_{\boldsymbol{\theta}=\hat{\boldsymbol{\theta}}}\right]\right\}\left\{-\frac{1}{T}\sum_{t=1}^{T}\left[\frac{\partial L(R_t;\boldsymbol{\theta})}{\partial\boldsymbol{\theta}}\bigg|_{\boldsymbol{\theta}=\hat{\boldsymbol{\theta}}}\right]\right\}'\left\{-\frac{1}{T}\sum_{t=1}^{T}\left[\frac{\partial^2 L(R_t;\boldsymbol{\theta})}{\partial\boldsymbol{\theta}\partial\boldsymbol{\theta}'}\bigg|_{\boldsymbol{\theta}=\hat{\boldsymbol{\theta}}}\right]\right\}^{-1}, \tag{5.138}$$

where the $K\times 1$ vector $-T^{-1}\sum_{t=1}^{T}\partial L(R_t;\,\hat{\boldsymbol{\theta}})/\partial\boldsymbol{\theta}$ is called the sum of the sample gradients of the log-likelihood function, that is, the sum of first-partial derivatives of the log-likelihood evaluated in correspondence to $\boldsymbol{\theta} = \hat{\boldsymbol{\theta}}_T^{QML}$. Such a vector is also called the *sample score*. One can prove that $Var[\hat{\boldsymbol{\theta}}_T^{QML}] - Var[\hat{\boldsymbol{\theta}}_T^{ML}]$ is a semi-positive definite $K\times K$ matrix, $\mathbf{C} = Var[\hat{\boldsymbol{\theta}}_T^{QML}] - Var[\hat{\boldsymbol{\theta}}_T^{ML}]$, which goes to show that the QML covariance matrix is "larger" (in matrix sense) than $Var[\hat{\boldsymbol{\theta}}_T^{ML}]$. For instance, the denominator of the z-score statistics such as the ones in Eq. (5.131) will be larger when $Var[\hat{\boldsymbol{\theta}}_T^{QML}]$ is used versus when $Var[\hat{\boldsymbol{\theta}}_T^{ML}]$ is used:

$$\mathbf{r}'Var[\hat{\boldsymbol{\theta}}_T^{QML}]\mathbf{r} - \mathbf{r}'Var[\hat{\boldsymbol{\theta}}_T^{ML}]\mathbf{r} = \mathbf{r}'(Var[\hat{\boldsymbol{\theta}}_T^{QML}] - Var[\hat{\boldsymbol{\theta}}_T^{ML}])\mathbf{r} = \mathbf{r}'\mathbf{C}\mathbf{r} \geq 0. \tag{5.139}$$

By using QMLE, we trade-off theoretical asymptotic parameter efficiency with expediency:

RESULT 5.5 (Properties of the QMLE)

Assuming a unique maximizer for Eqs. (5.111) or (5.116) and that the conditional mean and variance functions, $\mu_{t+1|t}$ and $\sigma^2_{t+1|t}$, are both correctly specified in terms of their functional dependence of $\boldsymbol{\theta}\in\Theta$, the QMLE for the parameter vector $\boldsymbol{\theta}\in\Theta$, where Θ is the subset of admissible parameters, is consistent and asymptotically normal; however, in general, $\hat{\boldsymbol{\theta}}_T^{QML}$ is not asymptotically efficient.

In short, Result 5.5 implies that we can still use ML estimation *based on normality assumptions* even when the shocks are not normally distributed (or we simply do not know whether this makes sense), provided our choices of conditional mean and variance function are defendable, at least in empirical terms. However, because the maintained model still has that $R_{t+1} = \mu_{t+1|t} + \sigma_{t+1|t}z_{t+1}$ $z_{t+1} \sim$ IID $D(0,\, 1;\boldsymbol{\theta}_D)$, the shocks will have to be IID: you can just do without normality, but the convenience of IID-ness that allows you to operate with a likelihood function written as a product of likelihood contributions, is usually maintained. In practice, QMLE buys us the freedom to worry about the conditional distribution of the shocks in a second stage, focusing most of the initial effort on coming up with realistic and empirically sound models of the conditional mean—what we are used to do in regression and in Box–Jenkins analyses, see Chapters 1 and 2—and conditional variance. On the latter account, hopefully the task remains a challenging one but has stopped being unsurmountable after working through this chapter.

How does QMLE perform in practice? Bollerslev and Wooldridge (1992) have performed extensive simulation experiments to show that for symmetric departures from conditional normality, the QMLE is generally close to the exact MLE, in terms of resulting point estimates. However, as noted by Engle and Gonzalez-Rivera (1991), for nonsymmetric conditional distributions both the asymptotic and the finite sample loss in efficiency may be quite large.

5.6.4 Misspecification Tests

The treatment of QMLE naturally leads us to ask how can we mature any legitimate concerns on any assumption that could have been initially made on the parametric, joint density of the errors that drive the model in Eq. (5.133). In particular, if a finance empiricist starts out, as it seems to be as typical as convenient, with an assumption of normally distributed errors, $z_{t+1} \sim \text{IID}N(0, 1)$, how can she test whether this assumption is backed by her data?

The first, rather crude, method consists of applying standard *univariate tests of normality*, that aim at checking whether data from a given stochastic process—in this case, the empirical standardized residuals from some CH model—are compatible with a normal data-generating process. In practice, if you have estimated the parameters of a conditional volatility model ($\hat{\sigma}_{t+1|t}$) by MLE and exploited the assumption that $z_{t+1} \sim \text{IID } N(0, 1)$ in, say,

$$R_{t+1} = \mu_{t+1|t} + \sigma_{t+1|t} z_{t+1} \quad z_{t+1} \sim \text{IID } N(0, 1), \tag{5.140}$$

this implies that the standardized model residuals, $\hat{z}_{t+1} \equiv R_{t+1}/\hat{\sigma}_{t+1|t}$, should have a normal distribution with zero mean and unit variance. Moreover, because a standard normal distribution is symmetric around 0 and the thickness of its tails are used as benchmarks to measure tail fatness of all distributions (i.e., the excess kurtosis of a normal is set to 0 by construction), the empirical (unconditional, overall) distribution of $\hat{z}_{t+1}$ should be characterized by zero skewness and zero excess kurtosis. Exploiting these properties, a typical approach consists of using *Jarque and Bera's (JB) test* that we have discussed in Chapter 2: despite not being the only way to test for normality, it is certainly the most popular in finance. There are also more general ways, compared to JB test, to investigate whether the standardized residuals from a CH model may be consistent with a different, assumed distribution. We refer readers to Davis and Stephens (1989) for an introduction to such more advanced, so-called *goodness of fit tests*, based on empirical distribution functions.

A second method echoes our earlier tests of time series independence of the filtered standardized residuals: this derives from the fact that even though normality has not been assumed (this is the case of QMLE) so that the model for returns is the general one in Eq. (5.135), correct specification requires that the *standardized residuals must be IID*. As already discussed in Section 5.2.4, independence implies that $\hat{Q}_k^g(z) \simeq 0$ for all $k \geq 1$ where

$$\hat{Q}_k^g(z) \equiv T \sum_{\tau=1}^{k} (\hat{\rho}_\tau^g)^2 \overset{asy}{\sim} \chi_k^2 \quad \hat{\rho}_\tau^g \equiv \frac{\sum_{t=1}^{T-\tau} (g(z_t) - \overline{g(z_t)})(g(z_{t+\tau}) - \overline{g(z_t)})}{\sum_{t=1}^{T-\tau} (g(z_t) - \overline{g(z_t)})^2} \tag{5.141}$$

is the *Box–Pierce Q statistics* already presented in Chapter 2 and $g(\cdot)$ is any (measurable) function. Because we are testing the correct specification of a conditional volatility model, it is typical to set $g(x) = x^2$, that is, to test whether the squared standardized residuals display any autocorrelation patterns.[29] Although we already showed some applications of the JB and Box–Pierce tests in Chapter 2, at this point, the Reader is invited to peruse an online example dealing with GARCH modeling.

5.6.5 Sequential Estimation and QMLE

There is one special case in which we may indulge into QMLE estimation even though our key problem is not really the correct specification of the joint density of the shocks to returns (or other variable of interest), that is, when we may need to invoke the QMLE result even though we have a precise idea on the parametric structure of the PDF in Eq. (5.133). This occurs when estimation of some vector of parameters $\boldsymbol{\theta} \in \Theta \subseteq \mathbb{R}^K$ is conveniently—this is the only reason why we would do that, because we understand that QMLE implies an efficiency loss—split up in a number of *sequential estimation* stages. For instance, if $\boldsymbol{\theta} \equiv [\boldsymbol{\theta}_1' \boldsymbol{\theta}_2']' \in \Theta$, the idea is that one would first estimate by regular, fully specified MLE the first sub-vector $\boldsymbol{\theta}_1$ and then, conditional on the $\hat{\boldsymbol{\theta}}_1$ obtained during the first stage, estimate—again, at least in principle by full MLE—$\boldsymbol{\theta}_2$. Why would we do that? Sometimes because of the enhanced tractability of the problem, since estimation would be otherwise much harder; in other occasions, to avoid numerical optimization altogether, which may be advantageous.

29. As noted in Example 5.11, we can also use sample autocorrelations to test the null of IID standardized residuals, possibly on the basis of rejection regions based on Bartlett's asymptotic standard errors.

EXAMPLE 5.25

In this example, we perform an operation that, especially in light of the online example just cited, may appear odd—in fact it is so: we try and estimate a Gaussian AR(1)–ARCH(1) model just by using OLS. Please let us not try this at home (or in our term papers)! We know that estimation should be performed by (Q)MLE. One premise is crucial: remember from Chapter 1 that, under specific but tight assumptions that define the so-called *classical linear regression model*, the OLS estimators of the coefficients in a linear regression models are identical to the ML estimators of the same coefficients. Therefore, under appropriate assumptions and *just for linear regressions*, OLS and MLE are identical methods. Given our daily sample of 1963–2016 excess stock returns data, we know from Section 5.6.1 what we ought to be doing, that is, solving:

$$\max_{\theta\in\Theta}\left\{-\frac{1}{2}\ln 2\pi-\ln\sqrt{\omega/(1-\alpha)}-\frac{1}{2}\frac{(R_1-\phi_0/(1-\phi_1))^2}{\omega/(1-\alpha)}\right.$$
$$\left.-\frac{T-1}{2}\ln 2\pi-\frac{1}{2}\sum_{t=2}^{T}\ln\left[\omega+\alpha(R_t-\phi_0-\phi_1R_{t-1})^2\right]-\frac{1}{2}\sum_{t=2}^{T}\frac{(R_t-\phi_0-\phi_1R_{t-1})^2}{\omega+\alpha(R_t-\phi_0-\phi_1R_{t-1})^2}\right\},$$

where $\Theta=\mathbb{R}\times(-1,1)\times\mathbb{R}_+\times[0,1)$. Note that the log-likelihood function jointly and simultaneously depends on all four parameters that characterize the model. ML estimation in E-Views in fact returns (the numbers in parenthesis below the estimates are standard errors):

$$x_{t+1}=\underset{(0.0067)}{0.039}+\underset{(0.0033)}{0.101}x_t+\varepsilon_{t+1}\quad \varepsilon_{t+1}\ \text{IID}\ N(0,\sigma^2_{t+1|t})$$
$$\sigma^2_{t+1|t}=\underset{(0.0046)}{0.669}+\underset{(0.0081)}{0.315}\varepsilon_t^2.$$

One may be tempted to follow a different route: why not obtain the estimated OLS residuals $\{\hat{\varepsilon}_t^2\}_{t=2}^T$ from a simple regression as:

$$\hat{\varepsilon}_t=R_t-\hat{\varphi}_0-\hat{\varphi}_1R_{t-1}$$

(which incidentally already gives estimates for φ_0 and φ_1) and then separately estimate ω and α from maximization of:

$$\max_{\omega,\alpha\in\Theta}\ -\frac{T-1}{2}\ln 2\pi-\frac{1}{2}\sum_{t=2}^{T}\ln(\omega+\alpha\hat{\varepsilon}_{t-1}^2)-\frac{1}{2}\sum_{t=2}^{T}\frac{\hat{\varepsilon}_t^2}{\omega+\alpha\hat{\varepsilon}_{t-1}^2},$$

where $\{\hat{\varepsilon}_t^2\}_{t=2}^T$ are considered as if they were data even though these are obtained conditional on the OLS estimates $\hat{\varphi}_0$ and $\hat{\varphi}_1$? Incidentally, note that because the residuals $\{\hat{\varepsilon}_t^2\}_{t=2}^T$ cannot be computed for $t=1$ (i.e., the first observation is "lost"), the equivalence between two-step OLS estimation and full MLE is already broken here, even though how good the approximation provided by MLE applied to $t=2,3,\ldots T$ will depend on T and to be sample-specific. Crucially though, under the assumption of normally distributed errors in the original AR(1) model, we have that $\hat{\varphi}_0$ and $\hat{\varphi}_1$ are also ML estimates. In this case, given $\boldsymbol{\theta}\equiv[\boldsymbol{\theta}'_1\boldsymbol{\theta}'_2]'$, we have $\boldsymbol{\theta}_1\equiv[\varphi_0\ \varphi_1]'$ and $\boldsymbol{\theta}_2\equiv[\omega\alpha]'$. If we apply such a two-step procedure in E-Views, we obtain:

$$x_{t+1}=\underset{(0.0084)}{0.024}+\underset{(0.0086)}{0.053}x_t+\varepsilon_{t+1}\quad \varepsilon_{t+1}\ \text{IID}\ N(0,\sigma^2_{t+1|t})$$
$$\sigma^2_{t+1|t}=\underset{(0.0049)}{0.663}+\underset{(0.0083)}{0.330}\varepsilon_t^2.$$

The estimates are rather different, especially those of the AR(1) model, and even though not all p-values reveal it, the standard errors have remarkably grown when the two-step method has been adopted. Clearly, there is no illusion: this is a QMLE and the loss of efficiency versus full MLE may be substantial, as we shall see below. In fact, you even suspect that the very estimation of φ_0 and φ_1 by OLS in the first stage may be problematic, as in the case of an AR process we know that MLE does not correspond to OLS. In short, OLS estimation of GARCH models should be avoided in favor of MLE.

Let us now dig a bit deeper by making our "mistake" even worse. Because we know that in ARCH models $\sigma^2_{t+1|t}=E_t[\varepsilon^2_{t+1}]$ so that $\varepsilon^2_{t+1}=E_t[\varepsilon^2_{t+1}]-\eta_{t+1}=\sigma^2_{t+1|t}-\eta_{t+1}$, we may even conceive to perform the second step of the ARCH(1) estimation as a regression, estimating by OLS:

$$\sigma^2_{t+1|t}+\eta_{t+1}=\hat{\varepsilon}_t^2=\omega+\alpha\hat{\varepsilon}_{t-1}^2+\eta_{t+1}\quad t=2,3,\ldots,\ T.$$

In E-Views, this gives:

$$\sigma^2_{t+1|t}=\underset{(0.0046)}{0.669}+\underset{(0.0081)}{0.315}\,\varepsilon_t^2,$$

which is even more imprecisely estimated than both the models analyzed above.

The problem with sequential estimation is simply stated: successive waves of (seemingly) partial ML estimators that may even, at least on the surface, fully exploit the assumed structure of a model will not deliver the optimal statistical properties and characterization of the MLE. On the contrary, *a sequential ML-based estimator may be characterized as a QMLE* and as such it will be subject to the same limitations as all QMLEs: loss of asymptotic efficiency, as already noted in Example 5.25. Intuitively, this is due to the fact that when we split $\boldsymbol{\theta}$ into $\boldsymbol{\theta} \equiv [\boldsymbol{\theta}_1^{'}\ \boldsymbol{\theta}_2^{'}]'$ to separately estimate $\boldsymbol{\theta}_1$ and $\boldsymbol{\theta}_2$, this very separation in a sequential estimator will imply that for all $\hat{\theta}_{1i} \in \hat{\boldsymbol{\theta}}_1$ and $\hat{\theta}_{2j} \in \hat{\boldsymbol{\theta}}_2$, $Cov[\hat{\theta}_{1i}, \hat{\theta}_{2j}] = 0$ is implicitly imposed even though empirically there is no guarantee that this should or might be the case. A few examples will help to clarify this point but also to appreciate the potential advantages from sequential estimation.

EXAMPLE 5.25 (continued)

The initial, full ML estimation reveals for instance that $Cov[\hat{\varphi}_1, \hat{\alpha}] = -5.30E-06$ so that $Corr[\hat{\varphi}_1, \hat{\alpha}] = (-5.30E-06)/(1.08E-05 \cdot 6.56E-05) = -0.20$, which cannot be simply arbitrarily set to 0 and ignored.

There is one common example of sequential estimation that frequently appears in practice and that we have already encountered in Example 5.10 and in Section 5.2.3. Consider for concreteness the case of the most common model, the GARCH(1,1). Because we know that the long-run (ergodic) variance from a GARCH(1,1) is $\overline{\sigma}^2 = \omega/(1-\alpha-\beta)$, instead of jointly estimating ω, α, and β, we can simply set

$$\tilde{\omega} = (1-\alpha-\beta)\left[\frac{1}{T}\sum_{t=1}^{T}\varepsilon_t^2\right] \tag{5.142}$$

for whatever values of α and β, where the term in square brackets is the sample variance of the residuals to be estimate beforehand, on the basis of the sample. In this case, given $\boldsymbol{\theta} \equiv [\boldsymbol{\theta}'_1\ \boldsymbol{\theta}'_2]'$, we have $\boldsymbol{\theta}_1 \equiv [\alpha\ \beta]'$ and $\theta_2 = \omega$. Here the sample variance estimator for $\overline{\sigma}^2$, $\hat{S}^2 \equiv T^{-1}\sum_{t=1}^{T}\varepsilon_t^2$ is itself a first-step MLE. Of course, the fact that we perform a pre-MLE run of estimation concerning the sample variance to scale down the dimension of $\boldsymbol{\theta}$ makes the resulting estimate $\hat{\boldsymbol{\theta}}_T$ a QMLE. There are, as usual, two advantages from this approach: (1) as already discussed in Section 5.2.3, you impose the long-run variance estimate on the GARCH model directly and avoid that the model may yield nonsensical estimates;[30] (2) you have reduced the number of parameters to be estimated by 1. These benefits must be carefully contrasted with the well-known costs, the loss of efficiency caused by QMLE. An example available as an online material provides a less compelling but realistic case in which one may want to use QMLE in the form of sequential ML estimation to purse a simplification of the problem.

5.6.6 Data Frequency in Estimation and Temporal Aggregation

In the examples so far, we have mixed a variety of sampling frequency choices: daily equity portfolio returns, weekly bond returns and interest rates, and monthly international stock returns. In all cases, we have often ended up specifying GARCH-type models. One naturally wonders whether the choice of the frequency of the data may have any importance. On the one hand, sometimes we shall have little choice: the problem will be characterized by a typical decision horizon and the data frequency will match such a horizon. On the other hand, think of a pension fund manager with a 10-year, long horizon: can she afford to use cumulative, 10-year return data? And even if this were possible, at what costs?

When deciding on the most appropriate sampling interval for inference purposes, more efficient parameter estimates for low-frequency processes may be available from the model estimates obtained with high-frequency data. For

30. MLE is not set up to match the sample moments of the data: this means that once $\hat{\boldsymbol{\theta}}_T^{ML}$ is obtained, if the implied moments of the process (mean and variance included) were computed, this may differ from those in the data because of the structure of the log-likelihood function that in general weighs means and variances in a highly nonlinear fashion. Even in the QMLE case, to correctly specify the conditional mean and variance function does not imply that the estimated model must match sample mean and variance in the data. If we wanted to match the moments, we should be using MM estimators.

instance, our portfolio manager may perform her estimation of GARCH models on monthly series and then find ways to aggregate such estimates to represent the implied process for 10-year cumulative returns. Conversely, in some instances, high-frequency processes may be of primary interest, while only low-frequency data are available. For instance, in several examples, we have examined weekly bond returns but we might have a use for their daily volatility forecasts. The nonlinearities in ARCH models severely complicate a formal analysis of *temporal aggregation*. In contrast to the linear ARIMA class of models for conditional means, most parametric ARCH models are only closed under temporal aggregation subject to specific qualifications. To examine such qualifications, it is useful to introduce the following.

DEFINITION 5.10 (Weak GARCH process)

$\{\varepsilon_{t+1}\}$ is a weak GARCH(p, q) process if $\{\varepsilon_{t+1}\}$ is serially uncorrelated with zero mean and $\sigma^2_{t+1|t}$ that follows Eq. (5.30) corresponds to the best linear projection of $\{\varepsilon^2_{t+1}\}$ on the space spanned by $\{1, \varepsilon_t, \varepsilon_{t-1}, \ldots, \varepsilon_t^2, \varepsilon_{t-1}^2, \ldots\}$, in the sense that:

$$E[(\varepsilon^2_{t+1} - \sigma^2_{t+1|t})] = E[(\varepsilon^2_{t+1} - \sigma^2_{t+1|t})\varepsilon_{t+1-i}] = E[(\varepsilon^2_{t+1} - \sigma^2_{t+1|t})\varepsilon^2_{t+1-i}] = 0; \quad i = 1, 2, \ldots \tag{5.143}$$

Here Eq. (5.143) means that all the information contained in past residuals and past squared residuals is efficiently used by $\sigma^2_{t+1|t}$ (otherwise the conditional expectations would not be 0). Based on our treatment in Section 5.2, we know that a conventional GARCH model in Eq. (5.30) is a weak GARCH process, but other processes may exist that are weak GARCH but do not fit Eq. (5.30), for instance:

$$\varepsilon^2_{t+1} = \omega + \sum_{i=1}^{p} \alpha_i \varepsilon^2_{t-i+1} + \sum_{j=1}^{q} \beta_j \sigma^2_{t-j+1|t-j} + v_{t+1}, \tag{5.144}$$

where v_{t+1} is *not* a white noise but it has mean 0 and $E[v_{t+1}\varepsilon_{t+1-i}] = E[v_{t+1}\varepsilon^2_{t+1-i}] = 0$; $i = 1, 2, \ldots$

The important fact about weak GARCH is that, while the conventional GARCH(p, q) class of models is not closed under temporal aggregation, Drost and Nijman (1993) show that *classical temporal aggregation of ARIMA models with weak GARCH*(p,q) *errors lead to another ARIMA model with weak GARCH*(p′, q′) *errors*, where the expressions for p' and q' are known. The orders of this temporally aggregated model and the model parameters depend on the original model characteristics.

The leading case is represented by a weak GARCH(1,1) with parameters ω, α, and β, where the series $\{\varepsilon_{t+1}\}$ concerns residuals from some ARMA model. Let $\left\{\varepsilon^{(m)}_{t+1}\right\}$ denote the discrete time temporally aggregated process defined at t, $t + m$, $t + 2m$, etc. For instance, if the original $\{\varepsilon_{t+1}\}$ was the residual of a *stock variable* (say, number of floating shares of a stock), then $\left\{\varepsilon^{(m)}_{t+1}\right\}$ is obtained by sampling $\{\varepsilon_{t+1}\}$ every mth period; in the case of a *flow variable*, such as stock returns (in continuous time), then $\left\{\varepsilon^{(m)}_{t+1}\right\}$ simply cumulates by summing m consecutive values of $\{\varepsilon_{t+1}\}$. In both cases, it is possible to show that the temporally aggregated process, $\left\{\varepsilon^{(m)}_{t+1}\right\}$, is also weak GARCH(1,1) with parameters:

$$\omega^{(m)} = \omega \frac{1 - (\alpha + \beta)^m}{1 - \alpha - \beta} \qquad \alpha^{(m)} = (\alpha + \beta)^m - \beta^{(m)} \tag{5.145}$$

so that the persistence index is $\alpha^{(m)} + \beta^{(m)} = (\alpha + \beta)^m$, where $\beta^{(m)}$ is a complicated function of the parameters of the original process that we spare ourselves to report here. Interestingly, under stationarity, $\alpha + \beta < 1$, the persistence index goes to 0 as $m \to \infty$, that is, as the sampling frequency decreases. This is the sense in which often we encounter the claim that *ARCH is property mostly characterizing high-frequency processes*, even though the proof of the claim requires the apparatus of weak GARCH to hold. Moreover, for covariance stationary GARCH(p, q) flow variables, the conditional kurtosis of the standardized residuals converges to the normal value of three for less frequently sampled observations and the entire process asymptotically convergences to normality. The extension of these aggregation results for the weak GARCH(p, q) model to other parametric specifications is in principle straightforward, but exact results are still scarce in the literature (at least to our knowledge).

EXAMPLE 5.26

A pension fund manager interested in the CH properties of 10-year, long-horizon (continuously compounded) stock excess returns could easily exploit Eq. (5.145) while performing estimation on daily data, were she ready to assume that daily excess returns follow a weak GARCH(1,1) process.

For instance, an application to daily excess equity returns gives ML estimates:

$$x_{t+1} = \underset{(0.0060)}{0.041} + \underset{(0.0092)}{0.124}x_t + \varepsilon_{t+1} \quad \varepsilon_{t+1} \text{ IID } N(0, \sigma^2_{t+1|t})$$
$$\sigma^2_{t+1|t} = \underset{(0.0007)}{0.008} + \underset{(0.0023)}{0.091}\varepsilon^2_t + \underset{(0.0028)}{0.904}\sigma^2_{t|t-1}$$

and an implied daily persistence index of 0.995. Because there are approximately 25,200 days in a 10-year period, it is then straightforward to compute:

$$\omega^{(10Y)} = 0.008\frac{1-(0.995)^{25200}}{1-0.995} = 1.600 \quad \alpha^{(10Y)} + \beta^{(10Y)} = (0.995)^{25200} = 1.39e^{-55},$$

which implies that at a 10-year horizon excess returns become essentially Gaussian IID with a variance of 1.6%, which is in fact rather modest.

However, a mutual fund manager with a typical 3-month horizon, faced with the same daily estimates would aggregate them in a moderately persistent GARCH process. Because there are approximately 64 trading days in a quarter, we have:

$$\omega^{(3M)} = 0.008\frac{1-(0.995)^{64}}{1-0.995} = 0.439 \quad \alpha^{(3M)} + \beta^{(3M)} = (0.995)^{64} = 0.726.$$

Interestingly, this implies a long-run variance of $0.439/(1-0.726) = 1.60$, which is exactly the approximately constant variance perceived by the 10-year horizon pension fund manager. This different perception of CH may lead to rather different asset allocation decisions.

The result in Eq. (5.145) has crucial implications for the way one scales up or down, that is, aggregates, variance forecasts over time. Suppose that using Eq. (5.102) on data at some baseline frequency, we have obtained a forecast $\hat{\sigma}^2_{t+1|t}$. How do we aggregate this forecast at a lower frequency that is an m multiple of the original one? For instance, how can we go from a daily variance forecast to a yearly one? In the case of a weak GARCH(1,1) process, the answer is implicit in Eq. (5.145):

$$\begin{aligned}\sigma^{2,(m)}_{t+1|t} &= \frac{\omega^{(m)}}{1-\alpha^{(m)}-\beta^{(m)}} + (\alpha^{(m)}+\beta^{(m)})\left(\sigma^{2,(m)}_{t|t-1} - \frac{\omega^{(m)}}{1-\alpha^{(m)}-\beta^{(m)}}\right) \\ &= \omega\frac{1-(\alpha+\beta)^m}{[1-(\alpha+\beta)^m][1-\alpha-\beta]} + (\alpha+\beta)^m\left[\alpha^{(m)}(\varepsilon^{2,(m)}_t - \bar{\sigma}^2) + \beta^{(m)}(\sigma^{2,(m)}_t - \bar{\sigma}^2)\right] \\ &= \bar{\sigma}^2 + (\alpha+\beta)^m\left[\alpha^{(m)}(\varepsilon^{2,(m)}_t - \bar{\sigma}^2) + \beta^{(m)}(\sigma^{2,(m)}_t - \bar{\sigma}^2)\right].\end{aligned} \tag{5.146}$$

Independently of the exact formula, note that $\sigma^{2,(m)}_{t+1|t} \neq m\sigma^2_{t+1|t}$. For instance, scaling monthly variance forecasts up to annual frequency just multiplying by 12 will be incorrect.

REFERENCES

Altman, N.S., 1992. An introduction to kernel and nearest-neighbor nonparametric regression. Am. Stat. 46, 175–185.

Backus, D., Gregory, A., 1993. Theoretical relations between risk premiums and conditional variance. J. Bus. Econ. Stat. 11, 177–185.

Bates, C., White, H., 1990. Efficient instrumental variables estimation of system of implicit heterogeneous nonlinear dynamic equations with non spherical errors. In: Barnett, W.A., Berndt, E.R., White, H. (Eds.), Dynamic Econometric Modeling. Cambridge University Press, Cambridge.

Black, F., 1976. Studies of stock price volatility changes. Proceedings of the 1976 Meetings of the American Statistical Association. Business and Economics Section.

Bollerslev, T., 1986. Generalized autoregressive conditional heteroskedasticity. J. Econom. 31, 307–327.

Bollerslev, T., 1988. On the correlation structure for the generalized autoregressive conditional heteroskedastic process. J. Time Ser. Anal. 9, 121–131.

Bollerslev, T., 2009. Glossary to ARCH/GARCH. In: Bollerslev, T., Russell, J., Watson, M. (Eds.), Volatility and Time Series Econometrics: Essays in Honour of Robert F. Engle. Oxford University Press, Oxford, UK.

Bollerslev, T., Wooldridge, J.M., 1992. Quasi-maximum likelihood estimation and inference in dynamic models with time-varying covariances. Econom. Rev. 11, 143–172.
Bollerslev, T., Engle, R.F., Nelson, D.B., 1994. ARCH models. In: Engle, R.F., McFadden, D. (Eds.), Handbook of Econometrics, vol. 4. North-Holland, Amsterdam.
Brock, W., Dechert, D., Sheinkman, J., LeBaron, B., 1996. A test for independence based on the correlation dimension. Econom. Rev. 15, 197–235.
Christoffersen, P., Jacobs, K., Ornthanalai, C., Wang, Y., 2008. Option valuation with long-run and short-run volatility components. J. Financ. Econ. 90, 272–297.
Davidson, R., MacKinnon, J.G., 2004. Econometric theory and methods. Oxford University Press, New York.
Davis, C.S., Stephens, M.A., 1989. Empirical distribution function goodness-of-fit tests. Appl. Stat. 38, 535–582.
Ding, Z., Granger, C.W., Engle, R.F., 1993. A long memory property of stock market returns and a new model. J. Emp. Fin. 1, 83–106.
Drost, F.C., Nijman, T.E., 1993. Temporal aggregation of GARCH processes. Econometrica 61, 909–927.
Engle, R., 1982. Autoregressive conditional heteroskedasticity with estimates of the variance of United Kingdom inflation. Econometrica 50, 987–1007.
Engle, R., Lee, G., 1999. A permanent and transitory component model of stock return volatility. In: Engle, R., White, H. (Eds.), Cointegration, Causality, and Forecasting: A Festschrift in Honor of Clive W.J. Granger. Oxford University Press, New York, NY, pp. 475–497.
Engle, R.F., Bollerslev, T., 1986. Modelling the persistence of conditional variances. Econom. Rev. 5, 1–50.
Engle, R.F., Gonzalez-Rivera, G., 1991. Semiparametric ARCH models. J. Bus. Econ. Stat. 9, 345–359.
Engle, R.F., Lilien, D.M., Robins, R.P., 1987. Estimating time varying risk premia in the term structure: the ARCH-M model. Econometrica 55, 391–407.
Flood, R.P., Rose, A.K., 1999. Understanding exchange rate volatility without the contrivance of macroeconomics. Econ. J. 109, 660–672.
Francq, C., Zakoïan, J.M., 2011. GARCH Models: Structure, Statistical Inference and Financial Applications. John Wiley & Sons, Chichester.
French, K., Schwert, W., Stambaugh, R.F., 1987. Expected stock returns and volatility. J. Financ. Econ. 19, 3–29.
Glosten, L.R., Jagannathan, R., Runkle, D., 1993. On the relation between the expected value and the volatility of the nominal excess return on stocks. J. Fin. 48, 1779–1801.
Gouriéroux, C., 1997. ARCH Models and Financial Applications. Springer Verlag, Cambridge.
Hall, P., Yao, Q., 2003. Inference in ARCH and GARCH models with heavy–tailed errors. Econometrica 71, 285–317.
Hamilton, J.D., 1994. Time Series Analysis. Princeton University Press, Princeton, NJ.
Hansen, P.R., Lunde, A., 2005. A forecast comparison of volatility models: does anything beat a GARCH (1, 1)? J. Appl. Econom. 20, 873–889.
Harris, L., 1986. A transaction data study of weekly and intradaily patterns in stock returns. J. Financ. Econ. 16, 99–117.
Heston, S., Nandi, S., 2000. A closed-form GARCH option pricing model. Rev. Financ. Stud. 13, 585–626.
Higgins, M.L., Bera, A., 1992. A class of nonlinear ARCH models. Int. Econ. Rev. 33 (1), 137–158.
Hsieh, D.A., 1991. Chaos and nonlinear dynamics: applications to financial markets. J. Fin. 46, 1839–1878.
Lee, S.W., Hansen, B.E., 1994. Asymptotic theory for the GARCH (1,1) quasi-maximum likelihood estimator. Econom. Theor. 10, 29–52.
Lumsdaine, R.L., 1996. Consistency and asymptotic normality of the quasi-maximum likelihood estimator in IGARCH (1, 1) and covariance stationary GARCH (1, 1) models. Econometrica 64, 575–596.
Merton, R.C., 1973. An intertemporal capital asset pricing model. Econometrica 41, 867–887.
Nelson, D.B., 1990. Stationarity and persistence in the GARCH(1,1) model. Econom. Theor. 6, 318–334.
Nelson, D.B., 1991. Conditional heteroskedasticity in asset returns: a new approach. Econometrica 59, 347–370.
Patell, J.M., Wolfson, M.A., 1979. Anticipated information releases reflected in call option prices. J. Account. Econ. 1, 117–140.
Poon, S.H., Granger, C.W., 2003. Forecasting volatility in financial markets: a review. J. Econ. Lit. 41, 478–539.
Poon, S.H., Granger, C.W., 2005. Practical issues in forecasting volatility. Financ. Anal. J. 61, 45–56.
Schwert, G.W., 1989. Why does stock market volatility change over time? J. Fin. 44, 1115–1153.
Shiller, R.J., 1979. The volatility of long-term interest rates and expectations models of the term structure. J. Polit. Econ. 87, 1190–1219.
Tauchen, G., Pitts, M., 1983. The price variability-volume relationship on speculative markets. Econometrica 51, 485–505.
Taylor, S.J., 1986. 2008 Modelling Financial Time Series, 1st ed. World Scientific, Singapore.
Taylor, S.J., Xu, X., 1997. The incremental volatility information in one million foreign exchange quotations. J. Emp. Fin. 4, 317–340.
Timmermann, A., 1996. Excess volatility and predictability of stock prices in autoregressive dividend models with learning. Rev. Econ. Stud. 63, 523–557.
Veronesi, P., 2000. How does information quality affect stock returns? J. Fin. 55, 807–837.
Zakoïan, J.M., 1994. Threshold heteroskedastic models. J. Econ. Dyn. Control 18 (5), 931–955.

APPENDIX 5.A NONPARAMETRIC KERNEL DENSITY ESTIMATION

The branch of statistics that deals with the task of estimating models in the absence of parameters is called *nonparametric* statistics (econometrics). Although its goals are ambitious, it is not appealing when applied to all the problems that applied users of econometrics face. For instance, in finance we care a lot for not only modeling objects of interest—such as mean and variances—but also for understanding their conditional dynamics over time, that is, how these react to the arrival of news. Usually this is because we would like to predict conditional means and variances. Unfortunately, nonparametric methods may turn problematic when they are employed in view of this second objective. Hence, parametric econometrics remains a crucial subject, and most work in applied finance and economics is still organized around parametric methods.

One useful bit of nonparametric econometrics that we have used a lot in this chapter are density estimators. A kernel density estimator (henceforth, KDE) is an empirical density smoother based on the choice of two objects: (1) the *kernel function* $K(x)$ and (2) the *bandwidth parameter*, h. The kernel function is defined as some smooth function (i.e., continuous and sometimes also differentiable) that integrates to 1:

$$\int_{-\infty}^{+\infty} K(x)\,dx = 1.$$

For instance, a typical kernel function is the Gaussian one,

$$K^{Gauss}(x) = \frac{1}{\sqrt{2\pi}} e^{-\frac{1}{2}x^2}$$

which also corresponds to the PDF of a standard normal variable. Here x represents any possible value that the generic random variable X_t may take. In our case, we shall deal either with asset returns and rate changes or with standardized residuals from some conditional mean model. The bandwidth parameter is instead used to allocate weight to values of x_t in the support of X_t that differ from a given x. This last claim can be understood only by inspecting the general definition of a *KDE*:

$$\hat{f}_X^{ker}(x) = \frac{1}{Th}\sum_{t=1}^{T} K\left(\frac{x - x_t}{h}\right),$$

where T is the number of points over which the estimation is based, usually the size of the sample at hand.

Two aspects need to be emphasized. First, we are using the sample to estimate not a parameter of the population (such as some elements of $\boldsymbol{\theta}$ that enter the mean, the variance, the slope coefficient in a regression or the GARCH coefficients), but the entire *density* of such a population. This means that $\hat{f}_X^{ker}(x)$ represents an estimator of the true but unknown $f_X(x)$. Second, the mechanics of the formula for a KDE is easy to understand: for each x_t in our data set, we compute $\hat{f}_X^{ker}(x)$ for any arbitrary value x in the support of X_t, by running through the entire sample and computing for each x_t the kernel scores $K\big((x - x_t)/h\big)$ and summing them. Note that because we have T observations in the sample and the differences $(x - x_t)$ are reweighted by the bandwidth h, the total sum is scaled by the factor Th. Additionally, a large (small) h tends to strongly (weakly) shrink any $(x - x_t) \neq 0$, which justifies our claim that the bandwidth parameter allocates weight to values of x_t in the support of X_t that differ from a given x.

Even though what precedes may sound rather technical, we are implicitly used to compute and use KDEs. As it turns out, however, we may have been trained to use a poor—in a statistical sense—KDE, the so-called *histogram estimator* that is obtained from the formula presented above when $h = 1$ (as we shall see, $h = 1$ is hardly optimal) and the kernel function is Dirac (usually denoted as $\delta(x)$), that is, an indicator function:

$$K_{hist}(x - x_i) = \delta(x_i) = \begin{cases} 1 & \text{if } x_i = x \\ 0 & \text{if } x_i \neq x \end{cases}.$$

As a result, every time we build a histogram, we are using a special case of the formula:

$$\hat{f}_X^{hist}(x) = \frac{1}{T}\sum_{t=1}^{T} \delta(x_t) = \frac{1}{T}\sum_{t=1}^{T} I_{\{x = x_t\}} = \text{Fraction of data equal to } x.$$

Of course, there is no good reason to set $K(x - x_i) = \delta(x)$ or $h = 1$. Next to the naive histogram estimator, the most common type of kernel function used in applied finance is the Gaussian kernel that we have displayed already. A $K(x)$ with optimal properties is instead Epanechnikov's:

$$K_{Epan}(x) = \frac{3}{4\sqrt{5}}\left(1 - 0.2x^2\right) I_{\{-\sqrt{5} \leq x \leq \sqrt{5}\}}.$$

Other popular kernels are the triangular and box kernels:

$$K_{Box}(x) = \frac{1}{2} I_{\{|x| < 1\}} \quad K_{Triang}(x) = (1 - |x|) I_{\{|x| < 1\}}.$$

The fact that Epanechnikov's kernel is optimal—in the sense that it minimizes the average squared deviations, $[f_X(x) - \hat{f}_X^{ker}(x)]^2$—while the Gaussian is not, illustrates one general point that to minimize the *Integrated Mean Squared Error*,

$$E \int_{-\infty}^{+\infty} [f_X(x) - \hat{f}_X^{ker}(x)]^2 dx,$$

kernel functions that are truncated and do not extend to the infinite right and left tails tend to be superior when compared to KDEs that do. However, the histogram kernel overdoes it in this dimension and seems to excessively truncate, because it prevents that any $x_t \neq x$ may bring any information useful to the estimation of $f_X(x)$. Finally, the bandwidth parameter h is usually chosen according to the rule $h^* = 0.9 \cdot \hat{S}_T \cdot T^{-1/5}$, which minimizes the integrated MSFE across kernels.

Do alternative choices of $K(x)$ functions make a big difference when it comes to assess deviations from normality? Although it is hard to give a definitive answer, experience suggests that with the length of the data sets that are typical in finance, implied differences in estimated KDEs are minor. For instance, in Fig. A.1, it seems that financial returns (in this case, value-weighted US excess stock returns) are easily assessed to be leptokurtic, that is, they have fat tails and highly peaked densities around the mean, independent of the specific KDE that is employed.

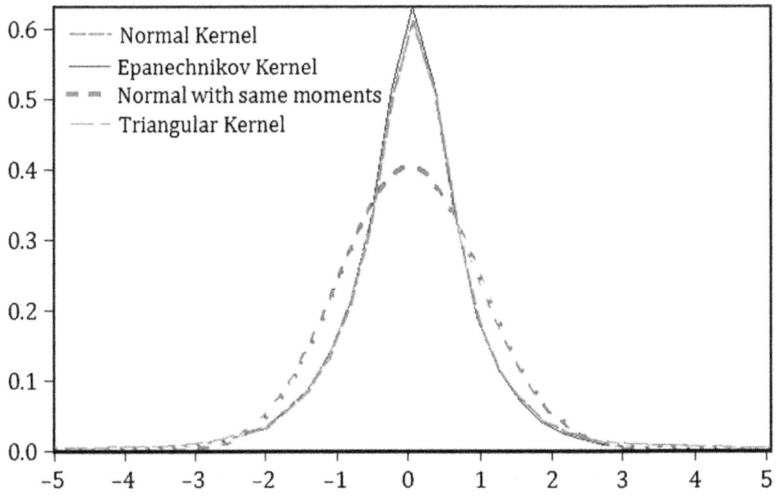

FIGURE A.1 Alternative KDEs versus normal density.

Chapter 6

Multivariate GARCH and Conditional Correlation Models

The world is generally multivariate.

Edward Tufte

6.1 INTRODUCTION AND PRELIMINARIES

As we have seen in Chapters 3 and 4, most relevant and realistic applications in empirical finance are *multivariate*, that is, they involve $N \geq 2$ assets/securities/portfolios. If you collect the returns on such N assets in an $N \times 1$ vector $\mathbf{R}_{t+1} \equiv [R^1_{t+1} R^2_{t+1} \ldots]$, then the variance of the random vector turns out to be a matrix of second moments, that is, variances and covariances:

$$Var[\mathbf{R}_{t+1}] \equiv E[(\mathbf{R}_{t+1} - E[\mathbf{R}_{t+1}])(\mathbf{R}_{t+1} - E[\mathbf{R}_{t+1}])'] = E\left\{ \begin{bmatrix} R^1_{t+1} - E[R^1_{t+1}] \\ R^2_{t+1} - E[R^2_{t+1}] \\ \vdots \\ R^N_{t+1} - E[R^N_{t+1}] \end{bmatrix} \begin{bmatrix} R^1_{t+1} - E[R^1_{t+1}] & R^2_{t+1} - E[R^2_{t+1}] & \ldots & R^N_{t+1} - E[R^N_{t+1}] \end{bmatrix} \right\} \tag{6.1}$$

$$= E\left\{ \begin{bmatrix} (R^1_{t+1} - E[R^1_{t+1}])^2 & (R^1_{t+1} - E[R^1_{t+1}])(R^2_{t+1} - E[R^2_{t+1}]) & \ldots & (R^1_{t+1} - E[R^1_{t+1}])(R^N_{t+1} - E[R^N_{t+1}]) \\ (R^1_{t+1} - E[R^1_{t+1}])(R^2_{t+1} - E[R^2_{t+1}]) & (R^2_{t+1} - E[R^2_{t+1}])^2 & \ldots & (R^2_{t+1} - E[R^2_{t+1}])(R^N_{t+1} - E[R^N_{t+1}]) \\ \vdots & \vdots & \ddots & \vdots \\ (R^1_{t+1} - E[R^1_{t+1}])(R^N_{t+1} - E[R^N_{t+1}]) & (R^2_{t+1} - E[R^2_{t+1}])(R^N_{t+1} - E[R^N_{t+1}]) & \ldots & (R^N_{t+1} - E[R^N_{t+1}])^2 \end{bmatrix} \right\}.$$

Clearly, all variances are collected on the main diagonal (they are N), while all covariances are collected off the main diagonal (they are $N(N-1)/2$. Moreover, because $Cov[R^i_{t+1}, R^j_{t+1}] = Cov[R^j_{t+1}, R^i_{t+1}]$ from simple properties of expectations, then $Var[\mathbf{R}_{t+1}]$ is by construction a *symmetric matrix*. For instance, any portfolio selection methodology is clearly based on the knowledge or estimation of $Var[\mathbf{R}_{t+1}]$ as it is well known that optimal portfolio shares will also depend on the covariance of asset returns considered in pairs. Because risk management concerns either portfolios of securities or investment projects, risk management is also intrinsically a multivariate exercise. Therefore, also with reference to the conditional second moment, we need to develop multivariate time series methods to model quantities of interest and, among them, dynamic covariances and correlations.

However, extending multivariate methods to model conditional heteroskedasticity opens up a new problem. While up to this point we have always assumed that given a CH framework, we would always have sufficient observations to proceed to estimation, when it comes to multivariate covariance matrix estimation and forecasting, the availability of sufficiently long-time series may become an issue. For instance, with only 15 assets in a portfolio—which is commonly seen in asset management—you will need (1) 15 volatility forecasts and (2) $15 \times 14/2 = 105$ correlation forecasts, for a total of 120 parameters or moments to forecast. Assume, for simplicity, that variances and covariances are constant over time. Then the 120 objects that you care for in this example simply become parameters to be estimated, $\{\hat{\sigma}_i\}^{15}_{i=1}$ and $\{\hat{\sigma}_{ij}\}^{N}_{i=1,}{}^{N}_{j>i}$. At this point, with 15 series of return data (with 15 assets you will have 15 time series), note that a total of 120 parameters to be estimated on 15 series, gives you $120/15 = 8$ data points per series. Even though you may think that 15 time series are a lot, for each of them you will need—because you need at least as many observations as parameters for estimation to be feasible—at least eight observations to proceed. However, would you ever estimate

Essentials of Time Series for Financial Applications. DOI: https://doi.org/10.1016/B978-0-12-813409-2.00006-6

120 parameters using exactly 120 observations? Hopefully not. In fact, as we have seen in Chapter 3, time series econometricians normally use a simple rule-of-thumb by which one should always have 20 observations *per parameter* before proceeding to any econometric analysis. We may recall that the ratio between the total number of observations and the number of parameters to be estimated is called saturation ratio. In this case, $20 \times 120 = 2400$ observations. This means that for each series, we should have $2400/15 = 160$ observations before seriously thinking of tackling this problem. For instance, 160 observations per series mean that we should have access to almost 14 years of monthly data. These requirements are moderate, but already not completely negligible when you deal with over-the-counter instruments or recently floated stocks in the aftermath of initial public offers (IPOs).

If you worked through the previous example afresh after having increased the number of assets to something even more realistic such as 100 or so assets, you will realize that there is a new dimension of multivariate time series problems that was unknown before: because the size of the covariance matrix grows as a function of N^2 (formally, $N + N(N-1)/2 = O(N^2)$), the size of the estimation problem and the corresponding data requirements grow as a quadratic function of the number of assets (i.e., very quickly). In fact, you can read most of the material that follows not only as an attempt to develop useful multivariate econometric methods to accurately forecast variances and covariances but also as a way to deal with the issue of excessively high number of parameters that estimating covariance matrices implies.

6.2 SIMPLE MODELS OF COVARIANCE PREDICTION

One early idea on modeling and forecasting covariances is that the concepts and tools introduced in the previous sections with reference to volatility forecasts can be extended to covariances (hence, to correlations). This of course starts with rather simple, almost naive techniques that we have introduced in Section 5.2 of Chapter 5. The simplest idea is to build time-varying estimates of covariances using *rolling (moving) averages*:

$$\sigma_{ij,t+1|t}(R) = \frac{1}{R}\sum_{\tau=1}^{R} \varepsilon_{i,t+1-\tau}\varepsilon_{j,t+1-\tau}, \tag{6.2}$$

where $\sigma_{ij,t+1|t}$ denotes *conditional covariance*, $\sigma_{ij,t+1|t} \equiv Cov_t[\varepsilon_{i,t+1-\tau}, \varepsilon_{j,t+1-\tau}]$, R is the window length and $\varepsilon_{i,t+1-\tau}$, $\varepsilon_{j,t+1-\tau}$ are the residuals from two conditional mean models, applied to quantities of interest concerning assets i and j. Clearly, when $i = j$, Eq. (6.2) becomes the rolling window variance estimator already analyzed in Section 5.2.1 of Chapter 5. The problems with this covariance predictor remain the same ones that we have encountered already: it is unclear how someone would go about picking the rolling window parameter R. Too long a window would make the estimator rather smooth but also increase the risk of including in the calculation data that may have been originated from a possibly different period or regime, in either a statistical or in an economic sense. The choice of a small R would lead to a jagged and quickly changing estimator. Moreover, the box-shaped spurious effects already discussed would also characterize this RW covariance estimator, with the risk of covariance prediction at time t changing not because of events recorded at time t, but because returns recorded R periods ago drop out of the rolling window. Finally, the rolling window estimator attaches equal weights to all past cross-products of the residuals, which may be highly questionable.

An alternative idea that has had some impact on the practice of risk and asset management consists of extending the *RiskMetrics* variance estimator to covariance, that is, the idea is that of an exponential smoother may also apply to covariances:

$$\sigma_{ij,t+1|t} = (1-\lambda)\varepsilon_{i,t}\varepsilon_{j,t} + \lambda\sigma_{ij,t|t-1}, \tag{6.3}$$

with $\lambda \in (0, 1)$. As we shall explain below, we need to set λ to be independent of i and j to ensure that the covariance matrix predicted from the model is semi-positive definite (SPD). As already discussed, JP Morgan had originally popularized a choice $\lambda = 0.94$, which turns out to work rather well also for covariances. However, the restriction that the coefficient $(1-\lambda)$ on the cross-product of residuals and the coefficient λ on past covariance sum to 1 is not necessarily desirable. To understand this, consider the GARCH(1,1) model:

$$\sigma_{ij,t+1|t} = \delta_0 + \delta_1\varepsilon_{i,t}\varepsilon_{j,t} + \delta_2\sigma_{ij,t|t-1}, \tag{6.4}$$

of which Eq. (6.3) represents a special case. Because when means are 0, the unconditional covariance $\overline{\sigma}_{ij} \equiv E[\varepsilon_{i,t}\varepsilon_{j,t}]$; we have that under covariance stationarity:

$$\begin{aligned}\overline{\sigma}_{ij} &\equiv E[\sigma_{ij,t+1|t}] = \delta_0 + \delta_1 E[\varepsilon_{i,t}\varepsilon_{j,t}] + \delta_2 E[\sigma_{ij,t|t-1}] \\ &= \delta_0 + \delta_1\overline{\sigma}_{ij} + \delta_2\overline{\sigma}_{ij} \Rightarrow \overline{\sigma}_{ij} = \frac{\delta_0}{1-\delta_1-\delta_2}.\end{aligned} \tag{6.5}$$

Comparing Eqs. (6.4) with (6.3) reveals that under RiskMetrics, $\delta_0 = 0$ and $\delta_1 + \delta_2 = 1$, and therefore $\overline{\sigma}_{ij} = 0/0$, that is, the long-run, unconditional covariance actually fails to exist. This implies that there is no mean reversion in covariance: based on the closing price of today, if tomorrow's covariance is high then it will remain high, rather than reverting back to its mean. Equivalently, we say that under Eq. (6.3), covariance follows a nonstationary, unit root process.

The RiskMetrics covariance predictive model can be easily rewritten in the equally familiar format:

$$\sigma_{ij,t+1|t} = (1-\lambda)\sum_{k=0}^{\infty} \lambda^k \varepsilon_{i,t-k}\varepsilon_{j,t-k}, \tag{6.6}$$

which shows that this forecast corresponds to an exponentially weighted, infinite moving average. To see this, we just need to rewrite the model in recursive fashion moving backward in time:

$$\begin{aligned} \sigma_{ij,t+1|t} &= (1-\lambda)\varepsilon_{i,t}\varepsilon_{j,t} + \lambda\sigma_{ij,t|t-1} \\ &= (1-\lambda)\varepsilon_{i,t}\varepsilon_{j,t} + \lambda(1-\lambda)\varepsilon_{i,t-1}\varepsilon_{j,t-1} + \lambda^2\sigma_{ij,t-1|t-2} \\ &= (1-\lambda)[\varepsilon_{i,t}\varepsilon_{j,t} + \lambda\varepsilon_{i,t-1}\varepsilon_{j,t-1}] + \lambda^2(1-\lambda)\varepsilon_{i,t-2}\varepsilon_{j,t-2} + \lambda^3\sigma_{ij,t-2|t-3} \\ &= (1-\lambda)[\varepsilon_{i,t}\varepsilon_{j,t} + \lambda\varepsilon_{i,t-1}\varepsilon_{j,t-1} + \lambda^2\varepsilon_{i,t-2}\varepsilon_{j,t-2}] + \lambda^3\sigma_{ij,t-2|t-3} \\ &= \cdots = (1-\lambda)\sum_{k=0}^{\infty} \lambda^k \varepsilon_{i,t-k}\varepsilon_{j,t-k} \end{aligned} \tag{6.7}$$

as $\lim_{k\to\infty} \lambda^k \sigma_{ij,t-k|t-k-1} = 0$ for $\lambda \in (0, 1)$.

EXAMPLE 6.1

We consider an example that will become pervasive throughout this section: we would like to model and forecast the dynamics of both covariances and correlations between weekly US value-weighted stock market returns (from Center for Research in Security Prices, CRSP) and weekly approximate returns on 10-year Treasury notes. The sample is January 1982–December 2016. This is a leading case study in applied asset management, where it becomes crucial to forecast whether and how much hedging opportunities will be offered by government bonds for the US aggregate stock market. In fact, even though one would naively expect that stocks and Treasuries were negatively correlated—because of a "flight-to-quality" effect—casual observation reveals that periods exist in which both markets are characterized by raising prices and hence positive realized returns, which however may not detract much from the overall hedging power of long-term bonds (they ought to hedge stock market losses, of course).

We start adopting rather straightforward models for the conditional mean—MA(1) for stock returns and AR(1) for bond returns—and the conditional variance, a simple Gaussian GARCH(1,1) model for both series. Neither of these models has been of course optimized nor is the result of a careful model specification search. Note that for the time being, the CH models only impact the estimation of the conditional mean parameters (because we use (Quasi) Maximum Likelihood Estimation—(Q)MLE) and the calculations of correlations displayed below, because the models presented so far are indeed models for covariances only and as such implied, time-varying correlation forecasts have to be computed as $\hat{\rho}_{ij,t+1|t} \equiv \hat{\sigma}_{ij,t+1|t}/(\hat{\sigma}_{ii,t+1|t} \times \hat{\sigma}_{jj,t+1|t})$. Using a stationary GARCH(1,1) model to predict standard deviation has one additional advantage: it makes the forecasts of conditional correlations from the model depend on differences in forecasts of covariances only, because the calculations are based on a common model for volatility.

Because these are weekly data, we implement three versions of the RW prediction model: for $R = 12$ weeks (an extremely reactive model), $R = 52$ weeks, and $R = 208$ weeks. Of course, in the three cases, 12, 52, and 208 observations out of an initial total of 1825 will be lost. As for the RiskMetrics model, after estimating the conditional mean models,

$$MKT_{t+1} = \underset{(0.000)}{0.613} - \underset{(0.046)}{0.049}\varepsilon_{MKT,t} + \varepsilon_{MKT,t+1} \qquad \varepsilon_{t+1} \text{ IID } N\left(0, \sigma^2_{MKT,t+1|t}\right)$$

$$\sigma^2_{MKT,t+1|t} = \underset{(0.000)}{0.237} + \underset{(0.000)}{0.153}\varepsilon^2_{MKT,t} + \underset{(0.000)}{0.806}\sigma^2_{MKT,t|t-1}$$

$$Bond_{t+1} = \underset{(0.169)}{0.032} + \underset{(0.099)}{0.230}\varepsilon_{Bond,t} + \varepsilon_{Bond,t+1} \qquad \varepsilon_{t+1} \text{ IID } N\left(0, \sigma^2_{Bond,t+1|t}\right)$$

$$\sigma^2_{Bond,t+1|t} = \underset{(0.003)}{0.023} + \underset{(0.000)}{0.073}\varepsilon^2_{Bond,t} + \underset{(0.000)}{0.910}\sigma^2_{Bond,t|t-1},$$

we obtain:

$$\sigma_{MKT-Bond,t+1|t} = \underset{(0.000)}{0.008}\varepsilon_{MKT,t}\varepsilon_{Bond,t} + \underset{(0.000)}{0.992}\sigma_{MKT-Bond,t|t-1}.$$

In this case, the estimate of λ turns out to be much higher than the classical 0.94. Fig. 6.1 shows the dynamics of predicted covariances obtained on the basis of these estimates/selections.

An estimate of λ in excess of 0.99 implies a very smooth path for the RiskMetrics covariance. Of course, per se covariance is hardly meaningful because it is a scaled measure (in this case, its unit of measurement is squared percentage returns, similarly to

(Continued)

EXAMPLE 6.1 (Continued)

a variance). Therefore, Fig. 6.2 presents the predicted, 1-week-ahead correlations computed from the covariances in Fig. 6.1 and the GARCH forecasts of volatility. We note a few interesting aspects. First, the RiskMetrics forecast of correlation reaches −1 and in fact goes below −1 in a few weeks of 2013. This is of course impossible and meaningless. The reason for this anomalous behavior is that by separately estimating one process for covariance and one for standard deviations, we have failed to impose adequate conditions to guarantee that $\hat{\rho}_{ij,t+1|t} \in [-1, 1]$. We shall return on this point later on.

One way to correct this problem is to estimate the RiskMetrics model on standardized residuals (and to predict correlations in the rolling window case using RW standard deviations forecasts). We will encounter again this idea of applying covariance modeling to standardized residuals in Section 6.4. If we do that with these data, we obtain a slightly inferior estimate of λ (exactly 0.990) and the forecast of correlations in Fig. 6.3.

Predicted correlations are now much less volatile. This occurs because extreme forecasts of covariance under a given method tend to occur when also forecasts of volatility are extreme, and GARCH(1,1) cannot always guarantee an adequate correction. Fig. 6.3 shows that in general, stock–bond correlations have been declining over time, especially over the 1999–2013 subsample. However, after 2014 they have been ticking up again, even though they remain negative and below −0.25. The general, long-standing perception that stock and bond returns are negatively correlated finds a shaky foundation: under all models (including the very unstable predictions obtained under $R = 12$ weeks), correlations have been structurally positive between the early 1980s and 1998. Since then they have mostly been negative and the big drop, almost a downward jump, has occurred in 1999; for instance, taking averages of weekly predictions, these are 0.001 and −0.013 for RiskMetrics and the 52-week RW models, respectively. Yet, even at a correlation of 0 or slightly negative, long-term US bonds do provide strong hedging to US stocks, of course.

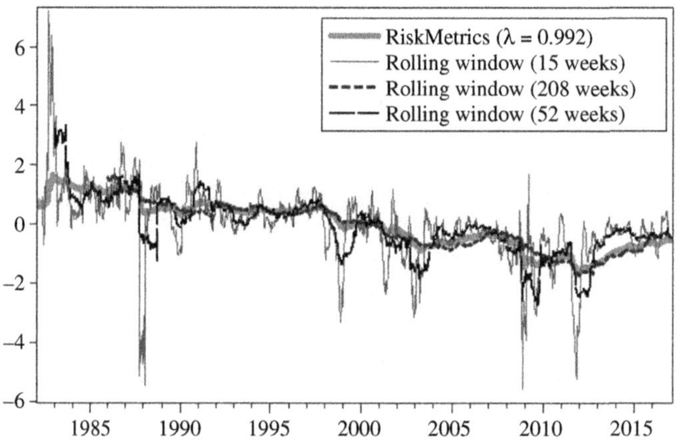

FIGURE 6.1 Rolling window versus RiskMetrics stock–bond covariances.

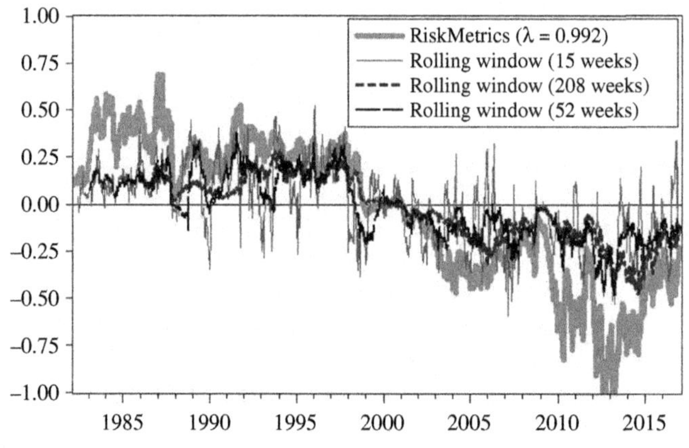

FIGURE 6.2 Rolling window and RiskMetrics stock–bond correlations.

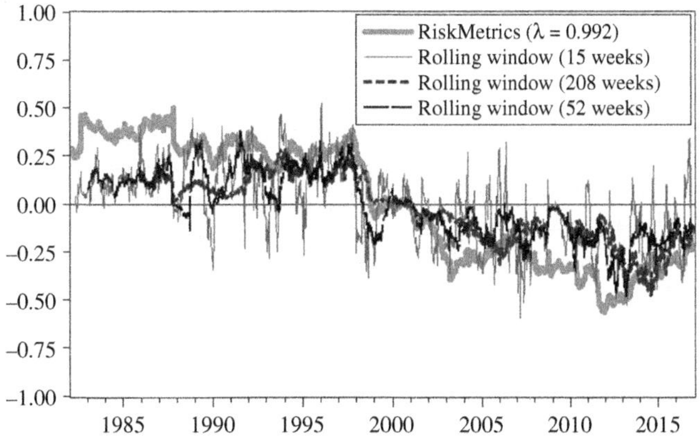

FIGURE 6.3 Rolling window and RiskMetrics stock–bond correlation forecasts under restrictions to keep them in [−1,1].

The model $\sigma_{ij,t+1|t} = \delta_0 + \delta_1\varepsilon_{i,t}\varepsilon_{j,t} + \delta_2\sigma_{ij,t|t-1}$, used above to work on the nonstationarity of the RiskMetrics estimator shows already an obvious direction in which we ought to be looking at, that is, extending GARCH(1,1) *style* variance models to predict covariances:

$$\sigma_{ij,t+1|t} = \omega_{ij} + \alpha_{ij}\varepsilon_{i,t}\varepsilon_{j,t} + \beta_{ij}\sigma_{ij,t|t-1}, \tag{6.8}$$

where α_{ij} and β_{ij} in principle depend on the pair of assets/portfolios i and j under examination. Similar to a GARCH (1,1), one needs $\alpha_{ij} + \beta_{ij} < 1$ for the process to be stationary, as:

$$\overline{\sigma}_{ij} = \frac{\omega_{ij}}{1 - \alpha_{ij} - \beta_{ij}} \tag{6.9}$$

which is derived from Eq. (6.5) is finite if and only if $\alpha_{ij} + \beta_{ij} < 1$ (you will recall that this condition ensures convergence of a series and that absente such a condition, the formula in Eq. (6.9) is not even defined). However, because covariances can be negative, one does not need to restrict any of the parameters to be estimated to be positive (or non-negative). Unfortunately, it is possible to show that unless $\alpha_{ij} = \alpha$ and $\beta_{ij} = \beta$ for all possible pairs $i \neq j$ (instead ω_{ij} is allowed to depend on the pair $i \neq j$), even though $\sigma_{ij,t+1}$ can be anyway estimated/predicted, when one organizes such estimates/predictions into a covariance matrix predicted at time t for time $t + 1$,

$$\hat{\boldsymbol{\Sigma}}_{t+1|t} \equiv \widehat{Cov}_t[\boldsymbol{\varepsilon}_{t+1}] = \begin{bmatrix} \hat{\sigma}^2_{1,t+1|t} & \hat{\sigma}_{12,t+1|t} & \cdots & \hat{\sigma}_{1N,t+1|t} \\ \hat{\sigma}_{12,t+1|t} & \hat{\sigma}^2_{2,t+1|t} & \cdots & \hat{\sigma}_{2N,t+1|t} \\ \vdots & \vdots & \ddots & \vdots \\ \hat{\sigma}_{1N,t+1|t} & \hat{\sigma}_{2N,t+1|t} & \cdots & \hat{\sigma}^2_{N,t+1|t} \end{bmatrix}, \tag{6.10}$$

the resulting $\hat{\boldsymbol{\Sigma}}_{t+1|t}$ is not guaranteed to be *SPD*, while it should be. Why do we need so desperately $\hat{\boldsymbol{\Sigma}}_{t+1|t}$ to be SPD? For once, the reason is not a purely statistical one, it also has an economic meaning: let us recall that any $N \times N$ square symmetric matrix $\mathbf{M}$ is SPD if and only if $\forall \mathbf{x} \in \mathbb{R}^N$, we have $\mathbf{x}'\mathbf{M}\mathbf{x} \geq 0$. When applied to our problem, this definition implies that for any vector of portfolio weights $\mathbf{w}_t \in \mathbb{R}^N$, $\mathbf{w}_t'\hat{\boldsymbol{\Sigma}}_{t+1|t}\mathbf{w}_t \geq 0$. Yet, such an expression has a very precise meaning to finance students and practitioners:

$$\widehat{Var}_t[R^{ptf}_{t+1}] = \mathbf{w}_t'\hat{\boldsymbol{\Sigma}}_{t+1|t}\mathbf{w}_t \geq 0, \tag{6.11}$$

that is, *the SPD nature of* $\hat{\boldsymbol{\Sigma}}_{t+1|t}$ *is necessary and sufficient to ensure that the variance of any portfolio is non-negative*, as it should be.

To get a feeling for why we need to prevent the GARCH-type coefficients to be a function of the pair of assets to ensure a good behavior of the covariance matrix, let us consider again the RiskMetrics case, which, as we know, it is just a case of zero-intercept, nonstationary GARCH model for covariances. We deal with RiskMetrics because thinking about this problem with reference to one parameter only (λ) delivers ready intuition with less algebra. Assume the exponential smoothing model is applied to both variances and covariances in the case of two assets, $N = 2$, that is, $\sigma_{ij,t+1|t} = (1 - \lambda)\varepsilon_{i,t}\varepsilon_{j,t} + \lambda\sigma_{ij,t|t-1}$ for $i, j = 1, 2$, so that the dynamic model also applies to variances when $i=j$. The exponential smoothing estimator of the entire conditional covariance matrix is then:

$$\mathbf{\Sigma}_{t+1|t}=\begin{bmatrix}\sigma^2_{1,t+1|t} & \sigma_{12,t+1|t}\\ \sigma_{12,t+1|t} & \sigma^2_{2,t+1|t}\end{bmatrix}=\begin{bmatrix}(1-\lambda)\varepsilon^2_{1,t}+\lambda\sigma^2_{1,t|t-1} & (1-\lambda)\varepsilon_{1,t}\varepsilon_{2,t}+\lambda\sigma_{12,t|t-1}\\ (1-\lambda)\varepsilon_{1,t}\varepsilon_{2,t}+\lambda\sigma_{12,t|t-1} & (1-\lambda)\varepsilon^2_{2,t}+\lambda\sigma^2_{2,t|t-1}\end{bmatrix}. \tag{6.12}$$

Assume now, by the sake of contradiction, that the smoothing parameters that apply to conditional variances and covariances were allowed to be different:

$$\begin{aligned}\sigma^2_{i,t+1|t}&=(1-\lambda_V)\varepsilon^2_{i,t}+\lambda_V\sigma^2_{i,t|t-1} \quad i=1,2\\ \sigma_{12,t+1|t}&=(1-\lambda_C)\varepsilon_{1,t}\varepsilon_{2,t}+\lambda_C\sigma_{12,t|t-1},\end{aligned} \tag{6.13}$$

with $\lambda_V \neq \lambda_C$ (both of them still belong to the interval (0,1)). It is relatively easy to use a simple example to show that $\lambda_V \neq \lambda_C$ may lead to a conditional correlation between returns on Assets 1 and 2 that fails to be in the interval $[-1,1]$. The idea is to work by focusing on few returns setting all other returns to 0, which may of course happen only by accident in reality—yet recall that you just need one example, not a general proof, to show that $\lambda_V \neq \lambda_C$ may cause problems. Suppose you have available a sample of $t+1$ pairs of return shocks, from some pre-estimated conditional mean model, that is, $\{\varepsilon_{1,\tau},\varepsilon_{2,\tau}\}_{\tau=0}^{t}$. The RiskMetrics processes can be rewritten in exponential smoothing form as:

$$\begin{aligned}\sigma^2_{i,t+1}&=(1-\lambda_V)\sum_{\tau=0}^{t}\lambda^{\tau}\varepsilon^2_{i,t-\tau}+\lambda_V^{t+1}\sigma^2_{i,0} \quad i=1,2\\ \sigma_{12,t+1}&=(1-\lambda_C)\sum_{\tau=0}^{t}\lambda^{\tau}\varepsilon_{1,t-\tau}\varepsilon_{2,t-\tau}+\lambda_C^{t+1}\sigma_{12,0}.\end{aligned} \tag{6.14}$$

Assume that at time 0, $\sigma_{ii,0}=\sigma_{12,0}=0$ for $i=1,2$ and that—just by accident—while $\varepsilon_{1,t-\tau}=\varepsilon_{2,t-\tau}=0$ for $\tau=0,1,\ldots, t-1$, at time t, the return shocks are potentially nonzero, call them $\varepsilon_{1,t}$ and $\varepsilon_{2,t}$. Then,

$$\begin{aligned}\sigma_{ii,t+1|t}&=(1-\lambda_V)\varepsilon^2_{i,t} \quad i=1,2\\ \sigma_{12,t+1|t}&=(1-\lambda_C)\varepsilon_{1,t}\varepsilon_{2,t}\end{aligned} \tag{6.15}$$

and the corresponding conditional correlation is:

$$\begin{aligned}\rho_{12,t+1|t}&=\frac{(1-\lambda_C)\varepsilon_{1,t}\varepsilon_{2,t}}{\sqrt{(1-\lambda_V)\varepsilon^2_{1,t}(1-\lambda_V)\varepsilon^2_{2,t}}}=\frac{(1-\lambda_C)\varepsilon_{1,t}\varepsilon_{2,t}}{(1-\lambda_V)|\varepsilon_{1,t}||\varepsilon_{2,t}|}\\ &=\frac{(1-\lambda_C)}{(1-\lambda_V)}sign(\varepsilon_{1,t}\varepsilon_{2,t}),\end{aligned} \tag{6.16}$$

where the sign function $sign(\varepsilon_{1,t}\varepsilon_{2,t})$ takes a value of $+1$ when the $sign(\varepsilon_{1,t}\varepsilon_{2,t})$ is positive and -1 otherwise. At this point, note that when $\lambda_V>\lambda_C$, then,

$$\rho_{12,t+1|t}\begin{cases}>1 & \text{if } sign(\varepsilon_{1,t}\varepsilon_{2,t})=+1\\ <-1 & \text{if } sign(\varepsilon_{1,t}\varepsilon_{2,t})=-1\end{cases} \tag{6.17}$$

which is clearly inadmissible. As argued above, this shows (although it is just a very special example) that $\lambda_V=\lambda_C$ is sufficient (not necessary, as $\lambda_V<\lambda_C$ works in this example, but other cases can be set up to show that other, different problems would ensue) for $\rho_{12,t+1|t}$ to be in $[-1,1]$ because in that case:

$$\rho_{12,t+1|t}=sign(\varepsilon_{1,t}\varepsilon_{2,t})=\begin{cases}+1 & \text{if } sign(\varepsilon_{1,t}\varepsilon_{2,t})=+1\\ -1 & \text{if } sign(\varepsilon_{1,t}\varepsilon_{2,t})=-1\end{cases}, \tag{6.18}$$

which is instead admissible. How does this example of $\rho_{12,t+1|t}\notin[-1,\ 1]$ map into our claim that when the coefficients are allowed to depend on either the assets (for instance, $\lambda_{12}\neq\lambda_{13}$ when $N=3$) or the moments (as in our example), then $\hat{\mathbf{\Sigma}}_{t+1|t}$ may fail to be SPD so that it cannot be a covariance matrix used in financial applications? Recall that if $\hat{\mathbf{\Sigma}}_{t+1|t}$ is SPD, then $\det(\hat{\mathbf{\Sigma}}_{t+1|t})\geq 0$. In our example, we have:

$$\mathbf{\Sigma}_{t+1|t}=\begin{bmatrix}(1-\lambda_V)\varepsilon^2_{1,t} & (1-\lambda_C)\varepsilon_{1,t}\varepsilon_{2,t}\\ (1-\lambda_C)\varepsilon_{1,t}\varepsilon_{2,t} & (1-\lambda_V)\varepsilon^2_{2,t}\end{bmatrix}, \tag{6.19}$$

The determinant of this matrix is simply:

$$\begin{aligned}\det(\boldsymbol{\Sigma}_{t+1|t}) &= [(1-\lambda_V)\varepsilon_{1,t}^2(1-\lambda_V)\varepsilon_{2,t}^2] - [(1-\lambda_C)\varepsilon_{1,t}\varepsilon_{2,t}(1-\lambda_C)\varepsilon_{1,t}\varepsilon_{2,t}] \\ &= (1-\lambda_V)^2\varepsilon_{1,t}^2\varepsilon_{2,t}^2 - (1-\lambda_C)^2\varepsilon_{1,t}^2\varepsilon_{2,t}^2 \\ &= \varepsilon_{1,t}^2\varepsilon_{2,t}^2[(1-\lambda_V)^2 - (1-\lambda_C)^2]\end{aligned} \tag{6.20}$$

which is nonnegative if and only if $[(1-\lambda_V)^2 - (1-\lambda_C)^2] \geq 0$ or

$$\frac{(1-\lambda_V)^2}{(1-\lambda_C)^2} \geq 1 \Rightarrow \frac{1-\lambda_V}{1-\lambda_C} \geq 1 \Rightarrow \lambda_C \geq \lambda_V. \tag{6.21}$$

Once more, should we be setting $\lambda_V > \lambda_C$, the outcome would be $\det(\hat{\boldsymbol{\Sigma}}_{t+1|t}) < 0$ which would show that $\hat{\boldsymbol{\Sigma}}_{t+1|t}$ is negative definite and hence it cannot be a covariance matrix.

In summary, setting $\alpha_{ij} = \alpha$ and $\beta_{ij} = \beta$ for all possible pairs $i \neq j$, that is, setting the coefficients in Eq. (6.8) to be identical across *all* pairs of assets and also across GARCH models for conditional variance versus covariance, one guarantees that for any portfolio that can be formed, $\widehat{Var}_t[R_{t+1}^{ptf}] \geq 0$:

$$\begin{aligned}\sigma_{i,t+1|t}^2 &= \omega_{ii} + \alpha\varepsilon_{i,t}^2 + \beta\sigma_{i,t|t-1}^2 \quad i = 1, 2, \ldots, N \\ \sigma_{ij,t+1|t} &= \omega_{ij} + \alpha\varepsilon_{j,t}\varepsilon_{j,t} + \beta\sigma_{ij,t|t-1} \quad i \neq j\end{aligned} \tag{6.22}$$

We call $\overline{\sigma}_{ij} \equiv E[\varepsilon_{i,t}\varepsilon_{j,t}] = \omega_{ij}/(1-\alpha-\beta)$ in Eq. (6.9) the unconditional covariance implied by a stationary GARCH (1,1) model in which $\alpha + \beta < 1$. Therefore, Eq. (6.8) can be rewritten as:

$$\sigma_{ij,t+1|t} = \overline{\sigma}_{ij} + \alpha(\varepsilon_{i,t}\varepsilon_{j,t} - \overline{\sigma}_{ij}) + \beta(\sigma_{ij,t|t-1} - \overline{\sigma}_{ij}). \tag{6.23}$$

This follows from

$$\begin{aligned}\sigma_{ij,t+1|t} &= \omega_{ij} + \alpha\varepsilon_{i,t}\varepsilon_{j,t} + \beta\sigma_{ij,t|t-1} = \overline{\sigma}_{ij}(1-\alpha-\beta) + \alpha\varepsilon_{i,t}\varepsilon_{j,t} + \beta\sigma_{ij,t|t-1} \\ &= \overline{\sigma}_{ij} + \alpha(\varepsilon_{i,t}\varepsilon_{j,t} - \overline{\sigma}_{ij}) + \beta(\sigma_{ij,t|t-1} - \overline{\sigma}_{ij}).\end{aligned} \tag{6.24}$$

This expression shows that forecasts of future covariance depend on three ingredients: (1) the baseline forecast is represented by the unconditional covariance $\overline{\sigma}_{ij}$, which depends on all the parameters, ω, α, β; (2) the deviation of the current cross-product of asset returns $\varepsilon_{i,t}\varepsilon_{j,t}$ from the unconditional covariance $\overline{\sigma}_{ij}$, weighted by the coefficient α; and (3) the deviation of the current conditional covariance $\sigma_{ij,t|t-1}$ from the unconditional covariance $\overline{\sigma}_{ij}$, weighted by the coefficient β. Interestingly, Eq. (6.23) can be equivalently rewritten as:

$$\sigma_{ij,t+1|t} = \overline{\sigma}_{ij} + (\alpha+\beta)(\sigma_{ij,t|t-1} - \overline{\sigma}_{ij}) + \alpha\sigma_{ij,t|t-1}\left(\frac{z_{i,t}z_{j,t}}{\rho_{ij,t|t-1}} - 1\right), \tag{6.25}$$

because (using a simple trick, i.e., adding and subtracting $\alpha(\sigma_{ij,t|t-1} - \overline{\sigma}_{ij})$ at the right stage and exploiting the fact that $\sigma_{ij,t|t-1} = \rho_{ij,t|t-1}\sqrt{\sigma_{ii,t|t-1}}\sqrt{\sigma_{jj,t|t-1}}$):

$$\begin{aligned}\sigma_{ij,t+1|t} &= \overline{\sigma}_{ij} + \alpha(\varepsilon_{i,t}\varepsilon_{j,t} - \overline{\sigma}_{ij}) + \beta(\sigma_{ij,t|t-1} - \overline{\sigma}_{ij}) \\ &= \overline{\sigma}_{ij} + \alpha(\varepsilon_{i,t}\varepsilon_{j,t} - \overline{\sigma}_{ij}) - \alpha(\sigma_{ij,t|t-1} - \overline{\sigma}_{ij}) + \beta(\sigma_{ij,t|t-1} - \overline{\sigma}_{ij}) + \alpha(\sigma_{ij,t|t-1} - \overline{\sigma}_{ij}) \\ &= \overline{\sigma}_{ij} + (\alpha+\beta)(\sigma_{ij,t|t-1} - \overline{\sigma}_{ij}) + \alpha(\varepsilon_{i,t}\varepsilon_{j,t} - \sigma_{ij,t|t-1}) \\ &= \overline{\sigma}_{ij} + (\alpha+\beta)(\sigma_{ij,t|t-1} - \overline{\sigma}_{ij}) + \alpha\sigma_{ij,t|t-1}\left(\frac{\varepsilon_{i,t}\varepsilon_{j,t}}{\sigma_{ij,t|t-1}} - 1\right) \\ &= \overline{\sigma}_{ij} + (\alpha+\beta)(\sigma_{ij,t|t-1} - \overline{\sigma}_{ij}) + \alpha\sigma_{ij,t|t-1}\left(\frac{\varepsilon_{i,t}\varepsilon_{j,t}}{\rho_{ij,t|t-1}(\sigma_{ii,t|t-1}\sigma_{jj,t|t-1})^{1/2}} - 1\right) \\ &= \overline{\sigma}_{ij} + (\alpha+\beta)(\sigma_{ij,t|t-1} - \overline{\sigma}_{ij}) + \alpha\sigma_{ij,t|t-1}\left(\frac{z_{i,t}z_{j,t}}{\rho_{ij,t|t-1}} - 1\right).\end{aligned} \tag{6.26}$$

At this point, the *H-step-ahead forecast for covariance* is:

$$\begin{aligned} E_t[\sigma_{ij,t+H}] &= \bar{\sigma}_{ij} + (\alpha+\beta)(E_t[E_{t+H-2}[\sigma_{ij,t+H-1}]] - \bar{\sigma}_{ij}) \\ &\quad + \alpha E_t\left[E_{t+H-2}\left(\sigma_{ij,t+H-1}\left(\frac{z_{i,t+H-1}z_{j,t+H-1}}{\rho_{ij,t+H-1}} - 1\right)\right)\right] \\ &= \bar{\sigma}_{ij} + (\alpha+\beta)(E_t[\bar{\sigma}_{ij} + (\alpha+\beta)(\sigma_{ij,t+H-2} - \bar{\sigma}_{ij})] - \bar{\sigma}_{ij}) \\ &= \bar{\sigma}_{ij} + (\alpha+\beta)^2(E_t[\sigma_{ij,t+H-2}] - \bar{\sigma}_{ij}) \\ &= \bar{\sigma}_{ij} + (\alpha+\beta)^2(E_t[E_{t+H-3}[\sigma_{ij,t+H-2}]] - \bar{\sigma}_{ij}) \\ &= \bar{\sigma}_{ij} + (\alpha+\beta)^3(E_t[\sigma_{ij,t+H-3}] - \bar{\sigma}_{ij}) = \cdots = \bar{\sigma}_{ij} + (\alpha+\beta)^H(\sigma_{ij,t} - \bar{\sigma}_{ij}), \end{aligned} \tag{6.27}$$

where we have exploited the *law of iterated expectations* by which, given a generic time series X_t, $E_t[X_{t+H-1}] = E_t[E_{t+H-2}[X_{t+H-1}]]$ and

$$\begin{aligned} E_{t+H-2}\left[\sigma_{ij,t+H-1}\left(\frac{z_{i,t+H-1}z_{j,t+H-1}}{\rho_{ij,t+H-1}} - 1\right)\right] &= E_{t+H-2}\left(\sigma_{ij,t+H-1}\right) \\ \times E_{t+H-2}\left(\frac{z_{i,t+H-1}z_{j,t+H-1}}{\rho_{ij,t+H-1}} - 1\right) &= 0, \end{aligned} \tag{6.28}$$

as $E_{t+H-2}\left(z_{i,t+H-1}z_{j,t+H-1}\right) = \rho_{ij,t+H-1|t+H-2}$ and $\sigma_{ij,t+H-1|t+H-2}$ is independent by construction of $z_{i,t+H-1}$ and $z_{j,t+H-1}$. This derives from the fact that this is a GARCH process and the filtered GARCH covariance just depends on past shocks.[1] Similar to what was found in Section 5.1 of Chapter 5, it is then simple to compute forecasts of future, H-step-ahead covariances from $E_t[\sigma_{ij,t+H}] = \bar{\sigma}_{ij} + (\alpha+\beta)^H(\sigma_{ij,t|t-1} - \bar{\sigma}_{ij})$.

Of course, there is nothing special about a GARCH(1,1), in the sense that—even though this is rarely encountered in practice—in principle Eq. (6.22) can be extended to more general GARCH(p,q) structures. Unfortunately, the restrictions $\alpha_{ij} = \alpha$ and $\beta_{ij} = \beta$ are empirically very odd and often contrary to the evidence in the data that require instead that the persistence parameters should be asset/portfolio-specific.

EXAMPLE 6.2

We return to investigate the dynamics of the correlation between stock and bond returns when variances and covariances all follow GARCH(1,1) with identical coefficients. In this case, we specify a restricted bivariate *VAR*(1) as a multivariate conditional mean model. In this model, only lagged government bond returns forecast both stock and bond returns. We have tried other specifications, including unrestricted *VARs* and models that only include a constant intercept, but these failed to minimize the information criteria. The Gaussian ML estimates of the restricted *VAR*(1) with GARCH(1,1) variances and covariances are:

$$MKT_{t+1} = \underset{(0.000)}{0.549} + \underset{(0.000)}{0.109}\,Bond_t + \varepsilon_{MKT,t+1} \quad \varepsilon_{t+1}\,\mathrm{IID}\,N\left(0, \sigma^2_{MKT,t+1|t}\right)$$

$$\sigma^2_{MKT,t+1|t} = \underset{(0.000)}{0.087} + \underset{(0.000)}{0.081}\,\varepsilon^2_{MKT,t} + \underset{(0.000)}{0.905}\,\sigma^2_{MKT,t|t-1}$$

$$Bond_{t+1} = \underset{(0.650)}{0.010} + \underset{(0.000)}{0.226}\,Bond_t + \varepsilon_{Bond,t+1} \quad \varepsilon_{t+1}\,\mathrm{IID}\,N\left(0, \sigma^2_{Bond,t+1|t}\right)$$

$$\sigma^2_{Bond,t+1|t} = \underset{(0.000)}{0.025} + \underset{(0.000)}{0.081}\,\varepsilon^2_{Bond,t} + \underset{(0.000)}{0.905}\,\sigma^2_{Bond,t|t-1}$$

$$\sigma_{MKT-Bond,t+1|t} = \underset{(0.039)}{-0.007} + \underset{(0.000)}{0.081}\,\varepsilon_{MKT,t}\varepsilon_{Bond,t} + \underset{(0.000)}{0.905}\,\sigma_{MKT-Bond,t|t-1}.$$

(Continued)

1. Note the notation: $E_{t+H-2}(z_{i,t+H-1}z_{j,t+H-1})$ is the time $t+H-2$ predicted conditional covariance between $z_{i,t+H-1}$ and $z_{j,t+H-1}$ that we denote as $\rho_{ij,t+H-1|t+H-2}$. Note that properties such as

$$E_{t+H-l}\left(\frac{z_{i,t+H-l+1}z_{j,t+H-l+1}}{\rho_{ij,t+H-l+1}} - 1\right) = 0,$$

with $l \geq H$ are used repeatedly in the proof.

EXAMPLE 6.2 (Continued)

The implied unconditional weekly second moments are 2.468, 1.314, and −0.142 for equity volatility, bond volatility, and covariance, respectively. The implied persistence index shared by the three processes is fairly high, 0.986. Among the information criteria, the Bayesian information criterion (BIC) for this model is 7.302. We have also tried GARCH(2,2) and a threshold GARCH(1,1,1) models obtaining BIC values of 7.871 and 7.286. We therefore settle for the latter model:

$$MKT_{t+1} = \underset{(0.000)}{0.535} + \underset{(0.004)}{0.093}\, Bond_t + \varepsilon_{MKT,t+1} \quad \varepsilon_{t+1} \text{IID } N\left(0,\ \sigma^2_{MKT,t+1|t}\right)$$

$$\sigma^2_{MKT,t+1|t} = \underset{(0.000)}{0.083} + \underset{(0.000)}{0.065}\, \varepsilon^2_{MKT,t} + \underset{(0.000)}{0.036}\, I_{\{\varepsilon_{MKT,t}<0\}} \varepsilon^2_{MKT,t} + \underset{(0.000)}{0.902}\, \sigma^2_{MKT,t|t-1}$$

$$Bond_{t+1} = -\underset{(0.708)}{0.008} + \underset{(0.000)}{0.231}\, Bond_t + \varepsilon_{Bond,t+1} \quad \varepsilon_{t+1} \text{IID } N\left(0,\ \sigma^2_{Bond,t+1|t}\right)$$

$$\sigma^2_{Bond,t+1|t} = \underset{(0.000)}{0.025} + \underset{(0.000)}{0.065}\, \varepsilon^2_{Bond,t} + \underset{(0.000)}{0.036}\, I_{\{\varepsilon_{Bond,t}<0\}} \varepsilon^2_{Bond,t} + \underset{(0.000)}{0.902}\, \sigma^2_{Bond,t|t-1}$$

$$\sigma_{MKT-Bond,t+1|t} = -\underset{(0.000)}{0.018} + \underset{(0.000)}{0.065}\, \varepsilon_{MKT,t}\varepsilon_{Bond,t} + \underset{(0.000)}{0.036}\, I_{\{\varepsilon_{MKT,t}\varepsilon_{Bond,t}<0\}} \varepsilon_{MKT,t}\varepsilon_{Bond,t} + \underset{(0.000)}{0.902}\, \sigma_{MKT-Bond,t|t-1}.$$

Note that the term $0.036 I_{\{\varepsilon_{MKT,t}\varepsilon_{Bond,t}<0\}}\varepsilon_{MKT,t}\varepsilon_{Bond,t}$ has a rather intriguing interpretation: when shocks had a different sign one period ago, this increases the negative impact of the current product of shocks on the predicted covariance, a sort of accelerator effect of markets moving in different directions (Fig. 6.4).

The forecasts of correlations confirm a declining trend between 2000 and 2013, a pattern that is interrupted only after 2014, when predicted correlations climb back toward 0.

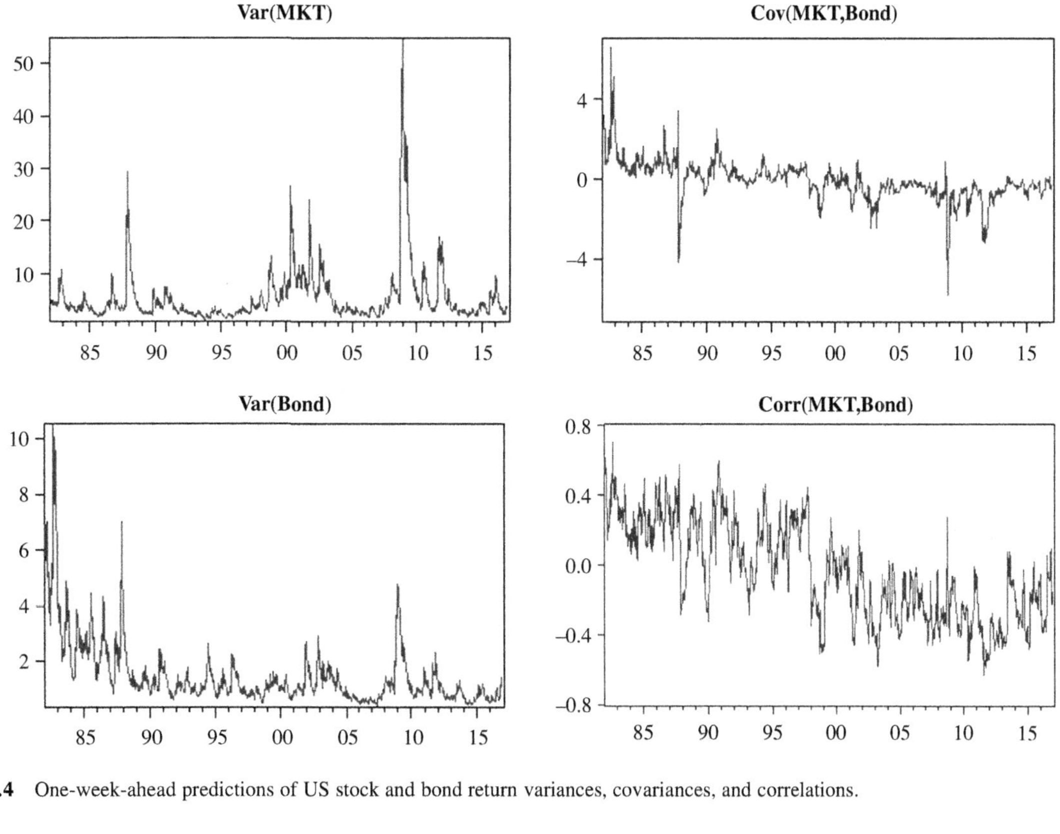

FIGURE 6.4 One-week-ahead predictions of US stock and bond return variances, covariances, and correlations.

Also with reference to covariance predictions, it is sensible to ask what are the effects of selecting a conditional model to be of a GARCH versus a RiskMetrics type. For concreteness, let us focus on the GARCH(1,1) case. As a starting point, we show that a GARCH model can be written in a format similar to RiskMetrics. We just need to rewrite the GARCH in a recursive fashion moving backward in time:

$$\begin{aligned}\sigma_{ij,t+1|t} &= \omega + \alpha\varepsilon_{i,t}\varepsilon_{j,t} + \beta\sigma_{ij,t|t-1}\\ &= \omega + \alpha\varepsilon_{i,t}\varepsilon_{j,t} + \beta\left[\omega + \alpha\varepsilon_{i,t-1}\varepsilon_{j,t-1} + \beta\sigma_{ij,t-1|t-2}\right]\\ &= \omega(1+\beta) + \alpha(\varepsilon_{i,t}\varepsilon_{j,t} + \beta\varepsilon_{i,t-1}\varepsilon_{j,t-1}) + \beta^2\sigma_{ij,t-1|t-2}\\ &= \omega(1+\beta+\beta^2) + \alpha(\varepsilon_{i,t}\varepsilon_{j,t} + \beta\varepsilon_{i,t-1}\varepsilon_{j,t-1} + \beta^2\varepsilon_{i,t-2}\varepsilon_{j,t-2}) + \beta^3\sigma_{ij,t-2|t-3}\\ &= \cdots = \omega\sum_{k=0}^{\infty}\beta^k + \alpha\sum_{k=0}^{\infty}\beta^k\varepsilon_{i,t-k}\varepsilon_{j,t-k} = \frac{\omega}{1-\beta} + \alpha\sum_{k=0}^{\infty}\beta^k\varepsilon_{i,t-k}\varepsilon_{j,t-k},\end{aligned} \tag{6.29}$$

where for simplicity ω does not depend on i and j. Clearly, Eq. (6.28) simplifies to RiskMetrics, $\sigma_{ij,t+1} = (1-\lambda)\sum_{k=0}^{\infty}\lambda^k\varepsilon_{i,t-k}\varepsilon_{j,t-k}$ when $\omega = 0$, $\alpha = 1-\lambda$, and $\beta = \lambda$. However, because the persistence of a GARCH (1,1) process is measured by the sum $\alpha+\beta$, now $\alpha = 1-\lambda$ and $\beta = \lambda$ imply that $\alpha+\beta = 1-\lambda+\lambda = 1$ which means that an exponentially smoothed process for conditional covariance implies that covariance is integrated of order 1. Equivalently, the covariance process has *infinite memory*, in the sense that any shock will have an impact on future, subsequent covariance that lasts forever. As a result, because under RiskMetrics $\alpha+\beta = 1$ and $E_t[\sigma^{RiskM}_{ij,t+H}] = \sigma^{RiskM}_{ij,t}$, we have:

$$\begin{aligned}E_t\left[\sigma^{RiskM}_{ij,t+H}\right] &= \overline{\sigma}_{ij} + \underbrace{(\alpha+\beta)}_{=1}E_t\left[E_{t+H-2}(\sigma_{ij,t+H-1} - \overline{\sigma}_{ij})\right]\\ &= E_t\left[E_{t+H-2}(\sigma_{ij,t+H-1})\right]\\ &= E_t[\sigma_{ij,t+H-2}] = E_t\left[E_{t+H-3}(\sigma_{ij,t+H-2})\right] = E_t[\sigma_{ij,t+H-3}] = \cdots = E_t[\sigma_{ij,t}] = \sigma_{ij,t}.\end{aligned} \tag{6.30}$$

This means that the forecast H-step-ahead in an exponential smoothing model is simply the current estimate of covariance. This is what we have alluded to early on when we have claimed that under Eq. (6.3) covariance follows a nonstationary, unit root process. On the contrary, because under GARCH, $E_t[\sigma_{ij,t+H}] = (\alpha+\beta)^H\sigma_{ij,t|t-1} + [1-(\alpha+\beta)^H]\overline{\sigma}_{ij}$, in the case of the GARCH(1,1) the current covariance receives a weight $(\alpha+\beta)^H$ which declines to 0 as $H\to\infty$ under covariance stationarity, so that the forecast simply converges to the unconditional covariance $\overline{\sigma}_{ij}$.

6.3 FULL, MULTIVARIATE GARCH MODELS

A fully-fledged extension and generalization of simple, univariate GARCH methods to the multivariate case presents many issues and problems related to the large scale of the resulting models and of their tendency to be over-parameterized. In any event, in this section, we take this task seriously and attempt to generalize the simple set-up $R_{t+1} = \mu_{t+1|t} + \sigma_{t+1|t}z_{t+1}z_{t+1}\text{IID } D(0,\, 1; \boldsymbol{\theta}_D)$, to the case in which returns on N assets or portfolios, collected in $\mathbf{R}_{t+1}$, are modeled as:

$$\mathbf{R}_{t+1} = \boldsymbol{\mu}_{t+1|t} + \boldsymbol{\varepsilon}_{t+1} = \boldsymbol{\mu}_{t+1|t} + \boldsymbol{\Sigma}^{1/2}_{t+1|t}\mathbf{z}_{t+1} \quad \mathbf{z}_{t+1}\text{IID } MD(\mathbf{0}, \mathbf{I}_N; \boldsymbol{\theta}_D), \tag{6.31}$$

where $\boldsymbol{\varepsilon}_{t+1} = \boldsymbol{\Sigma}^{1/2}_{t+1|t}\mathbf{z}_{t+1}$, MD indicates a generic multivariate density parameterized by $\boldsymbol{\theta}_D \subset \boldsymbol{\theta}, \mathbf{I}_N$ is an $N \times N$ identity matrix, and (similar to Chapter 3, $\boldsymbol{\Sigma}^{1/2}_{t+1|t}$ is the square-root, or *Cholesky decomposition*, of the covariance matrix, such that $\boldsymbol{\Sigma}^{1/2}_{t+1|t}(\boldsymbol{\Sigma}^{1/2}_{t+1|t})' = \boldsymbol{\Sigma}_{t+1|t} \equiv Var[\mathbf{R}_{t+1}|\Im_t]$. In this section, to make the distinction starker, we denote as $\boldsymbol{\Sigma}^{1/2}_{t+1|t}$ the *Cholesky factor* of $\boldsymbol{\Sigma}_{t+1|t}$.[2] Obvious examples of the generic multivariate distribution $MD(\mathbf{0}, \mathbf{I}_N; \boldsymbol{\theta}_D)$ are the multivariate normal that implies no other additional parameters and the *multivariate t-Student*:

2. Note that $\boldsymbol{\Sigma}^{1/2}_{t+1|t}$ is in no way the matrix of square roots of the elements of the full covariance matrix $\boldsymbol{\Sigma}_{t+1|t}$ (if so, how would we deal with potentially negative covariances?). $\boldsymbol{\Sigma}^{1/2}_{t+1|t}$ is a lower triangular matrix appropriately defined according to an algorithm that is implemented in most software packages.

$$f_t(\mathbf{z}_{t+1};\nu) = \frac{\Gamma\left(\frac{\nu+N}{2}\right)}{\Gamma(\nu/2)\sqrt[N]{\pi(\nu-2)}}\left(1+\frac{\mathbf{z}'_{t+1}\mathbf{z}_{t+1}}{\nu-2}\right)^{-\frac{\nu+N}{2}}. \tag{6.32}$$

As we have seen, skewed versions of Eq. (6.32) exist but they are even harder to work with, see the skewed PDF that has appeared in Chapter 5.

Given the general model in Eq. (6.31), our problem is then to write and estimate appropriate dynamic time series models for $\mathbf{\Sigma}_{t+1|t}$ knowing that this matrix contains $0.5N(N+1)$ distinct elements (because of symmetry these are less than N^2), which implies that in principle we would have to write and estimate dynamic models for each of these elements. However, as already discussed in Section 6.2, constructing SPD covariance matrix forecasts, which ensures that any portfolio variance will be always nonnegative, remains difficult. Appropriate structure needs to be imposed to guarantee the "SPD-ness" of the resulting forecast $\hat{\mathbf{\Sigma}}_{t+1|t}$. Here one thing needs to be carefully pondered: although much theoretical (econometric) literature has focused on relatively small multivariate cases of Eq. (6.31), for instance with $N=2$ or 3, practitioners need to access methods that apply to any value of the cross-sectional dimension N, including limit cases of N being large. In this respect, most of the models to be discussed in this section (possibly, with partial exception of BEKK, defined below), have to be approached with great caution. In fact, it is by now widely acknowledged that many of the models that we are about to introduce are rather interesting in a theoretical perspective and for small-scale applications (up to $N=4$ or 5) but rapidly become unwieldy or even impossible to estimate for realistic applications with hundreds of assets or securities to be modeled simultaneously.

This point is easily understood through the case of the straightforward, plain vanilla N-dimensional generalization of a GARCH(1,1) to *VEC(H) form*:

$$vech(\mathbf{\Sigma}_{t+1|t}) = vech(\mathbf{C}) + \mathbf{A}vech(\varepsilon_t\varepsilon_t') + \mathbf{B}vech(\mathbf{\Sigma}_{t|t-1}), \tag{6.33}$$

where $vech(\cdot)$("vector half") is the operator that converts the unique upper triangular elements of a symmetric matrix into a $0.5N(N+1)\times 1$ column vector that removes any duplicates (i.e., $0.5N(N-1)$ redundant covariances). For instance,

$$vech\left(\begin{bmatrix}\sigma^2_{1,t+1|t} & \sigma_{12,t+1|t}\\ \sigma_{12,t+1|t} & \sigma^2_{2,t+1|t}\end{bmatrix}\right) = \begin{bmatrix}\sigma^2_{1,t+1|t}\\ \sigma_{12,t+1|t}\\ \sigma^2_{2,t+1|t}\end{bmatrix}. \tag{6.34}$$

In this general, unrestricted *VEC(H) model, each element of $\mathbf{\Sigma}_{t+1|t}$ is a linear function of the lagged squared errors, the cross-products of past errors for all assets, and the lagged values of the elements of $\mathbf{\Sigma}_{t+1|t}$*. Note that while the $vec(\cdot)$ of an $N\times N$ symmetric matrix would simply be an $N^2\times 1$ vector, the $vech(\cdot)$ is instead a smaller, $0.5N(N+1)\times 1$ vector. In the VECH-GARCH(1,1) model above, $\mathbf{A}$ and $\mathbf{B}$ are $0.5N(N+1)$-dimensional square matrices, whereas $\mathbf{C}$ is an $N\times N$ symmetric matrix. Therefore, the structure of $\mathbf{C}$, $\mathbf{A}$, and $\mathbf{B}$ gives a total of:[3]

$$\begin{aligned}0.5N(N+1)+2[0.5N(N+1)]^2 &= 0.5N(N+1)[N^2+N+1]\\ &= 0.5N^4+0.5N^3+0.5N^2+0.5N^3+0.5N^2+0.5N\\ &= 0.5N^4+N^3+N^2+0.5N = O(N^4)\end{aligned} \tag{6.35}$$

parameters to be estimated. For instance, for $N=100$, which represents hardly a large portfolio or risk management problem, then the VECH-GARCH(1,1) model has 51,010,050 parameters to be estimated! If you need to have at least 20 observations available per estimable parameter, with $N=100$ assets, this means $20\times 51,010,050/100 = 10,202,010$ observations per series or a *daily* history of more than 40,484 years per series. This is not feasible. More generally, VECH-GARCH(p,q) models,

$$vech(\mathbf{\Sigma}_{t+1|t}) = vech(\mathbf{C}) + \sum_{i=1}^{p}\mathbf{A}_i vech(\varepsilon_{t+1-i}\varepsilon'_{t+1-i}) + \sum_{j=1}^{q}\mathbf{B}_j vech(\mathbf{\Sigma}_{t+1-j|t-j}), \tag{6.36}$$

that naively generalize the GARCH models of Section 5.2 in Chapter 5 to the multivariate case, tend to generate a serious *curse of dimensionality* problem, because—even when $p=q=1$—estimating as many free parameters as $0.5N^4+N^3+N^2+0.5N$ is obviously infeasible, both in terms of data availability and in numerical terms.[4] This is not the end of the problems: many of such $O(N^4)$ parameters shall need to be restricted for them to yield forecasts of the

3. In what follows, the notation $O(N^q)$ indicates that the quantity under examination grows at the same speed as the power N^{qq}.
4. The fact that over-parameterization represents the key obstacle in the generalization of GARCH to the multivariate case also explains why in what follows we mostly limit our treatment to the (1,1) case.

covariance matrix that are SPD, as expected. Such restrictions are even too complex and involved to be presented here (see, e.g., Gouriéroux, 1997, Section 6.1).[5]

As we know already, tricks—such as *covariance targeting*—are often invoked to deal with the curse of dimensionality in GARCH and also to make sure that the implied unconditional moments are consistent with what the model implies:

$$vech(\mathbf{C}_{VT}) = (\mathbf{I}_{0.5N(N+1)} - \mathbf{A} - \mathbf{B})vech\left(\frac{1}{T}\sum_{t=1}^{T} \varepsilon_t \varepsilon'_t\right), \tag{6.37}$$

(where "VT" stands for covariance targeting). Because by analogy to the univariate case, the unconditional, long-run covariance matrix from a VECH-GARCH(1,1) model is:

$$vech(\overline{\mathbf{\Sigma}}) = (\mathbf{I}_{0.5N(N+1)} - \mathbf{A} - \mathbf{B})^{-1} vech(\mathbf{C}), \tag{6.38}$$

setting $vech(\mathbf{C})$ in the way reported in Eq. (6.38), gives:

$$vech(\overline{\mathbf{\Sigma}}_{VT}) = vech\left(\frac{1}{T}\sum_{t=1}^{T} \varepsilon_t \varepsilon'_t\right). \tag{6.39}$$

This trick avoids cumbersome nonlinear estimation of $vech(\mathbf{C})$ and is also useful in a forecasting perspective to avoid that small perturbations in any of the elements of the matrices **A** and **B** may result in large changes in implied unconditional variances and covariances. However, although setting $vech(\mathbf{C})$ as in Eq. (6.38), does reduce the number of estimable parameters by $0.5N(N+1)$, the residual number $2[0.5N(N+1)]^2$ remains $O(N^4)$, which means that there are still too many parameters to be simultaneously estimated in **A** and **B** when N is large. As a result, further ideas have been explored in the literature to simplify VECH-GARCH models, besides covariance targeting.

One idea that has emerged early on (in the 1990s) in the literature is that appropriate restrictions on **A** and **B** would deliver a sensible reduction in the number of estimable parameters. One such possibility is offered by a *diagonal multivariate GARCH* (p, q), which is identical to Eq. (6.36), apart from the fact that all the $0.5N(N+1)$-dimensional square matrices $\{\mathbf{A}_i\}_{i=1}^{p}$ and $\{\mathbf{B}_j\}_{j=1}^{q}$ are diagonal matrices, in the sense that all of their off-diagonal elements equal 0. Typically, also in the diagonal case, the model is estimated by imposing that the **C** matrix is *triangular*, to allow a nonzero unconditional covariance. In fact, simple algebra reveals that each element of the covariance matrix follows a simple dynamics:

$$\begin{aligned}\sigma_{kl,t+1|t} = {} & \left(1 - \sum_{i=1}^{p}\alpha_{kl,i} - \sum_{j=1}^{q}\beta_{kl,j}\right)\frac{1}{T}\sum_{t=1}^{T}\varepsilon_{k,t}\varepsilon_{l,t} + \sum_{i=1}^{p}\alpha_{kl,i}\varepsilon_{k,t+1-i}\varepsilon_{l,t+1-i} \\ & + \sum_{j=1}^{q}\beta_{kl,j}\sigma_{kl,t+1-j|t-j}.\end{aligned} \tag{6.40}$$

Here covariance targeting was imposed already. This expression shows that conditional variances depend only on own lags and own lagged squared residuals, and conditional covariances depend only on own lags and own lagged cross-products of residuals. This is very restrictive because it prevents the detection of any *causality in variance*, the fact that past shocks to some variables forecast future variances of other variables. Even the diagonal GARCH framework, however, results in $O(N^2)$ parameters to be jointly estimated, which is computationally infeasible with large enough N; in fact, the number of parameters is:

$$p\,0.5N(N+1) + q\,0.5N(N+1) = 0.5(p+q)N(N+1). \tag{6.41}$$

We know of another issue that is likely to complicate estimation: because the coefficients $\alpha_{kl,i}$ and $\beta_{kl,j}$ for $k,l = 1, 2, \ldots, N$, and $i = 1, \ldots, p$, $j = 1, \ldots, q$ are not restricted to be the same across different assets and pairs of assets, constraints will have to be imposed to keep $\mathbf{\Sigma}_{t+1|t}$ that collects the forecasts $\sigma_{kl,t+1|t}$, (semi-) positive definite. In spite of the reduction in the number of parameters to be estimated, such constraints may represent a considerable drag on the estimation speed and ease. Example 6.3 puts these issues into context and offers some heuristic reasoning.

5. For instance, to avoid estimating **C**, **A**, and **B** jointly, Ledoit et al. (2003) estimate each variance and covariance equation separately. The resulting estimates do not necessarily guarantee an SPD $\mathbf{\Sigma}_{t+1|t}$. Therefore, in a second step, the estimates are transformed to ensure SPD-ness, keeping the disruptive effects as small as possible.

EXAMPLE 6.3

Consider the case of two assets ($N = 2$) and a simple diagonal multivariate ARCH(1) model,

$$vech(\boldsymbol{\Sigma}_{t+1|t}) = (\mathbf{I}_3 - \mathbf{A})vech\left(T^{-1}\sum_{t=1}^{T}\boldsymbol{\varepsilon}_t\boldsymbol{\varepsilon}_t{'}\right) + \mathbf{A}vech(\boldsymbol{\varepsilon}_t\boldsymbol{\varepsilon}_t{'}),$$

where the covariance targeting restriction has already been imposed and $\mathbf{A}$ is a diagonal matrix. Because we have set $N = 2$, $\boldsymbol{\Sigma}_{t+1|t}$ will be a 2×2 matrix, $\mathbf{A}$ is a 3×3 matrix, $vech(\boldsymbol{\Sigma}_{t+1|t})$ is a 3×1 vector of unique elements from $\boldsymbol{\Sigma}_{t+1|t}$, and $vech\left(T^{-1}\sum_{t=1}^{T}\boldsymbol{\varepsilon}_t\boldsymbol{\varepsilon}_t{'}\right)$ is a 3×1 vector of unique elements from the sum of cross-product matrices $\sum_{t=1}^{T}\boldsymbol{\varepsilon}_t\boldsymbol{\varepsilon}_t{'}$. The number of coefficients to be estimated is of course 3, a^{11}, a^{22}, and a^{33} in the representation:

$$\begin{bmatrix}\sigma^2_{1,t+1|t}\\ \sigma_{12,t+1|t}\\ \sigma^2_{2,t+1|t}\end{bmatrix} = \left(\begin{bmatrix}1&0&0\\0&1&0\\0&0&1\end{bmatrix} - \begin{bmatrix}a^{11}&0&0\\0&a^{22}&0\\0&0&a^{33}\end{bmatrix}\right)\begin{bmatrix}T^{-1}\sum_{t=1}^{T}\varepsilon^2_{1,t}\\ T^{-1}\sum_{t=1}^{T}\varepsilon_{1,t}\varepsilon_{2,t}\\ T^{-1}\sum_{t=1}^{T}\varepsilon^2_{2,t}\end{bmatrix}$$

$$+\begin{bmatrix}a^{11}&0&0\\0&a^{22}&0\\0&0&a^{33}\end{bmatrix}\begin{bmatrix}\varepsilon^2_{1,t}\\ \varepsilon_{1,t}\varepsilon_{2,t}\\ \varepsilon^2_{2,t}\end{bmatrix} = \begin{bmatrix}(1-a^{11})T^{-1}\sum_{t=1}^{T}\varepsilon^2_{1,t} + a^{11}\varepsilon^2_{1,t}\\ (1-a^{22})T^{-1}\sum_{t=1}^{T}\varepsilon_{1,t}\varepsilon_{2,t} + a^{22}\varepsilon_{1,t}\varepsilon_{2,t}\\ (1-a^{33})T^{-1}\sum_{t=1}^{T}\varepsilon^2_{2,t} + a^{33}\varepsilon^2_{2,t}\end{bmatrix}.$$

As for the conditions that guarantee that both $\sigma^2_{1,t+1|t}$ and $\sigma^2_{2,t+1|t}$ are positive at all times, that is, that help ensure semi-positive definiteness of $\boldsymbol{\Sigma}_{t+1|t}$, clearly, because under a continuous distribution past squared shocks are unbounded,

$$(1-a^{11})T^{-1}\sum_{t=1}^{T}\varepsilon^2_{1,t} + a^{11}\varepsilon^2_{1,t} > 0 \quad \text{if and only if } a^{11}\in(0,1)$$

$$(1-a^{33})T^{-1}\sum_{t=1}^{T}\varepsilon^2_{2,t} + a^{33}\varepsilon^2_{2,t} > 0 \quad \text{if and only if } a^{33}\in(0,1).$$

At this point, the filtered (predicted) correlation coefficient has an expression:

$$\rho_{12,t+1|t} = \frac{c^{22} + a^{22}\varepsilon_{1,t}\varepsilon_{2,t}}{\sqrt{c^{11} + a^{11}\varepsilon^2_{1,t}}\sqrt{c^{33} + a^{33}\varepsilon^2_{2,t}}},$$

where we have shortened the notation defining $c^{11} \equiv (1-a^{11})T^{-1}\sum_{t=1}^{T}\varepsilon^2_{1,t}, c^{33} \equiv (1-a^{33})T^{-1}\sum_{t=1}^{T}\varepsilon^2_{2,t}$, and $c^{22} \equiv (1-a^{22})T^{-1}\sum_{t=1}^{T}\varepsilon_{1,t}\varepsilon_{2,t}$. On focusing on the upper bound of the interval, this means that $(c^{22} + a^{22}\varepsilon_{1,t}\varepsilon_{2,t})^2 \le (c^{11} + a^{11}\varepsilon^2_{1,t})(c^{33} + a^{33}\varepsilon^2_{2,t})$ or

$$(c^{22})^2 + (a^{22})^2\varepsilon^2_{1,t}\varepsilon^2_{2,t} + 2c^{22}a^{22}\varepsilon_{1,t}\varepsilon_{2,t} \le c^{11}c^{33} + c^{33}a^{11}\varepsilon^2_{1,t} + c^{11}a^{33}\varepsilon^2_{2,t} + a^{11}a^{33}\varepsilon^2_{1,t}\varepsilon^2_{2,t}$$

which is equivalent to:

$$[a^{11}a^{33} - (a^{22})^2]\varepsilon^2_{1,t}\varepsilon^2_{2,t} + [c^{11}c^{33} - (c^{22})^2] + c^{33}a^{11}\varepsilon^2_{1,t} + c^{11}a^{33}\varepsilon^2_{2,t} - 2c^{22}a^{22}\varepsilon_{1,t}\varepsilon_{2,t} \ge 0'$$

which cannot hold for a continuous distribution for the two return series as, even imposing $[a^{11}a^{33} - (a^{22})^2] \ge 0$ and $[c^{11}c^{33} - (c^{22})^2] \ge 0$,

$$c^{33}a^{11}\varepsilon^2_{1,t} + c^{11}a^{33}\varepsilon^2_{2,t} - 2c^{22}a^{22}\varepsilon_{1,t}\varepsilon_{2,t} \ge 0$$

in general it does not hold for $a^{22} \neq 0$. However, notice that if one sets $a^{22} = 0$, then the inequalities simplify to:

$$a^{11}a^{33}\varepsilon^2_{1,t}\varepsilon^2_{2,t} + [c^{11}c^{33} - (c^{22})^2] + c^{33}a^{11}\varepsilon^2_{1,t} + c^{11}a^{33}\varepsilon^2_{2,t} \ge 0,$$

which has a chance to hold if a^{11} and a^{33} are such that:

$$\left[(1-a^{11})T^{-1}\sum_{t=1}^{T}\varepsilon^2_{1,t}\right]\left[(1-a^{33})T^{-1}\sum_{t=1}^{T}\varepsilon^2_{2,t}\right] \ge \left[T^{-1}\sum_{t=1}^{T}\varepsilon_{1,t}\varepsilon_{2,t}\right]^2,$$

which also means that:

$$\bar{\rho}_{12} = \frac{\bar{\sigma}_{12}}{\bar{\sigma}_{11}\bar{\sigma}_{22}} = \frac{T^{-1}\sum_{t=1}^{T}\varepsilon_{1,t}\varepsilon_{2,t}}{\sqrt{(1-a^{11})T^{-1}\sum_{t=1}^{T}\varepsilon^2_{1,t}}\sqrt{(1-a^{33})T^{-1}\sum_{t=1}^{T}\varepsilon^2_{2,t}}} \le 1,$$

the unconditional correlation implied by the data and the diagonal bivariate ARCH(1) process is well-behaved. Therefore, if $a^{11}\in(0,1)$ and $a^{33}\in(0,1)$, then $a^{22} = 0$ (and possibly some other restrictions on a^{11} and a^{33} such that the condition above holds)

(Continued)

EXAMPLE 6.3 (Continued)

must be imposed. This means that it is impossible to model the dynamics of volatilities and covariances simultaneously, while satisfying the positivity requirement for the volatilities and keeping the covariance matrix SPD at all times. Equivalently, if one wants to impose that the diagonal VECH-ARCH(1) model delivers a filtered covariance matrix $\boldsymbol{\Sigma}_{t+1|t}$ that is SPD at all times, the diagonal model itself must be turned into a constant covariance multivariate ARCH model, as you understand that $a^{22}=0$ implies $\sigma_{12,t}=T^{-1}\sum_{t=1}^{T}\varepsilon_{1t}\varepsilon_{2t}=\overline{\sigma}_{12}$, so that:

$$\rho_{12,t+1|t}=\frac{\overline{\sigma}_{12}}{\sqrt{c^{11}+a^{11}\varepsilon_{1,t}^{2}}\sqrt{c^{33}+a^{33}\varepsilon_{2,t}^{2}}},$$

and dynamics in conditional correlations will exclusively come from dynamics in volatilities.[6]

An even more drastic simplification of VECH-GARCH, that we have in fact already examined before, is represented by a *scalar GARCH(p, q)*:

$$\sigma_{kl,t+1|t}=\left(1-\sum_{i=1}^{p}\alpha_i-\sum_{j=1}^{q}\beta_j\right)\frac{1}{T}\sum_{t=1}^{T}\varepsilon_{k,t}\varepsilon_{l,t}+\sum_{i=1}^{p}\alpha_i\varepsilon_{k,t+1-i}\varepsilon_{l,t+1-i}+\sum_{j=1}^{q}\beta_j\sigma_{kl,t+1-j|t-j} \tag{6.42}$$

which means that ARCH and GARCH coefficients reduce to real scalar parameters common across assets. In matrix format, the model becomes:

$$\begin{aligned}vech(\boldsymbol{\Sigma}_{t+1|t})=&\left(1-\sum_{i=1}^{p}\alpha_i-\sum_{j=1}^{q}\beta_j\right)vech\left(\frac{1}{T}\sum_{t=1}^{T}\boldsymbol{\varepsilon}_t\boldsymbol{\varepsilon}_t'\right)\\&+\sum_{i=1}^{p}\alpha_i vech(\boldsymbol{\varepsilon}_{t+1-i}\boldsymbol{\varepsilon}_{t+1-i}')+\sum_{j=1}^{q}\beta_j vech(\boldsymbol{\Sigma}_{t+1-j|t-j}).\end{aligned} \tag{6.43}$$

These strong restrictions ensure that the resulting predicted covariance matrix is SPD because all coefficients are restricted to be the same across different pairs of assets. Moreover, the parametric simplification is obvious as the number of parameters now—when also covariance targeting is imposed—simply becomes $p+q$, which is in fact independent of N. However, one is left to wonder about the exact meaning of a model in which the speed of mean reversion is restricted to be common across N different assets or portfolios, and in fact all conditional variances and covariances share common dynamics as in examples in Chapter 5.

EXAMPLE 6.4

We now apply VECH-GARCH models to investigate the dynamics of the correlation between stock and bond returns. We specify a restricted bivariate VAR(1) as a multivariate conditional mean model. In this model, only lagged government bond returns forecast both stock and bond returns. Using the BIC to perform model selection, we find that a full VECH-GARCH(1,1) characterized by 25 parameters leads to a criterion of 7.304; a full **C** matrix diagonal VECH-GARCH(1,1) characterized by 13

(Continued)

6. The heuristic proof above is in itself sufficient to derive that $a^{22}=0$ from $a^{11}\in(0,1)$ and $a^{33}\in(0,1)$; we also need to deal with the lower bound of the filtered correlation coefficient derived from a^{11}, a^{22}, and a^{33}. For completeness, let us also consider the possibility to impose $0\geq\rho_{12,t}\geq-1\,\forall t\geq 1$. This lower bound means that $-(c^{22}+a^{22}\varepsilon_{1,t}\varepsilon_{2,t})\leq\sqrt{(c^{11}+a^{11}\varepsilon_{1,t}^2)(c^{33}+a^{33}\varepsilon_{2,t}^2)}$ or $(c^{22}+a^{22}\varepsilon_{1,t}\varepsilon_{2,t})^2\leq(c^{11}+a^{11}\varepsilon_{1,t}^2)(c^{33}+a^{33}\varepsilon_{2,t}^2)$
which implies

$$(c^{22})^2+(a^{22})^2\varepsilon_{1,t}^2\varepsilon_{2,t}^2+2c^{22}a^{22}\varepsilon_{1,t}\varepsilon_{2,t}\leq c^{11}c^{33}+c^{33}a^{11}\varepsilon_{1,t}^2+c^{11}a^{33}\varepsilon_{2,t}^2+a^{11}a^{33}\varepsilon_{1,t}^2\varepsilon_{2,t}^2$$

which is equivalent to

$$[a^{11}a^{33}-(a^{22})^2]\varepsilon_{1,t}^2\varepsilon_{2,t}^2+[c^{11}c^{33}-(c^{22})^2]+c^{33}a^{11}\varepsilon_{1,t}^2+c^{11}a^{33}\varepsilon_{2,t}^2-2c^{22}a^{22}\varepsilon_{1,t}\varepsilon_{2,t}\geq 0,$$

which is the same condition used above.

EXAMPLE 6.4 (Continued)

parameters reaches a BIC of 7.284; a full diagonal VECH-GARCH(1,1) characterized by 12 parameters leads to a BIC of 7.353, and a scalar VECH-GARCH(1,1) characterized by 9 parameters achieved a BIC of 7.320. Hence a full **C** matrix diagonal VECH-GARCH(1,1) is preferred.

Before settling on the full **C** matrix diagonal VECH-GARCH(1,1) ML estimates, we try three more specifications, always ranked on the basis of their BIC. First, we estimate a richer, triangular VECH-GARCH(2,2) model that under 21 parameters yields a BIC of 7.325, which marks a worse fit. Second, we try and impose covariance targeting on the full **C** matrix diagonal VECH-GARCH(1,1), obtaining a BIC of 7.345 under 10 parameters. Third, we estimate a full **C** matrix diagonal VECH-GARCH(1,1) with *t*-Student errors, which delivers a BIC of 7.222. As one may have expected, we end up selecting this very last model that delivers the estimates:

$$MKT_{t+1} = \underset{(0.000)}{0.574} + \underset{(0.003)}{0.098}\, Bond_t + \varepsilon_{MKT,t+1}$$

$$\sigma^2_{MKT,t+1|t} = \underset{(0.001)}{0.092} + \underset{(0.000)}{0.074}\, \varepsilon^2_{MKT,t} + \underset{(0.000)}{0.906}\, \sigma^2_{MKT,t|t-1}$$

$$Bond_{t+1} = -\underset{(0.888)}{0.003} + \underset{(0.000)}{0.247}\, Bond_t + \varepsilon_{Bond,t+1} \qquad [\varepsilon_{MKT,t+1}\varepsilon_{Bond,t+1}]' \ \text{IID}\ Mt\left(0,\ \boldsymbol{\Sigma}_{t+1|t}; \underset{(0.000)}{9.631}\right)$$

$$\sigma^2_{Bond,t+1|t} = \underset{(0.008)}{0.020} + \underset{(0.000)}{0.062}\, \varepsilon^2_{Bond,t} + \underset{(0.000)}{0.923}\, \sigma^2_{Bond,t|t-1}$$

$$\sigma_{MKT-Bond,t+1|t} = -\underset{(0.895)}{0.0002} + \underset{(0.000)}{0.028}\, \varepsilon_{MKT,t}\varepsilon_{Bond,t} + \underset{(0.000)}{0.963}\, \sigma_{MKT-Bond,t|t-1}.$$

All the estimated conditional second moment processes are highly persistent (the corresponding indices are 0.980, 0.985, and 0.991 for conditional stock variance, bond variance, and covariance, respectively), but there are differences across the three GARCH processes that a scalar model could not take into account. For instance, conditional variances react to shocks much more (0.074 and 0.062) than conditional covariances do (0.028); the latter process is indeed considerably smoother. Fig. 6.5 shows implied conditional second moments from VECH-GARCH(1,1), under *t*-Student errors. Even though the general patterns are rather similar, now predicted correlations are smoother in time and occupy a smaller range of values.

However, after duly printing ML parameter estimates and their standard errors, E-Views warns us that "Coefficient matrix is not SPD," and this remains a considerable reason for concern.

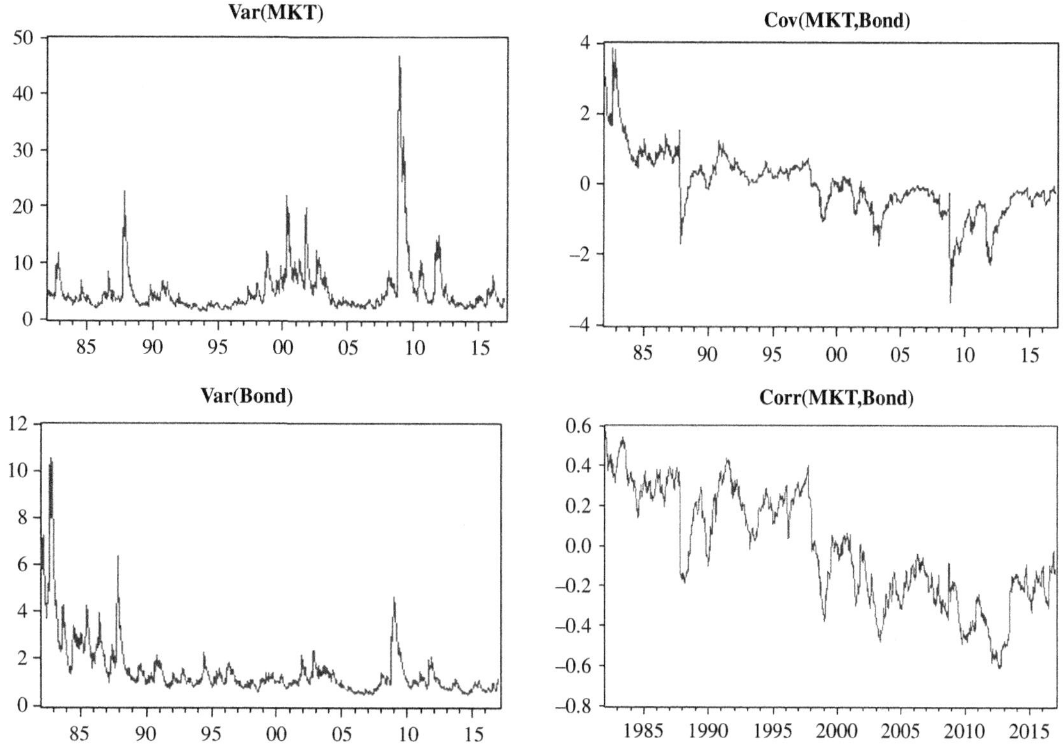

FIGURE 6.5 One-week-ahead predictions of US stock and bond return variances, covariances, and correlations.

However, there is one simple transformation of the model in Eq. (6.33) that—at the cost of sacrificing the direct interpretation of the estimated coefficients in the model—can guarantee the SPD nature of the predicted covariance matrix without restricting the model to become scalar: this is the *Full Rank* version of Bollerslev, Engle, and Wooldridge's (1988) *multivariate GARCH(p,q)* model:

$$\boldsymbol{\Sigma}_{t+1|t} = \mathbf{C}\mathbf{C}' + \sum_{i=1}^{p} \mathbf{A}_i\,\mathbf{A}'_i \odot \varepsilon_t\,\varepsilon'_t + \sum_{j=1}^{q} \mathbf{B}_j\,\mathbf{B}'_j \odot \boldsymbol{\Sigma}_{t|t-1}, \tag{6.44}$$

where $\odot$ denotes the *element-wise (Hadamard) matrix product.*[7] Note that the $\mathbf{C}$, $\{\mathbf{A}_i\}_{i=1}^{p}$, and $\{\mathbf{B}_j\}_{j=1}^{q}$ matrices can be $N \times M$ with $M \leq N$ and their maximum rank. The number of parameters to estimate is then $MN(p+q+1)$. When $M=1$, they simply become vectors of coefficients and allow the investigator to economize the number of parameters to $N(p+q+1)$ only. The full rank version is obtained when the model is reparameterized as:

$$\boldsymbol{\Sigma}_{t+1|t} = \mathbf{C}^{1/2}(\mathbf{C}^{1/2})' + \sum_{i=1}^{p} \mathbf{A}_i^{1/2}(\mathbf{A}_i^{1/2})' \odot \varepsilon_t\,\varepsilon_t' + \sum_{j=1}^{q} (\mathbf{B}_j^{1/2})(\mathbf{B}_j^{1/2})' \odot \boldsymbol{\Sigma}_{t|t-1}, \tag{6.45}$$

where given a generic matrix $\mathbf{M}$, $M^{1/2}$ denotes its Cholesky decomposition. In this case, each of the matrices in Eq. (6.45) includes $0.5N(N+1)$ coefficients, so that the total number is $0.5N(N+1)(p+q+1)$. However, because they are based on the Hadamard product representations, the models in Eqs. (6.44) and (6.45) still imply that the variance of the returns on asset i only depends on:

- its past squared residuals and
- its past cross-products between the residuals of asset i and the residuals of the $(N-1)$ other assets.

This means effects from past squared residuals of assets $j \neq i$ on the forecast of the variance of returns of asset i are impossible. The predicted covariance between the returns on assets i and j also only depends on the past residuals (in isolation, squared, and taken in pairwise products) of these assets, while any influence from other assets different from i and j is ruled out. This remains a bit restrictive. For instance, let us ask: during the European sovereign debt crisis of 2010–11, would the variance of returns on Italian government debt have depended on past news concerning Greek debt in isolation? It is very likely.[8] The cost of using Eqs. (6.44) and (6.45) instead of a VECH-GARCH is that none of the elements of the parameter matrices may be directly interpreted as carrying estimates (with related standard errors) of the effects of past shocks or their products on the forecasts of quantities of interest: it is the products $\mathbf{CC}'$, $\mathbf{A_iA_i'}$, and $\mathbf{B_jB_j'}$ only that matter.

EXAMPLE 6.4 *(continued)*

Here we simply extend our earlier example to a Full Rank multivariate *t*-Student GARCH(1,1), obtaining:

$$MKT_{t+1} = \underset{(0.000)}{0.587} + \underset{(0.003)}{0.098}\,Bond_t + \varepsilon_{MKT,t+1}$$

$$\sigma^2_{MKT,t+1|t} = \underset{(0.002)}{0.108} + \underset{(0.000)}{0.092}\,\varepsilon^2_{MKT,t} + \underset{(0.000)}{0.886}\,\sigma^2_{MKT,t|t-1}$$

$$Bond_{t+1} = \underset{(0.989)}{-0.0003} + \underset{(0.000)}{0.246}\,Bond_t + \varepsilon_{Bond,t+1} \quad [\varepsilon_{MKT,t+1}\varepsilon_{Bond,t+1}]' \ \text{IID}\ Mt\Big(0,\ \boldsymbol{\Sigma}_{t+1|t}; \underset{(0.000)}{9.359}\Big)$$

$$\sigma^2_{Bond,t+1|t} = \underset{(0.014)}{0.022} + \underset{(0.000)}{0.074}\,\varepsilon^2_{Bond,t} + \underset{(0.000)}{0.912}\,\sigma^2_{Bond,t|t-1}$$

$$\sigma_{MKT-Bond,t+1|t} = \underset{(0.531)}{-0.003} + \underset{(0.000)}{0.069}\,\varepsilon_{MKT,t}\varepsilon_{Bond,t} + \underset{(0.000)}{0.899}\,\sigma_{MKT-Bond,t|t-1}.$$

(Continued)

7. For instance, the (i,j) element of the product $\mathbf{M}_1 \odot \mathbf{M}_2$ is simply the product between the (i,j)-element of $\mathbf{M}_1$ and the (i,j)-element of $\mathbf{M}_2$.

8. Moreover, we may ask, would the predicted covariance between Italian and Spanish government debt returns have depended on past news concerning Greek debt? This also seems plausible. Yet, the models in Eqs. (6.44) and (6.45) fail to accommodate for these plausible channels of volatility and covariation spreading.

EXAMPLE 6.4 *(continued)* **(Continued)**

The estimates are very similar to what we had found in the diagonal VECH case. Yet, now the resulting time-varying covariance matrix is SPD at all times. However, even small differences are enough to generate differences between the two implied time series of predicted correlations that are not always negligible, as shown in Fig. 6.6.

In fact, even though the general dynamics of correlation forecasts is similar, the Full Rank estimates are spikier, more volatile, and yet more sensible because resulting from uniformly SPD covariance matrices.

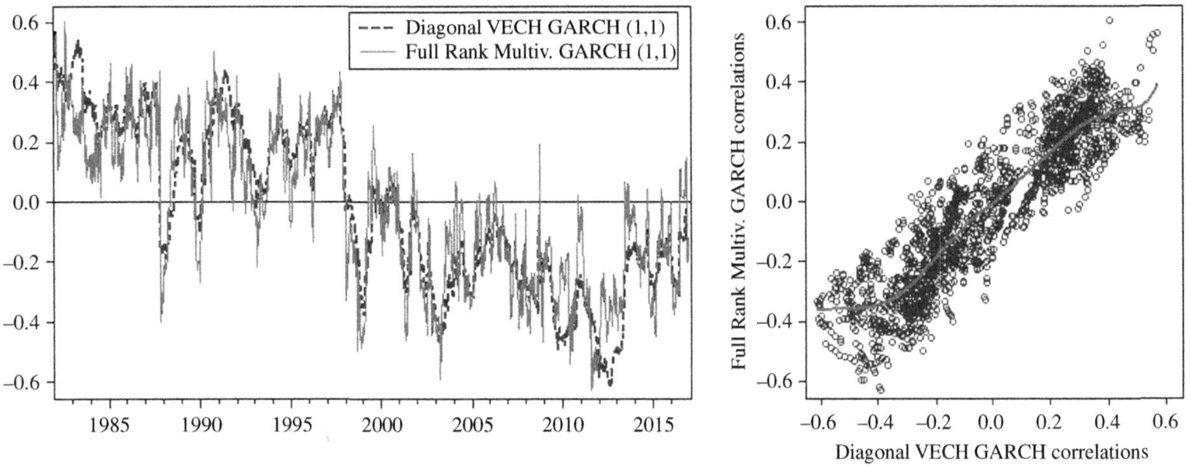

FIGURE 6.6 One-week-ahead predictions of US Stock–bond return correlations under diagonal VECH and full rank multivariate GARCH(1,1).

Because of the many limitations of VECH-GARCH, during the 1990s, one multivariate GARCH model that surged to popularity has been Engle and Kroner's (1995) *BEKK GARCH(p, q)*:[9]

$$\boldsymbol{\Sigma}_{t+1|t} = \mathbf{CC}' + \sum_{i=1}^{p} \mathbf{A}_i(\boldsymbol{\varepsilon}_{t+1-i}\boldsymbol{\varepsilon}'_{t+1-i})\mathbf{A}_i{}' + \sum_{j=1}^{q} \mathbf{B}_j\boldsymbol{\Sigma}_{t+1-j|t-j}\mathbf{B}_j{}', \tag{6.46}$$

where the collection of matrices, $\mathbf{C}$, $\{\mathbf{A}_i\}_{i=1}^{p}$, and $\{\mathbf{B}_j\}_{j=1}^{q}$ are composed of nonnegative matrices (but we often impose that they are also *symmetric*). This special *product-sandwich form* that is used to write the BEKK ensures the SPD property without imposing further restrictions, which represents the key reason for the success of BEKK models. In fact, this full matrix BEKK is easier to estimate than VECH-GARCH models. In practice, the popular form of BEKK that many empiricists have come to appreciate is a simpler (1,1) *diagonal BEKK* that restricts the matrices **A** and **B** to be diagonal. BEKK models possess three attractive properties:

- When symmetry is imposed, a BEKK is a truncated, low-dimensional application of a theorem by which all nonnegative, symmetric $N \times N$ matrices (say, **M**) can be decomposed (for instance) as:

$$\mathbf{M} = \begin{bmatrix} m_{11} & m_{12} \\ m_{21} & m_{22} \end{bmatrix} = \sum_{k=1}^{2N} \begin{bmatrix} \mathbf{m}'_{k,1}\mathbf{m}_{k,1} & \mathbf{m}'_{k,1}\mathbf{m}_{k,2} \\ \mathbf{m}'_{k,2}\mathbf{m}_{k,1} & \mathbf{m}'_{k,2}\mathbf{m}_{k,2} \end{bmatrix} \tag{6.47}$$

  for appropriately selected vectors $\mathbf{m_{k,j}}$. In this sense, mathematically at least, it is no surprise that BEKK models often offer a good fit to the dynamics of variance, even though empirically we tend to set p and q to values obviously much smaller than $2N$.

9. The acronym BEKK stands Baba–Engle–Kraft–Kroner, the names of the four econometricians who contributed to its development.

- BEKK easily ensures SPD-ness of the covariance matrix, because by construction, $\mathbf{CC}'$ is SPD, $\mathbf{A}_i(\boldsymbol{\varepsilon}_{t+1-i}\boldsymbol{\varepsilon}'_{t+1-i})\mathbf{A}_i' i=1,\ldots,p$ is SPD and sums of SPD matrices are SPD, $\mathbf{B}_j\boldsymbol{\Sigma}_{t+1-j|t-j}\mathbf{B}_j' j=1,\ldots,q$ is SPD if $\boldsymbol{\Sigma}_{t+1-j|t-j}$ is SPD and sums of SPD matrices are SPD.
- BEKK is *invariant to linear combinations*, for example, if $\mathbf{R}_{t+1}$ follows a BEKK GARCH(p,q), then any portfolio formed from the N securities or assets in $\mathbf{R}_{t+1}$ will also follow a BEKK.

However, the number of parameters in BEKK remains rather large even when the matrices $\{\mathbf{A}_i\}_{i=1}^p$ and $\{\mathbf{B}_j\}_{j=1}^q$ are assumed to be symmetric:

$$\begin{aligned}&0.5N(N+1)+0.5pN(N+1)+0.5qN(N+1)\\&\quad=0.5N(N+1)(1+p+q)=O(N^2).\end{aligned}\tag{6.48}$$

Nonetheless, the number of parameters in BEKK is substantially inferior to those appearing in a full VECH specification. This happens because the parameters governing the dynamics of the covariance equation in BEKK models are the products of the corresponding parameters of the two corresponding variance equations in the same model.

The third property of BEKK models can only be fully appreciated contrasting the features of BEKK under linear aggregation with the properties of alternative multivariate GARCH models, even a simple diagonal VECH-ARCH (i.e., a GARCH(1,0)): not all multivariate GARCH models are invariant with respect to linear transformations.[10] On the one hand, as far as BEKK models are concerned, it is easy to see that under BEKK the variance of portfolio returns, $\sigma^2_{p,t+1}\equiv Var_t[R_{p,t+1}]$, characterized by weights $\mathbf{w}$, $\sigma^2_{p,t+1}=\mathbf{w}'\boldsymbol{\Sigma}_{t+1|t}\mathbf{w}$:

$$\begin{aligned}\sigma^2_{p,t+1}&=\boldsymbol{w}'\boldsymbol{\Sigma}_{t+1|t}\boldsymbol{w}=\underbrace{\boldsymbol{w}'\mathbf{C}}_{\boldsymbol{c}'}\underbrace{\mathbf{C}'\boldsymbol{w}}_{\boldsymbol{c}}+\sum_{i=1}^{p}\underbrace{\mathbf{w}'\mathbf{A}_i}_{\mathbf{a}_i'}(\mathbf{R}_{t+1-i}\mathbf{R}'_{t+1-i})\underbrace{\mathbf{A}_i{}'\boldsymbol{w}}_{\boldsymbol{a}_i}\\&\quad+\sum_{j=1}^{q}\underbrace{\mathbf{w}'\mathbf{B}_j}_{\mathbf{b}_j'}\;\boldsymbol{\Sigma}_{t+1-j|t-j}\underbrace{\mathbf{B}_j{}'\boldsymbol{w}}_{\boldsymbol{b}_j}\\&=\boldsymbol{c}'\boldsymbol{c}+\sum_{i=1}^{p}\boldsymbol{a}_i'(\mathbf{R}_{t+1-i}\mathbf{R}'_{t+1-i})\boldsymbol{a}_i+\sum_{j=1}^{q}\boldsymbol{b}_j'\,\boldsymbol{\Sigma}_{t+1-j|t-j}\boldsymbol{b}_j.\end{aligned}\tag{6.49}$$

This is a rather odd univariate BEKK(p,q) model, but it is still in BEKK form. On the other hand, such invariant aggregation generally fails for other multivariate ARCH models. For instance, consider again the case of two assets ($N=2$) and a simple diagonal multivariate ARCH(1) model as in Example 6.1,

$$vech(\boldsymbol{\Sigma}_{t+1|t})=(\mathbf{I}_3-\mathbf{A})vech\left(T^{-1}\sum_{t=1}^{T}\boldsymbol{\varepsilon}_t\boldsymbol{\varepsilon}_t'\right)+\mathbf{A}vech\left(\boldsymbol{\varepsilon}_t\boldsymbol{\varepsilon}_t'\right),\tag{6.50}$$

where the covariance targeting restriction has already been imposed and $\mathbf{A}$ is a diagonal matrix. Consider a portfolio of the two assets, with weights w and $(1-w)$. We show that in spite of the fact that $\mathbf{R}_{t+1}$ is characterized by a diagonal bivariate ARCH(1), the portfolio returns $R_{p,t+1}=wR_{1,t+1}+(1-w)R_{2,t+1}$ have a variance process that fails to display the typical diagonal form, that is, $(1-a^{kk})T^{-1}\sum_{t=1}^{T}R_{p,t+1}+a^{kk}R^2_{p,t+1}$. Note first that:

$$\begin{aligned}\sigma^2_{p,t+1|t}&\equiv Var_t[wR_{1,t+1}+(1-w)R_{2,t+1}]\\&=w^2\sigma^2_{1,t+1|t}+(1-w)^2\sigma^2_{2,t+1|t}+2w(1-w)\sigma_{12,t+1|t}\\&=w^2(1-a^{11})T^{-1}\sum_{t=1}^{T}\varepsilon^2_{1,t}+w^2a^{11}\varepsilon^2_{1,t}+(1-w)^2(1-a^{33})T^{-1}\sum_{t=1}^{T}\varepsilon^2_{2,t}\\&\quad+(1-w)^2a^{33}\varepsilon^2_{2,t}+2w(1-w)(1-a^{22})T^{-1}\sum_{t=1}^{T}\varepsilon_{1,t}\varepsilon_{2,t}+2w(1-w)a^{22}\varepsilon_{1,t}\varepsilon_{2,t}\end{aligned}\tag{6.51}$$

10. By invariance of a model, we mean that a linear transformation applied to $\tilde{\mathbf{R}}_{t+1}=\mathbf{FR}_{t+1}$, where $\mathbf{F}$ is a square matrix of constants and $\tilde{\mathbf{R}}_{t+1}$ corresponds to the returns of a portfolio combining the original assets, yields a model in the same class. It is sensible that volatility models should be invariant, or a question would arise as to whether portfolio or asset returns should be modeled.

which cannot be written in diagonal form, $(1-a^p)T^{-1}\sum_{t=1}^{T}[w\varepsilon_{1,t}+(1-w)\varepsilon_{2,t}]^2+a^p[w\varepsilon_{1,t}+(1-w)\varepsilon_{2,t}]^2$, because for no definition of the coefficient a^p, it is possible to obtain that:

$$\begin{aligned}&w^2(1-a^p)T^{-1}\sum_{t=1}^{T}\varepsilon_{1,t}^2+(1-w)^2(1-a^p)T^{-1}\sum_{t=1}^{T}\varepsilon_{2,t}^2+2w(1-w)(1-a^p)T^{-1}\sum_{t=1}^{T}\varepsilon_{1,t}\varepsilon_{2,t}\\&=w^2(1-a^{11})T^{-1}\sum_{t=1}^{T}\varepsilon_{1,t}^2+(1-w)^2(1-a^{33})T^{-1}\sum_{t=1}^{T}\varepsilon_{2,t}^2+2w(1-w)(1-a^{22})T^{-1}\sum_{t=1}^{T}\varepsilon_{1,t}\varepsilon_{2,t}\end{aligned}\tag{6.52}$$

and especially that:

$$\begin{aligned}w^2a^{11}\varepsilon_{1,t}^2+(1-w)^2a^{33}\varepsilon_{2,t}^2+2w(1-w)a^{22}\varepsilon_{1,t}\varepsilon_{2,t}&=w^2a^p\varepsilon_{1,t}^2\\&+(1-w)^2a^p\varepsilon_{2,t}^2+2w(1-w)a^p\varepsilon_{1,t}\varepsilon_{2,t}.\end{aligned}\tag{6.53}$$

This means that the diagonal multivariate ARCH model fails to be invariant to linear combinations: if you start with N assets that each follows a diagonal VECH-ARCH model, the conditional variance of the resulting portfolio of assets will fail to follow a similar diagonal model, which is of course problematic if not confusing. As discussed by Bauwens et al. (2006), the problem with Eq. (6.36) that causes it not to display the invariance property is simple to visualize: while in Eq. (6.36), the fact that $\mathbf{A}$ is diagonal, $R_{p,t+1}$ can be written as $[w\ 1-w]'\mathbf{R}_{t+1}=\mathbf{w}'\mathbf{R}_{t+1}$, and $\sigma_{p,t+1}^2=\mathbf{w}'\mathbf{\Sigma}_{t+1|t}\mathbf{w}$ that jointly implies the need to use a vector of coefficients $\mathbf{w}'\mathbf{A}$ which is no longer a diagonal matrix (of course, it is not even a matrix). It is also easy to see what you need to do in order for the invariance property to hold: if you set $a^{11}=a^{22}=a^{33}$, then when $a^p=a^{11}$:

$$\begin{aligned}&w^2(1-a^p)T^{-1}\sum_{t=1}^{T}\varepsilon_{1,t}^2+(1-w)^2(1-a^p)T^{-1}\sum_{t=1}^{T}\varepsilon_{2,t}^2+2w(1-w)(1-a^p)T^{-1}\sum_{t=1}^{T}\varepsilon_{1,t}\varepsilon_{2,t}\\&=w^2(1-a^{11})T^{-1}\sum_{t=1}^{T}\varepsilon_{1,t}^2+(1-w)^2(1-a^{33})T^{-1}\sum_{t=1}^{T}\varepsilon_{2,t}^2+2w(1-w)(1-a^{22})T^{-1}\sum_{t=1}^{T}\varepsilon_{1,t}\varepsilon_{2,t}\\\text{and}\quad&w^2a^{11}\varepsilon_{1,t}^2+(1-w)^2a^{33}\varepsilon_{2,t}^2+2w(1-w)a^{22}\varepsilon_{1,t}\varepsilon_{2,t}\\&=w^2a^p\varepsilon_{1,t}^2+(1-w)^2a^p\varepsilon_{2,t}^2+2w(1-w)a^p\varepsilon_{1,t}\varepsilon_{2,t}\end{aligned}\tag{6.54}$$

will trivially hold. But this means that the only way for a diagonal VECH-ARCH to possess the invariance property is for it to actually be a scalar multivariate ARCH, in which the same ARCH coefficient applies to all conditional equations. Example 6.5 shows BEKK models in action.

EXAMPLE 6.5

We apply again several types of BEKK models to predict the correlation between weekly US stock and bond returns. When it is not otherwise stated, all details are identical to Examples 6.1 and 6.4. We use also in this case BIC to rank different models. A full BEKK(1,1) model with 13 parameters, leads to a BIC of 7.321. A diagonal BEKK(1,1) model with 11 parameters gives instead a BIC of 7.301. We also tried a diagonal BEKK(2,2) model that leads to a BIC of 7.320; a t-Student diagonal BEKK(1,1) leads to a BIC of 7.224 with 12 parameters. Therefore, we select this last model obtaining these ML estimates:

$$MKT_{t+1}=\underset{(0.000)}{0.582}+\underset{(0.001)}{0.103}\,Bond_t+\varepsilon_{MKT,t+1}$$

$$\sigma_{MKT,t+1|t}^2=0.080+0.068\varepsilon_{MKT,t}^2+0.915\sigma_{MKT,t|t-1}^2$$

$$Bond_{t+1}=-\underset{(0.935)}{0.002}+\underset{(0.000)}{0.242}\,Bond_t+\varepsilon_{Bond,t+1}\quad[\varepsilon_{MKT,t+1}\varepsilon_{Bond,t+1}]'\ \text{IID}\ Mt\left(0,\ \mathbf{\Sigma}_{t+1|t};\underset{(0.000)}{9.148}\right)$$

$$\sigma_{Bond,t+1|t}^2=0.014+0.044\varepsilon_{Bond,t}^2+0.945\sigma_{Bond,t|t-1}^2$$

$$\sigma_{MKT-Bond,t+1|t}=-0.002+0.055\varepsilon_{MKT,t}\varepsilon_{Bond,t}+0.930\sigma_{MKT-Bond,t|t-1}.$$

Note that the coefficients associated to conditional second moments do not carry p-values: this derives from the fact that when products are written in "sandwich form" as in Eq. (6.46), it is not the individual coefficient that provides the marginal impact effect on predicted variances and covariances of past residuals. Fig. 6.7 gives the standard representation of conditional variances, covariances, and correlations predicted by the best performing BEKK(1,1) model.

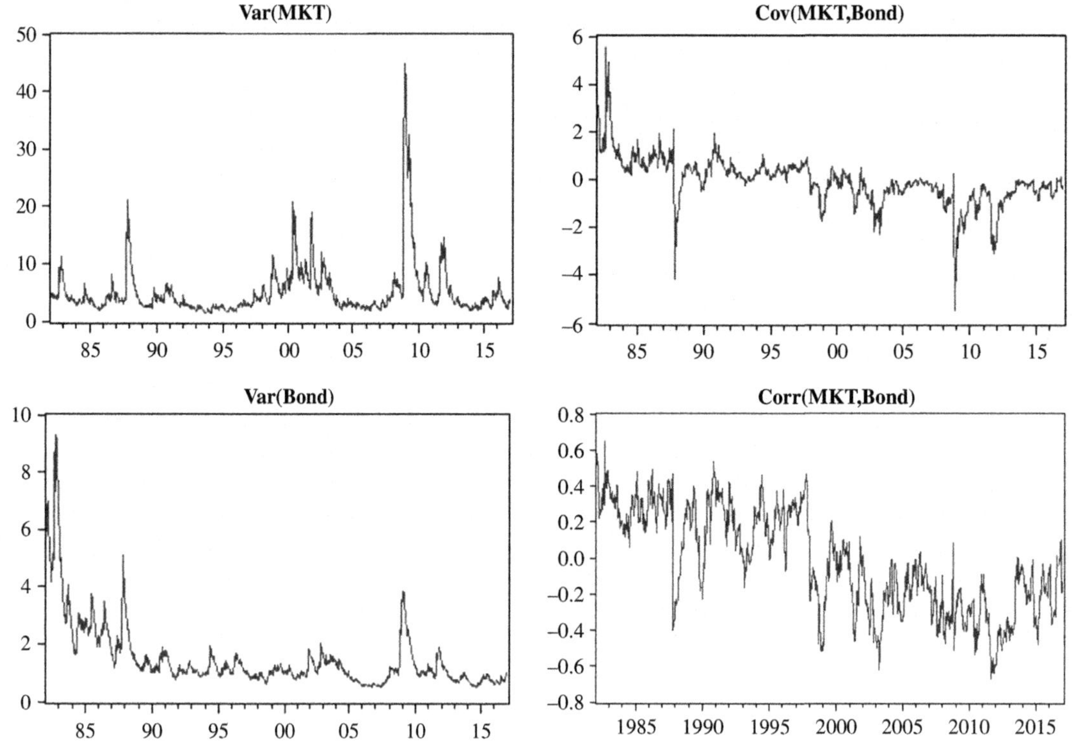

FIGURE 6.7 One-week-ahead predictions of US stock and bond return variances, covariances, and correlations.

The idea already discussed in Section 5.2.6 of Chapter 5—especially befitting to stock returns—that negative shocks may have a larger impact on volatility than positive shocks of the same absolute value (as we know, sometimes interpreted as a leverage effect) can be easily extended to multivariate ARCH models: both conditional variances and covariances may react differently to a positive than to a negative shock. For instance, in the case of a BEKK(p,q) model, we may add d threshold ARCH-type terms as in:

$$\begin{aligned}\mathbf{\Sigma}_{t+1|t} &= \mathbf{CC}' + \sum_{i=1}^{p} \mathbf{A}_i(\varepsilon_{t+1-i}\varepsilon'_{t+1-i})\mathbf{A}_i' + \sum_{i=1}^{d} \mathbf{D}_i(\varepsilon^-_{t+1-i}(\varepsilon^-_{t+1-i})')\mathbf{D}'_i \\ &+ \sum_{j=1}^{q} \mathbf{B}_j \mathbf{\Sigma}_{t+1-j|t-j}\mathbf{B}_j' \quad \boldsymbol{e}_l'\varepsilon^-_{t+1-i} \equiv \max\,[0, \; -\boldsymbol{e}_l'\varepsilon_{t+1-i}].\end{aligned} \tag{6.55}$$

The additional term $\mathbf{D}_i(\varepsilon^-_{t+1-i}(\varepsilon^-_{t+1-i})')\mathbf{D}_i'$ simply involves in the BEKK expression only past negative residuals that are however squared, as typical of ARCH models. Interestingly, there is sometimes evidence—and not only for stocks—that also predicted covariances may depend on the sign of past shocks, as shown in the following example, that compares the forecasts of correlations from a full rank Cholesky diagonal VECH GARCH(1,1) and BEKK(1,1) models with and without threshold asymmetries.

EXAMPLE 6.6

We simply consider the models in the continuation of Examples 6.4 and 6.5 to include threshold effects. In the case of the diagonal VECH GARCH(1,1) we adopt a Cholesky implementation that guarantees—on par with the diagonal BEKK(1,1) model—that the sequence of forecasts for the covariance matrix are all SPD. Consistent with earlier examples, the errors are assumed to be drawn from a multivariate *t*-Student distribution. In the case of Example 6.4, continued, we obtain:

$$MKT_{t+1} = \underset{(0.000)}{0.569} + \underset{(0.002)}{0.100}\, Bond_t + \varepsilon_{MKT,t+1}$$

(Continued)

EXAMPLE 6.6 (Continued)

$$\sigma^2_{MKT,t+1|t} = \underset{(0.000)}{0.157} + \underset{(0.001)}{0.067}\,\varepsilon^2_{MKT,t} + \underset{(0.001)}{0.076}\,I_{\{\varepsilon_{MKT,t}<0\}}\varepsilon^2_{MKT,t} + \underset{(0.000)}{0.859}\,\sigma^2_{MKT,t|t-1}$$

$$Bond_{t+1} = \underset{(0.954)}{0.001} + \underset{(0.000)}{0.245}\,Bond_t + \varepsilon_{Bond,t+1} \quad [\varepsilon_{MKT,t+1}\varepsilon_{Bond,t+1}]' \text{ IID } Mt\left(0,\ \boldsymbol{\Sigma}_{t+1|t};\underset{(0.000)}{9.928}\right)$$

$$\sigma^2_{Bond,t+1|t} = \underset{(0.014)}{0.023} + \underset{(0.000)}{0.080}\,\varepsilon^2_{Bond,t} - \underset{(0.731)}{0.006}\,I_{\{\varepsilon_{Bond,t}<0\}}\varepsilon^2_{Bond,t} + \underset{(0.000)}{0.907}\,\sigma^2_{Bond,t|t-1}$$

$$\sigma_{MKT-Bond,t+1|t} = -\underset{(0.643)}{0.003} + \underset{(0.000)}{0.073}\,\varepsilon_{MKT,t}\varepsilon_{Bond,t} - \underset{(0.867)}{0.003}\,I_{\{\varepsilon_{MKT,t}\varepsilon_{Bond,t}<0\}}\varepsilon_{MKT,t}\varepsilon_{Bond,t} + + \underset{(0.000)}{0.883}\,\sigma_{MKT-Bond,t|t-1}.$$

Clearly, the asymmetric effects concern only stock returns, as we would expect, but do not affect the dynamics of covariances. In the case of BEKK, we have:

$$MKT_{t+1} = \underset{(0.000)}{0.569} + \underset{(0.001)}{0.103}\,Bond_t + \varepsilon_{MKT,t+1}$$

$$\sigma^2_{MKT,t+1|t} = 0.101 + 0.051\varepsilon^2_{MKT,t} + 0.053 I_{\{\varepsilon_{MKT,t}<0\}}\varepsilon^2_{MKT,t} + 0.898\sigma^2_{MKT,t|t-1}$$

$$Bond_{t+1} = -\underset{(0.962)}{0.001} + \underset{(0.000)}{0.244}\,Bond_t + \varepsilon_{Bond,t+1} \quad [\varepsilon_{MKT,t+1}\varepsilon_{Bond,t+1}]' \text{ IID} Mt\left(0,\ \boldsymbol{\Sigma}_{t+1|t};\underset{(0.000)}{9.789}\right)$$

$$\sigma^2_{Bond,t+1|t} = 0.017 + 0.063\varepsilon^2_{Bond,t} + 0.0001 I_{\{\varepsilon_{Bond,t}<0\}}\varepsilon^2_{Bond,t} + 0.925\sigma^2_{Bond,t|t-1}$$

$$\sigma_{MKT-Bond,t+1|t} = -0.004 + 0.057\varepsilon_{MKT,t}\varepsilon_{Bond,t} + 0.003 I_{\{\varepsilon_{MKT,t}\varepsilon_{Bond,t}<0\}}\varepsilon_{MKT,t}\varepsilon_{Bond,t}$$
$$+ 0.911\sigma_{MKT-Bond,t|t-1}.$$

Our earlier conclusions on the asymmetric effects being limited to stocks are confirmed, even though note that dynamic correlations will be influenced via dynamic stock return standard deviations.

Fig. 6.8 plots the predicted correlations with and without asymmetric effects being taken into account. Because the two plots in Fig. 6.8 are hardly distinguishable from the dashed ones, we conclude that at least in this example, asymmetries have a rather limited impact.

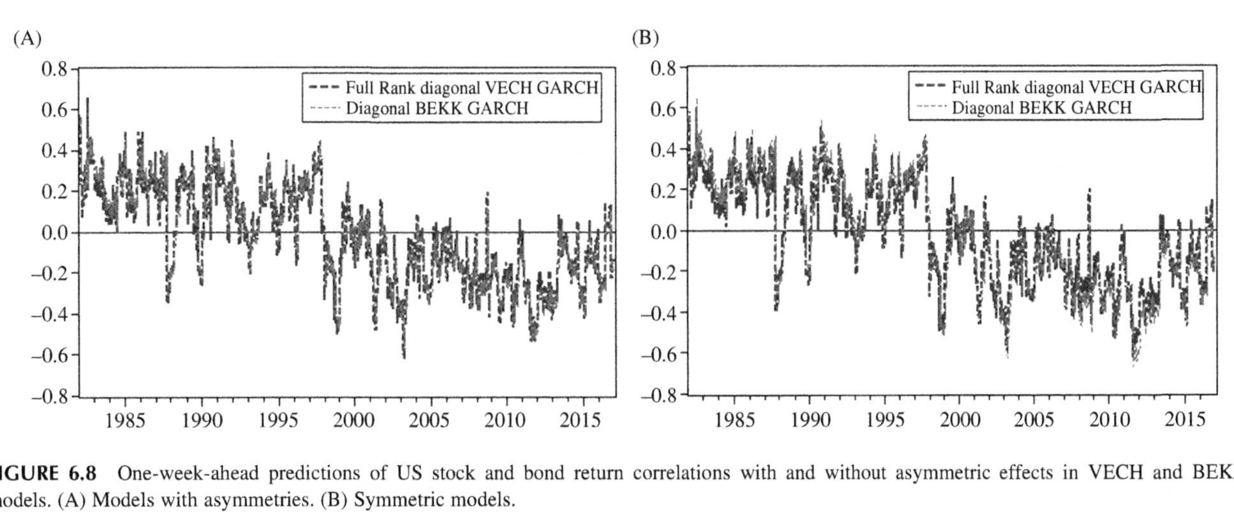

FIGURE 6.8 One-week-ahead predictions of US stock and bond return correlations with and without asymmetric effects in VECH and BEKK models. (A) Models with asymmetries. (B) Symmetric models.

Stationarity and moment convergence criteria for multivariate ARCH models are generally complex, and explicit results are only available for a few special cases. Just to provide a flavor, consider the VECH GARCH(1,1) model in Eq. (6.45). Similarly to the univariate GARCH(1,1) expression in Chapter 5, it is possible to write a time t forecast of the future covariance matrix as:

$$E_t[vech(\boldsymbol{\Sigma}_{t+s})] = vech(\mathbf{C})\left[\sum_{i=0}^{s-1}(\mathbf{A}+\mathbf{B})^i\right] + (\mathbf{A}+\mathbf{B})^s vech(\boldsymbol{\Sigma}_t), \tag{6.56}$$

where $(\mathbf{A}+\mathbf{B})^0 = \mathbf{I}_N$. Apply now a (*Jordan's*) decomposition of $(\mathbf{A}+\mathbf{B})$ into $\mathbf{V}\boldsymbol{\Lambda}\mathbf{V}^{-1}$, where $\boldsymbol{\Lambda}$ equals the diagonal matrix of eigenvalues, and $\mathbf{V}$ is the associated matrix of eigenvectors, so that $(\mathbf{A}+\mathbf{B})^i = \mathbf{V}\boldsymbol{\Lambda}^i\mathbf{V}^{-1}$. Therefore, $E_t[vech(\boldsymbol{\Sigma}_{t+s})]$ converges (almost surely) as $t\to\infty$ to the unconditional covariance matrix of the process, $vech(\mathbf{C})\left[\sum_{i=0}^{\infty}(\mathbf{A}+\mathbf{B})^i\right] = vech(\mathbf{C})(\mathbf{I}_N - \mathbf{A} - \mathbf{B})$ if and only if the norm of the largest eigenvalue $(\mathbf{A}+\mathbf{B})$ is strictly less than 1. A similar condition on the eigenvalues of the matrix polynomials defined by the sequences $\{\mathbf{A}_i\}_{i=1}^p$ and $\{\mathbf{B}_j\}_{j=1}^q$ rules the covariance stationarity of VECH GARCH(p,q) processes (see, e.g., Bollerslev and Engle, 1993). However, the exact conditions for strict stationarity and ergodicity for the multivariate GARCH(p,q) model are hard to establish, even in the VECH case.

6.4 CONSTANT AND DYNAMIC CONDITIONAL CORRELATION MODELS

If we listen to trading desks' and asset management lingo, they will hardly talk about covariances: instead their focus will be on correlations, besides volatility. For instance, one interesting (worrisome) phenomenon is that all *correlations tend to considerably increase during financial market crises* (bear regimes) and this—as we shall study in detail in Chapter 8—has recently attracted considerable attention. You may want to add this one as a fourth stylized fact to those in Section 5.1 of Chapter 5. On the one hand, as already exploited in a number of earlier examples, it is obvious that given any type of model to forecast covariances and variances jointly or separately, one can always compute the implied dynamic (prediction of) correlation, $\hat{\rho}_{ij,t+1|t} = \hat{\sigma}_{ij,t+1|t}/(\hat{\sigma}_{i,t+1|t}\hat{\sigma}_{j,t+1|t}), \forall i,j = 1,\ldots,N$. On the other hand, there is now a well-developed time series literature that strives to write and estimate models for dynamic conditional correlations (DCCs) *directly*, that is, when the model directly concerns the behavior of $\rho_{ij,t+1|t}$ over time. However, this task appears to be far from trivial for one obvious reason: $\rho_{ij,t+1|t}\in[-1,\ 1]$ and so any dynamic estimator would imply a need to constrain parameter estimates to avoid that at all times t, $|\rho_{ij,t+1|t}|$ may exceed 1. For instance, consider a simple GARCH(1,1)-type model $\rho_{ij,t+1|t} = \delta_0 + \delta_1(\varepsilon_{i,t}/\sigma_{i,t|t-1})\cdot(\varepsilon_{j,t}/\sigma_{j,t|t-1}) + \delta_2\rho_{ij,t|t-1}$ and ask yourself what kind of restrictions on δ_1 and δ_2 may keep $|\rho_{ij,t+1|t}|$ from exceeding 1 given that in the case of net returns, it must be $R_{i,t}\in[-1,\ +\infty)$, $i = 1,2,\ldots,N$.

A more fruitful approach is the one that leads to specify and estimate *DCC* models introduced by Engle (2002). This approach is based on the idea that it is more appealing to model an appropriate *auxiliary variable*, $q_{ij,t+1}$, than correlations directly. An auxiliary variable can be considered as just a by-product of modeling and estimation that has no direct immediate meaning but that can be used in subsequent steps. The DCC approach is based on a generalization to the vector/matrix case of the standard result that $\sigma_{ij,t+1|t} \equiv \rho_{ij,t+1|t}\sigma_{i,t+1|t}\sigma_{j,t+1|t} = \sigma_{i,t+1|t}\rho_{ij,t+1|t}\sigma_{j,t+1|t}$:

$$\boldsymbol{\Sigma}_{t+1|t} \equiv \mathbf{D}_{t+1}\boldsymbol{\Gamma}_{t+1|t}\mathbf{D}_{t+1}, \tag{6.57}$$

where $\mathbf{D}_{t+1}$ is an $N\times N$ matrix of predicted standard deviations, $\sigma_{i,t+1}$, on the ith element of the diagonal and 0 everywhere else ($i = 1,2,\ldots,N$), and $\boldsymbol{\Gamma}_{t+1|t}$ is a matrix of predicted correlations, $\rho_{ij,t+1|t}$ with 1s on its main diagonal. For instance, in the $N = 2$ case:

$$\begin{aligned}\boldsymbol{\Sigma}_{t+1|t} &\equiv \begin{bmatrix}\sigma^2_{1,t+1|t} & \sigma_{12,t+1|t}\\ \sigma_{12,t+1|t} & \sigma^2_{2,t+1|t}\end{bmatrix} = \begin{bmatrix}\sigma_{1,t+1} & 0\\ 0 & \sigma_{2,t+1}\end{bmatrix}\begin{bmatrix}1 & \rho_{12,t+1|t}\\ \rho_{12,t+1|t} & 1\end{bmatrix}\\ &\times\begin{bmatrix}\sigma_{1,t+1} & 0\\ 0 & \sigma_{2,t+1}\end{bmatrix}.\end{aligned} \tag{6.58}$$

The key step of the DCC approach is therefore based on the ability to disentangle the estimation and prediction of $\mathbf{D}_{t+1}$ from the estimation and prediction of $\boldsymbol{\Gamma}_{t+1|t}$. In particular, we proceed in two steps:

- The volatility of each asset is estimated/predicted through a GARCH or one of the other methods considered in Sections 5.2 and 5.3 of Chapter 5. For instance, one can think of using a simple NAGARCH(1,1) model for each of the N assets, $\sigma^2_{i,t+1|t} = \omega + \alpha(R_{i,t} - \delta\sigma_{i,t|t-1})^2 + \beta\sigma^2_{i,t|t-1}$.

- Model the conditional covariances of the resulting *standardized* residuals, $z_{i,t+1} \equiv R_{i,t+1}/\sigma_{i,t+1|t}$, derived from the first-step GARCH-type models. Here, we exploit the fact that *the conditional covariance of the standardized residuals equals the conditional correlation of original residuals*:

$$Cov_t\left[z_{i,t+1},\ z_{j,t+1}\right] = Cov_t\left[\frac{\varepsilon_{i,t+1}}{\sigma_{i,t+1|t}},\ \frac{\varepsilon_{j,t+1}}{\sigma_{j,t+1|t}}\right] = \frac{Cov_t[\varepsilon_{i,t+1},\ \varepsilon_{j,t+1}]}{\sigma_{i,t+1|t}\sigma_{j,t+1|t}} = \rho_{ij,t+1|t}. \tag{6.59}$$

However, a GARCH-type modeling in the second step will not concern directly the covariance of standardized residuals, but instead an auxiliary variable $q_{ij,t+1}$ to be estimated/predicted to be able to compute conditional correlations. Typically, the most popular model used in this second DCC step is:

$$q_{ij,t+1} = \overline{\rho}_{ij} + \alpha(z_{i,t}z_{j,t} - \overline{\rho}_{ij}) + \beta(q_{ij,t} - \overline{\rho}_{ij}) \quad \forall i,j \tag{6.60}$$

which is a GARCH(1,1) for the auxiliary variable, written in deviations from the unconditional, long-run mean, usually set to be equal to the unconditional sample covariance of the standardized residuals. An alternative that has been sometimes used is of a RiskMetrics type:

$$q_{ij,t+1} = (1-\lambda)z_{i,t}z_{j,t} + \lambda q_{ij,t} \quad \forall i,\ j \tag{6.61}$$

where $\lambda \in (0,1)$. Note that these models apply to all pairs of assets even when $i = j$ which is used in formula Eq. (6.62). Of course, nothing prevents that more complex, asymmetric or nonlinear (e.g., power) GARCH(p,q) models be assumed, or that more than one set of lags be employed in the GARCH case:

$$q_{ij,t+1} = \overline{\rho}_{ij} + \sum_{i=1}^{p} \alpha_i(z_{i,t+1-i}z_{j,t+1-i} - \overline{\rho}_{ij}) + \sum_{j=1}^{q} \beta_j(q_{ij,t+1-j} - \overline{\rho}_{ij}) \quad \forall i,j. \tag{6.62}$$

How do we go now from a forecast of the auxiliary variable $q_{ij,t+1}$ to a forecast of correlations? Here one uses the obvious transformation:

$$\rho_{ij,t+1|t} = \frac{q_{ij,t+1}}{\sqrt{q_{ii,t+1}}\sqrt{q_{jj,t+1}}}. \tag{6.63}$$

Note that Eq. (6.63) guarantees by construction that $\rho_{ij,t+1|t} \in [-1,\ 1]$. Clearly, in the GARCH(1,1) case, $\overline{\rho}_{ij} = \omega_{ij}/(1-\alpha-\beta)$. Interestingly, only the intercept parameter ω_{ij} is allowed to differ across different pairs of assets: also in this case, α and β are common across different pairs of assets; the same occurs for the single parameter λ in the RiskMetrics-type model. This implies that the persistence of the correlation between any two assets in the portfolio is the same, which is obviously very simplistic.[11] The RiskMetrics/DCC and GARCH/DCC models can also be written in matrix form as:

$$\begin{aligned} \mathbf{Q}_{t+1} &= (1-\lambda)\mathbf{z}_t\mathbf{z}_t{}' + \lambda\mathbf{Q}_t \\ \mathbf{Q}_{t+1} &= \mathbf{\Pi} + \alpha\mathbf{z}_t\mathbf{z}_t{}' + \beta\mathbf{Q}_t, \end{aligned} \tag{6.64}$$

where $\mathbf{z}_t \equiv \left[z_{1,t+1} \quad z_{2,t+1} \quad \cdots \quad z_{N,t+1}\right]'$, $\mathbf{\Pi}$ is either one estimable symmetric matrix of coefficients, or $\mathbf{\Pi} \equiv (1-\alpha-\beta)\overline{\boldsymbol{\Gamma}}$ with $\overline{\boldsymbol{\Gamma}}$ the unconditional, sample correlation matrix (it is positive definite by construction) and $\mathbf{Q}_{t+1}$ is an $N \times N$ symmetric SPD matrix that collects the values/predictions of the auxiliary variables $q_{ij,t+1}$:

$$\mathbf{Q}_{t+1} \equiv \begin{bmatrix} q_{11,t+1} & q_{12,t+1} & \cdots & q_{1N,t+1} \\ q_{12,t+1} & q_{22,t+1} & \cdots & q_{2N,t+1} \\ \vdots & \vdots & \ddots & \vdots \\ q_{1N,t+1} & q_{2N,t+1} & \cdots & q_{NN,t+1} \end{bmatrix}. \tag{6.65}$$

11. In any event, because ω_{ij} is allowed to differ across pairs of assets, the fact that α, β, or λ must be common across pairs does not imply that the level of the correlations at any time is the same across different pairs.

$\mathbf{Q}_{t+1}$ is SPD because it is a weighted average of SPD and positive definite matrices. This will in turn ensure that the correlation matrix $\mathbf{\Gamma}_{t+1|t}$ and the covariance matrix, $\mathbf{\Sigma}_{t+1|t}$, will be SPD, as desirable. When we set $\mathbf{\Pi} \equiv (1-\alpha-\beta)\overline{\mathbf{\Gamma}}$, we speak of DCC/GARCH under a *covariance targeting* constraint, which as usual guarantees that the unconditional correlation will be identical to the sample unconditional correlation of the data. Note that when $i=j$, $q_{ii,t+1}$ is in general different from $\sigma^2_{i,t+1}$ obtained in the first step. This represents the logical sacrifice, the minor "approximation burden" on which the two-step DCC estimation is based: the use of first-step predictions for variances that potentially differ from those that are then used to go from predictions of the $q_{ij,t+1}$ to predictions of correlations constrained to be in $[-1,1]$. As one would expect, covariance stationarity of all the GARCH processes that "populate" $\mathbf{D}_{t+1}$ along with covariance stationarity of the (matrix) process for $\mathbf{Q}_{t+1}$ are sufficient for a DCC model to be weakly stationary and for unconditional variances, covariances, and correlations to exist. Example 6.7 shows DCC models in action and compares RiskMetrics versus GARCH formulations

EXAMPLE 6.7

We consider once more our stock–bond application, holding all the assumptions we made on the conditional means. However, in this example, we assume all shocks to be normally distributed. In the case of a RiskMetrics/DCC, we estimate both the standardized residuals and the process for the auxiliary variable $q_{ij,t+1}$ using RiskMetrics. In the first step of estimation, we obtain:

$$MKT_{t+1} = \underset{(0.000)}{0.582} + \underset{(0.008)}{0.094}\, Bond_t + \varepsilon_{MKT,t+1}$$

$$\sigma^2_{MKT,t+1|t} = \underset{(0.000)}{0.112}\,\varepsilon^2_{MKT,t} + \underset{(0.000)}{0.888}\,\sigma^2_{MKT,t|t-1}$$

$$Bond_{t+1} = \underset{(0.169)}{0.032} + \underset{(0.000)}{0.230}\, Bond_t + \varepsilon_{Bond,t+1} \quad [\varepsilon_{MKT,t+1}\varepsilon_{Bond,t+1}]' \text{ IID } N(\mathbf{0}, \mathbf{I}_2),$$

$$\sigma^2_{Bond,t+1|t} = \underset{(0.000)}{0.066}\,\varepsilon^2_{Bond,t} + \underset{(0.000)}{0.934}\,\sigma^2_{Bond,t|t-1}.$$

In the second step (here we no longer iterate on the conditional mean parameters, see below for details on the estimation), we have:

$$q_{MKT-Bond,t+1} = \underset{(0.000)}{0.014}\,\hat{z}^{RiskM}_{MKT,t}\hat{z}^{RiskM}_{Bond,t} + \underset{(0.000)}{0.986}\, q_{MKT-Bond,t}.$$

This implies the predicted variances, covariances, and correlations shown in Fig. 6.9.

We repeat the exercise in the case when the conditional second moment processes are described by stationary GARCH(1,1) processes. In this case, both to illustrate the flexibility of DCC modeling and because we understand very well that this is required by the data, the process of stock index return variance is modeled as a threshold GARCH(1,1,1). In the first step, we obtain:

$$MKT_{t+1} = \underset{(0.000)}{0.507} + \underset{(0.000)}{0.125}\, Bond_t + \varepsilon_{MKT,t+1}$$

$$\sigma^2_{MKT,t+1|t} = \underset{(0.000)}{0.382} + \underset{(0.009)}{0.043}\,\varepsilon^2_{MKT,t} + \underset{(0.000)}{0.229}\, I_{\{\varepsilon_{MKT,t}<0\}}\varepsilon^2_{MKT,t} + \underset{(0.000)}{0.764}\,\sigma^2_{MKT,t|t-1}$$

$$Bond_{t+1} = \underset{(0.707)}{-0.000} + \underset{(0.000)}{0.226}\, Bond_t + \underset{(0.018)}{0.053}\, Bond_{t-1} + \varepsilon_{Bond,t+1} \quad [\varepsilon_{MKT,t+1}\varepsilon_{Bond,t+1}]' \text{ IID } N(\mathbf{0}, \mathbf{I}_2)$$

$$\sigma^2_{Bond,t+1|t} = \underset{(0.003)}{0.020} + \underset{(0.000)}{0.065}\,\varepsilon^2_{Bond,t} + \underset{(0.000)}{0.919}\,\sigma^2_{Bond,t|t-1}.$$

In the second step, we have:

$$q_{MKT-Bond,t+1} = \underset{(0.016)}{0.0001} + \underset{(0.000)}{0.009}\,\hat{z}^{GARCH}_{MKT,t}\,\hat{z}^{GARCH}_{Bond,t} + \underset{(0.000)}{0.986}\, q_{MKT-Bond,t}.$$

This implies the predicted variances, covariances, and correlations shown in Fig. 6.10.

As we would expect, also because the GARCH estimates reveal considerable persistence in the variance, the resulting dynamics is very similar when compared to Fig. 6.9. Moreover, we should not be surprised by the fact that the predicted correlations are smoother under GARCH: note that the estimated β coefficients are approximately identical across the RiskMetrics and GARCH(1,1) models, but α is instead smaller in the latter case, that is, past shocks affect predicted correlations 35% (from 0.009 to 0.014) less under a stationary GARCH.

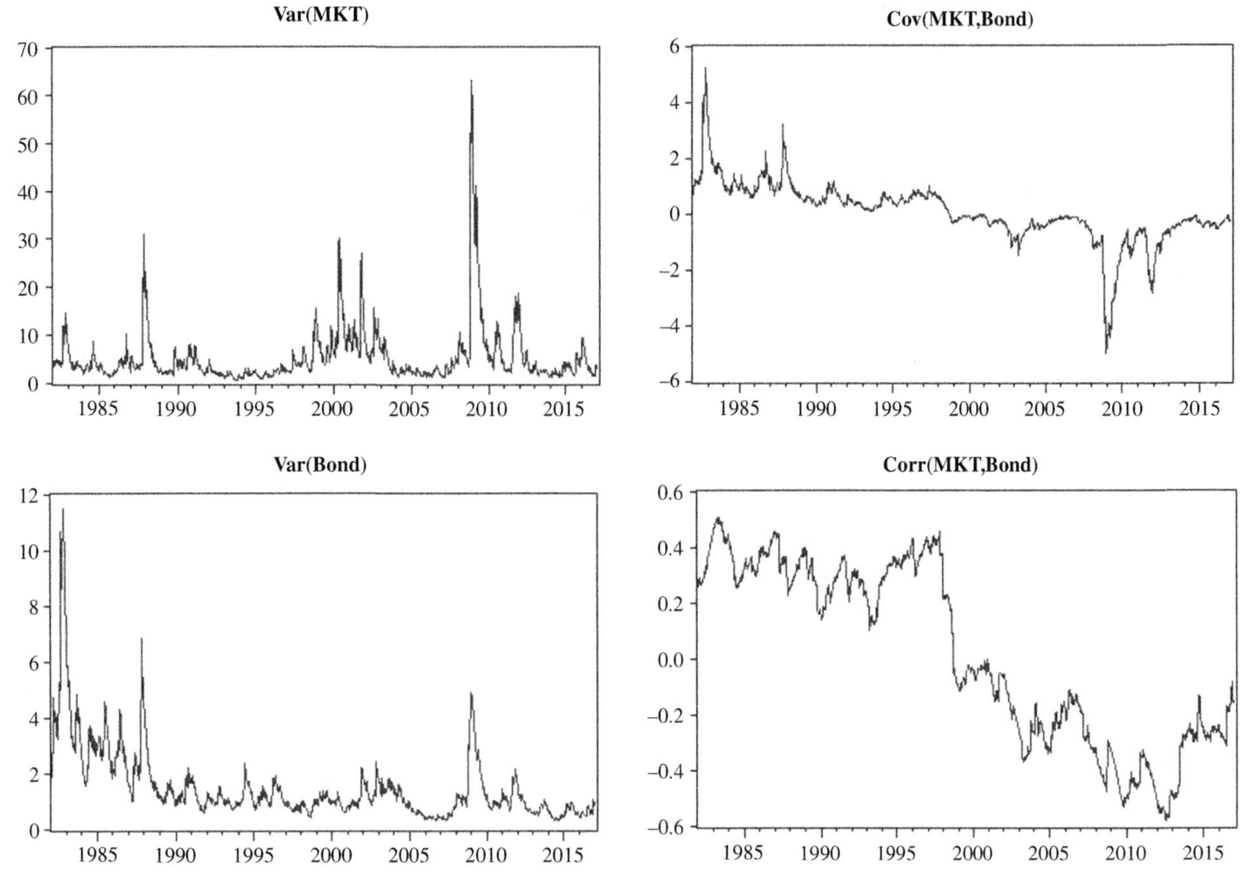

FIGURE 6.9 One-week-ahead predictions of US stock and bond return variances, covariances, and correlations from RiskMetrics/DCC(1) model.

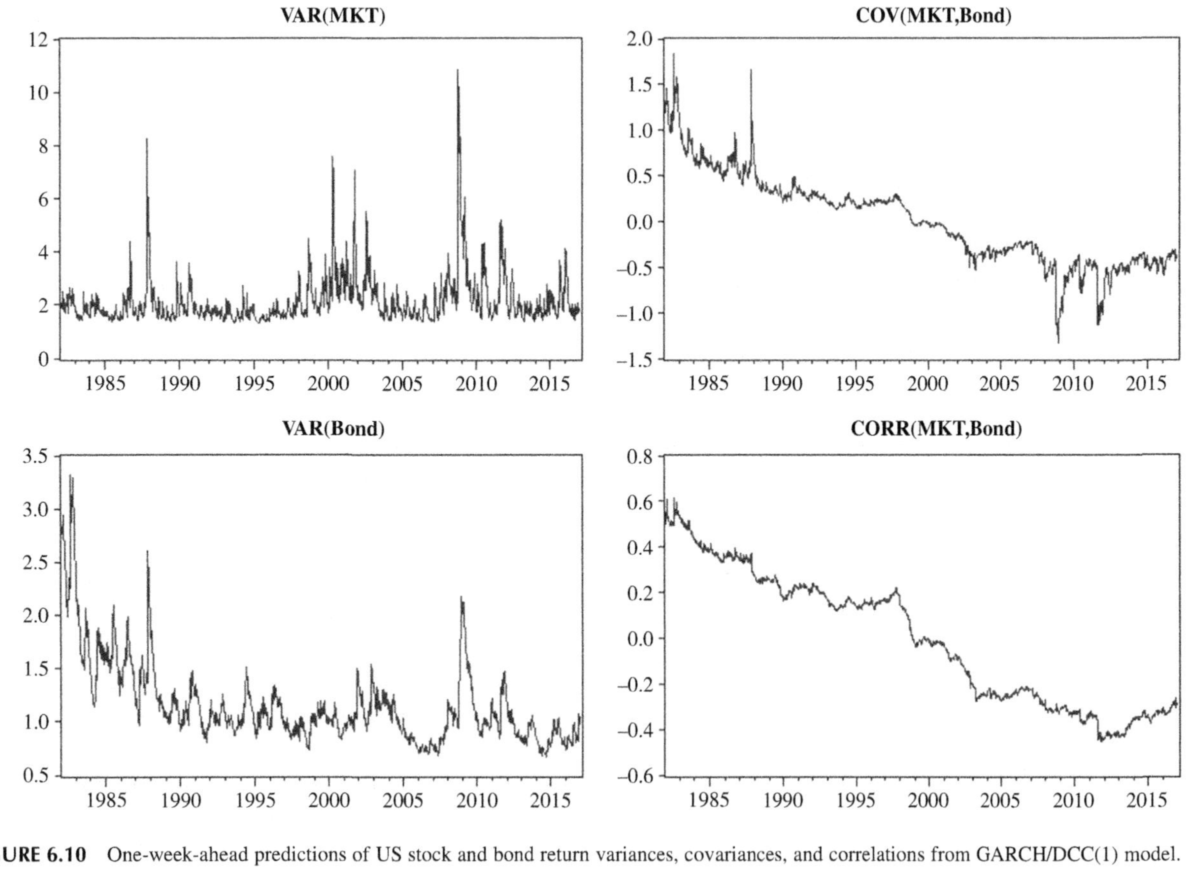

FIGURE 6.10 One-week-ahead predictions of US stock and bond return variances, covariances, and correlations from GARCH/DCC(1) model.

Especially in their covariance targeting variation, DCC models are enjoying a massive popularity because they are easy to implement in four steps:

- All the individual variance processes are estimated one by one, devoting as much effort and care for statistical details as appropriate.
- The returns or residuals (from some conditional mean model) are standardized and the unconditional correlation matrix is estimated.
- The correlation persistence parameters (α and β in the GARCH case, or sequences of related parameters when p and/or q exceed 1, λ under RiskMetrics) are estimated and hence the process of $q_{ij,t+1}$ is filtered.
- The filtered, time-varying predicted correlations are obtained from Eq. (6.62).

Interestingly, if the time series of dynamic covariances should be needed, when we wish to go back from knowledge of $\hat{\boldsymbol{\Gamma}}_{t+1|t}$ to the forecast of the covariance matrix, then we shall use $\hat{\boldsymbol{\Sigma}}_{t+1|t} \equiv \hat{\mathbf{D}}_{t+1}\hat{\boldsymbol{\Gamma}}_{t+1|t}\hat{\mathbf{D}}_{t+1}$, as we have repeatedly done in Example 6.7. Often practitioners will face this need because—even though as of recently an active over-the-counter market of correlation-related derivatives has arisen (see, e.g., Schofield, 2017)—correlations are seldom the final objective of a forecasting exercise: for instance, both the practice of dynamic portfolio choice and of portfolio market and credit risk management usually requires predictions of $\hat{\boldsymbol{\Sigma}}_{t+1|t}$ over time, not just of $\hat{\boldsymbol{\Gamma}}_{t+1|t}$.

One additional point that is worthwhile to make (see Bauwens et al., 2006, for additional details) is that the class of models that is based on nonlinear combinations of univariate GARCH models in which one can specify separately, on the one hand, the individual conditional variance processes and, on the other hand, the conditional correlation matrix (i.e., those based on a *hierarchical specification strategy*) is not composed of DCC models only. For instance, Tse and Tsui (2002) specify their multivariate DCC model as $\boldsymbol{\Sigma}_{t+1} \equiv \mathbf{D}_{t+1}\boldsymbol{\Lambda}_{t+1}\mathbf{D}_{t+1}$, where $\boldsymbol{\Lambda}_{t+1}$ follows a GARCH-like process, but it is not necessarily a time-varying correlation matrix and has instead a factor structure. In practice, in this case the DCC formulates the conditional correlation directly as a weighted sum of past correlations.

Another interesting case is the *copula-GARCH approach* that makes use of a theorem due to Sklar, stating that any N-dimensional joint distribution function may be decomposed into its marginal distributions and a copula function that completely describes the dependence between the N variables. These models are specified by separate GARCH equations for the conditional variances (possibly with each variance depending on the lag of the other variances and of the other shocks), marginal distributions for each series (e.g., t-Student or GED distributions), and a conditional copula function. The copula function may be time-varying through its parameters which can be functions of past data. In this respect, like the DCC model of Engle (2002), copula-GARCH models can be estimated by using a two-step QML approach, see Section 5.6 of Chapter 5.

As in Section 6.3, also all DCC models can be easily extended to incorporate asymmetries, that is, when the effect of two positive shocks is not the same as the effect of two negative shocks of the same magnitude or the effect of two shocks with different signs. This can be achieved by using an asymmetric DCC model where, for instance (also imposing correlation targeting),

$$\mathbf{Q}_{t+1} = (1-\alpha-\beta)\hat{E}[\mathbf{z}_t\mathbf{z}_t'] + \alpha\mathbf{z}_t\mathbf{z}_t' + \beta\mathbf{Q}_t + \zeta(\mathbf{g}_t\mathbf{g}_t'), \tag{6.66}$$

where hatted expectations will be estimated using sample moments, for instance $\hat{E}[\mathbf{z}_t\mathbf{z}_t'] = T^{-1}\sum_{t=1}^{T}\mathbf{z}_t\mathbf{z}_t'$, and the vectors $\mathbf{g}_t$ are defined as the negative part of $\mathbf{z}_t$ as follows:

$$g_{i,t} \equiv \begin{cases} z_{i,t} & \text{if } z_{i,t} < 0 \\ 0 & \text{if } z_{i,t} \geq 0 \end{cases}, \quad i = 1, \ldots, N. \tag{6.67}$$

The term $\zeta(\mathbf{g}_t\mathbf{g}_t')$ captures a *leverage effect in correlations*: When $\zeta > 0$, then the correlation between returns on assets i and j will increase more when $z_{i,t}$ and $z_{j,t}$ are both negative than in any other case. This captures a phenomenon sometimes observed in markets for risky assets: their correlation increases more in down markets ($z_{i,t}$ and $z_{j,t}$ both negative) than in up markets ($z_{i,t}$ and $z_{j,t}$ both positive). Note that even more complex cases can be built in which a separate effect, captured by a distinct linear term in Eq. (6.66), is assigned to cases in which past standardized shocks are not both negative but carry different signs. Example 6.8 offers one such example.

One special, restricted case of DCC in fact had appeared already in the late 1980s: Bollerslev's (1990) *constant conditional correlation (CCC)* multivariate covariance model. It can be just obtained from Eq. (6.56) by setting a constant correlation matrix, $\boldsymbol{\Sigma}_{t+1} \equiv \mathbf{D}_{t+1}\boldsymbol{\Gamma}\mathbf{D}_{t+1}$. Of course, the assumption of constant correlations over time is unrealistic. However, it simply avoids all the business of defining and modeling with GARCH-type processes the $q_{ij,t+1}$ auxiliary variable. In the early 1990s, when computational resources were scarce, this made sense. Example 6.8 shows CCC in action for the stock−bond returns case.

EXAMPLE 6.8

To provide an example of the role of asymmetries in the DCC/CCC world, we return again to our weekly US stock–bond return data, for a 1982–2016 sample. First of all, we perform a round of model selection that shows evidence is in favor of a parsimonious CCC/GARCH(1,1), as expected. However, when the error distribution is changed to a multivariate *t*-Student, we have a BIC of 7.286 (vs 7.357 of the CCC/GARCH(1,1)). Therefore, we adopt this fat-tailed distribution. Finally, an asymmetric, threshold CCC/GARCH(1,1,1) with *t*-Student shocks leads to a BIC of 7.282, showing some moderate evidence in favor of asymmetries. This model features 16 parameters, estimated by ML to be:

$$MKT_{t+1} = \underset{(0.000)}{0.558} + \underset{(0.001)}{0.113}\, Bond_t + \varepsilon_{MKT,t+1}$$

$$\sigma^2_{MKT,t+1|t} = \underset{(0.000)}{0.260} + \underset{(0.053)}{0.038}\, \varepsilon^2_{MKT,t} + \underset{(0.000)}{0.137}\, I_{\{\varepsilon_{MKT,t}<0\}}\varepsilon^2_{MKT,t} + \underset{(0.000)}{0.831}\, \sigma^2_{MKT,t|t-1}$$

$$Bond_{t+1} = \underset{(0.287)}{0.025} + \underset{(0.000)}{0.243}\, Bond_t + \varepsilon_{Bond,t+1} \quad \left[\varepsilon_{MKT,t+1}\varepsilon_{Bond,t+1}\right]' \text{ IID } Mt\left(0,\ \boldsymbol{\Sigma}_{t+1|t}; \underset{(0.000)}{9.485}\right)$$

$$\sigma^2_{Bond,t+1|t} = \underset{(0.011)}{0.026} + \underset{(0.000)}{0.063}\, \varepsilon^2_{Bond,t} + \underset{(0.854)}{0.003}\, I_{\{\varepsilon_{Bond,t}<0\}}\varepsilon^2_{Bond,t} + \underset{(0.000)}{0.916}\, \sigma^2_{Bond,t|t-1}$$

$$\rho_{MKT-Bond} = -\underset{(0.732)}{0.0085} \quad \sigma_{MKT-Bond,t+1|t} = \hat{\rho}_{MKT-Bond}\hat{\sigma}_{MKT,t+1|t}\hat{\sigma}_{Bond,t+1|t}.$$

As usual, the asymmetric term is statistically significant only for stock returns. The estimated, constant correlation is, as expected, very small and not statistically significant. However, Fig. 6.11 shows that the presence of asymmetries makes some difference for correlations forecasts. Obviously symmetric forecasts are always below the asymmetric ones, because they imply a lower forecast of unconditional correlation of the shocks: this is possible because under full maximum likelihood estimation (MLE), the estimation of the multivariate volatility models interacts with the estimation of the conditional mean functions and therefore of model residuals. Needless to say, the examples in this chapter all have shown that in the case of US stock and bond returns, correlations have been historically far from constant.

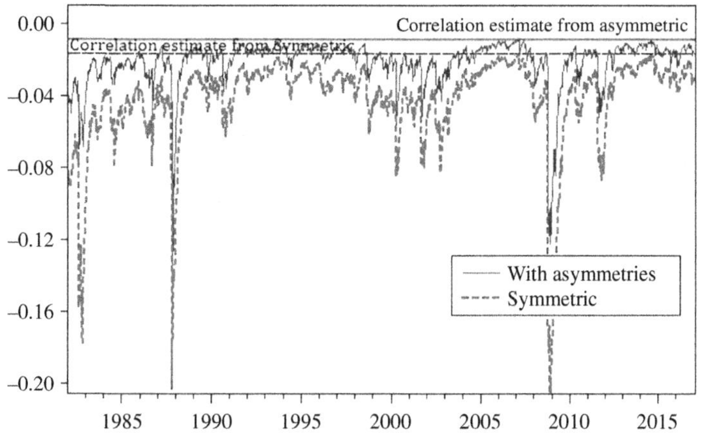

FIGURE 6.11 One-week-ahead predictions of US stock and bond return covariances with and without asymmetric effects in a threshold GARCH/CCC.

At a more philosophical level, one may ask what can be the point of adopting DCC models in which the same, few parameters govern the dynamics of all pairwise correlation of asset returns, or even CCC models that assume, for operational reasons, that correlation is constant over time. Here the key trade-off is the one between model parsimony—using technical jargon, the need to keep saturation ratios above acceptable levels—and realism. Example 6.9 uses a rather realistic, probably important to international equity fund managers, application to make us think a bit more about the trade-offs involved.

EXAMPLE 6.9

Before moving on in our treatment, it is time to become ambitious. We use ML in E-Views to try and estimate a multivariate GARCH model for a 17×1 vector of monthly, international stock returns for aggregate markets (Australia, Belgium, Canada, France, Germany, Hong Kong, Italy, Japan, the Netherlands, New Zealand, Norway, Singapore, Spain, Sweden, Switzerland, the

(Continued)

EXAMPLE 6.9 (Continued)

United Kingdom, and the United States) over the sample of 1988–2016, all expressed in USD. Because we suspect that asymmetries may appear in a number of series, we try and estimate a Gaussian VAR(1) threshold VECH-GARCH(1,1,1) multivariate model. The VAR(1) model is not subject to fine-tuning, but a number of series are either persistent or predicted by lags of the key national stock markets, such as the United States, Japan, and Germany. This model is to be estimated using $17 \times 347 = 5899$ observations but it implies the need to estimate 918 parameters! This implies a rather worrying saturation ratio of 6.4 only, well below the canonical threshold of 20 that is normally expected. In fact, E-Views seems to be concerned as much as we are and, with such a low saturation ratio, stops short from computing standard errors and performing a few other calculations that would normally be expected (Fig. 6.12).

The problem is that trying to estimate and forecast variances and correlations for 17 international stock markets around the globe using 30 years of monthly data does not strike us either as implausible or as pointless in terms of potential applications. Of course, we may try to economize on the number of parameters in a number of ways, for instance, by imposing restrictions on the VAR model, adopting a simpler diagonal VECH GARCH model or a BEKK. However, here the beauty of a DCC framework comes out in full. As we know, the steps would be simple and one can easily program up most software packages (starting from E-Views itself) to perform the two easy steps that follow. For instance, suppose a US-based investor cares for forecasting the correlation between Italian and Swiss stock returns. Exploiting a quantitative framework such as a GARCH DCC may appear to be a good idea because rarely the policy and business cycle news for these two countries (for many and perhaps opposing reasons) will be sufficiently memorable and significant to provide support to forecasts that could be only based on economics.

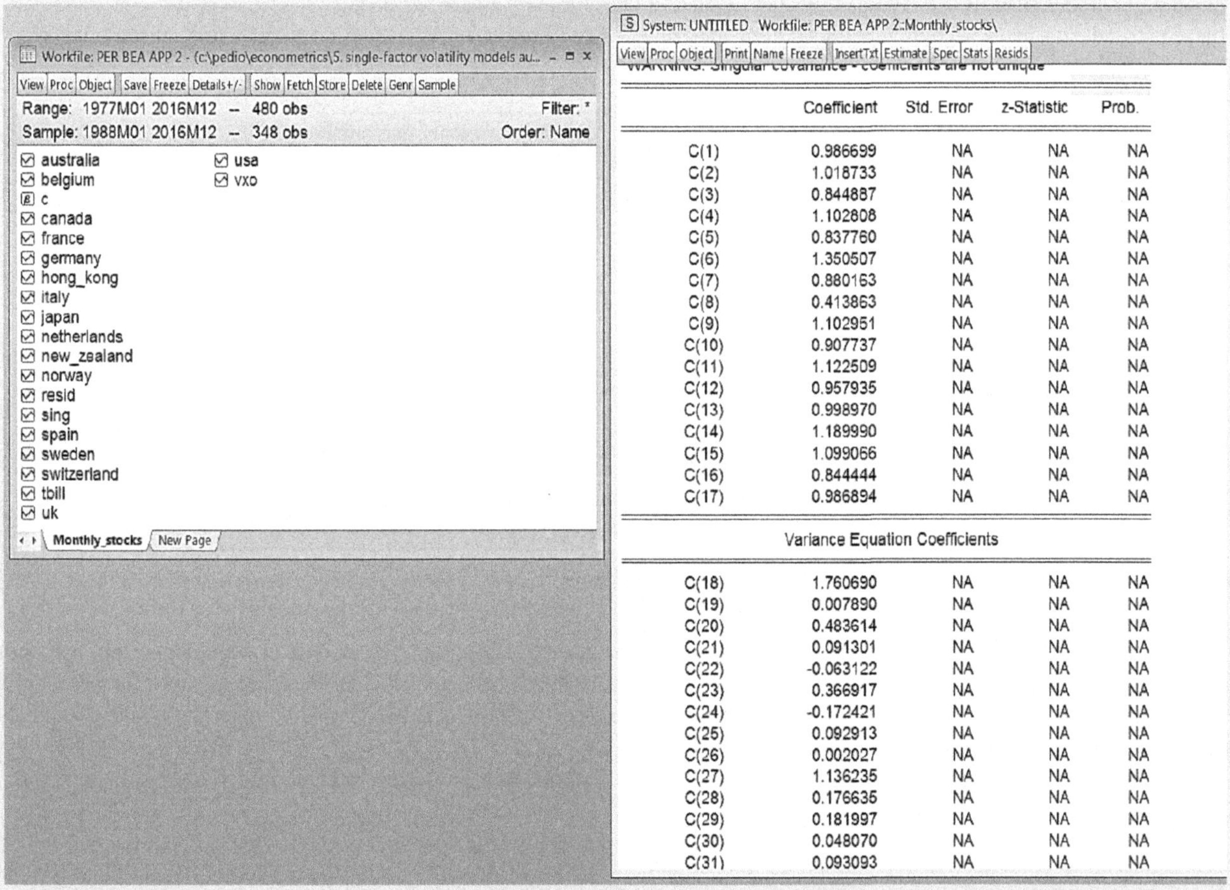

	Coefficient	Std. Error	z-Statistic	Prob.
C(1)	0.986699	NA	NA	NA
C(2)	1.018733	NA	NA	NA
C(3)	0.844887	NA	NA	NA
C(4)	1.102808	NA	NA	NA
C(5)	0.837760	NA	NA	NA
C(6)	1.350507	NA	NA	NA
C(7)	0.880163	NA	NA	NA
C(8)	0.413863	NA	NA	NA
C(9)	1.102951	NA	NA	NA
C(10)	0.907737	NA	NA	NA
C(11)	1.122509	NA	NA	NA
C(12)	0.957935	NA	NA	NA
C(13)	0.998970	NA	NA	NA
C(14)	1.189990	NA	NA	NA
C(15)	1.099066	NA	NA	NA
C(16)	0.844444	NA	NA	NA
C(17)	0.986894	NA	NA	NA
	Variance Equation Coefficients			
C(18)	1.760690	NA	NA	NA
C(19)	0.007890	NA	NA	NA
C(20)	0.483614	NA	NA	NA
C(21)	0.091301	NA	NA	NA
C(22)	-0.063122	NA	NA	NA
C(23)	0.366917	NA	NA	NA
C(24)	-0.172421	NA	NA	NA
C(25)	0.092913	NA	NA	NA
C(26)	0.002027	NA	NA	NA
C(27)	1.136235	NA	NA	NA
C(28)	0.176635	NA	NA	NA
C(29)	0.181997	NA	NA	NA
C(30)	0.048070	NA	NA	NA
C(31)	0.093093	NA	NA	NA

FIGURE 6.12 MLE output from E-Views for a Gaussian VAR(1) threshold VECH-GARCH(1,1,1) for 17 monthly series of stock returns.

(Continued)

EXAMPLE 6.9 (Continued)

In the first step of estimation, we obtain:

$$Italy_{t+1} = \underset{(0.234)}{0.442} - \underset{(0.317)}{0.070}\, Italy_t + \underset{(0.009)}{0.214}\, Switz_t + \varepsilon_{Italy,t+1}$$

$$\sigma^2_{Italy,t+1|t} = \underset{(0.169)}{1.954} + \underset{(0.141)}{0.035}\, \varepsilon^2_{Italy,t} + \underset{(0.028)}{0.095}\, I_{\{\varepsilon_{Italy,t}<0\}}\varepsilon^2_{Italy,t} + \underset{(0.000)}{0.877}\, \sigma^2_{Italy,t|t-1}$$

$$Switz_{t+1} = \underset{(0.002)}{0.902} + \underset{(0.911)}{0.004}\, Italy_t + \underset{(0.550)}{0.042}\, Switz_t + \varepsilon_{Switz,t+1} \quad [\varepsilon_{Italy,t+1}\varepsilon_{Switz,t+1}]' \text{ IID } N(\mathbf{0}, \mathbf{I}_2)$$

$$\sigma^2_{Switz,t+1|t} = \underset{(0.002)}{12.133} + \underset{(0.578)}{0.041}\, \varepsilon^2_{Switz,t} + \underset{(0.061)}{0.263}\, I_{\{\varepsilon_{Switz,t}<0\}}\varepsilon^2_{Switz,t} + \underset{(0.231)}{0.265}\, \sigma^2_{Switz,t|t-1}.$$

In the second step (here we no longer iterate on the conditional mean parameters, see below for details on the estimation), we have:

$$q_{Italy-Switz,t+1} = \underset{(0.000)}{0.005} + \underset{(0.000)}{0.070}\, \hat{z}_{Italy,t}\hat{z}_{Switz,t} + \underset{(0.000)}{0.907}\, q_{Italy-Switz,t}.$$

We have tested for asymmetries in the process of $q_{Italy-Switz,t+1}$, finding none. These QML estimates imply the predicted variances, covariances, and correlations shown in Fig. 6.13.

Although during the 1990s Swiss and Italian stock markets seem to have provided an excellent hedge to each other, this gradually stops after 2000. In fact, during the financial crisis, the estimated correlation comes close to 0.9.

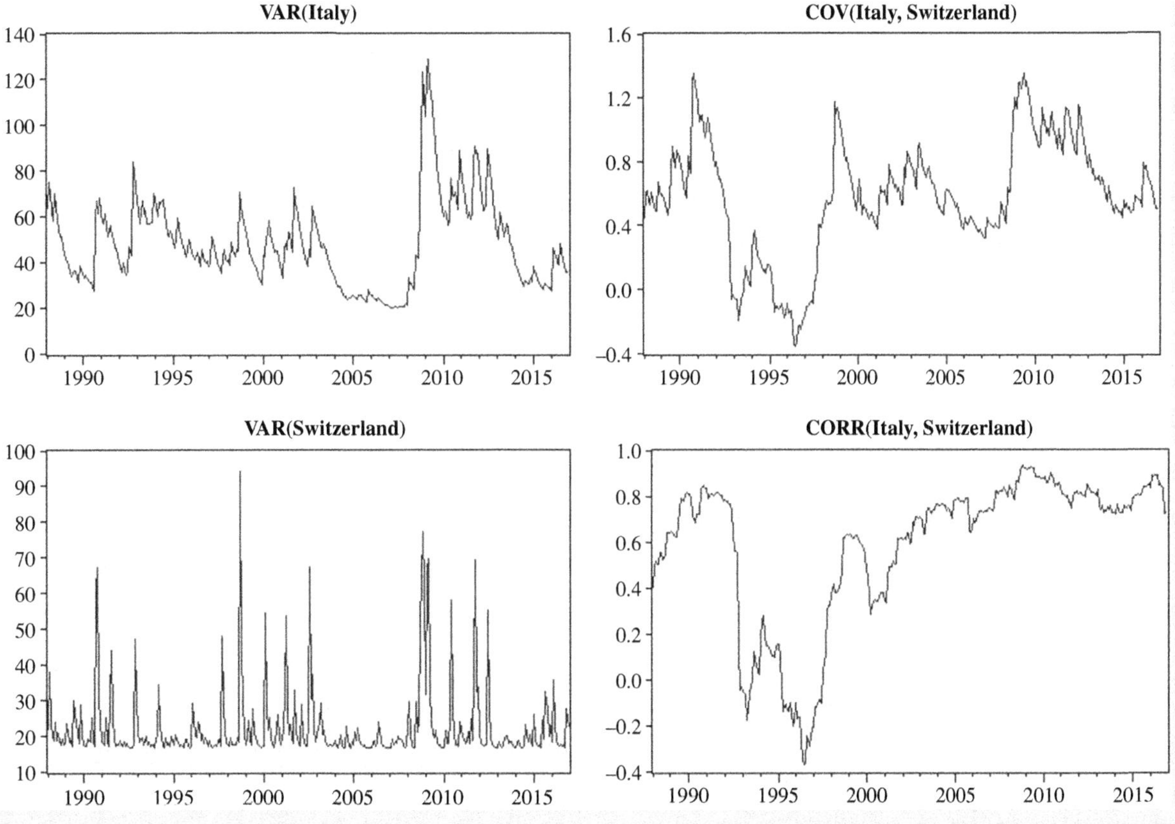

FIGURE 6.13 One-week-ahead predictions of Italian and Swiss stock return variances, covariances, and correlations from GARCH/DCC(1) model.

6.5 FACTOR GARCH MODELS

At the intersection between time series for financial modeling and empirical asset pricing lies the idea that factor models may greatly simplify the forecasting of conditional second moments. The difficulty when estimating a VECH or even a BEKK model is the high number of unknown parameters, even after imposing several restrictions. It is thus not surprising that these models are rarely used when N exceeds 3 or 4. *Factor and orthogonal models* circumvent this difficulty by imposing a *common dynamic structure* on all the series that affect $\boldsymbol{\Sigma}_{t+1|t}$. However, we shall see that doing so within a multivariate framework is not much different from building and estimating special, constrained BEKK models.

For concreteness, we shall present an example. Generalizing it should be simple enough. Suppose that the $N \times 1$ vector of returns $\mathbf{R}_{t+1}$ has a factor structure with two factors given by the 2×1 vector $\mathbf{f}_{t+1} \equiv [XMKT_{t+1}\ \hat{\eta}_{t+1}^{slope}]'$, the excess return on some proxy of the market portfolio and the change in the slope of the government bond yield curve, say 10-year yield minus 3-month not explained by excess market returns (i.e., the residuals $\hat{\eta}_{t+1}$ in the least-squares regression $\Delta Slope_{t+1} = \hat{a} + \hat{b}XMKT_{t+1} + \hat{\eta}_{t+1}^{slope}$) and time-invariant factor loadings given by the $N \times 2$ matrix $\mathbf{L}$:

$$\mathbf{R}_{t+1} = \mathbf{L}\mathbf{f}_{t+1} + \boldsymbol{\varepsilon}_{t+1}. \tag{6.68}$$

Although we consider the special case of two factors only, this example can be generalized to the case of any $F \geq 2$ factors, at the cost of a more involved algebra. Also assume that the idiosyncratic shocks in the vector $\boldsymbol{\varepsilon}_{t+1}$ have conditional covariance matrix $Var_t[\boldsymbol{\varepsilon}_{t+1}] = E_t[\boldsymbol{\varepsilon}_{t+1}\boldsymbol{\varepsilon}_{t+1}'] = \boldsymbol{\Psi}$ which is constant in time and SPD, and that the common factors are characterized by $E_t[\mathbf{f}_{t+1}] = \mathbf{0}$, $E_t[\mathbf{f}_{t+1}\boldsymbol{\varepsilon}_{t+1}'] = \mathbf{O}$ (a matrix of zeros of the appropriate dimensions), and $E_t[\mathbf{f}_{t+1}\mathbf{f}_{t+1}'] = diag\{\sigma^2_{XMKT,t+1}, \sigma^2_{\Delta Slope,t+1}\}$. Because $E_t[\boldsymbol{\varepsilon}_{t+1}] = \mathbf{0}$, then $E_t[\mathbf{R}_{t+1}] = \mathbf{0}$, which means that the returns have been demeaned beforehand. The expression for the conditional covariance matrix of $\mathbf{R}_{t+1}$ can then be written by explicitly disentangling the role played by the risk exposures, the variance of the risk factors, and the variance of idiosyncratic risk:

$$\begin{aligned}\boldsymbol{\Sigma}_{t+1|t} &= LE_t[\mathbf{f}_{t+1}\mathbf{f}_{t+1}']L' + E_t[\boldsymbol{\varepsilon}_{t+1}\boldsymbol{\varepsilon}_{t+1}'] + E_t[\mathbf{f}_{t+1}\boldsymbol{\varepsilon}_{t+1}'] \\ &= LE_t[\mathbf{f}_{t+1}\mathbf{f}_{t+1}']L' + \boldsymbol{\Psi} = \mathbf{b}_{Mkt}\mathbf{b}_{Mkt}'\sigma^2_{XMKT,t+1} + \mathbf{b}_{slope}\mathbf{b}_{slope}'\sigma^2_{slope,t+1} + \boldsymbol{\Psi},\end{aligned} \tag{6.69}$$

where $\mathbf{b}_{Mkt}$ is the $N \times 1$ vector that collects the factor loadings of each of the N assets on the market portfolio, and $\mathbf{b}_{slope}$ is the $N \times 1$ vector that collects the factor loadings of each of the N assets on the riskless yield curve slope factor. We may highlight the differential role played by variances and covariances of the assets through a simple bivariate example (i.e., at this point we have that $N = F = 2$):

$$\begin{aligned}&\begin{bmatrix}\sigma^2_{1,t+1} & \sigma_{12,t+1} \\ \sigma_{12,t+1} & \sigma^2_{2,t+1}\end{bmatrix} = \begin{bmatrix}(b_1^{Mkt})^2 & b_1^{Mkt}b_2^{Mkt} \\ b_1^{Mkt}b_2^{Mkt} & (b_2^{Mkt})^2\end{bmatrix}\sigma^2_{XMKT,t+1} + \begin{bmatrix}(b_1^{slope})^2 & b_1^{slope}b_2^{slope} \\ b_1^{slope}b_2^{slope} & (b_2^{slope})^2\end{bmatrix}\sigma^2_{Slope,t+1} \\ &+ \begin{bmatrix}\psi_{11} & \psi_{12} \\ \psi_{12} & \psi_{22}\end{bmatrix} = \\ &\begin{bmatrix}(b_1^{Mkt})^2\sigma^2_{XMKT,t+1} + (b_1^{slope})^2\sigma^2_{Slope,t+1} + \psi_{11} & b_1^{Mkt}b_2^{Mkt}\sigma^2_{XMKT,t+1} + b_1^{slope}b_2^{slope}\sigma^2_{Slope,t+1} + \psi_{12} \\ b_1^{Mkt}b_2^{Mkt}\sigma^2_{XMKT,t+1} + b_1^{slope}b_2^{slope}\sigma^2_{Slope,t+1} + \psi_{12} & (b_2^{Mkt})^2\sigma^2_{Mkt,t+1} + (b_2^{slope})^2\sigma^2_{Slope,t+1} + \psi_{22}\end{bmatrix}.\end{aligned} \tag{6.70}$$

Importantly, as Eq. (6.70) makes it clear, Eq. (6.69) implies that not only the dynamic variances of asset returns depend on the loadings of the asset on the factors and on the variance of the factors, for instance,

$$\sigma^2_{1,t+1} = (b_1^{Mkt})^2\sigma^2_{XMKT,t+1} + (b_1^{slope})^2\sigma^2_{Slope,t+1} + \psi_{11}, \tag{6.71}$$

but also that predicted covariances depend on factor loadings and factor variances:

$$\sigma_{12,t+1} = b_1^{Mkt}b_2^{Mkt}\sigma^2_{XMKT,t+1} + b_1^{slope}b_2^{slope}\sigma^2_{Slope,t+1} + \psi_{12} \tag{6.72}$$

In general, with N assets and F factors, Eq. (6.69) can be generalized to:

$$\boldsymbol{\Sigma}_{t+1|t} = \sum_{f=1}^{F}\mathbf{b}_f\mathbf{b}_f'\sigma^2_{f,t+1|t} + \boldsymbol{\Psi}. \tag{6.73}$$

The covariance stationarity and positivity of the F GARCH processes that enter this expression will be sufficient to ensure that also the overall process followed by $\boldsymbol{\Sigma}_{t+1|t}$ will be covariance stationary and the matrix SPD. This is another, notable payoff of a factor GARCH strategy compared to complex multivariate problems.

As we shall see below, heuristically Eq. (6.73) will provide useful forecasts when the factors will explain most of the variability captured by the covariance matrix. For instance, it would be sufficient that "most" equations in Eq. (6.68) provided relatively high R-square. This derives from the fact that the errors in Eq. (6.68) are assumed to be homoskedastic and they ought to be small for the factor model to provide accurate variance and covariance predictions.

At this point, especially when $F \ll N$, and assuming all the calculations to obtain/estimate F orthogonal factors have been performed already, it will be possible to estimate and predict large-scale $N \times N$ covariance matrices that would otherwise require formidable efforts, in three simple steps:

- Estimate, for instance by simple OLS applied to Eq. (6.68), the NF factor loadings required by Eq. (6.73), $\hat{\mathbf{b}}_1, \hat{\mathbf{b}}_2, \ldots, \hat{\mathbf{b}}_F$.

- Specify and estimate F models for the conditional variance of the factors; such models can be heterogeneous across factors, similarly to the DCC approach.
- Once the predictions $\sigma^2_{f,t+1|t} \forall t > 1$ have been obtained, proceed to predict variances and covariances of the N series of asset returns using Eq. (6.73).

Crucially, Eq. (6.73) exploits the structural *orthogonality across the factors* to reduce a complex $0.5N(N-1)$-dimensional problem of covariance prediction into a much simpler $(N+F)$-dimensional problem in which one estimates N least-square regressions and then FGARCH-type models. Needless to say, the advantage can be enormous because when $F < N$, $(N+F) < 2N < 0.5N(N-1)$ is satisfied for $N \geq 6$, that is, for estimation problems that are of relatively modest size in terms of number of univariate models to be estimated (i.e., we are not counting parameters, but instead estimable equations here).

Example 6.10 takes seriously the role of excess market returns and (orthogonalized) changes in the slope of the yield curve in forecasting the covariance matrix of stock and bond returns.

EXAMPLE 6.10

Because US stock returns data are to be used as one of the factors and 10-year US Treasury rates enter in the definition of US government bond returns, in this example we shall forecast the covariance matrix of the returns on weekly returns of two famous Fama–French US portfolios, HML and SMB, that represent the excess returns on value- and size-sorting. As a preliminary step, we compute by OLS the shocks to the change in the term spread that are uncorrelated with excess market returns, by estimating:

$$\Delta Slope_{t+1} = -\underset{(0.886)}{0.0005} + \underset{(0.708)}{0.0006}\, XMKT_{t+1} + \hat{\eta}^{slope}_{t+1}$$

As a first step, we estimate by OLS the two-factor model:

$$SMB_{t+1} = \underset{(0.941)}{-0.002} + \underset{(0.027)}{0.029}\, XMKT_{t+1} + \underset{(0.174)}{0.289}\, \hat{\eta}_{t+1} + \varepsilon^{SMB}_{t+1} \quad R^2 = 0.37\%$$

$$HML_{t+1} = \underset{(0.000)}{0.122} - \underset{(0.000)}{0.088}\, XMKT_{t+1} + \underset{(0.000)}{0.860}\, \hat{\eta}_{t+1} + \varepsilon^{HML}_{t+1} \quad R^2 = 3.18\%.$$

Interestingly, even though they are long–short portfolios, SMB and HML are not market-neutral portfolios, although the coefficients are rather small. They both positively correlate with the slope of the yield curve. As a result of the first step, we have $\hat{\mathbf{b}}_{XMKT} = [0.029 \;\; -0.088]'$ and $\hat{\mathbf{b}}_{Slope} = [0.289 \;\; 0.860]'$. However, the R^2 are modest.

In the second step, we work on the specification of the conditional variance models of the two factors. In the case of excess market returns, we specify a Gaussian MA(1) EGARCH(1,1) model. In the case of the shocks to the term spread—after picking a conditional mean model of AR(4) type—the use of BIC to sort the different models leads to the selection of the following threshold GARCH(1,1) model:

$$\ln\sigma^2_{MKT,t+1|t} = \underset{(0.000)}{-0.100} + \underset{(0.000)}{0.249}\, |z^{MKT}_t| - \underset{(0.000)}{0.126}\, z^{MKT}_t + \underset{(0.000)}{0.933}\, \ln\sigma^2_{MKT,t|t-1}$$

$$\sigma^2_{\eta,t+1|t} = \underset{(0.000)}{0.001} + \underset{(0.000)}{0.110}\, \varepsilon^2_{\eta,t} - \underset{(0.000)}{0.063}\, I_{\{\varepsilon_{\eta,t}<0\}}\varepsilon^2_{\eta,t} + \underset{(0.000)}{0.885}\, \sigma^2_{\eta,t|t-1}.$$

The plots in Fig. 6.14 show predictions of the variance of the two factors with evidence of some heteroskedasticity also in $\hat{\eta}^{slope}_{t+1}$.

In the last step, we compute:

$$\sigma^2_{smb,t+1} = (0.029)^2\sigma^2_{XMKT,t+1} + (0.289)^2\sigma^2_{Slope,t+1} + 1.296$$

$$\sigma^2_{hml,t+1} = (-0.088)^2\sigma^2_{XMKT,t+1} + (0.860)^2\sigma^2_{Slope,t+1} + 1.301$$

$$\sigma_{smb-hml,t+1} = (-0.088\cdot 0.029)\sigma^2_{XMKT,t+1} + (0.289\cdot 0.860)\sigma^2_{Slope,t+1} - 0.2979.$$

Fig. 6.15 shows the resulting predictions of variances, covariances, and correlations deriving from the two-factor model. Even though there is some discernible time variation, the results are rather unrealistic in the case of the variance of SMB and the correlation. However, this is hardly a surprise: the factor loadings of SMB are small enough that, when squared, almost no portion of the conditional heteroskedasticity in market excess returns and in the changes of the slope of the yield curve is copied in the time variation of SMB returns. Therefore, also the range of the predicted correlation between SMB and HML is modest, between −0.23 and −0.1.

To have an objective measurement of how much the two-factor model may be letting us down because of its low regression R^2, in Fig. 6.16, we have estimated a Gaussian threshold BEKK(1,1,1) model and reported the resulting forecasts of variances, covariances, and correlations. Clearly, a two-factor linear model did not manage to perform sensibly.

To show what the origin of the problem is, we use an artificial 50–50 US balanced portfolio composed by 50% by CRSP value-weighted stocks and by 50% by US 10-year Treasuries. We estimate by OLS the two-factor model:

$$PtfR_{t+1} = \underset{(0.013)}{0.034} + \underset{(0.000)}{0.498}\, XMKT_{t+1} - \underset{(0.000)}{1.819}\, \hat{\eta}_{t+1} + \varepsilon^{SMB}_{t+1} \quad R^2 = 80.85\%.$$

(Continued)

EXAMPLE 6.10 (Continued)

Almost by construction, now the model provides an excellent fit—clearly, 10-year Treasury returns respond strongly to changes in the yield curve, that they contribute to define. Now we have that:

$$\sigma^2_{ptf,t+1} = (0.498)^2 \sigma^2_{XMKT,t+1} + (-1.819)^2 \sigma^2_{Slope,t+1} + 0.324$$

$$\sigma_{ptf-hml,t+1} = (-0.088 \cdot 0.498)\sigma^2_{XMKT,t+1} + (-1.819 \cdot 0.860)\sigma^2_{Slope,t+1} - 0.247$$

and as a result, the resulting variances and also covariances are much more realistic (this does not mean that they will accurately forecast, which is beyond the point of this example) (Fig. 6.17).

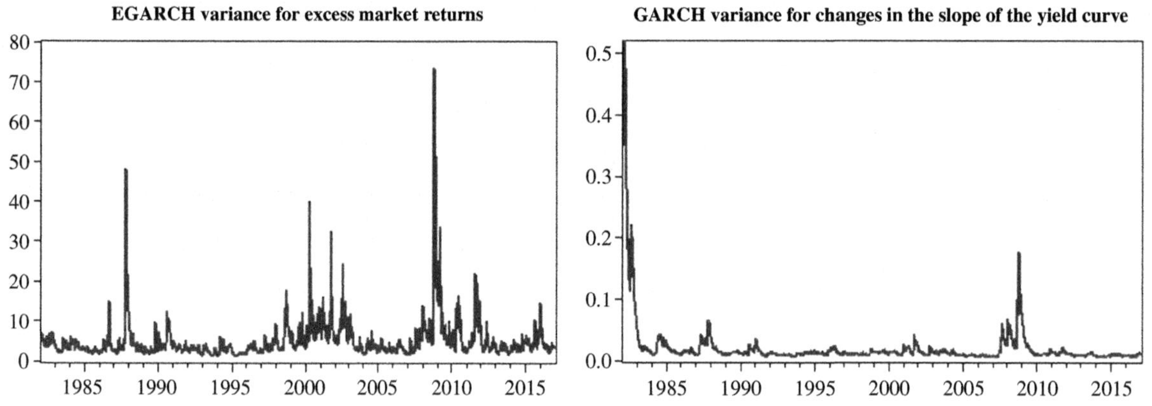

FIGURE 6.14 One-week predictions of variance for US excess stock returns and changes in the slope (10-year−3-month rates) of the riskless yield curve.

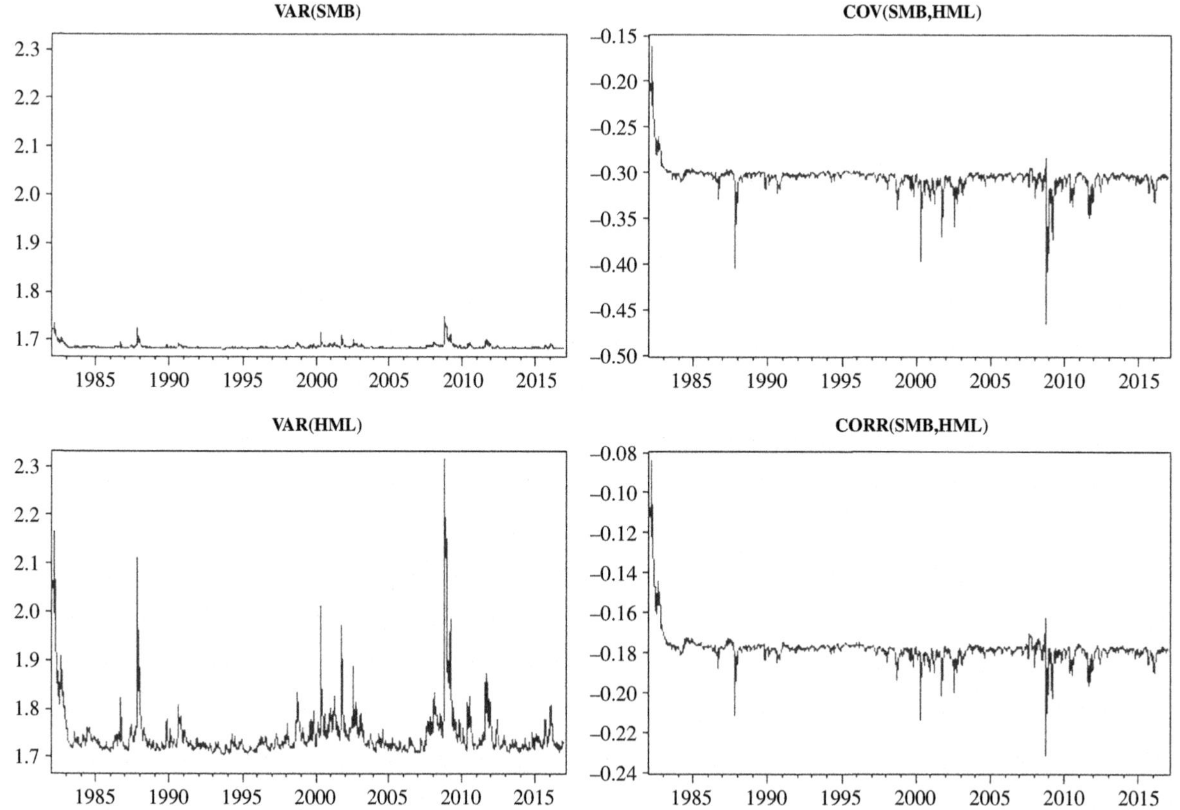

FIGURE 6.15 One-week predictions of US size and value mimicking portfolio return variances, covariances, and correlations from a two-factor model.

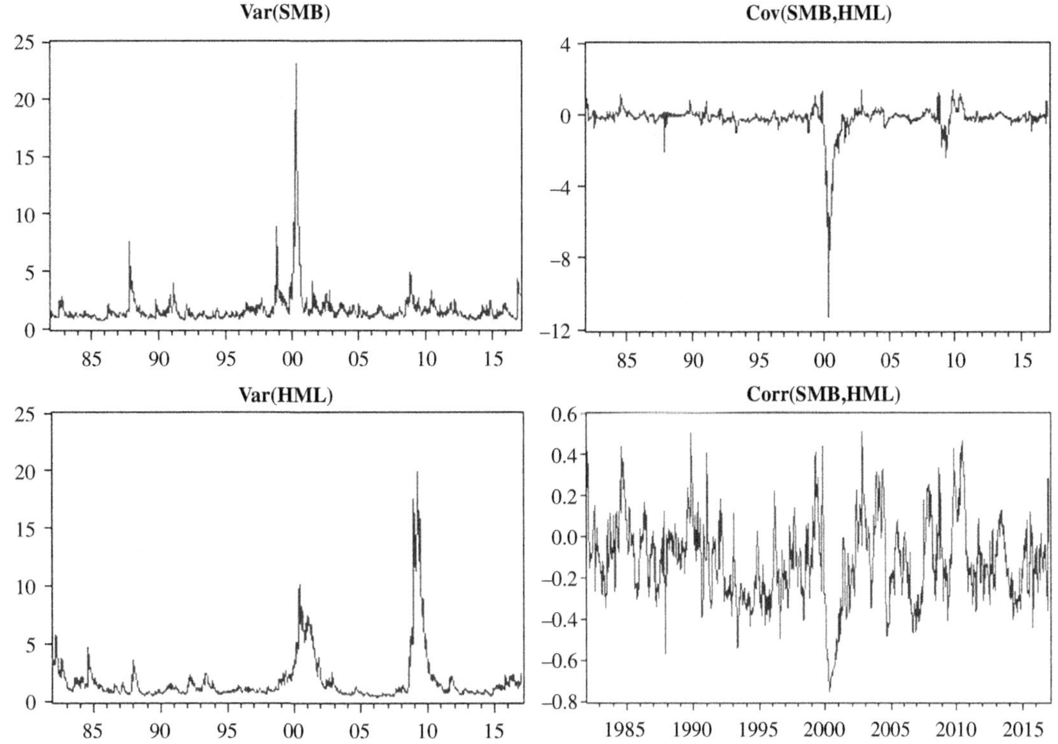

FIGURE 6.16 One-week predictions of US size and value mimicking portfolio variances, covariances, and correlations from a threshold BEKK(1,1,1)

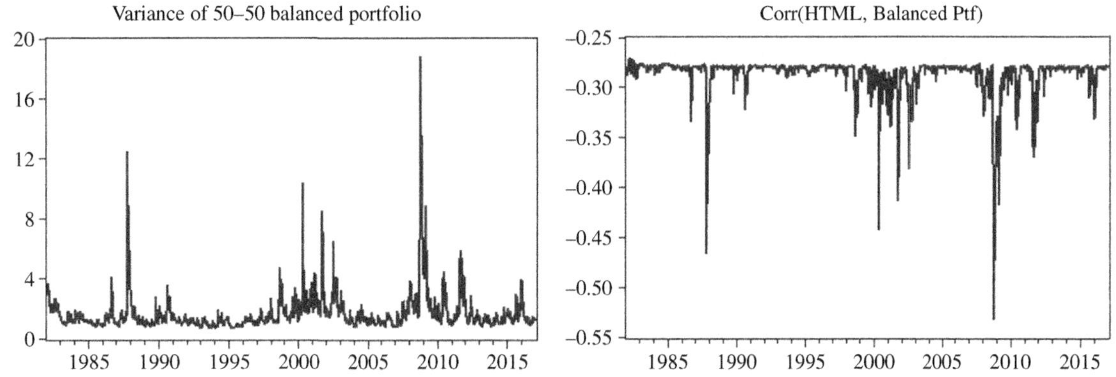

FIGURE 6.17 Predictions of variance for a 50–50 stock–bond balanced portfolio and of its correlation with HML returns from the two-factor model.

Example 6.10 makes a probably obvious point: because Eq. (6.73) derives from Eq. (6.68) and all the assumptions that came with it, when the latter turns out to be inconsistent with the data, it is not reasonable to expect the factor GARCH forecasts to be of any good quality. In particular, when (1) the regression residuals ε_{t+1} are heteroskedastic, that is, $Var_t[\varepsilon_{t+1}] = \Psi_{t+1|t}$, and/or (2) the regression residuals are generally "large," in the sense that the regressions in Eq. (6.68) all yield modest or even negligible R^2 (as in the first part of Example 6.10), then we cannot expect much from a factor approach.

In fact, in Example 6.10, a simple Gaussian threshold diagonal BEKK(1,1,1) reveals that the SMB and HML OLS residuals from the first-step regressions are "large" (as we have seen the R^2 fell between 0% and 3%) and contain a rich CH structure, as shown in Fig. 6.18. Therefore, just because imposing a homoskedastic Ψ turns out to be a false restriction, the poor performance of the model follows.

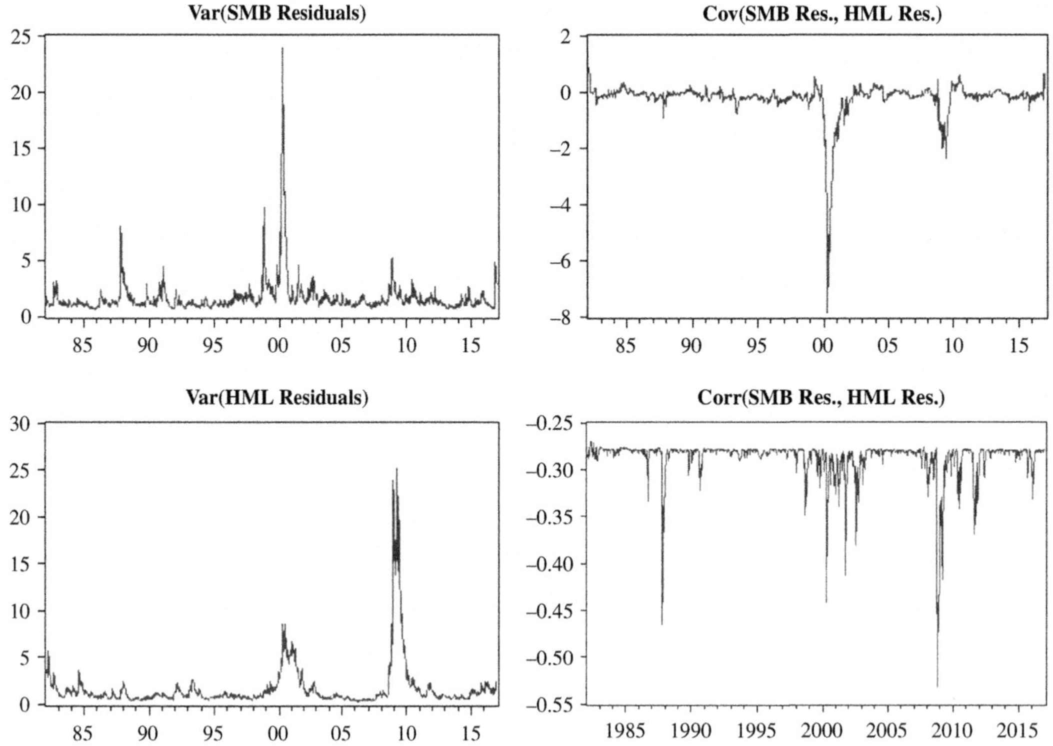

FIGURE 6.18 One-weekly predictions of US size and value mimicking portfolio variances, covariances, and correlations of regression residuals.

One wonders whether any quick fix can be found. On the one hand, it may seem sufficient to work on discovering—either by expanding the number of factors F, provided these remain much smaller than N, or by more carefully selecting the identity of such factors—multifactor models that imply high R^2, ideally as close to 100% as possible, so to constrain residuals to be sufficiently "small," when any residual CH stops mattering. Unfortunately, discovering such strong multifactor models is the task of one branch of empirical finance, asset pricing, on which the state of the art does not seem to be that promising (see, e.g., Fama and French, 2004, or Cochrane, 2009). On the other hand, we may naively think that—because the problem seems to be also posed by the fact that it is $Var_t[\boldsymbol{\varepsilon}_{t+1}] = \boldsymbol{\Psi}_{t+1|t}$ and not $Var_t[\boldsymbol{\varepsilon}_{t+1}] = \boldsymbol{\Psi}$—one may simply generalize Eq. (6.73) to become:

$$\boldsymbol{\Sigma}_{t+1|t} = \sum_{f=1}^{F} \mathbf{b}_f \mathbf{b}_f' \sigma^2_{f,t+1|t} + \boldsymbol{\Psi}_{t+1|t}. \tag{6.74}$$

Unfortunately, this is no fix: $\boldsymbol{\Psi}_{t+1|t}$ is an $N \times N$ symmetric and PD covariance matrix and predicting it would require us using the full thrust of the methodologies developed in Section 6.3. In other words, the whole point of adopting Eq. (6.73) and estimating only F processes for the variances (and no process for dynamic covariance) stops when $\boldsymbol{\Psi}_{t+1|t}$ acquires itself a CH structure.

There is one final transformation of Eq. (6.73) that is useful to illustrate the fact that *all factor GARCH(p,q) models are just special, restricted cases of diagonal BEKK models*. Suppose that the variance of all factors follows a GARCH (p,q) model:

$$\sigma^2_{f,t+1|t} = \omega_f + \sum_{i=1}^{p} \alpha_{f,i} \varepsilon^2_{f,t-i+1} + \sum_{j=1}^{q} \beta_{f,j} \sigma^2_{f,t-j+1|t-j}. \tag{6.75}$$

Then Eq. (6.73) may be rewritten as:

$$\boldsymbol{\Sigma}_{t+1|t} = \left(\sum_{f=1}^{F} \mathbf{b}_f \omega_f \mathbf{b}_f' + \boldsymbol{\Psi} \right) + \sum_{f=1}^{F} \sum_{i=1}^{p} \mathbf{b}_f \alpha_{f,i} \varepsilon^2_{f,t-i+1} \mathbf{b}_f' + \sum_{f=1}^{F} \sum_{j=1}^{q} \mathbf{b}_f \beta_{f,j} \sigma^2_{f,t-j+1|t-j} \mathbf{b}_f' \tag{6.76}$$

which appears to be in a (diagonal) BEKK form as in Eq. (6.46).

Before we storm out of this section thinking that factor GARCH models are too prickly because they seem to require a support from asset pricing theory that so far we understand it is unlikely to come, we emphasize one additional advantage they have. Because from standard principles of regression analysis (also used in elementary CAPM presentations), we know that the beta (concerning any factor $f = 1, 2, \ldots, F$) *of a portfolio is a weighted linear combination of the betas of each of the assets* concerning the same factor, $\hat{\mathbf{b}}_{ptf} = \sum_{n=1}^{N} w_n \hat{\mathbf{b}}_n$, then it follows that:

$$\begin{aligned} Var_t\left[R_{ptf,t+1}\right] &= \mathbf{w}'\boldsymbol{\Sigma}_{t+1|t}\mathbf{w} = \sum_{f=1}^{F} \underbrace{\mathbf{w}'\mathbf{b}_f}_{b_{ptf,f}} \underbrace{\mathbf{b}_f'\mathbf{w}}_{b_{ptf,f}} \sigma^2_{f,t+1|t} + \mathbf{w}'\boldsymbol{\Psi}\mathbf{w} \\ &= \sum_{f=1}^{F} b^2_{ptf,f}\, \sigma^2_{f,t+1|t} + Var[\varepsilon_{ptf,t+1}], \end{aligned} \tag{6.77}$$

where w is the $N \times 1$ vector of portfolio weights and $\varepsilon_{ptf,t+1}$ is the least-square residual of a simple regression of portfolio returns on the F factors. This result is worth the following:

RESULT 6.1 (Factor–GARCH Mapping Exposure)

In a factor–GARCH framework for the covariance matrix of N assets, $\boldsymbol{\Sigma}_{t+1|t}$, the forecast of the variance of a portfolio obtained from applying the framework to the factor model estimated directly on portfolio returns will be identical to the forecast obtained as $\mathbf{w}'\boldsymbol{\Sigma}_{t+1|t}\mathbf{w}$, where w is the $N \times 1$ vector of portfolio weights.

Special families of factor–GARCH models are the *orthogonal GARCH* and the *principal component (PC) GARCH* (see Chapter 1 for a review of PC analysis). In a PC GARCH model, the observed data are assumed to be generated by an orthogonal transformation of N univariate GARCH processes. The matrix of the linear transformation is the orthogonal matrix (or a selection) of eigenvectors of the population unconditional covariance matrix of the standardized residuals from the GARCH models. PC/orthogonal models can be considered as special cases of factor GARCH models, where the orthogonal factors are a subset of N original univariate GARCH-type processes. Equivalently, they represent factor GARCH models in which PC analysis is performed to find which combination of the starting asset return series explains most of the overall variation in the data.

In practice, after M of the N PCs have been retained (we usually focus on the M components that explain between 80% and 90% of total variance of the original N-variable set of series), we estimate a univariate GARCH model for each of the M components. Next, we use the $N \times M$ loading matrix $\mathbf{L}$ of these PCs (this collects the loading of all the original series on just the first M PCs) to rotate the PC variances back to variable space, computing at each point in time $\mathbf{C}_{t+1} = \mathbf{L}\mathbf{D}_{t+1}\mathbf{L}'$, where $\mathbf{D}_{t+1}$ is the time t diagonal matrix of the predicted variances of the PCs at time t; $\mathbf{C}_{t+1}$ is an approximate correlation matrix for the original variables at time t (however, there is no guarantee that the elements on the diagonal of $\mathbf{C}_{t+1}$ are equal to 1). At this point, we standardize $\mathbf{C}_{t+1}$, so that it is a correlation matrix with all of its diagonal elements equal to 1, call the result $Corr_{t+1}$. Finally, we scale $Corr_{t+1}$ with the estimated variances of the original GARCH models in $\mathbf{D}_{t+1}$ to get the covariance matrix, $\boldsymbol{\Sigma}_{t+1|t} = \mathbf{D}^{1/2}_{t+1} Corr_{t+1} \mathbf{D}^{1/2}_{t+1}$.

Although there are no compelling reasons for why it may work or accurately forecast variances and covariances, PC GARCH can handle any practically interesting value for N: computationally, a problem would need to have several thousand variables/assets before computing time becomes an issue. In the case of the PC GARCH, experiments have been performed to show that even when not obtaining GARCH estimates for the least important PCs (i.e., associated with smallest eigenvalues)—that is, those that explain a minor fraction of total variance—PC GARCH may perform well, in the sense that not only explaining the time variation of variances and covariances is not seriously impaired, but there is actually evidence of solid forecasting accuracy. For instance, Alexander (2001) illustrates the use of the PC GARCH model (that she calls orthogonal GARCH). She emphasizes that using a small number of PCs compared to the number of assets is the strength of the approach (in one example, she fixes M at 2 for $N = 12$ assets). However, note that the conditional covariance matrix will then have a reduced rank of $M < N$, which may be a problem for applications and for diagnostic tests which depend on the inverse of $\boldsymbol{\Sigma}_{t+1|t}$.

6.6 INFERENCE AND MODEL SPECIFICATION

Multivariate GARCH estimation is performed using *ML* to jointly estimate the parameters of the (conditional) mean and the variance equations in Eq. (6.31). Call $\theta \in \Theta \subseteq \mathbb{R}^K$ the $K \times 1$ vector collecting all parameters characterizing the conditional moment functions $\boldsymbol{\mu}_{t+1|t}$ and $\boldsymbol{\Sigma}_{t+1|t}^{1/2}$. Note that although the GARCH parameters do not affect the conditional mean, the conditional mean parameters generally enter the conditional variance specification through the residuals, $\varepsilon_{t+1} \equiv \mathbf{R}_{t+1} - \boldsymbol{\mu}_{t+1|t}(\boldsymbol{\theta})$. For instance, in the multivariate normal case, the log-likelihood contributions (i.e., the PDF values for each of the sample observations) for GARCH models are given by:

$$\ell(\mathbf{R}_{t+1};\ \boldsymbol{\theta}) \equiv -\frac{1}{2}N\ln(2\pi) - \frac{1}{2}\ln\det\boldsymbol{\Sigma}_{t+1}(\boldsymbol{\theta}) - \frac{1}{2}\boldsymbol{\varepsilon}_{t+1}'\,\boldsymbol{\Sigma}_{t+1}^{-1}(\boldsymbol{\theta})\boldsymbol{\varepsilon}_{t+1}. \tag{6.78}$$

In the case of a *t*-Student distribution, the contributions are of the form:

$$\begin{aligned}\ell(\mathbf{R}_{t+1};\ \boldsymbol{\theta},\nu) \equiv \ln\frac{\Gamma\left(\dfrac{N+\nu}{2}\right)}{\Gamma\left(\dfrac{\nu}{2}\right)\sqrt[N]{\pi(\nu-2)}} - \frac{1}{2}\ln\det\boldsymbol{\Sigma}_{t+1}(\boldsymbol{\theta})\\ - \frac{1}{2}(\nu+N)\ln\left[1+\frac{\boldsymbol{\varepsilon}_{t+1}'\,\boldsymbol{\Sigma}_{t+1}^{-1}(\boldsymbol{\theta})\boldsymbol{\varepsilon}_{t+1}}{\nu-2}\right],\end{aligned} \tag{6.79}$$

where $\nu > 2$ is the number of degrees of freedom. The asymptotic properties of ML (and QML) estimators in multivariate GARCH models are not yet firmly established, and are difficult to derive from low-level assumptions. While *consistency* has been proven by Jeantheau (1998), asymptotic normality of the QMLE is not established generally. However, applied researchers who use multivariate GARCH models have generally proceeded as if asymptotic normality holds in all cases.[12]

As in Chapter 5, we may often hesitate before introducing a specific parametric assumption on the distribution of the (standardized) residuals and may want to proceed instead under the weaker assumption in Eq. (6.31) that $\mathbf{z}_{t+1}$IID $MD(\mathbf{0},\ \mathbf{I}_N; \boldsymbol{\theta}_D)$, where *MD* is some multivariate distribution that is not yet specified. In this case you will be able to obtain QML estimates using the same logic illustrated in Chapter 5 in the case of univariate GARCH models: even though the conditional joint distribution of the shocks $\mathbf{z}_{t+1}$ is *not* normal (i.e., $\mathbf{z}_{t+1}$ IID $MD(\mathbf{0},\ \mathbf{I}_N)$ and *MD* does not reduce to a normal), *under some conditions*, an application of MLE based on the false assumption $\mathbf{z}_{t+1}$ IID $N(\mathbf{0},\ \mathbf{I}_N)$ will yield estimators of the conditional mean, variance, and covariance parameters which converge to the true parameters as the sample gets infinitely large, that is, that are consistent. The conditions mentioned above are that:

- The conditional covariance (matrix) function, $\boldsymbol{\Sigma}_{t+1|t}$, seen as a function of the information at, $\Im_t$, must be correctly specified.
- The conditional mean function, $\boldsymbol{\mu}_{t+1|t}$ seen as a function of the information at time, $\Im_t$, must be correctly specified.

In particular, DCC models are estimated by QMLE by construction: because the model is implemented in three different steps, even though in each of these stages a log-likelihood function is written and maximized, the overall outcome only represents a QMLE. In each of the stages, only few parameters are estimated simultaneously using numerical optimization. This feature makes DCC models extremely tractable for the risk management of large portfolios: in the first step, one only estimates univariate GARCH-type models; the resulting GARCH inferences are then used to compute the standardized residuals; in the final step, one only estimates few parameters (for instance, just α and β when covariance targeting has been imposed) that apply to all pairs of assets. For instance, in the case of $N = 2$, in the first stage, one solves (in the simple GARCH(1,1) case),

$$\begin{aligned}\max_{\omega_i,\,\alpha_i,\,\beta_i}\ -\frac{T}{2}\ln 2\pi - \frac{1}{2}\sum_{t=0}^{T-1}\ln(\omega_i + \alpha_i R_{i,t}^2 + \beta_i\sigma_{i,t|t-1}^2)\\ -\frac{1}{2}\sum_{t=0}^{T-1}\frac{\varepsilon_{i,t+1}^2}{\omega_i + \alpha_i R_{i,t}^2 + \beta_i\sigma_{i,t|t-1}^2}\qquad i = 1,\ 2,\end{aligned} \tag{6.80}$$

12. Gouriéroux (1997) (Section 6.3) proves it for a general formulation using high-level assumptions. Comte and Lieberman (2003) prove it for the BEKK formulation.

where $\sigma^2_{i,0}$ is initialized at the unconditional variance, $\omega_i/(1-\alpha_i-\beta_i)$. In the second step, given the time series $z_{1,t+1} \equiv R_{1,t+1}/\hat{\sigma}_{1,t+1|t}$ and $z_{2,t+1} \equiv R_{2,t+1}/\hat{\sigma}_{2,t+1|t}$, one solves:

$$\max_{\alpha,\beta} -\frac{T}{2}\log 2\pi - \frac{1}{2}\sum_{t=0}^{T-1}\ln[1-q^2_{12,t+1}/(q_{11,t+1}\,q_{22,t+1})] \\ -\frac{1}{2}\sum_{t=0}^{T-1}\frac{(z_{1,t})^2+(z_{2,t})^2-2\dfrac{q_{12,t+1}}{\sqrt{q_{11,t+1}}\sqrt{q_{22,t+1}}}\rho_{12,t+1|t}z_{1,t}z_{2,t}}{[1-q^2_{12,t+1}/(q_{11,t+1}\,q_{22,t+1})]}, \tag{6.81}$$

where the $q_{ij,t+1}$s follow either a GARCH or a RiskMetrics model, involving the parameters α and β in the former case (under covariance targeting), and λ in the latter. Note that the variables that enter the log-likelihood are the standardized residuals and not the original raw returns themselves. In Eq. (6.81) we are therefore treating the standardized residuals as actual observations, and this is an alternative way to appreciate the loss of estimation efficiency that QMLE implies in the estimation of DCC. In theory, we could obtain more precise estimators by estimating all the volatility models and the correlation model simultaneously, which would yield an ML estimator. In practice, this is not feasible for large portfolios, that is, for cases in which N exceeds three or four different assets/series.

Because estimating multivariate GARCH models is time-consuming, it is desirable to check *ex ante* whether the data present evidence of multivariate (G)ARCH effects. This is done both on the individual series by testing whether squared residuals are serially correlated for each individual series, but also testing whether squared residuals appear to display any *significant cross-correlations*, that is, $Corr[\varepsilon^2_{i,t},\ \varepsilon^2_{j,t-k}] \neq 0$ for $i \neq j$ and $k \neq 0$. Ex post, it is also of crucial importance to check the adequacy of any multivariate GARCH specification. However, few tests are specific to multivariate models. Univariate tests applied independently to each series of (standardized) residuals remain very common, but are not completely appropriate. For instance, as seen in Chapter 5, it is typical—when $\mathbf{z}_{t+1}$ IID $N(\mathbf{0},\ \mathbf{I}_N)$ has been assumed—to apply standard *univariate tests of normality* to the standardized residuals $\hat{z}_{i,t+1} \equiv R_{i,t+1}/\hat{\sigma}_{i,t+1|t}$, where $\hat{\sigma}_{i,t+1}$ denotes the time series of filtered standard deviations derived from the estimated volatility model, $\hat{\sigma}^2_{i,t+1|t} = \mathbf{e}_i{}'\hat{\boldsymbol{\Sigma}}_{t+1|t}\mathbf{e}_i$ $i=1,2,\ldots,N$, that is, the ith element on the main diagonal of $\hat{\boldsymbol{\Sigma}}_{t+1|t}$). Here, we are exploiting the fact that $\mathbf{z}_{t+1}$ IID $N(\mathbf{0},\ \mathbf{I}_N)$ implies that each of the elements $\mathbf{z}_{t+1}$ must have a marginal normal distribution.[13] As we know by now, one commonly used test is Jarque and Bera's, based on the idea of measuring departures from normality in terms of the skewness and kurtosis of standardized residuals. A second method exploits the fact that even though normality has not been assumed (this is the case of QMLE), in most applications, a correctly specified model anyway implies $\mathbf{z}_{t+1}$ IID $MD(\mathbf{0},\ \mathbf{I}_N)$. As we know, independence implies that $\hat{Q}^{g,h}_k(z_i,z_j) \simeq 0$ for all $k \geq 1$ where

$$\hat{Q}^{g,h}_k(z_i,z_j) \equiv \frac{T}{T+2}\sum_{\tau=1}^{k}\frac{(\hat{\rho}^{g,h}_{ij,\tau})^2}{T-k} \overset{a}{\sim} \chi^2_k \\ \hat{\rho}^{g,h}_{ij,\tau} \equiv \frac{\sum_{t=1}^{T-\tau}(g(z_{i,t})-\overline{g(z_{i,t})})(h(z_{j,t+\tau})-\overline{h(z_{j,t})})}{\sqrt{\sum_{t=1}^{T-\tau}(g(z_{i,t})-\overline{g(z_{i,t})})\sum_{t=1}^{T-\tau}(h(z_{j,t})-\overline{h(z_{j,t})})}} \tag{6.82}$$

and $g(\cdot)$ and $h(\cdot)$ are any two (measurable) function. Note that differently from Section 5.4 in Chapter 5, the ones in Eq. (6.82) are transformed cross-series, serial correlation coefficients. The transformations—typically, in applied work, these will be powers—consist of employing not the standardized residual series z_i and z_j but appropriately revealing functions, such as squares and cubes. Because we are testing the correct specification of conditional volatility models, it is typical to set $g(x)=h(x)=x^2$, that is, to test whether the squared standardized residuals display any systematic autocorrelation patterns. However, the existence of CH in covariances is normally tested by setting $g(x)=h(x)=x$, and the existence of asymmetric effects by setting $g(x)=x^2$ and $h(x)=x$.

Although univariate tests can provide some guidance, contemporaneous correlation of the residuals entails that statistics from individual equations will not be independent. Therefore, truly multivariate tests have been developed and are routinely applied in practice (see, for instance, the ones that we have reviewed in Chapter 3).

13. The opposite does not hold: $z_{i,t+1} \sim N(0,1)\forall i \nRightarrow \mathbf{z}_{t+1} \sim \text{IID } N(0,\mathbf{I}_N)$.

REFERENCES

Alexander, C., 2001. Market Models. John Wiley, New York.

Bauwens, L., Laurent, S., Rombouts, J., 2006. Multivariate GARCH models: a survey. J. Appl. Econom. 21, 79–109.

Bollerslev, T., 1990. Modelling the coherence in short-run nominal exchange rates: a multivariate generalized ARCH model. Rev. Econ. Stat. 72, 498–505.

Bollerslev, T., Engle, R.F., 1993. Common persistence in conditional variances. Econometrica 61, 166–187.

Bollerslev, T., Engle, R.F., Wooldridge, J.M., 1988. A capital-asset pricing model with time-varying covariances. J. Polit. Econ. 96, 116–131.

Cochrane, J.H., 2009. *Asset Pricing*:(Revised Edition). Princeton University Press, Princeton, NJ.

Comte, F., Lieberman, O., 2003. Asymptotic theory for multivariate GARCH processes. J. Multivar. Anal. 84, 61–84.

Engle, R.F., 2002. Dynamic conditional correlation: a simple class of multivariate generalized autoregressive conditional heteroskedasticity models. J. Bus. Econ. Stat. 20, 339–350.

Engle, R.F., Kroner, K.F., 1995. Multivariate simultaneous generalized ARCH. Econom. Theory 11, 122–150.

Fama, E.F., French, K.R., 2004. The capital asset pricing model: theory and evidence. J. Econ. Perspect. 18, 25–46.

Gouriéroux, C., 1997. ARCH Models and Financial Applications. Springer-Verlag, New York.

Jeantheau, T., 1998. Strong consistency of estimators for multivariate ARCH models. Econom. Theory 14, 70–86.

Ledoit, O., Santa-Clara, P., Wolf, M., 2003. Flexible multivariate GARCH modeling with an application to international stock markets. Rev. Econ. Stat. 85, 735–747.

Schofield, N.C., 2017. Equity valuation. In: Schofield, N.C. (Ed.), Equity Derivatives. Palgrave Macmillan, London, United Kingdom.

Tse, Y.K., Tsui, A., 2002. A multivariate GARCH model with time-varying correlations. J. Bus. Econ. Stat. 20, 351–362.

Chapter 7

Multifactor Heteroskedastic Models, Stochastic Volatility

As far as the laws of mathematics refer to reality, they are not certain; and as far as they are certain, they do not refer to reality.

Albert Einstein

Most financial economists and practitioners refer to the fact that the variances and covariances of asset returns are time-varying (and to the whole lot of stylized facts discussed in Chapter 5), by saying that the data contain glaring evidence of *stochastic volatility* (that we shall often abbreviate as SV). Autoregressive conditionally heteroskedasticity (ARCH) processes are often also described as SV models, but we do not follow that nomenclature in this book. The essential feature of ARCH models is that they explicitly model the conditional variance of returns only as a function of past returns observed by the econometrician. This one-step-ahead prediction approach to volatility modeling is very powerful, particularly in the field of risk management. It is convenient from an econometric viewpoint as it immediately delivers the likelihood function as the product of one-step-ahead predictive densities. On the other hand, under the SV approach, volatility is a random variable characterized by shocks that do not simply reflect past asset returns. As a result, the predictive distribution of returns is specified indirectly, via the structure of the model, rather than directly. Even though for a small number of SV models (henceforth, SVMs) this predictive distribution can be calculated explicitly, invariably, for empirically realistic representations, it can only be evaluated numerically.

Such difficulties with the computation of the likelihood function has been a source of frustration for econometricians in the late 1980s and early 1990s. Indeed, even though since the mid-1980s continuous-time SV has dominated the option pricing literature, in those early days, econometricians struggled with the difficulties of estimating and testing these models. Only in the 1990s novel simulation strategies were developed to efficiently estimate SV models. As one would hope, a virtuous cycle has ensued: the advances in the econometrics of SVMs have led to refinements of the models, with many early models adopted because of their tractability being rejected from an empirical viewpoint. The resulting enriched SV literature has brought us much closer to the empirical reality we face in financial markets.

In today's practice of econometrics, we face a distinction between:

- ARCH-type models, in which only one random source of shocks drives the innovations in both asset returns and in conditional variances and covariances, hence called *single-factor volatility* models,[1] and
- genuine (here we follow the definition in Andersen and Benzoni, 2009) SVMs, in which two or more sources of random shocks drive asset returns and conditional variances and covariances (at least one for both), hence called *multi-factor volatility* models.

The distinguishing feature of genuine SV specifications is that volatility, being inherently unobservable and subject to its own random shocks, is not measurable with respect to observable information. That is, the current volatility state

1. Let us add that ARCH models, in which past return innovations govern the one-period-ahead conditional mean and variance and in which the volatility is known, or deterministic, at a given point in time, but the random evolution of the processes renders volatility stochastic for any horizon beyond the present period, are not the only widespread types of single-factor models. Another example is the one-factor continuous-time Cox et al. (1985) celebrated model in which the (stochastic) level of the short-term interest rate governs the dynamics of both the (instantaneous) drift and of the volatility diffusion term of all zero-coupon yields.

Essentials of Time Series for Financial Applications. DOI: https://doi.org/10.1016/B978-0-12-813409-2.00007-8

is not known for sure, conditional on the true data generating process and the past history of all available discretely sampled data. Therefore, *an estimate of the current volatility state must be filtered* from a noisy environment and the estimate will change as future observations become available. Hence, in-sample estimation typically involves smoothing techniques, not just filtering. In contrast, the conditional variance in GARCH models is observable given past information, which renders (quasi-) maximum likelihood techniques for inference rather straightforward while smoothing techniques have no role. As such, GARCH models are easier to estimate and to use in real-time forecasting.

However, this departure from direct one-step-ahead predictions that are typical of GARCH models yields two main advantages. First, much asset pricing theory (APT) is built around continuous-time models. Within this class, SVMs tend to fit more naturally with a wide array of applications, including the pricing of options, swaps, and other derivatives, as well as the modeling of the term structure of interest rates. In particular, SVMs provide a basis for realistic modeling of option prices. For instance, Hull and White (1987) assumed that volatility risk was unrewarded and showed that SV models could produce smiles and skews in option prices, which are frequently observed in market data. Second the increasing use of high-frequency intraday data for the construction of so-called realized volatility measures (see Chapter 10) is also starting to inject new life and practical applicability to SVMs as the realized volatility approach is naturally linked to the continuous-time SV framework.

Even though Clark (1973) had made important advances toward what we now consider SV modeling by introducing his time-changed Brownian motion processes, Taylor (1982) first introduced a (discrete-time) SVM for continuously compounded, demeaned returns written as the product $\sigma_t\xi_t$, where ξ_t was a unit-variance AR(p) process and $\sigma_t = \exp(0.5h_t)$ was some non-negative process in which h_t is a nonzero mean Gaussian linear process.[2] In fact, Taylor's model is a discretized case of Rosenberg's (1972) continuous-time product processes, of the type:[3]

$$\varepsilon_t = \int_0^t \sigma_s dW_{1,s}, \tag{7.1}$$

where the non-negative spot volatility σ_s may display jumps. Interestingly, Eq. (7.1) applies not only to univariate processes, but also admits elegant multivariate generalizations in which σ_s is a matrix process and $dW_{1,s}$ is a vector multivariate Brownian motion.

There are some unique challenges in dealing with genuine SVMs. For example, volatility is truly latent and this feature complicates estimation and inference. The main difficulty in conducting efficient inference for a continuous-time model from discretely sampled data is that closed-form expressions for the discrete-transition density generally are not available, especially in the presence of unobserved and serially correlated state variables. The latter is usually the case for SVMs. Although maximum likelihood estimation (MLE) is, in principle, feasible via numerical methods, see, for example, Lo (1988), the computational demands are typically excessive if latent variables must be integrated out of the likelihood function. Section 7.1 provides tools to address some of the challenges posed by the latent nature of SV. Section 7.2 uses such methods to develop rather intuitive, but inefficient, quasi-maximum likelihood estimators. Section 7.3 extends the simple SVMs presented in Section 7.2, reviewing a number of novel issues and estimation methodologies that have been developed in the literature. Section 7.4 concludes by attempting a brief summary of an on-going debate on the relative merits and empirical performance of single-factor ARCH versus multifactor SVMs.

7.1 A PRIMER ON THE KALMAN FILTER

7.1.1 A Simple Univariate Example

Although a general treatment is possible, here we just consider an example to convey the intuition for what a filter is about and defer to more complete and formal treatments to Hamilton (1994). Suppose that one observable time series of returns R_t depends on a variable which is unobservable or *latent*. For instance, this variable could be the *SV* of R_t.

---

2. In Clark's model the risky portion of the log of an asset price is written as W_{τ_t}, where W is a standard Brownian motion, t is continuous time, τ is a random time-shifting variable, and τ_t and W_τ are independent. In practice, W_{τ_t} is a standard Brownian motion that has realization at random times.

3. Hull and White (1987) have shown that σ_t^2 follows the solution to the univariate stochastic differential equation $d\sigma^2(t) = \nu(\sigma^2(t))\cdot dt + \kappa(\sigma^2(t))\cdot dW_{2,t}$, where $dW_{2,t}$ is a Brownian motion and $\kappa(\cdot)$ is a non-negative deterministic function.

Because h_t is unobservable, we can at most simulate it from its own stochastic process. Assume that the variance of h_t denoted by W_t is also unobservable and time-varying. Say the model can be represented as:

$$R_t = \gamma_1 + \gamma_2 h_t + \varepsilon_t \tag{7.2}$$

$$h_t = \gamma_3 + \gamma_4 h_{t-1} + \eta_t, \tag{7.3}$$

where γ_1, γ_2, γ_3, and γ_4 are unknown parameters, and ε_t, η_t are zero-mean white noise Gaussian processes with variances v_1 and v_2, respectively: ε_t IID $N(0,\ v_1)$ and η_t IID $N(0,\ v_2)$. For the time being, assume that $\text{Cov}(v_1, v_2) = 0$, an assumption that we shall relax in Section 7.1.2. This means that shocks to the two factors are uncorrelated. Eq. (7.2) is called the *measurement or observation equation* whereas Eq. (7.3) is the *state or transition equation.* In fact, Eq. (7.3) visibly displays an exquisite dynamic nature. Eqs. (7.2) and (7.3) jointly taken are called the *state-space representation of the model.* Assume that the initial values of h_0 and w_0 are given and fixed, for instance to zero and some large value (just to emphasize that h_0 is indeed unknown), respectively.

The Kalman filter exploits the assumed normality of the shocks and is organized around three steps: *filtering, forecasting, updating, and parameter estimation.* To illustrate the three steps, suppose to be at time $t-1$. In the *forecasting step,* we predict $h_{t|t-1}$, that is, the expectation of h_t conditional on the available information at time $t-1$, and $w_{t|t-1}$, that is, the expectation of w_t conditional on the available information at time $t-1$. These forecasts, that under normality of the shocks also represent optimal forecasts in a mean-squared error sense, are computed as:

$$\begin{aligned} h_{t|t-1} &= \gamma_3 + \gamma_4 h_{t-1} \\ w_{t|t-1} &= \gamma_4^2 w_{t-1} + v_2. \end{aligned} \tag{7.4}$$

The second step is the *updating* one. At time t, we have a new observation available on the observable variable, R_t; we can thus compute the *prediction error* u_t:

$$\begin{aligned} u_t &= R_t - \gamma_1 - \gamma_2 h_{t|t-1} = (\gamma_1 + \gamma_2 h_t + \varepsilon_t) - \gamma_1 - \gamma_2 h_{t|t-1} \\ &= \gamma_2(h_t - h_{t|t-1}) + \varepsilon_t. \end{aligned} \tag{7.5}$$

The variance of u_t, denoted by ψ_t, is given by:

$$\psi_t = \gamma_2^2 w_{t|t-1} + v_1. \tag{7.6}$$

At this point, we can use Eqs. (7.5) and (7.6) to update h_t and its variance w_t as follows (see Hamilton, 1994, for a proof of the optimality of these formulae):

$$\begin{aligned} h_t &= h_{t|t-1} + \frac{\gamma_2 w_{t|t-1}}{\psi_t} u_t \\ w_t &= w_{t|t-1} + \frac{(\gamma_2 w_{t|t-1})^2}{\psi_t}. \end{aligned} \tag{7.7}$$

The updating equations in Eq. (7.7) are conditionally unbiased and efficient estimators of the latent variables h_t and w_t, which then become available for a subsequent step of forecasting, based on the two formulae in Eq. (7.4). However, before proceeding, one needs to deal with *parameter estimation*: to estimate the parameters γ_1, γ_2, γ_3, γ_4, v_1, and v_2, we use the maximum likelihood method. The (partial, conditioning on given initial values h_0 and w_0) log-likelihood function can be written as:

$$\begin{aligned} \ell(\gamma_1, \gamma_2, \gamma_3, \gamma_4, v_1, v_2) &= -\frac{1}{2}\ln 2\pi - \frac{1}{2}\sum_{t=1}^{T} \ln \psi_t - \frac{1}{2}\sum_{t=1}^{T} \frac{u_t^2}{\psi_t} \\ &\propto -\frac{1}{2}\sum_{t=1}^{T} \ln(\gamma_2^2\gamma_4^2 w_{t-1} + \gamma_2^2 v_2 + v_1) - \frac{1}{2}\sum_{t=1}^{T} \frac{(R_t - \gamma_1 - \gamma_2\gamma_3 - \gamma_2\gamma_4 h_{t-1})^2}{\gamma_2^2\gamma_4^2 w_{t-1} + \gamma_2^2 v_2 + v_1}. \end{aligned} \tag{7.8}$$

The log-likelihood can be recursively evaluated by iterating the forecasting and updating steps between $t = 1$ and T. This filter, originally due to Kalman (1960), therefore returns not only estimates of the unknown parameters, but also the time series of the latent variable $\{h_t\}_{t=1}^T$, its variance $\{w_t\}_{t=1}^T$, the prediction error $\{u_t\}_{t=1}^T$, and its variance $\{\psi_t\}_{t=1}^T$, even though the modeling/prediction problem remains univariate in the sense that only a time series $\{R_t\}_{t=1}^T$ is effectively available. The operation that allows us to reconstruct the time series $\{h_t\}_{t=1}^T$, given h_0 and parameter estimates, is the *filtering step.*

7.1.2 The General Case

A linear state-space representation of the dynamics of the $N \times 1$ vector $\boldsymbol{y}_t$ is given by the system of equations:

$$\boldsymbol{y}_t = \boldsymbol{\gamma}_t + \boldsymbol{\Gamma}_t \boldsymbol{h}_t + \boldsymbol{\varepsilon}_t \tag{7.9}$$

$$\boldsymbol{h}_t = \boldsymbol{\delta}_t + \boldsymbol{\Delta}_t \boldsymbol{h}_{t-1} + \boldsymbol{\eta}_t, \tag{7.10}$$

where $\boldsymbol{h}_t$ is an $M \times 1$ vector of possibly unobserved state variables, $\boldsymbol{\gamma}_t$, $\boldsymbol{\Gamma}_t$, $\boldsymbol{\delta}_t$, and $\boldsymbol{\Delta}_t$ are conformable vectors and matrices of potentially time-varying parameters, and $\boldsymbol{\varepsilon}_t$ and $\boldsymbol{\eta}_t$ are vectors of zero mean *Gaussian disturbances*. When the parameters are themselves time-varying and random (time-variation may also be deterministic), they of course represent additional state variables. In the following, we disregard this additional source of latency in the system (7.9) and (7.10). Under the law of motion (7.10) the unobserved state vector $\boldsymbol{h}_t$ (where "h" may be interpreted to stand for "hidden") is assumed to move over time as a p-th order vector autoregression (VAR). It is often assumed that such a VAR is first-order, stationary, and ergodic by imposing the same conditions that we have discussed in Chapter 3. However, the Kalman filter is general enough to deal with the case of a nonstationary VAR model for the hidden state, for instance, when $\boldsymbol{h}_t = \boldsymbol{\delta}_t + \boldsymbol{h}_{t-1} + \boldsymbol{\eta}_t$. As early on, Eq. (7.9) represents the system of observation equations and Eq. (7.10) is the vector of state equations. We generalize the treatment in Section 7.1.1, assuming the disturbance vectors to be serially independent, with contemporaneous variance structure:

$$\boldsymbol{\Omega}_t = Var\begin{bmatrix} \boldsymbol{\varepsilon}_t \\ \boldsymbol{\eta}_t \end{bmatrix} = \begin{bmatrix} \boldsymbol{H}_t & \boldsymbol{G}_t \\ \boldsymbol{G}'_t & \boldsymbol{Q}_t \end{bmatrix}, \tag{7.11}$$

where $\boldsymbol{G}_t$ is an $N \times M$ matrix of covariances across shocks to the observation and state systems, and $\boldsymbol{H}_t$ and $\boldsymbol{Q}_t$ are the covariance matrices of the $\boldsymbol{\varepsilon}_t$ and $\boldsymbol{\eta}_t$ vectors of errors, respectively. Also, these matrices may be time-varying in either a deterministic or random fashion, even though the former case remains prevalent because it is easy to handle: for instance, some or all these matrices may depend on a vector of predetermined variables, subject to constraints to keep the matrix $\boldsymbol{\Omega}_t$ positive definite.

The first step of the Kalman filter that it is convenient to present in this general case is *forecasting*. Consider the conditional distribution of the state vector given information available at time $t-s$: we can define the mean and covariance matrix of the conditional distribution as $h_{t|t-s} \equiv E_{t-s}[h_t]$ and $P_{t|t-s} \equiv E_{t-s}[(h_t - \mathbf{h}_{t|t-s})(h_t - \mathbf{h}_{t|t-s})']$. In the case of $s = 1$, these are the one-step-ahead mean and one-step-ahead covariance matrix of the states, and standard statistical theory yields that, under our Gaussian error assumption, $\mathbf{h}_{t|t-1}$ is also the *minimum MSE estimator* of $\mathbf{h}_t$ and $\mathbf{P}_{t|t-1}$ is the MSFE of $\mathbf{h}_{t|t-1}$ interpreted as a forecast of the vector of states.[4] Given the one-step-ahead state conditional mean, we can also form the (linear) minimum MSFE one-step-ahead estimate of $\mathbf{y}_t$:

$$y_{t|t-1} \equiv E_{t-1}[y_t] = \boldsymbol{\gamma} + \boldsymbol{\Gamma}\boldsymbol{h}_{t|t-1}, \tag{7.12}$$

while the one-step-ahead prediction error is given by:

$$\varepsilon_{t|t-1} \equiv \boldsymbol{y}_t - E_{t-1}[y_t] = \boldsymbol{\Gamma}(\boldsymbol{h}_t - \boldsymbol{h}_{t|t-1}) + \varepsilon_t, \tag{7.13}$$

and the prediction error variance is given by:

$$\boldsymbol{F}_{t|t-1} \equiv Var[\varepsilon_{t|t-1}] = \boldsymbol{\Gamma} Var[\boldsymbol{h}_t - \boldsymbol{h}_{t|t-1}]\boldsymbol{\Gamma}' + Var[\varepsilon_t] = \boldsymbol{\Gamma}\boldsymbol{P}_{t|t-1}\boldsymbol{\Gamma}' + \boldsymbol{H}. \tag{7.14}$$

Given Eqs. (7.12)−(7.14), it is useful to introduce the following definitions.

DEFINITION 7.1 (Kalman filter)

The Kalman (Bucy) filter is a recursive algorithm for sequentially *updating* (also called filtering) the one-step-ahead estimate of the state mean and variance has given new information.

Given initial values for the state mean and covariance, values (either estimated or assigned) for the matrices of parameters $\boldsymbol{\gamma}$, $\boldsymbol{\Gamma}$, $\boldsymbol{\delta}$, $\boldsymbol{\Delta}$, $\boldsymbol{G}$, $\boldsymbol{H}$, $\boldsymbol{Q}$ (that we henceforth collectively indicate as $\boldsymbol{\theta}$), and time series observations on the vector $\{\mathbf{y}_t\}$ $t = 1, 2, \ldots, T$ the filter may be used to compute one-step-ahead estimates of the state and the associated mean

4. If the normality assumption is dropped, $h_{t|t-1}$ is still the minimum mean-squared linear estimator of $\mathbf{h}_t$.

square error matrix $\{h_{t|t-1}, P_{t|t-1}\}$, the contemporaneous or *filtered state mean and variance*, $\mathbf{h}_t, \mathbf{F}_t$ and the one-step-ahead prediction, prediction error, and prediction error variance, $\{\mathbf{y}_{t+1|t}, \varepsilon_{t+1|t}, \mathbf{F}_{t+1|t}\}$.[5]

Of course, to implement the Kalman filter, we must first replace any unknown elements of the system matrices by their estimates. Under the assumption that the shocks are Gaussian, the sample log-likelihood is:

$$\ell(\boldsymbol{\theta}) \propto -\frac{1}{2}\sum_{t=1}^{T}\ln|\boldsymbol{F}_{t|t-1}(\boldsymbol{\theta})| - \frac{1}{2}\sum_{t=1}^{T}(\boldsymbol{y}_t - \boldsymbol{y}_{t|t-1}(\boldsymbol{\theta}))'\boldsymbol{F}_{t|t-1}^{-1}(\boldsymbol{\theta})(\boldsymbol{y}_t - \boldsymbol{y}_{t|t-1}(\boldsymbol{\theta})), \tag{7.15}$$

where $\propto$ indicates that constant terms that do not depend on $\boldsymbol{\theta}$ have been dropped and $\boldsymbol{y}_{t|t-1}(\boldsymbol{\theta})$, and $\boldsymbol{F}_{t|t-1}(\boldsymbol{\theta})$ depend on $\boldsymbol{\theta}$ through Eqs. (7.12)–(7.14) and may be evaluated using the Kalman filter. Using numeric derivatives, standard iterative techniques may be employed to maximize the log-likelihood with respect to the unknown parameters. As always, evaluation of the Kalman filter and forecasting all require that we provide the initial one-step-ahead predicted values for the states and covariance matrix, $\mathbf{h}_{1|0}$ and $\mathbf{P}_{1|0}$. In some cases, when the model is stationary, steady-state conditions for the system allow us to use the estimated vectors and matrices to solve for the optimal $\mathbf{h}_{1|0}$ and $\mathbf{P}_{1|0}$, that therefore become matrices of parameter estimates themselves. Of course, for sufficiently long-time series, and because of stationarity and ergodicity of the model (when this is either imposed in estimation or verified ex-post), the initial values of $\mathbf{h}_{1|0}$ and $\mathbf{P}_{1|0}$ progressively lose importance and stop affecting both the parameter estimates and the predictions from the model.

Eqs. (7.12)–(7.14) are naturally extended to compute H-period ahead predictions, as:

$$\boldsymbol{y}_{t+H|t} \equiv E_t[\boldsymbol{y}_{t+H}] = \boldsymbol{\gamma}_t + \boldsymbol{\Gamma}_t\boldsymbol{h}_{t+H|t}, \tag{7.16}$$

$$\boldsymbol{F}_{t+H|t} = \boldsymbol{\Gamma}_t\boldsymbol{P}_{t+H|t}\boldsymbol{\Gamma}'_t + \boldsymbol{H}_t, \tag{7.17}$$

where $h_{t+H|t}$ and $P_{t+H|t}$ carry obvious definitions. Importantly, these predictions of the MSE matrix do not account for the additional variability introduced in the estimation of any unknown parameters. Therefore, $F_{t+H|t}$ will understate the true variability of the forecast and should be viewed as being computed conditional on the specific value of the estimated parameters.[6]

7.2 SIMPLE STOCHASTIC VOLATILITY MODELS AND THEIR ESTIMATION USING THE KALMAN FILTER

In this section, we introduce a rather basic and yet powerful SVM and illustrate how the Kalman filter techniques surveyed in Section 7.1 can be used to address estimation and prediction issues.

7.2.1 The Economics of Stochastic Volatility: The Normal Mixture Model

APT contends that asset prices reflect the discounted value of future expected cash flows, implying that all news relevant for either discount rates or cash flows should induce a shift in market prices. Since economic news items appear almost continuously, this perspective rationalizes the ever-changing nature of financial prices. The process linking news arrivals to price changes may be complex, but if it is stationary in a statistical sense, it will yield a robust relationship between news arrivals, market activity, and return volatility. However, if the number of news arrivals is very large, a standard central limit theory implies that asset returns are approximately normally distributed conditional on the news count. Therefore, specifications such as $R_t|S_t \sim N(\mu S_t, \sigma^2 S_t)$ may be used, where for simplicity we focus immediately on asset returns (but also yields, yield changes, or currency rates may be modeled in the same way) and S_t is a positive intensity process reflecting the rate of news arrivals. This is a *normal mixture model*, where the S_t process governs or "mixes" the scale of the distribution across periods. For instance, Clark (1973) used the trading volume as a proxy for the activity variable, a choice motivated by the high contemporaneous correlation between return volatility and volume.

5. Related quantities are the *smoothed* estimates of the states, of their covariance matrix, and as a result of the observable variables (and the associated smoothed errors). Smoothing uses all of the information in the sample $t = 1, 2, \ldots, T$ to provide estimates, such as $h_{t|T} \equiv E_T[h_t]$, $P_{t|T} \equiv E_T[(h_t - \boldsymbol{h}_{t|T})(h_t - \boldsymbol{h}_{t|T})']$, $y_{t|T} = \gamma + \boldsymbol{\Gamma}\boldsymbol{h}_{t|T}$, $\varepsilon_{t|T} = \boldsymbol{\Gamma}(\boldsymbol{h}_t - \boldsymbol{h}_{t|T})$, and $\boldsymbol{F}_{t|T} = \boldsymbol{\Gamma}\boldsymbol{P}_{t|T}\boldsymbol{\Gamma}'$. Lastly the smoothing procedure allows us to compute smoothed disturbance estimates and a corresponding smoothed disturbance covariance matrix.

6. Alternatively, we can compute *smoothed forecasts* which use all available observable data over the forecast sample. These forward-looking forecasts may be computed by initializing the states at the start of the forecast period, and performing "Kalman smoothing" over the entire forecast period using all relevant signal data. This technique is useful in settings where information on the entire path of the signals is used to interpolate values throughout the forecast sample.

If S_t is constant, the mixture model degenerates to a simple Gaussian IID process for returns which—as we know from previous chapters—is clearly at odds with the empirical evidence. Therefore, S_t is typically assumed to follow a separate (subordinated) stochastic process with random innovations. Hence, in each period the return series is subject to two separate shocks, namely the usual idiosyncratic error associated with the (normal) return distribution, and also a shock to the variance or volatility process, S_t. This endows the return process with genuine SV, reflecting the random intensity of news arrivals. Moreover, it is typically assumed that only returns, transactions, and quotes are observable, but not the actual value of S_t itself, implying that the variance/diffusion process σ^2 cannot be separately identified. Because it cannot be identified, it is typical to set σ^2 at unity.

As shown in Clark (1973), the time variation in the information flow series induces a fat-tailed unconditional distribution, consistent with the stylized facts for financial returns described in Chapters 5 and 6: intuitively, days with many news display more rapid price fluctuations and trading activity than days with a low news count. In addition, if the S_t process is positively serially correlated, then shocks to the conditional mean and variance processes for returns will be persistent. This is consistent with the observed clustering in financial markets, where return volatility and trading activity are contemporaneously correlated and each displays pronounced positive serial dependence.

The structural randomness and unobserved nature of the news arrival process makes the true mean and variance series latent. As already discussed, this property of SV is the major difference with the ARCH class, in which the one-step-ahead conditional mean and variance are known functions of observed variables at time t. As such, for genuine SV models, we must distinguish the full, but infeasible, information set in which $S_t \in \Im_t$ and the observable information set that does not include the news signal, S_t. The fact that econometricians typically perform estimation using the second, smaller information set causes filtering and smoothing of the unobservable S_t to be of technical interest, and tools exist to deal with it, for instance the Kalman filtering approach discussed in Section 7.1.

7.2.2 One Benchmark Case: The Log-Normal Two-Factor Stochastic Volatility Model

For concreteness, we follow the seminal paper by Harvey and Shephard (1996) and consider the following, simple differential equation for the logarithm of the price ($P(t)$) of an asset of interest:

$$d \ln P(t) = \frac{dP(t)}{P(t)} = \mu \cdot dt + \sigma(t) dz_{1,t}, \tag{7.18}$$

where the shock $dz_{1,t}$ is standard IID normal. For short horizon returns, μS_t from Clark's mixture model will be nearly negligible and can reasonably be fixed at a constant value. A simple discretization then delivers:

$$R_t \equiv \Delta \ln P(t) = \mu + \sigma_t dz_{1,t}, \tag{7.19}$$

where $R(t)$ indicates a continuously compounded return (defined as the difference in logarithmic prices at two adjacent points) and $dz_{1,t}$ is a standardized random shock with zero mean and unit variance such that $E_{t-1}[R_t] = E[R_t] = \mu$ and $Var_{t-1}[R_t] = \sigma_t^2$. In line with typical finance applications, assume that the process followed by the log-conditional variance is:

$$h_t \equiv \ln \sigma_t^2 = \gamma_1 + \gamma_2 h_{t-1} + dz_{2,t}, \quad dz_{2,t} \text{ IID } N(0, \sigma_{z2}^2), \tag{7.20}$$

for $|\gamma_2| < 1$ (γ_2 is generally found to be positive in empirical applications). This implies that $\sigma_t = \exp(0.5h_t)$ and that the long-run log-variance is $\gamma_1/(1 - \gamma_2)$. Although the assumption of normality of log-variance may seem ad hoc at first sight, Andersen et al. (2003) have shown that empirically the log-variance process can be well approximated by a normal distribution (we shall return to this empirical fact in Chapter 10). If $\sigma_{z2}^2 = 0$, the model is not identified. γ_2 is a measure of persistence of the log-variance process; when γ_2 is close to 1 and σ_{z2}^2 is close to 0, the evolution of variance over time is very smooth; in the limit, if $\gamma_1 \to 1$, $\gamma_2 \to 1$, and $\sigma_{z2}^2 \to 0$, variance is constant over time. Eqs. (7.19) and (7.20) make it clear why we may refer to this SVM as a *two-factor model*: there are two shocks, two random drivers of asset returns:

- $dz_{1,t}$ which enters directly in the model, in a conditionally linear fashion.
- $dz_{2,t}$ which enters instead through the (transformed, nonlinear) process for the multiplicative factor σ_t that appears in Eq. (7.20).

Sometimes Eqs. (7.19) and (7.20) are called the *log-normal, two-factor SVM* or the autoregressive SVM, ARSV(1) model. This model is in fact close to the discrete-time SVM originally introduced by Taylor (1986).

Taylor (2008) proves that the process for the continuously compounded returns is a martingale difference; that if $|\gamma_2| < 1$, then the entire model is stationary and in this case, the log-run, unconditional variance of continuously compounded returns is given by:

$$\overline{\sigma}^2 = \exp\left[\frac{1}{2}\frac{\sigma_{z2}^2}{1-\gamma_2^2}\right]. \tag{7.21}$$

While the model is clearly symmetric and returns display zero skewness (but see below for an extended version that deals with this limitation), the unconditional kurtosis of returns is:

$$Kurt(R_t) = Kurt(dz_{1t})\exp\left[\frac{\sigma_{z2}^2}{1-\gamma_2^2}\right], \tag{7.22}$$

where $Kurt(dz_{1t})$ is the kurtosis of the marginal distribution of the log-price shocks, for example, $Kurt(R_t) = 3\exp\left[\sigma_{z2}^2/(1-\gamma_2^2)\right]$ in the log-normal case, and $\exp\left[\sigma_{z2}^2/(1-\gamma_2^2)\right]$ is the coefficient of variation of the log-variance process. Therefore, if $Kurt(dz_{1t})$ is finite, the kurtosis of returns exists if $|\gamma_2| < 1$ and by construction $Kurt(R_t) > Kurt(dz_{1t})$, as one would expect of SVM: the model creates arbitrarily thick tails. Therefore, as long as the model is stationary, the dynamic evolution of the volatility does not need to be further restricted to guarantee the existence of the fourth order moment. This is to be contrasted with what we have reported in Chapter 5, where we saw that in the case of models in the ARCH family, strong parametric restrictions on the conditional heteroskedasticity (CH) process need to be imposed for kurtosis to exist. The decomposition in Eq. (7.22), first noted by Clark (1973), shows that there are two ways to accommodate well documented leptokurtic features of financial time series: either contemplating probability distributions for the standardized innovations with a large kurtosis coefficient, or specifying a volatility process with a large coefficient of variation.

Finally, even though in this model returns are uncorrelated, they are far from an independent sequence because, as always with CH models, the dynamics of the series appear in the squared returns. Their autocorrelation function can be shown to be:

$$Corr(R_t^2, R_{t-\tau}^2) = \frac{\exp[(\sigma_{z2}^2/(1-\gamma_2^2))\gamma_2^\tau] - 1}{Kurt(dz_{1t})\exp[(\sigma_{z2}^2/1-\gamma_2^2)] - 1} \quad \tau = 1, 2, \ldots \tag{7.23}$$

Even though the expression in Eq. (7.23) shows that this is technically not completely correct, γ_2 tends to be considered the coefficient driving the persistence of the autocorrelations of squared returns.

Although it is rather common to assume that all the errors have a normal distribution, there are examples of SVMs based on heavy-tailed distributions for price shocks, see for example, Mahieu and Schotman (1998). However, and differently from ARCH, even when the shocks are assumed to be Gaussian, the distribution of time t returns conditional on past observations up to time $t-1$ is not normal, because the stochastic model for log-variance provides a mixture of normal distribution (see Chapter 9 for a definition) in the log-price equation, that is, a weighted sum of normal densities, with random weights.

To simplify the algebra, it is now useful to linearize the first stochastic difference equation (SDE). Assume that $\mu = 0$ (which is an empirically plausible assumption for high-frequency data, for instance for daily series) so that the model in Eq. (7.19) becomes:

$$R_t = \exp(0.5h_t)dz_{1,t}, \tag{7.24}$$

which implies

$$\ln R_t^2 = h_t + \ln(dz_{1,t})^2. \tag{7.25}$$

The distribution of $\ln(dz_{1,t})^2$ is therefore a logarithmic χ^2 distribution with 1 degree of freedom and therefore with an expectation of -1.27. Therefore, we can write Eq. (7.25) as:

$$\begin{aligned}\ln R_t^2 &= \gamma_0 + E[\ln(dz_{1,t})^2] + h_t + \underbrace{(\ln(dz_{1,t})^2 - E[\ln(dz_{1,t})^2])}_{v_t} \\ &= (\gamma_0 - 1.27) + h_t + v_t,\end{aligned} \tag{7.26}$$

where γ_0 is a small sample correction that can be dropped for large estimation samples, and v_t is a zero mean χ^2 shock with 1 degree of freedom such that $Var[v_t] = 0.5\pi^2 \simeq 4.93$ (see Broto and Ruiz, 2004). Eventually, the equation system that we want to estimate is the following:

$$\begin{aligned} \ln R_t^2 &= (\gamma_0 - 1.27) + h_t + v_t \quad v_t \text{ IID } \chi_1^2 \\ h_t &= \gamma_1 + \gamma_2 h_{t-1} + dz_{2,t} \quad dz_{2,t} \text{ IID } N(0, \sigma_{z2}^2) \end{aligned} \quad (7.27)$$

This linearized model is non-Gaussian due to the long left tail of $\ln R_t^2$, which generates outliers when squared returns are small. For the time being, also assume that v_t and $dz_{2,t}$ are uncorrelated, that is, shocks to the variance of returns carry no information on shocks to the level of the same.

The two equations in Eq. (7.27) are now in appropriate form for the Kalman filter presented in Section 7.1 to be applied, subject to an approximation:[7] the first is the measurement equation, since the variable $\ln R_t^2$ is observed; the second equation is the state or the transition equation, since h_t, the log-variance state variable, is not observed. Note that both the log-squared returns and the log-variance of returns are driven by two stochastic shocks, v_t and $z_{2,t}$ so that the model for asset returns and their variance in Eq. (7.27) is a *two-factor SVM*. The following example shows how this model, and therefore the Kalman filter, may be implemented on actual, relevant data.

EXAMPLE 7.1

Consider a comparison between the SVM in Eq. (7.27) and a standard GARCH(1,1) model, similar to the one used in Chapter 5, both estimated on US value-weighted Center for Research in Security Prices (CRSP) total stock returns over a 1963–2016 daily sample. Quasi-maximum likelihood (QML) estimation in EViews of the SVM (the initial state, here represented by log-variance, is solved to be −1.92, simply exploiting the AR(1) nature of the state equation) when v_t IID χ_t^2 is replaced by a v_t IID $N(0, 4.935)$ approximation yields (*P*-values are computed using the estimated Hessian matrix and are in parenthesis):

$$\begin{aligned} \ln R_t^2 &= (\underset{(0.998)}{-0.005} - 1.27) + h_t + v_t \quad v_t \text{ IID } N(0, 4.935) \\ h_t &= \underset{(0.716)}{-0.004} + \underset{(0.000)}{0.993} h_{t-1} + dz_{2,t} \quad dz_{2,t} \text{ IID } N(0, \exp(\underset{(0.000)}{-4.629})). \end{aligned}$$

The estimators are of QML type because they derive from maximizing a quasi log-likelihood function that approximates—by replacing χ^2 shocks in the first equation with normal disturbances—the true log-likelihood. Interestingly the model is covariance stationary: a Wald test of the null hypothesis $\gamma_2 = 1$ is rejected with a *p*-value of 0.001. On the same data, maximum likelihood (ML) estimation of a plain vanilla Gaussian GARCH(1,1) model gives (*p*-values are in parenthesis):

$$\begin{aligned} R_{t+1} &= \underset{(0.000)}{0.065} + \sigma_{t+1|t} dz_{1,t+1} \quad dz_{1,t+1} \text{ IID } N(0,1) \\ \sigma_{t+1|t}^2 &= \underset{(0.000)}{0.008} + \underset{(0.000)}{0.090} \sigma_{t|t-1}^2 (dz_{1,t})^2 + \underset{(0.000)}{0.904} \sigma_{t|t-1}^2. \end{aligned}$$

Interestingly the implied GARCH persistence is almost identical to the one found in the case of the SVM, 0.994 (but the latter refers to the latent SV $h_t = \ln \sigma_t^2$); also in this case, however, we can reject the null of a unit persistence, that is, of an IGARCH (1,1) model. The leftmost panel of Fig. 7.1 compares the one-step-ahead volatility from the GARCH model with a transformation of the filtered state obtained through the Kalman filter, that is, $\sigma_t = \exp(0.5 h_t)$. The right panel compares instead predicted and smoothed volatility derived from the SVM.

The right panel shows that whether the latent state variable in the SVM is smoothed or predicted one-day ahead makes some visible difference, even though the most striking aspect is that, at least in the SVM estimated in this example, Black Monday on October 19, 1987 is not entirely picked up as a high volatility spike, or at least not as the highest spike ever occurred, contrary to some related literature (see, e.g., Ineichen, 2000).

Finally, Fig. 7.2 compares the observed values of the log-squared S&P 500 index returns with the fitted values from the model (the two dashed curves around predicted variance from the model represent the 95% confidence interval, although only the upper bound of the confidence interval may be visible). Even though in this case the fitted series is just a downward shifted version of the latent volatility state, such a plot is less interesting in the same way in which in an ARCH model it would not be that revealing to look at the plot of past squared residuals (or their weighted average).

7. Fridman and Harris (1998) proposed an ML estimator that evaluates the likelihood function directly by means of a recursive numerical integration procedure useful for non-Gaussian filtering problems. This method can be considered as an extended Kalman filter. However, such methods are characterized by slow computational convergence.

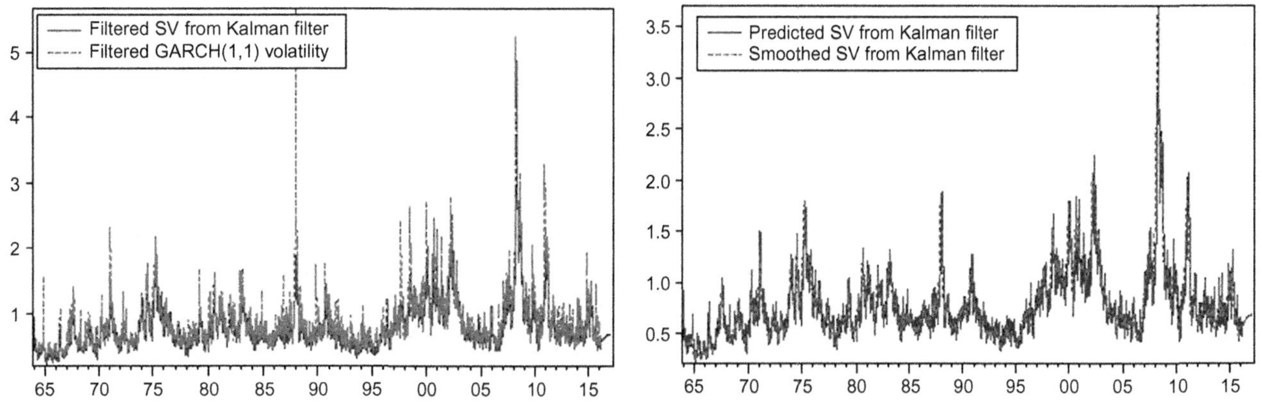

FIGURE 7.1 Comparing volatility filtered and smoothed from an SVM versus GARCH(1,1) filtered volatility.

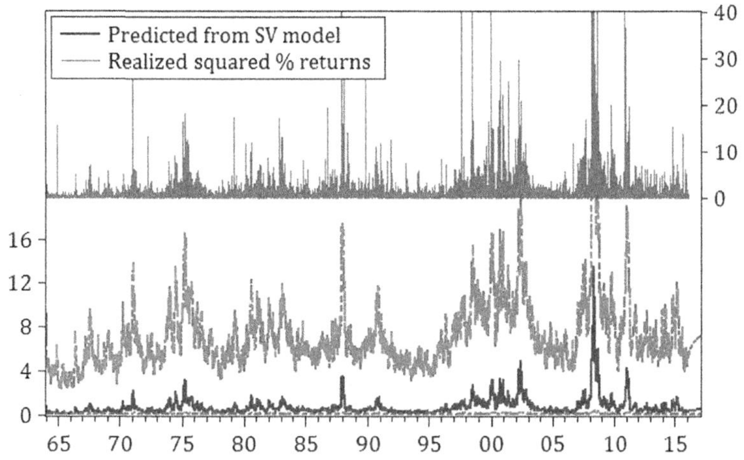

FIGURE 7.2 Observed and fitted log-squared S&P 500 returns.

Ruiz (1994) shows that the QML estimator applied to Eq. (7.25), when υ_t IID χ^2_1 is replaced by υ_t IID $N(0, 4.935)$, is consistent and asymptotically normal. However, the QML procedure is inefficient, as the method does not rely on the exact likelihood of $\ln R_t^2$. The approximation may occasionally be poor because, when returns are very close to 0, the log-squared transformation yields large negative numbers. To solve this (so-called inlier) problem, Broto and Ruiz (2004) suggest the following modification of the log-squared transformation:

$$\ln\left(R_t^2 + \tau\widehat{Var}[R_t]\right) - \frac{\tau\widehat{Var}[R_t]}{R_t^2 + \tau\widehat{Var}[R_t]}, \tag{7.28}$$

where $\widehat{Var}[R_t]$ is the sample variance of returns and τ a small constant commonly set to 0.02. The following example extends Example 7.1 when the adjustment in Eq. (7.28) is applied.

EXAMPLE 7.2

We perform afresh QML estimation of the autoregressive stochastic volatility (ARSV(1)) model in Eq. (7.27) already performed in Example 7.1, when squared returns are adjusted as in Eq. (7.28). In this case, the initial log-variance state is solved to be −1.56 and the estimated model is:

$$\ln\left(R_t^2 + \tau\widehat{Var}[R_t]\right) - \frac{\tau\widehat{Var}[R_t]}{R_t^2 + \tau\widehat{Var}[R_t]} = \left(\underset{(0.982)}{0.040} - 1.27\right) + h_t + \upsilon_t, \quad \upsilon_t \text{ IID } N(0, 4.935)$$

$$h_t = -\underset{(0.807)}{0.002} + \underset{(0.000)}{0.997}\, h_{t-1} + dz_{1,t}, \quad dz_{1,t} \text{ IID } N\left(0, \exp\left(-\underset{(0.000)}{5.660}\right)\right).$$

In fact, the adjustment seems to make some small difference to the estimates, as the process for the latent log-variance becomes more persistent but less volatile (which is to be expected, when large negative outliers are removed).

Of course, also in the light of the empirical and predictive evidence reported in Chapter 5, it is natural to wonder why an asymmetric GARCH model, for instance a simple threshold GARCH(1,1), may not be a more sensible benchmark. In order for this intuition to make sense, we shall modify the SVM in Eq. (7.13) to remove one restrictive assumption we have held up to this point: that the two factors (shocks) driving asset returns, and therefore their squares, are simultaneously uncorrelated. For instance, it is empirically plausible that when a large shock to $dz_{1,t}$ generates large positive or negative asset returns (hence a large squared shock υ_t), it becomes more likely (in a linear sense, i.e., in a regression of $dz_{2,t}$ on υ_t) that also shocks driving the time-varying variance of $dz_{2,t}$ are large. For instance, as shown in Chapter 2, for the US case, in many developed countries the realized inflation dynamics between the 1970s and the 1980s has delivered us time series of government bond yields that feature high volatility when interest rates were higher (in general before the early 1990s), so that volatility clustering is stronger exactly when the shocks to nominal rates were generally larger, both when rates were climbing up and later, when inflation was reabsorbed and rates started to decline.

Following Harvey and Shephard (1996), it is very simple to modify the SVM in Eq. (7.27) to take such commonalities between shocks into account: it is enough to add a new parameter ρ to capture just such correlation,

$$\begin{aligned} \ln R_t^2 &= (\gamma_0 - 1.27) + h_t + \upsilon_t, \quad \upsilon_t \text{ IID } \chi_1^2 \\ h_t &= \gamma_1 + \gamma_2 h_{t-1} + dz_{2,t}, \quad dz_{2,t} \text{ IID } N(0, \sigma_{z_2}^2), \quad \rho = Cov[\upsilon_t, dz_{2,t}]. \end{aligned} \tag{7.29}$$

Essentially, Eq. (7.27) is then a restricted version of Eq. (7.29) in which $\rho = 0$ has been imposed. Should $\rho < 0$ be estimated, this would give a form of *leverage effect*: because we recall that the first stochastic equation in Eq. (7.27) is implied by $R_t \equiv \Delta \ln P(t) = \mu + \sigma_t dz_{1,t}$ in Eq. (7.19), when shocks to latent log-variance are positive (negative) and variance increases (declines), this tends to correlate with negative (positive) shocks to asset returns.

EXAMPLE 7.3

We extend Example 7.1 to the estimation of the model in Eq. (7.29) and compare results with the symmetric, uncorrelated two-factor SVM in Eq. (7.27):

$$\begin{aligned} \ln R_t^2 &= (\underset{(0.998)}{-0.022} - 1.27) + h_t + \upsilon_t, \quad \upsilon_t \text{ IID } N(0, 4.935) \\ h_t &= \underset{(0.944)}{-0.004} + \underset{(0.000)}{0.994}\, h_{t-1} + dz_{2,t}, \quad dz_{2,t} \text{ IID } N(0, \exp(\underset{(0.000)}{-4.562})), \quad \hat{\rho} = \underset{(0.025)}{0.143}. \end{aligned}$$

This model yields a maximized log-likelihood of −30,535.9, which exceeds by 2.6 the maximized log-likelihood of −30,538.5 obtained in Example 7.1. Indeed, the Hannan–Quinn information criterion (modestly) values the additional parameter represented by ρ, because it is 4.50117 in the case of the asymmetric, five-parameter SVM and 4.50122 in the case of the simpler, symmetric four-parameter SVM of Example 7.1. Fig. 7.3 performs a comparison between the 1-day-ahead predicted latent volatility from the two SVMs in Eqs. (7.27) and (7.29). Clearly, the differences are rather small and rarely visible, which intuitively derives from the fact that, albeit significant, the QML estimate of ρ turns out to be rather small.

Even though the series of the 1-day predicted variances obtained from the Kalman filter seem to be very close independently of whether asymmetries are taken into account or not, one wonders whether any of the two models may predict squared returns better than the other or, for that matter, better than a simple GARCH(1,1), with or without threshold effects. To test whether this is the case, we perform the standard predictive regressions introduced in Chapter 5:

$$R_{t+1}^2 = \underset{(0.084)}{-1.710} + \underset{(0.098)}{3.410} \exp(0.5 h_{t+1|t}^{SV}) + e_{t+1|t} \quad R^2 = 8.14\%.$$

In this case, even without formal tests, it is clear that the intercept is significantly negative and that the slope significantly exceeds 1. Therefore, SVM forecasts are biased and inefficient. Matters are hardly better when an SVM that incorporates asymmetries is selected:

$$R_{t+1}^2 = \underset{(0.085)}{-1.709} + \underset{(0.091)}{3.382} \exp(0.5 h_{t+1|t}^{SV,\,Asy}) + e_{t+1|t} \quad R^2 = 8.04\%.$$

Finally, as it has occasionally been reported in the forecasting literature, a plain vanilla GARCH(1,1) outperforms both SVMs:

$$R_{t+1}^2 = \underset{(0.038)}{0.127} + \underset{(0.019)}{0.851} (\sigma_{t+1|t}^{GARCH})^2 + e_{t+1|t} \quad R^2 = 13.13\%.$$

Fig. 7.4 shows how different the variance forecasts from GARCH and SVMs can be.

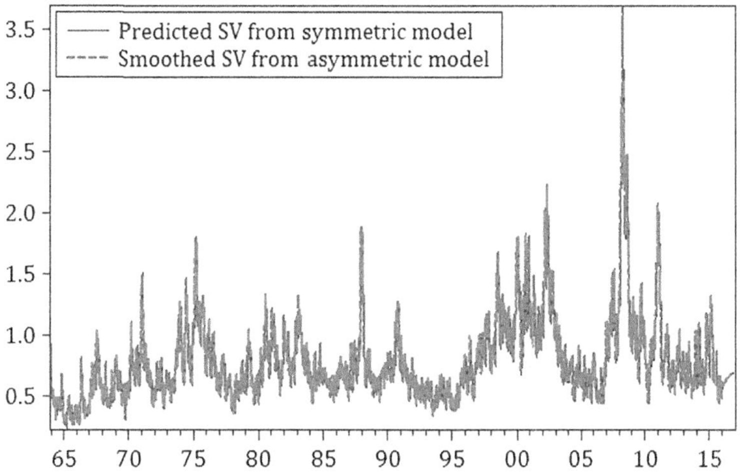

FIGURE 7.3 Comparing 1-day-ahead predicted variance from two alternative SVMs.

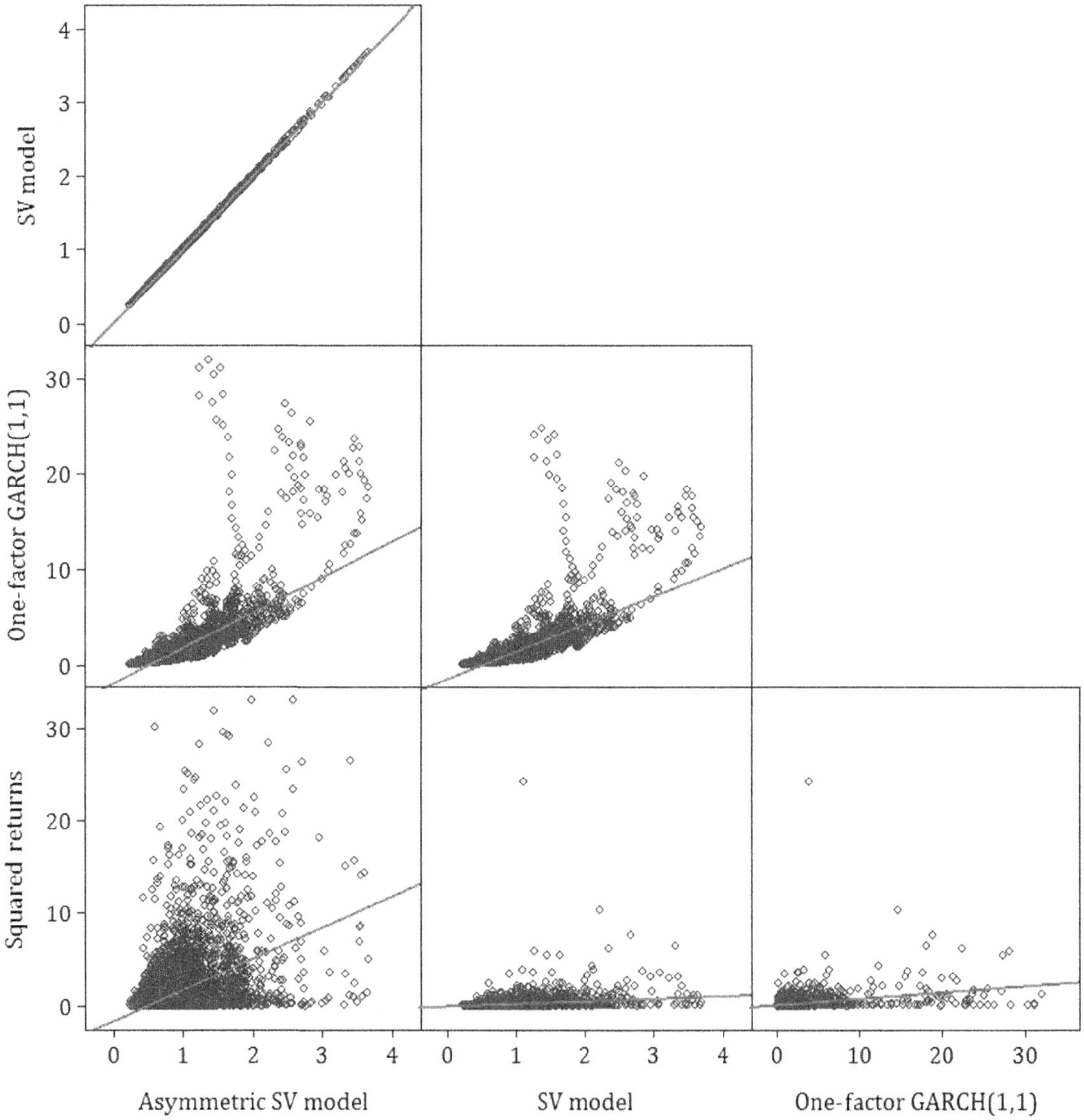

FIGURE 7.4 One-day-ahead predicted variance from three models.

One final extension of the ARSV model in Eq. (7.27) consists of incorporating *"SV-in mean" effects*, following the intuition in Koopman and Hol-Uspensky (2002), in which a third equation relating returns to stochastic log-variance is introduced:

$$\begin{aligned} \ln R_t^2 &= (\gamma_0 - 1.27) + h_t + \upsilon_t \quad \upsilon_t \text{ IID } \chi_1^2 \\ h_t &= \gamma_1 + \gamma_2 h_{t-1} + dz_{2,t} \quad dz_{2,t} \text{ IID } N(0, \sigma_{z2}^2), \quad \rho = Cov[\upsilon_t, dz_{2,t}] \\ R_t &= \gamma_3 + \gamma_4 h_t + \exp(0.5h_t) dz_{1,t}, \end{aligned} \tag{7.30}$$

where γ_4 measures the impact of log-variance on expected returns. As already commented in Chapter 5, this represents a stylized way to capture a volatility feedback effect. Of course, it is the need to use a linear Kalman filter that "advises us" to relate stock returns not to latent return variance or volatility but to log-variance, with the result that the standard interpretation of γ_4 as a coefficient of relative risk aversion does not apply. Moreover, it is clear that the first and third equations may be inconsistent with each other because in general $\ln[\gamma_3 + \gamma_4 h_t + \exp(0.5h_t)dz_{1,t}]^2$ is not the same as $\gamma_0 + h_t + \ln(dz_{1,t})^2$ (implicitly the link between $dz_{1,t}$ and υ_t is broken). Therefore one alternative strategy foresees the estimation of:

$$\begin{aligned} R_t &= \gamma_3 + \gamma_4 h_t + dz_{1,t} \quad dz_{1,t} \text{ IID } N(0, \exp(h_t)) \\ h_t &= \gamma_1 + \gamma_2 h_{t-1} + dz_{2,t} \quad dz_{2,t} \text{ IID } N(0, \sigma_{z2}^2), \quad \rho = Cov[dz_{1,t}, dz_{2,t}]. \end{aligned} \tag{7.31}$$

This model is linear, it imposes no approximation, and therefore it can be estimated by full MLE, supplemented by the Kalman filter. However, it is a purely empirical model un-hinged from the martingale APT that had originally led to the SVM in Eq. (7.27). The following example shows a few of the difficulties arising from these facts.

EXAMPLE 7.4

Using again US CRSP total stock returns over a 1963–2016 daily sample, QML estimation of the SVM in Eq. (7.30) (initial log-variance is solved to be −0.66 by exploiting the AR(1) nature of the state equation) when υ_t IID χ_1^2 is replaced by a υ_t IID $N(0, 4.935)$ approximation, we obtain (p-values computed using the estimated Hessian and are in parenthesis):

$$\begin{aligned} \ln R_t^2 &= (\underset{(0.976)}{-0.005} - 1.27) + h_t + \upsilon_t \quad \upsilon_t \text{ IID } N(0, 4.935) \\ h_t &= \underset{(0.086)}{-0.002} + \underset{(0.000)}{0.997}\, h_{t-1} + dz_{2,t} \quad dz_{2,t} \text{ IID } N(0, \exp(\underset{(0.000)}{-4.673})), \quad \widehat{\rho} = \underset{(0.000)}{-0.474} \\ R_t &= \underset{(0.775)}{-0.003} - \underset{(0.000)}{0.075}\, h_t + \exp(0.5h_t) dz_{1,t}. \end{aligned}$$

Interestingly, when a direct "SV-in mean" channel is considered, the correlation between variance and return shocks becomes stronger, in the sense of turning more negative. This seems to indicate that both large expected (from the second equation, given its high and precisely estimated persistence coefficient of 0.997) variance increases, and large unexpected shocks to variance are associated with lower stock returns, which is a classical leverage effect. Of course, such negative associations will cause asymmetries by allowing SV to inflate the left tail of the unconditional density of returns more than the right tail. Additionally, because the sample mean of the smoothed state h_t is negative (−0.625), the unconditional expected return turns out to be 0.044% per day, that is, approximately 11.8% per year, which is in fact close to the historical mean of these data. Interestingly the persistence of the log-variance process is even higher than what had been estimated in Example 7.3.

The maximized pseudo log-likelihood in this case is −49,587.5, with a Hannan–Quinn information criterion of 7.2965. One wonders whether, given the evidence of a negative estimated coefficient γ_4, it is really necessary to allow the shocks to prices and the log-variance to be correlated. We therefore proceed to reestimate the model after restricting $\rho = 0$:

$$\begin{aligned} \ln R_t^2 &= (\underset{(0.978)}{0.025} - 1.27) + h_t + \upsilon_t \quad \upsilon_t \text{ IID } N(0, 4.935) \\ h_t &= \underset{(0.456)}{-0.005} + \underset{(0.000)}{0.993} h_{t-1} + dz_{2,t} \quad dz_{2,t} \text{ IID } N(0, \exp(\underset{(0.000)}{-4.541})) \\ R_t &= \underset{(0.745)}{0.013} - \underset{(0.000)}{0.046} h_t + \exp(0.5h_t) dz_{1,t}. \end{aligned}$$

The maximized pseudo log-likelihood is −49,620.3, to which we can associate a Hannan–Quinn criterion of 7.3023. The fact that the maximized log-likelihood is significantly lower and the information criterion higher, indicates that the $\rho = 0$ restriction can be rejected.

Finally, we also estimate the version of the model in Eq. (7.31), obtaining:

$$\begin{aligned} R_t &= \underset{(0.692)}{0.061} + \underset{(0.874)}{0.242}\, h_t + dz_{1,t} \quad dz_{1,t} \text{ IID } N(0, \exp(h_t)) \\ h_t &= \underset{(0.873)}{-0.031} + \underset{(0.040)}{0.575}\, h_{t-1} + dz_{2,t} \quad dz_{2,t} \text{ IID } N(0, \exp(\underset{(0.817)}{-2.898})). \end{aligned}$$

(Continued)

EXAMPLE 7.4 (Continued)

Unfortunately, this model leads to ML coefficient estimates (in this case no approximation is applied) that are mostly not significant.

Fig. 7.5 shows that in the perspective of computing forecasts of 1-day-ahead volatility, the difference between imposing $\rho = 0$ or not is modest, even though this becomes rather visible in correspondence to a few major volatility spikes, in particular in September 2008.

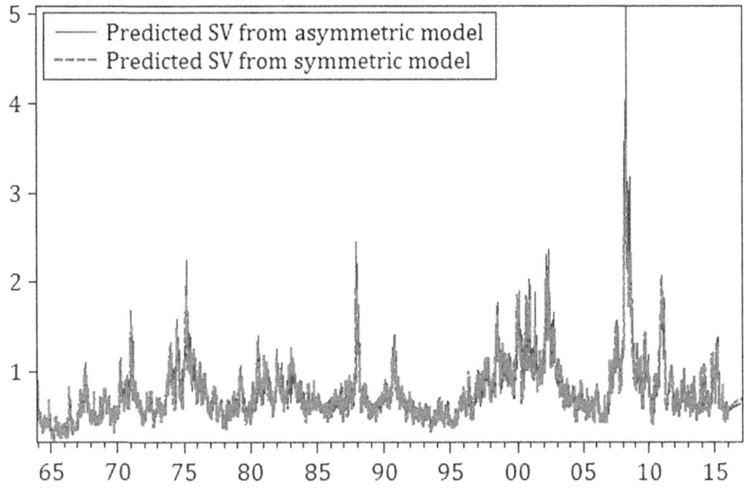

FIGURE 7.5 Comparing 1-day-ahead predicted variance from two alternative SVMs.

So far, we have tackled all of our estimation problems by (quasi) maximum likelihood methods. The QML feature derives from the fact that often—for instance, when going from Eq. (7.27) to the Gaussian model actually estimated in Examples 7.1–7.4—we approximate highly non-Gaussian shocks with normal ones. As explained in Chapter 5, inference is valid as long as the standard errors are appropriately adjusted. One major drawback of the Kalman filter approach is that the finite sample properties can be quite poor because the error terms are highly non-Gaussian, as shown by Andersen et al. (1999). One additional limitation of the Kalman filter is that it requires the existence of an explicit transition density transforming the vector of states into observables, like in Eq. (7.27). However, the majority of empirically relevant continuous-time models do not possess explicit transition densities and alternative approaches to evaluate the log-likelihood may be necessary.[8] Even though an extensive review of all the techniques that have been developed to overcome this limitation is out of the scope of this book, the reader finds a short overview of the approaches that have become popular in the literature.

- *Inverse-mapping.* A simple and popular approach is to invert the mapping between the state vector and a subset of the observables, assuming that the model prices specific securities exactly. In applications to equity markets, this has been done, for example, by assuming that one option contract is priced without error; in applications to fixed income markets it is sometimes stipulated that certain bonds (e.g., for a subset of maturities) are priced without error. This approach yields an estimate for the latent variables through an inverse-mapping that transforms known prices into latent quantities. Of course, such a state vector inversion procedure requires ad hoc assumptions regarding the choice of the securities that are error-free vis-a-vis those observed with error.
- *Generalized method of moments (GMM).* Starting with Taylor (1982), some researchers have estimated their models using the (generalized) *method of moments*. As already commented in Chapter 5, a primary attraction of this method is that it is well suited for identifying and estimating volatility models without a complete parametric specification of the probability distribution involved. However, a difficulty with using moment-based estimators for continuous-time

8. Lo (1988) has warned that the common approach of estimating parameters of an Ito process by applying maximum likelihood to a discretization of the stochastic differential equation yields inconsistent estimators. In contrast, he characterizes the likelihood function as a solution to a partial differential equation.

SVMs is that it is not always straightforward to compute the moments. As usual, (generalized) method of moments estimators tend to display poor finite sample properties, and their efficiency is suboptimal with respect to ML methods. As it is natural, the quality of (finite sample) GMM inferences is sensitive to both the choice of the number of moments to include and the exact choice of moments. Furthermore, the GMM criterion surface—the objective computed as a weighted sum of the selected moments to measure how these are empirically matched for a given set of estimates—for the ARSV(1) model is often highly irregular. Therefore, optimization may fail to converge, especially for small sample sizes. Even though it is always the case that under appropriate conditions GMM delivers asymptotically efficient estimators, because our interest often lies in estimating the latent volatility series at every time period, asymptotic arguments are of limited value. An estimator of variance does not converge to the true unobserved state variable as the sample size diverges: the Kalman filter produces the best linear estimator of h_t, but if the innovations to the SDE of log-squared returns are non-normal, accurate estimation of the time series of volatilities would require the entire conditional distribution of h_t, given the data and the parameters. Finally, given that GMM estimators do not generate estimates of the latent volatilities, other procedures as, for example, the Kalman filter should be used to make inference on them, which is often awkward.

- *Simulated method of moments (SMM).* Because in the case of nonlinear models characterized by latent variables, such as SVMs, efficiency is hardly achievable in practice (as emphasized by Renault, 2009), tractable analytic expressions for moments are no longer an issue since simulations may provide accurate Monte Carlo counterparts to any moment of interest, through the *SMM* approach. In fact, financial loss functions are typically less concerned with efficient inference than with robust estimation of some moments of interest related for instance to risk premiums, Value at Risk, and expected shortfall.[9]
- *Simulated maximum likelihood estimator (SML).* Danielsson (1994) has proposed the *SML estimator* as a general method for estimation of SVMs. In essence the unknown likelihood function that the model implies is evaluated by simulation, specifying some approximating auxiliary density whose expectation equals the true, joint multivariate density of the observables. By taking N draws from the auxiliary density at each point in time t, a natural estimator of the true but unknown likelihood is then the average of such simulations. Once the likelihood is evaluated by simulation, estimates are obtained using a standard optimizer. The SML estimator has the same asymptotic distribution as the ML estimator. However, in the case of SML, it may be hard to measure the accuracy of the proposed approximation and hence to assess the quality of the resulting estimates.
- *Simulated expectation maximization.* QML-type methods exist that try to approximate the likelihood of log-squared returns with the likelihood from some other distributions. For instance, Kim et al. (1998) proposed a *simulated expectation maximization* (SEM, similar to the EM algorithm that will be covered in Chapter 9) using a mixture of seven normal distributions to match the first four moments of the χ^2 that describes the log-squared returns. A *mixture of normal distributions* is obtained when at all times, an additional random variable governs the selection of the normal distribution from which the data will be drawn. The main advantage of approximating the distribution of log-squared returns with normal mixtures is that, conditional on the mixture component, the state-space models in Eqs. (7.27) and (7.28) are Gaussian. The performance of SEM estimators in finite samples has been studied by Fridman and Harris (1998), who show that this method is similar to Markov Chain Monte Carlo (MCMC) and SML in terms of efficiency.
- *Monte Carlo likelihood (MCL).* Sandmann and Koopman (1998) have proposed an *MCL* method that approximates the likelihood function of log-squared returns with a standard Gaussian portion constructed via the Kalman filter plus a correction for departures from the normality assumption relative to the true unknown model.
- *Empirical characteristic function (ECF).* Recently, Singleton (2001) has proposed a new estimation procedure based on the *ECF* that circumvents the issues related to the impossibility of writing down and computing the log-likelihood in simple ways: because log-squared returns are driven by a process that is the convolution of an AR(1) and an independent log-variance process, while there is no simple expression for the log-likelihood, there is a closed-form expression for the characteristic function, so that the model is fully and uniquely parameterized by it (see Andersen and Benzoni, 2009, for additional details). The method consists of evaluating the ECF and then finding the corresponding values of the log-likelihood by numerical integration. Knight and Yu (2002) have established the strong consistency and asymptotic normality of ECF estimators.

9. Moreover, the Cramer-Rao lower bound efficiency of the MLE is reached by MM whenever the chosen moments are rich enough to span the likelihood score vector, which variations of the SMM method (such as the efficient method of moments by Gallant and Tauchen, 1996) have exploited.

7.3 EXTENDED, SECOND-GENERATION STOCHASTIC VOLATILITY MODELS

In the early diffusion-based SVMs covered in Section 7.1, volatility was assumed to be Markovian (for instance, to follow a simple AR(1) model) with continuous sample paths. Research in the late 1990s and early 2000s has shown that more complicated volatility dynamics compared to the standard model in Eq. (7.27) written in continuous time (i.e., over very small time intervals and assuming that some regularity conditions apply), such as:

$$\begin{aligned} dP(t) &= \mu P(t)\,dt + \sigma(t)\,P(t)\,dW_{1,t} \\ d\ln\sigma^2(t) &= \beta\left(v - \ln\sigma^2(t)\right)dt + \kappa dW_{2,t}, \end{aligned} \tag{7.32}$$

(two Brownian motions, $dW_{1,t}$ and $dW_{2,t}$, potentially correlated) are needed to model either options data or high-frequency return data. Leading extensions to the model are:

- To allow *jumps* into the stochastic differential equation (henceforth, SDE) followed by volatility (see, e.g., Merton, 1976), like in the two-factor model:

$$\begin{aligned} dP(t) &= (\mu - \lambda\bar{\xi})\,P(t)\,dt + \sigma P(t)\,dW_{1,t} + \xi(t)\,dq_t \\ \Pr(dq_t = 1) &= \lambda\cdot dt, \qquad \xi(t) \sim N(\bar{\xi}, \sigma_\xi^2), \end{aligned} \tag{7.33}$$

  where q follows a *Poisson process* uncorrelated with the Brownian motion $dW_{1,t}$ and parameterized by a constant jump intensity λ, $\lambda\bar{\xi}$ compensates for the price of jump risk, and the scaling factor $\xi(t)$ denotes the normally distributed magnitude of the jump in the return process when a jump occurs at time t, so that jumps can be both positive and negative (however $\bar{\xi} < 0$ will create left asymmetries); jump-diffusion models produce returns that are leptokurtic and asymmetric so that the model can reproduce asymmetric implied volatility smiles and accurately price options;
- To model the volatility process as a function of a number of separate diffusive stochastic processes or *factors* (e.g., Chernov et al., 2003), of the type:

$$\boldsymbol{\varepsilon}_t = \sum_{j=1}^{J} \int \boldsymbol{B}_{j,s} d\boldsymbol{F}_{j,s} + d\boldsymbol{W}_t, \tag{7.34}$$

  where the factors $\mathbf{F}_1, \mathbf{F}_2, \ldots, \mathbf{F}_J$ are independent univariate SV models and $\mathbf{W}_t$ is a correlated multivariate Brownian motion;[10]
- To specify a *long-memory model* for σ in discrete or continuous time, where the log of volatility is modeled as a *fractionally integrated* process (Brownian motion), as in Breidt et al. (1998), in opposition to first generation SVMs in which the volatility process was just diffusive as driven by a standard Brownian motion, which implies—contrary to widespread empirical evidence—that the dependence in the volatility structure always decays at a rapid rate.

Of course, there are many variations of these models that have been documented in the literature and that have been used to make the process of jumps increasingly compatible with the notion that economically, jumps reflect the discrete but uncertain arrival of new information that induces an instantaneous revision of asset prices. For instance, in some empirical papers, the log-jump size follows a double exponential distribution instead of a normal one. Without giving the fine details, for finite samples, it is hard to distinguish a double exponential distribution from a Student's t-distribution. However, a double exponential distribution is more tractable analytically and can generate a higher probability concentration (e.g., higher peak) around its mean value. It represents a way to take a mixture process with t-Student features which, as we have seen also in a few examples in Chapter 5, seems to be required by financial data. Alternatively, the jump intensity λ could be made itself an affine function of the latent instantaneous variance, like in $\lambda(t) = \lambda_0 + \lambda_1\sigma^2(t)$.

It is often desirable to include regression effects in the specification of an SVM. For instance, Tsiakas (2006) has introduced dummy effects to account for seasonal patterns in volatility; Koopman et al. (2005) have considered a regression variable that contains information on the unobserved log-variance process. Such regression effects can be incorporated into the SVM by simply extending the log-variance signal specification to include predetermined regressors. The estimation of regression effects in the volatility process can be carried out in two ways. First the regression coefficients can be treated as unknown but fixed parameters to be estimated; second the state vector can be augmented so that it

10. Harvey et al. (1994) proposed the model $\boldsymbol{\varepsilon}_t = \mathbf{C}\int_0^t \boldsymbol{\sigma}_s d\mathbf{W}_s$, where $\boldsymbol{\sigma}_s$ is a diagonal matrix process and $\mathbf{C}$ is a fixed matrix of constants with a unit leading diagonal. This means that returns are simply a rotation of an N-dimensional vector of independent univariate SV processes.

includes the regression coefficients, that become part of the definition of the state. Needless to say, regressors for the expected return observed specification can also be included, which turns the model into a regression model with SV errors.

As seen in Eq. (7.22), to capture the high sample excess kurtosis often found in financial time series, the model can be generalized by assuming that the innovations to the price process come from a fat-tailed distribution, such as a scaled t-distribution. In this way, the dynamic properties of the log-variance and the thickness of the tails are modeled separately, as in Fridman and Harris (1998). Of course, QML estimation based on a standard linear Gaussian Kalman filter then becomes impossible, but estimation methods exist that allow us to circumvent this issue.

Multivariate SV models have been often used to represent systems of financial returns related, for example, to the APT. For instance, Harvey et al. (1994) have proposed the following *multivariate diagonal SVM* which allow the variances and covariances to evolve through time with possibly common trends but that restricts correlations to be constant:

$$\begin{aligned} R_{i,t} &= \gamma_{1,i} + dz_{1i,t}, \quad dz_{1,i,t} \text{ IID } N(0, \exp(h_{i,t})) \\ h_{i,t} &= \gamma_{2,i} + \gamma_{3,i} h_{i,t-1} + dz_{2,i,t} \quad dz_{2i,t} \text{ IID } N(0, \sigma_i^2), \end{aligned} \tag{7.35}$$

where $h_{i,t} = \ln\ \sigma_{i,t}^2$, the shocks to individual asset returns, $[dz_{1,1,t}\ dz_{1,2,t}\ \cdots\ dz_{1,N,t}]'$ have an joint multivariate normal distribution with covariance matrix $\boldsymbol{\Omega}_1$, the shocks to individual covariances $[dz_{2,1,t}\ dz_{2,2,t}\ \cdots\ dz_{2,N,t}]'$ have a joint multivariate normal distribution with covariance matrix $\boldsymbol{\Omega}_2$, and the correlation matrix between the two vectors of shocks is some constant $\boldsymbol{\Gamma}$, so that the overall covariance matrix is:

$$\begin{bmatrix} \boldsymbol{\Omega}_1 & diag(\boldsymbol{\Omega}_1)\boldsymbol{\Gamma} diag(\boldsymbol{\Omega}_2) \\ diag(\boldsymbol{\Omega}_1)\boldsymbol{\Gamma} diag(\boldsymbol{\Omega}_2) & \boldsymbol{\Omega}_2 \end{bmatrix}, \tag{7.36}$$

in which the $diag(\cdot)$ operator extracts the main diagonal of a covariance matrix into an $N \times N$ diagonal matrix.

Alternatively, Jacquier et al. (1994) and Aguilar and West (2000) (among others) have extended these models to factor SVMs for a vector of observable returns over time, $\mathbf{R}_t$:

$$\begin{aligned} \boldsymbol{R}_t &= \mathbf{D}\mathbf{f}_t + dz_{1,t}, \quad dz_{1,t} \text{ IID } N\left(\mathbf{0}, diag\left\{\sigma_{1,1}^2, \sigma_{1,2}^2, \ldots, \sigma_{1,N}^2\right\}\right) \\ f_{i,t} &= \gamma_{1,i} + dz_{2,i,t} \quad dz_{2,i,t} \text{ IID } N(0, \exp(h_{i,t})) \\ \boldsymbol{h}_t &= \boldsymbol{\gamma}_2 + \boldsymbol{\Gamma}_3 \boldsymbol{h}_{t-1} + d\mathbf{z}_{3,t}, \quad dz_{3,t} \text{ IID } N(\mathbf{0}, \boldsymbol{\Omega}). \end{aligned} \tag{7.37}$$

Here, $\mathbf{D}$ is the matrix of factor loadings and $d\mathbf{z}_{1,t}$ is the vector of price shocks uncorrelated with $d\mathbf{z}_{2,t} \equiv [dz_{2,1,t}\ dz_{2,2,t}\ \cdots\ dz_{2,N,t}]'$. Simultaneous correlation between the shocks to asset log-variances and shocks to the factors is allowed in a way similar to Eq. (7.29). One of the goals of factor SVMs is to generate time-variation in the implied conditional correlation matrix between returns without resorting to more complex multivariate SVMs.

7.4 GARCH VERSUS STOCHASTIC VOLATILITY: WHICH ONE?

7.4.1 Some GARCH Models Are (Asymptotically) Stochastic Volatility Models

Contrary to what one may have inferred in our discussion so far, ARCH and SV models are not orthogonal to each other in the following sense: although the two classes of models are very rich and bigger than their "intersection," they also overlap in the sense that a few specific types of SVMs may be discretized to become ARCH and especially the continuous-time limit of a few specific GARCH models is a precise type of SVM! Of course, this means that cases exist in which the two or more factors driving the conditional variance in an SVM degenerate to a single factor. In fact, given that ARCH models are systems of nonlinear SDEs—and this makes their probabilistic and statistical properties (e.g., stationarity) more difficult to establish than in the case with linear models, see for example, Davis and Mikosch (2009)—one well-known way to simplify the analysis of ARCH models is to *approximate the SDEs with more tractable stochastic differential equations* of the SVM type.[11] In this section, we investigate in-depth the mathematical relationships that may be exploited to turn ARCH into SV models and vice versa.

11. However, for certain purposes, for instance point estimation, ARCH models remain more convenient than the stochastic differential equation models of the SV literature.

For concreteness, consider the continuous-time SVM for log-asset prices given by Eq. (7.32) for fixed starting values P_0 and σ_0^2. By Ito's lemma the log-price process in Eq. (7.32) may be equivalently written as $d\ln P(t) = (\mu - 0.5\sigma^2(t))\cdot dt + \sigma(t)\cdot dW_{1,t}$. It turns out that it is possible to formulate an ARCH model that is similar to such a process. This means that the distribution of the sample paths generated by the ARCH and the diffusion model become "close" for increasingly finer discretizations starting from a standard Euler approximation:

$$\begin{aligned} \ln P_{t+\Delta t} &= \ln P_t + (\mu - 0.5\sigma_t^2)\,\Delta t + \sqrt{\Delta t}\sigma_t dz_{1,t+\Delta t}, \\ \ln \sigma_{t+\Delta t}^2 &= \ln \sigma_t^2 + \beta(v - \ln \sigma_t^2)\,\Delta t + \sqrt{\Delta t}\kappa dz_{2,t+\Delta t}, \end{aligned} \tag{7.38}$$

for $t = \Delta t,\ 2\Delta t,\ 3\Delta t, \ldots,$ and $[dz_{1,t}\ dz_{2,t}]'$ is IID bivariate standard normal with zero mean vector and covariance matrix is given by:

$$Cov\begin{bmatrix} dz_{1,t+\Delta t} \\ dz_{2,t+\Delta t} \end{bmatrix} = \begin{bmatrix} 1 & \rho \\ \rho & 1 \end{bmatrix}. \tag{7.39}$$

Convergence of this set of SDEs to the diffusion in Eq. (7.32) as $\Delta t \to 0$ may be verified using results reported, for instance, in Bollerslev et al. (1994).

While conditionally heteroskedastic, the model defined by the stochastic difference Eqs. (7.38) and (7.39) is not yet an ARCH model. In particular, for $\rho \neq 1$, σ_t^2 is not simply a function of the discretely observed sample path of asset prices combined with some initial value σ_0^2. However, Nelson (1990) shows that to create an ARCH approximation to the diffusion in Eq. (7.32), we can simply replace Eq. (7.38) by:

$$\begin{aligned} \ln P_{t+\Delta t} &= \ln P_t + (\mu - 0.5\sigma_t^2)\Delta t + \sqrt{\Delta t}\sigma_t dz_{1,t+\Delta t} \\ \ln \sigma_{t+\Delta t}^2 &= \ln \sigma_t^2 + \beta(v - \ln \sigma_t^2)\Delta t + \sqrt{\Delta t} g(dz_{1,t+\Delta t}), \end{aligned} \tag{7.40}$$

where $g(\cdot)$ is a measurable function with $E[|g(dz_{1,t+\Delta t})|^{2+\delta}] < \infty$ for some $\delta > 0$ and

$$Cov\begin{bmatrix} dz_{1,t+\Delta t} \\ g(dz_{1,t+\Delta t}) \end{bmatrix} = \begin{bmatrix} 1 & \rho\kappa \\ \rho\kappa & \kappa^2 \end{bmatrix}. \tag{7.41}$$

In particular, Nelson proposes the function

$$g\,(dz_{1,t+\Delta t}) = \rho\kappa dz_{1,t+\Delta t} + \kappa\sqrt{\frac{1-\rho^2}{1-(2/\pi)}}\left(|dz_{1,t+\Delta t}| - \sqrt{2/\pi}\right). \tag{7.42}$$

This corresponds to the EGARCH model presented in Chapter 5. Alternatively, also the specification

$$g\,(dz_{1,t+\Delta t}) = \rho\kappa dz_{1,t+\Delta t} + \kappa\sqrt{\frac{1-\rho^2}{2}}\left[(dz_{1,t+\Delta t})^2 - 1\right] \tag{7.43}$$

yields the same result. Therefore, the SVM in Eqs. (7.38) and (7.39) can be discretized to the GARCH models in Eqs. (7.40) and (7.41) when $g(\cdot)$ takes the functional form in either Eq. (7.42) or (7.43) and that in this case the Euler discretization converges to the starting SVM.

Now consider the opposite question, that is, how to best approximate a discrete time ARCH model with a continuous-time diffusion. This is not only a matter of intellectual curiosity because in some occasions representing an ARCH model as a diffusive, continuous-time model may bring benefits to our understanding. For instance, provided $\beta < 0$ and $v > 0$ in Eqs. (7.38) and (7.39), we know that the SVM is stationary and that the stationary distribution of $\ln\sigma_t^2$ is $N(v, -\kappa^2/2\beta)$ and this may help establish the stationarity of the (exponential) GARCH model that the SVM helps representing. In fact, Nelson (1990) shows that this is also the limit as $\Delta t \to 0$ of the $\ln\sigma_t^2$ in the sequence of EGARCH models in Eqs. (7.40) and (7.41), when $g(\cdot)$ takes the functional form in either Eq. (7.42) or (7.43). Moreover, different ARCH models will generally result in different limit diffusions, some of them well-known and used in asset pricing and in the econometrics of continuous-time processes, and others not so frequently used.

For instance, consider a simple Gaussian GARCH(1,1) model written in a form similar to Eqs. (7.40) and (7.41):

$$\begin{aligned} \ln P_{t+\Delta t} &= \mu + \ln P_t + \sqrt{\Delta t}\sigma_t dz_{1,t+\Delta t} = \mu + \ln P_t + \varepsilon_{t+\Delta t} \\ \sigma_{t+\Delta t}^2 &= \omega\Delta t + (1 - \theta\Delta t - \alpha\sqrt{\Delta t})\sigma_t^2 + \alpha\Delta t\sigma_t^2 (dz_{1,t+\Delta t})^2 \\ &= \omega\Delta t + (1 - \theta\Delta t - \alpha\sqrt{\Delta t})\sigma_t^2 + \alpha\sqrt{\Delta t}\varepsilon_{t+\Delta t}^2, \end{aligned} \tag{7.44}$$

where given time t information, $dz_{1,t+\Delta t} \sim N(0,1)$. Note that as $\Delta t \to 0$, $(1-\theta\Delta t - \alpha\sqrt{\Delta t}) \to 1$ so that for increasing sampling frequencies, the parameters of the process approach an IGARCH(1,1) boundary, $\sigma^2_{t+\Delta t} \to \sigma^2_t + \varepsilon_{t+\Delta t}$. Nelson (1990) shows that as $\Delta t \to 0$,

$$\begin{aligned} dP(t) &= \mu P(t)\cdot dt + \sigma(t)P(t)\cdot dW_{1,t} \\ d\sigma^2(t) &= (\omega - \theta\sigma^2(t))\cdot dt + \sqrt{2}\alpha\sigma^2(t)\cdot dW_{2,t}, \end{aligned} \tag{7.45}$$

where $W_{1,t}$ and $W_{2,t}$ are independent standard Brownian motions. The SVM in Eq. (7.45) is quite different from the model in Eqs. (7.32): for instance, the second diffusion features a mean-reverting dynamic for σ^2_t and not for $\ln \sigma^2_t$. However, Eq. (7.45), often termed the *GARCH-diffusion model*, is strictly related to the seminal work by Hull and White (1987) in option pricing theory and therefore plays a key practical role. Clearly, in the case of a homoskedastic IID Gaussian model in which $\omega = \theta = \alpha = 0$ and

$$\ln P_{t+\Delta t} = \mu + \ln P_t + \varepsilon_{t+\Delta t} \quad \text{with } \sigma^2_{t+\Delta t} = \sigma^2_t = \sigma^2, \tag{7.46}$$

the continuous-time limit is represented by the classical, Black-Scholes Geometric Brownian motion-with drift model:

$$dP(t) = \mu P(t)\cdot dt + \sigma P(t)\cdot dW_{1,t} \qquad d\sigma^2(t) = 0. \tag{7.47}$$

7.4.2 Stressing the Differences: What Have We Learned So Far?

The literature that has used SV models with jumps (also known as SVJMs) to jointly fit the time series of the underlying asset returns and the cross-section of option prices written on them has established that SVJ models dramatically improve the fit to underlying index returns and options prices compared to the Black and Scholes model (see Andersen et al., 2002) that is an extension of a homoskedastic IID Gaussian model to the continuous-time limit, as in Eq. (7.47). SV alone has a first-order effect and low-frequency, rare jumps further enhance model performance by generating fatter tails in the return distribution and reducing the pricing error for short-dated options (e.g., Bakshi et al., 1997). Indeed, if volatility follows a pure diffusion, the implied continuous sample path may be incapable of generating a sufficiently volatile return distribution over short horizons to justify the observed prices of derivatives. Adding a jump component improves the fit to the observed time series of returns because the jumps may help accommodate outliers as well as asymmetry in the return distribution. The presence of outliers depends upon the magnitude and variability of the jump component, while the asymmetry is controlled by the average magnitude of the jumps. Also, a pronounced negative correlation between return and volatility innovations appears necessary to capture the skewness often present in asset returns.

Interestingly, since Andersen et al. (2002), it has been observed that estimates of the model parameters directly obtained from asset returns data and ignoring option information (what is called the *physical process*) are generally similar to those obtained exploiting only options. In fact, relatively small premia for the uncertainty associated with volatility and jumps are sufficient to replicate most of the salient features of the term structure of implied volatility in derivative prices. This implies that a large number of characteristics of the price process, which seem to be implied or priced by derivative contracts (i.e., under the so-called *risk neutral, or equivalent martingale measure*), are independently identified as highly inherent features of the underlying dynamics of prices themselves, when sufficiently rich SVJMs are specified.

The literature on the pure comparative performance of SVMs versus ARCH models in forecasting the volatility of asset returns as a prerequisite for many risk management tasks in finance is oddly scarce. However, the evidence is rather mixed. For instance, early work by Heynen and Kat (1994) found that SV was able to outperform ARCH models on a range of international stock return series, but less for the log-rate of change in exchange rates. Additionally, Dunis et al. (2001) have compared GARCH and SV models using a group of six foreign exchange rates, finding that GARCH gave more accurate predictions in five out of the six rates over a 1-month horizon and for four out of the six rates for a 3-month horizon. Sadorsky (2005) has then found that for a variety of assets, an equity index, crude oil, bonds, and foreign exchange rates, SV forecasts were less accurate than RiskMetrics. Poon and Granger (2005) have summarized this early literature writing that "Based on the forecasting results, option implied volatility dominates time series models because the market option price fully incorporates current information and future volatility expectations. Between historical volatility and ARCH models, we found no clear winner, but they are both better than the SVM. *Despite the added flexibility and complexity of SV models, we found no clear evidence that they provide superior volatility forecasts.*" (p. 54, emphasis added). Recently, Ding and Meade (2010) have used a simulation experiment (with data generated from SVMs) to study the comparative forecasting performance of SV versus GARCH. They report that SV model forecasts are significantly more accurate than GARCH in scenarios with very high volatility of volatility in the generating SVM; otherwise, GARCH (often RiskMetrics) tends to perform fairly well in spite of the fact that the simulations are generated from SV. The same results are obtained from a wide set of time series selected from FX rates, equity indices, equities, and commodities. All in all, consistently with our earlier Examples 7.1 and 7.4, some doubts on the actual predictive accuracy of SV models remain, in spite of little doubts on their crucial role in asset pricing.

REFERENCES

Aguilar, O., West, M., 2000. Bayesian dynamic factor models and variance matrix discounting for portfolio allocation. J. Bus. Econ. Stat. 18, 338–357.

Andersen, T.G., Benzoni, L., 2009. Stochastic volatility. Encyclopedia of Complexity and Systems Science. Springer, New York.

Andersen, T.G., Chung, H.J., Sorensen, B.E., 1999. Efficient method of moments estimation of a stochastic volatility model: a Monte Carlo study. J. Econometr. 91, 61–87.

Andersen, T.G., Benzoni, L., Lund, J., 2002. An empirical investigation of continuous-time equity return models. J. Finan. 57, 1239–1284.

Andersen, T.G., Bollerslev, T., Diebold, F.X., Labys, P., 2003. Modeling and forecasting realized volatility. Econometrica 71, 579–626.

Bakshi, G., Cao, C., Chen, Z., 1997. Empirical performance of alternative option pricing models. J. Finan. 52, 2003–2049.

Bollerslev, T., Engle, R.F., Nelson, D.B., 1994. ARCH models, Handbook of Econometric, 4. North-Holland, Amsterdam, pp. 2959–3038.

Breidt, F.J., Crato, N., de Lima, P., 1998. On the detection and estimation of long memory in stochastic volatility, J. Econometr. 83. pp. 325–348.

Broto, C., Ruiz, E., 2004. Estimation methods for stochastic volatility models: a survey. J. Econ. Surv. 18, 613–649.

Chernov, M., Gallant, A.R., Ghysels, E., Tauchen, G., 2003. Alternative models of stock price dynamics. J. Econometr. 116, 225–257.

Clark, P.K., 1973. A subordinated stochastic process model with fixed variance for speculative prices. Econometrica 41, 135–156.

Cox, J.C., Ingersoll, J.E., Ross, S.A., 1985. A theory of the term structure of interest rates. Econometrica 53 (2), 385–408.

Danielsson, J., 1994. Stochastic volatility in asset prices: estimation with simulated maximum likelihood. J. Econometr. 64, 375–400.

Davis, R., Mikosch, T., 2009. Probabilistic properties of stochastic volatility models. In: Mikosch, T., Kreiß, J.P., Davis, R., Andersen, T. (Eds.), Handbook of Financial Time Series. Springer, Berlin, Heidelberg, pp. 255–266.

Ding, J., Meade, N., 2010. Forecasting accuracy of stochastic volatility, GARCH and EWMA models under different volatility scenarios. Appl. Finan. Econ. 20, 771–783.

Dunis, C., Laws, J., Chauvin, S., 2001. The use of market data and model combination to improve forecast accuracy. In: Dunis, C., Timmermann, A., Moody, J. (Eds.), Developments in Forecast Combination and Portfolio Choice. John Wiley & Sons, London, pp. 45–80.

Fridman, M., Harris, L., 1998. A maximum likelihood approach for non-Gaussian stochastic volatility models. J. Bus. Econ. Stat. 16, 284–291.

Gallant, A.R., Tauchen, G., 1996. Which moments to match. Econometr. Theory 12, 657–681.

Hamilton, J.D., 1994. Time Series Analysis. Princeton University Press, Princeton, NJ.

Harvey, A.C., Shephard, N., 1996. Estimation of an asymmetric stochastic volatility model for asset returns. J. Bus. Econ. Stat. 14, 429–434.

Harvey, A.C., Ruiz, E., Shephard, N., 1994. Multivariate stochastic variance models. Rev. Econ. Stud. 61, 247–264.

Heynen, R., Kat, H., 1994. Volatility prediction: a comparison of the stochastic volatility, GARCH(1,1), and EGARCH(1,1) models. J. Derivat. 94 (50-65).

Hull, J., White, A., 1987. The pricing of options on assets with stochastic volatilities. J. Finan. 42, 281–300.

Ineichen, A.M., 2000. Twentieth century volatility. J. Portf. Manag. 27, 93–101.

Jacquier, E., Polson, N.G., Rossi, P.E., 1994. Bayesian analysis of stochastic volatility models. J. Bus. Econ. Stat. 12 (371-417), 1994.

Kalman, R.E., 1960. A new approach to linear filtering and prediction problems. J. Basic Eng. Trans. ASME Ser. D 82, 35–45.

Kim, S., Shephard, N., Chib, S., 1998. Stochastic volatility: likelihood inference and comparison with ARCH models. Rev. Econ. Stud. 45, 361–393.

Knight, J.L., Yu, J., 2002. The empirical characteristic function in time series estimation. Econometr. Theory 18, 691–721.

Koopman, S.J., Hol-Uspensky, E.H., 2002. The stochastic volatility in mean model: empirical evidence from international stock markets. J. Appl. Econometr. 17, 667–689.

Koopman, S.J., Jungbacker, B., Hol- Uspensky, E., 2005. Forecasting daily variability of the S&P 100 stock index using historical, realised and implied volatility measurements. J. Empiric. Finan. 12, 445–475.

Lo, A.W., 1988. Maximum likelihood estimation of generalized Ito processes with discretely-sampled data. Econometr. Theory 4, 231–247.

Mahieu, R.J., Schotman, P.C., 1998. An empirical application of stochastic volatility models. J. Appl. Econometr. 13, 333–360.

Merton, R.C., 1976. Option pricing when underlying stock returns are discontinuous. J. Finan. Econ. 3, 125–144.

Nelson, D.B., 1990. Stationarity and persistence in the GARCH(1,1) model. Econometr. Theory 6, 318–334.

Poon, S.H., Granger, C.W., 2005. Practical issues in forecasting volatility. Finan. Anal. J. 61, 45–56.

Renault, E., 2009. Moment-based estimation of stochastic volatility models. In: Mikosch, T., Kreiß, J.P., Davis, R., Andersen, T. (Eds.), Handbook of Financial Time Series. Springer, Berlin, Heidelberg, pp. 269–311.

Rosenberg, B., The behaviour of random variables with nonstationary variance and the distribution of security prices. Working paper No. 11, University of California, Berkeley, 1972.

Ruiz, E., 1994. Quasi-maximum likelihood estimation of stochastic volatility models. J. Econometr. 63, 289–306.

Sadorsky, P., 2005. Stochastic volatility forecasting and risk management. Appl. Finan. Econ. 15, 121–135.

Sandmann, G., Koopman, S.J., 1998. Estimation of stochastic volatility models via Monte Carlo maximum likelihood. J. Econometr. 87, 271–301.
Singleton, K.J., 2001. Estimation of affine asset pricing models using the empirical characteristic function. J. Econometr. 102, 111–141.
Taylor, S.J., 1982. Financial returns modelled by the product of two stochastic processes: a study of daily sugar prices 1961–79. In: Anderson, O.D. (Ed.), Time Series Analysis: Theory and Practice, 1. North-Holland, Amsterdam.
Taylor, S.J., 2008. *Modelling Financial Time Series*. World Scientific, Singapore, first edition 1986.
Tsiakas, I., 2006. Periodic stochastic volatility and fat tails. J. Finan. Econometr. 4, 90–135.

Chapter 8

Models With Breaks, Recurrent Regime Switching, and Nonlinearities

Life is not an orderly progression, self-contained like a musical scale or a quadratic equation... If one is to record one's life truthfully, one must aim at getting into the record of it something of the disorderly discontinuity which makes it so absurd, unpredictable, bearable.

Leonard Woolf

In this chapter, we study statistical models that accommodate non-recurring (often called *structural breaks*) as well as *recurrent regimes* of a particular (threshold) type in time series data. Therefore, the material covered in the following sections is characterized by considerable connections with Chapter 9, where the dynamic process followed by the key "features" will display recurrent regimes but governed by a Markov state variable. The difference is that in this chapter, such dynamic properties (e.g., the conditional mean and/or variance functions or the shape of the marginal distribution of the shocks) will be entirely, endogenously driven by the variable(s) under the investigation; in Chapter 9 the variable (s) of interest will be allowed to take a finite number of *recurrent states* that tend to persist over time as a result of some exogenously given, directing stochastic process that controls whether and when the regime shifts occur.

8.1 A PRIMER ON THE KEY FEATURES AND CLASSIFICATION OF STATISTICAL MODEL OF INSTABILITY

In an economic perspective, choosing between the case of structural shifts and recurrent regimes means has far-reaching implications, as it implies a logical shift from analyzing a question such as

"Did the demise of Lehman in September 2008 cause the statistical relationships involving a number of financial variables to morph and assume a new balance?"

to ask instead

"Does a market state similar to the one that marked the demise of Lehman in September 2008 and that caused the statistical relationships involving a number of financial variables to morph into a new balance recur over time? If such a state does not represent a new permanent, normal state, how long will it persist once we enter in such crisis conditions? Will it happen again and, if so, can we predict when this will occur again and for how long?"

As a result, the sequence of models that, at least ideally, this book has (and is about to have) featured is:

- Univariate and multivariate *constant-parameter* (i.e., time homogeneous) *time series models*, such as linear regressions, (Vector) Autoregressive Moving Average ((V)ARMA) homoskedastic models, VARX GARCH-type models, and VAR models with stochastic volatility (SV).
- Models subject to *breaks* (also multivariate, when one can examine cobreaking), that is, sudden and unpredictable instances of time heterogeneity that lead to a structural change in the dynamics of the series.
- Models subject to *recurrent shifts* in their properties that may also be conceived as breaks of repetitive nature as drawn from a finite set of possible states, often called regimes, both endogenous and exogenous.

Needless to say, when a (vector) time series process turns out not to be affected by either breaks or recurrent regimes, then it will be of a constant-parameter type. Therefore, standard, constant-parameter models may be considered just as a special, simpler case of many of the tools and concepts that we shall be developing in this chapter and Chapter 9. However, our goals in this portion of our treatment remain the same as the rest of the book, that is, to be able to specify, estimate, and perform classical inference (such as hypotheses tests) on models subject to either breaks

Essentials of Time Series for Financial Applications. DOI: https://doi.org/10.1016/B978-0-12-813409-2.00008-X

or regime switching (henceforth, RS), and to forecast a variety of quantities of interest—often not only the conditional moment functions (typically, the mean and/or the variance) that are directly subject to structural or regime changes, but also the entire *conditional (multivariate) density* of the time series under investigation—with a keen interest in financial applications.

Because we have now built the necessary apparatus for us to be able to do so, the theoretical treatment in this chapter and Chapter 9, will be often multivariate in nature when the models admit a natural generalization to the N-variable case, given the state of the art in time series econometrics. As such this part of the book connects directly to Chapters 3, 6, and (part of) Chapter 4 which were also multivariate in nature. However, to develop stronger insights, we shall often offer examples which are based on univariate applications. In fact, to provide some preliminary intuition on goals and contents ahead, we offer here a univariate example. Consider a simple two-state, RS Gaussian autoregressive of order one (AR(1)) process for the returns on some asset or portfolio:

$$R_{t+1} = \phi_{0,S_{t+1}} + \phi_{1,S_{t+1}} R_t + \sigma_{S_{t+1}} z_{t+1} \quad z_{t+1} \text{ IID } N(0,1), \tag{8.1}$$

where S_{t+1} is a discrete random variable that takes only two values, $S_{t+1} = 1, 2$ (or "bad" and "good," or A and B, as we shall see the exact labels assigned do not matter). In Eq. (8.1) the unconditional mean, the persistence, and the conditional variance of the AR(1) process, all depend on some state variable, S_{t+1}.

This simple model allows to preview the work that awaits us. First, one shall need to specify the probability law followed by S_{t+1}, for instance whether S_{t+1} follows either a simple two-point process (say, either Bernoulli or finite memory, of Markov type) or depend on (say) a finite number of past returns. Second, we will need to clarify what is the specific role that, given the fact that S_{t+1} may take (say) two values, is played by the parametric distribution of the random, standardized shocks, z_{t+1}, here assumed to follow a simple Gaussian process. Third, either the data at hand or economic/financial models may suggest that Eq. (8.1) may fail to be sufficiently parsimonious, so that it may be worthwhile to investigate simpler models, such as:

$$R_{t+1} = \phi_{0,S_{t+1}} + \phi_{1,S_{t+1}} R_t + \sigma z_{t+1} \quad z_{t+1} \text{ IID } N(0,1), \tag{8.2}$$

in which the variance is constant over time, or

$$R_{t+1} = \phi_{0,S_{t+1}} + \phi_1 R_t + \sigma z_{t+1} \quad z_{t+1} \text{ IID } N(0,1), \tag{8.3}$$

in which only the unconditional mean of the process depends on the state. One particularly meaningful case of Eq. (8.2) occurs when $\phi_{1,1} = 1$ and $|\phi_{1,2}| < 1$, that is, a nonstationary regime exists. Although by construction Eq. (8.1) buys us considerable flexibility, for instance because a model like

$$R_{t+1} = \begin{cases} \phi_{1,1} R_t + \sigma_1 z_{t+1} & z_{t+1} \text{ IID } N(0,1) \\ \phi_{0,2} + \sigma_2 z_{t+1} & z_{t+1} \text{ IID } N(0,1) \end{cases}, \tag{8.4}$$

becomes possible (i.e., in state 1 the unconditional mean of the process is restricted to be 0, while in state 2 the persistence of the process is 0), in the literature more complex models of the type:

$$R_{t+1} = \phi_{0,S_{t+1}} + \phi_{1,S_{t+1}} R_t + \sigma_{Q_{t+1}} z_{t+1} \quad z_{t+1} \text{ IID } N(0,1), \tag{8.5}$$

in which different state variables (here S_{t+1} and Q_{t+1}) capture different regime dynamics in means and variances, have appeared (see, e.g., Kim and Nelson, 1999).

Of course, when the state variables are nonrecurrent in the sense that

$$S_t = \begin{cases} 1 & \text{for } t < B \\ 2 & \text{for } t \geq B \end{cases}, \tag{8.6}$$

we obtain that Eq. (8.1) is sufficiently general to nest the case of the nonrecurrent, once-and-for-all structural *break*, a true kind of statistical discontinuity: in this case the break occurs at time B and it may affect simultaneously all the parameters of the model. Finally, when the regime variable collapses to assume only one value over the entire sample (or better, for all times t), then Eq. (8.1) simplifies to a standard Gaussian AR(1) process, already investigated in Chapter 2. Given that Eq. (8.1) nests many other models covered before, including a model written as

$$R_{t+1} = \phi_{0,S_{t+1}} + \phi_{1,S_{t+1}} R_t + \left(\sqrt{\omega_{S_{t+1}} + \alpha_{S_{t+1}} R_t^2}\right) z_{t+1} \quad z_{t+1} \text{ IID } N(0,1), \tag{8.7}$$

(for instance, this is an RS AR(1)-ARCH(1)), the issue is then how can we formally test whether S_{t+1} and/or Q_{t+1} will take only one value, two, or more.

At the heart of the detection and modeling of structural change and recurring regimes there are two closely related motivations. On the one hand, there is a simple, almost innate need to look back at history and classify the past on the basis of whether and how a given, time-heterogeneous statistical relationship among a range of possible ones, evolved and applied. Although with different, qualitative and more complex tools, this is one of the many tasks that economic historians perform within society. On the other hand, in financial applications, we care not just for modeling the past of a set of variables but also about forecasting their future; if and when such relationships are subject to instability over time, then such instability also needs to be modeled and predicted. In particular, RS models are a set of relatively innovative statistical tools that have been proposed exactly to detect and predict repeated instability in econometric models, exploiting the fact that even time variation in the series may display sufficient structure to make its modeling fruitful.

It is easy to give a number of popular examples of how such instability may manifest itself: in this chapter and Chapter 9, we shall discuss in depth the idea of bull and bear regimes alternating in financial markets, and their economic meaning; the 2008–09 financial crisis has shown that most markets are characterized by variations in their state of liquidity over time and this has profound pricing implications; it is well known that exchange rates tend to alternate protracted periods of depreciation and appreciation, which means that it is often possible to detect visible, persistent swings in their trends; there is an ever expanding literature on the presence and the origins of regimes in monetary policy (e.g., as dictated by the personality of governors and chairmen, think of Janet Yellen taking over Ben Bernanke's chair in 2014, or Mario Draghi taking the helm of the ECB from Jean-Claude Trichet in 2011).

One aspect that is worth emphasizing is that all models of breaks and RS represent powerful cases of *nonlinear time series models*. The nonlinearity arises from the fact that the model contains parameters that change, also abruptly, over time. This means that while the model

$$R_{t+1} = \phi_0 + \phi_1 R_t + \sigma z_{t+1} \quad z_{t+1} \text{ IID } N(0,1) \tag{8.8}$$

is a linear AR(1) model, as we have seen in Chapter 2, it is enough to turn even only one of its parameters to incorporate a dependence on the same switching state variable, S_{t+1}, like in

$$R_{t+1} = \phi_{0,S_{t+1}} + \phi_1 R_t + \sigma z_{t+1} \quad z_{t+1} \quad \text{IID } N(0,1), \tag{8.9}$$

for the model to become nonlinear, because it will then switch over time between

$$R_{t+1} = \begin{cases} \phi_{0,1} + \phi_1 R_t + \sigma z_{t+1} & z_{t+1} \quad \text{IID } N(0,1) \\ \phi_{0,2} + \phi_1 R_t + \sigma z_{t+1} & z_{t+1} \quad \text{IID } N(0,1) \end{cases}. \tag{8.10}$$

As we have seen in Chapter 2, a purely stochastic (stationary) time series (but extending the definition to a nonzero conditional mean depending on exogenous variables, time, or periodic functions is straightforward) is said to be *linear* if it can be written as $R_{t+1} = \mu + \sum_{i=0}^{\infty} \phi_i z_{t+1-i}$ where the coefficients are finite real numbers with $\phi_0 = 1$ and $\{z_{t+1}\}$ an identically and indipendently distributed (IID) sequence from some distribution function with 0 mean and finite variance. By exclusion, any stochastic process that does not satisfy such a condition is said to be *nonlinear* and can be represented as $R_{t+1} = f(z_{t+1}, z_t, \ldots,)$, where $f(\cdot)$ is any, possibly nonarithmetic (that cannot even be written in closed form), nonlinear function. However, while this general nonlinear model is not directly applicable because it contains too many parameters, the models that we shall introduce in this chapter and Chapter 9 will be made specific enough (one may say, very specific) to have actual implementation. In particular, the RS models that we are about to cover, they all belong to the following family.

DEFINITION 8.1 (Location-scale nonlinear family)

The location-scale family of nonlinear models is characterized by the conditional moments as in

$$R_{t+1} = \underbrace{E[R_{t+1}|\Im_t]}_{g(\Im_t)} + \underbrace{(Var[R_{t+1}|\Im_t])^{1/2}}_{h(\Im_t)} z_{t+1} \quad z_{t+1} \quad \text{IID } D(0,1), \tag{8.11}$$

where $\Im_t$ is the time t information set and $g(\cdot)$, $h(\cdot)$ are well-defined nonlinear functions with $h(\cdot) > 0$.

In the case of a linear time series, $g(\cdot)$ is a linear function of the elements in $\Im_t$ and $h(\cdot)$ is simply a constant. The development of nonlinear models involves extending $g(\cdot)$ and $h(\cdot)$ to nonlinear functions: if $g(\cdot)$ is nonlinear, the series is said to be *nonlinear in mean*; if $h(\cdot)$ is time-varying, then is *nonlinear in variance*. Therefore, the conditional heteroskedastic models examined in Chapters 5 and 6, were nonlinear in variance (and covariances, in the multivariate case). However, ARCH-in-mean models feature at the same time nonlinearities in both mean and variance. Because nonlinearities in the conditional variance function have been already addressed, in the following, we focus mostly on nonlinearities in the mean function.

In general, the RS models covered in portion of the book may be viewed as parsimonious approximations to general nonlinear autoregressions. While linear autoregressions dominate the field of applied time series, there is no compelling, a priori reason to presume that the true dynamic structure is linear as in Chapters 2 and 3. The primary argument for linearity is simplicity (estimation, interpretation, forecasting), and yet considerable research has shown that the analysis of threshold and MS models can be made reasonably straightforward. Furthermore, there is no convincing theoretical reason to focus exclusively on linear models. Finance models derived from first-principles (say, investors' utility and production functions of firms) will only display simple linear dynamics under narrow functional form restrictions and heroic distributional assumptions. Nonlinearities become in fact especially important in the presence of asymmetric costs of adjustment, irreversibilities, transactions costs, liquidity constraints, and other forms of rigidities that are increasingly popular in economic and financial models.

8.2 DETECTING AND EXPLOITING STRUCTURAL CHANGE IN LINEAR MODELS

The first case that we investigate in detail is when an otherwise standard, linear model is subject to abrupt, unpredictable, and nonrecurrent parameter shifts. Note at once the key postulate: the model is otherwise linear and usually rather simple, apart from the suspected occurrence of one or more breaks, especially in the conditional mean function.

A first interesting aspect is that tests of *specific* kinds of structural change are hardly distinguishable from one class of unit root tests which we have briefly hinted at in Chapter 4: unit root tests derived under the null hypothesis of stationarity. For instance, consider a univariate time IID series, $\{y_t\}_{t=1}^{T}$, which under the null hypothesis has mean μ and variance σ^2. Under the alternative hypothesis, y_t is subject to a one-time change in its mean at some unknown date T_b, that is,

$$y_{t+1} = \mu_1 + \mu_2 I_{\{t \geq T_b\}} + \varepsilon_{t+1} \quad z_{t+1} \quad \text{IID } N(0, \sigma^2). \tag{8.12}$$

A simple test introduced as early as in Quandt (1960), the *Sup-F-test* (which is the same as an Loglikelihood ratio, LR, test for a change in parameters evaluated at the break date T_b that maximizes the likelihood function),

$$Q = \frac{1}{T\hat{\sigma}^2}\sum_{t=1}^{T}\left[\sum_{j=t+1}^{T}(y_j - \bar{y})\right]^2, \tag{8.13}$$

has a limiting distribution that is nonstandard but ends up displaying the same limiting distribution as the Kwiatkowsky, Phillips, Schmidt, and Shin Lagrange multiplier (KPSS LM) test for the null hypothesis of stationarity versus the alternative of a unit root, already discussed in Chapter 4. The case of Quandt's test is a famous example of a more general concept, that the same (or at least, closely related) statistics can be often applied to tests for stationarity versus either unit root or structural change because the two issues are linked in important ways: *evidence in favor of unit roots can be a manifestation of structural changes and vice versa*, because level shifts induce persistent features in the data. We shall return on this concept in Section 8.2.4.

Following Bai (1997) and Bai and Perron (1998) the framework of analysis is the following *(partial structural change) linear model* with K breaks (implicitly defining $K+1$ nonrecurrent regimes as the intervals of time delimited by two consecutive break dates):

$$y_t = \boldsymbol{x}_t'\boldsymbol{\beta}_j + \boldsymbol{z}_t'\boldsymbol{\delta} + \varepsilon_t \quad t = T_{j-1},\ T_{j-1}+1, \ldots, T_j - 1, \tag{8.14}$$

where $\boldsymbol{x}_t$ is the subvector of covariates whose coefficients ($\boldsymbol{\beta}_j$) are subject to breaks, and $\{\varepsilon_t\}_{t=1}^{T}$ satisfies restrictions on its time series dependence patterns, even though for the time being we can simply assume the extreme case of $\varepsilon_t \sim \text{IID } N(0, \sigma^2)$. We call $\dim(\boldsymbol{\theta}_j)$ the total number of (conditional mean) parameters that appear in the model, where $\boldsymbol{\theta}_j \equiv [\boldsymbol{\beta}_j' + \boldsymbol{\delta}']'$, $j = 1, 2, ..., K$. The indices $(T_1, T_2, ..., T_K)$, the break point dates, are unknown and we set $T_0 = 1$, $T_{K+1} = T$. Our goal is to estimate the unknown regression coefficients together with the break points when T observations are available. Of course, when $\mathbf{z}_t = 0$, we obtain a pure structural change model where all the coefficients are subject to change. The intercept, when present, may be subject to breaks when $\boldsymbol{x}_t$ is assumed to include a column of ones. Either $\boldsymbol{x}_t$ or z_t or both may include lagged values of y_t and therefore Eq. (8.14) nests AR(p) models. When we estimate the model by Ordinary Least Square (OLS), using this framework, we are now able to discuss a range of potential tests, sometimes applied to the dates of the breaks besides the coefficients.

8.2.1 Chow Tests for Given Break Dates

As we discussed already in Chapter 1, Chow's (1960) represents the baseline approach with which most applied econometricians are familiar. When a hypothesis for the break date(s) is available—and this represents the major limitation of this tool, *it assumes that the alternative hypothesis specifies one or more exogenously given break dates*—the idea of Chow's test is to fit the equation separately for each subsample as defined by the conjectured breakpoint(s) and to see whether there are significant differences in the estimated (conditional mean) equations. The only requirement is that each subsample must contain more observations than the number of coefficients in the equation so that it can be estimated. A significant difference indicates a structural change in the relationship. In particular, the test is based on the comparison between the sum of squared residuals (SSR) obtained by fitting a single equation to the entire sample with the SSR obtained when separate equations are fit to each subsample as defined by the assumed break dates. The Chow test statistic may be written as:

$$\text{Chow}_T(K) = \frac{T - K\,\dim(\boldsymbol{\theta}_j)}{\dim(\boldsymbol{\theta}_j)} \frac{\sum_{t=1}^{T} \varepsilon_t^2 - \sum_{j=1}^{K} \sum_{t=T_{j-1}}^{T_{j-1}-1} \varepsilon_{j,t}^2}{\sum_{j=1}^{K} \sum_{t=T_{j-1}}^{T_{j-1}-1} \varepsilon_{j,t}^2}, \tag{8.15}$$

which has a clear interpretation as the relative, scaled increase in the SSR when one removes the assumed break dates $(T_1, T_2, ..., T_K)$ and estimates a standard, constant-coefficient linear model. The test statistic in Eq. (8.15) can be interpreted in three equivalent ways, in the sense that it leads to numerically equivalent p-values in large samples:[1]

- As an F-statistic of the null hypothesis that restricts K to equal 0, which has an exact finite sample F-distribution with $\dim(\boldsymbol{\theta}_j)$ and $T - K\dim(\boldsymbol{\theta}_j)$ degrees of freedom if the errors are indeed IID normal random variables.
- As an LR statistic based on the comparison of the restricted and unrestricted maximum of a (Gaussian) log-likelihood function, which has an asymptotic chi-square distribution with degrees of freedom equal to $(K-1)\dim(\boldsymbol{\theta}_j)$, the number of restrictions under the null hypothesis of no structural change.
- As a standard Wald test of the restriction that the coefficients in the mean equation are the same in all subsamples defined by the break points $(T_1, T_2, ..., T_K)$, which also has an asymptotic chi-square distribution with $(K-1)\dim(\boldsymbol{\theta}_j)$ degrees of freedom.

One example shall quickly familiarize us with the use of Chow's test.

EXAMPLE 8.1

In this example, we consider whether the predictive relationship between the classical Fama–French factor monthly US portfolio returns that we have already encountered in previous chapters for a 1953:03–2016:12 sample. The predictors are represented by three traditional state variables that are supposed to capture or predict the state of the business cycle, that is, the 12-month moving average of the dividend yield on the Standard and Poors' index, the term spread (the difference between the annualized yields on 10-year and 3-month Treasury notes and bills), and the default spread (the difference between the annualized yields on Bbb- and Aaa-rated corporate bonds with a maturity close to 10 years, as classified by Moody's). We would like to test whether the forecasting model has been subject to breaks in correspondence to three major, well-known economic events:

- The October 1973 first oil crisis (when Organization of the Petroleum Exporting Countries, OPEC, proclaimed an oil embargo targeting the United States, among other countries).
- The stock market crash in October 1987.
- Lehmann Brother's bankruptcy in September 2008.

These events and, to some extent also the dates that are going to be tested, are of course arbitrary and selected just to provide an example.

We start by estimating a baseline predictive regression in which the dividend yield is used in first differences because the series turns otherwise out to be $I(1)$ using a variety of unit root tests. Even though, strictly speaking, stationarity of the predictors is not assumed in deriving Chow's test, this avoids that the residuals may inherit statistical properties incompatible

(Continued)

1. This is due to the fact that as $T \to \infty$, $(T - K\dim(\boldsymbol{\theta}_j))/\dim(\boldsymbol{\theta}_j) \to 1$ and an F random variable with diverging degrees of freedom at the denominator becomes a chi-square.

EXAMPLE 8.1 (Continued)

with Eq. (8.14) and will allow us to extend this example later on. The resulting estimates are (Heteroskedasticity and Autocorrelation Consistent, HAC, p-values are in parenthesis):

$$x^{mkt}_{t+1} = \underset{(0.895)}{0.078} - \underset{(0.576)}{5.541}\,\Delta dy_t + \underset{(0.014)}{0.343}\ term_t + \underset{(0.998)}{0.002}\ default_t + \varepsilon_{t+1} \quad \varepsilon_{t+1} \sim \left(0, \left(\underset{(0.000)}{4.300}\right)^2\right)$$

$$x^{SMB}_{t+1} = -\underset{(0.185)}{0.382} - \underset{(0.401)}{5.983}\,\Delta dy_t + \underset{(0.262)}{0.092}\ term_t + \underset{(0.058)}{0.419}\ default_t + \varepsilon_{t+1} \quad \varepsilon_{t+1} \sim \left(0, \left(\underset{(0.000)}{2.902}\right)^2\right)$$

$$x^{HML}_{t+1} = \underset{(0.016)}{0.600} - \underset{(0.463)}{4.868}\,\Delta dy_t + \underset{(0.747)}{0.028}\ term_t - \underset{(0.205)}{0.293}\ default_t + \varepsilon_{t+1} \quad \varepsilon_{t+1} \sim \left(0, \left(\underset{(0.000)}{2.687}\right)^2\right).$$

The (predictive, in-sample) R^2 are 0.91%, 0.73%, and 0.31%, respectively: it is hard to argue that any of the three instruments has any predictive power for the three portfolio returns. However, we suspect that this result may be hiding the presence of a few structural breaks.

Table 8.1 presents the results of the Chow structural change tests. There is apparently no evidence of breaks, apart from excess market returns that however seem to be only affected by a break in the intercept and not in the forecasting relationships linking returns to the three predictors. In particular, it appears that the intercept charactering excess market returns shifts in an abrupt way after the crash of October 1987 that imparts a shift strong enough to lead to a rejection of the null also when the three break dates are jointly considered.

In particular, the model for excess market returns shifts before and after October 1987 as follows:

$$x^{mkt}_{t+1} = -\underset{(0.275)}{0.565} - \underset{(0.768)}{3.309}\,\Delta dy_t + \underset{(0.001)}{0.670}\ term_t + \underset{(0.432)}{0.388}\ default_t + \varepsilon_{t+1} \quad \varepsilon_{t+1} \sim \left(0, \left(\underset{(0.000)}{4.144}\right)^2\right) \quad \text{(before October 1987)}$$

$$x^{mkt}_{t+1} = \underset{(0.196)}{1.503} - \underset{(0.516)}{12.103}\,\Delta dy_t + \underset{(0.935)}{0.017}\ term_t - \underset{(0.420)}{0.983}\ default_t + \varepsilon_{t+1} \quad \varepsilon_{t+1} \sim \left(0, \left(\underset{(0.000)}{4.427}\right)^2\right) \quad \text{(on and after October 1987).}$$

The two in-sample predictive R^2 are now 4.07% and 0.86%. Here the interpretation is that while before 1987 excess US market returns were weakly predictable, especially using the lagged term spread, after October 1987 this stopped being the case, as also shown by the coefficient associated with the term spread that drops from 0.670 to 0.017, that is, essentially 0. Likewise the coefficient on the changes in the dividend yield grows in magnitude but remains imprecisely estimated.

In the case of excess market returns, Fig. 8.1 compares the predictive performance of the benchmark linear regression to the case in which *all* the breaks are exogenously imposed. The evidence of improvement is weak but somewhat visible in correspondence to the market busts of 1974 and 2009. In fact the overall R^2 of the model increases from 0.91% to 4.20%. Correspondingly, the SSR declines from 14,052 in the absence of breaks to 13,586 when breaks are imposed, leading to an F-statistic of 2.135 and an LRT of 25.734.

TABLE 8.1 Results of Chow Break Tests for Three Selected Dates

	All Break Dates		First Oil Shock (October 1973)		Black Monday Crash (October 1987)		Lehman's Default (September 2008)	
	F-Test	LR Test	*F*-Test	LR Test	*F*-Test	LR Test	*F*-Test	LR Test
Tests of Breaks Affecting All Coefficients, Intercept Included								
Market	**0.013**	**0.012**	0.420	0.415	**0.015**	**0.014**	0.200	0.196
SMB	0.609	0.596	0.335	0.330	0.260	0.255	0.805	0.802
HML	0.290	0.277	0.302	0.297	0.281	0.276	0.261	0.257
Tests of Breaks Affecting Only Coefficients on Predictors								
Market	0.229	0.220	0.272	0.268	0.102	0.100	0.294	0.290
SMB	0.572	0.562	0221	0.218	0.215	0.212	0.655	0.652
HML	0.139	0.133	0.197	0.193	0.277	0.273	0.271	0.267

Note: Test statistics significant at a size of 5% or less.

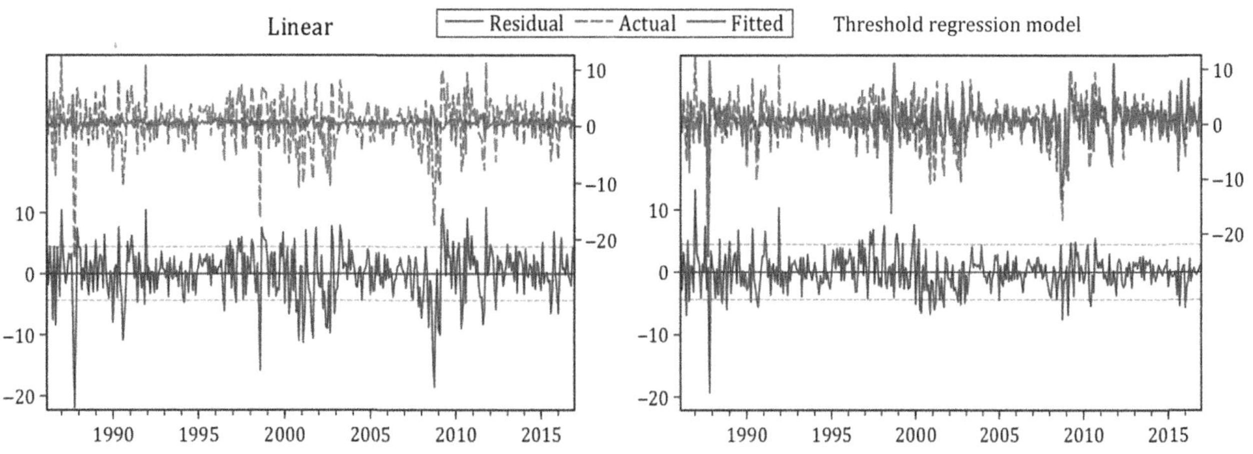

FIGURE 8.1 In-sample performance of linear versus breaking models.

8.2.2 CUSUM and CUSUM Square Tests

Needless to say, not always we shall know or at least be able to conjecture the dates of breaks. In fact, Example 8.1 has shown that sometimes, even well-known and historically important dates may not represent a firm reference to find break dates. Indeed, historically, tests for structural change were first devised based on procedures that did not assume or even estimate a break point explicitly. The main reason, as we shall soon see, is that the distribution theory for the estimates of the break dates (obtained using the least squares or likelihood principles) has become available only recently. Most of these early tests were of the form of *partial sums of residuals*. The most famous among them is the CUSUM test proposed by Brown et al. (1975). This test is based on the maximum of the partial sums of recursive residuals:

$$CUSUM_T = \max_{k+1\leq j\leq T}\left(1+2\frac{j-\dim(\boldsymbol{\theta})}{T-\dim(\boldsymbol{\theta})}\right)^{-1}\left|\frac{\sum_{t=k+1}^{j}\tilde{u}_t}{\hat{\sigma}\sqrt{T-\dim(\boldsymbol{\theta})}}\right|, \tag{8.16}$$

where $\hat{\sigma}$ is a consistent estimator of the variance of the residuals (usually the sum of squared OLS residuals although, to increase power, one can use the sum of squared demeaned recursive residuals, as suggested by Harvey, 1976) and the $\tilde{u}_t$ are the *recursive residuals* defined by:[2]

$$\tilde{u}_t = \frac{y_t - \boldsymbol{x}'_t\hat{\beta}_{t-1}}{\sqrt{(1+\boldsymbol{x}'_t(\boldsymbol{X}'_{t-1}\boldsymbol{X}_{t-1})\boldsymbol{x}_t}}, \tag{8.17}$$

for $t = 2, 3, ..., T$, where $\boldsymbol{X}_{t-1}$ contains the observations on all the regressors up to time $t-1$, $\hat{\sigma}\sqrt{(1+\boldsymbol{x}'_t(\boldsymbol{X}'_{t-1}\boldsymbol{X}_{t-1})\boldsymbol{x}_t}$ is the typical forecast error variance from a linear model, and $\hat{\beta}_{t-1}$ is the OLS estimate of $\boldsymbol{\beta}$ using data up to time $t-1$. Implicitly, Eq. (8.17) differs from Eq. (8.14) because it assumes that all regressors are subject to structural change. The limit distribution of the CUSUM test can be expressed in terms of the maximum of a weighted combination of Wiener processes, which can be at least numerically characterized. Another popular alternative, also suggested by Brown et al. (1975), is the *CUSUM of squares test*:

$$CUSUMSQ_T = \max_{k+1\leq j\leq T}\left|\frac{\sum_{t=k+1}^{j}\tilde{u}_t^2}{\sum_{t=k+1}^{T}\tilde{u}_t^2} - \frac{j-\dim(\boldsymbol{\theta})}{T-\dim(\boldsymbol{\theta})}\right|. \tag{8.18}$$

However, Ploberger and Krämer (1990) have shown that while the CUSUM test tends to display good local asymptotic power, that is, for small deviations from the null hypothesis, the CUSUM square test has only trivial local power for one-time parameters changes. However, the CUSUM test is subject to a problem: for a given sample size the power function can be nonmonotonic in the sense that it can decrease and even reach a zero value as the alternative considered becomes further

2. Ploberger and Krämer (1992) have shown that using OLS residuals instead of recursive residuals yields a valid test though its limit distribution under the null hypothesis is different. Their simulations showed that the OLS-based CUSUM test has higher power except for shifts that occur early in the sample (the standard CUSUM has instead low power for late shifts).

away from the null of no breaks, that is, exactly when one would expect the starkest rejections. The reason for this feature is the need to estimate the variance of the errors $\hat{\sigma}$ to properly scale the statistics. Because no break is directly modeled, one needs to estimate this variance using least squares or recursive residuals that are contaminated by the shift under the alternative. As the shift gets larger the estimate of the scale gets inflated with a resulting loss in power.[3] This is a troubling feature because tests that are consistent and have good local asymptotic properties can perform rather badly globally. In Deng and Perron's (2008) simulations, this problem does not occur for the CUSUM of squares test, which leads to the peculiar conclusion that the test with the worst local asymptotic properties has the best global behavior. This suggests using both the CUSUM and CUSUM squares tests jointly as a matter of routine. The example shows how this can deliver good payoffs.

EXAMPLE 8.1 (continued)

We extend Example 8.1 to investigate whether there is any evidence of breaks coming from CUSUM and CUSUM square tests. Fig. 8.2 shows the results for each of the three factors investigated earlier.

Fig. 8.2A shows that the linear model for excess market returns does contain breaks, even though the CUSUM points to a recent break in early 2009, in the aftermath of Lehman's default, and CUSUM square indicates instead a structural shift in the mid-1960s already, and in any event rather early in the sample. Fig. 8.2B shows that, differently from Chow-type tests, where however we had to specify the break dates in advance, the CUSUM square test shows breaks in the model for SMB returns occurring as early as in the early 1960s. In fact, conditioning on a break in 1965:01, the CUSUM square test applied again to the predictive linear model for SMB returns features another break in early 2000; however, none of these dates correspond to any of the break points previously tested using Chow's methodology. Similarly, in Fig. 8.2C no breaks in the linear predictive model for HML returns are revealed by a CUSUM test, but a CUSUM square test gives evidence of breaks since the late 1960s. Conditioning on a break in 1969:01 the CUSUM square test applied again to the predictive linear model for HML returns features another break in late 1999.

8.2.3 Andrews and Quandt's Single-Break Test

The odd properties of CUSUM tests suggest that to have better (e.g., globally more powerful) tests for the null hypothesis of no structural change versus the alternative hypothesis that changes are present, one should consider statistics that are based on a regression that allows for at least one break. As we saw in Eq. (8.13), Quandt (1960) proposed to build tests centered around the LR statistics derived at the break date that maximizes the likelihood function. However, as we shall also comment in Section 8.3 and in Chapter 9, this represents a nonstandard problem because at least one parameter is only identified under the alternative hypothesis, namely the break date (see Davies, 1977, 1987). One of the many solutions to this problem, already advocated by Davies (1977) for the case in which a nuisance parameter is present only under the alternative, is to use as a test statistic the maximum of the LR test overall possible values of the parameter in some prespecified set. In the case of a single structural change occurring at some unknown date, this translates into the following statistic:

$$\sup_{\lambda_1 \in \Lambda_\tau} LR_T(\lambda_1), \tag{8.19}$$

where $LR_T(\lambda_1)$ denotes the value of the likelihood ratio evaluated at some break point T_1 equal to the integer part of $T\lambda_1$ and the maximization is restricted over break fractions that are in $\Lambda_\tau \equiv [\tau, 1-\tau]$ some subset of the unit interval [0, 1] with τ being the lower bound and $1-\tau$ the upper bound. Asymmetric intervals Λ_τ are also possible but rarely used in practice. One can see Eq. (8.19) as a single Chow breakpoint test performed at every observation over a sample or between two previously determined break dates; Eq. (8.18) then summarizes the sequence of Chow tests into one test statistic for a test against the null hypothesis of no break points.

The limit distribution of the statistic in Eq. (8.19) is given by the sum of q squares of independent Wiener processes when q regression coefficients are allowed to change. Not surprisingly the limit distribution depends on both q and τ. This is crucial because the restriction that the search for a maximum value be restricted to Λ_τ represents not only a computational constraint, but it also influences the properties of the test. In particular, Andrews (1993) has shown that when $\tau = 0$, so that no restrictions are imposed and the break can occur at the very edges of the sample, the test will diverge to infinity under the null hypothesis and critical values grow and the power of the test decreases, as the break shifts toward the edges of the sample. Hence, the range over which we search for a maximum of the LR statistic must be small enough for the critical values not to be too large and for the test to retain useful power, yet large enough to include

3. With a lagged dependent variable the problem is exacerbated because the shift induces a bias of the autoregressive coefficient toward one (see Perron, 1989, 1990).

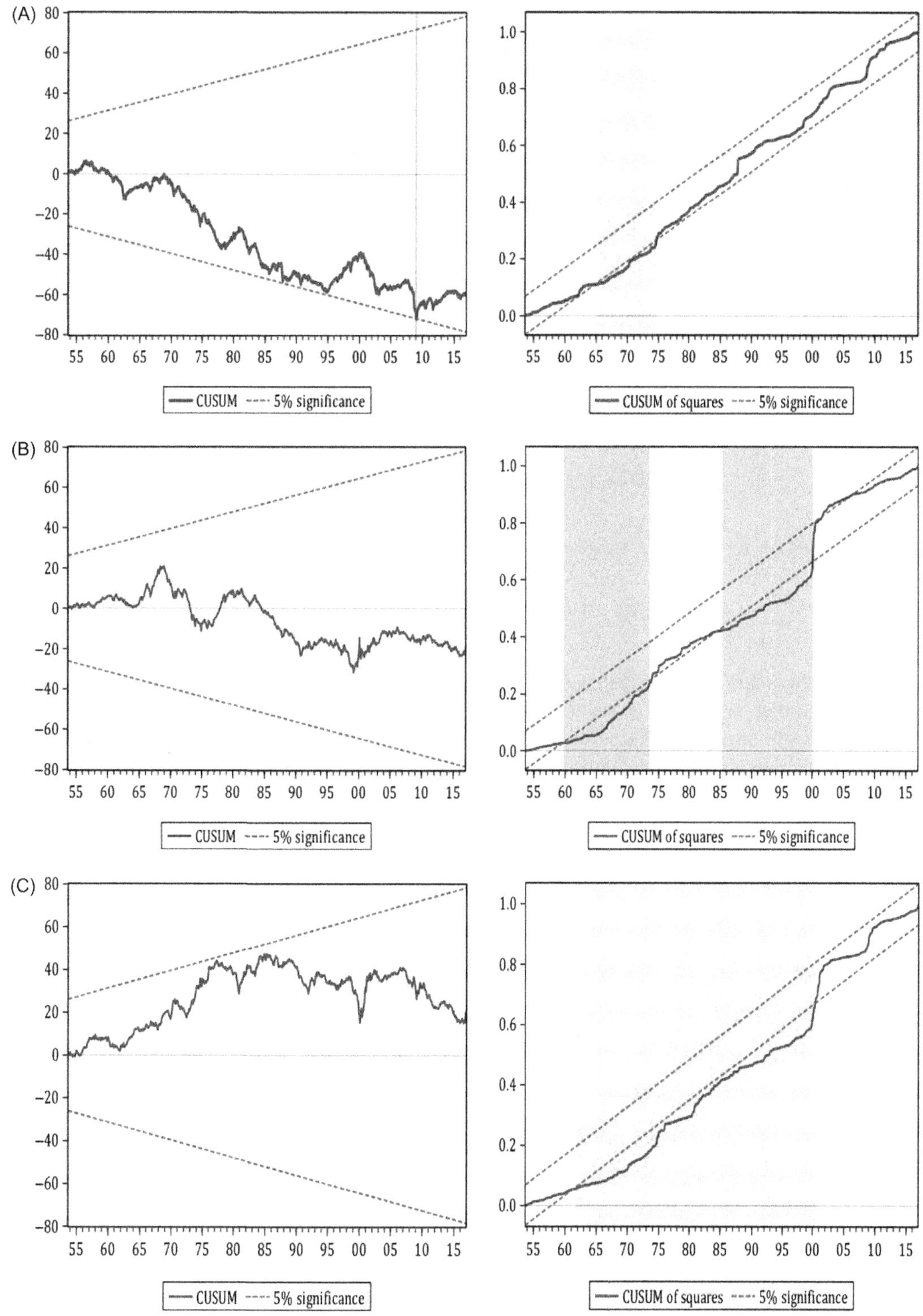

FIGURE 8.2 CUSUM and CUSUM square tests applied to a predictive linear model for Fama–French portfolio returns. (A) Excess market returns. (B) Small-minus-Big (SMB) factor. (C) High-minus-Low (HML) portfolio.

break dates that are potential candidates. In the single-break case a popular choice is $\tau = 0.15$. Because Andrews (1993) has also considered tests based on the maximal value of the Wald and LM tests and shows that they are asymptotically equivalent under the null hypothesis, the test is often called *Andrews–Quandt Sup-LR tests* to emphasize the complete generality of the LR version.[4] The tests are consistent and have nontrivial local asymptotic power against a wide range of alternatives, namely for which the parameters of interest are not constant over the interval specified by Λ_τ. One final property of Eq. (8.19) that is useful in practice is that under IID shocks and for a single break, the structural change date that solves Eq. (8.19) corresponds to the estimate of the break point, so that $\sup_{\lambda_1 \in \Lambda_\tau} LR_T(\lambda_1) = LR_T(\hat{\lambda}_1)$. However, when the errors are not IID because they feature serial correlation and/or heteroskedasticity, the test must be adjusted to account for this. Unfortunately *the sup-LR and sup-Wald tests are in general not optimal, in the sense that they fail to maximize power for a given size*. The class of optimal statistics is instead of the following exponential form:

$$Exp - LR_T(c) = (1+c)^{-q/2} \int \exp\left[\frac{1}{2}\frac{c}{1+c} LR_T(\lambda_1)\right] dJ(\lambda_1), \tag{8.20}$$

where q is the number of parameters that are subject to change. To implement this test, we need to specify the weighting function $J(\lambda_1)$ and the parameter c. A natural choice for $J(\lambda_1)$ is to specify it, so that equal weights are given to all break fractions in the trimmed interval $\Lambda_\tau \equiv [\tau, 1-\tau]$. As for c, one possibility is to set $c \to 0$ to put higher weight on alternatives close to the null value, that is, on small shifts; the alternative is $c \to \infty$, in which case greatest weight is put on large changes. This leads to two statistics that have found wide appeal: when $c \to \infty$, the test is of an exponential form:

$$Exp - LR_T(\infty) = \ln \frac{1}{T} \sum_{T_1 = \text{int}(T\tau)+1}^{T-\text{int}(T\tau)} \exp\left[\frac{1}{2} LR_T\left(\frac{T_1}{T}\right)\right]; \tag{8.21}$$

when $c \to 0$, the test takes the form of an average of the LR tests and is often referred to as the Mean-LR test:

$$Mean - LR_T = \text{Exp} - LR_T(0) = \frac{1}{T} \sum_{T_1 = \text{int}(T\tau)+1}^{T-\text{int}(T\tau)} LR_T\left(\frac{T_1}{T}\right). \tag{8.22}$$

The distribution of these test statistics is nonstandard. Andrews (1993) developed their true distribution, and Hansen (1997) provided approximate asymptotic p-values. Simulations in Andrews et al. (1996) show that the tests perform well in practice. Relative to other tests discussed earlier the Mean-LR has the highest power for small shifts and Exp-LR performs best for moderate to large shifts. However, none of them uniformly dominates the Sup-LR test in Eq. (8.14). Moreover, while the Sup-LR and Exp-LR tests have monotonic power when only one break occurs under the alternative, Vogelsang (1999) shows that the Mean-LR test can exhibit a nonmonotonic power function.

EXAMPLE 8.1 (Continued)

We now apply the Andrews–Quandt's tests further extending Example 8.1 to investigate whether there is any evidence of breaks in the predictive regressions linking the classical three Fama–French factor portfolio returns to changes in the aggregate stock market dividend yield, the term spread, or the default spread. The results for each of the three factors investigated are as follows:

Excess mkt:	Sup-LR = 4.360 (0.032) in correspondence to 1983:07
	Exp-LR = 1.136 (0.076), Mean-LR = 2.175 (0.023)
SMB:	Sup-LR = 3.780 (0.075) in correspondence to 1969:01
	Exp-LR = 0.567 (0.517), Mean-LR = 1.023 (0.395)
HML:	Sup-LR = 3.399 (0.127) in correspondence to 2000:03
	Exp-LR = 0.670 (0.389), Mean-LR = 1.275 (0.228).

The p-values were computed using Hansen's (1997) bootstrap and imposing $\tau = 0.15$, which delivers 535 alternative break dates. For simplicity, we just present LR-type tests even though, because the model estimated consisted of a regression, in this case the p-values are numerically identical. Consistently with earlier results, only excess market returns contain a structural break (as revealed by the Sup-LR and the Mean-LR tests) that is however now identified in correspondence to 1983:07, that is, a date we had not experimented with before under Chow's framework. Moreover, the CUSUM and CUSUM square tests had failed to identify this date as a significant break date. On the contrary, and under all tests, SMB and HML returns fail to show any evidence of a break in the predictive relationships, consistently with earlier results. Fig. 8.3 shows the recursively computed LR tests for each possible date.

4. One may wonder whether the equivalence between Wald, LR, and LM tests has broken down. Even though one may also use a Sup-LM test, the simulations of Vogelsang (1999) showed that this sup test is seriously affected by the problem of nonmonotonic power, in the sense that, for a fixed sample size, the power of the test can rapidly decrease to 0 as the change in the parameter increases. This is again because the variance of the errors is estimated under the null hypothesis of no change.

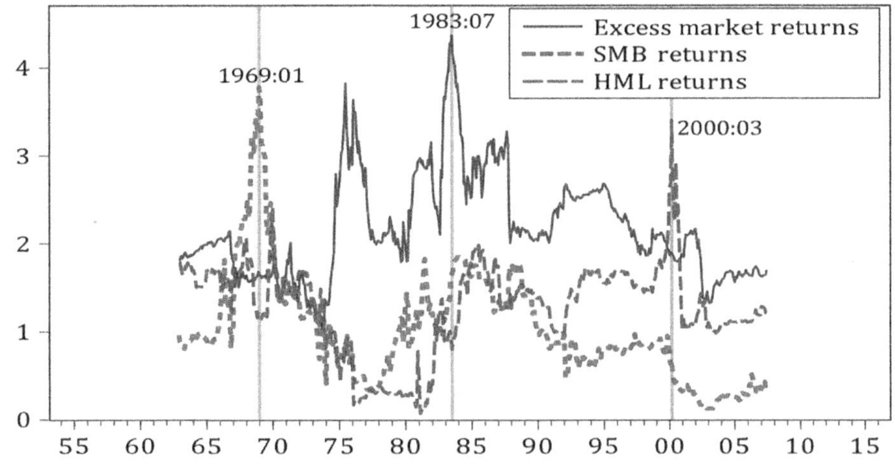

FIGURE 8.3 Andrews–Quandt Sup-LR tests over the subinterval fractions [0.15, 0.85].

All of these tests, however, suffer from important power problems when the alternative is one that involves two breaks. This suggests that any (or most) tests will exhibit nonmonotonic power functions if the number of breaks present under the alternative hypothesis is greater than the number of breaks explicitly accounted for in the construction of the tests. Therefore, substantial power gains can be derived from using tests for multiple structural changes. It is then natural to think of ways to generalize the Andrews–Quandt's tests to multiple structural changes. However, we still know little on this point. Andrews et al. (1996) studied a class of optimal tests. The Avg-LR and Exp-LR tests remain asymptotically optimal. However, the problem with these tests in the case of multiple structural changes is practical implementation as they require the computation of the LR test (or of the equivalent Wald test) overall permissible partitions of the sample as defined by the break dates in Λ_T; hence, the number of tests that need to be evaluated is of the order $O(T^K)$, which is already very large with $K=2$ and prohibitively large when $K>2$. Consider instead the simpler Sup-LR test. With IID errors, maximizing the LR statistic with respect to admissible break points is equivalent to minimizing the SSR when the search is restricted to the same possible partitions of the sample. As we shall discuss in Section 8.2.4, this maximization problem can be solved with an efficient algorithm. Of course, using the Sup-LR test in place of Avg-LR or Exp-LR entails a loss of power, but in the literature there are not many studies quantifying such a loss, at least in simulations.

8.2.4 Bai and Perron's Multiple, Endogenous Breaks Test

In a series of papers, Bai and Perron have offered a different approach to *estimating multiple breaks using efficient algorithms*. With reference to the regression in Eq. (8.14), for each K-partition $(T_1, T_2, ..., T_K)$, the associated least squares estimates of β_j and δ are obtained by minimizing the sum of squared residuals,

$$SSR(T_1, T_2, ..., T_K) = \sum_{j=1}^{K} \sum_{t=T_{j-1}}^{T_{j-1}-1} (y_t - x'_t\beta_j - z'_t\delta)^2. \tag{8.23}$$

Let $\left\{\hat{\beta}_j(T_j)\right\}$ and $\left\{\hat{\delta}(T_j)\right\}$ denote the estimates based on the given K-break partition. Substituting these break dates in the objective function and denoting the resulting SSR as $SSR(T_1, T_2, ..., T_K)$, the estimated break points $(\hat{T}_1, \hat{T}_2, ..., \hat{T}_K)$ are global minimizers of the objective function such that:

$$(\hat{T}_1, \hat{T}_2, ..., \hat{T}_K) = \underset{(T_1, T_2, ..., T_K)\in T}{\operatorname{argmin}} \; SSR(T_1, T_2, ..., T_K), \tag{8.24}$$

where the minimization is taken over some set of admissible partitions T; when lagged dependent variables are included among the regressors, the additional condition that $T_j - T_{j-1}$ should exceed some constant fraction of the overall sample size T is added. A standard grid search procedure would require least squares operations of an order of magnitude of T^K and becomes prohibitive when the number of breaks is greater than 2, even for relatively small samples. However, fast methods based on a dynamic programming algorithms turn out to be efficient. The basic idea becomes fairly intuitive once it is realized that, with a sample of size T, the total number of possible segments is at most $T(T+1)/2$ and is therefore of an order proportional to T^2; one then just needs a method to select which combination of segments (i.e., which partition of the sample) yields a minimum value of the objective function. The partial structural change regression parameter estimates are the estimates associated with the K-partition, $\left\{\hat{\beta}_j(T_j)\right\}$ and $\left\{\hat{\delta}(\hat{T}_j)\right\}$.[5]

Under some conditions detailed in Perron and Qu (2006), essentially equivalent to:

- weak stationarity of the regressors (that however does not need to rule out conditional heteroskedasticity), so that IIDness appears sufficient but also unnecessarily strong, and
- that the break dates are asymptotically distinct and that breaks will keep occurring when all segments of time separating breaks were to increase in length in the same proportions to each other when asymptotically $T\rightarrow\infty$ (this rules out the absurd implication that if we were able to collect more and more data, the last regime should increase in length while all other segments would become a negligible proportion of the total sample),

A key theoretical result is as follows.[6]

RESULT 8.1

The true but unknown break fractions $\lambda_j \equiv T_j/T$ ($j = 1, 2, ..., K$) are consistently estimated by solving Eq. (8.24), $p\lim \hat{\lambda}_j \equiv \hat{T}_j/T = \lambda_j$, the resulting rate of convergence is T, and the estimators are independent of each other. Conditioning on the estimated break dates, the OLS estimator of the regression coefficients is also consistent at rate T.

Without reporting complex expressions the limit distribution of the estimates of the multiple break dates depends on:

- the magnitude of the change in the coefficients (with larger changes leading to higher precision, as expected);
- the (limit) sample moment matrices of the regressors (quantities similar to $\boldsymbol{X}_t'\boldsymbol{X}_t$) for the segments prior to and after the true break date (on which they are allowed to be different);
- the so-called long-run variance, which involves potential serial correlation in the errors (and which again is allowed to be different prior to and after the break); and
- whether the regressors are trending or not.

A feature of interest is that the confidence intervals need not be symmetric given that the data and that errors can have different properties before and after the break.

Interestingly, because of the definition of probability limits (see the mathematical and statistical Appendix to this book), the estimates of the break dates are not themselves consistent, but the differences between the estimates and the true values are bounded by some constant, in probability. However, Result 8.1 still implies that the estimates of the other parameters have the same distribution that would prevail if the break dates were known.[7] The independence of the estimated break dates result is very helpful: for each break date, the analysis becomes exactly the same as if a single break has occurred. The intuition behind this feature is that the distance between each break increases at rate T as the sample size increases.

Perron and Qu (2006) have dealt with a broader framework whereby *arbitrary linear restrictions on the parameters of the conditional mean can be imposed* in the estimation:

$$y_t = \boldsymbol{x}_t'\boldsymbol{\beta}_j + \varepsilon_t \quad \boldsymbol{R\beta} = \boldsymbol{r}, \qquad t = T_{j-1}, T_{j-1}+1, ..., T_j - 1, \tag{8.25}$$

where $\boldsymbol{R}$ is a matrix with rank r that imposes the restrictions, r is a column vector with size equal to number of restrictions r that are imposed, and $\boldsymbol{\beta} \equiv [\boldsymbol{\beta}_1' \; \boldsymbol{\beta}_2' \; ... \; \boldsymbol{\beta}_K']'$. Eq. (8.25) has the advantage that there is no need for a distinction between variables whose coefficients are allowed to change and those whose coefficients are not allowed to change. A partial structural change model can be obtained as a special case by specifying restrictions that impose some coefficients to be identical across all break-implied regimes. Moreover, a number of practically interesting cases become

---

5. Our use of OLS to estimate the model implies that if changes in the variance of the errors were allowed, provided they occur at the same dates as the breaks in the parameters of the regression, such changes cannot be exploited to increase the precision of the break date estimators.

6. With a sample of size of 1000 observations and four breaks occurring at dates 200, 400, 600, and 800, all segments are a fifth of the total sample. It therefore makes sense to use an asymptotic framework whereby this feature is preserved.

7. Chong (2001) has considered an AR(1) model where the AR coefficient takes a value less than one before some break date and value one after, or vice versa. He showed consistency of the estimate of the break date and derived the limit distribution. When the move is from stationarity to unit root, the rate of convergence is the same as in the stationary case (though the limit distribution is different), but interestingly, the rate of convergence is faster when the change is from a unit root to a stationary process.

possible in which we specify a number of states less than the number of regimes (i.e., states are partially recurrent for a limited number of times or a subset of coefficients may be allowed to change over only a limited number of regimes). Under the same assumptions described earlier, Perron and Qu show that the same consistency and rate of convergence results as in Result 8.1 hold. Moreover, the limit distribution of the estimates of the break dates is unaffected by the imposition of valid restrictions.

Another as interesting as useful result is that *it is possible to consistently estimate all break fractions sequentially, that is, one at a time*. This is due to the fact that when we estimate a single-break model in the presence of multiple breaks, the estimate of the break fraction will converge to one of the true break fractions, the one that is dominant in the sense that taking it into account allows the greatest reduction in the sum of squared residuals. Then, allowing for a break at the estimated value, a second single-break model can be applied which will consistently estimate the second dominating break, and so on (in the case of two breaks that are equally dominant, the estimate will converge with probability 1/2 to either break). However, Bai (1997) has derived the limit distribution of the estimates and shows that they are not the same as those obtained when estimating all break dates simultaneously. In particular, except for the last estimated break date, the limit distributions of the estimates of the break dates depend on the parameters in all segments of the sample (when the break dates are estimated simultaneously, the limit distribution of a particular break date depends on the parameters of the adjacent regimes only). To remedy this problem, Bai (1997) suggested a procedure called *repartition*. This amounts to reestimating each break date conditional on the adjacent break dates. For example, if the initial estimates of the break dates are $(\hat{T}_1^0, \hat{T}_2^0, \ldots, \hat{T}_K^0)$, the second round estimate for the ith break date is obtained by fitting a one break model to the segment starting at date $\hat{T}_{i-1}^0$ and ending at date $\hat{T}_{i+1}^0 - 1$ (with $\hat{T}_0^0 = 1$ and $\hat{T}_{K+1}^0 = T$). The estimates obtained from this repartition procedure have the same limit distributions as those obtained simultaneously.

The last point worth covering concerns testing for the presence of structural change when we do not wish to prespecify a particular number of breaks to make inference. In such instances, two approaches can be used:

- *Global tests* of the null hypothesis of no structural break against an unknown number of breaks given some upper bound K, also called *double maximum tests*;
- *Sequential tests*, which are tests of L versus $L+1$ breaks, which can be used as the basis of a sequential testing procedure that stops when the null of L breaks cannot be rejected against the alternative of $L+1$ breaks.

There are two well-known double maximum tests. The first is an equally weighted version defined by:

$$UD\,max\,LR_T(K, q) = \max_{1 \le j \le K} LR_T(\hat{\lambda}_1, \hat{\lambda}_2, \ldots, \hat{\lambda}_K; q), \tag{8.26}$$

where $\hat{\lambda}_j = \hat{T}_j / T$ are the estimates of the break points obtained using the global minimization of the sum of squared residuals, and K is the maximum number of admissible breaks. The UD max test (the U stands for unweighted) can be given a (Bayesian) interpretation in which the prior assigns equal weights to the possible number of changes. The second test applies weights to the individual tests such that the marginal p-values are equal across values of j prior to taking the "external maximum" and is denoted the weighted $WDmax\ F_T(\mathrm{K}, q)$. Its analytical formulation is complex enough to discourage us to copy it here and we refer to Bai and Perron (1998) for details. In both simulations and applications, it is found that usually $K = 5$ should be sufficient, or other models (such as Markov switching (MS), see Chapter 9) may appear better suited. Double maximum tests have shown to have good power in simulations: Bai and Perron (2006) show that the power of the double maximum tests is almost as high as the best power that can be achieved using the test that accounts for the correct number of breaks.

As for the sequential tests, for a model with L breaks, the estimated break points denoted by $\hat{T}_1, \hat{T}_2, \ldots, \hat{T}_L$ are obtained by a global minimization of the SSR. The strategy proceeds then by testing for the presence of an additional break in each of the $(L+1)$ segments (obtained using the estimated partition $\hat{T}_1, \hat{T}_2, \ldots, \hat{T}_L$). The test amounts to the application of $(L+1)$ tests of the null hypothesis of no structural change versus the alternative hypothesis of a single change, applied to each segment defined by two adjacent break dates. We conclude in favor of a rejection in favor of a model with $(L+1)$ breaks if the overall minimal value of the sum of squared residuals (overall segments where an additional break is included) is sufficiently smaller than the sum of squared residuals from the L breaks model. The break date selected is the one associated with this overall minimum. More precisely, the test is of a Wald/F-type and is defined by:

$$W_T(L+1|L) = \frac{SSR_T(\hat{T}_1, \hat{T}_2, \ldots, \hat{T}_L) - \min\limits_{L \le j \le L+1} \inf\limits_{\eta \in \Lambda_{j,\tau}} SSR_T(\hat{T}_1, \ldots, \hat{T}_{j-1}, \eta, \hat{T}_j, \ldots, \hat{T}_L)}{\hat{\sigma}^2} \tag{8.27}$$

$$\Lambda_{j,\tau} = \left\{\eta; \hat{T}_{j-1} + (\hat{T}_j - \hat{T}_{j-1})\tau \le \eta \le \hat{T}_j - (\hat{T}_j - \hat{T}_{j-1})\tau\right\},$$

where $\hat{\sigma}^2$ is a consistent estimate of σ^2 under the null hypothesis and also, preferably, under the alternative. Note that for $j=1$ the second SSR at the numerator is understood as $SSR_T(\eta, \hat{T}_1, \ldots, \hat{T}_j, \ldots, \hat{T}_L)$ and for $j = \text{T}$ as $SSR_T(\hat{T}_1, \ldots, \hat{T}_j, \ldots, \hat{T}_L, \eta)$. Importantly, one can and often needs to allow different distributions across segments for the regressors and the errors. The limit distribution of the test in Eq. (8.27) is related to the limit distribution of a test for a single change.

Bai (1999) attacks the problem in a slightly different way and considers the same problem of testing for L versus $L+1$ breaks while allowing the breaks to be global minimizers of the SSR under both the null and alternative hypotheses. This leads to the likelihood ratio test defined by:

$$Sup\ LR_T(L+1|L) = \frac{SSR_T(\hat{T}_1, \hat{T}_2, \ldots, \hat{T}_L) - SSR_T(\hat{T}_1^*, \hat{T}_2^*, \ldots, \hat{T}_{L+1}^*)}{SSR_T(\hat{T}_1^*, \hat{T}_2^*, \ldots, \hat{T}_{L+1}^*)/T}, \tag{8.28}$$

which has a limit distribution equal to a weighted sum of Brownian bridges that are amenable to computing asymptotic critical values.

As already emphasized, both tests can support a sequential procedure. One simply needs to apply the tests successively starting from $L=0$, until a nonrejection occurs. The estimate of the number of breaks thus selected will be consistent, provided the significance level used decreases at an appropriate rate, to keep into account the data snooping problem caused by repeated, non-independent testing. The simulation results in Bai and Perron (2006) show that the resulting estimate of the number of break points is more accurate than those obtained using information criteria, including a few that have been proven to be particularly suitable to select the number of breaks in linear models.[8] However, they report a percentage of cases in which the procedure stops too early and under-reports the number of breaks. Their recommendation is then to first use a double maximum test to ascertain if any break is at all present. The sequential tests can then be used starting at some value greater than 0 to determine the number of breaks. It is now time to put these tools to work by concluding Example 8.1.

EXAMPLE 8.1 (Continued)

We apply the Bai and Perron's technology to investigate once more, from a different perspective, whether there is any evidence of breaks in the predictive regressions linking the classical three Fama–French factor returns to standard predictors. As a first step, we try to use information criteria under a variety of choices, such as $\tau = 0.15$ and 0.10, allowing the error distributions and standard errors to differ across break-implied regimes (this provides robustness of the test to error distribution variation at the cost of power if the error distributions are the same across regimes); in all cases, we set the maximum number of breaks to five. All tests are robust to heteroskedasticity and autocorrelation in the residuals because based on HAC variance estimates (with Bartlett's kernel and Newey–West bandwidth). We always find that none of the linear predictive models contains breaks, which is somewhat surprising in the case of excess market returns data.

Next, we apply global tests based on both the unweighted and the weighted double maximum tests, $WDmax\ F_T(K)$ and $UDmax\ LR_T(K)$. We set $\tau = 0.10$ and we use in the selection *p*-values of 0.05, allowing the error distributions and standard errors to differ across break-implied regimes. When the $UDmax\ LR_T$ test is applied, we find evidence of four breaks in the case of excess market returns (1968:12, 1975:07, 1994:12, and 2009:03), of three breaks in the case of SMB returns (1969:01, 1976:11, and 1983:08), and of no breaks in HML returns. When the $WDmax\ F_T$ test is applied, we find evidence of the same four breaks in the case of excess market returns, of the same three breaks in the case of SMB returns, and of five breaks (1970:01, 1985:03, 1993:08, 2000:03, and 2009:03) in the case of HML returns. The contrast between unweighted and weighted double maximum tests in the case of HML returns is striking.

Finally, we deploy sequential tests, using at first a sequential strategy that applies $(L+1)$ tests of the null hypothesis of no structural change versus the alternative hypothesis of a single change, applied to each segment defined by two adjacent break dates. Interestingly, we find no evidence of breaks in any of the series under investigation for a wide range of parameter choices as to the trimming factor and the *p*-values sequentially applied. However, when also apply Bai's (1999) approach by testing for L versus $L+1$ breaks while allowing the breaks to be global minimizers of the SSR under both the null and alternative hypotheses, the resulting LR tests indicate that two breaks are present in excess market returns data (1987:09 and 2009:03), but again no breaks in SMB and HML returns.

(Continued)

8. Yao (1988) has shown that under relatively strong conditions, the number of breaks that minimizes the SBIC is a consistent estimator of the true number of breaks in a breaking mean model. Liu et al. (1997) have proposed a modified SBIC for determining the number of breaks showing consistency of the estimated number of break points.

EXAMPLE 8.1 (Continued)

All in all, one lesson is that even within Bai and Perron's multiple breaks framework, different approaches may lead to rather heterogeneous conclusions. Specifically, we find hard evidence of breaks in excess market returns, even though their exact identity is considerably uncertain. There is some sporadic, fleeting evidence of breaks in SMB and hardly any evidence of structural shifts in HML returns. Just to document how Bai and Perron's sequential tests of $L+1$ versus L globally determined breaks works, we report here the estimates for the excess market return predictive regression obtained conditioning on the two breaks reported earlier:

$$x_{t+1}^{mkt} = \underset{(0.275)}{-0.566} - \underset{(0.779)}{3.153}\,\Delta dy_t + \underset{(0.000)}{0.686}\; term_t + \underset{(0.442)}{0.380}\; \text{default}_t + \varepsilon_{t+1} \quad \text{(before September 1987)}$$

$$x_{t+1}^{mkt} = \underset{(0.000)}{3.202} + \underset{(0.696)}{8.636}\,\Delta dy_t - \underset{(0.771)}{0.071}\; term_t - \underset{(0.000)}{3.052}\; default_t + \varepsilon_{t+1} \quad \text{(between September 1987 and February 2009)}$$

$$x_{t+1}^{mkt} = \underset{(0.060)}{-2.430} - \underset{(0.176)}{33.195}\,\Delta dy_t + \underset{(0.336)}{0.418}\; term_t + \underset{(0.001)}{2.646}\; default_t + \varepsilon_{t+1} \quad \text{(after March 2009).}$$

Table 8.2 presents a portion of the break point sequential specification analysis that uses Bai and Perron's tests produced by E-Views.

As Table 8.2 presents, the test statistic is written as an *F*-test and, because of the global spin given to the sequential search, even though the null of no breaks is not rejected against the alternative of one break, the null of one break is rejected against two and in correspondence to such a rejection, the scaled *F*-statistic takes a value of 18.81. Fig. 8.4 completes the analysis showing the forecasts and the prediction errors for excess market returns when the two breaks isolated above are taken into account. Even though the eye-balling is always dangerous in econometrics, the ability of the predictive model to forecast positive and negative excess returns of 8%–9% per month in absolute value during the Great Financial Crisis is impressive.

TABLE 8.2 Results of Bai–Perron's Sequential Multiple Break Tests

Breakpoint Specification

Estimated number of breaks: 2
Method: Bai–Perron tests of $L+1$ versus L globally determined breaks
Maximum number of breaks: 5
Breaks: 1987M09, 2009M03

Sample: 1953M05, 2016M12
Included observations: 764
Breaking variables: C DELTA_DY(-1) TERM(-1) DEFAULT(-1)
Break test options: Trimming 0.10, max. breaks 5, sig. level 0.05
Test statistics employ HAC covariances (Bartlett kernel, Newey–West fixed bandwidth)
Allow heterogeneous error distributions across breaks

Break Test	*F*-Statistic	Scaled *F*-Statistic	Critical Value[a]
0 versus 1	3.596	14.383	16.76
1 versus 2*	**4.703**	**18.810**	**18.56**
2 versus 3	4.679	18.717	19.53
3 versus 4	5.028	20.114	20.24
4 versus 5	4.728	18.912	20.72

Estimated break dates:
(1) 1983M07
(2): 1987M09, 2009M03
(3) 1982M08, 1991M07, 2009M03
(4) 1968M12, 1975M07, 1994M12, 2009M03
(5) 1968M12, 1975M07, 1982M08, 1991M07, 2009M03
[a]*Bai–Perron (Econometric Journal, 2003) critical values.*
**Significant at the 0.05 level.*

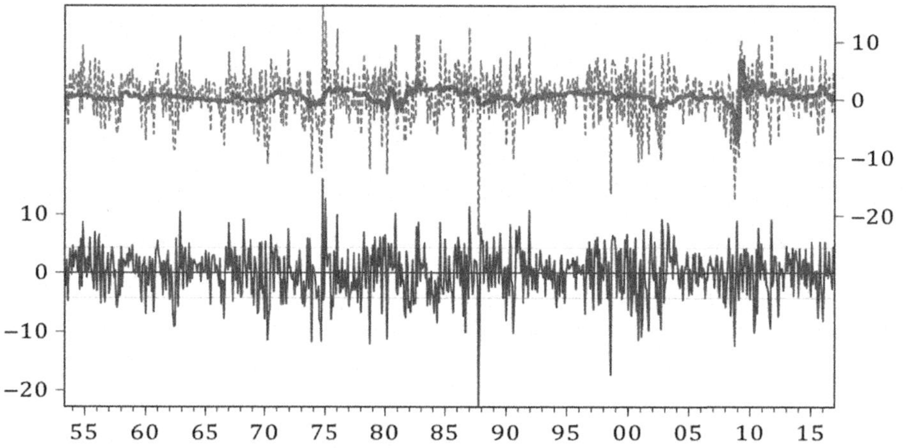

FIGURE 8.4 In-sample performance of a linear model subject to two breaks.

There has also been some work on multiple structural changes in multivariate systems, such as VAR(p) models, see, that is, Qu and Perron (2007) who consider the case of $\boldsymbol{y}_t$ $N \times 1$ vector of endogenous variables where only a subset of the coefficients is allowed to change, whether it be the parameters of the conditional mean, the covariance matrix of the errors, or both. Their test is once more based on the maximized value of the likelihood ratio overall permissible partitions assuming uncorrelated and homoskedastic errors. The results are similar to those obtained in Bai and Perron (1998).

8.2.5 Testing for Breaks When Testing for Unit Roots and Cointegration, and Vice Versa

Another interesting set of methods concerns testing the null hypothesis of a unit root in the presence of structural changes in the drift and/or trend functions. Of course, this is technically far from trivial because we know that structural changes and unit root nonstationarity share similar features in the sense that most tests for structural change will reject in the presence of a unit root in the errors, and vice versa, tests of stationarity versus unit root will reject in the presence of structural changes. In particular, Perron (1989) has made the compelling point that *conventional unit root tests are biased toward a false unit root null when the data are trend-stationary but contain a structural break.* He shows that, when the true process involves structural changes in the trend function, the power of unit root tests may dramatically be reduced. In particular, if a level shift occurs, the estimate of the autoregressive coefficient (α) is asymptotically biased toward 1. If a change in the trend slope is present, its limit value is actually 1. This translates into substantial power losses of standard unit root tests. Worse, simulations in Perron (1994) emphasize that such power reduction increases as the number of lags p in the augmentation portion of DF tests are increased; Montañés and Reyes (2000) show that the power problems also plague the Phillips-Perron type unit root tests while Lee et al. (1997) point out that the presence of structural breaks in the trend function affects tests of the null hypothesis of stationarity (e.g., the KPSS test) by inducing size distortions toward rejecting the null hypothesis too often. In short the presence of structural changes induces a bias in favor of a unit root representation that empirically researchers ought to take into account.

These results have spurred a large literature on *modified unit root tests that may remain valid in the presence of a break.* In essence the point is to amend the standard augmented Dickey–Fuller test to allow for levels and trends that differ across (at least) a single break date. This has occurred through the development of testing tools that concern four different types of models:

- Nontrending data with a one-time change in level.
- Trending data with a one-time change in level.
- Trending data with a one-time change in trend slope.
- Trending data with a one-time change in both level and trend slope.

These are applied to evaluate the null hypothesis that the data follow a unit root process, possibly with *one break*, against a trend stationary with break alternative. Moreover, each of the four types can be formulated as *innovational outlier (IO) models*, when the break occurs gradually, with the breaks following the same dynamic path as the innovations of the regression, or as an *additive outlier (AO) model*, which assumes that the break occurs abruptly. Even though it is possible to assume that the break date is known, the most interesting case is when the break date is to be estimated endogenously.

For the IO model, under the (drifting random walk) null we have:

$$y_t = \mu + y_{t-1} + \varphi(L)[\theta I_{\{t=T_b\}} + \gamma I_{\{t \geq T_b\}} + \varepsilon_t], \tag{8.29}$$

where ε_t is IID and $\varphi(L)$ is a lag polynomial representing the dynamics of the stationary and invertible ARMA error process. Under the alternative hypothesis, we assume a trend-stationary model with breaks in the intercept and trend:

$$y_t = \mu + \beta t + \varphi(L)[\theta I_{\{t=T_b\}} + \varsigma I_{\{t \geq T_b\}}(t - T_b + 1) + \varepsilon_t]. \tag{8.30}$$

We therefore construct a generalized Dickey–Fuller test equation that nests the two hypotheses:

$$y_t = \mu + \beta t + \theta I_{\{t=T_b\}} + \gamma I_{\{t \geq T_b\}} + \varsigma I_{\{t \geq T_b\}}(t - T_b + 1) + \alpha y_{t-1} + \sum_{i=1}^{p} \varphi_i \Delta y_{t-i} + u_t, \tag{8.31}$$

and use the t-statistic of the estimate of α comparing it to 1 to evaluate the null hypothesis. As in Chapter 4, the lagged differences are included in Eq. (8.31) to eliminate the effect of the error correlation structure on the asymptotic distribution of the t-statistic. Within this general framework, we may specify different models for the null and alternative hypotheses by placing zero restrictions on one or more of the trend and break parameters, $\beta, \theta, \gamma, \varsigma$. When we consider nontrending data with a one-time change in level, we have:

$$y_t = \mu + \theta I_{\{t=T_b\}} + \gamma I_{\{t \geq T_b\}} + \alpha y_{t-1} + \sum_{i=1}^{p} \varphi_i \Delta y_{t-i} + u_t, \tag{8.32}$$

a test of a random walk against a stationary model with a breaking intercept. When the data are trending and we suspect a break in the intercept:

$$y_t = \mu + \beta t + \theta I_{\{t=T_b\}} + \gamma I_{\{t \geq T_b\}} + \alpha y_{t-1} + \sum_{i=1}^{p} \varphi_i \Delta y_{t-i} + u_t, \tag{8.33}$$

a test of a random walk with drift against a trend-stationary model with intercept break. However, the same test may accommodate a break in the slope of the trend:

$$y_t = \mu + \beta t + \gamma I_{\{t \geq T_b\}} + \varsigma I_{\{t \geq T_b\}}(t - T_b + 1) + \alpha y_{t-1} + \sum_{i=1}^{p} \varphi_i \Delta y_{t-i} + u_t, \tag{8.34}$$

which tests a random walk with drift null against a trend stationary with trend break alternative. Finally the general alternative in Eq. (8.31) tests the random walk with drift against a trend stationary with intercept and trend breaking alternative. Note that if the break date is known, while Eqs. (8.31)–(8.33) allow for breaks under the null hypothesis of stationarity Eq. (8.30), this is not the case in Eq. (8.34) because $\varsigma \neq 0$ implies itself nonstationarity (a breaking trend). This represents a problem with the derivation of the limit distribution of the relevant test statistics (basically, the t-statistics for α) when the break dates need to be estimated that has kept theorists busy for a decade.

In the case of the general AO model the random walk with drift null hypothesis is:

$$y_t = \mu + y_{t-1} + \theta I_{\{t=T_b\}} + \gamma I_{\{t \geq T_b\}} + \varphi(L)\varepsilon_t, \tag{8.35}$$

where ε_t is IID and $\varphi(L)$ is a lag polynomial representing the dynamics of the stationary and invertible ARMA error process. The alternative hypothesis is of a trend-stationary model with possible breaks in the intercept and trend:

$$y_t = \mu + \beta t + \gamma I_{\{t \geq T_b\}} + \varsigma I_{\{t \geq T_b\}}(t - T_b + 1) + \alpha y_{t-1} + \varphi(L)\varepsilon_t. \tag{8.36}$$

Testing for a unit root in the AO framework is a two-step procedure where we first use the intercept, trend, and breaking variables to detrend the series using OLS, and then use the detrended series to test for a unit root using a modified Dickey–Fuller regression. Even though the AO case may appear simpler, is the technically more involved one and in fact, it leads us to a two-step procedure.

In the first step of the AO test, we detrend the data using a model with appropriate trend and break variables:

- Nontrending data with a one-time change in the intercept, $y_t = \mu + \gamma I_{\{t \geq T_b\}} + u_t$.
- Trending data with a one-time change in level, $y_t = \mu + \beta t + \gamma I_{\{t \geq T_b\}} + u_t$.
- Trending data with a one-time change in trends slope, $y_t = \mu + \beta t + \varsigma I_{\{t \geq T_b\}}(t - T_b + 1) + u_t$.
- Trending data with a one-time change in both level and trend slope Eq. (8.36).

In the second step, we apply a further, modified Adjusted Dickey-Fuller (ADF) unit root test equation to the residuals obtained from the detrending step:

$$\hat{u}_t = \sum_{i=0}^{p} I_{\{t-i=T_b\}}\kappa_i + \alpha\hat{u}_{t-1} + \sum_{i=1}^{p} \varphi\Delta\hat{u}_{t-i} + v_t, \tag{8.37}$$

where we use the t-statistic for comparing the estimate of α to 1, to evaluate the null hypothesis. These are standard ADF equations with the addition of break dummy variables to eliminate the asymptotic dependence of the test statistic on the correlation structure of the errors and to ensure that the asymptotic distribution is identical to that of the corresponding IO specification. The number of lags p can be selected with a variety of methods, for instance, so that the coefficient on the last included dependent variable lag difference is significant at a specified probability value, using F-tests of the joint significance of the lag coefficients for a given p_0 against all higher lags up to some $p_{\max}$, or by minimizing some information criterion for models with number of lags from 0 to $p_{\max}$. While sometimes the break dates may be fixed a priori, this has raised concerns. The argument is that the choice of the break date is inevitably linked to the historical record and, hence, involves an element of data-mining. Unfortunately, it has been shown that if one performed a systematic search for a break when the series is actually a unit root process without break, using fixed break critical value would entail a test with substantial size distortions. Therefore, methods have been studied to select the break dates endogenously from the data, for example:

- Minimizing the Dickey–Fuller t-statistic, to select the date providing the strongest evidence against the null hypothesis of a unit root and in favor of the breaking trend alternative hypothesis.
- Choose the date that gives the strongest evidence of a type of break that is considered particularly plausible, say in either γ or ς (or we can use F-test to minimize the p-value coming from both types of breaks).

In these cases, for each possible break date, the optimal number of lags is chosen using the specified method, and the test statistic of interest is computed. The procedure is repeated for each possible break date, and the optimal break date is chosen from the set of candidate dates, which may have to be restricted to be smaller than the full sample. Perron and Vogelsang (1992) have derived the limit distributions for testing break dates for both the IO and AO cases and conveniently tabulated critical values although rather tricky assumptions are required in order to make any claims on the optimality of the resulting tests. While these methods lead to tests with the correct asymptotic size, they obviously imply a reduction in power because of the joint need to estimate dates and parameters jointly.

Of course, also the fact that we test and take into account one break only may represent a problem. However, as argued by Perron (2006), it is mostly major changes in level and/or slope that induce a reduction in the power of standard unit root tests. Small shifts, especially in level, are likely to reduce power only slightly. Hence, what is important is to account for the large shifts, and not all of them if the others are small. Therefore, starting with one break may already provide a large payoff. Example 8.2 reexamines one result obtained in Chapter 4, that is, that aggregate dividends and earnings in the United States contain a unit root.

EXAMPLE 8.2

In Chapter 4, we concluded that monthly US aggregate dividends and earnings contain a unit root with reference to a long, 1871:01–2016:12 sample. In this example, we examine whether such a conclusion from standard ADF tests may have been contaminated by the presence of at least one break in the time series.

As a first step, we copy in Table 8.3 the results from standard ADF tests that assume the absence of breaks in both the drift and, if any, the trend of the series. For both series, and under a variety of choices concerning the specification of the model and the selection and the number of lags, we conclude that both series are nonstationary.

Next, we apply breakpoint-adjusted ADF tests on the basis of IO models, in which the break is allowed to occur gradually, through the realizations of the model shocks. Because we have no priors in this regard, we allow the breaks to affect both the intercepts and the slope of the trend. We select the number of lags using a modified Schwarz Bayesian Information criterion, SBIC, (but the results discussed later are robust to this choice) appropriate to ADF applications, with a maximum of 24. As for the estimation of the breakpoint, we initially aim at minimizing the t-statistic for α in the ADF test. Table 8.4 presents the estimation results. In the case of dividends the break is estimated to occur in October 2009, just in the aftermath of the financial crisis. The break date is highly significant, at least in the sense that the OLS estimates of γ and ς in Eq. (8.34) command p-values of 0.000. However, accounting for this break hardly affects the test results, in the sense that dividends remain a unit root process. Results are very different in the case of the earnings series: a break is estimated to have occurred in July 1987, a few months

(Continued)

EXAMPLE 8.2 (Continued)

before the October 1987 crash (and this could make us ponder whether the extreme market correction of that Fall may have reflected the change in the dynamics of companies' earnings, but this would require testing whether the break had been perceived in real time). In particular, estimation leads to a precisely estimated break in the trend slope. When the break is taken into account, the aggregate US earnings series turns out to be stationary.

Table 8.5 details results obtained from applying the AO model to the same series and under the same selection of parameters. Even though the ADF t-statistics associated with α change, and there is generally more evidence against the null of a unit root, it remains the case that dividends follow a random walk with drift, while earning appear to follow a stationary process.

TABLE 8.3 Results of Standard ADF Tests Applied to Aggregate US Dividends and Earnings

Null hypothesis: Dividends have a unit root Exogenous: Constant, linear trend Lag length: 16 (automatic—based on modified SIC, maxlag = 24)			
		***t*-Statistic**	**Probability***
Augmented Dickey–Fuller test statistic		3.1761	1.000
Test Critical Values	1% level	−3.9633	
	5% level	−3.4124	
	10% level	−3.1281	
Null hypothesis: Earnings have a unit root Exogenous: Constant, linear trend Lag length: 24 (automatic—based on modified SIC, maxlag = 24)			
		***t*-Statistic**	**Probability***
Augmented Dickey–Fuller test statistic		0.6893	0.9997
Test Critical Values	1% level	−3.9634	
	5% level	−3.4124	
	10% level	−3.1282	

**MacKinnon (1996) one-sided* p-values.

TABLE 8.4 Results of Breakpoint-Modified ADF Tests for Aggregate Dividends and Earnings—Innovational Outliers

Null hypothesis: Dividends have a unit root Trend specification: Trend and intercept Break specification: Trend and intercept Break type: Innovational outlier Break date: 2009M10 Break selection: Minimize Dickey–Fuller *t*-statistic Lag length: 16 (automatic—based on Schwarz information criterion, maxlag = 24)			
		***t*-Statistic**	**Probability***
Augmented Dickey–Fuller test statistic		−2.3438	>0.999
Test Critical Values	1% level	−5.7191	
	5% level	−5.1757	
	10% level	−4.8940	

(Continued)

TABLE 8.4 (Continued)

Null hypothesis: Earnings have a unit root
Trend specification: Trend and intercept
Break specification: Trend and intercept
Break type: Innovational outlier

Break date: 1987M07
Break selection: Minimize Dickey–Fuller *t*-statistic
Lag length: 16 (automatic—based on Schwarz information criterion, maxlag = 24)

		t-Statistic	Probability*
Augmented Dickey–Fuller test statistic		−8.7615	**<0.010**
Test Critical Values	1% level	−5.7191	
	5% level	−5.1757	
	10% level	−4.8940	

Note: Test statistics significant at a size of 5% or less.
**Vogelsang (1997) asymptotic one-sided* p-values.

TABLE 8.5 Results of Breakpoint-Modified ADF Tests for Aggregate Dividends and Earnings—Additive Outliers

Null hypothesis: Dividends have a unit root
Trend specification: Trend and intercept
Break specification: Intercept only
Break type: Additive outlier

Break date: 2009M10
Break selection: Minimize Dickey–Fuller *t*-statistic
Lag length: 10 (automatic—based on Schwarz information criterion, maxlag = 24)

		t-Statistic	Probability*
Augmented Dickey–Fuller test statistic		−4.0996	0.313
Test Critical Values	1% level	−5.3476	
	5% level	−4.8598	
	10% level	−4.6073	

Null hypothesis: Earnings have a unit root
Trend specification: Trend and intercept
Break specification: Trend and intercept
Break type: Additive outlier

Break date: 1987M07
Break selection: Minimize Dickey–Fuller *t*-statistic
Lag length: 13 (automatic—based on Schwarz information criterion, maxlag = 24)

		t-Statistic	Probability*
Augmented Dickey–Fuller test statistic		−8.8834	**<0.010**
Test Critical Values	1% level	−5.7191	
	5% level	−5.1757	
	10% level	−4.8940	

Note: Test statistics significant at a size of 5% or less.
**Vogelsang (1997) asymptotic one-sided* p-values.

We conclude this section by briefly mentioning that breakpoint tests similar to those covered in Section 8.2.3 are available with reference to cointegrated VAR models written in error correction form:

$$\Delta \boldsymbol{y}_t = \boldsymbol{\mu} + \boldsymbol{\alpha B}' \boldsymbol{y}_{t-1} + \sum_{i=1}^{p} \boldsymbol{\Gamma}_i \Delta \boldsymbol{y}_{t-i} + \boldsymbol{u}_t, \tag{8.38}$$

where $\boldsymbol{u}_t$ is a vector white noise, $\boldsymbol{B}$ is the $N \times r$ cointegrating matrix, and $\boldsymbol{\alpha}$ is the adjustment matrix (hence, there are r cointegrating vectors). Under the null hypothesis, both are assumed constant, while under the alternative either one or both are assumed to exhibit a (or at least) one-time change at some unknown date. Here the results available in the literature are quite fragmentary and much of them pertain to a single break at a known date. Also, different treatments are possible by allowing for a change in the trend function of the original series (i.e., the marginal processes), or in allowing for a change in the cointegrating relation. Indeed, one of the difficulties is that standard methods to analyze system cointegration covered in Chapter 4 are not easily extended to the case of breaks, when their date is unknown.

When the break date is unknown, the tests are of an Andrews–Quandt type but tend to be Sup, Mean, and Exp versions of the LM test, they concern special cases (for instance, Seo (1998) considers the case of triangular VARs), and their limit distribution is complicated by the appearance of μ in Eq. (8.38), that is, on whether the series are assumed to be drifting. Also the tests are valid if the cointegrating rank is correctly specified. As usual, being LM tests, these can be expected to have nonmonotonic power since they do not explicitly allow for any breaks. To escape these limitations, Hansen and Johansen (1999) have exploited the fact that any instability in $\boldsymbol{\alpha}$ and/or $\boldsymbol{B}$ will manifest itself in the form of instability in the eigenvalues estimates for the special expression involving matrices that depend on the residuals from a regression of $\Delta \boldsymbol{y}_t$ (or $\boldsymbol{y}_t$) on a constant and lags of $\Delta \boldsymbol{y}_t$, when evaluated using different samples. They propose to assess the presence of breaks using the recursive estimates of such sample eigenvalues through a fluctuations test. Interestingly, there is simulation evidence that such tests over-reject the null hypothesis of no structural change when the cointegrating rank is over-specified, that is, when the number of stochastic trends, or unit root components, is under-specified. This is the multivariate equivalent of the problem discussed early on, that structural change and unit roots can easily be confounded.

Of course, in the special cases in which cointegration may be assessed by estimating a univariate regression (see Chapter 4, because cointegration tests boil down to testing whether the regression residuals contain a unit root, then the material just covered is normally applicable and may support the applied work.[9]

8.3 THRESHOLD AND SMOOTH TRANSITION REGIME SWITCHING MODELS

As we saw in Section 8.2, an intuitive and always appealing approach to statistical instability is to simply use dummy variables in classical regression analysis: say, one regime applies before the break or regime shift, the other(s) afterward. For instance, one estimates (say, by OLS)

$$\begin{aligned} y_{t+1} &= [\phi_{0,1} I_{\{t<T_b\}} + \phi_{0,2} I_{\{t\geq T_b\}}] + [\phi_{1,1} I_{\{t<T_b\}} + \phi_{1,2} I_{\{t\geq T_b\}}] y_t + \varepsilon_{t+1} \\ \varepsilon_{t+1} &\sim N(0, [\sigma_1^2 I_{\{t<T_b\}} + \sigma_2^2 I_{\{t\geq T_b\}}]), \end{aligned} \tag{8.39}$$

where $I_{\{t<B\}}$ and $I_{\{t\geq B\}}$ are standard indicator variables that separate the pre- and postregime change periods, and B is the time of the regime change. Eq. (8.39) can be generalized to any number of regime changes (breaks). However, this way of proceeding makes sense if and only if T_b (more generally, the dates of the regime changes) were known for sure. This has two implications:

- Dummy regressions can only be used to estimate RS parameters conditioning on some other method having been used to infer that (an event on) date T_b has triggered a regime or structural shift in parameters; as we saw in Section 8.2, the nature of such a method remains rather involved and subject to limits, while any argument that regime changes must be accompanied by visible alterations in the recorded dynamics of the series turns soon tautological, in the sense that one would then be expected to learn from the data the dates of the regime shifts that need to be imposed on the same data, in order to estimate the nature of such regime shifts.
- Even assuming that such a method to isolate RS dates is fully valid and with associated uncertainties, using dummy variables will not allow us to predict future instability, that is, regime changes, for instance to derive data-driven indications as to the average duration of the current regime (i.e., when it is likely to end).[10]

9. However, structural changes can also manifest themselves through changes in the long-run relationship, either in the form of a change in the intercept, or a change in the cointegrating vector and this may cause substantial reductions in the power of standard tests for the null hypothesis of no-cointegration as documented by Gregory et al. (1996). Unfortunately, in many cases the resulting break date associated with the minimal value of a given statistic to test for unit roots/cointegration is not, in general, a consistent estimate of the break date if a change is present.

10. Absent better methods, in financial applications, either T_b is obvious to predict, which is however an embarrassing claim because the change in parameter values would then have been discounted by all traders in the market a long time before, or T_b becomes completely unpredictable which is equivalent to surrender to the randomness of market regimes.

When forecasting financial data is our objective, estimating simple regressions supplemented by dummy variables that capture instability will often prove insufficient.

In fact, at least since the 1970s, econometricians have developed methods in which statistical instability is stochastic, it has structure, and as such it can be predicted. This reflects the intuition that the regime shifts are caused by some imperfectly predictable forces that produce the changes that are reflected by the dynamic process of financial time series. In particular, it is often elegant to assume that there is some larger model encompassing all regressions (more generally, dynamic time series models) across all possible regimes. For instance, using the same example already proposed in Section 8.1, a new framework may be written as in Eq. (8.1):

$$y_{t+1} = \phi_{0,S_{t+1}} + \phi_{1,S_{t+1}} y_t + \sigma_{S_{t+1}} z_{t+1} \quad z_{t+1} \text{ IID } N(0,1), \tag{8.40}$$

where S_{t+1} is a discrete, stochastic variable that may take $K \geq 1$ values, $S_{t+1} = 1, \ldots, K \ \forall t \geq 0$. We generally assume that S_{t+1} and z_{t+1} are independent, in the sense that current shocks affect the variable of interest only directly and not also through induced shifts in regimes (however, it will be the case that S_{t+1} depends on past values of the innovations). Of course, when $K = 1$, the model simplifies to a standard single-regime Gaussian AR(1).

However, simply specifying Eq. (8.40) provides at this point only a partial description of the time series properties of the data: a complete description of the probability law governing the series requires *a probabilistic model of what causes any time variation in* S_{t+1}. In fact, this very effort can be of key importance to determine the most appropriate form of the nonlinearity. After all, adopting an incorrect nonlinear specification may be more problematic than simply ignoring the nonlinearity altogether. Since selecting the proper nonlinear model can be difficult, it is not surprising that this remains an important area of research. However, some special forms of nonlinearity have proven to be particularly useful in applied time series analysis. The econometrics literature offers three leading examples of frameworks with regimes:[11]

1. *Threshold RS (TRS) models*, when S_{t+1} is *deterministically* driven by the (combination of) current and past value(s) of the variables of interest, often the very past values of the dependent variable in a regression model.
2. *Smooth transition RS (STRS) models*, when S_{t+1} is determined by the (combination of) current and past value(s) of the variables of interest, in the sense that the weight (interpretable as a probability) assigned to the statistical relationship corresponding to alternative values of S_{t+1} conditions on such current and past values.
3. *MS models*, when S_{t+1} follows a *finite-order Markov chain variable* that does not directly or purely depend on a (combination of) current and past value(s) of the variables of interest, which brings into the model an additional degree of randomness that is absent in TRS and STRS models.

There is an intuitive analogy between the contrast TRS/STRS versus MS models and the opposition between GARCH and stochastic volatility models: TRS and STRS feature the same source(s) of randomness twice, the first time directly, for instance in Eq. (8.40) time $t+1$ returns depend on their past, and the second time indirectly, through the regime variable S_{t+1}, that in Eq. (8.40) may be assumed to depend on past values of the series. However, the source of any random dynamics is purely represented by the time series $\{y_t\}$. On the contrary, MS models feature two (simultaneously independent) sources of randomness, for instance, in Eq. (8.40) past returns are supplemented by the influence of one (simultaneously) independent Markov chain, S_{t+1}. As a result, MS models allow more flexibility in fitting the available data than TRS and STRS do, even though they all are examples of nonlinear time series models.

8.3.1 Threshold Regression and Autoregressive Models

In a threshold model, S_{t+1} assumes K distinct values (these do not have to be numbers, but can also be letters or descriptions of the corresponding economic characterization, such as "bull" and "bear" markets) in dependence of the value taken at time t by some *threshold variable*, x_t which may also correspond to some exogenous, but always observable variable, for instance:

11. This is just a heuristic classification: once you leave the special case of linear models, there are infinite nonlinear model—among them, RS and MS specifications—you can choose from. For instance, Enders (2008) provides a readable introduction to a large family of nonlinear models such as nonlinear ARMA, generalized autoregressions, bilinear models, artificial neural networks, etc.

$$S_{t+1} = \begin{cases} 1 & \text{if } x_t \leq x_1^* & \Leftrightarrow y_{t+1} = \phi_{0,1} + \phi_{1,1}y_t + \varepsilon_{t+1} & \varepsilon_{t+1} \sim N(0, \sigma_1^2) \\ 2 & x_1^* < x_t \leq x_2^* & \Leftrightarrow y_{t+1} = \phi_{0,2} + \phi_{1,2}y_t + \varepsilon_{t+1} & \varepsilon_{t+1} \sim N(0, \sigma_2^2) \\ \vdots & \vdots & & \vdots \\ K & x_{K-1}^* < x_t & \Leftrightarrow y_{t+1} = \phi_{0,K} + \phi_{1,K}y_t + \varepsilon_{t+1} & \varepsilon_{t+1} \sim N(0, \sigma_K^2) \end{cases}, \tag{8.41}$$

where $x_1^*, x_2^*, \ldots, x_{K-1}^*$ are estimable threshold parameters that are simply required to exceed the minimum value in the sample for x_t and to be inferior to the maximum for x_t. Note that K regimes require defining and estimating $K-1$ such parameters. When a TRS model has $x_t = y_{t+1-d}$ where $d \geq 1$, we write of *self-exciting threshold models*, in the sense that past (often extreme) realizations of the variable of interest will cause regime shifts and hence cause nonlinearities to appear in the series; d is called the *delay parameter* of the model. The economic intuition of self-excitement is rather intriguing: for instance, $x_t = y_t$ may capture the fact that when in a given periods asset returns are high, this may trigger a shift to a regime of high mean and high variance, so that large returns today lead larger returns and also higher volatility in the future, and vice versa, as typical of bubbles, for instance.

Apart from the self-exciting case, what else may x_t be? An example could be some key financial indicator, capturing the overall state of financial markets that persistently affects them. For instance, x_t could be the Federal Funds Rate (FFR), used in a TRS model of US stock returns with, say, $K = 2$.

EXAMPLE 8.3

Consider the following two-state threshold autoregressive AR(1) model, often shortened as TAR(1):

$$R_{t+1} = \phi_{0,LowFFR} + \phi_{1,LowFFR}R_t + \sigma_{LowFFR}z_{t+1} \quad z_{t+1} \text{ IID } N(0,1),$$

when $FFR \leq FFR^*$, rates are low (or quantitative easing is active or increasing) and monetary policy lose, and

$$R_{t+1} = \phi_{0,HighFFR} + \phi_{1,HighFFR}R_t + \sigma_{HighFFR}z_{t+1} \quad z_{t+1} \text{ IID } N(0,1),$$

when $FFR > FFR^*$, rates are high (or quantitative easing is not present or tapering is under way) and monetary policy tight. One may expect to find that $\phi_{0,LowFFR}/(1-\phi_{1,LowFFR}) > \phi_{0,HighFFR}/(1-\phi_{1,HighFFR})$ and $\sigma_{LowFFR} < \sigma_{HighFFR}$ even though these are just empirically testable hypotheses. Interestingly, besides estimating $\phi_{0,LowFFR}$, $\phi_{1,LowFFR}$, $\phi_{0,HighFFR}$, $\phi_{1,HighFFR}$, σ_{LowFFR}, and $\sigma_{HighFFR}$, also FFR^* becomes an estimable parameter.

The same example can easily be adapted and be instructive in empirical terms when one replaces FFR with the VIX (an indicator of the level of expected volatility by market participants and often labeled the market's "fear gauge"), or be extended to any sensible number of alternative regimes, $K > 2$.

More generally, the *threshold regression model* (TRM) of Tong (1983)—that nests threshold ARMA models as a special case—allows for abrupt switching depending on whether the transition variable is above or below a threshold. For instance, for concreteness and in the case of two regimes and a predictive regression (i.e., in which the RHS time t-indexed variables forecast y_{t+1}), we have:

$$y_{t+1} = [I_t\alpha_1 + (1-I_t)\alpha_2] + [I_t\beta_1 + (1-I_t)\beta_2]'\mathbf{X}_t + \varepsilon_{t+1}$$
$$\varepsilon_{t+1} \sim N(0, [I_t\sigma_1^2 + (1-I_t)\sigma_2^2]) \quad I_t = \begin{cases} 1 \text{ if } g(\mathbf{X}_t) < c \\ 0 \text{ if } g(\mathbf{X}_t) \geq c \end{cases} \quad \text{or } I_t = \begin{cases} 1 \text{ if } -\infty < g(\mathbf{X}_t) < c \\ 0 \text{ if } c \leq g(\mathbf{X}_t) < +\infty, \end{cases} \tag{8.42}$$

that is, each of the two regimes applies in dependence on whether some function of the regressors $g(\mathbf{X}_t)$ exceeds or not a threshold c (to be estimated), where $g(\cdot): \mathbb{R}^M \to \mathbb{R}$ is a function that converts the current values of the M predictors in $\mathbf{X}_t$ into a value to be compared with the threshold c.[12] Note that even though the model for y_{t+1} is *piecewise linear* within each of the K regimes, the mere possibility of RS means that the entire time series $\{y_t\}_{t=1}^T$ is nonlinear.

12. Of course, when the function $g(\cdot)$ reduces to a selector that extracts one variable from $\mathbf{X}_t$, then the regime is defined simply on the basis of the extracted variable. ε_{t+1} does not need to be IID, it is sufficient to assume it is a uniformly square integrable martingale difference sequence, so that $E_t[\varepsilon_{t+1}] = 0$ and its variance is finite. However, $g(\cdot)$ may be more general, for instance $g(\mathbf{X}_t, \ldots, \mathbf{X}_{t+1-d}) = \mathbf{X}_t - \mathbf{X}_{t+1-d}$ for $d \geq 2$, which is what Enders and Granger (1998) call the momentum-TAR(p) model.

DEFINITION 8.2 (TRM)

Given a set of predetermined variables collected in the matrix $\mathbf{X}_t$, a TRM is defined as:

$$\begin{aligned} y_{t+1} &= \sum_{k=1}^{K} I_t(k)\alpha_k + \sum_{k=1}^{K} I_t(k)\boldsymbol{\beta}_k{}'\mathbf{X}_t + \varepsilon_{t+1} \\ \varepsilon_{t+1} &\sim N\left(0, \sum_{k=1}^{K} I_t(k)\sigma_k^2\right) \quad I_t(k) = \begin{cases} 1 \text{ if } c_k < g(\mathbf{X}_t, \ldots, \mathbf{X}_{t+1-d}) \leq c_{k+1} \\ 0 \text{ otherwise,} \end{cases} \end{aligned} \tag{8.43}$$

where $c_1 = -\infty$ and $c_{K+1} = +\infty$, and $g(\cdot): \mathbb{R}^M \to \mathbb{R}$ is a function that converts the current and past values of the M predictors in $\mathbf{X}_t, \ldots, \mathbf{X}_{t+1-d}$ into a value to be compared with the thresholds $c_2 < c_3 < \cdots < c_K$. When $\mathbf{X}_t$ collects $p \geq 1$ lags of the dependent variable y_{t+1}, then Eq. (8.43) turns into a TAR model, TAR(p); when $g(\mathbf{X}_t, \ldots, \mathbf{X}_{t+1-d})$ collects $p \geq 1$ lags of the dependent variable y_{t+1}, then Eq. (8.43) turns into a self-exciting threshold autoregressive model, SETAR(p).

In what follows, we shall assume that in each of the K regimes featured by a TAR(p) model, the associated AR(p) submodels (within regimes) are stationary. In fact, conditions for global stationarity (usually implied by geometric ergodicity) of SETAR(p) models

$$\begin{aligned} y_{t+1} &= \sum_{k=1}^{K} I_t(k)\alpha_k + \sum_{k=1}^{K} I_t(k)\sum_{j=1}^{p} \phi_{j,k} y_{t+1-j} + \varepsilon_{t+1} \\ \varepsilon_{t+1} &\sim N\left(0, \sum_{k=1}^{K} I_t(k)\sigma_k^2\right) \quad I_t(k) = \begin{cases} 1 \text{ if } c_k < y_{t+1-d} \leq c_{k+1} \\ 0 \text{ otherwise} \end{cases} \end{aligned} \tag{8.44}$$

have been studied but apart from the simple $K = p = 1$ case (i.e., $|\phi_{1,1}\phi_{1,2}| < 1$ that obviously always follows when $|\phi_{1,1}| < 1$, $|\phi_{1,2}| < 1$) they are rather tedious. There is also a small set of results on testing the hypothesis of a unit root (linear nonstationarity) against a stationary TAR (nonlinear stationary) and on testing the hypothesis of linearity against the alternative of nonlinearity while allowing for the possibility of nonstationarity under the null hypothesis that follow a logic similar to Section 8.2.4 and that we shall not deal with again (see Hansen, 2011, for an introduction and references).[13]

Note that Eq. (8.44) can be rewritten as:

$$y_{t+1} = \alpha_t + \boldsymbol{\beta}_t{}'\mathbf{X}_t + \varepsilon_{t+1}, \tag{8.45}$$

which is a *time-varying parameter model* with $\alpha_t \equiv \sum_{k=1}^{K} I_t(k)\alpha_k$ and $\boldsymbol{\beta}_t{}' \equiv \sum_{k=1}^{K} I_t(k)\boldsymbol{\beta}_k$, also known as nonlinear transfer function model. When $\mathbf{X}_t$ simply includes lags of y_t and the variable controlling the regime switches is also some dth lag of the dependent variable, the model in Eq. (8.45) becomes in fact an example of a *nonlinear autoregression model*. Note that in Eq. (8.44), K regimes always originate $K-1$ estimable threshold parameters, $c_2 < c_3 < \cdots < c_K$, so that we are in regime k if the value of the threshold variable is at least as large as the kth threshold value, but does not exceed the $(k+1)$th threshold. It is easy to envision extensions of Eqs. (8.44) and (8.45) to a mixed TRM/TAR model in which the slope coefficients of some of the regressors fail to be switching:

$$y_{t+1} = \alpha_t + \boldsymbol{\beta}_t{}'\mathbf{X}_t + \boldsymbol{\delta}'\mathbf{Z}_t + \varepsilon_{t+1}. \tag{8.46}$$

Here $\boldsymbol{\delta}$ is a fixed $Q \times 1$ vector of constant parameters. For instance, thinking of our earlier Example 8.3, one may envision a model in which while past VIX always affects stock returns with the same slope coefficients across regimes,

13. The techniques of Chapter 4 can be extended to encompass a threshold framework. For instance, Balke and Fomby (1997) have introduced a "threshold cointegration" multivariate Vector Error Correction Model (VECM) which allows a discontinuous adjustment to a long-run equilibrium; Enders and Siklos (2001) have extended the Engle and Granger's test for cointegration to allow for threshold adjustment. In the case of nonlinear time series the notion of a $I(1)$ series is replaced by a long-memory concept and cointegration by the existence of possibly nonlinear attractors, see Granger and Hallman (1991).

past stock returns predict subsequent returns in ways the depend on the FFR_t, used as a threshold variable with a delay parameter of one period.

Nonlinear least squares (see Chapter 1), conditional on some assumed initial conditions where appropriate, represent a natural approach to estimating the parameters of the models in Eqs. (8.45) and (8.46). When the errors are IID normal, this is equivalent to Maximum Likelihood estimation (MLE). Defining the sum of squares objective function as:

$$SSR(\alpha_1,...,\alpha_K,\boldsymbol{\beta}_1,...,\boldsymbol{\beta}_K,c_2,...,c_K,\boldsymbol{\delta}) = \sum_{t=1}^{T}\left(y_{t+1} - \sum_{k=1}^{K} I_t(k)\alpha_k - \sum_{k=1}^{K} I_t(k)\boldsymbol{\beta}_k{}'\mathbf{X}_t - \boldsymbol{\delta}'\mathbf{Z}_t\right)^2$$
$$I_t(k) = \begin{cases} 1 \text{ if } c_k < g(\mathbf{X}_t,...,\mathbf{X}_{t+1-d}) \leq c_{k+1} \\ 0 \text{ otherwise} \end{cases} \quad k = 1,...,K, \quad c_1 = -\infty, \ c_{K+1} = +\infty. \tag{8.47}$$

We may obtain consistent TRM/TAR/SETAR estimates by minimizing Eq. (8.47) with respect to the parameters. In fact, taking advantage of the fact that for a given set of thresholds $c_2,...,c_K$, say $\hat{c}_2,...,\hat{c}_K$, the minimization of the *concentrated objective*—that is, $SSR(\alpha_1,...,\alpha_K,\boldsymbol{\beta}_1,...,\boldsymbol{\beta}_K,\boldsymbol{\delta};\hat{c}_2,...,\hat{c}_K)$—is a simple least squares problem, we can view estimation as finding the set of thresholds and corresponding OLS coefficient estimates that minimize the sum-of-square residuals across all possible sets of threshold partitions.[14] Normally, as described in Hansen (1999), the algorithm proceeds iteratively: given some initial set of thresholds arbitrarily picked, we minimize $SSR(\alpha_1,...,\alpha_K,\boldsymbol{\beta}_1,...,\boldsymbol{\beta}_K,\boldsymbol{\delta};\hat{c}_2^0,...,\hat{c}_K^0)$ to obtain OLS parameters $\hat{\alpha}_1^1,...,\hat{\alpha}_K^1,\hat{\boldsymbol{\beta}}_1^1,...,\hat{\boldsymbol{\beta}}_K^1,\hat{\boldsymbol{\delta}}^1$; at this point, we estimate by grid search a new set of thresholds, $\hat{c}_2^1,...,\hat{c}_K^1$ (usually, these simply coincide with a subset of K sample observations, sufficiently spaced) and proceed again to minimize the residual sum of squares conditioning on these values, etc. In general, at step j, for given threshold parameter estimates from step $j-1$, one solves an OLS problem to minimize $SSR(\hat{\alpha}_1^j,...,\hat{\alpha}_K^j,\hat{\boldsymbol{\beta}}_1^j,...,\hat{\boldsymbol{\beta}}_K^j,\hat{\boldsymbol{\delta}}^j;\hat{c}_2^{j-1},...,\hat{c}_K^{j-1})$; this can be iterated until convergence. For a given K, global estimation of thresholds compares the SSRs for all possible sets of threshold values. In fact, with reference to one analogous estimation problem that we have tackled in Section 8.2, threshold regressions and TAR models may be thought of as breakpoint least squares regression with data reordered with respect to the threshold variable(s). Chan (1990) has shown (in the univariate case) that if the model is stationary and ergodic, the iterative NLS parameter estimates, including those of the thresholds, are strongly consistent; of course, not all of the estimators can be asymptotically normal, think of delay parameter that is by construction a nonnegative integer, so that their joint distribution is best estimated by simulation methods.

There are several approaches available to select the value of the delay parameter, d. The standard one is to estimate a TRM/TAR for each potential value of d. The one with the smallest value of the residual sum of squares delivers the most appropriate value of the delay parameter. Alternatively, we can choose d that leads to the smallest value of our favorite information criterion. This second approach has been proven to be the most useful when the optimal number of lags or the selection of predictors in the different regimes turns out to severely depend on the choice of d.

As for the choice of the number of regimes K, they and the associated threshold values may be known a priori or they may be estimated using a variety of approaches that, at least in general terms, can be classified as:

- global maximizer
- sequential testing methods.

For instance, as already described in Section 8.2, Bai and Perron (1998) describe global optimization procedures for identifying the number of regimes and associated threshold parameters which minimize the SSR in Eq. (8.47). If K is known, the globally optimizing breaks are defined by the set of estimated thresholds and corresponding coefficient estimates that minimize the overall SSR. If K is not known, one typically specifies a maximum number of regimes and employs testing to determine the optimal number. The test of $K-1$ versus Kregime-procedure may be applied sequentially beginning with a $K=2$ until the null is not rejected. Additionally, selection of the number of regimes based on information criteria may be used as in Yao (1988), where we minimize a specified criterion with respect to the number of regimes. Alternatively, we can use sequential estimation, based on finding one initial threshold value that minimizes the associated concentrated SSR, followed by a search of additional values (given the initial value) and hence of the number of regimes that minimizes the SSR, until the desired number of thresholds, possibly determined through testing, is obtained.[15]

14. Because if a threshold is to be meaningful, the series must actually cross it a sufficient number of times, the search for the monotonically ordered thresholds occurs applying a trimming factor $\tau \in (0,1)$ to the sorted data, such that no thresholds are estimated on the data after excluding the lowest and the highest $(\tau/2)T$ observations.

15. In applied work, it is common to use the Bai–Perron Sup-F-test statistic described in Section 8.2. We caution that in the case of TARs that include lagged endogenous variables, the conditions required for the distributional results in Bai and Perron's tests may be violated, see Hansen (1999).

Example 8.4 shows the potential that a TAR(p) with K states has for modeling financial data.

EXAMPLE 8.4

We start by estimating a (homoskedastic) TRM for value-weighted monthly US excess returns (x_t) for the sample 1986:01–2016:12, in which one and two lags of the change in the effective FFR (roughly speaking, the interest rate at which US banks and credit unions lend reserve balances to each other overnight, on an uncollateralized basis; the reserve balances are amounts held at the Federal Reserve to maintain depository institutions' reserve requirements) forecast the conditional equity risk premium in ways that potentially differ according to one- and two-lags (i.e., $d = 1$ or 2) of FFR itself. Moreover, we admit that the monthly changes in the VXO (an index of the level of implied volatility on the S&P 100 index) may also forecast excess stock returns. We apply a standard trimming factor $\tau = 0.1$.

Using sequential Bai–Perron tests (with a test size of 5%) of $L + 1$ versus L regimes starting with $L = 1$ and going up to six regimes, we obtain evidence in favor of $L = 2$ (i.e., the null of $L = 2$ is not rejected in favor of three regimes) and of a delay parameter $d = 1$, that is, it is month t FFR that affects the regime prevailing at time $t + 1$. The estimated threshold is at an annualized FFR of 0.54%. In light of the fact that FFR displays a sample average of 3.62%, with first and fourth quartiles of 0.40% and 5.56%, we basically isolate a regime of extremely low, below-mean, and median policy rates from medium and high rates. Table 8.6 presents how E-Views proceeds to apply sequential Sup-F-tests.

Empirically the first regime includes 97 observations, mostly at the end of the sample period, and the second regime includes 273 observations. The estimated model is (HAC p-values are in parentheses):

$$x_{t+1} = \begin{cases} \underset{(0.000)}{1.093} - \underset{(0.002)}{28.493}\Delta FFR_t + \underset{(0.000)}{30.023}\Delta FFR_{t-1} - \underset{(0.000)}{0.654}\Delta VXO_t + \varepsilon_{t+1} & \text{if } FFR_t < 0.54 \\ \underset{(0.004)}{0.563} - \underset{(0.498)}{1.471}\Delta FFR_t + \underset{(0.282)}{2.245}\Delta FFR_{t-1} - \underset{(0.000)}{0.654}\Delta VXO_t + \varepsilon_{t+1} & \text{if } FFR_t \geq 0.54 \end{cases}$$

with an overall estimate of the standard deviation of the errors of 3.118. Therefore, when money market rates are low, excess stock returns strongly and precisely respond to FFR changes, even though with a typical over-reaction pattern: for instance, a 1 standard deviation increase (by 0.197%) in the FFR today decreases excess stock returns over the following month by −5.61%, which is a considerable move, in excess of 1 standard deviation of excess stock returns; however, such an effect appears to be retracked in 2 months, because the overall change is then 0.301%. In the second regime of high rates the effects are instead between 10 and 15 times smaller in absolute value and never precisely estimated, even though a weak over-reaction pattern also appears. Instead, an increase in market-implied volatility is always followed by a statistically significant stock market downturn: for instance, a 1 standard deviation increase (4.864%) in VXO is always followed by a negative excess return of -0.79%, which has been restricted to be constant across the two regimes.

The adjusted R^2 of the model, measured in conventional ways, is a rather impressive 50.9%. In fact, it is interesting to compare this two-state TRM with a single-state model:

$$x_{t+1} = \underset{(0.008)}{0.634} - \underset{(0.558)}{1.395}\,\Delta FFR_t + \underset{(0.611)}{1.133}\,\Delta FFR_{t-1} + \underset{(0.006)}{0.139}\,\Delta VXO_t + \varepsilon_{t+1}$$

with an estimated standard error of 4.411 and an adjusted R^2 of 1.64% only! Moreover, a simple regression would lead us to conclude that changes in the FFR have no impact on the conditional equity risk premium, which we have seen not to be the case. Worse, it appears that an increase in implied market volatility would precisely forecast a higher conditional risk premium, contrary to what we have found earlier. However, as revealed by the reported adjusted R^2, this simple, single-state, linear model provides a poor fit to the data, as emphasized by the two panels of Fig. 8.5.

However, this TRM has one limitation: while we have introduced RS models as models of recurrent regimes, the estimated model almost ends up featuring a structural break in correspondence to October 2008, when the Great Financial Crisis sets foot in the United States and the system switched to the first, crisis regime. Yet, as shown in Fig. 8.6, regime 1 does not persist until the end of the sample, because we face a switch out of regime 1 and back to regime 2 in October 2016, exactly 9 years later.

A first modification of the TRM estimated above also allows recent changes in the VXO to have effects that switch across regimes. We obtain the evidence of three regimes in this case with estimated thresholds $\hat{c}_2 = 0.40\%$ and $\hat{c}_3 = 6.92\%$. The three regimes, characterized by very low, intermediate, and very high money market rates, include 93, 239, and 38 observations, respectively. The estimated model is:

$$x_{t+1} = \begin{cases} \underset{(0.000)}{1.090} - \underset{(0.010)}{34.47}\Delta FFR_t + \underset{(0.000)}{30.37}\Delta FFR_{t-1} - \underset{(0.000)}{0.682}\Delta VXO_t + \varepsilon_{t+1} & \text{if } FFR_t < 0.40 \\ \underset{(0.001)}{0.677} - \underset{(0.089)}{3.104}\Delta FFR_t + \underset{(0.018)}{4.283}\Delta FFR_{t-1} - \underset{(0.000)}{0.712}\Delta VXO_t + \varepsilon_{t+1} & \text{if } 6.92 > FFR_t \geq 0.40 \\ \underset{(0.702)}{0.213} + \underset{(0.164)}{6.962}\Delta FFR_t - \underset{(0.174)}{6.923}\Delta FFR_{t-1} - \underset{(0.000)}{0.463}\Delta VXO_t + \varepsilon_{t+1} & \text{if } 6.92 \leq FFR_t \end{cases}$$

which shows that while the dynamic relationship between lagged implied volatility changes and excess equity returns is always negative and precisely estimated, the patterns of over-reaction to changes in FFR commented earlier are much more widespread and in fact just fail to characterize the third regime of very high FFR. However, the adjusted R^2 does not increase by much, now reaching 53.0%.

Another interesting experiment consists of returning to the original specification, in which past VXO changes affect subsequent excess stock returns (SESR) always with the same strength, but in which the number of regimes is selected according to a different criterion. In particular, Table 8.7 presents a specification analysis now based on information criteria. We find again evidence of two regimes, as in Table 8.6.

(Continued)

EXAMPLE 8.4 (Continued)

Finally, we make one final attempt investigating the same series but using a pure STAR(2) approach, in which we use Bai–Perron's sequential testing using a size of 5% to decide which past lags of the excess stock returns between 1 and 12 (which implicitly corresponds to the delay parameter) should be best used as the threshold variable. We find evidence in favor of $K=2$ when the threshold is driven by one lag of the very market returns. The first regime is active when $x_t < 4.77\%$ on a monthly basis, a market crash that includes only 39 observations, so that the second regime obtains most of the time, for 331 observations. The estimated model is:

$$x_{t+1} = \begin{cases} \underset{(0.026)}{-1.154} + \underset{(0.433)}{3.822}\Delta FFR_t + \underset{(0.952)}{0.380}\Delta FFR_{t-1} - \underset{(0.000)}{0.649}\Delta VXO_t + \varepsilon_{t+1} & \text{if } x_t < -4.77 \\ \underset{(0.000)}{0.916} - \underset{(0.010)}{4.290}\Delta FFR_t + \underset{(0.020)}{3.947}\Delta FFR_{t-1} - \underset{(0.000)}{0.649}\Delta VXO_t + \varepsilon_{t+1} & \text{if } x_t \geq -4.77 \end{cases}$$

which shows that changes in the FFR fail to forecast SESR during a market crash (but changes in implied volatility keep having predictive power), while they do—according to the typical over-reaction patterns already discussed—in normal times, including moderate bear states. The estimated standard error of the model residuals is 3.068% and the adjusted R^2 is 52.4% that is intermediate versus what has been obtained before. Fig. 8.7 computes dynamic, recursive forecasts between 2001 and 2016, where the threshold variable is simulated (on the basis of 10,000 independent draws) to produce regimes switches according to the estimated STAR(2) dynamics and the reported 95% confidence bands for the forecasts are produced from this parametric bootstrap. Although it is hard to tell from the figure whether the model yields high-quality predictions when compared to actual realized returns, we do note that when returns become more volatile so do the forecasts. Moreover, in very few occasions (these are less than in 5% of the forecasts we have back-tested), the actual realized returns fall outside the 95% confidence bands so showing only modest evidence of model failure. These are all encouraging signs.

TABLE 8.6 Threshold Specification Analysis Based on Sequential Tests

Multiple threshold tests
Bai–Perron tests of $L+1$ versus L sequentially determined thresholds
Threshold variable: FFR(−1)
Threshold varying variables: C DELTA_FFR(−1) DELTA_FFR(−2)
Nonthreshold varying variables: DELTA_VXO(−1)
Threshold test options: Trimming 0.10, max. thresholds 5, sig. level 0.05
Test statistics employ HAC covariances (Bartlett kernel, Newey–West fixed bandwidth)

Sequential F-statistic Determined Thresholds: 1

Threshold Test	F-Statistic	Scaled F-Statistic	Critical Value[a]
0 versus 1*	13.12207	39.3662	14.6
1 versus 2	2.111643	6.334929	16.53

[a]*Bai–Perron (Econometric Journal, 2003) critical values.*
**Significant at the 0.05 level.*

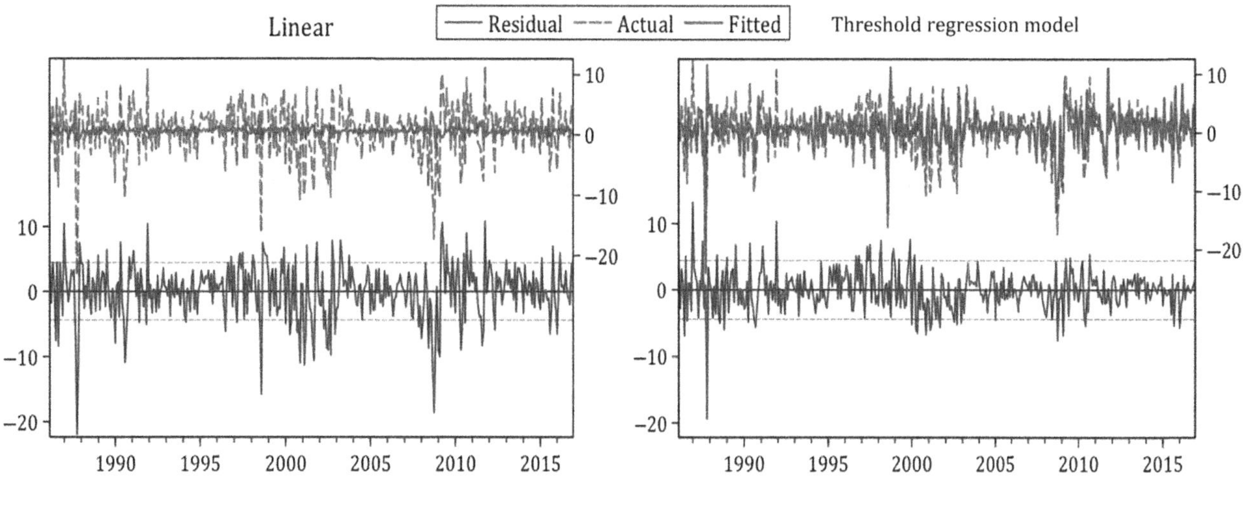

FIGURE 8.5 In-sample fit of linear versus threshold regression models.

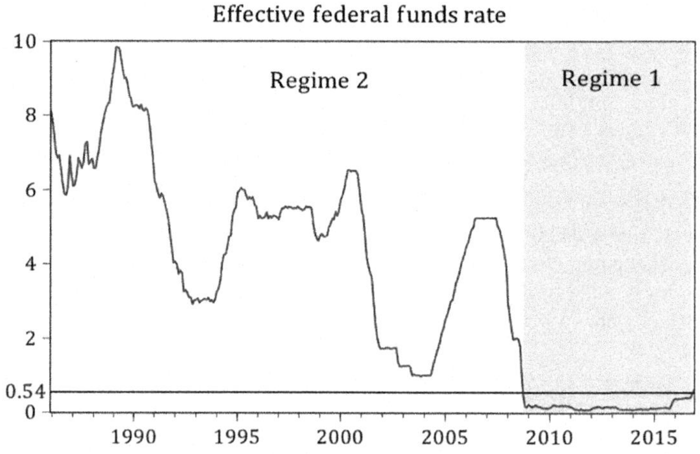

FIGURE 8.6 Regime classification from threshold regression model.

TABLE 8.7 Threshold Specification Analysis Based on the SBIC

Multiple threshold tests
Compare info. criteria for 0 to M globally determined thresholds
Threshold variable: FFR (−1)
Threshold varying variables: C DELTA_FFR(−1) DELTA_FFR(−2)
Nonthreshold varying variables: DELTA_VXO(−1)
Threshold test options: Trimming 0.10, Max. thresholds 5
Test statistics employs HAC covariances (Bartlett kernel, Newey−West fixed bandwidth)

Schwarz Criterion Selected Thresholds

Thresh.	# of Coefs.	Sum of Sq. Resids.	Log-*L*	Schwarz[a] Criterion
0	4	3769.236	−954.42	2.3851
1	8	3528.972	−942.23	***2.3831***
2	12	3382.776	−934.4	2.4047
3	16	3174.931	−922.67	2.4053
4	20	3048.468	−915.15	2.4285
5	24	3006.144	−912.57	2.4785

Estimated threshold values:
(1) 0.5
(2) 1.26, 6.51
(3) 0.54, 4.29, 6.51
(4) 0.54, 4.25, 5.29, 6.51
(5) 0.2, 1.26, 4.25, 5.29, 6.51
[a]*Minimum information criterion values are displayed in bold.*

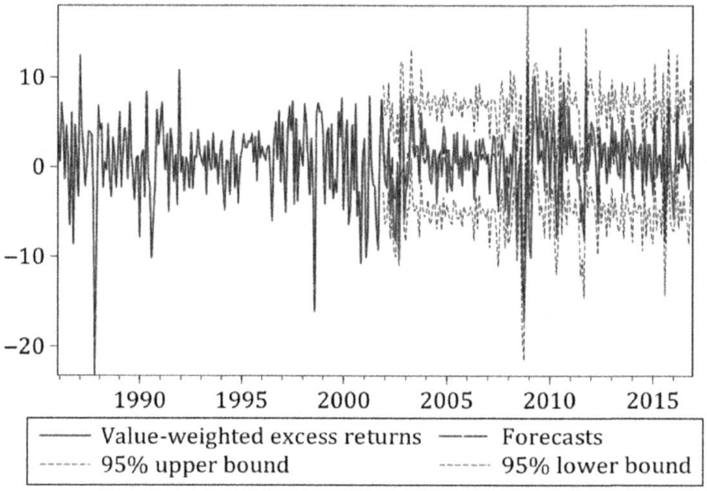

FIGURE 8.7 Back-tested actual and forecast excess returns.

The model in Example 8.4 is homoskedastic. Even though it is possible, as shown in Definition 8.2, to extend TRMs and TARs to encompass heteroskedastic models through the component $\sum_{k=1}^{K} I_t(k)\sigma_k^2$, in practice, when regimes are allowed, the ARMA component or the regression function in Eq. (8.43) tends to be so richly specified, that considerable time variation in the volatility of the dependent variable can be accommodated through the RS dependence of the $\{\alpha_k\}_{k=1}^{K}$ and $\{\beta_k\}_{k=1}^{K}$ coefficients/vectors, see, e.g., Teräsvirta (2006). In any event, in Chapter 5, we have already analyzed the structure and predictive power of threshold GARCH models.

As hinted at in Example 8.4, a popular application of TAR and STAR models has been forecasting. The common goal has been to compare the relative forecasting performance of TAR models with traditional linear and random walk forecasts. In this literature the models are typically compared using out-of-samplemean-square forecast error summary measures. The overall evidence is mixed. Some authors find improvements using TAR models, whereas others find no clear improvements. Chapter 9 surveys some of this evidence.

SETAR models have been often extended to become multivariate models when we shall speak of (self-exciting, homoskedastic) *threshold vector autoregressions*, SETVAR(p) models,

$$\begin{aligned} \mathbf{y}_{t+1} &= \sum_{k=1}^{K} I_t(k)\boldsymbol{\Phi}_{0,k} + \sum_{k=1}^{K} I_t(k)\sum_{j=1}^{p} \boldsymbol{\Phi}_{j,k}{}' \mathbf{y}_{t+1-j} + \boldsymbol{\varepsilon}_{t+1} \\ I_t(k) &= \begin{cases} 1 \text{ if } c_k < g(\mathbf{y}_{t+1-d}) \leq c_{k+1} & k = 1,\ldots,K \\ 0 \text{ otherwise,} \end{cases} \end{aligned} \tag{8.48}$$

where $\mathbf{y}_t$ is a $N \times 1$ random vector, $\boldsymbol{\varepsilon}_{t+1}$ is usually assumed to be IID from some multivariate distribution, $\boldsymbol{\Phi}_{0,k}$ is a $N \times 1$ vector of intercepts, and $\boldsymbol{\Phi}_{j,k}$ ($j = 1,2,\ldots,p; k = 1,2,\ldots,K$) are pK $N \times N$ matrices of coefficients to be estimated. The remaining portions of the model are identical to Definition 8.2, apart from a need posed by the threshold function $g(\mathbf{y}_{t+1-d})$ to either select one variable from $\mathbf{y}_{t+1-d}$ or to combine them to allocate observations across the K alternative regimes. In the empirical finance literature, Eq. (8.48) has been often proposed to study (also in its threshold VAR cointegrating variant, with $K = 3$) whether there are separate regimes in whether and how market forces, net of transaction costs and frictions, work to correct mispricings or even arbitrage opportunities toward some parity. Statistically, it is often the case that three regimes can be found so that in the two "outer" regimes, the deviations of prices from equilibrium or no-arbitrage relations follow mean reverting processes that reflect pricing corrections, while in the "central" regime, mispricing or arbitrage deviations persist but asset prices may follow a random walk. Example 8.5 illustrates an application of a SETVAR(p) model.

EXAMPLE 8.5

We resume Example 8.4, concerning the influence of lagged changes in the FFR and market-implied volatility on subsequent US excess equity returns. However, differently from Example 8.4, in which we had estimated a range of univariate threshold regressions, in this case we shall estimate a trivariate TVAR(2) in which excess returns, changes in FFR, and in VXO are all endogenous and in which two lags of each variable forecasts the others. We set the threshold function to make the regimes depend on one lag of returns and obtain:

$$x_{t+1} = \begin{cases} \underset{(0.004)}{1.555} - \underset{(0.974)}{0.007}x_t + \underset{(0.013)}{0.185}x_{t-1} - \underset{(0.006)}{6.450}\Delta FFR_t + \underset{(0.024)}{5.722}\Delta FFR_{t-1} \\ \quad - \underset{(0.000)}{0.733}\Delta VXO_t - \underset{(0.006)}{0.459}\Delta VXO_{t-1} + \varepsilon_{t+1}^{x} \quad \text{if } x_t < -2.06 \\ \underset{(0.394)}{0.581} + \underset{(0.094)}{0.088}x_t + \underset{(0.447)}{0.054}x_{t-1} - \underset{(0.042)}{3.174}\Delta FFR_t + \underset{(0.014)}{3.458}\Delta FFR_{t-1} \\ \quad - \underset{(0.000)}{0.656}\Delta VXO_t - \underset{(0.149)}{0.056}\Delta VXO_{t-1} + \varepsilon_{t+1}^{x} \quad \text{if } x_t \geq -2.06 \end{cases}$$

$$\Delta FFR_{t+1} = \begin{cases} \underset{(0.016)}{0.022} + \underset{(0.744)}{0.015}x_t + \underset{(0.983)}{0.002}x_{t-1} + \underset{(0.000)}{0.510}\Delta FFR_t + \underset{(0.746)}{0.031}\Delta FFR_{t-1} - \underset{(0.574)}{0.011}\Delta VXO_t \\ \quad + \underset{(0.248)}{0.066}\Delta VXO_{t-1} + \varepsilon_{t+1}^{x} \quad \text{if } x_t < -2.06 \\ - \underset{(0.008)}{0.025} + \underset{(0.647)}{0.009}x_t + \underset{(0.938)}{0.003}x_{t-1} + \underset{(0.001)}{0.419}\Delta FFR_t + \underset{(0.030)}{0.208}\Delta FFR_{t-1} - \underset{(0.903)}{0.005}\Delta VXO_t \\ \quad - \underset{(0.989)}{0.001}\Delta VXO_{t-1} + \varepsilon_{t+1}^{x} \quad \text{if } x_t \geq -2.06 \end{cases}$$

(Continued)

EXAMPLE 8.5 (Continued)

$$\Delta VXO_{t+1} = \begin{cases} \underset{(0.000)}{1.151} + \underset{(0.001)}{0.390}x_t + \underset{(0.007)}{0.290}x_{t-1} - \underset{(0.000)}{4.042}\Delta FFR_t + \underset{(0.017)}{1.965}\Delta FFR_{t-1} - \underset{(0.000)}{0.371}\Delta VXO_t \\ \quad - \underset{(0.006)}{0.254}\Delta VXO_{t-1} + \varepsilon^x_{t+1} \quad \text{if } x_t < -2.06 \\ \underset{(0.005)}{0.823} - \underset{(0.074)}{0.100}x_t - \underset{(0.220)}{0.036}x_{t-1} + \underset{(0.008)}{2.753}\Delta FFR_t - \underset{(0.025)}{2.756}\Delta FFR_{t-1} - \underset{(0.374)}{0.024}\Delta VXO_t \\ \quad + \underset{(0.042)}{0.159}\Delta VXO_{t-1} + \varepsilon^x_{t+1} \quad \text{if } x_t \geq -2.06 \end{cases}.$$

Obviously the model includes a large number of estimated parameters even though a good portion of the same fails to be statistically significant, on an individual basis. Interestingly the two piecewise regressions for excess stock returns are characterized by the same qualitative features that have emerged in Example 8.4. For instance, in both the bear and bull regimes, changes in the FFR forecast a decline in excess stock returns within a month, followed by a rebound of comparable size. In both regimes, increases in implied market variance forecast subsequent lower (negative) excess stock returns. Moreover, there is evidence that changes in FFR are somewhat persistent (this may be explained by monetary policy smoothing and several policy rates changes in the same direction being enacted gradually over time) but hardly affected by past changes in VXO.

It may be also of interest to contrast the estimated single-state, linear VAR(2) model applied to the same quantities:

$$x_{t+1} = \underset{(0.001)}{0.556} + \underset{(0.114)}{0.036}\, x_t + \underset{(0.039)}{0.095}\, x_{t-1} - \underset{(0.000)}{3.286}\, \Delta FFR_t + \underset{(0.000)}{4.294}\, \Delta FFR_{t-1}$$
$$- \underset{(0.000)}{0.684}\, \Delta VXO_t - \underset{(0.000)}{0.216}\, \Delta VXO_{t-1} + \varepsilon^x_{t+1}$$
$$\Delta FFR_{t+1} = -\underset{(0.134)}{0.012} + \underset{(0.042)}{0.006}\, x_t + \underset{(0.374)}{0.002}\, x_{t-1}$$
$$+ \underset{(0.000)}{0.445}\, \Delta FFR_t + \underset{(0.030)}{0.138}\, \Delta FFR_{t-1} - \underset{(0.002)}{0.008}\, \Delta VXO_t + \underset{(0.003)}{0.009}\, \Delta VXO_{t-1} + \varepsilon^{FFR}_{t+1}$$
$$\Delta VXO_{t+1} = -\underset{(0.547)}{0.145} + \underset{(0.063)}{0.122}\, x_t + \underset{(0.106)}{0.113}\, x_{t-1} + \underset{(0.104)}{2.468}\, \Delta FFR_t - \underset{(0.847)}{0.244}\, \Delta FFR_{t-1}$$
$$- \underset{(0.000)}{0.156}\, \Delta VXO_t - \underset{(0.833)}{0.061}\, \Delta VXO_{t-1} + \varepsilon^{VXO}_{t+1}.$$

As one would expect, most of the coefficients are smaller in absolute value because their estimates are in a way simply "averaging" across two distinct regimes, an indication of the potential misspecification of the single-state VAR(2).

8.3.2 Smooth Transition Regression and Autoregressive Models

A criticism of threshold models is that the conditional mean (and variance) equation that they imply is not continuous. The thresholds represent indeed the discontinuity points of the conditional moment functions. In a *smooth transition model* the state variable S_{t+1} is drawn from some cumulative probability distribution (CDF), $F(\cdot)$, whose domain may be suitably partitioned into K nonoverlapping subintervals to allow us to track the dynamics of the regime S_{t+1}. One occasionally pursued (again, nonlinear) modeling strategy is that in practice S_{t+1} is drawn from a discrete probability distribution $F(S_{t+1};\ g(\boldsymbol{X}_{t+1-d}))$ that can take K values and that also depends on some set of threshold variables through a $g(\cdot)\colon \mathbb{R}^M \to \mathbb{R}$ transformation. $F(S_{t+1};\ g(\boldsymbol{X}_{t+1-d}))$ is usually some type of CDF that delivers $\Pr(S_{t+1}=1; g(\boldsymbol{X}_{t+1-d}))$, $\Pr(S_{t+1}=2; g(\boldsymbol{X}_{t+1-d}))$, ..., $\Pr(S_{t+1}=K; g(\boldsymbol{X}_{t+1-d}))$ as:

$$\begin{aligned} &\Pr(S_{t+1}=1; g(\boldsymbol{X}_{t+1-d})) = F(1; g(\boldsymbol{X}_{t+1-d})) \\ &\Pr(S_{t+1}=2; g(\boldsymbol{X}_{t+1-d})) = F(2; g(\boldsymbol{X}_{t+1-d})) - F(1; g(\boldsymbol{X}_{t+1-d})) \\ &\vdots \\ &\Pr(S_{t+1}=K; g(\boldsymbol{X}_{t+1-d})) = 1 - F(K-1; g(\boldsymbol{X}_{t+1-d})). \end{aligned} \tag{8.49}$$

The idea is then that the shape of $F(S_{t+1};\ g(\boldsymbol{X}_{t+1-d}))$, and as a result the probabilities of the different regimes, change as $g(\boldsymbol{X}_{t+1-d})$ changes over time. Usually, $F(S_{t+1};\ g(\boldsymbol{X}_{t+1-d}))$ depends on a vector of parameters that will have to be estimated. For instance, $F(S_{t+1}; g(\boldsymbol{X}_{t+1-d}), \rho, \kappa)$ may depend on some parameters ρ and κ to be introduced later. The reason for why this TRS model is said to be "smooth" is that in Eq. (8.49), $\boldsymbol{X}_{t+1-d}$ no longer deterministically determines the state, but it simply affects the CDF of the regime variable that, on its turn, affects the assessment of the probability of the regimes. $g(\boldsymbol{X}_{t+1-d})$ can also be a linear combination of several variables. One interesting special case is $g(\boldsymbol{X}_{t+1-d}) = t+1-d$, which yields a linear model with deterministically changing parameters.

DEFINITION 8.3 (Smooth TRM)

Given a set of predetermined variables collected in the matrix $\boldsymbol{X}_t$, a STRM is defined as:[16]

$$\begin{aligned} y_{t+1} &= \sum_{k=1}^{K} \Pr(S_{t+1}=k; g(\boldsymbol{X}_{t+1-d}))\alpha_k + \sum_{k=1}^{K} \Pr(S_{t+1}=k; g(\boldsymbol{X}_{t+1-d}))\boldsymbol{\beta}_k{}'\boldsymbol{X}_t + \varepsilon_{t+1} \\ \varepsilon_{t+1} &\sim N(0, \sum_{k=1}^{K} \Pr(S_{t+1}=k; g(\boldsymbol{X}_{t+1-d}))\sigma_k^2) \\ \Pr(S_{t+1}=k; g(\boldsymbol{X}_{t+1-d})) &= F(k; g(\boldsymbol{X}_{t+1-d})) - F(k-1; g(\boldsymbol{X}_{t+1-d})), \end{aligned} \tag{8.50}$$

where $F(0; g(\boldsymbol{X}_{t+1-d}))=0$, $F(Q; g(\boldsymbol{X}_{t+1-d}))=1$ for $Q \geq K$, and $g(\cdot):\mathbb{R}^M \rightarrow \mathbb{R}$ is a function that converts the current and past values of the M predictors in $\mathbf{X}_t, \ldots \mathbf{X}_{t+1-d}$ into regime probabilities through the *transition function* $F(k; g(\boldsymbol{X}_{t+1-d}))$. When $\mathbf{X}_t$ collects $p \geq 1$ lags of the dependent variable y_{t+1}, then Eq. (8.50) turns into a smooth threshold autoregressive model, STAR(p); when $g(\boldsymbol{X}_t, \ldots \boldsymbol{X}_{t+1-d})$ collects $p \geq 1$ lags of the dependent variable y_{t+1}, then Eq. (8.50) is a self-exciting smooth threshold autoregressive model, SESTAR(p).

While threshold regressions impart an abrupt nonlinear behavior depending on whether the threshold variable(s) is above or below the threshold value, the smooth-transition variant allows for possible gradual shifts among regimes and is able to capture two types of adjustment. First the parameters of the model change depending upon whether the transition variable(s) is above or below the transition value. Second the parameters of the model change depending upon the distance between the transition variable and the transition value. We also say that STR/STAR models are *locally linear but globally nonlinear*.

For instance a rather general smooth transition regression model is written as:

$$\begin{aligned} y_{t+1} &= \alpha_1 + \boldsymbol{\beta}_1{}'\mathbf{X}_t + [\alpha_2 - \alpha_1 + (\boldsymbol{\beta}_2 - \boldsymbol{\beta}_1)'\mathbf{X}_t]F(\mathbf{e}_i{}'\boldsymbol{X}_{t+1-d}) + \varepsilon_{t+1} \\ \varepsilon_{t+1} &\sim N(0, \sigma_1^2 + (\sigma_2^2 - \sigma_1^2)F(\mathbf{e}_i{}'\boldsymbol{X}_{t+1-d})), \end{aligned} \tag{8.51}$$

where $0 \leq F(\mathbf{e}_i'\mathbf{X}_{t+1-d}) \leq 1$ is the transition function and the dth lag of the ith variable in $\mathbf{X}_t$ (selected by the product $X_{i,t+1-d} = \mathbf{e}_i'\mathbf{X}_{t+1-d}$) acts as the only transition variable with a delay factor of d periods. The RS model in Eq. (8.51) is smooth because as $X_{i,t+1-d}$ grows—and this is occurring in a continuous and differentiable way for most of the CDF-type transition functions that are typically used—then $F(\mathrm{X}_{i,t+1-d})$ grows, say by $dF(\mathrm{X}_{i,t+1-d})$ so that the expected return and residual variance smoothly change as

$$\begin{aligned} dE[R_{t+1}] &= (\alpha_2 - \alpha_1)dF(\mathrm{X}_{i,t+1-d}) + (\boldsymbol{\beta}_2 - \boldsymbol{\beta}_1)'\mathbf{X}_t dF(\mathrm{X}_{i,t+1-d}) \\ dVar[\varepsilon_{t+1}] &= (\sigma_2^2 - \sigma_1^2)dF(\mathrm{X}_{i,t+1-d}), \end{aligned} \tag{8.52}$$

where $dF(\mathrm{X}_{i,t+1-d}) = (\partial F(\mathrm{X}_{i,t+1-d})/\partial \mathrm{X}_{i,t+1-d})d\mathrm{X}_{i,t+1-d}$. Because of this feature, STR (as well as STAR and SESTAR) models are perhaps theoretically more appealing—at least as far as financial applications are concerned—versus the simple threshold models that impose an abrupt switch in parameter values, because only if all traders act simultaneously this will be the plausible outcome. For a market of many traders acting at slightly different times a smooth transition is normally more realistic. For instance, echoing Example 8.4, it may be true that a higher FFR has a negative effect on future stock returns only when monetary policy is strongly tightening, meaning that $\mathbf{e}_i'\mathbf{X}_{t+1-d}$ selects FFR_t (say) and that $F(FFR_t) \cong 1$ for very high values of FFR_t; the story would be that at the end of an expansion, an initial policy tightening may lead to a slower subsequent growth. At the same it may be sensible that a higher FFR forecasts positive future stock returns only for extremely low values of FFR_t for which $F(FFR_t) \cong 0$. For intermediate levels of the policy rates, $F(FFR_t)$ may take intermediate values so that the effect of a change in FFR_t on subsequent stock returns will be captured by a weighted combination of elements in $\boldsymbol{\beta}_1$ and $\boldsymbol{\beta}_2$. This additional flexibility derives from the smoothness of the model and is impossible under a simpler (two-regime) TRM/TAR model: either the FFR is high enough to imply a negative effect of FFR increases on stock returns, or the opposite occurs. In practice, one may obtain STR/STAR effects from a TRM/TAR model when the number of regimes K becomes very large. For instance, in our example, a weighted combination of the slope coefficients $\boldsymbol{\beta}_1$ and $\boldsymbol{\beta}_2$ may appear if we define at least three regimes. However, the fact that as K grows large, TRM/TAR models may approximate the smoothness of STR/STAR is just a special case of a general

16. Also in this case, it is possible to augment the model by including also regressors or ARMA components, the coefficients of which are constant over time, as in Eq. (8.46).

result, by which a large class of nonlinear functions may always be approximated arbitrarily well by a piecewise linear function in which an infinite number of linear segments are modeled although at the cost of a substantial increase in the number of estimable parameters.

The STR/STAR model allows different types of time series behavior depending on the nature of the transition function. Among the possible transition functions the *logistic* has received considerable attention in the literature and is given by the following specification, where the full model is referred to as the logistic STR/STAR (or LSTR/LSTAR) model:

$$F(\mathbf{e}_i'\mathbf{X}_{t+1-d}) = \frac{1}{1+\exp(-\rho(\mathbf{e}_i'\mathbf{X}_{t+1-d}-\kappa))} \quad \rho>0,\ d\geq 1, \tag{8.53}$$

where ρ is called the smoothing parameter, and κ is the transition parameter, both to be estimated. The logistic function allows the parameters to change monotonically with $\mathbf{e}'_i\mathbf{X}_{t+1-d}$. As $\rho\rightarrow\infty$, $F(\mathbf{e}_i'\mathbf{X}_{t+1-d})$ becomes a standard dummy function:

$$F(\mathbf{e}_i'\mathbf{X}_{t+1-d}) = \begin{cases} 1 & \text{if } \mathbf{e}_i'\mathbf{X}_{t+1-d} > \kappa \\ 0 & \text{if } \mathbf{e}_i'\mathbf{X}_{t+1-d} \leq \kappa \end{cases} \tag{8.54}$$

and the STR/STAR model supplemented by Eq. (8.53) reduces to a standard TRM. Moreover, because as $\rho\rightarrow 0$, $1/1+\exp(-\rho(\mathbf{e}_i'\mathbf{X}_{t+1-d}-\kappa))\rightarrow 1/2$, the STR/STAR model simply turns into a linear regression/AR(p) model because switching becomes impossible. This flexibility of the model, that is said *to nest* both the nonlinear threshold and the linear models as special cases depending on the value taken by the parameter ρ, is a source of attractiveness of the LSTR/LSTAR because such special cases all become testable hypotheses. Extensions to the case in which multiple Q lags of the variables in $\mathbf{X}_{t+1-d}$ affect the smooth transitions exist, for instance:

$$F(\mathbf{e}_i'\mathbf{X}_{t+1-d}) = \frac{1}{1+\exp\left(-\rho\prod_{i=1}^{Q}(\mathbf{e}_i'\mathbf{X}_{t+1-d}-\kappa_i)\right)} \quad \rho>0,\ d\geq 1, \tag{8.55}$$

where the threshold parameters become now Q, $\kappa_1, \kappa_2, \ldots, \kappa_Q$. Interestingly, in the case $Q=1$ in Eq. (8.55), the parameters in the STRM change monotonically as a function of $\mathbf{e}_i'\mathbf{X}_{t+1-d}$ from α_1 and β_1 to α_2 and β_2; when $Q=2$, the parameters change symmetrically around the midpoint $(\kappa_1+\kappa_2)/2$, where the logistic function attains its minimum value. The LSTR model with $Q=1$ is capable of characterizing asymmetric behavior when $\kappa_1\neq 0$; the LSTR with $Q=2$ is instead appropriate in situations where the local dynamic behavior of the process is similar for both large and small values of the threshold and different "in the middle" (smooth band threshold).

An alternative choice of the transition function consists of assuming a *normal* CDF:

$$F(\mathbf{e}_i'\mathbf{X}_{t+1-d}) = \frac{1}{\sqrt{2\pi}}\int_{-\infty}^{\mathbf{e}_i'\mathbf{X}_{t+1-d}} \exp(-0.5\rho(z-\kappa)^2)dz \quad \rho>0,\ d\geq 1 \tag{8.56}$$

or $F(\mathbf{e}_i'\mathbf{X}_{t+1-d})=\Phi(\rho(z-\kappa))$. Also in this case, when $\rho\rightarrow\infty$, $\mathbf{F}(\mathbf{e}_i'\mathbf{X}_{t+1-d})$ becomes a standard dummy function as in Eq. (8.54) and the model degenerates to a standard TRM/TAR model. As $\rho\rightarrow 0$, $\mathbf{F}(\mathbf{e}_i'\mathbf{X}_{t+1-d})$ becomes the CDF of a uniform distribution with infinite support, and a subtle mathematical argument shows that also in this case, the model degenerates to a single-state regression or AR(p) model. Both the logistic and normal CDF transition functions are monotonically increasing in $\mathbf{e}_i'\mathbf{X}_{t+1-d}$, so that regimes can be ordered in correspondence to high and low values of the threshold variable. The threshold value κ determines the point at which the regimes are equally weighted, while ρ controls the speed and smoothness of the transition.

A final choice of the functional form governing the smooth transition is represented by the *exponential* function, with the resulting model referred to as the exponential STR/STAR (or ESTR/ESTAR) model:

$$F(\mathbf{e}_i'\mathbf{X}_{t+1-d}) = 1-\exp(-\rho(\mathbf{e}_i'\mathbf{X}_{t+1-d}-\kappa)^2) \quad \rho>0,\ d\geq 1, \tag{8.57}$$

where the weight assigned to the regime-specific parameters change symmetrically around κ with $\mathbf{e}_i'\mathbf{X}_{t+1-d}$. If $\rho\rightarrow\infty$ or $\rho\rightarrow 0$, the ESTR/ESTAR model becomes linear, while nonlinearities require intermediate values for ρ. Interestingly the ESTR/ESTAR model does not nest the TRM/TAR model. This model implies that the dynamics obtained for values of the transition variable close to κ differ from those obtained for values that strongly differ from κ: the exponential transition function is increasing in absolute deviations of $\mathbf{e}_i'\mathbf{X}_{t+1-d}$ from the threshold κ. The model is also symmetric around κ. The smooth *band-threshold effect* that Eq. (8.57) captures is a common theme in the application of (S)TAR models to financial prices because of the presence of transaction costs: economic arbitrage requires that the prices of related goods and securities move together, but the presence of transaction costs can produce a band-threshold effect, where only deviations above or below a threshold will have an effect on price adjustments. For instance, Yadav et al. (1994) have estimated an ESTAR model for the difference between the price of an index futures contract and the equivalent underlying cash index.

Even though, in principle at least, any CDF can be used as a transition function, the logistic and exponential transition functions are by far the most commonly used and they are both characterized by a parameter ρ that carries a similar meaning. A peculiar issue in estimating all STR/STAR models concerns such smoothing parameter ρ, the estimation of which may turn problematic. The estimation is performed by MLE even though it is typical to use (quasi-maximum likelihood) iterative algorithms that rely on the sequential application of generalized NLS to converge to final parameter estimates. Also in this case, estimation is not always straightforward because local minima may occur, so that estimation with different starting-values is recommended. A few issues are typically encountered with the yet popular LSTR/LSTAR model, in which a large ρ results in a steep slope of the transition function at the point κ; thus a large number of observations in the neighborhood of κ are required to estimate ρ accurately. As a result, the convergence of any estimator of ρ, say of ML type, may be very slow, with relatively large changes in ρ having only a minor effect upon the shape of the transition function.[17] Because of these numerical issues, even though logistic specifications are most often encountered, in applied work, it is sometimes advised to also estimate Gaussian or exponential STR/STAR models as a robustness check.

Example 8.6 shows STR models and different transition functions in action.

EXAMPLE 8.6

We resume the analysis in Example 8.4 on predicting value-weighted monthly US excess returns (x_t) for a sample 1986:01–2016:12 using one and two lags of the change in the effective FFR and monthly changes in the VXO. We apply a standard trimming factor $\tau = 0.1$ as in Example 8.5. The starting parameter values are chosen by grid search when the regression coefficients are concentrated out of the likelihood function and grid search is performed over the transition parameters.

Starting with a logistic two-state STRM the first step is to select between one and three lags ($d = 1,2,3$) of FFR as the variable governing the transition dynamics. The E-Views package informs us that FFR_t, that is, $d = 1$, is the selection that minimizes the SSR and hence maximizes the log-likelihood function. In fact the differences in SSR are rather large, 3528 when versus 3543 for $d = 2$ and 3559 for $d = 3$. Given this selection the estimated model is:

$$x_{t+1} = \left(\underset{(0.000)}{1.093} - \underset{(0.002)}{28.493}\,\Delta FFR_t + \underset{(0.000)}{30.023}\,\Delta FFR_{t-1}\right) + \left(-\underset{(0.075)}{0.531} + \underset{(0.004)}{27.022}\,\Delta FFR_t - \underset{(0.000)}{27.778}\,\Delta FFR_{t-1}\right)\frac{1}{1+\exp\left(-\underset{(1.000)}{333.25}\left(FFR_t - \underset{(1.000)}{0.470}\right)\right)} - \underset{(0.000)}{0.654}\,\Delta VXO_t + \varepsilon_{t+1}.$$

Interestingly, in spite of our STR specification, we obtain an estimate of the transition slope ρ so large (and as a result imprecisely estimated, because the shift of regime occurs very abruptly, see Teräsvirta et al., 1994) that this reveals that what the data require is indeed a threshold predictive regression model, given that any smoothness is rejected by the data. The estimated threshold occurs at 0.47%, which is indeed very close to the 0.54% estimate obtained in Example 8.4. Fig. 8.8 shows this result.

Consistently with our threshold regression findings the first regime of strongly reacting excess stock returns to changes in FFR characterizes the 1986–2008 subsample and has appeared again in the last few months of 2016. Note that this STRM (implicitly, TRM) reaches an SBIC of 5.237 and an adjusted R^2 of 50.6%.

One may wonder whether there may be anything special about the logistic transition function. Therefore, we have estimated afresh this nonlinear model assuming an exponential transition function, obtaining, subject to the same technical choices made above, a completely different set of ESTR results!

$$x_{t+1} = \left(-\underset{(0.348)}{1.628} + \underset{(0.146)}{9.744}\,\Delta FFR_t - \underset{(0.000)}{15.413}\,\Delta FFR_{t-1}\right) + \left(\underset{(0.183)}{2.340} - \underset{(0.057)}{13.188}\,\Delta FFR_t + \underset{(0.000)}{21.289}\,\Delta FFR_{t-1}\right)\left[1-\exp\left(-\underset{(0.085)}{4.614}\left((FFR_{t-2} - \underset{(0.000)}{7.226})^2\right)\right)\right] - \underset{(0.000)}{0.646}\,\Delta VXO_t + \varepsilon_{t+1}.$$

First of all, a SSR-minimizing specification search reveals that the preferred threshold variable, to enter the transition function, is represented by three lags of the FFR: SSR is 3366 when $d = 3$ versus 3522 for $d = 1$, and 3527 for $d = 2$. Even though it is not obvious to interpret the fact that the smooth transitions may be governed by the monetary policy indicator of 3 months before,

(Continued)

17. Slow convergence of an estimator means that in simulation experiments, there is evidence that with increasing sample sizes, the recovery of the parameters from which the data were generated happens at a slow pace.

EXAMPLE 8.6 (Continued)

the statistical SSR measures give stark indications. Fig. 8.9 shows the estimated transition function and the time series of the probabilistic regime weights obtained from the exponential transition.

The shape of the estimated exponential transition implies a high, positive sensitivity of excess stock returns to recent increases in FFR followed by a movement in an opposite direction—which is normally interpreted as evidence of an initial over-reaction—for rates around 7%–7.5% 3 months before the change in FFR; such levels of FFR are historically quite high and have occurred in our sample only between 1987 and 1988. For past values of FFR well below 7% or above 8%, the effects of changes in FFR on excess stock returns are weaker and a current increase in FFR causes a decline in excess stock returns followed by a subsequent increase. Remarkably, an increase in market-implied volatility always forecasts subsequently lower excess stock returns and the size of the coefficient is almost unchanged versus the TRM model estimated earlier.

This ESTRM reaches an SBIC of 5.196 which is sensibly lower (hence, better) than the criterion for the TRM reported earlier and a higher adjusted R^2 of 52.6%. Therefore, there is some evidence of the ESTRM out-performing a more abrupt TRM.

Fig. 8.10 shows that, albeit not perfect, the ESTRM provides an appreciable fit to excess stock return data. Given these encouraging results, we test whether a superior fit may be achieved by changing the initial conditions, and in particular we use an OLS regression on the linear portion of the model while setting the nonlinear coefficient values to 0, and use sample moments to obtain the starting values for the slope and threshold parameters. However, we find convergence to a considerably lower value of the log-likelihood function.

We have also estimated a model in which also lagged implied volatility follows a smooth transition model, obtaining:

$$x_{t+1} = \Big(\underset{(0.213)}{1.510} + \underset{(0.150)}{1.869}\,\Delta FFR_t - \underset{(0.000)}{15.422}\,\Delta FFR_{t-1} + \underset{(0.001)}{0.527}\,\Delta VXO_t\Big)$$
$$+ \Big(-\underset{(0.501)}{0.833} - \underset{(0.013)}{4.898}\,\Delta FFR_t + \underset{(0.000)}{20.872}\,\Delta FFR_{t-1} - \underset{(0.150)}{1.223}\,\Delta VXO_t\Big)$$
$$\left[1-\exp\left(-\underset{(0.000)}{7.367}\left(FFR_{t-2}-\underset{(0.000)}{7.300}\right)^2\right)\right]+\varepsilon_{t+1}.$$

Now also the sign of the effects of changes in implied volatilities on subsequent excess returns switches, in the sense that there is a regime, characterized by three lags of FFR close to 7.3% in which increases in implied volatility forecast increases in excess returns, as if the risk measured by implied volatility would be simply compensated by the market. The resulting adjusted R^2 increases to 55.1% and the SBIC is 5.154, marking some further improvement versus the STRM analyzed earlier. The shape of the transition function is similar to Fig. 8.9, for instance with a trough still centered around a value slightly in excess of 7%, but with a region around such value in which the first regime applies that is less wide because the estimate value for the transition slope ρ is now higher, 7.37 versus 4.62. Therefore, there is evidence of smooth RS both in the predictive power of changes in FFR and of changes in implied market volatilities for SESR.

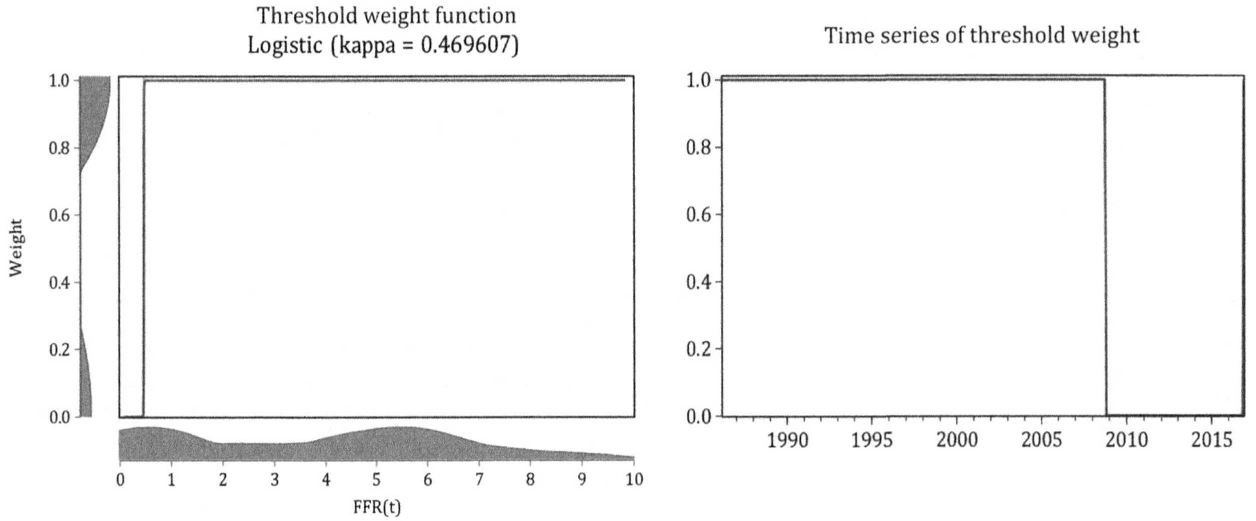

FIGURE 8.8 Estimated logistic transition function and time series of estimated $F(\text{FFR}_t)$.

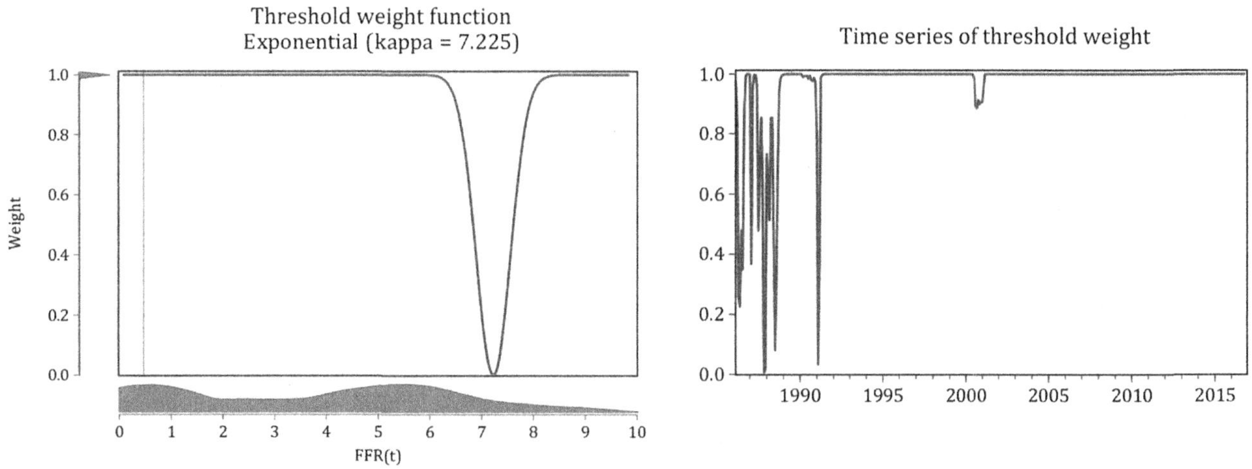

FIGURE 8.9 Estimated exponential transition function and time series of estimated $F(\text{FFR}_{t-2})$.

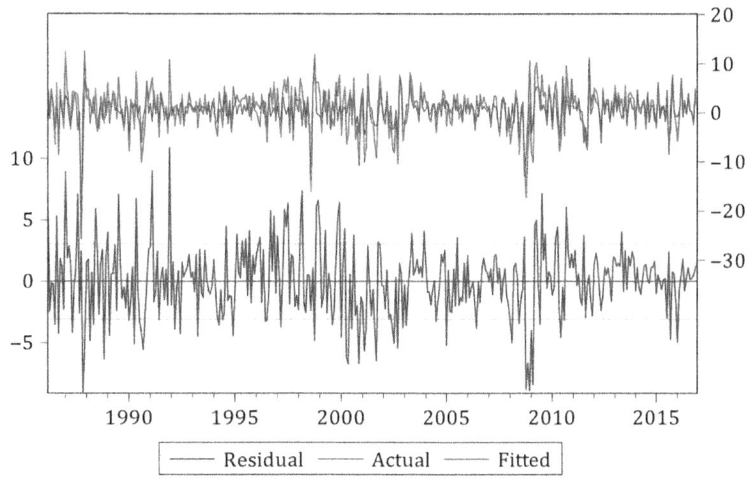

FIGURE 8.10 In-sample fit of an exponential smooth threshold regression.

The SESTAR models admit an interesting and famous generalization: *artificial neural networks* (ANNs). In its simplest form, an ANN can be derived from a SESTAR(p) model as:

$$y_{t+1} = \sum_{k=1}^{K} F_k(y_{t+1-d}; \boldsymbol{\theta}_k)\alpha_k + \sum_{j=1}^{p} \phi_j y_{t+1-j} + \varepsilon_{t+1} \quad \varepsilon_{t+1} \sim N(0, \sigma^2) \tag{8.58}$$

and can be useful to model nonlinear processes that have an unknown functional form. Eq. (8.58) can be seen as a smooth self-exciting AR(p) model in which the intercept is a mixture of K alternative smoothing functions. As in STR and STAR models, $F_k(y_{t+1-d}; \boldsymbol{\theta}_k)$ is a cumulative distribution or a logistic function such as Eq. (8.55), where the $\boldsymbol{\theta}_k$ $(k = 1, 2, \ldots, K)$ are vectors of parameters, but the ANN uses K different functions (called *nodes*). Kuan and White (1994) have proven that as $K \to \infty$, the ANN can approximate any first-order nonlinear model arbitrarily well. One then wonders why should we waste any time with threshold or smooth AR(p) models if ANN can do such an excellent job. Even though Eq. (8.58) can fit many complex time series well, the K nodes usually fail to carry any economic interpretation. Moreover, because as $K \to \infty$ ANNs have a tendency to involve an extremely large number of parameters, there is a danger of *overfitting the data*, which means that a researcher may end up fitting their noise component; the fact that the R^2 grows toward 1 as $K \to \infty$ should not be especially comforting if the goal is to forecast a series. In fact, just to avoid overfitting the data, it is common to select K using parsimonious information criteria, such as the SBIC. ANN also pose interesting estimation challenges, because it is usually hard to identify the parameters that appear in

Eq. (8.58): as $K \to \infty$, the same effects on the R^2 may be alternatively obtained by changing in appropriate ways many different constellations of parameters. Therefore, numerical optimization routines may encounter a difficulty in finding the parameter values that minimize the sum of squared residuals since many local minima often exist.

8.3.3 Testing (Non-)Linearities

It is interesting to also introduce to how one can *test the null of linearity*—i.e., of no smooth transition RS effects—versus the alternative hypothesis of smooth regimes, in the form of a $F(\mathbf{e}_i'\mathbf{X}_{t+1-d})$ that fails to be constant. Such a test is of particular importance in finance and economics as there is a presumption among most analysts that applications should use linear models unless there is convincing evidence to support a specific nonlinear specification. Moreover, models such as TRMs and STRMs often nest a linear model and are not identified if the data-generating process is linear. Therefore, fitting one of these models to a linear series leads to inconsistent parameter estimates, and forecasts from the estimated model are bound to be poor. Testing linearity first, as an essential step of the modeling process, considerably reduces the probability of this occurrence. An implication often neglected is that this step implies that the process must then always start with the construction of an adequate linear model on which nonlinearity tests ought to be based, to avoid the risk the misspecifications of the linear model that differ from neglected nonlinearities may be erroneously confused with nonlinearities. For instance, Pitarakis (2006) has shown that the lag order selection can seriously influence the power properties of linearity tests since the linear model will be misspecified if the true data generating process (DGP) is actually nonlinear.

Let us focus for concreteness on the two-regime model:

$$y_{t+1} = (\alpha_1 + \boldsymbol{\beta}_1'\mathbf{X}_t) + [\alpha_2 - \alpha_1 + \boldsymbol{\beta}_2'\mathbf{X}_t - \boldsymbol{\beta}_1'\mathbf{X}_t]F(\mathbf{e}_i'X_{t+1-d}; \rho, \kappa) + \varepsilon_{t+1} \tag{8.59}$$

and assume without loss of generality that $F(\mathbf{e}_i'X_{t+1-d}; \rho, \kappa) = 0$. From now on, we shall assume homoskedasticity to keep things as simple as possible. Given Eq. (8.59), we can test for linearity under the null hypothesis using either the null of $\rho = 0$, given that for all the transition functions examined, as $\rho \to 0$, the STR/STAR model becomes a single-state linear model, or the null $[\alpha_2 - \alpha_1 + \boldsymbol{\beta}_2'\mathbf{X}_t - \boldsymbol{\beta}_1'\mathbf{X}_t] = 0$, because in this case the model simplifies to a linear regression. However, it seems more convenient to test $\rho = 0$, even though, under the null hypothesis, the parameters κ and $[\alpha_2 - \alpha_1 + \boldsymbol{\beta}_2'\mathbf{X}_t - \boldsymbol{\beta}_1'\mathbf{X}_t]$ will not be identified (as we shall see in Chapter 9 these become *nuisance parameters in estimation*), so that standard theory cannot be used to obtain the null distribution of the test statistic.

Because of the nuisance parameters problem, Luukkonen et al. (1988) propose an approach which replaces (a differentiable) $F(\mathbf{e}_i'X_{t+1-d}; \rho, \kappa)$ by a Taylor series expansion under the null of $\rho = 0$, which is estimable. The resulting test procedure involves taking the linear portion of the model and adding terms representing the interaction of the linear regressors with the polynomial terms in the Taylor expansion and then testing for the statistical significance of sets of interaction coefficients. Teräsvirta et al. (1994) show that such Taylor expansion tests are just regression-based implementations of score-based tests in which an analyst aims at testing whether the weighted vector of the sum of the squared scores of the (pseudo, in a Quasi-Maximum Likelihood, QML, set-up) log-likelihood for a sample is statistically significantly different from 0. If this were to be the case, it would indicate that the linear log-likelihood cannot represent a (global) maximum as otherwise presumed when nonlinearities are ignored. In other words, if a component of a model $F(\mathbf{e}_i'X_{t+1-d}; \rho, \kappa)$ is to be excluded from it, the derivatives of the log-likelihood function with respect to $F(\mathbf{e}_i'X_{t+1-d}; \rho, \kappa)$ ought to be negligible, when adequately weighted. Of course the resulting Taylor series expansion and therefore the outcomes of this linearity test will differ depending on the form assumed by the transition function $F(\mathbf{e}_i'X_{t+1-d}; \rho, \kappa)$, because the specific terms of the Taylor expansion that are asymptotically relevant under the alternative hypothesis differ across $F(\mathbf{e}_i'X_{t+1-d}; \rho, \kappa)$.

For instance, defining $\delta_t \equiv [\alpha_2 - \alpha_1 + \boldsymbol{\beta}_2'\mathbf{X}_t - \boldsymbol{\beta}_1'\mathbf{X}_t]$, one tests the null of zero coefficients in the expanded, approximate model:

$$\begin{aligned} y_{t+1} &= (\alpha_1 + \boldsymbol{\beta}_1'\mathbf{X}_t) + F'(\mathbf{e}_i'X_{t+1-d}; 0, \kappa)\rho(\mathbf{e}_i'\mathbf{X}_{t+1-d} - \kappa)\delta_t \\ &\quad + F''(\mathbf{e}_i'X_{t+1-d}; 0, \kappa)\rho(\mathbf{e}_i'\mathbf{X}_{t+1-d} - \kappa)^2\delta_t + F'''(\mathbf{e}_i'X_{t+1-d}; 0, \kappa)\rho(\mathbf{e}_i'\mathbf{X}_{t+1-d} - \kappa)^3\delta_t \\ &\quad + F''''(\mathbf{e}_i'X_{t+1-d}; 0, \kappa)\rho(\mathbf{e}_i'\mathbf{X}_{t+1-d} - \kappa)^4\delta_t + v_{t+1} \\ &= (b_0 + \boldsymbol{\beta}_1'\mathbf{X}_t) + b_1\mathbf{e}_i'\mathbf{X}_{t+1-d}\delta_t + b_2(\mathbf{e}_i'\mathbf{X}_{t+1-d})^2\delta_t + b_3(\mathbf{e}_i'\mathbf{X}_{t+1-d})^3\delta_t \\ &\quad + b_4(\mathbf{e}_i'\mathbf{X}_{t+1-d})^4\delta_t + v_{t+1}, \end{aligned} \tag{8.60}$$

where the second equality is derived after collecting all terms of similar order to have common coefficients, b_1, b_2, b_3, and b_4 that are of course a complex function of the primitive parameters ρ, κ, and the partial derivatives of the smoothing functions evaluated at $\rho = 0$. For instance, in the logistic case, it is straightforward to check that $F'(\mathbf{e}_i'\boldsymbol{X}_{t+1-d}; 0, \kappa) = 1/4, F''(\mathbf{e}_i'\boldsymbol{X}_{t+1-d}; 0, \kappa) = 0, F'''(\mathbf{e}_i'\boldsymbol{X}_{t+1-d}; 0, \kappa) = -1/8$ and $F''''(\mathbf{e}_i'\boldsymbol{X}_{t+1-d}; 0, \kappa) = 0$ so that $b_2 = b_4 = 0$ by construction, even though b_1 and b_3 are estimable.[18] Of course, if $F(\mathbf{e}_i'\boldsymbol{X}_{t+1-d}; \rho, \kappa) = \text{const.}$ and there are no regimes, then $b_1 = b_2 = b_3 = b_4 = 0$. Luukkonen et al. (1988) linearity tests are joint hypothesis tests of this null. Usually the hypotheses are tested conditioning on the fact that the higher order terms are restricted to be 0, which has been proven to produce tests with better power. For example, it is convenient to test $b_1 = b_2 = 0$ assuming that $b_3 = b_4 = 0$. Clearly the test depends on the delay parameter d: when we are not sure about the choice of d, the recommendation is to apply the test using all plausible values of d; the value of d that results in the smallest p-value (i.e., the value providing the best fit from the Taylor expansion) is reasonably the relevant one.

Interestingly, the linearity test methods featured in Eq. (8.60) responds to an important prerequisite: because estimation of nonlinear models is generally more difficult than that of linear models, it is natural to look for linearity tests which do not require estimation of any nonlinear alternative. As already commented in Chapter 5, when the nonlinearity concerned the second conditional moment, the *Lagrange multiplier principle* thus appears useful for the construction of linearity tests. In fact the F-tests just illustrated can be interpreted as LM tests.

Tests similar to those in Eq. (8.60) can be used to test the null of K versus $K+1$ regimes. For concreteness, consider the case of two regimes versus three regimes. The latter model can be written as:

$$y_{t+1} = (\alpha_1 + \boldsymbol{\beta}_1'\mathbf{X}_t) + \delta_{1,t}F(\mathbf{e}_i'\boldsymbol{X}_{t+1-d}; \rho_1, \kappa_1) + \delta_{2,t}[F(\mathbf{e}_i'\boldsymbol{X}_{t+1-d}; \rho_2, \kappa_2) - F(\mathbf{e}_i'\boldsymbol{X}_{t+1-d}; \rho_1, \kappa_1)] + \varepsilon_{t+1} \tag{8.61}$$

and can be approximated as:

$$\begin{aligned} y_{t+1} = {} & (\alpha_1 + \boldsymbol{\beta}_1'\mathbf{X}_t) + [\delta_{1,t}F(\mathbf{e}_i'\boldsymbol{X}_{t+1-d}; \rho_1, \kappa_1) - \delta_{2,t}F(\mathbf{e}_i'\boldsymbol{X}_{t+1-d}; \rho_1, \kappa_1)] \\ & + b_1\mathbf{e}_i'\mathbf{X}_{t+1-d}\delta_{2,t} + b_2(\mathbf{e}_i'\mathbf{X}_{t+1-d})^2\delta_{2,t} + b_3(\mathbf{e}_i'\mathbf{X}_{t+1-d})^3\delta_{2,t} \\ & + b_4(\mathbf{e}_i'\mathbf{X}_{t+1-d})^4\delta_{2,t} + v_{t+1}. \end{aligned} \tag{8.62}$$

Testing the null of $b_1 = b_2 = b_3 = b_4 = 0$ jointly or sequentially, represents one way to test the null of two regimes versus three regimes. Although variation exists (for instance, likelihood ratio tests are possible), all these tests are typically set-up as F-tests of a composite, joint hypothesis. The following example shows how these tests are applied by E-Views.

EXAMPLE 8.7

We resume the analysis in Examples 8.4–8.6 on predicting value-weighted monthly US excess returns (x_t) for a sample 1986:01–2016:12 using one and two lags of the change in the effective FFR and monthly changes in the VXO. In this case, we consider self-exciting models (SESR) and, just to show what the results may look like, consider the case of a $F(\mathbf{e}_i'\boldsymbol{X}_{t+1-d}; \rho, \kappa)$ function of cumulative standard normal type. As in Examples 8.5 and 8.6, we apply a standard trimming factor $\tau = 0.1$. The starting parameter values are chosen by grid search, when the regression coefficients are concentrated out of the likelihood function and grid search is performed over the transition parameters. Because it delivered a better in-sample fit, we set changes in VXO to have an RS marginal effect over time.

The ML estimates of a self-exciting SRM reveal that the best threshold variable is represented by two lags of excess stock returns; the estimated model is:

$$\begin{aligned} x_{t+1} = {} & \Big(\underset{(0.067)}{0.491} + \underset{(0.543)}{2.037}\Delta FFR_t + \underset{(0.385)}{2.717}\Delta FFR_{t-1} - \underset{(0.000)}{0.609}\Delta VXO_t\Big) \\ & + \Big(\underset{(0.285)}{0.356} - \underset{(0.092)}{7.132}\Delta FFR_t + \underset{(0.829)}{0.907}\Delta FFR_{t-1} - \underset{(0.352)}{0.093}\Delta VXO_t\Big)\Phi\Big[\underset{(0477)}{2.203}\Big(x_{t-1} + \underset{(0.796)}{0.175}\Big)\Big] + \varepsilon_{t+1}. \end{aligned}$$

The estimated transition function is shown in Fig. 8.11 along with the regime weights allocated on the basis of the values taken by x_{t-1} and plugged in $\Phi(2.203(x_{t-1} + 0.175))$. Unfortunately the estimates give evidence of weak significance of the parameters and a confusing time series of regime weights, also shown in Fig. 8.11. This emphasizes the existence of one bear regime characterized by low or negative excess returns (that occurs in approximately 37% of the sample), well below 0.175%, in which

(Continued)

18. The Taylor expansion of an ESTAR model implies zero odd partial derivatives and nonzero even partial derivatives. Teräsvirta (1994) emphasizes that the auxiliary equation (8.60) for the ESTAR model is nested within that of an LSTAR model. If the ESTAR is appropriate, it should be possible to exclude all the terms in the cuSBIC expression term, while if the LSTAR is appropriate, all the even terms ought to disappear. This suggests a natural way to test LSTAR versus ESTAR, after rejecting the null of linearity.

EXAMPLE 8.7 (Continued)

changes in policy rates have no impact on excess stock returns, that are predicted only by past changes in implied volatility with a negative sign. The bull regime, which is very likely for positive excess returns, features a weak negative impact of recent FFR changes on excess stock returns, while volatility declines. The resulting adjusted R^2 is 51% and the SBIC attained is 5.267, not the smallest achievable for this series.

Even though the model is far from perfect, we anyway apply the linearity tests examined earlier, as shown in the output obtained from E-Views and displayed in Table 8.8.

On top of Table 8.8 the first batch of Luukkonen et al. (1988) joint linearity tests show that collectively, there is no doubt that the null of a constant $F(\mathbf{e}_i'\mathbf{X}_{t+1-d}; \rho, \kappa)$ (hence of a linear model, with constant and unit weight on one regime only) can be rejected with a negligible p-value; however, there are some indications that when $b_4 = 0$ is imposed, the null of $b_2 = b_3 = 0$ cannot be rejected. This may give us some indications as to the likely shape of the transition function. In the bottom portion of Table 8.8, the tests are performed in an explicitly conditional way and they also point to the fact that at least the term $b_1(\mathbf{e}_i'\mathbf{X}_{t+1-d})\delta_t$ gives a significant contribution to explaining/predicting the target variable.

As we have briefly discussed, similar tests can be used to test the null of two versus more than two regimes. Table 8.9 displays the results. Both types of tests support a need to increase the number of regimes that are entertained by the selected SESRM. However, we shall not pursue this task here.

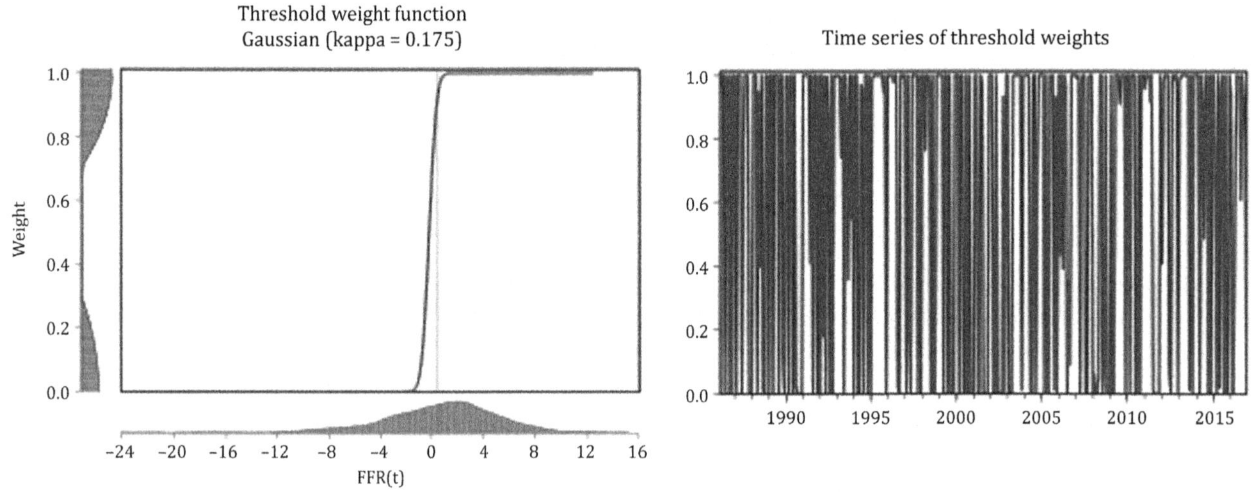

FIGURE 8.11 Estimated cumulative normal self-exciting transition function and time series of estimated $F(x_{t-2})$.

TABLE 8.8 Linearity Tests Based on (up to) the Fourth-Order Taylor Expansion

Test for Nonlinearity Using RET(−2) as the Threshold Variable
Taylor Series Alternatives: $b0 + b1*s$ [$+ b2*s^2 + b3*s^3 + b4*s^4$]

Linearity Tests Null Hypothesis	F-Statistic	d.f.	p-Value
H04: $b1 = b2 = b3 = b4 = 0$	3.5132	(15,351)	**0.000**
H03: $b1 = b2 = b3 = 0$	1.6346	(12,354)	0.080
H02: $b1 = b2 = 0$	1.8709	(8,358)	0.064
H01: $b1 = 0$	3.0060	(4,362)	**0.018**

The H0i Test Uses the ith Order Taylor Expansion ($bj = 0$ for all $j > i$)

Terasvirta Sequential Tests Null Hypothesis	F-Statistic	d.f.	p-Value
H3: $b3 = 0$	1.1554	(4,354)	0.330
H2: $b2 = 0 \| b3 = 0$	0.7443	(4,358)	0.562
H1: $b1 = 0 \| b2 = b3 = 0$	3.0060	(4,362)	**0.018**

All tests are based on the third-order Taylor expansion ($b4 = 0$).
Linear model is not rejected at the 5% level using $H03$.
Note: Test statistics significant at a size of 5% or less.

TABLE 8.9 Additional Nonlinearity Tests Based on (up to) the Fourth-Order Taylor Expansion

Encapsulated Nonlinearity Test Using RET(−2) as the Threshold
Taylor Series Alternatives: $b0 + b1*s\ [+ b2*s^2 + b3*s^3 + b4*s^4]$

Null Hypothesis	*F*-Statistic	d.f.	*p*-Value
H04: $b1 = b2 = b3 = b4 = 0$	1.8283	(28,332)	**0.008**
H03: $b1 = b2 = b3 = 0$	1.9137	(24,336)	**0.007**
H02: $b1 = b2 = 0$	1.8139	(16,344)	**0.028**
H01: $b1 = 0$	0.5450	(8,352)	0.822
The H0*i* Test Uses the *i*th Order Taylor Expansion ($bj = 0$ for all $j > i$)			
Terasvirta Sequential Tests			
Null Hypothesis	***F*-Statistic**	**d.f.**	***p*-Value**
H3: $b3 = 0$	2.0268	(8,336)	**0.043**
H2: $b2 = 0 \mid b3 = 0$	3.0574	(8,344)	**0.002**
H1: $b1 = 0 \mid b2 = b3 = 0$	0.5450	(8,352)	0.822

All tests are based on the third-order Taylor expansion ($b4 = 0$).
Original model is rejected at the 5% level using H03.
Note: Test statistics significant at a size of 5% or less.

The linearity tests mentioned earlier are not easily extended to TRM and TAR models because in these cases $F(\mathbf{e}_i' \boldsymbol{X}_{t+1-d}; \rho, \kappa)$ is not a continuous function of the parameters if the thresholds are unknown. This makes the likelihood function irregular and the score principle inapplicable. On the one hand, some researchers have proposed to use the same methods developed for STR and STAR models adopting a simple trick: a TRM/TAR may be approximated by a STR/STAR model with a large fixed value for the slope parameter ρ; the idea is then to first apply the linearity test and then the test of no residual nonlinearity sequentially, to find the number of regimes holding ρ constant (say, at 1000). This gives the modeler an approximate control over the significance level, and the technique appears to work reasonably well in simulations. Ertel and Fowlkes (1976) suggested instead the use of cumulative sums of recursive residuals for testing linearity against the presence of hard thresholds:

- Order the variables in ascending (or descending) order according to the selected transition variable with delay parameter d, $\mathbf{e}_i' \boldsymbol{X}_{t+1-d}$.
- Estimate the parameters recursively to compute the cumulative sum of recursive residuals.

The test is then analogous to the CUSUM test discussed in Section 8.2, in this case to detect structural breaks that are one special case of TRS behavior.

The earlier linearity tests are the tests against a well-specified nonlinear alternative. There exist other tests that are intended as *general tests without a specific alternative*. Probably the most famous one is the regression error specification test (RESET) briefly covered in Chapter 1 in which we ended up performing an LM-style F-test comparing the SSR of some linear model with the SSR from an augmented model including the $m+1$ powers of the fitted values from the original linear model. Tsay (1986) recommends to implement the RESET also using powers of the cross-products of the regressors of the lagged values in the case of TAR and STAR model tests, which can be simply described as using as the RESET regressors $vech(\mathbf{X}_t \mathbf{X}_t')$, where vech$(\cdot)$ denotes the half-stacking vector of a matrix, as in Chapter 6. For example, in the case of a TAR or STAR model with $p = 2$, the RESET may be implemented through the Lagrange multiplier auxiliary regression:

$$y_{t+1} = \beta_0 + \beta_1 y_t + \beta_2 y_{t-1} + \beta_3 y_t y_{t-1} + \alpha_1 \hat{y}_t^2 + \alpha_2 \hat{y}_t^3 + \cdots + \alpha_m \hat{y}_t^{m+1} + u_{t+1}. \tag{8.63}$$

Under special conditions and for self-exciting models at least, such RESET tests are similar to the F-tests based on Taylor expansions suggested by Luukkonen et al. (1988).

Of course, the two important types of tests presented earlier—*Ljung–Box portmanteau tests applied to powers of standardized residuals* (typically, their squares) and *BDS tests* based on sample estimation of correlation integrals, see Chapter 5—can also be constructed as tests of linearity without a specific alternative hypothesis. The idea is that, under the null hypothesis of linearity, the residuals of a properly specified linear model should be independent. Any violation of independence in the residuals may indicate inadequacy of the entertained model, *including* the linearity assumption. However, a warning is in order: the BDS test is able to detect serial correlation, parameter instability, neglected nonlinearity, structural breaks, and other misspecification; therefore rejecting the null hypothesis of independence does little to help identify the nature of the problem, that is, the alternative hypothesis is *very* general.

Finally, it is also possible to use information criteria, both to test linearity ($K = 1$ vs $K > 1$) and to select the number of regimes. Strictly speaking, information criteria could not be employed in order to select among linear and nonlinear models, because they are developed under the assumption that all models under consideration belong to the same parametric family; nevertheless, this approach can be a valuable alternative to linearity tests since it does not depend on a (possibly misspecified) lag order estimate under the assumption of linearity and will always lead to a definite model choice. Gonzalo and Pitarakis (2002) have proposed to select sequentially the number of regimes: expanding the model by adding another regime is discontinued when the value of the model selection criterion, such as SBIC or H-Q (see Chapter 2 for their definition), stop decreasing. As always, a drawback of this technique is that the significance level of each individual comparison (K regimes vs $K + 1$) is a function of the size of the model and cannot be controlled by the analyst. This is due to the fact that the size of the penalty in model selection criteria is a function of the number of parameters.

REFERENCES

Andrews, D.W.K., 1993. Tests for parameter instability and structural change with unknown change point. Econometrica 61, 821–856.

Andrews, D.W.K., Lee, I., Ploberger, W., 1996. Optimal change point tests for normal linear regression. J. Econometr. 70, 9–38.

Bai, J., 1997. Estimation of a change point in multiple regression models. Rev. Econ. Stat. 79, 551–563.

Bai, J., 1999. Likelihood ratio tests for multiple structural changes. J. Econometr. 91, 299–323.

Bai, J., Perron, P., 1998. Estimating and testing linear models with multiple structural changes. Econometrica 66, 47–78.

Bai, J., Perron, P., 2006. Multiple structural change models: a simulation analysis. In: Corbae, D., Durlauf, S., Hansen, B.E. (Eds.), Econometric Theory and Practice: Frontiers of Analysis and Applied Research. Cambridge University Press, Cambridge, pp. 212–237.

Brown, R.L., Durbin, J., Evans, J.M., 1975. Techniques for testing the constancy of regression relationships over time. J. R. Stat. Soc. B 37, 149–163.

Chan, K.S., 1990. Testing for threshold autoregression. Ann. Stat. 18 (4), 1886–1894.

Chong, T.T.L., 2001. Structural change in AR(1) models. Econometr. Theory 17, 87–155.

Chow, G.C., 1960. Tests of equality between sets of coefficients in two linear regressions. Econometrica 28, 591–605.

Davies, R.B., 1977. Hypothesis testing when a nuisance parameter is present only under the alternative. Biometrika 64, 247–254.

Davies, R.B., 1987. Hypothesis testing when a nuisance parameter is present only under the alternative. Biometrika 74, 33–43.

Deng, A., Perron, P., 2008. A non-local perspective on the power properties of the CUSUM and CUSUM of squares tests for structural change. J. Econometr. 142, 212–240.

Enders, W., 2008. Applied Econometric Time Series. John Wiley & Sons, Hoboken, NJ.

Enders, W., Granger, C.W.J., 1998. Unit-root tests and asymmetric adjustment with an example using the term structure of interest rates. J. Bus. Econ. Stat. 16, 304–311.

Enders, W., Siklos, P., 2001. Cointegration and threshold adjustment. J. Bus. Econ. Stat. 19, 166–176.

Ertel, J.E., Fowlkes, E.B., 1976. Some algorithms for linear spline and piecewise multiple linear regression. J. Am. Stat. Assoc. 71, 640–648.

Gonzalo, J., Pitarakis, J.-Y., 2002. Estimation and model selection based inference in single and multiple threshold models. J. Econometr. 110, 319–352.

Granger, C.W.J., Hallman, J., 1991. Long-memory processes with attractors. Oxford Bull. Econ. Stat. 53, 11–26.

Gregory, A.W., Nason, J.M., Watt, D.G., 1996. Testing for structural breaks in cointegrated relationships. J. Econometr. 71, 321–341.

Hansen, B.E., 1997. Approximate asymptotic *p* values for structural-change tests. J. Bus. Econ. Stat. 15, 60–67.

Hansen, B.E., 1999. Testing for linearity. J. Econ. Surv. 13, 551–576.

Hansen, B.E., 2011. Threshold autoregression in economics. Stat. Interface 4, 123–127.

Hansen, H., Johansen, S., 1999. Some tests for parameter constancy in cointegrated VAR-models. Econometr. J. 306–333.

Harvey, A.C., 1976. Estimating regression models with multiplicative heteroskedasticity. Econometrica 44, 461–465.

Kim, C.J., Nelson, C.R., 1999. State-Space Models With Regime Switching: Classical and Gibbs-Sampling Approaches With Applications. MIT Press, Cambridge, MA.

Kuan, C.M., White, H., 1994. Artificial neural networks: an econometric perspective. Econometr. Rev. 13, 1–91.

Lee, J., Huang, C.J., Shin, Y., 1997. On stationary tests in the presence of structural breaks. Econ. Lett. 55, 165–172.

Liu, J., Wu, S., Zidek, J.V., 1997. On segmented multivariate regressions. Stat. Sin. 7, 497–525.

Luukkonen, R., Saikkonen, P., Teräsvirta, T., 1988. Testing linearity against smooth transition autoregressive models. Biometrika 75, 491–499.

MacKinnon, J.G., 1996. Numerical distribution functions for unit root and cointegration tests. J. Appl. Econometrics 11 (6), 601–618. Nov. - Dec., 1996.

Montañés, A., Reyes, M., 2000. Structural breaks, unit roots and methods for removing the autocorrelation pattern. Stat. Prob. Lett. 48, 401–409.

Perron, P., 1989. The great crash, the oil price shock and the unit root hypothesis. Econometrica 57, 1361–1401.

Perron, P., 1990. Testing for a unit root in a time series with a changing mean. J. Bus. Econ. Stat. 8, 153–162.

Perron, P., 2006. Dealing with structural breaks. In: Mills, T.C., Patterson, K. (Eds.), Palgrave Handbook of Econometrics, Vol. 1: Econometric Theory. Palgrave Macmillan, New York.

Perron, P., Qu, Z., 2006. Estimating restricted structural change models. J. Econometr. 134, 373–399.

Perron, P., Vogelsang, T.,J., 1992. Testing for a unit root in a time series with a changing mean: corrections and extensions. J. Bus. Econ. Stat. 10, 467–470.

Perron, P., 1994. Trend, unit root and structural change in macroeconomic time series. In: Rao, B.B. (Ed.), Cointegration for the Applied Economist. Macmillan Press, Basingstoke, pp. 113–146.

Pitarakis, J.Y., 2006. Model selection uncertainty and detection of threshold effects. Stud. Nonlinear Dyn. Econometr. 10 (1). Available from: http://dx.doi.org/10.2202/1558-3708.1256.

Ploberger, W., Krämer, W., 1990. The local power of the CUSUM and CUSUM of squares tests. Econometr. Theor. 6, 335–347.

Ploberger, W., Krämer, W., 1992. The CUSUM test with OLS residuals. Econometrica 60, 271–285.

Qu, Z., Perron, P., 2007. Estimating and testing structural changes in multivariate regressions. Econometrica 75, 459–502.

Quandt, R.E., 1960. Tests of the hypothesis that a linear regression system obeys two separate regimes. J. Am. Stat. Assoc. 55, 324–330.

Seo, B., 1998. Tests for structural change in cointegrated systems. Econometr. Theor. 14, 222–259.

Teräsvirta, T., 1994. Specification, estimation and evaluation of smooth transition autoregressive models. J. Am. Stat. Assoc. 89, 208–218.

Teräsvirta, T., 2006. Forecasting economic variables with nonlinear models. In: Elliott, G., Timmermann, A. (Eds.), Handbook of Economic Forecasting, vol. 1. Elsevier, Amsterdam.

Teräsvirta, T., Tjøstheim, D., Granger, C.W.J., 1994. Aspects of modelling nonlinear time series, Handbook of Econometrics, vol. 4. Elsevier, Amsterdam, pp. 2917–2957.

Tong, H., 1983. Threshold Models in Non-linear Time Series Analysis. Lecture Notes in Statistics, vol. 21. Springer, Berlin.

Tsay, R.S., 1986. Nonlinearity tests for time series. Biometrika 73, 461–466.

Vogelsang, T.J., 1997. Wald-type tests for detecting breaks in the trend function of a dynamic time series. Econometric Theory 13 (6), 818–848.

Vogelsang, T.J., 1999. Sources of nonmonotonic power when testing for a shift in mean of a dynamic time series. J. Econometr. 88, 283–299.

Yadav, P.K., Pope, P.F., Paudyal, K., 1994. Threshold autoregressive modeling in finance: the price differences of equivalent assets. Math. Finance 4, 205–221.

Yao, Y.C., 1988. Estimating the number of change-points via Schwarz'criterion. Stat. Prob. Lett. 6, 181–189.

Chapter 9

Markov Switching Models

History repeats itself, but in such cunning disguise that we never detect the resemblance until the damage is done.

Sidney J. Harris

In this chapter, we introduce the structure and mechanics of estimation, inference, and forecasting for Markov switching (henceforth, MS) models, in which a latent state governs how part or all the parameters of a time series framework may change over time. MS represents the most widely applied and best-known case of regime switching (RS) model in both finance and macroeconomics. To uncover (filter) from financial data, the underlying but unobservable "general state" of the economy or more specifically of asset markets through MS models has become one of the leading methods through which applied researchers try and recover important and yet unobservable (missing) data that have proven the key to successfully understand and also forecast a variety of financial phenomena.

Because in earlier chapters we have already generously dealt with dynamic, multivariate time series methods, and because, in the case of MS models, univariate approaches really just represent special cases of the multivariate ones, in this chapter, we present the general, *N*-variable case, even though our examples will also be univariate, to provide a reader with additional intuition.

9.1 DEFINITIONS AND CLASSIFICATIONS

Consider the case of a $N \times 1$ random vector of variables of interest, when all variables are jointly considered to be endogenous, but *regimes are exogenous*. The following definition formalizes the nature of an MS model.

DEFINITION 9.1 (Markov Switching VAR Model)

$\mathbf{y}_t$ that follows a *K*-state heteroskedastic MS *VAR(p)* process, compactly *MS(I)VARH(K, p)*,

$$\mathbf{y}_{t+1} = \boldsymbol{\mu}_{S_{t+1}} + \sum_{j=1}^{p} \mathbf{A}_{j,S_{t+1}} \mathbf{y}_{t+1-j} + \boldsymbol{\Sigma}_{S_{t+1}}^{1/2} \mathbf{z}_{t+1} \quad S_{t+1} = 1, 2, \ldots, K, \tag{9.1}$$

with $\mathbf{z}_{t+1} \sim \text{IID } D(\mathbf{0}, \mathbf{I}_N)$ and S_{t+1} independent of $\mathbf{z}_{t+1}$ and $\boldsymbol{\Sigma}_1^{1/2}, \boldsymbol{\Sigma}_2^{1/2}, \ldots, \boldsymbol{\Sigma}_K^{1/2}$ lower triangular matrices. The unobservable state S_{t+1} is generated by a discrete-state, homogeneous, irreducible, and ergodic *M*-order Markov chain (MC) such that:

$$\Pr\left(S_{t+1} = j | \{S_\tau\}_{\tau=1}^{t}, \{\mathbf{y}_\tau\}_{\tau=1}^{t}\right) = \Pr\left(S_{t+1} = j | \{S_{t-j}\}_{j=0}^{M-1}, \{\mathbf{y}_{t-j}\}_{j=0}^{M-1}\right) \in (0, 1). \tag{9.2}$$

When $M = 1$ (first-order MC process) and $\Pr\left(S_{t+1} = j | \{S_\tau\}_{\tau=1}^{t}, \{\mathbf{y}_\tau\}_{\tau=1}^{t}\right) = \Pr\left(S_{t+1} = j | S_t\right)$ (the MC is time invariant), we call the $K \times K$ matrix collecting the probabilities $p_{ij} \equiv \Pr\left(S_{t+1} = j | S_t = i\right)$, $i = 1, \ldots, K, j = 1, \ldots, K$ such that $\sum_{j=1}^{K} p_{ij} = 1$, the *transition matrix* of the *K*-state Markov process. Of course, the transition matrix can be defined for general *M*th-order Markov process, but this requires an adequate redefinition of the regimes that we describe in Section 9.4. Note the meaning of $p_{ij} \equiv \Pr\left(S_{t+1} = j | S_t = i\right)$; this is the probability that, starting in regime *i*, the model may move to regime *j*.

The fact that the *regime is unobservable* (*latent*) means that even with unlimited time series information made available, estimation will never reveal the actual, true state S_{t+1} in the time series. However, a reader should already be

Essentials of Time Series for Financial Applications. DOI: https://doi.org/10.1016/B978-0-12-813409-2.00009-1

familiar with this state of affairs, because volatility is typically unobservable in finance (we shall return again on this principle in Chapter 10. Sometimes, with reference to MS models, we write of *hidden state RS*. The regime variable is latent in the sense that even at time t, both the agents/investors of our models and the econometrician will fail to observe S_t: at most they can use the methods that will be described below to produce data-driven inferences on the identity of S_t over time. The same sample data concerning the N variables in $\mathbf{y}_t$ are used also to produce inferences on the sample path followed by $\{S_t\}_{t=1}^T$, besides producing standard inferences on the parameters, see Section 9.5. Differently from Chapter 8, and leaving aside any efforts to provide economic interpretation for any econometric results, no attempt is made to provide a formal structural model of either the reason that regime changes occur or to explain the timing of such changes.

In addition to the structure that appears in Definition 9.1, we shall assume the absence of roots outside the unit circle in all regimes, thus making the process stationary. In the following, we shall use the terms *regimes* and *states* indifferently, without any special implication. The acronym MS(I)VARH means MS, Vector AutoRegressive, Heteroskedastic model.[1] K is the number of regimes that we are free to specify (or test for, when needed, see Section 9.5) and p is the number of autoregressive lags that we can select (or again, test for).

In Definition 9.1, the $N \times 1$ vector $\boldsymbol{\mu}_{S_{t+1}}$ collects the N regime-dependent intercepts, while the p alternative $N \times N$ $\{\mathbf{A}_{j,S_{t+1}}\}_{j=1}^p$ vector autoregressive matrices capture regime-dependent VAR effects at lags $j = 1, 2, \ldots, p$. This means that with p VAR lags and K regimes, there are a total of pK matrices to deal with, each potentially containing (unless restrictions are imposed) N^2 parameters to be estimated. The (lower triangular) matrix $\boldsymbol{\Sigma}_{S_{t+1}}^{1/2}$ represents the factor applicable to *latent* (unobservable) state S_{t+1} in a state-dependent Cholesky factorization of the covariance matrix of asset returns, $\boldsymbol{\Sigma}_{S_{t+1}}^{1/2}$,

$$\boldsymbol{\Sigma}_{S_{t+1}}^{1/2}(\boldsymbol{\Sigma}_{S_{t+1}}^{1/2})' = \boldsymbol{\Sigma}_{S_{t+1}} \equiv Var[y_{t+1}|\Im_t,\ S_{t+1}], \tag{9.3}$$

where $\Im_t$ denotes time t information composed of all past observations and states (filtered states, see below). Note that in Eq. (9.1) the conditional covariance matrix depends on the time $t+1$ state and that $\boldsymbol{\Sigma}_{S_{t+1}}^{1/2}$ is in no way the matrix of square roots of the elements of the actual covariance matrix $\boldsymbol{\Sigma}_{S_{t+1}}$ (if so, how would you deal with potentially negative covariances?).[2] Obviously, a nondiagonal $\boldsymbol{\Sigma}_{S_{t+1}}$ makes the N variables contemporaneously cross-correlated, thus capturing simultaneous comovements between them. Finally, $D(\mathbf{0}, \mathbf{I}_N)$ is a generic distribution, even though, for reasons that we also explore later, much of the literature has resorted to the simple assumption that $\mathbf{z}_{t+1} \sim \text{IID } N(\mathbf{0}, \mathbf{I}_N)$. A recent literature has occasionally generalized Eq. (9.1) to models in which different Markov state variables (usually assumed to be independent, of orders M_S and M_Q) drive the conditional mean and the conditional covariance matrix functions, respectively:

$$\mathbf{y}_{t+1} = \boldsymbol{\mu}_{S_{t+1}} + \sum_{j=1}^{p} \mathbf{A}_{j,S_{t+1}} \mathbf{y}_{t+1-j} + \boldsymbol{\Sigma}_{Q_{t+1}}^{1/2} \mathbf{z}_{t+1}, \tag{9.4}$$

where $S_{t+1} = 1, 2, \ldots, K_S$ and $Q_{t+1} = 1, 2, \ldots, K_Q$, such that $\Pr\left(S_{t+1} = j|\{S_{t-j}\}_{j=0}^{t-1}, \{y_\tau\}_{\tau=1}^{t}\right) = \Pr\left(S_{t+1} = j|\{S_{t-j}\}_{j=1}^{K_S-1}\right)$ and $\Pr\left(Q_{t+1} = j|\{Q_{t-j}\}_{j=0}^{t-1}, \{y_\tau\}_{\tau=1}^{t}\right) = \Pr\left(Q_{t+1} = j|\{Q_{t-j}\}_{j=0}^{K_Q-1}\right)$, respectively. In case of independence of the two-state variables, clearly the total number of regimes is the product of K_S and K_Q, so that the minimal total number of regimes characterizing Eq. (9.4) is four, because as a minimum $K_S = 2$ and $K_Q = 2$.

Conditionally on the unobservable state S_{t+1}, Eqs. (9.1) and (9.2) define a standard Gaussian reduced form VAR(p) model, which is implied by the simple structure of $\mathbf{z}_{t+1} \sim \text{IID } D(\mathbf{0}, \mathbf{I}_N)$ and the triangular nature of $\boldsymbol{\Sigma}_{S_{t+1}}$. This means that if one were to take S_{t+1} as given and observable (we shall not of course, in practice), then between time t and time $t+1$, Eq. (9.1) turns into a VAR(p) similar to the models that we have studied in Chapter 3. Implicitly, Definition 9.1 assumes that all the $K \geq 2$ alternative hidden states are possible and that they influence the conditional mean, the conditional variance, and the conditional correlation structures characterizing the multivariate process in Eq. (9.1).

Several special cases of Eq. (9.1) are very popular in applied finance, for instance the simple MSVARH(K,1) case:

$$\mathbf{y}_{t+1} = \boldsymbol{\mu}_{S_{t+1}} + \mathbf{A}_{S_{t+1}} \mathbf{y}_t + \boldsymbol{\Sigma}_{S_{t+1}}^{1/2} \mathbf{z}_{t+1} \quad S_{t+1} = 1, 2, \ldots, K, \tag{9.5}$$

which is a simple *VAR*(1) with K regimes. Of course, in the literature, the case of $K = 2$ tends to be the most common, even though it is easy to understand there is nothing special or compelling about setting $K = 2$, especially when

1. The "I" in parenthesis is probably superfluous, but it stands there to emphasize that in Eq. (9.1) also the intercept is regime-dependent. We shall simplify the acronym omitting the I when this causes no ambiguity.
2. $\boldsymbol{\Sigma}_{S_{t+1}}^{1/2}$ is a lower triangular matrix appropriately defined according to an algorithm that is implemented in most software packages.

N is large.[3] Another model that has found some popularity (see Guidolin and Ono, 2006) is a mixed MSIH(K)-VAR(p) model in which all parameters but the p VAR matrices are RS:

$$\mathbf{y}_{t+1} = \boldsymbol{\mu}_{S_{t+1}} + \sum_{j=1}^{p} \mathbf{A}_j \mathbf{y}_{t+1-j} + \boldsymbol{\Sigma}_{S_{t+1}}^{1/2} \mathbf{z}_{t+1} \quad S_{t+1} = 1, 2, \ldots, K. \tag{9.6}$$

Interestingly, especially when daily and weekly returns data are used, it is not uncommon to find that they support a choice of $p = 0$, which reduces the model to a simpler MSIH(K) (or, to be precise, MSIH(K,0)):

$$\mathbf{y}_{t+1} = \boldsymbol{\mu}_{S_{t+1}} + \boldsymbol{\Sigma}_{S_{t+1}}^{1/2} \mathbf{z}_{t+1} \quad S_{t+1} = 1, 2, \ldots, K. \tag{9.7}$$

However, in the literature you also find many cases in which $p = 0$ works at all frequencies. The reason is that when there are many regimes, $K >> 2$, it is possible that the need of a vector autoregressive structure ($p > 1$) in single-state VAR(p) models arises from the omission of regimes in the dynamics of asset returns.[4]

The general model in Definition 9.1 simplifies in obvious ways in univariate applications, when $N = 1$, where we write of MS AR(K,p) models that are just one special case of the general family of nonlinear ARMA:

$$y_{t+1} = \mu_{S_{t+1}} + \sum_{j=1}^{p} a_{j,S_{t+1}} y_{t+1-j} + \sigma_{S_{t+1}} z_{t+1} \quad S_{t+1} = 1, 2, \ldots, K, \tag{9.8}$$

where $z_{t+1} \sim \text{IID } D(0, 1)$ and $\sigma_{S_{t+1}}$ is a regime-specific volatility. It is now time for a first set of empirical examples.

EXAMPLE 9.1

In this example, we train ourselves to understand the typical MS outputs and to appreciate the relationships between univariate MS models and multivariate ones on a monthly data set (the sample is 1986:01–2016:12) of international excess equity returns for the United States, Japan (denominated in US dollars) and the rate of monthly change of the VXO volatility index, for a total of $N = 3$.

As a first step, we analyze *for each series* what type of first-order MSIVARH(K,p) model may be required by estimating a range of models, collecting, and reporting in Table 9.1 the corresponding summary statistics from maximum likelihood (ML) estimation. In the table, the saturation ratio is simply the ratio between the total number of observations and the number of parameters to be estimated in each model. Winning models according to each criterion have been boldfaced.

Table 9.1 uses information criteria, an aspect of MS model selection that we shall deal with in Section 9.5. However, as always, the point is to minimize such criteria, as already seen in the case of a single-state VAR (see Chapter 3). The evidence from all the three series is in favor of multiple regimes in the sense that various linear ARMA-type models (including the simple Gaussian IID benchmark in which only mean and variance can be estimated as time invariant over our sample) always yield information criteria that grossly exceed those typical of MSIARH(K,p) models with $K = 2$ and 3. However, the precise model favored by each information criterion in the case of each series may differ. As it is usually the case, Akaike information criterion (AIC) tends to favor larger models with more parameters and in the case of US excess returns and VXO rates of growth, the criterion favors models with three regimes over models with two regimes. However, a simple heteroskedastic MSIH(2,0) model with no AR components and two states is always picked, for all three series, by at least one criterion, the most parsimonious Schwarz bayesian information criterion (SBIC). The implication is that even though in a linear world (i.e., when $K = 1$ is imposed) the data may give some indications in favor of ARMA components in the conditional mean (this is particularly evident in the case of the rates of change in VXO), these lose importance when nonlinearities are accommodated through an MS framework.

Because for all three series, the SBIC selects it as the best model trading-off in-sample fit with parsimony, in the following we report the three sets of estimates for MSIH(2,0). Details on estimation methods are provided in Section 9.5; p-values are in parentheses and are obtained through a sandwich form that will be described in the following:

(Continued)

3. Think about collecting in $\mathbf{y}_{t+1}$ three different assets or portfolios, each characterized by two specific, not perfectly synchronous regimes. Then one ought to expect to find $2^3 = 8$ regimes if the assets or portfolios are characterized by truly different sets of regimes.

4. To complete the list of possibilities, Ang and Bekaert (2002) have used weekly data to support the fit of a simple MSH(K) model, $\mathbf{y}_{t+1} = \boldsymbol{\mu} + \boldsymbol{\Sigma}_{S_{t+1}}^{1/2} \mathbf{z}_{t+1}$. In principle it is also possible to envision the use of homoskedastic MSI(K) models, $\mathbf{y}_{t+1} = \boldsymbol{\mu}_{S_{t+1}} + \sum^{1/2} \mathbf{z}_{t+1}$ with constant covariance matrix. However, the evidence of conditional heteroskedasticity is empirically so overwhelming that the instances in which MSI(K) has been found to appropriately fit the data are rare.

EXAMPLE 9.1 (Continued)

$$x_{t+1}^{US} = \begin{cases} \underset{(0.000)}{1.096} + \underset{(0.000)}{2.649}\, z_{t+1}^{US} & \text{if } S_{t+1}^{US} = 1 \text{ (bull)} \\ \underset{(0.751)}{0.206} + \underset{(0.000)}{5.662}\, z_{t+1}^{US} & \text{if } S_{t+1}^{US} = 2 \text{ (bear)} \end{cases} \qquad \hat{P}^{US} = \begin{bmatrix} 0.966 & 0.034 \\ 0.035 & 0.965 \end{bmatrix}$$

$$x_{t+1}^{Japan} = \begin{cases} \underset{(0.298)}{0.462} + \underset{(0.000)}{3.806}\, z_{t+1}^{Japan} & \text{if } S_{t+1}^{Japan} = 1 \text{ (bull)} \\ \underset{(0.709)}{0.196} + \underset{(0.000)}{7.433}\, z_{t+1}^{Japan} & \text{if } S_{t+1}^{Japan} = 2 \text{ (bear)} \end{cases} \qquad \hat{P}^{Japan} = \begin{bmatrix} 0.984 & 0.016 \\ 0.012 & 0.988 \end{bmatrix}$$

$$rvxo_{t+1} = \begin{cases} -\underset{(0.434)}{2.758} + \underset{(0.000)}{14.363}\, z_{t+1}^{VXO} & \text{if } S_{t+1}^{VXO} = 1 \text{ (vol down)} \\ \underset{(0.169)}{30.496} + \underset{(0.000)}{35.872}\, z_{t+1}^{VXO} & \text{if } S_{t+1}^{VXO} = 2 \text{ (vol up)} \end{cases} \qquad \hat{P}^{VXO} = \begin{bmatrix} 0.867 & 0.133 \\ 0.823 & 0.177 \end{bmatrix}.$$

In terms of excess returns, the two stock markets feature by typical bull (characterized by high-risk premia and low volatility) and bear (low or even 0, in the sense of not statistically significantly, risk premia and high volatility) phases. Both regimes are highly persistent, in the sense that for both United States and Japan, $\Pr(S_t = bull|S_{t-1} = bull)$ is between 0.97 and 0.98, and the equivalent probability estimates for the bear regime are 0.97 and 0.99; in short, regime shifts occur but are rare. The estimates give instead rather different indications as far as growth rates in VXO are concerned. The state-dependent means are never precisely estimated, even though one implies modestly falling implied volatility and the other sharply increasing VXO; in the latter regime, the volatility of implicit volatility is almost double than in the former state. This means that when volatility falls, it does so slowly and following a low-variability path, while when it increases, it does so in an abrupt and in an extremely erratic way. In fact, the estimated transition matrix of the MSIH process for the VXO confirms this story: the regime of declining implied volatility is rather persistent with a "stayer" probability of 0.87, whereas the regime of increasing implicit market volatility is not persistent and may even last 1 month only.

We now approach the problem of building a three-variable MS model. It is useful to ask ourselves—given that all the individual series seem to contain evidence of regimes—how many Markov states should we expect from these data when the three series are jointly modeled. Fig. 9.1 shows that in a multivariate exercise, it seems naïve to expect $K = 2$, because the univariate state probability series that one recovers from the models estimated early on seem not to be sufficiently synchronized to support an expectation of $K = 2$. In fact, the sample Spearman rank correlations (this is just the standard correlation of the ranks of two series of data, that is, of their relative standing from the largest to the smallest) for each pairs of state probabilities that is filtered out of the univariate models (we shall explain in detail what is the meaning of such a filtering operation in Section 9.5) are 0.46 (p-value is 0.000) between the two bull state probabilities for United States and Japanese excess returns, but only -0.05 (p-value 0.308) and -0.13 (p-value 0.011) for the pairs formed by excess stock returns and VXO growth rate filtered state probabilities. Using rank correlations is in fact warranted by the fact that state probabilities must by construction fall in the interval [0, 1] which would make the use of standard linear correlations. In fact, this evidence could make us expect as many as $2 \times 2 \times 2 = 8$ regimes. Table 9.2 reports evidence exactly on such effort of model specification search.

To some surprise, the AIC and Hannan–Quinn (H-Q) information criteria converge on the choice of a rather richly parameterized MSIVARH(3,1). The model implies the estimation of as many as 51 parameters and a saturation ratio of 21.8 which is just above the classical threshold of 20 typically required in nonlinear estimation problems. Unsurprisingly, the number of regimes equals three, even though it does not reach an absurdly high value such as eight. In fact, we were not able to achieve convergence in estimation for an MS VAR heteroskedastic model with eight regimes that would be characterized by 200 parameters. These three regimes are likely to represent an attempt to accommodate the different features of the state process for the two excess equity returns series versus those of the VXO series.

The estimated model is (the square matrices that premultiply the standardized shocks list standard errors on their main diagonal, pairwise linear correlations above the main diagonal, and covariances below):

$$\begin{bmatrix} x_{t+1}^{US} \\ x_{t+1}^{Japan} \\ rvxo_{t+1} \end{bmatrix} = \begin{cases} [\underset{(0.000)}{-2.088}\ \underset{(0.000)}{-6.157}\ \underset{(0.000)}{-6.785}]' & \text{if } S_{t+1} = 1 \\ [\underset{(0.000)}{0.958}\ \underset{(0.424)}{0.296}\ \underset{(0.019)}{-3.780}]' & \text{if } S_{t+1} = 2 \\ [\underset{(0.000)}{2.256}\ \underset{(0.000)}{4.227}\ \underset{(0.000)}{20.226}]' & \text{if } S_{t+1} = 3 \end{cases} + \begin{cases} \begin{bmatrix} \underset{(0.000)}{0.237} & \underset{(0.592)}{0.033} & \underset{(0.000)}{-14.914} \\ \underset{(0.875)}{0.018} & \underset{(0.788)}{0.028} & \underset{(0.271)}{-1.891} \\ \underset{(0.000)}{0.002} & \underset{(0.389)}{0.002} & \underset{(0.304)}{-0.050} \end{bmatrix} & \text{if } S_{t+1} = 1 \\ \begin{bmatrix} \underset{(0.007)}{0.167} & \underset{(0.767)}{0.011} & \underset{(0.000)}{-12.254} \\ \underset{(0.064)}{0.204} & \underset{(0.704)}{0.027} & \underset{(0.000)}{-7.586} \\ \underset{(0.213)}{0.004} & \underset{(0.457)}{0.002} & \underset{(0.000)}{-0.390} \end{bmatrix} & \text{if } S_{t+1} = 2 \\ \begin{bmatrix} \underset{(0.265)}{-0.135} & \underset{(0.864)}{0.011} & \underset{(0.143)}{-8.715} \\ \underset{(0.864)}{0.235} & \underset{(0.071)}{0.214} & \underset{(0.136)}{-6.385} \\ \underset{(0.000)}{0.015} & \underset{(0.045)}{0.008} & \underset{(0.370)}{-0.136} \end{bmatrix} & \text{if } S_{t+1} = 3 \end{cases} \cdot \begin{bmatrix} x_{t}^{US} \\ x_{t}^{Japan} \\ rvxo_{t} \end{bmatrix}$$

(Continued)

EXAMPLE 9.1 (Continued)

$$+\left\{\begin{array}{ll}\begin{bmatrix}3.104 & -0.154 & -0.151\\ -2.269 & 4.746 & -0.321\\ -5.118 & -16.64 & 10.92\end{bmatrix} & \text{if } S_{t+1}=1\\ \begin{bmatrix}2.332 & 0.312 & 0.097\\ 3.067 & 4.215 & -0.009\\ 2.914 & -0.489 & 12.88\end{bmatrix} & \text{if } S_{t+1}=2\\ \begin{bmatrix}3.661 & 0.118 & -0.335\\ 2.924 & 6.768 & -0.468\\ -36.45 & -94.14 & 29.72\end{bmatrix} & \text{if } S_{t+1}=3\end{array}\right\}\cdot\begin{bmatrix}z^{US}_{t+1}\\ z^{Japan}_{t+1}\\ rvxo_{t+1}\end{bmatrix}\qquad \hat{P}=\begin{bmatrix}0.397 & 0.055 & 0.548\\ 0.000 & 0.841 & 0.159\\ 0.392 & 0.340 & 0.268\end{bmatrix}.$$

The first, nonpersistent regime ($\Pr(S_t = 1|S_{t-1} = 1) = 0.40$) is characterized by negative risk premia and quickly declining implied market volatility, even though additional VXO increases strongly depress subsequent excess stock returns. The second regime is instead rather persistent ($\Pr(S_t = 2|S_{t-1} = 2) = 0.84$) and features a positive and significant US equity risk premium, a small and not statistically significant Japanese premium, and a slowly declining aggregate implicit volatility. The third regime is once more not persistent but characterized by high international equity premia but also rapidly growing forward-looking volatility. Finally, note that while in general from any of the three regimes it is possible to switch to any of the three regimes (which includes "staying" in the initial regime), this characterization admits one exception as $\Pr(S_{t+1} = 1|S_t = 2)$ is estimated to be 0: from the second, tranquil state, it is not possible to switch to the first, turbulent bear regime. As in earlier papers, for instance Guidolin and Pedio (2017), it is frequent to find that high-volatility regime only "communicate" with other high-volatility regimes. Such instances of "failure" to communicate among Markov regimes are rather frequent when $K = 3$ or 4 and carry interesting economic interpretations.

TABLE 9.1 Univariate MS Model Selection

Type of Model	K	p	Heteroskedasticity	No. of Parameters	Saturation Ratio	AIC	Hannan–Quinn	BIC
US Excess Stock Returns								
Linear IID	1	0	No	2	185.0	5.826	5.830	5.836
Linear AR(1)	1	1	No	3	123.3	5.828	5.836	5.849
Linear AR(2)	1	2	No	4	92.5	5.827	5.840	5.859
Linear ARMA(1,1)	1	1	No	4	92.5	5.828	5.840	5.859
MSI	2	0	No	5	74	5.746	5.767	5.799
MSIH	2	0	Yes	6	61.7	5.687	**5.712**	**5.751**
MSIH	3	0	Yes	12	30.8	**5.667**	5.718	5.794
MSIAR	2	1	No	7	52.9	5.754	5.783	5.828
MSAR	2	1	No	6	61.7	5.794	5.819	5.857
MSI-AR(1)	2	1	No	6	61.7	5.753	5.778	5.816
MSIARH	2	1	Yes	8	46.3	5.682	5.715	5.766
MSARH	2	1	Yes	7	52.9	5.683	5.713	5.757
MSIH-AR(1)	2	1	Yes	7	52.9	5.694	5.724	5.768
MSARH	2	2	Yes	9	41.1	5.688	5.723	5.783
MSARH	3	1	Yes	13	28.5	5.723	5.778	5.861

(Continued)

TABLE 9.1 (Continued)

Type of Model	K	p	Heteroskedasticity	No. of Parameters	Saturation Ratio	AIC	Hannan–Quinn	BIC
Japanese Excess Stock Returns in USD								
Linear IID	1	0	No	2	185.0	6.495	6.499	6.507
Linear AR(1)	1	1	No	3	123.3	6.492	6.500	6.513
Linear AR(2)	1	2	No	4	92.5	6.491	6.503	6.522
Linear ARMA(1,1)	1	1	No	4	92.5	6.478	6.490	6.509
MSI	2	0	No	5	74	6.479	6.500	6.531
MSIH	2	0	Yes	6	61.7	6.397	**6.422**	**6.460**
MSIH	3	0	Yes	12	30.8	6.417	6.468	6.544
MSIAR	2	1	No	7	52.9	6.479	6.509	6.553
MSAR	2	1	No	6	61.7	6.475	6.500	6.538
MSI-AR(1)	2	1	No	6	61.7	6.477	6.502	6.540
MSIARH	2	1	Yes	8	46.3	6.401	6.434	6.485
MSARH	2	1	Yes	7	52.9	**6.396**	6.425	6.469
MSIH-AR(1)	2	1	Yes	7	52.9	6.397	6.426	6.471
MSARH	2	2	Yes	9	41.1	6.400	6.438	6.496
MSARH	3	1	Yes	13	28.5	6.422	6.476	6.559
Percentage Rate of Change of VXO								
Linear IID	1	0	No	2	185.0	9.035	9.039	9.045
Linear AR(1)	1	1	No	3	123.3	9.014	9.022	9.035
Linear AR(2)	1	2	No	4	92.5	9.017	9.029	9.048
Linear ARMA(1,1)	1	1	No	4	92.5	8.988	9.000	9.019
MSI	2	0	No	5	74	8.815	8.836	8.868
MSIH	2	0	Yes	6	61.7	8.762	8.787	**8.762**
MSIH	3	0	Yes	12	30.8	8.719	8.770	8.846
MSIAR	2	1	No	7	52.9	8.731	8.760	8.805
MSI-AR(1)	2	1	No	6	61.7	8.767	8.792	8.831
MSIARH	2	1	Yes	8	46.3	8.709	8.743	8.794
MSARH	2	1	Yes	7	52.9	8.750	8.779	8.824
MSIH-AR(1)	2	1	Yes	7	52.9	8.704	8.733	8.778
MSIH-AR(1)	2	2	Yes	8	46.3	8.693	8.726	8.777
MSIH-AR(1)	3	1	Yes	13	28.5	**8.665**	**8.720**	8.802
MSIH-AR(2)	3	2	Yes	13	28.5	8.683	8.742	8.831

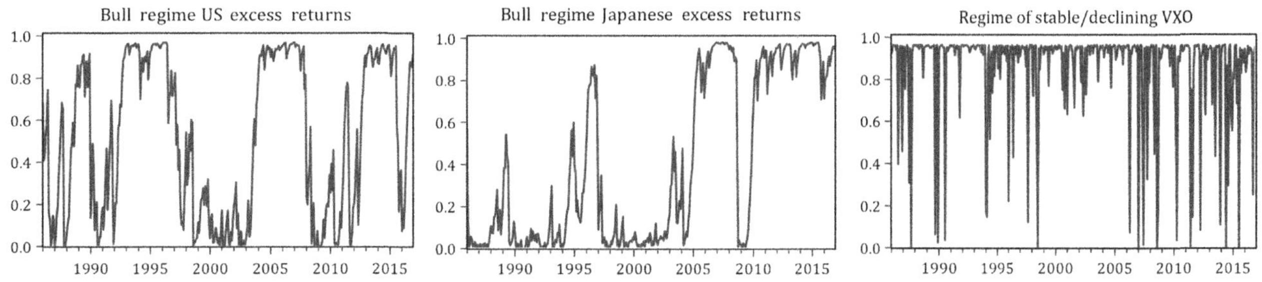

FIGURE 9.1 State probabilities from three univariate MSIH models.

TABLE 9.2 Multivariate MS Model Selection

Type of Model	K	p	Heteroskedasticity	No. of Parameters	Saturation Ratio	AIC	Hannan–Quinn	BIC
Linear IID	1	0	No	9	123.3	11.990	12.027	12.084
Linear VAR(1)	1	1	No	18	61.7	11.426	11.501	11.616
Linear VAR(2)	1	2	No	27	41.1	11.389	11.503	11.675
MSI	2	0	No	14	79.3	11.831	11.889	11.978
MSIH	2	0	Yes	20	55.5	11.635	11.719	11.846
MSIH	3	0	Yes	33	33.6	11.364	11.503	11.712
MSIH	4	0	Yes	48	23.1	11.236	11.436	11.741
MSIVAR	2	1	No	32	34.7	11.358	11.492	11.695
MSIVAR	3	1	No	48	23.1	10.956	11.157	11.463
MSIVAR	4	1	No	66	16.8	10.969	11.246	11.666
MSVAR	3	1	No	42	26.4	11.361	11.537	11.804
MSI-VAR(1)	3	1	No	30	37.0	11.183	11.309	11.500
MSI-VAR(2)	3	2	No	39	28.5	11.122	11.286	11.535
MSI-VAR(1)	4	1	No	39	28.5	11.124	11.287	11.536
MSIVARH	2	1	Yes	38	29.2	11.073	11.233	11.475
MSIVARH	2	2	Yes	56	19.8	11.037	11.272	**11.269**
MSIVARH	3	1	Yes	60	18.5	11.006	11.257	11.629
MSIH-VAR(1)	3	1	Yes	42	26.4	10.862	11.038	11.305
MSIH-VAR(1)	4	1	Yes	57	19.5	10.872	11.111	11.473
MSIH-VAR(2)	3	1	Yes	51	21.8	**10.806**	**11.020**	11.345
MSIH-VAR(1)	4	1	Yes	84	13.2	10.887	11.239	11.773

The MSIVARH(3,1) in Example 9.1 was characterized by 51 estimable parameters, quite a large model. This is a constant issue: when N is large, MSIVARH(K,p) implies the estimation of a large number of parameters, given by the formula:

$$K[N + pN^2 + N(N+1)/2 + (K-1)]. \tag{9.9}$$

In this formula, KN is the number of regime-specific intercepts that need to be estimated; KpN^2 is the total number of regime-specific VAR matrix parameters; $KN(N+1)/2$ is the total number of regime-specific lower triangular Cholesky factor parameters that are needed; finally, $K(K-1)$ is the number of elements that can be estimated from the transition matrix, when the by-row summing up constraints that have appeared in Definition 9.1 are taken into account. Because the *saturation ratio* is simply the ratio between the total number of observations available for estimation (NT) and the total number of parameters, an MSIVARH(K,p) implies a saturation ratio of:

$$\frac{NT}{K[N+pN^2+N(N+1)/2+(K-1)]}. \tag{9.10}$$

For instance, for $K=2$, $N=8$, and $p=1$ (which is not such an extreme case, see e.g., the application in Guidolin and Ono, 2006), this implies the estimation of 218 parameters. Especially when one works with monthly data, it is not difficult to imagine situations in which one ends up with saturation ratios well below what is usually recommended, such as ratios of 20. Moreover, as one may suspect on the basis of our treatment of maximum likelihood estimate (MLE) from Chapters 5 and 6, when there are hundreds of floating parameters, ML estimation may pose serious numerical as well as statistical problems:

- The log-likelihood function may present flat regions so that convergence of standard algorithms becomes slow or even impossible;
- *Identification issues* may appear, that is, numerical optimization algorithms may get "confused" because multiple, alternative configurations that are of course well possible when so many parameters have to be estimated may all deliver identical values of the log-likelihood function to be optimized.

Of course, some readers will object that these two difficulties are strictly related, and they would be correct (in fact, flat regions of the log-likelihood may reflect poor identification, but the problem may be more general or reflect the limitations the numerical optimization tools that are employed). However, Section 9.5 will introduce an iterative estimation scheme (called Expectation–Maximization (EM) algorithm) that often makes ML estimation possible even in the presence of a large number of parameters.

One special case of Definition 9.1 that has had some historical importance is the *simple switching model* (also called IID normal mixture model) which obtains when

$$\Pr\left(S_t=j|\{S_{t-j}\}_{j=1}^{t-1},\{y_\tau\}_{\tau=1}^{t-1}\right)=\Pr(S_t=j)=p_j\in(0,\ 1), \tag{9.11}$$

for $j=1,\ldots,K$ and $\sum_{j=1}^{K}p_j=1$. In words, the probability of accessing a given state j does not depend on the M-period history of the regimes visited in the past, which is equivalent to say that the MC process is memoryless, that is, a simple multinomial process. Equivalently, and focusing for concreteness on first-order MCs, while in general the transition matrix implied by an MS model has a structure:

$$\begin{bmatrix} p_{11} & p_{12} & \cdots & 1-\sum_{j=1}^{K-1}p_{1j} \\ p_{21} & p_{22} & \cdots & 1-\sum_{j=1}^{K-1}p_{2j} \\ \vdots & \vdots & \ddots & \cdots \\ p_{K1} & p_{K2} & \cdots & 1-\sum_{j=1}^{K-1}p_{Kj} \end{bmatrix}, \tag{9.12}$$

in this case, we have:

$$\begin{bmatrix} p_1 & p_2 & \cdots & 1-\sum_{j=1}^{K-1}p_j \\ p_1 & p_2 & \cdots & 1-\sum_{j=1}^{K-1}p_j \\ \vdots & \vdots & \ddots & \cdots \\ p_1 & p_2 & \cdots & 1-\sum_{j=1}^{K-1}p_j \end{bmatrix}, \tag{9.13}$$

that is, all the columns of the transition matrix will be identical. An example that is available online as supplementary material shows that unless of odd situations, simple switching is normally rejected by financial data in favor of richer Markov process that have memory.

9.2 UNDERSTANDING MARKOV SWITCHING DYNAMICS THROUGH SIMULATIONS

To better understand the mechanics of MS models, let us now return to our initial toy model, that we copy here for your convenience:

$$R_{t+1} = \phi_{0,S_{t+1}} + \phi_{1,S_{t+1}} R_t + \sigma_{S_{t+1}} z_{t+1} \quad z_{t+1} \text{ IID } N(0,1), \tag{9.14}$$

where S_{t+1}, is a discrete, first-order Markov state variable that takes K values, $S_{t+1} = 1, 2, \ldots, K$. For concreteness, let us say that this is an MSIARH(K) for percentage asset returns, R_{t+1}. Let us first simulate a time series of 1000 values from two models to help us represent in a stark way what MS models do. First, we set $K = 1$ and $\phi_0 = 0.50, \phi_1 = 0, \sigma = 5.50$, where the regime-specific subscripts have been dropped because this is just a *single-state Gaussian IID model* with no predictability or structure in either the conditional mean or the conditional variance. These are sensible parameterizations when applied to US excess equity returns data, delivering an annualized mean of $0.5 \times 12 = 6$, or 6% per year, and an annualized volatility of $5.5 \times \sqrt{12} = 19.1$, approximately 19% per year. Second, we simulated from an MSI(2,0) model and set $\phi_{0,1} = -6.6$, $\phi_{0,2} = 2.275, \phi_{1,1} = \phi_{1,2} = 0, \sigma_1 = \sigma_2 = 4.3$, where the transition matrix is simply characterized by "stayer" probabilities $\Pr(S_t = 1|S_{t-1} = 1) = 0.92$ and $\Pr(S_t = 2|S_{t-1} = 2) = 0.98$ (the remaining elements are pinned down by the sum-up constraints mentioned in Definition 9.1). As we shall see in Section 9.4, the resulting transition matrix, yields unconditional, long-run probabilities for the two regimes of 0.2 and 0.8, respectively. Using such unconditional probabilities, it is possible to check that the parameters above still yield an unconditional mean of 6% per year and a volatility of approximately 19% per year. For instance, $0.2 \times (-6.600) + 0.8 \times 2.275 = 6$. The relevant formulas are presented in Section 9.4, but for the time being it appears to be of greater importance to develop adequate intuition for MS models. Using the same 1000 random draws of the white noise process z_{t+1} IID $N(0, 1)$, Fig. 9.2 compares the Gaussian IID and the MSI(2) realizations.

In the MS case, we superimpose a dashed plot of the regime shifts (to be compared to the right scale, in which only two values are possible). The two series display a qualitatively different behavior because in the rightmost plot there are protracted periods in which returns are systematically above or below the long-run mean, that is by construction the same as in the leftmost plot. It seems fair to note that most observers would probably manage to detect the presence of "more structure" in the rightmost plot versus the leftmost, but would have a hard time detecting exactly an MSI(2) model; probably some additional "variability" would be guessed, but we know that this would be incorrect, as the two series in the two plots are generated to have identical variance. After all, this failure to simply "eyeball" the right model is why we study econometrics.

It turns out that one of the key drivers of the visual appearance of the simulated MS process in Fig. 9.2 is represented by the difference $\phi_{0,2} - \phi_{0,1} = 8.875$. In Fig. 9.3, we copy to the left the same MSI(2,0) process as in Fig. 9.2 but now add to the right a new MSIH(2,0) simulation in which $\phi_{0,2} - \phi_{0,1} = 6.25$ (in particular, $\phi_{0,1} = -4.50, \phi_{0,2} = 1.75, \phi_{1,1} = \phi_{1,2} = 0, \sigma_1 = \sigma_2 = 4.87$, where the transition matrix is again characterized by "stayer" probabilities $\Pr(S_t = 1|S_{t-1} = 1) = 0.92$ and $\Pr(S_t = 2|S_{t-1} = 2) = 0.98$).

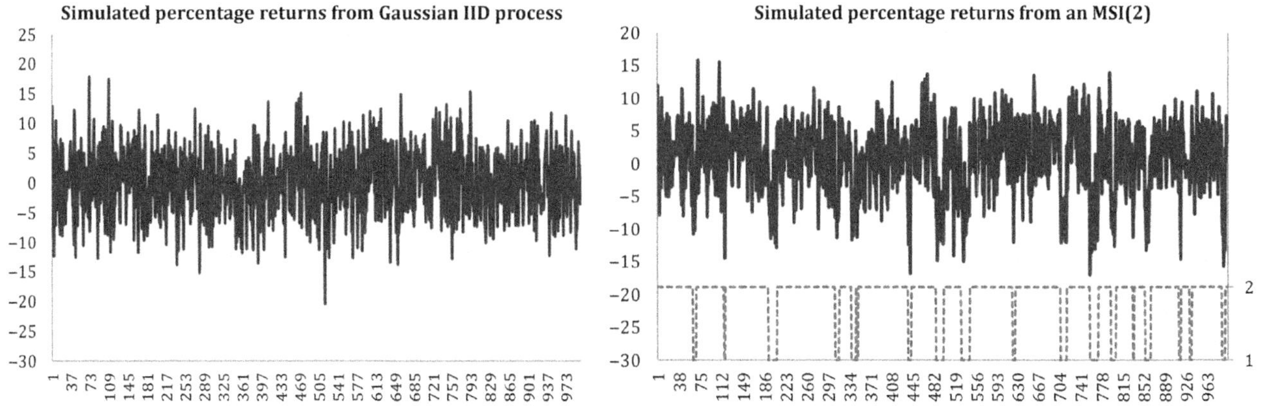

FIGURE 9.2 Comparing single- and two-state MS models.

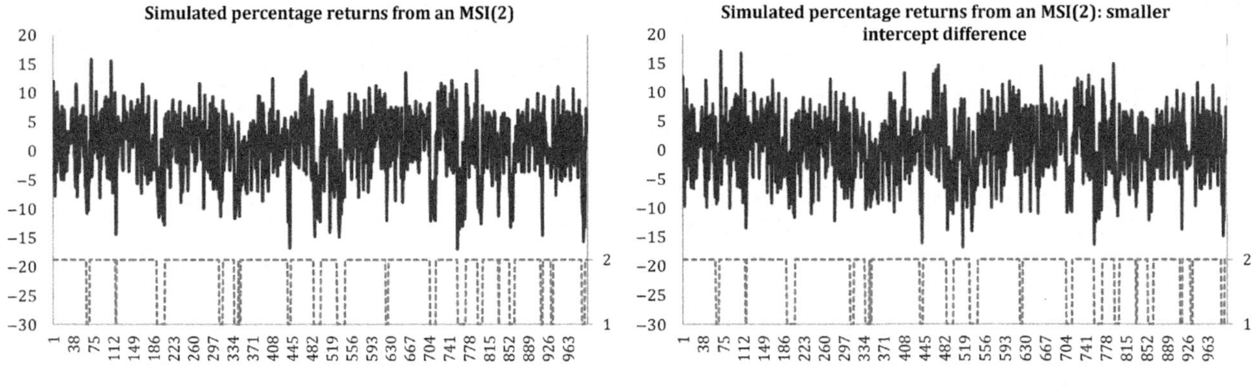

FIGURE 9.3 Comparing two alternative MSI(2,0) models.

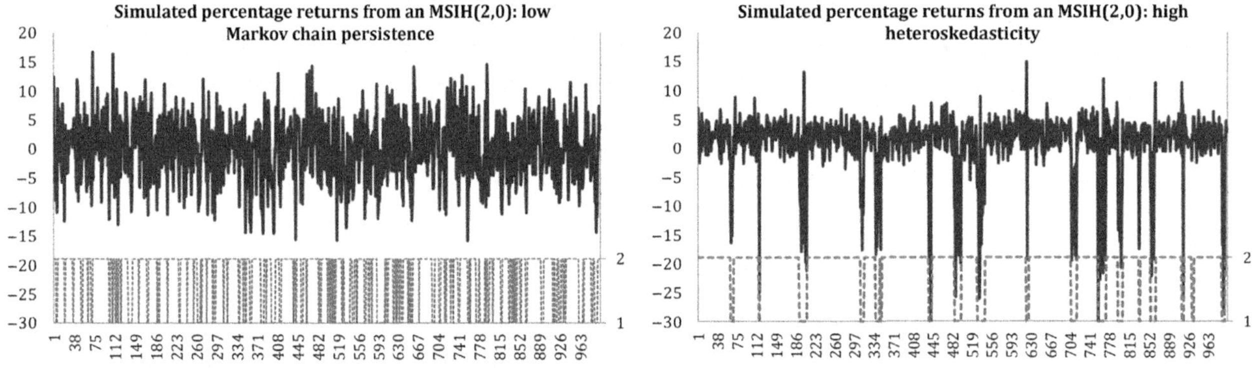

FIGURE 9.4 Comparing two alternative MSIH(2,0) models.

Given that the random realizations of the white noise z_{t+1} IID $N(0,1)$ and also of the first-order MC are held to be identical by construction, to enhance comparability, in spite of the different parameterization, it is striking to note that the left and right panels of Fig. 9.3 are rather similar. This indicates that is the switch in sign that drives most of the visible dynamics in the MS-generated series and not the exact values of the coefficients, in this case the spread in intercepts.

In Fig. 9.4, we operate two changes. The leftmost plot carries the same parameterization as the right plot in Fig. 9.3, when we reduce the persistence of the MC to $\Pr(S_t = 1|S_{t-1} = 1) = 0.6$ and $\Pr(S_t = 2|S_{t-1} = 2) = 0.88$ (we will see that a simple formula delivers unconditional, long-run regime probabilities of 0.23 and 0.77, respectively, that is, very similar to those underlying Figs. 9.2 and 9.3). The right plot uses instead different parameters and a fully-fledged MSIH (2,0) model in which also the regime-dependent differences in variances are of first-order magnitude. We use the parameters $\phi_{0,1} = -6.600, \phi_{0,2} = 2.275, \phi_{1,1} = \phi_{1,2} = 0, \sigma_1 = 10, \sigma_2 = 2.08$, where the transition matrix is again characterized by "stayer" probabilities $\Pr(S_t = 1|S_{t-1} = 1) = 0.92$ and $\Pr(S_t = 2|S_{t-1} = 2) = 0.98$. This is a model in which state-specific volatility may switch from a modest 7.2% per year to a regime of raging turmoil, 34.6% per year.

In the plot to the left, regime shifts are frequent and given the lower unconditional frequency of the first, bear-like regime, this tends to give the resulting simulated series an appearance that may remind some readers of the occurrence of frequent (negative) "jumps" in stock returns. In the rightmost plot, the presence of considerable heteroskedasticity—in fact, displaying "leverage-type" effects as returns tend to be negative when volatility is higher, so that downward spikes obtain—is glaring and yields a time series of considerable realism.

Fig. 9.5 generalizes this set of simulation exercises to two different MSIARH(2,1) models that include an autoregressive component. The leftmost plot concerns a nonlinearly persistent RS AR model ($\Pr(S_t = 1|S_{t-1} = 1) = 0.95$ and $\Pr(S_t = 2|S_{t-1} = 2) = 0.98$) with negative (positive) unconditional mean and low (high) linear persistence in the first (second) regime. The parameters are in fact $\phi_{0,1} = -6.45, \phi_{0,2} = 1.00, \phi_{1,1} = 0.4, \phi_{1,2} = 0.8, \sigma_1 = 6, \sigma_2 = 4$. It is easy to check using the results in Chapter 2 that the unconditional means

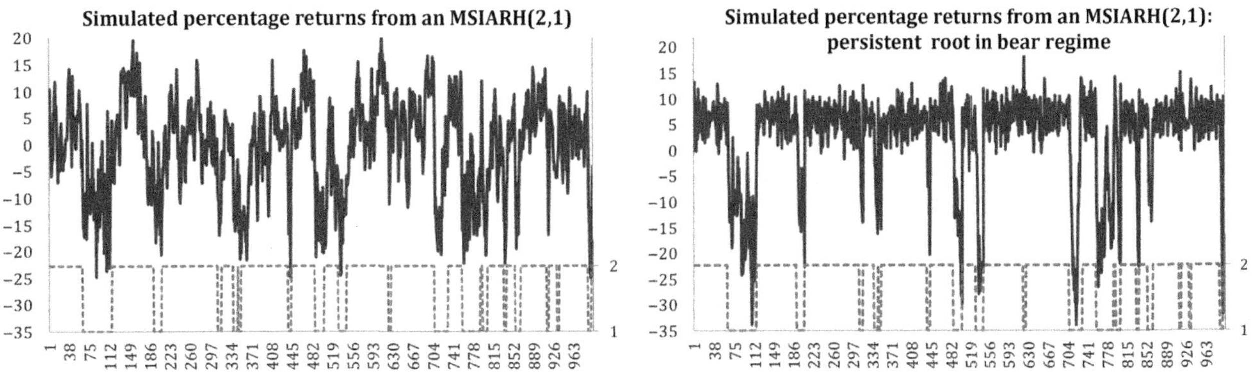

FIGURE 9.5 Comparing two alternative MSIARH(2,0) models.

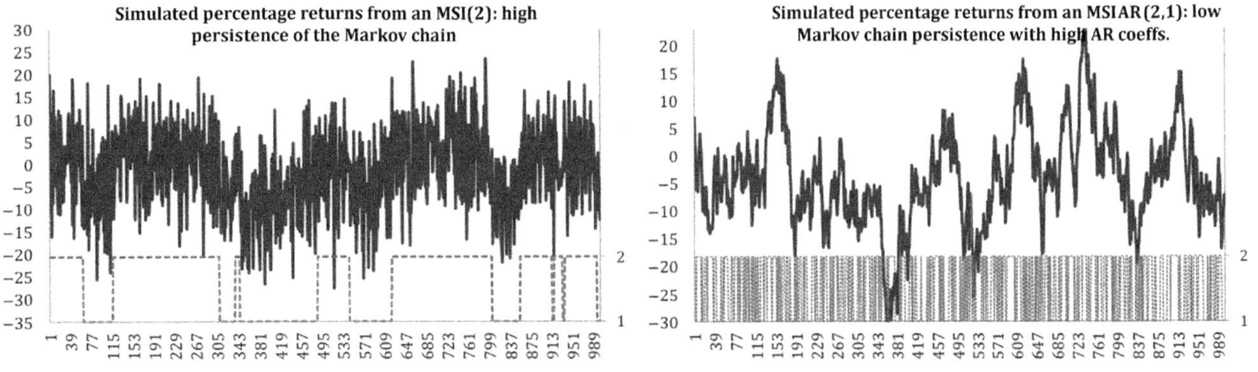

FIGURE 9.6 Comparing linear versus nonlinear persistence in MSIAR(2,1) models.

(standard deviations) are −10.75 and 5 (7.14 and 11.11) in the first and second regime, respectively.[5] The higher (double) linear persistence in the second regime is probably visible to many also from the plot, as the series tends to "wiggle" on the spot in correspondence to large, positive values.

The rightmost plot represents instead an MSIARH(2,1) characterized by identical unconditional mean and standard deviation as in the plot to the left (these are 6% and 9% in annualized terms, respectively) but in which the bear, negative mean regime is now characterized by a persistent root (the MC governing the process is characterized by the same parameters as in the leftmost plot). In particular, we assume $\phi_{0,1} = -2.000, \phi_{0,2} = 7.056$, $\phi_{1,1} = 0.88, \phi_{1,2} = -0.1, \sigma_1 = 6.0, \sigma_2 = 2.8$. The intercepts and standard error parameters need to be adjusted to allow the process to be characterized by the same unconditional mean and standard deviation as the leftmost plot. The increased tendency of the series to "wander off," as typical of highly persistent series, in correspondence to the bear state becomes quite visible.

Fig. 9.6 reports one last set of simulations, as usual the random white noise error z_{t+1} IID $N(0, 1)$ as well as the first-order MC draws originating the realizations for the regime variable S_t, are held fixed as in the previous plots. The figure wants to clarify the difference between *linear and nonlinear persistence* in MS models. In both panels, the parameters have been adjusted to yield an overall, unconditional mean of 6% per year (i.e., summing over groups of 12 observations) and a standard deviation of 31% per year, obviously inflated by either the high linear persistence or by the large shifts in the level of the series. In the left plot, we use the same parameters as in Fig. 9.4, but then we set $\Pr(S_t = 1|S_{t-1} = 1) = \Pr(S_t = 2|S_{t-1} = 2) = 0.99$ and $\sigma_1 = \sigma_2 = 7.84$. This implies, as we shall compute later on, that in the long run, the two regimes have the same probability, 0.5, and that nonlinear persistence is extremely high. Of course, an MSI(2,0) model represents an extreme case of an MSIAR(2,1) in which $\phi_{1,1} = \phi_{1,2} = 0$, that is, all linear persistence is assumed away.

5. These simple calculations are just an approximation because they implicitly assume that each regime is absorbing, that is, that the system will remain in each of the two states forever, once they are accessed.

The leftmost plot shows highly visible intercept switches, around which we then find the typical "no structure" patterns of a white noise. On the opposite, in the rightmost plot, we simulate 1000 draws from homoskedastic MSIAR(2,1) process in which nonlinear persistence is low, we set $\Pr(S_t = 1|S_{t-1} = 1) = \Pr(S_t = 2|S_{t-1} = 2) = 0.7$ (this implies again equal long-run frequencies of the two regimes), and $\phi_{0,1} = -0.42, \phi_{0,2} = 0.09, \phi_{1,1} = 0.90, \phi_{1,2} = 0.98, \sigma_1 = \sigma_2 = 2.871$. In this case, the presence of near-unit roots in each of the two regimes becomes visible and in fact tends to cloud the fact that there are rather frequent regime shifts. However, the few protracted occurrences of regime 1 that can be detected from the right plot are also marked by simulated percentage returns that drop at levels of -20% or even lower and persistently so, as one would expect given that $\phi_{1,1} = 0.9$.

Overall, the simulated series in Figs. 9.2–9.6 help us visualize the enormous flexibility that MS models allow us, in terms of the time series properties of the process to substantially differ across different regimes.

9.2.1 Markov Switching Models as Normal Mixtures and Density Approximation

MS models are known to capture central statistical features of asset returns. Marron and Wand (1992) have emphasized that *mixtures of normal distributions* provide a flexible family that can be used to approximate many distributions.

DEFINITION 9.2 (Mixture of normal distributions)

A mixture of normal densities is a weighted sum of normal densities, in which the weights are themselves random variables and may change over time.

In the case of MS models, such weights are given by the random state probabilities inferred over time. Mixtures of normals can also be viewed as a limit of a *nonparametric approach* to modeling the distribution of the variable of interest when the number of states, K, is allowed to diverge to infinity and hence grows with the sample size, as $T \to \infty$.

For instance, differences in conditional means across regimes enter the higher moments such as variance, skewness, and kurtosis. In particular, in an MS model, variance is not simply the average of the variances across the two regimes: intuitively, the differences in means also impart an effect because the switch to a new regime contributes to volatility; these differences in regime-dependent means also generate nonzero conditional skewness. An online appendix performs these calculations in detail. Finally, differences in means in addition to differences in variances can generate persistence in levels as well as squared values akin to volatility persistence observed in many financial return series. Again, differences in means play an important role in generating autocorrelation in first moments: without such differences, the autocorrelation will be 0. In contrast, volatility persistence can be induced either by differences in means or by differences in variances across regimes. In both cases, the persistence tends to be greater, the stronger the combined persistence, as measured by the diagonal transition probabilities collected in **P**.

To see such features in action, in Fig. 9.7 we show the kernel density estimator (using an Epanechnikov kernel and a standard bandwidth choice) of the homoskedastic MSIAR(2,1) model characterized by high linear persistence but frequent regime changes already represented in the rightmost plot of Fig. 9.6. The ability of MS to generate nonzero skewness and excess kurtosis appears, even though the deviations from a matching Gaussian density with identical mean and variance are modest (skewness is 0.16 and excess kurtosis 0.50). However, it is interesting that a simple difference in intercepts, $\phi_{0,2} - \phi_{0,1} = 0.00429$, and regime-dependent AR coefficients, $\phi_{1,2} - \phi_{1,1} = 0.1$, with nonpersistent regimes may generate such realistic density.

In fact, MS models are flexible enough to even generate negative excess kurtosis, provided that the model is homoskedastic, as in the case of the MSI(2,0) already used in the leftmost plot of Fig. 9.6, the (kernel) density of which is now plotted in Fig. 9.8. The resulting skewness is -0.09 and the excess kurtosis is -0.26, even though a hint at the density becoming bimodal becomes somewhat obvious.

Finally, in Fig. 9.9 that uses the same simulations as in the rightmost plot in Fig. 9.4, the departure from normality caused by the mixture is so strong to take the form of an obvious multimodality. The implicit asymmetries (skewness is -1.78) and thick tails are massive (excess kurtosis is 2.62). However, a mixture of two Gaussian random variables need not have a bimodal appearance: Gaussian mixtures can also produce a unimodal density, as in Figs. 9.7 and 9.8, and still allow skewness and kurtosis to differ from those of a single-regime Gaussian benchmark. Therefore MS models can clearly capture nonnormalities in the data and can be useful in many asset pricing and risk management applications, exactly for this reason.

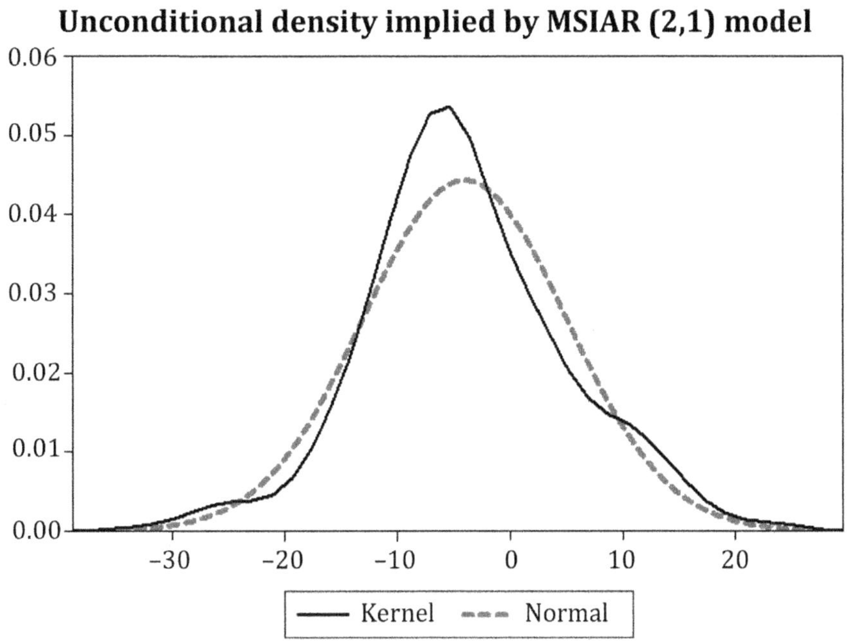

FIGURE 9.7 Unconditional density implied by an MSIAR(2,1) model.

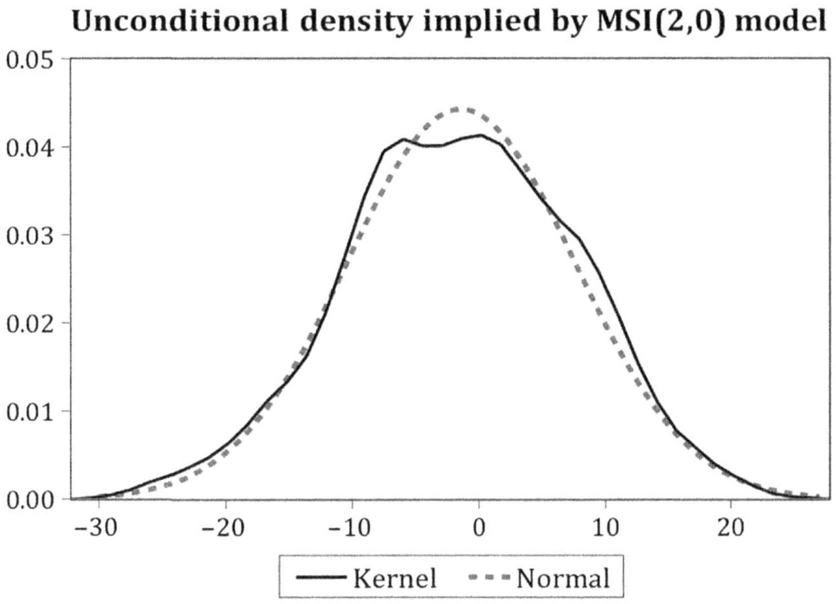

FIGURE 9.8 Unconditional density implied by an MSI(2,0) model.

9.3 MARKOV SWITCHING REGRESSIONS

It is useful to generalize Definition 9.1, when specialized to $N = 1$, to reflect a more general form that also includes:

- exogenous, fixed predictors (or explanatory variables, when the relationship is contemporaneous), and
- predictors whose coefficient does not follow an MS process, such as:

$$\mathbf{y}_{t+1} = \boldsymbol{\mu}_{S_{t+1}} + \sum_{j=1}^{p} a_{j,S_{t+1}}\mathbf{y}_{t+1-j} + \check{\boldsymbol{\beta}}'_{S_{t+1}}\check{\mathbf{X}}_t + \boldsymbol{\delta}'\mathbf{Z}_t + \sigma_{S_{t+1}}z_{t+1} \quad S_{t+1} = 1, 2, \ldots, K, \tag{9.15}$$

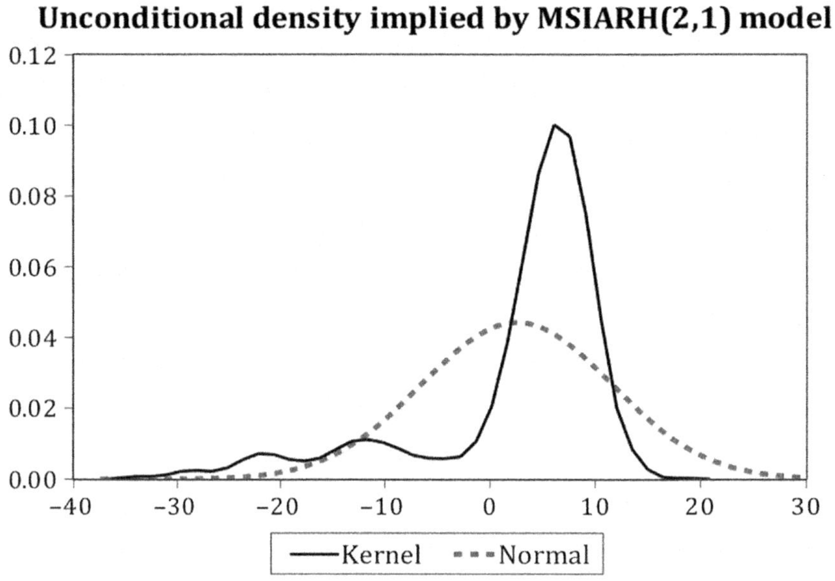

FIGURE 9.9 Unconditional density implied by an MSIARH(2,1) model.

where the notation has standard meaning. However, if one defines $\mathbf{X}_t \equiv [y_t y_{t-1} \ldots y_{t-p} \check{\mathbf{X}}_t]$ and $\boldsymbol{\beta}_{S_{t+1}} \equiv [a_{1,S_{t+1}}\ a_{2,S_{t+1}} \ldots a_{p,S_{t+1}}\ \check{\boldsymbol{\beta}}'_{S_{t+1}}]'$ then Eq. (9.15) may be rewritten as:

$$\mathbf{y}_{t+1} = \boldsymbol{\mu}_{S_{t+1}} + \boldsymbol{\beta}'_{S_{t+1}}\mathbf{X}_t + \boldsymbol{\delta}'\mathbf{Z}_t + \sigma_{S_{t+1}}\mathbf{z}_{t+1} \quad S_{t+1} = 1, 2, \ldots, K. \tag{9.16}$$

This is an *MS regression model*. MS regressions come in very handy when we suspect that a set of exogenous variables/predictors may be related (in causal sense, even affect) a variable of interest with variable sign and strength in different regimes. Example 9.2 elaborates further on Example 9.1 when a researcher is not ready to consider all the variables as simultaneously endogenous.

EXAMPLE 9.2

Suppose you are just interested in forecasting monthly Japanese excess aggregate stock returns using one lag of the same, one lag of US excess stock returns, and one lag of S&P 100 implied volatility. Table 9.3 shows the different sets of fit/predictive performance that may be obtained from different combinations of choices concerning which coefficients are MS and which are not. Note that we only assume in all cases an MS intercept coefficient.

Table 9.3 shows that all information criteria unanimously select an MS regression in which all the coefficients are time invariant but the standard error of the regression follows an MS process. All attempts to extend such model to three regimes are rejected by the information criteria that increase. In the following, we report estimates of the linear benchmark in which all coefficients are constant and of the selected MS heteroskedastic regression. To provide additional information, we also show estimates of an MS regression in which all coefficients are driven by the same two-state MC (p-values are in parentheses):

$$x_{t+1}^{Japan} = \underset{(0.325)}{0.312} + \underset{(0.154)}{0.078}\, x_t^{Japan} + \underset{(0.063)}{0.144}\, x_t^{US} - \underset{(0.000)}{0.068}\, rvxo_t + 6.020\varepsilon_{t+1}^{Japan} \quad \overline{R}^2 = 0.072$$

$$x_{t+1}^{Japan} = \begin{cases} \underset{(0.186)}{0.416} & \text{if } S_{t+1} = 1 \\ \underset{(0.706)}{0.206} & \text{if } S_{t+1} = 2 \end{cases} + \underset{(0.706)}{0.071}\, x_t^{Japan} + \underset{(0.011)}{0.182}\, x_t^{US} - \underset{(0.000)}{0.073}\, rvxo_t$$

$$+ \begin{cases} \underset{(0.186)}{3.854} & \text{if } S_{t+1} = 1 \\ \underset{(0.706)}{7.265} & \text{if } S_{t+1} = 2 \end{cases} z_{t+1}^{Japan} \quad \hat{P} = \begin{bmatrix} 0.997 & 0.003 \\ 0.004 & 0.996 \end{bmatrix} \quad \overline{R}^2 = 0.057$$

(Continued)

TABLE 9.3 MS Regression Model Selection

	Number of Regimes	Lagged Japanese EXRET	Lagged US EXRET	Lagged VXO Rate of Change	Standard Error	No. of Parameters	Saturation Ratio	Max Log-Likelihood	Adj. R^2	AIC	Hannan–Quinn	BIC
Linear	1	Constant	Constant	Constant	Constant	5	74.20	−1190.4	0.0720	6.439	6.456	6.481
Model 1	2	MS	Constant	Constant	Constant	9	41.22	−1180.9	0.0565	6.415	6.452	6.510
Model 2	2	Constant	MS	Constant	Constant	9	41.22	−1178.0	0.0416	6.399	6.435	6.494
Model 3	2	Constant	Constant	MS	Constant	9	41.22	−1179.1	0.0569	6.405	6.443	6.500
Model 4	2	Constant	Constant	Constant	MS	9	41.22	−1161.7	0.0573	**6.311**	**6.349**	**6.406**
Model 5	2	MS	MS	Constant	Constant	10	37.10	−1180.6	0.0543	6.418	6.460	6.524
Model 6	2	MS	Constant	MS	Constant	10	37.10	−1180.8	0.0540	6.419	6.461	6.525
Model 7	2	MS	Constant	Constant	MS	10	37.10	−1161.7	0.0550	6.316	6.358	6.422
Model 8	2	Constant	MS	MS	Constant	10	37.10	−1188.0	0.0558	6.458	6.500	6.564
Model 9	2	Constant	MS	Constant	MS	10	37.10	−1161.3	0.0558	6.314	6.356	6.420
Model 10	2	Constant	Constant	MS	MS	10	37.10	−1161.5	0.0564	6.315	6.357	6.421
Model 11	2	Constant	MS	MS	MS	11	33.73	−1161.1	0.0555	6.318	6.365	6.435
Model 12	2	MS	Constant	MS	MS	11	33.73	−1161.5	0.0542	6.321	6.367	6.437
Model 13	2	MS	MS	Constant	MS	11	33.73	−1161.3	0.0528	6.320	6.366	6.436
Model 14	2	MS	MS	MS	Constant	11	33.73	−1180.5	0.0519	6.423	6.469	6.539
Model 15	2	MS	MS	MS	MS	12	30.92	−1161.0	0.0525	6.324	6.374	6.450
Model 16	3	Constant	Constant	Constant	MS	15	24.73	−1156.4	0.0508	6.315	6.378	6.473
Model 17	3	MS	MS	MS	MS	21	17.67	−1140.9	0.0397	6.263	6.351	6.485

EXAMPLE 9.2 (Continued)

$$x_{t+1}^{Japan} = \begin{cases} \underset{(0.197)}{0.412} & \text{if } S_{t+1}=1 \\ \underset{(0.691)}{0.224} & \text{if } S_{t+1}=2 \end{cases} + \begin{cases} \underset{(0.595)}{0.050} & \text{if } S_{t+1}=1 \\ \underset{(0.279)}{0.082} & \text{if } S_{t+1}=2 \end{cases} \cdot x_t^{Japan} + \begin{cases} \underset{(0.013)}{0.238} & \text{if } S_{t+1}=1 \\ \underset{(0.483)}{0.088} & \text{if } S_{t+1}=2 \end{cases} \cdot x_t^{US} +$$

$$-\begin{cases} \underset{(0.000)}{0.078} & \text{if } S_{t+1}=1 \\ \underset{(0.024)}{0.057} & \text{if } S_{t+1}=2 \end{cases} \cdot rvxo_t + \begin{cases} 3.884 & \text{if } S_{t+1}=1 \\ 7.289 & \text{if } S_{t+1}=2 \end{cases} \cdot z_{t+1}^{Japan} \quad \hat{P} = \begin{bmatrix} 0.997 & 0.003 \\ 0.003 & 0.997 \end{bmatrix} \quad \overline{R}^2 = 0.053.$$

Even though we have imposed everywhere that the intercepts would be time-varying, we obtain no evidence that they are significantly different in any of the regimes or of the differences being statistically significant at standard size levels. There is weak evidence of rates of change in VXO having a different predictive power across regimes, but once more a zero difference between coefficients in the two states (−0.078 vs. −0.057) is not rejected in a Wald test. So, what really makes the MS regression superior to a simpler, linear regression is the regime shifts in the standard errors, that in fact—as we should expect when heteroskedasticity is dealt with in regression models (see Chapter 1 for an introduction)—allow us to obtain more precise estimates for the predictive impact of lagged US excess returns versus the linear case that incorrectly assumes homoskedasticity. Finally, all the MS regressions estimated are characterized by highly persistent MCs, an indication of very strong evidence of regimes.

9.4 MARKOV CHAIN PROCESSES AND THEIR PROPERTIES

So far, our treatment and examples of MS models have focused on elementary models, as defined by a very simple type of discrete MC processes, that is:

- *Homogeneous*, in the sense that $\Pr\left(S_{t+1}=j|\{S_\tau\}_{\tau=1}^{t-1}, \{\mathbf{y}_\tau\}_{\tau=1}^{t-1}\right) = \Pr\left(S_{t+1}=j|\{S_{t-j}\}_{j=0}^{M-1}\right)$, the probability of transitioning to state j at time t just depends on the most recent M-period history of the states and not on the past values of the vector of variables of interest.
- *First-order*, meaning that $\Pr\left(S_{t+1}=j|\{S_{t-j}\}_{j=0}^{M-1}\right) = \Pr(S_{t+1}=j|S_t)$, or that all the memory of the past of series is retained by just one lag of the very state S_t, as far as the linear components of the process are concerned.

While both these restrictions may be removed below, it is important to familiarize the reader with the mechanics of MC processes in some more detail. MS models are defined as driven by a *hidden, discrete Markov state* that is also latent, ergodic, and irreducible.

We proceed to define and discuss each of these properties. S_t is *latent* because it cannot be extracted from the data with perfect precision, but at most the time series of the states $\{S_\tau\}_{\tau=1}^{T}$ may be inferred from the observed, available data $\{\mathbf{y}_\tau\}_{\tau=1}^{T}$. Heuristically, this is caused by the fact that in the time domain, the length of the time series for $\{S_\tau\}_{\tau=1}^{T}$ that is to be inferred grows with the sample size T, while in the cross section, each single S_τ is independent of the shocks to the vector $\mathbf{y}_\tau$.

Ergodicity implies the existence of a stationary $K \times 1$ vector of probabilities $\overline{\boldsymbol{\xi}}$ satisfying

$$\overline{\boldsymbol{\xi}} = \mathbf{P}'\overline{\boldsymbol{\xi}}. \tag{9.17}$$

The probabilities in $\overline{\boldsymbol{\xi}}$ are called *ergodic probabilities.*

DEFINITION 9.3 (Ergodic probabilities)

The vector $\overline{\boldsymbol{\xi}}$ of a K-state discrete MC is the special K-dimensional vector (proportional to the eigenvector of the transition matrix $\mathbf{P}$ associated to the unit eigenvalue) that satisfies the *stationarity condition* $\overline{\boldsymbol{\xi}} = \mathbf{P}'\overline{\boldsymbol{\xi}}$, which means that when the chain is initialized at $\overline{\boldsymbol{\xi}}$, the predicted state probabilities implicit in the chain are identically $\overline{\boldsymbol{\xi}}$.

Eq. (9.17) implies that all the information needed to compute $\overline{\boldsymbol{\xi}}$ is contained in the transition matrix. The meaning of the matrix product in Eq. (9.17) is easily seen when $\overline{\boldsymbol{\xi}}$ is replaced by a elementary vector $\mathbf{e}_j$, $j = 1, 2, \ldots, K$:[6]

6. Note that Eq. (9.18) uses the transpose of **P** and not **P** itself. Therefore, because the rows of **P** need to sum to 1 by construction, obviously the same applies to sums across columns of **P′**, which is used in what follows.

$$\mathbf{P}'\boldsymbol{\pi} = \begin{bmatrix} p_{11} & p_{21} & \cdots & p_{K1} \\ p_{12} & p_{22} & \cdots & p_{K2} \\ \vdots & \cdots & \ddots & \vdots \\ p_{1K} & p_{2K} & \cdots & p_{KK} \end{bmatrix} \mathbf{e}_j = \begin{bmatrix} p_{j1} \\ p_{j2} \\ \vdots \\ p_{jK} \end{bmatrix}, \tag{9.18}$$

that is, the product gives the vector of (predicted) probabilities of switching from a fixed, initial regime j to each of the other possible regimes, besides the (predicted) probability of the model to remain in regime j, p_{jj}. This example illustrates the sense in which Eq. (9.17) defines a $K \times 1$ vector of ergodic, also called *long-run or unconditional state probabilities*: if you start the system from a configuration of current state probabilities equal to $\bar{\boldsymbol{\xi}}$, then your prediction for the probabilities of the regimes one-period forward is identical to $\bar{\boldsymbol{\xi}}$ itself, that is, it is as if the MS model had reached a *steady-state*. This is why all the information required to compute $\bar{\boldsymbol{\xi}}$ is contained in the transition matrix, because this is the object that contains all the information concerning the dynamics of the MC and whether and how such dynamics may eventually vanish. Interestingly, it is the entire matrix $\mathbf{P}$ that matters to compute the ergodic probabilities and not only—as one may be lured into thinking—the values on the main diagonal of $\mathbf{P}$, $p_{jj} \equiv \Pr(S_{t+1} = j | S_t = j)$, $j = 1, 2, \ldots, K$. However, given the estimates of the "stayer probabilities", $\hat{p}_{jj} < 1$, the *average estimated duration*, that is, the expected time spent in each regime, can be computed as:

$$1 + \sum_{\tau=1}^{\infty} (\hat{p}_{jj})^{\tau} = \sum_{\tau=0}^{\infty} (\hat{p}_{jj})^{\tau} = \frac{1}{1 - \hat{p}_{jj}}, \tag{9.19}$$

where the "1" added at the beginning of the expression counts the regime j in which the system is initially assumed to be. Appendix 9.A shows that $\bar{\boldsymbol{\xi}}$ can also be interpreted as the average, long-run time of occupation of the different regimes by the MC, that is (at least heuristically), as:

$$\lim_{T \to \infty} \frac{1}{T} \sum_{t=1}^{T} I_{\{S_t = j\}} = \bar{\boldsymbol{\xi}}' \mathbf{e}_j \quad j = 1,\ 2,\ \ldots,\ K, \tag{9.20}$$

where $\bar{\boldsymbol{\xi}}' \mathbf{e}_j$ simply selects the jth element of the ergodic probability vector $\bar{\boldsymbol{\xi}}$.

An alternative way to think about ergodicity can be developed by first defining $\boldsymbol{\xi}_t$ as a $K \times 1$ vector made of zeros except for the jth element that equals 1 to signal $S_t = j$ and 0 otherwise, $\boldsymbol{\xi}_t \equiv [I(S_t = 1) I(S_t = 2) \ldots I(S_t = K)]'$, where $I(S_t = i)$ is a standard indicator variable. In practice the sample realizations of $\boldsymbol{\xi}_t$ will always consist of *elementary vectors* $\mathbf{e}_i$ characterized by a 1 in the ith position and by 0 everywhere else. Then, when S_t follows a first-order MC, it is possible to show (see Hamilton, 1994) that:

$$\boldsymbol{\xi}_{t+1} = \mathbf{P}' \boldsymbol{\xi}_t + \boldsymbol{v}_{t+1}, \tag{9.21}$$

where $\boldsymbol{v}_{t+1}$ is some vector of error terms with $E_t[\boldsymbol{v}_{t+1}] = E_t[\boldsymbol{v}_{t+H}] = \mathbf{0}$, $\forall H \geq 1$.[7] Eq. (9.21) represents a sort of VAR(1)-like representation of (a function of) the Markov state variable, $\boldsymbol{\delta}_t$. Eq. (9.21) is useful because it gives you an easy way to forecast the state in an MS model:

$$E_t[\boldsymbol{\xi}_{t+1}] = E_t[\mathbf{P}' \boldsymbol{\xi}_t + \boldsymbol{v}_{t+1}] = \mathbf{P}' \boldsymbol{\xi}_t \tag{9.22}$$

which is exactly the $\mathbf{P}'\boldsymbol{\pi}$ predictive multiplication used in Eq. (9.18). Moreover, note that:

$$E_t[\boldsymbol{\xi}_{t+2}] = E_t[\mathbf{P}' \boldsymbol{\xi}_{t+1} + \boldsymbol{v}_{t+2}] = \mathbf{P}' E_t[\boldsymbol{\xi}_{t+1}] = (\mathbf{P}'\mathbf{P}') \boldsymbol{\xi}_t, \tag{9.23}$$

so that one can establish by induction that:

$$E_t[\boldsymbol{\xi}_{t+H}] = (\mathbf{P}')^H \boldsymbol{\xi}_t, \tag{9.24}$$

where $(\mathbf{P}')^H \equiv \prod_{j=1}^{H} \mathbf{P}'$. At this point, an MC (hence, the associated MS model) is ergodic if and only if

$$\text{plim}(\mathbf{P}')^H \boldsymbol{\delta}_t = \bar{\boldsymbol{\xi}}, \tag{9.25}$$

that is, if a constant limit for the prediction as the forecast horizon diverges can be found, which does not depend on the initial time t. By construction, $\bar{\boldsymbol{\xi}} \boldsymbol{\iota}_K = 1$, where $\boldsymbol{\iota}_K$ is a $K \times 1$ vector of ones (Appendix 9.A provides details on this calculation). Note that $(\mathbf{P}')^H$ as defined above does not yield the same result as taking powers of each individual element of $\mathbf{P}'$. For instance, while the matrix of squares of a transposed transition matrix gives:

---

7. Technically, $\boldsymbol{v}_{t+1}$ is a martingale difference sequence.

$$\begin{bmatrix} 0.95^2 & 0.19^2 \\ 0.05^2 & 0.81^2 \end{bmatrix} = \begin{bmatrix} 0.9025 & 0.0361 \\ 0.0025 & 0.6561 \end{bmatrix}, \tag{9.26}$$

the product of the transposed transition matrix with itself yields:

$$\begin{bmatrix} 0.95 & 0.19 \\ 0.05 & 0.81 \end{bmatrix} \cdot \begin{bmatrix} 0.95 & 0.19 \\ 0.05 & 0.81 \end{bmatrix} = \begin{bmatrix} 0.9120 & 0.3344 \\ 0.0088 & 0.6656 \end{bmatrix} \neq \begin{bmatrix} 0.9025 & 0.0361 \\ 0.0025 & 0.6561 \end{bmatrix}. \tag{9.27}$$

Irreducibility of an MC implies that $\bar{\boldsymbol{\xi}} > \mathbf{0}$, meaning that all unobservable regimes are possible and remain possible over time and no *absorbing states or cycles* among states exist. Consider for instance the case $K = 3$, then the transition matrix

$$\mathbf{P} = \begin{bmatrix} p_{11} & p_{12} & 0 \\ p_{21} & p_{22} & 0 \\ 0 & p_{32} & p_{33} \end{bmatrix} = \begin{bmatrix} p_{11} & 1-p_{11} & 0 \\ 1-p_{22} & p_{22} & 0 \\ 0 & 1-p_{33} & p_{33} \end{bmatrix} \tag{9.28}$$

implies that it is impossible to reach state 3 from the other two states. In fact, as soon as one leaves regime 3, which will occur almost surely as $p_{33} \in (0,1)$ but $p_{i3} = 0$ for $i = 1, 2$, it becomes impossible to ever return again to state 3. Therefore the third element of $\bar{\boldsymbol{\xi}}$ will have to be 0 because $\lim_{T\to\infty}\frac{1}{T}\sum_{t=1}^{T} I_{\{S_t=3\}} = 0$.

In practice, the matrix $\mathbf{P}$ is unknown and hence $\bar{\boldsymbol{\xi}}$ can be at most estimated given the estimates of $\mathbf{P}$ extracted from the (full-sample) information set $\Im_T = \{\mathbf{y}_\tau\}_{\tau=1}^{T}$ and exploiting the definition, $\bar{\boldsymbol{\xi}} = \mathbf{P}'\bar{\boldsymbol{\xi}}$. In fact, Appendix 9.A emphasizes that, given Eq. (9.17), $\bar{\boldsymbol{\xi}}$ is the eigenvector of $\mathbf{P}'$ associated with the unit eigenvalue, that is, the vector of ergodic probabilities $\bar{\boldsymbol{\xi}}$ is normalized to sum to unity (i.e., $\bar{\boldsymbol{\xi}}\boldsymbol{\iota}_K = 1$). Moreover, besides representing the vector of ergodic probabilities, $\bar{\boldsymbol{\xi}}$ also represents the *vector of unconditional probabilities*, that is, the average frequencies of the K different regimes as the sample size $T \to \infty$. For instance, in the case of $K = 3$, if we have obtained an estimate of the transition matrix equal to:

$$\hat{\mathbf{P}} = \begin{bmatrix} 0.88 & 0.09 & 0.03 \\ 0.01 & 0.96 & 0.03 \\ 0.23 & 0 & 0.77 \end{bmatrix}, \tag{9.29}$$

the ergodic probabilities $\bar{\boldsymbol{\xi}}$ characterizing this three-state model can be derived by resorting to many software packages (for instance, MATLAB). It turns out that $\hat{\mathbf{P}}$ and $\hat{\mathbf{P}}'$ share the same eigenvalues, that is, 1, 0.87, and 0.74. Here we care only for the unit eigenvalue. Your math software will also inform you that the eigenvector of $\hat{\mathbf{P}}'$ associated to the first, unit eigenvalue is [0.3926 0.8834 0.1664]'. However, this eigenvector is not yet $\bar{\boldsymbol{\xi}}$ because it fails to have unit length. In fact, the eigenvector ends up summing to 1.4424 while it should be $\bar{\boldsymbol{\xi}}'\boldsymbol{\iota}_K = 1$ by definition. However, it is now sufficient to scale the eigenvector so to have unit length, which is done by simply dividing its entries by their sum 1.4424. The resulting estimated (because implied by $\hat{\mathbf{P}}$) vector of ergodic probabilities is:

$$\bar{\boldsymbol{\xi}} = [0.272 \;\; 0.613 \;\; 0.125]'. \tag{9.30}$$

As shown in Appendix 9.A, in the special case of $K = 2$, one obtains explicit solutions for the ergodic probabilities by solving Eq. (9.17):

$$\bar{\xi}_1 = \frac{1-p_{22}}{2-p_{11}-p_{22}} \qquad \bar{\xi}_2 = \frac{1-p_{11}}{2-p_{11}-p_{22}}, \tag{9.31}$$

where obviously $\bar{\xi}_1 + \bar{\xi}_2 = 1$. We now use these concepts to return to Example 9.2 to compute ergodic probabilities.

EXAMPLE 9.2 (Continued)

In the example, a careful model specification search on a monthly data set (the sample is 1986:01–2016:12) of international excess equity returns for the United States, Japan (denominated in US dollars), and the rate of monthly change of the VXO volatility index had led to estimate an MSIVARH(3,1) model. While the estimates have been reported early on, the estimated transition matrix is:

$$\hat{\mathbf{P}} = \begin{bmatrix} 0.397 & 0.055 & 0.548 \\ 0.000 & 0.841 & 0.159 \\ 0.392 & 0.340 & 0.268 \end{bmatrix}.$$

Solving the system $\bar{\boldsymbol{\xi}} = \mathbf{P}'\bar{\boldsymbol{\xi}}$ looking for the eigenvector associated with the highest, unit eigenvalue gives:

(*Continued*)

EXAMPLE 9.2 (Continued)

$$\bar{\xi} = [0.162\ 0.589\ 0.249]'.$$

As one would have expected from its persistence, the tri-variate system spends on average almost 60% of the time in the second regime. However, in spite of their very low persistence, regimes 1 and 3 also occur on average 16% and 25% of the time; these positive rates at which they are visited are helped by the fact that regimes 1 and 3 also "communicate with each other", in the sense that $\Pr(S_{t+1}=3|S_t=1)=0.392$ and $\Pr(S_{t+1}=1|S_t=3)=0.548$. Such unconditional probabilities can be also interpreted as long-run frequencies. As a result, with 371 observations available for estimation, regime 1 characterizes 61 observations; regime 2, 217 observations; and regime, 3 93 observations. Estimating the properties of a VAR(1) for $N=3$ variables on the basis of a minimum of 61 observations seems at the limits of feasibility but cannot be called off because absurd.

The corresponding average durations of the three regimes are 1.7, 6.3, and 1.4 months. Of course, regimes 1 and 3 have low durations, even though in the case of regime 1, it is safe to expect the same regime to last another month, which in applications may be of considerable importance.

The MC process followed by the state variable S_t is time homogeneous when $\mathbf{P}$ is a constant matrix over time, that is, $\Pr(S_{t+1}=j|\{S_\tau\}_{\tau=1}^{t-1},\{\mathbf{y}_\tau\}_{\tau=1}^{t-1}) = \Pr\left(S_{t+1}=j|\{S_{t-j}\}_{j=0}^{M-1}\right)$ or more generally, no set of variables (including exogenous ones) $\{\mathbf{Z}_\tau\}_{\tau=1}^{t-1}$ can be found to drive the probabilities that govern system transitions. However, a richer, more sophisticated class of MS models exists in which the driving MC is instead heterogeneous over time or, equivalently, we say that the model features *time-varying transition probabilities*. Note that such time variation is applied to a framework that has been set up to feature time variation: the MS model that is used to capture instability in the statistical relationships becomes itself unstable, that is, we are modeling and forecasting the "instability of instability", that is, instability-square! However, Guidolin (2013) has reviewed the field of modern asset pricing subject to MS to find that modern papers that root MS in the properties, empirical or theoretical, of the stochastic discount factor, often come up with solid reasons to assume that the transition probabilities may be time-varying. If we call $\{\mathbf{g}_\tau\}_{\tau=1}^{t-1}$ the time series of the vector of predetermined variables (either exogenous or lagged endogenous) that drive the variation in transition probabilities, the literature, since the seminal papers by Diebold et al. (1994) and Filardo (1994), has used a multinomial logit parameterization, similar in spirit to LSTRM/LSTAR models:

$$\Pr\left(S_{t+1}=j|S_t=i,\{\mathbf{y}_\tau\}_{\tau=1}^{t-1},\{\mathbf{z}_\tau\}_{\tau=1}^{t-1},\mathbf{g}_t;\boldsymbol{\delta}_{ij}\right) = \frac{\exp(\mathbf{g}'_t\boldsymbol{\delta}_{ij})}{\sum_{j=1}^{K}\exp(\mathbf{g}'_t\boldsymbol{\delta}_{ij})}, \tag{9.32}$$

subject to the identifying normalization that $\boldsymbol{\delta}_{iK}=\mathbf{0}$. In Eq. (9.32), the variables in $\mathbf{g}_t$ may consist of (lags of) $\mathbf{y}_t$ or $\mathbf{z}_t$, or of both, while by construction $\sum_{j=1}^{K}\Pr\left(S_{t+1}=j|S_t=i,\{\mathbf{y}_\tau\}_{\tau=1}^{t-1},\{\mathbf{z}_\tau\}_{\tau=1}^{t-1};\boldsymbol{\delta}_{ij}\right)=1$. The standard case of a time homogeneous MC and of constant transition probabilities is obtained (and can therefore be tested) by imposing $\mathbf{g}_t=1$.

In a time-varying MS model, because the "stayer" transition probabilities are time-varying, the same occurs to the implied average durations, as the formula becomes $1/[1-\Pr(S_{t+1}=j|S_t=j,\{\mathbf{g}_\tau\}_{\tau=1}^{t-1};\boldsymbol{\delta}_{jj})]$ for $j=1,2,\ldots,K$. Example 9.3 asks whether, in a (potential) MS regression, there is potential for a variable to affect a variable of interest through the transition matrix and not directly.

EXAMPLE 9.3

Extending Example 9.2, let us keep investigating the possibility to predict monthly Japanese excess aggregate stock returns by using one lag of the same, one lag of US excess stock returns, and one lag of S&P 100 implied volatility. In Example 9.2 we saw that a heteroskedastic mixed MS ARX regression model,

$$x_{t+1}^{Japan} = \begin{cases} \underset{(0.186)}{0.416} & \text{if } S_{t+1}=1 \\ \underset{(0.706)}{0.206} & \text{if } S_{t+1}=2 \end{cases} + \underset{(0.706)}{0.071}\,x_t^{Japan} + \underset{(0.011)}{0.182}\,x_t^{US} - \underset{(0.000)}{0.073}\,rvxo_t$$

$$+ \begin{cases} \underset{(0.000)}{3.854} & \text{if } S_{t+1}=1 \\ \underset{(0.000)}{7.265} & \text{if } S_{t+1}=2 \end{cases}\varepsilon_{t+1}^{Japan} \quad \hat{P} = \begin{bmatrix} 0.997 & 0.003 \\ 0.004 & 0.996 \end{bmatrix} \quad \bar{R}^2 = 0.057,$$

delivers a better adjusted fit than a simple predictive regression, at least in terms of the information criteria, that penalize the whole maximized log-likelihood with a function that depends on the number of parameters. We now drop all predictors from the regression and ask whether it may not provide a better set of (in-sample) forecasts to include lagged Japanese and US excess

(Continued)

EXAMPLE 9.3 (Continued)

returns or lagged percentage changes in VXO as predictors of time variation in transition probabilities. Because one can try seven different permutations of these three variables (jointly and isolation) as part of a specification of $\mathbf{g}_t$, we use SBIC to select the best trade-off between in-sample predictive power and parsimony. We obtain a striking result: SBIC is minimized (at 6.406) by our original model keeping transition probabilities constant. The best performing model with time-varying transition probabilities (it achieves a BIC of 6.427) is the following:

$$x_{t+1}^{Japan} = \begin{cases} \underset{(0.179)}{1.208} & \text{if } S_{t+1}=1 \\ \underset{(0.609)}{0.132} & \text{if } S_{t+1}=2 \end{cases} - \underset{(0.000)}{0.070}\, rvxo_t + \begin{cases} \underset{(0.000)}{8.824} & \text{if } S_{t+1}=1 \\ \underset{(0.000)}{4.524} & \text{if } S_{t+1}=2 \end{cases} \varepsilon_{t+1}^{Japan} \quad \bar{R}^2 = 0.048$$

$$\hat{\boldsymbol{P}} = \begin{bmatrix} \dfrac{\exp\left(\underset{(0.000)}{6.259} + \underset{(0.005)}{0.503}\, x_t^{US}\right)}{\exp\left(\underset{(0.000)}{6.259} + \underset{(0.005)}{0.503}\, x_t^{US}\right) + \exp\left(\underset{(0.000)}{6.259}\right)} & \dfrac{\exp\left(\underset{(0.000)}{6.259}\right)}{\exp\left(\underset{(0.000)}{6.259} + \underset{(0.005)}{0.503}\, x_t^{US}\right) + \exp\left(\underset{(0.000)}{6.259}\right)} \\ \dfrac{\exp\left(-\underset{(0.000)}{6.618} - \underset{(0.002)}{0.653}\, x_t^{US}\right)}{\exp\left(-\underset{(0.000)}{6.618} - \underset{(0.002)}{0.653}\, x_t^{US}\right) + \exp\left(-\underset{(0.000)}{6.618}\right)} & \dfrac{\exp(-\underset{(0.000)}{6.618})}{\exp\left(-\underset{(0.000)}{6.618} - \underset{(0.002)}{0.653}\, x_t^{US}\right) + \exp\left(-\underset{(0.000)}{6.618}\right)} \end{bmatrix}.$$

In this model, past excess US returns do not directly predict Japanese ones, but they affect the persistence of the MC: a recent positive performance of the US stock market makes both regimes more persistent and hence increases their average duration; however, even though −0.653 exceeds in absolute value 0.503, we cannot claim that past positive US performance increases more the duration of the bear regime (here note that while the derivative of δx with respect to x is just δ, the derivative of $1/(-\delta x)$ is $\delta/(-\delta x)^2$ and the two will differ unless $(-\delta x)^2 = 1$), as the result will depend on the precise values taken by lagged US excess returns. By using the implied transition probabilities plotted in Fig. 9.10, one can compute that the model implies a (sample) mean for $\Pr\left(S_{t+1} = 1 | S_t = 1, [1 x_t^{US}]'; \hat{\boldsymbol{\delta}}_{11}\right)$ of 0.982 with a (sample) standard deviation of 0.089, and a mean for $\Pr\left(S_{t+1} = 2 | S_t = 2, [1 x_t^{US}]'; \hat{\boldsymbol{\delta}}_{22}\right)$ of 0.973 with a standard deviation of 0.114. The implied durations are instead very large, almost implausible, but it is easy to understand why: given their formula $1/[1 - \Pr(S_{t+1} = j | S_t = j, \{\mathbf{g}_\tau\}_{\tau=1}^{t-1}; \boldsymbol{\delta}_{jj})]$, when $\Pr(S_{t+1} = j | S_t = j, \{\mathbf{g}_\tau\}_{\tau=1}^{t-1}; \boldsymbol{\delta}_{jj})$ becomes very close to 1, as it seems to occur on the basis of what Fig. 9.10 shows, the time $t+1$ duration diverges to infinity and any sample average that involves a few very large numbers will inevitably be skewed to the right. Fig. 9.10 plots the "stayer" transition probabilities and uses as a (trivial because) constant benchmarks the transition probabilities from the homogeneous MC model reported in Example 9.3.

The two plots show that spectacular stock market busts (rallies) in the United States considerably lower the probability that 1 month later the Japanese stock market may have remained in a bull (bear) market; in correspondence to a few famous US market drops (October 1987, the Asian flu and the collapse of Long-Term Capital Management in June 1998, and Lehman's filing for Chapter 8 in September 2008), the probability of Japanese stocks to remain bullish in the subsequent month drops to 0.

As one would expect, adopting a heterogeneous MC framework makes a difference for all the reported inferences. For instance, the volatility of residuals is now higher in the first, bull state than in the bear state. Therefore Fig. 9.11 shows how the (filtered, see Section 9.5) state probabilities inferred from estimation are affected by the choice constant versus time-varying transition probabilities.

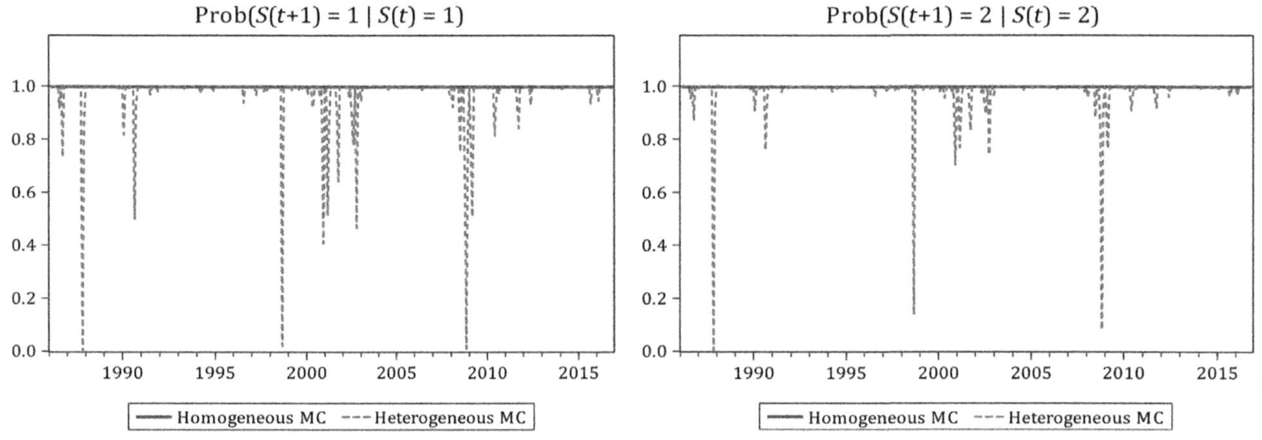

FIGURE 9.10 Constant versus time-varying transition probabilities.

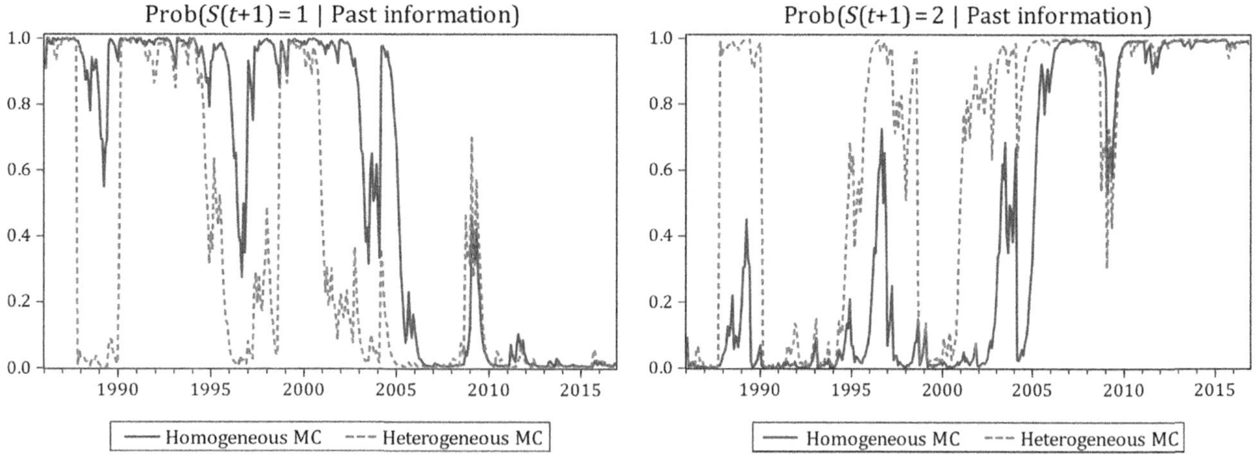

FIGURE 9.11 Filtered state probabilities under constant versus time-varying transition probabilities.

The assumption of a first-order MC can be easily generalized at the cost of some additional complexity: any $M \geq 2$-order K-state discrete MC can be rewritten as an equivalent chain with $K^M > K$ regimes; in this case, we say that we are expanding the set of regimes to accommodate the higher order nature of the MC. To make this point concrete, let us consider the case of a three-state, second-order MC, $K = 3$ and $M = 2$, that is, when $\Pr\left(S_{t+1} = j|\{S_\tau\}_{\tau=1}^{t-1}, \{y_\tau\}_{\tau=1}^{t-1}\right) = \Pr(S_{t+1} = j|S_t = i, S_{t-1} = q) = p_{qij}$, to show that it can be written as a $(3^2 = 9)$-state MC. The strategy is simple: given the original Markov state S_t, define a new state $\breve{S}_t$ such that $\breve{S}_t \equiv [S_t \; S_{t-1}]'$ and the MC for $\breve{S}_t$ follows a first-order MC characterized by $\Pr\left(\breve{S}_{t+1} = j|\breve{S}_t = i\right) = \breve{p}_{ij}$. Clearly, $\breve{S}_{t+1} \equiv [S_{t+1} \; S_t]'$ and $\breve{S}_t \equiv [S_t \; S_{t-1}]'$ share one common realization of the original state variable S_t but this represents no problem. In fact:

$$\Pr\left(\breve{S}_{t+1} = j|\breve{S}_t = i\right) = \Pr(S_{t+1} = j, S_t = q_2|S_t = q_1, S_{t-1} = i)$$
$$= \begin{cases} p_{iqj} = \breve{p}_{ij} & \text{if } q_1 = q_2 = q \\ 0 & \text{if } q_1 \neq q_2. \end{cases} \tag{9.33}$$

Eq. (9.33) imposes 54 zero restrictions on the transition matrix of the expanded $(K^M = 9)$-state MC as follows:

	$S_t=1, S_{t+1}=1$	$S_t=1, S_{t+1}=2$	$S_t=1, S_{t+1}=3$	$S_t=2, S_{t+1}=1$	$S_t=2, S_{t+1}=2$	$S_t=2, S_{t+1}=3$	$S_t=3, S_{t+1}=1$	$S_t=3, S_{t+1}=2$	$S_t=3, S_{t+1}=3$
$S_{t-1}=1, S_t=1$	p_{111}	p_{112}	$1-p_{111}-p_{112}$	0	0	0	0	0	0
$S_{t-1}=1, S_t=2$	0	0	0	p_{121}	p_{122}	$1-p_{121}-p_{122}$	0	0	0
$S_{t-1}=1, S_t=3$	0	0	0	0	0	0	p_{131}	p_{132}	$1-p_{131}-p_{132}$
$S_{t-1}=2, S_t=1$	p_{211}	p_{212}	$1-p_{211}-p_{212}$	0	0	0	0	0	0
$S_{t-1}=2, S_t=2$	0	0	0	p_{221}	p_{222}	$1-p_{221}-p_{222}$	0	0	0
$S_{t-1}=2, S_t=3$	0	0	0	0	0	0	p_{231}	p_{232}	$1-p_{231}-p_{232}$
$S_{t-1}=3, S_t=1$	p_{311}	p_{312}	$1-p_{311}-p_{312}$	0	0	0	0	0	0
$S_{t-1}=3, S_t=2$	0	0	0	p_{321}	p_{322}	$1-p_{321}-p_{322}$	0	0	0
$S_{t-1}=3, S_t=3$	0	0	0	0	0	0	p_{331}	p_{332}	$1-p_{331}-p_{332}$

(9.34)

This is a 9×9 matrix that in principle contains 81 different transition probabilities; however, because of the sum-up constraints concerning the probabilities (for each row) and of the very structure of the transition process in Eq. (9.33), it is clear that the matrix in Eq. (9.34) only contains 18 estimable parameters. This example clearly shows that, for a fixed K, assuming $M > 1$ is an implicit way to extend the state space, even though this occurs only subject to restrictions. Whether, say, starting from $K = 3$, it may be more sensible to specify a higher order MC or for fixed $M = 1$ it may be more sensible to increase K in an unrestricted way remains of course an empirical issue that may be subject to adequate testing. Of course, the fact that an Mth-order MC may be represented in this way that imply rich restrictions on the transition matrix $\mathbf{P}$ does nothing to remove that fact that with $K^M > K$ regimes, estimation will have to deliver—unless additional restrictions are imposed—K^M sets of parameter estimates and this is often unwieldy or even impossible with nine or more states. Example 9.4 shows the implied difficulties and how such Mth-order MC-driven MS models may be harshly penalized by standard information criteria.

EXAMPLE 9.4

Let us resume Example 9.3 and investigate the usefulness of extending the MSIARH(2)-X regression for the prediction of monthly Japanese excess stock returns to a second-order MS model. We keep a two-state specification as above, obtaining the following four-state, restricted estimates (p-values are in parentheses):

$$x^{Japan}_{t+1} = \begin{cases} \underset{(0.752)}{0.184} & \text{if } S_{t+1}=1, S_t=1 \\ \underset{(0.000)}{-4.504} & \text{if } S_{t+1}=2, S_t=1 \\ \underset{(0.039)}{6.103} & \text{if } S_{t+1}=1, S_t=2 \\ \underset{(0.213)}{0.400} & \text{if } S_{t+1}=2, S_t=2 \end{cases} + \underset{(0.136)}{0.089}\, x^{Japan}_t + \underset{(0.006)}{0.214}\, x^{US}_t - \underset{(0.000)}{0.084}\, rvxo_t$$

$$+ \begin{cases} \underset{(0.000)}{7.369} & \text{if } S_{t+1}=1, S_t=1 \\ \underset{(0.000)}{1.301} & \text{if } S_{t+1}=2, S_t=1 \\ \underset{(0.000)}{4.264} & \text{if } S_{t+1}=1, S_t=2 \\ \underset{(0.000)}{3.523} & \text{if } S_{t+1}=2, S_t=2 \end{cases} \varepsilon^{Japan}_{t+1} \quad \hat{P} = \begin{bmatrix} 0.997 & 0.003 & 0 & 0 \\ 0 & 0 & 0.001 & 0.999 \\ 0.052 & 0.948 & 0 & 0 \\ 0 & 0 & 0.070 & 0.930 \end{bmatrix} \quad \bar{R}^2 = 0.043.$$

The estimated transition probabilities for the second-order MC are interesting. For instance, $\Pr(S_{t+1}=1|S_t=1, S_{t-1}=1) = 0.997 > \Pr(S_{t+1}=2|S_t=1, S_{t-1}=2) = 0.948$ indicates that when the regime has persisted for two periods in state 1, leaving state 1 becomes much harder than when state 1 has been visited for only one period. Also note that $\Pr(S_{t+1}=2|S_t=2, S_{t-1}=1) = 0.999$, when regime 2 has been recently reached, it is almost impossible for the system to leave it, even though after one additional period, we find $\Pr(S_{t+1}=2|S_t=2, S_{t-1}=2) = 0.930$; jointly, these estimates imply that when the system switches from regime 1 to 2, then a stay of at least two periods in state 2 "is guaranteed". Even though this second-order MC-driven model allows us to tell interesting stories, it is not the model favored by the data: an identical selection of switching versus nonswitching variables in the MS regression with $K=2$ leads to an SBIC of 6.406 versus 6.473 when the restricted four-state model deriving from the second-order MC is specified. Of course, even under the transition matrix restrictions that we have imposed, the reason for such a deterioration of the SBIC is that this model implies a large number of estimable parameters (17 vs. only 9 in the two-regime case).

9.5 ESTIMATION AND INFERENCE FOR MARKOV SWITCHING MODELS

9.5.1 Maximum Likelihood Estimation and the Expectation-Maximization Algorithm

MSIVARH(K,p) models are estimated by maximum likelihood. However, some assumptions have to be imposed to guarantee at least the local identifiability of the parameters (collected in a vector $\boldsymbol{\theta}$) under estimation.[8] The vector $\boldsymbol{\theta}$ collects all regime-dependent parameters in $\{\boldsymbol{\mu}_k\}_{k=1}^{K}$, $\{\boldsymbol{A}_{j,k}\}_{j=1}^{p}{}_{k=1}^{K}$, and $\{\boldsymbol{\Sigma}_k^{1/2}\}_{k=1}^{K}$. Roughly speaking, local identifiability means that at least in a neighborhood of the true but unknown vector of parameters $\boldsymbol{\theta}_0$ that defines the assumed data generating process (DGP), it must be the case that $\boldsymbol{\theta}_0$ is also the vector of parameters that maximizes the log-likelihood function. Krolzig (1997) has generalized results in Leroux (1992) to show that under the assumption of multivariate Gaussian shocks (to the measurement equation, see Appendix 9.B), MS models are identifiable up to any arbitrary relabeling of unobservable states, which should be then reassuring to us.

Estimation is performed through the *EM algorithm* proposed by Dempster et al. (1977) and Hamilton (1990), a filter that allows the iterative calculation of the one-step-ahead forecast of the state vector $\boldsymbol{\xi}_{t+1|t}$ given the information set $\Im_t$ and the consequent construction of the log-likelihood function of the data. The algorithm is divided in two logical steps, the Expectation and the Maximization steps.

Start from the MS model written in state-space form (see Chapter 7 and Appendix 9.B for an explanation of what this means, but even a very superficial understanding of this aspect will not prevent you from following the argument below):

$$\begin{aligned} \mathbf{y}_t &= \mathbf{X}_t \boldsymbol{A}\boldsymbol{\xi}_t + \boldsymbol{\Omega}_K(\boldsymbol{\xi}_t \otimes \mathbf{I}_N)\varepsilon_t. \\ \boldsymbol{\xi}_{t+1} &= \mathbf{P}'\boldsymbol{\xi}_t + \mathbf{v}_{t+1}. \end{aligned} \tag{9.35}$$

8. Later on, $\boldsymbol{\theta}$ will be expanded to include the elements of the transition matrix $\mathbf{P}$, to form a new vector γ that collects all the parameters of the MS model.

Here $\mathbf{X}_t$ is a $N \times (Np+1)$ matrix of predetermined variables with structure $[1\mathbf{y}'_{t-1} \ldots \mathbf{y}'_{t-p}] \otimes \iota_N$, $\mathbf{A}$ is a $(Np+1) \times NK$ matrix collecting the VAR parameters, both means or intercepts and autoregressive coefficients, in all regimes:

$$\mathbf{A} = \begin{bmatrix} \boldsymbol{\mu}'_1 & \boldsymbol{\mu}'_2 & \cdots & \boldsymbol{\mu}'_K \\ \mathbf{A}_{11} & \mathbf{A}_{12} & \cdots & \mathbf{A}_{1K} \\ \vdots & \vdots & \ddots & \vdots \\ \mathbf{A}_{p1} & \mathbf{A}_{p2} & \cdots & \mathbf{A}_{pK} \end{bmatrix}, \tag{9.36}$$

and $\boldsymbol{\Omega}_K$ is a $N \times NK$ matrix collecting all the possible K square root (Cholesky-factorized) covariance matrix factors $[\boldsymbol{\Sigma}_1^{1/2}, \boldsymbol{\Sigma}_2^{1/2}, \ldots \boldsymbol{\Sigma}_K^{1/2}]$ such that $\forall t$, $\boldsymbol{\Omega}_K(\boldsymbol{\xi}_t \otimes \mathbf{I}_N)\,(\boldsymbol{\xi}_t \otimes \mathbf{I}_N)'\boldsymbol{\Omega}'_K = \boldsymbol{\Sigma}_{S_t}$, the regime-dependent covariance matrix of the asset return innovations $\boldsymbol{\varepsilon}_t$.

The *expectation step* consists of taking parameter estimates from the previous maximization step as given (call it $\boldsymbol{\theta}$) and in computing both the time series sequence of *filtered probability* vectors, $\{\hat{\boldsymbol{\xi}}_{t|t}\}_{t=1}^{T}$, and the time series sequence of *smoothed probability* vectors, $\{\hat{\boldsymbol{\xi}}_{t|T}\}_{t=1}^{T}$, with the latter depending on the former. These two concepts are now formally defined.

DEFINITION 9.4 (Filtered probabilities)

The K-dimensional vector time series $\{\hat{\boldsymbol{\xi}}_{t|t}\}_{t=1}^{T}$ of filtered probabilities associated to a K-state ergodic MC collects at all times $t = 1, 2, \ldots, T$ is the optimal, *real-time inference* on the state probabilities

$$\hat{\boldsymbol{\xi}}_{t|t} \equiv \Pr(\boldsymbol{\xi}_t | \Im_t) \tag{9.37}$$

given all information on the time series $\{\mathbf{y}_\tau\}_{\tau=1}^{t}$ up to time t (more generally, given the information set $\Im_t$).

DEFINITION 9.5 (Smoothed probabilities)

The K-dimensional vector time series $\{\hat{\boldsymbol{\xi}}_{t|T}\}_{t=1}^{T}$ of filtered probabilities associated to a K-state ergodic MC collects at all times $t = 1, 2, \ldots, T$ is the optimal, *full-sample inference* on the state probabilities

$$\hat{\boldsymbol{\xi}}_{t|T} \equiv \Pr(\boldsymbol{\xi}_t | \Im_T) \tag{9.38}$$

given all the available information on the time series $\{\mathbf{y}_\tau\}_{\tau=1}^{T}$ (more generally, given the information set $\Im_T$).

The fact that one needs to use $\{\hat{\boldsymbol{\xi}}_{t|t}\}_{t=1}^{T}$ and $\{\hat{\boldsymbol{\xi}}_{t|T}\}_{t=1}^{T}$ to extract inferences concerning the dynamics of regimes over time (technically, concerning $\{\boldsymbol{\xi}_t\}_{t=1}^{T}$) derives from the latent nature of $\{S_t\}_{t=1}^{T}$ in an MS model. Algorithmically, the expectation step is the outcome of a few smart applications of *Bayes' law* that allow us to recursively derive at first a sequence of filtered probabilities and then (going backward) a sequence of smoothed probabilities. Starting from a *prior distribution* on the $K \times 1$ vector of probabilities $\boldsymbol{\xi}_t$, $\forall t \geq 1$, defined as:[9]

$$\Pr(\boldsymbol{\xi}_t | \Im_{t-1}) = \sum_{\boldsymbol{\xi}_{t-1}} \Pr(\boldsymbol{\xi}_t | \boldsymbol{\xi}_{t-1}) \Pr(\boldsymbol{\xi}_{t-1} | \Im_{t-1}). \tag{9.39}$$

9. $\sum_{\boldsymbol{\xi}_{t-1}}$ denotes the summation over all the elements of $\boldsymbol{\xi}_{t-1}$. For instance, when $K = 2$, for regime 1:

$$\Pr(\xi_t^1 | \Im_{t-1}) = \sum_{k=1}^{2} \Pr(\xi_t^1 | \xi_{t-1}^k) \Pr(\xi_{t-1}^k | \Im_{t-1}).$$

A prior distribution on some random vector $\boldsymbol{\xi}_t$ simply collects your initial views on what sensible values for the elements of $\boldsymbol{\xi}_t$ are.

This prior distribution simply takes the time $t-1$ posterior $\Pr(\xi_{t-1}|\Im_{t-1})$ defined below and turns it into a new prior, $\Pr(\xi_t|\Im_{t-1})$. Note that the elements of $\Pr(\xi_t|\xi_{t-1})$ are simply the elements of the transition matrix $\mathbf{P}$. The *posterior distribution* of ξ_t given $\Im_t = \{\Im_{t-1}, \mathbf{y}_t\}$, $\Pr(\xi_t|\Im_t)$, is then given by:[10]

$$\Pr(\xi_t|\Im_t) = \frac{\Pr(\mathbf{y}_t|\xi_t, \Im_{t-1})\Pr(\xi_t|\Im_{t-1})}{\Pr(\mathbf{y}_t|\Im_{t-1})}, \tag{9.40}$$

where $\Pr(\mathbf{y}_t|\Im_{t-1}) = \sum_{\xi_t}\Pr(\mathbf{y}_t, \xi_t|\Im_{t-1}) = \sum_{\xi_t}\Pr(\mathbf{y}_t|\xi_t, \Im_{t-1})\Pr(\xi_t|\Im_{t-1})$ is the unconditional likelihood of the current observation given its past. For compactness, Eq. (9.40) can also be expressed as $\eta'_t\hat{\xi}_{t|t-1} = \iota'_K(\eta_t \odot \hat{\xi}_{t|t-1})$ where $\odot$ denotes the element-by-element (*Hadamard*) product (see the Statistical and Mathematical Appendix to the book) and the $K \times 1$ vector η_t collects the possible log-likelihood values as a function of the realized state:

$$\eta_t \equiv \begin{bmatrix} p(\mathbf{y}_t|\xi_t = \mathbf{e}_1, \Im_{t-1}) \\ p(\mathbf{y}_t|\xi_t = \mathbf{e}_2, \Im_{t-1}) \\ \vdots \\ p(\mathbf{y}_t|\xi_t = \mathbf{e}_K, \Im_{t-1}) \end{bmatrix} = \begin{bmatrix} (2\pi)^{-1/2}|\boldsymbol{\Sigma}_1|^{-1/2}\exp\left[(\mathbf{y}_t - \mathbf{X}_t\mathbf{A}\mathbf{e}_1)'\boldsymbol{\Sigma}_1^{-1}(\mathbf{y}_t - \mathbf{X}_t\mathbf{A}\mathbf{e}_1)\right] \\ (2\pi)^{-1/2}|\boldsymbol{\Sigma}_2|^{-1/2}\exp\left[(\mathbf{y}_t - \mathbf{X}_t\mathbf{A}\mathbf{e}_2)'\boldsymbol{\Sigma}_2^{-1}(\mathbf{y}_t - \mathbf{X}_t\mathbf{A}\mathbf{e}_2)\right] \\ \vdots \\ (2\pi)^{-1/2}|\boldsymbol{\Sigma}_K|^{-1/2}\exp\left[(\mathbf{y}_t - \mathbf{X}_t\mathbf{A}\mathbf{e}_K)'\boldsymbol{\Sigma}_K^{-1}(\mathbf{y}_t - \mathbf{X}_t\mathbf{A}\mathbf{e}_K)\right] \end{bmatrix}. \tag{9.41}$$

Of course Eq. (9.40) is nothing but Bayes' rule applied to our problem. At this point, the vector of filtered probabilities, $\hat{\xi}_{t|t}$, corresponds to the discrete probability distribution of the possible states perceived on the basis of the information set $\Im_t$:

$$\hat{\xi}_{t|t} = \frac{\eta_t \odot \hat{\xi}_{t|t-1}}{\iota'_K\left(\eta_t \odot \hat{\xi}_{t|t-1}\right)}. \tag{9.42}$$

A filtered probability is the best assessment of (inference on) the current state, based on real-time information. Of course, $\hat{\xi}_{t|t}\iota_K = 1$, that is, the filtered probability at time t they all sum up to 1. The expressions in Eqs. (9.40) and (9.42) emphasize that the filtered probability of being in a regime k at time t is the ratio between the sum of the probabilities of reaching regime k from each of the K possible regimes, including k itself, divided by the total probability of $\mathbf{y}_t$, given all past information.

The expectation step is completed by the transition Eq. (9.35), by which $E_t[\xi_{t+1}|\Im_t] \equiv E_t[\xi_{t+1}] = \hat{\xi}_{t+1|t} = \mathbf{P}'\hat{\xi}_{t|t}$, which defines the vector one-step-ahead predicted probabilities.

DEFINITION 9.6 (Predicted probabilities)

The K-dimensional vector time series $\{\hat{\xi}_{t+1|t}\}_{t=1}^{T}$ of one-step-ahead predicted probabilities associated to a K-state ergodic MC collects at all times $t = 1, 2, \ldots, T$ is the optimal, *real-time, recursive inference* on the state probabilities

$$\hat{\xi}_{t+1|t} \equiv \Pr(\xi_{t+1}|\Im_t) = \mathbf{P}'\hat{\xi}_{t|t} \tag{9.43}$$

given the information on the time series $\{y_\tau\}_{\tau=1}^{t}$ up to time t (more generally, given the information set $\Im_t$). More generally, the vector $\{\hat{\xi}_{t+H|t}\}_{t=1}^{T}$ of H-step-ahead predicted probabilities can be found as $\hat{\xi}_{t+H|t} \equiv \Pr(\xi_{t+H}|\Im_t) = (\mathbf{P}^H)'\hat{\xi}_{t|t}$.

Note that because we are generally uncertain about the identity of the initial state vector as of time t, we use the inferred filtered state probabilities $\hat{\xi}_{t|t}$ from the previous step of the algorithm. Assuming that the initial state probability vector $\hat{\xi}_{1|0}$ is unknown and must be estimated, Eqs. (9.42) and (9.43) define an iterative algorithm that allows one to generate a sequence of filtered state probability vectors:[11]

10. In a Bayesian problem, the posterior distribution of the random vector ξ_t collects your views after you have observed the data up to time t (here, $\Im_t$), and therefore reflects a mixture between the initial priors and the data, as summarized by the likelihood function, $\Pr(\mathbf{y}_t|\xi_t, \Im_t)$.

11. This assumption implies that $\hat{\xi}_{1|0}$ is a $K \times 1$ vector that must be estimated. A simpler alternative is postulated that the stochastic process had started from a deterministic but unknown state S_0 that must be estimated along with the remaining parameters (in practice, it is ξ_0 that is estimated). In these two cases, the EM algorithm returns a complete information MLE. Alternatively, $\hat{\xi}_{1|0}$ may be assumed to correspond to the stationary unconditional probability distribution $\bar{\xi}$, but the resulting estimator will be a QMLE (this simplifying assumption is similar to a variance targeting approach).

$$\hat{\boldsymbol{\xi}}_{1|1} = \frac{\boldsymbol{\eta}_1 \odot \hat{\boldsymbol{\xi}}_{1|0}}{\boldsymbol{\iota}'_K \left(\boldsymbol{\eta}_1 \odot \hat{\boldsymbol{\xi}}_{1|0} \right)}, \quad \hat{\boldsymbol{\xi}}_{2|2} = \frac{\boldsymbol{\eta}_2 \odot \mathbf{P}' \hat{\boldsymbol{\xi}}_{1|1}}{\boldsymbol{\iota}'_K \left(\boldsymbol{\eta}_2 \odot \mathbf{P}' \hat{\boldsymbol{\xi}}_{1|1} \right)}, \ldots, \quad \hat{\boldsymbol{\xi}}_{T|T} = \frac{\boldsymbol{\eta}_T \odot \mathbf{P}' \hat{\boldsymbol{\xi}}_{T-1|T-1}}{\boldsymbol{\iota}'_K \left(\boldsymbol{\eta}_T \odot \mathbf{P}' \hat{\boldsymbol{\xi}}_{T-1|T-1} \right)}. \tag{9.44}$$

The filtered probabilities are the product of a *limited information recursive technique*, because despite the availability of a sample of size T, each $\hat{\boldsymbol{\xi}}_{t|t}$ is filtered out of the information set $\Im_t$ only, ignoring $\{\mathbf{y}_\tau\}_{\tau=t+1}^T$. However, once the full-time series of filtered probabilities $\{\hat{\boldsymbol{\xi}}_{t|t}\}_{t=1}^T$ has been calculated, Kim's (1994) algorithm is easily implemented to recover the sequence of smoothed probability distributions $\{\hat{\boldsymbol{\xi}}_{t|T}\}_{t=1}^T$ by iterating the following algorithm backward. Starting from the filtered (in this case, identical by construction to the smoothed) probability distribution $\hat{\boldsymbol{\xi}}_{T|T}$ produced by Eqs. (9.42) and (9.43), observe that:

$$\begin{aligned}
\hat{\boldsymbol{\xi}}_{t|T} = \Pr\left(\boldsymbol{\xi}_t | \Im_T\right) &= \sum_{\boldsymbol{\xi}_{t+1}} \Pr\left(\boldsymbol{\xi}_t, \boldsymbol{\xi}_{t+1} | \Im_T\right) \quad \text{(by the definition of probability)} \\
&= \sum_{\boldsymbol{\xi}_{t+1}} \Pr\left(\boldsymbol{\xi}_t | \boldsymbol{\xi}_{t+1}, \Im_T\right) \Pr\left(\boldsymbol{\xi}_{t+1} | \Im_T\right) \quad \text{(by the definition of joint probability)} \\
&= \sum_{\boldsymbol{\xi}_{t+1}} \Pr\left(\boldsymbol{\xi}_t | \boldsymbol{\xi}_{t+1}, \Im_t, \{\mathbf{y}_\tau\}_{\tau=t+1}^T\right) \Pr\left(\boldsymbol{\xi}_{t+1} | \Im_T\right) \\
&= \sum_{\boldsymbol{\xi}_{t+1}} \frac{\Pr\left(\boldsymbol{\xi}_t | \boldsymbol{\xi}_{t+1}, \Im_t\right) \Pr\left(\{\mathbf{y}_\tau\}_{\tau=t+1}^T | \boldsymbol{\xi}_t, \boldsymbol{\xi}_{t+1}, \Im_t\right)}{\Pr\left(\{\mathbf{y}_\tau\}_{\tau=t+1}^T | \boldsymbol{\xi}_{t+1}, \Im_t\right)} \Pr\left(\boldsymbol{\xi}_{t+1} | \Im_T\right) \\
&= \sum_{\boldsymbol{\xi}_{t+1}} \Pr\left(\boldsymbol{\xi}_t | \boldsymbol{\xi}_{t+1}, \Im_t\right) \Pr\left(\boldsymbol{\xi}_{t+1} | \Im_T\right) = \sum_{\boldsymbol{\xi}_{t+1}} \frac{\Pr\left(\boldsymbol{\xi}_t | \Im_t\right) \Pr\left(\boldsymbol{\xi}_{t+1} | \boldsymbol{\xi}_t, \Im_t\right)}{\Pr\left(\boldsymbol{\xi}_{t+1} | \Im_t\right)} \Pr\left(\boldsymbol{\xi}_{t+1} | \Im_T\right)
\end{aligned} \tag{9.45}$$

because the first-order MC structure implies that $\Pr(\{\mathbf{y}_\tau\}_{\tau=t+1}^T | \boldsymbol{\xi}_t, \boldsymbol{\xi}_{t+1}, \Im_t) = \Pr(\{\mathbf{y}_\tau\}_{\tau=t+1}^T | \boldsymbol{\xi}_{t+1}, \Im_t)$. Hence, $\hat{\boldsymbol{\xi}}_{t|T}$ can be rewritten as:

$$\hat{\boldsymbol{\xi}}_{t|T} = (\mathbf{P}'(\hat{\boldsymbol{\xi}}_{t+1|T} \div \hat{\boldsymbol{\xi}}_{t+1|t})) \odot \hat{\boldsymbol{\xi}}_{t|t}, \tag{9.46}$$

where $\div$ denotes element-by-element division and $\Pr\left(\boldsymbol{\xi}_{t+1} | \boldsymbol{\xi}_t, \Im_t\right)$ equals by construction the transition matrix driving the first-order MC. Eq. (9.46) is initialized by setting $t = T-1$ thus obtaining $\hat{\boldsymbol{\xi}}_{T-1|T} = (\mathbf{P}'(\hat{\boldsymbol{\xi}}_{T|T} \div \hat{\boldsymbol{\xi}}_{T|T-1})) \odot \hat{\boldsymbol{\xi}}_{T-1|T-1}$, to then compute $\hat{\boldsymbol{\xi}}_{T-2|T-1} = (\mathbf{P}'(\hat{\boldsymbol{\xi}}_{T-1|T-1} \div \hat{\boldsymbol{\xi}}_{T-1|T-2})) \odot \hat{\boldsymbol{\xi}}_{T-2|T-2}$ ($\hat{\boldsymbol{\xi}}_{T|T}$ and $\hat{\boldsymbol{\xi}}_{T-1|T-1}$ will be known from the application of Hamilton's filtering algorithm in Eq. (9.42), and $\hat{\boldsymbol{\xi}}_{T|T-1} = \mathbf{P}' \hat{\boldsymbol{\xi}}_{T-1|T-1}$), and so forth, proceeding backward until $t = 1$.

What is the deep difference between filtered and smoothed probabilities? Clearly, while filtered probabilities condition on information up to time t, the smoothed probabilities condition on the entire sample and hence reflect more information. Therefore *a smoothed probability represents an ex-post measure of the state of the model at time t*, where $t \ll T$ is possible. A filtered probability provides instead a recursive, real-time assessment (filter) on the current state. One example that may ease you into an understanding of the difference comes from comparing the two questions:

- Given what I know about what the weather has been like during the past few weeks, what is chance of recording a high atmospheric pressure today (also given observed conditions today)? This requires a real-time, recursive assessment akin to the calculation of a *filtered probability*.
- Given the information on the weather in the past 12 months and up to today, what was the chance of a high atmospheric pressure to have been recorded 4 months ago? This requires a full-information, but backward-looking assessment that employs data that were not yet available 4 months ago.

Obviously, in financial applications we tend to operate in real time, to focus on forecasting future market conditions, and as such we tend to care more for filtered probabilities than for smoothed ones, even though it is clear that the two concepts coincide by construction at the end of all available sample data. In fact, using Eq. (9.43), the focus frequently goes to the vector of predicted H-step-ahead probabilities. On the contrary, the smoothed probabilities correspond to the logical approach of historians to assess events: by using all the available information at time T, a researcher wants to understand what the probability of the K different regimes had been at time $t < T$. Clearly, using information posterior to time T may easily make our understanding of events more accurate and interesting. Yet, the fact remains that such a probabilistic assessment would not have been available to investors and traders at time $t < T$, that is, in real time. Moreover, we shall see soon how smoothed probabilities also play a crucial role in ML estimation of MS models.

The *maximization step* is rather complex and involved. Therefore, some technical or boring details can be found in Appendix 9.C. The point of taking a look at the conditions and results that follow is that it is important to have some idea for what happens behind the curtains of the typical software code (say E-Views or MATLAB's routines). Call ρ the vector collecting the transition probabilities in **P**, that is, $\boldsymbol{\theta} \equiv [vec(\mathbf{A})|vec(\boldsymbol{\Omega}_K)]$ and $\boldsymbol{\rho} \equiv vec(\mathbf{P})$. Write the likelihood function of our sample of N asset returns as:

$$L\left(\{\mathbf{y}_t\}_{t=1}^T | \{\boldsymbol{\xi}_t\}_{t=1}^T, \boldsymbol{\theta}, \boldsymbol{\rho}\right) = \sum_{\{\boldsymbol{\xi}_t\}_{t=1}^T} \prod_{t=1}^T p(\mathbf{y}_t|\boldsymbol{\xi}_t, \Im_{t-1}; \boldsymbol{\theta}) \Pr\left(\boldsymbol{\xi}_t|\boldsymbol{\xi}_0; \boldsymbol{\rho}\right), \tag{9.47}$$

where $\Pr\left(\boldsymbol{\xi}_t|\boldsymbol{\xi}_0; \boldsymbol{\rho}\right) = \sum_{s_0=1}^K \xi_{s_0} \prod_{t=1}^T p_{S_{t-1},S_t}$ and the first summation spans the space defined by $\boldsymbol{\xi}_1 \otimes \boldsymbol{\xi}_2 \otimes \cdots \otimes \boldsymbol{\xi}_T$ for a total of K^T possible combinations. In words, this means that in principle computing the likelihood function forces us to sum over all possible paths/evolutions of regime probabilities between $t=1$ and $t=T$. As we know, when the shocks to the MS model are assumed to be multivariate normal (as they are in our treatment, also to attain identification), then the density function is $p(\mathbf{y}_t|\boldsymbol{\xi}_t, \Im_{t-1}; \boldsymbol{\theta}) = \boldsymbol{\eta}_t \odot \boldsymbol{\xi}_t$ where the kth element of $\boldsymbol{\eta}_t$ is defined as:

$$(2\pi)^{-1/2}|\boldsymbol{\Sigma}_k|^{-1/2}\exp\left[-1/2(\mathbf{y}_t - \mathbf{X}_t\mathbf{A}\mathbf{e}_k)'\boldsymbol{\Sigma}_k^{-1}(\mathbf{y}_t - \mathbf{X}_t\mathbf{A}\mathbf{e}_k)\right], \tag{9.48}$$

that is, the multivariate normal density. At this point, the parameters $[\boldsymbol{\theta}' \; \boldsymbol{\rho}']'$ can be derived by maximization of Eq. (9.47) subject to the natural constraints:

$$\begin{gathered} \mathbf{P}\boldsymbol{\iota}_K = \boldsymbol{\iota}_K \text{ (rows sum to 1)}, \quad \boldsymbol{\xi}'_0\boldsymbol{\iota}_K = 1 \text{ (probabilities sum to one)} \\ \boldsymbol{\rho} \geq \mathbf{0}, \boldsymbol{\xi}_0 \geq \mathbf{0}, \text{and } \boldsymbol{\Omega}_K\mathbf{e}_k \text{ is (semi-) positive definite } \forall k = 1, 2, \ldots, K. \end{gathered} \tag{9.49}$$

At this point, it is common to assume that the nonnegativity constraints in Eq. (9.49) are satisfied and to take the first-order conditions (FOCs) of a Lagrangian function that explicitly enforces the adding-up constraints:

$$\begin{aligned} L^*\left(\{\mathbf{y}_t\}_{t=1}^T | \{\boldsymbol{\xi}_t\}_{t=1}^T, \boldsymbol{\theta}, \boldsymbol{\rho}\right) = & \sum_{\{\boldsymbol{\xi}_t\}_{t=1}^T} \prod_{t=1}^T p(\mathbf{y}_t|\boldsymbol{\xi}_t, \Im_{t-1}; \boldsymbol{\theta}) \Pr\left(\boldsymbol{\xi}_t|\boldsymbol{\xi}_0; \boldsymbol{\rho}\right) \\ & - \boldsymbol{\lambda}'_1(\mathbf{P}\boldsymbol{\iota}_K - \boldsymbol{\iota}_K) - \lambda_2(\boldsymbol{\xi}'_0\boldsymbol{\iota}_K - 1). \end{aligned} \tag{9.50}$$

However, additional work on the FOCs derived from Eq. (9.50) in Appendix 9.C shows a few interesting aspects of the ML estimator. If you differentiate the logarithm of Eq. (9.50) with respect to $\boldsymbol{\theta}$, this gives the so-called *score function* already encountered in Chapter 5:

$$\begin{aligned} \frac{\partial \ln L^*(\boldsymbol{\theta}, \boldsymbol{\rho})}{\partial \boldsymbol{\theta}'} &= \frac{1}{L(\boldsymbol{\theta}, \boldsymbol{\rho})} \sum_{\{\boldsymbol{\xi}_t\}_{t=1}^T} \frac{\partial \prod_{t=1}^T p(\mathbf{y}_t|\boldsymbol{\xi}_t, \Im_{t-1}; \boldsymbol{\theta})}{\partial \boldsymbol{\theta}'} \Pr\left(\boldsymbol{\xi}_t|\boldsymbol{\xi}_0; \boldsymbol{\rho}\right) \\ &= \frac{1}{L(\boldsymbol{\theta}, \boldsymbol{\rho})} \sum_{\{\boldsymbol{\xi}_t\}_{t=1}^T} \frac{\partial \ln\left[\prod_{t=1}^T p(\mathbf{y}_t|\boldsymbol{\xi}_t, \Im_{t-1}; \boldsymbol{\theta})\right]}{\partial \boldsymbol{\theta}'} \prod_{t=1}^T p(\mathbf{y}_t|\boldsymbol{\xi}_t, \Im_{t-1}; \boldsymbol{\theta}) \Pr\left(\boldsymbol{\xi}_t|\boldsymbol{\xi}_0; \boldsymbol{\rho}\right) \\ &= \sum_{\{\boldsymbol{\xi}_t\}_{t=1}^T} \sum_{t=1}^T \Pr\left(\boldsymbol{\xi}_t|\Im_T; \boldsymbol{\theta}, \boldsymbol{\rho}\right) \frac{\partial \ln p(\mathbf{y}_t|\boldsymbol{\xi}_t, \Im_{t-1}; \boldsymbol{\theta})}{\partial \boldsymbol{\theta}'}. \end{aligned} \tag{9.51}$$

This proves that:

$$\sum_{t=1}^T \hat{\boldsymbol{\xi}}_{t|T}(\hat{\boldsymbol{\theta}}, \hat{\boldsymbol{\rho}}) \frac{\partial \ln \boldsymbol{\eta}_t(\hat{\boldsymbol{\theta}})}{\partial \boldsymbol{\theta}'} = \mathbf{0}' \tag{9.52}$$

provides the first set of FOCs with respect to $\boldsymbol{\theta}$. Note that these conditions involve the smoothed probabilities of the state vector, $\{\hat{\boldsymbol{\xi}}_{t|T}\}_{t=1}^T$ and not the filtered probabilities as one may naively come to expect. The reason lies in the math shown above. At this point, Eq. (9.52) simply represents a smoothed probability-weighted standard ML vector FOC, $\partial \ln \boldsymbol{\eta}_t(\boldsymbol{\theta})/\partial \boldsymbol{\theta}' = \mathbf{0}'$. This means that in practice, the special structure of the MS model allows us to perform standard, multivariate normal probability density function (PDF) based estimation, with the only caution that because each observation $\mathbf{y}_t$ carries a different vector of probabilities for the K regimes, when the log-likelihood is computed, it must be weighted by the time series of the smoothed probabilities. Importantly, the FOCs Eq. (9.52) as well as those reported in Appendix 9.C, all depend on smoothed probabilities $\hat{\boldsymbol{\xi}}_{t|T} \equiv \Pr\left(\boldsymbol{\xi}_t|\Im_T; \boldsymbol{\theta}, \boldsymbol{\rho}\right)$ and therefore they all present a high degree of nonlinearity in the parameters $[\boldsymbol{\theta}' \; \boldsymbol{\rho}']'$. Therefore the FOCs have to be solved numerically, by using methods identical or similar to those surveyed in Chapter 5. In special cases, for instance MSIH(K) − VAR(p), in which the vector autoregressive coefficients are constant over time, one can use the FOCs (as in Krolzig, 1997) to prove that estimates of $vec(\boldsymbol{A})$ can be easily obtained in closed form by appropriately setting up the log-likelihood function as in a GLS problem (see Chapter 1). As for the estimates of $vec(\boldsymbol{\Omega}_K)$, because the (expected) log-likelihood function can be expressed as:

$$\ell(\boldsymbol{\theta}|\{\mathbf{y}_t\}_{t=1}^T) \propto \frac{1}{2}\sum_{k=1}^{K^T}\sum_{t=1}^{T}\ln|\boldsymbol{\Sigma}_k^{-1}|\hat{\xi}_{kt|T} - \frac{1}{2}\sum_{k=1}^{K^T}\sum_{t=1}^{T}(\mathbf{y}_t - \mathbf{X}_t\boldsymbol{A}_k)'\boldsymbol{\Sigma}_k^{-1}(\mathbf{y}_t - \mathbf{X}_t\boldsymbol{A}_k)\hat{\xi}_{kt|T}; \tag{9.53}$$

this leads to:

$$\frac{\partial\ell(\boldsymbol{\theta}|\{\mathbf{y}_t\}_{t=1}^T)}{\partial\boldsymbol{\Sigma}_k^{-1}} = \frac{1}{2}\boldsymbol{\Sigma}_k\sum_{t=1}^{T}\hat{\boldsymbol{\xi}}_{kt|T} - \frac{1}{2}\sum_{t=1}^{T}(\mathbf{y}_t - \mathbf{X}_t\boldsymbol{A}_k)(\mathbf{y}_t - \mathbf{X}_t\boldsymbol{A}_k)' = \mathbf{O} \tag{9.54}$$

and

$$\hat{\boldsymbol{\Sigma}}_k(\boldsymbol{A}_k) = \left(\sum_{t=1}^{T}\hat{\boldsymbol{\xi}}_{kt|T}\right)^{-1}\sum_{t=1}^{T}(\mathbf{y}_t - \mathbf{X}_t\boldsymbol{A}_k)(\mathbf{y}_t - \mathbf{X}_t\boldsymbol{A}_k)'. \tag{9.55}$$

The expectation and maximization steps can be combined and used in an iterative fashion with the objective of solving numerically the FOCs. The result is the EM algorithm. Starting with arbitrary initial values $\tilde{\boldsymbol{\theta}}^0$, $\tilde{\boldsymbol{\rho}}^0$, and $\tilde{\boldsymbol{\xi}}_{1|0}^0$, the expectation step is applied first, thus obtaining a time series sequence of smoothed probabilities, $\{\hat{\boldsymbol{\xi}}_{t|T}^1\}_{t=1}^T$. Given these smoothed probabilities, the FOCs are numerically solved to calculate $\tilde{\boldsymbol{\theta}}^1$, $\tilde{\boldsymbol{\rho}}^1$, and $\tilde{\boldsymbol{\xi}}_{1|0}^1$. Based on $\tilde{\boldsymbol{\theta}}^1$, $\tilde{\boldsymbol{\rho}}^1$, and $\tilde{\boldsymbol{\xi}}_{1|0}^1$, the expectation step can be applied again to find a new sequence of smoothed probabilities, $\{\hat{\boldsymbol{\xi}}_{t|T}^2\}_{t=1}^T$. This starts the second iteration of the algorithm. The algorithm keeps being iterated until convergence, that is, until $[\tilde{\boldsymbol{\theta}}^l\tilde{\boldsymbol{\rho}}^l]' \simeq [\tilde{\boldsymbol{\theta}}^{l-1}\tilde{\boldsymbol{\rho}}^{l-1}]'$, or $[\tilde{\boldsymbol{\theta}}^l\tilde{\boldsymbol{\rho}}^l]' - [\tilde{\boldsymbol{\theta}}^{l-1}\tilde{\boldsymbol{\rho}}^{l-1}]' \simeq \mathbf{0}$. This means that tests will have to be applied to check whether two subsequent iterations have essentially left the corresponding estimates unaltered, so that (for instance, using a standard Euclidean norm):

$$\sqrt{\sum_j(\tilde{\theta}_j^l - \tilde{\theta}_j^{l-1})^2 + \sum_i(\tilde{\rho}_i^l - \tilde{\rho}_i^{l-1})^2} < \overline{\kappa}, \tag{9.56}$$

where $\overline{\kappa}$ is a number chosen to be small (e.g., typically, 1E-04). Note that these conditions normally exclude the estimate for $\boldsymbol{\xi}_{1|0}$ from the convergence test in Eq. (9.56). At that point one simply sets $\hat{\boldsymbol{\theta}}_T^{MLE} = \tilde{\boldsymbol{\theta}}^l$, $\hat{\boldsymbol{\rho}}^{MLE} = \tilde{\boldsymbol{\rho}}^l$, and $\hat{\boldsymbol{\xi}}_{1|0}^{MLE} = \tilde{\boldsymbol{\xi}}_{1|0}^1$. Importantly, by construction, when the EM iterations are applied, the likelihood function increases at each step and reaches an approximate maximum in correspondence to convergence (see Baum et al., 1970). It is now time to see these concepts in action by returning to Example 9.4 and examining further a few details.

EXAMPLE 9.4 (Continued)

We are interested in forecasting monthly Japanese excess aggregate stock returns by using their own lag, one lag of US excess stock returns, and one lag of S&P 100 implied volatility. We have already used information criteria to specify a two-state MS heteroskedastic regression model driven by a first-order, homogeneous MC, and reported the corresponding quasi-ML (QML) estimates, which we copy again for completeness:

$$x_{t+1}^{Japan} = \begin{cases} \underset{(0.186)}{0.416} & \text{if } S_{t+1} = 1 \\ \underset{(0.706)}{0.206} & \text{if } S_{t+1} = 2 \end{cases} + \underset{(0.706)}{0.071}\, x_t^{Japan} + \underset{(0.011)}{0.182}\, x_t^{US} - \underset{(0.000)}{0.073}\, rvxo_t$$
$$+ \begin{cases} \underset{(0.000)}{3.854} & \text{if } S_{t+1} = 1 \\ \underset{(0.000)}{7.265} & \text{if } S_{t+1} = 2 \end{cases} \cdot \varepsilon_{t+1}^{Japan} \quad \hat{P} = \begin{bmatrix} 0.997 & 0.003 \\ 0.004 & 0.996 \end{bmatrix} \quad \overline{R}^2 = 0.057.$$

(Continued)

EXAMPLE 9.4 (Continued)

The resulting, maximized log-likelihood is −1161.68. We now proceed first to show filtered, smoothed, and 1-month-ahead predicted regime probabilities, shown in Figs. 9.12 and 9.13. Of course, because regime probabilities always sum to 1, it is largely redundant to present plots for both regimes, but for the time being we shall do that.

In Fig. 9.12, also to contrast them, we plot together both filtered and smoothed probabilities. By construction, filtered probabilities are more erratic and record considerably more time variation than "smoothed" (indeed) regime probabilities do. This is because an econometrician inferring the state in real time is prone to occasionally get "confused" in the light of the recent evidence collected, as to the nature of the state. On the opposite—one may say with the benefit of hindsight—smoothed regime probabilities record much less uncertainty because ex-post, in the light of the full sample, it becomes easier to classify the observation(s) from a given time in the sample generated by one state versus another. For instance, in real time, the MS regression faces difficulties at classifying the data from early 2009 and attributes a filtered probability of 0.4 to regime 1 and of 0.6 to regime 2. However, ex-post, when the full sample is available, an analyst would have revised to 0 or just above 0 the full-sample estimate of the probability of regime 1.

It is legitimate to wonder whether Fig. 9.13 may plot again by mistake the filtered probabilities from Fig. 9.12 because the two series are largely similar. However, this is not a surprise because we know from Definition 9.6 that $\hat{\boldsymbol{\xi}}_{t+1|t} \equiv \Pr(\boldsymbol{\xi}_{t+1}|\Im_t) = \mathbf{P}'\hat{\boldsymbol{\xi}}_{t|t}$, while in this case we have reported:

$$\hat{P} = \begin{bmatrix} 0.997 & 0.003 \\ 0.004 & 0.996 \end{bmatrix}.$$

Clearly whatever $\hat{\boldsymbol{\xi}}_{t|t}$ may be, if this vector is multiplied by a transition matrix that is basically almost an identity matrix, one will obtain $\hat{\boldsymbol{\xi}}_{t+1|t} \simeq \hat{\boldsymbol{\xi}}_{t|t}$ which explains the similarity between one-step-ahead predicted and filtered state probabilities.

We have also seen that a number of choices is available when it comes to the initial state vector $\boldsymbol{\xi}_{1|0}$. The QML estimates above have been computed by setting $\boldsymbol{\xi}_{1|0} = \bar{\boldsymbol{\xi}}$, the vector of ergodic/stationary probabilities which in this case are equal to 0.533 and 0.467, respectively. Therefore using E-Views, we have also tried to test the robustness of the estimates to changes in this assumption. When $\boldsymbol{\xi}_{1|0}$ is treated as unknown vector of parameters to be estimated by ML, we easily achieve convergence using $\bar{\kappa} = 1\text{E-}04$, but we cannot (in spite of hundreds of random starts) get any estimates of the covariance matrix of the estimates and hence of the standard errors. The same occurs when we try to set $\boldsymbol{\xi}_{1|0}$ to a range of alternative values. Therefore QML estimation seems to be highly sensitive to a specific way in which $\boldsymbol{\xi}_{1|0}$ is initialized. However, when $\boldsymbol{\xi}_{1|0}$ is set to $[0.5 \quad 0.5]'$, we find regular QML estimates that differ from those reported above and are instead:

$$x_{t+1}^{Japan} = \begin{cases} \underset{(0.171)}{0.425} & \text{if } S_{t+1} = 1 \\ \underset{(0.737)}{0.197} & \text{if } S_{t+1} = 2 \end{cases} + \underset{(0.198)}{0.071}\, x_t^{Japan} + \underset{(0.010)}{0.183}\, x_t^{US} - \underset{(0.000)}{0.073}\, rvxo_t$$

$$+ \begin{cases} \underset{(0.000)}{3.871} & \text{if } S_{t+1} = 1 \\ \underset{(0.000)}{7.269} & \text{if } S_{t+1} = 2 \end{cases} z_{t+1}^{Japan} \quad \hat{P} = \begin{bmatrix} 0.999 & 0.001 \\ 0.005 & 0.995 \end{bmatrix}$$

which features an almost absorbing state. The estimated coefficients are rather similar (in economic terms these are probably indistinguishable) but their statistical significance seems to increase somewhat. The resulting, maximized log-likelihood is −1161.20. Therefore given that setting $\boldsymbol{\xi}_{1|0}$ instead of estimating it will just deliver a QML estimate, it seems preferable to initialize $\boldsymbol{\xi}_{1|0}$ to $[0.5 \quad 0.5]'$ and not to $\bar{\boldsymbol{\xi}}$.

Above we have emphasized that often the FOCs have to be solved numerically. As always, and beyond what we have investigated above with reference to $\boldsymbol{\xi}_{1|0}$, when the log-likelihood (or the implied FOCs) has to be numerically maximized, the initial conditions matter. Moreover, it is advisable that a range of alternative initial conditions be tried, to settle to a "best set" under some sensible criterion. We return to $\boldsymbol{\xi}_{1|0} = \bar{\boldsymbol{\xi}}$ and investigate whether the initial conditions concerning the remaining parameters, $\tilde{\boldsymbol{\theta}}^0$ and $\tilde{\boldsymbol{\rho}}^0$, may matter. First, we note that the estimates reported above were achieved (from high-quality initial conditions) starting from this model:

$$x_{t+1}^{Japan} = \begin{cases} 0.423 & \text{if } S_{t+1} = 1 \\ 0.720 & \text{if } S_{t+1} = 2 \end{cases} + 0.088 x_t^{Japan} + 0.141 x_t^{US} - 0.065 rvxo_t$$

$$+ \begin{cases} 7.473 & \text{if } S_{t+1} = 1 \\ 4.127 & \text{if } S_{t+1} = 2 \end{cases} \cdot z_{t+1}^{Japan} \quad \hat{P} = \begin{bmatrix} 0.997 & 0.003 \\ 0.001 & 0.999 \end{bmatrix}.$$

As a first experiment, we have divided all coefficients above by a factor of 2 and proceed to reestimate the model from such different conditions. Reassuringly, we reach the same QML estimates as those reported above. We also initialize the maximization problem starting from zero initial conditions and reach the same conclusions. Interestingly, while setting $\boldsymbol{\xi}_{1|0}$ seems to matter a lot, the initialization of the remaining parameters does not seem to matter much for the estimation of the model. Finally, we have also tested the robustness of the QML estimation by trying a massive amount of initial conditions, as many as 250: for each of

(*Continued*)

EXAMPLE 9.4 (Continued)

them, we perform 50 iterations of the EM algorithm and eventually retain the best set, in terms of achieving the highest level of the log-likelihood function. However, we do not simply use such set of parameter values to represent new initial conditions, we proceed instead to apply a further set of 50 perturbations (with scale equal to 1 standard deviation of the estimated parameters) and eventually retain only the set of values reaching the highest log-likelihood. In any event, the resulting QML estimates are those reported early on. Even though all the experiments are interesting because they corroborate the robustness of the estimates reported above to perturbations, unfortunately this finding does not have a general value, in the sense for each data set and application, these "stress tests" of QML estimation will have to be applied afresh, hoping in similar (or more reassuring results).

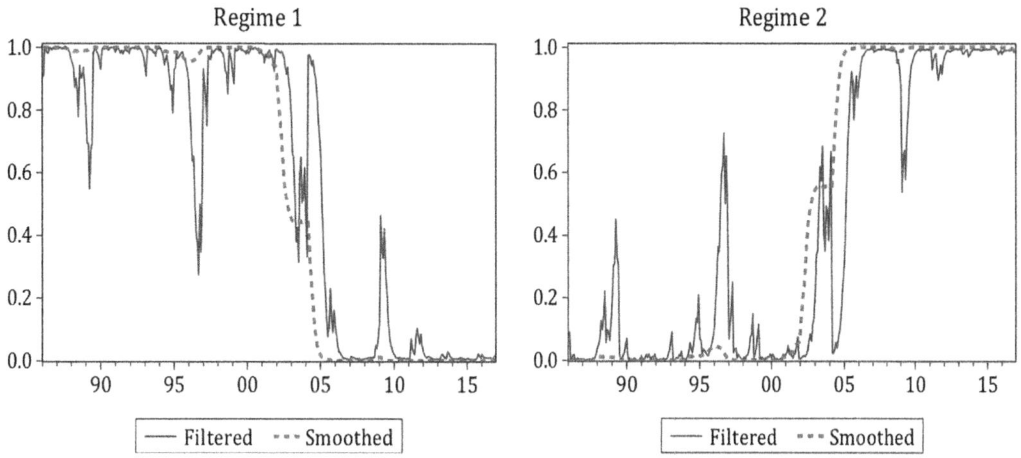

FIGURE 9.12 Filtered and smoothed state probabilities from two-state MS heteroskedastic regression.

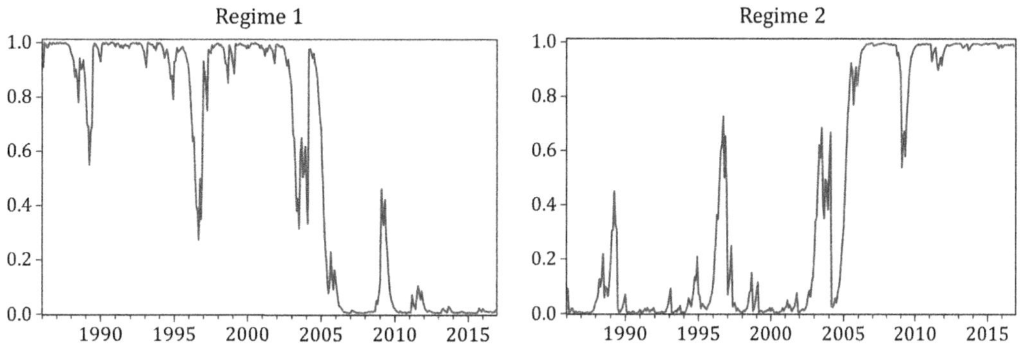

FIGURE 9.13 One-month predicted state probabilities from two-state MS heteroskedastic regression.

As for the properties of the ML estimators, for ergodic, univariate MS models with autoregressive components, it has been proven by Karlsen (1990) that in an MSIARH(K,p),

$$y_{t+1} = \mu_{S_{t+1}} + \sum_{j=1}^{p} a_{j,\, S_{t+1}} y_{t+1-j} + \sigma_{S_{t+1}} z_{t+1} \quad S_{t+1} = 1, 2, \ldots, K, \tag{9.57}$$

where $z_{t+1} \sim \text{IID } N(0, 1)$ fulfills some technical conditions (it follows a strong mixing process), because stationarity is implied by the stationarity of the homogenous MC $\boldsymbol{\xi}_t$, a functional central limit theorem may be used to derive the asymptotic distribution of $\hat{\gamma}_T^{MLE} \equiv [\hat{\boldsymbol{\theta}}_T^{MLE} \; \hat{\rho}^{MLE}]'$. Leroux (1992) has formally proved the consistency of MLE for MSIH(K,0) processes. More generally, under standard regularity conditions (such as identifiability, ergodicity, and the fact that the true parameter vector does not fall on the boundaries established by the constraints in Eq. (9.49)), we can at least speculate (and under some conditions, prove) the consistency and asymptotic normality of the ML estimator (see Douc et al., 2004):[12]

$$\sqrt{T}(\hat{\gamma}-\gamma) \xrightarrow{D} N\left(\mathbf{0},\ I_a(\gamma)^{-1}\right), \tag{9.58}$$

where $I_a(\gamma)$, is the asymptotic information matrix,

$$I_a(\gamma) \equiv \lim_{T\to\infty} -T^{-1}E\left[\frac{\partial^2 \ln \prod_{t=1}^{T} p(\mathbf{y}_t|\gamma)}{\partial\gamma\partial\gamma'}\right]. \tag{9.59}$$

Three alternative sample estimators of $I_a(\gamma)$ providing estimates for $\widehat{Var}(\hat{\gamma})$ are available and commonly employed:

- An estimator based on the outer product of the conditional scores (also called *OPG estimator*):

$$I_1(\hat{\gamma}) = T^{-1}\sum_{t=1}^{T}[\mathbf{h}_t(\hat{\gamma})]\,[\mathbf{h}_t(\hat{\gamma})]' \quad \mathbf{h}_t(\hat{\gamma}) = \frac{\partial \ln p(\mathbf{y}_t|\Im_{t-1};\ \hat{\gamma})}{\partial\gamma}. \tag{9.60}$$

- Alternatively, it is possible to numerically calculate the second partial derivative (the *Hessian*) of the log-likelihood function with respect to the estimated parameters, simply as:

$$I_2(\hat{\gamma}) = -T^{-1}\sum_{t=1}^{T}\left[\frac{\partial^2 \ln p(\mathbf{y}_t|\Im_{t-1};\ \hat{\gamma})}{\partial\gamma\partial\gamma'}\right]. \tag{9.61}$$

In fact, it may happen that Eqs. (9.60) and (9.61) widely differ in finite samples. Although this might simply reveal a poor numerical approximation of the second partial derivative of the log-likelihood function, it might also be a sign of model misspecification. In this case, the sandwich quasi-maximum likelihood estimator of the information matrix proposed by White (1982) may be preferable:

$$\widehat{Var}(\hat{\gamma}) = T^{-1}\left[I_2(\hat{\gamma})(I_1(\hat{\gamma}))^{-1}I_2(\hat{\gamma})\right]. \tag{9.62}$$

We now further extend Example 9.4 to show whether the different methods may have major economic implications.

EXAMPLE 9.4 (Continued)

The standard errors of the model reported early on were based on the estimated Hessian matrix in Eq. (9.61). When we use instead the OPG estimator, we have:

$$x_{t+1}^{Japan} = \begin{cases} \underset{(0.238)}{0.416} & \text{if } S_{t+1}=1 \\ \underset{(0.695)}{0.206} & \text{if } S_{t+1}=2 \end{cases} + \underset{(0.163)}{0.071}\,x_t^{Japan} + \underset{(0.008)}{0.182}\,x_t^{US} - \underset{(0.000)}{0.073}\,rvxo_t$$

$$+\begin{cases} \underset{(0.000)}{3.854} & \text{if } S_{t+1}=1 \\ \underset{(0.000)}{7.265} & \text{if } S_{t+1}=2 \end{cases} .z_{t+1}^{Japan} \quad \hat{P} = \begin{bmatrix} 0.996 & 0.003 \\ 0.004 & 0.997 \end{bmatrix} \quad \overline{R}^2 = 0.057.$$

In fact, a few of the standard errors are now different, even though there is no clear direction. Although the standard errors reported do not clearly demand such a step (i.e., a few standard errors are identical under the Hessian- and OPG-based methods), it is always safer to consider reported White-corrected standard errors as in Eq. (9.62):

$$x_{t+1}^{Japan} = \begin{cases} \underset{(0.153)}{0.416} & \text{if } S_{t+1}=1 \\ \underset{(0.620)}{0.206} & \text{if } S_{t+1}=2 \end{cases} + \underset{(0.246)}{0.071}\,x_t^{Japan} + \underset{(0.018)}{0.182}\,x_t^{US} - \underset{(0.000)}{0.073}\,rvxo_t$$

$$+\begin{cases} \underset{(0.000)}{3.854} & \text{if } S_{t+1}=1 \\ \underset{(0.000)}{7.265} & \text{if } S_{t+1}=2 \end{cases} z_{t+1}^{Japan} \quad \hat{P} = \begin{bmatrix} 0.996 & 0.003 \\ 0.004 & 0.997 \end{bmatrix} \quad \overline{R}^2 = 0.057.$$

12. Notice though that the estimator for $\hat{\xi}_{1|0}$ is inconsistent due to the binary nature of its components.

9.5.2 Tests of Hypotheses

As a consequence of the results on consistency and asymptotic normality, and with one important exception, standard inferential procedures are available to test statistical hypotheses with relevant economic content. Starting with the usual aspects of testing procedures, assuming asymptotic normality for $\hat{\gamma}$, as implied by Eq. (9.58), the three classical tests are available. Call $\varphi:\mathbb{R}^q \to \mathbb{R}^r$, a function that imposes $q - r$ restrictions on the q-dimensional parameter vector $\boldsymbol{\theta}$. Note that $\boldsymbol{\theta}$ is a subvector of γ. We want to test H_0: $\varphi(\gamma) = \mathbf{0}$ vs. H_1: $\varphi(\gamma) \neq \mathbf{0}$ under the assumption that under both hypotheses, *the number of regimes K is identical.*[13] Such a null hypothesis—in fact this may be a vector of hypotheses, as emphasized by the fact that $\varphi(\gamma) = \mathbf{0}$ is $\mathbb{R}^q \to \mathbb{R}^r$—may be tested by using three alternative procedures. First, *Lagrange Multiplier (LM) tests* are undoubtedly the preferred tests as they only require the estimation of the restricted model. While the cumulative scores,

$$\mathbf{s}_T(\hat{\boldsymbol{\theta}}) \equiv \sum_{t=1}^{T} \mathbf{h}_t(\hat{\boldsymbol{\theta}}) = \sum_{t=1}^{T} \frac{\partial \ln p(\mathbf{y}_t|\Im_{t-1};\, \hat{\gamma})}{\partial \gamma} \tag{9.63}$$

of an *unrestricted* model have zero mean vector by construction, as these correspond to the FOCs for the vector $\boldsymbol{\theta}$, the scores of the *restricted* model obtained by ML and imposing $\varphi(\gamma) = \mathbf{0}$ can be used to obtain the standard test statistic:

$$LM \equiv \mathbf{s}_T(\tilde{\boldsymbol{\theta}}_r)' \left[\widehat{Var}(\tilde{\boldsymbol{\theta}}_r)\right]^{-1} \mathbf{s}_T(\tilde{\boldsymbol{\theta}}_r) \overset{D}{\to} \chi^2_r, \tag{9.64}$$

where $r \equiv rank\left(\partial\varphi(\boldsymbol{\theta})/\partial\boldsymbol{\theta}'\right)$ and $\tilde{\boldsymbol{\theta}}_r$ denotes the restricted estimator. The idea is that if the restriction is rejected by the data, while $\mathbf{s}_T(\hat{\boldsymbol{\theta}}) = \mathbf{0}$ by construction, $\mathbf{s}_T(\tilde{\boldsymbol{\theta}}_r)$ will be large. Therefore a suitable weighted sum of squares of such restricted, nonzero scores over your sample ought to be large. Here the weighting is performed using the estimated covariance matrix of the restricted estimates, $\widehat{Var}(\tilde{\boldsymbol{\theta}}_r)$, which can be computed in one of the three ways listed above. If such a weighted sum of squares deviations of the restricted scores from 0 is large, then given some prespecified size of the test, the sample statistic Eq. (9.64) will exceed the critical value under a χ^2_r and cause a rejection of the null hypothesis.

As an alternative, the *likelihood ratio (LR) test* may be employed,

$$\mathrm{LR}(r) \equiv 2\left[\ln L(\hat{\boldsymbol{\theta}}) - \ln L(\tilde{\boldsymbol{\theta}}_r)\right] \overset{D}{\to} \chi^2_r, \tag{9.65}$$

where $\ln L(\hat{\boldsymbol{\theta}})$ is the maximized log-likelihood under the unrestricted model and $\ln L(\tilde{\boldsymbol{\theta}}_r)$ is the maximized log-likelihood under the restricted one. Although very simple to compute and understand, this test requires the estimation of both the restricted and the unrestricted models, which for N large enough, can be quite cumbersome and requires a host of diagnostic checks on the performance of the EM algorithm in locating a truly global maximum of the likelihood function. However, it remains the case that an LR test is logically very simple: under the null hypothesis H_0: $\varphi(\gamma) = \mathbf{0}$ imposes a restriction involving $\boldsymbol{\theta}$. If these restrictions are rejected by the data, then maximizing the log-likelihood subject to a false constraint will prevent us from reaching the true maximum of the log-likelihood. It is like running carrying a heavy weight—you will end up being much slower than you otherwise would. Therefore $\ln L(\tilde{\boldsymbol{\theta}}_r)$ will be considerable inferior to $\ln L(\hat{\boldsymbol{\theta}})$, and $2[\ln L(\hat{\boldsymbol{\theta}}) - \ln L(\tilde{\boldsymbol{\theta}}_r)]$ will be large. If this is the case, given some prespecified size of the test, $2[\ln L(\hat{\boldsymbol{\theta}}) - \ln L(\tilde{\boldsymbol{\theta}}_r)]$ will exceed the critical value under a χ^2_r and lead to a rejection of the null hypothesis.

Finally, standard t- and F-statistics can be calculated using a *Wald test*: under asymptotic normality of the unrestricted ML estimator, $\hat{\boldsymbol{\theta}}$, and assuming the function $\varphi(\boldsymbol{\theta})$ is "smooth" and one-to-one, one can prove that:[14]

$$\begin{aligned} &\sqrt{T}\left[\varphi(\hat{\boldsymbol{\theta}}) - \varphi(\boldsymbol{\theta})\right] \overset{D}{\to} N\left(\mathbf{0}, \left.\frac{\partial\varphi(\boldsymbol{\theta})}{\partial\boldsymbol{\theta}}\right|_{\boldsymbol{\theta}=\hat{\boldsymbol{\theta}}} \widehat{Var}(\hat{\boldsymbol{\theta}})\left.\frac{\partial\varphi'(\boldsymbol{\theta})}{\partial\boldsymbol{\theta}'}\right|_{\boldsymbol{\theta}=\hat{\boldsymbol{\theta}}}\right) \text{ and} \\ &\mathrm{Wald} \equiv T(\varphi(\hat{\boldsymbol{\theta}}))' \left[\left.\frac{\partial\varphi(\boldsymbol{\theta})}{\partial\boldsymbol{\theta}'}\right|_{\boldsymbol{\theta}=\hat{\boldsymbol{\theta}}} \widehat{Var}(\hat{\boldsymbol{\theta}})\left.\frac{\partial\varphi'(\boldsymbol{\theta})}{\partial\boldsymbol{\theta}'}\right|_{\boldsymbol{\theta}=\hat{\boldsymbol{\theta}}}\right]^{-1} \varphi(\hat{\boldsymbol{\theta}}) \overset{D}{\to} \chi^2_r. \end{aligned} \tag{9.66}$$

Interestingly, also a Wald test has an asymptotic chi-square distribution with a number of degrees of freedom equal to the number r of restrictions that we want to test. However, this is not surprising, because asymptotically, as the

13. Hypotheses involving elements of ρ set equal to 0 cannot be entertained as simply as the ones in the main text as they fall on the boundaries of the parameter space and may imply a change in the number of the regimes. However, other hypotheses involving ρ can be tested without special cautions.

14. This follows from the fact that if $\hat{\boldsymbol{\theta}}$ is an ML estimator, under suitable technical conditions, also $\varphi(\hat{\boldsymbol{\theta}})$ is one ML estimator of $\varphi(\boldsymbol{\theta})$ and as such it is consistent and asymptotically normal.

number of degrees of freedom goes to infinity, a t -statistic will converge in distribution to a normal; moreover, the definition of the Wald statistic provided above employs a quadratic form that is a weighted square of normals and it is well known that a weighted sum of r squared normal distributions has a χ_r^2 distribution. The idea is that if the restrictions captured by H_0: $\varphi(\gamma)=\mathbf{0}$ are satisfied by $\hat{\boldsymbol{\theta}}$, then in correspondence to $\varphi(\hat{\boldsymbol{\theta}})\simeq\mathbf{0}$ and as such the quadratic form

$$(\varphi(\hat{\boldsymbol{\theta}}))'\left[\frac{\partial\varphi(\boldsymbol{\theta})}{\partial\boldsymbol{\theta}'}\bigg|_{\boldsymbol{\theta}=\hat{\boldsymbol{\theta}}}\widehat{Var}(\hat{\boldsymbol{\theta}})\frac{\partial\varphi'(\boldsymbol{\theta})}{\partial\boldsymbol{\theta}'}\bigg|_{\boldsymbol{\theta}=\hat{\boldsymbol{\theta}}}\right]^{-1}\varphi(\hat{\boldsymbol{\theta}})\simeq\mathbf{0}, \tag{9.67}$$

so that the null will not be rejected for most/all choices of size of the test under a χ_r^2. If, on the contrary, the quadratic form defined above were to give large values, then given some prespecified size of the test, it will exceed the critical value under a χ_r^2 and lead to a rejection of the null hypothesis. For instance, the hypothesis that in MSIVARH(K,p) the matrices of autoregressive coefficients are regime independent can be written as:

$$\begin{bmatrix} \mathbf{O}_N & \mathbf{O}_N & \cdots & \mathbf{I}_N & -\mathbf{I}_N & \mathbf{O}_N & \cdots & \mathbf{O}_N \\ \mathbf{O}_N & \mathbf{O}_N & \cdots & \mathbf{O}_N & \mathbf{I}_N & -\mathbf{I}_N & \cdots & \mathbf{O}_N \\ \vdots & \vdots & \ddots & \vdots & \vdots & \vdots & \ddots & \vdots \\ \mathbf{O}_N & \mathbf{O}_N & \cdots & \mathbf{O}_N & \mathbf{O}_N & \mathbf{O}_N & \cdots & \mathbf{O}_N \end{bmatrix}\begin{bmatrix} \boldsymbol{\mu}_1 \\ \boldsymbol{\mu}_2 \\ \vdots \\ \mathbf{A}_{11}'\mathbf{e}_1 \\ \vdots \\ \mathbf{A}_{1K}'\mathbf{e}_N \\ \vdots \\ \mathbf{A}_{pK}'\mathbf{e}_N \end{bmatrix} = \mathbf{R}vec(\mathbf{A})=\mathbf{0} \tag{9.68}$$

and implies the test statistic

$$T\hat{\boldsymbol{\theta}}'\mathbf{R}'\left[\mathbf{R}\widehat{Var}(\hat{\boldsymbol{\theta}})\mathbf{R}'\right]^{-1}\mathbf{R}\hat{\boldsymbol{\theta}} \tag{9.69}$$

is a simple F-statistic because in this case $\varphi(\boldsymbol{\theta})$ defines a linear function, as shown by the use of linear algebra to express the constraints.

What is the difference between LM, LR, and Wald tests? Which one should we be using, given a set of null hypotheses $\varphi(\boldsymbol{\theta})=\mathbf{0}$ that we would like to test? First, note that all the inferential results concerning the distribution of the test statistics listed above simply hold asymptotically, as $T\to\infty$, which was the meaning of the claim that LM, LR, Wald $\to^D \chi_r^2$. Second, this automatically answers our question, because we know how the test statistics behave only as the sample size grows without bounds, and therefore the idea is to assume that this is the case, using any of the three specific test procedures, becomes a matter of indifference. However, as already mentioned, there has been a time in which—because an LM test implies a need to estimate the MS model only under the restrictions implied by $\varphi(\boldsymbol{\theta})=\mathbf{0}$ (which often means to estimate less parameters than one would find in $\boldsymbol{\theta}$)—applied econometricians with scarce but costly computing power at their disposal developed a strong preference for LM tests.[15] Yet, it turns out that in general LM tests have rather poor small sample properties, which means that among the three tests, these are the ones converging in distribution to the χ_r^2, more slowly than the other test statistics do. Finally, when it comes to a choice between LM and Wald tests, it must be added that we still lack of sufficient knowledge for which of these two tests may perform best in small samples for MS models. However, because of their clear intuitive meaning and their direct reliance on the maximized log-likelihood function, many applied researchers tend to have a preference for LR tests, even though these imply estimating two different MS models, one unrestricted, and the other one restricted. Example 9.5 provides a few illustrations of how testing can be applied.

EXAMPLE 9.5

We now study how weekly excess returns on 10-year US Treasuries (over 1-month T-bill rates) over a 1986–2016 sample may depend on lagged implicit aggregate uncertainty (as proxied by the VXO) and the lagged slope of the US riskless yield curve, as proxied by the difference between 10-year and 1-month Treasury yields. A few asset pricing theories exist that imply that the ex-post excess returns on long-term Treasury should positively relate to volatility but be unrelated to the lagged term spread, for instance, the celebrated expectations hypothesis.

(Continued)

15. You may object that also under Wald tests, we shall need to estimate only the unrestricted model. This is correct, but the complication here arises from the need to estimate the quantity $\partial\varphi(\boldsymbol{\theta})/\partial\boldsymbol{\theta}'|_{\boldsymbol{\theta}=\hat{\boldsymbol{\theta}}}$.

EXAMPLE 9.5 (Continued)

A simple linear regression reveals that the lagged term spread surely forecasts higher excess returns while there is a bit more of uncertainty as to whether higher volatility may predict higher excess returns (*p*-values computed using White's sandwich form are in parentheses):

$$x_{t+1}^{10Y} = -\underset{(0.000)}{0.569} + \underset{(0.000)}{0.098}\, spread_t + \underset{(0.145)}{0.008}\, VXO_t + \underset{(0.000)}{1.112}\, z_{t+1}^{10Y} \quad \bar{R}^2 = 0.017.$$

Such results are a bit embarrassing to standard finance theory. However, an MS regression may reveal whether such an embarrassment may possibly characterize just one specific regime. We therefore generalize the regression to two- and three-state models and find that an MS regression with $K = 2$ provides the best trade-off between fit and parsimony. We find:

$$x_{t+1}^{10Y} = \begin{cases} -\underset{(0.000)}{1.121} & \text{if } S_{t+1} = 1 \\ -\underset{(0.000)}{0.604} & \text{if } S_{t+1} = 2 \end{cases} + \begin{cases} \underset{(0.277)}{0.062} & \text{if } S_{t+1} = 1 \\ \underset{(0.000)}{0.149} & \text{if } S_{t+1} = 2 \end{cases} spread_t + \begin{cases} \underset{(0.002)}{0.019} & \text{if } S_{t+1} = 1 \\ \underset{(0.000)}{0.018} & \text{if } S_{t+1} = 2 \end{cases} \mathrm{VXO}_t$$

$$+ \begin{cases} \underset{(0.000)}{1.355} & \text{if } S_{t+1} = 1 \\ \underset{(0.000)}{0.799} & \text{if } S_{t+1} = 2 \end{cases} z_{t+1}^{10Y} \quad \hat{\mathbf{P}} = \begin{bmatrix} \dfrac{\exp\left(\underset{(0.000)}{2.822}\right)}{1+\exp\left(\underset{(0.000)}{2.822}\right)} & \dfrac{1}{1+\exp\left(\underset{(0.000)}{2.822}\right)} \\ \dfrac{\exp\left(-\underset{(0.000)}{3.164}\right)}{1+\exp\left(-\underset{(0.000)}{3.164}\right)} & \dfrac{1}{1+\exp\left(-\underset{(0.000)}{3.164}\right)} \end{bmatrix} = \begin{bmatrix} 0.943 & 0.057 \\ 0.040 & 0.960 \end{bmatrix}.$$

The adjusted R^2 raises to 0.022 and the maximized log-likelihood is −2379.0443. There is a first regime characterized by high variance and in which excess bond returns are not predictable using past term spread values; in the second regime, however, the puzzling predictability power of past term spreads for excess bond returns reemerges. In both regimes, it remains the case that past VXO forecasts subsequent, higher excess long-term Treasury returns. Note that the transition probabilities have been indirectly estimated through the reparameterization:

$$\Pr\left(S_{t+1} = j \mid S_t = i; \delta_{ij}\right) = \frac{\exp(\delta_{ij})}{\exp(\delta_{i1}) + \exp(\delta_{i2})} \quad \exp(\delta_{12}) = \exp(\delta_{22}) = 1,$$

which leads to estimate δ_{11} and δ_{21}, both defined over the real line, but has the advantage of allowing us to compute standard errors (this is hard in the case of the original transition probabilities because, being probabilities, they are just defined over [0,1] and inference becomes problematic when the point estimates fall close to the boundaries).

Faced with the estimates reported above, one wonders whether there is enough evidence of an RS effect in the coefficient that maps VXO into predicted excess bond returns. First, we can do that by performing a Wald test. We obtain a Wald statistic of type Eq. (9.69) that equals 0.00446 which commands a *p*-value of 0.947, such that the null that the same coefficient applies in the two regimes cannot be rejected. If instead we perform an LR test, we need to estimate the restricted model that carries one coefficient less than the unrestricted model:

$$x_{t+1}^{10Y} = \begin{cases} -\underset{(0.000)}{1.113} & \text{if } S_{t+1} = 1 \\ -\underset{(0.000)}{0.608} & \text{if } S_{t+1} = 2 \end{cases} + \begin{cases} \underset{(0.274)}{0.063} & \text{if} S_{t+1} = 1 \\ \underset{(0.000)}{0.149} & \text{if} S_{t+1} = 2 \end{cases} \cdot spread_t + \underset{(0.000)}{0.019}\, VXO_t$$

$$+ \begin{cases} \underset{(0.000)}{1.355} & \text{if } S_{t+1} = 1 \\ \underset{(0.000)}{0.799} & \text{if } S_{t+1} = 2 \end{cases} \cdot z_{t+1}^{10Y} \quad \hat{\mathbf{P}} = \begin{bmatrix} 0.944 & 0.056 \\ 0.040 & 0.960 \end{bmatrix}.$$

The maximized log-likelihood is essentially the same, −2379.0441. As a result, the LRT statistic is a meager 0.0006 which, under a chi-square with 1 degree of freedom implies a *p*-value of 0.999 and leads again to a failure to reject the null of no regime shifts in the coefficient associated to lagged VXO.

We also use Wald and LR tests to check instead whether there is statistically significant evidence against the restriction that the term spread predicts subsequent excess Treasury returns with the same coefficient across the two regimes. We find a Wald statistic of 1.648 which, by using the critical value of an *F*-statistic 1 and 1607 degrees of freedom, yields a *p*-value of 0.199; the associated LRT statistic is instead 2(2379.7211−2379.0441) = 0.677 which gives a *p*-value of 0.411. This leads to respecify the following, even more parsimonious, two-state MS model:

$$x_{t+1}^{10Y} = \begin{cases} -\underset{(0.000)}{1.279} & \text{if } S_{t+1} = 1 \\ -\underset{(0.000)}{0.578} & \text{if } S_{t+1} = 2 \end{cases} + \underset{(0.000)}{0.132}\, spread_t + \underset{(0.000)}{0.019}\, VXO_t + \begin{cases} \underset{(0.000)}{1.359} & \text{if } S_{t+1} = 1 \\ \underset{(0.000)}{0.808} & \text{if } S_{t+1} = 2 \end{cases} \varepsilon_{t+1}^{10Y}$$

$$\hat{\mathbf{P}} = \begin{bmatrix} 0.939 & 0.061 \\ 0.041 & 0.959 \end{bmatrix}.$$

(Continued)

EXAMPLE 9.5 (Continued)

At this point, the model cannot be further simplified. For instance, the restriction that the intercept is the same across the two regimes implies a Wald statistic of 50.281, which has a *p*-value of 0.000 under an *F* with 1 and 1608 degrees of freedom, and an LR statistic of 2(2399.4462−2379.7211) = 39.450, which gives a *p*-value of 0.000 under a chi-square with 1 degree of freedom. This model poses the initial puzzle in its fullness: even in the presence of regimes, the term spread always forecasts excess long-term bond returns. Note how misleading it would be to think that the term spread actually has a regime-specific impact on excess returns just contrasting the *p*-values (one is 0.274 and the other 0.000) obtained for different coefficient estimates. However, modeling regimes has a desirable effect: it helps to flesh out the full forecasting power of volatility for future excess returns. For completeness, Fig. 9.14 plots filtered and smoothed regime 1 probabilities of the restricted model shown above. This is a regime of negative and volatile excess long-term bond returns that characterizes on average 40.2% of any long sample and has an average duration of 4 months. Because state probabilities must sum to 1 and there are only two regimes, the plots for regime 2 are easily inferred and it is common not to report them.

The implied state probabilities frequently switch between the extremes and spend little time around intermediate values, which is a positive indication for the quality of the fit of an MS model. Of course, it remains questionable whether the number of featured shifts between regimes may be plausible.

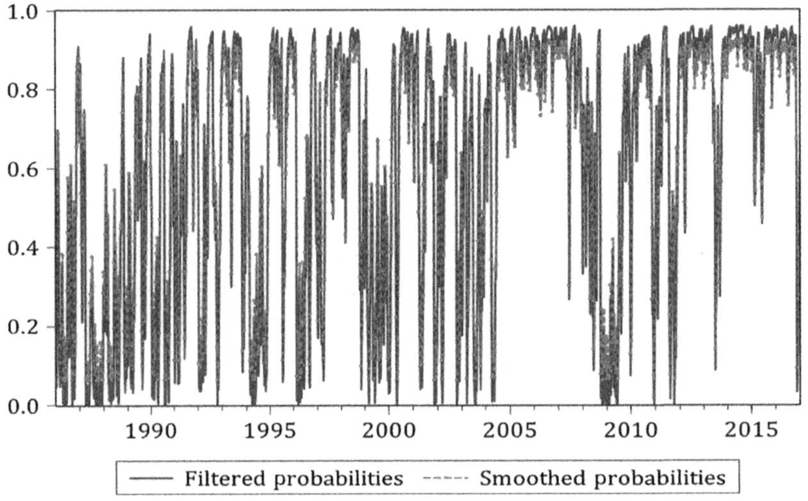

FIGURE 9.14 Filtered and smoothed state probabilities of regime 1 from two-state MS heteroskedastic regression.

9.5.3 Testing and Selecting the Number of Regimes and the Nuisance Parameters Problem

The only exception to the methods to test hypotheses that we have just introduced concerns the number of nonzero columns of the transition matrix **P**, that is, *the number of regimes*, K. In this case, even under the assumption of asymptotic normality of the ML estimator $\hat{\gamma}$, standard testing procedures suffer from nonstandard asymptotic distributions of the test statistics due to the existence of *nuisance parameters* under the null hypothesis. As we saw already, when $K = 1$, an MS model boils down to a standard, homoskedastic VAR(p) in standard form. Therefore a first important divide occurs in correspondence to the choice as to whether $K = 1$ or $K \geq 2$. Once $K \geq 2$ has been established, then one may even worry about whether more than two regimes may be needed. The problem is then how do we test for the appropriate number of regimes or in any event proceed to select them?

The problem with the choice of the number of states is that under any number of regimes smaller than some "starting" (alternative) hypothesis value K^*, there are a few structural parameters of the unrestricted model—the elements of the transition probability matrix associated with the rows that correspond to disappearing states—that can take any value without influencing the resulting likelihood function. For instance, for $K^* = 2$, the transition matrix is—in the light of the sum-up constraints that apply in each row—characterized by the parameters p_{11} and p_{22}, both constrained in [0,1]. When the number of states is restricted to 1, then the transition matrix **P** collapses to $p_{11} = 1$ only: at this point

p_{22} stops affecting the likelihood function and therefore under the null of a single-state can take any values without this being recorded by the optimization algorithms. Similarly, when $K^* = 3$ we know that:

$$\boldsymbol{P} = \begin{bmatrix} p_{11} & p_{12} & 1-p_{11}-p_{12} \\ p_{21} & p_{22} & 1-p_{21}-p_{22} \\ 1-p_{32}-p_{33} & p_{32} & p_{33} \end{bmatrix}. \tag{9.70}$$

When the null hypothesis of $K = 2$ is tested, then **P** just includes p_{11} and p_{22}, so that p_{12}, p_{21}, p_{32} and p_{33} become unidentified and stop affecting the log-likelihood. We say that *these parameters become a nuisance to the estimation.* Mathematically, the result is that the presence of these nuisance parameters gives the likelihood surface so many degrees of freedom that computationally one can never reject the null that the nonnegative (better, positive) values of those parameters were purely due to sampling variation.[16] For instance, suppose that we start with an MSIH(3) model,

$$\mathbf{y}_{t+1} = \boldsymbol{\mu}_{S_{t+1}} + \boldsymbol{\Sigma}_{S_{t+1}}\boldsymbol{\varepsilon}_{t+1} \quad \boldsymbol{\varepsilon}_{t+1} \sim \text{IID } N(\mathbf{0}, \mathbf{I}_N), \tag{9.71}$$

but we would like to test whether $K = 2 < K^* = 3$ may be optimal. Suppose you are to compare the maximized log-likelihood obtained from the three-state model, $\ell(\hat{\boldsymbol{\gamma}}|\{\mathbf{y}_t\}_{t=1}^T; K = 3)$, to the log-likelihood of the restricted model in which $K = 2$ so that $\boldsymbol{\mu}_3$, $\boldsymbol{\Sigma}_3$ and especially the (1,2), (2,1), (3,2) and (3,3) elements of the transition matrix can be set to any value without affecting $\ell(\hat{\boldsymbol{\gamma}}|\{\mathbf{y}_t\}_{t=1}^T; K = 2)$.

Unfortunately, the nuisance parameter problem makes the standard Wald and LR tests invalid, in the sense that even in expanding samples, the distribution of the corresponding statistics fail to converge to a χ_r^2, where r is the number of restrictions implied from passing from some K^*-regime model to a model with a lower number of regimes. In fact, even in the simple classical case of Gaussian mixture models, it has been long known that the LR statistic diverges to infinity at the rate of $\ln(\ln T)$. There are, however, a number of ideas in the literature on how to deal with such identification issues.

As already mentioned in Chapter 8, Hansen (1996) has proposed to treat the log-likelihood as a function of the unknown and nonestimable nuisance parameters so that the asymptotic distribution is generated in each case numerically (i.e., by simulation) from a grid of transition and regime-dependent nuisance parameters. This test belongs then to the so-called *sup class of tests*, for instance:

$$\sup_{\boldsymbol{\lambda} \in \Lambda} LR(\boldsymbol{\lambda}|\{\mathbf{y}_t\}_{t=1}^T) \tag{9.72}$$

(but "sup" versions of LM and Wald tests can also be applied, see Altissimo and Corradi, 2002), where $\boldsymbol{\lambda}$ is the subset of the parameters that become a nuisance and Λ is a suitably chosen compact subset of the parameter space; under regularity conditions, Eq. (9.72), will indeed have a limiting distribution for which asymptotic p-values and critical values can be obtained by simulation. The resulting LR test statistic converges in distribution to a complex function and in most cases a closed-form expression cannot be found and an upper bound for the true critical value of the test statistic can be calculated by simulation and therefore becomes data-dependent. Hansen's way to empirically compute the p-values of LR tests is logically straightforward but computationally intensive because it requires a good command of *bootstrap methodologies*, see the Appendix to chapter 1.

Instead, Davies (1977) had already reported *bounds for the LR statistic, by using approximations:*[17]

$$\Pr(\text{LR}(r) > x) \leq \Pr(\chi_1^2 > x) + \sqrt{2x}\exp\left(-\frac{x}{2}\right)\left[\Gamma\left(\frac{1}{2}\right)\right]^{-1}. \tag{9.73}$$

Davidson and MacKinnon's (1981) *J-test for nonnested models* can be also applied, because MS models with K versus $K-1$ regimes are logically nested but cannot be treated as such on a statistical basis.[18] The test is implemented by estimating both the models with K and $K-1$ regimes and calculating their full information fitted values on the basis of the smoothed probabilities, $\hat{\mathbf{y}}_t^{(j)} = \mathbf{X}_t\hat{\mathbf{A}}^{(j)}\hat{\boldsymbol{\xi}}_{t|T}^{(j)}$, for $t = 1, 2, \ldots, T$, $j = K-1$ and K, and where the notation is identical to the one used above. At this point, the J-test is based on the regression:

$$\mathbf{y}_t = \mathbf{c} + (\mathbf{I}_N - \boldsymbol{\Upsilon})\hat{\mathbf{y}}_t^{(K-1)} + \boldsymbol{\Upsilon}\hat{\mathbf{y}}_t^{(K)} + \boldsymbol{\varepsilon}_t. \tag{9.74}$$

16. Formally, the presence of unidentified nuisance parameters implies that the scores become identically 0 and their covariance matrix is singular.
17. Davies' bound applies if the log-likelihood function has a single peak (i.e., only one stationary point).
18. Two models are nested if one can go from Model A to Model B just by turning off (i.e., setting to 0) a few of the parameters.

The p-value of an F-test applied to the $N \times 1$ vector of intercepts $\hat{\mathbf{c}}$ and the $N \times N$ matrix of estimated coefficients $\hat{\boldsymbol{\Upsilon}}$ (each row of coefficients can be simply estimated by OLS) gives the p-value for the null of $K-1$ regimes against the alternative hypothesis of K regimes. The intuition is that if a joint F (hence, Wald) test cannot reject the null that $\boldsymbol{c} \simeq \mathbf{0}$ and $\boldsymbol{\Upsilon} \simeq \mathbf{O}$, then this means that once the fitted return values produced by a $(K-1)$-state model have been computed, no significant explanatory power may be further derived from the fitted values of a larger, K-state MS model. On the opposite if the null hypotheses that $\boldsymbol{c} = \mathbf{0}$, $\boldsymbol{\Upsilon} = \mathbf{O}$ can be rejected at a given size of the F-test, then it means that there is evidence of the fact that one also needs the last, additional Kth regime in order to explain returns, so that K regimes may be preferred to $K-1$.

A practical alternative to these formal statistical test procedures to select the number of regimes most appropriate in an MS model consists of the use of information criteria that we have already discussed and employed multiple times also in this chapter. The general structure of the information criteria is $-\max_{\boldsymbol{\gamma}} \ell(\boldsymbol{\gamma} | \{\mathbf{y}_t\}_{t=1}^{T}; K) + f(\dim(\hat{\boldsymbol{\gamma}}))$, where $f(\cdot)$ is a penalty function, and $\dim(\hat{\boldsymbol{\gamma}})$ is the notation of a counter of the number of different parameters to be estimated in $\boldsymbol{\gamma} \in \Gamma$, which in the case of MS models will include both the elements of transition matrix and the variances and covariances of the errors. Because the maximized log-likelihood is multiplied by -1 while the penalty has been added, it is clear that empirically we shall select models that actually *minimize information criteria*, not maximize them. We now extend Example 9.5 to show how these measures and statistical procedures can be implemented in practice.

EXAMPLE 9.5 (Continued)

We now worry about two issues: first, should a simple regression model for the excess returns on 10-year US Treasuries be specified in place of the MSIH(2) regression investigated above; second, given an MSIH(K) selection, is there evidence of a need of three instead of two regimes?

In terms of LR tests, the linear, single-state model achieves a maximized log-likelihood of -2382.99, while the MSIH(2) regression on which we have settled early on, achieves a maximized log-likelihood of -2379.21; the corresponding maximized log-likelihood for an MSIH(3) model is -2343.91. Therefore the LRT for two versus one regime is a modest 7.56, which leads to a failure to reject the null of a single-regime, with or without taking into account the nuisance parameter problem (the p-values are respectively 0.161, by using Davies' approximation and 0.109, considering that four restrictions are imposed). This is exceedingly interesting: both Wald and LR tests led to rejecting the null that $\mu_1 = \mu_2$ and $\sigma_1 = \sigma_2$, but when we formally test for the presence of regimes, the evidence is very faint in the available data. The oddity grows when we perform two more tests. The LRT of the null of $K = 1$ versus the alternative of $K = 3$ implies an LRT of $2(2382.99 - 2343.91) = 70.60$ that, under 10 restrictions, implies a rejection regardless of whether identification issues are ignored or not. Similarly, the LRT of the null of $K = 2$ versus the alternative of $K = 3$ implies an LRT of $2(2379.21 - 2343.91) = 78.16$ that, under six restrictions, implies a rejection regardless of whether identification issues are ignored or not. This shows the vagaries of sequential testing methods: there is clear-cut evidence of three regimes versus two or one, but no evidence of two regimes and one may be lured into the conclusion that a simple regression model may be sufficient.

Let us now check what the information criteria may reveal, even though one needs little calculations when faced with cases in which the log-likelihood hardly climbs when parameters are added, as in the case in which we go from $K = 1$ to $K = 2$. For the single-, two-, and three-regime MS regressions, the SBIC values are 2.9901, 2.9818, and 2.9694, respectively; the H-Q values are 2.9691, 2.9650, and 2.9400, respectively. Under both criteria (but the conclusions are the same when AIC is considered), one should specify a three-state MSI regression, as the criteria are minimized. However, according to the information criteria, it is remarkable that a two-state model is preferred over a single-state one, which was already our remark in the first part of this example. Even though it is not simple to make sense or attach a meaning to the difference between information criteria scores, we note that the improvement (decline) when going from two to three regimes remains substantial. We therefore perform estimation of the three-state model (p-values are in parentheses and computed using White's version of the ML covariance matrix):

$$x_{t+1}^{10Y} = \begin{cases} \underset{(0.001)}{-0.377} & \text{if } S_{t+1} = 1 \\ \underset{(0.000)}{-1.598} & \text{if } S_{t+1} = 2 \\ \underset{(0.009)}{-0.922} & \text{if } S_{t+1} = 3 \end{cases} + \underset{(0.000)}{0.129}\ spread_t + \underset{(0.007)}{0.013}\ VXO_t + \begin{cases} \underset{(0.000)}{0.799} & \text{if } S_{t+1} = 1 \\ \underset{(0.000)}{0.906} & \text{if } S_{t+1} = 2 \\ \underset{(0.000)}{2.030} & \text{if } S_{t+1} = 3 \end{cases} z_{t+1}^{10Y} \qquad \hat{\boldsymbol{P}} = \begin{bmatrix} 0.904 & 0.089 & 0.007 \\ 0.254 & 0.742 & 0.004 \\ 0.015 & 0.058 & 0.927 \end{bmatrix}.$$

The estimated MC has a special structure: it is very hard (but not impossible, as the chain is irreducible) to access the highly volatile regime 3, but when this occurs, the implied duration is almost 14 weeks.

It is now time to apply Davidson's J-test. For all the three models invoked, we compute the time series of the fitted values implied by the smoothed probabilities. We then regress the actual data for the 10-year excess bond returns on such values,

(Continued)

EXAMPLE 9.5 (Continued)

restricting the sum of the two coefficients to be equal to 1. We do so separately for one- and two-state, one- and three-state, and two- and three-state models obtaining (robust standard errors are in parentheses):

$$\text{Linear versus MSIH(2)}: x_t^{10Y} = \underset{(0.0309)}{-0.0008} + (1 - \underset{(0.7539)}{0.6096})\hat{x}_t^{Linear} + \underset{(0.7539)}{0.6096}\,\hat{x}_t^{K=2} + u_t$$

$$\text{Linear versus MSIH(3)}: x_t^{10Y} = \underset{(0.0293)}{0.0016} + (1 - \underset{(0.1882)}{0.9818})\hat{x}_t^{Linear} + \underset{(0.1882)}{0.9818}\,\hat{x}_t^{K=3} + u_t$$

$$\text{MSIH(2) versus MSIH(3)}: x_t^{10Y} = \underset{(0.0292)}{0.0017} + (1 - \underset{(0.2167)}{1.0281})\hat{x}_t^{K=2} + \underset{(0.2167)}{1.0281}\,\hat{x}_t^{K=3} + u_t.$$

Confirming earlier evidence, the coefficient on the two-state model in the first regression is different from 1 so that the coefficient on the linear model is positive, even though none of the coefficients is significantly different from 0, and doubts exist as to whether a two-state model is actually needed. In the remaining two regressions, the coefficient on the largest MS model is not significantly different from 1 so that the coefficient on the smallest MS model (linear in the second regression) is not significantly different from 0: therefore we reject a linear model in favor of $K=3$, and we reject $K=2$ in favor of $K=3$. Fig. 9.15 compares actual excess returns to the in-sample predictions from each of the models that were used in the *J*-test regressions. The superiority of the three-state MS model is probably visible, even though all models offer a variability of the forecasts largely inferior to the actual data.

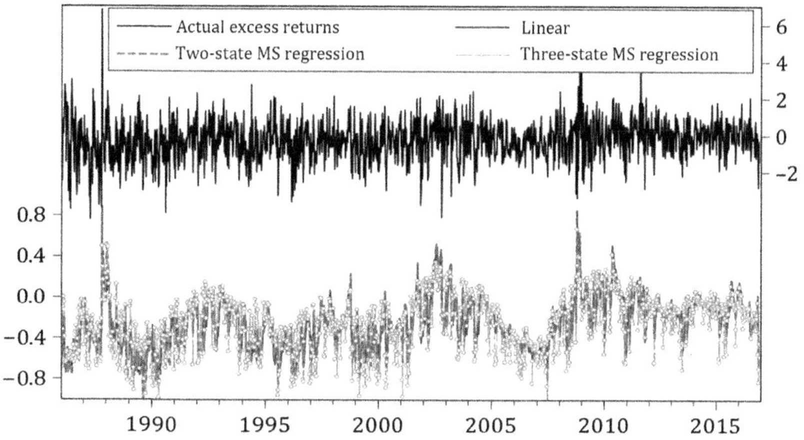

FIGURE 9.15 In-sample predictions of 10-year treasury excess returns from three alternative models.

An online appendix shows how to deal with the fact that an MS model has been estimated, the need of further improvements could arise that requires performing a few diagnostic checks.

9.6 FORECASTING WITH MARKOV SWITCHING MODELS

Under a mean squared forecast error (MSFE) criterion, the required algorithms are relatively simple in spite of the non-linearity of the MS class of processes. An MSFE criterion has a simple meaning: you care for minimizing the *square* of the forecast errors, $\eta_{t+H} \equiv y_{t+H} - y_t^f(H|\Im_t)$, where $y_t^f(H|\Im_t)$ is a $N \times 1$ vector of forecasts that simply conditions on the information available at time t. Under such MSFE criterion and appealing once more to the state-space representation in Appendix 9.B, we obtain rather intuitive results. Ignoring for the time being the issue of parameter uncertainty, that is, the fact that the parameters of the MS process are unknown and must therefore be estimated, the prediction function minimizing MSFE is the standard conditional expectation, $y_t^f(H|\Im_t) = E[y_{t+H}|\Im_t]$. For instance, in the case of one-step-ahead forecasts, we have:

$$E[\mathbf{y}_{t+1}|\Im_t] = \mathbf{X}_{t+1}\hat{\mathbf{A}}(\hat{\boldsymbol{\xi}}_{t+1|t} \otimes \boldsymbol{\iota}_N), \tag{9.75}$$

where the notation is by now standard and $\hat{\boldsymbol{\xi}}_{t+1|t}$ is the vector of one-step-ahead, predicted state probabilities to be filtered out of the available information set $\Im_t$ according to the known transition equation $\hat{\boldsymbol{\xi}}_{t+1|t} = \hat{\mathbf{P}}'\hat{\boldsymbol{\xi}}_{t|t}$, where also the transition matrix $\mathbf{P}$ will have to be estimated. Note that because $\mathbf{X}_t$ is a $N \times (Np+1)$ matrix of predetermined variables with structure $[1\ \mathbf{y}'_{t-1}\ldots\mathbf{y}'_{t-p}]\otimes\iota_N$ and $\mathbf{A}$ is a $(Np+1)\times NK$ matrix collecting the VAR parameters, both intercepts and autoregressive coefficients, in all regimes, then

$$\mathbf{X}_{t+1}\hat{\mathbf{A}} = \underbrace{([1\,\mathbf{y}'_t\ldots\mathbf{y}'_{t-p+1}]\otimes\iota_N)}_{N\times(Np+1)}\underbrace{\begin{bmatrix}\hat{\mu}'_1 & \hat{\mu}'_2 & \cdots & \hat{\mu}'_K\\ \hat{\mathbf{A}}_{11} & \hat{\mathbf{A}}_{12} & \cdots & \hat{\mathbf{A}}_{1K}\\ \vdots & \vdots & \ddots & \vdots\\ \hat{\mathbf{A}}_{p1} & \hat{\mathbf{A}}_{p2} & \cdots & \hat{\mathbf{A}}_{pK}\end{bmatrix}}_{(Np+1)\times NK}$$
$$= \begin{bmatrix}\hat{\mu}'_1+\sum_{j=1}^{p}\mathbf{y}'_{t+1-j}\hat{\mathbf{A}}_{j1} & \hat{\mu}'_2+\sum_{j=1}^{p}\mathbf{y}'_{t+1-j}\hat{\mathbf{A}}_{j2} & \cdots & \hat{\mu}'_K+\sum_{j=1}^{p}\mathbf{y}'_{t+1-j}\hat{\mathbf{A}}_{jK}\\ \hat{\mu}'_1+\sum_{j=1}^{p}\mathbf{y}'_{t+1-j}\hat{\mathbf{A}}_{j1} & \hat{\mu}'_2+\sum_{j=1}^{p}\mathbf{y}'_{t+1-j}\hat{\mathbf{A}}_{j2} & \cdots & \hat{\mu}'_K+\sum_{j=1}^{p}\mathbf{y}'_{t+1-j}\hat{\mathbf{A}}_{jK}\\ \vdots & \vdots & \ddots & \vdots\\ \hat{\mu}'_1+\sum_{j=1}^{p}\mathbf{y}'_{t+1-j}\hat{\mathbf{A}}_{j1} & \hat{\mu}'_2+\sum_{j=1}^{p}\mathbf{y}'_{t+1-j}\hat{\mathbf{A}}_{j2} & \cdots & \hat{\mu}'_K+\sum_{j=1}^{p}\mathbf{y}'_{t+1-j}\hat{\mathbf{A}}_{jK}\end{bmatrix} \tag{9.76}$$

and Eq. (9.75) follows. For instance in the univariate case of $N=1$ and assuming $p=1$, that is, in the case of an MS(I) ARH(K,1) model, we have:

$$E[y_{t+1}|\Im_t] = \sum_{k=1}^{K}(\mu_k + a_k y_t)\hat{\xi}^k_{t+1|t}. \tag{9.77}$$

This expression means that one forecasts conditioning on each of the K regimes, and then each of these state-specific predictions is weighted by the appropriate predicted probabilities.

As usual, when it comes to forecasting conditional means, the regime-specific second moments are irrelevant because under a standard MS setup, the errors are IID $N(\mathbf{0},\ \boldsymbol{\Sigma}_{S_{t+1}})$ and hence have zero mean (vector). However, for $h>$ one-step-ahead forecasts the task is much more challenging as:

- $\mathbf{X}_{t+H}$ is unknown and must be predicted itself.
- $E[\mathbf{X}_{t+H}|\Im_t]$ involves sequences of predictions $\{E[\mathbf{y}_{t+1}|\Im_t],\ \ldots, E[\mathbf{y}_{t+H-1}|\Im_{t+T-2}]\}$ and as such the sequence $\{\hat{\xi}_{t+1|t},\ldots,\ \hat{\xi}_{t+H-1|t}\}$ which are likely to impress patterns of cross-correlation to the forecasts, because of the very presence of switching among persistent states. For instance, for $H=2$, $p=1$, and ignoring the presence of an intercept term, we have:

$$\begin{aligned}E[\mathbf{y}_{t+2}|\Im_t] &= E\left[(\mathbf{y}'_{t+1}\otimes\iota_N)\hat{\mathbf{A}}\left(\boldsymbol{\xi}_{t+2}\otimes\iota_N\right)|\Im_t\right]\\ &= E\left[\left(\left((\mathbf{y}'_t\otimes\iota_N)\hat{\mathbf{A}}\left(\boldsymbol{\xi}_{t+1}\otimes\iota_N\right)+\hat{\boldsymbol{\Sigma}}_K\left(\boldsymbol{\xi}_{t+1}\otimes\mathbf{I}_N\right)\boldsymbol{\varepsilon}_t\right)\otimes\iota'_N\right)\hat{\mathbf{A}}\left(\boldsymbol{\xi}_{t+2}\otimes\iota_N\right)|\Im_t\right]\\ &= E\left[\left((\mathbf{y}'_t\otimes\iota_N)\hat{\mathbf{A}}\left(\boldsymbol{\xi}_{t+1}\otimes\iota_N\right)\otimes\iota'_n+\hat{\boldsymbol{\Sigma}}_K\left(\boldsymbol{\xi}_{t+1}\otimes\mathbf{I}_N\right)\boldsymbol{\varepsilon}_t\otimes\iota'_N\right)\hat{\mathbf{A}}\left(\boldsymbol{\xi}_{t+2}\otimes\iota_N\right)|\Im_t\right]\\ &= E\left[\left((\mathbf{y}'_t\otimes\iota_N)\hat{\mathbf{A}}\left(\boldsymbol{\xi}_{t+1}\otimes\iota_N\right)\otimes\iota'_N\right)\hat{\mathbf{A}}\left(\boldsymbol{\xi}_{t+2}\otimes\iota_N\right)|\Im_t\right]\end{aligned} \tag{9.78}$$

which is not simply the product of the conditional expectations $[(\mathbf{y}'_t\otimes\iota_N)\hat{\mathbf{A}}(\hat{\boldsymbol{\xi}}_{t+1|t}\otimes\iota_N)\otimes\iota'_N]\hat{\mathbf{A}}(\hat{\boldsymbol{\xi}}_{t+2|t}\otimes\iota_N)$ as the future state vectors $\boldsymbol{\xi}_{t+1}$ and $\boldsymbol{\xi}_{t+2}$ are correlated, $\boldsymbol{\xi}_{t+2}=\mathbf{P}'\boldsymbol{\xi}_{t+1}+\mathbf{v}_{t+2}$. However, in applied work it is customary to follow the suggestion of Doan et al. (1984) consisting in the substitution of the sequence of predicted values $\{E[\mathbf{y}_{t+1}|\Im_t],\ldots,\ E[\mathbf{y}_{t+H-1}|\Im_t]\}$ in place of $\{E[\mathbf{y}_{t+1}|\Im_t],\ldots, E[\mathbf{y}_{t+H-1}|\Im_{t+T-2}]\}$. This case (one-step-ahead forecast) generalizes to generic $H>$ two-step-ahead predictions:

$$\breve{E}[\mathbf{y}_{t+H}|\Im_t] = E[\mathbf{X}_{t+H}|\Im_t]\hat{\mathbf{A}}\left[(\hat{\mathbf{P}}')^H\hat{\boldsymbol{\xi}}_{t|t}\otimes\iota_N\right], \tag{9.79}$$

which in practice gives a recursive formula since $E[\mathbf{X}_{t+H}|\Im_t]$ forces one to forecast a sequence of future $\mathbf{y}_{t+i}$ values, $i=1,\ldots, H-1$. For instance, in the univariate case of $N=1$ and assuming $p=1$, that is, for an MS(I)ARH(K,1) model, we have that:

$$E[y_{t+2}|\Im_t] = \sum_{k=1}^{K}(\mu_k + a_k E[y_{t+1}|\Im_t,\ \hat{\xi}^k_{t+1|t}])\hat{\xi}^k_{t+2|t+1}, \tag{9.80}$$

and this is not the same as

$$\begin{aligned}
\breve{E}[y_{t+2}|\Im_t] &= \sum_{k=1}^{K}(\mu_k + a_k E[y_{t+1}|\Im_t])\hat{\xi}^k_{t+2|t} \\
&= \sum_{k=1}^{K}\mu_k\hat{\xi}^k_{t+2|t} + \sum_{k=1}^{K}a_k E[y_{t+1}|\Im_t]\hat{\xi}^k_{t+2|t} \\
&= \sum_{k=1}^{K}\mu_k\hat{\xi}^k_{t+2|t} + \sum_{k=1}^{K}a_k\left(\sum_{k=1}^{K}(\mu_k + a_k y_t)\hat{\xi}^k_{t+1|t}\right)\hat{\xi}^k_{t+2|t} \\
&= \sum_{k=1}^{K}\mu_k\hat{\xi}^k_{t+2|t} + \sum_{k=1}^{K}a_k\left(\sum_{j=1}^{K}\mu_j\hat{\xi}^j_{t+1|t}\right)\hat{\xi}^k_{t+2|t} + \sum_{k=1}^{K}a_k\left(\sum_{j=1}^{K}a_j y_t\hat{\xi}^j_{t+1|t}\right)\hat{\xi}^k_{t+2|t}.
\end{aligned} \tag{9.81}$$

However, $\breve{E}[y_{t+2}|\Im_t]$ and similar formulas are what are reported in most applied work. In Example 9.6 we offer one leading, famous example that assesses the forecasting power of MS models.

EXAMPLE 9.6

Are MS models useful to forecast monthly S&P 500 stock index returns? We tackle this question by using 564 observations spanning the period January 1970–December 2016. On the one hand, we know from Chapters 2 and 5, that the answer tends to be disappointing as far as time series models of the conditional mean are concerned. In fact, also in this case, a preliminary analysis reveals that both AR and MA terms are never statistically significant and that all information criteria select a simple ARMA(0,0), that is, an IID, model, characterized by an SBIC of 5.797 and an H-Q criterion of 5.792. On the other hand, there is strong evidence of MS in the variance of S&P 500 index returns: even a simple MSH(2) model yields an SBIC of 5.737 and an H-Q criterion of 5.714. This fact is well known in the literature since seminal work by Turner et al. (1989). In fact, a carefully conducted model specification search leads to settle on MSIH(2) model with time-varying transition probabilities (in which lagged returns affect transition probabilities 1 month later), for which the SBIC is 5.712 and the H-Q criterion is 5.674. The estimated model is (sandwich-form standard errors are in parentheses):

$$R^{S\&P}_{t+1} = \begin{cases} \underset{(0.723)}{0.200} & \text{if } S_{t+1}=1 \\ \underset{(0.000)}{0.901} & \text{if } S_{t+1}=2 \end{cases} + \begin{cases} \underset{(0.000)}{6.147} & \text{if } S_{t+1}=1 \\ \underset{(0.000)}{3.141} & \text{if } S_{t+1}=2 \end{cases}\varepsilon^{S\&P}_{t+1},$$

$$\hat{\mathbf{P}} = \begin{bmatrix} \dfrac{\exp\left(\underset{(0.903)}{1729.2} - \underset{(0.914)}{248.43}R^{S\&P}_t\right)}{\exp\left(\underset{(0.903)}{1729.2} - \underset{(0.914)}{248.43}R^{S\&P}_t\right) + \exp\left(\underset{(0.903)}{1729.2}\right)} & \dfrac{\exp\left(\underset{(0.903)}{1729.2}\right)}{\exp\left(\underset{(0.903)}{1729.2} - \underset{(0.914)}{248.43}R^{S\&P}_t\right) + \exp\left(\underset{(0.903)}{1729.2}\right)} \\ \dfrac{\exp\left(-\underset{(0.002)}{3.567} - \underset{(0.085)}{0.594}R^{S\&P}_t\right)}{\exp\left(-\underset{(0.002)}{3.567} - \underset{(0.085)}{0.594}R^{S\&P}_t\right) + \exp\left(-\underset{(0.002)}{3.567}\right)} & \dfrac{\exp\left(-\underset{(0.002)}{3.567}\right)}{\exp\left(-\underset{(0.002)}{3.567} - \underset{(0.085)}{0.594}R^{S\&P}_t\right) + \exp\left(-\underset{(0.002)}{3.567}\right)} \end{bmatrix}.$$

Clearly, regime 1 is a bear state with zero mean return and high variance, while regime 2 is a bull state in which variance is modest. In case you are puzzled by the association between negative mean returns and high risk, which seems to contradict the first principles in standard finance theory, an online supplement provides additional insights using MS technology. Low or negative current stock returns make the bear regime more persistent and the bull regime less persistent. Figs. 9.16 and 9.17 show the smoothed and transition probabilities implied by the model.

We finally come to the forecasting performance. Fig. 9.18 compares the forecasts derived from an IID model with those under MS. Of course, in an IID framework, the forecasts are just equal to the sample mean that is recursively adjusted over time. The plot shows that even though an MS model features a remarkable capability to adapt to produce small forecasts close to 0, it has no chance to anticipate extreme market swings in the order of $\pm 10\%$.

As often found in earlier literature, an MS model that is mostly (only?) fitting dynamics in the second moment has no chance to do a good job with the first moment. For instance, simple calculations reveal that while the linear model implies an RMSFE of 4.366 and a mean absolute error of 3.296, the two-state MS model scores 4.367 and 3.295, respectively. In essence, the MS model fails to improve much over a recursive mean forecast. Of course, matters may be different were the MS model applied to forecast the variance, see Guidolin (2009) for a related application.

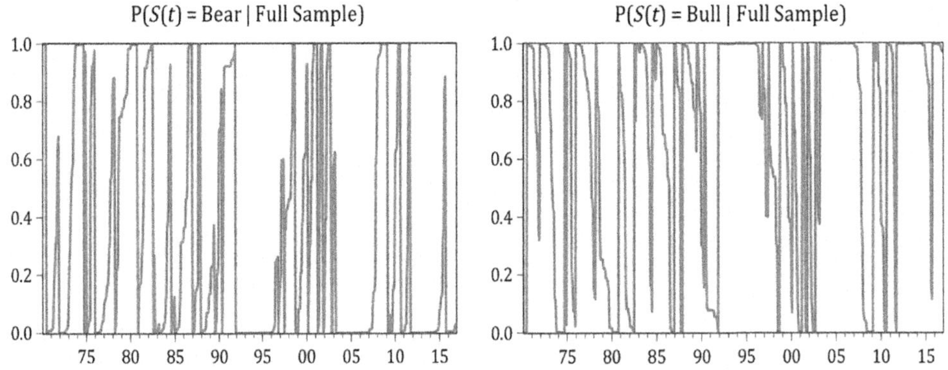

FIGURE 9.16 Smoothed probabilities from MSIH(2) model with time-varying probabilities.

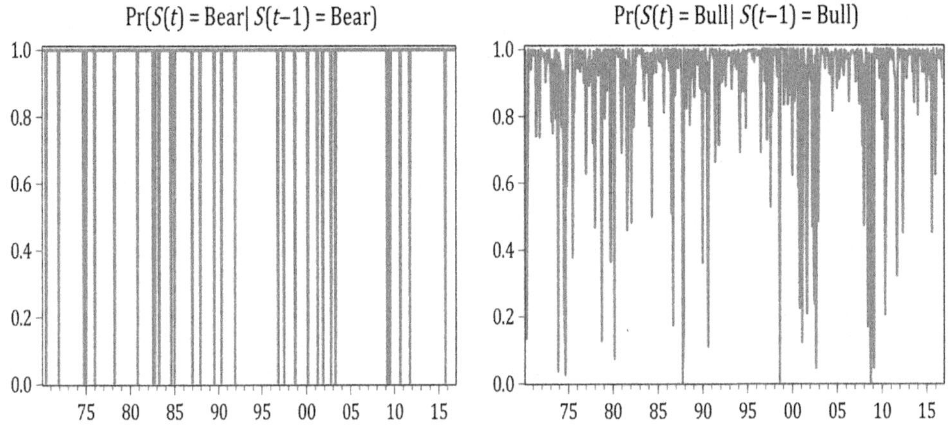

FIGURE 9.17 Time-varying probabilities from MSIH(2) model.

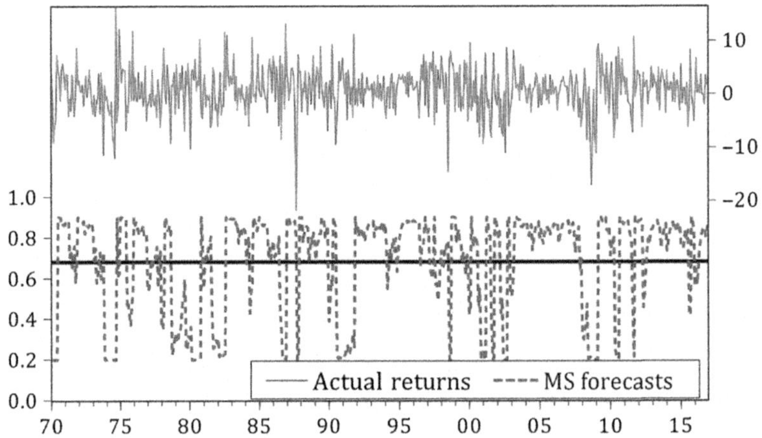

FIGURE 9.18 In-sample forecasts from MSIH(2) model with time-varying probabilities.

MS models are also powerful tools to forecast conditional higher order moments. In Section 9.2, we have generically argued that *mixtures* of normals driven by MS models may lead to capture strong nonnormalities in financial data. This makes MS an interesting alternative to other routes explored in Chapter 5 to generate realistic skewness and excess kurtosis (see Timmermann, 2000). Moreover, under MS predicted variance is not simply the weighted, predicted-probability average of the variances across the K regimes: the difference in means also contribute to variance because the switches among regimes generate important variations; these differences in regime means may also generate non-zero conditional skewness and kurtosis. Finally, differences in means in addition to differences in variances can generate persistence in levels as well as squared values akin to volatility persistence observed in many return series. An online appendix provides additional details on these aspects.

9.7 MARKOV SWITCHING ARCH AND DCC MODELS

One may wonder about the positioning of MS models within the logical path covered so far in Chapters 5–7. The path was marked by three incremental steps:

- Even after fitting relatively sophisticated GARCH models, standardized residuals from financial returns often remain non-Gaussian with evidence of thick tails and asymmetries, so that in Chapter 5, we have developed methods to model non-Gaussian returns.
- To deploy active risk and asset management methods, you need to model correlations, besides variances.
- DCC models are the most promising multivariate models of heteroskedastic dynamics in second moments.

Instead of representing a separate approach, MS models perfectly fit the logical sequence illustrated above, in at least two ways. MS models represent distinct, practical, and powerful solutions to these problems because an MS framework can be easily combined with everything else we have seen in Chapters 5 and 6. In fact, we have already seen in Section 9.2 that MS models generate strong nonnormalities in the series, such as nonzero skewness and excess kurtosis. Moreover, Example 9.6 has shown that multivariate MS models may lead to the estimation of RS correlations, which is clearly relevant to our case here.

In fact, a recent literature (see the review in Guidolin, 2011) has shown that although at some frequencies—usually monthly, quarterly, and annual, when the residuals of well-specified MS models often reject the need of also introducing ARCH effects—MS directly competes with GARCH, at higher (daily, weekly) frequencies MS, ARCH, DCC, and t-Student modeling tools are fully compatible with MS assumptions. For instance, efforts have been made to produce MS models with switching ARCH and GARCH effects; the same applies to DCC models. Although GARCH models driven by normally distributed innovations and their numerous extensions can account for a substantial portion of both the volatility clustering and excess kurtosis found in financial return series, a GARCH-type model has yet to be constructed for which the filtered residuals consistently fail to exhibit clear-cut signs of nonnormality. On the contrary, it appears that the vast majority of GARCH models, when fitted to returns over weekly and shorter horizons, imply quite heavy-tailed conditional innovation distributions. A natural solution has consisted of developing GARCH frameworks that incorporate the original assumption of normal innovations but in which the conditional distribution is a mixture of normals, as it is the case under MS. As for the frequency, the result that seems to rule in most of applied econometrics holds: the higher the frequency, the higher the chances that MS GARCH may genuinely be needed, with little peril of overfitting the data. As a rule of thumb, most papers that analyze daily or weekly data normally specify some form of MS GARCH process; at a monthly frequency, there is much more uncertainty as to what the right choice may be;[19] at quarterly or annual frequencies, strong evidence of both regimes and ARCH is unlikely.

What does an MS GARCH look like? Cai (1994) has developed probably the first MS ARCH model to examine the issue of volatility persistence in monthly excess returns of 3-month T-bills. He was concerned that the high volatility persistence commonly reported from ARCH models might be spuriously inflated by the presence of a small number of regime shifts. Therefore he has proposed to model occasional shifts in the long-run, ergodic variance of an MS ARCH process. In this case, the conditional variance is no longer determined by an exact linear combination of past squared shocks, as in a standard ARCH: the intercept in the conditional variance is allowed to change in response to occasional discrete shifts. Thus the model is able to retain the volatility-clustering feature of ARCH and, in addition, to capture the discrete shifts in the intercept in the conditional variance that may cause spurious persistence in the process. In the simplest of the two-regime cases explored by Cai (1994), his MSIAR(2,1) ARCH process is:

$$\begin{aligned} y_{t+1} &= \mu_{S_{t+1}} + \varphi(y_t - \mu_{S_{t+1}}) + \varepsilon_{t+1} \quad \varepsilon_{t+1} \sim \text{IID } N(0, \sigma^2_{t+1}) \\ \sigma^2_{t+1} &= \omega_{S_{t+1}} + \sum_{i=1}^{q} \alpha_i \varepsilon^2_{t+1-i}, \qquad \omega_{S_{t+1}}, \ \alpha_i \geq 0, \end{aligned} \tag{9.82}$$

where $S_{t+1} = 1, 2$ follows a first-order, homogeneous and irreducible two-state MC. A related, but slightly different approach is Hamilton and Susmel's (1994) who have proposed a *Switching GARCH* (SWARCH) model in which changes in regime are captured as changes in the scale of the ARCH process,

19. For instance, using UK equity and bond data, Guidolin and Timmermann (2005) have formally tested for (bivariate) ARCH effects in a three-state MSIH model and found that the null of no ARCH cannot be rejected. On US monthly equity data, Guidolin and Timmermann (2007) have reported similar evidence from a four-state model.

$$\begin{aligned} y_{t+1} &= \mu + \varepsilon_{t+1} \quad \varepsilon_{t+1} \sim \text{IID } N(0,\ \delta_{S_{t+1}}\sigma^2_{t+1}) \\ \sigma^2_{t+1} &= \omega + \sum_{i=1}^{q} \alpha_i \varepsilon^2_{t+1-i}, \quad \alpha_i \geq 0,\ S_t = 0,\ 1,\ 2, \end{aligned} \tag{9.83}$$

so that ε_{t+1} follows a standard ARCH(p) process and the MS component concerns the scaling factor $\delta_{S_{t+1}}$. This is obviously different (and in some sense more powerful) than Cai's MS ARCH in which a shift to the volatile regime only affects the unconditional (long-run) variance, whereas in Hamilton and Susmel's SWARCH, also the dynamic process of conditional variance is affected. This model is flexible enough to attribute most of the persistence in the volatility of stock returns to the persistence of the low-, moderate-, and high-volatility regimes, which typically last for several years.

Both of these models simply focus on augmenting ARCH with regimes. In a way, this is natural because the point of the literature has been to show that the high persistence of asset return volatilities often reported in the GARCH literature may have been spuriously inflated by the presence of regime shifts and/or breaks. As we have seen in Chapter 5, the very reason for why Bollerslev had proposed the GARCH generalization of ARCH was to increase the persistence of the ARCH conditional heteroskedastic family within a parsimonious parameterization. Therefore the early prominence of MS ARCH models over MS GARCH models should not come a surprise. However, one may still wonder how we should go about specifying and estimating MS GARCH models. Unfortunately, combining the MS model with GARCH induces tremendous complications in estimation. As a result of the particular lag structure of a GARCH model—by which all past lags of squared shocks affect conditional variance—the standard equations characterizing the EM algorithm for MS parameter estimation would depend on the entire history of the Markov states through the smoothed probabilities. Because each of the Markov states may take K values, this implies a total of K^T probabilities that need to be computed and stored, which would make most MS GARCH models extremely difficult to estimate for sample sizes of more than 100 observations. Direct maximum likelihood estimation (i.e., not based on the EM algorithm) via a nonlinear filter also turned out to be practically infeasible. Gray (1996) has instead developed a two-state generalized MS ARCH model for the US short-term riskless nominal interest rate,

$$\begin{aligned} y_{t+1} &= \mu_{S_{t+1}} + \varphi_{S_{t+1}} y_t + \varepsilon_{t+1} \quad \varepsilon_{t+1} \sim \text{IID } N(0,\ \sigma^2_{t+1}) \\ \sigma^2_{t+1} &= \omega_{S_{t+1}} + \alpha_{S_{t+1}} \varepsilon^2_t + \beta_{S_{t+1}} \sigma^2_t, \end{aligned} \tag{9.84}$$

($S_{t+1} = 1,\ 2$) which implies an infinite memory because $Var_t[y_{t+1}|S_{t+1}] = \omega_{S_{t+1}} + \alpha_{S_{t+1}}\varepsilon^2_t + \beta_{S_{t+1}} Var_{t-1}[y_t|S_t]$, which can be solved backward to show that conditional variance depends on the entire history of shocks to the short-term rate, ε_0, $\varepsilon_1, \ldots, \varepsilon_t$. This would cause the log-likelihood function to have an exponentially (in T) growing number of terms. Gray has tackled the problem of path dependence in MS GARCH by adopting an approach that preserves the essential nature of GARCH and yet allows tractable estimation. Under conditional normality, the variance of y_t is:

$$\begin{aligned} \overline{\sigma}^2_t &= E_{t-1}[(y_t)^2] - \{E_{t-1}[y_t]\}^2 = \Pr(S_t = 2|\Im_{t-1})[\mu_2^2 + \sigma^2_t(S_t = 2|\Im_{t-1})] \\ &+ [1 - \Pr(S_t = 2|\Im_{t-1})][\mu_1^2 + \sigma^2_t(S_t = 1|\Im_{t-1})] - \{\Pr(S_t = 2|\Im_{t-1})\mu_2 \\ &- [1 - \Pr(S_t = 2|\Im_{t-1})]\mu_1\}^2, \end{aligned} \tag{9.85}$$

which is not path-dependent and corresponds to a difference of averages across regimes (with probabilities given by filtered probabilities) of the first and second moments. This value of $\overline{\sigma}^2_t$ can be used in the specification Eq. (9.84) to replace $\sigma^2_t(S_t)$.

EXAMPLE 9.7

We follow Guidolin (2009) and compare the 1-month-ahead volatility forecasts for excess stock and bond returns derived over a monthly sample 1953–2007. He estimates a three-state version of the bivariate Hamilton and Lin's (1996) t-Student MSVAR(2) VECH ARCH(2) model, in which the number of VAR lags is assumed to be a prespecified at 2. We do not report his complete estimates to save space, but the attempt to impose either a restriction of zero correlation between stock and bond shocks across all regimes or, on the opposite, that stock and bond excess returns be driven by two independent MCs were both rejected. However, although there is some evidence of ARCH in covariance, the effect is mild (the coefficient is 0.147 only at lag 1, and the other coefficients are practically 0). The regime-specific estimates of the t-Student degrees of freedom parameter (see Chapter 5) ν (9.97, 8.80, and 6.80) imply nonnegligible departures from bivariate normality, with thicker tails in spite of having accommodated ARCH effects. Fig. 9.19 plots the 1-month-ahead forecasts of volatility and correlation produced by the single-state t-Student VAR(2) VECH ARCH(2) versus the three-state MS model.

As far as equity volatility is concerned, while the single-state volatility has in practice a lower bound at around 3.4% per month, this is not the case for the three-state model. Otherwise, the two forecasts appear to be correlated (0.65), with a much higher standard deviation for the MS forecasts (1.4% vs. 1%). In the case of bond volatility, the main difference lies in the heterogeneous level of the forecast series in the periods 1953–70 and 1989–2007, when single-state forecasts are considerably lower (although they

(Continued)

EXAMPLE 9.7 (Continued)

still strong comove, the overall correlation is 0.69), at around 2%, than three-state forecasts, which oscillate around 2.5%. Finally, the panel devoted to correlation predictions offers an unusual perspective: in this case, single-state forecasts are in fact more volatile (0.21) than three-state ones (0.14), as the latter tend to simply oscillate in a narrow range around 0 with only two exceptions: the late 1980s and early 1990s when predicted correlation becomes positive and averages almost 0.2 and 2000–04, when the predicted correlations turn negative and gravitate around −0.2. Guidolin (2009) shows that recursive volatility forecasts obtained that incorporate RS are considerably more accurate than those estimated from single-state methods but results are more mixed when it comes to forecast covariances.

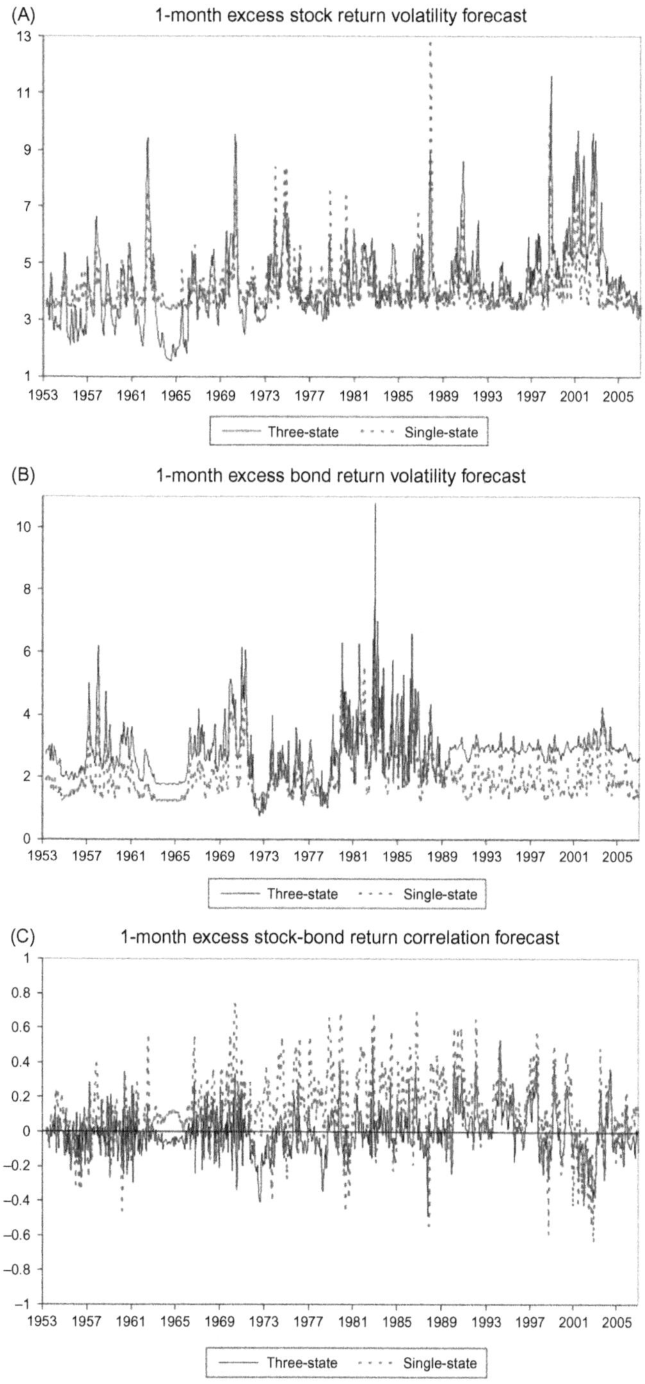

FIGURE 9.19 Forecasts from three-state MSIVAR(2)-VECH ARCH(2) model.

For MS ARCH processes conditions for stationarity, existence of moments, autocorrelation functions, and ergodicity have been studied in Francq et al. (2001), and Francq and Zakoïan (2005) under the assumption of independence of S_t and the shocks assumed to be IID. For example, in the MS GARCH(1,1) case with two regimes, a sufficient condition for stationarity and finite second-order moments can be related to the eigenvalues of the matrix

$$\begin{bmatrix} p_{11}(\alpha_1+\beta_1) & (1-p_{11})(\alpha_2+\beta_2) \\ (1-p_{22})(\alpha_1+\beta_1) & p_{22}(\alpha_2+\beta_2) \end{bmatrix}, \tag{9.86}$$

in the sense that the highest eigenvalue must be less than 1 in module. This generalizes the well-known condition for classical GARCH(1,1), $\alpha_1+\beta_1<1$, and allows for one of the regimes to violate this condition. Thus switching between persistent IGARCH, even explosive, and nonpersistent volatility regimes is not excluded.

The extensions discussed above only concern univariate ARCH and GARCH models. What about their multivariate counterparts? Pelletier (2006) has proposed an extension of Bollerslev's (1990) constant conditional correlation multivariate framework to incorporate MS dynamics in the conditional variance and covariance functions. Similarly to a standard DCC model, Pelletier's (2006) *regime switching dynamic correlation (RSDC) model* decomposes the covariances into standard deviations and correlations, but these correlations are allowed to change over time as they follow an MS model:

$$\mathbf{y}_{t+1} = \boldsymbol{\Sigma}_{t+1}^{1/2}\mathbf{z}_{t+1} \quad z_t \text{IID}(\mathbf{0}, \mathbf{I}_N) \quad \boldsymbol{\Sigma}_{t+1} = \mathbf{D}_{t+1}\boldsymbol{\Gamma}_{S_{t+1}}\mathbf{D}_{t+1}, \tag{9.87}$$

where $\mathbf{D}_{t+1}$ is a diagonal matrix composed of the standard deviations (Pelletier simply suggests that each of them may follow a standard univariate GARCH(1,1) process) of N return series and the regime-dependent matrix $\boldsymbol{\Gamma}_{S_{t+1}}$ contains the correlations that are assumed to be constant within a regime but different across regimes. This feature implies that in the evaluation of the likelihood, the correlation matrix can only take K possible values so we only have to invert K times a $N \times N$ matrix, which—especially when the number of time series is large—can be a computational advantage over models such as a DCC, where a different correlation matrix has to be inverted for every observation. Pelletier shows that the RSDC model has many interesting properties. First, it is easy to impose that the variance matrices are SPD. Second, by modeling time variation in correlations as an MS model, the variances and covariances are not bounded which is the case when they are the ones following an RS. Estimation is made simpler by adopting a two-step QMLE procedure as in Chapter 6.

9.8 DO NONLINEAR AND MARKOV SWITCHING MODELS WORK IN PRACTICE?

As planned, we conclude this chapter by asking the most important among all questions: whether and under what conditions do the nonlinear RS models covered in Chapter 8 and the MS models just entertained in this chapter work in the practice of applied econometrics? In fact, there is a large literature composed of detailed and ingenious economic forecast-driven comparisons involving nonlinear models with purpose of finding out whether, for a given time series or a set of series, nonlinear models are worth the while of an empiricist. In many cases, the answer from *out-of-sample* (OOS) tests appears to be negative, even when the nonlinear model in question fits *in-sample* the data better than the corresponding linear model (see a review in Clements and Hendry, 1998). Many reasons for this outcome have been discussed in the literature:

- Nonlinear models may sometimes explain features in the data that do not occur very frequently; if these features are not present in the series during the period to be forecast, then there is no gain from using nonlinear models; this may easily be the case at least when the number of OOS forecasts is relatively small.
- It may be that a nonlinear model predicts better than a linear one in particular regimes only; for example, a nonlinear model may be useful in forecasting stock returns only in bear markets but not in bull markets.
- Another potential reason for the inferior performance of nonlinear models compared to linear ones is overfitting, even though careful modeling, including testing linearity before fitting a nonlinear model, should reduce the likelihood of overfitting.
- Another possibility is that even if linearity is rejected upon testing, the nonlinear model fitted to the time series is misspecified to the extent that its forecasting performance does not match the performance of a linear model containing the same variables; in other words, a standing misspecification of an ARMA model or of a regression can be made worse by the fact that regimes are introduced.

- The potential gains from forecasting with nonlinear models can be strongly reduced because of parameter estimation; Psaradakis and Spagnolo (2005) show that (for both threshold and MS models, with linear cointegration), even when the DGP is nonlinear and the model is correctly specified, the linear model may yield more accurate forecasts than the correct nonlinear one because of overwhelming parameter uncertainty; short time series are thus a disadvantage, but the results also suggest that considerable attention should be paid to adopting efficient estimation methods.

These empirical evidences and remarks are well-established when applied to threshold RS models. For instance, Bradley and Jansen (2004) find that a range of threshold models fail to forecast US excess stock returns better than linear ones when the criterion is the RMSFE. Kilian and Taylor (2003) have concluded that in forecasting nominal exchange rates, ESTAR models are superior to the random walk model, but only at long horizons, 2–3 years. The results in Stock and Watson (1999) indicate that using a large number of nonlinear models to produce direct forecasts and combining forecasts from them is much better than using single nonlinear models. It also seems that this way of exploiting nonlinearity may lead to better forecasting performance than what is achieved by linear models. Marcellino (2004) suggests that nonlinear models are uneven performers but that they can do well in some types of macroeconomic series such as unemployment rates.

The balance of the existing evidence seems to be relatively more encouraging when it comes to MS models, especially when applied to long time series of financial data, see Guidolin (2011) for a survey of the literature. The seminal paper by Engel and Hamilton (1990) had already accounted for a strong OOS forecasting performance of MS models of exchange rate changes, even when compared with the random walk that had traditionally dominated in previous forecasting work. More recently, Ang and Bekaert (2002) have reported encouraging results for multivariate MS applied to international interest rates, showing that what makes the difference for the predictive performance is not represented by uni- versus multivariate modeling. Interestingly, in their paper, MS models with time-varying probabilities outperform their constant probability counterparts. Guidolin and Ono (2006) have performed systematic multivariate comparisons of single-state VARs versus MSVARs with reference to US equity and bond returns, when standard macroeconomic aggregates are used as predictors. They report that a relatively parsimonious four-state MSIH-VAR(1) model predicts well and that the performance differential is statistically significant when formal tests of superior predictive accuracy are applied, especially at intermediate and long horizons. Guidolin et al. (2009) have reported mixed evidence from univariate MS models of stock and bond returns for the G7 countries, but with stronger results as far as the US, Canadian, and the UK returns are concerned. In a similar vein, Henkel et al. (2011) use Bayesian MSVAR methods to capture time variation in stock market return predictability from the dividend yield and commonly used term structure variables (the short rate, the slope of the term structure, and the default premium) in the G7 countries. Their key finding is that standard predictors in the finance literature are effective exclusively during recessions.

A different but equally interesting strand of the literature has examined the performance of MS at predicting volatilities, which are key inputs in risk management and derivative pricing. Papers estimating MS GARCH models generally report OOS prediction results that are promising. For instance, Haas et al. (2004) have re-examined the forecasting performance of MS-GARCH(1,1) against a range of alternative benchmarks, including both standard GARCH(1,1) as well as ARCH models with nonstandard innovations. For daily NASDAQ return data, they report that the OOS performance of the mixture GARCH is superior to both simpler MS (like a plain MSIH) and GARCH. Calvet and Fisher (2001) have developed a MS multifractal model, which is a stochastic volatility model (see Chapter 7) characterized by a small number of parameters but an arbitrarily large number of frequencies, in the sense that volatility is hit by exogenous shocks with heterogeneous durations, which range from one day to more than a decade in empirical applications. The number of components and their frequencies can be inferred directly from returns data. MS multifrequency models are sufficiently flexible to account for market conditions that change considerably over a long-time span and captures the outliers, volatility persistence, and power variation of financial series. This has guaranteed a rather strong forecasting performance in a range of empirical application, see Calvet and Fisher (2008).

One interesting concern is whether or not there would be evidence that the key challenge of MS model would lie in the chances of incorrectly inferring and predicting regime shifts; the alternative consists of thinking of MS models not only (or mostly) as devices to anticipate regime shifts but as a flexible class of nonlinear tools that, besides predicting future regimes, may imply useful density and higher moment forecasts as we have seen in Section 9.2. For instance, Lettau and Van Nieuwerburgh (2007) have argued that the real challenge with MS is not really dating or predicting the switches, but instead precisely estimating the shifts in the conditional mean function. Although there is no specific paper on this point, possibly too much time has been devoted to using MS as a way to forecast regimes and too little as devices to forecast the density of variables of interest.

Guidolin (2011) also reviews the literature asking whether there is a sampling frequency below/above which it is obvious that MS models would stop being useful, to be replaced by other dynamic econometric frameworks (such as richer nonlinear models or copulas). Even though MS regimes are routinely thought of as ways to predict recession/expansion dates, and the fact that MS originated in the macroeconomics literature, the dominant frequency at which MS seems to be most effective is the monthly one. However, there is also a substantial body of research that has applied MS to daily data, and therefore Guidolin concludes that MS tools seem in the end to work well at all possible frequencies. Yet, it is typical to observe that the higher the frequency, the higher the chances that MS GARCH will be needed, with little peril of overfitting the data.

Finally, because MS models are simply (Gaussian) mixtures with finite MC memory, starting from the late 1990s, the focus on testing their predictive performance has shifted away from point forecasts toward density forecasts. Moreover, because most economic-based loss functions depend on a range of features of the predictive density (usually not only on its mean, think of mean–variance portfolio choice problems), the literature has increasingly translated the assessment of the performance of MS models from a purely statistical domain to an economic one, in which specific decision problems are solved both under single-state and MS, to compare in OOS experiments their average payoffs. For instance, Hong et al. (2004) have considered a wide variety of popular short-term (spot) interest rate models—including single-factor diffusions, GARCH, MS, and jump-diffusion models—to conclude that although previous studies have shown that simpler models, such as the random walk, tend to provide better forecasts for the conditional mean of interest rates, MS (with time-varying probabilities) and models with jumps significantly improve density modeling. A few papers (among others, Guidolin and Timmermann, 2006, and Haas et al., 2004) have investigated the forecasting performance of MS using a Value-at-Risk criterion popular in risk management. The general conclusion is that MS models, with and without GARCH components, tend to give accurate predictions, especially for VaR at 1% level.

As for the assessment of the predictive accuracy of MS models under economic loss functions, there has been considerable progress by a new dynamic portfolio choice literature based on nonlinear processes that has shown that findings in standard linear VAR frameworks—for example, that the equity allocation should be higher the longer the horizon—may have to be re-examined. As early as in Ramchard and Susmel (1998) who have examined mean–variance asset allocation among international equity portfolios under MS ARCH, the finding has been that accounting for regimes easily leads to higher in-sample Sharpe ratios versus linear models. Dal Pra et al. (2017) have recently extended results and intuitions in Ang and Bekaert (2004) to characterize in closed form the dynamic process of the mean-variance efficient frontier in the presence of MS dynamics in returns (with observable regimes), and have shown that simply tracking such simple dynamics might have improved considerably realized OOS performances relative to textbook, naive static mean–variance strategies.

Because we know from Section 9.2 that MS Gaussian mixtures impress strong patterns of time variation in conditional skewness and excess kurtosis, unless restrictive assumptions on preferences are enforced, simple mean–variance asset allocation may be logically inconsistent with the very nature of MS. Ang and Bekaert (2002) is the seminal paper on the effects of MS on optimal dynamic portfolio choice, a contribution that has spurred a substantial volume of additional refinements and applications. Their paper assumes a power utility function that—by depending on the entire joint predictive density of returns—allows optimal portfolios to depend on all the conditional moments implied by MS. Under the assumption that regimes are known to the agent (which is counterfactual) and using international equity data, they show that the costs of ignoring MS may be substantial when a conditionally risk-free asset exists. When regimes are not observable, which is of course the case, and when an investor may only filter the nature of regimes out of the data, Guidolin and Timmermann (2007) have applied MS-based asset allocation tools to a typical strategic asset allocation problem and show that the costs of ignoring MS may be equivalent to losses of up to 3% at short horizons—when investors can exploit market timing more aggressively—whereas at the longest horizons the loss is around 1.3% per annum. Using a similar (Bayesian) framework Tu (2010) reports an annualized certainty-equivalent cost associated with ignoring RS in excess of 2% per year and as high as 10%. Guidolin and Timmermann also evaluate the economic significance of heteroskedastic MS by examining real-time OOS performance of asset allocation rules based on both standard VARs that use the dividend yield as a predictor variable, simple MSIH, MSVAR models for the joint dynamics of US stock and bond returns. The VAR(1) model performs the best over short investment horizons but for longer horizons, an MSIH model produces the highest mean realized utility and the difference is statistically significant.

REFERENCES

Altissimo, F., Corradi, V., 2002. Bounds for inference with nuisance parameters present only under the alternative. Econ. J. 5, 494–519.

Ang, A., Bekaert, G., 2002. International asset allocation with regime shifts. Rev. Finan. Stud. 15, 1137–1187.

Ang, A., Bekaert, G., 2004. How regimes affect asset allocation. Finan. Anal. J. 60, 86–99.

Baum, L., Petrie, T., Soules, G., Weiss, N., 1970. A maximization technique occurring in the analysis of probabilistic functions of Markov chains. Ann. Math. Stat. 41, 164–171.

Bollerslev, T., 1990. Modelling the coherence in short-run nominal exchange rates: a multivariate generalized ARCH model. Rev. Econ. Stat. 72, 498–505.

Bradley, M.D., Jansen, D.W., 2004. Forecasting with a nonlinear dynamic model of stock returns and industrial production. Int. J. Forecast. 20, 321–342.

Cai, J., 1994. A Markov model of switching-regime ARCH. J. Bus. Econ. Stat. 12, 309–316.

Calvet, L., Fisher, A., 2001. Forecasting multifractal volatility. J. Econometr. 105, 27–58.

Calvet, L., Fisher, A., 2008. Multifractal Volatility: Theory, Forecasting, and Pricing. Academic Press, Cambridge, MA.

Clements, M., Hendry, D., 1998. Forecasting Economic Time Series. Cambridge University Press, Cambridge.

Dal Pra, G., Guidolin, M., Pedio, M., Vasile, F., 2018. Regime shifts in excess stock return predictability: an out-of-sample portfolio analysis. J. Portfol. Manage. 44 (3), 10–24.

Davidson, R., MacKinnon, J., 1981. Several tests for model specification in the presence of alternative hypothesis. Econometrica 49, 781–793.

Davies, R.B., 1977. Hypothesis testing when a nuisance parameter is present only under the alternative. Biometrika 64, 247–254.

Dempster, A., Laird, N., Rubin, D., 1977. Maximum likelihood from incomplete data via the EM algorithm. J. R. Stat. Soc. B 39, 1–38.

Diebold, F.X., Lee, J.H., Weinbach, G.C., 1994. Regime switching with time-varying transition probabilities. In: Hargreaves, C. (Ed.), Nonstationary Time Series Analysis and Cointegration. Oxford University Press, Oxford, pp. 283–302.

Doan, T., Littermann, R., Sims, C., 1984. Forecasting and conditional projection using realistic prior distributions. Econ. Rev. 3, 1–14.

Douc, R., Moulines, E., Rydén, T., 2004. Asymptotic properties of the maximum likelihood estimator in autoregressive models with Markov regime. Ann. Stat. 32, 2254–2304.

Engel, C., Hamilton, J., 1990. Long swings in the dollar: are they in the data and do markets know it? Am. Econ. Rev. 80, 689–713.

Filardo, A.J., 1994. Business-cycle phases and their transitional dynamics. J. Bus. Econ. Stat. 12, 299–308.

Francq, C., Roussignol, M., Zakoïan, J., 2001. Conditional heteroskedasticity driven by hidden Markov chains. J. Time Ser. Anal. 22, 197–220.

Francq, C., Zakoïan, J., 2005. The L2-structures of standard and switching-regime GARCH models. Stoch. Process. Appl. 115, 1557–1582.

Gray, S., 1996. Modeling the conditional distribution of interest rates as a regime switching process. J. Finan. Econ. 42, 27–62.

Guidolin, M., 2009. Detecting and exploiting regime switching ARCH dynamics in US stock and bond returns. In: Gregorious, G. (Ed.), Stock Market Volatility. Chapman Hall, London, pp. 92–133.

Guidolin, M., 2011. Markov switching models in empirical finance. Missing Data Methods: Time-Series Methods and Applications. Emerald Group Publishing Limited.

Guidolin, M., 2013. Markov switching models in asset pricing research. In: Bell, A.R., Brooks, C., Prokopczuk, M. (Eds.), Handbook of Research Methods and Applications in Empirical Finance. Edward Elgar, Cheltenham, pp. 3–44.

Guidolin, M., Hyde, S., McMillan, D., Ono, S., 2009. Nonlinear predictability in stock and bond returns: when and where is it exploitable? Int. J. Forecast. 25, 373–399.

Guidolin, M., Ono, S., 2006. Are the dynamic linkages between the macroeconomy and asset prices time-varying? J. Econ. Bus. 58, 480–518.

Guidolin, M., Pedio, M., 2017. Identifying and measuring the contagion channels at work in the European financial crises. J. Int. Finan. Markets Inst. Money 48, 117–134.

Guidolin, M., Timmermann, A., 2005. Economic implications of bull and bear regimes in UK stock and bond returns. Econ. J. 115, 111–143.

Guidolin, M., Timmermann, A., 2006. Term structure of risk under alternative econometric specifications. J. Econ. 131, 285–308.

Guidolin, M., Timmermann, A., 2007. Asset allocation under multivariate regime switching. J. Econ. Dyn. Contr. 31, 3503–3544.

Haas, M., Mittnik, S., Paolella, M., 2004. A new approach to Markov-switching GARCH models. J. Finan. Econ. 2, 493–530.

Hamilton, J.D., 1990. Analysis of time series subject to changes in regime. J. Econom. 45, 39–70.

Hamilton, J.D., 1994. Time Series Analysis. Princeton University Press, Princeton, NJ.

Hamilton, J.D., Lin, G., 1996. Stock market volatility and the business cycle. J. Appl. Econom. 11, 573–593.

Hamilton, J., Susmel, R., 1994. Autoregressive conditional heteroskedasticity and changes in regime. J. Econom. 64, 307–333.

Hansen, B.E., 1996. Inference when a nuisance parameter is not identified under the null hypothesis. Econometrica 64, 413–430.

Henkel, S., Martin, J., Nardari, F., 2011. Time-varying short-horizon predictability. J. Finan. Econ. 99, 560–580.

Hong, Y., Li, H., Zha, F., 2004. Out-of-sample performance of discrete-time spot interest rate models. J. Bus. Econ. Stat. 22, 457–473.

Karlsen, H., 1990. Existence of moments in a stationary stochastic difference equation. Adv. Appl. Probab. 22, 129–146.

Kilian, L., Taylor, M.P., 2003. Why is it so difficult to beat the random walk forecast of exchange rates? J. Int. Econ. 60, 85–107.

Kim, C.-J., 1994. Dynamic linear models with Markov-switching. J. Int. Econ. 60, 1–22.

Krolzig, H.-M., 1997. Markov-Switching Vector Autoregressions. Springer-Verlag, Berlin.

Leroux, B., 1992. Maximum likelihood estimation for hidden Markov models. Stoch. Process. Appl. 40, 127–143.

Lettau, M., Van Nieuwerburgh, S., 2007. Reconciling the return predictability evidence. Rev. Finan. Stud. 21, 1607–1652.

Marcellino, M., 2004. Forecasting EMU macroeconomic variables. Int. J. Forecast. 20, 359–372.

Marron, J.S., Wand, M.P., 1992. Exact mean integrated squared error. Ann. Stat. 20, 712–736.

Pelletier, D., 2006. Regime switching for dynamic correlations. J. Int. Econ. 131, 445–473.

Psaradakis, Z., Spagnolo, F., 2005. Forecast performance of nonlinear error-correction models with multiple regimes. J. Forecast. 24, 119–138.

Ramchard, L., Susmel, R., 1998. Volatility and cross correlation across major stock markets. J. Empirical Finan. 5 (4), 397–416.

Stock, J.H., Watson, M.W., 1999. Business cycle fluctuations in US macroeconomic time series. In: Taylor, J.B., Woodford, M. (Eds.), Handbook of Macroeconomics, first ed. Elsevier, Amsterdam, pp. 3–64.

Timmermann, A., 2000. Moments of Markov switching models. J. Int. Econ. 96, 75–111.
Tu, J., 2010. Is regime switching in stock returns important in portfolio decisions? Manage. Sci. 56, 1198–1215.
Turner, C., Startz, R., Nelson, C., 1989. A Markov model of heteroskedasticity, risk, and learning in the stock market. J. Finan. Econ. 25, 3–22.
White, H., 1982. Maximum likelihood estimation of misspecified models. Econometrica 50, 1–25.

APPENDIX 9.A SOME NOTIONS CONCERNING ERGODIC MARKOV CHAINS

Consider a K-state, first-order MC with transition matrix with generic element $p_{ij} \equiv \Pr(S_{t+1} = j|S_t = i)$. In general $\mathbf{P} \neq \mathbf{P}'$ although many of the claims that follow shall refer to $\mathbf{P}'$. Suppose that one of the eigenvalues of $\mathbf{P}'$ is unity and that all the other eigenvalues of $\mathbf{P}'$ are inside the unit circle (i.e., they are less than 1). Then, the MC is said to be ergodic and the $K \times 1$ vector of ergodic probabilities for the chain is denoted as $\bar{\boldsymbol{\xi}}$. This vector $\bar{\boldsymbol{\xi}}$ is defined as the eigenvector of $\mathbf{P}'$ associated with the unit eigenvalue, that is, the vector of ergodic probabilities $\bar{\boldsymbol{\xi}}$ satisfies $\mathbf{P}'\bar{\boldsymbol{\xi}} = \bar{\boldsymbol{\xi}}$ and it is normalized to the sum to unity (i.e., $\bar{\boldsymbol{\xi}}'\boldsymbol{\iota}_K = 1$).

First, noting that the eigenvalues of $\mathbf{P}$ and $\mathbf{P}'$ are identical by construction and using the standard properties of a (discrete) probability law (measure), it is easy to prove that $\mathbf{P}\boldsymbol{\iota}_K = \boldsymbol{\iota}_K$, so that at least one eigenvalue of $\mathbf{P}'$ is equal to 1:

$$\mathbf{P}\boldsymbol{\iota}_k = \begin{bmatrix} p_{11} & p_{12} & \cdots & p_{1K} \\ p_{21} & p_{22} & \cdots & p_{2K} \\ \vdots & \cdots & \ddots & \vdots \\ p_{K1} & p_{K2} & \cdots & p_{KK} \end{bmatrix} \begin{bmatrix} 1 \\ 1 \\ \vdots \\ 1 \end{bmatrix} = \begin{bmatrix} p_{11} + p_{12} + \cdots + p_{1K} \\ p_{21} + p_{22} + \cdots + p_{2K} \\ \vdots \\ p_{K1} + p_{K2} + \cdots + p_{KK} \end{bmatrix} = \begin{bmatrix} 1 \\ 1 \\ \vdots \\ 1 \end{bmatrix}, \tag{A1}$$

where the last equality derives from the law of total probability, that is, the fact that starting from any state $S_t = i$, the sum of the probabilities of either staying in regime i or of switching to any other regime must always be 1:

$$\Pr(S_{t+1} = 1|S_t = i) + \Pr(S_{t+1} = 2|S_t = i) + \cdots + \Pr(S_{t+1} = K|S_t = i) = 1.$$

Recall now from your math courses that the expression $\mathbf{P}\boldsymbol{\iota}_K = \boldsymbol{\iota}_K$ is equivalent to the definition of one specific set of eigenvector/eigenvalue of a matrix $\mathbf{P}$, in the sense that $\mathbf{P}\boldsymbol{\iota}_K = \boldsymbol{\iota}_K$ identifies 1 as one of the eigenvalues of $\mathbf{P}$. Also notice that if $\mathbf{P}\boldsymbol{\iota}_K = \boldsymbol{\iota}_K$ holds, then also $\zeta\mathbf{P}\boldsymbol{\iota}_K = \zeta\boldsymbol{\iota}_K$, with $\zeta \in \mathbb{R}$ some scalar, which means that ζ will be an eigenvalue of $\mathbf{P}$ as well.

At this point, if $\mathbf{P}$ is the transition matrix for an ergodic MC with K distinct eigenvalues, then

$$\lim_{T\to\infty} (\mathbf{P}')^T = \bar{\boldsymbol{\xi}}\boldsymbol{\iota}_K' = \begin{bmatrix} \xi_1 & \xi_1 & \cdots & \xi_1 \\ \xi_2 & \xi_2 & \cdots & \xi_2 \\ \vdots & \cdots & \ddots & \vdots \\ \xi_K & \xi_K & \cdots & \xi_K \end{bmatrix}, \tag{A2}$$

where $(\mathbf{P}')^T$ is the matrix $\mathbf{P}'$ multiplied by itself T times, that is, $(\mathbf{P}')^T \equiv \prod_{\tau=1}^{T} \mathbf{P}'$. Recall that when the K eigenvalues are distinct, $\mathbf{P}'$ can always be written in the form $\mathbf{P}' = \mathbf{Q}\boldsymbol{\Lambda}\mathbf{Q}^{-1}$ where $\mathbf{Q}$ is a $K \times K$ matrix whose columns are the eigenvectors of $\mathbf{P}'$ and $\boldsymbol{\Lambda}$ is a diagonal matrix whose diagonal contains the corresponding eigenvalues of $\mathbf{P}'$, sorted in descending order (so 1 will occupy the (1,1) position). It is elementary (try it with a $K = 2$ example) to show that $(\mathbf{P}')^T = \mathbf{Q}\boldsymbol{\Lambda}^T\mathbf{Q}^{-1}$. Because the (1,1) element of $\boldsymbol{\Lambda}$ is unity and all other elements of $\boldsymbol{\Lambda}$ are inside the unit circle, $\boldsymbol{\Lambda}^T$ converges to a matrix with unity in the (1,1) position and 0s elsewhere. For instance:

$$\lim_{T\to\infty} \begin{bmatrix} 1 & 0 & \cdots & 0 \\ 0 & \lambda_2^T < 1 & \cdots & 0 \\ \vdots & \cdots & \ddots & \vdots \\ 0 & 0 & \cdots & \lambda_k^T < 1 \end{bmatrix} = \begin{bmatrix} \lim_{T\to\infty} 1 & 0 & \cdots & 0 \\ 0 & \lim_{T\to\infty} \lambda_2^T & \cdots & 0 \\ \vdots & \cdots & \ddots & \vdots \\ 0 & 0 & \cdots & \lim_{T\to\infty} \lambda_k^T \end{bmatrix} = \begin{bmatrix} 1 & 0 & \cdots & 0 \\ 0 & 0 & \cdots & 0 \\ \vdots & \cdots & \ddots & \vdots \\ 0 & 0 & \cdots & 0 \end{bmatrix}. \tag{A3}$$

Hence, $\lim_{T\to\infty} (\mathbf{P}')^T = \mathbf{x}\mathbf{y}'$ where $\mathbf{x}$ is the first column of $\mathbf{Q}$ and $\mathbf{y}'$ is the first row of $\mathbf{Q}^{-1}$. The first column of $\mathbf{Q}$ is the eigenvector of $\mathbf{P}'$ corresponding to the unit eigenvalue, whose eigenvector was defined as $\bar{\boldsymbol{\xi}}$ in $\mathbf{P}'\bar{\boldsymbol{\xi}} = \bar{\boldsymbol{\xi}}$, so $x = \bar{\boldsymbol{\xi}}$. Here we have used without proof the fact that the first row of $\mathbf{Q}^{-1}$, when expressed as a column vector, corresponds to the eigenvector of $\mathbf{P}$ associated with the unit eigenvalue, whose eigenvector was seen to be *proportional* to the vector 1 in $\zeta\mathbf{P}\boldsymbol{\iota}_k = \zeta\boldsymbol{\iota}_k$, with ζ some scalar. Therefore $\mathbf{y} = \zeta\boldsymbol{\iota}_k$. At this point, by substituting $x = \bar{\boldsymbol{\xi}}$ and $\mathbf{y} = \zeta\boldsymbol{\iota}_k$ into the limit expression for $(\mathbf{P}')^T$ as $T \to \infty$, we have $\lim_{T\to\infty} (\mathbf{P}')^T = \zeta\bar{\boldsymbol{\xi}}\boldsymbol{\iota}'_k$.

Because $(\mathbf{P}')^T$ can be interpreted as a matrix of (predicted) transition probabilities, each column must sum to unity. Thus because the vector of ergodic probabilities $\bar{\boldsymbol{\xi}}$ was normalized by the condition that $\bar{\boldsymbol{\xi}}'\iota_k = 1$, it follows that the normalizing −constant ζ must be unity, establishing that:

$$\lim_{T\to\infty} (\mathbf{P}')^T = \bar{\boldsymbol{\xi}}\iota'_k. \tag{A4}$$

This means that as the forecast horizon for predicted transition probabilities T diverges, all the elements of the resulting T-step-ahead transition matrix $\mathbf{P}^T$ will simply collapse to be identical to the ergodic, unconditional probabilities.

For instance, in the special case of $K = 3$, if you have obtained an estimate of $\mathbf{P}$ equal to:

$$\hat{\mathbf{P}} = \begin{bmatrix} 0.88 & 0.09 & 0.03 \\ 0.01 & 0.96 & 0.03 \\ 0.23 & 0 & 0.77 \end{bmatrix}, \tag{A5}$$

the ergodic probabilities $\bar{\boldsymbol{\xi}}$ characterizing this three-state model can be derived by resorting to a statistical package. It turns out that both $\hat{\mathbf{P}}$ and $\hat{\mathbf{P}}'$ share the same eigenvalues, that is, 1, 0.87 and 0.74. Here we care only for the unit eigenvalue. Your software of choice will also inform you that the eigenvector of $\hat{\mathbf{P}}'$ associated to the unit eigenvalue is [0.3926 0.8834 0.1664]′. This eigenvector is not yet $\bar{\boldsymbol{\xi}}$ because it fails to have unit length. In fact the eigenvector ends up summing to 1.4424, while $\bar{\boldsymbol{\xi}}'\iota_K = 1$ by definition. However, it is now sufficient to scale the eigenvector so to have unit length, which is done by simply dividing its entries by their sum, 1.4424. The resulting estimated (because implied by $\hat{\mathbf{P}}$) $\bar{\boldsymbol{\xi}}$ is $\bar{\boldsymbol{\xi}}$ = [0.272 0.613 0.125]′.

In particular, straightforward algebra shows that when $K = 2$, we have:

$$\bar{\xi}_1 = \frac{1-p_{22}}{2-p_{11}-p_{22}} \qquad \bar{\xi}_2 = \frac{1-p_{11}}{2-p_{11}-p_{22}} \tag{A6}$$

which is as simple as useful a formula to have. Interestingly, by construction, for any $p_{11} = p_{22} \in (0, 1)$, we have then $\bar{\xi}_1 = \bar{\xi}_2 = (1-p_{11})/2(1-p_{11}) = 1/2$, which reveals that what carries information on the ergodic frequency of the regimes is not their individual "stayer" probabilities, but instead their relative probabilities of not leaving the two regimes.

Finally, the vector of ergodic probabilities can also be viewed as indicating the unconditional probability ($\boldsymbol{\pi}$) of each of the K states, $\boldsymbol{\pi} = \bar{\boldsymbol{\xi}}$. We have seen in Section 9.5, in Eq. (9.43), that if we define $\boldsymbol{\delta}_{t+1}$ to be a $K \times 1$ vector that lists a 1 in its jth position if the MC is in state j at time t and 0 otherwise, then $E_t[\boldsymbol{\delta}_{t+1}] = E[\boldsymbol{\delta}_{t+1}|S_t] = \Pr(S_{t+1}|S_t)$ and will equal the jth column of the matrix $\mathbf{P}'$ if $S_t = j$. This is the vector of conditional probabilities of all possible K states, given $S_t = j$. Correspondingly, the unconditional probabilities of each of the K regimes may be defined as a vector $\Pr(S_{t+1})$:

$$\begin{aligned} E[\boldsymbol{\delta}_{t+1}] &= \Pr(S_{t+1}) = E[\mathbf{P}'\boldsymbol{\delta}_t + \mathbf{v}_{t+1}] \\ &= \mathbf{P}'\Pr(S_t) + E[\mathbf{v}_{t+1}] = \mathbf{P}'\Pr(S_t). \end{aligned} \tag{A7}$$

It is clear that the vector $\Pr(S_{t+1})$ satisfies $\Pr(S_{t+1}) = \mathbf{P}'\Pr(S_t)$. At this point, please compare with the definition of ergodic probabilities $\bar{\boldsymbol{\xi}} = \mathbf{P}'\bar{\boldsymbol{\xi}}$: clearly $\bar{\boldsymbol{\xi}} = \Pr(S_{t+1})$ so that $\bar{\boldsymbol{\xi}}$ can also be interpreted as the vector of long-run, unconditional probabilities for each of the K regimes. Alternatively, as seen in Section 9.4, because $\lim_{T\to\infty} (\mathbf{P}')^T = \boldsymbol{\pi}\iota'_K$ and $\Pr(S_t) \equiv E[\boldsymbol{\delta}_t] = \lim_{T\to\infty} E[\boldsymbol{\delta}_{t+T}|S_t] = \lim_{T\to\infty} (\mathbf{P}')^T\boldsymbol{\delta}_t$, then $\Pr(S_t) = \boldsymbol{\pi}\iota'_K\boldsymbol{\delta}_t = \boldsymbol{\pi}$, as by construction $\iota'_K\boldsymbol{\delta}_t = 1$. As a result, $\bar{\boldsymbol{\xi}}$ = [0.272 0.613 0.125] will also give the long-run, unconditional frequencies of the bear, normal, and bull phases of the market. As one would expect, the normal regime occurs the majority of the time, in excess of 60% of any long sample. The finding above that $\Pr(S) = \mathbf{P}'\Pr(S)$ extends more generally to show that:

$$\begin{aligned} E_t[\boldsymbol{\delta}_{t+1}] &= \boldsymbol{\xi}_{t+1|t} = \Pr(S_{t+1}|\Im_t) = E[\mathbf{P}'\boldsymbol{\delta}_t + \mathbf{v}_{t+1}|\Im_t] \\ &= \mathbf{P}'\Pr(S_t|\Im_t) + E[\mathbf{v}_{t+1}|\Im_t] = \mathbf{P}'\boldsymbol{\delta}_t. \end{aligned} \tag{A8}$$

APPENDIX 9.B STATE-SPACE REPRESENTATION OF AN MARKOV SWITCHING MODEL

This appendix offers a heuristic idea of what it means to write an MSIVARH(K,p) in its state-space form (see also Chapter 7). Let us collect the information on the time t realization of the MC in a random vector

$\boldsymbol{\xi}_t \equiv [I(S_t = 1)I(S_t = 2)...I(S_t = K)]'$, where $I(S_t = i)$ is a standard indicator variable. In practice, the sample realizations of $\boldsymbol{\xi}_t$ will always consist of elementary vectors $\mathbf{e}_i$ characterized by a 1 in the ith position and by 0 everywhere else. As we have seen in Section 9.4, an important property is that $E[\boldsymbol{\xi}_t|\boldsymbol{\xi}_{t-1}] = \mathbf{P}'\boldsymbol{\xi}_{t-1}$. The state-space form is composed of two equations:

$$\begin{aligned} \mathbf{y}_t &= \mathbf{X}_t A\left(\boldsymbol{\xi}_t \otimes \iota_N\right) + \boldsymbol{\Sigma}_K\left(\boldsymbol{\xi}_t \otimes \mathbf{I}_N\right) \mathbf{z}_t \quad \text{(measurement equation)} \\ \boldsymbol{\xi}_{t+1} &= \mathbf{F}\boldsymbol{\xi}_t + \mathbf{v}_{t+1} \quad \text{(transition equation)}, \end{aligned} \tag{B1}$$

where the symbols have been defined in the main text. Moreover, $\mathbf{z}_t \sim$ IID $N(\mathbf{0}, \mathbf{I}_N)$, and in the transition equation $\boldsymbol{v}_{t+1}$ is a zero mean discrete random vector that can be shown to be a martingale difference sequence. Also, the elements of $\mathbf{v}_{t+1}$ are uncorrelated with $\mathbf{z}_{t+1}$ as well as $\boldsymbol{\xi}_{t-j}$, $\mathbf{z}_{t-j}$, $\boldsymbol{y}_{t-j}$, and $\mathbf{X}_{t-j}$ $\forall j \geq 0$. To operationalize the dynamic state-space system (B1), assume that the multivariate process started with a random draw from the unconditional probability distribution $\bar{\boldsymbol{\xi}}$. Finally, from the definition of transition probability matrix, it follows that because $E[\mathbf{v}_{t+1}|\boldsymbol{\xi}_t] = \mathbf{0}$ by assumption, $E[\boldsymbol{\xi}_{t+1}|\boldsymbol{\xi}_t] = \mathbf{F}\boldsymbol{\xi}_t$ implies that $\mathbf{F}$ corresponds to the transpose of the transition probability matrix, $\mathbf{P}'$. Note that in general, this dynamic state-space model is neither linear (as the state vector $\boldsymbol{\xi}_t$ also influences the covariance matrix of the process) nor Gaussian, as the innovations driving the transition equation are non-Gaussian random variables.

APPENDIX 9.C FIRST-ORDER CONDITIONS FOR MAXIMUM LIKELIHOOD ESTIMATION OF MARKOV SWITCHING MODELS

The FOCs with respect to the transition probabilities are determined as follows. Because

$$\begin{aligned} \frac{\partial \ln L(\boldsymbol{\theta}, \boldsymbol{\rho})}{\partial \boldsymbol{\rho}'} &= \frac{1}{L(\boldsymbol{\theta}, \boldsymbol{\rho})} \sum_{\{\boldsymbol{\xi}_t\}_{t=1}^T} \frac{\partial \Pr\left(\boldsymbol{\xi}_t|\boldsymbol{\xi}_0; \boldsymbol{\rho}\right)}{\partial \boldsymbol{\rho}'} \prod_{t=1}^T p(\mathbf{y}_t|\boldsymbol{\xi}_t, \Im_{t-1}; \boldsymbol{\theta}) \\ &= \frac{1}{L(\boldsymbol{\theta}, \boldsymbol{\rho})} \sum_{\{\boldsymbol{\xi}_t\}_{t=1}^T} \frac{\partial \ln \Pr\left(\boldsymbol{\xi}_t|\boldsymbol{\xi}_0; \boldsymbol{\rho}\right)}{\partial \boldsymbol{\rho}'} \prod_{t=1}^T p(\mathbf{y}_t|\boldsymbol{\xi}_t, \Im_{t-1}; \boldsymbol{\theta}) \Pr\left(\boldsymbol{\xi}_t|\boldsymbol{\xi}_0; \boldsymbol{\rho}\right) \\ &= \sum_{\{\boldsymbol{\xi}_t\}_{t=1}^T} \sum_{t=1}^T \frac{\partial \ln \Pr\left(\boldsymbol{\xi}_t|\boldsymbol{\xi}_0; \boldsymbol{\rho}\right)}{\partial \boldsymbol{\rho}'} \Pr\left(\boldsymbol{\xi}_t|\Im_T; \boldsymbol{\theta}, \boldsymbol{\rho}\right), \end{aligned} \tag{C1}$$

for each component p_{ij} of $\boldsymbol{\rho}$, this implies:

$$\begin{aligned} \frac{\partial \ln L(\boldsymbol{\theta}, \boldsymbol{\rho})}{\partial p_{ij}} &= \sum_{t=1}^T \sum_{\boldsymbol{\xi}_{t-1} = \mathbf{e}_i} \sum_{\boldsymbol{\xi}_t = \mathbf{e}_j} \frac{\partial \ln \Pr\left(\boldsymbol{\xi}_t|\boldsymbol{\xi}_{t-1}; \boldsymbol{\rho}\right)}{\partial p_{ij}} \Pr\left(\boldsymbol{\xi}_t, \boldsymbol{\xi}_{t-1}|\Im_T; \boldsymbol{\theta}, \boldsymbol{\rho}\right) \\ &= \sum_{t=1}^T \sum_{\boldsymbol{\xi}_{t-1} = \mathbf{e}_i} \sum_{\boldsymbol{\xi}_t = \mathbf{e}_j} \frac{1}{p_{ij}} I_{\{\boldsymbol{\xi}_{t-1} = \mathbf{e}_i,\, \boldsymbol{\xi}_t = \mathbf{e}_j\}} \Pr\left(\boldsymbol{\xi}_t, \boldsymbol{\xi}_{t-1}|\Im_T; \boldsymbol{\theta}, \boldsymbol{\rho}\right) \\ &= \sum_{t=1}^T \sum_{\boldsymbol{\xi}_{t-1} = \mathbf{e}_i} \sum_{\boldsymbol{\xi}_t = \mathbf{e}_j} \frac{\Pr(\boldsymbol{\xi}_{t-1} = \mathbf{e}_i, \boldsymbol{\xi}_t = \mathbf{e}_j|\Im_T; \boldsymbol{\theta}, \boldsymbol{\rho})}{p_{ij}}, \end{aligned} \tag{C2}$$

which originates the vector expression

$$\frac{\partial \ln L(\boldsymbol{\theta}, \boldsymbol{\rho})}{\partial \boldsymbol{\rho}'} = \left(\sum_{t=1}^T (\hat{\boldsymbol{\xi}}_{t|T}^{(2)})'\right) \div \boldsymbol{\rho}', \tag{C3}$$

where $\hat{\boldsymbol{\xi}}_{t|T}^{(2)}$ is a $K^2 \times 1$ vector of (smoothed) probabilities concerning the matrix of state perceptions $\hat{\boldsymbol{\xi}}_{t-1|T}(\hat{\boldsymbol{\theta}}, \hat{\boldsymbol{\rho}}) \otimes \hat{\boldsymbol{\xi}}_{t|T}(\hat{\boldsymbol{\theta}}, \hat{\boldsymbol{\rho}})$, capturing how these regime beliefs move between $t-1$ and t. Because the K adding-up restrictions in $\mathbf{P}\iota_K = \iota_K$ can equivalently be written as $(\iota'_K \otimes \mathbf{I}_K)\boldsymbol{\rho} = \iota_K$, it follows that the FOCs are:

$$\frac{\partial L^*(\boldsymbol{\theta}, \boldsymbol{\rho})}{\partial \boldsymbol{\rho}'} = \left(\sum_{t=1}^T (\hat{\boldsymbol{\xi}}_{t|T}^{(2)})'\right) \div \hat{\boldsymbol{\rho}}' - \hat{\boldsymbol{\lambda}}'_1(\iota'_K \otimes \mathbf{I}_K) = \mathbf{0}'. \tag{C4}$$

In other words,

$$\hat{\rho} = \left(\sum_{t=1}^{T} (\hat{\boldsymbol{\xi}}_{t|T}^{(2)}) \right) \div (\boldsymbol{\iota}_K \otimes \hat{\boldsymbol{\lambda}}_1), \tag{C5}$$

implying

$$(\boldsymbol{\iota}'_K \otimes \mathbf{I}_K) \left(\sum_{t=1}^{T} \hat{\boldsymbol{\xi}}_{t|T}^{(2)} \right) \div (\boldsymbol{\iota}_K \otimes \hat{\boldsymbol{\lambda}}_1) = \left(\sum_{t=1}^{T} \hat{\boldsymbol{\xi}}_{t|T} \right) \div \hat{\boldsymbol{\lambda}}_1 = \boldsymbol{\iota}_K \tag{C6}$$

so that $\hat{\boldsymbol{\lambda}}_1 = \sum_{t=1}^{T} \hat{\boldsymbol{\xi}}_{t|T}$ obtains. $(\boldsymbol{\iota}'_K \otimes \mathbf{I}_K) \sum_{t=1}^{T} \hat{\boldsymbol{\xi}}_{t|T}^{(2)}$ produces a $K \times 1$ vector with ith element $\sum_{t=1}^{T} \hat{\boldsymbol{\xi}}_t$ and $(\boldsymbol{\iota}'_K \otimes \mathbf{I}_K)$ is a communication (conversion) matrix that converts probability distributions over $\boldsymbol{\xi}_{t-1|T}(\hat{\boldsymbol{\theta}}, \hat{\rho}) \otimes \boldsymbol{\xi}_{t|T}(\hat{\boldsymbol{\theta}}, \hat{\rho})$ into a distribution over $\boldsymbol{\xi}_t$ only. Finally, we have:

$$\hat{\boldsymbol{\rho}} = \left(\sum_{t=1}^{T} \hat{\boldsymbol{\xi}}_{t|T}^{(2)} \right) \div \left(\boldsymbol{\iota}_K \otimes \sum_{t=1}^{T} \hat{\boldsymbol{\xi}}_{t|T} \right), \tag{C7}$$

which is a highly nonlinear function of estimated smoothed probabilities.

When the initial state probability vector $\boldsymbol{\xi}_{1|0}$ is an unknown $K \times 1$ vector of parameters that must be estimated, note that the likelihood function can be alternatively be written as:

$$\begin{aligned} L\left(\{\mathbf{y}_t\}_{t=1}^{T} | \{\boldsymbol{\xi}_t\}_{t=1}^{T}, \boldsymbol{\theta}, \boldsymbol{\rho}\right) &= \prod_{t=1}^{T} \sum_{\{\boldsymbol{\xi}_t\}_{t=1}^{T}} p(\mathbf{y}_t | \boldsymbol{\xi}_t, \Im_{t-1}; \boldsymbol{\theta}) \Pr\left(\boldsymbol{\xi}_t | \Im_{t-1}; \boldsymbol{\theta}, \rho\right) \\ &= \prod_{t=1}^{T} \boldsymbol{\eta}'_t \boldsymbol{\xi}_{t|t-1} = \prod_{t=1}^{T} \boldsymbol{\eta}'_t \mathbf{P}' \boldsymbol{\xi}_{t-1|t-1} \\ &= \boldsymbol{\iota}'_K \prod_{t=1}^{T} \text{diag}(\boldsymbol{\eta}_t) \mathbf{P}' \hat{\boldsymbol{\xi}}_{t-1|t-1} = \boldsymbol{\iota}'_K \prod_{t=1}^{T} \mathbf{K}_t \boldsymbol{\xi}_{1|0}, \end{aligned} \tag{C8}$$

where $\mathbf{K}_t(\boldsymbol{\theta}) \equiv \text{diag}(\boldsymbol{\eta}_t)\mathbf{P}'$ (see Krolzig, 1997, p. 81, for a proof of the last line). Because the likelihood function is linear in $\boldsymbol{\xi}_{1|0}$, the solution is a boundary one:

$$\hat{\boldsymbol{\xi}}_{1|0} = \underset{1 \le i \le K}{\arg\max}\, \boldsymbol{\iota}'_K \prod_{t=1}^{T} \boldsymbol{K}_t(\boldsymbol{\theta}, \rho) \boldsymbol{e}_i. \tag{C9}$$

Chapter 10

Realized Volatility and Covariance

The world is noisy and messy. You need to deal with the noise and uncertainty.

Daphne Koller

As we have emphasized earlier in this book, the variance of asset returns (together with the correlations among them) plays an essential role in a number of practical financial applications, from risk management to asset pricing. In addition, it should also be clear that the conditional variance is *latent*, in the sense that it is not directly observable. In Chapter 5, we have presented the riskmetrics methodology and the (G)ARCH family of models as a framework to estimate and predict volatility, while in Chapter 7, we have introduced the notion of stochastic volatility. However, these models need to rely on parametric assumptions, in the sense that they write out complete function form and distributional specifications for all the random quantities of interest. Moreover, as observed by Bollerslev (1986) and Carnero et al. (2004), among the others, most of the standard parametric, latent volatility models fail to satisfactorily capture a number of stylized facts observed empirically, such as the low, but persistent autocorrelations in squared returns that are associated with high excess kurtosis of returns (see Chapter 5 for a discussion of this stylized fact).

Notably, if continuously observed prices were available and transaction costs did not exist, realized returns and therefore their variation over time would be measured without error. In other words, their realized variance (RV) could be treated as an observable variable, similar to the returns themselves. Although in reality, prices may of course only be observed in discrete time, Merton (1980) had already noted that the variance over a fixed interval can be estimated fairly accurately as the sum of squared returns, provided that returns are available at a sufficiently high-sampling frequency (we say that they are *finely sampled*).[1] For instance, the daily variance can be estimated as the sum of squared high-frequency (say, 1-min) intraday returns. Obviously, the daily volatility is then just the square root of the daily variance.

Given the increase in the availability of high-quality transaction asset price data that we have experienced in recent years across a range financial markets, the use of high-frequency returns to construct ex post (realized) measures of (daily) volatility has gained popularity. Therefore, in this chapter, after introducing the concept of *realized volatility*, we discuss how it can be constructed and how it should be adjusted in order to reduce the impact of microstructure effect, that tend to plague high-frequency data making them noisy. In addition, we discuss how future realized volatility can be forecasted using univariate linear and nonlinear models. Finally, we briefly discuss how realized correlations can be measured.

10.1 MEASURING REALIZED VARIANCE

10.1.1 Quadratic Variation and Its Estimators

Suppose that, during a day t, the logarithmic price process of a given asset follows the *continuous-time semi-martingale* (to rule out arbitrage opportunities) diffusion process

$$dp(t) = \mu(t)dt + \sigma(t)dW(t), \tag{10.1}$$

1. Throughout the chapter we shall often refer to high versus low sampling frequency. Therefore, it is fundamental that the Reader understands that the shortest the length of the subintervals, the larger the number of observations collected during the period of interest, and therefore the higher the sampling frequency is.

Essentials of Time Series for Financial Applications. DOI: https://doi.org/10.1016/B978-0-12-813409-2.00010-8

where $0 \leq t \leq T$, $p(t) = \ln P_t$, $\mu(t)$ is the drift component, $\sigma(t)$ is the strictly positive and square integrable *return instantaneous volatility*, and $W(t)$ is a standard Brownian motion. Hence, the continuously compounded return over the time interval from $t-k$ to t (where k is the length of the interval) is:

$$R(t,k) = p(t) - p(t-k) = \int_{t-k}^{t} \mu(\tau)d\tau + \int_{t-k}^{t} \sigma(\tau)dW(\tau). \tag{10.2}$$

The term $\int_{t-k}^{t} \sigma^2(\tau)d\tau$ that is implied by Eq. (10.2) represents the diffusive sample path variation over the interval $[t-k, t]$ and it is generally known as *integrated variance* (IV, also denoted as $IV_{t,k}$). Notably, under the process in Eq. (10.1), the IV is equal to the *quadratic variation* (QV, also denoted as $QV_{t,k}$). QV is a measure of the *true ex post variation* in continuously compounded returns over the period $[t-k, t]$. Although if we assume that Eq. (10.1) represents the price process, the terms QV and IV can be used interchangeably, we warn the reader that this does not need to be always the case, as we shall see in Section 10.1.4.

As we already anticipated, if we were able to observe the price continuously, we would also be able to treat return variation as an observable variable. However, because we only observe prices at discrete intervals, we can only estimate RV defined as follows.

DEFINITION 10.1 (Realized variance)

RV is the sum of squared returns over a period t (usually 1 day):

$$RV_{t,k} = \sum_{j=1}^{m} R^2_{t-k+j/m}, \quad j = 1, \ldots, m, \tag{10.3}$$

where $R_{t-k+j/m} = p_{t-k+j/m} - p_{t-k+(j-1)/m}$ is the return in the subinterval $[t-k+(j-1)/m, t-k+j/m]$, where $\left\{t-k+\frac{j}{m}, j = 1, \ldots, m\right\}$ is the partition of the interval $[t-k, t]$.

For instance, suppose that we want to compute the daily (where the day is assumed to contain 6 trading hours, that is 360 min, which is quite a common assumption in the literature) RV of the return on a given asset, using a sampling frequency of 5 min. We often say that we are collecting the prices (and thus computing the returns) on a 5-min grid. This means that we need to divide the 360 min in 72 periods with length equal to 5 min and to measure the return over each of them. Next, in order to compute the RV, we shall sum the 72 squared returns. Therefore, in this example, $m = 72$ and the length of the interval, let us call it δ_m, is simply k (equal to 1 day, that is 360 min) divided by m, which in this example yields 5 min. This sampling scheme that implies intervals that are equidistant in calendar time is also known as *calendar time sampling*. Of course, alternatives to this sampling scheme also exist, such as RV estimators that deal directly with the irregularly spaced tick-by-tick data. However, calendar time sampling is by far the most common approach and we shall assume this scheme throughout our discussion.

Although in principle different time horizons (e.g., weekly or monthly RV) are possible, the term RV is typically used in the literature to indicate a measure of daily variance constructed from intraday returns and, unless differently stated, we shall adopt this terminology in the rest of this chapter. Usually, when daily variation is estimated using the prices on a 1-min grid, its estimator is called the *all RV estimator*.

Needless to say, realized volatility is simply the square root of the RV. Under fairly general assumptions (see Aït-Sahalia and Jacod, 2014, for a discussion of convergence conditions), RV_t is a consistent estimator of QV, such that $RV_{t,k} \rightarrow^{P} QV_{t,k}$.

The attentive reader may have noticed that the sample path variation of returns is not affected by innovations to the drift component, so that in Eq. (10.3) we do not need to subtract the mean of the intraday returns. This is because the mean term $\mu(t)dt$ is of a lower order in terms of second-order properties than the diffusive innovations, $\sigma(\tau)dW(t)$. This means that the second moment dominates the first moment in influencing the high-frequency squared returns; therefore, the nonparametric estimate of the variance can be based on uncentered squared returns. This is very convenient as the expected daily return cannot be estimated with precision even when a sample of high-frequency data is collected. This should become clear if we recall that the estimator of the mean return is:

$$\hat{\mu} = \frac{1}{T}\sum_{t=1}^{T}(\ln(P_t) - \ln(P_{t-1})), \tag{10.4}$$

which yields

$$\hat{\mu} = \frac{1}{T}(\ln P_T - \ln P_{T-1} + \ln P_{T-1} - \ln P_{T-2} + \cdots + \ln P_2 - \ln P_1 + \ln P_1 - \ln P_0) = \frac{1}{T}(\ln(P_T) - \ln(P_0)). \tag{10.5}$$

It is evident that all the intermediate prices cancel out so that only the first and the last observation of the sample matter when estimating the mean of returns. We know that this is not the case for the variance estimator, as the return observations are squared before they are summed in the average. For instance, when $T = 2$, we can contrast

$$\hat{\mu} = \frac{1}{2}(\ln(P_1) - \ln(P_0)) + \frac{1}{2}(\ln(P_2) - \ln(P_1)) = \frac{1}{2}(\ln(P_2) - \ln(P_0)) \tag{10.6}$$

with

$$\begin{aligned}\hat{\sigma}^2 &= \frac{1}{2}(\ln(P_1) - \ln(P_0))^2 + \frac{1}{2}(\ln(P_2) - \ln(P_1))^2 \\ &= \frac{1}{2}(\ln(P_0))^2 + (\ln(P_1))^2 + \frac{1}{2}(\ln(P_2))^2 - \ln(P_0)\ln(P_1) - \ln(P_1)\ln(P_2).\end{aligned} \tag{10.7}$$

10.1.2 Microstructure Noise and the Choice of the Sampling Frequency

Theoretically, an arbitrary precision in the estimate of the QV can be reached by increasing the frequency of the observations. In other words, the accuracy of the QV estimator is optimized using the highest possible sampling frequency. However, high-frequency data are generally plagued by microstructure noise that may arise from the bid-ask bounce, asynchronous and infrequent trading, gradual and slow response of prices to block trading, etc. (see, for instance, Madhavan, 2000 and Biais et al., 2005 for surveys). These *microstructure effects* may induce spurious autocorrelations in (ultra) high-frequency returns, which can in turn unduly inflate the RV measure over what "pure" measures of asset prices would justify.

To understand this effect, suppose, as in Zhang et al. (2005), that the logarithmic prices p_t of an asset are observed with noise, that is,

$$p_{t,j} = p^*_{t,j} + \varepsilon_{t,j}, \tag{10.8}$$

where $p^*_{t,j}$ is the latent, true price process and ε_t is the microstructure noise. Consequently, the intraday asset return $R_{t,j}$ can be written as:

$$R_{t,j} = R^*_{t,j} + \varepsilon_{t,j} - \varepsilon_{t,j-1} = R^*_{t,j} + v_{t,j}, \tag{10.9}$$

exploiting the fact that $R_{t,j} = p_{t,j} - p_{t,j-1}$. It is not difficult to see that such a return process must be autocorrelated. Therefore,

$$RV_t = \sum_{j=1}^{m}(R^*_{t,j})^2 + 2\sum_{j=1}^{m}R^*_{t,j}v_{t,j} + \sum_{j=1}^{m}v^2_{t,j}, \tag{10.10}$$

and thus, conditioning on true (unobserved) returns we obtain that:

$$E\left[RV_t | R^*_t\right] = RV^*_t + \underbrace{2mE\left[\varepsilon^2_{t,j}\right]}_{\text{upward bias}}. \tag{10.11}$$

In practice, as shown by Bandi and Russel (2008) and Zhang et al. (2005), in the presence of a noise of empirically reasonable size, RV is a biased estimator of QV.

One way of dealing with microstructure noise is to construct a grid of intraday returns that are sampled at a frequency that is lower than 1-min, as biases tend to cancel out as one decreases the sampling frequency. For instance, Andersen et al. (2001a, b) have suggested to select a frequency between 5 and 15 min to trade off accuracy against the biases introduced by microstructure noise. This simple procedure is known as *sparse sampling*.

DEFINITION 10.2 (Sparse realized variance)

When the sampling frequency is lower than 1-min, it is common to denote as RV_t^s (or sparse RV, in opposition to the "all" RV), the sum of squared returns over a trading day

$$RV_t^s = \sum_{j=1}^{m/s} R_{t-1+js/m}^2, \tag{10.12}$$

sampled at frequency $s \neq 1$.

It is important to realize that there is nothing but the sampling frequency that differentiates Eq. (10.12) from Eq. (10.3). The choice of the frequency s obviously depends on the specific asset or market that we are considering. For instance, for very liquid assets, we shall use a frequency as close as possible to 1 min, while for less actively traded and deep markets, the optimal sample frequency is likely to be much lower. To accomplish the (difficult) task of striking a balance between the highest efficiency obtainable using the highest possible sampling frequency with the presence of microstructure noise, it is common to use the so-called *volatility signature plot*, that depicts the sample average of the RV estimator over a long-time span as a function of the sampling frequency. Because taking the average over a long-time span mitigates sample variation, in the absence of microstructure effects, the plot should be close to a horizontal line (i.e., daily realized volatility should be the same irrespective to the sampling frequency that we select). Therefore, one common strategy is to choose s^* such that the average RV does not change much for $s > s^*$. In other words, we want to set s^* equal to the smallest sampling frequency for which the average RV stabilizes. Example 10.1 compares the realized volatility measures at a frequency of 5 and 10 min for the S&P 500 index.

EXAMPLE 10.1

Fig. 10.1 plots the daily realized volatility (i.e., the square root of RV) of the S&P 500 over the period January 3, 2000–November 30, 2017, estimated using 5- and 10-min intervals. To make the plot easier to read, we have cut both the left and the right scales at 8%, thus removing from the plot part of the spike experienced by S&P 500 returns and hence variance, in 2008. To give an idea of the magnitude of this volatility "jump," consider that on October 10, 2008, in the aftermath of Lehman Brothers' default, the square root of the daily RV_t^5 reached a peak of 8.88% (vs a sample average equal to 0.84%)! Such a spike is of course economically interesting, and we are omitting it only to keep the plot interpretable.

Even if a visual comparison of the two RV frequencies is not easy (when plotted against each other they would be hardly distinguishable), note that the (square root of) RV_t^{10} (right axis) is slightly noisier than its 5-min counterparty (left axis). This shall not surprise us, as it is a consequence of the variance-bias trade-off. Indeed, when we try to remove microstructure noise from the data by choosing a lower sampling frequency, we discard information, thus reducing the efficiency of the estimator. Therefore, in Section 10.1.3, we shall propose some alternatives to the sparse RV estimator.

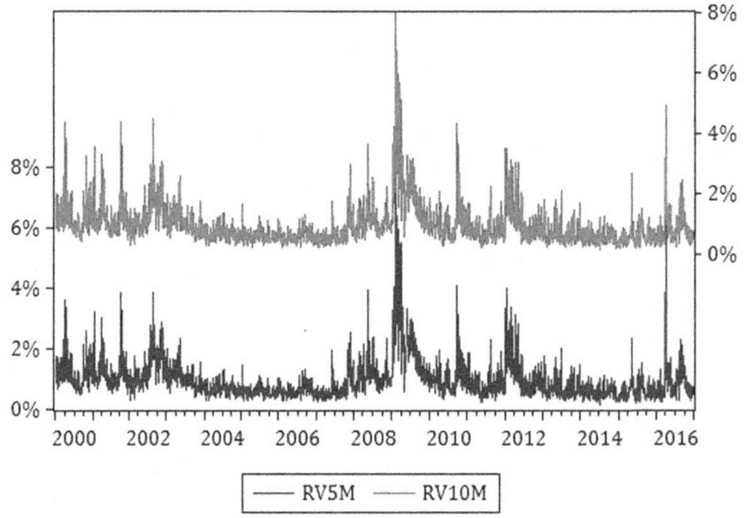

FIGURE 10.1 S&P 500 realized volatility at 5- and 10-min sampling frequency.

10.1.3 Other Bias-Adjusted Measures of Realized Volatility

As we have discussed in Section 10.1.2, while sparse sampling helps to reduce microstructure biases, the cost is to lose (potentially important) information, thus reducing the efficiency of the estimator. Therefore, we shall now discuss a number of alternatives, more efficient RV estimators, starting from the rather simple and intuitive average RV estimator.

Let us suppose, for instance, that a careful analysis of the volatility signature plot has led us to select an RV_t^{10} estimator, similar to the one that we have plotted in Fig. 10.1 for S&P 500 returns. As it shall be now clear, this means that we are summing up 10-min squared return to compute the daily RV. In addition, imagine that we have also a finer, 1-min pricing grid at our disposal. In principle, we can then compute 10 overlapping sparse RV estimators. To compute the first estimator, we start, say, at 8 a.m. and use a 10-min grid to sample the next price at 8:10 a.m. and to compute the first return. Next, instead of starting at 8:00 a.m. to compute the second estimator, we shall start at 8:01 a.m., and use again the 10-min grid, by sampling the price to compute the first return at 8:11 a.m. We repeat this procedure till we have computed the 10th sparse RV estimator that starts at 8:09 a.m. (and use the price recorded at 8.19 a.m. to compute the return). Our first 10-min RV estimator is then obtained by averaging the 10 overlapping RV_t^{10} estimators. This algorithm is iterated until the end of the trading day. Of course, once the mechanism is clear, nothing prevents us from computing the 5-min RV estimator by averaging five overlapping estimators that start every minute, or, say, the 40-min one using 40 overlapping estimators, shall the volatility signature plot indicate that 40-min is the sampling frequency that first stabilizes RV. Formally, we have that:

$$RV_t^{Avg} = \frac{1}{S}\sum_{i=1}^{S} RV_t^{s,i}. \tag{10.13}$$

The discernible strength of this simple but yet powerful method is that we compute the estimator at a frequency that is lower than 1-min, thus overcoming the problem of microstructure noise, but we also exploit the information from the finest available price grid.

EXAMPLE 10.1 (continued)

Coming back to our previous example on the S&P 500 data over the period January 3, 2000–November 30, 2017, in Fig. 10.2 we compare the 10-min realized volatility estimator with the one obtained using the subsampling, average RV method.

It is apparent (a glance at the 2008 spike is enough) that the (square root of the) average RV estimator, computed at a 10-min frequency but subsampling at a 1-min one as suggested by Eq. (10.13), is much smoother than its nonaveraged counterpart.

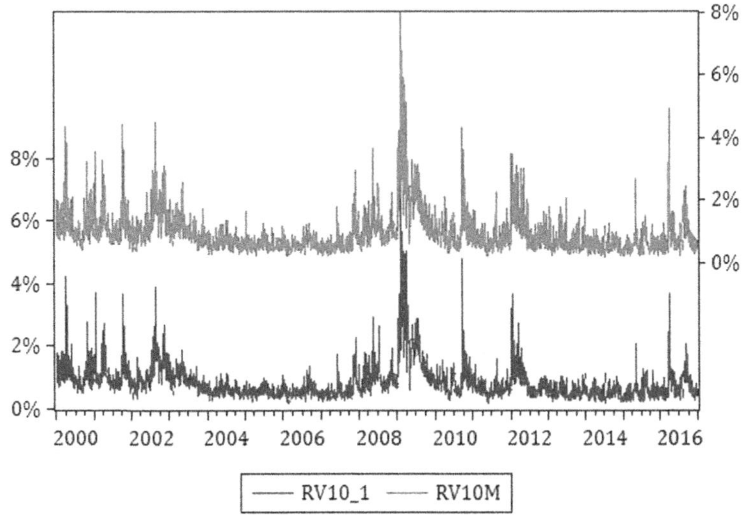

FIGURE 10.2 S&P 500 realized volatility at 10-min frequency versus average realized volatility at 10-min with 1-min subsampling.

A number of other, more sophisticated RV estimators have been suggested. For example, instead of using a lower sampling frequency in the attempt to remove the autocorrelation among intraday returns induced by microstructure noise, we may try to model it. For instance, if we were persuaded that return generating process was the one described in Eq. (10.9), we could correct the RV estimator as follows:

$$\begin{aligned} RV_t^{AR(1)} &= \sum_{j=1}^{m}(R_{t-1+j/m})^2 + \sum_{j=2}^{m} RV_{t-1+j/m}RV_{t-1+(j-1)/m} \\ &+ \sum_{j=1}^{m-1} RV_{t-1+j/m}RV_{t-1+(j+1)/m}, \end{aligned} \tag{10.14}$$

where $\mathrm{RV}_{t-1+j/m}$ is simply the RV computed as in Eq. (10.3).

That is, by adding the cross products from the adjacent intraday returns.

Alternatively, *realized kernel estimators of QV* have been proposed. Indeed, the problem of consistently estimating QV in presence of autocorrelations induced by microstructure noise is somehow similar to the estimation of the long-run variance of stationary time-series and therefore similar techniques can be employed (see for instance our notes in Chapter 4 on estimating the spectral variance at frequency 0). Among many others, Zhou (1996), who first introduced the idea of using kernel (weighting) functions to deal with the issue of microstructure noise in high-frequency data, suggested to use the following estimator:

$$RV_t^K = RV_t + 2K\left(\frac{m}{m-1}\right)\hat{\gamma}_1, \tag{10.15}$$

where $\hat{\gamma}_1$ is the first realized autocovariance $\hat{\gamma}_1 = (m/(m-1))\sum_{j=1}^{m-1} R_{t,j}R_{t,j+1}$, RV_t is the "all RV" estimator computed as in Eq. (10.3), $K(\cdot)$ is a kernel function, and m has the same meaning as earlier, that is, it is the number of intraday observations that are being summed up in the calculation of RV. Despite being unbiased, this estimator is not consistent, that is, rather oddly, it has the right expectation for finite m, but it diverges away from true, unobserved QV as $m \to \infty$, that is, when we truly move to continuous time.

Extending the early work by Zhou (1996), Hansen and Lunde (2006) (henceforth, HL) have developed the following estimator:

$$RV_t^{HL} = RV_t + 2\sum_{h=1}^{H} K\left(\frac{m}{m-h}\right)\hat{\gamma}_h, \tag{10.16}$$

where $\hat{\gamma}_1$ is the hth realized autocovariance, $\hat{\gamma}_h = m(m-h)^{-1}\sum_{j=1}^{m-h} R_{t,j}R_{t,j+h}$. Notably, Zhou's estimator in Eq. (10.15) is just a version of Eq. (10.16) in which $H=1$. Consequently, despite being more efficient than Zhou's version, also HL's estimator is unbiased but inconsistent. However, HL have shown that it is a more efficient estimator.

More recently, again extending these seminal papers on RV kernel-based estimators, Barndorff-Nielsen et al. (2008) (henceforth BNHLS) have proposed a class of unbiased and consistent estimators, the *flat-top kernel-based estimators* that we define the following.

DEFINITION 10.3 (Flat-top kernel-based estimator)

The flat-top, kernel-based estimator is computed as:

$$RV_t^{BHLS} = RV_t + \sum_{h=1}^{H} K\left(\frac{h-1}{H}\right)(\hat{\gamma}_h + \hat{\gamma}_{-h}), \tag{10.17}$$

where the kernel $K(x)$ for $x \in [0,1]$ is a nonstochastic weighting function such that $K(0)=1$ and $K(1)=0$, $h=-q,\ldots,q$, RV_t is RV, and $\hat{\gamma}_h$ is again the hth realized autocovariance, computed as earlier.

In their work, BNHLS compared three different kernels:

- Bartlett's kernel, $K(x) = 1 - x$ (already used in Chapter 4).
- Second-order kernel, $K(x) = 1 - 2x - x^2$.
- Epanechnikov's kernel, $K(x) = 1 - x^2$.

They found that the second-order kernel dominated the other two in terms of efficiency and that Bartlett's kernel dominated Epanechnikov's. Of course, other kernel functions, such as the Tukey–Hanning's kernel, can and have been employed in applied work, although it may remain unclear how and whether these may be optimal. More generally, a large number of realized volatility estimators that deal with the variance-bias trade-off have appeared in the literature, but a complete review of all of them is beyond the scope of this book. The interested reader may refer, for example, to McAleer and Medeiros' (2008) survey article.

10.1.4 Jumps and Bipower Variation

Up to this point, we have assumed that the return process is continuous, as expressed by Eq. (10.1). However, this is quite a strong assumption, as it is common knowledge that asset prices tend to show sudden discrete movements, when an unexpected news hits the market and induces trading flows. To take this fact into account, as already briefly mentioned in Chapter 7, the stochastic differential equation (SDE) in Eq. (10.1) can be modified to accommodate the presence of *jumps*:

$$dp(t) = \mu(t)dt + \sigma(t)dW(t) + \xi(t)dq_t, \tag{10.18}$$

where q is a Poisson process uncorrelated with the Brownian motion dW and governed by the jump intensity λ_t, that is, $\text{Prob}(dq_t = 1) = \lambda_t dt$, with λ_t positive and finite (this means that only a finite number of jumps per time period are allowed); $\xi(t)$ represents the magnitude of the jump at time t, should a jump occur. The attentive reader may recall that we have already encountered the model in Eq. (10.18) in Chapter 7. However, in contrast with stochastic volatility, the realized volatility approach is fully nonparametric and therefore it does not need any explicit distributional assumptions to be imposed.

Under the SDE in Eq. (10.18) the QV of returns over the interval $[t-k, t]$, $0 \le k \le t \le T$, is given by the sum of the diffusive IV ($IV_{t,k}$) and the cumulative squared jumps, that is,

$$QV_{t,k} = \underbrace{\int_{t-k}^{t} \sigma^2(\tau)d\tau}_{IV_{t,k}} + \sum_{t-k \le \tau \le t} J^2(\tau), \tag{10.19}$$

where $J(t) \equiv \xi(t)dq(t)$ is nonzero only if there is a jump at time t.

Although the RV estimator in Eq. (10.3) remains a consistent measure of the *total QV* also in presence of jumps (see the discussion in Andersen et al., 2004), the diffusive and jump volatility components generally (i.e., for the most typical price series) display different persistence properties. As a consequence, Barndorff-Nielsen and Sheppard (2004) suggest to separately estimate the IV_t and the jump components in Eq. (10.19). In particular, they introduced the h-skip bipower variation measure (henceforth BV) to estimate IV:

$$BV(t,k,h,m) = \frac{\pi}{2} \sum_{j=h+1}^{mk} \left| R\left(t-k+\frac{jk}{m}, \frac{1}{m}\right) \right| \left| R\left(t-k+\frac{(j-h)k}{m}, \frac{1}{m}\right) \right|. \tag{10.20}$$

Setting $h = 1$ in Eq. (10.20), we obtain the *realized bipower variation*, $BV(t,k,m)$, that provides a consistent estimate of the IV component, by construction robust to the presence of jumps. Therefore, if we subtract realized BV from RV, we obtain a consistent estimate of the cumulative squared jump component:

$$RV(t,k,m) - BV(t,k,m) \xrightarrow{m \to \infty} QV(t,k) - IV(t-k) = \sum_{t-k \le \tau \le t} J^2(\tau). \tag{10.21}$$

The decomposition featured in Eq. (10.21) is useful when we aim at using today's RV to forecast h-step-ahead RV. Indeed, intuitively, if the diffusive and the jump component display different persistence properties, separately forecasting each component should lead to better predictions. This has been empirically demonstrated, for instance, by Andersen et al. (2007).

10.2 FORECASTING REALIZED VARIANCE

10.2.1 Stylized Facts About Realized Variance

As we have emphasized so far, RV is an estimate of the true, unobserved *ex post (daily) return variation*. This means that we will be able to compute the RV of day t only after the market has closed and the last price has been posted and recorded. Although it is of course of interest to have an ex post measure of market volatility, it will be often practically more useful to traders and risk managers (among others) if it were possible to forecast the h-step-ahead RV. For instance, at day $t-1$ an analyst may be interested in forecasting the volatility that the market for a security will experience by the end of day t. Therefore, in this section, we shall discuss a number of forecasting models for RV. However, before we proceed, it is important to note a number of interesting empirical stylized facts about RV. For instance, let us consider the RV_t^5 of the S&P 500 returns that we have introduced in Example 10.1 and observe its main statistical properties.

EXAMPLE 10.2

Table 10.1 shows the sample autocorrelations and partial autocorrelations of the daily RV (we do not take its square root here) of the S&P 500 returns at a 5-min sampling frequency. The original sample that we consider is the same as in Example 10.1, index prices sampled at a 1-min frequency for the period January 3, 2000–November 30, 2017. We plot autocorrelations up to lag 20 (i.e., approximately 1 month, in terms of trading days).

From Chapter 2, we should be able to easily read the output in Table 10.1: the autocorrelations are quite high and decay very slowly remaining statistically significant for all the 20 lags that we have examined (that means for approximately 1 month!). Although the interpretation of the PACF is a bit more difficult, it could be that RV_t^5 has been originated from a very persistent ARMA process (or from a fractionally integrated process that we have briefly mentioned in Chapter 7). However, the relevant AR order is difficult to identify: from what we see in the sample correlogram, we may need more than 20 lags to capture the features of the RV. Of course, a specification search similar to the ones that we presented in Chapter 2 would be necessary to determinate the model that best fits the data.

TABLE 10.1 SACF and SPACF of S&P 500 RV at 5-min Sampling Frequency

Autocorrelation	Partial Correlation		AC	PAC	Q-Stat	Probability
		1	0.665	0.665	1976.54	0.000
		2	0.648	0.368	3850.46	0.000
		3	0.546	0.061	5183.91	0.000
		4	0.567	0.182	6619.98	0.000
		5	0.524	0.083	7848.33	0.000
		6	0.495	0.016	8943.05	0.000
		7	0.472	0.048	9938.75	0.000
		8	0.486	0.104	10993.79	0.000
		9	0.536	0.190	12280.11	0.000
		10	0.490	−0.006	13353.97	0.000
		11	0.465	−0.030	14321.91	0.000
		12	0.467	0.074	15298.69	0.000
		13	0.462	0.023	16255.94	0.000
		14	0.439	−0.021	17119.95	0.000
		15	0.439	0.054	17982.87	0.000
		16	0.413	0.002	18747.92	0.000
		17	0.406	−0.018	19488.15	0.000
		18	0.409	0.019	20240.19	0.000
		19	0.408	0.038	20987.98	0.000
		20	0.405	0.033	21723.57	0.000

Example 10.2 has illustrated a very important property of RV: it is *highly persistent*. Of course, this is good news, as this suggests that volatility can be forecastable over horizons of one or of a few months, once that the information contained in intraday prices is efficiently summarized.

A second stylized fact concerns the distribution of RV or, better, of its logarithmic transformation. Indeed, as RV is computed summing up squared returns and as such can only be positive, we cannot expect it to be normally distributed. However, once the logarithm of the RV is considered, we can show that in general this is approximately normally distributed with mean μ_{RV} and variance σ^2_{RV} (in other words, RV is well approximated by a log-normal distribution).

EXAMPLE 10.2 (continued)

As an example of this second stylized fact, Fig. 10.3 shows that the distribution of the natural logarithm of the 5-min RV for S&P 500 returns is close to a normal, although slightly positively (right) skewed. Indeed, the sample skew is equal to 0.32.

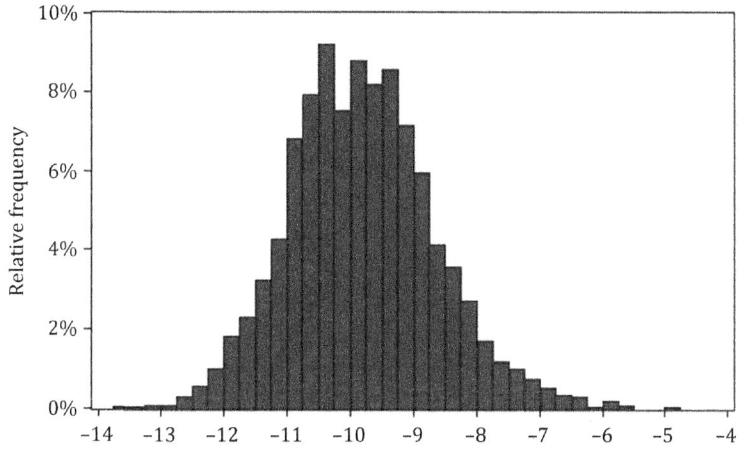

FIGURE 10.3 Distribution of the logarithm of S&P 500 5-min RV.

A third stylized fact concerns the distribution of standardized returns (i.e., in this case, returns divided by their realized standard deviation). A well-known result in the financial econometrics literature is that, when GARCH or stochastic volatility models are used, the standardized returns are often not normally distributed, but instead they keep display excess kurtosis in spite of the fact that in principle GARCH and SV models ought to help to capture these features. As we have discussed in Chapters 5 and 7, this result has led to the use of heavy-tailed distributions, such as the *t*-Student or the GED. On the contrary in the empirical high-frequency literature, it has been often reported that, when realized volatility is used, the distribution of standardized returns is approximately normal (see, for instance, Andersen et al., 2001a, for an application to equity and Andersen et al., 2001b, for an application to exchange rate data).

EXAMPLE 10.2 (continued)

The third stylized fact that we have just discussed also applies to the S&P 500 returns from our sample in Example 10.2. Fig. 10.4 shows that the distribution of S&P 500 returns that have been standardized using 5-min realized volatility is approximately normal, although the resulting empirical density displays a marginally negative skewness (−0.017) and a kurtosis that is slightly below the Gaussian threshold of three (2.580).

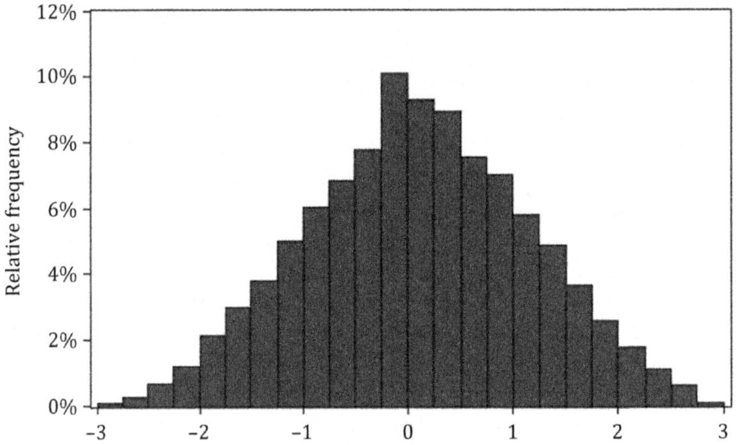

FIGURE 10.4 Distribution of standardized S&P 500 returns using 5-min RV.

10.2.2 Forecasting Realized Variance: Heterogeneous Autoregressions

From Example 10.2, we have learned an important empirical feature of RV, that is its positive persistence. As a result, it would be completely sensible to think of simple AR or ARMA models, similar to those discussed in Chapter 2, as appropriate tools to model and forecast RV. In particular, because we know that RV is observed with a measurement error, ARMA models could probably provide the best fit for the data, for instance incorporating MA terms that capture the delayed reaction to news due to microstructure effects. However, Example 10.2 has emphasized another empirical property of RV: it is highly persistent, much more than what can be accommodated by standard, parsimonious ARMA models. As an implication, a large number of lags would be probably necessary in order to capture the *long-memory feature of the RV process*. Moreover, if we think that in our example more than 20 lags seemed to be needed for an AR (p) framework to capture the properties of RV, it becomes evident that to estimate such a model would require a large number of observations. To deal with the extreme persistence of realized volatility while at the same time preserving some parsimony to the model, that is of course always welcome in forecasting applications, Corsi (2009) has proposed the *heterogeneous autoregressive (HAR) model*. In practice, he suggests adding to the predictive model or RV also weekly and monthly moving averages of RV to capture the long-memory dynamics of the RV process. The HAR (or HAR-RV) model is defined as follows.

DEFINITION 10.4 (HAR model)

Given the weekly and the monthly moving averages of RV, that is $RV_{W,t}$ and $RV_{M,t}$, respectively, and daily RV such that $RV_{D,t} \equiv RV_t$, according to the HAR model, the one-step-ahead forecast is:

$$RV_{t+1} = \phi_0 + \phi_D RV_{D,t} + \phi_W RV_{W,t} + \phi_M RV_{M,t} + \varepsilon_{t+1}, \tag{10.22}$$

where

$$RV_{W,t} \equiv RV_{t-4,t} = \frac{[RV_{t-4} + RV_{t-3} + RV_{t-2} + RV_{t-1} + RV_t]}{5},$$

$$RV_{M,t} \equiv \frac{[RV_{t-20} + RV_{t-19} + \cdots + RV_t]}{21},$$

assuming 5 trading days in a week and 21 trading days in a month.

Interestingly, the HAR model has only four parameters, ϕ_0, ϕ_D, ϕ_W, and ϕ_M, and enjoys the additional advantage that it can be estimated simply by OLS, as it does not contain the MA component (as we know from Chapter 2 an ARMA model must be estimated by MLE). However, because it features long lags of past RV through the monthly and weekly RV estimates as of time t, although very simple—clearly the model in Eq. (10.22) is just a type of AR(p) so that all the coverage given in Chapter 2 to h-step-ahead forecasts will apply—it is powerful enough to capture very high and slowly decaying persistence, as typical of fractionally integrated models. For instance, the one-step-ahead forecast of RV is simply:

$$RV_{t+1|t} = \phi_0 + \phi_D RV_{D,t} + \phi_W RV_{W,t} + \phi_M RV_{M,t}, \tag{10.23}$$

while the h-step-ahead forecasts can then be obtained by iteration. However, considering the (approximate) log-normality of RV, we may prefer to estimate HAR models of the log transformation of RV (to obtain more precisely estimated coefficients by OLS), as in

$$\ln(RV_{t+1}) = \phi_0 + \phi_D \ln(RV_{D,t}) + \phi_W \ln(RV_{W,t}) + \phi_M \ln(RV_{M,t}) + \varepsilon_{t+1}, \tag{10.24}$$

where ε_{t+1} IID $N(0, \sigma_\varepsilon^2)$. Obviously, in order to obtain h-step-ahead forecast, we should carefully "undo" the log transformation, that is:

$$\begin{aligned} RV_{t+1|t} &= \exp[\phi_0 + \phi_D \ln(RV_{D,t}) + \phi_W \ln(RV_{W,t}) + \phi_M \ln(RV_{M,t})] \\ &\times \exp(\sigma_\varepsilon^2/2) = (RV_{D,t})^{\phi_D}(RV_{W,t})^{\phi_W}(RV_{M,t})^{\phi_M}\exp(\phi_0 + \sigma_\varepsilon^2/2). \end{aligned} \tag{10.25}$$

EXAMPLE 10.3

In this example, we estimate a HAR model for the daily RV of the returns of the (net of dividends and other cash distributions) NYSE Index, for the sample January 3, 2000–December 30, 2016. Clearly, we are going to lose the initial 21 observations of the sample, because we need five of them to compute the first weekly moving average of RV and all of them to calculate the first monthly moving average. The model estimated is as follows:

$$RV_{t+1} = \underset{(0.003)}{2.18E-05} - \underset{(0.000)}{0.15}\, RV_{D,t} + \underset{(0.000)}{0.51}\, RV_{W,t} + \underset{(0.000)}{0.49}\, RV_{M,t} + \varepsilon_{t+1},$$

where p-values are reported in parenthesis. The R^2 of the regression is equal to a rather interesting 0.26. To evaluate forecast accuracy, we perform a rather simple backtesting exercise: we reestimate the HAR model using observations up to December 31, 2010 and then we compute the forecasts of RV from January 03, 2011 to December 30, 2016. The model estimated on this shorter dataset is

$$RV_{t+1} = \underset{(0.019)}{2.48E-05} - \underset{(0.000)}{0.17}\, RV_{D,t} + \underset{(0.000)}{0.50}\, RV_{W,t} + \underset{(0.000)}{0.52}\, RV_{M,t} + \varepsilon_{t+1},$$

with an R^2 equal again to 0.26 (interestingly, all the estimated coefficients turn out to be rather stable).

To oppose some (admittedly, naïve) benchmark to the HAR framework, we have also estimated a simple AR(1) model for the daily RV over the same in-sample period:

$$RV_{t+1} = \underset{(0.000)}{0.0001} + \underset{(0.000)}{0.21}\, RV_{D,t} + \varepsilon_{t+1}.$$

In this case, the R^2 is equal to 0.045, much lower than the one of the HAR regression.

Fig. 10.5 plots daily realized volatility (in this case, we plot the square root of RV to make the diagram easier to read) from the HAR and from the naïve AR(1) model against the actual realizations. Interestingly, the AR(1) model (scale on the right axis) tends to predict lower realized volatility than the HAR. To compare the predictive accuracy of the two models, we also computed the mean squared forecast error of each of them. As we expected, the HAR model has a lower MSFE than the simple AR(1) model: 105.20 versus 171.74 and the difference appears to be as major as reported in the literature before.

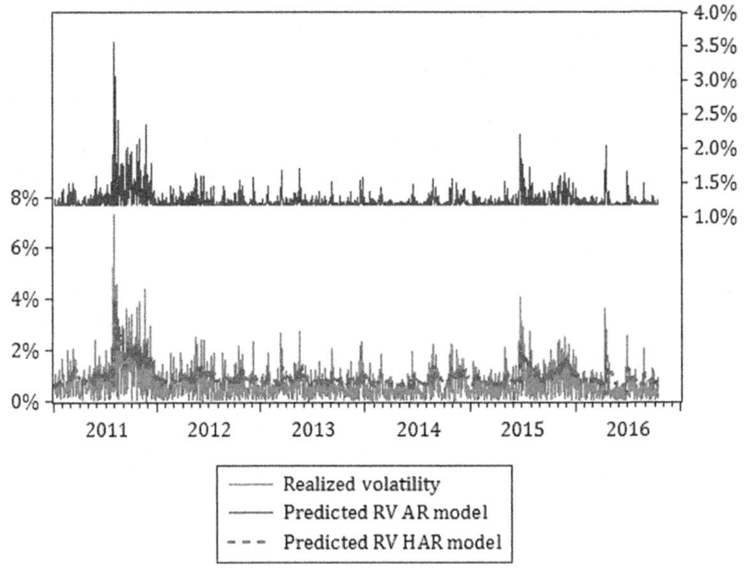

FIGURE 10.5 Plots of realized volatility forecasts for NYSE returns from HAR versus AR(1) models.

10.2.3 Range-Based Variance Forecasts

As we have seen in Section 10.2.2, the construction of RV measures requires the availability of good quality, high-frequency data. For instance, building a 1-min price grid requires that the security trades at least once every minute. While this can be reasonable for very liquid assets, it can become a problem for less liquid ones. As a consequence, we shall now introduce range-based variance (volatility) proxies, which are by far easier to compute than RV.

Range-based variance measures, introduced by Parkinson (1980) and Garman and Klass (1980), are based on the highest and the lowest prices observed during the trading day. More specifically, these measures are computed as follows.

DEFINITION 10.5 (Range-based variance measures)

Given the highest and lowest prices recorded during the trading day, that is, P_t^{High} and P_t^{Low}, respectively, the range statistic is defined as:

$$D_t = \ln(P_t^{High}) - \ln(P_t^{Low}) = \ln\left(\frac{P_t^{High}}{P_t^{Low}}\right). \tag{10.26}$$

If the log return on the asset is normally distributed with 0 mean and variance σ^2, the expected value of the range is $E[D_t^2] = 4\ln(2)\sigma^2$, so that a range-based measure of variance is:

$$\sigma^2 = \frac{1}{4\ln(2)}\frac{1}{T}\sum_{t=1}^{T} D_t^2, \tag{10.27}$$

where T is the number of observations. Therefore, a range proxy of daily, time-varying variance, call it RP_t, can be simply constructed as:

$$RP_t = \frac{1}{4\ln(2)} D_t^2. \tag{10.28}$$

Notably, $1/(4\ln(2))$ is a constant and is approximately equal to 0.361. A more accurate range-based variance proxy can be computed when we consider also the daily open and close log prices. Again, assuming that log returns are normally distributed with mean 0 and variance σ^2, we obtain:

$$RP_t = \frac{1}{2}D_t^2 - (2\ln(2) - 1)\ln\left(\frac{P_t^{Close}}{P_t^{Open}}\right)^2. \tag{10.29}$$

If the mean return cannot be assumed to be equal to 0, a more general range-based variance proxy is instead

$$\begin{aligned} RP_t = {} & \ln\left(\frac{P_t^{High}}{P_t^{Open}}\right)\left[\ln\left(\frac{P_t^{High}}{P_t^{Open}}\right) - \ln\left(\frac{P_t^{Low}}{P_t^{Open}}\right)\right] \\ & + \ln\left(\frac{P_t^{Low}}{P_t^{Open}}\right)\left[\ln\left(\frac{P_t^{Low}}{P_t^{Open}}\right) - \ln\left(\frac{P_t^{Close}}{P_t^{Open}}\right)\right], \end{aligned} \tag{10.30}$$

where the nature of the correction derives from tedious but straightforward algebra.

EXAMPLE 10.4

Fig. 10.6 plots the range-based volatility proxy (computed as the square root of Eq. 10.29) of S&P 500 returns for a sample January 3, 2000–December 30, 2016 and compares it with the square root of squared returns (the absolute value). Clearly, squared returns are a natural, although biased, proxy for daily variance when intraday prices are not available. It is easy to see that the range-based proxy is much less noisy than squared returns (although it is noisier than RV measures).

In Fig. 10.7, we also plot the distribution of the logarithm of the two variance estimators. It is obvious that the log transformation of the range-based variance proxy resembles to a normal much more than the logarithm of squared returns.

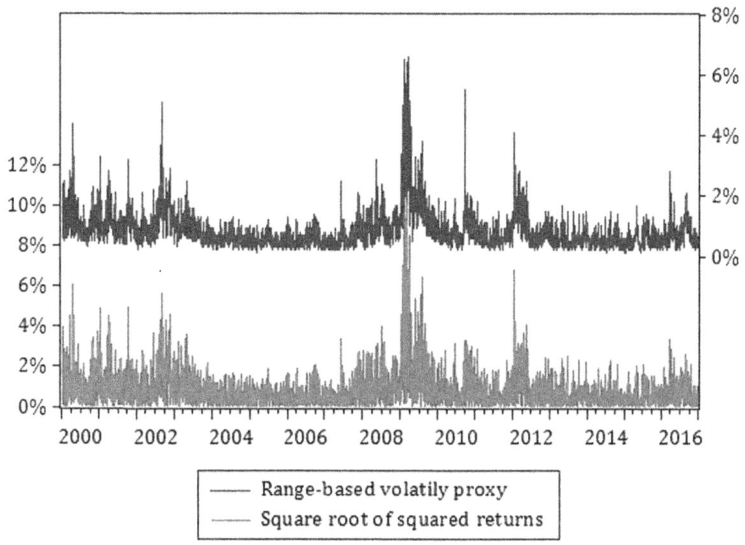

FIGURE 10.6 Range-based volatility and square root of squared returns for S&P 500 data.

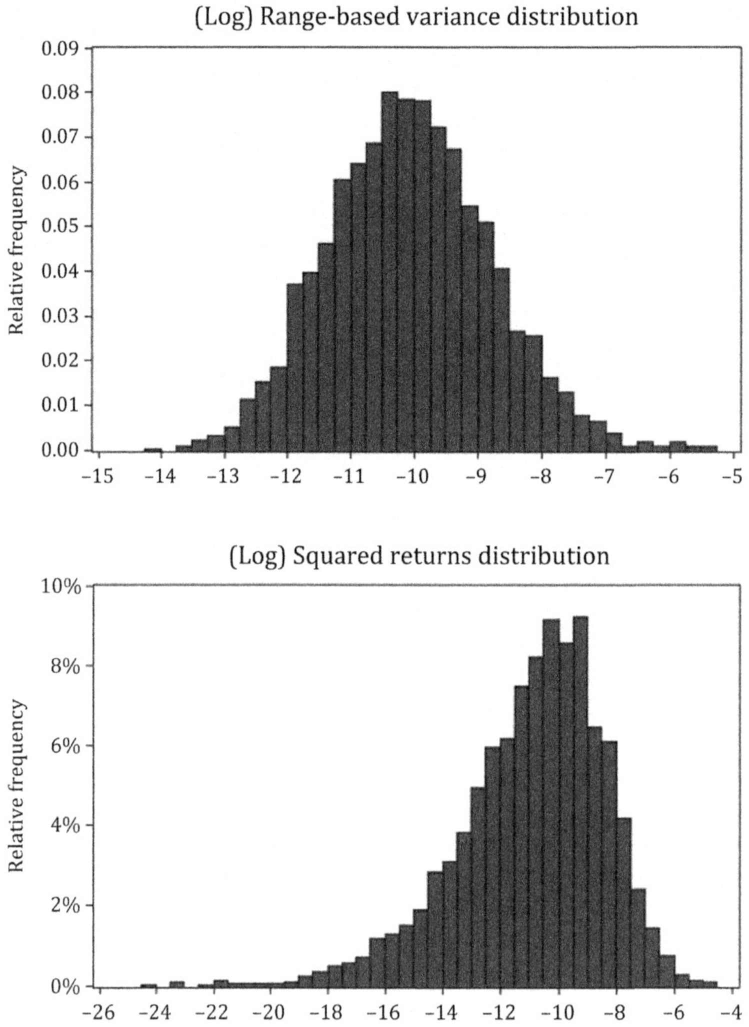

FIGURE 10.7 Empirical distribution of the logarithm of a range-based variance proxy versus squared returns.

Noticeably, also RP can be predicted using a HAR model like the one presented in Section 10.2.2, such as:

$$RP_{t+1} = \phi_0 + \phi_D RP_{D,t} + \phi_W RP_{W,t} + \phi_M RP_{M,t} + \varepsilon_{t+1}, \tag{10.31}$$

where

$$RP_{W,t} \equiv \frac{[RP_{t-4} + RP_{t-3} + RP_{t-2} + RP_{t-1} + RP_t]}{5}$$

$$RP_{M,t} \equiv \frac{[RP_{t-20} + RP_{t-19} + \cdots + RP_t]}{21}.$$

Of course, considering that the log-transform of RP seems to be approximately distributed as a normal, as we have seen in Example 10.4, the logarithmic HAR model in Eq. (10.24) would make sense to forecast RP as well.

A final remark on range-based volatility proxies is that they seem to be less affected by microstructure noise; however, despite being quite useful for illiquid markets, range-based volatility measures have generally been found to be less efficient than RV, that should always be preferred by an analyst when a sufficiently dense grid of high-frequency price data is available.

10.3 MULTIVARIATE APPLICATIONS

10.3.1 Realized Covariance Matrix Estimation

Up to this point, we have limited ourselves to the discussion of ex post variance measures. However, many applications, such as portfolio choice (see, e.g., Bandi et al., 2008) and risk management (see, e.g., Bollerslev and Zhang, 2003), require measuring and also forecasting correlations. Unfortunately, multivariate applications are made difficult by delayed reactions of one security to changes in the prices of related assets and by nonsynchronous trading effects. In particular, the asynchronous nature of intraday prices tends to bias realized covariances toward 0, unless an appropriate approach is used to further apply adjustments. The downward bias occurs because when trading is infrequent, news that affect a pair of assets will be incorporated in prices at different times not because their news do not matter for both assets, but simply as a result of asynchronous trading. Despite in the literature the debate on the issues involved appears to be far from settled, in this section we shall illustrate a simple procedure to estimate realized covariance (correlations) from intraday prices.

Let us consider a pair of assets and suppose that we can observe their prices at exactly the same time intervals. Following the same reasoning that we applied in deriving RV measures, an estimate of the realized daily covariance will be the following.

DEFINITION 10.6 (Realized covariance)

The daily realized covariance between two assets computed from intraday returns recorded at m subintervals of length $1/m$ is simply obtained as the sum of the cross products of the intraday returns, that is:

$$RCov_{12,t}^{m} = \sum_{j=1}^{m} R_{1,t-1+j/m} R_{2,t-1+j/m}. \tag{10.32}$$

Therefore, the realized correlation can be computed as:

$$RCorr_{12,t}^{m} = \frac{RCov_{12,t}^{m}}{\sqrt{RV_{1,t}^{m} RV_{2,t}^{m}}}, \tag{10.33}$$

where $RV_{1,t}^{m}$ and $RV_{2,t}^{m}$ are the daily RVs of the two assets.

As already discussed in the case of RV, the higher the sampling frequency we use, the more efficient the forecast that we will obtain. However, we already know from Section 10.1.2 that high-frequency data will be plagued by microstructure noise; in addition, now that covariances are under scrutiny, asynchronous trading is likely to represent an even more challenging issue. Recently, a number of approaches have been used to tackle the problem of asynchronous trading and its effects on realized covariance estimators. Such strategies can be broadly divided into two strands:

- The first approach consists into fixing a time interval, for instance 5 mins, and uses the last quote prior to the 5-min mark, or, alternatively, the interpolation of the first and the last price in the 5-min subinterval. Needless to say, at least one quote should be available for both assets in the chosen time interval for this algorithm to be applicable.
- The second approach consists instead of denoting as $\tau(1)$ the first point in time when both assets have changed their price at least one time since market opening; as soon as we have identified $\tau(1)$ we repeat the exercise and denote by $\tau(2)$ the first point in time when both assets have changed their prices again, after $\tau(1)$. We iterate this time labeling algorithm until the end of the day, obtaining $\tau(j)$ data points with $j = 1, \ldots, M$.

To offer a simple example, imagine that, after the market opening at 8:00 a.m., we record a price for the first asset at 8:02. However, we get a price for the second asset only at 8:04; therefore $\tau(1)$ will be 8:04. Similarly, if we next get a quote for the second asset at 8:06, and a quote for the first asset at 8:09, $\tau(2)$ will be equal to 8:09. We can proceed in this way, until we exhaust the available 1-min price grid for both assets. At the end of the trading day, the synchronized intraday returns for the two assets will be computed as follows:

$$\begin{aligned} R_{1,\tau(j)} &= \ln(P_{1,\tau(j)}) - \ln(P_{1,\tau(j-1)}) \\ R_{2,\tau(j)} &= \ln(P_{2,\tau(j)}) - \ln(P_{2,\tau(j-1)}). \end{aligned} \tag{10.34}$$

Therefore, the realized daily covariance between the assets can now be computed simply as:

$$RCov_{12,t}^{\text{Sync}} \equiv \sum_{j=1}^{M} R_{1,\tau(j)} R_{2,\tau(j)}. \tag{10.35}$$

Notably, in order to obtain the covariance matrix and the realized correlation, it is necessary to compute the RV estimates for the assets on the same time grid $\tau(j)$ that has been employed for the covariance.

Clearly, this approach can be generalized to the case of any number $N \geq 3$ assets; of course, the more are the assets involved, the more will be the burden coming from asynchronicity in trading, as measured by the difference between the number of recorded prices on the high-frequency grid recorded for each of the assets and M. In fact, when all the assets are highly illiquid, and N becomes very large, it is possible for M to decline to a very small number, which entails a considerable loss of efficiency.

10.3.2 Range-Based Covariance Estimation

It is possible to extend the range-based modeling approach of Section 10.2.3 also to covariance prediction, although this may not be immediately intuitive: in fact, the cross product of ranges does not provide an estimate of covariance. Therefore, it is necessary to exploit no-arbitrage restrictions—if any can be found of course—among the assets in order to be able to obtain range-based covariance and correlations measures. For instance, Christoffersen (2012) shows how range-based covariances can be computed in the case of exchange (henceforth, FX) rates. Let us denote the USD/YEN rate as P_1, the EUR/USD rate as P_2, and the EUR/YEN rate as P_3. By no-arbitrage, we can write that the cross-rate between two currencies should always equal the product of the FX rates of the two currencies against a fixed notional currency:

$$S_{3,t} = S_{1,t} S_{2,t}. \tag{10.36}$$

When Eq. (10.36) fails, it is possible to show that an arbitrage opportunity exists. Because of Eq. (10.36), by taking logs of both sides, we have that:

$$R_{3,t} = R_{1,t} + R_{2,t}. \tag{10.37}$$

Because

$$\frac{S_{3,t}}{S_{3,t-1}} = \frac{S_{1,t}S_{2,t}}{S_{3,t-1}} = \frac{(S_{1,t}S_{2,t})}{(S_{1,t-1}S_{2,t-1})} = \frac{S_{1,t}}{S_{1,t-1}}\frac{S_{2,t}}{S_{2,t-1}} \tag{10.38}$$

and

$$\sigma_{3,t}^2 = \sigma_{1,t}^2 + \sigma_{2,t}^2 + 2\sigma_{12,t}. \tag{10.39}$$

Rearranging, we find that the covariance between USD/YEN and EUR/USD from Eq. (10.39) as:

$$\sigma_{12,t} = \frac{(\sigma_{3,t}^2 - \sigma_{1,t}^2 - \sigma_{2,t}^2)}{2}. \tag{10.40}$$

Therefore, the range-based covariance proxy can be computed as:

$$RPCov_{12,t} \equiv \frac{(RP_{3,t} - RP_{1,t} - RP_{2,t})}{2}, \tag{10.41}$$

where $RP_{3,t}$, $RP_{2,t}$, and $RP_{1,t}$ are computed as in Section 10.2.3.

REFERENCES

Aït-Sahalia, Y., Jacod, J., 2014. High-Frequency Financial Econometrics. Princeton University Press, Princeton, USA.

Andersen, T.G., Bollerslev, T., Diebold, F.X., Ebens, H., 2001a. The distribution of realized stock return volatility. J. Finan. Econom. 61, 43–76.

Andersen, T.G., Bollerslev, T., Diebold, F.X., Labys, P., 2001b. The distribution of exchange rate volatility. J. Am. Stat. Assoc. 96, 42–55.

Andersen, T.G., Bollerslev, T., Diebold, F.X., 2004. Parametric and nonparametric volatility measurement. In: Hansen, L.P., Aït-Sahalia, Y. (Eds.), Handbook of Financial Econometrics. North-Holland, Amsterdam.

Andersen, T.G., Bollerslev, T., Dobrev, D., 2007. No-arbitrage semi-martingale restrictions for continuous-time volatility models subject to leverage effects, jumps and i.i.d. noise: theory and testable distributional implications. J. Econometr. 138, 125–180.

Bandi, F.M., Russell, J.R., 2008. Microstructure noise, realized variance, and optimal sampling. Rev. Econom. Stud. 75, 339–369.

Bandi, F.M., Russell, J.R., Zhu, Y., 2008. Using high-frequency data in dynamic portfolio choice. Economet. Rev. 27, 163–198.

Barndorff-Nielsen, O.E., Shephard, N., 2004. Power and bipower variation with stochastic volatility and jumps. J. Finan. Econometr. 2, 1–37.

Barndorff-Nielsen, O.E., Hansen, P., Lunde, A., Shephard, N., 2008. Designing realised kernels to measure the ex-post variation of equity prices in the presence of noise. Econometrica 76, 1481–1536.

Biais, B., Glosten, L., Spatt, C., 2005. Market microstructure: a survey of microfoundations, empirical results, and policy implications. J. Finan. Markets 8, 217–264.

Bollerslev, T., 1986. Generalized autoregressive conditional heteroskedasticity. J. Econometr. 21, 307–328.

Bollerslev, T., Zhang, L., 2003. Measuring and modeling systematic risk in factor pricing models using high -frequency data. J. Empirical Finan. 10, 533–558.

Carnero, M.A., Peña, D., Ruiz, E., 2004. Persistence and kurtosis in GARCH and stochastic volatility models. J. Finan. Econometr. 2, 319–342.

Christoffersen, P.F., 2012. Elements of Financial Risk Management, second ed. Academic Press, Waltham, USA.

Corsi, F., 2009. A simple approximate long memory model of realized volatility. J. Finan. Econom. 7, 174–196.

Garman, M.B., Klass, M.J., 1980. On the estimation of security price volatilities from historical data. J. Bus. 53, 67–78.

Hansen, P.R., Lunde, A., 2006. Consistent ranking of volatility models. J. Econometr. 131, 97–121.

Madhavan, A., 2000. Market microstructure: a survey. J. Finan. Markets 3, 205–258.

McAleer, M., Medeiros, M.,C., 2008. Realized volatility: a review. Economet. Rev. 27, 10–45.

Merton, R.C., 1980. On estimating the expected return on the market: an exploratory investigation. J. Finan. Econom. 8, 323–361.

Parkinson, M., 1980. The extreme value method for estimating the variance of the rate of return. J. Bus. 53, 61–65.

Zhang, L., Mykland, P.A., Aït-Sahalia, Y., 2005. A tale of two time scales: determining integrated volatility with noisy high-frequency data. J. Am. Stat. Assoc. 100, 1394–1411.

Zhou, B., 1996. High frequency data and volatility in foreign-exchange rates. J. Bus. Econom. Stat. 14, 45–52.

Appendix A: Mathematical and Statistical Appendix

A FUNDAMENTAL STATISTICAL DEFINITIONS

A.1 Random Variables

Every bit of data that we may collect to implement one of the empirical analyses described in this textbook is seen in statistics and econometrics, as a realization of a *random variable*, which is a function that may assume one among different values as a result of a random experiment or phenomenon, according to some structure, a *probability law*. Consider for instance the daily closing return on a stock. In statistics, analysts consider the observed return as a realization of a corresponding random variable, meaning that, before the closure of the market, there exist many possible values for the stock return and, when the market closes, we will observe only one of them, called a *realization* of the random variable. The individual values actually assumed by a random variable are called *outcomes*, while sets of elementary realizations are called *events*. Random variables are used to model the outcomes of random experiments or phenomena, i.e., when their results are ex ante uncertain but the chances of their occurrence are subject to the laws of probability.

Random variables can be either *discrete* or *continuous*. The former type is composed by random variables whose set of possible outcomes (also called the support) is discrete (i.e., outcomes are finite in number or at least infinitely countable). Continuous random variables are those whose set of possible outcomes is an interval of $\mathbb{R}$ or $\mathbb{R}$ itself. An example of a discrete random variable could be the result of rolling a dice; an example of a continuous random variable could be the annual rate of GDP growth. In this book, we will in general use continuous random variables, because financial and economic data rarely assume a finite number of discrete values only. A discrete random variable that turns out to be occasionally useful in time series analysis of financial data is the *binary* (also called *dummy*) *variable*, which can assume only the realized values 0 and 1. A dummy variable is used to indicate the occurrence or nonoccurrence of a particular event, or the presence vs absence of a particular characteristic of the random experiment or phenomenon under investigation.

To describe a random variable, we commonly employ the concept of *probability*. Probability can be defined in a classical vs a frequentist way. The classical definition of probability is that the probability of an event is the ratio between the number of favorable outcomes and the number of all possible outcomes from an experiment or uncertain phenomenon. According to the frequentist definition, the probability of an event is its relative frequency computed on a sufficiently large number of trials that elicit realizations from the random experiment or phenomenon. In simple words, a random variable is then described by the probabilities of the events that may take place under the variable. If the random variable is discrete, we can describe it by associating a probability to each one of its possible values in the support; such probability values will be between 0 and 1 and their sum will be 1. If a random variable is continuous, we will describe it by using a *probability density function* (PDF), which, for a given random variable X, is a function $f(x)$ such that:

$$\Pr(a \leq X \leq b) = \int_a^b f(x)dx,$$

where $\Pr(a \le X \le b)$ is the probability that the random variable X assumes a value between a and b, and these are values in the support of the variable. A continuous function f can be used as PDF to describe a continuous random variable, if it is nonnegative and if the whole area below the curve is equal 1, that is:

$$f(x) \ge 0 \ \forall x;$$

$$\int_{-\infty}^{+\infty} f(x)dx = 1.$$

Both conditions are needed to ensure that any computable value of the probability of an event (in this case, defined as the interval [a, b]) lies between 0 and 1. Fig. A.1 graphically shows one example of a very important PDF, which is the PDF of a standard normal variable, a crucial density, to which we shall return later in this appendix.

The same information carried by the PDF can be usefully represented also through the so-called *cumulative distribution function* (CDF), which is a function F such that:

$$P(X \le a) = F(a),$$

where $P(X \le a)$ indicates the probability that the random variable X assumes a value smaller or equal to a. Notice that the CDF of a random variable is the integral of the PDF of the same variable:

$$F(a) = \int_{-\infty}^{a} f(x)dx.$$

A continuous function F can be used as CDF to describe a random variable, if it is nondecreasing (i.e., the corresponding PDF is nonnegative) and if the following two conditions hold:

$$\lim_{x \to -\infty} F(x) = 0; \qquad \lim_{x \to +\infty} F(x) = 1.$$

From the definition of CDF and the stated properties, it follows that

$$P(X > a) = 1 - F(a),$$
$$P(a \le X \le b) = F(b) - F(a)$$

and that the probability of a continuous variable assuming a specific single value is equal to 0,

$$P(X = a) = 0.$$

Fig. A.2 shows the normal CDF that is computed from the PDF in Fig. A.1.

The key features of a given random variable X are often described through the so-called *moments*, which are scalar values representing some features of the PDF/CDF that are commonly believe to be of importance of significance, such

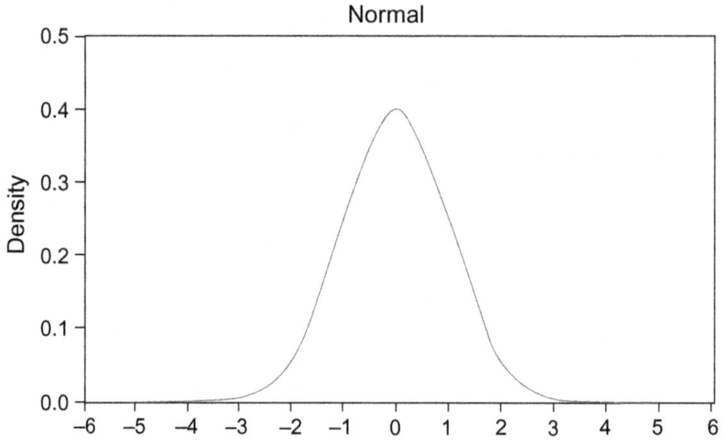

FIGURE A.1 PDF of a standard normal variable.

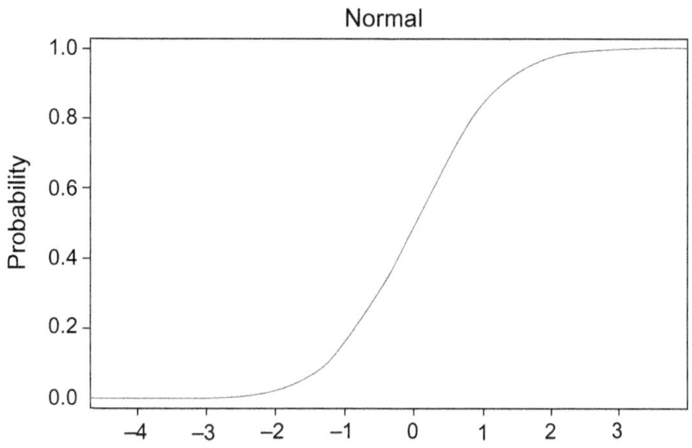

FIGURE A.2 CDF of a standard normal variable.

as location, dispersion, and asymmetry. Moments can be *uncentered* or *centered.* The kth *uncentered moment* of a distribution is defined as

$$M_k(X) = \int_{-\infty}^{+\infty} x^k f(x)dx,$$

while the kth *central moment* is defined as

$$\mu_k(X) = \int_{-\infty}^{+\infty} [x - M_1(X)]^k f(x)dx.$$

The values assumed by (all) the moments, at least heuristically speaking, describe the shape of the distribution as represented by PDF/CDF (technically the correspondence is imperfect in the sense that there are distributions for which no moments exist).

Particular attention is normally paid to the first uncentered moment, which is called *expected value* (or mathematical expectation or just expectation or mean) of the random variable X, and it is indicated as $E[X]$ (occasionally, with μ):

$$E[X] = M_1(X) = \int_{-\infty}^{+\infty} xf(x)dx.$$

This is the continuous counterpart of summing the products between each possible outcome of a discrete random variable and the corresponding probability, $E[X] = M_1(X) = \sum_{s=1}^{S} x_s \Pr(X = x_s)$ (where $S \rightarrow \infty$ can also be accommodated). The expectation of a random variable carries information on the location of its distribution on the real line. Moreover, if the PDF of a variable is symmetric, as in Fig. A.1, the expected value is highly informative because it represents the value around which the distribution is symmetric. Notice that in the case in which the expected value is equal to 0, then there is no difference between the central and noncentral moments.

Another important moment index often used to characterized random variables (especially in finance) is the second central moment, also called *variance* and denoted as $Var[X]$ (sometimes also as σ^2):

$$Var[X] = \int_{-\infty}^{+\infty} (x - E[X])^2 f(x)\, dx = E[(X - E[X])^2].$$

The variance, which is simply the expected value of the squared deviations from the mean, tells us how the possible outcomes are dispersed around the expected value of the distribution. The higher the variance, the higher the dispersion of the values around the mean. Higher moments add further information about the shape of the PDF: for instance, the third moment gives information about the level of asymmetry of a distribution. We will say that the kth (central or noncentral) moment m_k of a distribution exists if $m_k < \infty$. It can be shown that if the kth moment exists, then there exist also the first $k - 1$ moments.

A frequently used distribution in applied work is the *normal (or Gaussian) distribution*, which is indicated with $N(\mu, \sigma^2)$. If the random variable X is distributed according to a normal distribution, its PDF is then

$$f(x) = (2\pi\sigma^2)^{-1/2}\exp\left\{-\frac{(x-\mu)^2}{2\sigma^2}\right\},$$

where μ is the expectation and σ^2 is the variance of X, and we write $X \sim N(\mu, \sigma^2)$. If X is normally distributed, it can assume any real value (meaning that both positive and negative outcomes are possible) and its PDF is a "bell-shaped" curve. All the moments of a normal distribution exist, and they can be expressed in terms of the parameters μ and σ^2 only. Therefore when we know these two moments, we are actually able to describe the entire distribution. The standard normal distribution, $N(0, 1)$, which also is indicated with Z, is a normal distribution with zero expected value and unit variance, and can be simply obtained from $X \sim N(\mu, \sigma^2)$, by subtracting the mean to all its possible values and then scaling such demeaned values by standard deviation, σ.

The random variables that have been described so far are *univariate random variables* because they can only take scalar values/outcomes. However, the concept can be easily extended to a multivariate framework defining a *multivariate random variable* as a list (mathematically, a vector or a matrix) of univariate random variables. The outcome of a multivariate random variable will be a vector. Both the definitions of PDF and CDF can be extended to the multivariate case. Consider for simplicity the bivariate case, when we can define the joint PDF of X_1 and X_2 as the function f such that:

$$\Pr\{(a_1 \le X_1 \le b_1) \cap (a_2 \le X_2 \le b_2)\} = \int_{a_1}^{b_1}\int_{a_2}^{b_2} f(x_1, x_2)dx_1dx_2.$$

The corresponding univariate PDFs f_{X_1} and f_{X_2} are the *marginal PDF*. Similarly, the joint CDF is the function F such that:

$$\Pr\{(X_1 \le a_1) \cap (X_1 \le a_2)\} = F(a_1, a_2).$$

The corresponding univariate CDFs F_{X_1} and F_{X_2} are here the *marginal CDF*. If the joint PDF f is equal to the product of the two marginal density functions f_{X_1} and f_{X_2}, then we shall say that the two random variables are *independent*. If two variables are independent, the same relation holds also between the joint CDF F and the two marginal cumulative distributions, F_{X_1} and F_{X_2}:

$$f(x_1, x_2) = f_{X_1}(x_1) \cdot f_{X_2}(x_2) \quad \forall x_1, x_2,$$
$$F(x_1, x_2) = F_{X_1}(x_1) \cdot F_{X_2}(x_2) \quad \forall x_1, x_2.$$

If the variables are not independent, this means that there exists some relation between them and in general we will be interested also in knowing the *conditional PDF* and *conditional CDF*, which are the PDF and the CDF of one variable, having observed a particular value for the other variable. For instance, the conditional PDF and the conditional CDF of X_1 given that the value assumed by X_2 is x_2 are defined by:

$$\Pr\{a \le X_1 \le b | X_2 = x_2\} = \int_a^b f(x_1|x_2)dx_1 \qquad \text{where} \quad f(x_1|x_2) = \frac{f(x_1, x_2)}{f(x_2)}$$

$$\Pr\{X_1 \le a | X_2 = x_2\} = F(a|x_2) \qquad \text{where} \quad F(a|x_2) = \int_{-\infty}^{a} f(x_1|x_2).$$

Note that if the two variables are independent, then the conditional PDF is equal to the marginal PDF. To describe the shape of a conditional PDF, we can of course also use the moments, which in this case will be characterized as conditional moments. The *conditional expected value* of X_1 given that the value assumed by X_2 is x_2 which is simply the first uncentered moment calculated using $f(x_1|x_2)$, and it is indicated as $E[X_1|x_2]$, which is a scalar. In fact, we are often interested in studying how the conditional expectation depends on the different possible values assumed by X_2. Therefore the conditional expectation becomes a function that for any possible value of X_2 returns the conditional expectation of X_1. We indicate this function as $E[X_1|X_2]$, that is, the expected value of X_1 given X_2. To compute conditional expected values, it is often useful to use the *law of iterated expectation*, which states that

$$E\left[E[X_1|X_2]\right] = E[X_1].$$

Identical concepts apply to conditional variances, defined as $Var[X_1|X_2]$ and interpretable as functions that for any possible value of X_2 return the conditional variance of X_1.

A.2 Stochastic Processes

When working with time series data, which means using observations sampled over regularly points in time (e.g., daily returns on some stock index over one year) over a period of total length T, we are actually dealing with an *ordered sequence* of random variables, and each one of them corresponds to a single date and we obtain a single observation for each random variable. A series of random variables $X_1, X_2, \ldots$ is defined as a *stochastic process*, $\{X_t\}_{t=1}^{T}$; it is a scalar one if the random variables that compose it are univariate, otherwise it is said to be of a multivariate type. We often (but not always) assume that the variables included in the sequence defining a stochastic process are *independent and identically distributed* (IID), which means that they have the same marginal PDF/CDF at all points in time and that they are mutually independent. When this assumption holds, the variables clearly have the same moments and, in particular, the same expected values and variances, i.e., $E[X_1] = E[X_2] = \ldots = E[X_T] = \mu$, $Var[X_1] = Var[X_2] = \ldots = Var[X_T] = \sigma^2$. This property enables us to investigate the features of their joint distribution using simple methods, because we observe many outcomes corresponding to the same PDF. When working with IID random variables, we can rely on some important theorems that help describe them. Before stating such results, we need to introduce two basic definitions.

A.2.1 Convergence in Probability

A sequence of random variables Z_t with $t = 1, 2, \ldots$ converges in probability to a value z, if $\lim_{t \to \infty} \Pr(|Z_t - z| < \varepsilon) = 0$, for every $\varepsilon > 0$. In this case, we write $plim(Z_t) = z$.

A.2.2 Convergence in Distribution

A sequence of random variables Z_t with $t = 1, 2, \ldots$ converges in distribution to a random variable Z, if $\lim_{t \to \infty} F_{Z_t}(\cdot) = F_Z(\cdot)$. In this case, we write $Z_t \xrightarrow{d} Z$, where F_{Z_t} and F_Z represent the CDFs of Z_t and of Z.

At this point, note that if we have a finite sequence of random variables X_t with $t = 1, 2, \ldots, T$, we can define a new random variable

$$\overline{X}_T = T^{-1} \sum_{t=1}^{T} X_t,$$

which is called the *sample mean*. It is a random variable because it will assume different values based on the outcomes of the variables X_t with $t = 1, 2, \ldots, T$ and as the sample size expands. Moreover, if we consider the simple mean as the sample size expands, $T = 1, 2, \ldots$, we have built a sequence of sample mean variables, which can assume different values as T increases. When T goes to infinity, the behavior of $\overline{X}_T$ follows the so-called Law of Large Numbers.

A.3 Key Theorems Concerning Stochastic Processes

A.3.1 Law of Large Numbers

The sample mean $\overline{X}_T$ of an IID sequence of random variables, $\{X_t\}_{t=1}^{T}$, converges in probability to the expected value $E[X_t] = \mu$ of the IID variables, i.e., $plim(\overline{X}_T) = \mu$.

Thanks to this rule, we have exactly pinned down the value to which the sample mean converges. However, it is also useful to identify the distribution of $\overline{X}_T$ and to do so we need the central limit theorem.

A.3.2 Lindeberg–Lévy's Central Limit Theorem

If a sequence of IID variables $\{X_t\}_{t=1}^{T}$ has expected value equal to μ and variance $\sigma^2 < \infty$, then as T increases, $\sqrt{T}\overline{X}_T$ converges in distribution to a normal random variable with expected value equal to μ and variance equal to σ^2.

Notice that this result does not depend on the distribution of the variables X_t, and that the only condition assumed is that $\{X_t\}_{t=1}^{T}$ are IID with finite first and second moments.

B MATRIX ALGEBRA

A *matrix* is a two-dimensional array of elements, which can be scalars or random variables. A is said to be a $M \times N$ matrix, if it has M rows and N columns and therefore $M \cdot N$ elements. A single element of a matrix A is in general denoted as a_{ij}, where i and j are the indices of the row and the column that define the position of a_{ij} in the matrix, respectively. For instance, a generic 3×3 matrix A can be represented as:

$$A = \begin{bmatrix} a_{11} & a_{12} & a_{13} \\ a_{21} & a_{22} & a_{23} \\ a_{31} & a_{32} & a_{33} \end{bmatrix}.$$

When the number of rows equals the number of columns, the matrix is said to be a *square matrix*. The elements a_{ij} with $i = j$ of a square matrix lie on what is called the main diagonal of the matrix. Any square matrix where $a_{ij} = a_{ji} \quad \forall i,j$ is said to be *symmetric*. A special kind of symmetric matrices are those where all the elements off the main diagonal are equal to 0 and these are called *diagonal matrices*. Instead, a square matrix in which only all the elements above (below) the main diagonal are equal to 0 and the others are unconstrained is said to be a lower triangular (upper triangular) matrix.

The transpose of a matrix A is a matrix that has as rows the columns of A, while it has as columns the rows of A; it is denoted as A'. Therefore if A is a $M \times N$ matrix, then A' is a $N \times M$ matrix, the element in the ith row and jth column of A will be equal to the element in the jth row and ith column of A': $a_{ij} = a'_{ji}$, and the main diagonal of A is also the main diagonal of A'. Finally, note that the transpose of a symmetric matrix is equal to the matrix itself and that by the definition of transposition, it follows that:

$$(A')' = A.$$

B.1 Rank of a Matrix, Eigenvalues, and Eigenvectors

The *rank* of a matrix $\mathbf{A}$ is the number of linearly independent columns (or rows) of $\mathbf{A}$, and it is denoted as *rank*($\mathbf{A}$). A $M \times N$ matrix is said to have full rank if *rank*($\mathbf{A}$) $= \min(M, N)$.

Let $\mathbf{A}$ be a $N \times N$ square matrix and let $\mathbf{x}$ be a $N \times 1$ vector. $\mathbf{x}$ may differ from a vector of zeroes. The scalar λ is called a characteristic root or *eigenvector* of $\mathbf{A}$ if it satisfies the equation

$$\mathbf{Ax} = \lambda \mathbf{x}$$

$\mathbf{x}$ is the eigenvector associated to the eigenvalue λ. Note however that this defining equation may be written as

$$(\mathbf{A} - \lambda \mathbf{I}_N)\mathbf{x} = \mathbf{0}$$

Because $\mathbf{x}$ is a vector containing values not identically equal to zero, this system of equations requires that the rows of $(\mathbf{A} - \lambda \mathbf{I}_N)$ be linearly dependent, i.e., a linear combinations of the rows of $(\mathbf{A} - \lambda \mathbf{I}_N)$ must give one of the rows that as such becomes redundant. Equivalently, the system of equations $(\mathbf{A} - \lambda \mathbf{I}_N)\mathbf{x} = \mathbf{0}$ requires that the determinant of the matrix $(\mathbf{A} - \lambda \mathbf{I}_N)$ be zero, $\det(\mathbf{A} - \lambda \mathbf{I}_N) = 0$. Thus we can find the characteristic root(s) of $\mathbf{A}$ by finding the value(s) of λ that satisfy $\det(\mathbf{A} - \lambda \mathbf{I}_N) = 0$. The reason why eigenvalues are also called characteristic roots is that the determinant equation $\det(\mathbf{A} - \lambda \mathbf{I}_N) = 0$ is also called the *characteristic equation* of the square matrix $\mathbf{A}$. Notice that the characteristic equation will be an Nth-order polynomial in λ. The reason is that the determinant $\det(\mathbf{A} - \lambda \mathbf{I}_N)$ contains the Nth degree term λ^N resulting from the expression:

$$(a_{11} - \lambda)(a_{22} - \lambda) \cdots (a_{NN} - \lambda)$$

From this fact, it immediately follows that an $N \times N$ square matrix will necessarily have N characteristic roots. Some of the roots may be repeating and some may be complex. In fact, the determinant of an $N \times N$ matrix is equal to the product of its characteristic roots, $\det(\mathbf{A}) = \lambda_1 \cdot \lambda_2 \cdot \cdots \cdot \lambda_N$.

At this point, the rank of a square $N \times N$ matrix $\mathbf{A}$ is the number of linearly independent rows (columns) in the matrix and the matrix $\mathbf{A}$ is said to be of full rank if *rank*($\mathbf{A}$) $= N$. From the discussion above, it follows that the rank of $\mathbf{A}$ is equal to the number 0 (its nonzero eigenvalues). If rank($\mathbf{A}$) $=$ 0, then each element of $\mathbf{A}$ must equal zero.

B.2 Matrix Operations

B.2.1 Addition

Given two $M \times N$ matrices A and B, the matrix $A + B$ is a $M \times N$ matrix such that its generic element is equal to $a_{ij} + b_{ij}$. Note that A and B must be exactly of the same size for them to be *conformable*.

B.2.2 Subtraction

Given two $M \times N$ matrices A and B, the matrix $A - B$ is a $M \times N$ matrix such that its generic element is equal to $a_{ij} - b_{ij}$. Note that A and B must be exactly of the same size for them to be *conformable*.

B.2.3 Multiplication by a Scalar

Given a $M \times N$ matrix A and a scalar c, the matrix cA is a $M \times N$ matrix such that its generic element is equal to $c \cdot a_{ij}$.

It is always possible to multiply a matrix by a scalar, whereas the addition and the subtraction between two matrices exist only if the two matrices have the same dimension, as noted. All the standard properties of these operations hold, meaning that matrix addition is commutative and associative and the distributive property holds,

$$A + B = B + A,$$
$$(A + B) + C = A + (B + C),$$
$$c(A + B) = cA + cB.$$

Moreover, the following identities are satisfied.

$$(A + B)' = A' + B',$$
$$(cA)' = cA'.$$

B.2.4 Multiplication

Given a $M \times N$ matrix A and a $N \times P$ matrix B, the matrix AB is a $M \times P$ matrix such that its generic element is $(ab)_{ij} = \sum_{h=1}^{N} a_{ih} b_{hj}$.

Note that the product between two matrices exists only when the number of columns of the first matrix is equal to the number of columns of the second matrix. The multiplication between two matrices does not satisfy the commutative propriety, because not only in general $\mathbf{AB} \neq \mathbf{BA}$, but also if $\mathbf{AB}$ exists, this does not imply the existence of $\mathbf{BA}$. When we refer to $\mathbf{AB}$, we say that we are *premultiplying* $\mathbf{B}$ by $\mathbf{A}$, while in the case of $\mathbf{BA}$ we say that we *postmultiplying* $\mathbf{B}$ by $\mathbf{A}$. Matrix multiplication satisfies the distributive property over addition and the associative property:

$$\mathbf{A(B + C) = AB + AC},$$
$$\mathbf{(B + C)A = BA + BC},$$
$$\mathbf{(AB)C = A(BC)}.$$

Moreover, the following identity holds

$$\mathbf{(AB)' = B'A'}.$$

B.3 Trace of a Matrix

The trace of an $N \times M$ square matrix is defined as the sum of the elements along the principal diagonal:

$$tr(\mathbf{A}) = a_{11} + a_{22} + \cdots + a_{NN}.$$

If $\mathbf{A}$ is an $M \times N$ matrix and $\mathbf{B}$ is an $N \times M$ matrix, then $\mathbf{AB}$ is a $M \times M$ matrix whose trace is

$$tr(\mathbf{AB}) = \sum_{j=1}^{N} a_{1j} b_{j1} + \sum_{j=1}^{N} a_{2j} b_{j2} + \cdots + \sum_{j=1}^{N} a_{Mj} b_{jM} = \sum_{k=1}^{M} \sum_{j=1}^{N} a_{kj} b_{jk}$$

$$tr(\mathbf{BA}) = \sum_{k=1}^{M} b_{1k}a_{k1} + \sum_{k=1}^{M} b_{2k}a_{k2} + \cdots + \sum_{k=1}^{M} b_{Nk}a_{kN} = \sum_{j=1}^{N}\sum_{k=1}^{M} b_{jk}a_{kj} = \sum_{k=1}^{M}\sum_{j=1}^{N} a_{kj}b_{jk}.$$

Thus $tr(\mathbf{AB}) = tr(\mathbf{BA})$. Moreover, if $\mathbf{A}$ and $\mathbf{B}$ are both $N \times N$ matrices, then

$$tr(\mathbf{A} + \mathbf{B}) = tr(\mathbf{A}) + tr(\mathbf{B}).$$

B.4 Identity and Inverse Matrices

The *identity matrix*, often denoted as $\mathbf{I}$, is a diagonal matrix, with all the elements on the main diagonal equal to 1. It can be easily proven that by multiplying any matrix $\mathbf{A}$ by a conformable $\mathbf{I}$, the resulting matrix is again equal to $\mathbf{A}$. Therefore $\mathbf{I}$ is a neutral matrix in multiplications in the same way in which the zero matrix $\mathbf{O}$ is neutral in sums of matrices, when these operations are possible.

The *inverse* of a square $N \times N$ matrix $\mathbf{A}$ is a $N \times N$ matrix $\mathbf{A}^{-1}$ such that

$$\mathbf{A} \cdot \mathbf{A}^{-1} = \mathbf{A}^{-1} \cdot \mathbf{A} = \mathbf{I}.$$

Note that the inverse of a matrix does not always exist. It exists if and only if it has full rank. $rank(\mathbf{A}) = N$. When $\mathbf{A}$ is a noninvertible matrix, it is said to be *singular*.

B.5 Kronecker and Hadamard (Dot) Products

For $\mathbf{A}$ an $N \times M$ matrix and $\mathbf{B}$ a $P \times Q$ matrix, the Kronecker product of $\mathbf{A}$ and $\mathbf{B}$ is defined as the following $NP \times MQ$ matrix:

$$\mathbf{A} \otimes \mathbf{B} = \begin{bmatrix} a_{11}\mathbf{B} & a_{12}\mathbf{B} & \dots & a_{1N}\mathbf{B} \\ a_{21}\mathbf{B} & a_{22}\mathbf{B} & \dots & a_{2N}\mathbf{B} \\ \vdots & \dots & \ddots & \vdots \\ a_{N1}\mathbf{B} & a_{N2}\mathbf{B} & \dots & a_{NN}\mathbf{B} \end{bmatrix}.$$

The following properties of the Kronecker product are readily verified: $(\mathbf{A} \otimes \mathbf{B})' = \mathbf{A}' \otimes \mathbf{B}'$ and $(\mathbf{A} \otimes \mathbf{B}) \otimes \mathbf{C} = \mathbf{A} \otimes (\mathbf{B} \otimes \mathbf{C})$.

As for the Hadamard product, this simply the product of the corresponding elements of two matrices $\mathbf{A}$ and $\mathbf{B}$ of identical dimensions, say $N \times M$:

$$\mathbf{A} \odot \mathbf{B} = \begin{bmatrix} a_{11}b_{11} & a_{12}b_{12} & \dots & a_{1N}b_{1N} \\ a_{21}b_{12} & a_{22}b_{22} & \dots & a_{2N}b_{2N} \\ \vdots & \dots & \ddots & \vdots \\ a_{N1}b_{N1} & a_{N2}b_{N2} & \dots & a_{NN}b_{NN} \end{bmatrix}.$$

C UNCORRELATEDNESS AND INDEPENDENCE

In probability theory, two real-valued random variables, $X$and Y, are said to be uncorrelated if their covariance, $E[XY] - E[X]E[Y]$, is zero. A set of two or more random variables is defined as *uncorrelated* if each pair of them is uncorrelated. If two variables are uncorrelated, there is no linear relationship between them.

If X and Y are *independent*, with finite second moments, then they are uncorrelated. However, not all uncorrelated variables are independent; in fact uncorrelatedness does not imply independence. One example will help to shed light on this important lack of equivalence between the two concepts.

Let X be a random variable that takes the value 0 with probability 1/2 and the value 1 with probability 1/2. Let Z be a random variable, independent of X, which takes the value -1 with probability 1/2, and the value 1 with probability 1/2. Finally, let U be a random variable constructed as $U = XZ$. The claim is that U and X have zero covariance (and thus are uncorrelated) but are not independent. Therefore it is true that if two random variables are independent, then they are uncorrelated, and this holds for all random variables, both continuous and discrete.

THEOREM: If the two random variables X and Y are independent, then they are uncorrelated.

Proof: Uncorrelated means that their correlation is 0, or, equivalently, that the covariance between them is 0. Therefore we need to show that for two generic random variables that are independent, their covariance is 0. However, the two terms cannot be used interchangeably.

Let us order the pairs of possible values of the two random variables in correspondence to the coordinates $(-1,1)$, $(0,0)$, and $(1,1)$ with probabilities 1/4, 1/2, and 1/4, respectively. Then

$$\begin{aligned} E[X] &= -1\cdot(1/4)+0\cdot(1/2)+1\cdot(1/4)=0 \\ &= E[X]E[Y] = -1\cdot(1/4)+0\cdot(1/2)+1\cdot(1/4)=0=E[Y] \\ E[XY] &= -1\cdot(1/4)+0\cdot(1/2)+1\cdot(1/4)=0 \\ &= E[X]E[Y] = -1\cdot(1/4)+0\cdot(1/2)+1\cdot(1/4) \end{aligned}$$

and thus X and Y are uncorrelated.

Now let us look at the marginal distributions of X and Y. X can take values -1, 0, and 1, and the probability it takes each of those is 1/4, 1/2, and 1/4. The same is true of Y. Then looping through the possibilities, we have to check whether $\Pr(X=x, Y=y)=\Pr(X=x)\Pr(Y=y)$. But it is immediate to verify that

$$\Pr(X=-1, Y=1)=1/4 \neq 1/16=\Pr(X=-1)\Pr(Y=1).$$

Therefore X and Y fail to satisfy the definition of independence.

Now suppose that two random variables, X and Y, are *jointly normally distributed*. This is the same as saying that the random vector $[XY]'$ has a multivariate normal distribution. It means that the joint probability distribution of X and Y is such that any linear combination of X and Y is normally distributed, i.e., for any two constants (i.e., nonrandom) scalars a and b, the random variable $aX+bY$ is normally distributed. In just this case, if X and Y are uncorrelated, i.e., their covariance $Cov[X,Y]=0$, then they will also be independent. However, it is possible for two random variables X and Y to be distributed jointly such that each random variable in isolation is marginally normally distributed, and they are uncorrelated but they are not independent.

Therefore when the T random variables in a stochastic process $\{X_t\}_{t=1}^{T}$ are mutually independent and multivariate normal, then all their pairwise correlations are zero, as are the pairwise covariances and thus their covariance matrix will be diagonal and there is no serial correlation.

D BOOTSTRAPPING

Bootstrapping is a way of providing a *nonparametric* estimate of statistical parameters (e.g., the population expectation and its confidence intervals) from a sample by means of *resampling with replacement*. It is often used as an alternative to statistical inference based on the assumption of a parametric model when that assumption is in doubt or where parametric inference is impossible or requires complicated formulas for the calculation of standard errors.

Like other nonparametric approaches, bootstrapping does not make any assumptions about the distribution of the sample (e.g., whether the series are normally distributed and hence can be simply characterized by mean and variance parameters). The major assumption behind bootstrapping is that the sample distribution is a good approximation of the population distribution, i.e., that the sample is representative of the population, which will require at most strict stationarity. In the case where a set of observations can be assumed to be from an IID population, the bootstrap can be simply implemented by constructing a number of resamples with replacement from the observed data, of equal size vs the observed data.

Therefore the idea behind the bootstrap is to use the data in a given sample as a "surrogate population," for the purposes of approximating the sampling distribution of a statistic (a moment, a parameter, a confidence interval, a test statistic, etc.); i.e., to resample (with replacement, according to some optima scheme) from the data at hand and create a large number of "replica samples" known as *bootstrap samples*. The sample summary that is of interest is then computed on each of the bootstrap samples (usually, at least a few thousands). A histogram of the set of these computed values is referred to as the bootstrap distribution of the statistic. From this bootstrapped distribution of the statistic of interest, one can then compute point estimates (the average of the histogram), confidence intervals (a pair of percentiles from the histogram), some standardized ratio to compute the critical region of a test of hypothesis, etc. Bootstrapping allows us to assign measures of accuracy (defined in terms of bias, variance, confidence intervals, prediction error or some other such measure) to sample estimates. This technique allows the estimation of the sampling distribution of almost any statistic using random sampling methods.

One major advantage of bootstrap is its operational simplicity (its statistical properties, i.e., why it may work is instead rather complex). It gives a straightforward way to derive estimates of standard errors and confidence intervals for convoluted estimators of complex parameters of the distribution, such as percentiles, proportions, odds ratio, and correlation coefficients. Although for most problems it is impossible to know the true value of a statistic of interest, simulation studies have shown that the bootstrap is asymptotically more accurate than the inference obtained using sample statistics under the (often, false) assumption of normality. However, even though bootstrapping is (under some conditions) asymptotically consistent, it does not provide general finite-sample guarantees. Its apparent simplicity may conceal the fact that important assumptions are being made when undertaking a bootstrap analysis (e.g., independence or limited, asymptotically vanishing dependence of the observations), whereas these could be more formally stated under alternative approaches.

The basic steps of a bootstrap resampling procedure are:

1. Construct an empirical distribution, $\hat{F}_T$, from a given sample by attaching a probability $1/T$ to each observation $x_1, x_2, ..., x_T$ of the sample. This is the empirical distribution function (EDF) of the sample, which can be shown to be the *nonparametric maximum likelihood estimate of the population distribution F*.
2. From the EDF, $\hat{F}_T$, draw a random sample of size T with replacement. This is a resample. Special resampling schemes may be required when the stochastic process that is assumed to have generated the data is not IID and the series are instead dependent (e.g., it may be optimal to draw not one observation at the time, but blocks of D observations, to preserve the dependence structure that is present in the data).
3. Calculate the sample statistic of interest, $\hat{\Upsilon}_T$ (say, the sample mean), from this resample, called $\hat{\Upsilon}_T^b$.
4. Repeat Steps 2 and 3 B times, where B is a large number, to create B resamples. To each resample is then associated a bootstrap sample−derived statistic, $\hat{\Upsilon}_T^b$, $b = 1, 2, \ldots, B$. The practically advised size of B depends on the type of statistics that are under investigation. Typically, B is at least equal to 2000 when an estimate of confidence intervals around $\hat{\Upsilon}_T$ is required.
5. Construct the relative frequency histogram from the B generated values of $\hat{\Upsilon}_T^b$ by placing a probability of $1/B$ in correspondence to the generated values $\hat{\Upsilon}_T^1, \hat{\Upsilon}_T^2, ..., \hat{\Upsilon}_T^B$. The distribution thus obtained represents the bootstrapped estimate of the sampling distribution of $\hat{\Upsilon}_T$. This distribution can now be used to make inferences about either the population statistic Υ directly or to use it to estimate other quantities of interest that may depend on Υ, such as some vector of parameters, θ.

As we have claimed, the conceptual justification of the bootstrap procedure rests on the fact that the sample EDF is optimal (in fact, ML estimate) of the population distribution function. The theoretical justification for this result is based on a two-level asymptotics:

- As the original sample size T approaches the population size, the EDF approaches the true distribution, PDF. This makes intuitive sense, in that as a sample increases in size, it contains more and more information about the population until converging (at least abstractly) to the population.
- If the original sample size T is large enough, then, as the number B of resamples increases to infinity, the bootstrapped estimate of the sampling distribution approaches the sampling distribution of the original statistic.

Index

Note: Page numbers followed by "*f*" and "*t*" refer to figures and tables, respectively.

A

ACF. *See* Autocorrelation function (ACF)
Additive outlier model (AO model), 302–303
ADF test. *See* Augmented Dickey–Fuller test (ADF test)
Adjusted R^2, 6
Advanced univariate volatility modeling, 190–198. *See also* Simple univariate parametric models
  empirical estimates of distribution of 1-year T-bill rates, 196*f*
  GARCH models augmented by exogenous factors, 197–198
  non-Gaussian marginal innovations, 190–196
  volatility forecasts from Gaussian *vs. t*-Student threshold GARCH(1,1), 194*f*
Akaike's information criterion (AIC), 64, 331
Alternative hypothesis, 14
Andrews and Quandt's single-break test, 294–297, 297*f*
Andrews–Quandt Sup-LR tests, 294–296
AO model. *See* Additive outlier model (AO model)
APT. *See* Asset pricing theory (APT)
AR processes. *See* Autoregressive processes (AR processes)
AR(*p*). *See p*th order AR process (AR(*p*))
ARCH models. *See* Autoregressive conditional heteroskedastic models (ARCH models)
ARCH(*p*) model, 153, 202, 207
ARCH(*W*) model, 210
ARMA models. *See* Autoregressive Moving Average models (ARMA models)
Asset pricing theory (APT), 268, 271
Asset returns, 163
Asymmetric CH effects, 167
Asymptotic covariance matrix, 10
Asymptotic distribution of MLE, 214
Asymptotic efficiency, 10
Asymptotic normal distribution, 65–66
Asymptotic normality, 10
  of OLS estimator of regression coefficients, 18
  of MLE, 213
Asymptotic theory for linear regressions, 16–18
Augmented Dickey–Fuller test (ADF test), 126–130
Autocorrelated errors, 34
Autocorrelation, 153
  of errors, 32–34
Autocorrelation function (ACF), 43, 115–116, 116*t*, 118*f*, 124*f*, 164–165
Autocovariance function, 43
Automatic variable selection procedures, 27
Autoregression, 126–127
Autoregressive conditional heteroskedastic models (ARCH models), 161–168, 188, 248, 267, 381
  CGARCH model, 186–189
  GARCH-in-mean model, 189–190
  in-sample volatility forecasts from C-GARCH *vs.* GARCH, 188*f*
  in-sample volatility forecasts from T-GARCH and PARCH, 185*f*
  information criteria-based model selection, 181*t*, 185*t*, 189*t*
  KDEs of model residuals, 191*f*
  power ARCH and NAGARCH models, 182–186
  testing for, 198–205
    empirical nonparametric impact curve for HML returns, 204*f*
    empirical nonparametric impact curve for US equity returns, 205*f*
    Lagrange multiplier ARCH tests, 199–201
    news impact curves and testing for asymmetric ARCH, 202–205
  threshold GARCH (TARCH) model, 182
  transitory variance components, 186–189
  variance forecasts, 167*t*
    from asymmetric component GARCH (1,1,1), 189*f*
Autoregressive conditionally heteroskedasticity. *See* Autoregressive conditional heteroskedastic models (ARCH models)
Autoregressive Moving Average models (ARMA models), 6–7, 34, 41, 58–60, 77–79, 82–83, 87, 96, 288–290, 326, 338–339, 367, 388–392. *See also* Linear regression model; Vector Autoregressive Moving Average models (VARMA models)
  AR processes, 52–58
  estimation methods, 65–67, 67*t*
  MA process, 49–60
  plots and correlogram of ARMA (1,1) simulated data, 61*f*
  residual diagnostics, 67–70, 69*f*
  rolling one-step-ahead forecasts for US inflation, 74*f*
  selection, 61–70
    characteristics, 62*t*
    plot of monthly percentage changes, 62*f*
    selection of model and role of information criteria, 61–64
    serial correlation structure of changes in US CPI, 63*t*
  time series analysis, 41–48
Autoregressive processes (AR processes), 41, 52–58
  autoregressive moving average processes, 58–60
  estimation methods, 65–67, 67*t*
  plots and correlogram, 56*f*, 57*f*
  residual diagnostics, 67–70, 69*f*
  rolling one-step-ahead forecasts for US inflation, 74*f*
  selection, 61–70
    characteristics, 62*t*
    plot of monthly percentage changes, 62*f*
    selection of model and role of information criteria, 61–64
    serial correlation structure of changes in US CPI, 63*t*
Autoregressive SVM, 273
Auxiliary regression, 196
Average estimated duration, 344–345

B

Baba-Engle-Kraft-Kroner models (BEKK models), 239, 245–248
Backward elimination algorithm, 28, 29*t*
Backward shift. *See* Lag operator
Bai and Perron's multiple, endogenous breaks test, 297–302, 301*t*
Bartlett–Kernel estimation method, 130
Bayes' law, 351–352
Bayesian information criterion (BIC), 152, 347–348
Bayesian MSVAR methods, 373
BDS portmanteau test for independence, 197
BEKK models. *See* Baba-Engle-Kraft-Kroner models (BEKK models)
Best linear unbiased estimator (BLUE), 4

Beta of portfolio, 263
BIC. *See* Bayesian information criterion (BIC)
Binary variable, 192, 399
"Black Swan" type of complacency, 169
Block-causality tests. *See* Block-exogeneity tests
Block-exogeneity tests, 109
BLUE. *See* Best linear unbiased estimator (BLUE)
Bootstrapping methods, 103–104, 363, 407–408
Box-Jenkins procedure, 65, 114–115
Box-Pierce test, 46
"Box-shaped" effects, 179
Box–Jenkins type techniques, 161
Box–Pierce Q statistics, 220
Break points, 291, 294, 299–300
Breakpoint-adjusted ADF tests, 304–305
Breakpoint-modified ADF tests, 305*t*, 306*t*
Breusch–Godfrey test, 34
Bucy filter. *See* Kalman filter

C

Calendar time sampling, 382
Capital asset pricing model (CAPM), 182
Capture departures, 163
CBOE. *See* Chicago Board Options Exchange (CBOE)
CCC models. *See* Constant conditional correlation models (CCC models)
CDF. *See* Cumulative distribution function (CDF)
Centered moment, 400–401
CGARCH model. *See* Component GARCH model (CGARCH model)
CH. *See* Conditional heteroskedasticity (CH)
CH models. *See* Conditionally heteroskedastic models (CH models)
Characteristic equation, 52–53, 60, 404
χ^2 statistics, 110
Chicago Board Options Exchange (CBOE), 198
Choleski decompositions, 85, 103, 238–239
Choleski factor, 238–239
Chow Breakpoint Test, 25, 25*t*
Chow tests for given break dates, 291–292, 292*t*
Classical DF tests, 124–126
Classical linear regression model, 2, 220–221
Classical temporal aggregation of ARIMA models, 224
Clusters, 164
Coefficient of determination, 6, 161
Coefficient of variation, 156
Cointegrating regression Durbin–Watson test (CRDW test), 139
Cointegration, 134–135
  cointegrating rank, 138
  cointegrating vector, 134
  relationship between economic theory and, 133–134
  testing for, 138–148, 147*f*, 147*t*, 148*f*
Common dynamic structure, 257–258
Common stochastic trends, 135
Companion matrix, 90
Component GARCH model (CGARCH model), 186–189
Conditional correlation model
  constant and dynamic conditional correlation models, 250–257
  factor GARCH models, 257–263
  inference and model specification, 264–265
  simple models of covariance prediction, 230–238
  VARMA models, 229
Conditional covariance, 230
Conditional density, 210, 287–288
Conditional expectations, 89
Conditional forecast, 202
Conditional heteroskedasticity (CH), 7–8, 273
Conditional mean
  function, 219
  process, 202
Conditional probability distribution function, 402
Conditional variance function, 219
Conditionally heteroskedastic models (CH models), 158
Confidence intervals, 10–15
  with confidence level, 215
Consistency, 10
  of OLS estimator of regression coefficients, 18
  of OLS estimator of residual variance, 18
Consistent estimators, 214
Constant conditional correlation models (CCC models), 250–257, 255*f*
Consumer Price Index (CPI), 62
Contemporaneous feedback effects, 83
Continuous random variables, 399
Continuous-time product processes, 268
Continuous-time semimartingale diffusion process, 381–382
Contribution to total likelihood of sample. *See* Conditional density
Convergence
  in distribution, 17, 403
  in probability, 17, 403
Copula-GARCH approach, 254
Correctly selected regressors, 3
"Correctly specified" expression, 219
Correlations, 250, 253*f*, 257, 257*f*, 261*f*, 262*f*
  forecasts, 229–230
  integrals, 197
Covariances, 115, 229, 233–234, 243*f*, 248*f*, 257, 257*f*, 260*f*, 261*f*, 262*f*
  matrix, 4
  prediction models, 230–238
  stationary, 43
  targeting, 240
    constraint, 252–254
CPI. *See* Consumer Price Index (CPI)
Cramér–Rao lower variance bound, 10
CRDW test. *See* Cointegrating regression Durbin–Watson test (CRDW test)
Cross-correlation matrices, 78–80, 81*t*
Cumulative distribution function (CDF), 399–400, 401*f*
Cumulative probability distribution, 316, 400
Cumulative response, 101–102
Current volatility state, 267–268
CUSUM test, 24–25, 25*f*
  odd properties, 294
  square tests, 293–294, 295*f*

D

Daily volatility, 381
Data frequency in estimation, 223–225
Data generating process (DGP), 1, 18, 45
DCCs. *See* Dynamic conditional correlations (DCCs)
Decomposition, 387
"Degree-of-freedom adjusted" version of covariance matrix estimator, 91
Delay parameter, 308–309
Dependent variable, 1
Descriptive statistics of one-month and 10-Year US treasury yield series, 80*t*
Determinant equation, 404
Deterministic detrending, 116
Deterministic regressors, 125–126
Deterministic trends, 113–115, 114*f*
  deterministically trending series, 116
Detrended process, 116
  unit root process, 118
DGP. *See* Data generating process (DGP)
Diagonal BEKK, 245–247, 262
Diagonal matrices, 404
Diagonal multivariate GARCH, 240
Differencing/difference
  to (deterministic) trend-stationary series, 119–120, 120*f*
  operators, 52
  to stationary series, 120
Differentiating trend-stationary processes, 119
Direct maximum likelihood estimation, 370
Discounted dividend/earnings growth model, 133–134
Discrete random variable, 399
Discretely sampled time series, 41–42
Distance parameter, 197
Distribution hypothesis, mixture of, 163
Drift process, 113–114, 118–119
*d*th order integration, 116
Dummy regressions, 307
Dummy variable. *See* Binary variable
Durbin–Watson test (DW test), 68, 139
Dynamic conditional correlations (DCCs), 250–257
Dynamic econometric frameworks, 373–374
Dynamic error-correction model, 135–136

E

ECF. *See* Empirical characteristic function (ECF)
Economic(s)

of stochastic volatility, 271–272
theory, 105–106, 125, 133–134
EDF. *See* Empirical distribution function (EDF)
EGARCH model. *See* Exponential GARCH model (EGARCH model)
Eigenvalues, 8, 38, 144, 404
of companion matrix, 90
decomposition, 31
of matrix, 87
Eigenvectors, 38, 404
Element-by-element product, 352
Element-wise (Hadamard) matrix product, 244
Elementary vectors, 345–346, 377–378
Elliott, Rothenberg, and Stock method (ERS method), 129–130
EM algorithm. *See* Expectation–Maximization algorithm (EM algorithm)
Embedding dimension, 197
Empirical characteristic function (ECF), 280
Empirical distribution function (EDF), 408
Empirical NIC, 199
Engle–Granger tests, 141, 142*t*
regression, 138–139
univariate methodology, 138
Epanechnikov kernel, 340
Equilibrium error process, 134
Equivalent martingale measure, 284
Ergodic Markov chains, notions concerning, 376–377
Ergodic probabilities, 344, 377
explicit solutions for, 346–347
vector, 346, 377
Ergodicity, 250, 344–346
Error-correction models, 133–148
ERS method. *See* Elliott, Rothenberg, and Stock method (ERS method)
ESM. *See* Exponential smoothing models (ESM)
ESTAR models, 318–319, 323, 373
Estimation methods, 1, 65–67, 206–207
Estimation of and inference on GARCH models, 210–225
data frequency in estimation and temporal aggregation, 223–225
misspecification tests, 221
MLE, 212–214
properties of MLE, 214–218
QMLE, 218–221
sequential estimation and QMLE, 221–223
Estimator, 206–207
Events, 399
E-views, 171, 215, 353–354, 356
Ex post return variation, 388–389
Excess kurtosis, 165
Excess market returns (Excess MKT), 11
Exogenous variables, 329
Exp-LR tests, 296–297
Expectation step, 351–352, 355–357
Expectation–Maximization algorithm (EM algorithm), 336, 350–358, 357*f*
Expected value, 2, 12, 18, 401
conditional, 402–403
of constant, 49
of dependent variable, 35
of OLS estimator, 26
of squared deviations, 401
Explained sum of squares (SSE), 6, 36
Explanatory variables, 1, 5–6, 15, 18, 21–22
deterministic, 129–130
importance, 36
selection and properties, 25
Explosive autoregressive process, 117
Exponential function, 318–319
Exponential GARCH model (EGARCH model), 171–172, 181*f*
Exponential smoothing models (ESM), 184
Exponential smoothing variance forecasts, 160–161
Extended stochastic volatility models, 281–282

F

Factor and orthogonal models, 257–258
Factor GARCH models, 257–263
Fama–French factors, 7, 15*t*, 291
Federal fund's rate (FFR), 309
Filtered probabilities, 349*f*, 351–353
Filtering step, 269
Final prediction error (FPE), 96–97
Finance models, 290
Finite order moving average processes, 49–51
Finite-order Markov chain variable, 308
First-order conditions (FOCs), 354
for ML estimation of MS models, 378–379
First-order MC process, 344
Fitted values, 3
Fixed costs, 167
Flat-top kernel-based estimator, 386
Flow variable, 224–225
FOCs. *See* First-order conditions (FOCs)
Forecast accuracy measures, 98, 99*t*
Forecast error variance decomposition, 105, 106*t*, 108*t*
Forecast out-of-sample, 71
Forecasting, 270
with MS models, 365–369, 368*f*
realized variance, 390–391, 390*f*
range-based variance forecasts, 392–394, 394*f*
stylized facts on RV, 388–389
step, 269
Forecasting ARMA processes, 71–74. *See also* Autoregressive Moving Average models (ARMA models)
evaluating accuracy of forecast function, 73–74
forecasting AR(p) process, 71–72
forecasting future value of MA(q) process, 72–73
rolling one-step-ahead forecasts, 75*f*
standard principles, 71
Forward selection algorithm, 27
FPE. *See* Final prediction error (FPE)
Fractionally integrated process, 281
F-statistics, 93, 359
F-test, 18, 29, 127, 301, 323, 364
Full, multivariate GARCH models, 238–250
Full-sample inference, 351
Fundamental statistical definitions, 399
Future conditional log-variance, 171

G

GARCH model. *See* Generalized autoregressive conditional heteroskedasticity model (GARCH model)
Gaussian distribution, 402
Gaussian disturbances, 270
Gaussian mixture models, 340, 363
Gaussian threshold diagonal BEKK(1,1,1) model, 261
Gaussian WN process, 44, 44*f*
Gaussian-type likelihood function, 211
Gauss–Markov theorem, 4, 8, 10
GED. *See* Generalized error distribution (GED)
General-to-simple approach, 95
Generalized ARCH models and statistical properties, 171–180
Generalized autoregressive conditional heteroskedasticity model (GARCH model), 58, 158, 173*t*, 188, 248, 267–268, 282–284, 369, 381, 389–390
augmented by exogenous factors, 197–198
estimation of and inference, 210–225
forecasting with, 205–209
forecasts of variance for sums of returns or shocks, 208–209
long-horizon, point forecasts, 206–208
recursive, in-sample mean and variance forecasts, 208*f*
GARCH-diffusion model, 283–284
GARCH-in-mean model, 189–190
predicted conditional volatility, 177*f*, 181*f*
Generalized error distribution (GED), 190
distributions, 389–390
Generalized Least Squared estimator (GLS estimator), 7–9
Generalized method of moments (GMM), 209, 279–280
Generalized normal distribution. *See* Generalized error distribution (GED)
GFC. *See* Great Financial Crisis (GFC)
Global tests, 299
GLS estimator. *See* Generalized Least Squared estimator (GLS estimator)
GMM. *See* Generalized method of moments (GMM)
Goodness of fit
measures, 5–7
tests, 220
Gradient, 3
Granger causality, 108–110, 110*t*
Granger's representation theorem, 138
Granger–Sims causality tests, 79
Great Financial Crisis (GFC), 169

H

HAC estimators. *See* Heteroskedasticity/autocorrelation-consistent estimators (HAC estimators)
Hadamard product, 352
Hannan-Quinn's information criterion (HQIC), 64, 332
HAR model. *See* Heterogeneous autoregressions model (HAR model)
Heavy tailed distributions, 389–390
Hessian matrix, 212
Hessian of likelihood function, 214
Hessian-OPG based methods, 358
Heterogeneous autoregressions model (HAR model), 390–391, 394
  HAR-RV model, 390
Heteroskedastic errors, 32–33
Heteroskedasticity
  heteroskedasticity-consistent SEs, 32, 34
  issues with, 32–34
Heteroskedasticity/autocorrelation-consistent estimators (HAC estimators), 9
H-horizon GARCH forecasts, 203–204
H-horizon return GARCH forecasts, 205–206
Hidden, discrete Markov state, 344
Hidden state RS, 329–330
Hierarchical specification strategy, 254
High minus low (HML), 7
High-frequency data, 381, 383, 395
Higher order moments, 159
HML. *See* High minus low (HML)
Homogeneous MC process, 344
Homoskedasticity, 2
HQIC. *See* Hannan-Quinn's information criterion (HQIC)
H-step-ahead forecast for covariance, 236, 391–392
Hypotheses testing, 10–15, 94–97

I

IC. *See* Information criterion (IC)
Identification
  asymmetry, 101–103
  issues, 336
Identity matrix, 4, 356, 406
IGARCH(*p*,*q*) model. *See* Integrated GARCH (p;q) model (IGARCH(*p*, *q*) model)
IID. *See* Independent and identically distributed (IID)
Impact multipliers, 101
Impulse response function (IRF), 77, 100–104, 102*f*, 104*f*
In-sample
  forecasts, 71, 207
  tests, 372–373
Independent and identically distributed (IID), 159, 403
  distributed matrix, 8
  normal mixture model, 336
  random variables, 42
Independent variables, 1, 25–32, 41
  correlation matrix, 30*t*
  measurement errors in, 31–32
  multicollinearity, 29–31
  selection, 26–28
  variance inflation factors, 31*t*
  VIFs after dropping one regressor, 31*t*
Individual *t*-type Wald statistics, 196
Inference and model specification, 264–265
Infinite memory, 238, 370–372
Information criteria, 300–302, 326, 364, 367
  for alternative models used to CPI inflation, 64*t*
  multivariate version, 96
  selection of model and role, 61–64
Information criterion (IC), 63–64, 64*t*
Information matrix, 214
  equality, 214
Innovation accounting, 106–108
Innovational outlier models (IO models), 302–303
Instruments, 209
Integrated GARCH(p;q) model (IGARCH(*p*, *q*) model), 169–171
Integrated variance (IV), 382
Interpretation of regression results, 34–36
Intertemporal capital asset pricing model, 182
Invariance, 10
  invariant to linear combinations, BEKK, 246–248
Inverse-mapping, 279
Invertibility condition, 58
Invertible MA(*q*) model, 58
IO models. *See* Innovational outlier models (IO models)
IRF. *See* Impulse response function (IRF)
Irreducibility of MC, 346
Iterative numerical algorithm, 23
IV. *See* Integrated variance (IV)

J

Jacobian term, 210–211
Jarque–Bera test (JB test), 67–68, 220
Joint PDF of data, 209
J-test for non-nested models, 363–364
Jumps and bipower variation, 387

K

K regressors, 2
Kalman filter, 270
  primer on, 268–271
  simple stochastic volatility models and estimation using, 271–280
    economics of stochastic volatility, 271–272
    log-normal two-factor stochastic volatility model, 272–280
Kalman smoothing, 271
Kernel density estimator model, 340
Kernel density plots, 183–184
Kernel functions, 386–387
Kitchen-sink regressions, 27
Known break date, Chow test, 24–25
Kwiatkowski, Phillips, Schmidt, and Shin method (KPSS method), 131–132

L

Lag operator, 52, 58–59, 75–76, 87–90, 117
Lagged polynomial, 160–161
Lagrange multiplier (LM), 359
  ARCH tests, 199–201
  principle, 323
  tests, 195, 359
Latent variables, 159
Latent volatility models, 381
Law of iterated expectations, 236, 402–403
Law of large numbers, 17
Leaps, 182
Leptokurtic asset returns, 163–164
Leverage effect, 167, 182–183, 276–278
  in correlations, 254
Likelihood function, 9–10, 209, 267
Likelihood ratio (LR), 95, 359, 361–362
  statistic, 363
  test, 359, 361–362
Limited information recursive technique, 353
Lindeberg–Lévy's central limit theorem, 17, 403
Linear and nonlinear persistence, 339
Linear dependence, 45
Linear models
  Andrews and Quandt's single-break test, 294–297, 297*f*
  Bai and Perron's multiple, endogenous breaks test, 297–302, 301*t*
  Chow tests for given break dates, 291–292, 292*t*
  CUSUM and CUSUM square tests, 293–294, 295*f*
  detecting and exploiting structural change in, 290–307
  testing for breaks and testing for unit roots and cointegration, 302–307
Linear predictions, 71
Linear process, 42
Linear regression model, 1, 91, 93, 344. *See also* Autoregressive Moving Average models (ARMA models)
  asymptotic theory for, 16–18
  inference in, 1–18
    confidence intervals, 10–15
    Fama–French linear regression model for US oil stock returns, 12*t*
    GLS estimator, 7–9
    goodness of fit measures, 5–7
    hypotheses testing, 10–15
    MLE, 9–10
    OLS procedure, 3–5
    output of linear regression model with three regressors, 7*t*
    predictive intervals, 10–15
  interpretation of regression results, 34–36
  issues with heteroskedasticity and autocorrelation of errors, 32–34
  specifying regressors, 25–32
  with stochastic regressors, 15–16
  testing for violations of linear regression framework, 18–25
    linearity, 18–23

structural breaks and parameter stability test, 23–25
Linear variable, 4
Linearity, 2, 18–23
Ljung–Box portmanteau tests, 326
Ljung–Box test statistics, 62
LM. *See* Lagrange multiplier (LM)
LM test. *See* Lagrange multiplier test (LM test)
Location-scale nonlinear family, 289
Log-likelihood function, 9–10, 211, 269, 336, 363
Log-normal model, 273
Log-normal two-factor stochastic volatility model, 272–280
Logarithmic HAR model, 394
Long-horizon
point forecasts, 206–208
returns, 205
Long-memory model, 281
Long-run
covariance of random vector, 34
multipliers, 101
state probabilities, 344–345
Long-term components. *See* Permanent variance components
Loss function, 71
LR. *See* Likelihood ratio (LR)

M

MA models. *See* Moving average models (MA models)
MA(q). *See* qth order MA (MA(q))
MAE. *See* Mean absolute error (MAE)
MAPE. *See* Mean absolute percentage error (MAPE)
Marginal CDF, 402
Market model, 2, 25
Markov chain (MC), 329
processes and properties, 344–350, 349*f*
Markov state variables, 330
Markov switching (MS), 299, 329
ARCH model, 369–372
comparing two alternative MSI(2,0) models, 338*f*
DCC models, 369–372, 371*f*
definitions and classifications, 329–336
dynamics through simulations, 337–340
as normal mixtures and density approximation, 340
estimation and inference
MLE and EM algorithm, 350–358, 357*f*
nuisance parameters problem, 362–365, 365*f*
testing and selecting regimes, 362–365, 365*f*
tests of hypotheses, 359–362, 362*f*
FOCS for ML estimation, 378–379
forecasting with, 365–369, 368*f*
Markov chain processes and properties, 344–350
models, 308
work in practice, 372–374
MS regression model selection, 343*t*
multifractal model, 373
multivariate MS model selection, 335*t*
nonlinear and MS models work in practice, 372–374
notions concerning Ergodic Markov chains, 376–377
regressions, 341–344
state probabilities from three univariate MSIH models, 335*f*
state-space representation, 377–378
univariate MS model selection, 333*t*
VAR Model, 329
Markovian nature of financial and macroeconomic data, 52
Martingale difference, 273
MATLAB, 346, 353–354
Matrix, 404
algebra, 404
Maximization step, 353–354
Maximum likelihood (ML), 9
Maximum likelihood estimator/estimation (MLE), 9–10, 171, 206, 212–214, 255, 268, 336, 350–358, 357*f*
properties, 214–218
quasi, 218–221
sample variance estimator, 157–158
MC. *See* Markov chain (MC)
Mean absolute error (MAE), 98
Mean absolute percentage error (MAPE), 73, 98
Mean response, 12
Mean reversion, 72
Mean square forecast error (MSFE), 71, 73, 97
Mean squared prediction error criterion, 365–366
Mean-squared error (MSE), 188
Measurement errors in regressors, 31–32
Measurement or observation equation, 268–269
Method-of-moment estimator (MM estimator), 206
Microstructure effects, 383
Microstructure noise, 383–384
Minimum MSE estimator, 270
Misspecification tests, 219, 221
Mixtures of normal distributions, 280, 340
ML. *See* Maximum likelihood (ML)
MLE. *See* Maximum likelihood estimator/ estimation (MLE)
MM estimator. *See* Method-of-moment estimator (MM estimator)
Modified unit root tests, 302
Monte Carlo likelihood (MCL), 280
Monte Carlo techniques, 81, 124
Most efficient estimators, 214
Moving average model for squared residuals, 157–158
Moving average models (MA models), 41, 49–60. *See also* Vector Autoregressive Moving Average models (VARMA models)
estimation methods, 65–67, 67*t*
finite order moving average processes, 49–51
plots and correlogram of MA simulated data, 51*f*, 52*f*
residual diagnostics, 67–70, 69*f*
rolling one-step-ahead forecasts for US inflation, 74*f*
selection, 61–70
characteristics, 62*t*
plot of monthly percentage changes, 62*f*
selection of model and role of information criteria, 61–64
serial correlation structure of changes in US CPI, 63*t*
Moving-average processes, testing for unit roots in, 132–133
MS, Vector AutoRegressive, Heteroskedastic model (MS(I)VARH), 330
MS. *See* Markov switching (MS)
MS VAR heteroskedastic model, 332
MS(I)VARH. *See* MS, Vector AutoRegressive, Heteroskedastic model (MS(I)VARH)
MSE. *See* Mean-squared error (MSE)
MSFE. *See* Mean square forecast error (MSFE)
MSVAR models, 374
Multicollinearity, 29–31
Multifactor volatility models, 267
Multiple, endogenous
breaks test, 297–302, 301*t*
Multiplicity of cointegrating vectors, 138
Multistep-ahead forecast, 71
Multivariate
applications
range-based covariance estimation, 396
realized covariance matrix estimation, 395–396
constant-parameter, 287
covariance model, 254–255
diagonal SVM, 282
GARCH model
factor GARCH models, 257–263
full, multivariate GARCH models, 238–250
inference and model specification, 264–265
simple models of covariance prediction, 230–238
VARMA models, 229
Ljung–Box statistic, 82
methods, 229–230
normal density, 353–354
portmanteau tests, 81–82
random variable, 402
SV models, 282
t-Student, 238–239
time series analysis, 77
foundations of, 77–82
weak stationarity of, 77–78
VECM-based tests, 138
weak stationarity of multivariate time series, 77–78
white noise process, 82
Multivariate density. *See* Conditional density

N

NAGARCH model. *See* Nonlinear asymmetric GARCH model (NAGARCH model)
N-dimensional vector stochastic process, 77
Near-unit root, 115–116
Newey–West covariance estimator, 34
News impact curve (NIC), 202–205
  from alternative GARCH models, 203*f*
  and testing for asymmetric ARCH, 202–205
News response, 12–13
Newton's method, 212
NIC. *See* News impact curve (NIC)
NLS estimator. *See* Nonlinear least squares estimator (NLS estimator)
Nodes, 321–322
Non-Gaussian marginal innovations, 190–196
(Non-)linearities testing, 322–326, 325*t*
Non-stochastic regressors, 3
Nonlinear asymmetric GARCH model (NAGARCH model), 178, 184
Nonlinear autoregression model, 310
Nonlinear least squares estimator (NLS estimator), 22–23
Nonlinear time series models, 289
Nonlinear work in practice, 372–374
Nonnormal shocks, 219
Nonparametric
  approach, 339
  bootstrap, 103–104
  method of controlling for serial correlation, 131
Nonparametric GARCH model, 191
Nonpersistent regime, 333
Nonstationarity, 116–117, 139
Nonstationary series, 122
Nonsynchronous trading effects, 395
Normal CDF, 318
Normal distribution, 402
Normal mixture model, 271–272
Normalized autocorrelation coefficient, 138–139
Normally distributed errors, 2–3
Not reject the null hypothesis, 13
Nuisance parameters problem, 321–322, 362–365, 365*f*
Null hypothesis, 13, 68, 215
Numerical methods, constrained optimization, 212

O

Observed time series, 42
OLS. *See* Ordinary least square (OLS)
Omitted variable bias, 26
One-sided tests, 14
One-step-ahead forecast, 71
OOS tests. *See* Out-of-sample tests (OOS tests)
OPG estimator, 358
Optimal prediction function, 97
Option implied volatilities, 198
Ordered sequence of random variables, 403
Ordinary least square (OLS), 46, 198
  estimator, 4–5, 46
  procedure, 3–5
Orthogonal matrix, 8
Orthogonality conditions of GMM, 209
Out-of-sample tests (OOS tests), 372–373
Outliers, 195
Overfitting, 63–64

P

PACF. *See* Partial autocorrelation function (PACF)
Parameter estimation step, 269
Parameter stability test, 23–25
Parametric bootstrap, 103–104
Parametric models, 210
Parametric specification, 191–192
Partial autocorrelation function (PACF), 46, 116, 152, 388
Partial R^2 coefficients, 30, 36
Partial structural change, 290
PC. *See* Principal component (PC)
PCA. *See* Principal component analysis (PCA)
PDF. *See* Population distribution function (PDF); Probability density function (PDF)
Per-period variance from GARCH model, 206
Percentage of correct signs prediction statistic, 73–75
Perfect multicollinearity, 29
Permanent variance components, 186–189
Persistence level/index of model, 204
Phillips and Perron method (PP method), 131, 139
Phillips-Ouliaris' test, 139, 141
Physical process, 284
Point prediction, 12
Poisson process, 281
Polynomial of degree, 52–53
Population, 1
Population distribution function (PDF), 408
Portfolio choice, 395
Positive conditional excess kurtosis, 190
Post-weekend or holiday (PWH), 192
Posterior distribution, 352
Power ARCH models, 182–186
PP method. *See* Phillips and Perron method (PP method)
Predicted probabilities, 352
Predictions, 12
  error, 269
    decomposition, 210
Predictive intervals, 10–15
Primer on Kalman filter, 268–271
Principal component (PC), 263
Principal component analysis (PCA), 31
Prior distribution, 351–352
Probability, 399–400
  law, 399
Probability density function (PDF), 184–186, 399–400
Product-sandwich form, 245–246
pth order AR process (AR(p)), 52, 390
P-values, 296
  of test, 14
PWH. *See* Post-weekend or holiday (PWH)

Q

QARCH model. *See* Quadratic ARCH model (QARCH model)
QMLE. *See* Quasi maximum likelihood estimator (QMLE)
QQ plot. *See* Quantile–quantile plot (QQ plot)
Q-statistics, 46, 69
qth order MA (MA(q)), 49
Quadratic ARCH model (QARCH model), 176–178
Quadratic variation (QV), 382
Quadratic variation and estimators, 381–383
Quantile–quantile plot (QQ plot), 191
Quasi maximum likelihood estimator (QMLE), 218–223
Quasi-differenced series, 129–130
(Quasi) Maximum Likelihood Estimation ((Q) MLE), 65–66, 95, 231, 275–276, 352

R

Random variables, 1, 399
Random walk (RW), 113–114
  with drift process, 165
Range-based covariance estimation, 396
Range-based variance forecasts, 392–394, 392*f*
Range-based volatility proxy, 393
Rank of matrix, 14, 404
Realization of random variable, 399
Realized bipower variation, 387
Realized covariance matrix estimation, 395–396
Realized variance (RV), 381
  estimators, 382
  forecasting, 388–394
  kernel-based estimators, 386
  measuring
    bias-adjusted measures of RV, 385–387
    jumps and bipower variation, 387
    microstructure noise and choice of sampling frequency, 383–384
    quadratic variation and estimators, 381–383
  multivariate applications, 395–396
  stylized facts on, 388–389
Realized volatility, 268, 381
Recurrent regime switching
  threshold and smooth transition regime switching models, 307–326
    smooth transition regression and autoregressive models, 316–322, 321*f*
    testing (non-)linearities, 322–326, 325*t*
    threshold regression and autoregressive models, 308–316, 313*f*
Recurrent regimes, 287
Recurrent shifts, 287
Recurrent states, 287
Recursive Choleski triangularization, 84
Recursive regression residuals, 24–25
Recursive relationship, 202
Recursive residuals, 293
Reduced-form VAR, 83–84, 94, 103
  forecast error variance decompositions, 105–106

from structural to, 82–86
Regime model, 363
Regime switching (RS), 287–288, 329. *See also* Recurrent regime switching
Regime switching dynamic correlation model (RSDC model), 372
Regime variable, 329–330
Regressand. *See* Dependent variable
Regression
coefficients, 2
errors, 122
Regression error specification test. *See* Regression Specification Error Test (RESET)
Regression Specification Error Test (RESET), 20–21, 22*t*, 23*t*, 325
Regressors. *See* Independent variables
Replica samples, 407–408
RESET. *See* Regression Specification Error Test (RESET)
Residual(s), 3, 5
diagnostics, 67–70
residual-based regression statistics, 66–67
Return instantaneous volatility, 381–382
Risk, 158
management, 395
measure of, 159
neutral, 284
RiskMetrics model, 160–161, 208, 284–285
calculations, 167*t*, 173*t*
covariance predictive model, 231–233
processes, 234
variance estimator to covariance, 230–231
RMSE. *See* Root mean squared error (RMSE)
RMSFE, 367, 373
Rolling window
forecasts, 157–159
plots of rolling window forecasts of mean and variance, 160*f*
worked out calculations, 159*t*
models, 157–158
vs. RiskMetrics
stock–bond correlations, 232, 232*f*, 233*f*
stock–bond covariances, 231–232, 232*f*
Root mean squared error (RMSE), 98
Root mean squared prediction error, 192
RS. *See* Regime switching (RS)
RSDC model. *See* Regime switching dynamic correlation model (RSDC model)
RV. *See* Realized variance (RV)
RW. *See* Random walk (RW)

S

S&P. *See* Standard & Poors (S&P)
Sample autocorrelation function (SACF), 45, 70*t*, 116, 128, 128*f*
Sample autocorrelations, 45–48
Sample cross-covariance matrices, 79–80, 81*t*
Sample moments, 206
Sample partial autocorrelations, 45–48
Sample score, 219
Sampling frequency, 383–384
Sandwich quasi-maximum likelihood estimator, 358
Saturation ratio, 96–97, 336
SBIC. *See* Schwarz's Bayesian information criterion (SBIC)
Scalar matrix, 3, 7–8
Scatter plot, 18–19, 19*f*, 20*f*
to investigating linearity assumption, 20*f*
matrix, 19, 21*f*
Schur criterion, 54
Schwarz's Bayesian information criterion (SBIC), 64, 347–348
threshold specification analysis based on, 314*t*
Score function, 10, 354
SD. *See* Standard deviation (SD)
SDE. *See* Stochastic difference equation (SDE)
SE. *See* Standard error (SE)
Second-generation stochastic volatility models, 281–282
Self-exciting models (SESR), 323, 324*f*
Self-exciting threshold models, 308–309
SEM. *See* Simulated expectation maximization (SEM)
Semi-positive definite (SPD), 230–231
Semiparametric GARCH model, 191
Sequential Bai-Perron tests, 312
Sequential estimation, 221–223
Sequential ML-based estimator, 223
Sequential tests, 299
SESR. *See* Self-exciting models (SESR)
SESTAR models, 321–322
SETAR models, 315–316
Simple switching model, 336
Simple univariate parametric models, 157–190. *See also* Advanced univariate volatility modeling
ACF/PACF for residuals and squared standardized residuals, 176*t*
ARCH models, 161–168
comparing performance of alternative variance forecast models, 168–171
exponential smoothing variance forecasts, 160–161
few additional, popular ARCH models, 181–190
generalized ARCH models and statistical properties, 171–180
rolling window forecasts, 157–159
sample ACF and PACF
for squared residuals, 166*t*
for squared residuals and cross-correlogram, 170*t*, 171*t*
for US excess stock returns, 165*t*
Simulated expectation maximization (SEM), 280
Simulated maximum likelihood estimator (SML), 280
Simulated method of moments (SMM), 280
Single-break test, 294–297, 297*f*
Single-factor conditionally heteroskedastic models, 92, 158, 239, 248, 381
advanced univariate volatility modeling, 190–198
comparing ML estimates of Gaussian *vs.* *t*-student GARCH, 193*t*
estimation of and inference on GARCH models, 210–225
forecasting with GARCH models, 205–209
sample ACF and PACF for squared stock returns, 155*t*
scatter plots of squares *vs.* levels for two series, 156*f*
simple univariate parametric models, 157–190
stylized facts and preliminaries, 151–157
testing for ARCH, 198–205
time series and scatter plots of squared returns/yield changes, 157*f*
Single-factor volatility models, 267
Single-state Gaussian IID model, 337
Size of test, 14
Slutsky's theorem, 17
Small Minus Big (SMB), 7
SML. *See* Simulated maximum likelihood estimator (SML)
SMM. *See* Simulated method of moments (SMM)
Smooth band-threshold effect, 318–319
Smooth function, 3
Smooth transition
model, 316
regression and autoregressive models, 316–322, 321*f*
Smooth transition RS models (STRS models), 308
Smoothed probability, 351, 353
vectors, 351
Snedecor's F random variable, 14
Sparse realized variance, 384
Sparse sampling, 383–384
SPD. *See* Semi-positive definite (SPD)
"Spectral estimator", 130
"Spectral" decomposition, 8
Spurious regression problem, 121–124, 123*f*
Square matrix, 404
SSE. *See* Explained sum of squares (SSE)
SSR. *See* Sum of squared residuals (SSR)
SST. *See* Total sum of squares (SST)
Standard & Poors (S&P), 127, 128*f*, 131*f*, 141*f*, 145*f*
S&P 500 index, 41–42
S&P 500 realized volatility, 384*f*, 385*f*
standardized S&P 500 returns, 390*f*
Standard Brownian motion, 381–382
Standard deviation (SD), 11–12
Standard error (SE), 11–12, 157
Standard Euclidean norm, 355–357
Standard linear VAR frameworks, 374
Standard regularity conditions, 357–358
Standard *t*-statistics, 359
Standard VAR models, 94
State or transition equation, 268–269
State-space representation
of model, 268–269
of MS model, 377–378
Stationarity, 41–44
conditions, 52–53, 86–89, 344

Stationarity (*Continued*)
  and moment convergence criteria, 250
  weak stationarity of multivariate time series, 77–78
Stationary process, 114, 129
Stationary series, 117, 122
  autocovariances, 50
  differencing to, 120
  sums of stationary and, 120
Statistical model, 1
  primer on key features and classification of instability, 287–290
Statistical parametric models of NIC, 201
"Stayer" probabilities, 337
Stepwise regression method, 28
Stochastic difference equation (SDE), 273, 281, 387
Stochastic process, 41–42
Stochastic regressors, linear regression model with, 15–16
Stochastic trends, 113–114, 165
Stochastic volatility (SV), 267, 282–285, 381
  extended, second-generation SV models, 281–282
  GARCH models, 282–284
  models with jumps, 284
  primer on Kalman filter, 268–271
  simple stochastic volatility models and estimation, 271–280
  stressing differences, 284–285
Stochastic volatility models (SVMs), 267, 389–390
Stochastically trending series, 116
Stock variable, 224–225
Stress tests, 356–357
Strict stationarity, 78, 161
STRS models. *See* Smooth transition RS models (STRS models)
Structural analysis with vector autoregressive models
  Granger causality, 108–110, 110*t*
  impulse response functions, 100–104
  variance decompositions, 105–107
Structural breaks, 23–25, 287
  detecting and exploiting structural change in linear models, 290–307
  primer on key features and classification of statistical model of instability, 287–290
Structural VAR, 83
Stylized facts and preliminaries, 159
Sum of squared residuals (SSR), 3, 6, 63–64
Sums of returns or shocks, forecasts of variance for, 208–209
Sup-F-test, 290
Sup-LR tests, 294–296
Sup-Wald tests, 294–296
"Sup" class of tests, 363
Superconsistent estimator, 138
SV. *See* Stochastic volatility (SV)
"SV-in mean" effects, 278
SVJMs. *See* Stochastic volatility (SV)—models with jumps
SVMs. *See* Stochastic volatility models (SVMs)
Switching GARCH model (SWARCH model), 369–370
Symmetric matrix, 229, 404
Symmetric *t*-Student, 191–192

T

Temporal aggregation, 223–225
Test statistic, 13
Tests of hypotheses, 29, 34–35, 359–362
Theory of hypothesis testing, 13
Threshold autoregressive models, 308–316, 313*f*
"Threshold cointegration" multivariate VECM, 311
Threshold GARCH (TARCH) model, 182
Threshold model, 308–309, 316
Threshold regression model (TRM), 308–316, 313*f*
Threshold RS models (TRS models), 308
Threshold vector autoregressions, 315–316
Time invariant distribution, 43
Time series, 113–114
  analysis, 41–48
    correlograms of two times series with alternative persistence properties, 46*f*
    Gaussian WN process, 44*f*
    plots of two times series with alternative persistence properties, 44*f*
    properties, 41–42
    sample autocorrelations and sample partial autocorrelations, 45–48
    serial correlation structure of simulated AR(1) data, 47*t*
    serial correlation structure of simulated WN data, 48*t*
    stationarity, 42–44
  models, 287
  process, 118, 132–133
Time-varying
  coefficient model, 184
  MS model, 347–349
  parameter model, 310
  transition probabilities, 347
Total sum of squares (SST), 5–6
Transition equation, 365–366
Transition matrix, 329
Transitory variance components, 186–189
Trend stationary model, 113
Triangularization, 85
Trimming, 195
TRM. *See* Threshold regression model (TRM)
TRS models. *See* Threshold RS models (TRS models)
True ex post variation, 382
t-student, 254, 389–390
  diagonal BEKK(1,1) model, 247
  distribution, 187, 264
  modeling tools, 369
  MSVAR(2) VECH ARCH(2) model, 370
Tukey-Hanning's kernel function, 387
Two-factor model, 259, 272–273
Two-factor SVM model, 273–275
Two-sided tests, 14
Two-state MS heteroskedastic regression model, 355–356, 357*f*, 361–362
Two-step QMLE procedure, 372
TXT covariance matrix, 8

U

Ultinomial logit parameterization, 347
Unbiased predictor of squared residuals, 161
Unbiased variable, 4
Uncentered moment, 400–401
Unconditional covariance matrix, 87
Unconditional state probabilities, 344–345
Uncorrelatedness and independence in probability theory, 406
Unfeasible GLS, 9
Uniformly most efficient estimator, 9–10
Unit roots
  cointegration and error-correction models, 133–148
  processes, 113–121
    detrends unit root series, 118–119
    differencing d + r times to *I*(*d*) series, 121, 121*f*
    differencing to (deterministic) trend-stationary series, 119–120
    differencing to stationary series, 120
  spurious regression problem, 121–124
  testing for unit roots and cointegration, 302–307
  tests
    ADF, 126–130
    classical DF, 124–126
    other, 131–132
    testing for unit roots in moving-average processes, 132–133
Univariate
  constant-parameter, 287
  GARCH methods, 238–239
  model, 359
  random variables, 402
  regression-based tests, 138
Updating step, 269

V

Value-at-Risk criterion, 374
VAR models. *See* Vector autoregressive models (VAR models)
VAR(*1*) model
  estimation output, 93, 93*t*
  population moments of VAR(*1*) process, 86–89
VAR(*p*) model, 302
  estimation, 91–94
  estimation output of VAR(*1*) model, 93*t*
  generalization to, 89–90
Variance(s), 159, 229, 233–234, 243*f*, 248*f*, 257, 257*f*, 260*f*, 262*f*, 340, 401
  of asset returns, 381
  decompositions, 105–107
  inflation factors, 30, 31*t*
    after dropping one regressor, 31*t*
  targeting, 153

VARMA models. *See* Vector Autoregressive Moving Average models (VARMA models)
VECM. *See* Vector error-correction model (VECM)
Vector autoregressive analysis
  estimation of VAR(*p*) model, 91–94
  estimation output of VAR(*1*) model, 93*t*
  forecasting with vector autoregressive model, 97–99
  generalization to VAR(*p*) model, 89–90
  specification of vector autoregressive model and hypothesis testing, 94–97
  stationarity conditions and population moments of VAR(*1*) process, 86–89
  from structural to reduced-form vector autoregressives, 82–86
  VAR selection criteria, 97*t*
Vector autoregressive models (VAR models), 77, 82. *See also* Moving average models (MA models)
  forecasting with, 97–99
  selection criteria, 97*t*
  specification, 94–97
  structural analysis with
    Granger causality, 108–110, 110*t*
    impulse response functions, 100–104
    variance decompositions, 105–107
Vector Autoregressive Moving Average models (VARMA models), 27, 41, 77, 229–230, 238–239, 265, 270, 288, 290, 330–331. *See also* Autoregressive Moving Average models (ARMA models)
foundations of multivariate time series analysis, 77–82
  cross-covariance and cross-correlation matrices, 78–79
  descriptive statistics of one-month and 10-year US treasury yield series, 80*t*
  multivariate portmanteau tests, 81–82
  multivariate white noise process, 82
  sample cross-covariance and cross-correlation matrices, 79–80, 81*t*
  weak stationarity of multivariate time series, 77–78
structural analysis with VAR models, 100–110
VAR analysis
  estimation of VAR(*p*) model, 91–94
  estimation output of VAR(*1*) model, 93*t*
  forecasting with vector autoregressive model, 97–99
  generalization to VAR(*p*) model, 89–90
  selection criteria, 97*t*
  specification of vector autoregressive model and hypothesis testing, 94–97
  stationarity conditions and population moments of VAR(*1*) process, 86–89
  from structural to reduced-form vector autoregressives, 82–86
vector moving average and, 110–112
Vector error-correction model (VECM), 136
Vector error-correction representation, 136
Vector moving average (VMA), 77, 110–111
Vector of unconditional probabilities, 346
Volatility, 159, 267–268, 392–393
  feedback effect, 182–183

W

Wald test, 359, 361–362, 364
Weak GARCH process, 224
Weak stationarity, 43, 77–78
White covariance estimator, 32
White heteroskedasticity test, 33, 33*t*
White noise process (WN process), 44
White test, 32–33
White's version of ML covariance matrix, 364
WN process. *See* White noise process (WN process)
Wold's decomposition theorem, 53–54
Wold's representation theorem, 87, 217

Y

Yule-Walker equations, 54–55

Z

Zero serial correlation, 2
Zero-mean errors, 2

Printed in the United States
By Bookmasters